PACIFISM IN THE UNITED STATES
From the Colonial Era to the First World War

PACIFISM
IN THE UNITED STATES
From the Colonial Era to the First World War

BY PETER BROCK

PRINCETON, NEW JERSEY
PRINCETON UNIVERSITY PRESS
1968

Copyright © 1968 by Princeton University Press

ALL RIGHTS RESERVED

Library of Congress Catalog Card Number: 68-11439

Printed in the United States of America
by Princeton University Press, Princeton, New Jersey

This book has been composed in Linotype Caledonia

✧

Portions of chapter 8 originally appeared
as "The Peace Testimony in 'a Garden Enclosed' "
in *Quaker History*, vol. 54, no. 2 (Autumn 1965),
and are reprinted here with the
permission of the editor.

TO CARMEN

Preface

This history of pacifism in British colonial America and in the American Republic to the outbreak of war in Europe in 1914 has not been conceived as a general history of the American peace movement during this period. Its aim is narrower: to tell the story of the religious groups whose members refused military service on the basis of their objection to war, and of that section of the organized peace movement which from its beginnings in 1815 repudiated all war. But it is not always easy to define the limits within which a study of this kind should be pursued, and to a large extent it must remain a matter for individual judgment to assess how much background material should be included in order to show clearly the subject's bearing within a wider framework.

In most cases, the spelling, but not the punctuation, of the documents cited has been modernized. Shortened references have been used in the footnotes, but I trust no ambiguity has resulted. Except for a few items of peripheral importance mentioned only in the footnotes, the bibliography includes full details concerning the sources used in the text, as well as information on a few additional volumes, not cited in the footnotes, that relate directly to the subject of this book. General reference works, bibliographical aids, and books used solely for preparing the broad historical background have not been included. Lastly, I doubt if I have been able in the text to take into consideration all relevant items published during the year preceding the date of this preface.

I hope my bibliography may be generally useful as a guide to the printed sources for the history of American pacifism before 1914. I have made no attempt, however, to utilize the full range of archival materials bearing on the subject. Its bulk, covering, as it does, a span of over two and a half centuries and a wide variety of groups and personalities, made such an effort virtually impossible. Still, I could not resist taking samplings from this store from time to time.

Whatever shortcomings the book may have are solely my responsibility. That these are not more numerous than they are is due to the generous help of a number of scholars and scholarly institutions. First of all, I should like to thank three friends and fellow workers in the field who read large portions of the typescript of the book's first draft: Larry Gara of Wilmington College, Guy F. Hershberger of Goshen College, and Frederick B. Tolles of Swarthmore College. Their pertinent criticisms and timely advice have saved me from innumerable errors of fact and judgment. Next, my thanks are due to the John

vii

Simon Guggenheim Memorial Foundation for a fellowship that enabled me to concentrate a year's uninterrupted work on research and writing, and to Columbia University, which, while I was a member of its faculty, provided funds for typing large parts of the manuscript. I owe much, also, to the courtesy and efficiency of the staff of the reference desk at Columbia University Library, who obtained a number of items for me on interlibrary loan and who answered my numerous queries. And the magnificent array of materials available on the Library's shelves proved invaluable.

Moreover, without the services supplied by the staffs of a large number of other libraries and archives, this book could not have been written. I should like to mention in particular the Friends Historical Library and the Peace Collection at Swarthmore College, the Quaker Collection at Haverford College, the Mennonite Historical Library and Archives at Goshen College, Bethel College Historical Library (North Newton, Kan.), and Moravian College Library and Moravian Archives (Bethlehem, Pa.), as well as the grand collections of Harvard University Library and of the New York and Boston Public Libraries. Among other institutions that have assisted me in the course of my researches are: American Antiquarian Society (Worcester, Mass.); American University (Washington, D.C.); Boston Athenaeum; Brethren Historical Library (Elgin, Ill.); Bridgewater College Library (Va.); British Museum (London); Butler University Library; Cornell University Library; Department of Records of Philadelphia Yearly Meeting of the Society of Friends; Disciples of Christ Historical Society (Nashville, Tenn.); Eastern Mennonite College Historical Library (Harrisonburg, Va.); Free Library of Philadelphia; Friends House Library (London); German Society of Pennsylvania (Philadelphia); Historical Society of Pennsylvania (Philadelphia); Library Company of Philadelphia (Ridgeway Branch); Library of Congress (Washington, D.C.); Maine Historical Society (Portland); Massachusetts Historical Society (Boston); Public Record Office (London); Schwenkfelder Library (Pennsburg, Pa.); Smith College Library; State Historical Society of Wisconsin (Madison); Union Theological Seminary Library; University of Pennsylvania Library; University of Toronto Library; William L. Clements Library, University of Michigan; Yale University Library. I should also like to thank the Department of History of the University of Toronto, which assisted me in the last stage of preparing my manuscript. In addition, I am much indebted to Sanford G. Thatcher, of Princeton University Press, for the care with which he has made my manuscript ready for publication. It has greatly benefited from his rigorous insistence on clarity and good style.

Finally, this preface would be incomplete if I did not mention the continual help and encouragement that my wife has given me while I have been writing this book. The dedication on a previous page represents a small expression of my gratitude.

P. de B. B.

Toronto, Ontario, Canada
31 December 1967

Contents

xi

CONTENTS

PACIFISM IN THE UNITED STATES
From the Colonial Era to the First World War

KEY TO ABBREVIATIONS
(in footnotes and bibliography)

AHR	*American Historical Review*
B.P.L.	Boston Public Library
BFHA	*Bulletin of Friends' Historical Association*
C.O.	conscientious objector
EHR	*English Historical Review*
F.H.L.S.C.	Friends Historical Library, Swarthmore College
H.C.Q.C.	Haverford College Quaker Collection
MAM	*Minutes of the Annual Meetings of the Church of the Brethren*
MHB	*Mennonite Historical Bulletin* (Scottdale, Pa.)
M. M.	Monthly Meeting (Quaker)
MQR	*Mennonite Quarterly Review* (Goshen, Ind.)
NEQ	*New England Quarterly*
PMHB	*Pennsylvania Magazine of History and Biography* (Philadelphia)
Q. M.	Quarterly Meeting (Quaker)
S.C.P.C.	Swarthmore College Peace Collection
TMHS	*Transactions of the Moravian Historical Society* (Nazareth, Pa.)
Y. M.	Yearly Meeting (Quaker)

Introduction

On the North American continent pacifism, the renunciation of war by the individual, represented at first a transplantation into these new and open territories of an attitude that had originated among religious groups in the European homeland. Antimilitarism and the refusal to participate personally in any warlike activity formed, as it were, part of the intellectual baggage brought over the ocean by emigrants from their midst. The attempt to maintain these ideas, the transmutations and accretions that resulted from life in a new and often strange environment, and the eventual widening of the ideal of peace held by these sects to embrace members of other denominations constitute the content of the history of pacifism as it developed in North America.

The major pacifist sects that were transplanted to America had begun as outgrowths of the great religious movements that transformed the intellectual climate of large parts of northern and central Europe in the sixteenth and seventeenth centuries. Mennonitism and its offshoots formed the radical wing of the Protestant Reformation, which at the beginning was collectively known as Anabaptism, and the Quaker Society of Friends, for all the differences that set it apart from the parent movement, was a genuine child of mid-seventeenth-century English Puritanism. A half century later, German Pietism produced both the Dunkers and the Moravian Church. Even the nonsectarian peace movement which took root in the United States from about 1815 on and which included among its adherents an influential minority who adopted the full pacifist position had one of its main sources in the eighteenth-century European Enlightenment, with its reasonable religion and its humanitarian abhorrence of war—however much the more evangelically minded peace men might have repudiated such an affinity.

The origins of American pacifism, then, must be traced back at least as far as the outset of the Protestant Reformation. Nevertheless, Luther, after he had issued his call in 1517 for a return to the doctrine and practice of the apostolic church, came finally to assert the permissibility of Christian participation in war at the command of the lawful magistrate. And this rejection of pacifism was ultimately shared, too, by Luther's contemporary Zwingli, who had begun a somewhat similar reformation in the Swiss city of Zürich in the early 1520's, and by Calvin, who set up his presbyterian polity in Geneva in the 1540's. Thus, Christian pacifism was excluded as a tenable doctrine for the faithful in the various churches that derived from Luther and Calvin,

3

as well as in the Church of England that was established as a result of the Anglican Reformation.

However, from the beginning a more rigorous Christian discipleship was adopted toward war, as it was toward other aspects of social and religious life, by certain groups among the early reformers. This "Anabaptist Vision" contrasted nowhere more markedly with the mainstream of the Reformation than in its position regarding the state. True, the Anabaptists believed that the state, even when it came under the control of an evil tyrant, was an institution ordained by God that had been established by him since the Fall as an instrument essential for man's well-being on this earth, to punish the wicked, protect the weak, and maintain good order in society. Christians, they held, must willingly obey the state in all matters rightfully pertaining to the state's competence. Although armed rebellion against a bad government runs directly counter to God's will, the state, so they believed, needs to wield the power of the sword to fulfill its task of maintaining domestic order and protecting the land from foreign invaders. Thus far, indeed, the Anabaptist *Weltanschauung* corresponded with that of the major Reformation churches. Yet Anabaptist support for the state was circumscribed by significant reservations which the other reformers did not share and which they regarded with alarm and abhorrence.

In the first place, Anabaptists categorically denied that the magistrate had any right to exercise authority in spiritual matters: in questions of religion, the Christian must refuse obedience and suffer the consequences rather than act against his conscience. Membership in the church, for them, was not to be conterminous with citizenship but voluntary, something for the individual to decide for himself and for the congregation to approve (although salvation, they held, lay with their church alone). Adult baptism, hence baptism of the believer, was to take the place of baptism of the unthinking infant and to become the outward symbol of entry into their church community. Here, indeed, existed in embryo the modern ideas of the separation of church and state and of the voluntary church.

Secondly, and equally categorically, the Anabaptists asserted the incompatibility of political office with true Christian discipleship. Only after the purity of the primitive church had been soiled and Christian faith corrupted, they claimed, did church members begin to participate in government. Acceptance of office, far from being a duty incumbent on the conscientious, inevitably required the performance of actions diametrically opposed to the teaching and example of Christ and his apostles. It is of the very essence of the magistrate's office, so they believed, to wage war, to deal out harsh punishments, and to impose oaths, all of which had been expressly forbidden by Christ. A Christian should therefore avoid participation in the state, not merely by refusing to accept any government post but by refraining from law suits and from taking oaths and becoming a soldier or policeman.

In the eyes of the Anabaptists, then, the way of Christ and the way of the "world" were seen to be quite separate, indeed antithetical: Christians, always a minority on this earth (for Anabaptist theology was essentially pessimistic), must remain nonconformed to the world until the coming of Christ's kingdom. Among those who consider themselves Christ's followers, discipline should be maintained only through the disfellowshipping of any who refuse to show proper contrition for sin—not, as in the world, by the force of arms. For the Anabaptists, the Sermon on the Mount and the various New Testament texts that they quoted in support of their position formed, as it were, a code of legislation that in their view had supplanted the Mosaic law, the covenant contained in the Old Testament books, which are replete with bloody wars and harsh views on punishment. "Resist not evil" was the kernel of the new dispensation introduced by Christ.

The Anabaptists and their Mennonite successors called themselves "defenseless Christians." In the early decades, it is true, there were some connected with the movement who either never adopted or later abandoned the nonviolent attitude outlined above. (Indeed, the bloody tragedy of Münster in 1534-1535 imprinted on Anabaptism for several centuries afterward the stigma of violent revolution.) It is also true that, at first, the movement represented to some extent an upsurge of social and economic discontent on the part of the peasantry and the lower urban strata. Yet, as a whole, its followers continued to adhere to a philosophy of nonresistance.

The genesis of the Anabaptists' nonresistance is still an open question in historiography. Possibly, the pacifist teachings of Erasmus and other humanist writers exerted an influence on the thinking of Conrad Grebel (ca. 1498-1526) and the Swiss Brethren, whose break with Zwingli in January 1525, in effect, marked the beginning of organized Anabaptism. Or it may have been derived from earlier medieval sects, like the Czech Brethren or the Waldenses, whose antipolitical nonresistance closely parallels that of the Anabaptists; but no genetic connection has yet been proved. In any case, the main inspiration of the Swiss Brethren, and of their successors down through the centuries, was undoubtedly the New Testament, interpreted in a literalist spirit and freed from the glosses appended by Catholic and Protestant exegetes alike. For Anabaptists and, later, Mennonites, participation in war and violence was wrong, both because it had been forbidden in the New Testament and because spiritual weapons alone were thought to be consistent with Christian discipleship.

The problem of conscientious objection to military service—a subject that will be the focus of considerable attention in the subsequent chapters of this book—even though it did occur quite early, remained of secondary importance in Europe before the era of universal military conscription inaugurated by the French Revolution and the Napoleonic wars. In the sixteenth century, while the communistic Hutterite groups founded in Moravia in the 1530's refused either to pay war taxes or to make weapons of war or gunpowder, the Dutch Mennonites showed a less uncompromising disposition when they gratefully accepted the exemption from military duties granted by William of Orange in 1577 in exchange for the payment of commutation money. This remained the pattern for Mennonite communities in Europe and North America into the nineteenth century. But, though such commutation was regarded as an acceptable rendering to Caesar of his due, direct hiring of a substitute to take the place of a conscripted man, which in many countries the law permitted, was condemned as connivance at the shedding of innocent blood.

Nonresistance, indeed, occupied a central place in the teachings of Menno Simons (1496-1561), a Dutch Roman Catholic priest who was converted to Anabaptism in 1536. It was Menno who was chiefly responsible for the reconstitution of the movement, disorganized after the disastrous debacle at Münster. Eventually, with the exception of the Hutterites and, also, the Silesian Schwenkfelders who emigrated to Pennsylvania in the second quarter of the eighteenth century, all who fell broadly within the Anabaptist tradition, whether Dutch or German or English, came to bear the name of Mennonites.

Although its pacifism may have contributed to the authorities' suspicions that Anabaptism was a subversive movement, the savage persecution that its adherents encountered—both in its original cradle in Switzerland and in Germany and the Netherlands where it had soon spread—came as a reaction primarily against other aspects of the movement. Theological unorthodoxy and radical separation from the state church, as well as an element of latent violence in some sections of the movement, account for the fury with which the Anabaptists were pursued by Protestant and Catholic rulers alike in the period from 1527 until at least the 1560's. The Christian answer, peaceful Anabaptists believed, was to suffer without resisting: that had been the way of the Cross. A long chain of martyrs was forged to bind subsequent generations in Europe, as in the New World, to the concept of their

6

people as the Lord's suffering servants, who should expect no better fate on this earth at the hands of the world's followers. The doctrinal aspects of Christian nonresistance were constantly restated during frequent theological disputations with opponents and in the confessions of faith and polemical tracts of the German and Dutch Mennonites of the sixteenth to eighteenth centuries. Many of these documents were reprinted by the American Mennonites and are still accepted by them today as basic statements of their beliefs.

During the sixteenth century, first in Moravia and in Polish Pomerania, then in Calvinist Holland, and finally in the German lands, Anabaptists were granted limited toleration. Toward the end of the eighteenth century, Catherine II of Russia invited their Mennonite descendants to settle in her realm, thus repeating the pattern of protectorship on the part of rulers of alien faith who were anxious to profit by the settlement of such excellent farmers on their territories. It was in Holland, however, that the Mennonites enjoyed greatest freedom. Increasing material prosperity and urbanization made the seventeenth century a golden age for the Dutch Mennonites. Yet, as a result, Dutch Mennonitism contributed little directly to swell the tide of Mennonite emigration to the New World. Moreover, gradual acculturation within secular society created insidious dangers for the traditional way of life of the church. From the early eighteenth century on, numbers rapidly declined. Growing religious liberalism and a relaxed attitude toward the prohibition of participation in politics and toward many aspects of social life led among the *Doopsgezinden* (as Dutch Mennonites were now called) to a narrowing of the gap between the church and the world. Among the Mennonite testimonies that finally lapsed was the profession of nonresistance, enforced for over two centuries by exercise of the ban against any who deviated from it. In Holland, nonresistance was abandoned in the first half of the nineteenth century.

Pacifism was also almost entirely given up by the Mennonites in the new Imperial Germany (it disappeared altogether in twentieth-century Germany), as well as by the few surviving communities in Switzerland and France. But in Russia, where both Pomeranian Mennonites of Dutch extraction and refugee Hutterites found a home, pacifism, along with much of the traditional Mennonite culture, survived into the Communist era. It was, indeed, fear regarding the fate of the collective military exemption granted by the Tsarist government to their ancestors that prompted the great emigration of Russian Mennonites to the United States and Canada in the mid-1870's.

On the whole, however, pacifism formed only a minor component

7

in the complex of motives that led German-speaking Mennonites, as well as the even more rigorous Amish who split away in Alsace, South Germany, and Switzerland in the mid-1690's, to emigrate to the New World, a migration that began in the 1680's and has continued sporadically into the middle of the twentieth century. The most cogent reasons for emigration have been, first, economic—the desire for new lands for a rapidly increasing population and wider possibilities for new generations—and, then, religious—the desire to escape persecution and the imposition of disabilities by a state that looked askance at religious dissidence. By the beginning of the nineteenth century, Mennonitism in Germany and in the surrounding lands was on the decline in respect to both its numerical strength and its spiritual energy, and the Soviet Revolution destroyed the prosperous and expanding Mennonite communities of the former Russian Empire. Thus the center of Mennonitism has shifted from the Old to the New World. Yet traditional nonresistance, a basic article of faith in the mainstream of Anabaptism, though discarded almost entirely by the Mennonite communities surviving in Europe, remains as an important element in Mennonite doctrine on the North American continent.

The first of the European pacifist sects to send emigrants to North America in any large numbers was not the Mennonites, however, but the British Quakers, the origins of whose Society of Friends date back to the middle of the seventeenth century. For early Friends, it was not the legalistic injunction "Resist not evil" but rather an intuitional view of the wrongness of war and violence when held up to the Inner Light of Christ which shone within all men that became the source of their refusal to fight. Yet belief in the inadmissibility of war was only gradually arrived at, belief in the permissibility of fighting in a righteous cause only slowly abandoned. The final crystallization of the Quaker peace testimony may be dated to their declaration of January 1661 against taking up arms, either on behalf of an earthly kingdom or to inaugurate the kingdom of Christ. By this time the Commonwealth era, which had seen the birth and early expansion of Quakerism under the leadership of George Fox (1624-1691), was at an end. The restored Stuart monarchy was soon to begin a period of renewed persecution of Quakers and other religious nonconformists, when the Clarendon Code was enacted against all who dissented from the established Church of England.

The faith of the early Quakers was experiential, enthusiastic, and perfectionist. The pioneers of the movement were filled with an apocalyptic belief in the imminence of a new age of history, which would commence with their own victory in the "Lamb's War" (a phrase

8

early Quaker writers liked to use to denote the struggle against sin and the "world"). For, unlike Anabaptists and Mennonites, the early Quakers did not expect the true church to remain always, to the end of time, a small and outcast minority in this world. Instead, they believed in the transforming power of the Holy Spirit, a power that would enable them to convert and remold the peoples of the whole earth. Theirs was to be a total victory. And their rapid spread during the 1650's, despite fierce persecution by the English government, seemed to confirm their optimism. It was only in the last decade of the century, after religious toleration had been granted by the English Parliament in 1689, that the Lamb's War was finally abandoned; only then was the attempt to conquer the world by the power of the Spirit replaced by the desire to maintain righteousness within the Quaker community.

A second point at which the Quaker *Weltanschauung* from the beginning diverged from that of the Anabaptist-Mennonite was in the Quaker's attitude toward the state—an area of great importance, therefore, in any discussion of the pacifism of the two groups. Quakers never regarded the state as at best merely a necessary evil and rulers as men who must by the very nature of their office stand outside the pale of the true Christian community. For Quakers, the godly ruler was no contradiction in terms. Rulers also could be guided by the Spirit. The role of the state had its positive aspect as well as the purely negative one of maintaining order among the ungodly; some measure of force in upholding righteousness in the community did not deprive the authorities of their Christian character. Early Friends, however, did not attempt to relate too closely the role of the Christian magistrate wielding the sword to suppress evil and unrighteousness within the state and their own abandonment of carnal weapons to withstand the external aggressor or the personal assailant. In fact, in Britain, it was not until the nineteenth century that the law permitted a Quaker to take an active role in politics or government. The problem of the pacifist magistrate was faced by Friends only in the New World—in Pennsylvania and, to a lesser degree, in Rhode Island, too.

Although Friends were always ready to quote scripture, particularly the New Testament, in support of their repudiation of armed force, as in defense of all their beliefs, and although their pacifism was certainly to some extent an attempt at restitution of what they believed was the practice of primitive Christianity, the Quaker peace testimony at the outset did not stem from any "notions" (to use the Quaker term). It derived essentially from their view that, in the grand crusade against evil they had been called by God to wage, only inner

9

spiritual weapons were consistent with the leadings of the Spirit. Unrighteousness must be cast down, but not with the weapons of unrighteousness. The Quakers, indeed, may be described as nonviolent resisters rather than as nonresisters in the Mennonite style.

Later, humanitarian and even economic arguments were used by Quaker writers in pleading their case against war. Nonetheless, pragmatic considerations of this kind were considered as supplements, rather than as substitutions for the fundamental principle derived from the guidance of the Inner Light that had to be followed regardless of the cost. For Quakers, peace came to mean following the way of love that begins in the hearts of individuals and through them leavens society until all men are won.

The apocalyptic visions of the "First Publishers of Truth" were, however, replaced by a growing emphasis on gradualism. Thus, we find Robert Barclay (1648-1690) in his famous *Apology for the True Christian Divinity*, which from its first publication in 1676 remained for over a century and a half the most systematic and the most generally accepted statement of Quaker faith, putting forward in his treatment of peace contained in Proposition XV (Sections XIII-XV) a conditional justification of war for non-Quaker Christians, whose political ethic remained sub-Christian, as well as for non-Christians. And a little later William Penn (1644-1718) and John Bellers (1654-1725) elaborated schemes for establishing concord between the nations without requiring them to accept the lofty ideals of the Quakers.

Thus, the original testimony of Friends against war—which, like their other testimonies in such matters as the refusal to swear judicial oaths or to pay tithes, simplicity of attire and plainness of speech, and denial of hat honor and maintenance of strict honesty in business, had at first been regarded as part and parcel of their general strategy in the Lamb's War against sin throughout the world—then became the distinguishing mark of a sect, of a body, which, in spite of having now won toleration and even respect from society at large, did not expect that its peculiarities would gain universal acceptance in the world, much less that this world would ever come to embrace Quakerism. This devotional quietism that blanketed the early eighteenth-century Society of Friends was matched by an equally inward-looking witness for peace, which entailed personal renunciation of violence on the part of every Quaker but which lacked a more positive approach toward peace.

Early Friends in Britain had been, for the most part, country folk: farmers, shepherds, mechanics of one kind or another. A few of the well-to-do, even some gentlemen, had joined the movement. But its rural character, and especially its North-country origins (it was from the ranks of seekers and separatists in this area that Fox recruited his first adherents in the early 1650's), gave its stamp to emergent Quakerism, which to this day has remained a lay movement. But, by the end of the seventeenth century, its social composition had been transformed. Though a rural element continued within the Society, it was now the prosperous bourgeoisie that set the tone, even before townsmen had come to form a majority of the membership.

In Fox's own lifetime—and largely due to his efforts and organizational skill—a loose association of Friends was transformed into a Quaker Society with its established pattern of silent worship, written discipline, and formal membership. Birthright membership was not finally accepted until 1737, but by the late 1660's and early 1670's Fox had succeeded in setting up a Quaker organization for administration and for religious worship by establishing for these purposes a hierarchy of "meetings," from the monthly meetings at the bottom through quarterly meetings up to London Yearly Meeting at the top. The so-called Meeting for Sufferings, set up in 1676 during a period of acute persecution, eventually developed into an executive committee for the English Society as a whole. Much of this organizational framework had, in fact, come into existence during the previous decades. But by establishing it on a permanent footing, by, so to speak, institutionalizing the religion of the Spirit, Fox put an end to the threat of anarchy that had dogged Quakers from the outset. In most respects, the new organization became a model for the transplanted Quakerism of British North America and the West Indian islands.

The same institutionalization that created a Society of Friends was applied, also, to the Quaker repudiation of war. The peace testimony became a branch of the Society's discipline. As the old Quaker warriors in the Lamb's War died off, they were succeeded by a new generation for whom pacifism had become part of a traditional faith, albeit a faith that was often cherished with a genuine devotion. Anyone who deviated from the peace testimony by supporting military activities was now promptly disowned. However, in Britain, Quaker "sufferings" on account of refusal of militia or army service were never severe, although Friends in coastal areas encountered periodic trouble from attempts to impress them into the Royal Navy. In 1693, London Yearly Meeting passed the first of a series of resolutions condemning the arming of vessels owned or captained by Quakers (a prohibition not always obeyed, as minutes of local meetings had to acknowledge "sorrowfully" over the course of the succeeding century). In regard to taxes, though the position was not in all respects clear, almost every Quaker willingly rendered taxes "in the mixture," that is, where only an indeterminate proportion went to support war; and many eminent British Friends urged payment even when the money would be allocated wholly for military purposes, since this allocation might be construed as being solely Caesar's responsibility.

If we may judge by the small amount of space (in comparison to other subjects treated) which was devoted to the subject of peace in the mass of polemical, expository, and devotional literature produced by Friends in the course of the first two and a half centuries of the Society's existence, the Quaker testimony against war did not figure as a primary concern of the Society in this period. However, allegiance to it remained as an essential requirement for a loyal Quaker.

In the course of the eighteenth century, American Quakerism outstripped the British Society in numbers. It had originated in the efforts of missionaries who, beginning in the mid-1650's, crossed the ocean to publish the "Truth" in the struggling little settlements on the new continent. It grew thereafter with the influx of Quaker immigrants, who left their native land either to escape the religious persecution that lasted until the Glorious Revolution of 1688 or to seek better economic conditions in the New World, and it grew, too, with the conversion of colonists. The American Society of Friends remained, however, closely bound to Quakers in the British Isles, even after the overwhelming majority of Friends were American-born. Whereas ties between the immigrant Mennonites and Amish and their coreligionists in Europe became increasingly tenuous as time passed, it was not until the nineteenth century—when the great westward movement placed Friends in the same frontier conditions that had served to isolate the rural German peace sectaries earlier and when the American Quaker schisms shattered the unity of the Society—that the close Anglo-American Quaker connection was relaxed for a time.

Apart from the continuous and massive Quaker migration that continued for half a century and more (greatly augmented, of course, after Penn had acquired his province in 1682), it was the institution of traveling ministers that did more than anything else to cement ties between the two branches of Quakerism. By the end of the seventeenth century the exchanges had become two-way, for not only did Friends from the British Isles come to visit and encourage the struggling Quaker communities in the New World, but now the latter had grown strong enough to send their own concerned members for pastoral work in Britain. On the roster of ministers visiting America we find, besides George Fox, the names of many other leading British

Friends. The itinerant Quaker minister may, indeed, be reckoned as one of the most effective builders of the spiritual empire of Friends.

Unity among Friends was also reinforced by other agencies. There was, for instance, the voluminous and often intimate correspondence between London Yearly Meeting and the various yearly meetings on the American continent, as well as between individual Friends on different sides of the ocean. Trade relations were usually close between British and American Quaker merchants, who often wielded an influence in their respective societies commensurate with their wealth rather than with their numerical strength. In addition, British and American Friends enjoyed a common religious culture and read the same devotional books and pamphlets. They came to share, too, from early in the eighteenth century on in joint humanitarian endeavors: such concerns as antislavery, penal reform, and the relief of material suffering exercised the conscience and imagination of the more sensitive spirits among Friends equally on both continents. Above all, London Yearly Meeting retained its position as a center of Quakerism as much for American as for British Friends, a position that it continued to enjoy even after the American colonies had established their independence. London's decisions, as we shall see later, were often accepted without argument by American yearly meetings and incorporated into their books of discipline.

The stout English and Welsh yeomen who made up the early generations of Quaker immigrants and, later, their descendants stressed proudly their rights as freeborn English citizens and were ready, in spite of their belief in nonviolence, to assert them even against their fellow Quaker, Proprietor William Penn. A quite different attitude, however, was displayed by the German peasants and craftsmen from whom were drawn the first members of two new religious groups that sprang up on the radical wing of German Pietism in the first quarter of the eighteenth century. These Dunkers and Inspirationists sooner or later were driven to emigrate to the more hospitable lands of the new continent in search of greater religious freedom and economic opportunity. Although they shared with the Quakers the unwillingness to participate in any kind of military activity, they more closely resembled their fellow countrymen of Mennonite and Amish persuasion in their aloofness from the world. German Pietism, like English Quakerism, was essentially a religion of spiritual renewal, but the differing circumstances that gave birth to the two movements left their imprint on the different ways they regarded society outside them. Quakers sought first to conquer, then to leaven the world; the radical

Pietists, like the Mennonites, aimed rather at first saving the individual and thereafter nurturing those who had been redeemed out of the world from contamination by an unredeemable world.

Like the more conservative Pietists, the radicals had emphasized religious feeling at the expense of doctrinal orthodoxy and ecclesiastical authority and had attached great importance to the experience of conversion, which they believed would transform the life patterns of those who underwent it. But intense study of the Bible had also convinced them of the utter depravity of existing state churches. With *sola scriptura* as their touchstone, they called on the converted to separate from the established church, which since Constantine's day had become irremediably corrupted by its connection with government. They called on men to refuse to undertake military service or to swear oaths on the pattern of the early church. The individualistic strain in the radical Pietists' beliefs was strengthened by imbibing the mystical doctrines of the Silesian mystic, Jakob Boehme (1575-1624). Like the sixteenth-century spiritualists, many radical Pietists opposed the formation of new sects. To others, however, some form of organization, an attempt to recreate the primitive Christian community, seemed essential if pristine Christian faith were to be effectively revived.

In 1708 a group of eight of the "Brethren," as the radical Pietists liked to style themselves, took the first step by baptizing themselves by immersion in the river Eder near Schwarzenau in central Germany. This event marked the beginning of the Dunkers, later known officially as the German Baptists and finally, in this century, as the Church of the Brethren. The contacts of the first Brethren with German Mennonites a little earlier, though by no means altogether harmonious, had led to their acceptance of a large part of the Anabaptist view of the state.

A second German separatist group arose half a decade later under the influence of missionaries from the ecstatic French Camisards. Whereas the latter were remarkable for their fighting spirit, their German converts (like their more remote spiritual descendants, the English Shakers) adopted a nonresistant stance. The Community of True Inspiration, which formally came into being in 1714 under the leadership of Eberhard Ludwig Gruber (1665-1728) and Johann Friedrich Rock (1687-1749), was built up around the divinely inspired messages received through the instrumentality of a series of prophets, or *Werkzeuge*. Unlike the Dunkers, who emigrated en masse to Pennsylvania within a quarter of a century after their founding, the Inspirationists did not move to the New World until 1842, after having endured periods of alternate spiritual decline and renewal and suffered frequent harassment from church and state on account of their separatist and pacifist position. In the United States, like several other small, German-speaking immigrant groups with a similar background and outlook, they adopted a community way of life.

Whereas Dunkers and Inspirationists drew leadership as well as rank and file from the lower middle-class and peasantry, the Renewed Moravian Church (whose origins reveal the strong influence of both radical and more conservative Pietism) had a count of the Holy Roman Empire for its founder, although many of its members at the beginning came from the same social background as the radical Pietist sectaries. Nicolaus Ludwig von Zinzendorf (1700-1760), a devout Lutheran, had not at first intended to found a new church; his object was simply the old Pietist goal of establishing an *ecclesiola in ecclesia*. Circumstances, rather than his own inclinations, pushed him finally into separation. This ambivalence was reflected both in his own personality, which combined a broad ecumenicity with a drive toward dominance, and in the church which he founded and led, with its leadership cult and, at the same time, its undenominational missionary evangelism.

In 1722 a group of German-speaking fugitives from Catholic Moravia who were descendants of the suppressed Unity of Brethren (*Unitas Fratrum*), a predominantly Czech denomination that dated back to the middle of the fifteenth century, had crossed the border into Saxony and been given refuge there on the estate of Count Zinzendorf, who granted them permission to erect a settlement they called Herrnhut. The refugees, and their fathers before them, had nurtured the hidden seed of evangelical religion through a century of fierce religious persecution. During the next few years more families succeeded in escaping across the frontier. German sympathizers in increasing numbers joined them and the count in the new religious fellowship that now began to center on Herrnhut. These activities not unnaturally aroused considerable opposition from the Lutheran state church. Outside hostility and pressure from the strong separatist element within the group pushed the count in the direction of an open breach with his church. In 1735, David Nitschmann the carpenter (1696-1772) was consecrated a bishop by the Prussian court preacher, Daniel Ernst Jablonski, one of the two remaining clergymen who held episcopal orders deriving from the Unity of Czech Brethren. This step, taken not long before Nitschmann's departure with a group of Moravian brothers for the newly established British colony of Georgia

15

where a Moravian settlement had recently been set up, marked a turning point in the brotherhood's history—a step that was completed two years later when Zinzendorf himself accepted episcopal rank.

Famous in the centuries to come for their missionary activities throughout the world, the Moravians placed a personal devotion to Christ and the obligation to win souls for him, irrespective of the niceties of doctrine, in the center of their church program. In addition to their German homeland and the overseas mission stations, Moravian communities arose in the British Isles and in Scandinavia, Holland, and Switzerland, as well as among German settlers in Russia. In North America the Moravian Church, after an unsuccessful start in Georgia, took root in the Quaker commonwealth of Pennsylvania and later in North Carolina. The German language of the first generation of immigrants, reinforced by the close ties that, even after Zinzendorf's death, continued for many decades to bind the American provinces to the mother church at Herrnhut, was preserved among their American-born descendants into the nineteenth century. Gradually, however, the partition that existed between the sect and the alien world was dismantled as the process of acculturation proceeded. Among Moravians in America, as on the European continent, the early objection to military service (which seems, anyhow, to have been accepted more as a symbol of, and protection for, otherworldliness than as an integrated element in the group ethos) was jettisoned in the course of their assimilation to society.

In the case of the pacifist sects with which we have dealt in the preceding pages, it was the relaxation of earlier rigorism, brought about by increased acculturation, that eventually led in some instances to a partial or total abandonment of their pacifism. In the case of New England Calvinism, on the other hand, precisely this same tempering of a previously severe rigorism made possible the adoption of pacifism in the first half of the nineteenth century by a number of clergymen and laymen in New England who were not connected with any pacifist sect. Released from the rigid matrix of Calvinist orthodoxy, New England churchmen of Unitarian, Congregationalist, Presbyterian, and Baptist persuasion formed a majority in the membership of both radical and conservative wings of the American peace movement that, starting in 1815, was to lose momentum only in the third quarter of the century.

Their impulse to agitate and organize on behalf of peace, as in the case of other philanthropic reforms of the nineteenth century, derived in large part from the influence of the powerful evangelical movement. But the intellectual roots of American pacifism lay rather in the eighteenth-century Enlightenment. Belief in the possibility of abolishing international conflict and establishing perpetual and universal peace in the world, along with attacks on war as inhumane and contrary to the ideal of human unity and brotherhood, formed the core of the Enlightenment's case against war. Beginning with the projects of the English Quakers, Penn and Bellers, around the turn of the seventeenth century (to go no further back) and continuing on through a series of peace plans proposed by such writers as the Abbé de Saint-Pierre, Jean-Jacques Rousseau, Jeremy Bentham, and Immanuel Kant, the rationalist pacifism of the Enlightenment was reinforced at the end of the eighteenth century by the universalist ideals of the French Revolution. True, the French Revolution with its concomitant French nationalism and imperialist expansionism ushered in a long era of global warfare that lasted almost without interruption from 1792 until 1815. But this, too, contributed to an increased desire for peace in warweary Europe and America. Now, while conservative peace men campaigned against the custom of war, their more radical colleagues in America (as in Britain where, at first, Friends formed the backbone of the peace movement) attacked war as sin and urged Christians to refuse participation in it, after the manner of the Quakers and other peace sectaries.

In the first half of the nineteenth century the declining Anglo-American Quaker connection was even in some measure replaced by a flourishing transatlantic pacifist communication that formed merely one section of a wider transatlantic community of the reform-minded. Beginning with the years 1814-1816, which saw the emergence, independently of each other, of the major peace societies in the United States and Britain (nondenominational but religiously motivated), the peace movements in both countries, despite minor differences in emphasis or divergencies in outlook, shared a common literature, common policies, and common activities. In periods of tension between the two countries (in 1838-1846, for instance), there was joint action among their peace men to try to prevent war from breaking out. On both sides of the Atlantic, too, there was a widespread belief that the new American Republic had a special role to play in bringing about world peace. In 1846, with the founding of Elihu Burritt's League of Universal Brotherhood, a common Anglo-American peace organization with a membership pledge renouncing participation in all wars actually came into existence, although it lasted only a few years.

The third quarter of the nineteenth century witnessed the decline of the old peace movement on both sides of the Atlantic. Close collaboration continued as before between the London Peace Society and its

17

counterpart, the American Peace Society. But these bodies, having become increasingly conservative and uncreative, now lacked the energy to pursue in an era of *Realpolitik* the kind of peace crusade that they had led half a century earlier. As for radical pacifism, which renounced all war instead of merely seeking the more moderate goal of war's ultimate abolition, scarcely any organized form of it existed at this time. The Crimean War in Britain and the Civil War in the United States may each be considered a watershed in the evolution of the peace movement in these lands.

Such, in outline, is the story of the transplantation of the pacifist impulse and idea from the Old to the New World in the centuries before a world pacifist movement came gropingly into existence out of the holocaust of the First World War. It would not be complete, however, without passing mention of the quasi-pacifism professed by certain apocalyptic sects. The Adventists and most of the late nineteenth-century pentecostal groups, as well as the International Bible Students (Jehovah's Witnesses), constituted a native American growth; Christadelphians and the Plymouth Brethren, on the other hand, originated in Great Britain in the first half of the last century. Like the selective objectors of the twentieth century (though on the basis of quite different premises), members of these sects chose to stand aside from certain wars. Their tenets forbade participation in the strife generated by the kingdoms of this world; they meant to conserve their combatancy instead for the eventual struggle that would usher in Christ's kingdom on earth.

American pacifism, then, was rooted in the intellectual soil of Europe. From the beginning the peace sects and, later, the nondenominational peace movement that sprang up in the nineteenth century—in both its conservative and radical branches—continued to nurture ties with the Old World. Yet the fresh environment, the new physical setting as well as the changed mental context, subtly and gradually produced alterations in both the expression and organization of American pacifism. This process of acculturation over the years up to 1914 forms the theme of the chapters that follow.

Part One

*Pacifism in Colonial America
and the American Revolution*

"We are agreed as follows concerning the sword: The sword is ordained of God outside the perfection of Christ. It punishes and puts to death the wicked, and guards and protects the good. . . . In the perfection of Christ, however, only the ban is used for a warning and for the excommunication of the one who has sinned, without putting the flesh to death,—simply the warning and the command to sin no more."

—From Article 6 of the Schleitheim Confession of Faith (1527)

"There is hardly one frame of government in the world so ill-designed by its first founders that in good hands, [it] would not do well enough. . . . Governments rather depend upon men than men upon governments. Let men be good and the government cannot be bad: if it be ill, they will cure it. But if men be bad, let the government be never so good, they will endeavour to warp and spoil it to their turn."

—From William Penn, *Preface to the First Frame of Government for Pennsylvania* (1682)

Chapter 1

The Society of Friends
in the Colonial Period outside
Pennsylvania

The peace testimony of the colonial Quakers was, we have seen, as much an outgrowth of the parent society in Britain as were the other elements of the faith, which the "First Publishers of Truth" brought with them on their journey across the ocean. This Anglo-American Quaker connection remained lively and close well into the nineteenth century. Yet, despite the manifold similarities in belief and practice, the peace witness of the colonial Quakers was never an exact reflection of that of Friends back in Britain, for in this New World the Quaker pioneers, like their fellow citizens of other faiths, had to face a complex of factors—geographical, political, economic, and religious—differing in many important respects from that existing back home. For the Quakers, a greater share in affairs of state (and this not only in Pennsylvania) and also, in many cases, greater insecurity in daily life introduced new problems in their attempt to create a fellowship of men and women dedicated to the achievement of a society without violence.

Quakerism was brought to the New World in the second half of the 1650's. Within a few decades adherents of the "Truth" (as its followers boldly called their faith) were to be found organized in compact meetings in most of the Atlantic coast colonies as well as in a number of the islands of the British West Indies. Important Quaker settlements soon arose in the existing colonies of Massachusetts, Plymouth, New Hampshire, Rhode Island, New York (then New Netherlands), Maryland, Virginia, and the Carolinas and also, with their opening to colonization, in New Jersey and Pennsylvania (along with Delaware). In the eighteenth century small Quaker groups came into being in Georgia as well as in Maine, to which Friends had found their way in the previous century. Only in Connecticut did Quakerism meet with scarcely any response during this period. Indeed, "by the middle of the eighteenth century there were more Quakers in the Western hemisphere than in Great Britain,"[1] even though by this date the early

---

[1] Rufus M. Jones, *The Quakers in the American Colonies*, p. xv. At the end of the colonial period there were probably about 50,000 Quakers on the American continent out of a total population of approximately 2,500,000.

missionary vigor that had aimed at bringing the whole world speedily into the spirit of Christian truth had given way to the cultivation of a narrower sectarian ethos, which sought to preserve intact the virtues of a "peculiar people."

Among the colonial Quakers, as in Britain, strict adherence to the peace testimony was maintained by the imposition of sanctions against those who deviated from it. Those members who strayed and would not express regret for their offense were dealt with in the same way as those who transgressed other precepts of the discipline, expulsion from the Society being the final step against any who remained impervious to admonition and exhortation. At this time there were still very few Friends who urged that, although pacifism should remain a collective witness of the Society, it would be better for the individual to decide exactly what stand he should take in regard to military service or self-defense. A nonpacifist Quaker like Penn's secretary, James Logan, or Anthony Benezet, the pacifist expatriate Frenchman who favored a relaxation of the discipline in regard to the peace testimony, remained isolated figures, and it was not until the twentieth century that the Society finally came to adopt their position (at least unofficially).

The main issue dominating the history of the Quaker peace testimony in colonial America was, of course, military service. Outside Pennsylvania, conscription for the local militia was in force in all the provinces for almost the whole period. Only in Rhode Island did the law give Friends complete exemption. Elsewhere, exemption, where provided for, was granted only on terms that were usually unacceptable to them, for Quakers would neither pay the required fine in commutation of service which they believed to be wrong in itself nor hire another man to perform it in their stead, as the law also sometimes permitted.[2] Obduracy of this kind often brought distraint of property—frequently far in excess of the amount of the fine—and sometimes imprisonment. However, there existed considerable variation in the rigor with which the law was enforced. In times of peace, and in small communities where the sincerity of Quaker objections

---

[2] Of course, Friends did not always live up to their principles in this as in other respects. To give just one example, in 1760 we find New England Y. M. lamenting: "We are sorrowfully affected, by the answers to the queries, that some Friends have failed in the maintenance of our Christian testimony against wars and fighting, by joining with others to hire substitutes, and by the payment of money to exempt themselves from personal service in the militia. . . . Let therefore the care of Friends, in their several monthly-meetings, be exerted to prevent any contributions for hiring substitutes, or other methods of exempting themselves from the militia, inconsistent with our well-known testimony" (The Book of Discipline [1785], p. 148).

was well known to their neighbors, law enforcement was mild, and delinquents often escaped without penalty. Indeed, the drills of the militia were at times more social than martial affairs. But, when a war scare occurred or when actual fighting had broken out, the Quakers often suffered considerable hardship as a result of their refusal to fight; and such occasions were not rare in seventeenth- and eighteenth-century America, for, with the Indian border not too far from any of the settlements and with the long coastline and the Caribbean islands open to attack from Britain's European enemies, whether Dutch or Spanish or French, and from marauding privateers who were also active in periods of nominal peace, war conditions were present most of the time. On such occasions, too, men of military age might be called out by special decree to participate in expeditions against the enemy outside their province.

Periodic musterings of the local militia and occasional summonses to active service at a distance did not exhaust the military demands that might be made of young Quaker males. They could also be required to take their turn in armed watches to guard against foreign invaders or indigenous marauders and could be called up for labor in building fortifications and military encampments. Moreover, in the New England coastal areas Quakers, especially those who had chosen the sea as their career, were sometimes subjected to impressment into the royal navy. Occasionally, too, cases are recorded where soldiers, coming under the influence of Quaker ideas while in the service, developed a conscientious objection to further military duties.[3]

[3] One of the most curious instances of this kind is contained in the memoirs of the eighteenth-century English-born Friend, Elizabeth Ashbridge (1713-1775), printed in the next century in *The Friends' Library*, vol. IV. She had emigrated to America as an indentured servant and had there married a young schoolmaster, who proved to be a hard drinker, an irreligionist, and a frequenter of bad company. The couple eventually settled in New Jersey, where she was converted to Quakerism and was recognized as a minister in the Society. Her religious views were, however, very unpopular with her husband, who ridiculed them and subjected his wife to blows and oaths on their account. Her attempts to reform him proved unavailing, and her efforts to interest him in Friends appeared at the time to be without effect. At last, in 1741 during a drinking bout in Burlington, her husband enlisted as a common soldier to fight in the expedition against Spanish-held Cuba. The rest of the story may be told in Elizabeth's own words: "I have since had cause to believe that he was benefited by the rash act, as in the army, he did what he could not at home; he suffered for the testimony of Truth. When they came to prepare for an engagement, he refused to fight; he was whipped and brought before the general, who asked him why he enlisted if he would not fight. 'I did it,' said he, 'in a drunken frolic, when the devil had the better of me; but now my judgment is convinced I ought not to fight, neither will I, whatever I suffer. I have but one life, and you may take that if you please, for I'll never take up arms.' He adhered to this resolution. By their cruel usage of him in consequence, he was

23

Quakers who were not liable to direct military service also had to face problems in adjusting their pacifist beliefs to the demands of Caesar. Here, perhaps, taxation was the most trying issue.[4] From the beginning, as we have seen, most Friends had felt that there was nothing inconsistent with their peace testimony in paying what they called taxes "in the mixture," that is, taxes of which only a part went for the support of war. They dutifully paid ordinary taxes to the government in time of war, too. There was less unanimity, however, in the case of special war taxes, where it was known that the whole sum paid would be used to carry on war. "George Fox himself paid war taxes," and so did a number of other leading Friends in the early days. Others refused. (And, of course, payment of any kind of assessment that could be at all construed as an alternative to direct military service was forbidden to Friends.[5]) The tax issue in its relation to the peace testimony was, as we shall see, to be vigorously debated among colonial Friends, some of whom advocated nonpayment not only of war taxes but of mixed ones, too. Finally, in the American Revolution, nonpayment of most taxes to an administration engaged in waging war against the traditionally established government became the official policy of the whole Society.

In their businesses many Friends took great care to avoid all support of warmaking, although there were still others whose laxness in this regard became a matter of concern to the Quaker meetings and had to be dealt with by them. The chief offenses were the manufacturing and trading of articles of war, the arming of vessels, either owned by members of the Society or used for shipping Quaker goods, and involvement in privateering.

Behavior in consonance with the peaceful principles to which the Society laid claim was demanded of every individual member. Naturally, since American Quakerism was a society made up of ordinary human beings, and not saints (although it did, indeed, produce several saints of the caliber of John Woolman), harmony among its members and between members and nonmembers was not always maintained. But members of the Society were expected to show an example of nonviolence in their daily lives, even if lapses from this high

---

so much disabled that the general sent him to Chelsea Hospital, near London. Within nine months afterwards he died at this place, and I hope made a good end" (p. 22).

4 See Ernest R. Bromley, "Did Early Friends Pay War Taxes?" *Friends Intelligencer*, 16 Oct. 1948, pp. 591-93.

5 See, e.g., a minute of New England Y. M. in 1762, *The Book of Discipline* (1785), p. 148.

standard would inevitably occur.[6] And, if the dispute were one between fellow members, Friends were forbidden to go to law until every attempt had been made to settle the affair by arbitration.

However, at least during this period, Quaker pacifism differed from the Anabaptist-Mennonite variety in its positive attitude toward the nonmilitary functions of the state. Not merely in Pennsylvania during the years of Quaker rule, but in Rhode Island, and much more briefly in New Jersey, Maryland, and the Carolinas, Friends participated in the government and legislature. In this sphere the practice of the Society in America during this period differed radically from that of its parent Society in Britain, which, as a body of religious dissenters, was by the law of the land effectively excluded from all part in government. But politics meant compromise, and we shall find, both in Pennsylvania and in the other colonies where Friends had access to power, that their peace testimony became to some extent adjusted to the demands of expediency. Still, they continued as a body to bear witness to a nonviolent way of life.

Throughout the colonial period the question of self-defense against Indian attack, especially where Quakers were settled in frontier districts, constituted not merely an academic exercise in pacifist dialectic but an issue that all might be called upon to face at some moment in their lives. The same was true for the Caribbean islands, where the sometimes more bloodthirsty pirate or privateer took the place of the marauding Indian. The history of Quaker Indian policy falls outside the scope of the present study except insofar as it bears directly on their pacifism.[7] The essence of this policy, both as carried out by individual Friends and as expressed in the actions of the Quaker regime in Pennsylvania, lay in their desire to deal justly with the Indian peoples, giving a fair price for their lands and settling only with their prior assent, dealing equitably with them in trade, and refraining from corrupting them by the sale of hard liquor. When Pennsylvania de-

[6] See, e.g., the following declaration made to his meeting by a Rhode Island Friend in 1767: "A man came to me in my field and tho' I desired him to keep off, yet [he] made an attempt to beat or abuse me. To prevent which I suddenly and with too much warmth pushed him from me with the rake I was leaning on, which act of mine as it did not manifest to that Christian patience and example in suffering trials becoming my profession I therefore freely condemn it and desire that I may be enabled for the future to suffer patiently any abuse or whatever else I may be tried with and also desire Friends to continue their watchful care over me." Caroline Hazard, *The Narrangansett Friends' Meeting in the XVIII Century*, p. 101.

[7] See Rayner Wickersham Kelsey, *Friends and the Indians 1655-1917*, pp. 19-24, 27-29, 38-47, 51, 52, 55-62, 70-74, for Quaker-Indian relations outside Pennsylvania during the period up to 1775.

parted from this policy (against the wishes of its Quaker legislators), bitter warfare eventually followed.

The American Indians with whom colonial Friends came into contact apparently remained unmoved by the Quaker message, despite occasional attempts by men like William Penn and John Woolman to reach them. Although there were Indians who showed some understanding of the indwelling God of the Quakers ("the good Spirit"), no converts were made. At times Quakers not only attempted to let their actions toward the Indians explain the nature of Quaker pacifism without the intermediacy of words, but tried also to expound the nature of the Society's nonviolent faith to them. A moving example of this latter approach is recorded in the autobiography of Samuel Bownas (1676-1753), a traveling minister, who in 1702 found himself in jail on Long Island (N.Y.) for speaking out against the Church of England. During his incarceration he was visited by "an Indian King" and three of his chiefs, who were able to converse in English. When the king inquired of Bownas what the differences were between Quakers and other Christians, Bownas sought among other things to elucidate the Quaker peace testimony. Christians outside the Society, he told his inquirers,

... held it *lawful* to kill and destroy their enemies; but we cannot think that good and right in us; but rather endeavour to overcome our enemies with courteous and friendly offices and kindness, and to assuage their wrath by mildness and persuasion, and bring them to consider the injury they are doing to such as can't in conscience revenge themselves again. He assented, *that this was good: but who can do it?* said he; *when my enemies seek my life, how can I do other than use my endeavour to destroy them in my own defence?* My answer was, That unless we were under the government of a better spirit than our enemies, we could not do it; but if we are under the government of the good Spirit, which seeks not to destroy men's lives, but to save them, and teaches us to do good for evil and to forgive injuries, then we can submit to *Providence*, putting our trust in the great God to save us from the violence and wrath of our enemies. The King said, *Indeed this is very good; but do you do thus when provoked by your enemies?* I said, sundry of our Friends had done so, and been saved from the rage of their enemies, who have confessed our Friends to be good men. *Ay,* said he, *they are good indeed; for if all came into this way, there would then be no more need of war, nor killing one the other to enlarge their kingdoms, nor one nation want to overcome another.* I then asked him, if this was not a right principle; and what would much add to the happiness of mankind? They all four said, *it was very good indeed; but feared few would embrace this doctrine.* I said, all things have their beginnings; and 'tis now our duty to embrace this truth, hoping that others by this example may do the same. They lifted up their eyes as a token of their assent, shewing by their words their desire that this good spirit might prevail in the world: *Then,* said they, *Things will go well.*[8]

The records of the period contain plentiful illustrations of the kind of nonviolent approach to personal defense that Bownas describes here as being the practice of members of his Society. Far more frequently than his coreligionists back in Britain, the American Friend was to find himself in situations of potential violence that would test this belief.[9]

Quaker pacifists at their best, whether in America or in Europe, bore witness to their beliefs in both a negative and a positive fashion—in the one case, by an uncompromising refusal to meet the military demands of Caesar and, in the other, by an outflow of love for their fellowmen, whether heathen Indians or Christians belonging to "enemy" nations. This witness remained circumscribed in its dimensions, however. There was little attempt, until the arrival of John Woolman and a handful of Friends who shared his outlook, to think through the social aspects of the peace testimony, to understand how Friends' protest against war and their refusal to resist attack by violence were related to shortcomings in the existing political and social order, in particular to the evil of slavery and to inequalities in wealth. With the exception of the practical experiment in peaceable government carried out in Pennsylvania, the American Quaker communities of the colonial period failed to examine the possibilities of creating a peaceful international order; no works were produced on this continent to parallel the schemes for international peace of the English Quakers, William Penn and John Bellers. In neither Britain nor America at this time had thinking within the Society matured to the point of exploring ways and means of setting up a nonviolent technique of dealing with aggression, whether inside society or from outside invasion.

Sources for the history of Quaker pacifism in the colonial period are

---

[8] *An Account of the Life and Ministry of Samuel Bownas,* pp. 79-81.

[9] The journals of visiting ministers from Britain (e.g., those of Thomas Story and Thomas Chalkley, who traveled in the West Indies and on the American continent during the first half of the eighteenth century, which have been used extensively in this chapter) also provide examples of a courageous upholding of Quaker nonviolence in situations of conflict.

27

plentiful enough, but (except for those relating to the Pennsylvania experiment) they do not easily lend themselves to a chronological treatment, nor can they readily be used to give an overall picture of the colonial scene. Each colony, after all, enjoyed a completely autonomous existence, dependent only upon the mother country; each had its own separate constitution and political and religious institutions, though derived from the same British roots; each moved to a large extent along separate lines of historical and economic evolution. Yet common factors there certainly were, factors which, developing in the course of the eighteenth century, led eventually with the war as catalyst to the creation of a united Republic out of these disparate provinces. In colonial Quakerism, likewise, there were common threads present which knit the Society throughout the different colonies into a community with, in this case, virtually one mode of worship and similar ways of life. On the other hand, here also the divergence in development, which dominated the overall American picture, was mirrored in the life of the Society of Friends. Autonomous organizations sprang up in New England, New York, Pennsylvania (together with Delaware and New Jersey), Maryland, Virginia, and North Carolina. In these areas the peace witness of Friends, though it followed roughly the same pattern in each, can best be illustrated by separate treatment. This, therefore, will be the method adopted in the more detailed account given below.

I

Probably the first Quakers to reach the American continent were two English women missionaries, Mary Fisher and Ann Austin, who landed in Boston on 11 July 1656. The alarmed magistrates drove them from the town within a month after their arrival. But on 7 August, a couple of days after their expulsion, eight more Quakers from England succeeded in making a landing. Despite the passing, soon after, of the first of a series of anti-Quaker laws of mounting severity that the Massachusetts colony (followed by its sister colony, Plymouth) directed against the "cursed sect," converts began to be made among the local people. Spreading also to unorthodox Rhode Island in the following year, the vigorous new faith, strong in its belief that it held the truth that would soon peaceably conquer the whole world, continued to gather new adherents in the Puritans' New England stronghold until "by the year 1660 . . . the whole southern part . . . was . . . honeycombed with Quakerism."[10] Neither the heavy fines, whippings of men

[10] Jones, The Quakers, p. 62.

28

and women stripped to the waist, ear croppings and tongue borings, nor even the death penalty imposed by law in 1658, which took the lives of three men and one woman in the course of the subsequent two years, were effective in stemming the tide of conversion. The year 1661 marked the foundation of New England Yearly Meeting, which still exists today. In that year, too, the most savage phase of persecution came to an end with an order procured by Quakers in England from King Charles II preventing any further executions for professing Quakerism (though it did not stop the passing of the barbarous "Cart and Whip Acts" of 1661 and 1662). Apart from a brief resuscitation of persecution in the years 1675-1677, the Quakers in Massachusetts won virtual toleration after the death of Governor John Endecott in 1665; and in the early 1670's, stimulated by the visit of George Fox and several other leading English Friends to this continent in 1672, Quakerism underwent considerable expansion throughout all of New England (except in Connecticut, which proved infertile soil for the new sect).

In Massachusetts the Puritan theocracy, at least in the beginning, successfully excluded the nonelect from all share in government. Thus, even after the cessation of persecution, Quakers there were never faced, as they were to be in neighboring Rhode Island and later in Pennsylvania, with the problems involved in squaring Christian pacifism with the requirements of Christian magistracy. Only remotely, by some vague and confused association of Quakerism with subversive Anabaptism in the minds of populace, priesthood, and magistracy alike, had their pacifism been responsible for the ferocious legislation that the civil authorities erected against them at the beginning in their unsuccessful attempt to exclude the sect altogether from the Bay colony. The roots of persecution lay elsewhere, above all in the challenge which early Quakerism presented to the church establishment in the colony.

After the fires of persecution had died down and the ardent enthusiasm of the first missionary effort had ebbed, the Massachusetts Quakers, who numbered over 3,000 in the first half of the eighteenth century, were content to pursue their way of life as a "peculiar people," worshipping God in their own fashion and living quiet lives apart from affairs of state. Compulsory service in the militia seems to have presented a serious problem only in wartime or during an invasion scare; at other times Friends usually either paid the comparatively small sums imposed as fines for nonattendance at drills or allowed their property to be distrained for failure to pay these fines (for among most New England Friends payment of commutation money was regarded as a dereliction of duty). Thus, in August 1675 during King Philip's War when an Indian attack on Boston was feared, we read, for instance, of "several men, some whereof are Quakers, [who] will not go out on command, and for their disobedience thereunto, are forced to run the gauntlet."[11] A second period of crisis came early in the next century after the outbreak of the War of the Spanish Succession, when preparations were on foot for an invasion of Canada from New England. A law was passed by the commonwealth of Massachusetts imposing a term of imprisonment on any who refused to bear arms and who were also unwilling to pay a fine in lieu of service; in addition, the law provided that delinquents were subsequently to be bound out to work for such time as was necessary to cover the cost of fine and imprisonment.

One of those Quakers who suffered under the law has left an account of his experiences. John Smith was born of Quaker parents in Dartmouth, Bristol County (Mass.), in 1681. In June 1703, then aged 22, Smith received a summons to join the militia, which he refused. At first, no action was taken against him. But in January of the following year, a year of intense Indian warfare, when the Massachusetts clergy were proclaiming the Indian atrocities to be God's way of punishing the colony's inhabitants for suffering Quakers to live in their midst—when, therefore, hostility toward the still unpopular sect was widespread—John Smith and a second young objector, Thomas Maccomber, were tried and fined at Bristol. Upon their refusal to pay this fine, the magistrate first attempted, unsuccessfully, to hire them out for up to four years in order to cover the cost and then sentenced them to hard labor in the fort at Boston for as long as would be necessary for them to work off the fine and incidental expenses.

While in prison at Bristol, the two men were visited by the weighty traveling minister from Britain, Thomas Story (1662-1742), and another Friend from Rhode Island. Story attempted to intervene on their behalf with the judge, Colonel Nathaniel Byfield. The judge proved not unfriendly, although he felt that only "ignorance, and a perverse nature," could lead anyone to refuse to fight against such dangerous enemies as the French and Indians had proved themselves to be. At the trial Story spoke on behalf of the two Friends. In reply to Colonel Byfield's query why Friends who willingly paid ordinary taxes

---

[11] *Narratives of the Indian Wars 1675-1699*, 1952 edn., p. 44. "Running the gauntlet" was a form of punishment frequently used by the Indians, in the course of which a man could actually be beaten to death. The quotation is from a contemporary eyewitness account, "The Present State of New-England with Respect to the Indian War."

could not pay in this instance, Story drew a distinction between a "general tax," which Christ had required his followers to pay regardless of the fact that Caesar might apply a part for war purposes, and a tax imposed in lieu of personal military service, an activity which Quakers believed to be contrary to their Christian profession. For their part, the young men stated that "'it was not obstinacy, but duty to God, according to their consciences, and religious persuasions, which prevailed with them to refuse to bear arms, or learn war.'"

Soon after arriving at Boston, Smith and Maccomber were sent to the fort, where they were supposed "to work as pioneers." Despite their unwillingness to perform labor of a military nature, they were on the whole treated well as prisoners: "the people behaved civilly towards me," Smith writes, "as believing I acted from a religious principle."

Story had followed the two men to Boston, and shortly after his arrival he paid a visit, along with two other Friends, to the governor of Massachusetts. To him he endeavored to explain the basis of Friends' objections to war. The governor was sympathetic, but he told Story "'that he was no disputant about religion; . . . to tell you the truth, said he, seeing the judges have given such a judgment, I cannot tell how to dispense with it; especially now in time of war, when every body thinks there is both so much need of help, and just cause of war.'" When Story mentioned the prophecy concerning the time when swords would be beaten into plowshares, the governor replied: "'That day . . . is not come; for you see many nations are at war at this time.'" In any event, he continued, if he were to release the young men before their time was up, he would set the whole community against him. If the judge had erred in sentencing them, then recourse should be had to the law to rectify the mistake. But we are poor people, Story now insisted, and cannot afford the costly process of appeal; we believe that you do possess the authority to release them if you wish. To this objection the governor responded as before, "'that the country would be about his ears if he should do that; but, said he, it is a harmless thing to work at the castle; they need not fight there.'" Story protested, "'that is an erection for war, and we cannot be active in such works as may be thought necessary there.'" Unfortunately, neither these arguments nor the petition Story later composed asking for the prisoners' release succeeded in gaining their object. The men remained in the fort for four months more until the governor finally relented and ordered them to be sent home.[12]

[12] John Smith, *A Narrative of Some Sufferings for His Christian Peaceable Testi-*

31

Thanks to young Smith's own narrative and the journal of the older Friend, Thomas Story, we can follow the details of the debate between Quaker conscience and the military establishment. Normally, as Henry J. Cadbury has written, "while today we are kept carefully informed of Friends in prison for refusal of military service, cases of the same sort two centuries ago existed uncollected and unlisted. A mere accident brings now one or another to our attention."[13] One such case, uncovered by Professor Cadbury himself, is that of Hatsell O'Kelley, a "husbandman" from the village of Yarmouth on Cape Cod who in 1748, at the end of the War of the Austrian Succession, was drafted for military service. However, the captain "by whose warrant he was impressed" was unable to "find any estate of the said Hatsell O'Kelley's whereby to make distress upon for said ten pounds," which was the penalty imposed for his refusal to serve. O'Kelley was therefore sentenced to six months' imprisonment in the Barnstable County jail and assessed the costs of prosecution. Nevertheless, O'Kelley did not have to languish for long in prison, for the monthly meeting at Sandwich raised the necessary funds to obtain his release. This meeting, at least in this period, apparently had no scruples about the payment of fines in lieu of service.

Quakers in the seacoast districts of New England, who often chose the sea rather than the farm as their source of livelihood, were subject to the danger of impressment into the British navy, as well as to the other perils of the seafaring life of that day. In time of war the chances of impressment occurring were, of course, greatly increased. Again, it is the young Quaker, John Smith, who provides us with a fully authenticated example of the impressment of a Quaker into the royal navy. Smith, after being released from his Boston prison, joined the crew of a ship bound for London that was owned by a well-to-do New England Quaker merchant. All went well on the voyage until

---

mony, pp. 6-10; A Journal of the Life of Thomas Story, pp. 264-70, 309-12, 339. Jones (The Quakers, p. 150) cites details from the minutes of New England Y. M. for 1712 concerning four young Massachusetts Quakers who were imprisoned for refusing to serve in the expedition to Canada of the previous year. Two of the men were well treated, but two, who had been imprisoned in Boston fort, were given such "hard usage" after they had been "thence conveyed by force on board transport under ye command of Major Roberton" that, as a result, one of them, John Terry, died "within twenty-four hours after their return to Boston." During the Seven Years War, in 1759 (the year the British captured Quebec), an act was passed by the Massachusetts assembly "for the speedy levying of soldiers for an intended expedition against Canada," in which Quakers were specifically exempted by name from the draft. They were, however, to be additionally taxed in a rather roundabout manner for the privilege of such exemption.

[13] Friends Intelligencer, 23 July 1949, p. 409 ("Letter from the Past—102" by "Now and Then").

April 1704 when, on arrival at Plymouth (England), they were met by British men-of-war who seized Smith and a second young Quaker sailor, Thomas Anthony, for service in the royal fleet. Several days later the vessel to which they were assigned met with a French ship. "When they were going to engage," Smith writes, "they placed us to a gun, and commanded us to fight, but we told them we could not, for Christ and the apostles spoke to the contrary; but they not regarding what we said, hauled us about deck to make us work, but we signified we could not on any such account." Realizing that they might inadvertently be trapped into some seemingly innocent but compromising action, the two Quaker seamen were careful not to do anything that might be construed as compliance with the fighting. Their conduct soon earned them the anger of one of the lieutenants, who ordered that they be given the "cat." As they were being whipped in this barbarous fashion, which was customary in the British navy during the eighteenth century, Smith prayed for his persecutors. Later, a rough but kindly boatswain's mate remarked to them concerning their punishment: "You have been beat enough to kill an ox." Their trials, however, were by no means over, for, all the while the ship was involved in further engagements, the captain and officers continued their endeavors to make the Quakers work. "They sent for us to make points for reefing the sails," Smith relates in one place, "which I refusing to do, some mocked and scoffed, while others filled with envy and malice, could scarce keep their hands from me." The two men were not released from the ship until over a year later when the captain, allowing them to go ashore at Plymouth, made it clear that he never wanted to see his two recalcitrant tars back on board again. English Friends cared for the young men, who needed time to recuperate after their thirteen months of rough treatment in Her Majesty's navy. In London, which they visited before returning to America, they lodged with old Thomas Lurting, the former fighting sailor turned Quaker.[14]

We do not know how many other Quaker John Smiths over the years were seized on board ship and taken off to serve in the royal navy, nor whether some yielded to threats and ill-treatment and others remained firm in upholding their Society's peaceable testimony. That impressment, at least in wartime, remained a peril for the Quaker sailors of New England is certain. One writer has unearthed nineteen certificates of membership issued by local meetings during the Seven Years War to Friends "bound on a whale voyage" in an attempt to protect them against impressment or at least to provide them,

[14] Smith, *A Narrative*, pp. 10-18.

if taken, with evidence to show that their protest against fighting was a genuine one.[15]

The onus of opposing military requirements and naval impressments was carried by the younger men. But all Quakers might at some moment of their lives have to face the issue of war taxes or have to decide what stand they should take in case of Indian attack on themselves and their families. In regard to special war taxes, whether intended for raising troops and war equipment or for paying for the erection of fortifications, no unanimity existed among New England Friends. There were certainly some who refused to pay and as a consequence had their property distrained or, if this were insufficient to cover the amount demanded, were thrown into jail. But many more, it would seem, paid in good conscience (the matter was finally left undecided by yearly meeting), and the example of such weighty English visitors as Thomas Story, who urged Friends to pay without compunction, must have exercised an influence in the direction of compliance.

In 1702 during the sessions of New England Yearly Meeting, discussion at one point turned to a minute concerning "what Friends might do, in case there should be a lay or tax laid upon the inhabitants for building some fortifications, and to provide men and arms for the security of the island [of Rhode Island]." A British visitor, John Richardson (1666-1753), found himself appealed to by Friends present to explain how the Society in England dealt with this knotty problem. New England Friends, one of them said (according to Richardson's account), "looked upon themselves but as the daughter, and Friends . . . in old England as their mother, and they were willing to act consistent with us as far as they could, and would know how we did there in that matter, whether we could pay to that tax which was for carrying on a vigorous war against France?" Despite Richardson's obvious reluctance to get involved in the debate, Friends remained insistent on hearing his views, refusing to proceed further with the discussion until he had spoken. "At last," Richardson goes on, "when I could not well do otherwise, I signified to that large Meeting, that I had heard the matter debated both in superior and inferior meetings, and privately, and the most general result was this; Friends did not see an effectual door opened to avoid the thing, that tax being mixed [i.e., in England] with other taxes; although many Friends are not so easy as they could desire." However, he added, "there is a great disparity between our circumstances and yours here." Above all, in Rhode Island at least, he told them, "you have . . . a great share in the

15 Robert J. Leach, "Nantucket Quakerism 1661-1763" (MS in F.H.L.S.C.), chap. XIII.

government" and may thus be able in this part of the country to prevent the imposition of a tax of the kind now being discussed. Finally, he concluded by warning American Friends not to be overeager to look to the parent society for a pattern of behavior, which might actually not be applicable in the transatlantic environment; instead, he advised them, "mind your own way in the Truth, and look not out."[16]

For the problem of Indian defense, indeed, the practice of British Friends could offer little that was immediately relevant, except in the way of general principle. Living as a small minority among the hardheaded Puritan settlers, Quakers in New England became enmeshed in the Puritans' often unfair and harsh policies toward the indigenous population, the unhappy results of which constituted a negation of Friends' methods in dealing with these peoples. When the Indians in retaliation went on the warpath and proceeded to burn outlying settlements and massacre their inhabitants, threatening as well the less accessible towns and villages, Quakers in these areas were as much exposed to atrocities as their non-Quaker fellow settlers. This Indian danger lessened as the eighteenth century passed by, but in earlier days Indian attacks occurred periodically. So far as the somewhat exiguous record indicates, Friends—with a few exceptions—remained loyal to their peace testimony despite the temptation to resort to arms in self-defense, and their peaceable demeanor seems on most occasions to have been recognized by the Indians, who left them alone. During King Philip's War (1675-1676), for instance, we hear of the visiting minister, William Edmundson (1627-1712), traveling without weapons up and down the country, which was then infested by hostile Indians on the warpath. Despite frequent scalpings of whites and the burning of homesteads, the unarmed Quakers whom he visited were apparently not harmed.[17]

We know more about the situation of Friends during the Indian troubles of 1704 because two English-born Friends, Thomas Chalkley (1675-1741) and Thomas Story, were traveling in the area at this time. "It was a dismal time indeed in those parts," writes Story, "for no man knew, in an ordinary way . . . on lying down to sleep, but his first waking might be in eternity, by a salutation in the face with a hatchet, or a bullet from the gun of a merciless savage." Most of the white settlers went on about their business during the day with their guns cocked ready for immediate use, and at night they took refuge within the fortified garrisons established up and down the country. "And some professing truth [i.e., Quakers] also went into the same

[16] An Account of the Life of John Richardson, pp. 128, 129.
[17] A Journal of the Life of William Edmundson, sec. IX.

with their guns, and some without them." The matter was debated in meetings: "the unfaithful," records Story, "not being content in their unfaithfulness, nor satisfied in their forts and guns, sought to justify themselves in that unworthy practice, condemning the faithful as wilful and presumptuous." But on the whole, according to the testimony of the two visiting Friends, their coreligionists refused to resort to arms in their defense and were left untouched by the Indians. One of the Friends whom Chalkley visited at this time told him of his own experiences.

> As he was at work in his field the Indians saw, and called him, and he went to them. They told him, that they had no quarrel with the Quakers, for they were a quiet, peaceable people and hurt nobody, and that therefore none should hurt them. But they said, that the Presbyterians in these parts had taken away their lands, and some of their lives, and would now, if they could, destroy all the Indians.

On the other hand, we hear of another Quaker living nearby, who had decided to carry a gun, being shot and killed by Indians as he went to his work along with a second Quaker, who was unarmed and unharmed by them. "When they knew that the young man they had killed was a Friend," writes Story, "they seemed to be sorry for it, but blamed him for carrying a gun: for they knew the Quakers would not fight, nor do them any harm; and therefore, by carrying a gun, they took him for an enemy."[18]

The most striking incident which took place among the Massachusetts Quakers at this time was that involving the Doe (or Dowe) family. Mary and Henry Doe lived, together with their small children and Mary's widowed mother, in an isolated farmstead in the forest not far from the town of Salisbury, "a place of as much seeming danger as any: being within pistol-shot of a great swamp, and thicket, where Indians formerly inhabited." All three were Friends. At first, they refrained from seeking shelter at night in the nearest fortified place, as their non-Quaker neighbors were doing. But after a while the old lady became increasingly nervous and eventually persuaded the young couple, who apparently were only partially convinced of the rightness of this step, to accompany her to spend the nights in the stockade

---

[18] Chalkley relates a similar story of two Quaker farmers who for a long time refused to follow the example of their neighbors and arm themselves when they went to work in the fields. Finally, yielding to fear, they decided to take guns with them. "And the Indians, who had seen them several times without them, and let them alone, saying, 'They were peaceable men, and hurt nobody, therefore they would not hurt them,'" now took alarm and killed both men.

under protection. One day, according to Mary Doe's own account, her mother decided to visit a friend outside the fort, but she was ambushed and killed on the way by "the bloody cruel Indians." This event, regarded as a judgment by God, convinced first the daughter and then (somewhat reluctantly) her husband that they should return home for good and "stand in a testimony for truth, and trust in the name of the Lord." Although their non-Quaker neighbors considered their action deluded and certain to end in disaster for the whole family, they stayed on in their lonely homestead "when the Indians were at our doors and windows," the children being left alone in the house when the parents went to meeting.[19]

Massachusetts Friends seem thus to have been able successfully to dissociate themselves in the eyes of the Indians from the Indian policy of the colonial government. In Rhode Island for many decades government was largely in the hands of the Quakers, who eventually came to form a considerable section of the colony's population.[20] This oasis of religious toleration in the harsh environment of Puritan New England had come into being toward the end of the 1630's as a refuge for the "Antinomian" opponents of Massachusetts theocracy, who had gathered around Mrs. Anne Hutchinson. In some ways forerunners of Quakerism, the members of the group—at least some of them— seem to have held pacifist beliefs. John Winthrop wrote that "divers of them . . . would not wear any arms," and, according to an entry in the colonial records of Rhode Island, Nicholas Easton (1593-1675), a later convert to Quakerism who was to hold the office of governor of the colony, in 1639 "was fined five shillings . . . for coming to meeting without his weapons."[21]

Within a few years after the arrival of the Quaker missionaries in New England in 1656, a number of the colony's leading citizens joined the movement, and almost immediately the colonial capital of Newport became the center of New England Quakerism. The colony's tolerant policy toward religious unorthodoxy, as well as the similarity in belief between its founding fathers and the newcomers, led Rhode Island to provide shelter to the sect that was being so fiercely persecuted in the neighboring colonies. Thus, when in the autumn of 1657

---

[19] *A Journal of the Life of Thomas Chalkley,* pp. 40-45; Story, *Journal,* pp. 315, 316, 318; *John Farmer's First American Journey 1711-1714* (ed. H. J. Cadbury), pp. 7, 8. These three accounts, although they vary slightly in detail, are in substantial agreement with each other.

[20] The best study of Quaker government in Rhode Island is to be found in Jones, *The Quakers,* bk. I, chap. VIII.

[21] Jones, *The Quakers,* p. 23.

the commissioners of the United Colonies wrote from Boston requesting the authorities in Rhode Island to take steps to prevent the spread of Quakerism within its boundaries, the latter, while being careful to state their dislike of Quaker tenets, sent back a polite refusal. In the following spring the commissioners tried their hand at persuading the General Assembly of the Providence Plantations (which eventually joined Rhode Island) to expel all Quakers from their midst—again without success. The fellow citizens of Roger Williams (who, however, was no friend to Quaker doctrines) answered the request by stating that freedom of conscience was a fundamental tenet of their charter. They noted, too, that the sect was allowed to exist in peace in England itself. In their colony, however, Quakers would be required to fulfill all their civil obligations according to the law. "And in case they the said Quakers which are here, or who shall arise or come among us, do refuse to subject themselves to all duties aforesaid, as training, watching, and such other engagements, as other members of civil societies, for the preservation of the same in justice and peace," they will consult the English government as to "how to carry ourselves in any further respect towards these people so, that therewithall there may be no damage, or infringement of that chief principle in our charter concerning freedom of conscience."[22]

Quaker participation in governing Rhode Island commenced at the end of the Commonwealth period with the acceptance of the faith of Friends by many of its leading men. From 1663 (the date of the Rhode Island charter) until 1714, Quakers were almost uninterruptedly in control of the colony, and even thereafter, until the eve of the American Revolution, Quakers were still to be found in high office, although their influence on politics was less. The first phase of Quaker rule in particular, which came to an end with the death in 1714 of that Quaker stalwart in government, Walter Clarke (ca. 1638-1714), was a period of incessant warfare: the two Dutch wars of 1664-1667 and 1672-1674, King Philip's War of 1675-1676, and the French and Indian wars during the reigns of William and Mary and of Anne, paralleling the great struggles which were taking place on the European continent, all brought the little seacoast colony into the orbit of the fighting. The behavior of the Quaker politicians in Rhode Island, however, is in striking contrast to that of their brethren who ruled Pennsylvania during roughly the same period. Despite certain tacit compromises and rather devious devices, Penn's colony, as we shall see later in this story, attempted to steer clear of all direct military commitments; the Quaker rulers of Rhode Island, on the other hand, while

[22] *Records of the Colony of Rhode Island and Providence Plantations,* I, 374-80.

following a general policy of peace, took measures of a military character in their administrative capacity. "Cette conduite," writes a French historian of early American Quakerism, "n'était pas d'une exacte orthodoxie et d'une parfaite limpidité."[23] Yet it was never censured by any of the meetings or by George Fox or the other leading Friends who visited Rhode Island during this period.

The explanation of this apparent inconsistency actually seems to be fairly simple. Pennsylvania, in the eyes of Friends, was the "Holy Experiment," where—so far as its position as a possession of the British Crown would allow—Quaker pacifism could be worked out as a practical policy, as an example to the nations in peaceable living. True, Quakers were soon outnumbered there by men of different faiths. But the province owed its origin and long continued to draw its general tone from the religious Society which dominated its political life. The situation was different in Rhode Island, to which Quakerism had come as a guest and where Friends, though numerous,[24] never came to possess the special position that they held in Pennsylvania. If there were to be Quaker magistrates in Rhode Island—and, as we know, most Quakers rejected the Anabaptist view of the state—Friends could lay no claim to the colony as a fitting place for carrying out an experiment in their own "peculiar" views on the use of violence. Love, they believed, is the sole weapon that, in consonance with Christ's commands, his disciples ("a holy nation," Thomas Story calls them) may use in dealing with their fellowmen. In civilized society the awe in which the magistrate's office is held should be sufficient to maintain peace and order. Nevertheless, since in their view law functions under the old dispensation and not the new, they also believed that in extreme circumstances (to use Story's words) "force may be allowed . . . in the hand of a proper officer, whose business and duty it is to apprehend and bring to justice furious and incorrigible transgressors of righteous laws and ordinances of men, for the just rule of countries and nations."[25] Thus, the Quaker officers of Rhode Island felt it their

[23] Pierre Brodin, *Les Quakers en Amérique au dix-septième siècle et au début du dix-huitième*, p. 153. Cf. Thomas G. Sanders, *Protestant Concepts of Church and State*, p. 133: "The Quaker leadership in Rhode Island did not absolutize the principle of pacifism, but saw in public office an opportunity for Christian vocation and felt that some dimensions of political life by their very nature required coercion."

[24] Around 1700, for instance, half the population of Newport was Quaker. Half the population of the country districts of the South Narragansett shore during the first half of the eighteenth century was Quaker, too.

[25] See Story, *Journal*, pp. 364-67, for an exposition of this standpoint, which he presented in an argument with a Baptist preacher during his travels in New England in 1704. Such views were common among early Friends in Britain.

39

duty in their role as magistrates of a non-Quaker polity to take on occasion forcible measures against those who threatened the internal or external security of the little colony, whether they be Indians, French, or Dutch.

In 1667, for instance, Nicholas Easton (the same Nicholas Easton who had refused to carry arms in 1639) when deputy-governor acted as chairman of a committee appointed to levy a tax for the defense of Newport. Again, in 1671, Easton, now governor, assisted by a council that was predominantly Quaker, took steps to put the colony in a posture of defense against expected attack. Further military measures received the approval of governor and council in the course of this second Anglo-Dutch war. The Quaker administration did its utmost, however, to avert the bloodthirsty struggle with the Indians known as King Philip's War, which broke out on the mainland in 1675, largely owing to the aggressive policy of the colonial government of Massachusetts. Just prior to hostilities, the Rhode Island leaders attempted to prevent bloodshed by direct negotiations with the Indian leader; going unarmed to the latter's headquarters, they proposed that arbitration of grievances be substituted for fighting. But war came—an unnecessary war in the eyes of the Rhode Island's rulers—and the colony's mainland settlements were exposed to attack and destruction.

The Quaker politicians were now faced with their most acute dilemma since their access to power: involvement in a war that was neither one that they sought nor one that they could feel was just, even under the old dispensation.[26] William Edmundson, visiting Rhode Island around this time, speaks of the "great troubles" attending Friends "by reason of the wars" raging outside the colony between Indians and white settlers. "The people, that were not Friends, were outrageous to fight; but the Governor being a Friend, (one Walter Clarke) could not give commissions to kill and destroy men."[27] True, despite strong pressure for increasing military commitment from the non-Quaker inhabitants on the exposed mainland and from the other New England colonies, the Quaker-dominated administration and legislature did their best to avoid direct involvement in fighting the Indians. But—Edmundson's assertion to the contrary—they did once again sanction military preparedness, though in a rather halfhearted manner. On 12 April 1676, Clarke, on the eve of his election as governor to succeed the old pioneer of Rhode Island Quakerism, William Coddington (1601-1678), wrote to the Providence authorities: "We well

[26] Jones, *The Quakers*, pp. 173-79, 181-84.
[27] Edmundson, *Journal*, p. 81.

approve your advice and willingness to maintain a garrison, and have agreed to bear the charge of ten men upon the colony's account." The general assembly, which Quakers also dominated, had resolved that "there appears absolute necessity for the defence and safety of this colony" and therefore "for the orderly managings of the militia this Assembly do agree to choose a major to be chief captain of all the colony forces." Although naturally a non-Quaker was appointed to this post, his commission summoning him to do his utmost "to kill, expulse, expel, take and destroy all and every the enemies of this His Majesty's colony" was signed by Coddington, the Quaker governor. And, what is more, the two emissaries that the assembly had dispatched forthwith to Providence with instructions "to determine whether a garrison or garrisons shall be kept there at the charge of the colony and the place or places where they shall be kept and whether at all" were also Quakers.[28]

Clarke and a number of the other Quaker politicians took a leading part in the life of their meeting, serving as ministers and in other responsible functions. For a long period there is little evidence that either they or their fellow Quakers saw any inconsistency between their governmental activities and their profession as Friends (though it is interesting to note that they apparently stood aside when capital punishment was inflicted in court). Individual Friends had been exempted in 1673 from the military service that continued to be obligatory in the colony even after the Quakers came into virtual control of its government. (This was, incidentally, the first piece of legislation in America granting the right of conscientious objection to war.) The terms of the act were generous, for not merely did it exempt all who had genuine religious scruples against bearing arms but in peacetime demanded no alternative in the way of fine or civilian service from those who became conscientious objectors. In time of danger, however,

When any enemy shall approach or assault the colony or any place thereof, . . . then it shall be lawful for the civil officers for the time being, as civil officers (and not as martial or military) to require such said persons as are of sufficient able body and of strength (though exempt from arming and fighting), to conduct or convey out of the danger of the enemy, weak and aged impotent persons, women and children, goods and cattle, by which the common weal may be the better maintained, and works of mercy manifested to distressed, weak persons; and shall be required to watch to inform

[28] Jones, *The Quakers*, pp. 184-89. See also Douglas Edward Leach, *Flintlock and Tomahawk*, pp. 196, 197.

of danger (but without arms in martial manner and matters), and to perform any other civil service by order of the civil officers for the good of the colony, and inhabitants thereof.[29]

Thus, apart from a brief anti-Quaker reaction in 1676 after King Philip's War when exemption was withdrawn, Friends in Rhode Island, like their brethren in colonial Pennsylvania, remained untroubled by the problem of militia service, which on occasion proved so bothersome in the other provinces where the Society was established.

In the French and Indian conflict during William and Mary's reign, successive Quaker governors excused themselves under various pretexts from sending, in the shape of men and military supplies, the aid that the governor of New York was demanding. Although their peaceable principles may have contributed to their reluctance in the matter, these principles did not appear among the ostensible reasons given in their correspondence. The struggle around this time to prevent Massachusetts from gaining control over the colony's militia did not arise from pacifist scruples; it was rather the result of the Quaker politicians' ardent local patriotism, which had shown itself earlier in their championship of local autonomy against James II's attempt to convert Rhode Island into a royal colony.

Quaker participation in Rhode Island politics was less evident in the eighteenth century. But the leading Quaker family of this period, the Wantons, whose prominence in the Society was not unconnected with the fortune they had derived from their shipbuilding activities, contributed several outstanding local politicians. Like their predecessors, they too had to face the difficult task of squaring political necessity with their Quaker conscience. This dilemma is illustrated by the case of John Wanton (1672-1742). In his younger days he had, along with his elder brother, revolted against his father's Quakerism (the father Edward had been among the early converts in Boston) and had taken up amateur soldiering. In this pursuit John had acquired the rank of colonel of the militia. In 1712, however, having reached

[29] *Records of Rhode Island*, II, 495-99. In late 1675 a number of the wounded colonial troops were sent to Rhode Island to be nursed. A contemporary account relates: "Governor William Coddington received the wounded soldiers kindly, though some churlish Quakers were not free to entertain them until compelled by the Governor." Coddington would appear to have been acting within the rights accorded the governor by this act of 1673, which required pacifists in wartime "to perform any other civil service" that the nonmilitary authorities deemed beneficial. Jones (*The Quakers*, p. 186) makes an apt comment: "These Quakers believed the war thoroughly unjust, and desired to withhold from all acts which might seem like taking part in the war, though in declining to nurse wounded soldiers they were surely pushing their scruples too far."

the age of 40, he regained his Quaker faith and became an active and respected minister in Newport Meeting. An English Friend who visited the town in that year writes: "This John Wanton had been a valiant colonel: But now has ceased from carnal wars and is employed in Christ's service against the devil and his works."[30]

John's accession to Quakerism not only brought out his talents as a preacher but eventually opened the way to a political career in the province. From 1729 until his death in 1742, he served uninterrupt- edly first as deputy-governor and then, from 1733, as governor of the province. When, toward the end of his career, war with Spain (which developed subsequently into war with France) led the legislature, now no longer predominantly Quaker, to pass in 1740 an act providing for the defense of the colony and for dispatching volunteers to fight in the West Indies, the responsibility for the execution of these meas- ures lay with the governor—John Wanton, the Quaker minister. Wan- ton continued to fulfill the duties of his office, despite strong criticism from his meeting, and defended himself vigorously against charges of inconsistency and violation of his obligations as a Friend. Times had evidently changed. Although John Wanton's conduct as an executive officer of the colony followed exactly in the pattern of a whole line of Quaker predecessors back to the days of George Fox, feeling in the Society at large had grown more sensitive (as it was also beginning to do on the question of slavery) to the implications of the peace testi- mony in public as well as in private life, and on this occasion a meet- ing committee was appointed to interview their friend, the governor. Even so, Wanton successfully asserted his right to behave as he was doing before his meeting, and there were several more Quakers in high office in the colony before the conclusion of the colonial period. John's nephew Gideon Wanton, who was governor in the mid-1740's, for instance, was responsible for sending reinforcements to serve in the expedition against Cape Breton Island in 1745. True, Stephen Hopkins was no longer a Friend when he signed the Declaration of Independ- ence. But he was only disowned in 1774, and for an offense against the discipline unconnected with his disregard in public life for his So- ciety's peace testimony. Altogether, indeed, the record of the political Quakers of Rhode Island makes an interesting contrast to the role played by their counterparts in Pennsylvania.[31]

Public life was not the only sphere in which Rhode Island Friends showed a certain ambivalence in their attitude toward their peace

[30] *John Farmer's First American Journey*, pp. 8, 18, 19.
[31] Jones, *The Quakers*, pp. 202-5, 207-12; John Russell Bartlett, *History of the Wanton Family*, pp. 53-55, 69-76.

testimony. Not infrequently during the eighteenth century, members in good standing—including scions of such prominent Quaker families as the Wantons, Pitts, and Hazards, to name a few—were implicated in privateering activities.[32] (In the early decades of the century some Friends on the little island of Nantucket belonging to Massachusetts, an island whose population at this time was largely Quaker, had also engaged in privateering.) In this case, however, public duty could scarcely be pleaded in exoneration of action that was so obviously in contradiction with Quaker pacifism: the arming of Quaker-owned or Quaker-captained vessels had been strongly condemned by the parent society in Britain as well as by Pennsylvania Friends. In 1774, New England Yearly Meeting renewed its disapproval of such conduct in an official minute. "Some professing to be of our Society," it stated sorrowfully, "have of late slighted and neglected this our ancient and Christian testimony to that degree as to be concerned in privateering, or as owners in ships going with letters of marque, which is a flagrant and lamentable departure from our peaceable principle." The minute then went on to call for the disownment of all who continued their connection with privateering after being summoned by their meetings to mend their ways.[33]

Nevertheless, despite the solemn ban on this activity, there is evidence that some of the Quaker merchants of Rhode Island (as well as some in England and a few in Philadelphia) had engaged in privateering during the Seven Years War, too, when Quaker-owned vessels were sometimes armed for protection against attack. That individual Friends put profit before precept is not surprising, but that, despite the official policy of yearly meeting, their local meetings apparently took no action against them sheds an interesting light on the state of the peace testimony at this date—particularly in view of the alacrity with which what seem to us today minor infringements of the discipline were punished by disownment.

Newport not only became the center of New England Quakerism but was also in the 1670's the birthplace of the small sect of Rogerenes (a movement that had broken away from the Baptists) whose religious doctrines and practice were shaped to a considerable degree under Quaker influence. Their pacifism, too, probably derived from the inspiration of Friends. We hear of "divers persons [in Rhode Island] of several societies, who are one in that point of conscience, of not training and not fighting to kill" (to quote the words of the colony's

[32] A. T. Gary [Pannell], "The Political and Economic Relations of English and American Quakers (1750-1785)," D.Phil. thesis, Oxford (1935), pp. 112-14.
[33] New England Y. M. MS Discipline, in the H.C.Q.C., pp. 116, 117.

militia act of 1673).[34] This may be a reference to Rogerenes as well as Quakers. The sect's founder, John Rogers, Sr. (d. 1721), was a prosperous and well-educated farmer and tradesman, who gained his first adherents among well-to-do townsmen and country folk. Fiercely persecuted for many decades outside tolerant Rhode Island, they eventually became centered in Connecticut around New London where, as a slowly dwindling group, they survived to the end of the nineteenth century, remaining throughout firmly devoted to their pacifist witness.[35] At the beginning of the eighteenth century Samuel Bownas had written of them: "They bore a noble testimony against fighting, swearing, vain compliments and the superstitious observation of days."[36] They protested, too, against slavery and, considering their very small numbers, remained remarkably active to the end in their advocacy of humanitarian causes.

Their founder, however, had preached an otherworldly nonresistance that was perhaps more akin to the Anabaptist-Mennonite tradition than to the Quaker position (with which the Rogerenes differed also in regard to their views on baptism and the sacraments). "We are of another kingdom," he told his followers, "and therefore are not to be concerned in the kingdom we do not belong to, either to sit in judgment with them, or to fight and kill under their kingdom," being ready however "to pay them tribute for the carrying on the affairs of their kingdom and government" according to Christ's and the apostles' precepts. His disciples, he said, must stand aside from the work of government, which is tainted with blood, refusing not only to bear arms but to serve as "governor, judge, executioner or juryman, or to be active in the making any laws which may be useful in the body of the kingdoms of this world."[37]

II

Across the sound from the Rogerene settlements in Connecticut lies Long Island, where Quakerism had already taken root among English colonists before the Dutch lost it in 1664. In fact, "the first Quaker in the American colonies" was probably a Long Island resident, Richard Smith, who had been converted during a visit to England in 1654.[38] Later, Quakerism spread to the mainland of the province of New York,

---

[34] *Records of Rhode Island*, II, 496.
[35] See Ellen Starr Brinton, "The Rogerenes," *NEQ*, XVI, no. 1 (March 1943), 3-19.
[36] *An Account of the Life of Samuel Bownas*, p. 85.
[37] Quoted in John R. Bolles and Anna B. Williams, *The Rogerenes*, pp. 349-51.
[38] Jones, *The Quakers*, p. 219.

first to Westchester County and Manhattan and then slowly up the left bank of the Hudson. Apart from the Quaker merchants, tradesmen, and artisans of New York City, Friends in the province during the colonial period consisted mainly of farming folk and village craftsmen.

Under Dutch rule at the beginning there was a short period of persecution, but thereafter the Quakers were left more or less in peace. As New York Yearly Meeting wrote in an epistle, dated 1701, to London Yearly Meeting: "The government is kind to Friends and we enjoy our liberty."[39] Occasionally, however, there were clashes over the question of military duties. In 1672, for instance, at the outset of the second Anglo-Dutch war (in which the Dutch succeeded in regaining control of the province for a brief period), Friends, along with their fellow citizens, were asked to contribute "voluntarily" toward the repair of the fortifications of New York. Eight members of Flushing Monthly Meeting thereupon sent a letter of explanation to the English governor, in which they wrote:

> It is not unknown to the Governor how willing and ready we have been to pay our customs, county rates, etc., needful town charges, etc., how we have behaved ourselves peaceably and quietly amongst our neighbors, and are ready to be serviceable in any thing which doth not infringe upon our tender consciences. But being in measure redeemed out of wars and strifes we cannot for conscience-sake be concerned in upholding things of that nature. As you yourselves well know it hath not been our practice in old England or elsewhere since we were a people. And this in meakness we declare in behalf of ourselves, and our Friends, having love, and goodwill to thee, and to all men.[40]

Although on this occasion the administration appears to have been satisfied (at least no further steps were taken to enforce payment), Friends continued to suffer some hardship for their stand as conscientious objectors. The case of young John Underhill, son of the well-known English soldier of fortune of the same name, is typical of the experiences of young Friends at that date. Underhill, who had emigrated from England, settled eventually at Oyster Bay where he and his whole family became Quakers. In 1676 we find him being put in prison for refusing either "to train in the militia" or "to work on the

---

[39] *Ibid.*, p. 252.

[40] John Cox, Jr., *Quakerism in the City of New York*, pp. 70-72. The letter is also quoted in Jones, *The Quakers*, pp. 249, 250, in a slightly different version dated 10 October. Cox's volume is based directly on the New York meeting records.

fort."[41] A number of other Friends suffered distraint of goods for such offenses.[42] Despite the protests of the Quaker communities of the province that this action was contrary to the guarantee of religious liberty enjoyed by all the colony's inhabitants, the governor and his council refused to relent. To a Quaker petition asking for exemption from compulsory militia training, delivered in February 1686, the reply was given, "That no man can be exempted from that obligation and that such as make failure therein, let their pretence be what they will, must submit to the undergoing such penalties as by the said act is provided." From an account that Friends drew up in the following year, we learn that property valued at anything between 6s. and £15, and even higher, was seized for nonpayment of militia fines. The goods taken included not only sheep, cattle, and swine, but articles of farm equipment, household utensils, bed linen, and clothing.[43] The leading New York Friend of the period, John Bowne (1628-1695) of Flushing, originally an immigrant from England, was among those who were thus penalized: "Taken from John Bowne for his son Samuel not training, two sheep by John Harrison, the 3rd of the 7th month, 1687, worth £1.0.0.," runs the record, a typical entry for the late seventeenth century.[44] In the eighteenth century the same routine of fining Quakers for their failure to attend militia musterings and subsequently distraining the goods of the delinquents continued, though in a somewhat more moderate form.

Throughout the colonial period Quakers in New York, small in numbers and humble in station, were consistently excluded from political office.[45] The situation was different in the neighboring Jerseys where Friends were in political control until 1702, when the two parts were handed over to become a united colony under the Crown, and where, in West Jersey, they had been thickly settled from its beginnings in 1675. (In East Jersey, even though William Penn and a group of

[41] Quoted in Anna Davis Hallowell, *James and Lucretia Mott*, p. 8. (The Underhills were ancestors of the Motts.)

[42] Brodin, *Les Quakers en Amérique*, pp. 268, 269.

[43] XV. *Papers relating to Quakers and Moravians*, pp. 1003-7.

[44] Quoted in *Bulletin of Friends' Historical Society of Philadelphia*, vol. 9, no. 1 (1919), p. 42.

[45] The visiting English minister, James Dickinson (1659-1741), records in his *Journal*, p. 106, the convincement on Long Island in the year 1696 of "a captain in the army, and a justice of the peace, who were afterwards called before the Governor of New York, and because they could neither swear nor fight any longer, they laid down their commissions, having received the truth in the love of it." A Quaker could, without being inconsistent, serve as a justice of the peace in colonies like Pennsylvania, however, where office was not directly associated with oathtaking and armed force.

Friends obtained possession as proprietors in 1681, Quaker influence and settlement were on a considerably smaller scale.) In the late seventeenth century, especially in the western province, we find Friends filling the office of governor and sitting in the councils and in the assemblies. Many became wealthy men as planters, merchants, and shipowners. In the eighteenth century they often succeeded in adding culture to wealth; the Quaker gentlemen of New Jersey were the match of the Quaker grandees of Philadelphia across the river, with whom, indeed, they were united not only by the fact that New Jersey Friends shared the same yearly meeting (established in 1681) with those of Pennsylvania but also by close ties of marriage and social intercourse.

Nevertheless, the overwhelming majority of Quakers in New Jersey, as in the other colonies, were countryfolk, simple farmers and artisans for the most part, who did not always easily find a common language with the cultured and wealthy upper crust of their Society. When the colony passed into the possession of the Crown, it was the rank-and-file Quakers who had to face (what was a new issue for them) the question of militia conscription. Although Friends were guaranteed under the new order both freedom of worship and the right to make an affirmation in place of an official oath, they became liable for training in the militia and for service with it in time of war or danger of invasion. As in most of the other colonies, the authorities here, too, considered it quite sufficient for assuaging Quaker consciences to allow bona fide members of the Society the privilege of paying a fine in lieu of drilling or of hiring a substitute if the militia were mobilized for active service. The meeting records, therefore, begin to show from that point on a long series of distraints on property that parallels the story in other provinces. Perhaps because of the Quaker origins of the colony, however, Friends rarely appear to have been subjected to imprisonment for nonpayment. We hear, too, on occasion of reluctance on the part of the local constables to enforce distraint upon Quaker neighbors.[46]

[46] Brodin, Les Quakers en Amérique, p. 294. The records of Burlington M. M. contain the following rather involved entry for 1706: "It was ordered by this meeting, that there should be persons appointed out of each particular meeting belonging to this meeting, to speak to every Friend belonging to their respective meetings, to bring in an account to the next monthly meeting, of the goods strained from them for refusing to pay to the upholding of the militia" (Ezra Michener [ed.], A Retrospect of Early Quakerism, p. 372). There is a record of an amusing case in the next decade involving a member of Newtown M. M. who was disciplined by this meeting for threatening the constable who had come to distrain his property for an unpaid militia fine. The unruly Friend pledged himself in the future "not to give such occasion of offense but to make orderly as becoming his profession" (quoted in John E. Pomfret, "West New Jersey: A Quaker Society

But in wartime, as always, Friends' difficulties increased. In 1740, for instance, Governor Lewis Morris, who estimated the number of Quakers in West Jersey at that time to be as high as a third of the total population,[47] wrote somewhat testily of the negative response of members of the Society to his efforts to raise troops for the newly begun war: Friends were, he complains, "generally a laborious, honest and industrious people, but want not their share of craft; and they are unaccountable [sic] obstinate and tenacious."[48]

During the next round in the great Anglo-French contest of the eighteenth century, in 1757, a special call was made, first, for 1,000 and, then, for 3,000 militiamen "to go off as soldiers, to the relief of the English at Fort William Henry" in the province of New York. Among those chosen were a number of young Quakers from Burlington County. Of them John Woolman writes in his *Journal*:

> Some [of those drafted] were at that time in great distress, and had occasion to consider that their lives had been too little conformable to the purity and spirituality of that religion which we profess, and found themselves too little acquainted with that inward humility, in which true fortitude to endure hardness for the truth's sake is experienced. Many parents were concerned for their children, and in that time of trial were led to consider, that their care to get outward treasure for them, had been greater than their care for their settlement in that religion which crucifieth to the world, and enableth to bear a clear testimony to the peaceable government of the Messiah.

1675-1775," *William and Mary Quarterly*, 3rd ser., VIII, no. 4 [Oct. 1951], 510). A later case of un-Quakerlike belligerency in dealing with a military officer making a distraint is cited in Lois V. Given, "Burlington County Friends in the American Revolution," *Proceedings of the New Jersey Historical Society*, vol. 69, no. 3 (July 1951), p. 202. In 1782 a member of Evesham M. M. in that county was disowned for striking the officer with a stick. In this case the man's acknowledgment of error was not accepted by his meeting. We also find occasional record of New Jersey Friends being disciplined for having taken up arms especially during an emergency. After an invasion scare in 1704, for instance, four young members of Burlington M. M. submitted an acknowledgment of error to their meeting for having done so. "It seemed best," they said ingenuously in extenuation of their conduct, "for those that had guns [presumably, for the purpose of hunting], to take them, not with a design to hurt, much less to kill, man, woman or child; but we thought that if we could meet these runaways [who had escaped from an enemy vessel], the sight of the guns might fear them" (quoted in Amelia Mott Gummere, *Friends in Burlington*, p. 38; see also pp. 38-41, 44).

[47] Jones, *The Quakers*, p. xvi, gives an estimate of nearly 6,000 Quakers in New Jersey by 1775.

[48] Pomfret, "West New Jersey," p. 494.

A few of the Quaker conscripts expressed their willingness to march or to provide substitutes. Several more slipped away across the borders of the province to wait until the emergency had passed. Others decided to stand by their church's position and went to the militia captain, telling him the reasons for their refusal either to serve themselves or to get a substitute to go in their stead and stating at the same time that they would not try to run away. The captain, who was probably well acquainted with the Quaker attitude toward war, agreed to allow them to return home, warning them that they were still liable to be called up if the need arose. As things turned out, they were left in peace.[49] (One of those who refused to serve on this occasion later recorded in his journal: "Although my part might appear but as a drop in the ocean, yet the ocean, I considered, was made up of many drops.")[50] Earlier in the year, however, Quaker draftees in other parts of the province do not appear to have been quite so lucky. Woolman relates that "in some places they were [drafted], and such who stood true to their principles though they were taken away and nearly tried I have not heard that the officers were inclining to severity."[51]

Where fines had been imposed for failure to muster and distraint of property followed on nonpayment of fine, Friends in New Jersey had been warned by Yearly Meeting in 1755 not to accept money returned by kindly officers as "the overplus," that is, the difference between the amount of the fine and the proceeds of the sale of the delinquent's goods. Acceptance of such a sum would, it was felt, diminish "our peaceable testimony in its primitive authority and purity."[52]

Among those who were most concerned to reinvigorate the languishing peace testimony of Philadelphia Yearly Meeting (in which New Jersey Friends were included) was the Quaker tailor of Mount Holly, John Woolman (1720-1772), whose *Journal*—from which we have already quoted—was to become a religious classic. Love, the love of all created things, was the overriding emotion which inspired this naturally rather timid and sensitive man to courageous and outspoken defense of all God's creatures—"all animal sensible creatures"—suffering in one form or another from injustice or cruelty or oppression, whether they were African slaves or American Indians

49 *The Journal and Essays of John Woolman* (ed. A. M. Gummere), pp. 211, 212, 224, 225.

50 *A Journal of Joshua Evans*, p. 19.

51 Letter from John Woolman to Abraham Farrington, dated 1 Oct. 1757, in *PMHB*, XVII (1893), no. 3, 371.

52 Minutes of the Y. M. of Friends at Philadelphia for 1749-1779, pp. 77, 78 (printed in part in *Rules of Discipline* [1797], p. 131).

or English postboys, or the dumb animals who had few champions in those times.[53] "I rejoice, that I feel love unfeigned toward my fellow-creatures," he wrote to his wife.[54] He saw a natural harmony in the universe as the only possible condition for a creation emanating from an all-loving God. War, therefore, whether among civilized nations or between the more advanced and the less advanced peoples of the world, was an overturning of God's order. Woolman, therefore, put special value on the Quaker peace testimony and strove to keep his fellow Friends faithful to it, as fervently as he did in leading them to renounce their legal rights to property in men. But for him pacifism meant far more than a refusal to fight: it was part and parcel of a non-violent philosophy of life which, drawing its inspiration from Christian belief, sought to relate all man's activities in a coordinated whole. Thus Woolman, almost alone among eighteenth-century Quakers, attempted—one might say—to socialize the Society's peace testimony. This witness, he believed, was inadequate if Friends did not also try to remove the causes of war that lay concealed in the economic system, in such social institutions as the slave system, and in political relations with their Indian neighbors.

Basic to Woolman's economic theory was the idea of trusteeship: wealth is a trust with which a man is endowed by God, and he is responsible for using it to forward God's purposes. Desire to amass riches is wrong because in it—"like a chain in which the end of one link encloseth the end of another"—lies strife and, ultimately, war. In a striking passage in the essay which he significantly entitled "A Plea for the Poor" (which was published after his death as *A Word of Caution and Remembrance to the Rich*), he writes:

Wealth is attended with power, by which bargains and proceedings contrary to universal righteousness are supported; and here oppression, carried on with worldly policy and order, clothes itself with the name of justice, and becomes like a seed of discord in the soul: and as this spirit which wanders from the pure habitation prevails, so the seed of war swells and sprouts and grows and becomes strong till much fruit are ripened. Then cometh the harvest . . . Oh! that we who declare against wars, and acknowledge our trust to be in God only, may walk in the light, and therein examine our foundation and motives in holding great estates. May we look upon our treasures, the furniture of our houses, and our garments in which

[53] A good instance of Woolman's sensitivity to animal suffering is provided by H. J. Cadbury in "Some Anecdotes of John Woolman: Recorded by John Cox," *Journal of the Friends Historical Society* (London), XXXVI (1946), 49, 50.

[54] Woolman, *Journal*, p. 232. See also pp. 156, 157.

we array ourselves, and try whether the seeds of war have nourishment in these our possessions, or not.[55]

This doctrine was strong meat indeed for the Quaker grandees of Philadelphia and the Jersey shore (as, in fact, it has since remained also for the more modestly affluent). Woolman himself always strove to testify in his own daily life to a simple way of existence, one in which the seeds of war could not easily take root, and examined carefully all that he did in an effort to rid himself of anything that might possibly contribute, even remotely, to fostering war. It was this self-scrutiny that led him to abandon his career as a successful shopkeeper, for in that business he found it difficult to prevent himself from becoming prosperous. Later we find him giving up wearing dyed clothing and hats—at the risk of seeming eccentric—because (although his reasoning here appears rather devious) their use appeared to him an unnecessary luxury.[56]

His concern for the fair treatment of Negroes and Indians and for the recognition of their human dignity on the part of white Americans is a story that has often been told and need not be repeated here, except insofar as it bears directly on Quaker pacifism. Whereas Friends from the beginning had attempted to carry out a policy of justice and goodwill toward the Indians with whom they came in contact, an awareness of inconsistency between Friends' principles and the practice of slaveholding only ripened slowly (unlike the obligation to treat their Negroes kindly, which was always insisted upon). Woolman was one of those most responsible for bringing about the abolition of slaveholding among Friends and for launching the Society on its antislavery career. In all his contacts with his fellow members up and down the country, and in his public ministry, he was always careful to point out —gently, but insistently—the implicit hypocrisy of asserting the wrongfulness of all wars and at the same time holding in bondage fellow-men whose subjection was the result of armed force. As he told Virginia Yearly Meeting during one of his visits to that colony—by no means pleasing all those present who heard him—"as purchasing any merchandise taken by the sword, was always allowed to be inconsistent with our principles, negroes being captives of war, or taken by stealth, those circumstances make it inconsistent with our testimony to buy them; and their being our fellow-creatures, who are sold as slaves, adds greatly to the [difficulty]."[57]

The same painstaking exploration of all implications of the Quaker

[55] *Ibid.*, p. 419.   [56] *Ibid.*, p. 246.
[57] *Ibid.*, p. 195. See also pp. 255, 256.

objection to war, in order to discover where, in actions that previously had gone unnoticed, a possible source of conflict might be hidden, can be seen in Woolman's reactions to calls to pay war taxes or to billet soldiers in his house. In 1758, when an officer came to place one of his soldiers in Woolman's house, Woolman, after thinking the matter over, decided to submit without complaint "in a passive obedience to authority" but to refuse the legal compensation for this service, for reasons that he explained to the officer.[58] The question of taxation and its relation to the peace testimony exercised Woolman's thoughts, too, especially after the outbreak of the French and Indian War had made the matter once again topical. He was aware that (as we have already seen) both in the past and in his own day many weighty Friends on both sides of the Atlantic, men whose opinions he respected, had paid not only taxes "in the mixture" but also those that were specifically imposed to subsidize warlike measures. Yet, he writes, "[I] could not see that their example was a sufficient reason for me to do so," for the circumstances in which early Friends in Britain had found themselves, separated as they were from all participation in government, were quite different. However unpleasant it might be to run counter to the accepted view of the Society, this stand was still preferable to one which went against the voice of conscience within. "The spirit of truth required of me as an individual to suffer patiently the distress of goods, rather than pay actively." In December 1755, with the cooperation of a small group of Friends of Philadelphia Yearly Meeting whom he found to his surprise—after believing at first that his was a quite isolated opinion—to be of like mind, Woolman was instrumental in getting an unofficial declaration issued advising against the payment of war taxes, even though in their views on this point Friends were by no means unanimous.[59]

The danger that Woolman and his colleagues detected in Friends' acquiescence in this matter was twofold. In the first place, they feared that the easy circumstances in which Friends in the two provinces lived (especially in Pennsylvania, where there was no militia conscription), with persecution for any tenet of their religion a matter of past history, had bred an insensitivity to the call of conscience when obedience to it threatened to bring material loss—"a carnal mind" Woolman calls it in his *Journal.* Secondly, with Friends still holding the reins of political power in Pennsylvania and impelled by their position toward increasing compromise with the exigencies of power, these early Quaker absolutists felt the need, more acutely than most of their brethren, to

[58] *Ibid.,* pp. 81, 82. See Janet Whitney, *John Woolman,* pp. 225-30.
[59] See below, chap. 3.

reassert the compelling force of Friends' belief in nonviolence in order to override the demands of political expediency whenever the two should clash. Moreover, they asked, how could the Friends in office be expected to express Quaker principles in the commonwealth's policy if the Society at large failed to take a clear stand on the issue of contributions to war? The danger here was—to quote the *Journal* once more—that "by small degrees, there might be an approach toward that of fighting, till we came so near it, as that the distinction would be little else but the name of a peaceable people."

Woolman in this instance—as, indeed, in all that he said and did that relates to peace—stood for a renewal of the Society's witness for a nonviolent world. He was not content to follow unthinkingly in the footsteps of earlier generations or to repeat their precepts mechanically in a changed situation that called for new methods of action if the testimony were to remain a live one. The points where he took issue with the opinion prevailing among Quakers sometimes appear forced or extreme. But it is really not so much the form of his protest that is important as its spirit, the spirit that reneweth. The fervor of Woolman's advocacy of a peaceable creation, his all-embracing concept of peace as a total way of life instead of a specialized Quaker profession, stands out in contrast to the often arid and negative pacifism of eighteenth-century Quakerism. The essence of Woolman's pacifism is summed up in one passage from his *Journal*:

> It requires great self-denial and resignation of ourselves to God to attain that state wherein we can freely cease from fighting when wrongfully invaded, if by our fighting there were a probability of overcoming the invaders. Whoever rightly attains to it, does in some degree feel that spirit in which our Redeemer gave his life for us, . . . Many [Quakers] . . . having their religion chiefly by education, and not being enough acquainted with that cross which crucifies to the world, do manifest a temper distinguishable from that of an entire trust in God.[60]

Woolman, the apostle of antislavery within his Society, often felt called to journey into the Southern colonies to take his message to the small groups of Friends there. His reception, though usually polite,

---

[60] Woolman, *Journal*, pp. 204-10. Cf. the epistle composed by Woolman in 1772 just before leaving for England (*Journal*, p. 486): "The principle of peace, in which our trust is only on the Lord, and our minds weaned from a dependence on the strength of armies, to me hath appeared very precious; and I often feel strong desires that we who profess this principle may so walk as to give just cause for none of our fellow-creatures to be offended at us, and that our lives may evidently manifest that we are redeemed from that spirit in which wars are."

was not always too cordial; for a hard core of Quaker slaveholders in both North and South did not take kindly to the idea of emancipation, and it required many decades of quiet but firm insistence on the part of Woolman and other concerned Friends, as well as some disowning in the last resort, to finally eradicate this "seed of war" from the life of the Society. In their profession of the peace testimony, however, the Southern meetings showed the same degree of faithfulness as their Northern brethren: the pattern of war resistance, its achievements and defects, were roughly similar in both sections of colonial America.

III

The earliest cases recorded of Quakers on the American continent being penalized for their stand as conscientious objectors to service in the militia come from the province of Maryland, where the first Quaker, Elizabeth Harris, arrived in late 1655 (or in 1656), shortly before (or just after) Mary Fisher and Ann Austin landed in Boston. Elizabeth Harris and the early Maryland missionaries soon gathered converts.[61] As early as 1658 we read of one "Richard Keene, refusing to be trained as a soldier had taken from him the sum of 6l.15s. and was abused by the sheriff, who drew his cutlass, and therewith made a pass at the breast of the said Richard, and struck him on the shoulders, saying *You dog, I could find in my heart to split your brains.*" Fines in money or in tobacco continued to be imposed on Friends not only for their refusal to train in the militia but, in addition, for their objection to taking oaths. The poorer members of the Society suffered considerable hardship on this account. In the early times, before this usually tolerant colony had come to regard Quakers as a respectable if somewhat peculiar sect, severer penalties were sometimes imposed: Edward Coppedge, for instance, not only had property distrained to the value of £5.7.0 for his refusal to train or to pay fines in lieu thereof, but he "was also whipped by order of the military officers." In 1662 a number of Quaker objectors were given two months in prison for not paying a fine of "five hundred pounds of cask-tobacco."[62] One John Everitt is reported as having run "from his colors when pressed to go to the Susquehanna Fort, pleading that he could not bear arms for conscience's sake," for which offense he was ordered to be "kept in chains

---

[61] Among these converts were a sprinkling of men who remained active in political life (although by the end of the seventeenth century Friends had ceased to play an active role in this sphere). The beginnings of what became Baltimore Y. M. arose out of a visit George Fox paid to the area in 1672.

[62] Joseph Besse, *A Collection of the Sufferings of the People called Quakers,* II, 378-82.

55

and [to] bake his own bread" until such time as his trial could be arranged.[63]

After the first few years Quakers in Maryland seem to have suffered few disabilities for their pacifist beliefs. In time a routine came to be established: as each young Friend reached military age, his local meeting would supply him with a certificate of membership to show to the militia authorities. Then, upon refusal to pay the small statutory fine, the property of the objector or his family was distrained: probably, at least in peacetime, this penalty did not amount to much and was not a serious inconvenience to those concerned. From time to time a young man would break with family tradition and attend muster. His monthly meeting in that case would appoint some trusted Friends to labor with him to bring him to see the error of his ways. Sometimes they succeeded. To take just one case out of many hundreds: Henry Pratt from Third Haven Monthly Meeting in Talbot County, records an early eighteenth-century minute, "hath of late gone to training" despite the attempts of Friends to dissuade him. A committee of four members of the meeting was appointed, and after some time their efforts were crowned with success. "They dealt with him," they were able to report finally, "in the love of God as from the meeting, letting him know how inconsistent it is with the universal testimony of truth to go to training, which he acknowledged and said he kindly accepted of Friends' love and care towards him and that he was really convinced he ought not to go to training and for the time to come hoped he should stand clear of it."[64] Sometimes, however, Friends had to admit failure, the young man remaining adamant in his decision even when faced with the inevitable disownment, which would entail a difficult break with the family faith and often bring sadness to his parents and relatives, too.

If the question of militia service among Maryland Friends, as throughout the whole community of Friends in America, remained a fairly straightforward one—a consistent Quaker must neither serve himself, nor hire a substitute, nor send his servant in his place, nor pay the fine imposed for refusal to train—there were other questions

[63] Quoted in Jones, *The Quakers*, p. 279. Kenneth L. Carroll ("Persecution of Quakers in Early Maryland [1658-1661]," *Quaker History*, vol. 53, no. 2 [Autumn 1964], p. 75) quotes an order issued by governor and council in 1659 against Quaker missionaries—"vagabonds and idle persons"—who had been attempting to dissuade settlers both "from giving testimony or becoming jurors" and "from complying with the military discipline in this time of danger." The justices were told to have them "apprehended and whipped from constable to constable until they shall be sent out of the province."

[64] Carroll, "Talbot County Quakerism in the Colonial Period," *Maryland Historical Magazine*, vol. 53, no. 4 (Dec. 1958), p. 345.

where the connection with the military was not so clear. In the middle of the eighteenth century during the French and Indian War, when war came directly to many of the provinces, Friends did not always find it easy to know where to draw the line—or perhaps they were under greater temptation or stronger pressures to connive at some semi-military activity. In 1759, for instance, a minute of East Nottingham Preparative Meeting notes:

> That divers members thereof have some time ago, inadvertently or otherwise, been concerned in contributing to the furnishing (in some measure) of wagons, horses and provisions for conveying military stores for the use of the army. Such a contribution being declared by the last Yearly Meeting to be a military service and by our last quarterly meeting enjoined on each monthly meeting to report for the same, is taken notice of and cleared up (they having been respectively spoken to on the subject).

A couple of years later, Little Britain Preparative Meeting disowned a couple of young apprentices who had consented to work under military direction on the fort at frontier Pittsburgh, along with their master, who was not a Friend.[65]

The seven years and more of the French and Indian War, as we shall soon see, were also to bring their trials to the Friends in neighboring Virginia, where by the end of the colonial period there were nearly 5,000 Quakers scattered in meetings over a wide area, a figure somewhat larger than the estimated 3,000 Friends in Maryland at this date. Quakerism came to Virginia in 1657, barely a year after its commencement in Maryland and New England. In Virginia, however, where government throughout the colonial period continued to be controlled mainly by members of the established Anglican church, Friends took little part in affairs of state. Yet some of them in the course of time became quite affluent as owners of large plantations (like the Pleasants family at Curles) and owners of many slaves, too—until eventually the ferment generated by Woolman and his like led to the abandonment of slaveholding within the Society.[66]

---

[65] *Bi-Centennial of Brick Meeting-House, Calvert, Cecil County, Maryland, 1701-1901*, pp. 53, 54. (Little Britain is in Pennsylvania, but the meeting came to be associated with East Nottingham Q. M. in Maryland.)

[66] Among those who followed in Woolman's footsteps was Robert Pleasants, who after his conversion to abolition freed all his slaves at considerable financial loss and thenceforward devoted much of his energies to the antislavery cause. "We as a people are principled against fighting," he wrote in May 1775 at the commencement of the Revolutionary War in a passage reminiscent of the writing of Woolman

In 1666 the Virginia legislature made provision for having a fine of 100 pounds of tobacco (which passed as currency in the province) imposed for each time a person refused to attend militia musters. Although not mentioning them specifically by name, the legislators undoubtedly had Quakers in mind when drafting this clause.[67] For more than a century afterward, with minor variations in the nature of the fines demanded for refusal of service, there was a long record of heavy distresses levied upon Quaker conscientious objectors. There were even occasional cases of arrest and imprisonment, although as usual the degree of severity with which the law was implemented varied from one period to another and from district to district. Gradually, however, the earlier antagonism toward Quakers died down, so that at the beginning of the new century, in 1702, Virginia Yearly Meeting could write to London: "Friends doth here keep our meetings peacefully and quietly, blessed be the Lord for it, but Friends are generally fined for not bearing arms and that grand oppression of priests' wages, though the magistrates are pretty moderate at present and truth gains ground."[68]

A serious crisis arose for Friends in 1711, during the War of the Spanish Succession, when, upon hearing a rumor that the French were about to invade the province by sea from the West Indies, Governor Alexander Spotswood prevailed on the assembly to order an emergency mobilization of the militia for labor service on the coastal fortifications. The governor's pleasure at his success in persuading the colonial legislators to take action was, however, marred by one setback: the resistance of the little community of Quakers to what must have appeared to him to be the quite legitimate demands of national defense against impending enemy attack. As he wrote home to Lord Dartmouth in a letter dated 15 October 1711:

> I have been mightily embarrassed by a set of Quakers who broach doctrines so monstrous as their brethren in England never owned, nor, indeed, can be suffered in any government. They have not only refused to work themselves, or suffer any of their servants to be employed in the fortifications, but affirm that their consciences will not permit them to contribute in any manner of way to the defence of the country even so much as trusting the government with

---

himself. "Should we not be equally concerned to remove the cause of it?" (Quoted in Adair P. Archer, "The Quaker's Attitude Towards the Revolution," *William and Mary Quarterly*, 2nd ser., I, no. 3 [July 1921], 175.)

[67] Stephen B. Weeks, *Southern Quakers and Slavery*, p. 171.

[68] Quoted in *Encyclopedia of Quaker Genealogy*, VI: *Virginia*, ed. W. W. Hinshaw *et al.*, 94.

provisions to support those that do the work, tho' at the same time they say that being obliged by their religion to feed the enemies, if the French should come hither and want provisions, they must in conscience, supply them. As this opinion is quite different from practice in Carolina, where they were most active in taking arms to pull down the government,[69] tho' they now fly again to the pretence of conscience to be excused from assisting against the Indians, I have thought it necessary to put the laws of this country in execution against this sect of people, which empowered me to employ all persons as I shall see fit for the defence of the country in times of danger, and impose fines and penalties upon their disobedience.

Angrily, the governor went on to say that he expected loud protests from the Quakers because of his brusque treatment of them, as well as attacks on himself from the Society in England. "But I'm persuaded I shall not incur my sovereign's displeasure so long as I act by the rule of law, and it is absolutely necessary to discourage such dangerous opinions as would render the safety of the government precarious." Moreover, he added, if members of the Society were to be granted exemption from their duties as citizens, all the lazy and cowardly of the province would soon be found under cover of the Quaker name.[70]

Among those with whom the governor had taken counsel "concerning what should be done with obstinate Quakers" was William Byrd, the wealthy owner of Westover plantation on the James River and a justice of the peace. When earlier in the same month in which Governor Spotswood had written to London several Quakers appeared before Squire Byrd in court, along with other militia delinquents, they were fined. "I spoke gently to the Quakers," wrote the squire in his diary, "which gave them a good opinion of me and several of them seemed doubtful whether they would be arrested or not for the future. I told them that they would certainly be fined five times in a year if they did not do as their fellow subjects did."[71] In fact, some Quakers were kept in prison for periods of ten days for nonpayment of fines.[72] Others, however, cooperated, according to the yearly meeting records —either because they feared the consequences of not obeying the authorities or because they did not see anything contrary to Quaker

---

[69] For the Cary Rebellion of 1711, see below, p. 65.

[70] *The Official Letters of Alexander Spotswood*, I, 120, 121. See also pp. 85, 95, 100, 101, 108, for assertions by Spotswood that the North Carolina Quakers had taken up arms against the government in the Cary Rebellion.

[71] *The Secret Diary of William Byrd*, pp. 409, 415, 416.

[72] *John Farmer's First American Journey*, p. 6.

principles in doing so (in which view they might, indeed, have found some support in the writings of earlier Friends). These Quakers consented to carry out the labor assigned them, or else hired someone to work in their stead, or paid the fine imposed by the court—and thus had to be dealt with later by their meetings.[73]

The imposition of fines, distraints, and imprisonment continued even after the conclusion of the great struggle against France in 1713 and the inauguration of several decades of peace. In 1742, after the British empire had once again become involved in war, Virginia Quakers reported on their situation: "The men in military power act toward us in several counties with as much lenity and forbearance as we can reasonably expect, as they are ministers of the law; tho' in some places they are not so favourable." Indeed, as usual, several young Quakers were in jail as conscientious objectors at the time this report was written.[74]

The outbreak of the French and Indian War—"the commencement of a war with a most barbarous and savage enemy in this our late peaceful colony"—began a period of renewed trials for Virginia Quakers, as it did for some of their brethren in other provinces, as well as for members of the German peace sects. One settlement of Friends (at Goose Creek) was abandoned on account of the constant threat of Indian attack, but most Quakers living in the exposed frontier areas held their ground, though appearing "to the outward eye to be in imminent danger" (again, to use the words of the yearly meeting's epistle to London in 1758).[75] No Friend is known to have been attacked or killed by the Indian raiders. On the other hand, some members of the Society collaborated with the military in defense measures, either by helping with the construction of fortifications or by carrying weapons themselves for use against attack. Of Providence Preparative Meeting it was afterward reported: "All of them have been concerned in building a fortification and dwelling therein for defence against the Indian enemy." This constituted one of the reasons for later discontinuing this meeting; its members having departed so gravely from Friends' peaceable witness, its further existence appeared to many to cast a slur on the sincerity of the Quaker peace testimony.[76] And, of course, all who participated in military measures of

[73] Hinshaw, Encyclopedia, VI, 94; Weeks, Southern Quakers, pp. 173, 174.

[74] Margaret E. Hirst, The Quakers in Peace and War, pp. 348, 349; Weeks, Southern Quakers, p. 174; Jones, The Quakers, p. 319. Jones cites the case of a slave worth £9 being taken for nonpayment of militia fines from a Quaker named Thomas Ellyson.

[75] Hinshaw, Encyclopedia, VI, 292.

[76] Hopewell Friends History 1734-1934, p. 58.

this kind were subsequently dealt with and disowned, unless they displayed suitable contrition.

However, perhaps because a greater backsliding from the rigid position usually required by Quaker pacifism seems then to have taken place, greater leniency was apparently shown to those who were liable to be called up under a special militia act passed on 1 May 1756. According to the terms of this act, a ballot was to be held to choose one out of every twenty men for active service with the forces defending the province's frontiers. A representative meeting of Friends gathered immediately and decided against Friends' participation in the ballot or, in case any were chosen to serve without their consent, against payment of fine or the hiring of a substitute (these last two procedures, of course, having always been contrary to Quaker practice). Yet, despite this decision, the older members of the Society in fact mostly advised compliance, "under an apprehension of the consequence which might ensue to our young men, who by a refusal would be liable to be taken away as soldiers and either compelled to act in that station, or be made great sufferers in bearing a faithful testimony against it." As a result, many drew lots along with non-Quakers and, if the ballot went against them, acquiesced in the fine that was imposed on those unwilling to march.

Only seven young men had the courage to resist: five from Henrico County and two from New Kent County in the area around Richmond. They soon found themselves under arrest. After a week in jail, they were brought before the court. While refusing to make the required affirmation of allegiance or to take off their hats before the justices— actions which hardly won the favor of the court—they asserted their readiness to comply with the laws in all things not against their conscience. But, they said, "to bear arms or fight we could not." Thereupon one of the judges told them: "Then . . . you must work at the forts." Naturally, they refused to obey this order, too, and were sent back to prison. On the following day they were dispatched under escort to Fredericksburg and from there to Winchester, then a frontier post under the command of young Colonel George Washington. The journey lasted over four days, a long and weary tramp under trying conditions. The seven men suffered severely from hunger, due not to the harshness of their guards but rather to the meticulousness of their Quaker consciences: "For as we could not do any service, we had not freedom to eat of the king's victuals and having depended in a great measure on buying on the road where provisions proved so scarce, and the demand from our company so great that we being under some restraint had not an equal chance, so was [sic] obliged sometimes to

61

go with hungry stomachs." Their refusal to answer their names at roll call, which took place thrice daily—since answering might be construed as an acknowledgement of their status as soldiers—so infuriated the captain in charge of the company that he threatened to take one of the youths and have him whipped as an example to the rest. The sentence would have been carried out but for the protest of one of the soldiers (who were, indeed, becoming increasingly well disposed toward their prisoners) at the idea of punishing a man for his religious scruples. After this incident the Quakers informed the captain "that if he called us on any other occasion we were ready and willing to answer but not as soldiers, which we could not submit to be."

After arriving finally at Winchester, the Quakers were placed in the guardhouse along with a number of deserters and petty offenders, "a parcel of dirty lousy wicked and profane creatures." They were kept there for five weeks. Although the soldiers guarding them proved friendly and allowed them various minor privileges, the officers continually attempted—sometimes by persuasion, at other times by threats of whipping to the measure of 500 strokes each—to get them to accept service, if only to work on the fortifications. A short while later, a Quaker minister and leader in the Virginia community of Friends, Edward Stabler, arrived in Winchester with greetings and encouragement from the brethren. Stabler was able to get an interview with Colonel Washington, who had just returned from a tour of inspection on the frontier. Not overly friendly on this occasion, Washington told Stabler that he had received orders from Governor Robert Dinwiddie to whip the men until they agreed to work on the fort. He intended, he said, to carry out these instructions shortly, unless the men changed their minds. However, impressed perhaps by the Quakers' unwillingness to compromise their principles, Washington subsequently relented and agreed to release them from the guardhouse on parole, allowing them to lodge in the town with local Friends. Since Governor Dinwiddie refused to sanction their release before their legal term of service had expired, the men remained at Winchester until near the end of the year. Before their departure they went to thank Washington for his generous treatment of them. Wishing them "a good journey home," the colonel in answer to their expressions of thanks "told them they were welcome, and all he asked of them in return was that if ever he should fall as much into their power as they had been in his, they would treat him with equal kindness."[77]

[77] See my article "Colonel Washington and the Quaker Conscientious Objectors," *Quaker History*, 53, no. 1 (Spring 1964), 12-26. [Quotations from this article made here are reprinted by permission of *Quaker History*.] There I have printed

Barely a decade before the Revolutionary War, Friends in Virginia at last obtained temporary relief from the century-long round of distraints and imprisonments (as well as from the occasional backslidings, as in 1756, when, in spite of the Society's official testimony against this practice, fines were paid by so many that no disciplinary action appears to have been taken against the offenders). In 1766, after the yearly meeting had petitioned the assembly in the matter, this body passed a new law exempting bona fide Quakers in peace time (though not in time of war) from all obligations connected with militia training. Although on some occasions colonial Quakers objected to the necessity of having to produce certificates of membership in order to obtain exemption from militia service, the Virginia Quakers, feeling perhaps that they had already proved their sincerity in the cause of peace by a century and more of sporadic suffering, do not appear to have balked at this requirement under the present act. Rufus Jones cites a typical entry from meeting records:

At our monthly meeting held at the Western branch in Isle of Wight County in Virginia the 27th of the 6 month 1767: The overseers of each meeting are desired to collect the names of each of their members that are liable by a late act of assembly to be enlisted in the militia against our next monthly meeting, that a list may be given to the colonel or chief commanding officer of each county as by act of assembly directed; and have the indulgence granted by the same.[78]

The most southerly province in which Quakers were represented in any considerable numbers during the colonial period was North Carolina.[79] The establishment of Quakerism there dates back to 1671; in subsequent decades, in the absence of any serious competition from other denominations until the end of the seventeenth century, a large number of the unchurched in this still rather wild frontier area were

---

an account of their experiences by one of the men entitled "A Brief Narrative of the Conduct and Sufferings of Friends in Virginia, respecting an Act of Assembly passed the 1st day of the 5th month 1756 for drafting the Militia" from the manuscript in the H.C.Q.C. Woolman records in his *Journal*, p. 193: "I lodged at James Standley's, father of William Standley, one of the young men who suffered imprisonment at Winchester last summer on account of their testimony against fighting, and I had some satisfactory conversation with him concerning it."

[78] Jones, *The Quakers*, p. 320.

[79] In the eighteenth century small Quaker groups were formed in South Carolina and Georgia. But Quakerism in these provinces remained very weak; no provision for conscientious objection existed there, nor apparently is anything known about local Quakers who may have successfully or unsuccessfully maintained a pacifist stand.

gathered into the Society of Friends. By the end of the colonial period there were nearly 5,000 Quakers in the province.

The first recorded collision between Quakers and authority resulting from their conscientious objection to war occurred in the spring of 1680. In that year, to quote from a Quaker manuscript, "the government made a law that all that would not bear arms in the musterfield, should be at the pleasure of the court fined." Therefore, it goes on, "Friends not bearing arms in the field; they had several Friends before the Court, and they fined them, he that had a good estate a great sum and the rest according to their estates; and cast them into prison, and when they were in prison, they levied their fines upon their estates." Nine men in all suffered in this manner, and they were kept in jail for about six months. Weeks considers that this treatment, unusually harsh for North Carolina, was due to the resentment of the popular antiproprietary party then in power at the earlier opposition Quakers displayed against them at the time of the Culpepper Rebellion in 1677. Several of the Friends imprisoned in 1680 had signed a protest three years before against what was considered the seditious conduct of the popular party at that time. Anyhow, for the rest of the colonial period the North Carolina Quakers were treated leniently by the authorities. True, distresses on their property for nonpayment of militia fines and war taxes (such as the ones imposed in 1740 to cover the cost of erecting powder magazines in each county and to buy provisions for the troops)[80] were levied, but these were usually small in amount and were only imposed sporadically. The penalty of imprisonment appears to have been administered more rarely than in neighboring Virginia.[81]

Indeed, for a time Quakers were virtually exempt altogether from any obligations in regard to militia service. This circumstance resulted from the appointment in 1694 of a fellow Quaker, the English squire from Wycombe in Buckinghamshire, John Archdale (1642-1717), to the post of governor of the Carolinas. As governor—and at the

---

[80] In the French and Indian War apparently almost all Quakers in the province paid war taxes. Woolman in his *Journal* (pp. 200, 201) relates how, when journeying through North Carolina in 1757, he met a Friend, a minister and a working farmer possessing no slaves, who had refused to pay a recently imposed war tax, preferring to have his goods distrained rather than contribute in this way to an activity he believed inconsistent with Quaker ways. "And as he was the only person who refused it in those parts, and knew not that any one else was in the like circumstance, he signified that it had been a heavy trial upon him, and the more so, for that some of his brethren had been uneasy with his conduct in that case."

[81] Weeks, *Southern Quakers*, pp. 172, 173. See also Francis Charles Anscombe, *I have Called You Friends*, pp. 149-51.

64

same time "admiral, captain general and commander-in-chief of all the forces raised . . . both by sea and land within our said province" (to give the exact wording of the proprietors' letter of appointment)[82]— Archdale had the responsibility for enforcing conscription into the militia. However, in 1696 he was successful in getting the assembly to pass an act exempting from service all Friends whom the governor should certify as being motivated in their refusal to bear arms by genuine religious scruples. Archdale, unfortunately, returned to England in the same year, and a few years later, in 1703 during the governorship of Sir Nathaniel Johnson, the existing generous exemption was withdrawn. Quakers once again became liable to the old alternatives of service or fines. During the same period, as a result of the imposition of an oath of allegiance on all public servants, Friends were gradually removed both from the assembly and from all responsible offices within the province, which during Archdale's term they had largely controlled.

This change from the previously tolerant policy that had prevailed in the province resulted from efforts of the Anglican establishment to gain the upper hand there, efforts that were backed both by the Crown and by a majority of the proprietors. Once again, an antiproprietary party was formed, and this time it enjoyed a great deal of support from the Quakers—at least until 1711, when its leaders resorted to arms in order to turn the tide. The acting governor, Robert Cary, who headed the rebellion, was Archdale's son-in-law but was not himself a Friend. Several Quakers did join it as individuals, including Emmanuel Lowe, another son-in-law of Archdale's. The revolt, however, was easily suppressed. Lowe's case—his "stirring up a parcel of men in arms and going to Pamlico and from there to Chowan in a barkentine with men and force of arms contrary to our holy principles"—came up before North Carolina Yearly Meeting shortly afterward. As a result, Lowe was removed from the yearly meeting's executive committee for "having acted diverse things contrary to our ways and principles." But, presumably because he expressed suitable regret for his actions and promised to refrain from warlike behavior in the future, he was not disowned by the Society.[83]

Conscription for the provincial militia continued in force during the decades that followed. The French and Indian War, which began in 1755, was the only period when the colony was immediately threatened by enemy attack, however. In 1757 the yearly meeting, which was unsuccessful in its attempts at this time to obtain relief from its

[82] Quoted in Jones, The Quakers, p. 344.
[83] Weeks, Southern Quakers, pp. 165, 166.

militia obligations, appointed a standing committee to assist those who became entangled with the military, and in the following year two Friends were delegated in each of the counties where Quakers were settled to attend court martials "there to give the reason for our non-appearance as required by law."[84] But no Friends in North Carolina appear to have been called out on active service, as they were in Virginia.

The Regulator Movement—led by a former Quaker, Hermon Husband—which expressed the grievances of the underrepresented back counties over excessive taxation and official corruption, disturbed the peace of the Carolinas between 1766 and 1771. Although the view, sometimes put forward, that the Society backed the "regulators" is without foundation, several Friends were later dealt with by their meetings for complicity in the movement. Demands were made from time to time by the government's forces for provisions and equipment. "The people commonly called Quakers living in Rocky River and Cane Creek and thereabouts in Orange River," for instance, were required by Governor Tryon "to furnish for His Majesty's troops now marching under my command six wagonloads of flour . . . and also six able wagons and teams with sufficient drivers to attend the troops with the said flour." Although the governor promised that "the wagons and teams will be returned when the service is over," it is doubtful if the Friends in question complied—at least voluntarily—with the order.[85] In 1771, after these disturbances had ended, the legislature at last gave the Quakers in North Carolina the same status vis-à-vis the militia as Virginia had given its Quakers half a decade earlier: provided they could produce a certificate of membership in good standing, Friends in the colony were now granted complete exemption.[86]

IV

No account of American pacifism in the colonial period would be complete without a brief survey of the Quaker communities established in the British islands of the West Indies, which during that pe-

---

[84] Julia S. White, "The Peace Testimony of North Carolina Friends prior to 1860," *BFHA*, vol. 16, no. 2 (1927), p. 61.

[85] *Ibid.*, p. 62.

[86] Lists of members were compiled by local meetings in this connection. See, e.g., M. P. Littrell, M. E. Outland, J. O. Sams, *A History of Rich Square Monthly Meeting of Friends*, p. 21. But cf. the opposite practice recommended by Philadelphia Y. M. in 1742 in regard to certificates of exemption from compulsory militia service in the Three Lower Counties (see *Rules of Discipline of the Yearly Meeting of Friends for Pennsylvania and New Jersey* [1797], p. 130).

66

riod enjoyed close trading relations with the American mainland.[87] Here, in an area where sorties by Great Britain's European enemies (France, Spain, and Holland were all near neighbors in the Caribbean), semi-official privateering and raids by common pirates, and attacks by the aboriginal inhabitants or by revolting Negro slaves were not infrequent occurrences, Quaker pacifists faced some of their most trying experiences and difficult dilemmas. It is not surprising, therefore, that the local authorities occasionally lost patience with Quaker objectors and dealt harshly with them for their resistance to accepting a share in the common defense. Sometimes, however, the powers that be seemed to understand their position and were reluctant to force men to act contrary to religious scruples they might have against bearing arms. This fact, surely, must be placed in the balance alongside the severity and even cruelty that were often meted out, especially in the early days, to Quaker objectors.[88]

Quakerism came to the British West Indies in the second half of the 1650's, and soon meetings were established in a number of islands as a result of the work of the Quaker evangelists among their white inhabitants. Quakers eventually numbered several thousand in Barbados, and even more in Jamaica. Small communities existed also on Antigua, Nevis, and Montserrat in the Leeward islands and on "the remote Bermudas" out in the Atlantic far to the north of the Caribbean islands. Finally, at a time when Quakerism was already beginning to decline elsewhere in the West Indies, the seed was transplanted in the late 1720's to the very small island of Tortola in the Virgin Islands.

It was Barbados that, in George Fox's schemes to found a missionary empire across the Atlantic, provided the link between the continental

[87] A good account of the Quaker peace testimony as practiced by Friends in the British West Indies is given in Hirst, *The Quakers in Peace and War*, chap. XII. This chapter is based largely on manuscripts in the Public Record Office (London) and in the collections of London Y. M.

[88] An interesting illustration of the above remarks is to be found in a conversation related by Story in his *Journal* (p. 444) between himself and a high-ranking naval officer, Charles Wager, Rear Admiral of the Blue, which took place in April 1709 during the Quaker's visit to Jamaica. The admiral, whom Story describes as "a person of a calm, sedate temper, naturally courteous, and no way elevated," received his unusual visitor politely. "As he is a man of war," Story goes on, "we discoursed on that subject; and as I am a man of peace, we conversed religiously, and not martially; he for the punishment of privateers and pirates, as dogs, wolves, lions, bears and tigers; and invaders and breakers of the peace, and robbers; but I was rather for saving the life, that poor sinners might have time to repent and be saved: though what passed between us, was with the greatest civility and temper; the meekness of Christianity being more apparent in his deportment, than any martial harshness."

settlements and those on the islands of the southern sea. The "island of Barbados," writes Rufus Jones, "was, during the seventeenth century, the great port of entry to the colonies in the western world, and it was during the last half of that century, a veritable 'hive' of Quakerism. Friends wishing to reach any part of the American coast, sailed most frequently for Barbados and then reshipped for their definite locality. They generally spent some weeks, or even months, propagating their doctrines in 'the island' and ordinarily paying visits to Jamaica and often to Antigua, Nevis and Bermuda." A Quaker missionary in 1661 called Barbados "the nursery of truth."[89]

In 1660 the council, worried at the effect that the growth of Quaker doctrines among the islanders might have on the state of military preparedness, passed an act punishing refusal of service in the militia with a fine of "five hundred pounds of sugar for the first offence," to be raised to a thousand pounds for each subsequent failure to muster. The objector was to be confined to prison until the fine was paid. The rate of fining gradually increased over the following decades as a result both of a decline in the price of sugar and a rise in the frequency of militia musterings. Quakers now had to face a number of problems. As freemen, they were required to attend musterings in person and to take up arms when there was an alarm, and they were liable, if owners of landed property, to provide a certain number of foot soldiers and horsemen, depending upon the size of their property. In addition, Quakers (including men not otherwise liable for military service and women, too) encountered trouble for their refusal to permit the authorities to requisition either their Negro slaves or their horses for labor service on the island's fortifications, although these were sometimes taken off by force against their master's wishes. Petitioning by the Society failed to move the administration to abandon its policies of distraining the property of the well-to-do (which usually resulted in the confiscation of goods of considerably more value than the amount of the fine) and of putting those who had little on which to levy a distress in prison for periods lasting from a few days to over a year. Besse gives details of a number of cases of hardship from this period. William Piersehouse, for instance, was sentenced to four months' "hard imprisonment, to the great impairing of his health," for refusing to send any of his "servants" to work on the fortifications. Thomas Hunt, Sr., was fined 360 pounds of sugar "for not appearing in arms, though his age might reasonably have excused him." Most of those who were punished by fines or imprisonment or both, however, were young men, who were most liable to be called to train.

[89] Jones, *The Quakers*, pp. 26, 41.

68

A not unusual experience for Barbados Quakers of military age at this time was that which befell John Gittings in the years 1668-1669. Besse tells the story:

John Gittings, in the year 1668. Then taken from him by John Higginbotham Lieutenant-Colonel, one iron pot, for not bearing arms, worth 100 lb. of sugar. Afterward the aforesaid Gittings was sent for into the field by a file of musquetiers, by order of the said Higginbotham, who made his *mittimus* and sent him to gaol from constable to constable, where he remained twelve days, but was then set at liberty by Daniel Searl, Governor at that time. Ferdinando Bushel, Captain of Foot, sent a drummer with soldiers, and took from him a fat hog, for not serving in arms, which was worth 500 lb. of sugar. Nathaniel Trevanyan, Captain, sent a soldier with a Sergeant, and took from him a sow worth 250 lb. of sugar. Ferdinando Bushel, Captain of Horse, sent Thomas Perry, his Deputy-Marshal, who demanded of the said Gittings 2000 lb. of sugar for not trooping, for which he took away his horse, and never returned any thing again, which horse was worth 4000 lb. By order of a court of war he was committed to prison for a year and one day for not appearing at an alarm. The said Ferdinando Bushel, Major, sent Samuel Buckley, Marshal, to him the said Gittings, who demanded of him 630 lb. of sugar for not trooping, for which he took away a mare-colt appraised at 1500 lb. and returned no overplus. John Jennings, William Goodall, and other commissioners for the fortifications, sent Matthew Pinket, Constable, who took away from him in cotton to the value of 840 lb. of sugar, for not sending seven negroes one week to help him build forts.

On the 26th of the eighth month 1669. Then Joshua Chapell, Deputy-Marshal to Samuel Buckley, together with George Maggs and William Clark, took from him three sheep, for not trooping, worth 500 lb. of sugar. Taken from him in all to the value of 7690 lb.

The comparatively mild treatment accorded Gittings in 1669 was clearly attributable to the fact that he spent most of that year in jail.

In 1675 the penalties for conscientious objection were made more rigorous as a result of complaints from governor and council that Quaker noncombatancy was having an adverse effect on the efficiency of the militia. Three years later an 18-year-old Quaker apprentice, Richard Andrews, died as a result of ill-treatment while in the hands of the military, when on several occasions he was "tied neck and heels so straight that he could hardly speak."

69

The new governor, Sir Jonathan Atkins, was particularly vehement in his dislike of the Quakers. As he told the Committee for Trade and Plantations in London in 1680, Quakers "to the great discontent of the people, to their own great ease and advantage, . . . neither will serve upon juries, find arms, or send to the militia nor bear any office, shifting it off with their constant tricks 'they cannot swear,' when profit is the end they aim at." In the same year Sir Jonathan, forwarding a map of the island to the commissioners, was forced to explain that it was not entirely accurate with regard to detail since the mapmaker, being a Quaker, had omitted to mark on it either the churches or the fortifications!

At first, the reign of the Catholic King James II, William Penn's friend, brought an even severer militia act, passed in 1685. The continuing drop in the price of sugar led the authorities to seek another medium in which to measure their militia fines. Now, the Quakers complained, "they levy their execution upon our most serviceable negroes, both men, women and children, taking away, parting and selling husbands, wives, and children one from another, to the great grief, lamentation and distraction of our negro families." Seizure of valuable cattle and horses and the extension of the liability for militia service in a household to include the apprentice as well as the master added to the Quakers' distress. As a result, "the young people go off the island to their own hurt and parents' grief." At last, however, owing to the intervention of London Meeting for Sufferings with the king, probably through Penn's contacts at court, the government in London instructed the island authorities to show greater leniency in dealing with Quakers who had scruples against bearing arms. Some relaxation ensued, but it was followed again by bouts of severity, including further occasions on which recalcitrant Quakers were tied "neck and heels" for their objection against war, a practice that continued into the reign of William and Mary. The situation eased during the eighteenth century. But by the third quarter of the century Quakerism had died out entirely on the island.

A complicating factor in the situation here as in the other Caribbean islands was the possession of slaves by Quaker planters, many of them men of affluence. Although the movement for emancipation within the Society had scarcely got under way before Quakerism disappeared from the area, good treatment of their bond servants was a fundamental point of Quaker practice that George Fox and ministering Friends had insisted upon since the earliest days. The fact of their owning slaves, of course, involved the planters to a considerable degree in the support of a system based upon force and terror. We have just seen, too, that their conscientious scruples against war sometimes led to misery for their slaves rather than to personal hardship for themselves, apart from the loss of their Negroes' labor. At the same time their humanitarianism aroused the ire of the authorities as well as the anger of their fellow planters, who were afraid that the Quakers' attitude might incite the Negroes to revolt. Fear of an armed Negro uprising seems to have been ever present in the minds of the islanders, both within the administration and among the ordinary white citizenry. Thus, we find Friends doing all they could to show that, in fact, they had no ill designs in this respect. In their "Representation" of 1675 they point to "our readiness and diligence in watching, and warding, and patrolling in our persons and horses which for some time was accepted, since the late wicked contrivance of the Negroes, which the Lord by his witness in the heart made known for the preservation of the island and inhabitants." However, the willingness of Friends on the island to perform part of their duties, if allowed to do so unarmed, evidently failed to persuade the authorities to relax either their require-ments or the penalties consequent upon disobedience.[90]

The story in Jamaica, where Quakers were considerably more nu-merous than elsewhere in the British West Indies, followed much the same pattern of distraints and imprisonments as in Barbados. Al-though a proclamation of 1662 granted Quakers personal exemption from bearing arms "provided they shall contribute for the same," sub-sequent legislation withdrew this concession until 1670, when the gov-ernor and council, baffled by the passive resistance offered by the Quakers, once again granted them conditional exemption; the alterna-tive offered was to contribute a sum sufficient to furnish three substi-tutes in place of each Quaker objector. The imposition of fines and distresses continued unabated. According to Margaret Hirst, however, "the fines cannot have been very strictly enforced."[91] One case of cruel treatment is reported. This took place in 1687 when a young man, Peter Dashwood, was twice forced "to ride the wooden horse with a musket at each leg" for his refusal to train in arms.

In the Leeward islands Quaker communities grew up on Antigua and Nevis. Several prominent citizens were converted to the new faith, and there seems to have been the same kind of apprehension on the

[90] Hirst, The Quaker in Peace and War, pp. 309-14; Besse, Sufferings, II, 278-95, 314-18, 322, 330-33, 337-40, 342-49; Charles D. Sturge, "Friends in Barbados," Friends Quarterly Examiner, XXVI, no. 104 (Oct. 1892), 493.

[91] Hirst, The Quakers in Peace and War, pp. 314, 315. See also Besse, Suffer-ings, II, 388-91; H. J. Cadbury, "History of Quakers in Jamaica" (MS in micro-film, F.H.L.S.C.), pp. 72-83.

part of the authorities here, as in Barbados and elsewhere, that the spread of Quakerism would mean a serious depletion of the islands' military potential. So, in 1671, after William Edmundson and another traveling Friend were refused permission to land on Nevis, the governor of neighboring Montserrat, who visited their ship, told Edmundson: "We hear since your coming to the Carribee-Islands [i.e., the Leewards], there are seven hundred of our militia turned Quakers, and the Quakers will not fight, and we have need of men to fight, being surrounded with enemies, and that is the very reason why Governor Wheeler [of Nevis] will not suffer you to come on shore."[92]

Nevis had first received the Quaker message between the years 1656 and 1658. Thereafter a number of cases were recorded concerning Friends who were in prison for failing to appear at musters or on guard duty, "for not appearing in arms at an alarum," or "for refusing to go with their men to assist in making trenches and bulwarks to fortify the island." In some cases the punishment was repeated many times. There were instances, too, of the application of the familiar "neck and heels" treatment to recalcitrants. In 1674 the governor received a petition from ten Quaker objectors which had been smuggled out of prison. The men had been confined in different parts of the fort in order (so the authorities hoped) to prevent communication between them. In it they state:

> It is now twelve days since we were confined here, and there are some of us who have wives and children, and have nothing to maintain them but our labours. Now, General, the reason why we are thus imprisoned we do not well understand, unless for keeping the commandment of Christ, which we dare not disobey. . . . We desire that He would order thy heart that thou mightest discern betwixt us, who are in scorn called Quakers, a peaceable people, who fear God and make conscience of our ways, and those who run wilfully on their own heads and disobey thee.[93]

This forthright declaration had its effect, for the governor ordered the men to be released.

In the following year a new crisis occurred as a result of the Nevis Quakers' efforts to practice Christian pacifism in the lawless environment of those danger-infested seas. Previously, as in Barbados, the governor had permitted Friends to perform their statutory duty of watching for enemies, pirates, and other marauders, without carrying arms as the other white inhabitants on the island were obliged to do.

[92] Edmundson, *Journal*, p. 55.
[93] Besse, *Sufferings*, II, 352-54, 360, 366.

72

Now some members of the Society began to have reservations as to whether this practice was in fact consistent with a strict observance of the Quaker peace testimony, considering the close connection such an activity, though noncombatant, had with the all-pervading atmosphere of war on the island. Word of these doubts reached the ears of George Fox, who in November 1675 dispatched an epistle from his home at Swarthmore Hall in Lancashire "to Friends at Nevis and the Carribbee Islands concerning Watching." In it he upheld the views of those who believed it right to comply with the order to watch, pointing out that it was "a very civil thing, and to be taken notice of" that the governor had allowed them to perform this service unarmed and that, in addition, this was a privilege that Friends in Jamaica and Barbados (where it had been granted for only a brief period when a slave uprising threatened) would have been only too glad to obtain. Ordinarily, he went on, Friends in both town and country took precautions not to be surprised by bandits and housebreakers, as Quakers who owned sailing vessels did to guard against attack by pirates or enemy warships, and they were ready to have recourse to the magistrate if they suffered damage from the enemies of society. Watching without arms, therefore, in no way compromised Friends' testimony against all wars.

It seems that Fox's advice did not find acceptance with the majority of the Nevis meeting, for a little later we find the governor reporting home concerning its members: "They will neither watch nor ward, not so much as against the Carib Indians, whose secret, treacherous and most barbarous inroads, committing murders, rapes and all other enormities, discourages the planters in the Leeward Islands more than any one thing, knowing how they have been made use of in the last war by our neighbours."

So unpopular in fact did the Quakers now become with the islanders that in July 1677 the assembly passed a law imposing a heavy fine on anyone privy to the entry into the island of a Quaker and providing for that Quaker to be forthwith expelled. The reason alleged for this severity was that the Quakers had become a subversive element because they persuaded people to refuse to bear arms in defense of king and native soil. As soon as this act had been passed, Friends on the island drew up a statement declaring the assertions contained in it to be untrue. Pledging their loyalty to the Crown, they maintained that their sole object was to turn men toward the light of Christ, which takes away the need for defense by carnal weapons and for all killing. "If any are convicted by the Spirit of God in their own hearts, that fighting with any carnal weapon to the destroying of any man,

73

although their greatest enemy, be sin, then to him it is sin, if he do it."[94]

Turning from Nevis, where (so far as the surviving records show) the authorities apparently began from the end of the 1670's to regard Friends' noncombatancy more leniently, we need not linger in surveying the Quaker settlement on the neighboring island of Antigua over the by now familiar story of distraints and imprisonments, which were the lot of the male Quakers eligible for military duties from the first conversions around 1660 until near the end of the century.[95] Two incidents involving the peace witness of Antigua Friends are, however, worth brief mention. The first took place in 1664 when the island came briefly into the possession of the French. The commander of the fleet which had captured the island allowed any of its male inhabitants who took an oath of allegiance to the King of France to remain on the island; the rest were to be removed as prisoners of war. Fear concerning the fate of their families, who, left without assistance, would be exposed to the attacks of hostile Indians after the French had withdrawn, led all but four of the menfolk to take the oath. These four were the heads of the four families which then made up the little Quaker community on the island. The English governor, who had himself sworn allegiance (although he later went back on his oath, adds Besse), tried to persuade the men to conform by pointing out the dire consequences of refusal. After they had explained to the French commander that their religion prevented them from taking an oath, he told them that he was willing to accept their word alone that they would not fight against the French King for the remainder of the war. Then one of the Quakers replied: "We desire to be rightly understood in this our promise, for we can freely promise not to fight against the King of France, nor for him, nor indeed against the King of England, nor for him; for we can act no more for the one than the other in matter of war; only as the King of England is our natural prince, we must owe allegiance to him."[96] This display of loyalty to the English crown did not, however, protect the Quakers on the island from being continually harried for their pacifist scruples after the English had regained possession.

[94] Hirst, *The Quakers in Peace and War*, pp. 316-18, 323.

[95] Besse, *Sufferings*, II, 370-74, 376-78. In the seventies and eighties, under the command of a certain Major Thomas Mallet, physical manhandling of Quaker objectors by other militiamen was not infrequent on the island. Mallet, however, not long afterward came to a sudden and bad end according to Besse, who is fond of pointing out (see, e.g., pp. 344-49) that those who persecuted Friends for their peaceable principles—as well as on other grounds—were frequently struck down by God's vengeance!

[96] *Ibid.*, II, 371.

The second incident concerned the controversy which split Antigua Friends beginning in the year 1705, which, though it involved only one or two dozen persons at the most, provides a vivid illustration of the problems facing Quakers in these exposed islands. In 1705, when a French fleet appeared in the area and ravaged the neighboring islands of Nevis and St. Kitts, emergency defense measures were taken on Antigua. The authorities permitted Friends to make their contribution in the form of noncombatant auxiliary service, and they were not obliged to carry arms. Duties included "building of watch-houses, clearing common roads, making bridges, digging ponds," carrying "messages from place to place in the island, in case of danger by an enemy," as well as appearing at the place of muster without weapons. A difference of opinion soon arose between the older members, including the clerk of the little meeting, who found the compromise acceptable (perhaps, as Margaret Hirst suggests, because they could recall the stringent measures applied against Quaker objectors in former days), and the younger men, who regarded it as an impermissible watering down of their peace testimony and, indeed, as "all one" with the performance of directly military duties. By 1708 the conflict had grown so sharp that both parties proceeded to write to London Yearly Meeting for its opinion both on this matter and in regard to the payment of church rates, which was also in dispute between the two groups.

In the statement they submitted, the older men cited in their support George Fox's epistle written in 1675 to Friends in Nevis, who had faced a similar problem some thirty years earlier (as discussed above). The young men, in turn, declared in their letter:

> Whereas it is often ordered by the Government that fortifications are to be built, for the accomplishments whereof ponds for holding water (for the use of these persons who defend these places and inhabit them) are also to be dug, now the same Friends do think that if the Government will excuse them from carrying of great guns to these places, and digging of trenches, building of bulwarks, and such warlike things, and instead thereof employ them in digging these ponds, building of bridges, repairing of highways, building of guard-houses, and such things, they can freely do them, yet we do think that in such a case to dig ponds or the like to be excused from carrying of guns, etc., is not bearing a faithful testimony against such things, but below the nobility of that holy principle whereof we make profession, and (at best) but doing a lawful thing upon an unlawful account and bottom. Yet we are very will-

75

ing to dig ponds, repair highways, and build bridges, or such convenient things when they are done for the general service of the island and other people at work therein equal with us, and not to balance those things which for conscience' sake we cannot do. . . . And as concerning alarms or invasion of an enemy, we are free to give notice to the magistrate of an approaching danger or be serviceable as far as we can at such times, in going to see what vessels may be off or giving them information in such things, though as to carrying of permits for vessels of war "quietly to pass" such and such forts, when we are sensible their commissions are to kill, sink, burn, and destroy the enemy, we are scrupulous and not free in that case. And as concerning watching, we are free to do it in our own way [that is to say, by appearing without weapons].

But to appear on the musterfield, even without weapons, would be totally inconsistent with their peace witness, a view which, they added, the monthly meeting had finally come to share with them.

Margaret Hirst has rightly described the reply to these two epistles sent by London Meeting for Sufferings in the following year as "a temporizing document . . . instinct with that spirit of timidity and caution, combined with a genuine loyalty to the tolerant English Government, which marked Quaker leadership in the first half of the eighteenth century." Among its signatories were George Whitehead (after Penn perhaps the most influential figure in the Society of Friends) and Fox's son-in-law, Thomas Lower. This document went even further than the Antigua elders had done in urging compliance with the "intentions of love and favour granted by the magistrates" of the island. "As for digging ditches and trenches and making walls," it went on, "they are of like use with doors, locks, bolts and pales, to keep out bloody wicked and destructive men and beasts; and to give warning and to awake our neighbours by messengers or otherwise to prevent their being destroyed, robbed or burnt, doubtless is as we would desire should in the like nature be done and performed to us." The London Friends warned their overseas brethren against appearing to the authorities "a self-willed and stubborn people." Their definition of what action was "not an evil in its own nature, but service and benefit to our neighbours," ran directly counter, however, to that given by the young men in their letter. Unfortunately, there is a break in the record, so that it is not known what effect the missive from London had on the opposition group in the Antigua meeting. Within a couple of decades Quakerism had ceased to exist on the island.[97]

97 Hirst, *The Quakers in Peace and War*, pp. 322-26.

Even more remote than this "dark and barren island" was Bermuda, far out in the Atlantic, where in 1660 two Quaker preachers began to spread their message among its sparse inhabitants. A small meeting was set up in a private house, as was so often done in the early days of transatlantic Quakerism. The new converts do not appear to have encountered difficulties vis-à-vis the militia until 1665, when a certain Captain Dorrell with a troop of eight militiamen broke into the house where Friends were holding a meeting, dragged two of its members out by force, and carried them off to the musterfield. There the captain charged one of the two whom he had arrested, Francis Estlake, "with neglect of duty in not appearing among them in arms, and under that pretence tied him neck and heels together, which punishment the said Captain Dorrell threatened to inflict on him and others of his persuasion as often as they should neglect what he called their duty." However, instead of further tortures of this nature, the worst that was in fact inflicted on Friends in the future was either a fine of one shilling for each failure to muster or to appear in arms on an alarm or distress for nonpayment thereof, that was the outcome of a law passed in the following year.[98] Still, Quakerism never took deep root in Bermuda; by the early years of the next century there were only two Friends left on the island.

Indeed, the fact that the severity practiced against Quakers on account of their conscientious objection to military service[99] on the whole grew less from the turn of the century on may in part have been due to the declining numbers and vigor of the little societies lodged so precariously in this uncongenial soil. Not only on Bermuda but also on Antigua and Nevis, Friends practically disappeared in the course of the first two decades of the eighteenth century; and on Jamaica, too, the downward trend had already begun. Only on Barbados did the Society continue to flourish for a time.

Nevertheless, West Indian Quakerism did expand to one new area in the eighteenth century: the tiny island of Tortola in the Virgin Islands, which measured only about twenty-four square miles. Tortola was first settled as late as 1720. At the outset its inhabitants numbered a mere 100 persons, a figure which rose to around 5,000, the majority of whom were Negro slaves, before the disappearance of Quakerism from the island. Quakerism was implanted on Tortola in 1727

[98] Besse, *Sufferings*, II, 366, 367.

[99] The Quakers' opposition to taking oaths or to paying tithes—the two other major points at which Quaker practice on the islands clashed with authority—was a further cause of their ill-treatment by the latter.

as the result of a brief visit of a London merchant and traveling minister, Joshua Fielding. Among those who soon joined the Society of Friends was the lieutenant-governor of the island, John Pickering, whose father had been a Quaker, although Pickering himself had lapsed from the faith. During the 1730's a meeting was held regularly in the governor's house, and eventually as many as five meetinghouses were established on the island. Most of those who joined were slave-owning planters; Pickering himself possessed over 500 Negroes at his death in 1768. Pickering's conversion to Quakerism soon created difficulties for him, since in his capacity as governor he was in charge of the island's defense, holding the rank of major in its militia. As he wrote to a Quaker acquaintance in London of the first few years after becoming a Friend, when he still could not quite accept a fully pacifist position for himself:

> The thing soon made a great noise that I had turned Quaker, and was soon buzzed in the General's ear,[100] on which he wrote me, he heard that I had turned Quaker and if so, he thought me not a proper person to govern an island: In answer to which I wrote him, that it was a religion or Society I owned and loved above all others, and that I was endeavouring with God's assistance to live up to, tho' I had not yet got over or seen beyond that of self preservation or defending my country or interest in a just cause . . . and that if he did not like my holding the commission on these terms, he might give it to whom he pleased, for I should not alter my opinion or religion for all the honours he could confer on me nor all he could take away.

To this letter Governor Matthew gave a most friendly reply, confirming him in his position and even going so far as to say "that he believed a good Quaker bid fairer for Heaven than a wicked Protestant of his own religion."[101]

But with the coming of the wars of mid-century, when the island was in constant danger of attack from enemy ships, first Spanish and then French, and from these nations' privateers, and with the ripening of his own views into a full-fledged acceptance of Quaker pacifism, Pickering's position became untenable, and in June 1742—undoubtedly much to Pickering's relief—Governor Matthew finally relieved him of his office.

---

[100] A reference to Governor-General William Matthew of the Leeward Islands, under whose command Tortola lay.

[101] Charles F. Jenkins, *Tortola: A Quaker Experiment of Long Ago in the Tropics*, pp. 7-9, 51.

A year earlier the well-known English-born Quaker minister, Thomas Chalkley, had come to Tortola on a pastoral visit from his Philadelphia home. Shortly before his sudden and unexpected death on the island, he wrote home to his wife in a letter dated 16 August 1741: "The governor, his wife and her sister are dear tender hearted Friends, and he seems to be better satisfied as to defence since I came than he was before."[102] He notes with satisfaction—"to the mortification of all the great swordsmen"—Governor Matthew's continued confidence in Pickering, despite the latter's growing pacifist proclivities. And, indeed, for a while Matthew appears to have been willing to allow the overwhelmingly Quaker population (that is, if we leave the Negro majority out of account) to remain in a state of disarmedness. For Chalkley reports: "The General hath sent for the warlike arms here, saying if the people were Quakers they would have no need of them, that he should want them at Antigua. . . . If they could trust Providence with their interest, they had a right to do what they would with their own."

The arrival on the island of a new, non-Quaker governor signified that, in fact, the regional authorities were unwilling to risk the loss of the island to the enemy as a result of Quaker defenselessness. In 1748, Friends reported on the likelihood of their incurring penalties for disobeying both a recent requirement that all islanders keep firearms in their homes in readiness for use in case of alarm and an order from the governor to contribute money to build forts and protective turrets around the island. But, unlike their brethren on the other islands, neither in this case nor in regard to their unwillingness to serve with the island's miniature militia do Tortola Friends seem to have come into any serious collision with the authorities over their noncombatancy.[103] The reason probably lies in the preponderant influence Quak-

[102] In his *Journal* (p. 207) Chalkley describes the hesitation—likewise finally overcome—of an earlier convert to Quakerism in Barbados (called "P. M." in Chalkley's account) in accepting the pacifist element in Friends' message. In a conversation with this man, Chalkley had reminded him of the injunctions contained in the Sermon on the Mount: nonresistance to evil, turning the other cheek, loving enemies, going the second mile, etc. "After I had used these arguments," Chalkley goes on, "he asked me, *If one came to kill me, would I not rather kill than be killed?* I told him, *No; so far as I know my own heart, I had rather be killed than kill.* He said, *That was strange, and desired to know what reason I could give for it.* I told him, *That I being innocent, if I was killed in my body, my soul might be happy; but if I killed him, he dying in his wickedness, would, consequently, be unhappy; and if I was killed, he might live to repent; but if I killed him, he would have no time to repent; so that if he killed me, I should have much the better, both in respect to myself and to him.*" The argument set forth here by Chalkley is typical of those used by early Friends and some later non-Quaker pacifists discussed in this book.

[103] Jenkins, *Tortola*, pp. 19, 38, 85, 89.

79

ers wielded in the island's affairs, even after their leader Pickering had been replaced as governor.

"Things are yet young and tender here," wrote Chalkley in 1741.[104] And, indeed, Quakerism on Tortola, to an even greater degree than in the other West Indian islands, was a tender plant which fairly soon succumbed to its harsh and unfriendly environment. The isolated little Quaker group, even though it had gained fellowship for a time from the existence of a second community of Friends settled on the nearby island of Jost Van Dyke, began to decline in the 1760's, especially after Pickering's death, and it vanished altogether in the next decade.

Quakerism in the West Indies, like the Society of Friends on the American mainland, was at the beginning a manifestation of the dynamic missionary outreach of early English Quakerism. The new faith, however, failed to take permanent root on the Caribbean islands: its uncompromising pacifism, one cannot help feeling, was probably among the main factors accounting for the disappearance of Quakerism from this area within a century or so of its promising beginning.

On the American continent, too, the peace testimony brought its dilemmas and its hardships to the Quaker communities scattered along the coastal areas from Maine to Georgia and sometimes gave rise to conflict between the colonial authorities and these stubborn sectaries. But here the loyalty of the Quakers to their principles did not, after the first few decades of fierce persecution that greeted them in some areas had passed, prevent the acceptance of the Society into the texture of American life. In most provinces, indeed, Quakers were content to remain to a large extent a people apart, a community set off both from the state church and from the unchurched by the character of the severe discipline which the Society imposed on its members. In one province, however, the province of Pennsylvania, Quakers long held a position of authority, owing to the circumstances of its founding, and were for many decades leaders in political, social, and economic life. Thus, though Pennsylvania Quakerism exercised an influence on the remaining societies of colonial America second only to that wielded by the parent body in England, it differed in many important respects from these other branches of overseas Quakerism. We must now turn, then, to a consideration of the "Holy Experiment" and its aftermath.

104 *Ibid.*, p. 85.

Chapter 2

The Pacifist as Magistrate:
The Holy Experiment in Quaker Pennsylvania

I

William Penn's colony on the banks of the Delaware was intended to be a "Holy Experiment" in the wilderness, a Quaker Eden almost, set down in the forests of a new and scarcely explored continent. Hopes were high at the beginning that here at last God's children, after fighting valiantly in the Lamb's War back in the Old World, might establish a peaceable kingdom where Friends could dwell in amity with each other and with the rest of the world. And that world too, it was still believed, would eventually be won over to the Quaker faith. Pennsylvania, as the colony was called in honor of its founder's father, Admiral Sir William Penn, would in its internal institutions and its external relations constitute, as it were, a blueprint of a world to come, a new society from which war would be banished and where physical force would be contained within the limits of police action. For such a commonwealth of peace and justice, as Penn expressed it, "the nations want a precedent."[1]

Quaker control of Pennsylvania lasted seventy-four years. Yet long before this period had run out, the Holy Experiment was seen to have failed. The reasons for its failure and, even more, the conclusions to be drawn concerning the viability of pacifism as practical politics have been keenly debated ever since by historians and political scientists. This chapter is not intended as a study of Quaker Pennsylvania in all its manifold aspects: it will confine itself solely to discussing the relationship of Quaker pacifism to the domestic and external policies of the province.

The enormous expanse of forest land that was to become the province of Pennsylvania (along with Delaware formed from the three Lower Counties within Penn's grant), which until then was very

---

[1] Quoted in Guy F. Hershberger, "The Pennsylvania Quaker Experiment in Politics, 1682-1756," *MQR*, X, no. 4 (Oct. 1936), 197. I am extremely grateful to Professor Hershberger for allowing me to read a typescript draft of his forthcoming monograph on pacifism in Quaker Pennsylvania (referred to below in the notes to this and the succeeding chapter as "Ms book"). This is based on a wide array of sources in both printed and manuscript form and will undoubtedly constitute the standard work on the subject for many years to come.

sparsely inhabited except for the indigenous Indian tribes, had been assigned to William Penn by King Charles II probably, at least in part, as repayment of an old debt owed by the Crown to the late Admiral Penn. Penn and other English Quakers, as we have seen, had already been involved in the founding of the Jerseys, and Quaker immigration to America already went back almost three decades. The most important factor in Penn's plans for the new colony now was his desire to create a refuge for his persecuted coreligionists: Pennsylvania would prove to a skeptical world what Quakers could achieve in a primitive but friendly environment. True, Penn also hoped with the profits accruing from his overseas landholding to restore his financial stability, which was already declining in large part because of his generous support of the Quaker cause; but this was a factor of secondary importance for his scheme.[2] Finally, in his negotiations with the Crown, Penn had also urged the advantages that England would gain from the expansion of British settlement in this area.

Penn arrived in his new province in October 1682, seven months after the issue of the royal charter granting him his title to the land. His first sojourn in the New World lasted only two years; his departure earlier than he had expected was necessitated by his affairs in England. On returning home, he reported with satisfaction to a leading English Quaker, Stephen Crisp, that there was "not one soldier, or arms borne, or militia man seen, since I was first in Pennsylvania."[3]

The practice of nonviolence in the relations of man with man, whether savage or civilized, was as much a part of Penn's personal philosophy as it was a central tenet of the Quaker religious faith. Although some writers have concluded from certain of his utterances that Penn's condemnation of international war admitted of exceptions, that his pacifism was relativist, this claim surely is a misconception.

[2] E.C.O. Beatty, *William Penn as Social Philosopher*, pp. 43, 45, 46, 83, 175.

[3] Quoted in Catherine Owens Peare, *William Penn*, p. 283. An attempt by the mystically minded near-Quaker Thomas Tryon (1634-1703), pacifist, health reformer, and teetotaler, to persuade Quaker immigrants to adopt vegetarianism in their new homeland obviously failed. In his *Planter's Speech to his Neighbours & Country-Men of Pennsylvania* Tryon urged the Quakers to banish all lethal weapons from their settlements, even if used only to obtain food. For him, the animal kingdom was included in the precepts of Christian nonviolence. "Does not bounteous Mother Earth furnish us with all sorts of food necessary for life?" he inquired. "Though you will not fight with, and kill those of your own species, yet I must be bold to tell you, that these lesser violences (as you call them) do proceed from the same root of wrath and bitterness, as the greater do." He warned the Quaker settlers that, if they brought up their children to kill animals for food, they might become so accustomed to handling weapons that they would finally be reluctant to renounce their use against their fellow men (see pp. 17-28). Tryon did not himself visit the American continent.

Admittedly, in his famous *Essay towards the Present and Future Peace of Europe* (1693) he included (presumably) military sanctions as a last resort against a country that refused to accept the arbitration of the European diet of nations which his peace scheme postulated. It is true, too, that in the plan for intercolonial union that he propounded in 1696 provision was made for military defense. But these proposals applied only to the non-Quaker world: they represented interim recommendations that were necessary for the time being until the Quaker remnant had transformed the world. The New Testament and the Inner Light revealed to Penn as much as to the other Friends of this age a higher path, a condition of being difficult to attain yet to be prayerfully sought after, where the wearing of a sword became impossible. Penn, observes Henry J. Cadbury, "repudiated . . . any reliance upon the methods of war" in framing the government of Pennsylvania.[4] Although the establishment of religious toleration and constitutional government was the main goal of the province's founder, the creation there of a weaponless state "in accordance with the peace principles enunciated in . . . [the] sermon on the mount"[5] was also among his objectives.

The elevation of what was a personal, almost vocational pacifism into a political policy was, however, fraught with danger. Here, indeed, lay the seeds of later misfortune. For built into the very foundation of the Quaker commonwealth was the element of dependency on a higher authority that had by no means renounced the use of force in international relations, that was, moreover, soon to become engaged with its French imperial rival in a long drawn out, if intermittent, struggle which was to outlast Quaker government in Pennsylvania. Pennsylvania remained a colony of the English Crown; Quaker rule always had to function within this limitation. After Penn's death in 1718 and the conversion of his children to the Church of England, the proprietorship, too, slipped from Quaker hands. Thenceforward, the home authorities, the Penn proprietors, and increasing numbers of the inhabitants of the province that had hospitably opened its doors to the hosts of non-Quaker immigrants seeking admittance (who already began to outnumber members of the Society there by around the turn of the century) were all to a greater or less degree out of sympathy with the pacifist ideals of the Society of Friends.

At the very outset Penn had to accept titular military rank in his province, even though he did not intend to institute defensive meas-

---

[4] H. J. Cadbury, "Penn as a Pacifist," *Friends Intelligencer*, 21 Oct. 1944.
[5] Samuel M. Janney, *Peace Principles exemplified in the Early History of Pennsylvania*, p. 162.

ures within its borders—the military provisions of the royal charter of 4 March 1682 being to some extent a device to make English claims over the territory legally secure.[6] The charter, indeed, contained the following clause:

> And because in so remote a country, and situate near many barbarous nations, the incursions as well of the savages themselves, as of other enemies, pirates and robbers, may probably be feared. Therefore, we have given and for us, our heirs and successors, do give power by these presents unto the said William Penn, his heirs and assigns, by themselves or their captains or other, their officers, to levy, muster and train all sorts of men, of what condition, or wheresoever born, in the said province of Pennsylvania, for the time being, and to make war and pursue the enemies and robbers aforesaid, as well by sea as by land, yea, even without the limits of the said province, and by God's assistance to vanquish and take them, and being taken, to put them to death by the law of war, or to save them at their pleasure, and to do all and every other act and thing, which to the charge and office of a Captain-General of an army, belongeth or hath accustomed to belong, as fully and freely as any Captain-General of an army, hath ever had the same.[7]

As a result, we find "Captain-General" Penn during the greater part of his prolonged absences from the province delegating his military duties to a series of deputy- or lieutenant-governors who, some being soldiers by profession, did not share the Quaker scruples concerning war.[8]

At first, Penn had experimented with the appointment of prominent local Quakers to head the administration while he was away; "Quaker deputies, however, found it difficult to deal with the exigencies of government."[9] As Penn himself wrote in 1688 upon appointing the English Civil War veteran, Captain John Blackwell, as his deputy: "Being not a Friend, [he] could deal with those that were not and stop their mouths, and be stiff with neighbors upon occasion. This was my motive to have him."[10] Ever present in the background of Penn's thought must have been the possibility of the Crown's depriving him

[6] E. Dingwall and E. A. Heard, Pennsylvania 1681-1756: The State without an Army, p. 25.

[7] Charter to William Penn and Laws of the Province of Pennsylvania, p. 88.

[8] Cf. Charles P. Keith, Chronicles of Pennsylvania . . . 1688-1748, I, 156; II, 418.

[9] Hershberger, "Quaker Pacifism and the Provincial Government of Pennsylvania, 1682-1756," University of Iowa Studies: Studies in the Social Sciences, X, no. 4 (1937), 9.

[10] Hershberger, MQR, p. 198.

84

of his province if he were unable—or unwilling—to provide for its defense in time of war or threat of invasion. This possibility was in fact realized in 1692 when administration of the province was placed in the hands of Governor Benjamin Fletcher of New York.[11]

Although Penn regained possession two years later, he did so only at the price of a seeming renunciation of the pacifist position on his part. Promising to transmit to the provincial council and assembly all requests from the Crown in respect to defense measures, Penn told the Committee of Trade and Plantations: "He doubts not but they will at all times dutifully comply with and yield obedience thereunto." Even Sharpless, who tends to give a somewhat idealized picture of Quaker rule, is forced to describe Penn's words as "disingenuous." "For," he goes on, "he must have known that these Quaker bodies would do nothing of the kind."[12] True, Penn had not explicitly committed his own individual conscience; but he had compromised the Quaker reputation for straightforward dealing. Hershberger, while sympathetically describing the hard choice Penn had to face between probable extinction of all his hopes for the Quaker province and the possibility of regaining control at the cost of a compromise on principle, rightly speaks here of "a certain flirting with deception, which does not quite fit in with the ethical standard of a pious and spiritual Quaker."[13] Yet, in extenuation of Penn's action, it should be said that Penn's promise was probably adopted by the two parties as a face-

[11] Joseph E. Illick, *William Penn the Politician*, p. 117. See also pp. 125, 127, 128.

[12] Isaac Sharpless, *A Quaker Experiment in Government*, I, 191, 192. Margaret E. Hirst describes this incident as "the least satisfactory moment of Penn's career" (*The Quakers in Peace and War*, p. 359).

[13] Hershberger, *MQR*, p. 200. Cf. the story told to Benjamin Franklin (*Autobiography*, 1964 edn., p. 188) by the nonpacifist Quaker James Logan, who as a young man had accompanied Penn in the capacity of private secretary on the latter's second journey to Pennsylvania in 1699. "It was war time," Franklin relates, "and their ship was chased by an armed vessel supposed to be an enemy. Their captain prepared for defence, but told William Penn and his company of Quakers, that he did not expect their assistance, and they might retire into the cabin; which they did, except James Logan, who chose to stay upon deck, and was quartered to a gun. The supposed enemy proved to be a friend; so there was no fighting. But when the secretary went down to communicate the intelligence, William Penn rebuked him severely for staying upon deck and undertaking to assist in defending the vessel, contrary to the principles of Friends, especially as it had not been required by the Captain. This reproof being before all the company, piqued the secretary, who answered, *I being thy servant, why did thee not order me to come down; but thee was willing enough that I should stay and help to fight the ship when thee thought there was danger.*" Logan's most recent biographer, Frederick B. Tolles, states that Franklin's account, though possibly inaccurate in some details, may be regarded as substantially correct (*James Logan and the Culture of Provincial America*, p. 13).

saving formula, for the home authorities must surely have been well acquainted with the intransigent pacifism of the Quaker sect. The recovery of the province from the dangers which Crown rule posed for the continued existence of the Holy Experiment perhaps seemed to Penn worth a merely verbal concession. As he told his Pennsylvania Friends: "Things are not just now . . . as you may reasonably desire. . . . Accept this part of the goodness of God, and wait for the rest. We must creep where we cannot go, and it is as necessary for us, in the things of life, to be wise as to be innocent."[14]

Thus, in the relationship of Quaker pacifism to both the domestic government and the external affairs of the Quaker province, Penn and his fellow Friends strove to maintain a nicely adjusted balance between relativist "wisdom" and absolutist "innocence." The attempt frequently ran into difficulties and was finally abandoned in the middle of the next century. Let us begin our examination of the history of the Holy Experiment by considering the problem of the maintenance of internal order by a government whose members were almost all pledged by their religious belief to uphold nonviolent policies.

Unlike the nonresistant Mennonites who were soon to come out from Central Europe to settle in the Quaker colony, the Society of Friends from its inception had adopted a positive attitude toward civil government. Friends made a clear distinction between the waging of war by the state against an external enemy and the state's function of law enforcement against the domestic lawbreaker. Although they repudiated all participation in armies and the organization of military defense and practiced nonresistance in personal relations, Quakers were active in politics and in the magistracy and, moreover, became increasingly vocal in their new home in maintaining the rights belonging, as they believed, to true born Englishmen.[15] They did not share the pessimistic *Weltanschauung* of those reared in the Anabaptist tradition, the conviction that the godly would always constitute a small remnant on this earth. For Quakers, the Inner Light illumined all men, to however small a degree; all mankind, therefore, might sooner or later be reached by the redeeming spirit. "The result," writes Hershberger, "was an optimistic hope for the imminent Christianization of the social order."[16]

Although this underlying optimism led Quakers to undertake the establishment of a Christian commonwealth, they also shared with the

[14] Hershberger, *MQR*, p. 199.

[15] "We are Englishmen ourselves, and freeborn, although in scorn called Quakers," stated Maryland Friends in 1681 (Rufus M. Jones, *The Quakers in the American Colonies*, p. 333).

[16] Hershberger, *MQR*, p. 193.

rest of the Christian church a belief in the depravity of human nature in general when not restrained by government, a condition that had existed since the Fall when God had instituted civil government to suppress the evildoer and the impious as well as to promote the welfare of society. Penn, the friend of Algernon Sidney, would have included as well among the most important functions of the state the securing of liberty (though not egalitarian democracy), property, and religious toleration. These were the principles that animated Pennsylvania's founder and successive generations of its Quaker rulers.

In his preface to the final draft of the first Frame of Government which Penn issued as the province's constitution in April 1682 before his departure for America, the duties of magistrate and subject are clearly set forth: the former is exhorted "to terrify evil-doers . . . to cherish those that do well," while the latter is enjoined to render willing obedience "not only for wrath, but for conscience sake." "Government," wrote Penn, "seems to me a part of religion itself, a thing sacred in its institutions and end." It must not merely wield "coercive or compulsive means"; correction of evildoers is only "the coarsest part of it." "Kindness, goodness and charity" must be the methods employed to further the material and moral welfare of the community under its care.[17]

Pennsylvania's Quaker rulers, whether in the assembly and the executive council (which in the seventeenth century shared the legislative power) or in the lower magistracy, had no compunction in administering a police force and in imposing on malefactors the penalties laid down in the law. However, Penn and his people were successful in ameliorating some of the harshness and cruelty of the contemporary English penal code. Prisons were set up, but (at least in theory) these were to have a redemptive purpose. We read, for instance, in the "Laws agreed upon in England" in 1682 before the colony was formally established: "That all prisons shall be workhouses for felons, vagrants and loose and idle persons; whereof one shall be in every county."[18] At this date, an attitude of this kind was indeed a revolutionary advance in penology. Brandings and earcroppings are mentioned from time to time in the court records in the next century, but from the beginning "the favorite method of punishing was by whipping" and imprisonment,[19] with fines employed for less grave of-

[17] *Charter to William Penn etc.*, pp. 91, 92.

[18] *Ibid.*, p. 100.

[19] Pennsylvania, its founder states in a letter of 1701 (quoted in Beatty, *William Penn*, p. 231), had been "at great charge to build strong prisons, with high brick walls, grates, bolts, chains, etc., and one to watch and ward as well as" to seize dangerous malefactors. For Penn's zeal in urging the suppression in Pennsylvania

fenses.[20] "Some of these punishments," writes Lawrence H. Gipson, "may seem to our generation extreme and harsh, nevertheless, the Great Law [of 1682] was remarkable for its humaneness, especially as it existed side by side with codes loaded down with atrocious sanctions."[21] In many instances, the harsher penalties inscribed on the statute books seem to have been inflicted only infrequently. Apparently, however, neither Penn nor his fellow Quakers at this time held a testimony against capital punishment. At the beginning in Pennsylvania, in contrast to the mother country where according to English law a multitude of offenses were punishable by death, this penalty was retained for only two offenses: murder and treason. Although it is doubtful whether the Crown would have given its approval to the establishment of the Quaker colony if any punishment less than death had been made the penalty for these two crimes, its retention passed apparently without protest from any member of the Society. In a letter written from England in September 1688, for example, we find Penn directing his deputy-governor, Blackwell, "that the murderous woman's sentence should proceed, the case being notorious and barbarous."[22]

In the early decades of the eighteenth century we can observe a stiffening of the provincial penal code, a widening of the range of offenses for which harsh penalties were inflicted. In the so-called New Castle Code of 1700, "multilation and branding stand out among the new sanctions." "There was little of redemption in these punishments."[23] The climax in this process came in 1718 when the provincial assembly passed a law extending the death penalty to twelve more felonies, which were punished in this way in English law. In this case the abandonment to a large degree of the Quaker province's more enlightened attitude resulted from political maneuverings which had been going on for a number of years. The Quakers' enemies had

---

of pirates and of interlopers in respect to the English navigation laws, see *ibid.*, pp. 84, 217-27, 230, 231.

[20] H.W.K. Fitzroy, "The Punishment of Crime in Provincial Pennsylvania," *PMHB*, LX, no. 3 (July 1936), 260-64.

[21] Lawrence H. Gipson, "Crime and Its Punishment in Provincial Pennsylvania," *Pennsylvania History*, II, no. 1 (Jan. 1935), 6.

[22] *Pennsylvania Colonial Records*, I, 252. This, however, seems to be the only case of capital punishment inflicted in the province before 1700. It is interesting to note that Penn's more radical contemporary, the vegetarian pacifist Thomas Tryon, also did not disapprove of capital punishment. In his *Planter's Speech* (p. 31) he writes: "And if any wilfully commit man-slaughter, then let such perish by the same sword or weapon."

[23] Gipson, "Crime and Its Punishment," p. 9; Fitzroy, "The Punishment of Crime," p. 249.

been attempting to deprive them of their political predominance by forcing an oath on holders of judicial and administrative office within the province. These officials would then have been required to take a test oath themselves and to administer one to others. In order to prevent the consummation of their opponents' designs and to maintain their right to make an affirmation in place of an oath, the Quaker assembly finally agreed in a kind of bargain with the home government to a measure which would approximate the Pennsylvania penal code to that prevailing back in England. The Quaker bench acquiesced without a murmur in the law's increased stringency. In January 1730, we find David Lloyd (1656-1731), the former leader of the country party among Friends and an ardent upholder of the Quaker peace testimony insofar as it related to attack from without the state, supporting the execution of a convicted burglar. He "justly deserves to die," he then wrote, "and it may be of ill consequence to spare him."[24]

However, since harsher measures had begun to be introduced much earlier, the deeper reasons for this development must be sought elsewhere. During the time when almost all the inhabitants still belonged to the Society of Friends, few problems had arisen in connection with law enforcement. Those were the days when it was enough for Thomas Lloyd (1640-1694), when acting as chief executive of the province, to go out into the streets at night and deal out religious admonishment to any roisterous character he met with there. "Philadelphia became under his control the most decorous of cities."[25] But the influx of non-Quaker immigrants that began toward the end of the seventeenth century made the maintenance of law and order an increasingly complex problem. The preamble to an act of 1698 states that "many dissolute persons, notwithstanding the said laws [i.e., already on the statute book], have committed divers thefts and robberies within this government."[26] The idyllic conditions of the early days, when the strong arm of the law was only rarely needed to reinforce the meeting discipline of the religious Society to which most citizens belonged, soon passed, and the need grew for more effective police control, as did the clamor from the side of the non-Quaker settlers for more forcible action. In the case of moral offenses, the Puritan strain in Quakerism generated an impetus of its own in legislating against such things as profanity, drunkenness, and sexual

[24] Roy N. Lokken, *David Lloyd*, pp. 198, 237; Sharpless, *Political Leaders of Provincial Pennsylvania*, p. 103.
[25] Sharpless, *A Quaker Experiment*, I, 69.
[26] Fitzroy, "The Punishment of Crime," pp. 248, 249.

irregularity. "I recommend to you," Penn told Quaker officials in Pennsylvania in a letter dated 21 October 1687, "the vigorous suppression of vice, and that without respect to persons or persuasions. Let not foolish pity rob justice of its due and the people of proper examples."[27] And in 1727, for instance, we find that stalwart Quaker pacifist, Thomas Chalkley, reproving the largely Quaker magistracy for their alleged laxness in enforcing the law in this respect. "The Lord," he relates in his *Journal*, "was angry with the magistrates . . . because they use not their power as they might do, in order to suppress wickedness; and do not so much as they ought, put the laws already made in execution against profaneness and immorality: and the Lord is angry with the representatives of the people of the land, because they take not so much care to suppress vice and wickedness, . . . as they ought to do."[28]

For all its strictness, however, the Pennsylvania legal code throughout the period of Quaker rule undoubtedly continued to temper justice with mercy to a greater extent than other contemporary systems of law.[29] In civil disputes between members of the Society of Friends the parties were required to settle the affair by arbitration within the Society; recourse to courts of law was permitted only if arbitration were refused by one party, who would then suffer disownment for failure to abide by the discipline. Law suits involving a Friend and a non-Friend, however, could be settled in an ordinary court of law without endangering the member's status within the Society.[30] Thus, conciliation was combined with a relatively mild system of law enforcement in an effort to produce a commonwealth that was governed, be it only approximately, in the spirit of the Sermon on the Mount.

Church and state were formally separate. Nonetheless, despite the

[27] Beatty, *William Penn*, p. 35. See also pp. 290-92.
[28] Chalkley, *Journal*, 1754 edn., p. 203.
[29] Gipson, "Crime and Its Punishment," p. 16.
[30] See Appendix B in Tolles, *Meeting House and Counting House.* Complaints sometimes made about inconsistency between the Quakers' disapproval of taking their own disputes to the provincial courts and their willingness at the same time to serve as magistrates in these courts do not appear to me justified, especially in view of the fact that as early as 1683 (*Charter to William Penn etc.*, p. 128) provision was made (although apparently rarely put into effect subsequently) for appointing "common peacemakers" "in every precinct," the results of whose arbitration were given the force of law. Thus, not only was there no objection in principle to recourse on the part of Friends to the state machinery of justice; but, on the contrary, this machinery as framed by the province's Quaker rulers contained means of arbitration and extrajudicial conciliation open to all citizens, Friend and non-Friend alike. Of course, it is possible to argue that the Christian pacifism to which Quakers adhered is incompatible with participation in state affairs, including its judicial side. But this is a different question.

fact that the Society of Friends was granted no special privileges not possessed by other denominations, a close link existed between the government and the Quaker community. The same men who sat in the assembly (and at first in the council, too)—where, beginning as early as the mid-1680's, some of the Quaker representatives in fact from time to time displayed more heat than charity in the pursuit of their political goals—often took a prominent part also, at least during the early decades, in the deliberations of the yearly meeting, which until 1760 was held alternately in Philadelphia and Burlington (it has always included parts of New Jersey as well as strictly Pennsylvania territory). Weighty Quakers occupied most of the high judicial offices in the province, and the administration of justice in town and country was to a large extent carried out by members of the Society. A minute of Philadelphia Monthly Meeting in 1685 well illustrates the Quaker character of the state in practice:

> John Eckley and James Claypoole are appointed by this Meeting to request the magistracy of the county that they will please to keep their court on the first 5th day of every month, which, if they please to grant, then the weekly meeting, which hath hitherto been on the 5th day, shall be on the 4th day, that so the court and the meeting may not be on the same day.[31]

It was not always easy for the Quaker administrators to draw the line between police action, which could be carried out with a minimum of physical force, and measures where a degree of force that was scarcely consistent with a nonviolent philosophy appeared necessary. An incident of this latter type occurred in 1691 and aroused strong criticism—not from orthodox Friends but from a small dissident group that was to break away from the Society in the following year under the leadership of the Scotsman George Keith (1638-1716). The causes of the Keithite schism, however, were unconnected with pacifism or government: they stemmed from Keith's attempt to play down the doctrinal importance of the Inner Light in contrast to the authority of the Bible and the historic Jesus.

Early in 1691 a man named Babbitt and some associates stole a vessel from the harbor in Philadelphia and proceeded to commit a number of robberies on the river traffic. Upon receiving information of Babbitt's depredations, three magistrates—including a leading Quaker, Samuel Jenings—issued a warrant "in the nature of a hue and cry"[32]

---

[31] Quoted in Sharpless, *Quakerism and Politics*, p. 82.
[32] Samuel Smith, "The History of the Province of Pennsylvania," *The Register of Pennsylvania*, VI (1830), no. 16, 242. See also no. 18.

to apprehend the miscreants. Armed with this authority, and possibly (the accounts are contradictory) with no weapons more lethal than this, several young Quakers succeeded in capturing Babbitt's gang and bringing them to justice. The affair caused quite a stir, and it was their seizure and punishment that led Keith and his Christian Quakers (as his followers now called themselves) to denounce the Quaker magistracy for what they alleged was a dereliction of the Society's peace testimony.

In several tracts the Keithites now argued the inconsistency of Quaker participation in government. In their view, a Friend should refuse appointment as assemblyman or provincial councillor, justice of the peace or sheriff, constable or juryman, if their duties of office involved "the taking away of life or any other corporal punishment." In fact, they said, the magistracy was scarcely conceivable without the use of the sword "as the executive part of . . . office cannot in any ordinary way (and without miracles) be done without it." The application of force for police purposes within the state scarcely differed in principle from, or was in any way less reprehensible in a follower of Christian nonviolence than, the use of deadly weapons against an enemy from outside. "A pair of stocks, whipping post and gallows, are carnal weapons, as really as sword or gun, and so is a constable's staff, when used, as [it] hath been by some, to beat and knock down the bodies of some obstinate persons." If a constable might use physical violence against a domestic wrongdoer so as to lead to his death, why—asked the Keithites—was it unchristian to employ lethal weapons against an outside aggressor such as the French or Indians? Would not the Quaker magistrates eventually be brought to sanction the use of force against armed invaders? "For it is not the number being great or small that makes a thing to be right or wrong." The Keithites, like the Anabaptists and Mennonites, did not deny the divine sanction or practical need for the state to curb evildoers—even to the extent of waging defensive war. But the Quaker, the Christian, must have no part in such action.

To the arguments that Quakers in government could help to assuage its harshness and that their withdrawal would probably mean their replacement by cruel and evil rulers, the Keithites sternly replied that it could never be right to do evil that good might come and, moreover, that good and just men were to be found among non-Quakers, and even among the heathen, who would administer the state according to their natural lights. Let all who are convinced of the Truth, they advised, retire from the magistracy and leave government to those who have not yet reached a full awareness of the meaning of Christian nonviolence.[33]

The Keithites, however, went beyond a general criticism of Quaker involvement in running the state. Seizing upon the Babbitt affair, they accused Samuel Jenings, and those members of the Society who had aided and approved his forcible suppression of piracy, both of transgressing Friends' testimony against fighting and of undermining the position of Quakers in Britain, the American colonies, and the West Indian islands who at this very time were suffering for their refusal to accept service in the militia. "Is not their practice here," wrote Keith and his five colleagues in *An Appeal* which they drew up in the late summer of 1692 concerning the stance of Pennsylvania Quakerdom, "an evil precedent, if any change of government happen in this place, to bring sufferings on faithful Friends that for conscience sake refuse to contribute to the militia? And how can they justly refuse to do that under another's government, which they have done, or allowed to be done under their own?" They poured scorn on the Quaker magistrates "preaching one day, *Not to take an eye for an eye, Matt. 5.28*" in their capacity as Friends' ministers and on the next reversing their position "by taking life for life" in consequence of their obligations on the bench.[34]

Official Quakerdom, already irritated by the acrimonious dispute with Keith over theological matters, quickly struck back. The first edition of the *Appeal* was seized as a seditious publication tending to bring the magistracy—a predominantly Quaker magistracy—into disrepute, and its printer, the Keithite William Bradford, was arrested. Together with Keith and one other "Christian Quaker" who had signed the tract, he was then tried and found guilty. The penalty for Keith and his colleague was merely a £5 fine, which was not in fact collected from them.[35] But the spectacle of men, until recently prominent and respected members of the Friends' community, being arraigned and punished by Quaker judges for, among other offenses, propounding—in a manner, it is true, that these judges deemed offensive to the magistrate's office—what, in the Keithites' view, were true Quaker peace principles,[36] was extremely unedifying. Although the

[33] *A Testimony and Caution to such as do make a Profession of Truth, who are in scorn called Quakers*, pp. 1-10. This anonymous pamphlet was issued by the Keithite M. M. in Philadelphia on 28 December 1692.

[34] George Keith et al., *An Appeal from the Twenty Eight Judges to the Spirit of Truth & true Judgement in all faithful Friends*, pp. 7, 8.

[35] Ethyn Williams Kirby, *George Keith*, pp. 57-59, 72, 73, 81-85.

[36] In 1693 Keith wrote that he and his friends had been harried "by fines and imprisonment, for asserting the Quakers' principles against the use of the outward sword" (quoted in Kirby, *Keith*, p. 85).

Keithites obviously welcomed the opportunity that the Babbitt affair offered to add yet one more argument in their controversy with their opponents, there does not appear to be any reason to doubt the sincerity of their rigorist interpretation of Friends' peace testimony. In 1700, Keith, who had meanwhile returned to England, joined the established church, becoming an Anglican priest not long afterward, and his Christian Quaker group as a result soon dissolved. Whether the fervent episcopalian and still more rabid anti-Quaker that Keith now became retained anything of his Anabaptist views on war and government is not known.

Along with their uncompromising pacifism, Keith's Christian Quakers, it may be noted, adopted a critical attitude in regard to Quaker slaveholding. Though not explicitly urging the abolition of slavery within the province by law, the Keithites charged the Society of Friends with inconsistency in permitting ownership of slaves among its own members. This, argued the Keithite *An Exhortation and Caution to Friends Concerning Buying or Keeping of Negroes*, which William Bradford issued in August 1693 at his New York print shop, contravened the ban on "prize goods" which the Society maintained; for enslavement of Negroes resulted as much from "war, violence, and oppression; and theft and robbery of the highest nature," as did the seizure of property resulting from directly warlike actions.[37]

The Keithites, however, were not the first American Quakers to attack slaveholding by Friends for, among other reasons, its connection with war. The earliest protest of this kind had come five years before; its authors were members of the Germantown Friends meeting drawn from Dutch- and German-speaking Quakers who had joined the Society before their migration to the New World. Though mostly Nether-

[37] Thomas E. Drake, *Quakers and Slavery in America*, pp. 14, 15. Drake points out that this identification of the acquisition of prize goods and of slaves as both flowing from the same source, war, was common among Quaker antislavery advocates in the eighteenth century. They did not realize, of course, that the first to use this argument in their community had been the dissident Keithites. Cf. Sydney V. James, *A People Among Peoples*, pp. 127-29, 136, for the use made by American Quaker antislavery advocates in the first half of the eighteenth century of the general argument that slavery was incompatible with the Society's peace testimony. At first, many of these men encountered strong resistance from their meetings. Among the most devoted of the early abolitionists was the French-born Quaker Anthony Benezet, who in 1754 told Philadelphia Y. M.: "How can we, who have been concerned to publish the gospel of universal love and peace among mankind, be so inconsistent with ourselves as to purchase such who are prisoners of war, and thereby encourage this unchristian practice . . . ?" (George S. Brookes, *Friend Anthony Benezet*, pp. 80, 81, 475, 476). By this date the cause had made considerable headway among Friends and the buying, if not yet the keeping, of slaves was frowned on by the Society.

landers in origin, they had come out a few years before from the west German towns of Krefeld and Krisheim, where they had been converted from the Mennonite faith. The reasons for their emigration were mixed, economic and religious motives each having played a role.[38]

The protest against slavery was signed on the meeting's behalf by four of their number, including the intellectual leader of the Germantown settlement, Francis Daniel Pastorius (1651-1719).[39] Its authors declared the impossibility of maintaining slavery except through the threat of physical force: slavery's origins and its fruits were violence. Slaveholding in Quaker Pennsylvania was gaining Friends a bad reputation on the European continent. What would Friends do if their slaves combined together and revolted?

> If once these slaves . . . should join themselves, fight for their freedom, and handle their masters and mistresses as they did handle them before; will these masters and mistresses take the sword and war against these poor slaves, like, we are able to believe, some will not refuse to do? Or have these negroes not as much right to fight for their freedom, as you have to keep them slaves?[40]

The protest was premature. Forwarded up through monthly, quarterly, and yearly meeting in Pennsylvania, it was finally pigeonholed by London Yearly Meeting without any action having been taken. However, the ferment did not subside altogether, and the antislavery movement among American Friends slowly increased in strength during the course of the following decades.

Whereas an awareness of the seeds of war that lay within the institution of Negro slavery only matured among Pennsylvania Quakers slowly and painfully, the sensibility they displayed in their treatment of the indigenous inhabitants of the province was greater right from the beginning. It is not the purpose of this chapter to enter into a detailed study of Quaker relations with the Indians during the period

---

[38] See William I. Hull, *William Penn and the Dutch Quaker Migration to Pennsylvania*, chap. IV. Among the causes of their departure from Germany were difficulties encountered in connection with their objection to military duties. See pp. 237, 266, 289.

[39] One of the signatories, Abraham op den Graff, seems to have been of a rather obstreperous character. In December 1703, for instance, it was recorded that he "did mightily abuse the bailiff [Arent Klinken, also a Quaker, who in 1697 had provided stocks for punishing minor offenders and whose house in 1697 became a temporary prison] in open court wherefore he was brought out of it to answer for the same at the next Court of Record." Sometime after 1708 Op den Graff returned to the Mennonites. See C. Henry Smith, *The Mennonite Immigration to Pennsylvania in the Eighteenth Century*, pp. 113, 115.

[40] The protest is printed in full in Hirst, *Quakers in Peace and War*, Appendix E. See also Drake, *Quakers and Slavery*, pp. 11-14.

of Quaker rule.[41] Suffice it to say that from the start Friends strove to deal justly with the native inhabitants, to protect them from the corrupting influences in European civilization, and to live beside them in peacefulness. At the outset Penn made it a principle that all land should be purchased at a just price, and later deviations from fair practice in this respect which took place after Penn's death (and for which Quakers as a whole were not, in fact, responsible) were among the factors leading ultimately to a deterioration in relations with the Indians.

There was certainly an element of benevolent patriarchalism in the attitude of Brother Onas (as the Indians called Penn) toward the native inhabitants, unspoilt children of nature in the view of Penn and many of his contemporaries (as there was a similar element in Penn's relations with his own people in Pennsylvania). There was, too, some ambiguity in his treatment of the Indians as virtually sovereign owners of the land and in his simultaneous acceptance of his own monarch's claims to rule in the area. This ambiguity is revealed, for instance, in the famous letter he addressed to the Pennsylvania Indians in October 1681 when he was beginning preparations to visit his new patrimony across the waters. There is one all-powerful and all-loving God for all the peoples on earth, he told them. "Now this great God hath been pleased to make me concerned in your parts of the world; and the king of the country where I live hath given unto me a great province therein; but I desire to enjoy it with your love and consent, that we may always live together as neighbors and friends."[42] Whatever the theoretical implications of European settlement might have been, so long as the situation was not complicated by the intrusion of non-Quaker authorities and settlers, good relations were maintained between the Indians and the Quakers—even if the practice frequently followed by successive Quaker assemblies of appeasing the Indians with gifts may appear to us today of somewhat dubious value. As hunters primarily, the Indians were willing in principle, as Hershberger has pointed out, to coexist peacefully alongside the white-skinned cultivators of the soil. Although it has sometimes been asserted that the long peace was chiefly due to the unwarlike qualities of the Delawares and Shawnees, who were the tribes in closest contact with the Pennsylvania settlements, they were to give

[41] See Rayner Wickersham Kelsey, *Friends and the Indians 1655-1917*, pp. 24-27, 29-34, 47-57, 62-70, 74-83, for Pennsylvania Quakerdom's Indian policy up to the outbreak of the Revolution.
[42] Quoted in Peare, *Penn*, p. 223.

all too visible proof of their belligerence during the French and Indian War that ultimately brought Quaker rule to an end.

II

Although the Quaker government was fairly successful in bringing its Indian policy into line with the requirements of the Society's peace testimony, the problem of squaring the duties of administering the province within the framework of English imperial policy with a pacifist witness that would have at least some relevance in public life became increasingly difficult. In the far north and northwest the French were a potential menace even to the mid-Atlantic colonies, though the threat only became immediate toward the middle of the eighteenth century. In addition, the province was exposed to enemy attack by water and to the depredations of pirate and privateer. This situation gave rise to a running debate between successive Quaker-dominated assemblies and a long line of deputy-governors who, representing the absentee proprietors, had inherited the unenviable task of extracting support for war measures from the Quaker legislators. "Hosts of mosquitoes are worse than of armed men," said Captain John Blackwell, the first of these governors to attempt the task, in the course of the humid summer of 1689, "yet the men without arms worse than they."[43] His sentiments were to be echoed by his successors in similar circumstances. For, commingled with the straight pacifist issue, other factors were usually present to complicate the debate: obscure intrigues and countermaneuvers stemming from the assertion by provincial politicians of their constitutional rights against the claims of the proprietary interest or from the understandable reluctance, exhibited by the citizenry of all the colonies, to pay out money for purposes that seemed remote from their own concerns. As time passed and the pacifism of the Quaker-born politicians became more and more perfunctory, became in fact merely an inherited belief to which they made a formal bow of acknowledgement, political and economic opposition to defense measures began to predominate.

Pacifism became a public issue for the first time in the fall of 1689 soon after the outbreak of "King William's War" with his continental rival Louis XIV, which was to last until 1697 when the Treaty of Ryswick brought a short pause in the long Anglo-French struggle. At the beginning of November, Governor Blackwell came before the council with a request from the English government for defensive measures

---

[43] *Ibid.*, p. 312. See also Hershberger, MS book, chap. 4: "Worldly Power *versus* Christian Love," n. 28.

97

in the colony. At first, the Quaker members of the council hedged, alleging that such steps were in fact not needed. Said John Simcock: "I see no danger but from the bears and wolves. We are well, and in peace and quiet: let us keep ourselves so." However, one Quaker councillor, Griffith Jones, went so far as to urge qualified support of the governor's request. "Every one that will may provide his arms," he said. "My opinion is that it be left to the discretion of the governor to do what he shall judge necessary." These words brought Samuel Carpenter to his feet. Carpenter, a man of considerable spiritual stature whose growing affluence gave additional weight to his utterances, had suffered heavy distraints on his property for refusal of service in the militia earlier while a resident in Barbados.[44] He now spoke out plainly concerning the Quaker objection to war. "I am not against those that will put themselves into defense," he told the governor, "but it being contrary to the judgement of a great part of the people, and my own too, I cannot advise to the thing, nor express my liking it. The King of England knows the judgement of Quakers in this case before Governor Penn had his patent. But if we must be forced to it, I suppose we shall rather choose to suffer than to do it, as we have done formerly." This affirmation of willingness to suffer rather than compromise on principle, reminiscent of the earlier "heroic" age of Quakerism, was one that was only rarely to be heard in the official utterances of Quaker politicians in the decades to come. Much more frequent, as we shall see, were the attempts to ward off contributions for military purposes by appeals to expediency of various kinds.

On this occasion, however, Carpenter's example seems to have injected boldness into some of his colleagues. When the discussion was resumed two days later, we find John Simcock stating forthrightly: "We can neither offensively nor defensively take arms." At the same time, the Quaker councillors expressed their unwillingness "to tie others' hands" (to quote Simcock again) if they did not share Quaker scruples on this question. And they repeatedly stressed their loyalty to the Crown and their readiness to act as dutiful subjects in all matters which did not go against conscience. Finally, the five Quaker councillors, who formed a majority at that session, withdrew to consult among themselves. Their decision, which Blackwell's arguments were unable to shake, was to refuse active support to measures involving military preparedness, while at the same time giving the governor carte blanche (but with no money attached) to take on his own such defensive measures as he thought fit.[45] This was, indeed, about the

44 Hirst, Quakers in Peace and War, p. 357.
45 Pa. Col. Records, I, 306-11.

furthest that Quaker administrators of Pennsylvania could go in opposition to the warlike activities of the realm of which they still remained an integral part.[46]

In the following year the council approved the organization of an *ad hoc* militia within the province against possible French and Indian attack, provided that it was undertaken by private initiative without financial or other aid from the administration.[47] But such tepid support for preparedness did little to assuage the hostility of those who were pressing for the inclusion of Pennsylvania within the scheme of imperial defense. The governors of the other colonies, some of which were more exposed to enemy attack than Pennsylvania, were among the most severe critics of Quaker rule in Pennsylvania. In addition, Penn's friendship with the Catholic James II had brought suspicions of Jacobite sympathies down on his head after the Glorious Revolution of 1688; and, as we have seen, these doubts, along with fears of the military consequences of Quaker pacifism, were instrumental in bringing about the temporary conversion of Pennsylvania into a Crown colony under the authority of Governor Fletcher of New York in May 1692.[48]

The Quaker politicians, however, proved no more amenable to the Crown's representative, Governor Fletcher, than they had been earlier to Quaker William Penn's deputy, Governor Blackwell. We find Fletcher reporting to the Lords of Trade back home on his sojourn in the Quaker province:

> I have spent some weeks there but never yet found so much self-conceit. They will rather die than resist with carnal weapons, nay they would persuade me their province was in no danger of being lost from the crown, though they have neither arms or ammunition, nor would they suffer those few to be trained who were free for it, their minutes of council and assembly which we are now transcribing for you, will appear a farce.[49]

In 1693 the assembly was, in the end, persuaded to grant the sum of £760—but only after the governor, who attempted to convince the legislators that present defensive measures were analogous to such means

---

[46] Hershberger's remark, *MQR*, pp. 203, 204—"Their conscience still forbade military action, but they preferred not to use the moral argument against it if another could conveniently be found"—does not appear too stringent a comment on the Quaker contribution to debates on military measures on this and on subsequent occasions.

[47] Edwin B. Bronner, *William Penn's "Holy Experiment,"* p. 138.

[48] Winifred Trexler Root, *The Relations of Pennsylvania with the British Government*, pp. 261, 262.

[49] Quoted in Robert L.D. Davidson, *War Comes to Quaker Pennsylvania 1682-1756*, p. 13.

of protection as high walls, locked doors, and watchdogs that even Quakers used to guard their personal property, finally agreed to confirm their laws and privileges. The governor had at the same time offered a sop to the Quaker conscience by giving a somewhat vague assurance that money contributed by war objectors "shall not be dipt in blood." Yet it was clear that even if it would not be spent directly on the purchase of arms and ammunition, the appropriation was to be used for such scarcely less military purposes as the payment of officers' salaries.[50]

In the following year the assembly, now under the leadership of that ebullient Quaker constitutionalist, David Lloyd, expressed its willingness to vote money to purchase food and clothing for the Iroquois, who might otherwise go over to the side of the French.[51] Although the humanitarian guise of the request—"to feed the hungry and clothe the naked"—scarcely veiled the underlying military implications of the appropriation, the Quaker assemblymen were on this occasion prepared to swallow the pill when sugared in this way. After the province had been returned to Penn, further grants of money were passed by the assembly in 1695 and 1696 "to be made use of as he [the king] pleased." In 1696, Penn himself had intervened, urging David Lloyd and leading Pennsylvania Quaker politicians like Samuel Carpenter to use their influence in favor of a positive response to the Crown's requests for money. Refusal, Penn claimed, might endanger the existence of Quaker rule. At this date a further and extremely cogent reason for compromise lay in the desire of Lloyd and the Quaker politicians to obtain a revision of the second Frame of Government of 1683 in favor of an extension of the rights of the colonists. Penn's deputy, Governor Markham, finally acceded to their demands in November 1696, whereupon the assembly made their appropriation.[52]

Harmony on this issue was not of long duration, however. For in May 1697 the assembly turned down a request for at least £2000 to maintain Pennsylvania's quota of 80 men for colonial defense, which Governor Fletcher of New York had transmitted through Captain Markham's mediacy. The matter had been discussed at a joint meeting of council and assembly. The grounds given for rejection were, however, nonpacifist. "Considering the infancy and poverty of this government, which also lieth under other considerable debts," they felt that the province could not at this stage afford expenditure on such a

---

[50] *Pa. Col. Records*, I, 400.

[51] Roy N. Lokken, *David Lloyd*, pp. 56, 64-66. The bill was not accepted in the end by Governor Fletcher, because he had other objections to it.

[52] *Pa. Col. Records*, I, 490-92; Lokken, *David Lloyd*, pp. 70, 71.

scale. At the same time, they expressed their "readiness to observe the King's further commands, according to [their] religious persuasions and abilities."[53]

By the end of King William's War, it had become clear that the "religious persuasions" of the Quaker politicians concerning the inadmissibility of Christian participation in war of any kind, though undoubtedly genuine, were somewhat elastic. They might be stretched on occasion to meet the exigencies of practical politics: hope for a political concession, perhaps, if the legislators proved amenable, or anxiety over the possible curtailment of their rights if they remained adamant in refusing all compromise. During this period—and, indeed, virtually up to 1756—a saving clause or a significant vagueness in phraseology was used to cushion the full impact of such action on the continued validity of their peace testimony.

Certainly, critics like Guy F. Hershberger are right in pointing out the subtle but corrupting influence that Quaker involvement in the game of political power exerted on the Society's politicians and, indeed, on the Society as a whole. Parliamentary practice usually demands a certain give-and-take: "the Quakers found it very hard to reconcile their two ideals of representative government and pacifism."[54] Moreover, the maintenance of a Holy Experiment in living became increasingly identified with—indeed, slowly came to be replaced by —the political supremacy of the Quaker party in the province; it seemed worthwhile to guarantee this supremacy at the price of sacrificing some of the content, if not the form, of the Society's peace testimony. "The more they fought for power the more did they weaken their peaceful testimony. But to the political Quakers the struggle for power meant more than the cause of peace."[55]

Yet Quaker policy in the matter of war appropriations was by no means devoid of a certain logic, granted its basic premises. Friends' belief that a society patterned on the principles of the Sermon on the Mount was still achievable short of the millennium gave the original impulse to the creation of the Holy Experiment. Obedience to the powers that be, another central principle of Quakerism's political philosophy, meant in the context of colonial Pennsylvania not only obedience to the provincial Quaker authorities but to the Crown back in England. "And let none use their liberty by abusing of it," the New Jersey-Pennsylvania Yearly Meeting instructed its members, especially

[53] *Votes and Proceedings of the House of Representatives of the Province of Pennsylvania (Pennsylvania Archives*, 8th ser.), I, 195-97.

[54] Hershberger, "Quaker Pacifism and the Provincial Government of Pennsylvania, 1682-1756," Ph.D. diss., U. of Iowa (1935), p. 64.

[55] *Ibid.*, pp. 91-94.

the young people of its meetings, in 1694; they would be abusing it, among other ways, "by refusing to render to the government its lawful demands of tributes or assessments, for, according to scripture, we are to be subject to every ordinance of man for the Lord's sake."[56] If Caesar used this tribute for war, that was his concern; as we have seen, there does not appear to have been a testimony among early Friends against paying war taxes, let alone those "in the mixture." True, decade after decade we find the Quaker legislators displaying obvious reluctance to sanction the raising of money for war, a hesitation which did not stem solely from the pragmatic reasons, whether justified or not, that were alleged for refusal of requests of this kind. For it was one thing for English Friends excluded from Parliament and administration to pay whatever sums were demanded by their government willingly; it was quite another thing—even if in theory the distinction was somewhat unclear—for Quakers in the seat of government to take responsibility for raising taxation that would be spent on war. That the direct responsibility for expending the money was delegated to others and that the money was voted "for the use of" the Crown served, however, to veil the reality of Quaker complicity in the direction of military preparations, if only intermediately. From this practice flowed some of the ambiguities of Quaker "defense" policy in Pennsylvania. Nevertheless, although the assembly was not always able to prevent its nonpacifist fellow citizens from forming some kind of military association for defense, it did consistently refuse official consent to the organization of a militia on even a voluntary basis until a few months before the end of Quaker rule in the province. Here it did not seem possible to construct a viable bridge between civil obligation and religious conscience.

The conclusion of peace in 1697 did not mean an end to the military demands that the Quaker legislators had to face. The Atlantic seaboard colonies formed one long extended frontier where warfare was endemic on both land and sea. If Pennsylvania was relatively secure by virtue of her geographical position and the peaceful Indian policy of her rulers, other provinces continued to face danger and to demand defensive measures, too, in time of nominal peace. Thus, in June 1701 we find King William III requesting Penn, who was then in Pennsylvania, for £350 to be dispatched as his province's allocation of the costs of erecting fortifications on the New York frontier. In explanation of their refusal to grant this sum, the assembly, to whom the governor had passed on the royal demand, pleaded both the poverty

[56] "A General Testimony against all Looseness and Vanity" (1694), MS in F.H.L.S.C., typescript p. 18.

of a young colony already overburdened with taxes and quitrents and the tardiness of neighboring provinces to contribute their share to the common defense. Let His Majesty be assured, they told Penn, "of our readiness (according to our abilities) to acquiesce with, and answer his commands, so far as our religious persuasions shall permit, as becomes loyal and faithful subjects so to do." There was only a hint here of any conscientious scruples against contributing to military measures. However, Quaker views on war were well known in official circles. Yet why provoke royal anger by emphasizing the provincial rulers' unorthodoxy on this point if the requisition could be turned down on less controversial grounds? Writing home to his son in the following November, the governor told him:

> If they say, But you will not fight? I answer, King Charles, King James and King William knew that we are a Quaker colony, it was so intended . . . let us not be persecuted in our country when our consciences are tender, that came so far and have endured and spent so much that we might enjoy them with more ease than at home.[57]

Penn had stubbornly resisted growing pressure to set up a militia in the province. But he did give his approval at this time to the establishment at the entrance to the Delaware Bay of an armed watch against pirates and other possible invaders. In refutation of the complaints lodged at home against the province's alleged defenseless condition by the Anglican Colonel Robert Quarry, judge of the independent Vice-Admiralty Court in Pennsylvania and leader of the anti-Quaker faction there, Penn had asked what good a militia would be in the province "since by land there is none to annoy it"; "by sea, the position of the country and the manner of our settlements considered, . . . a small vessel of war would, under God's providence, be the best security."[58]

The Quaker political community faced the outbreak of Queen Anne's War in 1702 with its pristine idealism somewhat dimmed. In the previous year Penn's generous Charter of Privileges had vested all

[57] Votes and Proceedings, I, 278, 280, 289, 290; Pa. Archives, 2nd ser., VII, 12. See also Illick, Penn the Politician, pp. 187-89; Mary Maples Dunn, William Penn, pp. 180, 181.

[58] Correspondence between William Penn and James Logan, I, 27. See also Beatty, William Penn, pp. 113, 114; Bronner, Penn's "Holy Experiment," pp. 209, 211; Root, Relations of Pennsylvania with the British Government, pp. 274-79. At the conclusion of chap. 3, "William Penn and the Holy Experiment," MS book, Hershberger discusses another example, taken from the year 1710, of Penn's support of armed action by the English government against enemy attack on sea and river traffic.

legislative power in a unicameral legislative body based on a fairly wide electoral franchise and subject only to his deputy's veto, thereby reducing the provincial council to a merely advisory status.[59] Friends, although rapidly becoming a minority of the population, continued as before to dominate provincial politics through their heavy concentration in the geographical areas and in the social groups most liberally represented in the assembly, as well as through the high regard in which they were held by some of the new immigrants who gave them their political support. Yet Quakers on the whole showed little gratitude to Penn for his liberal attitude, quite exceptional at that date, and accepted what he had granted as simply the minimum rights and privileges due true-born Englishmen.

Indeed, Friends in politics had not shown themselves free from bitter factional strife. Slowly an antiproprietary party had coalesced under the leadership of the Welsh lawyer, David Lloyd, with its supporters drawn chiefly from the country Quakers. Against these country Friends were pitted the Quaker conservatives, small in numbers but eager to defend the proprietor against what they considered the "villainy" of Friend Lloyd and anxious to establish a stable society in which the increasingly affluent Quaker merchants of Philadelphia would exercise the same deserved authority within the province as they wielded in the counsels of Philadelphia Monthly Meeting. The acrimonious debates that took place during the last decade of the seventeenth century and during the first two of the eighteenth, both within the assembly and outside it, may have represented an important step in the evolution of American constitutional rights, but they were not an entirely edifying spectacle within a Society dedicated to the pursuit of brotherly love.

The place occupied by the peace testimony, although it still formed a vital part of the religious belief of almost all Pennsylvania Friends, became more and more anomalous. The political element, the argument from expediency, played an ever increasing role in the Quaker assembly's opposition to military measures. A recent Quaker historian states—perhaps a little too severely—that, by the time of Penn's final departure for England in 1701, already "the 'holy experiment' was nearly forgotten." But, as he admits, "a residue remained from the idealism of the early years, a residue that leavened the society as well

---

[59] By the second Frame of Government of 1683 the number of seats in the council had been reduced from (a theoretical) 72 to 18 and in the assembly from (a theoretical) 200 to 26. This size was retained for the two bodies in the Charter of 1701. By 1752 the number of assemblymen had been raised by stages to 36.

as the government of Pennsylvania during the remainder of the colonial period."[60] The history of the Quaker peace testimony, like many other aspects of the Society, over these years is to a large extent the story of the interplay between political expediency and the residual idealism that eventually became one of the factors leading to Quaker withdrawal from politics.

Quaker readiness within certain limits "to contribute for support of government,"[61] even if the use made of the money granted was for military purposes, usually provided a possible modus vivendi between assembly and home government (in the person of the proprietor's deputy) so long as the deputy-governor behaved with a modicum of tact. But in 1703, owing to a misjudgment of character that unfortunately was neither the first nor the last in his career, Penn appointed that rather foolish young man, John Evans, as his deputy (with instructions, incidentally, to see that "nothing may lie at my door in reference to the defence of the country").[62] The results were disastrous. In March 1706, for instance, believing with "the inexperience and assuming of youth," as an eighteenth-century Quaker historian expressed it,[63] that their pacifism was but a tender plant that could easily be uprooted, Evans attempted to panic the Quakers into approving the organization of a militia and other defensive measures by raising an alarm of a French invasion by sea threatening Philadelphia. Apparently Friends in the city almost to a man remained calm and did not budge in their determination to avoid taking any step that might compromise their peaceable principles. When the alarm proved false, relations between Evans and the assembly (even though the house was temporarily in control of the conservative party among the Quakers) became extremely strained. Tension increased when further acts of provocation from Evans's side followed within a few months.[64] As Hershberger aptly remarks: "The alarm did not cause the pacifism of the Quakers to break down. The break-down came when they learned the alarm was false. . . . What had been preserved of the spirit of love during the false alarm was now lost in the fight with the governor"

[60] Bronner, Penn's "Holy Experiment," p. 2.
[61] Votes and Proceedings, I, 477.
[62] Illick, Penn the Politician, p. 224. But Penn also instructed Evans that Quakers and other religious pacifists must not be "compelled in person or purse" in connection with defense measures. See Dunn, William Penn, p. 174.
[63] Robert Proud, The History of Pennsylvania, I, 468.
[64] Hirst, Quakers in Peace and War, p. 362. See also Pa. Col. Records, II, 243, where a minute of the council speaks of the proof that the assemblymen, who were all (with one exception) Friends, had given of their pacifist convictions "in the late alarm in not joining at all with the rest in bearing arms."

that became increasingly vehement after the victory of the Lloyd party in the October elections.[65]

Continued rumors of impending attack from enemy privateers during the summer months of 1706 were regarded skeptically by both council and assembly, and Governor Evans's requests for measures to meet the danger were received coldly. In September the assembly in a "Humble Address" to the governor turned down his requests categorically, pleading in extenuation of their refusal the poverty of the province and the tardiness of neighboring colonies to erect fortifications. Above all, however, they argued that in fact the menace was chimerical. "We hope," the Quaker politicians told Evans, "we are not in much danger of the enemy, considering our remoteness from the sea, and difficulty of access."[66] Once again in a situation of this kind, it was considered more prudent to make no mention of Friends' conscientious scruples against war.

The pacifist issue was certainly a delicate one for the Quaker rulers of an English colony. James Logan (1674-1751), who almost alone among the prominent Friends of this period did not share his sect's belief in nonviolence, was perhaps for this very reason acutely aware of the precarious nature of the existing compromise. "Friends can scarcely bear up under the difficulties they are oppressed with," he told Penn in 1703. If the Crown should insist that the province make an effective contribution to the war effort, "our government will be soon broken or miserably exposed." Logan's advice to his master was to rid himself, and Friends, of the burden of government, a load too heavy to bear in a world that was obviously not yet prepared to follow their peaceable example. "For my own part," he confided, "I am weary of government affairs as they must be managed."[67]

Penn, too, was evidently growing weary of his responsibilities in the New World since pressing business at home prevented his settling among his people across the waters and since, with each year, his lengthening absence from Pennsylvania widened still further the gap between the founder-proprietor and his independent-minded Quaker subjects and coreligionists. But it was his financial misfortunes, in part undeserved and in part due to his incompetence in money matters, that led Penn from 1703 on to begin negotiations with the Crown for the eventual surrender of his province. Penn naturally insisted on safeguards for the political rights of the provincials and for the special religious testimonies of his Friends. They would have to continue free

---

[65] Hershberger, Ph.D. diss., p. 106.
[66] Votes and Proceedings, I, 573-76.
[67] Penn-Logan Correspondence, I, 233-35.

from the obligation of taking oaths or of rendering military service or paying fines in lieu thereof. Agreement was at last reached in 1712, but Penn's sudden stroke which to a large extent deprived him of his mental powers put an end to the transaction before the final papers had been signed.

Chief among those who supported Penn's design was, of course, his former secretary Logan. In May 1708, for instance, we find Logan reporting to Penn, with the declared intent of proving the impossibility of combining pacifist beliefs and governmental responsibilities, that the depredations of enemy privateers on coastal traffic had recently become so severe that vessels were venturing out from the Delaware River only "under convoy of a small man of war from New York who comes round on purpose." Presumably, Philadelphia Quaker merchants were among those who took advantage of this paramilitary protection, though perhaps they may have regarded this as essentially police action. But the Friends' dilemma was a real one. As Logan went on: "This last business of the privateers upon our coasts infesting us above others, because unarmed, has brought Friends to a pretty general confession that a due administration of government, (especially in a time of war), under an English constitution is irreconcilable with our principles."[68]

In August, when the governor called a special meeting of the assembly to present a request for money to provide the wherewithal for eradicating enemy privateering, he compared such action to the forcible suppression of disorder within the state by the police, a not ineffective analogy in view of the Quaker support for government in this respect. "We have laws against thieves and robbers," he said, "and we have officers to put those laws into execution; if they resist, they are taken by force, and by force, when occasion, are obliged to submit to the last extremity; and without this there would be no such thing as government." It it were right to use physical force on the domestic wrongdoer even to the ultimate point of inflicting death, then were not similar measures justified against those who now aimed to destroy the whole state?

The argument was certainly plausible (it had Quaker Logan's agreement).[69] Yet it was not entirely convincing, for there were, indeed,

[68] Amelia M. Gummere, "Two Logan Letters," *Journal of the Friends' Historical Society*, IX, no. 2 (April 1912), 87-89.

[69] In the first half of 1709, when a French privateer had made a landing on the lower reaches of the Delaware and rumors of imminent invasion by a French fleet were rife, Logan was to tell Penn: "That a private murderer or robber should be taken and hanged, and yet public ones should be suffered to proceed without any resistance, is made the subject of so much banter and scorn, that 'tis very uneasy

107

significant differences between force to back law and war measures flowing from the absence of international law, differences that were to be urged by Quakers both within the assembly and outside it, as we shall see. But there was no hint of this line of argument in the reply drawn up by the assembly two days later in answer to Governor Evans's speech. Giving vent to indignation that trade should have been thus disrupted without Her Majesty's navy being able to take adequate steps to prevent it and, at the same time, setting out in review the financial support that the people of Pennsylvania had given the government in recent years "according to their abilities and circumstances," the assembly limited itself to a vague expression of willingness to grant money if it could really be proved that previous appropriations were insufficient to cover the present need. "For, as we partake of the Queen's gracious protection to all her subjects," the address (signed by David Lloyd, as speaker of the house) concluded, "so we hold ourselves obliged, in duty, to give supplies for supporting this government, according to the powers granted by the royal charter . . . altho' we do not pretend to direct the way and manner that the Governor . . . should dispose of those supplies."[70]

In the following year the incompetent Evans was replaced as Penn's deputy by Charles Gookin. A war atmosphere prevailed: threats of direct invasion by sea and talk of more distant conflict with the French on the northern frontiers disturbed the province's calm. Thus, one of the first actions of the new governor was to approach the assembly early in June 1709 with a request for the sum of at least £4,000, which would cover the cost of Pennsylvania's share in equipping its quota of men to the number of 150 in the proposed expedition against Canada. On the recommendation of a number of leading Quaker councillors and assemblymen, the request was refused as incompatible with the pacifist views of the overwhelming majority in the province's ruling bodies. Instead, as a gesture of goodwill insisted on by the more conservative councillors who had been drawn into the discussion, the assembly voted the Queen a mere £500 as "a present." This gift was disdainfully turned down by Governor Gookin, probably not least of all because of the proviso attached that the money should be paid out only when the legislature was quite sure that it would not be used for war purposes. Although the plea of poverty was not omitted on this occasion either as an explanation of the smallness of the sum voted, conscientious objection to war was now

---

to those concerned." He adds: "Those who differ from us in persuasion, as one half of Philadelphia does, are full of complaints, and Friends so uneasy under them" (*Penn-Logan Correspondence*, II, 344, 345; see also pp. 347, 348).

[70] *Votes and Prcoeedings*, II, 804-8.

given the most prominent place in the assembly's explanations.[71] The uncompromising character of this apologia for the assembly's conduct may have stemmed from the fact that the appropriation was being requested for an offensive campaign rather than for allegedly defensive, quasi-police action, assistance to which could be cloaked in suitably vague terminology. Two years later, however, Quaker consent was readily obtained for an expedition against Canada of an almost identical kind. The reason for this otherwise surprising change of attitude must be sought in the development of domestic politics in Pennsylvania.

In the elections of 1710 the Lloyd party was overwhelmingly defeated, and the Quaker conservatives gained complete control of the assembly. Their victory at the polls had been due largely to support given them by Philadelphia Yearly Meeting, where the well-to-do elements, who were alarmed at the vehemence with which the country party pressed their attacks against the proprietary interest, exercised great influence. These conservative Friends remained loyal to the Quaker peace testimony, although some among them—the elder Isaac Norris (1671-1735), for instance—seem to have entertained serious doubts about its compatibility with participation in government. All felt that their political opponents within the Society, driven on by their desire to assert provincial rights, had lost sight of the equally important testimony of rendering obedience to the powers that be. Thus, in July 1711 when Governor Gookin placed before the assembly a request from Her Majesty for £2,000 to help equip another expedition against the French in Canada, its consent was quickly given. Its address stated:

> That the majority of the inhabitants of this province being of the people called Quakers, religiously persuaded against war, and therefore cannot be active therein; yet are as fully persuaded, and believe it to be their bounden duty to pay tribute, and yield obedience to the powers God has set over them in all things, as far as their religious persuasions can permit; and therefore we take this occasion to express our duty, loyalty, and faithful obedience to our rightful and gracious Queen Anne.

The money being voted on this occasion "for the Queen's use" would, the assembly hoped, be considered "as a token of our duty" toward the Crown.[72]

As Isaac Norris had foreseen, the vote aroused "clamours and un-

---

[71] *Ibid.*, II, 860; *Pa. Col. Records*, II, 459-64. See also Tolles, *James Logan*, p. 49; Sharpless, *A Quaker Experiment*, I, 196-200.
[72] *Votes and Proceedings*, II, 990, 991.

easiness" among Friends in the province, who were now being required by their political and spiritual leaders (in this case, one and the same persons) to subsidize a military expedition. In fact, as we have seen, the policy and the motives behind it were not new: what was more novel perhaps was the unconcealed military purpose of the whole appropriation. But Norris argued that Friends had no business to be concerned with the use the Queen might make of the tax now to be paid by the province, "*that* being not our part, but hers."[73]

Among those who were most active in drumming up support for the tax among members of the Society was the English-born Thomas Story, a member of the provincial council at this time who, as we have already seen, was both a courageous exponent of Quaker pacifism and a proponent of rendering all war taxes to Caesar. In his sermons Story now exhorted Friends to pay the recent imposition willingly and with a clear conscience. In the Anglo-Dutch wars of the previous century, Dutch Friends, he told them, had contributed their share of the tribute demanded to carry on military operations, while Quakers in England at the same time had paid taxes to King Charles II to support his war effort against the Dutch. Friends in the two countries were not guilty of each other's blood because they had fulfilled their Christ-imposed duty of rendering tribute to Caesar. "The application," in Story's view, "is the business of kings and not of subjects" —words that echo those of his colleague, Isaac Norris.[74]

On the whole, apparently, Friends did pay the war tax of 1711; whether they did so as willingly as the conservatives hoped is not clear from the surviving sources. Indeed, we do hear of distraint being levied on the property of Quakers in Bucks County and in Chester County by order of the magistrates (who were also Friends, of course) for refusal, presumably on conscientious grounds, to pay the tax voted by the Quaker assembly. Moreover, several Friends were put in prison and at least one disowned by the Society for resistance to the tax. Thomas Story was himself strongly attacked in an anonymous pamphlet. The author, who described himself in the preface as "a plain rustic," approved payment of ordinary taxation but dissented from rendering straight war levies of the sort demanded in 1711. "Philalethes," which was the pseudonym the author adopted, may have been an adherent of the Lloyd party, which, in fact, returned to

---

73 *Penn-Logan Correspondence*, II, 436. Story was later to claim that the money then voted would be spent on "bread and flour" for the troops; but that its allocation for such directly nonlethal purposes was in the minds of the Quaker assemblymen when the appropriation was made is far from clear.

74 Emily E. Moore, *Travelling with Thomas Story*, pp. 124-27.

power in 1714; this connection is implied by Story in the rebuttal he drew up against the tract of his opponent, whom he identifies with a certain "turbulent" Quaker, William Rakestraw. Yet the doubts "Philalethes" cast on the compatibility of participation in the civil magistracy with maintenance of the Quaker peace testimony seem to disprove too close an association with the constitutionalist party.[75] At any rate, "Philalethes" in many ways appears as a forerunner of the radical peace men who were to bring great weight to bear on the Society in Pennsylvania early in the second half of the century.

III

A long period of peace and increasing prosperity for Pennsylvania followed the signing of the Treaty of Utrecht in 1713. The war issue did not crop up again in an acute form until the autumn of 1739 after the outbreak of war with Spain. But, during this quarter of a century of peace, tendencies already present in the development of the province's Quaker community were to grow in strength and to prove of fundamental importance in the trying decades of mid-century.[76]

In the first place, we find that increasing wealth among the Quaker bourgeoisie centered in Philadelphia considerably diminished the earlier idealism. As Frederick B. Tolles has shown, the countinghouse became a serious rival to the meetinghouse in the devotion of many Philadelphia Friends. Moreover, riches combined with political authority and the increasingly hereditary character of membership in the Society lessened the hold of Quaker pacifism on many members of the Society engaged at one or another level in the public affairs of the province.

[75] *Tribute to Caesar, How paid by the Best Christians, And to What Purpose*, preface and pp. 11-15, 26, 27. The tract bears no date of publication; however, it probably appeared between 1713 and 1715. Convincing evidence of Rakestraw's authorship is given by Hershberger in MS book, chap. 4. Rakestraw appears to have been disowned by Philadelphia M. M. in late 1713 for his campaign against Story. Story's reply (entitled "Treason against Caesar") to Rakestraw's pamphlet remained in manuscript. Emily Moore has published extracts from the copy deposited in the Quaker collections at Friends House (London), and it is discussed in Hershberger, MS book. See also Hershberger, *MQR*, pp. 207-9.

[76] This period is dealt with in two chapters of Hershberger, MS book: chap. 5, "Power, Prosperity, and Complacency," and part of chap. 6, "Unquakerly Indian Relations." Concerning the spiritual aspects of Pennsylvania Quaker development, Thomas G. Sanders has this to say: "In the early years of Quakerism it was assumed that a conversion underlay an individual's living a changed life, whereas in Pennsylvania it was believed that men have a natural inclination or capacity to conduct themselves in the way of the kingdom . . . the original eschatological element changed from a kingdom oriented to the will of God and guided by God's prophets to an essentially ethical realm of brotherhood, peace, and love" (*Protestant Concepts of Church and State*, p. 137).

Secondly, just as the Quaker virtues of sobriety and thrift had brought both the reward of material well-being and the danger of spiritual decay, so the Quaker tolerance which had led William Penn to open the doors of his province to all comers both "established a situation of cultural pluralism and thereby created the conditions for cultural growth," to use Tolles's words,[77] and at the same time exposed the Society to eventual engulfment in a sea of immigrants whose religious and political views were often quite alien to the Quaker ethos. True, the Germans for the most part, especially the small body of Mennonites and allied sects, proved reliable political allies of the Quaker interest. But the tough and restless "Scotch-Irish," as these northern Irish Presbyterian immigrants came to be called, remained almost wholly out of sympathy with Quaker ideals even though they proved to be enterprising pioneers. In conjunction with the adherents of the Episcopalian church, they provided the backbone of the anti-Quaker faction. But for a long time the frontier districts where the Scotch-Irish chiefly settled were underrepresented in the assembly: in 1752 they still had only 10 out of 36 seats. Along with the votes of the Germans, who looked on the Quakers as their benefactors for granting them a refuge in Pennsylvania and as their protectors against involvement in foreign war and oppressive conscription such as had blighted their lives back in Europe, this underrepresentation of the Scotch-Irish population served to shore up Quaker rule against the day when their position as a minority would make their continued political predominance impossible. Although under the Quakers restriction of the franchise was certainly no worse, indeed was considerably less illiberal, than in the mother country, the very conditions of colonial life made it inevitable that politically underprivileged elements would eventually demand political equality. And, in the struggle to achieve this equality, Quaker peace principles became an important issue, although in fact most of the Quaker politicians had virtually ceased before mid-century to regard pacifism as of relevance in the political realm.

A third area where, during the years of peace, changes beneath the surface of public life brought about conditions less favorable to a political witness of Quaker pacifism, lay in the sphere of Indian relations. These relations remained outwardly friendly, but such incidents as the notorious "Walking Purchase" of 1737, whereby Indians were deprived quasi-legally of considerable areas that they believed to be rightfully theirs, stored up trouble for administration and people in the years ahead when the French came into a position to utilize the

[77] *Quakers and the Atlantic Culture,* p. 131.

smoldering grievances of the Pennsylvania Indians. Although it is true that James Logan was involved in this shady transaction, it is also true that neither the Society as a whole nor the Quaker-dominated assembly was responsible in this instance for the bad faith of the province's proprietors, the former Quaker and now Episcopalian Penns. Yet this was, in fact, only one incident in a chain of events that originated in the deep conflict of interest between indigenous Indian and European settler over rights to the land. Quakers had consistently tried to resolve this conflict by fair practice in obtaining land. But the non-Quaker immigrants who began to stream into the province in increasing numbers as the eighteenth century advanced were not so particular as Friends were about the methods they used in their dealings with the Indians.[78] And the Quakers found it as difficult to control them as they had, in the case of the Walking Purchase, to prevent Crown or proprietary interest from doing things which ran counter to their own Indian policy. Gradually and almost imperceptibly, the tender plant of conciliation between Indian and white inhabitants of the Quaker colony that had sprung from the seed sown so hopefully by Penn and his early Friends was trodden under foot.

However, when war came to Pennsylvania again in the fall of 1739, it was not an Indian war, nor one that brought direct attack from internal or external enemies; as earlier, it meant only indirect involvement in the great imperial conflict that was shaping up between those old rivals, Great Britain and the Bourbon powers of France and Spain. The whole world was to become a battlefield now; eventually the struggle got entangled in the complicated rivalries of Central Europe, as well as in such distant spots as the Indian subcontinent. Pennsylvania's Quakers were thus caught up unwillingly in a long and bitter conflict of global dimensions.[79] However, their opposition to war, which for many Quakers active in politics on both the provincial and local level was by now somewhat lukewarm, was complicated by the fact that the provincial assembly was simultaneously engaged in a vehement contest with the proprietors of Pennsylvania. Thus, the issue over the decade and a half to come was rarely a straightforward one between simple adherence to the Society's traditional peace testi-

[78] See Sherman P. Uhler, *Pennsylvania's Indian Relations to 1754*, pp. 88ff., 108, 109, 111ff.

[79] Herbert L. Osgood writes of this period: "Quaker principles as to war became a question of large significance in general colonial politics, for the frontier and the struggle to maintain and defend it had now so far developed that Pennsylvania had become in a true sense a keystone of the structure" (*The American Colonies in the Eighteenth Century*, IV, 49). And general colonial politics, it may be added, formed only a part of the global policies of the major West European powers.

mony and wholehearted support for the war effort. Instead, party politics, the political power game, was subtly intermixed with considerations of Christian principle and absolute morality.

In October 1739, upon receiving news of the outbreak of war with Spain, Deputy-Governor George Thomas came before the assembly with a request to put the province in a condition of defense—in other words, to raise and equip a militia, erect fortifications, and provide the funds necessary for measures of this kind. If these measures were not taken, he told the Quaker legislators, their towns might be sacked and the colony ravaged by invaders.[80] However, the house showed no anxiety to discuss the matter and postponed its consideration to the end of the year. Then, on 5 January 1740, it drew up its reply in the traditional form of a "Humble Address," an answer that in fact was a straight refusal to comply with the governor's recommendations. They reminded him that liberty of conscience, the free exercise of religious scruple, had been by charter guaranteed to the inhabitants of the province by its founder and that his people, the Quakers, had always been "principled against bearing of arms in any case whatsoever." (During the previous autumn, in fact, Pennsylvania Yearly Meeting had issued a strongly worded call to its members to remain "vigilant" in upholding Friends' peace testimony and in keeping free from complicity in "warlike preparations, offensive or defensive.")[81] True, there were now many in the province who did not share Quaker principles concerning war, who "for ought we know" might think it necessary to take up arms in defense of country and hearth and who, should therefore be permitted to act as their consciences prompted them. Still, there could be no compulsion exercised in the matter. For, on one hand, to make conscription for militia service universal would not only be a violation of the colonial constitution but would also entail persecution of the numerous conscientious objectors in the province; while, on the other hand, the exemption of the latter from the working of the law would make an unfair distinction between members of the same commonwealth. In any event, no matter how its provisions were framed, the imposition of a militia law would constitute "an inconsistency" on the part of a body almost all of whose members were convinced pacifists. Let the governor take whatever steps he wished (although how he would find the money to implement his designs the address ignored), since he was legally entitled to institute military measures. "Morally speaking," the home government was chiefly responsible for seeing that the province was preserved "from the in-

80 *Votes and Proceedings*, III, 2512, 2513.
81 Ezra Michener, *A Retrospect of Early Quakerism*, p. 295.

sults of our enemies." Their trust, the assemblymen piously concluded, lay in the Almighty's arm, "which not only calms the raging waves of the sea, but sets limits beyond which they cannot pass."

A debate on the viability of pacifism as provincial policy ensued between the adroit governor and the assembly, which was now being led by the equally dexterous new speaker of the house, John Kinsey (1693-1750). This confrontation brought out the basic difference of viewpoint between the two sides. Governor Thomas's first reaction to the address of 5 January had been one of indignation. The very same day he wrote to the proprietors, exclaiming angrily: "Those who profess conscience, will not allow others to act agreeable to theirs, that is, to make use of the strength and courage God has given them to defend all that can be dear to a man in this world."[82] Behind the scenes he began to work for exclusion of the Quakers from the assembly by means of a test oath—a scheme that came to nothing owing to the influence of the Quaker parliamentary lobby in England and to the eventual granting by the assembly of money that could be employed for war purposes. However, in his exchanges with the assembly the governor spoke moderately, expressing consideration for Quaker scruples. His views were presented in two communications dated 10 and 23 January 1740 respectively.

Thomas in the first place stressed his desire to preserve constitutional freedoms and to avoid penalizing conscience. "I have always been a professed advocate for liberty, both civil and religious, as the only rational foundation of society," he stated. He agreed that there should be no attempt to coerce Quakers and other nonresistants to bear arms. Yet, in his view, a compulsory militia for nonpacifists was essential if the province was to protect itself effectively. The latter, indeed, formed the majority of the inhabitants of the province. And this fact led Thomas to make a second point, that the assembly, being "the representatives of the whole body of the people," should reflect, too, the needs and desires of the whole people, and not merely of the Society of Friends, to which almost all the assemblymen happened to be affiliated religiously. Thirdly, Thomas cleverly utilized Quaker approval of civil government and the mobilization of physical force behind the law, even to the point of inflicting the death penalty on thieves and murderers, in order to draw a parallel between this practice and the repulsion of the external enemies of society by force of arms. "You yourselves," he told the assembly, "have seen the necessity of acting in civil affairs as jurymen and judges, to convict and condemn such

[82] Quoted in Root, *Relations of Pennsylvania with the British Government*, p. 280.

little rogues to death as break into your houses, and acting in other offices where force must necessarily be used for the preservation of the public peace."

The governor appealed to Quaker precedent, too, in arguing his case for the assembly's support. He reminded them of the example of their English brethren dutifully paying taxes "for carrying on a war against the public enemy." He cited the minutes of the provincial council in the case of the military appropriation of 1711 (discussed above). Was not this tax imposed for the purpose of a military expedition against the French in Canada? The circumstance that the money was in fact misapplied by the governor at the time (as the assembly now asserted in reply) did not alter the principle. Thomas even attempted to prove that Penn, their founder, could have been only a very lukewarm pacifist since he had accepted the title of captain-general from the king and was known to have issued a commission—"which I have under his own handwriting"—for the officer in command of a fort at New Castle. Finally, the governor stated his opinion that God means for us to make provision to protect ourselves. Goodness and goodwill were not sufficient to ward off enemies. Moreover—and whatever the Quaker politicians might argue to the contrary—the safety of the province was endangered now that Pennsylvania was exposed to imminent attack both by land and by sea.

The Quaker assembly replied point by point to the governor's arguments and persuasion in messages dated 19 and 26 January. The assemblymen contended that there was in fact no need for the kind of measures the governor demanded. There was no war yet with the French, and they hoped there would not be one in the foreseeable future. By reason of its natural situation and its many inhabitants who, except for the Quakers, were willing to take to arms should an enemy invasion by ill chance occur, Pennsylvania was safe from danger. They believed their present peaceful policy, the governor's assertions notwithstanding, had the support of a large majority of Pennsylvania citizens, including many who did not in theory hold Quaker views on war. "Otherwise, why do they need to be compelled [i.e., to join a militia] who think it necessary for their common safety?" Again, the assembly reiterated its trust in divine protection for those who strove after righteousness, "even as the world is at present circumstanced." God, they told the governor, "for the sake of ten righteous persons, would have spared even the cities of Sodom and Gomorrah." They rejected Thomas's analogy between fighting and killing in war on one hand and police action and judicial execution on the other. To kill a soldier was to destroy a human being whose sole crime, per-

116

haps, was "obedience to the commands of his sovereign . . . who may . . . think himself in the discharge of his duty"; whereas to execute "a burglar who broke into our houses, plundered us of our goods, and perhaps would have murdered too, if he could not otherwise have accomplished his ends," was simply to apply the known judicial penalty for violating "laws human and divine."[83]

With some indignation the assembly sought to rebut the interpretation Thomas attempted to put on past Quaker actions. "The payment of taxes in carrying on a war by our Friends in England," they said, "is not parallel to the case under consideration." ("But as you have not been pleased to shew the difference, I must still conclude that there is not any," countered the governor.) The 1711 appropriation was granted simply as tribute to Caesar, as a token of their respect for Her Majesty the Queen, and not as approval of a military campaign. And as for the alleged belligerence of Penn himself, the assembly could only presume that the governor had not consulted his writings, for there he would have discovered that Penn "not only professed himself a Quaker and wrote in their favour, *but particularly against wars and fighting*, in which he has said so much and so well for himself . . . we need say little for him." His supposed approval of warlike measures stemmed solely from his recognition that some elements of the province's population did not subscribe to Quaker nonviolence. Surely, Friends' principles concerning war had for several generations been well enough known at home to both Crown and administration for there to be little need now of an elaborate defense.[84]

The discussion dragged on during the following months without much that was new being added to the argument. Although the Quakers' case was certainly weakened by approval of capital punishment, which watered down the consistency of its nonviolent witness, the distinction that they made between war and police action possessed greater validity than the governor was prepared to recognize. In his eyes, Quaker opposition to war was sufficient to incapacitate them for all part in public affairs. He asked them indignantly:

[83] This distinction is, indeed, a fundamental one in the Quaker position. Cf., e.g., Philadelphia Y. M.'s *The Ancient Testimony of the People called Quakers, reviv'd.* of 1722, where a sharp contrast is drawn between "the material or carnal sword, invented by men to execute their wrath and revenge upon their fellow-creatures," on one hand and "the sword of justice 'ordained of God for punishment of evil doers, and praise of them that do well'" on the other (p. 23).

[84] *Pa. Col. Records*, IV, 366-75, 380-84, 387, 388. For this whole controversy between Governor Thomas and the assembly, see also Sharpless, *Quakerism and Politics*, pp. 111-27; Osgood, *The American Colonies in the Eighteenth Century*, IV, 54-60; Brent E. Barksdale, *Pacifism and Democracy in Colonial Pennsylvania*, pp. 11-16, 44, 57.

If your principles will not allow you to pass a bill for establishing a militia, if they will not allow you to secure the navigation of the river by building a fort, if they will not allow you to raise men for His Majesty's service, and on His Majesty's affectionate application to you for distressing an insolent enemy, if they will not allow you to raise and appropriate money to the uses recommended by His Majesty, is it a calumny to say that your principles are inconsistent with the ends of government at a time when His Majesty is obliged to have recourse to arms . . . ?[85]

In the summer of 1740 the debate became involved with an extraneous issue, when in the middle of the harvest season the administration began to recruit indentured servants for service with the military. This action aroused the angry protests of Quaker merchants and farmers, who regarded it as an attack on the sanctity of contract. But, although the assembly remained adamant in refusing to sanction a militia and still continued to reiterate its repugnance to voting money for the purpose of killing, it did tentatively agree to make a grant ("a tribute to Caesar," as they put it) of £3,000 "for the king's use," provided these "redemptioners" were released from service and allowed to return to their masters.[86]

Meanwhile, no less a person than the distinguished Quaker minister, Thomas Chalkley, had come forward to defend the Friends' viewpoint and to strengthen assemblymen and other members of the Society in their passive resistance to the governor. Until then, he told them, the Lord had preserved the province from harm because his people had trusted in him and had renounced the ways of war. "Yet I would not be understood to be against the magistrates exercising the power committed to them, according to just law," Chalkley was careful to add, "but national wars, woeful experience teacheth, are destructive to the peaceable religion of Jesus, to trade, wealth, health and happiness." He warned them in prophetic strain that, if they were to backslide and sanction violence now, their enemies would overrun the country. Let them not excuse themselves by pleading the influx of non-Quakers, nonpacifists, into the province. The king had bestowed the land upon Penn as a refuge for Friends. Why, he demanded of those who disagreed with their views on war, "did they come among us, if they could not trust themselves with our principles, which they knew or might have known, if they would?"[87]

[85] Pa. Col. Records, IV, 465. Cf. p. 442.
[86] Ibid., pp. 425, 435, 436, 441.
[87] Chalkley, Journal, 1754 edn., pp. 317, 318.

The assembly's appropriation of 1740 had been turned down by the governor because of the strings attached to it. And so the trial of strength between the Quaker assembly and the military-minded governor continued. An English Friend, who was a careful observer of American affairs, wrote now of his coreligionists in Pennsylvania: "Your cause is undoubtedly good, but I am afraid you discover a little more warmth than is quite consistent with the moderation we profess." He chided their representatives in the legislature for the "acrimony" of their debates which, despite undoubted provocation on the governor's part, was unseemly in men of their religious profession.[88]

More critical of the assembly's stance was William Penn's former secretary, James Logan, who was still a prominent, if not particularly popular, member of the Society. Logan, indeed, seems at first to have given Governor Thomas support in his efforts to extract money from the assembly, for Logan, as we know, had always been out of sympathy with Friends' views on war, although out of loyalty to his people he had not publicly expressed his dissent. In fact, he tells us, he had refrained from taking a more active part in the Society's affairs because of his disagreement on this important article of faith. Early in his career he had even been disciplined by Philadelphia Monthly Meeting for accompanying the sheriff and an armed posse in an attempt to dislodge squatters from an island in the Delaware River and had been forced to present a somewhat grudging "acknowledgment" of error.[89] Logan has, in fact, been called "too good an imperialist to be a good Quaker."[90] His unscrupulous dealings in the fur trade—buying at a low price, selling at an exorbitantly high price, and trafficking in rum with the Indians—and the undefined yet undoubted role he played in the Walking Purchase of 1737 were certainly out of tune with the ethos of his first patron, William Penn, and of his Quaker coreligionists. In 1718, for instance, we find him working behind the scenes to establish a garrison settlement on the Indian frontier near Conestoga manned by pugnacious Scotch-Irish immigrants, and he continued to urge firm military measures on the frontier. Nevertheless, Logan claimed to regard offensive war as unchristian. A war of defense, however, was another matter (and, somewhat illogically, Logan regarded the imperialist conflicts of his time in this light). This type of war, in his view, was but an extension of police action, of which all Friends approved.

Thus, in September 1741, we find Logan composing a long letter for presentation at Yearly Meeting then convening in Philadelphia.

---

[88] R. Hingston Fox, *Dr. John Fothergill and His Friends*, p. 301.
[89] Printed in *Friends' Review*, XVI, no. 18 (3 Jan. 1863), 276.
[90] Tolles, *James Logan*, p. 157.

In it he urged Friends, in view of the threatening situation on the province's western frontiers along the Ohio River valley, where the French were already—in his opinion—a potential menace to security, to follow Governor Thomas's advice and withdraw from government, since they were obviously unwilling to shoulder its responsibilities. The dilemma of combining pacifist convictions and the duties of the magistracy, Logan reminded them, had troubled Penn to such an extent that he had concluded that his continued governorship was possible only by acting through a non-Quaker deputy. This dilemma, Logan claimed, echoing Thomas's arguments of the previous year, stemmed from the fact that "there is no difference, in the last resort, between civil and military government; and . . . the distinction that some affect to make, between the lawfulness of the one and of the other, is altogether groundless." Since Penn's day, now that Friends numbered at most a mere third of the province's inhabitants and its growing wealth offered a tempting prey to England's enemies, the situation had become even more untenable for a Quaker magistracy. Even though some of the newcomers might support Quaker defenselessness because it spared their pockets, those who had no religious scruples against it should be required to contribute to the defense of their land, either in their own persons or from their property. Moreover, contrary to what some now claimed (Logan must have been referring to Chalkley, although he did not mention him by name), Penn had never intended his colony to remain an exclusively Quaker dominion. Therefore, he entreated all Friends "who for conscience-sake cannot join in any law for self-defence" to recognize reality and, after the manner of their British brethren, who eschewed public positions "above those of the respective parishes where they live," to withdraw from government before they were driven out—or the enemy took over.

Logan, feeling perhaps that his presence at Yearly Meeting under the circumstances would be unwelcome, gave his epistle to his son William—the future provincial councillor—to deliver to Friends. A committee of five, which was thereupon appointed to advise "whether it contained matters which were fit for the meeting to take into consideration," decided in the negative, claiming that its contents were chiefly "of a military and geographical nature" and therefore unsuitable for a religious gathering. Only one dissenting voice was raised when the committee reported: the well-to-do Philadelphia merchant, Robert Strettell (disowned a few years later for refusing to remove the armaments he placed on a vessel he owned), pleaded that Logan's letter be read before the assembly. However—so the story runs—the

Friend sitting beside him plucked at his coat, saying peremptorily: "Sit thee down, Robert, thou art single in that opinion."[91]

Robert Strettell and James Logan were certainly not alone among Pennsylvania Friends in their rejection of Quaker pacifism. Among the politically inclined Quakers who filled the seats in the legislature and occupied the justices' bench in the civil courts, there must have been an increasing number of at least nominal Friends who (if the later record may be taken as presumptive evidence) had ceased to accept this tenet of their traditional faith. Not for another generation was the actual size of the minority opinion to be revealed, however, for with no compulsory militia—indeed, for most of the time with no militia at all—there was rarely an occasion when the Society's discipline had to be applied to deviants from its peace testimony. Then, too, the Revolution was to show that the bulk of members remained loyal to the pacifist position.

Every now and then, however, some particularly ebullient and vocal Friend, less discreet than the politic Logan, found himself at odds with his Society for some public disregard of the Quaker stance on war. Such a one, for instance, was Samuel Chew (1693-1743), chief justice of the Lower Counties and a member of Duck Creek Monthly Meeting near Dover (Delaware). On 21 November 1741, two months less a day after James Logan had penned his antipacifist letter, Mr. Justice Chew addressed a speech from the bench to the grand jury of the county of New Castle, which Benjamin Franklin published soon afterward. In his speech Chew, with rather un-Quakerly vehemence, launched a broadside not merely against the Pennsylvania assembly's recent opposition to the governor's policy of preparedness but against the basic concepts of his denomination's peace testimony.[92] He came down unequivocally in favor of "the lawfulness of defence against an armed enemy."[93] Pacifism he described as a doctrine without foundation either in human reason or in divine revelation, the consequences of

[91] "James Logan on Defensive War," *PMHB*, VI, no. 4 (1882), 402-11. See also Tolles, *James Logan*, pp. 27, 28, 39, 90, 153-56, 178-83, 218, 219. Logan, annoyed at the rejection of his epistle by Yearly Meeting, had thirty copies printed by Franklin under the title *To Robert Jordan, and other Friends of the Yearly Meeting for Business, now conven'd in Philadelphia*, but he was dissuaded from distributing them by his wife and prominent Friends in Philadelphia. A parallel effort to convince the German-speaking peace sects of the need for a complete divorce of religious pacifism from political activity was made by Conrad Weiser: his endeavors were as unsuccessful as Logan's, partly owing to the opposition of Christopher Saur, Sr., who urged continued support for the Quakers at the polls.

[92] Living up to this peace testimony was made more difficult in the three Lower Counties by the establishment of compulsory militia service.

[93] This was the title given to the speech when it was reprinted as an 8-page pamphlet "by desire of several gentlemen" in 1775 after Samuel Chew's death.

which were both "pernicious to society, and entirely inconsistent with, and destructive of all civil government," which would prove impossible if armed force were not the ultimate sanction for the enforcement of the law. And, pointing a finger at his fellow Quaker magistrates, Chew went on:

We see that these very people who assert the unlawfulness of all manner of defence, willingly serve in the legislature, consent to the enacting sanguinary and other penal laws, act as sheriffs, serve upon juries, sit in courts of judicature, and there try and condemn men to death. Is it not amazing, that any men should take it into their heads that it is lawful for one Christian forcibly to put another to death, after his hands are tied behind him, and yet think it unlawful to bind him by force, or even to kill him, in his unlawful resistance?

If constables in a Quaker province may use staves in an emergency to quell a riot even though death may result from a broken head, why, Chew asked, may not more lethal weapons be employed to oppose a more dangerous assailant? If some should be surprised to hear a Quaker argue in this fashion, said Chew, he "would have such to believe" that it was because he placed truth and the good of his country and of mankind above uniformity of religious belief or the interests of any one particular sect, even his own if it were mistaken. War, a "just and necessary war" with a dangerous enemy, had commenced, and, in his view, the behavior of the Quaker legislature in refusing full support to the country's war effort had transformed what before was merely an error of private judgment into public policy endangering the commonwealth.[94]

Judge Chew could scarcely have believed that, after this frontal attack on so central an element in the Quaker creed, he would escape censure by the Society. He probably did not care. The public nature of his statement, unlike the criticisms of Logan which were confided in proper form to the executive organ of the Society, constituted a challenge, which Friends did not hesitate to take up. After consideration of his case had commenced in his meeting, he launched a further attack on Quaker policy in Pennsylvania in August 1742, again equating it with a threat to the state and contrasting it with that of "the sensible Quakers in England." And now, he went on angrily, for speaking in the august capacity of one of His Majesty's judges he was being called to account by "a paltry ecclesiastical jurisdiction that calls it-

[94] *The Speech of Samuel Chew, Esq.; . . . Nov. 21. 1741*, pp. 3-16.

self a Monthly Meeting . . . of the people called Quakers." He complained of "insolent" behavior toward him, threats to expel him from the Society unless he withdrew what he had said. "An amazing instance this, of the intoxicating nature of power, and of the voracious unbridled appetite these meek self-denying Christians have after it." To this unwarrantable intervention in the affairs of justice, to this almost Romish tyranny, he had no intention of submitting. And, he added, he personally knew others in the Society (here we have no reason to doubt the veracity of Chew's statement) who shared his disagreement with the pacifist position and his conviction concerning the unfitness of Quaker pacifists to act as lawmakers and administrators.[95] It should hardly be surprising that shortly afterward the Quakers of Duck Creek proceeded to the final step of disowning their refractory member.

The validity of the case urged by both Logan and Chew against the Quaker position rested basically on their assertion that there was no real distinction between the force behind law and the violence stemming from international war. A difference in the degree and purpose of the force applied could not, they held, constitute a difference in kind; correcting a child by spanking was, in their view, essentially of one nature with killing an enemy soldier in battle.[96] To us today it is also clear that Quaker politicians, who at this time were becoming more and more deeply implicated in questionable compromises regarding war measures, did not envisage any techniques of nonviolent defense beyond sometimes expressing a vague readiness to conquer by suffering (an affirmation belied by the middle-class prosperity which was taking them even further from the spiritual atmosphere of the period of Quaker martyrdom) and that, in order to cover over an objection of principle that many of them no longer shared, they had come increasingly to rely on arguments drawn from expediency and from the party disputes in which they had become engaged in defending what they deemed their political rights.

Franklin, in an illuminating—and, in this instance, veracious—passage in his *Autobiography* concerning Pennsylvania's Quaker politicians, speaks of the "embarrassment" with which at this time they approached each request from the Crown or sister colony for a military appropriation. They were torn between two desires: on the one hand, to avoid provoking the government into retaliation by a clear refusal

[95] *The Speech of Samuel Chew, Esq.; . . . Aug. 20. 1742*, esp. pp. 8-13. See also Burton Alva Konkle, *Benjamin Chew 1722-1810*, pp. 31-35.

[96] Cf. Fothergill's comment on Logan's views quoted in Fox, *Dr. John Fothergill*, p. 301.

of aid—especially now that the proprietors, the governor, and influential sections of public opinion in the province had broached the possibility of removing Quakers from the assembly by a legal enactment; and, on the other, to escape an open repudiation of their denomination's peace testimony by an unqualified acceptance of the need for war. "Hence," Franklin writes, they employed "a variety of evasions to avoid complying, and modes of disguising when it became unavoidable."[97]

The evasiveness of the Quaker politicians in voting money usually, of course, took the form of resorting to the phrase "for the king's use"—an old device that dated back many decades. Thus, in October 1741, soon after Logan had made his unsuccessful attempt at pressuring the Society to withdraw from politics, the assembly voted the sum of £3,000 "to be applied to such uses as he [the king], in his royal wisdom, shall think fit to direct and appoint."[98] This offer was rejected by the governor. At last, however, after the elections in the following year, the two sides reached an accommodation on the various points at issue between them. Governor Thomas nevertheless could not refrain from venting his sarcasm at the assembly's changed attitude in his message of 17 August 1742:

> To declare their consciences could not allow them to raise or apply money for victualling and transporting soldiers, and yet to determine to give £4,000 to the king's use, that is, for victualling and transporting soldiers can, in my opinion, no otherways be accounted for, consistent with a good conscience, than upon a supposition of a new revelation intervening between the positive refusal and the determination to give.[99]

At the time of the Cape Breton expedition, in July 1745, when it was clear that the money the Crown was requesting would be used for purposes of war, the assembly in voting the sum of £4,000 added the proviso that the governor lay out the part allocated directly to him for the needs of the troops "in the purchase of bread, beef, pork, flour, wheat or other grain."[100] According to Franklin, who was clerk of the assembly during that period, Governor Thomas, upon receiving news of the appropriation, commented: "I shall take the money, for I understand very well their meaning; *other grain*, is gunpowder."[101] If, in-

[97] Franklin, *Autobiography*, 1964 edn., pp. 188-90.
[98] *Votes and Proceedings*, IV, 2709.
[99] *Pa. Col. Records*, IV, 591, 592.
[100] *Ibid.*, p. 769. See also Hershberger, "Pacifism and the State in Colonial Pennsylvania," *Church History*, VIII, no. 1 (March 1939), 67.
[101] *Autobiography*, p. 189.

deed, Thomas was correct in placing this interpretation on the phrase —and in his favor, as Franklin points out, stands the fact that the assembly, usually so quick to defend its privileges, raised no questions when the governor proceeded to act on this assumption—the assembly cannot be acquitted of a measure of hypocrisy; for, at the same time as they had voted this grant, they had informed the governor that "the peaceable principles professed by divers members of the present Assembly do not permit them to join in raising of men or providing arms and ammunition."[102] On the other hand, no positive proof of such double-talk on the part of the assembly has ever been discovered.

Whether or not Franklin erred on this occasion, it is indeed difficult to detect thenceforward any consistent and determined effort on the part of Quaker assemblymen (if, indeed, there really had ever been any such effort) to see that war taxes, when voted, would be used for some semi-noncombatant, rather than directly warlike, purpose. It is true that there was still to be frequent opposition to appropriations, either on the grounds that they were not in fact necessary for the safety of the province or because of the political squabbling between the assembly and the proprietary interest represented by the deputy-governor. In June 1746 we find the assembly expressing its readiness to donate money to buy presents for friendly Indians who might otherwise turn to the French, and at the same time stating "that men of our peaceable principles, cannot consistently therewith, join in persuading the Indians to engage in the war." Yet two months later the same body voted money to the amount of £5,000, which the governor at once laid out in raising and equipping "four companies of men, for an expedition against Canada." And no word of protest was raised.[103] The setting up of a compulsory provincial militia under the authority of the legislature was virtually the only military measure that the assembly balked at in principle.

During the invasion scare of 1747-1748 the establishment of a voluntary militia was once again tacitly approved. Rumors that the French and Spanish were about to descend on the province from its seaward side, backed by actual incursions of their privateers on the shores of

[102] *Pa. Col. Records*, p. 769. Additional evidence in favor of Franklin's assertion can be seen in the fact that the two commissioners appointed by the assembly to supervise the governor's expenditure of the money voted—John Pole and John Mifflin—were both Friends, although Mifflin, at least, was not a pacifist. "The two," writes Keith in his *Chronicles of Pennsylvania* (II, 873), "may have allowed Thomas to make the purchases." They would scarcely have done so, however, if they had not been assured of the assembly's approval.

[103] *Votes and Proceedings*, IV, 3104-6, 3109. See also Sharpless, *Political Leaders of Colonial Pennsylvania*, pp. 175, 176. The actual expedition proved abortive.

Delaware Bay, grew in volume during the summer months of 1747; agitation increased to organize militarily and strengthen the almost nonexistent defenses. While Philadelphia Yearly Meeting in July exhorted Friends to be vigilant in seeing that their conduct matched their "peaceable principles" and to avoid "joining with such as may be for making warlike preparations, offensive, or defensive,"[104] and while the Quaker-dominated assembly continued to reject the governor's pleas for military measures, public leaders like Benjamin Franklin (1706-1790), who advocated an active policy of preparedness, began to take steps to provide the province with armaments and a body of men trained to resist attack. That Franklin had some support for this move among members of the Society of Friends is clear. As he relates in his *Autobiography*, his scheme to use the funds of his recently formed Union Fire Company to buy tickets in a lottery, the proceeds of which would cover the cost of erecting and arming a river battery to protect Philadelphia, obtained the open or tacit approval of almost all its Quaker members. Still, his calculation that at that date the ratio of genuine Quaker pacifists to those who favored some measure of defense was one to twenty-one was undoubtedly a gross exaggeration. Not only does the subsequent behavior of Friends in the successive war crises that beset Pennsylvania disprove it, but at that very same moment in another fire insurance company almost all the Quaker members voted against buying lottery tickets for the battery (a fact not mentioned by Franklin in his account).[105] It is probable that Franklin's Quakers, although still members in good standing with the Society (according to his recollection, at any rate), were representative of the younger elements who were finding the Society's discipline in regard to peace, as in other matters, increasingly irksome and constraining.

There was one prominent representative of an older generation, however, who backed Franklin's endeavors to the hilt. This was James Logan, who had donated a considerable sum for purchasing lottery tickets. When in November of the same year Franklin published (anonymously) in a pamphlet which he entitled *Plain Truth* a plea for the organization of at least a voluntary militia, Logan wrote him in enthusiastic support. "Ever since I have had the power of thinking," wrote the Quaker, "I have clearly seen that government without arms is an inconsistency. Our Friends spare no pains to get and accumulate estates, and are yet against defending them, though these

---

[104] MS Additions to Philadelphia Y. M. Discipline, July 1747, p. 113 (typescript in F.H.L.S.C.).

[105] *Autobiography*, pp. 182, 183, 186, 187.

126

very estates are in a great measure the sole cause of their being invaded.[106]

Franklin's little tract, which went into a second edition after the first 2,000 copies quickly sold out, displayed all its author's skill as a propagandist. In it he presented the danger to Pennsylvania, now that all the other British colonies had put themselves in a posture of defense, of its proving a magnet to attract the enemy both on account of the wealth of its leading city and because of its openness to attack. He warned against what he considered a false sense of security resulting from the long peace on the Indian frontier, a calm that the machinations of the French might now cause to be shattered at any moment. In vivid colors he depicted the horrors of a sacking that might soon be visited on the city of Philadelphia: fire, slaughter, rapine, robbery. The wealthy proprietary party had proved its unreadiness to make adequate financial sacrifices for defense. And if the Quaker majority in the assembly, on whom the main responsibility for providing means to protect the province rested, was unwilling on grounds of conscience to shoulder the burden, they should retire "for a season" and give way during the emergency to persons who did not share their scruples. In the meantime, he appealed to "the middling people"—the traders, shopkeepers, and farmers—to take upon themselves the task of defense that had been neglected by the legislators and the upper-class and to organize themselves in "an Association" for this purpose.[107]

Franklin's *Plain Truth* was a challenge that Friends could not afford to pass by.[108] Other attacks on the Quaker position were appearing in the Philadelphia press, too. First to enter the lists was the well-to-do New Jersey Quaker historian, Samuel Smith (1720-1776), who entitled his reply *Necessary Truth*. Smith, it is true, was unwilling to censure those who sincerely and after consideration of the pros and cons of the case had concluded that armed defense was compatible with Christianity. But he took great pains to defend his Society from charges of inconsistency for upholding suppression of the domestic criminal while refusing support to war as a method of removing the external aggressor.

The difference between them is manifestly this; the one, to wit,

---

[106] *The Papers of Benjamin Franklin*, vol. 3, p. 219.

[107] *Ibid.*, pp. 180-204, where the whole of *Plain Truth* is reprinted.

[108] After a German version of *Plain Truth* had appeared along with other anti-Quaker pamphlets in German, this challenge was also seen as a threat to the Quaker hold on the German vote, a threat which might even cause some of the German peace sectaries to waver in their political allegiance. Christopher Saur, therefore, took up his pen in defense of Quaker pacifism and issued three pamphlets in German (discussed below in chap. 4) in reply to Franklin.

government, is ordained of God, and magistrates are said to be his ministers. But the other, to wit, war, is more or less the offspring of lust. The magistrate, in the execution of his office is to be in all respects upright, to know no revenge or lust of any kind, a thing exceedingly difficult, if not altogether impracticable in the execution of military exploits. The one of these God has seen meet to ordain for the benefit of mankind; but the other forbidden, to prevent their destruction.[109]

Underlying Smith's arguments is the assumption that no essential difference exists in the case of international conflicts between wars of aggression and wars of national defense. If it was right to condemn the former, then the arguments put forward by Franklin and his associates in favor of the latter were likewise groundless.

Franklin, though a layman and freethinker, soon gained stout reinforcement for his position from a number of clergymen of different denominations. Among them was the Presbyterian minister, the Rev. Gilbert Tennent, a leading Philadelphia churchman and one of the foremost figures in the Great Awakening. On Christmas Eve, 1747, Tennent preached a sermon on the text "The Lord is a man of war" (Exodus 15:3), which, when it was published soon after, bore the title: *The Late Association for Defence, Encourag'd, or The Lawfulness of a Defensive War.* On 1 January 1748, the well-to-do and cultured young Quaker merchant, John Smith (1722-1771), brother to Samuel, intimate friend of John Woolman, and (somewhat surprisingly) soon to be James Logan's son-in-law, wrote in his diary: "Gilbert Tennent's Sermon on the Lawfulness of War came out today, and I was so moved at the deceit and quirks in it that I determined to essay an answer and accordingly began one." It was finished within eight days. Submitted for the perusal of several leading members of Yearly Meeting, it soon received the Society's approval for publication and appeared in an edition of 1,000 copies on 30 January.[110] In fact, writes Tolles, "John Smith spoke semiofficially for the Society of Friends." His pamphlet was eagerly gobbled up by a public that throve on controversy, especially if it embraced—as in this instance —both politics and theology.

John Smith's vindication of Quaker pacifism is the most important item written by a Pennsylvania Friend in defense of the peace testimony during the period of Quaker control of the province. For the

[109] Samuel Smith, *Necessary Truth*, pp. 9, 10, 12-14. Smith's work was published anonymously.
[110] *Hannah Logan's Courtship*, pp. 139-41.

modern reader it appears, with its copious citing of scriptural texts and its attempt to answer Tennent point by point, to be a rather tedious and sterile compilation. Yet, to quote Tolles again, what to us seem defects "undoubtedly enhanced the effectiveness of Smith's reply in the minds of contemporaries." Its underlying sincerity is unmistakable.[111]

Smith centers most of his 56 pages on disproving Tennent's contention that war finds approval in the gospels (though he concedes that it had on occasion received divine sanction in the case of the Jews under the old dispensation). He uses the history of the early church to back up his argument for the pacifist nature of Christ's message and stresses the positive character of Christian pacifism—love of enemies and nonretaliation. At the same time, however, he points out that God's concern for his followers will not necessarily spare them persecution, loss of possessions, and even death itself. He defends Quakers against the charge of cowardice by citing their past record of courageous endurance of suffering for a righteous cause ("when many of the same profession with this sermon-writer hid themselves") and asserts their often impugned consistency in acting as magistrates[112] while refusing to participate in war. Finally, "in the present unhappy state of human affairs," he points to the unwillingness of Friends "to condemn [their] superiors engaging in war" if the latter felt it necessary. "We rather think it probable that as they have shewn a noble and Christian disposition, in granting liberty and protection to such as are of tender consciences, it may please God to bless their arms with success, and reward them for their kindness to his people, who desire to live in obedience to the inward appearance of his spirit.[113]

The Quaker politicians in the assembly were, indeed, prepared to give their unofficial blessing to the Voluntary Association of the People, as Franklin's organization was called.[114] It provided a convenient channel to drain off the energies of the more belligerent sections of the population, which might otherwise have proved dangerous to the administration; it quieted for the time being the demand for a compulsory militia bill which, even with a conscience clause at-

[111] Tolles, "A Literary Quaker: John Smith of Burlington and Philadelphia," *PMHB*, LXV, no. 3 (July 1941), 306.

[112] Smith himself was a justice of the peace and had participated in proceedings leading to the imposition of the death penalty.

[113] John Smith, *The Doctrine of Christianity*, esp. pp. iii, 3-6, 10, 12, 19-22, 32, 33, 40-45, 49-54. Tennent, among others, later published a lengthy reply to Smith.

[114] See Davidson, *War Comes to Quaker Pennsylvania*, chap. IV; Theodore Thayer, *Pennsylvania Politics and the Growth of Democracy*, pp. 20-23; Hershberger, MS book, chap. 9 ("The Voluntary Militia").

tached, was still unacceptable to the Quaker legislators; and it somewhat eased relations with the new deputy-governor, Anthony Palmer (who now bore the official title of President of Council). Of course, it was not expected that Quakers would join the Association; indeed, if they did, they could expect to be excluded from the Society for disregarding its discipline. As another Quaker pamphlet, written anonymously in answer to Franklin and Tennent, stated concerning such disownments: "Here is fully applied that saying of Scripture, *They that went out from us, because they were not of us.*" These deviants from the peace testimony had made their choice: there was no injustice in cutting them off.[115] Yearly Meeting and its subordinate bodies were, in fact, ready to take disciplinary action against such persons.[116]

In the spring of 1748 renewed fear of imminent invasion by an enemy fleet arose. A voluntary militia was now in existence, and batteries had been set up at suitable points along the river—all, however, at private expense, for, as the governor complained in a letter dated 5 March asking the British commander-in-chief at Cape Breton for the loan of some cannon, "we have the misfortune to have an Assembly consisting chiefly of Quakers." In reality, the assembly's stand was somewhat ambivalent. In a message sent in May to President

[115] *A Treatise shewing the Need we have to rely upon God as Sole Protector of this Province*, p. 20. The author's main argument against the Voluntary Association was that military preparations were both unnecessary and extremely costly to the province. He attempted to rebut Franklin's contention that Quakers whose consciences prevented them from providing for defense should resign during the war emergency: first, by asserting that it was not logical that they should "relinquish their power for a season, in order that others might act in that in which their conscience forbad them"; and, secondly, by pointing out that, if they did so, it was unrealistic to imagine that it would ever be possible for them to resume power after the emergency had passed. See pp. 18-22. The anonymous author also severely criticized the ill-treatment of Indians by neighboring provinces, comparing it unfavorably with Quaker policy in Pennsylvania (p. 15).

[116] Although Philadelphia merchants provided a better example in regard to arming their own ships than did their English brethren, they appear at this period to have practiced—and got away with—at least one other, rather less serious infraction of the peace testimony: permitting their vessels to travel under armed convoy of British men-of-war or privateers. Even a stout pacifist like Israel Pemberton II (1715-1779), who for fifteen years beginning in 1750 was clerk of Philadelphia Y. M., urged the necessity of this practice, since insurance rates would otherwise have been almost prohibitive. He added, somewhat sanctimoniously, "for my own part [I] confess I put little confidence in such help and protection." See Thayer, *Israel Pemberton*, pp. 18, 19. However, in his *Pennsylvania Politics* (pp. 22, 23) Thayer mentions that some Quakers who in 1747 had contributed toward financing a Pennsylvania privateer, the *Warren*, were disciplined by their meetings. Hershberger, MS book, also has illuminating sections in chap. 8 ("Quakers take stock") on "the privateering problem" during this period and on the policy followed by Philadelphia Y. M. of regularly disowning members who persisted in privateering and arming of their ships.

Anthony Palmer and his council, the assembly, having stated the difficulty it found in expressing its sentiments on the subject, reiterated the personal objection of most members, and many of their constituents, to bearing arms under any circumstances and their desire at the same time to leave others free to do their duty as they conceived it. In view of the fact that a large proportion of Pennsylvanians did not share their peace principles, the assemblymen did not hesitate to express their gratitude both to the British navy for its protection of commerce and to the governor of New York for his military aid, "as . . . it may have quieted the minds of divers of our inhabitants, tho' it is a favour we could not have asked, [being] intended for such a mode of defence in which we do not place our confidence."[117]

The dilemma confronting the assembly was twofold: it represented a minority opinion in the province on an issue of such vital importance as defense had now become, while within its own ideology Quakerism gave qualified support to the magistrate's sword. Quite apart from the need for circumspection in dealing with the demands of a superior authority at home, the theory of representative government and the Quaker view of the state created, therefore, a duality in the administration of Pennsylvania, two policies that were constantly in danger of cancelling each other out. The province was no longer an unarmed state relying on its very defenselessness and the accompanying goodwill, and the power of the Lord, to give it protection; forts and armaments were at hand, and a militia existed—albeit on a semi-voluntary basis. Yet, if we take the legislature to be its guiding force (and if we exclude the occasional sum voted "for the king's use"), Pennsylvania was still trying officially to follow in the footsteps of its founding fathers, who came to this land to tread the path of nonviolence toward all men, Europeans and Indians alike.

In this same summer of 1748, for instance, we find a radical country Quaker like John Churchman (1705-1775) exhorting the Quaker patricians of the assembly—to Speaker John Kinsey's alarm—to stand firm in their opposition to "carnal weapons and fortifications," remembering that God had preserved the province "in peace and tranquillity

---

[117] Pa. Col. Records, V, 204, 207, 208, 236. Even the strict pacifist John Smith, supported by James Pemberton (1723-1809), proposed at one point that a voluntary subscription be raised among Friends to reimburse councillors for expenses incurred in connection with the emergency defense measures, although he soon withdrew his approval after suffering pangs of conscience that he had acted without due consideration and in an un-Quakerly spirit. Pemberton also withdrew from the scheme, and other Quakers whom Smith had approached in the matter all indicated their disapproval. This incident is discussed in Hershberger, MS book, chap. 9, on the basis of Smith's manuscript diary.

for more than fifty years," and at the same time reminding the mayor of Philadelphia (an office frequently held by Quakers) of his obligations as an executant of God's wrath. He was, Churchman tells us in his journal,

> . . . engaged to lay before him the nature of his office as a magistrate, and exhorted him to take care that he bore not the sword in vain, but put the laws in execution against evil doers, such as drunkards, profane swearers, etc. and to be, in his authority, a terror to the wicked, and an encourager to them that do well.[118]

True, in this case "terror to the wicked" did not include waging war against an external "enemy." But we see the assembly, too, speaking of the president and the by now largely non-Quaker council as of "those whose duty it is to protect men in the enjoyment of their religious and civil liberties."[119] They had the duty, then, of extending such protection in the manner that answered their consciences. Let each tolerate the other, pleaded the assembly, which now denied any intention of restricting the military preparations of those without Quaker scruples in the matter. The actual outcome was confusion. Pennsylvania was living neither disarmed by the spirit that knows no evil nor strong according to the wisdom of this world.

Peace returned in October 1748 with the signing of the Treaty of Aix-la-Chapelle. Thus, the final crisis that was to end Quaker rule in Pennsylvania, and to resolve the dilemma created by the attempt of a (nominally) pacifist colonial administration to work within the framework of the imperial power politics of the mother country, was averted for a few years.

[118] *An Account of the Gospel Labours of John Churchman*, pp. 68-73. Churchman, like Chalkley a little earlier, argued that the non-Quaker settlers should accept Quaker pacifism as official policy, since its establishment in the province was known to them when they came over to Pennsylvania.

[119] *Pa. Col. Records*, V, 336.

Chapter 3

Quaker Pennsylvania: The Crisis of 1756 and Its Aftermath

The death in 1750 of John Kinsey—clerk of Philadelphia Yearly Meeting for the previous twenty years, speaker of the Pennsylvania assembly since 1739, and chief justice of the provincial supreme court after 1743—symbolized the passing of an epoch: the era of close integration of the affairs of meetinghouse and political assembly. True, Kinsey had engaged in some rather dubious financial transactions during his lifetime, including misappropriation of public funds[1] (conduct that was, indeed, not at all uncommon for a British politician reared in the age of Walpole yet was extremely unseemly for a Quaker dignitary). Nevertheless, Kinsey was, as Sharpless correctly states, "the last great Quaker political leader."[2] His successor as speaker of the assembly, Isaac Norris II (1701-1766), was also a Friend. However, Norris, who belonged to one of the leading Philadelphia Quaker families and remained a member in good standing until his death, did not, like Kinsey, take a prominent part in the affairs of the Society. Nor did he share Kinsey's absolute pacifism, even though he defended the position in his official utterances so long as this was the policy of the assembly he represented. In October 1754, for instance, we find him stating: "I am satisfied the Law of Nature, and perhaps the Christian system leaves us a right to defend ourselves as well against the enemies who are within the reach of our laws, as those who owe no subjection to them."[3] By this date a number of his fellow Quakers in the legislature were equally, if not more unequivocally, supporters of defensive war.

Until well into the second quarter of the century most Quaker legislators still personally adhered to pacifism (we have no reason to believe insincerely) even though they were perfectly prepared, as Speaker Kinsey himself said in 1744, "to let no expense be wanting proper to put the country into a posture of defence, in such manner as their known principles would admit of."[4] But opinion in the legisla-

---

[1] These transactions were revealed, to the shocked surprise of his executors, only at his death.

[2] Isaac Sharpless, *Political Leaders of Provincial Pennsylvania*, p. 179.

[3] Frederick B. Tolles, *Meeting House and Counting House*, p. 25.

[4] Theodore Thayer, *Israel Pemberton*, p. 50.

133

ture on this matter was gradually changing, so that eventually the house's Quaker majority for the most part came to share the standpoint of the younger Norris (which, indeed, was also that of his father-in-law, James Logan). When exactly this transition occurred is not clear, but it must have been around mid-century.

Its accomplishment did not, however, signify the end of the assembly's resistance to making regular appropriations for military purposes. For, even before this time, there had been a second factor responsible for generating resistance that was often more powerful than pacifism—the staunch antiproprietary attitude of the Whiggish Quaker party. This party, which had coalesced in the 1730's out of the former radical and conservative groupings of the early decades of the century after a long period when political allegiances were in a state of flux, remained unyieldingly opposed to the Tory and Anglican circles which now formed the Penn interest. Although very far from being social revolutionaries, these Quaker Whigs strove to defend the privileges of the assembly and of the well-to-do elements represented in it—which they tended to identify with the interests of the whole province—against what they considered the encroachments of the proprietors and their deputy, the governor. In this respect they were being true to one strand in their Quaker inheritance. Had not William Penn himself proudly told Governor Fletcher of New York in 1692 after the Crown had entrusted Pennsylvania to the latter: "I thought fit to caution thee that I am an Englishman"?[5] Pride in being Englishmen and in participating in the heritage of England's liberties was shared equally by Penn's Quaker settlers and their descendants, who cherished their "birthright as *English* subjects" even if, as their *Ancient Testimony* of 1722 stated, they eschewed "the protection by gun and sword which others make the terms of their allegiance."[6] The Quaker assemblymen of the early 1750's continued to stand up for their rights as Englishmen even after they had lost all but a nominal interest in injecting a Quaker flavoring into their resolutions on military measures.

Besides the paper currency problem, the great issue dividing assembly and proprietors during this period was the former's proposal to tax the estates of the latter, hitherto exempt, on an equal footing with property of ordinary citizens in the province. This dispute rendered nugatory the assembly's appropriation in 1754 of as large a sum as £15,000 to meet the impending danger to the western frontier from the French advance in the Ohio River valley and from hostile Indian attacks. Even now the assembly refused point-blank to impose com-

[5] E.C.O. Beatty, *William Penn as Social Philosopher*, p. 82.
[6] *The Ancient Testimony of the People called Quakers, reviv'd*, pp. 18, 19.

pulsory militia service on those not having a conscientious objection to fighting. And the old vague formula still appeared in the debates of the chamber, as in this citation from February 1754:

It is well known the Assemblies of this province are generally composed of a majority who are conscientiously principled against war, and represent a well-meaning peaceable people, deeply sensible of the great favours, protection and privileges they enjoy under the present royal family, and therefore ready and willing to demonstrate their duty and loyalty, by giving such sums of money to the King's use, upon all suitable occasions as may consist with our circumstances, or can be reasonably expected from so young a colony.[7]

The failure to reach accommodation on this occasion resulted from disagreement on an issue entirely unconnected with the peace principles of the Society of Friends. Isaac Norris in a letter to his brother Charles, dated 31 May 1754, summed up the situation in the following extremely revealing passage:

And indeed whatever difficulties our Assemblies may have in appropriating money to warlike purposes, when there is a good harmony and confidence in their governor, what they give may be made very effectual by leaving the disposition of it wholly to himself, and can be pretty easily obtained . . . on all suitable occasions, but when that confidence is lost the difficulties attending the granting money in that manner are very considerable with those who have otherwise a good influence in our house.[8]

The same crisis of confidence rather than any basic scruples of conscience on the assembly's part was responsible for the failure of the governor's efforts to obtain money in the course of the first half of the following year; for the bill to raise £50,000 for the king's use, which the assembly finally passed in July 1755, had a proviso attached stipulating that the proprietary lands should be taxable along with the

[7] Votes and Proceedings, V, 3654. "As I am well acquainted with their religious scruples," wrote Governor James Hamilton to Governor Dinwiddie of Virginia on 13 March 1754 (Pa. Col. Records, VI, 2), "I never expected they would appropriate money for the purpose of war or warlike preparations, but thought they might have been brought to make a handsome grant to the King's use, and have left the disposition of it to me, as they have done upon other occasions of the like nature." Did Hamilton, then, not realize the true complexion of the majority's views now on war? Or—as he had been in office since 1748 and should have been well informed on provincial politics—was this only a pretense to drum up feeling against the antiproprietary party?

[8] Quoted in William S. Hanna, Benjamin Franklin and Pennsylvania Politics, p. 66.

135

rest. A little earlier in the same month, General Braddock's disastrous defeat by the French near Fort Duquesne ushered in a period of Indian warfare on the frontier: Penn's old friends, the Delawares and Shawnees, had now become Pennsylvania's enemies. "The roots of the conflict," Tolles writes, "lay . . . in the harsh facts of imperial power, French expansionism and the land-hunger of Virginia planters and London merchants."[9]

The annual assembly elections of October 1755 coincided with the first Indian attacks on the frontier settlements. As usual, the Quaker party without difficulty won an overwhelming majority—owing in some measure to the inequitable franchise that underrepresented the frontier districts. "Quakers were only about a fifth of the total population of Pennsylvania, but they held two-thirds of the seats in the legislature."[10] As Indian marauders advanced into the more settled areas, attacking outlying farmsteads and killing their inhabitants, feeling rose against Friends. A correspondent from Reading reported: "The people exclaim against the Quakers, and some are scarce restrained from burning the houses of those few who are in this town."[11] Animosity was apparently directed more against members of the Society as such, where a new and more rigorous pacifist spirit was blowing, than against the politicians in the assembly who, though they bore the name of Friends, were now mostly out of touch with these vital currents that were infusing fresh life into an increasingly moribund Society.

Yearly Meeting, which was gathered at this time in Philadelphia, exhorted Friends to remain unmoved by "the commotions and stirrings of the earth . . . near us" and, instead, to put their trust "in the munition of that rock that all these shakings shall not move."[12] Men like John Woolman, Anthony Benezet, John Churchman, and John Pemberton (1727-1795)[13] were the most active here. These Friends from Pennsyl-

---

[9] "The Twilight of the Holy Experiment: A Contemporary View," *BFHA*, vol. 45, no. 1 (1956), pp. 30, 31. Tolles points out here that one of the chief figures in promoting the Ohio Company, the activities of which were in part responsible for exacerbating the Anglo-French conflict in the Ohio River valley, was none other than the English Quaker merchant, John Hanbury, a leading member of London Meeting for Sufferings. For Hanbury's role in this regard, see the detailed evidence marshalled in Hershberger, MS book, chap. 10: "John Hanbury, the Ohio Company, and the Beginning of the French and Indian War." See also Sherman P. Uhler, *Pennsylvania's Indian Relations to 1754*, chap. XIII.

[10] Brent E. Barksdale, *Pacifism and Democracy in Colonial Pennsylvania*, p. 16.

[11] *Pa. Col. Records*, VI, 705.

[12] Ezra Michener, *A Retrospect of Early Quakerism*, p. 297.

[13] He and his brothers—Israel, the merchant grandee, and James, the most politically inclined of the three—stood halfway between the old Quaker political past and the movement of Quaker renewal, of purification from worldliness, that,

vania and neighboring New Jersey were assisted in their efforts by visitors from England—Samuel Fothergill (1715-1772), Catherine Payton (later Phillips; 1727-1794), and Mary Peisley (1717-1757)—who were likewise zealously stirring their fellow members to a revived interest in the peace testimony. This tenet, they told Friends, was an essential part of their Quaker faith; if they abandoned it, they would lose a vital element of their religion and become indistinguishable from the mass of quasi-Christians. They spoke out against those Friends who now wished to approve of "defensive" war, and they warned sternly against repetition of the kind of compromises that had been made in the past by the Quaker politicians.[14]

Already in August the new governor, Robert Hunter Morris, had become alarmed at the activities of what may be described as the peace party within the Society of Friends. He complained about the pacifist sermons being preached by Quaker ministers and about the efforts of committees belonging to local meetings to instill loyalty to the peace testimony in their members. He feared the influence such a stand would have both upon the morale of the people at large and "even upon the Assembly, a great majority of which are Quakers." According to Morris, the Quaker pacifists had attributed Braddock's defeat to "a just judgment" of God "upon our forces."[15] The religious Society of Friends, if not yet the Quaker politicians, was on the way to being branded as a subversive element in the commonwealth that their ancestors had founded.

The events of the autumn revealed the widening chasm that existed between the outlook of the nominal Quakers who sat in the provincial assembly—even if they were still anxious to remove Indian grievances responsible for the conflict—and the new spiritual leaders whose influence in favor of nonviolent approaches was rising within the Society and who had been responsible for the insistently pacifist tone of Yearly Meeting's utterances that fall. The situation of the Society was indeed serious. As James Pemberton confided to his Quaker friend in England, Dr. John Fothergill (1712-1780), recent happenings had "produced a greater and more fatal change both with respect to the state of our affairs in general and among us as a Society than seventy preceding years."[16] Two measures of the assembly

---

gathering strength first among Friends of Pennsylvania Yearly Meeting, was eventually to embrace the whole Society in America.

[14] *Memoirs of the Life of Catherine Phillips*, pp. 131, 139, 140; Tolles, "The Twilight of the Holy Experiment," p. 37.

[15] *Pa. Archives*, 4th ser., II, 478, 489, 490.

[16] John J. Zimmerman, "Benjamin Franklin and the Quaker Party, 1755-1756," *William and Mary Quarterly*, 3rd ser., XVII, no. 3 (July 1960), 293.

in particular, both passed in November 1755, aroused strong opposition among Quaker peace men: the appropriation, after an uneasy accommodation had been reached concerning taxation of the proprietary lands, of the large sum of £60,000 "for the king's use" (which, of course, everyone knew meant military expenditure); and the establishment at last of a provincial militia. Resistance appeared even in the assembly. Seven Quakers voted against the supplies bill, and, even though a broadly framed conscience clause was included in the militia bill, placing that force, though now officially supported, on a virtually voluntary basis, there were four dissenters who voted against that bill, too—James Pemberton, Joshua Morris, Joseph Trotter, and Peter Worral.[17] The militia bill, which on account of its mildness was described by Governor Morris as "intended to answer no purpose but to amuse the people,"[18] was eventually quashed by the home government in the following July as unconstitutional. But the raising of a tax to implement the grant made for carrying on the undeclared war soon commenced.

While the tax measure was being debated in the assembly, twenty prominent personalities from Yearly Meeting—including members of well-to-do Philadelphia families like Israel and John Pemberton, John Reynell, John Smith, and Mordecai Yarnall and concerned ministers like Anthony Benezet, John Churchman, and Daniel Stanton—presented a strongly worded address to that body, protesting against "raising sums of money and putting them into the hands of committees who may apply them to purposes inconsistent with the peaceable testimony, we profess and have born to the world," and warning the house that many Friends would feel obliged in protest to refuse payment of such a tax that was in fact, they maintained, an infringement of religious liberty. The petitioners were careful to point out their approval of paying taxes for peaceful purposes "judged necessary towards the exigencies of government."[19] Yet they were actually reversing the long accepted practice of Pennsylvania Friends, who, whatever their particular political complexion, had not balked at paying tribute money that they knew would be applied in large measure to military ends, provided the transaction was cloaked (as, indeed, it still was in the present instance) with the threadbare phrase "for the king's use."

The assembly, with four members dissenting (one of whom was James Pemberton, brother to two of the signatories to the address),

---

[17] *Votes and Proceedings*, V, 4132.

[18] Winfred Trexler Root, *The Relations of Pennsylvania with the British Government*, p. 308.

[19] *Pa. Archives*, 1st ser., II, 487, 488. See also *An Account of the Gospel Labours of John Churchman*, pp. 169-71.

138

replied somewhat curtly to their coreligionists' plea, evidently regarding it as an uncalled-for intervention in what was none of their business. The address, they said,

. . . appears to us (however decent the language may be in respect to the house) assuming a greater right than they were invested with, and an indication that they had not duly considered what has been heretofore transacted in the Assemblies of this province, particularly in relation to the act for granting *two thousand pounds* for the Queen's use, passed in the year 1711, and is therefore an unadvised and indiscreet application to the house at this time.[20]

While their reference to the war appropriation of 1711 was a skillful move and the Quaker assemblymen could rightly fear the use the governor might make against them of the implied threat in the address to boycott war taxation if imposed,[21] the assembly's reply underlines the degree to which most of its Quaker members had drifted away from the Quaker views on war that were undergoing a revival in Yearly Meeting as a whole. Concerning this growing divergence between the assembly and Yearly Meeting, the proprietors' secretary, the Rev. Richard Peters, was correct when he wrote at this time: "Tho' the majority of them [i.e., the Quaker assemblymen] have been stiff in opposition against proprietor and government . . . they are for defence." And Israel Pemberton, who sternly criticized them from a standpoint exactly opposite to that of Peters, lamented the influence that these respected members of society and the Society might have on some of the weaker brethren. For him, the passing of a militia act was the last straw, the point of no return: "Their entering into these measures," he wrote, was "a manifest inconsistency and not to be reconciled to the profession" of the Society to which they belonged.[22]

The taxation now to be levied on the inhabitants of the province to provide the sinews of war—a war that would be waged on Pennsylvania territory rather than in some more distant spot outside its boundaries—also proved a landmark in the developing crisis. It created great uneasiness among Friends at large. Grave doubts arose, reports Israel Pemberton, "whether we could individually give our approbation to this measure by freely paying our assessments."[23]

[20] *Votes and Proceedings*, V, 4173, 4174.

[21] In fact, in a letter to the proprietor, Thomas Penn, dated 22 November, Morris attempts to discredit the assembly's good faith vis-à-vis defense measures by citing the address (*Pa. Col. Records*, VI, 739).

[22] Thayer, *Israel Pemberton*, pp. 88, 89.

[23] *Ibid.*, p. 90. Among those who shared such feelings was Israel Pemberton himself. Although some opponents of the Quakers, like Richard Peters, for instance,

The *spiritus movens* behind this opposition was undoubtedly John Woolman (whose thoughts on the subject of taxation have been touched on in the first chapter). Indeed, it was Woolman, supported by kindred spirits like John Churchman, Anthony Benezet, and Samuel Fothergill, who organized a protest against the new tax soon after it had been passed by the assembly. They raised the question in mid-December at a joint meeting in Philadelphia of two standing committees that had been appointed at the recent yearly meeting to deal with the current emergency. The conference was held at a moment of intense excitement in the city. As Woolman recorded in his *Journal*: "While these committees sat, the corpse of one . . . slain [by the Indians on the frontier] was brought in a wagon, and taken through the streets of the city, in his bloody garments, to alarm the people, and rouse them up to war." To Woolman and those who thought like him, this incident appeared as a symbol of the method of violence toward which members of the Society were now being required to contribute; moreover, this was a contribution that had been imposed by men who bore the name of Friends. Not all his colleagues, it is true, saw the matter quite in this light. "To refuse an active payment at such a time," they argued, "might be an act of disloyalty, and appeared likely to displease the rulers, not only here but in England." "Still there was a scruple so fastened upon the minds of many Friends, that nothing moved it." Therefore, after much discussion and prayer and several adjournments to give time for further thought, a group of those most concerned about the issue, numbering twenty-one, attached their signatures to a document whose chief author had been Woolman. It was entitled "An Epistle of Tender Love and Caution to Friends in Pennsylvania," and it bore the date 16 December 1755.

The epistle, which was not issued as an official declaration of the Society as a whole although the prominence of its signatories ensured it a respectful hearing by members, was a forthright declaration. It expressed pain at finding the assembly voting a sum of such magnitude almost exclusively for military uses, "for purposes inconsistent with our peaceable testimony." True, a small portion might be destined

---

attempted to cast doubt on Pemberton's sincerity in this case, insinuating that his reluctance to pay was due to the heavy assessment that would be made on his property, there is no reason to doubt the genuineness of his scruples, especially since he was prepared to endure burdensome distraints for nonpayment. (In 1740, Israel Pemberton had been among the "young fry of Quakers" whose strongly antiwar stand had aroused the anger of this same Peters; see Thayer, *Pennsylvania Politics and the Growth of Democracy*, p. 13). Some prominent English Friends opposed tax refusal as imprudent (Thayer, *Israel Pemberton*, pp. 114, 115).

for innocuous ends, for conciliating the Indians, for instance, or for relieving war sufferers. "We could most cheerfully contribute to those purposes if they were not so mixed" with the support of war. Therefore, its authors intimated their intention of refusing payment of the tax on grounds of conscience, "though suffering be the consequence of our refusal." This, if it should come, "we hope to be enabled to bear with patience."[24]

It is doubtful whether most of the substantial Quaker bourgeois who signed the document realized its novel implications, although they were apparent to such religious radicals as Woolman and Churchman. For the epistle reversed previous Quaker practice in sanctioning payment at least of taxes "in the mixture," if there was some doubt about direct military imposts. It now said in effect that, where any considerable portion of the money was destined for war, tax objection was the only consistent policy for Friends to follow, just as they had refused payment of tithes to an established church where these were demanded from them. But apprehension about the effect that the quasi-military policy of a nominally Quaker assembly might have on the integrity of the Society as a whole probably served to hide from some of the signatories the radical nature of the policy now being recommended in their epistle.

The early months of 1756 saw an intensification of the political crisis. The tax boycott now being threatened, added to the traditional Quaker pacifism, provided plentiful ammunition for use by the Quaker party's political opponents of the proprietary group in an effort to dislodge their rivals from their position of supremacy in the assembly. "Pacifism was not the real reason, of course, for removing the Quakers from the Assembly,"[25] because most of the nominal Quakers in that body were not pacifists; those few who were for the most part interpreted their pacifism as a purely individual credo that should not preclude approving war measures in their public capacity. But the pacifism professed by the Society as a whole provided an excellent excuse for getting rid of the core of the antiproprietary party. And a convenient lever lay ready to hand for the anti-Quaker group to effect this ejection: impose a test oath on all candidates for office, including seats in the assembly, and their political enemies would be broken (or so they expected, at least). This scheme was, as we have seen, over half a century old and had been contemplated at intervals when the policies of the Quaker-dominated assembly clashed with the interests

---

24 *The Journal of John Woolman* (ed. A. M. Gummere), pp. 205-10. See also Janet Whitney, *John Woolman*, pp. 207-12, 219.
25 Hanna, *Franklin and Pennsylvania Politics*, p. 95.

of proprietors, home government, or adherents of the Anglican church. The threat of its implementation had been responsible, at least earlier, for the various compromises devised by Quaker politicians in respect to war and the penal code, in particular.

The first to raise this proposal during the present crisis seems to have been the doughty Dr. William Smith (1727-1803), provost of the College of Philadelphia and a leading Episcopalian, in a pamphlet he had published as early as February 1755 called *A Brief State of the Province of Pennsylvania*. In it he accused Quakers in the assembly and outside it of being responsible—rather from self-interest than conscientious scruples in the case of the Quaker legislators—for the unprotected state of the province, for its defenselessness in face of the French and Indian menace. "It is very plain," he wrote, "they have no mind to give a single shilling for the King's use, unless they can thereby increase their own power." He therefore called for the imposition on all assemblymen of a test oath together with a declaration of readiness to defend the country militarily, as well as for the disfranchisement of the Pennsylvania Germans, whom Smith depicted as a potential fifth column on account of their support of Quaker policies, and the curtailment of their cultural rights.[26] Smith's arguments appear to have won little favor with the Pennsylvania electorate, which had as usual returned the Quaker party to power in the autumn elections. But in London, where his pamphlet was printed, the idea made a greater impression and was taken up with enthusiasm a little later by Proprietor Thomas Penn.[27]

In the early months of 1756 it really seemed likely that the British Parliament would be persuaded to enact legislation requiring a test oath in Pennsylvania. However, the Quaker lobby and a number of prominent English Quakers at once took steps to prevent passage of such a measure. In close cooperation with the Lord President of the Council, Earl Granville, in particular, they were able to hammer out a compromise solution that averted the danger of a test oath, while at the same time promising in exchange a temporary withdrawal of Pennsylvania Friends from the political scene for the duration of

[26] William Smith, *A Brief State of the Province of Pennsylvania*, pp. 11-17, 22, 23, 26-42.

[27] Francis Jennings, "Thomas Penn's Loyalty Oath," *American Journal of Legal History*, vol. 8, no. 4 (Oct. 1964), pp. 303-13. See also Thayer, *Pennsylvania Politics*, pp. 39-41. On p. 24, Thayer writes: "Quaker government in the eyes of the people was synonymous with good government, freedom, and low taxes." It was in these virtues, and not in any sympathy with pacifism as such, that the attraction of Quaker rule for the non-Quaker electorate lay.

the war emergency.[28] That this was planned as "a strategic retreat"[29] rather than as a permanent withdrawal is obvious, if only from the pains that were taken to ensure the possibility of eventual return.

But what Hanna aptly calls "the exclusion crisis" was not so easily overcome. The stumbling block was the resistance of many Pennsylvania Friends to accepting the decision made by their London brethren.[30] The certainty expressed, for instance, by the London Quaker merchant, Robert Plumsted, who had both strong commercial ties with, and family relations in, Philadelphia, "that those who are really Quakers will be very glad to withdraw from the present scene of action"[31] was overoptimistic. True, the influential Philadelphia Quarterly Meeting, in the defense of its members' participation in affairs of state ("some allowance must . . . be made for human imperfections," it pleaded) which it addressed to London Meeting for Sufferings in April 1755, had hinted at the possibility of a general withdrawal from politics "whenever it may appear impracticable for us [otherwise] to preserve . . . those principles" of peace that Quakers had always held. The epistle mentioned, moreover, that some had already taken that step, believing that only in this way could they maintain "our Christian testimony in all its branches." But Philadelphia Friends went on to explain the reason for continuing Quaker participation in government: the lack of capable men to defend the liberties and constitutional rights of the province against the ever present threat of arbitrary power from the side of the proprietary interest. Until this obstacle was overcome, "we cannot after the most deliberate consideration judge we should be faithful to [the province], to ourselves, or to our posterity, to desert our stations and relinquish the share we have in the legislation."[32]

There, indeed, lay the rub. Abandoning political power appeared to many sincere Quakers as an abandonment of political responsibility. But to retain political power, at least while war was raging on Pennsylvania soil, came increasingly to mean a repudiation in practice, if not

---

[28] See Zimmerman, "Franklin and the Quaker Party," pp. 307-12; Hanna, *Franklin and Pennsylvania Politics,* pp. 97-99.

[29] Jennings, "Thomas Penn's Loyalty Oath," p. 304.

[30] As Hershberger points out (MS book, chap. 11), it was not primarily pacifism but concern for their "imperialistic interests" that accounts for the anxiousness of some leading lights in London Y. M., like John Hanbury, to see the Quaker pacifists withdraw from politics.

[31] C.A.J. Skeel, "The Letter-book of a Quaker Merchant, 1756-8," *EHR,* XXXI, no. 121 (Jan. 1916), 141.

[32] This epistle is given in full in Sharpless, *A Quaker Experiment in Government,* I, 234-40.

in name, of Friends' witness for a peaceful world. To say that the issue was simply political and economic power is to disregard the genuine dilemma in which politically minded Quakers, including many who were genuinely attached to the peace testimony, found themselves in this period of crisis.

One such political pacifist was James Pemberton, who provided a link between the movement of renewal within Yearly Meeting and the Quaker politicians in the assembly. It was to him, in particular, that Dr. John Fothergill addressed the appeals of London Friends. "You accept of a public trust, which at the same time you acknowledge you cannot discharge," Fothergill told him. "You owe the people protection, and yet withhold them from protecting themselves. Will not all the blood that is spilt be at your doors?"[33] The same question was being asked angrily and ever more insistently by men who, unlike the Quaker Fothergill, thereby sought to discredit the Society and all its works. Early in 1756 Provost Smith published a sequel to his pamphlet of the previous year. Demanding still more effective defense measures from the assembly, he accused the Quaker pacifists outside it —"infatuated enthusiasts," he called them—of responsibility for the rising tide of Indian atrocities and denounced (not altogether without justification) the backstage influence of Yearly Meeting and its subordinate bodies—"degenerated into political cabals"[34]—on the politics of the province. Meanwhile, for several months there had been circulating petitions and tracts of similar content. Addresses of this kind were being directed to the home government in London, to the Crown, and to the Lords of Trade, who were immediately responsible for relations with Pennsylvania.[35] All this material was eagerly seized upon by Thomas Penn and his cronies for use in their political maneuvers against the dominant party in the assembly. Although pure Quaker pacifism was probably widely unpopular at this juncture, the degree of opposition that existed in regard to the Quaker party which, as is clear, no longer objected to military preparations was undoubtedly grossly exaggerated in the propaganda of its enemies, as is shown by the hold that the party continued to exert on the (admittedly restricted) electorate over the years to come.

The back counties, of course, were suffering most severely from Indian sorties; therefore, the back inhabitants, particularly the Scotch-

[33] Letter dated 16 March 1756, R. Hingston Fox, *Dr. John Fothergill and His Friends*, p. 308.

[34] William Smith, *A Brief View of the Conduct of Pennsylvania, for the Year 1755*, pp. 21, 23, 72-81.

[35] See Charles J. Stillé (ed.), "The Attitude of the Quakers in the Provincial Wars," *PMHB*, X, no. 3 (1886), 294ff.

Irish frontiersmen, were most virulent in denouncing the Quakers and the Quaker assembly, which was supposedly following a Quaker policy.[36] In fact, during the winter months the province was being placed on a war footing, so that in May, shortly after the official declaration of war against the Delawares and Shawnees made by the governor and council on 12 April,[37] the assembly could claim that the province was militarily prepared, even if the organization of the militia left something to be desired ("we have indeed had little experience of a militia in this province, and a law for regulating it was a new thing to us," they pleaded in extenuation). "By the care of the Governor and the commissioners for disposing of the sixty thousand pounds by us granted for His Majesty's service," they stated, "the frontier of this province is now in a better state of defence than that of any other colony on the continent, being guarded by a line of forts at no great distance from each other, all strongly garrisoned."[38] There was no qualification now in the assembly's support of the war effort. Gone was the pretense that the disposition of funds granted "for the king's use" was no business of theirs, for here we see the assembly through its special commissioners directly supervising the expenditure of the military appropriation and taking responsibility for recruiting soldiers and for the organization of militia. And this was an assembly 28 of whose 36 members were at least nominally members of the Society of Friends.

It is not surprising, then, that on the eve of the declaration of war we find Philadelphia Friends reaffirming in messages to the assembly and the governor their renunciation of all war and their continued belief in a nonviolent way of settling affairs with the Indians. They protested, too, at the savage proclamation that accompanied the declaration of war, offering a reward for the scalps of enemy Indians, regardless of age or sex.[39] These steps, indeed, constituted a challenge that could not be glossed over: the Quaker peace testimony was at

[36] Their opponents were quick to point out that there were few Quakers living in the exposed frontier districts (see, e.g., Stillé, p. 301). We do, however, hear of one presumed Quaker family falling victim of Indian attack at the beginning of the year. In a letter dated 5 Feb. 1756, a clergyman reports: "One Sherridan, a Quaker, his wife, three children and a servant, were killed and scalped" (quoted in *The Journals and Papers of David Schultze*, I, 163). Cf. Barksdale, *Pacifism and Democracy*, p. 27. See also Churchman, *An Account*, p. 175, for the rising unpopularity of Quakers, even in Philadelphia, as knowledge of frontier atrocities spread during the early months of 1756.

[37] The declaration was approved with only one dissenting vote, which was cast by Quaker William Logan (1718-1776), son of James, who, although not an absolute pacifist, stood closer to the Quaker position than his father had.

[38] *Votes and Proceedings*, V, 4234, 4235.

[39] *Ibid.*, V, 4216-20; *Pa. Col. Records*, VII, 83-86.

145

stake. Twelve days later Benezet reported to an English Quaker: "Many of our Friends begin to rouse from that lethargy in which they have too long been plunged, thro' a love of this world, an endeavour to reconcile those two contrarities—the world and heaven." They were awakening to a realization of the incompatibility of the Quaker witness for peace with the politics of a state at war.[40] And this message was being effectively brought home to Friends throughout the province by the endeavors of Benezet himself, the visiting English ministers, and American Quaker preachers like Woolman, Churchman, and John Pemberton. The results of their efforts with the Quaker assemblymen were meager: among some assemblymen, as we have seen, they were simply regarded as an unwarranted intervention in matters that were not their concern.

"If the potsherds of the earth clash together, let them clash!" declared Samuel Fothergill.[41] Friends must now stand clear of all involvement in warlike activities. This message was reinforced by the repeated advice emanating from London Yearly Meeting that Friends must retire for a time at least from provincial politics, by the insistence of English Quakers that their own reputation would be tarnished if they failed to implement their pledge to the home government of Friends' withdrawal from the assembly for a season. London Yearly Meeting did not always find it easy to understand the obvious reluctance with which Pennsylvania Friends contemplated shedding the burden of direct political power, and it was, besides, genuinely concerned not merely with the threatened enactment of a test oath but with the integrity of the Society's peace witness in the Quaker province. The pressure it brought to bear on Friends in Pennsylvania, combined as it was with an increasing feeling of discomfort at their own position in the assembly, finally led to the resignation on 7 June of six of the most concerned Friends sitting in that body, headed by James Pemberton.[42] "Many of our constituents," they stated in their letter of resignation, "seem of opinion that the present situation of public affairs call upon us for services in a military way, which, from a conviction of judgment, after mature deliberation, we cannot comply

[40] George S. Brookes, *Friend Anthony Benezet*, p. 220.
[41] George Crosfield, *Memoirs of Samuel Fothergill*, p. 261.
[42] For a detailed account of English Friends' influence on their brethren during the 1755-1756 crisis, see A. T. Gary [Pannell], "The Political and Economic Relations of English and American Quakers (1750-1785)," D.Phil. thesis, Oxford (1935), pp. 85-101. See also Sharpless, *A Quaker Experiment*, I, 250-254; Barksdale, *Pacifism and Democracy*, pp. 30-35, 37, 39, 40. There is also much material on this subject in Hershberger MS book.

with." Their withdrawal would both be "conducive to the peace of our own minds, and the reputation of our religious profession."[43]

The resignations of 7 June symbolized the end of Quaker rule in Pennsylvania. They marked the point when the last fragile remnants of a Holy Experiment disintegrated. As Franklin wrote ironically a week later: "All the stiff rump except one that would be suspected of opposing the [military] service from religious motives have voluntarily quitted the Assembly."[44] These resignations did not, of course, eliminate at one stroke the presence of members of the Society of Friends in the assembly, for the majority of Quaker representatives not sharing the pacifist scruples of their six colleagues still clung to their seats. Still less did it mean the destruction of the popular party's political ascendancy since, as we shall see, this continued under Franklin's leadership for almost another two decades, that is, under non-Quaker auspices but still with the old name of the "Quaker party" in use in popular parlance. Again, these resignations did not signify the ending of all hope of a Quaker return to power, of the reinauguration of a peaceable commonwealth within the confines of the Quaker colony. As has been aptly observed, "the object of the move from the standpoint of Quaker politicians . . . was the preservation of power, not its relinquishment." And this intention became evident in the elections of the following October.

Then, even though pressure was brought to bear by Friends' meetings to prevent members from standing for the assembly, the Quaker influence was placed as usual behind the popular so-called Quaker party, and its candidates swept the field once again. "Quaker influence in Pennsylvania," states a recent writer with a shade of exaggeration, "had never been more apparent."[45] But, instead of exerting it directly from within the assembly, the leaders of the Society now hoped to operate as a pressure group acting on both provincial politics and social life.

Nevertheless, the new policy did not prove acceptable to all the Friends active in politics. Three Quakers did indeed refuse to run as candidates, and four more after election were brought to give up their seats—somewhat reluctantly and, as they stated in their letter of resignation, because they understood "that the Ministry have requested

---

[43] *Votes and Proceedings*, V, 4246. See also *ibid.*, pp. 4245-50; *Pa. Col. Records*, VII, 148-51.

[44] Quoted in Thayer, *Pennsylvania Politics*, p. 56.

[45] Ralph L. Ketcham, "Conscience, War, and Politics in Pennsylvania, 1755-1757," *William and Mary Quarterly*, 3rd ser., XX, no. 3 (July 1963), 431, 432.

the Quakers . . . to suffer their seats, during the difficult situation of the affairs of the colonies, to be filled by members of other denominations, in such manner as to prepare, without any scruples, all such laws as may be necessary to be enacted for the defence of the province."[46] Yet twelve Quakers, either actual members of the Society or generally considered as such, remained in the new house—a proportion amounting to as much as a third of the whole. Isaac Norris II remained as speaker, despite the efforts of the two delegates of London Meeting for Sufferings, John Hunt and Christopher Wilson, who had just arrived from England, to persuade him of the need to retire as an example to others; thus his name continues to appear on the military measures sanctioned by the assembly.

In the months and years to come the Society took steps to convince their recalcitrant politicians of the need to conform, but Friends were obviously unwilling to cut them off altogether. We hear, for instance, of the monthly meeting in Chester County laboring with old George Ashbridge, a country Quaker who had sat in the assembly since 1743, and being bluntly told by him (in the words of the meeting minute): "He do [sic] not feel himself culpable."[47] And, indeed, Ashbridge continued to sit in the assembly until his death in 1773. Samuel Foulke, who accepted election for the first time in 1761, long after the stricter brethren had withdrawn and while the war was still on, remained clerk of his Richland Monthly Meeting and a respected Quaker elder in spite of his failure to follow official Quaker policy.[48] In this instance, not even a mild censuring appears to have been administered to the aspirant to political office. When peace came, the way appeared open for the Society to return to politics, and even James Pemberton in 1765 accepted reelection to the assembly.[49] But, in fact, as we shall see, such hopes were illusory. True, Friends remained an influential factor in politics up to the outbreak of the Revolution, and even Quaker pacifism was still palely reflected in provincial policy, which never imposed a throughgoing militia organization and retained something of the Quaker spirit in its relations with Indians.[50] But the so-called Quaker party was firmly in the grip of the pro-war Benjamin Franklin, while the pacifist element was uppermost now in the councils of Philadelphia Yearly Meeting and in the lower Quaker meetings.

[46] Pa. Col. Records, VII, 292, 293.
[47] Sharpless, Political Leaders of Provincial Pennsylvania, pp. 193, 194.
[48] Gummere's notes to Woolman's Journal, pp. 553, 554. Foulke was disowned during the American Revolution for having taken the "test."
[49] See Sharpless, A Quaker Experiment, I, 269.
[50] Ketcham, "Conscience, War, and Politics," pp. 435, 436; Hanna, Franklin and Pennsylvania Politics, pp. 99, 103-7, 228.

Moreover, after 1764, when the assembly petitioned the Crown to remove Pennsylvania from the hands of the Penn family and transform it into a Crown colony, some conservative Friends like Isaac Pemberton, fearing that Anglican domination would result from such a transference, switched over support to the proprietary interest.[51] As a new and revolutionary era approached and more radical elements began to group themselves to the left of the old popular party, ancient political alignments were beginning to break up.

If in 1756 Pennsylvania Friends had not yet given up hopes of an eventual return to the political *status quo ante* 1755, they had already begun to seek out extrapolitical channels through which they could express their concern for reestablishing peaceful conditions within the province and for proving their readiness to make material sacrifices to achieve this aim[52] and through which also, perhaps, they might be able to satisfy their less Quakerly desire to discredit what they considered the disastrous Indian policies of the proprietaries which the governor represented. Thus there came into existence in the summer of 1756 the Friendly Association for Regaining and Preserving Peace with the Indians by Pacific Means.[53] The Association was nominally independent of the Society of Friends but, in fact, was sponsored semi-officially by Philadelphia Yearly Meeting. "Unfortunately," writes Thayer, "from the outset, the activities of the Friendly Association were involved with provincial politics."[54] That the Association was to some extent a political maneuver is probably true; that it was also conceived as an instrument whereby the Quaker peace testimony

[51] Zimmerman, "Franklin and the Quaker Party," p. 291.

[52] An earlier example of this kind of motive for Quaker philanthropy is suggested by Tolles, *Meeting House and Counting House*, p. 229. At the beginning of the decade, when Governor Hamilton and the anti-Quaker interest were agitating for defense appropriations which the Quaker assembly stubbornly refused to pass, the very considerable support given by wealthy Quaker merchants and by the assembly itself to the founding of the Philadelphia Hospital in 1751 was most probably due, at least in part, to the desire to prove that Friends could be generous where no scruples of conscience intervened.

[53] The Association was founded in July but did not really get going until the following autumn. It acquired its full name in December 1756. See esp. Thayer, "The Friendly Association," *PMHB*, LXVII, no. 4 (Oct. 1943), 356-76, and his *Israel Pemberton*, chaps. VIII, XI-XIII. The most recent treatment of the Friendly Association is to be found in the penultimate chapter of Hershberger, MS book. Israel was in fact the moving spirit behind the Association's activities; among his chief associates were his brother John, Jonathan Mifflin, and John Reynell, all of whom made generous financial contributions to its work. The collaboration of the nonresistant Mennonites and Schwenkfelders was also enlisted by the promoters of the Association.

[54] "The Friendly Association," p. 356. Sydney V. James (*A People called Quakers*, p. 178) calls the Association "this grandiose adventure in pressure politics."

could find practical expression, whereby pacifism could be shown to yield positive results where the opposite policy of military action proved sterile, is also correct. Although the governor and council regarded it as meddlesome interference,[55] they were forced by the Association's initiative in this respect to enter into negotiations with the Indians. Peace was in fact reached with the Delawares in August 1757 and was extended to include other tribes in the conference at Easton in 1758. In addition, before the Association finally folded soon after the conclusion of peace in 1763, Quakers had succeeded to some degree in transferring blame for the bitter frontier warfare from their own shoulders, where many in the early years of the conflict had tended to place it, onto those of the proprietors and their agents. Whether considered as a farsighted endeavor to promote peaceful coexistence or as a narrow attempt to regain by other methods the political influence lost by the Quaker withdrawal, the Friendly Association deserves at least brief mention in any account of the development of Quaker pacifism in Pennsylvania.

For all their backstage political influence and their efforts to prove the practical efficacy of a peaceable political policy, the events of the winter of 1755-1756 ushered in a time of troubles for Pennsylvania Quakers. Their hardships, of course, were slight in comparison with those endured by earlier generations of Friends on both sides of the ocean or in later periods of war and stress, or even at the present time of conflict by Friends in other and less tolerant colonies—not to speak of the sufferings of their fellow provincials of other faiths in the exposed frontier districts. But it was with sadness that many Quakers saw war come to Penn's patrimony and military requisitions being made on his people by a legislature that still contained a number of professing Friends. In three areas the Quaker conscience found itself confronted with the requirements of a state at war: militia service (compulsion, however, was confined to the Three Lower Counties that were to become Delaware), war taxation, and demands for various auxiliary services with the army.

Already in 1756 the assembly of the Three Lower Counties, following the example of their Pennsylvania counterpart, had enacted a

[55] A view that has been held, too, by some recent historians, e.g., Daniel J. Boorstin, *The Americans: The Colonial Experience*, 1964 edn., p. 57, and Hanna, *Franklin and Pennsylvania Politics*, pp. 107-10. It should be noted that in a letter, dated 9 July 1754, the Quaker Meeting for Sufferings in London had strongly urged Pennsylvania Friends to pay all taxes "for the support of civil government." Payment, London Friends thought, was "agreeable to the several advices of the Yearly Meeting founded on the precept and example of our Saviour" (quoted in H. J. Cadbury, "Nonpayment of Provincial War Tax," *Friends Journal*, 1 Sept. 1966, p. 441).

new militia law—but in this case, as earlier in this area, service was obligatory and penalties were attached for failure to obey, "without any exemption of persons who conscientiously scruple to comply therewith." Soon Quakers began to be fined for failure to muster, and, in accordance with the pattern elsewhere, their goods were distrained for refusal to pay. Early next year we find Philadelphia Yearly Meeting, which had oversight over Delaware Friends, appealing to the new deputy-governor, William Denny, for redress. Their petition singled out for special criticism the conduct of one of the New Castle County justices, David Bush, who along with his underlings had acted in a particularly offensive fashion. Most of those who suffered at the hands of these officials were simple farming folk, for whom the confiscation of livestock or farm equipment or household goods meant serious hardship, as well as losses usually in very considerable excess of the original fine. In one instance the cradle in which the man's infant child lay dying was seized; other goods worth £2 in all were taken along with the cradle for a fine of merely 10s.[56]

In Pennsylvania proper, the most difficult issue that had to be faced was whether or not to pay the taxes that were being used to carry on a war of which Friends disapproved both on principle and on grounds of political expediency. Most paid; some refused, and, relates Woolman, "in many places, the collectors and constables being Friends, distress was made on their goods . . . by their fellow members." James Pemberton wrote to Samuel Fothergill in November 1756:

> Our situation is indeed such as affords cause of melancholy reflection that the first commencement of persecution in this province should arise from our brethren in profession, and that such darkness should prevail as that they should be instruments of oppressing tender consciences which hath been the case. The tax in this county [Philadelphia] being pretty generally collected and many in this city particularly suffered by distraint of their goods and some being near cast into jail.

This was a painful situation indeed—but one which Yearly Meeting was unable to resolve satisfactorily. In the fall of 1757, for instance, a committee appointed to consider the question concluded that, since it was clear that there existed a wide "diversity of sentiments" among members, those of one opinion censuring those who took an opposite view, the matter should not be discussed publicly by Friends,

---

[56] *Pa. Col. Records*, VII, 403, 404; *Pa. Archives*, 1st ser., III, 165-70. See also W. R. Gawthrop, "Retrospect of Wilmington Friends" in *Friends in Wilmington 1738-1938*, p. 35.

who were adjured "earnestly to have their minds covered with fervent charity towards one another."[57]

In the privacy of Quaker meetings, however, the merits and demerits of tax refusal continued to be debated. Thus we hear of Woolman arguing the question with a Pennsylvania Quaker justice in the summer of 1758. According to Woolman, although Friends must approve of the general purposes of civil government, they should not give active support to it if the particular governmental measure was one which they deplored, as was the case now with taxes for war. The proper conduct in such a situation was to refuse payment and endure meekly the hardships consequent on the inevitable distraints: "this joined with an upright uniform life may tend to put men athinking about their own public conduct." The justice demurred. Not refusal of payment, he contended, but quiet remonstrance with the authorities whom they believed to be acting wrongly was the correct response. For him, a tax boycott was an unjustifiable act of civil disobedience. But, countered Woolman, surely no government has a right to our unconditional acquiescence, and, where it was bound on a wrong course, "an active obedience in that case would be adding one evil to another." For a man to suffer quietly the legal penalties for refusing to consent to evil appeared to him "most virtuous."[58]

Only the coming of peace stilled, for the time being, the controversy generated among Friends on this issue. Less debatable was the question of the response to be made to the various demands for helping the war effort that was being waged on Pennsylvania soil. As early as 1756, in answer to a query from Shrewsbury Quarterly Meeting in New Jersey, Yearly Meeting declared participation in the watch to be "a military service . . . that no Friend should either in person, or by paying others, be concerned therein."[59] Thus, performance of the kind of noncombatant services alongside the militia that, according to a new—and stiffened—militia act projected in 1757, might be demanded in an emergency of Quakers and other sectaries who conscientiously objected to bearing arms would also appear to have been ruled out

[57] Woolman, *Journal*, p. 210; Sharpless, *A Quaker Experiment*, I, 249. See also Minutes of the Yearly Meeting of Friends at Philadelphia for 1749-1779 (Dept. of Records of Philadelphia Y. M.), p. 110. This epistle is signed not only by the more radical tax objectors like Woolman, Churchman, and John Pemberton but also by Councillor William Logan and Samuel Wetherill, future leader of the Free Quakers of the Revolutionary era, neither of whom were pacifists, of course, let alone tax radicals. The decision was clearly a compromise between the two divergent wings of Pennsylvania Quakerism.

[58] Woolman, *Journal*, pp. 214, 215.

[59] A Collection of Christian and Brotherly Advices (1762), MS in F.H.L.S.C., p. 402.

for a consistent Friend. But the bill was vetoed by the governor before it could become law. Friends, the majority of whom were still farmers living in the country areas of the province, did have to face frequent requests to furnish wagons and horses to assist the military, and the Quaker merchants of Philadelphia were often faced with the problem of importing war supplies on their ships. In June 1758 a minute of the Meeting for Sufferings, which Yearly Meeting had set up in 1756 on the model of the London body of the same name to deal with the new and trying situation in which Pennsylvania Friends found themselves, declared unequivocally that voluntary assistance "with ships, waggons, or other carriages for transporting implements of war or military stores" was a dereliction of Friends' discipline. Deviants in this respect were to be dealt with by their meetings "in order to convince them of their error."[60]

In this same year 1758, Yearly Meeting took a decisive step in their strategic retreat from the political arena, second in importance only to the withdrawal from the assembly two years earlier. For, although this withdrawal had encompassed almost all the Quaker assemblymen who remained close to the Society, there were still many devoted Friends in the subordinate magistracy, functioning as justices of the peace or as constables in the towns and in the country districts or participating in the various other lesser offices of government. Most of these men held to the Society's peace testimony, as they did to its other tenets. A few were even militant pacifists, like Justice Aaron Ashbridge (1712-1776), a prosperous farmer in Chester County, of whom complaint was made by the military early in 1757 that he "not only refused to attest his recruits, but discouraged the men that were brought to him for that purpose from entering into the king's service."[61] That Quaker magistrates, as this remark implies, were being required in their official capacity to administer oaths and collaborate in military matters—and thus deviate from two of Friends' most cherished testimonies—was placing the Society in an increasingly anomalous situation.

In 1758, therefore, under the compelling spiritual influence of John Woolman and his co-workers (for the purely political motives for withdrawal that had been apparent in regard to the assembly no longer

[60] Gummere's introduction to Woolman's *Journal*, p. 53; *Rules of Discipline of the Yearly Meeting of Friends of Pennsylvania and New Jersey* (1797), p. 131.

[61] Quoted in Gummere's notes to Woolman's *Journal*, p. 585. Aaron, surprisingly enough, was the son of George Ashbridge, who had stubbornly refused to resign his seat in the assembly in 1756. His second wife, who had died in 1755, was Elizabeth Ashbridge (whose first husband's strange story is told above in n. 3, chap. I). Aaron Ashbridge's term of office came to an end in 1757, perhaps as a result of his forthright antimilitarism.

applied to anything like the same degree), Yearly Meeting strongly advised members against continuance in, or acceptance of, civil offices where they would in any way be involved in "enjoining or enforcing the compliance of their brethren or others with any act which they conscientiously scruple to perform." (At the same time, the meeting also took the momentous step of excluding Friends who purchased slaves from holding positions of trust within the Society.) Members who, after being lovingly "labored with" by their meetings, refused to resign office should henceforward be debarred from sitting "in our meetings for discipline" or from employment "in the affairs of truth, until they are brought to a sense and acknowledgement of their error." Henceforth, the Quaker magistrate, though not actually disowned, would continue as a semi-outcast in the community of Friends.

Yet even this measure was not completely effective in drawing Friends out of the magistracy. In the following year, for instance, a traveling English minister, William Reckitt (1706-1769), after visiting Friends at Darby reported that "several had been meddling and concerning themselves" with military matters and that there was considerable confusion about how Friends should behave in respect to participation in administration. He complained generally of "a grievous refractory libertine spirit" among them. Even as late as 1763, the caution of 1758 was being repeated on account of "the painful occasion of uneasiness, which still continues to subsist in divers places," from members continuing to hold office; and in the following year Friends were warned not to be "accessory in promoting or electing any of our brethren to such offices."[62] Thus, in the lower magistracy, as in the central legislature, the Quaker withdrawal was carried through only slowly and painfully and with much soul-searching and hesitancy on each side. Although not brought to final completion before the end of the colonial period, the withdrawal nevertheless was widespread enough, when combined with the new religious currents in the Society, to transform Pennsylvania Quakerdom from a vitally important element in the political establishment into a group that lay merely on the periphery of provincial politics. The final stage in the process came only as a result of the Society's experiences in the Revolutionary War.

The settlement of 1763 brought twelve years of official peace to the American colonies. The growing colonial movement against the policies of the home government, in the early stages of which Pennsylvania

[62] Michener, A Retrospect, pp. 274, 275; Some Account of the Life and Gospel Labours of William Reckitt, pp. 143, 144.

Friends played an important part, introduced new problems for the Quaker peace witness, problems which were intensified as resistance deepened and relations between the colonies and the mother country deteriorated until finally they issued in open and armed conflict.

One incident in this period must be dealt with here, for in a way it provides a link between the crisis of Quaker pacifism in 1755-1756, when the alleged failure of Quaker government to provide for the province's defense was used to remove Quaker politicians from power, and the crisis which resulted from the outbreak of the American Revolution exactly two decades later, when the issue was the justifiability of armed opposition to allegedly tyrannous rule. This incident was the famous Paxton Riot of 1764,[63] which represented a reaction on the part of frontier elements in Pennsylvania to the Indian uprising further north known to history as Pontiac's Conspiracy (the Pennsylvania Indians were suspected by many frontiersmen of being in league with hostile Indians). In November the Moravians had the Indians under their care removed to Philadelphia since they felt that these Indians were not safe in the Bethlehem area. In the following month the government-protected Conestoga Indians, who lived not far from Lancaster, were massacred almost to the last man, woman, and child by groups of armed frontiersmen—many of them Scotch-Irish—who called themselves the "Paxton Boys"; and in February the Paxton Boys marched on Philadelphia, which thereupon put itself in a posture of defense. Among those elements most culpable in the eyes of the Paxton Boys and their supporters in promoting what they considered policies of appeasement toward the Indians were, of course, the Quakers, some of whose members still sat in the assembly and whose name was still given colloquially to the majority party in that body. Isaac Pemberton, not unnaturally, was their particular bête noire. As it happened, the whole affair soon petered out: on approaching Philadelphia, the Paxton Boys, instead of attacking, contented themselves with placing a list of grievances in the administration's hands and then returned home without further trouble.

In the excitement of the moment, however, and with the intention of protecting the Indian refugees in the city who, it was feared, might also be massacred by the irate Paxton Boys, some 200 young Philadelphia Quakers took up arms. To them the choice seemed to lie between passive acquiescence in "the progress of horrid murderers" and active resistance to their further advance. Even though few, if any, of the older members were involved, and even with due allowance

[63] For the incident's effect on Quakers, see Sharpless, A Quaker Experiment, vol. II, chap. III.

155

made for what James Pemberton described as "the instability of youth," still it constituted—in the words of Samuel Fothergill—"a sorrowful defection from our religious testimony."[64]

The Society's enemies seized upon the activities of these young enthusiasts in an effort to discredit the sincerity of Friends as a whole. We find the German Lutheran pastor in Philadelphia, the Rev. Henry Melchior Mühlenberg, commenting sarcastically: "What increased the wonder was, that the pious lambs in the long French, Spanish and Indians Wars had such tender consciences, and would sooner die than raise a hand in defence against these dangerous enemies, and now at once . . . rushing upon a handful of our poor distressed and ruined fellow citizens and inhabitants of the frontiers."[65] A whole series of pamphlets issued from the press during the following year arguing the case for or against both the Paxton Boys and their chief butt, the Quakers.[66] One of the anti-Quaker items—*The Conduct of the Paxton-Men, Impartially Represented*—even cites the Babbitt incident of 1691 (see above) to prove that Quakers had never in fact been principled against bearing arms. And today, the anonymous author went on, "did not your Philadelphia Quakers take up arms, and declare they would fight in one case, namely, in defence of Friend Indians?"[67]

This, of course, was a libel. But the care with which local meetings in Philadelphia for the next three years endeavored to bring their delinquent members to acknowledge the error of their recent conduct shows the concern felt in the Society lest this episode should cast doubt on the sincerity of its pacifism. They sternly rejected any attempt to equate the action of their young militants with quasi-police action, a legitimate exercise of force which might be squared with Friends' testimony against war. Success was achieved in most instances, but, it was reported, "some appear rather in a disposition to vindicate their conduct." A few did indeed remain recalcitrant, justifying the use of arms in defense, until the action was finally dropped in mid-1767. No one was disowned.[68]

The "war" Quakers of 1764 were forerunners of the Free Quakers of the American Revolution. However, the animus of their adversaries,

---

[64] Crosfield, *Samuel Fothergill*, p. 443.

[65] *The Paxton Papers* (ed. John R. Dunbar), p. 41.

[66] These tracts have been collected and published in the volume entitled *The Paxton Papers*, which also contains material on the Quakers' response during and after the emergency.

[67] *Ibid.*, pp. 275-77.

[68] Sharpless, *A Quaker Experiment*, II, 50-54. On the other hand, some who participated in the "Quaker" brigade of 1764 became firm pacifists in later years, among them its leader Edward Penington, who was one of the Virginia exiles in 1777.

the Paxton Boys, was directed mainly against the now vanishing political Quaker of an earlier age. For by this date, although neither Quaker nor non-Quaker was always aware of it, Quaker Pennsylvania had become a part of past history.

Quaker Pennsylvania, from the heyday of the Holy Experiment through the successive epochs of David Lloyd and John Kinsey up to the concluding phases of the rule of the Quaker party, has been evaluated in quite different ways by subsequent historians. For some writers it has seemed to be proof of the failure of a philosophy of nonviolence and of its fatuity, at least in the political arena. For others it has stood as a blueprint for a better and more peaceable world, an example of farsighted idealism to which future generations can look back for inspiration. Still others have regarded its record as illustrating, above all, the thoroughly inadequate expression given to the pacifism that its rulers professed, at least in theory; not doctrinaire pacifism, then, or "the curse of perfectionism,"[69] but lack of steady adherence to right principle and a tendency to compromise were the sources of its decline. On the other hand, the contradiction between Quaker law enforcement inside the state and Quaker noncombatancy in the face of external foes is held by some to have invalidated the whole experiment *ab initio*. That the idea of the Holy Experiment did become tarnished in the course of the years and with the growing affluence of the Society of Friends is a point on which almost all are in agreement, though there is no unanimity concerning the date when it effectually came to an end. It is also generally recognized that, apart from the moot question of defense policy, the Quaker legislators did achieve considerable success in such areas as civil and religious liberties, constitutional government, penal reform, Indian relations, and commercial development. An estimate of its relative success or failure cannot, therefore, be based on one facet of its policy alone.

In fact, it seems extremely doubtful whether Quaker Pennsylvania can be taken either to prove or disprove the validity of pacifism as a practical political policy, even if we consider only the earlier decades of its history before the idealism generated at its foundation had begun to wear thin. For from the very beginning its pacifist legislators, as we have seen, were not free agents in shaping the province's external relations; enmeshed in Britain's imperial strategy, they became increasingly unable to detach Pennsylvania from the worldwide ramifications of the power struggle among the great European states. This impotency was as potentially limiting in the early days as it was in

[69] Boorstin, *The Colonial Experience*, p. 63.

157

later decades, when the Quaker assembly's opposition to military measures in the colony was caused more by considerations relating to their own power struggle with internal political antagonists than by their ethico-religious scruples concerning war. Pennsylvania's pacifism, therefore, was always closely circumscribed by the mother country's dependence on military means to maintain its position in international politics.

Moreover, the failure of Quakerism to remain the majority creed and Friends' inability to impart their belief in nonviolence to any but a fraction of the non-Quaker immigrants who crowded into the province from the end of the seventeenth century presaged the final collapse of any attempt to impose a pacifist political policy on the colony. Quaker rule in the first half of the eighteenth century, hence, the continuation of Quaker policies on peace and war, came increasingly to depend on an inequitable electoral system.

Only if Pennsylvania had been as truly self-governing in its foreign policy as it actually was in its internal affairs, and only if it had remained a community which still shared for the most part Quaker views on war, could it have become a reliable testing ground for the political practicability of the pacifist precepts of the Sermon on the Mount.

Chapter 4

The German Peace Sects in Colonial America

The earliest settlers in the New World who held pacifist views[1] were probably Dutch Mennonites, who are known to have been living on Manhattan (then part of New Netherland) in the early 1640's. Others are reported on Long Island in the next decade. "However, no record of an organized congregation from this early time has been found, and no permanent settlement was made by them."[2]

A second venture involving Dutch Mennonites, although even more short-lived, has left a greater trace in the records. This is the settlement founded by the Dutchman Pieter Cornelis Plockhoy (ca. 1620-1700), a member of the liberal Lamist wing of the Mennonite church in Amsterdam who was closely associated with the influential Collegiant movement in Holland, the restitutionist ideas of which matched the Mennonites' in many respects. Not too much is known about Plockhoy. He was clearly a man of considerable culture, an exponent of religious toleration and ecumenicity and an advocate of a kind of communitarian socialism; all of these ideas he propounded in several pamphlets published in English during a visit to England in the late 1650's. With the restoration of the monarchy Plockhoy returned to Amsterdam. He then succeeded in enlisting the support of the city authorities in a scheme to plant a colony in New Netherland, where he could attempt to put his ideas into practice. In July 1663 he set sail with forty other settlers, apparently all Mennonites, for the shores of the Delaware in New Netherland. The moment chosen was unpropi-

---

[1] If, that is, we disregard the rather ambiguous instance from the year 1627 cited in Thomas Jefferson Wertenbaker, *The First Americans 1607-1690*, p. 224, of one Richard Bickley, who may have been a genuine conscientious objector to fighting. On the other hand, he may have been refusing military service for some other motive. All our source ("Decisions of Virginia General Court, 1626-1628," *Virginia Magazine of History and Biography*, IV, no. 2 [Oct. 1897], 159) tells us is that, on complaint by Ensign John Uty, Bickley was arraigned before the court held at James City on 7 May 1627. "Richard Bickley," the ensign complained, "hath resisted and opposed him, in his command, in denying to take arms and discharge his public duty." The minute concludes: "The Court hath ordered, that for this his offence he shall be laid neck and heels 12 hours, and at the crop by way of fine shall pay 100 l of tobacco." Is it just possible that Bickley had been influenced by Mennonite views on war which had percolated through to him by way, perhaps, of the English Baptists?

[2] *Mennonite Encyclopedia*, III, 863.

159

tious: undeclared war between England and the Dutch republic led to the destruction of the little colony even before open hostilities between the two great Protestant maritime powers broke out in 1665. A contemporary English account relates that in 1664 the British commander, Sir Robert Carr, a bare year after the colony's foundation, "destroyed the Quaking society of Plockhoy to a nail."[3] Some, if not all, of the members of the community, including Plockhoy himself, evidently survived the attack, for we learn that the founder continued to live on under British rule until his death around the end of the century.

Plockhoy had been granted considerable latitude by the Amsterdam authorities in making his arrangements. The colony was to be run on communitarian lines, and slavery was to be forbidden within it. It was to be armed against attack from hostile Indians and other enemies. But, as the colonists were drawn from the Mennonite community, all who had conscientious scruples were to be exempted from bearing arms or other military duties; in exchange for this privilege, they were to pay a special annual tax, which would be used for the maintenance of soldiers. Nonresistants, who at first, at any rate, would make up the overwhelming majority of the citizenry, were to be given special representation in the colony's legislative assembly. Thus, while Plockhoy, like Penn later, took into account the nonpacifist outlook of the home authorities and was ready to grant a place within society to the magistrate's sword—provided that those who were following the higher way were not called upon to share in this aspect of government—he saw to it that the scruples of his coreligionists against participation in warlike activities were safeguarded.

Power politics, the commercial rivalry between England and Holland that eventually led to open war, destroyed any possibility of a Mennonite "Pennsylvania" developing in Delaware. Indeed, such an outcome was unlikely anyway, not merely because Plockhoy's scheme was a private venture with no official backing from the Dutch Mennonites, but even more because of the difference in attitude between Mennonites and Quakers on the question of civil government. If Plockhoy's colony had eventually expanded, the Mennonite element in its administration would most likely have been eliminated very much sooner than the Quakers in Penn's colony were.

The first permanent settlement of Mennonites on this continent was not effected until just after the founding of Pennsylvania. In October 1683 a Dutch-speaking Mennonite family, along with twelve other families who had been converted from Mennonitism to Quakerism, arrived

---

[3] Leland and Marvin Harder, *Plockhoy from Zurik-see*, p. 35. See chap. IV for Plockhoy's colonization scheme.

from Crefeld in western Germany and located a few miles north of Philadelphia, where settlement had begun only in the previous year. The new township was called Germantown. In the period up to 1707 fifteen more Mennonite families from the lower Rhine area settled in Germantown along with the Quaker-Mennonite group and a few Mennonite settlers, both Dutch- and German-speaking, from other parts of Germany and from Amsterdam. At first, the little village was inhabited solely by Quakers and Mennonites, solely, that is, by adherents of religious groups professing a pacifist Christianity; hence, there could have been few problems of village administration at that time that would have led to a clash with the Mennonite principle of nonparticipation in affairs of state. The village magistrate did not need to wield the sword against the wrongdoer: minor offenses could easily be dealt with by public censure and nonviolent means. In 1689 Germantown obtained a charter from Penn, and in 1691 it became effectively incorporated as a borough. A General Court was set up to make village bylaws and a Court of Record to sit as a judiciary body, with its members acting as justices of the peace. The corporation was, in effect, a closed one, drawn from the leading members of the Quaker-Mennonite community.

"The Court [of Record] was chiefly concerned . . . with litigation relating to stray pigs, line fences, uncomplimentary adjectives, and such other matters as are likely to become causes for dispute between peaceful neighbors in a primitive settlement." But in the course of time, and with the gradual influx of other German settlers not belonging to the peace sects, who eventually considerably outnumbered Quakers and Mennonites combined, village proceedings began to take on a character not quite consistent with strict nonresistance as understood by (at least) the Mennonites. In 1693, for instance, stocks were erected "for evil doers," and in 1697 a makeshift prison was built. The Court of Record decided that henceforth all punishments meted out by it would be rigorously imposed.

Many of the Mennonite villagers soon began to have second thoughts about the compatibility of government, even under such halcyon conditions, with their nonresistant creed. Some refused fairly early to act as jurymen, and by the beginning of the new century it was becoming increasingly difficult to fill the other offices, too; according to the borough's charter, eligibility for these offices was confined to a narrow circle of Mennonites and Quakers. In 1701 Francis Daniel Pastorius, who had been the settlement's first bailiff, complained in a letter to Penn of the shortage of men to fill the General Court because of refusals to serve "for conscience sake." Finally, in 1707, the borough was deprived of its charter on account of the lack of candidates for office among those entitled to stand for them, and it was thenceforward merged with a larger administrative unit.[4] Since Quakers at this time did not object to participation in government, this boycott of office must have issued from the Mennonite element or been due to the influence of the Mennonite viewpoint on Quakers of Mennonite background.

This influence was probably responsible also for the well-known protest against slavery signed by Germantown Quakers of largely Mennonite origin in 1688. At this time (as we have seen in our discussion of the petition in an earlier chapter) British Quakers were not yet prepared to abandon slaveholding; hence, no action was taken on the petition by Philadelphia Yearly Meeting.[5]

Although its foundation marked the beginnings of continuous Mennonite settlement in America and although it gave birth to the first regularly organized Mennonite congregation in the New World, Germantown never played a particularly important role in the church's history. The community remained small, never rising above a hundred baptized members.

Religious persecution in Europe, which had prompted those (at least those from Germany) who settled in Germantown to brave the hardships of the ocean and a savage land, soon led other groups of Mennonites from both Germany and Switzerland to seek refuge in Pennsylvania, whose rulers shared much in common with their own religious faith. Whereas the Germantown Mennonites were mostly small craftsmen, the new wave of Mennonite immigrants, which started in 1710 and lasted until 1754, consisted mainly of peasants, who naturally settled in the countryside, clearing the virgin forest in many areas in order to farm. They came from the Palatinate and from Switzerland, having left their native land in large part for economic reasons, but also in part to escape the oppression which was the frequent lot of their barely tolerated faith in post-Reformation Central Europe. Only in the canton of Bern, where service in the citizen militia was compulsory, was a refusal to bear arms an important factor in emigration.[6] Some 3,000 Mennonites, including several hundred Amish, who began their immigration in the 1720's, crossed the Atlantic during this period. They settled to the north of Philadelphia in Montgomery and Bucks Counties, where the Mennonites formed the Franconia Conference, and to the west in Lancaster County and adjacent areas. By the outbreak of the

---

[4] C. Henry Smith, *The Mennonite Immigration to Pennsylvania in the Eighteenth Century*, pp. 110-19. See also *M.E.*, II, 481-83.
[5] Smith, pp. 107-10.   [6] *Ibid.*, p. 58.

American Revolution Mennonites and Amish combined may have numbered as many as 10,000 persons out of a total of about 100,000 Germans in Pennsylvania, which amounted to around a third of the province's population.[7]

During the period of Quaker rule in the colony, Mennonites and Amish enjoyed complete freedom of worship and were not subject to any form of military conscription. Special legislation relieved them of the obligation to take legal oaths. They were not required to participate in government, although the Mennonites, along with the other German sectaries, voted in elections and were one of the mainstays of Quaker government in the province.[8] As they wrote in an address to William Penn in 1718, the year of his death:

> We came to Pennsylvania to seek an asylum from the persecution to which we had been subjected in Europe. We knew the character of William Penn, and rejoiced God had made such a man. . . . We came to Pennsylvania to enjoy freedom of mind and body. . . . We ask you for permission to pass our lives in innocence and tranquillity. Let us pursue our avocations unmolested.[9]

Their tranquillity was seriously disturbed in Penn's province only after war broke out in 1739. Then both Mennonites and Amish became increasingly sensitive to the need to instruct their youth, especially, in their nonresistant faith in case they should once again be tested as they had been in Europe during the previous two centuries. In 1742 the German Pietist Christopher Saur (see below) had brought out at his Germantown press the Amish *Ausbund*, the hymnbook of the Swiss Brethren, with its portrayal of martyrdom and suffering as the lot of true Christians in this world of sorrow and sin. But the poor frontier communities did not possess their own printing press or the means to set one up. As the war progressed, the Mennonites began to consider the possibility of publishing a German translation of another classic of nonresistant martyrology which was available only in the original Dutch: Tieleman Jansz van Braght's *Martyrs' Mirror* (1660). A few copies of this bulky work had been brought over by the Dutch-speaking Mennonites that had settled in Germantown, but by this time the Dutch text was unintelligible to almost all the Pennsylvania Mennonites.

[7] *M.E.*, IV, 138.
[8] See Wilbur J. Bender, "Pacifism among the Mennonites, Amish Mennonites and Schwenkfelders of Pennsylvania to 1783," pt. I, *MQR*, I, no. 3 (July 1927), 29-32.
[9] E. K. Martin, *The Mennonite*, p. 11.

In October 1745, therefore, six ministers of the Skippack congregations appealed to the churches in Amsterdam and Haarlem for help in getting a translation published. With war raging, they were fearful, despite their present immunity from military demands, that in the near future "to the non-resistant Christians tribulation and persecution may come to their house." "We have no assurance," their letter went on, "in case there should be a hostile outbreak in this province, as has been the case in other provinces, that we would not be compelled against our consciences to bear arms, and with other provinces to meet an enemy armed, to the great burdening of our consciences." Attempts a few years earlier to get the provincial assembly to guarantee them exemption from military service, if it were ever imposed, had been received in a friendly spirit (not unnaturally, in view of its Quaker majority) but without positive results. The assembly had told them "that it was not in their power to grant their request, and that the right of liberty of conscience must be sought from his Royal Highness, the King of Great Britain." If trouble came, the *Martyrs' Mirror* would now help to strengthen the community's will to resist persecution. "We recognize the fact," they conclude, "that we have made a mistake in coming to this far off country with insufficient assurance in the matter of freedom of conscience."[10]

It was three years before the Dutch churches sent an answer to their brethren overseas, and then they had to report that the project, in their opinion, was unfortunately not practicable. Meanwhile, however, the American Mennonites had negotiated an agreement with the Ephrata Cloister (see below) to have the volume translated and printed by the fraternity there. It appeared in 1748-1749 in a large folio edition of over 1,500 pages.[11]

Whereas the Mennonites' alarm during the War of the Austrian Succession proved unfounded, the French and Indian War of 1755-1763, which brought Quaker rule in Pennsylvania to an end and fighting to the frontiers of the former Quaker province, tested for the first time in the New World the church's faith in its nonresistant principles —or at least the faith and constancy of some of its members. The ordeal, however, did not come, as they expected, as a result of their

[10] *Mennonite Year Book and Almanac*, pp. 25, 26, where the letter is printed in full. The Pennsylvania Mennonites had also tried unsuccessfully to enlist their Dutch brethren's help in getting their Estates General to intervene with the British Crown in favor of a guarantee of military exemption. See W. J. Bender, p. 33.

[11] Smith, pp. 324-30; *M.E.*, III, 527-29; Donald F. Durnbaugh, "Relationships of the Brethren with the Mennonites and Quakers, 1708-1865," *Church History*, XXXV, no. 1 (March 1966), 42, 43, 56, 57.

stand as conscientious objectors, for even after 1756 they continued to be exempt from military service along with the other pacifist groups.[12] It arose rather from the extension of the war to the borders of Pennsylvania, where Indian tribes in the pay of the French attacked exposed settlements and isolated homesteads, burning the dwellings, killing their inhabitants, or carrying them off into captivity. Mennonite communities deeper in the settled areas were not directly affected.

Before 1754 the frontier Mennonites and Amish had almost always enjoyed friendly relations with neighboring Indians. "With the Indians," writes C. Henry Smith, "the pioneer Mennonite lived in peace, profiting no doubt by the treaty made with the former William Penn only a few years before";[13] and successive generations of Mennonites continued to profit by the good relations long enjoyed by Quaker Pennsylvania with the province's indigenous inhabitants. On rare occasions a homestead might be attacked, but there is no record of any armed resistance being offered by Mennonites. True, there were a number of Mennonites among those who signed the petition drawn up by inhabitants of the Perkiomen Valley in 1728 asking the governor of Pennsylvania, on behalf of "your poor afflicted people," "for relief" from Indian attacks endangering themselves and their families.[14] But this appeal did not signify a retreat from personal pacifism on the part of the Mennonite signatories: armed protection of the state's citizens was among the duties of the powers that be, a function that was part of God's order for the world, though not one in which the faithful should participate themselves. In the French and Indian War, too, even though a few young Mennonites did volunteer for service, an act which automatically led to disownment, there is no evidence that any armed resistance was made against the Indian raiders.

The exact figure of those killed or captured in Mennonite or Amish communities is not known, "but a number of stories of Indian depredations have been preserved in various family histories." One of the best known instances is that of the Amishman Jacob Hochstetler, whose farm in Berks County was burned in September 1756. His wife and two of his children were killed, while Jacob himself and the remaining

---

[12] In a petition to the assembly in May 1755, Mennonites and Amish had given expression to their fears that, with war on the very frontiers of the province, naturalization might now be taken to have implied military obligations toward the state. Their refusal to fight, they had declared, was "not out of contempt to authority" but due solely to their desire to follow in Christ's footsteps. See Guy F. Hershberger, "A Newly Discovered Pennsylvania Mennonite Petition of 1755," *MQR*, XXIII, no. 2 (April 1959), 143-51.

[13] Smith, p. 378.

[14] John C. Wenger, *History of the Mennonites of the Franconia Conferences*, pp. 407, 408.

children were kept in Indian captivity for a period of seven years. The neighboring Amish settlement of Northkill, which was in close proximity to Indian routes, was destroyed in the following year, its inhabitants having taken refuge outside the danger zone. In the Shenandoah Valley of Virginia, where Mennonites settled in the second quarter of the eighteenth century, severe raiding took place during the war in 1758, forcing many to return to eastern Pennsylvania. The last raid in Virginia took place in 1764, after the official conclusion of hostilities, when a Mennonite preacher, John Rhodes, his wife, and six of their thirteen children were killed by an Indian raiding party led by a white man. Their scalps were then sold to the French.[15]

Killings, burnings, and scalpings were endemic all along the frontiers of the American colonies throughout the war period. The pacific attitude of the Mennonite communities, even in the face of death at the hands of the Indians, was apparently not looked upon kindly either by their neighbors or by provincial officialdom. In 1757 Governor Denny wrote to the proprietors of Pennsylvania concerning conditions on the frontiers of Lancaster County: "The poor inhabitants where these daring murders were committed, being without militia or associates, and living among Mennonites, a numerous sect of German Quakers, came supplicating me for protection."[16]

Yet, despite their trials with marauding Indians and some unpopularity in wartime with their nonpacifist fellow citizens, Mennonites and Amish did not as yet have to suffer any serious disabilities on account of their scruples against military service. The small communities in Virginia, where drilling with the militia was compulsory for able-bodied adult males, were able to obtain exemption by the payment of militia fines, against which—unlike the Quakers—they had no deep-seated scruples of conscience. In 1773 we find them petitioning the provincial government in Williamsburg to be excused from this requirement, not because of any fundamental objection to this alternative to service (for was it not merely rendering Caesar his due?) but on account of their poverty as frontiersmen eking out a bare subsistence.[17] In Pennsylvania, where most Mennonites and all the Amish were then located, no demands were in practice yet made of them in lieu of military service.

It should not be surprising, then, that the Mennonite communities

15 Smith, pp. 241, 380-85; L. J. Heatwole, *Mennonite Handbook of Information*, chap. XV; Glenn Weaver, "The Mennonites during the French and Indian War," *MHB*, vol. XVI, no. 2 (April 1955); Harry A. Brunk, *History of Mennonites in Virginia*, I, 32-36.

16 Martin, *The Mennonite*, p. 13.

17 Brunk, *History*, I, 34.

were filled with a sense of thankfulness as they compared their present lot with the sufferings they had endured in their European home-
lands before crossing the ocean. This feeling emerges strongly, for
instance, in a letter sent to their Dutch brethren by bishops of the
Franconia Conference in March 1773, on the eve of the revolution
that was to bring a new testing of their peace principles. They write
of their present situation: "Through God's mercy we enjoy unlimited
freedom in both civil and religious affairs. We have never been compelled to bear weapons. With yea and nay we can all testify before
our praiseworthy magistrates. We accept no office under the Government because force is used therein."[18]

The Brethren (or German Baptist Brethren or Dunkers, as they
are often known) were the second German pacifist group to leave
Europe for the New World in the early eighteenth century. Their migration took place between 1719 and 1736, with the main parties arriving in 1719 and in 1729. The earlier group came from Crefeld and was
headed by Peter Becker; the second contingent left Dutch Friesland,
to which it had migrated in 1720 from the birthplace of the movement in Schwarzenau in the little county of Wittgenstein in central
Germany. The denomination then numbered in all only several hundred adherents. Unlike the Mennonites, the Brethren neither possessed a long history in Europe before their migration nor left any
considerable following in the Old World. The few sympathizers who
stayed behind in the homeland soon melted away.

The year 1708 is usually taken as the date of foundation of the
Church of the Brethren. In that summer a group of eight men and
women under the leadership of Alexander Mack, Sr. (1679-1735), a
well-to-do miller, baptized each other by immersion in the river Eder
near Schwarzenau. They were all simple people, former members of
the Reformed Church who had come under the influence of the radical
Pietist movement. Most of them originated in the Rhenish Palatinate,
where religious persecution from the time the area had passed into the
hands of Catholic rulers in 1685, the devastation caused by recent
French invasions, and the economic exploitation of the peasantry had
given rise to a state of religious ferment that proved a fertile soil
for ideas directed against the establishment. The radical Pietists, like
all Pietists, strove to discover the meaning of the New Testament and
to shape their lives accordingly; they differed from the movement's
more conservative wing in believing that this effort entailed separation from the established Protestant churches. Mystically minded individualists, they feared that all organization of religion would kill

[18] Wenger, *Franconia Conference*, p. 400.

167

the true religious spirit. Mack's determination to establish a formal disciplined body in place of the loosely knit association of seekers that had existed hitherto brought a split with his closest mentor among the radical Pietists, the evangelizing former nobleman, Ernst Christoph Hochmann von Hochenau (1670-1721).

Radical Pietism, then, provided one source of Brethren pacifism.[19] The first Brethren studied the works of the great church historian associated with the Pietist movement, Gottfried Arnold (1666-1714). In particular, his *Die erste Liebe, das ist die wahre Abbildung der ersten Christen nach ihrem lebendigen Glauben und Leben* of 1696 and his still more famous *Unparteiische Kirchen-und-Ketzer-Historie*, published in four volumes in 1699-1700, depict the apostolic era, the early pre-Constantinian and the sectarian tradition thereafter, with their renunciation of military service as an unchristian way of life, as a pattern for later generations of believers to follow. At the turn of the century, too, another radical Pietist leader, Johann Konrad Dippel (1673-1734), had composed and published a tract entitled *Die Christen-Stadt auf Erden ohne gewöhnlichen Lehr-, Wehr-, und Nehr-Stand*. In the foreword to this tract, Dippel maintains that no one who has truly accepted Christ as his king could take part in war. Christians in office must resign if they found—as they most likely would—that they could not conduct themselves according to Christian precepts of love and humility. And, finally, Hochmann himself, the saintly and mild man with whom the first Brethren were in closest contact at the beginning, called upon those who had been awakened to follow Christ, to refuse military service if conscripted, and to renounce all use of force in their own defense. The magistracy, however, not being fully Christian, was in his view justified in using force for the protection of the state and for the maintenance of order.[20]

There may have been some Mennonite and Quaker influence shaping the pacifism of Hochmann and his associates. His views on war and magistracy, for instance, are almost identical with those expressed in the Scottish Quaker Robert Barclay's *Apology*, which Hochmann was reading in 1711 when he expressed himself most forcibly on the question of nonresistance.[21] But similar opinions, as we have seen, were being voiced among radical Pietists more than a decade earlier. That there was considerable Mennonite influence on the early Brethren is certain; possibly, there was some Quaker influence, too, for a

---

[19] See Chauncey David Ensign, "Radical German Pietism (ca. 1675-ca. 1750)," Ph.D. diss., Boston U. (1955), p. 418.

[20] Heinz Renkewitz, *Hochmann von Hochenau*, pp. 45, 335, 336, 354, 362, 363.

[21] *Ibid.*, p. 331.

Brethren group existed in Crefeld, which at that time was a center of German Quakerism. As Durnbaugh remarks: "The Brethren originally *came* out of radical Pietism, but they later *came out* of radical Pietism and accepted Anabaptism."[22]

That the Brethren, after absorbing so much of the Mennonites' theology, organization, and social ideology, did not merge with the Mennonites is attributable primarily to two causes. First, there were wide divergencies between the sects' methods of adult baptism: the Brethren accepted trine immersion, while the Mennonites baptized by pouring. More basic was the feeling of the first Brethren that contemporary Mennonitism had lost the drive and enthusiasm of the early days. The quality of Mennonite church life, in their opinion, had deteriorated. Nevertheless, the restitution of the early church among modern Christians and a close Christian discipleship remained among the Brethren's chief aims, as they did in the Mennonite church.

The Brethren's debt to the Anabaptist tradition insofar as their common pacifism is concerned, comes out in a passage in a polemical work of Alexander Mack's written in 1713, which at the same time forms the first statement of the Brethren faith. After castigating the willingness of the established churches, Protestant and Catholic alike, to use force in matters of religion, he adds: "What is more horrible, they go publicly to war, and slaughter one another by the thousands. All this is the fruit of infant baptism. No Baptist will be found in war. . . . The majority of them are inclined to peacefulness."[23]

The decision that was eventually reached to move to America was probably rooted as much in the attraction of free land for these peasants and small artisans eking out a precarious living near the subsistence level as in a desire to escape the periodic persecution of their faith and continuous uncertainty about the future that were the lot of the little church in Germany. Their pacifist views probably constituted only a minor factor in their decision to emigrate en masse to Quaker Pennsylvania. Since in those days soldiering was usually the affair of professional mercenaries and since where Brethren were located in towns they might be able to escape musterings of the citizen militias by monetary payments in lieu thereof, the question of military service did not threaten to become a major issue between them and the authorities.

However, at least one of the original eight Brethren, Andreas

[22] Durnbaugh, "Brethren Beginnings," Ph.D. diss., U. of Pennsylvania (1960), p. 173.
[23] Printed in Durnbaugh's anthology, *European Origins of the Brethren*, p. 343, from *Eberhard Ludwig Grubers Grundforschende Fragen, welche denen Neuen Täuffern, im Witgensteinischen, insonderheit zu beantworten, vorgelegt waren.*

Boni, a weaver from Basel in Switzerland, got into trouble with the city fathers over his refusal to bear arms or attend militia drillings. He had told them that, in his opinion, activity of this nature would be contrary to the teachings of the New Testament. The incident took place in 1705, after he had come under the influence of radical Pietist ideas during a recent sojourn in the Palatinate.[24] Later tradition also tells of two other of the early Brethren who suffered harsh imprisonment and torture because of their refusal to accept service after impressment by the King of Prussia's recruiting officers. One was a certain Johann Fischer, probably from Halle, and the other Elder Johann Naas (ca. 1670-1741), who was at the beginning second only to Alexander Mack in the Brethren leadership. Naas, according to the story, was "a head taller than most any other man in that vicinity and also of a very stout, athletic constitution," just the type of man, in fact, that King Frederick William I coveted for his famous bodyguard. After meekly enduring various torments for his refusal to accept enlistment, Naas—it is said—was brought before the king, who was so impressed by the man's steadfastness and courage that he ordered his immediate release.[25]

Before emigrating from Europe, the Brethren produced scarcely any literature of their own (and, indeed, for a long time they produced very little in their new homeland, too). They claimed simply to be living out the precepts of the gospels. Nonresistance, refusal of oaths, and avoidance of litigation and officeholding they viewed as merely the practical implementation of their Christian discipleship. These practices, along with trine immersion of adults, footwashing, the love feast, and a general nonconformity to the world, made up the faith for which they had broken with established religion in Europe. It was this faith that they strove to put into practice in the more hospitable atmosphere of colonial Pennsylvania.

The early Brethren who settled there found a home at first in Germantown but soon began spreading out into neighboring counties, with the largest settlements growing up in Lancaster County where much free land was available; a few scattered congregations arose in Maryland, New Jersey, and eventually in Virginia, too. By the time of the American Revolution the sect, still a very small group, numbered about 800 baptized members. During the colonial period they attracted little attention from their fellow citizens, living out laborious lives in rural obscurity.

[24] Durnbaugh diss., pp. 38, 39, 43.
[25] Ibid., pp. 114, 115. See also Rufus D. Bowman, The Church of Brethren and War, pp. 45, 46. It is not impossible—since they were written down only long after the event—that the stories about the two men in fact relate to one and the same person.

Several early accounts of the sect stress the fact that pacifism was one of the main tenets of their religious belief. For example, Morgan Edwards in his *Materials toward a History of the Baptists in Pennsylvania* writes of the Brethren:

> They use great plainness of language and dress, like the Quakers; and like them they will never swear nor fight. They will not go to law; nor take interest for the money they lend. They commonly wear their beards;[26] . . . Their acquaintance with the Bible is admirable. In a word they are meek and pious Christians; and have justly acquired the character of the harmless Tunkers.[27]

The New Jersey Quaker, Samuel Smith, paints a very similar picture of their attitude toward war and toward the state during this era. As well as bearing a testimony against oaths, he reports,

> They hold it not becoming a follower of Jesus Christ to bear arms or fight since their true Master has forbidden his disciples to *resist evil*. . . . They have a great esteem for the New Testament valuing it higher than all other books, and if they are asked about the articles of their faith, they know of no other than what is contained in this book, and therefore can give none. . . . They are a quiet inoffensive people.[28]

Almost entirely a farming community, the Brethren preserved their nonresistance as part of their whole traditional culture. Occasionally one of the handful of educated members, invariably a minister or elder, might commit his thoughts on religious questions to paper in order to edify the laity. The language employed was of course German, which was used by all congregations at this time. One of the Brethren who did so was Michael Frantz (1687-1747), a Swiss immigrant who was baptized by Peter Becker in 1734 and who became a leading figure in the important Conestoga (Lancaster County) congregation. His "Plain Instructive Considerations and Short Confession of Faith," which was not actually published until long after his death, contains among its curious rhymed verses some that deal with his church's pacifist beliefs. The author contrasts the two kingdoms existing side-by-side on this earth: Christians must reject the worldly realm and serve as citizens of Christ's kingdom alone. "Moreover you have heard that Christ taught not to re-

---

[26] The beard, like plain dress, appears to have been adopted by Brethren only after their arrival in America. Although the beard became obligatory for a time among all the German peace sectaries, the moustache was proscribed because of its association with soldiering. The ban was brought to America by Mennonites and Amish from Switzerland and southern Germany.

[27] Quoted in Bowman, *Brethren and War*, pp. 36, 37.

[28] Samuel Smith, *History of the Province of Pennsylvania*, pp. 180, 190.

sist evil, neither with weapon nor sword. Hence nobody ever heard that Christ waged worldly war with weapons of war." Spiritual combat was the only kind for which Christians were called.

> Wann Krieges Leut niemand thun G'walt,
> dann wird der Krieg aufhören bald;
> Sie sollen niemand unrecht thun,
> dass sie vom Kriege sollen ruhn.

In Old Testament times it was a sin not to destroy the enemy when the Lord so ordered.

> Nun aber soll Christi Gemein,
> von aussern Schwerdt ganz wehrlos seyn;
> Sie haben hier kein weltlich Recht,
> zu kriegen drum, ist viel zu schlecht.

The powers that be force men to slay their fellows in war. The Christian must refuse obedience.

> Kein Schwerdt soll man angreiffen nicht,
> und ob man schon werd mit Gericht,
> man muss Gott mehr gehorsam seyn,
> dann allen Menschen ins gemein.

> Wehrlosz, weltlosz und Sünden losz,
> im Hertzen klein und gar nicht gross,
> so will Gott haben ein Gemein,
> von Babels Fleck und Masern rein.[29]

[29] Michael Frantz, *Einfältige Lehr-Betrachtungen und Kurtz-gefasztes Glaubens-Bekantnisz*, pp. 20-25. Tr. in part in "Writings of Michael Frantz," *Schwarzenau*, II. no. 2 (Jan. 1941), 80, 81. The prose translation is mine:
> When men of war do violence to none,
> Then will war soon cease;
> You should not do wrong to anyone,
> So that you may rest from war./
> But now shalt Christ's community,
> Be quite defenseless against the outward sword;
> It has here no worldly right,
> To fight for such is much too wicked./
> One should not take up the sword,
> And, even if one has to face trial,
> One must be more obedient to God,
> Than to the rest of mankind together.
> Defenseless, free of the world and sinless,
> Of a humble heart and not at all puffed up,
> This is how God would have his community,
> Kept pure from Babel's stain and spots.

The guileless jingles of the country elder were, however, not the only written contribution to peace literature emanating from Brethren circles during the colonial period. On a far higher level and representing a much more sophisticated degree of culture was the work of the two Christopher Saurs, father and son, who had emigrated from Germany in 1724. The elder Saur (1693-1758) almost certainly never formally joined the Brethren, although as a radical Pietist he remained close to them in spirit. However, his son (1721-1784) was a full member of the church: "the most outstanding Brethren of colonial America" he has rightly been called.[30] Through their printing and publishing activities centered upon the Germantown press, which the father had set up in 1738, the two Saurs did indeed make a noteworthy contribution to German culture in Pennsylvania. Their German language newspapers and calendars, as well as the famous German Bible first issued in 1743, became the staple reading diet of the Pennsylvania "Dutch": not merely the sectarians but Lutherans, Calvinists, Catholics, and those belonging to no church. Politically, as we have seen, they were instrumental through their publications in rallying the German vote in support of Quaker policies, and thus they became one of the important factors in maintaining Quaker rule in the province long after Friends had ceased to form a majority of its inhabitants. Undoubtedly, the Saurs were swayed in this regard by their sympathy with the pacifist outlook of the Quakers and by their desire to prevent the rise to power of a party that would introduce war measures. They supported Quaker attempts at conciliating the Indians and stood for giving the latter a square deal. In their papers, pamphlets, and broadsides, they were able to play upon the antimilitarism of the nonpacifist German Pennsylvanians that they had brought with them from Europe, where war had often destroyed their homes and the lives of their kinfolk. Vote for the Quakers, the Saurs urged, and you will continue to enjoy peace in your new homeland. They emphasized that not only peace but prosperity and freedom from oppression, political as well as religious, had flowed from Quaker rule in the province under a distant, but benevolent English monarch.[31]

Right at the outset of his publishing career the elder Saur had made clear his opposition on religious grounds to all war.[32] The uncompromising character of his pacifism manifested itself again toward the

[30] Bowman, *Brethren and War*, p. 68.

[31] *Ibid.*, pp. 68, 69, 72, 74, 87-92. See also William Reed Steckel, "Pietist in Colonial Pennsylvania: Christopher Sauer, Printer 1738-1758," Ph.D. diss. Stanford U. (1949).

[32] Steckel, p. 153, quoting from *Der Hoch-Deutsch Pennsylvanische Geschicht-Schreiber*, 20 Aug. 1739.

end of the War of the Austrian Succession when, as we have seen, Franklin's Association attempted to put an end to the Quaker pacifist policy. The elder Saur had joined the Quaker John Smith in countering the antipacifist sermon of the Rev. Gilbert Tennent. In these same years, 1747 and 1748, Saur produced three short pamphlets in German which, although they were published anonymously by his press, were undoubtedly the fruits of his pen. In the first he lauded the humble, nonresistant disciples of Christ—*die Nachfolger Christi*— who had put aside carnal weapons in favor of the spiritual war, loving their enemies and crushing the lusts of the flesh from which all wars spring. He expressed his deep regret that some warmongers in the province were repaying the freedom of opportunity that Quaker government had given them by casting ridicule and hatred on its peaceable principles and by stirring up opposition to Quaker rule.[33] In the following year, 1748, Saur composed two further pamphlets both seeking to refute the arguments in favor of a policy of preparedness propounded in Franklin's *Plain Talk*, which had come out in a German translation. One was directed to German-speaking artisans; the author describes himself here as "ein Handwercksmann in Germanton." The other appears to have been aimed at the German farmers, since in this case the author is called "ein Teutsche Bauers-Mann in Pennsylvanien" ("a German farmer in Pennsylvania"). That Pennsylvania had prospered hitherto under the pious rule of William Penn and his successors, not least because of its freedom under their direction from the war spirit and the burden of military service, is the dominant theme of both pamphlets. A true follower of Christ, says the Germantown "craftsman," may not kill even "ein frantzoscher Morder" ("a French murderer") who is attacking him, since to do so is forbidden by Christ. "Wird er sich lieber lassen todten, wann er nicht entweichen kann, als dass er den Morder todten wolte." A Christian can only trust in God's protection.[34] Participation in war, therefore, is contrary to the gospel; Saur speaks of soldiers as military "slaves." And he appeals to the German countryfolk of the province:

O Pensylvanien! du hast einen gnadigen Gott, und auch einen leiblichen gutigen Konig [i.e., George II], welche beyde dir das Schwerdt zu ergreiffen, nicht gebiethen. Warum wilt du dich dann

[33] *Klare und gewisse Wahrheit* . . . (1747), pp. 4, 14.
[34] *Verschiedene Christliche Wahrheiten* . . . (1748), p. 26. The German passage cited runs in English as follows: "He should rather let himself be killed, if he cannot escape, than be willing to kill the murderer." (My translation.)

174

den Schwerd anvertrauen, und den Glauben (welcher all Dinge vermag) fahren lassen?[35]

Quaker government survived the crisis of 1747-1748, but it succumbed to the war party in 1756. The French and Indian War brought suffering to some of the Brethren as it did to all those, non-pacifists or nonresistants, who lived near the exposed frontiers of the province.[36] On the whole, however, the sect appears to have been comparatively undisturbed. Although unwilling to serve personally, the Brethren were prepared to meet the demands that the military might make from time to time on their property. For instance, the elder Saur in the columns of his *Pensylvanische Berichte* urged compliance with the requisition that took place in 1758 of wagons and horses from German farmsteads, and he "suggested the fairest means of apportioning the burden among the people."[37] This was not collaboration in the unchristian evil of war: Caesar must be aided in the things that pertained to him, and these included the protection of the state—provided, of course, that true Christians were not required to shed blood in its defense.

The Saurs in Germantown represented the very small cultured element in the early Brethren community in America. Another center of German language culture in colonial Pennsylvania was located at the Ephrata cloister, that rather eccentric offshoot of American Dunkerism. Its printing press, which was set up in 1745, was the equal of the Saurs's press in the quality of its products. The community's founder was Johann Conrad Beissel (1690-1768), an immigrant from Germany who had joined the Brethren in 1722 after his arrival in Pennsylvania two years earlier. Beissel, a self-educated man of humble peasant origin who was successively a baker and a weaver by trade, possessed outstanding gifts of leadership, which caused him not long after his conversion to be chosen as minister of the frontier congregation at Conestoga (Lancaster County); some have accused him of a lust for power. In Germany, like so many of the radical Pietists, he had come under the spell of the writings of the Silesian mystic, Jakob Boehme. His advocacy of celibacy, sabbatarianism, and community of goods brought a break with the Dunkers in 1728. In 1732 he and

---

[35] *Ein grundliches Zeugnusz* . . . (1748), pp. 6, 10, 11. "O Pennsylvania! Thou hast a merciful God as well as on earth a kind king, neither of whom commands thee to take up the sword. Why wilt thou, then, entrust thyself to the sword, and cast aside faith (which achieves all things)?" (My translation.)

[36] Bowman, *Brethren and War*, p. 74.

[37] Steckel, p. 210.

a few of his followers settled in the wilderness a few miles outside the town of Lancaster, where they were soon joined by other seekers after Christian perfection—Brethren, Mennonites, and others. Almost all the communitarians, who were organized by Beissel into two orders —the householders who were not expected to conform to the full rigors of the cloister rule and the celibate monks and nuns who formed a spiritual elite—were drawn from the German-speaking population. At its height the community numbered about 300 persons, of whom no more than 80 belonged to the strictly monastic order. Perhaps it was the spartan regimen more than the cloudy ideology of the community that proved the main obstacle to its expansion. At Beissel's death in 1768 the succession passed to a former Calvinist pastor, John Peter Miller (Müller; 1709-1796), a man of considerable learning but a poor leader. The cloister was already on the decline, and early in the nineteenth century the community way of life was abandoned altogether. All that remained was a dwindling sect, a few hundred of whom have survived until today under the denomination of Seventh Day German Baptists.

In their Confession of Faith the Seventh Day German Baptists have retained an article which forbids members "active participation by military service in the army or navy" as being "in violation of the sixth commandment and the teachings of Jesus Christ."[38] A prohibition of this kind was almost certainly a part of the discipline of the cloister from the beginning, since it was an article of faith for the Dunkers as well as for many other independent radical Pietists, from whose midst Beissel had originally come. We learn, for instance, that, when Conrad Weiser (1696-1760), who had joined the community in 1735 under the magnetic spell of Beissel's personality, was elected a local magistrate in 1741, his fellow communitarians advised him against accepting office since, in their view, such an act would be contrary to the community ethic. In this instance Beissel's attitude was rather ambivalent. In any event, Weiser, who probably never accepted the cloister's pacifism and nonconformity to the world, soon left Ephrata to start on a career that would bring him fame as the provincial government's adviser on Indian affairs.[39]

It is really not until the outbreak of the French and Indian War that we have clear documentary evidence on the cloister's attitude toward war. The community chronicle states for the year 1755: "At that time a good understanding existed between those at the head of government and the Solitary [as the monks were known], although the common

[38] Quoted in Walter C. Klein, *Johann Conrad Beissel*, p. 184.
[39] *Ibid.*, p. 88.

176

people were not well pleased with them, because they did not take up arms." "For many had bound themselves by oath not to march against the enemy until every non-combatant in the country had been massacred." Beissel, however, was prepared to pray "for the success of the king's arms"[40]—a point which perhaps explains why the authorities took a more lenient view of his sect's noncombatancy than its neighbors did.

The dynamic Beissel was already in his grave by the time the American Revolution broke out. His scholarly successor, John Peter Miller —or Brother Jabez as he was known to the fraternity—maintained the sect's previous pacifist stand. In a letter dated 10 October 1776 to James Read, a prominent South Carolina citizen, which was full of citations in Latin from classical writers and from the Vulgate, Miller expressed the point of view that war, whether defensive or offensive, is to be abhorred; it is better, he believed, to suffer at the hands of the enemy than to break Christ's injunctions. In his opinion, the province would have been much better off if it had continued the old Quaker policy of peace. A time of universal peace, as foretold in prophecy, was approaching. Nevertheless, he conceded that in the present age the magistracy was an unfortunate necessity for the ungodly. He went on: "I humbly conceive that the church should be under the sole government of the Holy Ghost, and therefore exempted from civil government: but I take here the word church in the strictest sense, having no possessions in this world"—a definition, of course, that would have placed outside the pale not merely Quaker pacifists but also his nonresistant neighbors of the Mennonite, Amish, and Dunker faiths. "I have hitherto been actuated by principles of love," he concludes, "and I hope not to deviate therefrom, let the consequence be what it will."[41]

Ephrata was not the only community of German solitaries in Pennsylvania during the first half of the eighteenth century. Less is known about the other communities, however—for instance, about the hermits of the Wissahickon River, just outside Germantown, who had gathered around the mystic Pietist, Johannes Kelpius, toward the end of the previous century. After their leader's death in 1708, their community, known as the "Woman in the Wilderness," which

---

[40] *Chronicon Ephratense*, pp. 235-37.

[41] "Letter of Peter Miller," *PMHB*, XXXVIII, no. 2 (1914), 227-31. Around this time Miller is reported to have told an inquirer interested in learning the principles of the community: "It is immoral to use violence at any time, but our duty to submit. We think going to law is not according to Christianity, and it is expressly forbidden" (Redmond Conygham, "An Account of the Settlement of the Dunkers at Ephrata," *Memoirs of the Historical Society of Pennsylvania*, II, pt. I, 139).

was composed entirely of male hermits, gradually disintegrated. In 1748, the year of his death, the last survivor of the group, the Swiss-born Conrad Matthai (1678-1748), was visited in his hermitage by the Quaker John Smith. When Matthai learned that Smith was the author of the reply to Tennent's pro-war sermon, the Quaker relates, "he expressed a great deal of gladness to see me, saying his mind has been often with me, and that he thanked God for giving me his grace in that service."[42] This response seems to indicate that Matthai at least, and probably others—if not all the deceased hermits of his community—shared the nonresistant views of their fellow German-Swiss immigrants of the Mennonite and Brethren churches.

The third nonresistant group to come to America in the first half of the eighteenth century was drawn from the Schwenkfelders of Lower Silesia. They were adherents of the teachings of the Silesian nobleman, Caspar Schwenckfeld (1489-1561), who had represented a spiritualistic trend in the radical Reformation. Severe persecution resulting from their refusal to attend Catholic worship had by the end of the seventeenth century reduced their numbers to less than a thousand. Although their founder was a nobleman and the movement at the beginning had enlisted the support of some gentry and prominent burghers, the group was confined by this time to peasants and artisans. Attempts in the early 1720's at forcible conversion to Catholicism and threats to remove the children from their parents and bring them up as Catholics had led in 1726 to the flight of some five hundred into Saxony, where they found refuge on the estate of Count Zinzendorf, founder of the Moravian church. A few hundred remained behind to face continued suppression, until Frederick the Great's annexation of the area to Prussia in 1740 brought them freedom of worship. "The last Schwenkfelder in Silesia died in 1826."[43] Relations between those who had migrated to Saxony and their benefactor Zinzendorf were not too harmonious, and, in addition, the imperial authorities were putting pressure on Saxony to extradite their former subjects. In the early and mid-1730's, therefore, with the assistance of Dutch and German Mennonites, just over two hundred of these Schwenkfelders decided on emigration to tolerant Pennsylvania; the main party arrived in Philadelphia in 1734 and settled in southeastern Pennsylvania. The church always remained small and today numbers about 2,500 members.

[42] *Hannah Logan's Courtship*, pp. 225, 226. For Matthai, see Julius Friedrich Sachse, *The German Pietists of Provincial Pennsylvania, 1674-1708*, pp. 388-401. At this date Matthai was in close touch with both the Moravians and the Ephrata cloister.

[43] Selina G. Schultz, "The Schwenkfelders of Pennsylvania," *Pennsylvania History*, XXIV, no. 4 (Oct. 1957), 302.

Schwenckfeld, although in sympathy with the Anabaptists and against the use of force in matters of religion, does not seem to have shared their pacifist and antistate views. "They teach," he wrote of them, "that a Christian may not be a civil ruler or official. But a Christian may be an official and an official can be a Christian."[44] At first, his followers included councillors and other city officials, who continued to hold office after their conversion. However, it is clear that the adoption of nonresistance as their official position, though not necessarily one that was obligatory on all members, had already occurred before their departure for the New World. The Quaker historian, Samuel Smith, writing only a few decades after the Schwenkfelders' arrival in Pennsylvania, states that prior to departure, in addition to religious persecution, they "were in fear concerning the military exercise."[45] And Zinzendorf, when in 1733 the abortive project of a Schwenkfelder emigration to Georgia was being mooted, took steps to see that *inter alia* a guarantee of exemption from military service would be given them by the trustees of the newly founded colony in exchange for the payment, in case of necessity, of "a double war tax."[46] It is possible that what had begun as a fear of involvement in the world and its evils rather than as an absolute objection to taking part in war or the state —a fear which would be understandable in a small religious group undergoing severe persecution at the hands of civil and church authorities alike—gradually consolidated into a prohibition based on nonresistance as a principle of conduct. That all the Schwenkfelder immigrants were not pacifists will be clear from what is written below. On the other hand, that by the middle of the eighteenth century nonresistance and nonparticipation in the state were accepted as incumbent on the church as a whole, if not on every individual member, is also certain. Quaker and Mennonite influence on the Schwenkfelders just prior to, and immediately after, emigration likewise cannot be excluded as a factor in strengthening, if not in originating, the group's antiwar stand.

Smith quotes from a Schwenkfelder confession of faith which declared "that the bearing and use of arms does not appertain to the new covenant and the kingdom of Christ." The wars of Old Testament times they interpreted figuratively as "spiritual wars and victories over the enemies of the Lord's people in the new covenant." They supported magistracy as an ordinance of God, although they held that Christ's disciples should refrain from holding office. Obedi-

[44] Schultz, *Caspar Schwenckfeld von Ossig*, pp. 199, 201, 202.
[45] Smith, *History of the Province of Pennsylvania*, p. 175.
[46] Adelaide L. Fries, *The Moravians in Georgia*, p. 33.

ence was incumbent on them except in matters "against God and his commandments," "which we also do hold of the use of arms, and desire to be understood after the same manner." They were forbidden, also, to swear oaths.[47]

The outbreak of violent frontier skirmishing in 1754 brought the problem of war home to the little Schwenkfelder community. Since most of them lived at some distance from the frontier, they were not so much exposed to direct Indian attack as many of the other German peace sectaries were. Nevertheless, they were, it would seem, under some pressure from the community to take part in local defense measures. A chronicle of the times written by the Schwenkfelder leader, the Rev. Christopher Schultz (1718-1789), which has been preserved in manuscript, records for the year 1755: "Die unsern haben alle Beschwerungen und Unkosten in den Townships willig tragen helfen was auf einen Jeden kommen ist, doch haben sich persönlicher Hand-Anlegung gegen die Feinde enthalten." If called upon to serve personally, they would be ready to hire a substitute in their place.[48] They also saw nothing inconsistent with their peace testimony in volunteering wagons and teams of horses for use by the army. A more humanitarian form of service was the relief in the form of food and clothing sent at the request of their fellow sectaries, the Moravians of Bethlehem, to help their refugees from Indian raids. Representatives of the Schwenkfelders collaborated with Quakers and Mennonites in the Friendly Association (discussed earlier), which strove to restore amicable relations again with the Indians, and the Schwenkfelder

[47] Smith, *History*, pp. 176, 177. It is possible that the Schwenkfelder confession from which Smith quotes is the one drawn up for presentation to the Quakers in 1751. It is referred to in an entry in the MS by Christopher Schultz, "Historische Anmerkungen was sich von Anno 1750 anfolgentlich bis 1775, mit den Schwenkfeldern merkliches vorlauffen," pp. 3, 4: "Im 1751 jahr ist auf Erfordern oder Begehren, an die Quäkker eine kurtze Bekäntnisz ausgefertiget worden, über 3 Puncte. I. Die Ursache unserer hiherkunfft in disz Land. II. Was wir vom Waffentragen oder Fechten und III. vom Eidschwören halten. Welches Ihnen in Englischer Sprache zugestellet, und freundlich angenohmen worden." This passage is printed in *Skizzen aus dem Lecha-Thale*, p. 46. In English it runs as follows: "In the year 1751, as required or wished, a short confession in three parts has been prepared for the Quakers. I. The grounds of our coming over into this land. II. What we hold concerning the bearing of arms or fighting and III. concerning the swearing of oaths. This was presented to them in the English tongue and in friendly fashion." (My translation.)

[48] "Historische Anmerkungen," p. 8 (reprinted in *Skizzen*, p. 47). The German passage cited runs in English as follows: "Our people willingly helped to carry all burdens and expenses in the townships that are laid on any individuals; however, they have abstained personally from violence against the enemy." (My translation.)

church contributed money to further the work of the Association. Schultz wrote of these efforts:

The Quakers as well as we and others who have scruples of conscience against taking up arms against an enemy were accused of not being willing to bear their due share of the common burdens. They took pity on the miserable condition of the inhabitants along the frontier and felt that the Indian war arose on account of the unjust treatment of the Indians and was carried on under unholy purposes to the serious detriment of the province. With these things in mind they formed a union among themselves and invited others to join them with the purpose of doing what was possible to restore peace with the Indians and to preserve the same in the future, knowing that such effort and object could only be accomplished by heavy labors and expense.[49]

Strangely enough, neither the Rev. Christopher Schultz nor his cousin David Shultze (1717-1797), a surveyor by profession, both of whom took a prominent part in the Friendly Association, were personally upholders of their church's pacifism, although they seem to have supported it when acting officially on the church's behalf. "As early as 1754 David Shultze . . . was active in organizing the home defences of the Perkiomen Valley."[50] His private view of the conscientious objector was not very sympathetic, as is disclosed in the following remarks written in his rather curious English: "As concerning the militia act," he says, "we don't see if much effectual will be done with, by reason of the continual disputes between those that are for and those that are or pretend to be principled against bearing arms, since the latter are not obliged thereby, to do at least something to the satisfaction of the former on that head." Despite his work in the Friendly Association, for him the Indians were "those beast-like creatures."[51] His cousin and several other Schwenkfelders had been among the German Pennsylvanians signing a declaration of November 1754 in favor of war measures. In March 1756 we again find the Rev. Christopher Schultz taking a similar stand: then, as the danger of Indian raids was approaching Schwenkfelder settlements, he urged the forma-

[49] Howard W. Kriebel, *The Schwenkfelders in Pennsylvania*, pp. 141, 146. The citation is based on "Historische Anmerkungen," pp. 9, 10. (*Skizzen*, p. 47). See also Glenn Weaver, *The Schwenkfelders during the French and Indian Wars*, pp. 10-16.

[50] Weaver, *The Schwenkfelders*, p. 10. See also *The Journals and Papers of David Shultze*, I, 157, 163-67, 169, 187, 190, 191.

[51] *David Shultze*, I, 165, 166.

tion of an Independent Company to act as a home guard in the area, and, after it was set up, he helped to equip it. However, such a belligerent stand on the part of one of the sect's leading ministers met with strong opposition from most of the Schwenkfelders, who continued to regard direct participation in war as a contravention of their religious principles.[52]

The development of the nonresistant views and practice of the German peace sects during the colonial period is not well documented. One reason for this exiguity of material is the almost complete absence of records, official or unofficial, in the case of all the groups concerned—a gap that lasts right down to the second half of the nineteenth century. A second reason is that, in fact, there is little to document, for in Quaker Pennsylvania—at least so long as the Society of Friends controlled the provincial legislature—these groups were unencumbered by demands for military service of any kind. Almost entirely a rural people, most of whom lacked a formal education, they had little inclination to put their pacifism down on paper. They had the Bible, and usually enough letters to read it. This seemed to them sufficient instruction for all who aimed to walk humbly in the footsteps of the nonresistant Savior.

[52] *Ibid.*, I, 169-73; Weaver, *The Schwenkfelders*, pp. 12-14.

Chapter 5

Quakers and the American Revolution

I

For all but one of the English-speaking provinces of the North American mainland the Revolutionary War brought the transition from colonial status to independence. This change was at first opposed officially by the Society of Friends and by a considerable proportion of those who remained members. Their opposition was based upon two grounds. First, and most fundamental, was Friends' rejection of the method of war and their personal objection to taking part in it, which prevented them from giving support to a cause that was being pressed by resort to arms. All those who remained in the Society, after it had been purged of members who did not share its peace testimony, assented to this point of discipline, including a minority in the Society who sympathized with the aims and final goal of the Continental cause. In the second place, alongside and reinforcing the Christian pacifism that Quakers had upheld since their crystallization as a denomination in the mid-seventeenth century, there now entered into their thinking and practice a political element (that was, however, still religiously inspired). Loyalty to the powers that be, a peaceable demeanor toward the rightful ruler of the land, had become as much part of the makeup of eighteenth-century Quakerism as it was of the churches which derived from the labors of the sixteenth-century Dutchman, Menno Simons. This, it was believed, was the pure doctrine inculcated by the teachings of the gospels and in the writings of Paul the apostle. In addition, as a factor buttressing sentiments of loyalty there arose a consciousness among many Friends of the manifold advantages to the Society on both sides of the Atlantic that had flowed from the British Crown over the past century and more.

Thus it came about that, in—and even before—the armed struggle that ensued from 1775 on, a church that was religiously pacifist took up a position that, politically, swung from attempted neutrality to a stance that at times was so close to loyalism that it was understandably mistaken for such by the great majority of the Quakers' fellow citizens. Among the immediate causes that led many Friends throughout the continent to mingle their pacifism with hostility, veiled or open, to the new governments that were ultimately set up in the former colonies by those who espoused, first, military resistance to the demands of the mother country within the framework of the imperial connection and, then, not many months after the first clashes at Lexington and Concord, a complete separation from the British monarchy, was the great prestige wielded in the whole American Quaker Society by Philadelphia Yearly Meeting. At the outbreak of the Revolutionary War this meeting, in fact, included over half the total number of Friends on the American continent. The various yearly meetings were autonomous bodies, but Friends everywhere, from Maine to Georgia, looked to the deliberations and decisions of the Quaker city for a lead in the policies they should adopt themselves.

During the decade before 1775, when the seeds of the Revolution were slowly ripening, the outlook of prominent Philadelphia Friends, of those circles of wealthy Quaker merchants who often gave the tone to the pronouncements of their yearly meeting (despite occasional rumblings of opposition from country Quakers, who by no means saw eye to eye on all subjects with their city brethren), veered from a restrained opposition to the stringent policy against the American colonies that the Grenville ministry had initiated at the end of the Seven Years War to an increasing distaste for the American movement of opposition that the home government's measures aroused. In 1765 a number of leading Quaker merchants in Philadelphia had, indeed, supported opposition to the hated Stamp Act, while attempting to dampen the violent emotions that were already beginning to come to the surface among irate colonials. Prominent Quaker merchants, like Israel and James Pemberton, Henry and James Drinker, John Reynell, Thomas Wharton, Thomas Clifford, and some fifty more participated in the ensuing economic boycott of British goods by using American manufactures whenever possible and by signing the Philadelphia nonimportation resolutions of that year.[1] The objectionable Townshend Acts of 1767, which marked a further step in Britain's attempt to raise taxes in the colonies for revenue purposes while not allowing the Americans to participate in framing legislation, likewise aroused opposition among Philadelphia Quakers. But, as the colonial movement gradually veered from a constitutional opposition that relied mainly on peaceful means to action that contained implications of violence, many Friends, like some other future "Tories" who had previously been sympathetic to the movement, began to draw back. And opinion among influential circles in Philadelphia Yearly Meeting became increasingly

[1] Among these Quaker "nonimporters" were nine who were in the party of allegedly pro-British Quakers deported to Virginia in 1777 (see below).

184

suspicious of the rightness of Friends' participation in the movement.

As early as 1765, at the time of the Stamp Act crisis, the meeting's epistle to New England Yearly Meeting contained the significant warning: "May we be watchful to keep out of those things."[2] This feeling grew stronger at the beginning of the seventies when the smuggling of tea, the chief item still taxed after the repeal of the Townshend duties in 1770 which formed the background of the famous Boston Tea Party of December 1773, constituted a leading weapon in the armory of colonial resistance. Although it might be pleaded that such activities were nonviolent for the most part, still they were clearly un-Quakerly, for they amounted, in effect, to defrauding the king of his lawful revenue and were therefore contrary to the Quaker testimony of honest dealings in all business matters. Members of the Society who partook in such activities—and they were fairly numerous, it would seem, from the evidence of local meeting records—were called to account. As agitation in the country grew, feeling within the Society began to harden. Typical of this trend was the state of mind revealed at a general meeting of Philadelphia Friends called in mid-October 1773 to discuss the current situation. According to the report sent to English Friends by one of the leading participants, James Pemberton, who was later to play a vital role in Philadelphia Yearly Meeting during the Revolution:

Altho' we are not insensible of the incroachments of powers and of the value of civil rights, yet in matters contestable we can neither join with nor approve the measures which have been too often proposed by particular persons and adopted by others for asserting and defending them, and such is the agitation of those who are foremost in these matters it appears in vain to interfere.[3]

Noninterference in political affairs and official disapproval of those of its members who continued active in the movement of colonial opposition thenceforward marked the policy of the Society of Friends both in Pennsylvania and in the other five yearly meetings on the continent. Throughout the over eighty monthly meetings into which the Society was grouped, a uniformity of conduct was enforced by dis-

[2] Quoted in Arthur J. Mekeel, "The Quakers in the American Revolution," Ph.D. diss., Harvard U. (1939), p. 18. This monograph, unfortunately not published, gives a comprehensive account of the Society of Friends during the war years, based on a wide variety of sources: manuscript Quaker meeting records and the unpublished papers of prominent individual Friends, contemporary newspapers, and official government documents. Mekeel's work has proved most useful in the preparation of this chapter.

[3] Letter dated 30 Oct. 1773, quoted by Mekeel.

ciplinary measures against those who deviated, in intent as well as in deed, from the peaceable standard set up.

The First Continental Congress, which met in Philadelphia in early September 1774, was dominated by the patriots, and the Continental "Association" which it adopted on 20 October for the purpose of enforcing more effectively the boycott of British goods amounted to a declaration of economic war against the home government, although few among the Congress's members were yet in favor of a complete break with Britain. There were Friends, and some near Friends, among the members of the Congress; however, those who continued on the path which the patriots had begun to tread soon either found themselves disowned or of their own accord ceased their connection with the Society of Friends. For the Society thenceforward set its face firmly against colonial resistance, feeling that the steps already taken constituted an illegal opposition against the sovereign power and would, if pursued further, result in armed rebellion and a state of war—suspicions that were confirmed by the development of events in Massachusetts during the winter months.

In January 1775, therefore, Philadelphia Yearly Meeting issued two declarations summing up its position in view of the impending conflict. The first was drawn up on 5 January by the Meeting for Sufferings and was designed primarily for use within the Society, for it was addressed (as the style was in such cases) "to our friends and brethren in these and the adjacent provinces." The epistle opened with a phrase describing the Anglo-American conflict that was repeatedly to crop up even after open war had broken out: it spoke of "the troubles and commotions which have prevailed" (a state of confusion "in this once peaceful land" that in the ensuing years would never be dignified with the name of war in the eyes of the more loyalistically inclined Friends, for wars took place only between legally constituted governments). The main tenor of the document was to warn all those members who had become entangled in the politics of resistance to withdraw, recollecting in time "that to fear God, honour the king, and do good to all men, is our indispensable duty."[4] In fact, it called on Friends to

---

[4] Thomas Gilpin (ed.), *Exiles in Virginia*, pp. 284-87. A preliminary warning directed against Friends who had publicly supported the resolves of the Continental Congress was issued by Meeting for Sufferings on 15 Dec. 1774 (printed in Isaac Sharpless, *A Quaker Experiment in Government*, II: *The Quakers in the Revolution*, 107). Cf. John A. Woods (ed.), "The Correspondence of Benjamin Rush and Granville Sharp 1773-1809," *Journal of American Studies*, I, no. 1 (April 1967), 14 (Rush to Sharp, 1 Nov. 1774): "The colonies are determined to carry all the resolutions of our Congress into execution. We shall wait with impatience to hear of the proceedings of the Parliament. But we are preparing for the worst. A military spirit is kindled among us. We talk with less horror than formerly of a

take a further step on the path toward complete disengagement from public life that had commenced in 1756.

The second document issued officially by Friends during this month, and likewise signed by James Pemberton in his capacity as clerk, was entitled "The Testimony of the People called Quakers" and was in the nature of a public declaration of their position. It was given wide publicity both within and outside the Society, and it was even translated into German for distribution chiefly among the Mennonites, who had sent delegates to Philadelphia to confer with the Quakers on the crisis.[5] The "Testimony" was short but left little doubt about where Friends—at least those who wielded most weight in the affairs of Philadelphia Yearly Meeting—stood in the mounting dispute between Britain and her colonies. Quakers, its framers claimed, had a religious duty "to discountenance and avoid every measure tending to excite disaffection to the King, as supreme magistrate, or to the legal authority of his government." It declared its complete confidence, as a result of past goodwill shown by the monarchy, in peaceful and loyal remonstrances as an effective method of righting any justifiable grievances that the colonies might entertain in respect to the home government. "We deeply lament," the "Testimony" goes on, "that contrary modes of proceeding have been pursued, which have involved the colonies in confusion, appear likely to produce violence and bloodshed, and threaten the subversion of . . . constitutional government, and of . . . liberty of conscience." It ended by an unequivocal declaration of opposition to the exercise of authority that was already being practised in some areas by colonial patriots; this it branded as a "usurpation of power," and it went on to condemn "all combinations, insurrections, conspiracies, and illegal assemblies."[6] The lines were fairly drawn: the other yearly meetings followed the lead given by Philadelphia, and henceforth there could be little doubt where official Quakerism stood in relation to the takeover of power that would be effected by the colonial forces during the ensuing months.

True, many among even the conservative Friends of Philadelphia, New York, and New England still retained inner reservations concerning the policies pursued by the English government. Even as loyal a British American as James Pemberton could write as late as May 1775

---

civil war. In two or three months there will be forty thousand men completely armed and disciplined in the Prov[ince of] Pennsylvania—many of whom [will be] Quakers. Thus you see a lively sense [of] public injuries has destroyed the strongest prejudices of education and religion."

[5] Mekeel, "The Quakers," pp. 76, 77.

[6] *Exiles in Virginia*, pp. 282-84.

of the "mistaken policy" of Britain "in the management of this unhappy contest."[7] Moreover, his correspondent in this instance, the wise and energetic English Quaker, Dr. John Fothergill, along with other British Friends, like David Barclay, who were in close touch with events across the Atlantic, considered that their American brethren had gone too far in opposition to the colonial cause which, in their view, had so much of right on its side. Commenting on the January "Testimony" of Philadelphia Friends, Barclay gently chided them for not having confined themselves to restating Friends' opposition to all warlike actions ("there on that ground your best friends wish you to remain," he wrote) and for having launched, instead, into a semi-political declaration. And Fothergill—"more American than the conservative American Friends themselves," as Sharpless has described him—was upset to think that a document such as the "Testimony" might only serve to strengthen the resolution of the court to continue a policy of strength in regard to the colonies, a policy that English Friends were doing their best to counter in favor of conciliation.[8] So we find the doctor telling James Pemberton in March 1775: "Submission to the prevailing power must be your duty. The prevailing power is the general voice of America."[9]

For men like Pemberton, however, and for the many Friends in town and country meetings up and down the continent who seemingly followed their lead, the general voice of America stood opposed to the still voice of Quaker conscience, which commanded loyalty to the established power and an exacting neutrality in the turmoil of war that was coming to their country. The overturning of kings and governments was God's business and not that of a people apart, as Friends were. As an epistle of North Carolina declared in the following October, they must not meddle in such affairs, "nor . . . be busybodies in matters above our station."[10] Already, before hostilities had formally broken out, Friends were gaining unpopularity for their refusal to sign the "Association," the declaration to abide by the nonintercourse agreements that, in effect, signified allegiance to the new authority represented by the Continental Congress and the local revolutionary committees. Already they were being branded as "Tories" in the eyes of neighbors who could not—or did not want to—distinguish between passive neutrality and active aid to the British interest, when in fact, as Tolles remarks with particular reference to the Quaker merchants of

[7] Sharpless, A Quaker Experiment, II, 121.
[8] Ibid., pp. 114, 118.
[9] Mekeel, "The Quakers," p. 81.
[10] Dorothy Gilbert Thorne, "North Carolina Friends and the Revolution," North Carolina Historical Review, XXXVIII, no. 3 (July 1961), 323.

Philadelphia who gave tone in many respects to the whole Society, "far from being Tories in the usual sense, [they] had stood for years as outspoken exponents of the Whig ideals of liberty and property."[11] In Virginia we find one quarterly meeting (Henrico) endeavoring to remove the stigma of disloyalty that was already being fixed on them by advising members to link their refusal to "associate" with the peace testimony: they were to explain to the new authorities that their religious principles prevented them from acting "in any matter which [might] have a tendency to the shedding of blood."[12]

In 1776, in two further statements of policy, Philadelphia Yearly Meeting, heedless of the sound advice given by Dr. Fothergill and his English associates, confirmed in even more categorical terms its previous negative attitude toward the new regime in the province. "The Ancient Testimony and Principles of the People called Quakers, renewed, with respect to the King and Government," which a representative meeting of Friends published on 20 January, was filled with nostalgia for the good old days under kingly rule and with lamentation at the unhappy changes in government which were taking place in the province and which the framers of the "Ancient Testimony" clearly hoped might be stemmed by a public protest of this kind on the part of such a highly influential group as Friends still were in Penn's commonwealth. "The inhabitants of these provinces [i.e., Pennsylvania and New Jersey] were long signally favoured with peace and plenty." In conclusion, Friends deplored—not unreasonably, it must be said—the impending break with Great Britain.

At the end of the year, after the Declaration of Independence had consummated the severing of ties between the colonies and mother country that Friends had so much feared and after Penn's constitution of 1701 had been swept away, Friends again appeared with an epistle, dated 20 December and directed this time "to our friends and brethren in religous profession, in these and the adjacent provinces." The letter was intended to strengthen the resolution of members in face of the rising hostility shown them—and all others who were suspected of friendly feelings toward the British cause—by the new authorities and the patriotic section of the community. It was also aimed at hardening their resistance to the various demands—for military service, special taxes, test oaths, etc.—that were being made on them. Its purpose, it said, was "to strengthen the weak, confirm the wavering, and warn and caution the unwary against being beguiled by the snares of the adversaries of truth and righteousness," lest "the fear of suffer-

[11] Frederick B. Tolles, *Meeting House and Counting House*, p. 28.
[12] Mekeel, "The Quakers," pp. 82, 83.

ing, either in person or in property, prevail on any to join with or promote any work or preparation for war." Friends were called upon to refuse obedience to these "arbitrary injunctions and ordinances of men, who assume to themselves the power of compelling others, either in person or by other assistance, to join in carrying on war," and to suffer the consequences of their disobedience to unlawful authority meekly.[13]

To the new regime, statements of this kind appeared as a challenge. Tom Paine (1737-1809), the Quaker-born rationalist, fulminated against what he called the "factional and fractional part" of Philadelphia Quakerdom responsible for its public utterances, accusing these persons of partiality to the British enemy and crypto-Toryism. Their pacifism, he contended, if it were genuine, should be able to distinguish between a commendable goal, independence, and the forcible means by which it was being achieved that would naturally incur their disapproval. "O! ye fallen, cringing, priest-and-Pemberton-ridden people!" he cried. "What more can we say of ye than that a religious Quaker is a valuable character, and a political Quaker a real Jesuit."[14]

The "Ancient Testimony" at the beginning of the year and Philadelphia Friends' epistle in December, combined with the momentous resolutions of their yearly meeting in September discussed below, were taken by the Second Continental Congress and by the radicals who were now in control of the provincial administration as a declaration of disloyalty to the new regime. In this belief they were, in fact, mistaken, for the statements expressed rather a traditional loyalty to the old order and passive, if unenthusiastic, obedience to the new. They did not represent a departure from the Quaker peace testimony but rather an extremely conservative interpretation of its implications. At its September sessions Yearly Meeting had enjoined Friends, among other things, to withdraw from all participation in the country's new political life and to refrain from paying fines or commutation in lieu of active service or from partaking in business activities connected with the war. These testimonies and resolutions, which were echoed in declarations of the other yearly meetings on the continent, formed the background both for the development of the Society during the remaining years of war and for the course of action pursued in regard to it by the various American authorities.

The discipline of the Society, which was exercised as vigilantly in wartime as in the previous years of peace, ensured "a fairly consistent

---

[13] *Exiles in Virginia*, pp. 287-93. See also p. 248.
[14] *The Writings of Thomas Paine*, I, 1894 edn., 126, 208. See also Robert P. Falk, "Thomas Paine and the Attitude of the Quakers to the American Revolution," *PMHB*, LXIII, no. 3 (July 1939), 306, 307.

and uniform conduct on the part of the Quakers throughout the continent."[15] Their peace witness during the Revolutionary War was collective and traditional; in some ways it lacked the stamp of individuality. There was little attempt on the part of private Friends to expound Quaker pacifism either by the published or the spoken word. In part this silence may be attributed to the difficulties always inherent in peace propaganda in wartime, in part, also, to the predominantly rural composition of a large section of the membership (although the Society did contain a highly cultured urban minority). But the main cause lay in the increasingly withdrawn character of Quaker pacifism, the pacifism now of a people apart—a transformation that was overtaking a number of its other traditional testimonies, too. A yearly meeting, as the mouthpiece of the Society, might need to publish from time to time a defense of its views on war for presentation to the authorities or before the general public in order to clear up the misunderstandings that were rife with regard to their position; such a body might feel called upon to restate its grounds for renouncing war in order to exhort its members to continued steadfastness in witnessing to this aspect of its faith or to bring support and comfort to Friends in other areas. But, unless we include a number of essays (most in manuscript form) devoted to the question of paying taxes in wartime and intended mainly for internal circulation among members of the Society, very few individual Friends felt called upon at this time, when one might have expected a crop of publications on the subject, to do battle in print for their peaceable principles.

Among the few, however, was Anthony Benezet (1713-1784), crusader against war, slavery, and spirituous liquors and a prolific pamphleteer on behalf of all these causes. Benjamin Rush describes in one of his essays an encounter he had with Benezet on a Philadelphia street corner. "In one hand," writes Rush, "he carried a subscription paper and a petition; in the other he carried a small pamphlet on the unlawfulness of the African slave-trade, and a letter directed to the King of Prussia upon the unlawfulness of war."[16] War and slavery, Benezet never ceased to insist, emanated from the same source: lust for wealth and for power over men, which constituted a direct contradiction of the Christian message. The fulfillment of the Christian message of peace was incumbent on nations as well as on individuals, "for a christian nation differs no otherwise from a christian person, than as the whole differs from one of the parts of which it essentially consists"—so he was telling his fellow Americans

[15] Mekeel, "The Quakers," p. 118.
[16] Quoted in George S. Brookes, *Friend Anthony Benezet*, p. 75.

in 1778.[17] And in the same year he published his "Serious Reflections affectionately recommended to the well-disposed of every religious denomination,"[18] in which in true Quaker fashion he advised his countrymen to look within themselves for the causes of the war rather than to seek them in the supposed faults of the enemy. "We fight against those we esteem our foes," he wrote, "and instead of labouring to overcome our sins, we basely yield to their temptations." Let us remember what Christianity means and pray for reconciliation with our enemies, he told both the contending sides.

Probably more effective in the long run than the kind of small-circulation pamphlet produced by the saintly, highly respected, but perhaps little heeded Benezet—and probably more telling, too, than the often platitudinous and uninspiring pronouncements of official Quakerism—were the efforts of simple men and women in the Society to argue with, and convince, neighbors and strangers concerning the validity of their views on war, which were so much out of line with those of the rest of the community, whether procolonial militants, dissident Tories, or even indifferent middle-of-the-roaders. Unfortunately, this kind of quiet propaganda for Quaker pacifism finds little reflection in surviving documents of the period: encounters of this sort passed for the most part unrecorded. Occasional insights do exist, however, in the Quaker journals. One of these is provided by the boyhood recollections of Henry Hull (1765-1834), who was then living in an isolated frontier area of upstate New York. A few Friends were settled there, and they had built themselves a small primitive log meetinghouse. In the absence of other places of religious worship in the neighborhood, services attracted non-Quakers, to whom many of the articles of Quaker belief—and especially, we might imagine, the Society's peace testimony—were new and sometimes strange at first. "The meeting was often attended," says Hull, "by a number of raw, rustic-looking people, most of whom were not Friends; and they would gather together near the house, before the meeting time, and engage in disputes about the war, sometimes with high words and angry looks." When time to go into meeting arrived, however, they quieted down. "There is good reason to believe," Hull goes on, "that

---

[17] Anthony Benezet, *Serious Considerations on Several Important Subjects*, pp. 2-12, 27. The section in the pamphlet devoted to war is, however, largely made up of extracts from *Address to the Clergy*, written by the early eighteenth-century Anglican clergyman William Law in 1760-1761, sections of which are directed against war and militarism.

[18] Reprinted in Brookes, *Benezet*, pp. 495-97. Benezet was also active in lobbying successive presidents of the Continental Congress, as well as other prominent personalities on both sides, on behalf of the Quaker peace testimony. See, e.g., Brookes, pp. 324, 325, 330, 331.

many of these persons were sincere-hearted, for some who were not then members of our Society, afterward joined in religious fellowship, and became united in bearing a Christian testimony against war, by patiently suffering the spoiling of their goods."[19] Thus, for all the occasional heated tempers and angry argument, and even in time of war when passions were aroused against talk of peace, we find these rough upcountry farmers, frontiersmen dwelling in the deep wilderness of the north, responding to the Quaker message of conciliation and love to all men.

A further instance of quiet and effective propaganda for peace occurs in the journal of another New York-born country Friend, Joseph Hoag (1762-1846). Around the year 1780 when still in his teens, Hoag while on a journey fell into conversation with a man who soon launched into a violent attack on Quakers because of their refusal to fight for the American cause. Embarrassed and tongue-tied at first and conscious of his shortcomings as a champion of his people, the boy finally plucked up courage. As he wrote later:

As I commenced all fear departed, words flowed rapidly, and I was enabled to . . . open to him our principles, give him our reasons for them, and to prove them by many Scripture passages; and finally, to show him it was impossible for a true Quaker, to be either whig or tory, for they implied opposite parties, and both believed in war, but Friends did not.

The man, visibly moved by the boy's eloquence and obvious sincerity, told him after he had concluded: "There must be great wisdom amongst the Quakers, for so young a man to know so much."[20]

A second positive expression of the Quaker witness for peace in wartime that can be put alongside the quiet working for peace of countless men like Benezet or Hoag whose names have not been recorded, and one that has become typical of the Society in this twentieth-century age of violence, is its relief work for the sufferers of war. One of the earliest examples of this Quaker humanitarianism was shown in the first years of the American Revolution. The work arose out of the British blockade of Boston in the second half of 1774 and the subsequent siege of the town by the American army after the outbreak of

---

[19] *Memoir of the Life and Religious Labours of Henry Hull*, pp. 25, 26.

[20] *A Journal of Joseph Hoag*, pp. 12, 13. (For the story of how, in 1777, Joseph's Quaker father, Elijah Hoag, found himself in the local jail because of his resistance to military orders, see pp. 17-21.) See also *Friends' Miscellany*, IX, no. 6 (Jan. 1837), 286, for the story of an encounter in Charleston in 1778 between the Lancaster Co. (Pa.) Quaker minister, Joshua Brown, and an Old Testament-minded South Carolina judge.

open hostilities in the following year. The organization of relief for those who were suffering as a result of warlike action was undertaken by the Meeting for Sufferings of Philadelphia Yearly Meeting, which grouped within its ranks a number of the most wealthy Quakers and which at that date had not yet come to feel the direct impact of the fighting. At first, assistance was limited to the small Quaker community in Boston, but the objective soon broadened to include—within the limits of Friends' resources—all who needed help, a pattern which was to become typical of later Quaker relief. When Washington, as commander of the army besieging the British in Boston, permitted only funds, and not Quaker personnel from outside the area, to pass through the lines, distribution became the responsibility of a group of New England Quakers, among the most active of whom was the famous Providence merchant, Moses Brown (1738-1836), a recent convert to Quakerism.[21] The British evacuated Boston in March 1776, and Quaker effort then turned to concentrate on the hapless refugees from the city and neighborhood scattered about the adjoining townships. Altogether over 3,000 families were aided, almost all of them non-Quakers, and over £4,000 was expended on relief, most of this money having been raised among members of Philadelphia Yearly Meeting. In its "Advices" issued at this time, we find it exhorting members, "and particularly . . . those who have received the increase of earthly possessions," to contribute liberally to the relief of the distressed by curtailing, if necessary, their outlay on themselves.[22]

Philadelphia Meeting for Sufferings noted, when the relief work drew to a close in the summer of 1776, that it had made "a good impression on the minds of some who have been prejudiced against Friends." In negotiations with Generals Washington and Howe, Friends had made it clear, not only that their help would be given "without distinction of sects or parties," but that their motives derived from the same source as their objection to war, that their action, indeed, reflected the positive side of this testimony. Relief, they stated to the contending generals, must be so administered "that our religious testimony against wars and fightings may be preserved pure."[23]

Quakers thereafter continued to aid the civilian victims of war, though only sporadically on a much smaller scale and with their own people primarily in view; help was given, for instance, to the desti-

[21] For Brown's part in the relief work, see Mack Thompson, *Moses Brown*, pp. 116-30.
[22] Sharpless, *A Quaker Experiment*, II, 140. See also p. 123.
[23] H. J. Cadbury, *Quaker Relief during the Siege of Boston*, p. 13.

tute islanders of Nantucket and in Virginia and Pennsylvania when war hit these provinces.[24] But for the most part, as was scarcely unavoidable in the circumstances of war when the Quakers formed a small and unpopular minority standing out, along with several even smaller and more obscure religious groups, against the tide of opinion on either side, their witness expressed itself in seemingly negative attitudes, in their refusal to participate in certain activities demanded of them by the public authorities or expected of them by public opinion. We must now survey in turn the various points at which the Quaker conscience clashed with a nation in arms and the disabilities they suffered as a result of their unwillingness to compromise. But first we should take a closer look at the machinery by which Friends supplemented the still small voice within by a discipline which assured the convinced, encouraged the fainthearted and the hesitant, and combed out those who failed, either through laxness or more often because of a different interpretation of what was right, to abide by the rules of the Society.

The main lines of Quaker policy were laid down by the various yearly meetings, primarily Philadelphia as we have seen; the implementation of policy was the responsibility of the local meetings, quarterly and monthly. Although quarterly meetings did act in a supervisory capacity, it was the monthly meetings that exercised direct control over members, and we find that most of these meetings were extremely active during the war period both in exhorting members to loyalty to "our Christian peaceable testimony" and in dealing with those who contravened it in some way. Most monthly meetings set up special committees of tried and trusted Friends whose business it was to visit all members who had strayed and to endeavor to bring them to a sense of error, in fact—to use the words of one such committee—"to strengthen the weak and confirm the wavering in this time of probation."[25] Varying success attended these efforts. A not untypical entry, taken from a Pennsylvania rural meeting, runs as follows: "They have gone through with respect to visiting their members, to inspect into their faithfulness, and . . . they had reason to believe divers have not been so upright in maintaining our testimony against military requisitions as becometh followers of Christ. But a considerable number they apprehend have en-

[24] See Mekeel, "The Quakers," chap. XIV, and Sydney V. James, *A People among Peoples*, pp. 258-64, for Quaker relief efforts during the Revolution. The best account of the Boston operation is given in H. J. Cadbury's pamphlet cited in the previous footnote.

[25] Radnor Monthly Meeting Minutes of Sufferings 1776-1779 (MS in F.H.L.S.C.), p. 21.

195

deavoured to be faithful therein so far as appeared."[26] Expulsion from the Society followed inexorably if no change could eventually be effected in a person being "dealt with," as, indeed, had always been the practice of the Society. A special committee was usually appointed, also, to collect details of Friends' "sufferings" on account of their opposition to the war: at its annual assembly in September 1776, Philadelphia Yearly Meeting, for instance, had required its constituent meetings to send up such accounts periodically to Meeting for Sufferings. These records, many of which have survived from all areas where Quakers were settled, provide much insight into the state of the Society during the Revolutionary period.

II

The strict control exercised by a local meeting over the conduct of its members brought with it the possibility of abuse, the ability of the Quaker community to impose an overall conformity by threat of cutting off a recalcitrant member and thus denying him the support of his Society if he were called up for military service. The outside world had (not unnaturally in this era) a stereotyped view of the Quaker and would give short shrift to any who did not fit this picture. The Pennsylvania "Dutchman," Jacob Ritter (1757-1841), who served in the Revolutionary War but later became a Quaker, tells an amusing story of the experiences of a "gay" young Friend at the hands of the military after he had been inducted into the Continental army. When the young man had explained his refusal to serve on the grounds that he was a Quaker,

> The presiding officer [Ritter used to relate in his Pennsylvania Dutch dialect] replied, "But you are no Quaker for you have not the 'cooterments'" (accoutrements). The young man then produced some written credentials by which he proved his right of membership. The officer now called for a shears that he might trim him; and so he cut off his capes and his lappels, and *sich a hair tail he had behind* (a cue), and then said to him, "now you may go, now you look more like a Quaker."[27]

The "gay" Quaker got off lightly in this instance because he had clear proof of membership. If his meeting had already dealt with him for his failure to conform to the Quaker norm of dress (or for marrying out or for dancing or for a dozen or more deviations in behavior that

[26] New Garden Monthly Meeting Committee on Sufferings, Minutes 1780-1782 (MS in F.H.L.S.C.), p. 17.
[27] Joseph Foulke, *Memoirs of Jacob Ritter*, p. 48.

—at least theoretically—might not exclude a perfectly genuine objection to war), the army would certainly not have released him so easily. Of course, at that date Quaker pacifism was much more an integral and indissoluble part of the whole Quaker religious ethos than it is today when there are Quaker nonpacifists and non-Quaker and unaffiliated pacifists. In many instances, those who then broke with custom on one issue broke with it on a number of others, and the pressure of community thought forged a quite genuine belief among most Quakers that conformity in cut of dress or style of hair or manner of speech was essential to a truly conscientious objection to war. Yet, even so, it is hard to believe that there were not some nonconformists in regard to Quaker externals (many of which have since been altogether abandoned)—whether they merely nursed their dissent in private or manifested it openly, suffering the penalty of disownment for daring to do so—who at the same time held as a result of their upbringing among Friends a quite sincere objection to war. One may suppose, moreover, that, since some in that century who were disowned for support of warlike activities still continued to worship with Friends thereafter and to associate themselves with the other points of their discipline apart from the matter of war, there would also be those who assented in regard to the peace testimony while dissenting on some other item then regarded as binding on all members. The records have little to say on the subject. We do hear, however, of a North Carolina man, Joseph Newby, who had been a member of the Society until his disownment for marrying out, objecting at the end of 1778 to the draft, which was ordered in connection with the British offensive in South Carolina. He was joined by nine other Quaker conscientious objectors, who were, however, more fortunate in being able to produce proof of membership. But after some discussion Newby, too, was finally released along with the rest.[28]

Proof of membership, then, was an extremely important matter for

---

[28] Mekeel, "The Quakers," pp. 231, 232. Two related cases from the same yearly meeting are discussed in Thorne, "North Carolina Friends and the Revolution," p. 329. The first is taken from Pasquotank M. M. where in 1782 one William Price, a young man of military age, "joined himself in marriage with a woman not of our Society." "As he hath lately obtained a certificate from this meeting," the minute continues, "in order to clear him from military services, Friends think it necessary to order a paper of denial against him." The second case is that of Caleb Goodwin of Perquimans M. M., a former soldier who had been admitted as a member in 1780 when he was given "a few lines setting forth that he is in unity" by his meeting in order to shield him from being drafted again. Three years later, however, Goodwin was disowned for wearing a ring, among other offenses of like nature. The war had already ended; otherwise, Goodwin would most likely have found himself in the same kind of difficulties as Newby had been in.

the potential Quaker objector, even when a special document for this purpose was not required by law. Sometimes, as we have seen, the authorities would in fact demand from the conscientious objector a certificate of membership drawn up in due form by his meeting before exemption from service in the militia was granted. Friends seem to have generally complied. But, at the outset of the Revolutionary struggle, New York Quakers had refused to supply the names of their male members between the ages of 16 and 60 on the grounds that it was not "consistent with our religious principles" to do so.[29] Their "truly conscientious scruple" in the matter, however, may have arisen at least in part from the fact that the request came from the local committee of safety, whose authority Quakers regarded as usurped. In Virginia, too, we find at least one of the meetings, Fairfax Monthly Meeting, refusing to supply its members when drafted with the certificates required by law on the grounds that this was an impermissible act of collaboration in war.[30] On the other hand, Friends in Rhode Island were prepared to issue certificates so long as militia service was required of them by law; yet they used the occasion to exclude from the benefit of the legal exemption not only those whom they did not consider genuine adherents of the peace testimony but also any who were felt to be wanting in regard to other facets of the discipline.

This policy emerges clearly in the following words of advice circulated among local meetings by the (New England) Meeting for Sufferings:

> Let it be remembered, Friends, that if we give certificates to any whose life and conversation does not well answer to our profession, we must bear the reproach, and shall mar our reputation as a Society; and very likely lose the indulgence we now have, through much labour, obtained. Therefore, dear Friends, let there be great care to inspect the conduct of such as require certificates, and also their principle respecting war; and we desire that none may be granted to any others but such who are of sober lives and conversations, and who are clear in our ancient testimony against wars and fightings; and that such certificates be inspected and directed by, and signed in open meeting.[31]

The Quaker objector, even when in good standing with the meeting, as the vast majority were, was still faced (except where the state

[29] John Cox, Jr., *Quakerism in the City of New York*, pp. 75, 76.
[30] Mekeel, "The Quakers," p. 225.
[31] Mekeel, "New England Quakers and Military Service in the American Revolution" in *Children of Light* (ed. Howard H. Brinton), p. 252.

198

granted complete exemption) with the familiar requirement either to pay a fine, varying in amount from province to province and often from year to year, or to hire a substitute to replace him in his statutory military duties, at a cost that might be greater even than repeated fining. When the assembly in Pennsylvania in November 1775 imposed a draft on all able-bodied men between the ages of 16 and 50, it provided that religious conscientious objectors should be excused service on payment of a fine of £2.10s.[32] This sum was later raised several times largely on account of the inflation of prices as the war proceeded, until at the end of 1778 it reached the figure of £40, with a penalty for nonpayment of distraint of goods or imprisonment for four months for those who had no property on which to distrain. In the following years fines went even higher, first up to £100 and then over that figure, reaching as much as £1,000 in some cases. In the other provinces the pattern is much the same: a rising scale of fines as the years went by and currency depreciated in value, with distraint or imprisonment following for any who refused to pay. In both New Jersey and New York additional sums of money were demanded in the event of an emergency when the militia went out on active service against an invasion. Effective conscription in Maryland did not come until 1777 and in Delaware until 1778. Certified religious objectors were exempt in Virginia, except when the province was threatened by actual invasion. North Carolina, where, as in Virginia, conscientious objectors had been virtually exempt from militia service at the time war broke out, from 1776 on followed the pattern of the middle provinces. The two New England states where Quakers were thickly settled, Rhode Island and Massachusetts, both imposed selective service laws after the proclamation of independence. In Massachusetts, by a law of September 1776, persons refusing the draft or the hiring of a substitute were to be fined £10 or imprisoned for up to two months; but at the end of November, as the result of an amendment, Quakers who had been

---

[32] A month earlier Philadelphia Y. M. had presented an address to the assembly protesting against its intention of introducing military conscription without giving complete exemption to religious objectors. This, the address claimed, conflicted with the guarantees of "liberty of conscience" set out in the fundamental laws of the commonwealth, to enjoy which the first Quaker settlers had left their native land. See *Votes of Assembly, Pa. Archives*, 8th ser., VIII, 7326-30. In the previous June the assembly had indeed generously recognized that "many of the good people of this province are conscientiously scrupulous of bearing arms." Associators, therefore, were asked to "bear a tender and brotherly regard towards this class of their fellow-subjects and country-men." The pacifists of the province, in their turn, were required to "cheerfully assist, in proportion to their abilities, such Associators as cannot spend their time and substance in the public service without great injury to themselves and families." (Quoted from VIII, 7249.)

in membership before 19 April 1775 were allowed complete exemption, although this was withdrawn for a brief time in 1780 during a period of acute manpower shortage. In Rhode Island, at first, Quakers were subject merely to the requirement included in prewar legislation of performing in an emergency certain auxiliary noncombatant but paramilitary duties, such as acting as scouts or messengers, watching, fire-fighting, etc. However, after a brief period during which they were completely exempted from all military obligations, the assembly in April 1777 imposed the draft on all citizens, including Quakers, without the benefit of a conscience clause. Those who would not find substitutes were to have a distress levied upon their property.

If Friends, then, had been willing to pay the statutory fine for refusing service, their conscientious objectors would in most cases—except for certain emergency situations or brief periods when the law was temporarily made more stringent in one or another province—have suffered little beyond a certain financial inconvenience for their opposition to soldiering. But, as in the preceding years, the Society turned its face sternly against any compromise on this issue. The advice issued by Philadelphia Yearly Meeting in September 1776 was, indeed, but a restatement of an old position; its contents were echoed in the declarations of Friends throughout the continent.

It is our judgment [it laid down] that such who make religious profession with us, and do either openly or by connivance, pay any fine, penalty, or tax, in lieu of their personal services for carrying on war; or who do consent to, and allow their children, apprentices, or servants [presumably also Quakers] to act therein do thereby violate our Christian testimony, and by so doing manifest that they are not in religious fellowship with us.[33]

Mekeel[34] has calculated that a total of 469 members of the Society were dealt with during the war for either paying militia fines themselves or conniving at others paying on their behalf:[35] 3 in New York, 125 in

[33] *Rules of Discipline and Christian Advices of the Yearly Meeting of Friends for Pennsylvania and New Jersey* (1797), p. 132. A curious case is cited in Frank H. Stewart, "The Quakers of the Revolution," *Year Book. The New Jersey Society of Pennsylvania, 1907-1921,* pp. 48, 49, of a member of Haddonfield M. M. who was disowned for allowing his apprentices, some aged less than 16, to serve in the militia in his stead.

[34] Mekeel, "The Quakers," p. 301.

[35] Thorne, "North Carolina Friends and the Revolution," pp. 325, 326, cites several examples of this practice. William Townsend of Perquimans M. M., for instance, was accused of "being a partner in hiring a man to serve in a military capacity to save himself from the penalty of the law in that case." John Charles of the same meeting was dealt with for "agreeing to repay a person for paying a draughted fine."

New Jersey, 321 in Pennsylvania, 4 in Delaware, 11 in Maryland, 2 in Virginia, and 3 in the Carolinas. No cases are reported from New England, where fining did not constitute a penalty imposed on Friends. It is not possible, either here or in regard to the other statistics given by Mekeel of "dealings" for offenses against the discipline connected with the war, to say how many of those dealt with were actually disowned and what percentage showed due contrition for their infringement of the rules and were reinstated in good standing with the Society. But probably well over half the cases ended in disownment. In addition, any Quaker found hiring a substitute—a more serious offense and a practice that, in fact, was also condemned by the more conformist German peace sects that did not object to paying fines in lieu of personal service—would be peremptorily disowned, unless he agreed to cancel the arrangement.

Under 500 members (most of whom were probably adherents—if somewhat faint-hearted ones—of Quaker peace principles rather than unconscientious draft dodgers hiding under the Quaker name) defaulted by paying fines. In contrast, 1,000 names are recorded of Friends who were dealt with by their meetings for accepting military service—for acting "in the quality of a soldier," as the quaint Quaker phrase ran. Mekeel gives a total figure of 1,149 dealings on this count: 109 for New England, 59 for New York, 226 for New Jersey, 542 for Pennsylvania, 32 for Delaware, 28 for Maryland, 54 for Virginia, 67 for the Carolinas. Very few of these cases represented enlistment in the British forces: the vast majority joined the Continental army or its auxiliary provincial militias. The number of able-bodied male Quakers of military age who abandoned the peace testimony at this juncture was indeed small, and the majority of such cases date from the first year or two of war when enthusiasm for the Revolutionary cause ran high, especially among the younger men,[36] and before the Society had had time to consolidate its ranks and clarify its position on the various issues connected with the war. In Philadelphia, where the falling away was greatest, Sharpless estimates that "about one-fifth of the [eligible]

---

[36] Among the older men who joined up at this time, some had already earlier shown a proclivity to martial affairs. A good example is John Blackburn, sometime judge of York Co. (Pa.), a Quaker of Irish extraction, who was dealt with on this account during the Indian troubles of 1755, when "at a report of Indians doing mischief at a great distance [he] went out in a warlike manner to meet them contrary to our peaceable principles." Since he finally, though reluctantly, was prevailed upon to express his regret at his action, he was not disowned on this occasion. But early in 1776 his meeting received a report that Judge Blackburn had "enlisted as a soldier," and this act finally brought an end to his career as a Quaker. See Albert Cook Myers, *Immigration of the Irish Quakers into Pennsylvania, 1682-1750*, pp. 231, 232.

adult male Friends . . . joined the American army, or [took] places under the revolutionary government."[37] In the country meetings of Pennsylvania and in the other more rural yearly meetings, the percentage was certainly less. Some of those who joined up were purely nominal Quakers, whose right to the name was limited to their birthright in the Society; some were young people who were in the process of emancipation from the rather narrow social mores of eighteenth-century Quakerism—and thus it is that a disownment for a military offense is often coupled in the records with other forms of deviation such as cardplaying, dancing, frequenting places of worldly amusement, non-Quakerly apparel, or marrying out. On the other hand, many who incurred the penalty of disownment for their soldierly activities were men who had a genuine attachment to the practices and worship of the Society of Friends, except for their disagreement with the peace testimony, and for them the break with Friends was a serious and often painful process.

That in the early months of the war Philadelphia Quakers were those most easily infected with a war spirit is not surprising, since in the provincial capital, with its close political and trading connections with Britain and the other colonies, a worldly spirit had already begun several generations back to seep into the Society. Early in May 1775, James Pemberton reported to his English friend, Dr. Fothergill: "It is too sorrowful and arduous a task to describe our present situation; a military spirit prevails, the people are taken off employment, intent on instructing themselves in the art of war, and many younger members of our Society are daily joining with them, so that the distresses of this province are hastening fast." And John Adams, writing in 1775 from Philadelphia, expressed his surprise at seeing "whole companies of armed Quakers in uniform going through the manual." Even the country meetings began to feel the effects of the mounting tension in the country, and some of their people were carried away. The clerk of Philadelphia Yearly Meeting, summarizing the reports sent in by constituent meetings at the annual assembly in 1775, stated sadly:

> All the accounts except that from Shrewsbury [New Jersey] lament the sorrowful deviation which has lately appeared in many members from our peaceable profession and principles in joining with the multitude in warlike exercise, and instructing themselves in the art of war which has occasioned painful labor to the faithful among us

[37] Sharpless, A Quaker Experiment, II, 151.

202

whose care has been extended to advise and admonish those who are concerned therein.[38]

In its epistle the yearly meeting, "in deep affliction and sorrow" at the failure of Friends "in this time of commotion and perils," admonished parents as well as Friends of experience and years to be more diligent in guarding the youth of the Society against the spirit of the world that had crept into it.[39]

However, within a comparatively short time the work of the local meetings in purging their ranks of "all backsliders and transgressors, who after being treated with in the spirit of meekness, cannot be reclaimed," had been completed. No one was spared because of previous distinction within the counsels of the Society or outside it. Among the earliest cases of disownment was that of the prominent Philadelphia merchant (and later general in the Continental army), Thomas Mifflin (1744-1800), whose home meeting, Philadelphia Monthly Meeting, first called him to account in March 1775. Owen Biddle was another prominent and respected Philadelphia Friend whose support of the war led to speedy disownment. He later returned to the Society ("the instance of O. Biddle shows that miracles are not ceased," commented James Pemberton with a touch of irony),[40] as did a few others similarly disowned, including the brothers Peter and Mordecai Yarnall, young men who were afterward to be active as Friends' ministers. But the greater number were lost to the Society for good.

The Society on the whole, however, emerged strengthened from the rather painful process of eliminating its nonpacifists. Philadelphia Yearly Meeting in 1776 noted the presence among its members of still "a large number of hopeful youth, [who] appear united with us in a living concern for the cause and testimony of truth, and the keeping to the good order of that excellent discipline which our ancestors were enabled to establish, and which as it is rightly administered, we have found to be as a hedge about us."[41] The only trouble was that the hedge

[38] *Ibid.*, pp. 120, 121, 128, 129; Margaret E. Hirst, *The Quakers in Peace and War*, p. 400.

[39] Philadelphia Y. M. MS Minutes for 1749-1779, p. 335. For all the shortcomings of the Philadelphia Quaker merchant class, there seems little justification in the assertion by A. T. Gary [Pannell] ("The Political and Economic Relations of English and American Quakers [1750-1785]," D.Phil. thesis, Oxford [1935], pp. 371ff.) that, in addition to the Society's traditional pacifism, the economic interests of wealthy Philadelphia Quakerdom gave an added stringency to the dealings with those participating in the war against Britain.

[40] Sharpless, *A Quaker Experiment*, II, 209.

[41] *Ibid.*, II, 139, 140.

might eventually become transformed into a prison wall. But most of those who had not been ejected from the Quaker plantation in the early period of the war were probably content to accept the Society's restrictive discipline as not merely a necessary cohesive force but as an essential part of Christian living.

Throughout the war, however, members continued to be cut off as a consequence of minor deviations from the peace testimony, although in many cases either unwillingness to suffer the penalties of disobedience to the new authorities or a lukewarm faith, rather than outright disagreement with Quaker pacifism, was responsible; and, as new members of the Quaker community grew to maturity each year, there were always some who saw their duty in service to their country in arms rather than in following the faith of their forefathers. For instance, to a young relative who was reported to have been attending militia musters, the distinguished Virginia Quaker, Robert Pleasants, wrote a letter of admonition in which he expressed the hope that the young man could be got to view his conduct as mistaken. Otherwise, he went on,

> Thou can't reasonably expect any other than to be excluded from a right of membership in a Society to whose discipline thou don't choose to conform. I wish, however, thou wouldst solidly consider the matter, and if thou canst not justify war from the doctrines and example of our Saviour, His apostles and the primitive Christians, would it not be a dangerous innovation, to set up thy own judgment in opposition to the highest authorities? Wherein, should thou be mistaken after having been favored with a different education, the greater will be thy condemnation.[42]

It is instructive to observe the author of this rather smug epistle appealing to "authorities" rather than inner personal conviction in his effort to recover the young brother for the Society.

As dangerous an innovation in the eyes of loyal Friends as compliance with the militia laws was submission to another demand of the Revolutionary authorities. By 1777 the legislatures of Pennsylvania, New Jersey, North Carolina, and most other states had imposed effective legislation requiring the taking of a test oath or affirmation, which included the renunciation of allegiance to the king and a statement of loyalty to the Continental cause. Severe penalties were attached for refusal, including fines (with distraint or imprisonment for nonpayment) and the loss of many civil rights. In Pennsylvania, where

[42] Adair P. Archer, "The Quaker's Attitude towards the Revolution," *William and Mary College Quarterly*, 2nd ser., I, no. 3 (July 1921), 181.

all schoolmasters were required to take the "test," many Quaker teachers preferred to sacrifice their means of livelihood rather than compromise on this issue. Refusal also entailed serious difficulty in traveling, which was so important an element in maintaining the close intercolonial relations of the Society of Friends, since the failure of a Friend to produce a certificate affirming that he had taken the test might lead the authorities to turn him back at the state or even the county boundary. Friends remained adamant in their refusal to take the test and systematically disowned all those who, for whatever reason, broke the discipline on this point. In 1783, for instance, a minute of Evesham Monthly Meeting in New Jersey recording the disownment of one of its members for this offense mentions that the man did so for "slavish fear of suffering imprisonment."[43] Mekeel gives a total figure of 353 dealings with members for having taken the test: 222 were from Pennsylvania and 49 from New Jersey, the two areas of greatest Quaker concentration. Both these states enforced the test with considerable strictness.

Two factors led Friends to refuse to cooperate with the authorities on this issue. In the first place, they were unwilling to give open recognition in this manner to the change in regime, for, as a minute of Philadelphia Yearly Meeting of 1778 expressed it, "we cannot be instrumental in setting up or pulling down any government."[44] This attitude was in line with all their political declarations since the outbreak of hostilities, and the authorities in Pennsylvania completely failed while the war was in progress to get their Quakers to come out with a clear-cut statement acknowledging president, executive council, and general assembly as the legal government of the state.[45] But there was a second source of Quaker objection to the test that was intimately linked with their whole peace testimony. If Friends were to take the test, it seemed to them that, quite apart from any question of disputed allegiance, they would thereby be giving tacit assent to the arbitrament of war. "We conceive," to quote this time from a statement by North Carolina Yearly Meeting, "that the proposed affirmation approves of the present measures, which are carried on and supported by military force." Later in the same document they optimistically expressed the hope that the administration would "consider our principles a much stronger security to any state than any test that can be required of us; as we . . . for conscience sake are submissive to the laws,

---

[43] Lois V. Given, "Burlington County Friends in the American Revolution," *Proceedings of the New Jersey Historical Society*, vol. 69, no. 3 (July 1951), p. 203.

[44] Ezra Michener (ed.), *A Retrospect of Early Quakerism*, p. 287.

[45] Sharpless, *A Quaker Experiment*, II, 197-200.

in whatsoever they may justly require." But, after the conclusion of peace when the issue was clearly settled in favor of independence and the taint of military means likewise disappeared, the Quaker objections were removed. And so we find North Carolina Friends, for instance, being advised: "Friends are at liberty either to take or refuse the said test according to the clear freedom of their minds."[46]

While there was unanimity among Friends concerning the test, there was more hesitation in issuing a categorical injunction in regard to two important aspects of war finance: the Continental paper currency and the payment of taxes of various kinds in a period of hostilities. Indeed, particularly in relation to the latter issue, members of the Society engaged in a long and sometimes heated controversy. Again, as in the case of the test, two basic reasons, one quasi-political and the other pacifist, lay at the source of Quaker opposition to the Continental authorities in this matter. The paper currency which Congress and state governments, acting on a timeworn principle of colonial administrations, began to issue from the outset of the struggle led inevitably to inflation and a very considerable depreciation in the value of the notes circulated. In the eyes of many Quakers, handling such currency—which, in addition, was the product of an authority whose legitimacy the Society did not acknowledge—was not financially honest, since transactions carried on with it, whether by the authorities or by private individuals, did not approximate the true values involved. Furthermore, Continental paper money was considered—not altogether unjustifiably—to be a covert means of taxation to finance the prosecution of the war.

At Philadelphia Yearly Meeting in the fall of 1775 the question was broached but no definitive conclusion reached. The scruples of those Friends who had "a religious objection" to handling paper money were to be respected. At the same time, Friends holding this position were to be tolerant of those who took a less radical view and were to refrain from censuring them.[47] Whereas Virginia Yearly Meeting, largely under the influence of the exacting Robert Pleasants, forbade its members to handle paper money, North Carolina after discussing the matter in early 1776 left it up to the conscience of every individual whether to accept the money or not. Currency objectors often met with opprobrium, and sometimes ill-treatment as well, from the populace and with the imposition of severe penalties by the

[46] Francis Charles Anscombe, *I have called you Friends*, p. 155; Thorne, "North Carolina Friends and the Revolution," pp. 330-33; Julia S. White, "The Peace Testimony of North Carolina Friends prior to 1860," *BFHA*, vol. 16, no. 2 (1927), p. 64.
[47] *A Retrospect of Early Quakerism*, p. 300.

authorities. Even the Quaker-born General Nathanael Greene (1742-1786), who had some understanding of Quaker views on war, considered such noncooperation an "effrontery" that quite naturally excited hostile sentiments among the people at large against those who practised it.[48]

One of those who objected to the use of Continental paper money was that earnest-minded Southern Quaker, Warner Mifflin (1745-1798). His decision not to handle it stemmed from an incident involving a fellow Quaker, John Cowgill, a farmer from Kent County (Del.), which he had read about in a newspaper. Cowgill had been proclaimed for his currency objection "an enemy of his country" by the county authorities. As a result, not only were his horses, cattle, sheep, and grain requisitioned, but an economic boycott was enforced against him, and his children were barred from attending school. On one occasion Cowgill himself was seized by some American troops and carried off to Dover, the state capital, where he was paraded up and down the town on a cart with a placard affixed to his back. Later, his daughter wrote of the family's experiences at this time: "When we went to bed at night, we did not know what would be the issue before day and in that way we lived for several years." Cowgill's protest started Mifflin thinking about the right Quakerly attitude in this matter. At first, he was torn first one way and then another by conflicting arguments in his own mind. He doubted, too, his strength to stand firm against the kind of persecution Cowgill was enduring. Finally one evening, greatly perturbed, as he relates, "under this exercise and concern I walked about my plantation after night, and seemed as if I never more should be able to make the stand, I thought if they took all my substance I could give that up, but the fear for the poor body prevailed." Returning to the house, he picked up his Bible and began to read in it. Slowly there took shape within him the resolution that it was his duty to refuse to have anything to do with this money.[49]

Another sensitive spirit who finally, after considerable travail of mind, adopted a similar line of conduct was the prominent Rhode Island minister, Job Scott (1751-1793). For a long time he worried over the various arguments pro and con. If he refused the currency, he knew that he would—not unnaturally—be suspected of pro-British sympathies and would have to face misunderstanding and considerable material hardship as well. Besides, many Friends evidently did

[48] Given, "Burlington County Friends," p. 206. See also Theodore Thayer, *Pennsylvania Politics and the Growth of Democracy*, p. 173.

[49] Warner Mifflin, "Statement concerning his Refusal to use and circulate Continental Currency" (1779), Misc. MSS, F.H.L.S.C.; John A. Munroe, *Federalist Delaware 1775-1815*, pp. 48, 49.

not entertain any scruples in the matter. Who was he to run counter to the opinion of those whom he respected? "Fears and reasonings of one kind or other prevailed on me to take it [i.e., Continental currency] for a season; and then it became harder than it would probably have been at first" to decide against acceptance. However, an increasing conviction that the use of such money was equivalent to aiding and abetting the war effort and to abandoning strict Quaker neutrality led him at last to decide to refuse the use of this money altogether. This decision brought financial difficulties, since scarcely any other currency was available, but, he tells us, he enjoyed an easy conscience thereafter.[50]

Mifflin and especially Scott were strict neutralists in their political views. As an example of a Quaker currency objector whose stand was motivated perhaps more by his hostility to the change in regime than by the money's association with the waging of war, we may take the case of the weighty Philadelphia burgher, Samuel Rowland Fisher (1745-1834), who, along with his father and brother, eschewed the use of the tainted paper currency. To accept it, in their view, would be to become a party "to . . . setting up and pulling down governments and the promotion of war in the land." Fisher's feelings emerge clearly in a remark he once made to a government official: "Your government," he told him, "if it can be so called, is exactly of a piece with the paper bills issued to carry on the war, which are the greatest lies, deception and hypocrisy and for these reasons I could not acknowledge their authority." Fisher would have liked all Friends to take the same course he did and boycott the Continental money. (In 1779, indeed, Philadelphia Yearly Meeting condemned its use as a dereliction of the peace testimony, while at the same time not making it actually a disciplinary matter and still leaving it up to the individual conscience to decide whether or not to discontinue handling it.)[51] In February 1776, as a result of their outspoken stand against the money, the two Fisher brothers were "advertised as enemies" of the American cause, and their stores were temporarily closed down by the authorities.[52]

---

[50] *Journal of Job Scott*, pp. 47-51.

[51] At Western Q. M. for Conference in August 1779, there arose a concern among some present "that Friends might exert themselves in laboring to have their brethren convinced of the pernicious consequences of continuing to circulate the Continental currency so called, it being calculated to promote measures repugnant to the peaceable principles we profess to be led by" (*A Retrospect of Early Quakerism*, p. 382).

[52] "Journal of Samuel Rowland Fisher, of Philadelphia, 1779-1781," *PMHB*, XLI (1917), no. 2, 149, 163, 193; no. 3, 291; no. 4, 401, 402, 431. Fisher was later one of the Virginia exiles of 1777-1778 and, in July 1779, was again arrested on charges—undoubtedly false, for Fisher for all his conservative loyalism was a

Among those Friends who disagreed with the view that Quaker pacifism required abstention from the use of Continental currency was Moses Brown, perhaps the most outstanding New England Friend of that day. "His position" on this issue, writes his most recent biographer, "was determined by sympathy for the American cause and by common sense." Brown believed that, in fact, no moral distinction could be made between handling paper money and using specie, which all Friends admitted to be necessary for carrying on everyday life. As a result largely of Brown's influence, New England Friends never made an issue of the Continental currency question; their unwillingness to do so, in turn, became a factor in creating better relations between the Society and the American authorities in this area than existed in most other parts of the continent.[53]

More intricate in its various ramifications than the paper money problem, and more apt to generate heat on both sides, was the controversy evoked within wartime Quakerdom by the tax question. As we know, this was by no means a new problem: indeed, it reached back to the early days of the Society. But the war had given it renewed urgency. Now, as earlier, there were really three questions at issue, although not all Friends seem to have been quite clear as to the distinction between them. In the first place came the question of "war taxes" for some quite specific military purpose: most Friends at this time agreed that such taxes should not be paid, but, as we shall see below, a small group in New England actively and publicly advocated compliance, a stand that led to their eventual separation from the main body of the Society. The next category was that of general taxes "in the mixture," where only a part—and usually a portion that was difficult to estimate exactly—went toward financing the war: about this issue there was less unanimity, indeed considerable confusion, in the minds of many Friends. Lastly came certain taxes and rates, for the upkeep of the highway, for example, or for the maintenance of the poor, where—except for the circumstance of their being levied by an administration that was waging a war—there was obviously no association with military objectives.

Most Friends at this date, then, had a clear sense that the payment of special taxes imposed for some military purpose was not compatible with the peace testimony and that both payment and collaboration with the machinery of levying such a tax[54] constituted a contravention

---

staunch Quaker pacifist—of having sent military intelligence to the British and was kept in prison for two years.

[53] Mack Thompson, *Moses Brown*, pp. 136, 137.

[54] As an example of a Friend who refused appointment as a collector of taxes,

of the discipline. Thus we find Friends being disowned for such offenses as "assisting in laying a tax for military purposes," "paying a fine for refusing to collect taxes for military purposes," or "paying taxes for hiring men to go to war."[55] As early as August 1775 we find a minute like the following appearing in the records of a New Jersey country meeting:

> John Gill, from Haddonfield Preparative Meeting, requested the sense of Friends respecting the present demand of money by the Provincial Committee for military purposes. The judgment of Friends was fully and clearly given. That paying it was a manifest deviation from our peaceable principles, and all under our name are desired deeply to attend to this principle which so distinguishes us as a people from other professions and seek for strength to live up thereto and not balk our testimony.[56]

The conviction expressed here of the incompatibility between assent to a demand of this kind on the part of Caesar and the Quaker profession of peace was typical of Friends' meetings up and down the country during the war years.

In the case of ordinary taxes which, especially in wartime, were obviously in part intended to finance military objectives, there prevailed in many parts of the Society a strong feeling that these, too, should be refused, despite the penalties that would follow for the tax objectors. As the war proceeded, Philadelphia Yearly Meeting and Virginia Yearly Meeting in particular, where perhaps—at least in influential Quaker circles—strong pro-British sentiment helped to exacerbate the reluctance to pay money to a rebellious administration, showed a widespread incidence of refusal to pay these mixed taxes, as well as specifically war ones. In 1778 Philadelphia Yearly Meeting passed a very sympathetic resolution concerning the increasing number of Friends who had scruples about paying general taxes in wartime. Although it did not state categorically that payment was con-

---

we may take the case of 26-year-old Eli Yarnall of Chester Co. (Pa.). In a letter explaining his rejection of the office, he stated: "I dare not do it, let my sufferings in consequence thereof be never so great," for many of the taxes he would be obliged to collect would be allocated for war purposes. As he expected, fine and distraint followed his action. See *Biographical Sketches and Anecdotes of Members of the Religious Society of Friends*, pp. 326-28.

[55] Cited in Sharpless, *A Quaker Experiment*, II, 134, 135, from the records of two monthly meetings within the city of Philadelphia.

[56] Stewart, "The Quakers of the Revolution," p. 42. On p. 44 Stewart cites the similar case of Woodbury Preparative Meeting, whose members in mid-1776 refused to pay a powder-tax imposed by the provincial convention and had their goods distrained as a result.

trary to Quaker principles, it did say that those Friends who felt "uneasiness to themselves" in paying should have the united support of the Society in their stand.[57] We hear of Pennsylvania Quakers spending periods of up to two years in prison for nonpayment of taxes.[58]

Philadelphia Monthly Meeting was later to claim, in reply to the assertions of the pro-war group of Free Quakers (see below), that "we know not of any of our members being disowned, for the payment of taxes, for the support of government, nor is there any rule of our discipline that requires it."[59] The latter part of the statement is undoubtedly correct, but it would seem that, if not in Philadelphia itself, at least in some of the rural meetings of Pennsylvania disciplinary action was taken against Friends who paid "mixed" taxes. The exact character of the various taxes referred to in meeting records is not always clear. But—to cite one case—the offense of the "ancient Friend" of London Grove Preparatory Meeting, Nathaniel Scarlet, who in 1779 was "dealt with" by New Garden Monthly Meeting for having "through weakness . . . paid a tax tending to the encouragement of war and commotion,"[60] surely concerned a "mixed" tax rather than a purely military one. The old man escaped disownment in this instance by expressing regret for his action, an acknowledgment of error that was accepted by the meeting. Or take the case of Kennett Monthly Meeting where we find this entry recorded for 15 January 1780:

> The Friends appointed to extend labour in order to strengthen their brethren against the payment of taxes report, that they have visited some members, to some degree of satisfaction, in some places; but as the service is not fully gone through, they are continued, and desired to attend thereto, and report to next meeting.[61]

In North Carolina legislation passed in 1778 requiring Friends on account of their refusal to take the oath of allegiance to pay three times the ordinary tax, combined with the knowledge that the money thus raised would be largely allocated to the prosecution of the war, led to a lively discussion of the issue within the Quaker community. Some Friends urged a united refusal to pay a mixed tax of this kind,

[57] *Rules of Discipline* (1797), pp. 132, 133.
[58] Mekeel, "The Quakers," p. 151.
[59] Quoted in Charles Wetherill, *History of the Religious Society of Friends called by some the Free Quakers*, p. 67, from "An Address and Memorial on Behalf of the People called Quakers" presented in February 1782 to the general assembly of Pennsylvania.
[60] Gilbert Cope, "Chester County Quakers during the Revolution," *Bulletins of the Chester County Historical Society* 1902-3, p. 24.
[61] Kennett Monthly Meeting Sufferings 1757-1791 (MS in F.H.L.S.C.), p. 29.

arguing that a divided witness now would "tend to weaken and discourage those who [conceived] it to be their duty to suffer the loss of life, liberty and property, rather than violate the testimony of a good conscience." In October 1778 in its epistle the yearly meeting advised members to have "a close and solid consideration whether the payment of taxes under the present commotions" was in fact consistent "with our peaceable principles." But it did not impose any clear ban on payment. The upshot was that Quakers in the western regions usually paid their taxes, while those in the eastern part of the state more often refused compliance and in most cases suffered distraint of property by the authorities.[62]

In other areas the story is much the same. In Delaware many Quakers refused to pay the ordinary taxes to the state because of the association of these taxes with the prosecution of the war. Among members of Baltimore Yearly Meeting, which covered Maryland and some adjacent districts, feeling also ran strong against compliance. The annual gathering in 1781 reported: "Most Friends appear to be careful in maintaining our testimony against war by refusing the payment of taxes."[63]

Another part of the country where the problem of tax payment in wartime was keenly debated was New England. There the small group that advocated the payment of all taxes, including specifically military ones, was, as we shall see, ejected from the Society without causing too much dissension. In regard to mixed taxes there was a genuine division of opinion, and the matter cropped up repeatedly at successive yearly meetings. The powerful influence of Moses Brown was exerted in the direction of granting tolerance to differing viewpoints: in Brown's view, an explicit ruling on the part of the highest authority among New England Friends against paying the ordinary taxes—taxes "in the mixture," to use the Quaker term for them—would only have excited additional hostility against the Society on the part of the Continental authorities and might as well engender a still more serious split in the Quaker ranks.[64] Some weighty New England Friends like Job Scott opposed him, hoping that Friends would issue a clear condemnation where any considerable amount of money was destined for use in war. But New England Yearly Meeting continued to urge tolerance of both these points of view, while explicitly requiring noncompliance in the case of "all taxes, expressly or specially for the support of war, whether called for in money, provisions or otherwise."

[62] Mekeel, "The Quakers," pp. 233-35.
[63] Kenneth S.P. Morse, *Baltimore Yearly Meeting 1672-1830*, p. 22.
[64] Thompson, *Moses Brown*, pp. 139, 141, 143-45.

"Such Friends as do actively pay such taxes," it laid down, should "be dealt with as disorderly walkers." And the scruples of the more radical members must be given all respect. "We also desire," the yearly gathering of 1781 told members, "that all Friends carefully avoid discouraging a tender scruple which may arise in the minds of our brethren respecting the payment of such taxes, a part whereof is evidently for the support of war." The hardships they might encounter for taking such a stand were to be reckoned as sufferings on account of Friends' principles. And so the same yearly meeting goes on to record:

> The testimony of many Friends in the nonpayment of taxes, part whereof goes for the support of war, coming under consideration of this meeting,—It is our sense and judgment that the several monthly meetings collect accounts of the sufferings of our brethren on account of said testimony, and send them up to the Meeting for Sufferings, there to be recorded after due inspection in Friends' Book of Sufferings as our brethren's testimony for the truth against the appropriation of any part thereof to the purposes of war and it is recommended to Friends, that labouring to be preserved unbiased herein, as to the powers which are or may be, they keep an eye single to the testimony of truth against war and fighting.[65]

At the same time, however, the validity of the position of the moderates within the Society, who felt no compunction in rendering government what they believed to be its normal due in the way of tribute, was safeguarded.

Moses Brown himself felt that, in the existing circumstances, he could not pay mixed taxes since such a large proportion was allocated to war. But at the same time he disagreed with the chief reason on which many of the tax objectors based their refusal. In a letter dated 2 October 1780 to his Pennsylvania friend, Anthony Benezet, he explained his point of view. "We fear," he wrote, "some take up the testimony [i.e., of nonpayment], more on account of the authority that demands the taxes than because they are used for war. Such we fear instead of forwarding will eventually retard the testimony." He stressed that of equal importance to their peace testimony was Friends' "testimony of supporting civil government by readily contrib-

---

[65] New England Y. M. MS Discipline, H.C.Q.C. (*BX 7617 N5C5 1781), p. 432; *The Book of Discipline, Agreed on by the Yearly-Meeting of Friends for New-England* (1785), pp. 148, 149. These debates and resolutions of 1781 seem to be the ones referred to in Job Scott's *Journal*, p. 63, but there they are mentioned as having taken place in 1779.

uting thereto," a fact the Quakers opposed to the Revolutionary regime had lost sight of. "I understand," he told Benezet, "that some Friends have fallen in with or been overpowered by the common argument that civil government is upheld by the sword, and therefore they decline paying to its support, which appears to me a great weakness, for I see a material distinction between civil government and military or a state of war and on this distinction our ancient testimonies were and remain to be supportable of paying tribute and custom for the support of the civil and yet to refuse paying trophy money and other expenses solely for war. Civil government is the restoring and supporting power." Brown did look forward, however, to a time when, peace having returned and the proportion of tax money devoted to military purposes being thus substantially reduced, Friends would be able to work out in cooperation with the government "a separation" between the amount that they were prepared in good conscience to contribute and the sum destined for war that, for all their approval of the civil power, they felt obliged to withhold. If such a separation were not permitted, then Friends should consider refusal to pay the whole tax, even where only a small part went toward war.[66]

A third tax problem, alongside direct war taxes which Friends were required to refuse to pay and taxes in the mixture toward which a considerable number of Friends adopted an attitude of noncooperation, concerned unquestionably nonmilitary taxes. Here no definite ruling was ever adopted by any of the yearly meetings. Most Friends saw nothing wrong in paying these taxes in wartime, even to a *de facto* authority in rebellion against the established government. But a small minority objected. We hear, for instance, of New England Friends taking this stand[67] and of some Quakers in Pennsylvania refusing to pay even the poor rate and the rate for the upkeep of the roads on the grounds that payment would constitute acknowledgment of an authority set up by violent revolution.[68] But, though generally recognized as a possible alternative for a concerned Friend to take, this form of protest was clearly a minority position.

"The consistency of paying tax for war," Benezet wrote to Virginia's most outstanding Quaker of the period, Robert Pleasants, in March 1781, "is becoming so interesting a subject to the Society" that he was sure his correspondent would be glad to hear the results of the most

[66] Brookes, *Friend Anthony Benezet*, pp. 431, 432.

[67] *Ibid.*, p. 432. Brown informed Benezet: "Some Friends [i.e., in New England] refuse all taxes even those for civil uses as well as those clear for war and others that are mixed."

[68] Mekeel, "The Quakers," p. 141.

recent consideration of the matter among Philadelphia Friends.[69] Pleasants himself had long been deeply concerned with the taxation issue and in 1779 had been largely instrumental in getting Virginia Yearly Meeting to take an antitax position. In December of that year he had stated his position in a letter to a friend. "It appears clear to my judgment that Friends can no more pay than take the test, for they are both calculated to promote the same ends and make us parties to the destruction, the violence and confusion consequent to such intestine commotion; and would it not be repugnant to reason to contribute by taxes to the support of either party who may happen to prevail, whom we could not, under the present unsettled state of affairs, be free to acknowledge."[70]

The tax issue had indeed occupied the thoughts and prayers of many of the most concerned members of the Society right from the early days of the war, and it became an increasing preoccupation with many as the war proceeded and the demands for money grew larger and more insistent. All the yearly meetings grappled with the problem at one time or another. We find the antitax party in New England Yearly Meeting in 1780 drawing up a lengthy "Apology," "running to over 60 quarto pages," elaborating their point of view, which they hoped to persuade their Meeting for Sufferings to publish. In the summer of the same year a prominent New Jersey Friend, Samuel Allinson, a lawyer by training and sometime surveyor general of his province, sat down and put his "Reasons against War, and paying Taxes for its Support" onto paper. The 24 pages of his manuscript exercise book, which contain his essay,[71] give perhaps the most trenchant statement of Quaker objections to paying mixed taxes in wartime. "The thoughts on paying taxes of Samuel Allinson," wrote Moses Brown after a copy had been sent for the perusal of New England Friends, "is well thought of even by those who yet pay them."[72] The essay is indeed well argued and shows a logical and well-trained mind at work, which, despite a certain legalistic cast, was free of excessive reliance on either scripture or the Quaker discipline. For this reason, and because of the important role tax objection played in the thought and practice of Friends during the Revolutionary War, the little work deserves some attention at this point.

Allinson's main argument was that the payment of all taxes which in any way contributed to the prosecution of war must be rejected by

---

[69] Brookes, *Benezet*, p. 353.
[70] Archer, "The Quaker's Attitude towards the Revolution," p. 179.
[71] Now in the H.C.Q.C.
[72] Brookes, *Benezet*, p. 435. Letters to Benezet, 24 Dec. 1780.

Friends on two counts, one general and one particular. In the first place, if Quakers felt that conscience forbade them to fight, then the same conscience should not lead them to contribute money willingly to assist others to do what they scrupled themselves to do. Secondly, in the present conflict taxes imposed by the Continental authorities differed in kind from those imposed by the government in past wars, for in levying them the regime was pursuing an objective that Friends must disapprove, namely, the overthrow of the king's authority and its replacement by one that was new. Moreover, Allinson pleaded, the destructiveness of war in their own land should now serve to bring home effectively to Friends its thoroughly evil nature. "Can we look at the dismal consequences of war," he asked, "and immediately reflect that we give our voluntary aid to it any way and be easy under it? or think we are consistent throughout?"

After stating his premises, Allinson went on to discuss in turn a number of objections that might be lodged against his position. Did not St. Paul, for instance, enjoin his fellow Christians to pay tribute to the authorities without mentioning any possible use that Caesar might make of the money? The Roman Empire was then at peace and the question of specifically war taxes was not involved, Allinson answered—not altogether convincingly. But anyhow, he went on, implicitly challenging—so it would seem—the right of St. Paul to speak authoritatively on all questions for later generations: "If tribute is demanded for a use that is antichristian it seems right for every Christian to deny it, for Caesar can have no title to that which opposes the Lord's command." Again, it was often argued, both within the Society and outside it, that Friends in the past had normally paid their taxes as a religious obligation without enquiring too closely about their later use. Although this assertion was true, Allinson admitted, yet might not the same be argued of the buying and owning of slaves, now generally admitted to be inconsistent with Quaker principles? Knowledge of good and evil is in some ways a progressive revelation. "This therefore seems to be the criterion; whenever an act strikes the mind with a religious fear that the voluntary performance of it will not be holding up the light of the Gospel of Peace, or be a *stumbling block* to others, it ought carefully to be avoided." A third argument frequently urged against the tax objectors was that payment represents the fulfillment of a debt that we owe our government in exchange for the services that it has rendered us, that, in fact, it is as obligatory on our conscience as the completion of a contract once entered into. In his answer Allinson, showing here his lawyer's deftness in making subtle distinctions, differentiated between a debt where the service for which payment was being made was in the past and the creditor was in no way obliged to render account of how he might spend the money repaid and a tax to be expended on future service to the state, where "he who gives has a right to *call to such an account* and therefore seems himself liable for and privy to the application." The citizen in a free polity, Allinson was arguing, has a responsibility for the actions of his government. If he does not approve morally of the purposes to which he knows his money will be put, he is under an obligation to withhold voluntary payment.

Considerations of this kind led Allinson on to a discussion of the vital and closely related problem of civil government. How did Quaker pacifism fit in with Friends' nice sense of obligation toward the powers that be (a dutifulness, we may add, that had led many to observe the strictest neutrality, if not to show considerable hostility toward the new American regime)? Since the first loyalty of man is to God, Allinson pointed out, a general approval of the institution of civil government "can never mean a compliance with every requisition." He went on:

> We pay our proportion to the support of the poor, the maintenance of roads and the support of civil order in government (if the demand is unmixed with war or tithes), these include every benefit we ask or receive. We desire not war or any of its consequences, nor do we apprehend any benefit arising from it.

He agreed that "the sword of municipal justice" can rightly, indeed on some occasions must, be used "against an internal malefactor." But this action is not the same as war, for "municipal justice is conducted by known rules agreed upon in stillness and quiet, and may be done without injury to any one." On the other hand, war represents the victory of lawless force, destroys innocent and guilty alike, and can usually be avoided by the application in good time of appropriate measures to remove its causes. "Civil justice is an innocent dispassionate remedy; this cannot be said of war."

In one passage Allinson made a sly allusion to the possible connection between the wealth and respectability that many Friends had acquired, "which sometimes seems to need the arm of power to secure," and their reluctance to take a firm stand on this question of war taxes. Yet at the same time, like Moses Brown and many of the wiser spirits of the Society, he refrained from calling for uniformity, for making the tax question a disciplinary matter, and instead urged tolerance of differing but sincerely held views among Friends. In both his rejection of precedent as obligatory on later generations of Friends and in his concept of a slow growth in awareness of truth, Allinson succeeded in instilling a certain freshness in what was in danger of becoming a rather sterile argument.

It was not in Allinson's yearly meeting, however, but among New England Friends that the tax issue had become a direct cause of schism within the Society. Late in 1775, at the very outset of the war, a prominent member of Sandwich (Mass.) Monthly Meeting, Timothy Davis, had composed a short tract strongly urging Friends to comply with all tax demands made on them by the new provincial authorities. Failing to secure the sanction of New England Meeting for Sufferings, which was then required for all publications bearing on any of the Quaker testimonies, he had gone ahead and brought the essay out on his own early the following year under the title *A Letter from a a Friend to Some of His Intimate Friends, on the Subject of paying Taxes &c*. Although the work was published anonymously, all Friends of course knew who the author was. The Meeting for Sufferings attempted to prevent the circulation of the pamphlet, fearing that it would "have a tendency to suppress tender and religious scruples, in the minds of those who are or may be exercised respecting the payment of taxes, for the purpose of war"; and it therefore started disciplinary action against both Davis and his printer, who was also a Quaker, the ostensible offense committed by the two being, of course, the publication of the tract without official permission and not the nature of its contents.[73] Meeting for Sufferings' fears were by no means groundless, for in fact New England Quakers were deeply divided on this question of paying taxes. Although it contained a number of tax radicals like Job Scott, the yearly meeting also included, to use Moses Brown's words, "a number of concerned Friends and leading members"[74] who took the opposite view. Public discussion of the issue would only lead, it was feared, to internal dissension before any general consensus among Friends had been reached.

Davis in his tract had not abandoned his Society's pacifism. This fact he was careful to point out early in his argument. "The peaceable profession," he writes, "which we have long made to the world (which constitutes a very amiable part of our religious character) will not ad-

[73] Mekeel, "Free Quaker Movement in New England during the American Revolution," *BFHA*, vol. 27, no. 2 (1938), p. 76.

[74] Quoted in Brookes, *Benezet*, p. 431. After Davis's disownment, Brown, who was making great efforts to reclaim him for the Society, reported that Davis had admitted that recently he had received a tax demand that he felt unable to pay. Brown contrasted this with the position of some Friends still within the Society, "even some who had been on appointment to treat with Timothy," "who had paid all." (They escaped disciplinary action, of course, because they had not made a public issue of it as Davis had done.)

mit of our taking up arms." On this point he differed from the dissident group in Philadelphia (discussed later in this chapter) which was to crystallize into the Free Quaker movement. But both were at one in their positive attitude toward the new Revolutionary regime, and it was largely this stance that brought down on the heads of both groups the wrath of many weighty members of the Society.

Davis could see no reason why Quakers should not be taxed along with their fellow citizens. While expressing his desire for a reconciliation between Great Britain and the colonies, he felt that Friends had no cause to withhold payment either because the government in control of their country had been set up as a result of revolution or because the money paid would be used for war purposes. Had not Friends in Cromwell's time paid taxes to the Commonwealth, which was the outcome of a successful rebellion against a lawful monarch? Or had a later generation of Quakers demurred from paying them to the governments which succeeded the Glorious Revolution of 1688? Indeed, almost any government was preferable to a condition of anarchy. Christ urged his fellow countrymen to pay to Caesar, even though they were in a state of subjection to Rome. Tax payment did not signify an overall approval of every aspect of government: it did not mean in the case of Friends that they were giving their blessing to either violent revolution or military defense. It simply showed that they appreciated that magistracy was an institution sanctioned by God. Besides, had not Friends regularly paid taxes in wartime as in periods of peace? "By all that I have been able to discover," he concluded, "our Society in England have ever made a point of being careful and exact in paying all taxes that are legally assessed, except the priest's rate." He quoted from that old Quaker stalwart of two continents, Thomas Story, to show that his own position had the sanction of the apostolic age of their Society. Although Davis, like many contemporary Quakers, did not clearly distinguish between direct war taxes and those "in the mixture" (his argument is directed toward showing that the necessity of government makes the question of the use to which taxes, once paid, are put irrelevant), he at least implicitly sanctioned the direct war tax along with the mixed ones. However, whatever had been the position of early Friends (and the surreptitious practice of some more recent ones), this was a viewpoint that was generally rejected by American Quakers in Davis's day.

The machinery for dealing with Davis's case moved slowly, partly because of the fact that he enjoyed a considerable following among the members of his own monthly meeting, with which prime responsibility rested in handling the matter. The case was shuttled back and forth from monthly meeting to yearly meeting until, finally, sentence of disownment was passed on Davis at the end of 1778. The delay may probably be attributed also to the hopes of reclaiming the erring minister that Moses Brown and other leading New England Friends who were not unsympathetic to Davis's point of view entertained, as well as to fears that, if Davis were ejected too precipitately, he might carry with him a considerable number of sympathizers. Delay was urged, too, by the tactful Anthony Benezet in Philadelphia.

In fact, the split when it came was on a small scale. Twenty-nine members of Sandwich Monthly Meeting followed Davis out in 1779, along with a dozen or so members from the neighboring monthly meeting at Dartmouth, where in 1781 the dissidents proceeded to set up their own separatist meeting. The usual disputes over meeting property ensued. The group enjoyed fairly close contacts with the more radically nonpacifist Free Quakers of Philadelphia. Even more quickly than the latter, however, the New England "Free Quakers" began to disintegrate.[75] In the mid-nineties Davis himself applied to be readmitted to the Society and was duly reinstated in membership after making acknowledgment of error.[76] After their leader had abandoned them, the tiny group disappeared altogether early in the next century.

As a pendant to the controversy that had at one time seemed to threaten to cause a severe breach in the Quaker ranks and in fact had made scarcely any impact on the Society, there was published in 1784, after the war had ended, a longish pamphlet by one Joseph Taber (1731-ca.1796) with the title *An Address to the People called Quakers*, in which the author set out to give a detailed defense of the views and conduct of his leader, Davis. Whereas Davis's original treatise had numbered a mere 8 pages, Taber's tract ran to 67. Taber had been angered by the Society's treatment of Davis, by what he considered their "impatience of dissent," behavior so inconsistent with the spirit of the "Christian liberty" that they professed.

Two points are worth bringing out in connection with Taber's pamphlet, which otherwise contains little that is of any special significance.[77] In the first place, in spite of their relations with the militant Philadelphia Free Quakers, Taber and, presumably, the group in whose name the pamphlet was issued (although the authorship is almost certainly Taber's) still adhered, as Davis had at the beginning, to the Quaker position on peace. The Society of Friends, stated Taber, has rightly been "called from the use of the sword . . . to hold the olive

---

[75] Mekeel, "Free Quaker Movement in New England," pp. 77-82.
[76] *Memoir of Henry Hull*, pp. 68, 69.
[77] See esp. pp. 22, 23, 30, 38-42, 44.

branch to the nations until it shall please infinite wisdom to call the rest of mankind in like manner from the use of the sword." Their role, however, he conceived as a strictly vocational pacifism; the sword-bearing magistracy was absolutely essential for the well-being of society in its present state, and it was imperative that Friends willingly support the magistracy by their taxes. Mankind in general, even Christians, would only be ready to adopt Quakerly peaceableness slowly, would have to grow gradually up to it; most men were not yet far enough advanced for this way of life. Secondly, while stating that his group opposed the antitax position, not because it was new, but because it appeared to them incorrect, Taber obviously felt that his strongest weapon against his opponents lay in his ability to marshal a whole array of proof texts in favor of tax payment, whatever the warlike implications. And indeed, with such authorities as George Fox, Isaac Penington, and London Yearly Meeting as late as 1756, it must be admitted that at this level at least Taber had the best of the argument, and it is clear that his claim that Davis's tract contained nothing "inconsistent with the ancient and approved practice of the Society, from their first appearance as such until very lately" was fully justified. The contention that Allinson had urged a few years earlier, that revelation even among Friends is progressive, was not a proposition that would have found assent among a number of Taber's and Davis's orthodox Quaker opponents. Equally, Taber's assertion that Timothy Davis was no more pro-American than a number of his opponents had been pro-British was also hard to deny. But, as we have seen, the root cause of disownment lay as much in the publicity which Davis chose to give his views and the decisiveness with which he endowed his pro-Continental sympathies as in his alleged failure in interpreting early Quaker practice in regard to tax payment.

The war had, in fact, ended by the time Taber wrote his apology for his group's defection, but the problem of war taxes continued to occupy the Quaker conscience for the rest of the decade (see Chapter VIII). The peace treaty had legitimized the regime of independence in the eyes of even the strictest Friend, and tax money was no longer destined for the prosecution of war. But were Friends to begin to pay up with an easy conscience when some taxes were designed specifically to help sink the considerable debt accumulated during the war? Some Quakers who had previously withheld payment of the more obviously military taxes now complied, arguing that payment was permissible now that peace had come. But the yearly meetings came out strongly against payment: Baltimore, Philadelphia, and New England meetings equated this kind of demand with a direct war tax and required their subordinate meetings to disown members who persisted in paying. New York Yearly Meeting, however, while also recommending noncompliance, did not call for disownment.[78]

The tax issue was one of the hardest problems that faced the Quakers during the war, for, unlike direct military service and its alternatives or the "Test," it was extremely difficult for them to know where to draw the line between the legitimate demands of the civil power and the rights of religious conscience. Here the sensitive Quaker conscience, which has so often been a cause of irritation to the Society's less sympathetic critics, had plenty of scope to expand. The aim of the tax objectors was to avoid the taint of hypocrisy that would seem to be implied by their contributing money to the war effort. Yet the actual result of their objection, where the objecting Friend owned any property, was in most cases a larger contribution by way of excessive distraint of goods, although, of course, this was extracted without the Friend's willing participation.

This same delicacy of conscience was exercised in a wide variety of other ways in connection with the wartime activities of Friends, usually without the agonizing dilemmas presented in the case of war taxes. A whole array of actions came up before the Society at one time or another and were duly disapproved, often on the basis of past decisions or administrative practice, with disownment following if the delinquent member refused to express contrition for his un-Quakerly conduct (except a few instances where a recommendation of disapproval of a milder sort replaced the more frequent categorical prohibition of some action). These quasi-military activities, which will now be discussed, may be divided into three broad (and overlapping) classes: actions which, although technically noncombatant, involved direct assistance to the military; business and trade activities that implied indirect support of war; and nonmilitary conduct that seemed to imply giving approval to war.

Direct assistance to the military, whether American or British, was always a disownable offense, although, owing to the congregational nature of the Society of Friends and the responsibility delegated with-

---

[78] Mekeel, "The Quakers," pp. 278-80. Baltimore Y. M. (Meeting for Sufferings) in 1784 resolved as follows: "We are unanimously of the judgment that notwithstanding the offering of human blood appears to be stayed Friends cannot be clear in paying taxes for sinking the debt incurred by the late war, and that Friends ought to be very careful how they act in all such cases as may have a tendency to lay waste our peaceable testimony, and especially those who have heretofore suffered the spoil of their goods rather than contribute towards the support of war, and that they give no occasion for the truth to be evilly spoken of" (quoted in Kenneth L. Carroll, "Talbot County Quakerism in the Colonial Period," *Maryland Historical Magazine*, vol. 53, no. 4 [Dec. 1958], pp. 347, 348).

in it to the local meetings to enforce the discipline, some offenders may have escaped the penalty. Mekeel has given the figure of 91 dealings with members who had assisted the armed forces. But certainly the number must have been considerably higher, the exact figure depending, of course, on the researcher's definition of assistance. Many of the cases concerned Quakers who had agreed to work for the army or to make munitions ("making weapons of war formed for the destruction of his fellowmen" was how a Philadelphia city meeting termed the latter offense).[79] We hear, for instance, of a member of Kennett Monthly Meeting (Pa.) confessing to having made "wheels for gun carriages";[80] in Maryland another Friend admitted that "two years since he did make four or five shot bags and cover [for] one cartridge box, for a neighbor, a military man." Meeting records contain many instances of action against members who had hired themselves out as workmen in camps or army. The temptation in country districts to accept temporary service as teamsters with one or other of the armies was considerable, since refusal was likely to have led to the requisitioning of horses and equipment. Friends were solemnly warned that, if the military authorities did seize these supplies, no payment that the army might afterward attempt to press on them should be accepted. We find Jeremiah Brown of Brick Meeting (Calvert, Md.) confessing in 1778:

> That when my wagon and team came back, which were forcibly taken to carry military stores, [I] did receive wages for the same and was paid for one of my horses which was lost in the journey, which compliance has not been easy to my mind, being convinced that the testimony of truth is against such, I do hereby acknowledge my weakness therein, hoping and desiring for the future to give closer attention to the inward principles which preserve out of error.[81]

And where a member of the family went along with the impounded horses to see that they were properly cared for, this action, too, was a matter of concern for the meeting.[82]

[79] Sharpless, *A Quaker Experiment*, II, 133.
[80] *A Retrospect of Early Quakerism*, p. 301.
[81] *Bi-Centennial of Brick Meeting-House, Calvert, Cecil County, Maryland, 1701-1901*, p. 55.
[82] Cope, "Chester County Quakers during the Revolution," p. 18. See also "Bucks County Quakers and the Revolution," *Pennsylvania Genealogical Magazine*, XXIV, no. 4 (1966), 297: "William Richardson offered a paper condemning his misconduct in sending a person to take care of his team that was pressed, expressing his sorrow for the same." This article prints extracts from the minutes of Middletown M. M., Bucks Co. (Pa.).

In the late seventies the American army frequently requisitioned foodstuffs and blankets for their ill-fed and ill-clad troops from among the well-stocked farms around Philadelphia. Although Quakers, as we have seen, were among the first to voluntarily assist the civilian victims of war, a demand of this nature came to them not as a humanitarian request but as a military imposition. Members, therefore, were forbidden to comply, and where they yielded, led either by a genuine wish to help or by a desire for gain, the discipline was rigorously enforced. Here is what the Committee on Sufferings of New Garden Monthly Meeting had to report for January 1777 of the reactions of their members in this situation:

> When military officers were going about collecting blankets for the use of soldiers, a number of Friends not being free to contribute to the support of war, had blankets taken from them for which they could not be free to receive any pay; others for want of due consideration received money themselves, or suffered some of their children or family to receive it; and some who received pay, and others who in their absence money was left at their houses, afterwards returned or sent the money to them that sent it.[83]

In similar fashion, Friends in New York City, then under British control, politely refused Governor Tryon's request made in 1777 to furnish money for the purchase of stockings for the army, explaining "that the proposed contribution is manifestly contrary to our religious testimony against war and fightings."[84] Later they were to refuse the rent, which the British authorities repeatedly attempted to make them accept, for the use of Quaker meetinghouses in the area that had been requisitioned for army use. In one instance, where the city meeting

---

[83] New Garden M. M. Committee on Sufferings, Minutes, p. 2. In the neighboring Kennett meeting we find the following rather complicated acknowledgment of error being accepted from a member in mid-1779: "To Kennet Monthly Meeting. Friends, I am free to acknowledge that when two armed men came to my house and demanded a blanket of me, that I ordered one to be handed to them, which they left pay for and I made use of it, but have had just cause to reflect on my misconduct therein; and some time afterwards complied to go with my team to draw fifty bushels of wheat to the mill, which they demanded of me; also consented for another person to take an order that was given for a horse that was pressed from me to answer a demand of substitute fine they had against him; altho' I forbad that any part of said order should go towards paying the demand they had against me, which he informed them, nevertheless when they received the order took it for satisfaction for both demands: which misconduct I have often to reflect on and acknowledge under others to my shame; with desires that I may be preserved from giving way when trials come. James Bennett" (quoted by Cope, p. 21).

[84] Rufus M. Jones, *The Quakers in the American Colonies*, p. 260.

had accepted some money on this account, the Meeting for Sufferings insisted on its refund; the army refused to take it, but eventually it was handed into the British Exchequer in London by the mediacy of an English Friend. The receipt he received ran as follows: "Paid by the Society of the People called Quakers of New York in America, by the hands of Daniel Mildred, being the money they had received for rent of their meeting house, which had been appropriated for the use of the army, as such they could not retain it consistently with their religious testimony against war."[85]

The same scrupulous care in avoiding the least contamination with military affairs as was shown in the case of those Friends who returned the money for their requisitioned blankets emerges, too, in the conduct of a young Quaker, Joseph Townsend, whose home was situated near the site of the battle of Brandywine. It was the British troops in this instance who tried to compel his collaboration as they marched past his house. His own account of the affair has been printed by Isaac Sharpless:

I arrived at the bars on the road [Townsend later related] where I was met by several companies of soldiers who were ordered into the field to form and prepare for the approaching engagement. The openings of the bars not being of sufficient width to admit them to pass with that expedition which the emergency of the case required, a German officer on horseback ordered the fence to be taken down, and as I was near to the spot had to be subject to his requiring as he flourished a drawn sword over my head with others who stood by. On a removal of the second rail I was forcibly struck with the impropriety of being active in assisting to take the lives of my fel-

---

[85] Mekeel, "The Quakers," pp. 204-7. When at the end of 1776 American forces took over Middletown meetinghouse for use as "an hospital for their sick," Friends protested vigorously that "it was not consistent with their minds nor their principles that their meetinghouse should be put to the use of the soldiery" (*Pennsylvania Genealogical Magazine*, XXIV, no. 4, 299). For a contemporary account of the efforts of New York Quakers—whose meetings were divided between the areas under American and British control, with contacts between Friends thus seriously impeded—to preserve a strict neutrality, see Mekeel (ed.), "New York Quakers in the American Revolution," BFHA, vol. 29, no. 1 (1940). According to one Long Island Friend, Elias Hicks (1748-1830), who later became famous as the leading figure in the Quaker separation of 1827, neutrality was possible because, Quakers being "friends to . . . all mankind, and principled against wars and fighting, the contending powers had such confidence in [them] that they let [them] pass freely on religious accounts" (quoted in Bliss Forbush, *Elias Hicks*, p. 46). For the distraints levied on Hicks by the British authorities in lieu of fines for his refusal to muster at an alarm or to contribute to the upkeep of the fortifications, see pp. 38, 44.

low beings and therefore desisted in proceeding any further in obedience to his commands.[86]

A more serious question than the removal of a fence to let the military pass (although the Roman pinch of incense had been a small matter, too, in its time) was the problem of the town watch in a period of war, which bothered several Quaker communities at one time or another during the conflict. In 1775 Friends in Lynn and Salem in Massachusetts had been troubled with the implications of their continued participation in watching in the troublous times that were then beginning. They referred the matter to the Meeting for Sufferings which New England Quakers had recently established. This body recommended complete abstention from the duty, which they held to be "inconsistent with our religious principles, being mixed with, if not wholly for military purposes, and we conceive will have a tendency to leaven you into the prevailing spirit thereof." Those who continued to serve should be dealt with and, if they did not show themselves amenable to tender persuasion, must finally be disowned, so "that the cause of truth and its followers do not suffer." It seems that the authorities (whose attitude in New England during the Revolutionary War was singularly mild if compared to that of their predecessors a hundred years earlier) accepted the Quakers' explanations and henceforward did not call upon them to do duty.[87]

The problem does not appear to have arisen again for Friends until near the end of the war. Then, in the spring of 1782, the British administration in New York demanded that Quakers—who had been exempted from military duties by a proclamation of the British commandant of the city of January 1780 on the proviso, however, that they would be expected nevertheless "to exert themselves in any cases of emergency"—should now take over complete responsibility for the city watch. In a letter to the British commandant, Friends, who in this case, too, were evidently willing to take their turn in the watch along with their fellow citizens, endeavored to explain the grounds of their present refusal of what they believed was a sincere effort on the part of the military to give recognition to their scruples against fighting. In the first place, they told the general, their compliance in the present circumstances, "when military works and labour are carried on by the rest of our fellow citizens who at other times share with us in common the business of the watch," would be equivalent to "a composition in lieu of military service," which was contrary to their

<hr/>

[86] Sharpless, A Quaker Experiment, II, 189.
[87] Mekeel, "New England Quakers and Military Service," p. 245.

principles: for at this time Quakers, as we know, rejected the acceptance of any alternative to a service they believed was essentially unchristian. The letter went on, secondly, to urge the incongruity of entrusting a public service of this kind to a group of men who not only were too few in numbers for the purpose but were by virtue of their whole attitude unsuited for the task. As they said:

> Our peaceable principles . . . render the business of a watch kept altogether by ourselves, attended with inconveniences, and perhaps so many that its end might be frustrated. Riotous and ill-disposed people would be under small restraint from persons who cannot submit even to bodily defense, and who would therefore more likely meet with injustice and abuse themselves than be able to control boisterous and unruly men.[88]

It is clear from this letter that these New York Friends had not thought through clearly the relationship of their pacifism to civil government, the kind of problem that Pennsylvania Friends had had to face during the period of their power.

Alongside activities that Friends prohibited as, in their view, giving direct assistance to the war effort must be placed the business and trade practices that, being a community very largely of merchants and farmers, they felt would compromise the purity of their testimony for peace. "We affectionately desire that Friends may be careful to avoid in engaging in any trade or business tending to promote war," Philadelphia Yearly Meeting testified in 1776, "and particularly against sharing or partaking of the spoils of war, by buying or vending prize goods of any kind."[89] This, like many of the Society's official declarations on war, was old advice; but the war situation gave it renewed relevance. Of course, all connection with privateering or its profits, all arming of Quaker-owned ships, and all participation of Quaker crews in manning armed vessels came under the ban. John Harris, a member of a North Carolina meeting near the coast, for instance, was disowned since, as the record goes, he "contrary to advice and counsel of his Friends made a cruise on board a privateer vessel of war, a practice so inconsistent with our principle and holy peaceable Christian profession that we can do no less than publicly testify against such antichristian practices." A Friend from Pasquotank Monthly Meeting journeying to the West Indies was refused a certificate by his meeting because "the vessel he intended to enter on board of is to carry guns in order to make some defense." At Perquimans one Solomon Elliott "who

---

[88] Cox, *Quakerism in the City of New York*, pp. 77, 79, 80.
[89] *Rules of Discipline* (1797), p. 132.

227

justified himself in consenting to his sons entering on board a privateer was disowned."[90] In the Narragansett district, another coastal area where the sea held snares for the unwary Quaker, we hear of a Friend being disowned because he bought books at an auction that had been taken from a captured ship as war booty.[91] The ultra-scrupulous Warner Mifflin finally came to a resolve to abandon for the duration the use of all imported products (except for salt in food he ate away from home, since it would scarcely have been possible to extract it), as he was later to give up using the products of slave labor. "In a time of national hostility," he wrote, "those sweets I am so fond of come . . . at a manifest risk of the lives of fellow men."[92]

On land as on sea the Quaker community watched over its members to see that, if possible, they did not either by their buying or their selling help contribute one iota to the prosecution of war—a concern that was increased by the element of personal profit frequently implicit in such transactions that served to compound the offense. In Maryland, for instance, we find Hezekiah and Elizabeth Rowles expressing their sorrow before their meeting that "they had not stood clear as they ought in selling some small matters to soldiers, and suffering some of their family to make and wash some of their clothes."[93] Or take this instruction, which Philadelphia Yearly Meeting in 1779 handed down to its subordinate meetings to carry out: "We are desirous and earnestly recommend, that Friends in every quarter be encouraged to attend to their tender scruples against contributing to the promotion of war, by grinding of grain, feeding of cattle, or selling their property for the use of the army, or other such warlike purposes."[94]

[90] Thorne, "North Carolina Friends and the Revolution," pp. 325, 326. In October 1780, Robert Pleasants wrote to a Quaker friend: "Thy son . . . tells me that he is going to sea in an armed vessel, and that he has the full consent of his father and mother for so doing. From a tender regard for his good and the reputation of his worthy parents, I was induced to query with him whether he thought, in case of an attack at sea, he would have resolution to withstand the scoffs and threats of the people on board so as not to give up the privilege of peace in which he had been favored with an education. And also whether he had been plainly explicit with the Captain. For it appears absolutely necessary, if he has an intention of preserving the unity of his friends that the Captain should not be deceived in time of action." (Quoted in Archer, "The Quaker's Attitude towards the Revolution," p. 180.)

[91] Caroline Hazard, *The Narragansett Friends' Meeting in the XVIII Century*, p. 169.

[92] *The Defence of Warner Mifflin*, pp. 19, 20. Mifflin once told his wife: "If every farthing we were possessed of, was seized for the purpose of supporting war, and I was informed it should all go, except I gave voluntarily one shilling . . . I was satisfied I should not so redeem it."

[93] *Bi-Centennial of Brick Meeting-House*, p. 56.

[94] *Rules of Discipline* (1797), pp. 133, 134.

Lastly, although the preceding account has by no means exhausted the list of activities forbidden to Friends as assisting more or less directly in the war, we must now turn briefly to certain other forms of conduct only remotely military, yet also disapproved on account of their implied sanction of the war. More than once American Quakers, like their English brethren, refused to illuminate their windows in celebration of an American victory, often having them smashed by angry crowds as a result;[95] many objected, also, to shutting up their shops on the public fast days or days of public penance proclaimed by the American authorities in connection with the war. In 1775 Philadelphia Yearly Meeting warned its members against seeming to give approval to war by attending military spectacles or watching the marching of troops. In the same year we find Providence (R.I.) Friends refusing the deputy-governor's order to produce their hunting guns for registration in connection with the impending war. All the men in the meeting signed a paper stating that to comply was against their conscience. (In reply the deputy-governor, instead of getting angry, told them that religious conscience was man's natural right—an answer that was in line with Rhode Island's tradition of toleration.)[96] Or again, to give still another instance of this type of Quaker peace witness, in the following year we find New York Friends refusing to give a bond of security to the local authorities that they would prevent their cattle from straying across into the British lines:[97] to do so, in their view, would have implied a certain degree of approval, however distant, to the prosecution of the war.

III

As a basic prerequisite to the whole Quaker wartime strategy that we have outlined, which constituted a withdrawal of collaboration in all aspects of public and private life connected in any way with either the British or American war effort,[98] the Society soon came to

[95] In extenuation of their brethren's behavior in the victory celebrations after Cornwallis's surrender at Yorktown in 1781, Philadelphia Meeting for Sufferings protested to the Pennsylvania assembly that, "as they could not fight with the fighters, neither could they triumph with the conquerors." (Their "Representation" is printed in *Pa. Archives*, 1st ser., IX, 450-54). In Virginia, on the other hand, Friends' refusal to participate in the official celebration on this occasion does not appear to have aroused serious ill-feeling among the populace (perhaps because Friends there did not live in towns, where nonconformity of this kind was more conspicuous). See Mekeel, "The Quakers," pp. 150, 151, 228.

[96] *Journal of Job Scott*, p. 47.

[97] Jones, *The Quakers*, pp. 259, 260.

[98] As a prominent Nantucket Quaker, William Rotch, expressed it during a hearing before the authorities in Boston: "Our principles are active obedience, or

posit a withdrawal starting at the top from all association with government. This was mainly a problem in Pennsylvania where, as we have seen, the Quaker retreat from politics begun in 1756 had only been partial, leaving a number of at least nominal Friends in the assembly (members of the so-called Quaker party) and a still larger proportion of members in good standing holding various lesser offices, especially at the local level. Thus the retreat was by no means a rout, and it is doubtful whether such orthodox Quakers as James Pemberton, who had accepted reelection in 1765 after the conclusion of the Seven Years War, had completely given up hopes of reasserting Quaker ascendancy in the province. Quakers were still to be found in the lesser ranks of officialdom in several other provinces; they also accepted election to the Second Continental Congress in 1774 and to some provincial conventions of that time. Indeed, the mild Benezet was driven to deplore "the violent spirit which some under our profession are apt to show, more particularly in the [Continental] congress."[99] Most of these fiery Quaker patriots, like the radical Assemblyman John Jacobs of Uwchlan Monthly Meeting (Chester County, Pa.) who "endeavoured to justify defensive war" to the committee appointed to labor with him and was finally disowned "for . . . having joined with things in the House of Assembly inconsistent with our testimony against wars and fightings,"[100] were of course weeded out as the disciplinary machinery of the Society went into action. Others, like Evan Thomas (1738-1826) of Baltimore who had participated in the first Maryland convention without feeling that his presence there conflicted with his obligations as a good Quaker, soon withdrew alto-

---

passive suffering" (*Memorandum*, p. 5)—i.e., active obedience to legitimate authority where religious conscience was not infringed and passive endurance of suffering for refusing the orders of illegitimate rulers or commands contrary to conscience.

[99] Brookes, *Benezet*, p. 322. Benezet, however, was an admirer of Quaker rule in Pennsylvania, when, as he wrote, government was "chiefly in the hands of a people principled against war." "They experienced the protecting hand of Providence, and enjoyed an uninterrupted tranquillity for more than sixty years." "The force used in the support of civil order, to regulate the weak and ill disposed" was not equivalent to war, in his view. Government was God-ordained and would always be necessary for the maintenance of order and man's happiness. Where good order was endangered, "restraint becomes necessary as mentioned in scripture." See Benezet, *The Plainness and Innocent Simplicity of the Christian Religion*, 1782 edn., pp. 14ff., 22, 23.

[100] Cope, "Chester County Quakers during the Revolution," p. 25. See Charles Francis Jenkins, "Joseph Hewes, the Quaker Signer" in *Children of Light* (ed. H. H. Brinton), pp. 211-39, for the story of a birthright Friend who was one of the signatories of the Declaration of Independence on behalf of North Carolina. However, Hewes (1730-1779), though never disowned, was by that date a purely nominal member of the Society.

gether from public life—a course of action that was not without sacrifice in the case of men like Thomas who nourished political ambitions.[101]

In the lower magistracy, where Friends had often served without clashes between their civil duty and their Quakerly conscience having been of too frequent occurrence, even before the fighting broke out many Friends had begun to doubt if they could in good conscience continue in service. In 1774, for instance, Warner Mifflin resigned as a justice of the peace, feeling that a post of this kind was too intimately bound up with both armed coercion and the slave system for a good Quaker to hold. "I revere magistracy," he wrote some years later, "confiding in the sacred text, that it is an *Ordinance of God*, and believing it a great benefit to mankind when executed under his holy and preserving fear. But in the present state of governments, I apprehend my brethren cannot be active therein consistent with our high profession . . . in the support of our principle against war, with which the various governments among men have so much affinity." Acting as exemplary citizens in every other respect, Quakers, he believed, would be permitted the enjoyment of their scruples on this point by government and community alike.[102]

The decisive moment came at the yearly meeting in Philadelphia in September 1776 when the assembled Friends declared categorically against continued participation in any kind of public office—legislative, executive, or administrative—which was even remotely connected with the prosecution of the present war. The minute ran as follows:

As we have for some years past been frequently concerned to exhort and advise Friends to withdraw from being active in civil government, it now appearing to us that the power and authority exercised at this time over the several provinces within the compass of our Yearly Meeting are founded and supported in the spirit of wars and fightings: We find it necessary to give our sense and judgment that if any making profession with us, do accept of or continue in public offices of any kind either of profit or trust under the present commotions, and unsettled state of public affairs, such are acting therein contrary to the profession and principles we have ever maintained since we were a religious Society: And we therefore think it necessary to advise, exhort, and caution our brethren in profession against being concerned in electing any person, or being them-

[101] *Friends' Miscellany*, II, no. 8 (July 1832), 360-62.
[102] *The Defence of Warner Mifflin*, pp. 7, 8.

selves elected to such places and stations . . . which is . . . recommended to the several quarterly and monthly meetings, and the members of our religious Society in general, in order for the promotion of our Christian peaceable testimony, by a life and conduct conformable thereto.[103]

This statement did not, indeed, mark a reversal of the positive attitude toward government taken up by Friends on both continents since the Society's beginnings more than a century before—the belief that somehow the state could be purged of its excessively coercive features, that pacifism and magistracy were not *ipso facto* incompatible. It did not mean that American Friends (for the other yearly meetings on the continent followed Philadelphia's initiative in this question) had gone over to the Anabaptist-Mennonite position, although in the decades to come the views of some influential Friends and of a wide cross section of the rank and file of the Society became almost identical with it. It did signify, however, that—so long, at any rate, as the war was being fought—the Quakerly withdrawal from politics must be complete, and it gave notice that all who refused to accept this situation would be cut off from the Society. Mekeel has calculated that 47 members of the Society were dealt with during the war period for accepting public office, 34 of whom came from Pennsylvania and 9 from New Jersey, the two provinces where Quaker participation in public life was most widespread; the complete figures may have been considerably higher than this.

Undoubtedly, the ban on politics put a strain on the loyalty of many members who still sympathized in general with their Society's pacifism. The ban seems to have had this effect particularly on Friends in rural areas where officeholding, even in wartime, was not so obviously connected with warmaking as it was in the centers of government like Philadelphia and where, too, a more positive attitude toward the American authorities seems to have existed. In rural New York, for instance, toward the end of the war when active fighting in the area had ceased, some Quakers began to take part in town meetings, considering such participation no longer in conflict with the peace testimony. But they met with stern disapproval from the Quaker leadership: "in the present commotions of public affairs," they were told, "Friends being in any ways active in government is inconsistent with our principles." Abstention from politics had to be absolute if the testimony "against wars and fightings" was to be "maintained and supported inviolate." In Pennsylvania we hear of Quakers during the war

---

[103] Philadelphia Y. M. MS Minutes for 1749-1779, pp. 356, 357.

refusing to serve even in the capacity of overseers of the poor and suffering fines and distraint of goods as a result. With the conclusion of war it once again became theoretically possible for a consistent Friend to hold public office. But feeling within the Society still ran strongly against such activity; the yearly and quarterly meetings issued advices underlining the dangers lurking in this region for the unwary and seldom endowed officeholding Friends with positions of trust within the Society.[104]

Friends in the city of Philadelphia had been the mainspring of the great movement of withdrawal from political life that took place in 1775-1776. The city was the scene, too, of the establishment of a small independent group of dissident Quakers, known as the Free Quakers, who supported the armed effort of the American revolutionaries. "The differences" between them and their orthodox brethren, their historian has claimed, "were not of faith, but of practice."[105] This assertion is true—if one does not count Quaker pacifism as an element of the Society's faith. The Free Quakers claimed complete toleration for all sincerely held religious opinion as their central tenet and the main body's abandonment of what they considered a basic component of primitive Quakerism as their chief reason for separation. But, in fact, the ranks of the new Society were filled exclusively by those who had abandoned the old Society's traditional pacifism: none who held to the latter felt sufficient attraction in the new body's liberty to take the step of joining it. In addition, only a small percentage of those who were disowned within the confines of Philadelphia Yearly Meeting for support of the war adhered thereafter to the Free Quakers.[106]

The *spiritus movens* behind the creation of the new group was Samuel Wetherill, Jr. (1736-1816), a minister of the Society and a prosperous cloth manufacturer by trade. From the outset of the struggle Wetherill, like the rest who eventually became Free Quakers, was heart and soul behind the struggle against Britain and was strongly set against the neutrality, if not mild loyalism, that marked most of his fellow Philadelphia Quakers. In particular, he opposed the policy of disowning Friends who gave active support to the colonial cause by entering military service or accepting public office or giving assistance of one kind or another to it. "Disowning is wrong in any case," he wrote, "but to disown a man for defending his life, or the life of his

[104] Mekeel, "The Quakers," pp. 204, 286-88; James, *A People among Peoples*, p. 244.

[105] C. Wetherill, *History of the Free Quakers*, p. 22. The author was a descendant of one of the founders of the group, Samuel Wetherill, Jr.

[106] Mekeel, "The Quakers," p. 271.

friend, or the government under which he lives, are extraordinary cases . . . the criterion of fellowship is made to consist, . . . in so acting, as not one man in an hundred thousand could act, were he brought to the test." And he made plain his belief that pacifism was a perfectionism such that only very, very few, even within the Quaker ranks, could meet its requirements. He pointed out the inconsistency between Quaker support of government, albeit now only passive, and their pacifist scruples. "The government cannot exist without defence, the sword being its sinews. Government in its essence is a defensive war; a defensive war of that kind is not sinful."[107] And for Wetherill and his associates, government meant the regimes set up by the Continental authorities in the various provinces.

Wetherill's disownment did not actually take place until August 1779 when he was dealt with for, among other charges of a similar nature, having taken the test in the previous year. Among those who labored—unsuccessfully—to keep such a valued member within the Society was Anthony Benezet, whose earnest devotion to the peace testimony did not preclude a recognition of the inadvisability of coercing those members who could not genuinely accept it for themselves. But Wetherill would evidently have been satisfied with nothing less than a complete abandonment of any official stand in the matter on the part of the Society. "I have repeatedly begged he would consider," wrote Benezet with a hint of exasperation, "that however he might think hardly of England's design with respect to us, in which he however might in part be mistaken; yet we, as a people, ought not to have taken any other part but mildly and tenderly to have exhorted people to follow after peace."[108]

In the fall of 1780 the first meetings of the emergent group began to be held in the homes of Wetherill himself and of Timothy Matlack (ca. 1735-1829), political radical, Revolutionary army colonel, and a member of the Pennsylvania Committee of Public Safety. The Religious Society of Friends "by some styled" the Free Quakers was formally set up in February 1781. Membership was confined almost entirely to the Philadelphia area, although tiny groups also emerged in Chester County (Pa.) and at West River (Maryland), and contact was of course maintained with the dissident Quakers of New England. After an unsuccessful attempt had been made to persuade the Pennsylvania legislature to give them the use of an existing Quaker

---

[107] Samuel Wetherill, *An Apology for the Religious Society, called Free Quakers, in the City of Philadelphia*, pp. 32-34. Although this pamphlet was published toward the end of the eighteenth century, Wetherill's views here substantially coincided with those he had expressed earlier.

[108] Brookes, *Benezet*, pp. 334, 335.

meetinghouse for their worship (the orthodox Society having replied to accusations of disloyalty made by the dissidents by pointing out that they had every right to remove the latter for violating the traditional rules of their body), the Free Quakers proceeded to build their own meetinghouse by public subscription, a brick building that still stands in Philadelphia today at the corner of Fifth Street and Arch Street, "erected," says a plaque on one of its walls, "in the year of our Lord, 1783, of the Empire 8."[109]

Among leading members of the Free Quakers, alongside Wetherill and Matlack, we may mention the names of Colonel Clement Biddle, quartermaster-general in Washington's army, William Crispin who acted as one of its commissaries, Christopher Marshall, a prominent member of the Pennsylvania Committee of Public Safety, Peter Thomson who helped to print the Continental paper money, and "Betsy" Ross who allegedly made the first American flag with its familiar stars and stripes. Some of the Free Quakers had not been expelled from the Society recently for their disagreement with its wartime stand but, like Christopher Marshall or Timothy Matlack who had been disowned as far back as 1751 and 1765, respectively, for what their meetings regarded as un-Quakerly business practices, had been forced to leave it in the prewar period. The group also attracted a few adherents, who had been hitherto unconnected with the Quakers. However, it remained a small group, never reaching more than about a hundred members, and in the early years of the next century it began to dwindle rapidly as the old members died off and new accessions became infrequent, until meetings for worship were finally discontinued in the mid-1830's. Descendants of the original members (many of them ultra-patriots) continued to maintain a formal organization, mainly for the purposes of property ownership, until this century. Thus ended the only schism within Quakerism that centered directly on the issue of its peace testimony.

The Free Quakers had modeled their discipline on that of the orthodox body in matters of worship and business, with the single difference that all mention of disownment for deviations in doctrine and practice was omitted. "No public censures shall be passed by us on any," they stated in the seventh article of their discipline. "Neither shall a member be deprived of his right among us, on account of his differing in sentiment from any or all of his brethren." However, al-

---

[109] Asked to explain the meaning of the somewhat cryptic phrase "Of the Empire," one of the Free Quakers answered: "I tell thee, Friend, it is because our country is destined to be the great empire over all the world" (quoted in Wetherill, *History of the Free Quakers*, p. 39).

though they claimed, not altogether without foundation, to be waging defensive war against "ecclesiastical tyranny" in the Quaker hierarchy because the Quaker nabobs would not "permit . . . that Christian liberty of sentiment and conduct which all are entitled to enjoy,"[110] rather than attempting to introduce innovations that were rejected by the vast majority in the Society, yet their separation was primarily a protest against the failure of Quakers as a body to come out squarely on the side of "the present great revolution."[111] In essence, not the virtues of religious tolerance and broadmindedness, but what they considered the sins of neutrality and passivity were the root causes of the schism.

The Free Quakers at the beginning had issued a goodly number of short pieces—addresses, testimonies, and declarations—setting forth their differences with orthodox Friends and pressing their legal rights against them. But although they included several members, like Wetherill himself, who were able at wielding the pen, they produced at this time no lengthy apology for their separation. In fact, the most considered statement of what may be called the Free Quaker position came from one who was never formally to become a member of the group. Its author, who tried to mask his unorthodoxy by anonymity, was Isaac Grey of New Garden Monthly Meeting; the publication without the official sanction of the Society of this defense of the Revolution and Quaker participation in it earned him speedy disownment. The pamphlet, a production which his meeting branded as likely "to spread discord and disunity in the Society"[112] and whose very title appeared as a challenge to official Quakerdom—*A Serious Address to Such of the People called Quakers, on the Continent of North-America, as profess Scruples relative to the Present Government: exhibiting the Ancient Real Testimony of that People, concerning Obedience to Civil Authority*—came out in 1778. The first edition was bought up by the yearly meeting in an effort to suppress its contents, but Grey and several friends (among whom, apparently, was Samuel Wetherill) succeeded in bringing out a second printing within a short time.[113]

Grey did not attempt directly to attack the Quaker peace testimony

[110] The spirit of Free Quakerism at its boldest and best was exemplified by young Thomas Ross, Jr., of Wrightstown M. M. in Pennsylvania. After the clerk had stood up in meeting and read a testimony of disownment against him for his part in military affairs, Ross got up and delivered his own statement claiming that Friends themselves had deviated from their traditional sense of liberty. "They are become," he told the meeting, "extremely partial, inconsistent, and hypocritical," and he had no desire to continue in membership.

[111] Wetherill, *History*, pp. 13, 27, 32, 47, 48.

[112] Cope, "Chester County Quakers during the Revolution," p. 23. Grey's disownment was also attributable to his having taken the test.

[113] Joseph Smith, *A Descriptive Catalogue of Friends' Books*, I, 71.

(although he leaves a distinct impression that he himself did not share it); he confines himself mainly to the task of persuading his fellow Friends that the Revolutionary government was the lawful one, to whom taxes of all kinds ("except those in lieu of personal service") and allegiance must be rendered willingly and in the fear of God, and that defensive war on the part of the magistracy was a duty, the refusal of which would be defiance of God's will. "If any man be appointed by God to defend my life," he asks, "is it possible that God can authorize me to call him a sinner for doing his duty; or is it possible that I can consistent with my duty, refuse him that tribute which is absolutely necessary to enable him thus to defend me?" Grey, like Timothy Davis of New England whom he quotes copiously, makes great play with the writings of early Friends like George Fox, Edward Burrough, Isaac Penington, Francis Howgill, William Penn, etc., which give a prominent place within God's order to the sword-wielding magistrate and stress the need for strict subordination to the latter. And, above all, Grey emphasizes that early Friends did not attach special importance "to any particular form of government merely as such": they had declared their loyalty first to the antimonarchical regime of Oliver Cromwell and then to the shifting changes in monarchical government which followed the Restoration. "It appears to me," he argues cogently, "that it is for those who choose not to have any hand in the formation of governments, to take governments as they find them, and comply with their laws, so far as they are clear of infringing rights and matters of faith toward God." Like the Free Quakers, Grey calls for tolerance of various standpoints within the Society on a level of equality, pro-war sentiments alongside pacifist scruples, and brotherly regard for the freedom of conscience of all.[114] Such views, however, could scarcely find acceptance within the carefully guarded seclusion of contemporary American Quakerism.

If by some chance the policy urged on the Society by the Free Quakers had been accepted by Friends, adherence to the peace testimony would have been reduced to a merely vocational pacifism, a transformation that has, indeed, almost been accomplished in our own day. As it was, the conscientious objector, nonconformist in regard to the community at large, was still the conformist in relation to his own Society.

IV

In the Revolutionary War the tax and the test objector were as prominent a feature of the Society of Friends as the straight conscien-

[114] Isaac Grey, *A Serious Address*, pp. 1-9, 12-15, 18, 21, 22.

tious objector to military service. But the wartime draft embraced a fair proportion of the younger men. Although, as we have seen, most consistent Friends of military age suffered fines and distraint for their refusal of service, as they had done before the war, a few among them nevertheless found themselves in jail or under arrest for a period of time.

Neither in the former Quaker commonwealth of Pennsylvania nor in any other place where we find a number of young Friends being put in prison for refusing service in the militia are any reliable statistics available, so that it is impossible to say even approximately how many persons suffered this penalty. Nor is it always possible in reported instances of imprisonment to tell whether the prisoner was a tax objector, test objector, or military service objector. Sometimes the offense was compounded of more than one form of protest. Since fine and distraint for nonpayment was the usual method of penalizing militia objectors, many of those who were put in prison were presumably propertyless men, whose goods did not suffice for repeated distraints. But undoubtedly in some cases the propertied also suffered, sometimes through local officers' ignorance of the law or through their animosity against a group that they considered unpatriotic or even sympathetic toward the enemy. In times of emergency, when the need to mobilize all available manpower overpowered all other considerations, Quakers' claims to exemption were liable to be overlooked along with the rights of their nonpacifist fellow citizens. Occasionally the imprisoned man may have only attended Quaker meetings but not been a full member of the Society and was therefore not literally entitled to the degree of exemption granted by the law.

The journal of John Pemberton, the unpolitical brother of Israel and James Pemberton, makes mention not infrequently of young Friends in prison as conscientious objectors from 1776 on. In December of that year, for instance, when a British attack on the city was expected and the Continental authorities were desperate for men to stem the enemy advance, two men from a Philadelphia meeting were jailed "for refusing to bear arms or work at the entrenchments near the city." They were released after Friends had intervened with General Israel Putnam. Again, to cite another instance in April 1778, when Pennsylvania was still the scene of battle, Pemberton noted in his journal: "At York, Henry Drinker and myself visited a young man [presumably a Friend] who was confined in jail for his religious testimony against war; we found him in a tender disposition."[115] In most cases the

[115] *Friends' Miscellany*, VIII, no. 2 (Jan. 1836), 61, 82. See *Exiles in Virginia*, pp. 296-99, for other examples of imprisonment of Pennsylvania and New Jersey

Quaker was released after several months in jail, if not before. In late 1779, however, two Friends were imprisoned in Lancaster jail, and, despite the efforts of the Meeting for Sufferings to gain their release, they were kept there for a period of over two years.[116]

One of the most detailed and graphic accounts from this period of the experiences of a Quaker conscientious objector in prison may be found in the manuscript minutes of New Garden Monthly Meeting. The report runs as follows:

Some account of the suffering of Stephen Howel, a young man belonging to New Garden Monthly Meeting. He was taken on the 17th of the 4th month 1778 by several armed men who were by order of Andrew Boyd called Sublieutenant collecting fines said to be to hire substitutes to serve two months in the militia in the room of such as refused to go themselves or send others. On which account they demanded fifty two pounds ten shillings of Stephen (tho' he had not been called upon to go nor had any account of such demand before) which he refusing to pay they had him before said Boyd and he ordered him under guard to a magistrate and being taken to Lancaster he was had before several under that character one after another who used many persuasions for him to pay the demand and not go to prison which he steadily refusing (as being inconsistent with his religious principles) was at last took [sic] to the house of the under-burgess and kept at the door by one of the guards while the other went in and procured the following order Viz "To the Gaoler for the County of Lancaster. This is to command you in the name of the Commonwealth of Pennsylvania to receive the body of Stephen Howel into your custody and him safely keep until you receive further orders. Given under my hand and seal this 19th day of April 1778. Henry Dehuff." (Seal) And being conducted there when he entered the prison he felt such sweetness of mind as encouraged him to persevere on in suffering for the testimony of a good conscience. He was kept close prisoner upwards

---

Friends taken from the year 1777. See also *Friends' Miscellany*, vol. I, no. 3 (June 1831), where an account (by John Hunt of Moorestown) is given of the trials of New Jersey Quakers during the last quarter of 1776. Not only did they have to face heavy requisitioning by the Continental troops, but, "about the middle of 12th month, there was great talk of pressing men to go to war, and very great fear fell on our young men in general; many strove to keep themselves hid for fear of being forced to go to war, for the [American] army now began to approach so near as Burlington and there away. It was said that many of our young men fled to barrens and cedar swamps at this time." In such circumstances those who refused to hide were sometimes caught up by the military.

[116] Mekeel, "The Quakers," p. 149.

of three months and favoured to bear his confinement with a good degree of patience and resignation. Several Friends being then on a visit to men in office found the said Dehuff under some exercise of mind for his conduct in this case and being treated with he readily ordered Stephen's release without any demand for fees or otherwise.[117]

Here we see on one hand the almost radiant joy of young Howel himself at being called to suffer "for the testimony of a good conscience," an attitude not too frequently found in sober eighteenth-century Quakerism and more reminiscent, indeed, of the ecstatic utterances of a seventeenth-century Friend like William Dewsbury, and on the other hand the sympathetic stance of the Lancaster County magistrate Dehuff, reluctant to hold a man in prison on account of religious scruples with which almost every educated Pennsylvanian was well acquainted from childhood.

The only cases recorded of severe ill-treatment of Quaker conscientious objectors come from the Southern states. We hear of a North Carolina Friend living in an isolated area "being drafted" in 1779 "to stand guard over part of Burgoyne's army, prisoners in Virginia" and, for his refusal to comply, being sentenced by a court-martial "composed of young officers" to forty lashes, "which [were] executed in the presence of some hundred spectators. Forty stripes were very heavily laid on, by three different persons, with a whip having nine cords; but the Friend, though much torn, was supported; and persuasions and threats were afterwards offered in vain, to prevail on him to yield to service." He refused to accept any kind of noncombatant duty, such as working as a medical orderly with the troops. After a little while, however, some of the officers became more sympathetic: "one captain, it was said, laid down his commission, declaring that if innocent conscientious men were thus treated, he would not serve any longer." The objector, however, was only released on the expiry of his draft period.[118]

In the summer of the previous year a milder instance of ill-treatment had occurred in regard to fourteen young men belonging to Hopewell Monthly Meeting in Frederick County (Va.). The cause of their summary drafting for active service in the Continental army lay in the

---

[117] New Garden M. M. Committee on Sufferings, Minutes, pp. 6-8.

[118] *The Life and Travels of John Pemberton*, pp. 97, 98; *A Journal of the Life of William Savery*, p. 6. There are small discrepancies in the two accounts, but both Pemberton and Savery visited the South in the ministry soon afterward, and it was then that they learned the story from local Friends. The conscripted Quaker may possibly have been from Virginia instead of North Carolina.

American reverses farther north, where the British army had recently occupied Philadelphia and a considerable part of Pennsylvania. The men were therefore marched northward, while unsuccessful efforts were made by the officers to force them to carry muskets. On one occasion "with drawn swords" they "pushed the Friends into rank threatening they would have their blood if they did not comply." Several had the muskets tied on their backs and were forced to march along in this way. The men also refused to draw army rations, considering that acceptance would compromise their resistance to military orders. Finally, after about half of them had been allowed to go back home on account of their poor physical condition, the remainder were brought, along with other draftees from Virginia, to Washington's encampment outside Philadelphia. Here Colonel Clement Biddle, the quartermaster-general, who was well acquainted with Quaker peace principles since he had himself been disowned by the Society in the previous year for his warlike activities, intervened with Washington to have the men released. The commander-in-chief, who, as we know, had already during a previous war come into contact with the Quaker conscientious objectors of his homeland, readily complied. As a result, "they were, by his order, discharged, and liberty given them to return home."[119]

In New York, Friends, although they suffered hardship in other ways, were not subjected to duress on account of their refusal of military service to the same extent as their brethren in other areas. We do hear of some young Quakers from Purchase Monthly Meeting on the left bank of the Hudson being put in prison in 1779 for this reason, but they were soon released. Many New York Friends lived in areas under British control, and the British military authorities did not impose conscription on Friends. (Indeed, some loyalist journals readily seized on instances of Quakers being imprisoned by the Continental regime for their refusal to fight as examples of military tyranny exercised on innocent victims.[120])

It was New England, and Massachusetts in particular, that seems to have provided the greatest number of cases of imprisonment of military service objectors, at least in proportion to the total number of Friends in the area. On the other hand, treatment under duress was not harsh on the whole, and imprisonment resulted from certain special circumstances and not from the settled policy of either central or local

[119] Mekeel, "The Quakers," p. 224; *Exiles in Virginia*, p. 181; Paul F. Boller, Jr., "George Washington and the Quakers," *BFHA*, vol. 49, no. 2 (1960), p. 73. More instances of Friends being drafted into the armed forces during this crisis period were reported from other Virginia monthly meetings.
[120] Mekeel, "The Quakers," pp. 161, 162.

officials. Mekeel, indeed, speaks rightly of "the sincere attempt made [by the Rhode Island and Massachusetts governments] to spare the Quakers and others with conscientious objections from suffering for their testimony against war." "The Quakers might have fared much worse," he adds. The two governments were careful to avoid impinging on religious conscience in this question wherever possible, only departing from this policy for a more rigorous one either where the demand for manpower became extremely acute or in communities with a large proportion of Quakers where the draft quota could not easily be filled. Referring to Massachusetts' wartime policy toward Friends, Mekeel comments: "In its consideration for the conscientious scruples of the Quakers against bearing arms the Puritan Commonwealth went far toward redeeming itself for the treatment accorded them a century before."

In Rhode Island a few Quakers suffered brief periods of imprisonment (as well as the more frequent distraints) during the early months of the Revolution for refusing the alternative service which was allowed objectors by law but which was unacceptable to the Quaker conscience. The stringent militia law of April 1777, which withdrew the recent very generous exemption, led to the jailing of at least one young Quaker, David Anthony of Greenwich Monthly Meeting. This caused New England Meeting for Sufferings to take the matter up with the general assembly, and Anthony was released after spending only nine weeks in prison. Although the law was not then repealed, as Friends had hoped, the situation became easier for them, especially after the British evacuation of Newport in 1779 removed the immediate threat to the province's security.

The Quaker community in Massachusetts, despite the generally well-disposed attitude of the government toward Friends, encountered greater difficulty in regard to military service requirements than did their Rhode Island brethren. When a selective service draft was established in September 1776 with a penalty of up to two months imprisonment for not paying the fine imposed for failure to muster or hire a substitute, three young Quakers from Worcester County soon found themselves behind bars. With the help of their elders they drew up a petition to the general court suitably larded with scriptural passages, in which they stated "that they profess themselves Friends and cannot in conscience take up arms on either side in the unnatural war subsisting between Great Britain and the American colonies or in any other wars whatever because they think it is contrary to the precepts of Christ as set forth in many places in the New Testament and in no ways lawful to such as will be the disciples of Christ." Their release and a blanket exemption for all who had been members of the Society prior to the war followed soon afterward. For several years the situation eased for Friends. But they were not altogether immune from the attentions of overofficious local authorities, for in January of the following year we hear that three more Worcester County Quakers were in jail for refusing the draft. They complained to the general court of their incarceration in "a crowded loathsome gaol in Worcester among prisoners of war and our health endangered by filth and vermin."

There were two classes of Quaker conscripts, however, who did not qualify for exemption under the recent law: those who joined the Society after 19 April 1775, the date set in the act, and those men who attended Quaker meetings but had not become full-fledged members. Cases of arrest and imprisonment of new Quakers and near-Quakers continued to occur, especially when, as in the summer of 1777, a general shortage of available troops made the need for fresh draftees urgent. Thus, in August 1777, four young men from East Hoosack in the northwest corner of Massachusetts (the meeting there was actually attached to Saratoga Monthly Meeting and thus formed part of New York Yearly Meeting) found themselves in prison for not answering the draft. With the support of their meeting they petitioned the general court, asking that the court "not for the bare want of certificates to leave us to suffer, although we do really believe the principles of truth as professed by our Friends." They were lucky in also being able to enlist the support of their local committee of safety, which backed their request for release on the grounds that it was a waste of time to try to force such men to serve and that in prison, too, they would be useless to the community. The committee confirmed the existence of "divers . . . persons within our township under the denomination of Friends (but not members of their Society) who profess with them, that it is against their consciences to take up arms either offensive or defensive." In all such cases the general court, upon receiving an appeal, ordered the release of the imprisoned men.

But in mid-1780, with the rising demand for new recruits, the existing Quaker exemption was withdrawn altogether. Now not only the fringe members of the Quaker community were threatened, in the words of the new act, with "all the penalties of the laws for desertion," but all who professed their peace principles. Almost at once arrests began: seventeen members of Dartmouth Monthly Meeting were taken, as well as some from the Quaker communities on Cape Cod. The New England Meeting for Sufferings was obliged to take the matter up with the Massachusetts executive council then in session, handing them a "Remonstrance" which asked "for redress in this interesting

243

matter from the lenient disposition of the Council." Quakers expressed their trust that the authorities in fact did not intend to treat Quaker objectors on a par with deserters or to oppress religious conscience. Once again we find local officials intervening on behalf of the Quaker conscripts. In this case the officer commanding the militia in Sandwich, obviously a local man who knew his neighbors well, sent a supporting letter along with the appeal of his Quaker draftees. In his letter he stated his conviction that these men could not be

> . . . marched unless by force, and if forced to camp I do not suppose they would be active in a single particular; nor do I think it would be practicable here to get any body to have any hand in dragging them off against their consciences. It was with reluctance the officers drafted them, but the resolve makes them as liable as others, and the towns here are called upon for men . . . in proportion to their polls, Quakers included, which makes such uneasiness among said poor distressed inhabitants this way that to draft of the non-Quakers much more than their proportion would be drawing the cords so as to break . . . the Quakers drafted are less than their proportion according to numbers.

The arrested men were all soon released, but the position of Friends remained anomalous. The root of the trouble lay in the dilemma touched on in the Sandwich militia commander's letter quoted above: while Quakers stubbornly refused to serve and their neighbors were loath to attempt the distasteful and probably fruitless task of coercing them to become soldiers, the statutory quota of militiamen remained and the gaps caused by Quakers' martial delinquency had to be filled by the township, if the law was not to be flouted. So we find the officer in charge of the Bristol County militia, where Friends were fairly numerous, grumbling to the authorities in Boston of his difficulties in getting together enough men in places where "more than half the number of the male inhabitants . . . had rather submit to be trampled on like the meanest reptile than by a vigorous exertion to defend himself." "Therefore," he concluded, "I desire the General Court will condescend to separate this burdensome class of men from the militia, in such a manner as their wisdom shall direct." And on Cape Cod the officer in charge of the militia of Barnstable County (another Quaker stronghold) bewailed: "The hardships of getting men among Quakers is inconceivable and what makes great uneasiness I cannot say unjustly." Several counties sent in requests to the executive council to excuse them from not filling the draft quota assigned them on account of the high proportion of Quakers among their inhabitants. As a result, to quote Mekeel's apt comment, "the very size of a large Quaker community was a strong reason for the difficulties of its members." However, the adoption of a new constitution for the commonwealth of Massachusetts in the same year, 1780, with a clause exempting Quakers from the duty of serving in the militia, resolved the difficulties and dilemmas of both Quakers and their military neighbors.[121]

For the first time almost during the wars of the seventeenth and eighteenth centuries, very few Quakers during the Revolution were subjected to the possibility of Indian attack. The only area settled by Friends in any numbers where this danger existed was Saratoga County in upper New York, which had only recently been opened to colonization. Here in 1777 the approach of the British army under Burgoyne, says a contemporary Quaker account,

. . . was preceded by very alarming reports of the scalping and devastation committed indiscriminately by the Indians, yet Friends were generally preserved quietly to await on their own habitations the trials that approached them, and not to neglect the assembling themselves for public worship, altho' to outward appearance the hazard was great from scouting parties from both sides, and at one of these times near the conclusion of the meeting, came a party of Indians with two Frenchmen [i.e., French Canadians], and surrounded the house. One of the Indians after looking in, withdrew and beckoned his hand, upon which a Friend went out, and was asked by signs whether there were soldiers there, the Indians upon being answered in the negative, shook hands with him, and the rest came into the house, they were marked, painted and equipt for war. And it being about the conclusion of the meeting, they shook hands with Friends and one Friend having [a knowledge of] the French tongue could confer with them, by the assistance of the two Frenchmen. When they understood Friends were at a religious meeting, they went to one of their houses, got some victuals, of which a prisoner with them partook, and they quietly departed.[122]

[121] Mekeel, "New England Quakers and Military Service," pp. 246, 248, 256, 257, 274, 275. The small community of Quakers in New Hampshire does not appear to have had any serious troubles connected with military service during the Revolution. The experiences of a Quaker attender in Maine, Moses Sleeper, who was arrested for refusing to join the militia, imprisoned in a fort, court-martialed and sentenced "to receive forty-five lashes on the naked back," are printed in the Philadelphia *Friend*, LII, no. 37 (1879), 272, 273. The sentence, however, was never carried out, and Sleeper soon afterward gained his release. Given the chance to escape, Sleeper had refused, explaining that, if he had accepted this offer, he would have acted contrary to Quaker principles; "though I am not a member of the Society of Friends," he stated, "yet I am one with them in profession, and by my acquaintance am considered as one of their number."

[122] Mekeel, "New York Quakers in the American Revolution," pp. 54, 55.

Another contemporary account of what is certainly the same incident[123] is given in the journal of a Quaker minister, who was then farming in the district, where there were about a dozen Quaker families living. He reports that, as the rival armies approached, "the skulking Indians seemed to strike the greatest dread, the more so because we could not converse with them: but they did not do so much damage by far, as to plundering, as our own people did." He tells of how a party of Indians arrived at their meeting "just as it was breaking up." "Their warlike appearance was very shocking, being equipped with their guns, tomahawks and scalping knives: they had a prisoner and one green scalp taken from a person they had killed but a few hours before: but they went away without doing any violence." General Burgoyne's defeat shortly afterward brought quiet back to the neighborhood again.[124]

Friends, like their non-Quaker neighbors, of course suffered from the plundering, requisitioning, and depredations the two conflicting armies inflicted on the settled population with whom they came into contact. On occasion Quaker pacifism seems to have served to aggravate the situation. We are told, for instance, of Thomas Lamborn, a farming Friend of Chester County (Pa.), that "his plainspoken advocacy of the principles of peace as held by Friends" did not appeal to the British troops when they were in the area. "They took everything available; almost everything that could be carried or driven away, beating the wheat battens against the posts in the barn to get the grain out, then throwing back the balance into the mow, saying 'there, Lamborn may have that.' At another time he was plowing in the field, when some officers of the [British] army detached the horses from the plow and unceremoniously appropriated them to the use of the army."[125]

This was, indeed, the first occasion when a major war was being fought on territory thickly populated by Friends; farmers in particular —and most Quakers during this period were country people—endured the most hardship on this account, exposed as they were to the

123 Mekeel (p. 55) considers that this episode was probably also the foundation of the story related by Violet Hodgkin in her popular *Book of Quaker Saints* (London-Edinburgh, 1917) under the title "Fierce Feathers," pp. 347-55.

124 *A Journal of Rufus Hall*, pp. 17, 18.

125 *Two Hundredth Anniversary of the Establishment of the Friends Meeting at New Garden, Chester County, Pennsylvania, 1715-1915*, pp. 24, 25. In addition, Lamborn suffered fines from the American authorities to the value of almost £760. As a result of his losses (the property taken in distraint having been, as in most cases, probably greatly in excess of the money demanded), Lamborn's farm had to be sold by the sheriff at a low price, only to be bought by a non-Quaker who returned it to him after paying off the debts.

marchings and counter-marchings of the often hungry, ill-disciplined, and ill-clad troops by their farms. New York Friends suffered a special trial in having to cross a kind of "no man's land," which separated the two occupying armies and, also, the several Quaker communities from each other. This zone had to be crossed frequently by groups of Friends wishing to attend monthly, quarterly, or yearly meetings, who thus not only risked interception by the authorities of either army but had to pass "over ground rendered still more perilous by desperate men" who lived by plundering unprotected travelers. In addition, about a hundred families lived in this border zone, refusing to flee as most of their neighbors had done and suffering considerably from the depredations of the gangs and desperadoes who infested the area. "Yet," as a Quaker report on their wartime experiences in New York, written shortly afterward, observed, "watchful providence preserved in these trying seasons, that we don't find the lives of any were suffered to be taken and the Friends thus tried were supported firm in this testimony committed them to bear."[126] The only recorded case of a Quaker meeting death at the hands of either of the armies is apparently the one reported from Rhode Island in the journal of a traveling Quaker minister from Maryland, George Churchman. He tells of a Friend there who was set upon by some looting German mercenaries in British pay who, accusing him—ironically—of being a rebel, "stabbed and killed [him] in his own house, his wife and small children present."[127]

The main hardship endured by Quakers during the Revolutionary War was neither loss of life nor harsh physical treatment nor imprisonment on the scale of the early "heroic" period of Quakerism of the third quarter of the seventeenth century. It consisted rather in the very considerable financial burden laid upon members of the Society

[126] Mekeel, "New York Quakers in the American Revolution," pp. 49, 50, 54, 55.
[127] H. J. Cadbury, "A Quaker Travelling in the Wake of War, 1781," *NEQ*, XXIII, no. 3 (Sept. 1950), 400. The case of the two Pennsylvania Quakers, John Roberts, a miller from Lower Merion, and Abraham Carlisle, a Philadelphia carpenter, who were executed in November 1778 on a charge of high treason for assisting the British military forces, is a special one. Their Meeting for Sufferings, while (quite correctly) considering their sentences unduly harsh and the result of "a party spirit" in the court trying them and while refraining, therefore, from passing the private Quaker sentence of disownment on them (particularly since the two Friends eventually expressed sorrow at their conduct), was at the same time unwilling to intervene officially on behalf of the two men, regarding their behavior (again correctly) to have been inconsistent with Friends' peace principles. See Sharpless, *A Quaker Experiment*, II, 192-97; Mekeel, "The Quakers," pp. 142, 143. It is interesting to note that John Roberts had suffered very severely from the requisitioning and confiscations of American troops: his losses, according to the Radnor M. M. Minutes of Sufferings, amounted on one occasion to as much as £500 worth of property.

by the confiscation of their property resulting primarily from distraints. Although some property losses stemmed from the general requisitioning of the armies mentioned above, a hardship that was shared by a large section of the non-Quaker population of varying political sympathies, the greater part was the outcome of Friends' loyalty to the demands of their peace testimony as they conceived them. As Mekeel has rightly remarked: "The record of disownments and dealings is a story of failure to abide by the religious ideals of the Society and is an indication of weakness. This record, however, is more than counterbalanced by the account of sufferings borne by the Friends in maintaining their principles. This latter story is a convincing testimony to the basic strength of the Society of Friends at that time."[128]

Undoubtedly, the witness was upheld by some Friends more imperfectly than by others. Apart from those members cut off for their obvious unwillingness to accept the peace testimony in part or in its entirety, there were occasionally serious backslidings because of a desire to escape the hardships of the war resister, as in the case of a wartime Quaker of Core Sound Monthly Meeting in North Carolina who, according to the meeting records, "for a small season sheltered himself under our holy profession, but could not stand in it and bear his testimony of the truth when suffering appeared at hand." Although he had, through joining Friends, been "screened from mustering . . . a few years past," he had now, in order to avoid having his goods distrained, consented to act "as commissary in supplying troops with provision."[129]

But we can see the impact that the collective witness for peace, borne consistently and often at considerable sacrifice on the part of the overwhelming majority of members, could make on a young and impressionable mind from the pages of the journal of Henry Hull. The son of a devout Quaker minister, Hull had revolted against the ancestral religion, and at the outbreak of war, although as yet much too young, he had wanted to go off to join the American forces. Later, in his teens, seeing the readiness with which his parents' people suffered the loss of their material possessions in their endeavor to uphold their pacifist witness, he underwent a change of heart.[130] Moreover, something of this respect for the Quaker willingness to suffer for their beliefs seems to have been felt by at least some of the officers entrusted with the task of enforcing the law against Friends; it was shown, too, in the course of the periodic visits Quaker representatives made to

[128] Mekeel, "The Quakers," p. 155.
[129] Thorne, "North Carolina Friends and the Revolution," p. 329.
[130] Memoir of Henry Hull, p. 27.

Continental officials in the government for the purpose of explaining the Society's point of view and of pointing out, in particular, that their own refractory conduct flowed not from partiality toward the British but from deep religious principle.[131]

The list of items seized from Quaker households—in the words of a contemporary Quaker account—"for not complying with the unjust requisition of men to become instrumental in shedding human blood"[132] would cover many pages of print. It would include livestock and farm equipment, furniture and household equipment, clothing, stocks of food and animal fodder; in very many cases the value of the goods taken far exceeded the amount of the fine on account of which the distraint was being made. Complaints were voiced by Friends about "the insolent conduct of collectors and others under them," of their arbitrary assessments and ruthless exactions, which had reduced many Quaker farmers to penury.[133] Friends were warned to "be careful not to balk our testimony against war, in giving way to collectors, either in letting them know what we can best spare, or by manifesting

[131] See, e.g., the following comment on the attitude of local magistrates and officials taken from the records of Western Q. M. (Philadelphia Y. M.) and printed in *A Retrospect of Early Quakerism*, p. 380: "They generally appeared friendly, and to receive our visit kindly, some of them particularly so; and most of them acknowledged that the prophecies concerning the disuse of carnal weapons, pointed to the gospel dispensation, and was much to be desired."

[132] James W. Moore, *Records of the Kingwood Monthly Meeting of Friends, Hunterdon County, New Jersey*, p. 25.

[133] *A Retrospect of Early Quakerism*, pp. 390-92. See also pp. 386-92. A "Memorial" of grievances presented by the Quakers of Chester Co., where the losses of Friends were among the highest, to the president and executive council of Pennsylvania has this to say about the behavior of the distraining officers: "Power has been put into the hands of rapacious and unreasonable men, who have sported with property; often selling and exposing goods to sale without having them present, representing them unfairly and purchasing them, themselves, at so low a rate as sometimes to double their money and more the same day; often seizing to the worth of double or treble their demand, and afterwards utterly refuse to give receipts, in some instances they have seized goods for the same fines over again, and when considerable overplus has been in their hands, fresh seizures have been made for others—to the whole amount, and often charging exorbitant fees. Fines have likewise been levied and collected for not marching where notice had not been given. And where goods have been taken for fines which had previously been obtained and the same made [to] appear they have seized and detained property to pay their costs. And when endeavours have been used to put a stop to those and like extravagances by laying it before superior officers we have been put off with 'Such conduct was not by their allowance,' also that the captain's return must be their rule of discrimination, and unless we have receipts we must suffer for requisitions which have been fully satisfied. Thus instead of being redressed or those covetous men restrained, who are endeavouring to enrich themselves by the ruin and spoil of their neighbours' goods, they have been encouraged by extending their jurisdiction over several townships and continuing them in office from year to year." (From an undated manuscript [possibly 1781] in the H.C.Q.C.)

a disposition contrary to the peaceable principle we profess."[134] Cases of Friends being disciplined both for conniving with the distraining officers at a lighter imposition as well as for un-Quakerly behavior toward them are met with in the records. New England Meeting for Sufferings in July 1776 adjured Friends in that area to remember "that they have enlisted themselves as soldiers under the Prince of Peace; for if any be so unwary as when distraint is made, and their goods taken from them, to be caught in that spirit, in which wars are fomented, and carried on, such instead of maintaining our peaceable testimony, will thereby wound the cause of truth, . . . and bring reproach on our holy profession."[135]

In the South we even find an occasional slave seized for his master's military delinquency, thereby giving an admirable opportunity for the latter's yearly meeting to deliver a timely warning on the bad effects of Friends' delaying manumission. In December 1779, for instance, the sheriff seized a 6-year-old Negro child from Robert Hunnicutt of Blackwater Monthly Meeting in Virginia "because of [his] testimony against war," and for not paying his war taxes in particular. This monthly meeting, despite the promptings of Virginia Yearly Meeting to make more rapid progress, was apparently extremely tardy in ridding itself of slaveownership, which had almost disappeared in most sections of the Society by this date. In official captivity the child, it was reported, had "suffered sorrowful neglect"; in addition, of course, it was now impossible to free him since he was no longer in Quaker hands.[136]

In coastal areas Quaker sailors and fishermen suffered loss of employment. Moreover, Quaker-owned vessels were frequently impounded by one or other belligerent on the pretext that their owners were trading with the enemy.[137]

The "crimes" for which Friends were thus penalized ranged from vague suspicions of Toryism (or, in some instances, of pro-colonial sympathies) to specific offenses such as refusal of military service and

[134] Kennett M. M. Sufferings, p. 54.

[135] Mekeel, "New England Quakers and Military Service," p. 250.

[136] *Encyclopedia of Quaker Genealogy*, VI: *Virginia*, ed. W. W. Hinshaw *et al.*, 95, 96.

[137] For the hardships inflicted on Nantucket Quakers on this account, see Rotch, *Memorandum*, pp. 5ff., 16-24, 36, 39, 82-89. Under the leadership of Rotch (1734-1828), a wealthy whaler and shipper, the island Quakers, who formed the majority of its inhabitants, attempted to steer a strictly neutral course between the two contestants. The non-Quaker minority backed this policy on grounds of expediency, except for a handful of pro-American enthusiasts. Despite their neutral stance, however, the islanders still had to endure plundering by British troops on land and by British privateers by sea and sporadic hostility and suspicion from the American side.

its alternatives in the way of fines or hiring of substitutes, failure to pay taxes of various kinds connected with the war, refusal to take a test oath or affirmation, "nonassociating," and, more rarely, refusal to handle the Continental paper currency.[138]

Just as Philadelphia and New York Yearly Meetings had established Meetings for Sufferings after the London model during the French and Indian War of mid-century, so similar meetings were set up during the Revolutionary War by the yearly meetings in New England, Baltimore, and Virginia, with an equivalent body, too, in North Carolina. Their prime function, as in the case of London Meeting for Sufferings in its early days, was to provide institutional support for members of the Society in a period of heavy trial. Abundant evidence of Friends' "sufferings" during the Revolutionary War exist in the Society's meeting records, since each meeting was required to keep a full and accurate account; excerpts have been published in such documentary compilations as Ezra Michener's *Retrospect of Early Quakerism*[139] and in histories of central and local meetings. However, no completely reliable statistics on the total losses in property incurred by American Quakers at this time are readily available. The figure given by Mekeel—£103,195. 8s. 11 3/4d.[140]—may be taken as reasonably close to the actual amount, even if hardly accurate to the last pound, shilling, and pence. For Pennsylvania, where the largest number of Friends were located and where army requisitioning and distraints for the various military and paramilitary delinquencies had been among the heaviest of all Quaker communities on the continent, Mekeel gives a figure of £38,550. 9s. 5 1/2d., with the greater part of the sum carried by Friends in Chester and Bucks Counties and with 1778 as the most burdensome year.[141] Indeed, everywhere it was naturally the pe-

---

[138] This last became a capital offense; no Friends, however, actually suffered the death penalty on this account. See *A Retrospect of Early Quakerism*, pp. 303-6, where details are given concerning the case of Thomas Watson, a prosperous Quaker farmer in Bucks Co., who during the winter of 1779-1780 became convinced that he must bear "a testimony against such money," as a hidden instrument of war, by refusing to handle it. After his refusal had been reported to the American military authorities, Watson was court-martialed and sentenced to be hanged; however, his wife's intercession with the commanding general, who had probably not realized the motives of Watson's conduct and mistook it for intent to help the enemy, brought about his pardon and release.

[139] See esp. chap. XXXII, which prints copious extracts concerning Friends' sufferings from the records of Western Q. M. of Philadelphia Y. M. and of its seven constituent monthly meetings covering Lancaster Co. and the western part of Chester Co., esp. for the period starting in 1777 when the systematic recording of "sufferings" was begun.

[140] Mekeel, "The Quakers," p. 299.

[141] *Ibid.*, pp. 155, 156. The losses of Philadelphia Friends amounted only to £1,283. 13s. 2d., thus illustrating once again the fact that it was the rural com-

riods when fighting was taking place in or near Quaker settlements that brought the severest strain between Quakers and the authorities, military and civilian.

It was in a period of serious military crisis, when Philadelphia was threatened by British troops (which soon afterward were to capture the city), that the *cause célèbre* occurred—the arrest by the Revolutionary authorities and subsequent detention of seventeen leading Philadelphia Quakers who, along with three well-known Anglicans (including that exacting critic of Quaker pacifism in the previous war, Provost William Smith), were accused of treasonable relations with the enemy.[142] Among those caught up in the net were the three Pemberton brothers, Israel II, James, and John—all of them among the foremost in the counsels of the Society—leading city merchants like Thomas Wharton, Henry Drinker, and Samuel Rowland Fisher, and prominent Quaker ministers like Thomas Gilpin and the English-born John Hunt. The arrests took place between 2 and 5 September 1777; on 9 September the men were removed for safekeeping to Winchester, Virginia, where they were held in honorable and not very onerous custody until April 1778. Two members of the group, Thomas Gilpin and John Hunt, died during their detention. The rest returned home.

The charge of Quaker complicity with the British was undoubtedly false; it was based in part on hearsay, in part on forged documents (the spurious Spanktown papers), and in part on the known neutralist and quasi-loyalist sentiments of these leading members of the Pennsylvania Society. The evidence against them was spiced by the rancor of Quaker renegades like the "Free Quaker" and Revolutionary radical, Timothy Matlack, who in his capacity as secretary of the supreme executive council of Pennsylvania was responsible for preparing the case against the men and for the decision to incarcerate them.

---

munities that suffered the heaviest losses in worldly possessions. In his *Quaker Experiment in Government*, II, 176, Sharpless estimates the aggregate losses of Pennsylvania Friends to have been at least £35,000; in his chapter in Jones, *The Quakers in the American Colonies*, p. 568, he gives an estimate of nearly £50,000, but this sum may include the losses incurred by New Jersey members of Philadelphia Y. M. For estimated losses among Friends of North Carolina Y. M., see Thorne, "North Carolina Friends and the Revolution," p. 335. The total for the period from 1778-1783 is given there as £9,888 in "good money." La Verne Hill Forbush provides some rather fragmentary information about the material losses suffered by Quakers belonging to Baltimore Y. M. during the Revolution ("The Suffering of Friends in Maryland," *The Maryland and Delaware Genealogist*, vol. 3, no. 2 [Winter 1961-1962], pp. 36, 37; vol. 3, no. 3 [Spring 1962], pp. 59, 60).

142 The main source for this episode is the compilation of documents edited by a later namesake of one of the exiles, Thomas Gilpin, under the title, *Exiles in Virginia*. See also Thayer, *Israel Pemberton*, pp. 215-31.

Whether one should class the hardships of the exiles as part of the "Tory" sufferings, which form such a deplorable chapter in the history of the Revolution, or as part of Quaker pacifist opposition to the war is a difficult question to resolve. The Revolutionary authorities obviously considered these Friends as "the Tories of the Quaker Society"[143] and would not have taken such action against them if they had believed them to be pure Quaker pacifists. In a resolution of late August 1777 issued by the Continental Congress, which had initiated the action against the Philadelphia Friends, the wartime "testimonies" of Philadelphia Yearly Meeting (discussed earlier in this chapter), especially the most recent of 20 December 1776, were quoted to show that "a number of persons of considerable wealth," who were in control of Yearly Meeting policy, had become "with much rancour and bitterness, disaffected to the American cause." Treasonable communication with the enemy was presumed to be an inevitable consequence of such an attitude.[144] On the other hand, the exiles themselves and Pennsylvania Yearly Meeting as a whole, which stood united behind its leaders both in its public utterances and by personal intervention with the Revolutionary authorities, maintained with at least equal sincerity that their behavior had not deviated from a strict adherence to Friends' peace testimony.

Protesting their innocence, the exiles in a number of remonstrances to Congress and the Pennsylvania authorities, which were permeated —it is worth noting—with the traditional Quaker insistence on their rights as citizens, branded their imprisonment as "arbitrary" and "illegal" and demanded a fair trial. "The testimony of the Quakers is against all wars and fightings, and against entering into military engagements of any kind," they expostulated; "surely then, it was the right of the representatives of the Society, to caution their members from engaging in any thing contrary to their religious principles." Their refusal to fight applied to both sides.[145] In denying that they harbored any hostility to the American cause, however, the exiles were undoubtedly a little disingenuous; although all convinced Quaker pacifists, the men formed an assortment of political views ranging from the religious apoliticism of John Pemberton to the cryptoloyalism of Samuel Rowland Fisher.

Among the efforts undertaken by Philadelphia Yearly Meeting in connection with the imprisonment of their brethren was the dispatch at the beginning of October 1777, just after the battle of Germantown,

---

143 *Exiles in Virginia*, p. 187.
144 *Ibid.*, p. 261. See also Sharpless, *A Quaker Experiment*, II, 151-53.
145 *Exiles in Virginia*, p. 101. See also pp. 58, 59, 75, 83, 240-45, 247, 248.

of a committee of six weighty Friends, including Warner Mifflin and Nicholas Waln (1742-1813), to interview the commanding generals on both sides, Howe and Washington.[146] Although at this time Washington shared the view, common among supporters of the Revolution, that identified Quakerism and Toryism,[147] he was convinced by the arguments of the delegation, at least of the inauthenticity of the Spanktown papers. As the delegation passed through the lines while moving from one camp to another without the support of either passports or armed backing to protect them from the overwhelming might of the two forces, which both in their different ways stood for principles in direct contrast to the quiet testimony of Friends, the six Quakers suddenly felt the powerlessness of their position, symbolic perhaps of the situation of the whole Society caught up in the turmoil of war and unable to identify itself with either of the contestants. One of their number, the ever sensitive Warner Mifflin, was thereby led to compare their present situation, at the mercy of arbitrary power, to the plight of the Negro slaves in their own land. "Herein," he writes, "I was brought into renewed sympathy with our oppressed African brethren, who are many of them exposed to the uncontrolled power of man, without any tribunal on all the earth whereunto they can appeal for redress of grievances."[148]

Suspicion of Friends' intentions continued on the part of the Pennsylvania Revolutionary authorities. On 14 November, for instance, we find the executive council telling its representative in Chester County "to watch the meetings and especially the Quarterly meetings of the Quakers. At these assemblies, agents of this nature [i.e., of a subversive

---

[146] *Ibid.*, pp. 52, 59-61. See also Sharpless, *A Quaker Experiment*, II, 160-71.

[147] See Boller, "George Washington and the Quakers," pp. 72-77. Washington spoke on one occasion of the "unfriendly Quakers and others notoriously disaffected to the cause of American liberty." On 20 March 1778 we find him writing to General Lacey from Valley Forge: "Sunday next being the time on which the Quakers hold one of their general meetings, a number of that Society will probably be attempting to go into Philadelphia. This is an intercourse that we should by all means endeavour to interrupt, as the plans settled at their meetings are of the most pernicious tendency" (quoted in Devere Allen, *The Fight for Peace*, pp. 559, 560). On the other hand, both the French general, de Choisy, who was in command of the troops of America's ally stationed in Rhode Island, and his officers spoke warmly of the Quaker peace testimony. "They knew our principle in that respect," they told some visiting Friends, "and allowed it to be good, that we were a people who were known and revered throughout the world on account of our peaceable sentiments and conduct, and that the French people had a very favorable opinion of us" (Cadbury, "A Quaker Travelling in the Wake of War, 1781," p. 399). The first comment perhaps only goes to show that the legend of the "good Quaker" was not one of the ideas of the French Enlightenment that easily found acceptance among the cultured class of Washington's Virginia.

[148] *The Defence of Warner Mifflin*, p. 17.

kind] will without doubt, be busy, and mischievous."[149] Fears that British spies lay concealed beneath the Quaker drab died hard; so, from the Quaker side, did Friends' hostility to the new political order.

Once the war was over, however, and American independence had been recognized by Britain in the Peace of Paris of September 1783, the Society of Friends, along with its brethren among the Mennonites, Dunkers, and Moravians who had likewise caviled at being privy to the overthrow of monarchies, soon accommodated itself to the new regime.[150] Some Friends, nevertheless, were unable to accept the transition from monarchy to republic. And so it happened that the earliest large-scale migration of Friends to Canada (if we except a small Quaker group that moved from Nantucket for economic reasons in 1762 and settled at Barrington, Nova Scotia) came about as a result of the American Revolution.

These immigrants were all loyalists. Some of them had abandoned their pacifism to fight or otherwise support the British cause and thereby earned disownment from the Society, along with their brethren who had espoused the Continental cause. Some were the wives and

[149] *Pa. Archives*, 1st ser., VI, 4.

[150] For the loyal address presented by Philadelphia Y. M. to Washington in October 1789 soon after his election as the country's first President, see *Exiles in Virginia*, pp. 235-37. It was signed by Nicholas Waln as clerk of the meeting and presented in person to the President by a delegation of Friends. "We can take no part in warlike measures on any occasion or under any power," the address stated, "but we are bound in conscience to lead quiet and peaceable lives." "As we are a people," it went on, "whose principles and conduct have been misrepresented and traduced, we take the liberty to assure thee, that we feel our hearts affectionately drawn towards thee, and those in authority over us, with prayers that thy presidency may, under the blessing of Heaven, be happy to thyself and to the people." Washington's reply to this address is printed on pp. 237, 238. Thanking Friends for their "affectionate address," he told them that their "principles and conduct" were well-known to him and "that (except their declining to share with others in the burthens of common defence) there is no denomination among us, who are more exemplary and useful citizens." Nonetheless, despite his disagreement with their pacifism, he stated it as his opinion that "the conscientious scruples of all men should be treated with great delicacy and tenderness" and as his earnest hope "that the laws may always be as extensively accommodated to them, as a due regard to the protection and essential interest of the nation may justify and permit." The well-known remark he made to Warner Mifflin (quoted in Boller, "George Washington and the Quakers," p. 68) when the latter was expounding Quaker pacifism in the course of his interview with the President—"Mr. Mifflin, I honor your sentiments; there is more in that than mankind have generally considered"—is just one more illustration of the fact that, if the Quakers subsequently moderated their wartime attitude toward the Revolutionary regime, the passing of the years also considerably mellowed the sentiments of the Revolution's great leader toward Friends. In the postwar years prosperous Quakers in Philadelphia and elsewhere gave their support to the Federalists; Quakers who sympathized with the Democrats were rare.

families of these men, who, though not held responsible for the delinquencies of their near relatives and therefore able to escape the penalty of expulsion from the Society, wished to accompany the latter in their exile from their native land. Still others were good Quaker pacifists whose sympathies, however, had been very decidedly with the old regime and had earned them a reputation for "Toryism" that made it inadvisable for them to remain in their old homes. Among such people those who still retained their Quaker membership were probably a minority.

Beginning their trek in 1783, more than 500 of these Quaker—or former Quaker—loyalists settled at Pennfield in New Brunswick. The settlers in this wilderness area experienced many difficulties and hardships at first. Quakerism among them was a tender plant that soon died off: it had disappeared altogether by the end of the century. Another group made for Upper Canada, where Quaker settlements sprang up in the Niagara district and at Adolphustown near the Bay of Quinte. There from the beginning the genuine Quaker element was stronger than in the New Brunswick settlement; and it soon began to be reinforced by newcomers from the United States, who were attracted to Canada by cheap land and generous terms of settlement. The earliest regular monthly meetings in Upper Canada date from 1797-1798. Probably some memory of the benefits Friends had enjoyed under British rule acted at first as a further incentive to move northward. However, this whole movement of Quaker settlers into Upper Canada (which later became the province of Ontario) that was to last into the 1820's should be regarded as one wing of the great "westward" movement of Friends—and many more thousands of others—into the free spaces of the continent that were now being gradually opened up for settlement.[151]

Friends in Upper Canada were first exempted from militia service by a law of 1793 (33 Geo.III c. 1), an exemption which was retained in subsequent legislation; this law, however, did not free them from payment of a fine in lieu of actual mustering. Thus the same pattern prevailed again here as in the land that they had left of distraint of goods and occasional imprisonment as a result of Friends' absolutist stand, with disownment for any members who consented to pay the fine or attended a militia muster. In 1809 and 1810 we hear of Friends being censured by their meetings for taking out government land set aside for United Empire loyalists. Since land of this kind was awarded ostensibly for services to the British Crown's military effort, its

[151] Arthur Garratt Dorland, A History of the Society of Friends (Quakers) in Canada, pp. 47-55.

256

acquisition was considered a contravention of the Quaker peace testimony. In the War of 1812, which saw fighting on Canadian territory, Friends who agreed to drive their teams of horses after they had been requisitioned for army use or who behaved, on the other hand, in an aggressive fashion when their animals were impressed for service were disciplined and required to make acknowledgment of faulty behavior. In the rebellion of 1837 a few young Quakers took up arms on the side of the insurgents; as usual, only by expressing regret for their conduct before their meeting could they escape disownment. In the second half of the nineteenth and on into the present century a steep decline in numbers became apparent in Canadian Quakerism. This, combined with the isolated rural character of the Canadian membership and the removal of any serious demands for military duties on the part of the government, made the peace witness of Canadian Friends during the half century and more before the First World War appear rather ineffective.[152]

In addition to the first Quaker migration to Canada, a second and, in the long run, more important legacy of the war period that was to influence the Society for many decades to come was a widespread aloofness from politics, a withdrawal from society which—apart from the Holy Experiment—had to a limited degree always been a feature of American Quakerism but which their wartime experiences had served greatly to intensify. A more compact body, more closely disciplined and more uniform in outlook, a body, too, that had become more sensitized to the needs of suffering humanity, emerged from the testing period of the Revolution. But, at the same time, the American Society of Friends as a whole, and the great concentration of Quakers comprising Philadelphia Yearly Meeting in particular, was in the post-Revolutionary period to be spiritually more narrow and culturally less variegated than it had been in the rather more relaxed years that had preceded the upheaval.

If the effects of the war years on the Society, with their subtle intermixing of positive and negative factors, are not always easy to assess, the verdict on Friends' role during the Revolutionary struggle is even more debatable. The interplay of forces within their ranks had been extremely diverse, and the gamut of opinions gathered under the overshadowing umbrella of the Society's peace testimony extraordinarily wide: it had ranged from the passivism of some of the Philadelphia Quaker grandees, scarcely distinguishable from authentic Toryism, through every neutral shade of pacifism to the pacific procolonialism of many country Friends and of such Quaker bourgeois as Moses

[152] *Ibid.*, pp. 308-23.

257

Brown in New England and old Elizabeth Shippen of Wilmington (Del.), who prophesied on her deathbed the ultimate expulsion under the Lord's power of "the invader of our land."[153] Genuine abhorrence of war and of all its fruits, traditional loyalty to the ancestral taboo on every activity connected with physical fighting, or a compound of the two might have provided the impulse toward the varied manifestations of Quaker war resistance. Their premises may have been incorrect; yet it was not partiality toward the enemy, as so many colonial enthusiasts thought, but a scrupulous regard to keep their conscience clear of what they believed was wrong that formed the basis of most Quaker conduct. The understanding verdict of a French observer, the future Girondin J. P. Brissot de Warville, who traveled widely in the United States half a decade after the end of the American Revolution, may be quoted as a suitable conclusion to this account of Friends' witness during the War of American Independence:

I believe that it was wrong to persecute them so ruthlessly for their pacifist neutrality. Had this been the first time they had refused to fight, had this refusal been dictated by devotion to the British cause, and had it been only a cloak to cover their true feelings, then they would have certainly been guilty and the persecution would have perhaps been justified. But their neutrality was dictated by religious beliefs which they had always professed and have continuously practiced. Whatever prejudiced or misinformed writers may say, the truth . . . is that the majority of Quakers did not favor more one side than the other, and that they helped anyone who needed help, no matter who he was. If a few Quakers did serve in the English army, a few . . . also served in the American army, and the Society expelled indiscriminately all who bore arms.[154]

[153] *Friends in Wilmington 1738-1938*, p. 36; Elizabeth Waterston, *Churches in Delaware during the Revolution*, pp. 47-49.

[154] J.P. Brissot de Warville, *New Travels in the United States of America 1788*, 1964 edn., pp. 328, 329.

258

Chapter 6

The Smaller Peace Sects
in the American Revolution

The outbreak of hostilities between the British government and the American colonists marked the commencement of a time of troubles for the German peace sectaries as well as for their fellow Quaker pacifists. Both were loath to compromise their loyalty to the Crown, an attitude that brought down on them accusations—in most cases unwarranted—of Toryism. But the religious pacifism of the Society of Friends, many of whom were city dwellers with a cosmopolitan culture, took a more militant, political character than that of the simple German-speaking farmers out in the rural counties, who wished to live withdrawn from all affairs of state, provided the authorities did not ask them to contravene their religious conscience. This it was—and not merely the fact that the Quakers formed a more conspicuous segment of the population and were therefore a more obvious target for belligerent American patriots—that explains why the Quakers suffered for their opposition to war more severely in terms of fines and imprisonment than did the Mennonites, Dunkers, or Schwenkfelders.

As the conflict expanded and demands for compulsory military service and forced monetary contributions to the war effort were voiced more widely among "associators," the outlook for the German peace sects became increasingly uncertain. True, neither the Continental Congress nor the Pennsylvania assembly required military service from religious conscientious objectors, but feeling in the province at large, and in the neighborhoods where they lived, was less tolerant. Accusations that conscience was being made a cloak for evading duty or even for hiding secret sympathies for the British enemy were rife. Outbreaks of mob violence against Mennonites were reported from parts of Lancaster County, though such action was deprecated by the Revolutionary authorities in the county.

It was this atmosphere of growing hostility that at an early stage in the struggle prompted Mennonites and Brethren to put aside those doctrinal and ritualistic differences that have made close cooperation between the two so infrequent until the present century, in order to present a common affirmation of their nonresistant creed to the newly elected provincial assembly. The statement was drawn up at first in German by a Mennonite minister, Benjamin Hershey (1697-1789), signed by a number of other Mennonite and Brethren elders, and then handed to the assembly in an English version on 7 November 1775. It lauded the assembly for its regard for conscience in the past. Alluding to the terms of the recent declaration of the assembly of 30 June 1775, which asked associators to tolerate religious objectors and asked the latter to give assistance to needy patriots, Mennonites and Brethren went on:

> The advice to those who do not find freedom of conscience to take up arms, that they ought to be helpful to those who are in need and distressed circumstances, we receive with cheerfulness towards all men of what station they may be—it being our principle to feed the hungry and give the thirsty drink; we have dedicated ourselves to serve all men in every thing that can be helpful to the preservation of men's lives, but we find no freedom in giving or doing, or assisting in any thing by which men's lives are destroyed or hurt. We beg the patience of all those who believe we err in this point.

They concluded by declaring their readiness, as Christ had taught, to pay taxes to Caesar and be subject to the authorities in all things lawful. But fight they would not. Their prayers would be offered for all —"for us and them."[1]

On the same day that the declaration was presented to the assembly, this body had passed a resolution requiring all able-bodied males between the ages of 16 and 50 either to become "associators" or to pay the annual sum of £2. 10s. This fine seems generally to have been paid by Mennonites and Amish throughout the war period: for them monetary commutation in lieu of actual military service had always been an acceptable agreement with Caesar. In their role as conscientious objectors to military service the German peace sects suffered little direct hardship during the war. Occasionally, there may have been cases of brief imprisonment owing to the excessive zeal of local military authorities. We hear, for instance, of the Quaker Benezet trying to persuade his friend Gérard, the French minister in Philadelphia, to exercise his "good offices in behalf of some Mennonites . . . who had been imprisoned and fined for not taking up arms."[2] But, in view of the lack of documentation, the whole matter remains obscure.

---

[1] *A Short and Sincere Declaration, to our Honorable Assembly, and all others in high or low Station of Administration, and to all Friends and Inhabitants of this Country, to whose sight this may come, be they English or Germans.* The German version has the title *Eine Kurze und aufrichtige Erklärung, an unsere wohlmeinende Assembly, ...* The declaration has been reprinted several times by modern authors, e.g., in C. Henry Smith, *The Mennonite Immigration to Pennsylvania in the Eighteenth Century,* pp. 285-87.

[2] Quoted from Gérard's report to the French foreign office in George S. Brookes, *Friend Anthony Benezet,* pp. 133, 134.

The Mennonites not merely paid their commutation money willingly; they were also ready to act as teamsters and to supply wagons and horses when the order came. We find some Mennonite farmers from Upper Saucon (Lehigh County), in a petition to the Pennsylvania assembly dated 9 September 1778, stating as evidence of their goodwill toward the Revolutionary cause that they had "furnished horses and teams for the continental service, whenever demanded, and some of them have gone with their teams as drivers to carry provisions to the army of the United States, for which service they have hitherto received no pay."[3] Mennonites were willing, too, to sell the produce of their richly stocked farms for the use of the army—a source of supply that was of utmost importance to the success of the Revolutionary cause. As W. J. Bender writes: "They raised the food and let God decide as to who should eat it." Nevertheless, they were wary of exchanging their products for the suspect paper money issued by the Revolutionary authorities so long as its value remained precarious. An official wrote to the Board of War in June 1777 concerning the Lancaster County community: "The Mennonites refuse to sell their produce unless for hard cash, and when they bring their market stuff to town will carry it from house to house and sell it very low for hard cash, but will carry it home sooner than sell it for Congress currency. I am informed this is done every market day."[4] There may also have been another factor contributing, though to a lesser degree, to the Mennonites' suspicions of the paper currency: like the Quakers, they may have been reluctant to handle the money of a rebel government.

There was no organized Mennonite relief work of the kind that New England Quakers had set up during the siege of Boston. Such action would have been difficult at that date in view of the sect's very loose organization. But there are examples of Mennonites volunteering to nurse the sick and wounded: for instance, the preacher, John Bear, and his wife died from an infection contracted during their nursing activities at the Ephrata cloister, which had opened its doors to give aid in this way. The provision of food and shelter by three Mennonite farmers in 1783 to some escaping British prisoners is known to have resulted in their arrest; however, through the intercession of Peter Miller, the head of Ephrata cloister, the authorities released the men when it became clear that the deed flowed from Christian charity rather than from sympathy with the enemy.[5]

---

[3] Smith, p. 301. See also John C. Wenger, *History of the Mennonites of the Franconia Conference*, p. 64.

[4] Wilbur J. Bender, "Pacifism among the Mennonites, Amish Mennonites and Schwenkfelders of Pennsylvania to 1783," pt. II, *MQR*, I, no. 4 (Oct. 1927), 32, 33.

[5] *Ibid.*, pp. 33, 34; Guy F. Hershberger, *War, Peace and Nonresistance*, 1944

There were really only two areas where the Mennonites came into conflict with the Revolutionary authorities during the war: the compulsory test oath imposed in June 1777, with severe penalties attached for refusal, and the payment of special war taxes. In regard to the test, it was, of course, not simply the Mennonite prohibition of oath-taking (for a simple affirmation might have been substituted) that was the source of their objection, but the transference of allegiance that it represented from the rightful monarch to newly constituted Revolutionary authorities, a change that was, moreover, being effected by the arbitrament of war. As in the case of the Quakers, whose opposition to the test we have described in the previous chapter, the subtle distinction between such a neutral stance and out-and-out Toryism was often not comprehended in the heat of conflict either by military men or by civilians. Yet the Mennonites were in fact not deviating from their traditional position. They had always been, as the Mennonites of the Franconia Conference had declared in 1776, "a defenseless people and could neither institute nor destroy any government, they could not interfere in tearing themselves away from the king."

Possibly, if the suggestion of a Lancaster County militia officer in 1778 to reframe the test in the case of the nonresistant sects so as to remove all hint of approval of warlike measures had been adopted (taking the test "appearing to us like joining our hands to the military service," in the words of a Mennonite group from Northampton County), Mennonite—if probably not Quaker—objection would have been softened. "They say, a good many at least," this officer reported to Philadelphia,[6] "that they would affirm to be faithful subjects to the state, endeavor nothing to its hurt, but discover all they knew doing so, etc., in consistence with their principles against bearing arms; to require more of them, they say, is persecution."

Refusal of the test did indeed bring down severe penalties on the heads of some Mennonites. Where they lived in large, compact communities and their peaceable principles were well-known to their neighbors—in Lancaster County, for example, or in the old Skippack settlements—delinquents were usually let off with nothing more serious than a small fine. In smaller settlements, where their pacifism was less familiar to the local population and where, therefore, there was

---

edn., pp. 93, 94. Miller's letter to Timothy Matlack, pleading the accused Mennonites' case, dated Ephrata, 9 Feb. 1783, is printed in *Pa. Archives*, 1st ser., IX, 751, 752.

   [6] *Pa. Archives*, 1st ser., VI, 572. His suggestion of imposing a bigger tax on pacifists than on the rest of the community would certainly have met with opposition from most Quakers. The officer concludes his letter: "And such as refuse qualifications, so framed, would have no excuse, but appear plainly to be enemies."

likely to be greater hostility toward their noncooperation, imprisonment, heavy fines, confiscation of property for nonpayment, and even the threat of banishment from the state were not infrequently their lot. The kind of harsh treatment sometimes meted out to these objectors emerges in a petition for relief sent in by eleven Upper Saucon farmers, stating that after their arrest

> . . . all their said personal estate, even their beds, bedding, linen, Bibles and books, were taken from them and sold by the Sheriff to the amount of about forty thousand pounds. That from some of them all their provisions were taken and even not a morsel of bread left them for their children. That as all their iron stoves were taken from them, though fastened to the freehold, they are deprived of every means of keeping their children warm in the approaching winter, especially at nights, being obliged to lie on the floor without any beds; that some of the men's wives were pregnant and near the time of deliverance, which makes their case the more distressing.

This incident took place despite the fact that in this case the men's nonpacifist neighbors vouched for their good character as citizens, adding that "their present blindness to their own essential interest proceeds from an unhappy bias in their education, and not from a disaffection to the present Government."[7]

The imprisonment of several Amish in Reading because of their refusal to take the test is also recorded. Tradition relates that they were eventually released through the intervention of a sympathetic Reformed Church minister, the Rev. Henry Hertzell.[8]

The second point of confrontation between Mennonites and the Revolutionary authorities lay in the policy adopted officially by the church of refusing to pay special war taxes. The grounds of their objection differed to some extent from the Quakers' in its emphasis. Whereas the latter were particularly concerned to avoid giving any support to the war effort, by contributions in money or kind as well as by personal service, the roots of the Mennonite refusal to pay special war taxes lay in their reluctance to concede legitimacy to what appeared to most of them a rebel government and thereby to renounce allegiance to an authority to which they had already pledged their loyalty.

Disagreement with this policy, so contrary—on the surface, at least—

[7] Smith, pp. 293-303.

[8] *Ibid.*, pp. 254, 255. See also C. Z. Mast, "Imprisonment of Amish in Revolutionary War," *MHB*, vol. XII, no. 1 (Jan. 1952), where the imprisonment of the men is attributed incorrectly to their refusal of military service. Mast also repeats the legend of their having been sentenced to be shot and then reprieved as a result of Hertzell's intervention.

to the usual Mennonite willingness to pay tribute to Caesar, certainly existed within the church. The leader of the opposition was a Franconia Conference bishop, Christian Funk (1731-1811), assisted by his brother Henry, a merchant and miller. Bishop Funk, though he had at first been suspicious of the Revolutionary authorities' credentials, soon came to feel that the new state constitution provided sufficient guarantees for freedom of worship and the church's nonresistant principles. He accused his fellow ministers of being swayed in their views by their feeling that the Revolutionary cause would be unsuccessful in the war. In his account of the controversy—which, despite its partial viewpoint, is the most complete source for the affair—he relates of the year 1777: "A tax of £3. 10s. was now laid, payable in congress paper money—my fellow ministers were unanimously of opinion, that we should not pay this tax to the government, considering it rebellious and hostile to the king; but I gave it as my opinion that we ought to pay it, because we had taken the money issued under the authority of congress, and paid our debts with it." Heated discussions ensued. "Were Christ here," Funk claimed, "he would say, Give unto *congress* that which belongs to congress, and to God what is God's." To this another minister, Andrew Zigler, replied angrily: "I would as soon go into war as to pay the £3. 10s." Accusations were bandied to and fro between the two sides, Funk claiming that his opponents were motivated by concern for their material interests and the latter in turn asserting (without foundation) that Christian had taken the test oath and that his brother Henry had accepted military service.

In 1778 Funk was disfellowshipped and forbidden to preach; thenceforward, he and his followers formed a separate sect, the first schism among the Pennsylvania Mennonites. In October 1781 a colonel in the Revolutionary army reported that Henry "and his brother Christian Funk (a remarkably strong whig) are preaching to the few well affected of that society," that is, the Mennonites.[9] The Funkites remained a small group, although undoubtedly there were laymen among the majority that did not secede who gave tacit assent to Funk's position by paying taxes when demanded by the powers that be, even if their claims to exercise authority were *de facto* rather than *de jure*. And, finally, we should note that, as in the case of the Quaker schism concerning payment of taxes which was taking place at the same time in New England, the issue of pacifism was not de-

---

[9] Christian Funk, A *Mirror for all Mankind*, pp. 9-18. The original German version, published in 1813 shortly after the author's death, was entitled *Ein Spiegel für alle Menschen*. See also Smith, pp. 295-99; Wenger, *Franconia Conference*, pp. 345-49; Bender, pp. 25-27, 30-32.

bated. In each case, both sides were at one in recognizing the validity of the traditional nonresistance. Argument centered rather on whether or not the Revolutionary authorities should be recognized as a legitimate government.

Apart from a handful who were carried away in the excitement of the Revolution and took up arms for the colonial cause, the Mennonites remained united in upholding their testimony against war.[10] On the whole, however, the lot of the Mennonite pacifist in wartime was not too onerous. Hardship there was in some cases resulting from fines and distraints and short periods of arrest, as well as from the seizure of provisions, horses, and equipment for the Revolutionary army—a practice to which, of course, their nonpacifist farmer neighbors fell victim, too. Economically, at least, the Pennsylvania Mennonites fared none too badly. The main strain was psychological: with the passing of the old tolerant regime of colonial times, uncertainty seized the Mennonites regarding their future fate under the rule of new and possibly unsympathetic masters. How these fears led to a new migration into the still unsettled wilderness of Upper Canada, where they once again came under the British Crown, will be told later. Those who remained under the new republic accommodated themselves fairly quickly to a change in rulers which they had at first regarded with suspicion.

Outside Pennsylvania, there were also during this period small Mennonite settlements in Maryland and Virginia and possibly a few scattered adherents in North Carolina. In the former two states Mennonites were exempted by law from direct military service. But in October 1777 the Virginia assembly required them to supply substitutes whose upkeep was made the responsibility of the church and not of the individual draftees. In Maryland they were subject to fines in lieu of service. Requisitioning of supplies and equipment from Mennonite farms was carried on by the Revolutionary army in this area also.[11]

In Virginia there existed in addition to the orthodox Mennonites a group of nonresistant Baptists, whose leader Martin Kauffman had originally been a Mennonite preacher until his conversion, along with some other members of his church, during a Baptist revival in Page County where he lived shortly before the Revolution. The group became known as the Mennonist Baptist Church and met at Kauffman's house at Mill Creek. Kauffman himself was accepted as its minister by

[10] For information concerning some Mennonites and Amish from the area covered by the Allegheny Mennonite Conference who accepted service in the Continental armies, see Sanford G. Shetler, *Two Centuries of Struggle and Growth 1763-1963*, pp. 17, 310.

[11] Smith, pp. 304-6; J. S. Hartzler and Daniel Kauffman, *Mennonite Church History*, p. 193.

the Baptists. When war broke out, the Baptists as a whole supported the colonial cause. Kauffman and his group, although they had split away from the Mennonites, still retained much of their church's heritage, including its belief in nonresistance. Their new church's support for war proved too much for the former Mennonites to stomach, even though this church was prepared to tolerate their peculiar pacifist views: Kauffman, therefore, announced their intention to secede. The other Baptists argued that a decision to participate in war or to take the oath of allegiance to the new government should be left to individual conscience. If we who now approve the use of arms are prepared to tolerate you who do not, they said, you should be ready in turn to tolerate us. But Kauffman and his congregation were not convinced. "To all these arguments they replied, that to them it appeared, that the points of difference were of primary importance, and that they could not, in good conscience, hold fellowship or communion with persons, who allowed such unlawful practices. All attempts to reconcile them failed." Kauffman now proceeded to form his own Separatist Independent Baptist Church on a platform of nonresistance, although he continued to have a high regard for the Baptist church. The little group remained virtually a one-man affair, never reaching more than about seventy members at its height. In 1793 Kauffman's group unsuccessfully petitioned the provincial legislature for the same exemption from militia duties that was granted to Mennonites and Quakers. By the end of the century the church had disintegrated almost completely. Kauffman died in 1805, and the sect disappeared altogether not long afterward. In May 1809 their petition to rejoin the main body of Baptists was rejected by the latter, who described the Kauffman group as separating "from us, in the time of the war, because they would keep no slaves, swear no oaths, nor bear arms in defence of their country."[12]

Just as the Virginia preacher Kauffman and his followers brought their Mennonite nonresistance with them when they joined the Baptists, so at least some of the Mennonites who formed, along with members of the Reformed Church, the most important ingredient in the creation of the United Brethren in Christ Church must have continued in their adherence to this tenet of their old faith. The United Brethren, though they finally crystallized into a formal church organization only in the year 1800, had arisen from the evangelistic movement among Pennsylvania Germans in the period of the American Revolution.

[12] Robert B. Semple, *A History of the Rise and Progress of the Baptists in Virginia*, pp. 184-89. See also the account in Harry A. Brunk, *History of Mennonites in Virginia*, I, 21, 22, 26, 37-39, which is based mainly on Semple.

Second in this movement only to the church's founder, the Reformed Church pastor Philip Otterbein, was the former Mennonite bishop from Lancaster County, Martin Boehm (1725-1812), who was disfellowshipped by the Mennonites in 1777 for his support of Methodist revivalism. Among the main charges brought against him was the following: "He had too much intercourse and fellowship with men (professors) who admit and allow war, and the swearing of oaths; and because these are directly opposed to the teachings of Christ."[13] At roughly the same time that Boehm and his associates were driven out of the Mennonite fellowship, there began a long period of spiritual travail for a young Lancaster County Mennonite, who eventually was also to break with the church in which he had been raised and to become a leader of the early United Brethren and the one chiefly responsible for giving the new body its organizational structure. This was Christian Newcomer (1749-1830), a man of little formal education who nonetheless became "the St. Paul of the United Brethren." In his autobiography composed at the age of more than 80, he has this to say about his early pacifist convictions:

About this time commenced the revolutionary war, between this country and England, which also created considerable distress with me, being conscientiously opposed to war and bearing arms, I was thereby placed in many instances in disagreeable situations, respecting both my temporal and spiritual concerns; I desired to have nothing to do with the war, and be at peace, bearing good will to all mankind.[14]

Nevertheless, despite the considerable Mennonite influence on the United Brethren, the church never adopted a pacifist position or, except during its earliest days, contained any considerable minority with pacifist views.[15]

The fate of the small Dunker community during the Revolutionary War was not unlike that of their fellow Germans of the Mennonite persuasion, with whom—as we have seen—they had joined forces at the outset of the conflict in presenting a statement of their nonresistant position for the legislature's consideration. During the course of the war the Brethren discipline was rigidly enforced in some congregations against those members who participated in the fighting. Several Brethren, including a deacon, Abraham Cable, for instance, were

[13] John F. Funk, *The Mennonite Church and Her Accusers*, p. 54.
[14] *The Life and Journal of the Rev'd Christian Newcomer*, p. 10.
[15] Jesse S. Engle, "The United Brethren and War," *Religious Telescope*, vol. 107 (1941), no. 18, pp. 4, 5.

expelled from the Brothersvalley church in western Pennsylvania, a part of the province where hostile Indians proved a continual menace.[16] However, in other congregations, even in the same area, a greater laxity seems to have prevailed. From the same western Pennsylvania district in which the Brothersvalley church was situated, a recent writer has given the names of at least six young Dunkers who enlisted, and yet, "according to the records, all of these brethren returned to become active members or leaders in their respective congregations."[17] Of course, it is possible that these men were as yet unbaptized and therefore not fully subject to the church discipline, or that they afterward expressed regret for their conduct which led them to be reinstated in membership: the exiguousness of Brethren records for this period leaves many details in doubt.

At any rate, it was the Brethren settlement at Morrison's Cove in the Juniata Valley of western Pennsylvania that provided a striking example of the practice of nonviolence comparable to the better known episode involving the Moravian Indians at Gnadenhütten in 1782. The date of the incident is uncertain, but it probably took place between 1777 and 1780, when a number of other Indian massacres occurred in the area. The Brethren refused either to flee or to offer resistance when the Indians finally invaded their settlement, repeating only the words "Gottes Wille sei gethan" as the killing proceeded.[18]

Such a dramatic stance, whether heroic or merely foolish as many must have thought it, was fortunately the lot of only a few of the Brethren. In fact, not only were the rest not confronted with this awesome test, but most, though unwilling to actually take up arms, were evidently prepared to compromise to some degree with the state in exchange for the freedom to contract out of the statutory obligation of military service. In 1780 the annual meeting of the church at Conestoga had forbidden members to pay "the substitute money"—a reference, presumably, to the choice that existed for those refusing military service to hire a substitute to go in their place instead of paying the statutory fine, which might in fact through repetition have proved more onerous. Paying a substitute was held to be wrong since it did not differ morally from personal participation in warfare. In the following year, however, it was reported that the previous meeting's decision had been widely disregarded. The annual meeting, therefore, repeated its warning against such practices, adding one, too,

[16] H. Austin Cooper, *Two Centuries of Brothersvalley Church of the Brethren 1762-1962*, pp. 83, 84, 87.

[17] W. J. Hamilton (ed.), *Two Centuries of the Church of the Brethren in Western Pennsylvania 1751-1950*, pp. 143-45.

[18] Rufus D. Bowman, *The Church of the Brethren and War*, pp. 74-76.

against collaboration with the authorities in extracting money for this purpose from fellow Brethren. "We exhort heartily, not to be scared [not] to do that which is not right." The heavy fines imposed for refusal of service should become a collective concern of each congregation. Nevertheless, "in case a brother or his son should be drafted, that he or his son should go to war, and he could buy himself or his son from it, such would not be deemed so sinful, yet it should not be given voluntarily, without compulsion." If it were so given, the brother must do penance, unless, indeed, he had first protested to the collector that to give willing consent was against his conscience.

The payment of taxes to the new government was in other respects legitimate "on account of the troublesome times . . . and in order to avoid offense." However, if some had scruples against doing so (whether on account of their association with war or with rebellion is not stated), they must be tolerated as they in turn should bear with their brethren who conformed in this respect, for "we deem the overruling of the conscience as wrong."

Although the Brethren were thus less uncompromising here than either Mennonites or Quakers, they were at one with them in their refusal to permit members to take "the attest." The annual meeting of 1778 threatened any member who took this oath of allegiance to the new regime with expulsion unless he was willing to formally recall it, apologize to the church, and do penance for his offense. In the following year the meeting repeated its stand against the test, explaining that "we could not, with a good conscience, repudiate the king and give allegiance to the state" until God's will in the matter had become clearly apparent.[19]

It is probably not merely the scarcity of Brethren records but the fact that the Brethren found a mutually acceptable *modus vivendi* with the military authorities which accounts for the apparent absence of hardships undergone as a result of a direct refusal to bear arms. Fines and confiscations of property there certainly were, but in most cases these originated in the Brethren's opposition to the test oath. In 1778, for instance, Christopher Saur, Jr., saw his Germantown press confiscated and then destroyed, while he himself underwent arrest and some ill-treatment at the hands of the Revolutionary army because of his refusal to take the oath of allegiance and, generally, because of his known opposition to war. The fact that his two sons, who did not follow in their father's Dunker faith, sided openly with the British brought down the suspicion of secret Tory leanings upon his head.

The destruction of the Saur press and the death of its owner in

[19] *MAM*, pp. 5-7.

269

1784 dealt the cultural life of the Brethren a severe blow. The uncertainties of the war years made an impact on them similar to the impact it made on the Mennonites. The church increasingly cut itself off from the world and became more and more completely a sect apart. Migration westward, prompted in part by their Revolutionary War experiences, emphasized these tendencies: the frontier congregations long remained isolated from the sources of the new nation's cultural life. A period of withdrawal set in and continued until the end of the nineteenth century.[20]

As in the earlier period the Schwenkfelders during the Revolution appear to have been less united in their nonresistant stand than either Mennonites or Brethren. Yet it remained the official policy of the church, and it continued to be upheld by most members. The two cousins, the Rev. Christopher Schultz and David Shultze, were again active supporters of military measures—on the colonial side.[21] But at the same time the former was diligent in his efforts to see that the sect's official noncombatancy was recognized by the authorities.

The outbreak of hostilities was greeted with alarm by most Schwenkfelders, who foresaw trouble ahead for a tiny group like theirs that wished to steer a neutral course between the two belligerents. As their chronicler recorded: "For those citizens of the province who at the breaking out of the war did not take up arms, the prospect was often full of fear and dread. The mad rabble said: 'If we must march to the field of battle, he who will not take up arms must first be treated as an enemy.'"[22] Although some members were forced to act as teamsters in the Revolutionary army, none were made to serve in a combatant capacity. Severe fines, however, were levied on those who were drafted and chose to stand as conscientious objectors[23]—the same treatment, in fact, as was meted out to members of the other nonresistant sects. As a result of the conscription—to quote the Schwenkfelder chronicle again—"musten solche, welche sich nicht dazu bequemten, entweder eine gewisse Straffe geben oder einer Mann an ihre Stelle dingen, welches letzere die Unsern meistentheils nicht gethan, doch haben sie ihre Straff bezahlt wenn es an sie begehrt worden."[24] Even

---

[20] Bowman, *Brethren and War*, pp. 84-86, 93-99.

[21] Selina G. Schultz, "The Schwenkfelders of Pennsylvania," *Pennsylvania History*, XXIV, no. 4 (Oct. 1957), 307; *The Journals and Papers of David Shultze*, II, 132.

[22] "Historische Anmerkungen was sich von Anno 1775 anfolgentlich mit den Schwenkfeldern merkliches zugetragen," p. 68, printed in *Skizzen aus dem Lecha-Thale*, p. 51. Tr. in Howard W. Kriebel, *The Schwenkfelders in Pennsylvania*, p. 151.

[23] Kriebel, *The Schwenkfelders*, p. 158; Schultz, "The Schwenkfelders," p. 307.

[24] "Historische Anmerkungen," p. 69 (printed in *Skizzen*, p. 51). "Such as did

heavier fines resulted from the reluctance of Schwenkfelders, like members of the other German peace sects, to take the oath of allegiance.

We learn from a document drawn up on 2 May 1777 and attached to another declaration of the previous day entitled "A Candid Declaration of Some So-Called Schwenkfelders concerning Present Militia Affairs" that the militia fines of members were paid from a common fund set up for that purpose. "Those on whom such burdens may fall will render a strict account to the managers of the Charity Fund in order that steps may be taken to a proper adjustment." The author of both documents was probably the Rev. Christopher Schultz, whom we find addressing a Pennsylvania assemblyman, Sebastian Levan, in August of the same year in explanation of the Schwenkfelder position. He states that he is not himself opposed either to a militia recruited on the voluntary system or to a standing army of professionals. But he reminds Levan that Pennsylvania was originally founded by men who were conscientiously opposed to war and to the swearing of oaths. Freedom of conscience is a basic condition of civil liberty in society. His own people, though unprepared to fight with carnal weapons, would make their contribution to the country's welfare by praying to God for its protection.[25]

Owing partly to the tactful statesmanship of their leader Schultz and partly to the fact that the consciences of its members were satisfied by the alternatives to military service permitted by the state legislature, the Schwenkfelders were subjected on account of their war resistance to little worse than suspicion and hostility on the part of some of their more patriotic neighbors and to an equal share in the common burden of the fines flowing from their disengagement from the war. Thus at the conclusion of hostilities one of their number could write to a correspondent in Germany concerning his church's war experi-

---

not feel at ease therein had either to present a certain fine or hire a man in their stead. This last our people for the most part have not done, rather have they paid their fine when it was demanded of them." (My translation.)

[25] Kriebel, *The Schwenkfelders*, pp. 152, 153, 208, 209, 212-15. The "Candid Declaration" had stated: "We who are known by the name Schwenkfelders hereby confess and declare that for conscience sake it is impossible for us to take up arms and kill our fellow men; we also believe that so far as knowledge of us goes this fact is well known concerning us. We have hitherto been allowed by our lawmakers to enjoy this liberty of conscience. We have felt assured of the same freedom of conscience for the future by virtue of the public resolution of Congress and our Assembly. We will with our fellow citizens gladly and willingly bear our due share of the common civil taxes and burdens excepting the bearings of arms and weapons. We can not in consequence of this take part in the existing militia arrangements, though we would not withdraw ourselves from any other demands of the government."

ences: "Without claiming undue praise to ourselves, we may still say that our people got through easier than others that also did not resort to the use of arms."[26]

A contrast to this conscientious "going the second mile" was the wartime witness of the little group of freshly arrived English immigrants who eventually crystallized into the body bearing the official title of "The United Society of Believers in Christ's Second Appearing" but who are better known simply as the Shakers. Here we have militant pacifism, a testimony more akin to that of the Quakers, from whose Society in England the original group of "Shaking Quakers" had emerged, than to the position of the Schwenkfelders or the other German immigrant peace sects.

The establishment of Shakerism in America was very largely the result of the efforts of one woman, Ann Stanley, née Lee (1736-1784). "Mother Ann," as she became known to her followers and all subsequent generations of Shakers, was an illiterate factory girl from Manchester who arrived in New York with eight companions in August 1774, on the very eve of the outbreak of the Revolution. The group originated in the Manchester area in the activities of two former English Quakers, James and Jane Wardley, whose reading of scripture had led them to expect the second coming of Christ on earth in the form of a woman. They eventually picked Ann Lee for this role. Ann herself shared in the visions and ecstatic dancing (probably derived originally from the influence of the French Camisards) that marked the little sect and brought down on it the derision of the populace, mob violence, and eventually imprisonment and other forms of persecution by the authorities. Its members were mostly people of little account in this world: factory workers and small shopkeepers. Ann herself entered enthusiastically into her role as the female incarnation of Christ with transparent sincerity and devotion to what she believed to be her duty as "Mother." Her unhappy marriage with the blacksmith Abraham Stanley, which provided her with numerous children but no love, engendered in her a hatred of sexual intercourse. Celibacy, along with ritual dancing and collective confession of sin, were tenets which the Shakers took over from their English background. Shakerism, writes one of its recent historians, "was a way of life leading to spiritual perfection over the dead body of man's physical nature."[27] This physical asceticism was to impart to its followers an immense drive toward its religious and economic goals.

[26] "The Conduct of the Schwenkfelders during the Revolutionary War," *The Pennsylvania-German*, XI, no. 11 (Nov. 1910), 659, 660.
[27] Marguerite Fellows Melcher, *The Shaker Adventure*, p. 9.

However, during the first six years after the party's arrival in America little seemed to be achieved. The group traveled north from New York and settled in the swampy and forested wilderness at Niska-yuna (later Watervliet) near Albany on land that was purchased by some well-to-do sympathizers back in England, who had also financed the party's voyage across the ocean. A few more persons came over from England, but at first no recruits were made from the indigenous population. This period of withdrawal appears to have been part of Mother Ann's strategy for her people; she planned a return to redeem the world in due course. The opportunity came in 1780, when some of the survivors of a recent revival in the area around New Lebanon (N.Y.), hearing of the little group of ecstatic pioneers in the wilderness not far away, decided to visit the prophetess and see if it was here that they could find the permanent source of inspiration that would prevent the spring of their religious enthusiasm from drying up. They were impressed by what they saw and became followers of "Mother."

And so began the great missionary campaign that filled the last four years of Mother Ann's life and was continued by her successors after her death. It took the early Shakers into the towns and villages of New York state and over into New England where they were joined by bands of men and women, ardent seekers after religious certainty whose spiritual longings had been stirred up by the great awakening during the previous decades. Loosely organized communities of Shakers arose in Massachusetts, Connecticut, and New Hampshire as well as back in New York, although community of goods—that most distinctive feature of Shaker polity—was not instituted until after Mother Ann's death. Most of these new adherents were simple people: farmers and rural craftsmen. But a few converts were made from the educated classes. There were, for instance, Joseph Meacham the former Baptist, who was to succeed Mother Ann in the leadership and accomplish the gathering of her disciples into closely knit societies of believers, and Samuel Johnson, a Yale graduate who was pastor of the Presbyterian church at New Lebanon until shortly before his conversion to Shakerism. Such men would provide the intellectual ballast to complement the amazing physical energy, dogged determination, and charismatic powers of the illiterate visionary Ann Lee.

One of the doctrines that Mother Ann inherited via the Wardleys from their Quaker roots was the belief in the wrongness of all warfare. However, although their new country became involved in war with Britain, their land of origin, less than a year after their arrival on the American continent, the first recorded clash between the new-

273

comers and the Revolutionary authorities on the question of their pacifism did not occur until 1780. Doubtless the little group of a dozen or so men and women squatting out in the wilderness easily escaped attention. But when in that year they began on their missionary activities and included agitation against war in their program, the authorities began to take alarm. Was this perhaps a Tory plot, a ruse of the British to wean the allegiance of the populace from the Revolutionary cause under the guise of religion? In July 1780 the state "Commissioners for detecting and defeating Conspiracies" took action after an angry mob had seized an American convert, David Darrow, as he was driving a herd of sheep from New Lebanon to Niskayuna. Darrow and two other Shakers were brought before the Albany County court. Here they stated it to be contrary to their religious convictions to fight. "It was their determined resolution," they said, "never to take up arms and to dissuade others from doing the same." The court was shocked at this defiant antimilitarism, recording in its minutes that "such principles at the present day are highly pernicious and of destructive tendency to the freedom and independence of the United States of America." It was also reported that "a certain Zadock Wright a prisoner of war . . . also pretends to be of the denomination of people called shaking Quakers and . . . dissuades people from taking up arms." Toward the end of the month six more Shakers—four men and two women, of whom one was Mother Ann herself—were arrested for endeavoring "to influence other persons against taking up arms," a charge to which the accused willingly pleaded guilty. Plans to remove Mother Ann to the territory held by the British army in the state did not materialize, although she was not released from prison until the end of the year. But by freeing the other accused earlier the authorities showed they realized that the group's opposition to war was not a plot to aid the enemy but merely one aspect of their unorthodox religious faith.[28]

Among those who had been arrested while Mother Ann was in prison in Albany was the former Presbyterian Samuel Johnson, who at the beginning of the war had been an ardent upholder of the Revolutionary cause. After resigning his pastorate and undergoing a period of spiritual stress, he began to have deepening doubts about the validity of Christian participation in war. This may have been one of the factors that led him to embrace Shakerism after his visit to Mother Lee's community in 1780. Not long afterward came his arrest. After spending ten days in the Albany town jail, he was released on the intercession

---

[28] *Minutes of the Commissioners for detecting and defeating Conspiracies in the State of New York. Albany County Sessions, 1778-1781*, II, 452, 453, 470, 471, 504; Melcher, *The Shaker Adventure*, p. 27.

of his brother, who provided evidence of Johnson's good character and his earlier efforts on behalf of the American cause. Of his brush with the authorities Johnson related later:

I was accused of speaking against the war . . . [and of] maintaining the principles of Ann Lee against the lawfulness of war. Such principles, they contended, were detrimental to the cause of the country, which was then engaged in the arduous struggle for liberty, against a powerful enemy, and forbad my preaching such doctrine. I replied, "I shall speak what God gives me to speak; for I feel it my duty to obey God rather than man. I did not receive the testimony against war from Ann Lee; but was taught by the revelation of God, before I ever saw Ann Lee, *that the followers of Christ could have nothing to do with wars and fightings.*" This declaration was so offensive to the commissioners that they gave orders for my imprisonment, declaring at the same time, that the Elect Lady was going to be banished to the British Army in New-York. I replied, "The *Elect Lady* she is, indeed and in truth; but whether she sinks or swims, I know the work is of God."

Persecution as a result of Shaker attacks, whether on the military or on the religious establishment, indeed, served rather to attract new followers by advertising the constancy and courage of its adherents than to frighten away any with deep religious convictions. "For many who received intelligence of these things, flocked to hear the testimony of a people who were persecuted and imprisoned for the cause of righteousness and peace."[29]

The early Shaker missionaries, however, on many occasions during their journeys had to endure the rigors of mob violence as fierce as any that attended the travels of George Fox and the early Quakers a century and more before. "They were hated as pacifists, religious innovators, as destroyers of families," writes the historian of early Shakerism.[30] They refused to appeal to the authorities for police protection or to accept it on the rare occasions when it was offered. A story was handed down in Shaker tradition that once, when a mob menaced Mother Ann during her visit in 1782 to the small Massachusetts town of Ashfield, a committee of citizens headed by the captain of the local militia approached her. "I am a poor, inoffensive, weak woman," she told them, thinking that they were on the side of the

[29] *Testimonies concerning the Character and Ministry of Mother Ann Lee and the First Witnesses of the Gospel of Christ's Second Appearing*, pp. 107, 109, 111, 112.

[30] Daryl Chase, *The Early Shakers: An Experiment in Religious Communism* (printed summary of 1936 U. of Chicago Ph.D. diss.), p. 4.

hostile crowd that had gathered. "I have suffered so much from the cruelty of mobs that it seems impossible that I could endure any more." "You need not fear, madam," the committee replied, "we have not come to hurt you, but to defend you." Ann thanked them for their goodwill but firmly refused the armed protection they wished to provide for her.[31] On this and many other occasions the early Shaker campaigners adopted a policy of nonviolence in the face of threats to life and limb.

By the time of the Revolution the German peace sects, and to a large extent the American Quakers as well, had lost much of their earlier dynamism and proselytizing zeal and had turned inward. Their pacifism, too, shared in the quietism which dominated their whole religious practice. In contrast, the Shakers, who were then only at the outset of their career, displayed a militant missionary spirit in spreading their pacifism as in propagating the other tenets of their somewhat strange faith. Mother Ann may not, indeed, have been the female incarnation of Jesus Christ, but she was certainly a feminine counterpart of George Fox.

A small religious group which was much more closely akin in many respects to the Society of Friends than were the Shakers and which had come into existence shortly before the Revolution was the rustic sect of Nicholites, followers of a Delaware farmer seer, Joseph Nichols (ca. 1730-1770). The church was constituted formally only in 1774 after its leader's death. It was never large: apart from a few members in the Carolinas, membership did not extend outside the "Delmarva" Peninsula. Although his original inspiration as a religious teacher had arisen independently of Friends, the similarity of Nichols's beliefs to the Quakers' was striking enough for contemporaries to refer frequently to his followers as "New Quakers." Silent meetings with impromptu ministry (though conducted in a more strongly emotional atmosphere than among eighteenth-century Quakers), Quakerly practice in carrying on business sessions, faith in the Inner Light (or "Inward Director," as the Nicholites termed it), absence of a paid ministry, austerity in dress and general conduct, pacifism and objection to oaths, and antislavery sentiments were the main points of identity between the two denominations.

The first authenticated contacts between Nichols and the Quakers occurred in the 1760's when Nichols, beginning then on his miniature revival—among the unchurched in particular—in Delaware and Maryland, met John Woolman and was further confirmed in his pacifist and antislavery views by the urgings of the New Jersey minister. The Nicholites were even more thoroughgoing than the Quakers in

[31] Henry C. Blinn, *The Life and Gospel Experience of Mother Ann Lee*, pp. 162-68.

the ban they imposed on members holding public office of any kind or voting in elections, though their historian, Kenneth L. Carroll, is of the opinion that the impulse toward this total political abstention arose from the partial Quaker withdrawal from politics that was in progress around this time. "The band that Nichols had gathered together," writes Caroll, "included all kinds of people: former slaves and ex-slaveowners, tenant farmers and landowners of moderate means, educated and uneducated"—in fact, a fairly representative cross section of the ordinary people living in this area.[32]

The Nicholites refused military service during the Revolution and suffered distraint of property, along with their Quaker brethren, for objecting to the payment of fines as an alternative to personal service. A few among them, like some Friends with especially scrupulous consciences, refused to handle the Continental paper money because of its connection with war. The Nicholites were mostly simple people, few of them with more than a smattering of letters; they have left little record, therefore, of their wartime witness. A petition protesting against the omission of their sect from the military exemption then granted to the other peace churches of the province that they presented in August 1778 to the general assembly of North Carolina, where a few of their number had migrated on the eve of the outbreak of war, has, however, survived. In it they stated that they were a peaceable people for whom active resistance against authority was against conscience. "We believe we can't be just before God," they went on, "to bear arms or lift the sword against our fellow creature, in justification of which we could mention sundry sayings of Christ and his apostles, and by a living sense of God's law written on our hearts." From the same motives they could not be privy to the death of a fellow human being by acting as a witness in cases involving the death penalty. "If so be you can feel bowels for us in the two above mentioned particulars," they concluded, "we desire to ever be thankful."[33]

In the post-Revolutionary period the Nicholites failed to expand—in part, perhaps, because after the death of their founder no leader of talent arose to give the little group cohesion and direction. Identity of doctrine and practice with the more flourishing Society of Friends eventually led most Nicholites around the turn of the century to apply for membership in the Society, either individually or in small groups. The few who remained outside it died in the course of the nineteenth century without leaving any successors.

Quaker views on war were also shared at the time of the Revolution

[32] Kenneth Lane Carroll, *Joseph Nichols and the Nicholites*, esp. pp. 16, 23, 29, 30, 33-36, 54, 55.
[33] *Ibid.*, p. 49.

by the followers of the Quaker-born Jemima Wilkinson (1752-1819), who, having been disowned by the Society of Friends in August 1776 for associating with the "New Light" Baptists and after having a mystical experience during a serious illness in the following autumn, now began her career as a prophetess and—as she called herself thenceforth—"the Universal Publick Friend." She appears to have been sincere in her claims to religious leadership, although she was something of a showman in the way she manipulated her visions and ecstasies to further the cult of her person. There was, indeed, little that was original in her ministry: in addition to the Quaker testimony against war, she retained much that she had learned as a result of her upbringing with Friends, including the plain dress and speech, plainness of worship, and antislavery views. The "Universal Friends," whom she recruited over the next few years in the course of a vigorous campaign centered in her home state of Rhode Island mostly from fellow Quakers and other well-to-do church people, firmly rejected participation in the war that was then raging between the mother country and her former colonies. In 1778 we read of Jemima preaching in British-occupied Newport against "sin, war, and fighting." Those among her early converts who had either fought or held office—usually on the Revolutionary side—resigned on joining her movement. At the end of the 1780's Jemima and her followers withdrew into the wilderness of northwestern New York. Numbering at its height several hundred devotees, the cult of the Universal Friends dwindled rapidly after this date and disappeared altogether soon after the death of its founder in 1819.[34]

The conscientious objectors and absolute pacifists of the Revolutionary War came almost exclusively from one or another of the old established or more recently established peace churches: from Quakers and closely related groups like the Rogerenes, Nicholites, and Shakers or from the German-speaking sectaries of Mennonite, Amish, Dunker, Schwenkfelder, or Moravian persuasion. There were, however, a few isolated instances of war resistance from religious principle that cropped up either among the great unchurched masses of the population or among members of nonpacifist denominations. How many such cases there were it is impossible to guess, for undoubtedly some remained unrecorded. That there were more than the eight chronicled in this chapter is virtually certain. Those instances most likely to be documented were the ones where—as was not infrequently the case in the two world conflicts of our century—the independent pacifist

[34] Herbert A. Wisbey, Jr., *Pioneer Prophetess: Jemima Wilkinson*, esp. pp. 35, 40, 95.

of wartime was later, in the postwar era, drawn to the largest pacifist denomination in the country, to the Society of Friends, whose passion for recording past and present for the benefit of the future has, indeed, frequently proved a boon for the historian of the highways and by-ways of religious life.

The nineteenth-century Quaker minister, Christopher Healy—to give one example of this Friendly historicism—has related the story of the experiences of his father, Joseph Healy, as a conscientious objector in the Revolutionary War. The elder Healy, who only joined the Society of Friends sometime after the conclusion of the war, lived at this time in Montville (Conn.). Connecticut in the colonial period, as we know, proved barren soil for the growth of Quakerism, and, apart from a period of apprenticeship to a Quaker shoemaker, Healy had had no contacts with Friends. Possibly, the boy may have learned Quaker views on war, as well as the cobbler's trade, in his master's workshop. But when war came, he does not appear to have been in touch with Friends or to have had any other close church affiliation. The neighborhood people were mostly Presbyterians or Baptists, keen supporters of the colonial cause and fiercely resentful of Healy's stubborn refusal of the call to bear arms. In these circumstances, as his son aptly comments in his account, it was "a little remarkable that he was strengthened to bear a consistent and faithful testimony against war—though too weak to live up to the doctrines of the gospel in other respects." So great, indeed, was the local feeling against him that the villagers began a boycott; as a result, he lost most of his custom as a shoemaker and began to experience great difficulty in supporting his wife and family.

On one occasion, when alarm of an imminent attack by a British fleet was raised, Healy was called upon to perform coastguard duty. He thereupon decided to take his case to the governor, Jonathan Trumbull. After walking some thirty miles to the temporary state capital at Lebanon and arriving disheveled and weary, the simple village craftsman had difficulty in persuading the state councillors then assembled, to whom he told his story, to allow him an audience with the governor. But the simplicity of his narrative and his obvious sincerity impressed them, as it did the governor, too, when he unexpectedly entered the council chamber as Healy was speaking. Governor Trumbull as a result gave Healy a letter to take back with him requiring the colonel of the local militia to respect the young man's scruples. The colonel, who of course was Healy's neighbor, appears to have taken the situation well. "I hope, Mr. Healy," he remarked jokingly, "you have no scruple against making shoes for your fighting neighbours."

"I am willing to work for anybody and everybody, according to my ability," Healy replied, and thereupon received an order from the colonel to make footwear for his whole family. This marked the end of Healy's troubles.[35]

It is from another Quaker journal—that of a Pennsylvania Friend, Phebe Speakman, who visited New England in the ministry in 1776—that we learn by a casual reference of another isolated war resister in this part of the country. During her travels she mentions meeting "one who was not a member," a former publican who had been brought up a Presbyterian but was not now attached to any denomination. "He told us," she writes, that "their ministers preached up war, and said God would be angry with them, if they would not fight for liberty. But he said he was convinced that all wars and fightings were wrong, and contrary to Christianity."[36] Phebe Speakman, unfortunately, gives no further details concerning the wartime experiences of this ex-publican pacifist.

A third instance of completely isolated conscientious objection in the Revolutionary War, and perhaps the most remarkable story of all, is that of the English-born trooper, Thomas Watson, who deserted from the British army a few months after the battle of Germantown because of his conviction, slowly reached, "that wars and fightings were from the wicked one." Watson had been born in a small English village in 1753 and had passed through a desperately poor childhood, having worked in the coal mines as a young boy and in various types of casual employment. Enlisting in the army, he was sent to America shortly before the outbreak of hostilities. Nothing in his career up to that time, no religious or other outside influence, appeared to presage the change which was maturing within him. Outwardly, he seemed the carefree and free-living young British trooper; inwardly, his thoughts began to turn more and more toward religious matters. When he made his decision to participate no further in fighting, he did not know—he tells us—of any other persons who had held a similar objection to war. His narrative is not quite clear on the point, but it seems that some of the officers who had come to appreciate the depth of his newly found scruples connived at his escape from the army, fearing that his example, if he were kept unwillingly in service, would spread disaffection in the ranks. From Philadelphia, where his regiment was then stationed, Watson made his way to New England, where he lived unmolested among his American neighbors for the rest of the war.

Something of a church hopper at the beginning, he attended Baptist

[35] *Friend*, LVI, no. 47 (30 June 1883), 372, 373.
[36] *Friends' Miscellany*, VI, no. 5 (Dec. 1834), 206, 207.

services first and then the meetings of the prophetess (and former Quakeress) Jemima Wilkinson before finally throwing in his lot with the Society of Friends. During the period of his religious seeking, he tells us, he read the Bible diligently. Indeed, it was probably his direct acquaintance with the New Testament message of peace, and not any external influence, that had first put the hard-living, hard-swearing British trooper Tom Watson on the path that eventually led to his transformation into Thomas Watson, the sober elder of the little Quaker meeting of Bolton, Massachusetts.[37]

The American Revolution had, of course, produced a powerful movement of political opposition to the prosecution of the war against Britain by the American colonists. Although the conscientious scruples of a Quaker, a Mennonite, or a Moravian against all war might sometimes be blended with a reluctance to resist the lawful sovereign, the genuine Tory loyalists were in most cases far from being pacifists. We know of at least one instance, however, of an amalgam of nonresistance and loyalism in a Church of England clergyman—the Rev. John Sayre (1736-1784) of Fairfield (Conn.), who refused to support the armed defense of American liberties on the grounds that this was contrary to the Christian gospel. "I dare not, therefore, promise to take up and use any carnal arms at all," he explained, even if the alternative were to be reduction to a state of slavery. How could he bind himself, as requested by his fellow townsmen, not to give any assistance to the enemies of the Revolutionary cause? Did not Christ command us to feed the hungry, give drink to the thirsty, clothe the naked? "Here it may be to no purpose to say, that such or such persons are mine enmies; because our Lord hath expressly, and that too in an especial manner, commanded me to extend my kind offices to mine enemies as such." But, despite his disavowal of any connection with politics and a declaration of his affection for his motherland—"America is my native country; all my connections are in it; I have enjoyed the liberty and plenty of it . . . too long and too thankfully, not to be sensible of the value of both, and to desire a continuance of them, if it be His will"—he was nevertheless branded as a traitor, his house was attacked by a mob, and finally—together with his wife and children —he was forced to take refuge on board a British man-of-war in order to escape further violence from his fellow countrymen.[38]

A somewhat similar experience was the lot of another isolated ob-

[37] Watson's autobiography is printed in *Some Account of the Life, Convincement, and Religious Experience of Thomas Watson*, pp. 17-49. See also my article, "The Spiritual Pilgrimage of Thomas Watson," *Quaker History*, vol. 53, no. 2 (Autumn 1964), pp. 81-86.

[38] John Sayre, *From the New York Journal*. See also Devere Allen, *The Fight for Peace*, p. 580; Merle E. Curti, *The American Peace Crusade*, p. 22.

jector to all war. John Baker was "a respectable farmer" residing in Brooklyn (Conn.), evidently a person of independence and courage, who was regarded by his neighbors, however, as "an odd and singular man, because he openly denounced all kinds of carnal warfare as contrary to the gospel." His refusal to serve, when conscripted into the Revolutionary army, brought accusations of "Tory" and "coward." His subsequent fate was later recounted by the son of a friendly farmer who lived nearby, the future peace pioneer, David Dodge:

> His neighbours determined he should serve by compulsion. He declared he would die before he would serve as a warrior, and consequently fled to the woods in the fall of 1779. The clergy and the laity urged his compulsion, and the populace turned out to pursue him, as hounds would a fox, and finally they caught and bound him, . . . placed him in a wagon, and sent two trusty patriots to convey him to Providence, to the troops stationed there. In the course of the night, however, he got hold of a knife, cut himself loose, and escaped to the woods.

Baker managed to survive the severity of winter in his hiding place.[39] We do not know the path by which he had, seemingly in isolation, reached the pacifist position. Possibly, he may have come under Quaker or Rogerene influence; more probably, his convincement arose out of his own unaided reading of, and meditation upon, the gospels. As in the case of the Anglican Sayre—as well as with many Quakers and Mennonites—the local community had mistaken religious scruples for political disloyalty, even treason.

Further evidence of independent pacifist witness in the Revolutionary War period is supplied by another later peace advocate, the Rev. Noah Worcester. He, too, in his youth had come in contact with absolute pacifism outside as well as inside the Quaker fold. He mentions a Baptist preacher, "a neighbor, who was educated among Quakers, and had imbibed their views of war." At the outbreak of the conflict, Worcester used to listen—unconvinced, for he was soon to go off to war himself—to the Baptist putting forward his case in argument with the boy's father and other farmers. A few years later, as the war was coming to a close, Worcester met the Rev. E. Estabrook, Congregational minister at Thornton (N.H.), whom he was eventually to succeed in this parish. Worcester writes of him: "He was known as a minister who denied the lawfulness of war. . . . [However, he] was prudent in regard to urging his views of war, seldom mentioning them in his discourses."[40]

[39] *Memorial of Mr. David L. Dodge*, pp. 25-27.
[40] Henry Ware, Jr., *Memoirs of the Reverend Noah Worcester*, p. 61.

The last case of an isolated war resister to be mentioned here is perhaps the most remarkable: a chaplain of the Congress of the United States during the war of 1812 who had been a conscientious objector in the Revolutionary War. This was the famous Methodist evangelist and circuit preacher, the Rev. Jesse Lee (1758-1816), who was ordained to the ministry in 1790 by Bishop Francis Asbury. Born and raised in Virginia, he had been converted at the age of 16 in a Methodist revival, along with his parents. In 1777 he had moved to work on a relative's farm in North Carolina where, although he was still young and had received scarcely any formal schooling during his childhood, his natural eloquence caused him to be chosen as a local preacher for his church, which was indeed still largely rural and without many educated members. In July 1780 the 22-year-old Lee was drafted into the state militia, which was then on a war footing. He writes: "I weighed the matter over and over again, but my mind was settled; as a Christian and as a preacher of the gospel, I could not fight. I could not reconcile it to myself to bear arms, or to kill one of my fellow creatures; however, I determined to go, and to trust in the Lord, and accordingly prepared for my journey" to the military camp to which he had been assigned. When Lee arrived, the sergeant presented him with a gun, which he refused. Continuing in his disobedience, he was summoned before the colonel ("a man of great humanity, although a profane swearer"), who tried unsuccessfully on several occasions to convince Lee that it was his duty as a Christian and a citizen to fight. "I told him," Lee relates, "that I could not kill a man with a good conscience, but I was a friend to my country, and was willing to do anything I could, while I continued in the army, except that of fighting. He then asked me if I would be willing to drive their baggage wagon? I told him I would, though I had never driven a wagon before."

Lee's willingness to cooperate led to his being released from temporary arrest. Accompanying the militia in its marches up and down the state, he spent the next three months mainly in preaching hellfire to the troops, organizing campfire revival meetings ("I wept much and prayed loud, and many of the poor soldiers also wept," writes Lee of the first one he held), holding religious singsongs, and ministering to the sick, wounded, and dying. By September, however, things began to look critical for the Revolutionary army in this area. "The Colonel told me, inasmuch as I was not willing to bear arms, I must join the pioneers. I was afterward appointed sergeant of the pioneers, which was a safe and easy berth; there were but few in that company and I had to direct them in their labours, which was not hard." On one occasion during a retreat, when the British were bearing down on them and the road was thronged with refugees fleeing before the

283

advancing army, "the colonel rode up and said to me, 'Well, Lee! don't you think you could fight now?' I told him I could fight with switches, but I could not kill a man." Shortly afterward, at the end of October, Lee received his discharge and started back home.[41] The lonely witness of the young Methodist, content to accept noncombatant status in the army provided that he was not called upon to actually shed human blood—a position that brings to mind that of the famous evangelist, Dwight L. Moody in the Civil War, discussed in a later chapter—was less dramatic but demanded more courage, perhaps, than the stand of the objector from one of the peace sects who refused induction into the armed forces.

[41] Minton Thrift, *Memoir of the Rev. Jesse Lee,* chap. III.

284

Chapter 7

The Peace Testimony
of the Early American Moravians:
An Ambiguous Witness

I

The Moravians emerged from somewhat the same Pietist milieu as the Dunkers. The episcopacy that they claimed derived from a church—the Unity of Czech Brethren or *Unitas Fratrum*—that had acknowledged back in the fifteenth century the pacifist and antistate *Weltanschauung* of the sixteenth-century Anabaptists and Mennonites (although it subsequently accommodated its political and social outlook more closely to that prevailing in society at large).[1] Like the Mennonites and Dunkers and Schwenkfelders, the first Moravians to reach America and their founder, Count von Zinzendorf, were Germans, and the church long retained the German language among its members; this difference in culture between them and their English-speaking environment served likewise to emphasize the trend toward nonconformity to the world that they had brought with them from Europe as part of their religious philosophy. Finally, the American Moravians of the eighteenth century shared Quaker views on the subject of war —or, at least, so it appeared to many of their fellow colonists. Yet, in fact, Moravian noncombatancy differed in many important respects in spirit both from the Anabaptist tradition of nonresistance among the other German peace sects and from Quaker pacifism, whose history we have already traced to the end of the Revolutionary War.

Although they frowned on direct participation of the brethren in war either as conscripts or, worse, as volunteers, Zinzendorf and his German Moravians saw no objection in hiring substitutes in the last resort, where there was no other way out of serving personally in the

---

[1] Some recollection of the early pacifism of the Czech Brethren seems to have existed among the eighteenth-century Moravians. John Ettwein refers to it several times. (See Kenneth Gardiner Hamilton, *John Ettwein and the Moravian Church during the Revolutionary Period* in TMHS, XII [1940], pts. III and IV, 215, 326.) During the American Revolution, Ettwein wrote to the pastor at Lititz referring to the foundation of the Czech Unity of Brethren in 1457-1458: "It was in Lititz that the first Brethren determined not to meddle in any war; God forbid that the Brethren in Lititz of today should stray from that course." Again in the early 1790's he says in a letter: "Since the time of John Huss [the United Brethren] have kept that religious principle," i.e., their refusal to bear arms. For the pacifism of the early Czech Brethren, see my book, *The Political and Social Doctrines of the Unity of Czech Brethren in the Fifteenth and Early Sixteenth Centuries*, The Hague, 1957.

army or in paying a special tax to buy freedom from military service. Their objections, as we shall see, seem to have stemmed as much from their otherworldliness as from a belief in the incompatibility of war with the Christian calling.

The first Moravians to arrive in the New World settled in General Oglethorpe's recently founded colony of Georgia in April 1735. On their way over from their German homeland the group had stopped for a short period in London. There, in conversations with Oglethorpe, they had explained to the general their church's objection to bearing arms, and he had promised them complete exemption from this obligation. Unfortunately, they received no written confirmation of this privilege to present to the colonial authorities in Savannah. Trouble was soon to arise on this score, since the struggling little colony was at this date beset on all sides with potential enemies: Spaniards in Florida to the south with claims to the colony's territories and Indians whose hostility might easily be aroused by conflicting claims to land. Therefore, all settlers were expected to be in readiness to answer the call to arms should an emergency arise; in addition, the freeholders were required to train at weekly drillings or find a substitute to perform this duty in their place. Land for the Moravian settlers had been taken out not only in Zinzendorf's name but in those of two other leading members: Augustus Gottlieb Spangenberg (1704-1792), a university-trained, former Lutheran theologian, and the unschooled brother, David Nitschmann (called "the Hausmeister" to distinguish him from the bishop of the same name).

For more than a year after their arrival no direct clash with the authorities on this subject of military service occurred. Spangenberg, who acted as leader of the group, excused himself from personal attendance at drilling—on grounds of health. The additional obligation, which was incumbent on him in his capacity as a freeholder, of taking his turn in the watch of ten men set up to patrol the town at all times of day and night had to be fulfilled, too. Spangenberg, indeed, acknowledged the necessity of this precautionary measure but still felt it preferable to pay a substitute to take his place rather than to serve in person. Presumably, the watch was furnished with some kind of arms; but the fact that it functioned rather as a police than as a military force probably led him to give it his qualified approval. Foreseeing trouble in the future, however, Spangenberg referred the whole problem back to the Moravian center at Herrnhut in Saxony for consideration in order to determine the course which their colonists should take.[2]

[2] Adelaide L. Fries, *The Moravians in Georgia 1735-1740*, pp. 87, 88. This volume is based mainly on the Herrnhut archives.

In February 1736 a second party of Moravians arrived in Savannah under the leadership of Bishop David Nitschmann. Bishop Nitschmann, a carpenter by trade and a man of simple but deep piety, had been one of the original refugees from Moravia. He had been disturbed by the lack of clarity in previous negotiations with the colony's trustees on the issue of bearing arms. Before embarking, therefore, he once again raised the matter with General Oglethorpe in London, seeking to get the matter defined more exactly. Again, no completely satisfactory agreement could be reached. Oglethorpe insisted that the three freeholders had the obligation, if unwilling or unable to serve themselves, to furnish three able-bodied men in their stead. This interpretation appeared unsatisfactory to Nitschmann, who among the early Moravian leaders seems to have been the one most concerned to uphold a strictly nonresistant position. Moravians, he told the general in conclusion, "could not and would not fight."

On account of these complications members of the second party decided not to take out any land individually, since this step would involve them as freeholders in military duties. Instead, they worked as Zinzendorf's "servants" and awaited clarification of the issue to result from further negotiations between Zinzendorf and the trustees.

Although Oglethorpe, during a visit he paid to his colony at this time, agreed that Moravians might take out tracts of land of up to twenty acres without incurring the obligation of military service, the situation continued to be uncertain. In the summer of 1736, Spangenberg and Bishop Nitschmann visited Pennsylvania. They were much impressed by what they observed there. The Quaker province appeared to them to offer more favorable prospects for a permanent settlement than did Georgia. In the first place, the proximity of large numbers of Indians there held out the hope that Pennsylvania might develop into a fruitful mission field for the Moravians. A second, and more immediately relevant, attraction was the similarity of the views of Pennsylvania's Quaker rulers on the subject of war and military service to those of the Moravian immigrants, a fact which would resolve the ticklish problem then facing them in Georgia.[3]

Indeed, within a few months after the departure of the two Moravian leaders, their community was subjected to a severe test. In February 1737 a scare of an imminent invasion of the colony by Spanish forces arose, and now the call went out to all able-bodied freemen to appear under arms to repel any attack. On 20 February three officers appeared at the chief Moravian dwelling house and demanded of a leading Moravian there, John Töltschig—a gardener by trade and, like Bishop Nitschmann, one of the original Moravian escapees—the names

[3] *Ibid.*, pp. 93, 94, 126, 141.

of all male Moravians capable of bearing arms, the servants along with the freeholders. "There was no one among them who could bear arms, and he would get no names from them," Töltschig replied boldly to one of the officers. To this response came the sarcastic reply: "It was remarkable that in a house full of strong men none could bear arms, —he should hurry and give them the names, they could not wait." Since Töltschig persisted in his refusal, the officers left him alone for the time being. The Moravian at once proceeded to the house of Savannah's chief magistrate, Mr. Causton, to clear the matter up. There the following dialogue took place between the two men:

CAUSTON: Everybody must go to the war and fight for his own safety, and if you will not join the army the townspeople will burn down your house and will kill you all.

TÖLTSCHIG: That may happen, but we can not help it, it is against our conscience to fight.

CAUSTON: If you do not mean to fight you had better go and hide in the woods, out of sight of the people, or it will be the worse for you; . . .

TÖLTSCHIG: You forget that General Oglethorpe promised us exemption from military service, and we claim the liberty he pledged.

CAUSTON: If the Count [Zinzendorf], and the Trustees and the King himself had agreed on that in London it will count for nothing here, if war comes it will be *fight or die*. If I were an officer on a march and met people who would not join me, I would shoot them with my own hand, and you can expect no other treatment from the officers here.

TÖLTSCHIG: We are all servants, and can not legally be impressed.

CAUSTON: If the Count himself were here he would have to take his gun on his shoulder, and all his servants with him. If he were living on his estate at Old Fort [i.e., in Georgia] it would make no difference, for the order of the magistrate must be obeyed. If the English, to whom the country belongs must fight, shall others go free?

Finally, Töltschig agreed to give the numbers of able-bodied men available, but he still persisted in withholding their names, explaining that they were conscientiously opposed to such service because it was incompatible with their religion. Therefore, as the brethren told

288

Causton at this time, bearing arms "being a thing against our conscience we cannot, dare not, will not do it." However, they added mollifyingly, "as we do not apprehend this to be the first, or the chief point of Christianity, we do not strive to bring over others to our persuasion, but leave every man to his own opinion and this is the liberty we desire for ourselves."[4]

By now the townsfolk were aroused against these foreigners, who refused to take their proper share in the community's defense—for reasons that must have been hard for most to grasp. The Moravians, however, stood firm, asserting their right to refuse service. They had explained their scruples to Oglethorpe, and he had accepted their noncombatancy. They believed that they had the right to expect that the authorities on the spot would also respect their position even if they did not understand it. About this time, too, specific instructions were received from Zinzendorf and their Herrnhut center, where the question had been referred in Biblical fashion to the lot, that "they should take no part in military affairs, but might pay any fines incurred by refusal."

At the end of the month the Moravians received an order from the authorities—who had evidently for the time being given up the idea of forcing them to perform direct military service—to haul supplies of wood for a fort that was being erected as protection against possible enemy attack. They replied that their wagons and oxen were at the officers' disposal and that they were ready to keep the oxen fed, but that they were unwilling to participate personally in this kind of indirect war activity. Such a refusal to collaborate with the machinery of war was a more uncompromising stand than the German-speaking peace sects of this period usually took. And, indeed, as the anger of their fellow townsfolk began to rise, some of the brethren began to have misgivings about whether they were acting rightly in taking this course. Would it not be possible, they argued, at least to assist in cutting logs for use in constructing the fort simply as a neighborly act? If they refused to accept pay for such work, would not this refusal make clear their motive and remove any taint of complicity in the waging of war? Recourse was then had, as usual, to the lot, and the answer received that such work was, indeed, entirely forbidden them. This proved to be a providential decision, as the historian of the Moravian settlement in Georgia points out, for it later transpired that the people had decided that, if the Moravians were ready to help with building fortifications, then their objections to fighting must be a sham.

[4] This last quotation is cited from the Moravians' petition to Causton, dated Savannah, 25 Feb. 1737, in the Public Record Office (London), C.O. 5/639.

As the tense situation continued in the colony, a second question was put to the lot on 2 March: should the community remain or withdraw altogether from the province, since Causton had intimated that they would be liable to military duties wherever they settled in Georgia? The answer received was: "Go out from among them." Now, however, Causton became alarmed at the prospect of losing these honest, industrious, and God-fearing settlers; there was probably a considerable amount of bluff in the threats he had directed at Töltschig a little earlier in the hopes of browbeating these outwardly meek and submissive peasants from Central Europe. It would be better to put up with their peculiarities than lose them altogether. So he now told them that he must refer the whole matter back to the trustees in England. Meanwhile, the invasion scare subsided, and things returned more or less to normal again. The brethren decided for the time being to postpone their resolve to migrate elsewhere.[5]

At first, some of the trustees received the news of the Moravians' behavior with alarmed surprise, thus indicating that perhaps not all of them had previously realized that the Moravians held a Quakerlike objection to war. "It were to be wished," Lord Egmont declared on 8 June, "they had never gone, for though they be a very religious and painstaking people, yet that principle of not fighting is a very bad one in a new erected colony." Soon Count Zinzendorf himself intervened to explain and expound his people's pacifism. They cannot be got to bear arms, he wrote on 19 August, even if force is used to this end and whatever the circumstances. "Je sais que nos Frères ne consentiront jamais ni de gré ni de force à aller tuer les gens dans des pays ou ils ne recherchent que le salut des âmes, parceque si les paroles de Notre Sauveur addressés à ses disciples n'ont pas ce sens, ils n'en ont aucun." And he concluded by stating his belief that the trustees would respect scruples of this kind. Indeed, the latter had already sent instructions to the authorities in Georgia that the Moravians should "not be troubled on that account," in the hope, apparently, that such tolerance might lead them to remain on in the colony even after the three years for which they had contracted to stay had ended. In answer to Zinzendorf's letter the trustees told the count:

We reply that we only require his two townships or lots to send each of them one man, who need not be a Moravian, but only paid by

[5] Fries, pp. 161, 163-67, 172. Spangenberg, writing from Philadelphia on 20 April 1737 (P.R.O., C.O. 5/639), had explained to the trustees the reasons why his brethren contemplated leaving Georgia. Their conduct there, he stated, had been beyond reproach apart from their conscientious objection "to bear arms or engage in war." There was really no cause, therefore, why they should be detained in the colony against their will.

them, and that our care of the province requires it: but we shall not oblige his people to fight, liberty of conscience being allowed to all within our province. That if this does not please him and he has altered his thoughts (for when in England he had agreed to this) then they shall have leave to withdraw upon his acquainting us that it is his desire.

These assurances seem to have satisfied Zinzendorf, even if his followers in Georgia continued to feel somewhat uneasy in their new home.[6]

In September 1737 they received a reply from Zinzendorf to their account of the events of the early months of the year. "You will not bear arms either defensive or offensive," the count told them. He went on to report his unsuccessful attempts to get a watertight declaration of exemption from the colony's trustees in England. The latter, as we have seen, were adamant in their demand that the Moravians hire the services of two armed men for the two town lots that were in their possession (they sent instructions to Causton to this effect). Zinzendorf therefore consented, feeling—like Spangenberg a little earlier— that, at least while they were employed on the night watch, the substitutes were performing a legitimate police duty necessary for the public welfare. But the count still continued to oppose, if at all possible, the hiring of substitutes for specifically military duties. In that case, he wrote, "there is nothing to do but to say *no*, and wait."

As the months passed, the feeling grew stronger among the Moravian colonists that their position in Georgia in regard to military service was unlikely to improve and that the best course would be to move elsewhere. The outbreak of war with Spain in October 1739—the War of Jenkin's Ear—reopened the old problem and renewed the group's unpopularity in the community. In fact, from the autumn of 1738, when the trustees refused all further concessions in regard to the brethren's military obligations, individuals and small parties began to leave the southern colony for Pennsylvania. The bulk of the Moravians left Savannah as a group in April 1740. This marked the end of their Georgian venture.[7]

The young and exposed colony had proved an uncertain resting place for a people that endeavored to steer clear of involvement in the affairs of the worldly community, for a brotherhood that wished to keep its hands from shedding human blood. They had met with hostil-

[6] *Diary of the First Earl of Egmont*, II, 412, 413, 422, 433, 470. Zinzendorf's letter (dated 19 Aug. 1737) is in P.R.O., C.O. 5/639.

[7] Fries, pp. 181-183, 215, 216. The total number of Moravian settlers in Georgia amounted to just under fifty.

ity from local officials and populace alike. Yet the obvious high qualities of the Moravians as pioneer settlers led not only the Quaker pacifists of Pennsylvania to give them shelter, but the nonpacifist rulers of other colonies to compete now in offering inducements to get them to settle within their boundaries. In Europe, even, the Prussian king, Frederick the Great, had exempted them from oathtaking and military service, and Holland and Denmark would have been prepared to grant the same privileges. Finally, in 1749 the British Parliament was to pass an act to the same effect (22 Geo. II c. 30, sect. IV).

In Pennsylvania—so long, at least, as Friends were in the seat of government—the Moravians were unlikely to be called upon to bear arms or to take a judicial oath. But from their experiences in Georgia they knew that, if they or their coreligionists in Europe were to accept any of the tempting offers from other colonies, they would first need to obtain clear-cut guarantees from the highest authority in the British dominions that they would be immune from molestation on this score. An act of Parliament incorporating these privileges would also act as a kind of charter for the foreign church throughout the realm of the English monarch.

The prosperity of the Moravian settlements in Pennsylvania, after only a few years of farming in the wilderness, provided an excellent argument for Zinzendorf and his coreligionists in their lobbying at Westminster. They were able, also, to enlist the support of General Oglethorpe in their efforts to gain exemption. In a letter to the Lords Commissioners of the Board of Trade and Plantations, dated 1 November 1746, the general described the difficulties the Moravians had encountered from the local inhabitants in his colony of Georgia because of their refusal to bear arms, "tho'," he added, "at the same time, they did the government service, in labour and other matters, equal and superior [to what] they could have done as militia." The Moravians, he went on, "are an industrious, sober, and quiet people." "I think, the greater number we could procure of them, the more would increase the welfare and cultivation of the country; . . . tho' they are indulged in not carrying arms. And indeed I take it to be one of the principal points of a new settlement to indulge all foreign Protestants in the full exercise of religion, as well with respect to any scruples they may have to carrying arms, as to public worship, and form of oaths."[8]

In pleading their case before Parliament, the Moravians, some of whom were now settled in England itself, were careful to emphasize that, apart from their objection to war and oaths (an aversion that they shared with the by now highly respectable British Quakers), they

8 *Acta Fratrum Unitatis in Anglia,* pp. 31, 32.

would behave as model citizens. In addition, states their petition: "Those of their people, who scruple the bearing of arms, will make no difficulty to pay, in lieu thereof, the sum or sums, which persons of the same estate, in the same province, who, by reason of age, sex, or other disabilities, cannot go to war in person, are assessed or rated at."[9]

Satisfied that the Moravian church since its inception a few decades earlier had held a genuine testimony against war and oaths and anxious, also, to encourage the settlement of these hardworking and frugal farmers in British America, Parliament passed the desired legislation. Then, to quote the words of a later Moravian document, "encouraged by that act and the glorious liberty in Pennsylvania most of the United Brethren [i.e., Moravians] now on this continent came from Germany in full trust and confidence that they and their children would enjoy here liberty of conscience without restraint."[10]

Freedom of worship they were indeed to have in their new home across the ocean. But their hopes of being able to live there in peace without recourse to arms were doomed to frustration within a short period of years. And it was by their own decision, under the impelling advice of their own leaders, that they—at least temporarily—abandoned the uncompromising nonresistance of their Georgian days.

In the autumn of 1755 bloody frontier warfare flared up, developing into the French and Indian War of 1755-1763. The Moravian settlements in Pennsylvania were at once exposed to the raids of hostile Indians, who were in the pay of the French and who, moreover, felt aggrieved at the way the white man had been treating them. A reign of terror ensued in the area, climaxing in the massacre of some ten unresisting Moravian settlers on the Mahoning River in November of that year. Refugees began to pour into the Moravian townships, among them Bethlehem and Nazareth, which were all situated slightly farther behind the line of Indian attack. A time of testing had arrived. Until then the Moravian brethren had lived peacefully alongside the

---

[9] *Ibid.*, p. 26. The implication that there were also some Moravians who did not have scruples against bearing arms, which appears to be the literal meaning of the wording, may not have been intended. However, although nonparticipation in military affairs appears as part of the discipline obligatory on the Moravians in the New World during this period, we read of church members in good standing in Europe serving as active soldiers in the Prussian and Saxon armies during the 1730's, 1740's, and 1750's. No objection seems to have been raised by the church authorities, even though presumably they were volunteers. At least some of these men later emigrated to America. See Otto Uttendörfer and Walther E. Schmidt, *Die Brüder: Aus Vergangenheit und Gegenwart der Brüdergemeine*, 2nd edn., pp. 102-10.

[10] Petition of 12 May 1778, Ettwein Papers 1299, Moravian Archives, Bethlehem (Pa.).

Indians, making converts among them where the way opened up, and remaining unarmed except for a few rifles for use in hunting game to supplement the meager food supplies of a frontier existence. Although as citizens of the Quaker province they were not liable to any military duties, they had always, from their first settlement in Georgia, stressed their noncombatancy. Were they now to abandon the peaceable principles which had been endorsed not only by the church leaders, including Zinzendorf, but by the ordeal of the lot expressing the divine will itself? If they did so, they would seem to stand condemned as hypocrites in the eyes of their neighbors.

Yet, as the situation became more menacing and as the main settlements came under danger of direct attack and the refugees—most of them non-Moravians—kept streaming in with stories of atrocities and acts of Indian savagery, doubts about the wisdom of their renunciation of all armed defense began to increase and more and more came to find vocal expression—perhaps chiefly because for most of the brotherhood pacifism had been mainly a negative creed, primarily a principle of noninvolvement rather than of outgoing love and a doctrine that had been imposed from above as part of the sectarian discipline. They were not indeed *kriegerisch*, but at the same time, they began to say, they were not *quäkerisch*. Could they abandon their womenfolk and children to the depredations of the Indians, not to speak of the hundreds of non-Moravian refugees who had sought shelter among them and who would not understand their scruples concerning the use of arms? Would not principle be mistaken for cowardice? Indeed, was it really contrary to their religion to take at least some measures in self-defense against a brutal and cruel enemy, especially when these precautions had no aggressive intent (even though they might in the last resort involve the handling of weapons)? Surely such steps did not mean the abandonment of their opposition to war—to wars between civilized nations carried on by mercenary or conscript armies—and to preparations for war?

It was, above all, Bishop Spangenberg who, by exercising a form of spiritual leadership in the American church that gave his advice immense prestige among the brethren, was responsible in the emergency that now faced the church for giving a peculiar twist, a novel interpretation, to his church's peace testimony. This testimony was not abandoned altogether, as we shall see: it was merely deemed inapplicable in the existing situation. That some still cleaved to a more rigorous interpretation and maintained a strictly nonresistant position seems probable from certain oblique references in the sources, but it is obvious that the overwhelming mass of brethren followed Spangenberg.

It was the bishop, then, who led in urging the Moravians to take measures to guard against attack by the approaching Indians. It was, he declared, "needful by all means to stand in defence of Bethlehem. . . . I think the best way is to keep guard and proper watches day and night." At his suggestion, small forts were built, each garrisoned by about fifty men, and stockades were erected around the settlements. Later, in his autobiography (written originally in German), he describes their situation around the turn of the year in the following words:

At night the watchmen shouted one to another at intervals of an hour, so that the sound rang out loudly into the forest. We also built block houses and mounted them with guns, and when a gun was discharged it was a signal to the vicinity that hostile Indians were near. Thus when the savages came spying at night, they always found us in readiness. Then I called all the Brethren together and begged them for Jesus' sake by all means to spare the life of every hostile Indian (shooting low if they were forced to shoot), and if one was, perchance, shot in the legs, we proposed to take him in for treatment and care for him with all faithfulness until he recovered. I fell upon my face and besought the Saviour to graciously prevent all bloodshed at our place, and, to Him be thanks, He heard our prayer.[11]

He insisted that the brethren continue to regard the Indians with love, not hatred—a difficult injunction in the trying situation in which the community then found itself. In December, referring to the Indian converts who had fled for safety from outlying Gnadenhütten, he told his congregation: "I have observed to my sorrow that some of you have somewhat of repugnance to the Indians. Cast out this leaven!" At the same time, he attempted to dampen the rising belligerency among his people. "I know that some of the Brethren say—Yes! had we but more guns! Had we but more people!" This attitude was a mistaken one, he said, for it deflected them from putting their trust solely in God and was therefore likely to arouse His anger and bring disaster upon them.[12]

Spangenberg's role in leading the Pennsylvania Moravians to modify, if not entirely to abandon, their previous noncombatancy seems to have been a decisive one;[13] so it is worthwhile to devote some atten-

[11] Joseph Mortimer Levering, A History of Bethlehem, Pennsylvania 1741-1892, pp. 319-21, 323, 324, 337, 338.

[12] John W. Jordan (ed.), "Bishop Augustus Gottlieb Spangenberg," PMHB, VIII, no. 3 (1884), 236.

[13] See Gerhard Reichel, August Gottlieb Spangenberg, pp. 201-5.

tion to his views on the subject of the use of force in society. Briefly, his reasoning was as follows. The state has the obligation to defend its citizens against evildoers from within and against attack from without. Where it failed to provide such protection (as was now the case in Quaker-ruled Pennsylvania), a Christian community—which otherwise had the obligation to refuse compliance with any demands that the state might make for military service—had a duty to step into the breach and give the protection that the authorities were incapable of providing. Nevertheless, the measures taken in this respect must approximate as nearly as possible to the gospel injunctions. Love must never give way before hatred—even of a brutal enemy. Defensive measures wherever possible should be noninjurious: stockades and forts and alarm shots caused no actual hurt, and shooting to wound was preferable to shooting to kill. The store of lethal weapons should be reduced to a minimum: overabundance of arms was dangerous, for it was likely to provoke an aggressive spirit. Finally, although communal measures of self-defense were legitimate even in a Christian people, this fact did not derogate from the binding force of personal nonresistance to evil in private life.[14] The state must be a terror to the wicked; the Christian community should be capable of acting in self-defense; but the individual, especially when he belonged to the pastorate, was called to an exact observance of the Christian law of love in regard to his own person.

Spangenberg's views, which bear strong traces of his Lutheran background, are well illustrated in a letter he wrote on 23 December 1755 to some Moravians in New York City, who had offered to transmit further supplies of arms and ammunition to their beleaguered brethren on the Pennsylvania frontier. This offer Spangenberg politely but firmly turned down. He noted, too, that the New York brethren were evidently deeply divided in their opinions concerning the justifiability of defensive measures. "Some of them," he remarks, "advised us to make no resistance to the barbarous enemy, but rather to come away

14 "This kind of love has prevailed upon many an enemy to reflect within himself, see, and own his injustice, and from an enemy, to become a friend. Oh how animating are such examples!" exclaimed the bishop in *An Exposition of Christian Doctrine, as taught in the Protestant Church of the United Brethren, or Unitas Fratrum* (2nd edn., p. 368) in a passage devoted to extolling the gospel injunction of turning the other cheek. Elsewhere (p. 58) he explains that wars between nations are "the righteous judgments of God." "He punishes one nation, on account of their sins, by means of another nation that is not much better; and this is again punished, as soon as it exalts itself, by means of other nations." The *Exposition* was originally published in German in 1779 (at Barby in Saxony) under the title *Idea Fides Fratrum . . .* ; the first English edition was issued in 1780.

from our settlements. Others write to us to stand upon our defence, and to oppose such wicked and abominable creatures." He goes on to give his own views on the relationship between government and force. Rulers are not merely permitted but are positively under an obligation to defend the weak and innocent against attack. "This sword given to them, they have not in vain. . . . [If] they neglect this their office, they will be answerable for it to their Master." On the other hand, a minister of religion may only use spiritual weapons: on no account must he wield a carnal weapon (unless, possibly, in defense of some innocent victim of evil). "He conquers by no other weapons than by the blood of the Lamb, by the sword of the Gospel, by faith in Christ, by prayers and tears etc." He is called to resist not evil, to turn the other cheek, to give his cloak to him who takes away his coat. If he agreed to become a soldier, he would be disloyal to "his commission" from God. However, Spangenberg went on,

> A common man, such as they call a layman, if he hath wife and children, he is to provide for his family, and to protect them against mischief. It would not be right in him, to see his wife ravished by a wicked fellow, and to sit still at it. It would be very wrong in him, if wicked wretches should fall upon his children, and he be indolent and patient at the murdering of them. If it is right in a pastor to kill rather the wolf, than to see the lamb killed, it is certainly right in a father, to stand up for the life of his children.

Lastly, the bishop returned to the situation in which he and the other brethren in and around Bethlehem, both the married men with families and single persons who carried on a community life during this period, then found themselves. Turning to the pacifists among the New York Moravians, he explained that at Bethlehem they were too many to just pull up and move to some other more secure spot. "Where should we go to be safer? Here we know Providence has placed us." Here it was their duty to remain. On the other hand, he also expressed his disagreement with the militants who were urging more aggressive measures against their assailants. "We do not trust in weapons nor in arms," he told them. "For we know for certain that if the Lord will have us suffer, no arms will keep us free. If he will have us safe, not all the devils will be able to hurt us in the least."

In another passage of the letter Spangenberg vividly and dramatically pointed to the terrible dilemma that faced them in this crisis: on the one hand, they naturally desired to afford protection to their families and the hundreds of innocent people not of their faith who had sought a refuge in their settlements; on the other hand, they were

297

at the same time anxious to remain loyal to their Christian noncombatancy. After the first decision, to appoint watchmen as a deterrent against a surprise attack, had been reached,

> The watchmen then proposed whether it would not be good to have some guns, partly to give a signal to the rest of the guard, partly to hinder the cruel enemy from falling upon the sisters and children, and using them after his abominable manner. They said, "What shall we do? If the savages would be satisfied with taking our lives it might be so; but shall we leave our sisters and our children a prey to their devilish designs?" I could not say, "Let the savages do what they please with our sisters and our children." No indeed! For how could a father or a husband do so and not think himself guilty of neglecting his duty? But this I have told my Brethren, "Pray rather to God that he may send fear and trembling upon the enemy and thereby keep him a great way from us, for I should neither like to see an Indian, nor one of my Brethren nor their wives and children, killed at Bethlehem, at Nazareth, or at any of our places."[15]

One historian has attributed to Spangenberg a major role in bringing to an end the period of Quaker rule in the province, which came about in June 1756.[16] Undoubtedly, this view is much exaggerated. It is unlikely that the opinions of the backwoods bishop could have carried so much weight in the counsels of the provincial capital. He may, however, be reckoned one of the most trenchant contemporary critics of the policies of the Quaker pacifists in office. In a letter written on 9 December 1755, for instance, he says:

> The Quakers have ruled the country up to now according to their particular doctrines of belief. What our Saviour said to His disciples about not resisting evil, they have applied to the authorities. And the words of the apostle: "it is the minister of God and beareth not the sword in vain," etc., have been forgotten.[17]

Early in 1756 the chief opponent of the Quaker peace policy, Benjamin Franklin, visited Bethlehem with a commission from the provincial governor to strengthen the military forces of the threatened northwestern frontier. Upon arriving in the town, Franklin relates, "I was surprised to find it in so good a posture of defence. . . . The prin-

---

[15] J. W. Jordan (ed.), "Bishop Augustus Gottlieb Spangenberg," *PMHB*, VIII, no. 3 (1884), 235-39; William C. Reichel (ed.), *Memorial of the Moravian Church*, I, 204-6; Hamilton, *John Ettwein*, pp. 218, 219.

[16] Hellmuth Erbe, *Bethlehem, Pa. Eine kommunistische Herrnhuter Kolonie des 18. Jahrhunderts*, pp. 111-13.

[17] Hamilton, *John Ettwein*, p. 219.

298

cipal buildings were defended by a stockade. . . . The armed brethren, too, kept watch, and relieved as methodically as in any garrison town." Having expressed to Spangenberg his astonishment that a people whom, on account of their parliamentary exemption from military service, he had previously supposed were "conscientiously scrupulous of bearing arms" were now manifesting such a belligerent spirit, he was told by the bishop that conscientious objection, in fact, "was not one of their established principles; but that, at the time of their obtaining that act, it was thought to be a principle with many of their people." In the present emergency they had discovered that few among them now held to an uncompromising pacifism. "It seems," Franklin concludes ironically, "they were either deceived in themselves, or deceived the Parliament. But common sense, aided by present danger, will sometimes be too strong for whimsical opinions."[18]

Naturally, the military authorities were pleased at this unexpected aid from a sect whom they had come to look upon as little better than the Quakers in its attitude toward defense. Spangenberg, too, was proud of the role that his people were playing as a bulwark preventing the whole province from being overrun by the Indians. As he reported to the brethren at Herrnhut in a letter of 24 July 1756:

Ja, ich dürfte wohl sagen, es würde in ganz Pennsylvania nicht besser gewacht als bei und von den Brüdern. Das glaubt auch nicht nur unser Gouvernement, sondern das ganze Land. Sie sehen deshalb Bethlehem und unsere settlements auf Nazareth als eine Vormauer der ganzen Provinz an. Würden die Brüder aus dem Wege geschafft, so wäre nichts, das den Strom aufhalten könnte.[19]

The brethren applied to the government for official sanction for the defensive steps they had taken, and approval was, of course, gladly given. In March 1757, in fact, the governor appointed several leading

---

[18] The Autobiography of Benjamin Franklin, 1964 edn., pp. 231, 232. Several details in this passage, not quoted here, are inaccurate. See Levering, A History of Bethlehem, p. 336. Franklin's concluding remarks evidently rather irritated the church's official historian, J. Taylor Hamilton, who writes: "Yet it ought not to have been difficult for a philosopher to discriminate between professional participation in military operations of an aggressive character and preparation for self-defence against savages in order that bloodshed might be averted by the very thoroughness of the preparation" (A History of the Moravian Church during the Eighteenth and Nineteenth Centuries, p. 174).

[19] Quoted in Erbe, Bethlehem, p. 114. This passage runs in English as follows: "Indeed, I may well say that in all Pennsylvania the watch is kept nowhere better than with and by the Brethren. Not only our government but the whole community thinks this. They, therefore, regard Bethlehem and our settlements around Nazareth as a bastion of the whole province. Should the Brethren be swept out of the way, then there would be nothing that could stem the torrent." (My translation.)

Moravian laymen "captains or overseers of ye watches."[20] And in July of the same year a government report spoke warmly of the "prudent circumspection of the Brethren" at Bethlehem in arming some of their Indians and using them as reconnoitering parties to discover anyone trying to creep up on a settlement; in this way a surprise attack could be forestalled.[21]

Clearly, the overwhelming majority of the Pennsylvania Moravians had followed Spangenberg's lead in approving the use of arms in a situation where the state had ceased to afford protection to its citizens. Yet the bishop was obviously reluctant to signal a complete retreat from their pacifism and to abandon the church's claim to a noncombatant position in case of war; and the laity, likewise, made up as they were for the most part of conservative-minded farmers of European peasant stock, were undoubtedly thankful that too radical a reversal of their earlier stand was not imposed upon them even in this critical time. The halfway position that they now occupied is described in a petition which Spangenberg had drawn up "for appointment of officers for the Moravian civil guard—Bethlehem, March 14, 1757." In it he states:

> Tho' we conscientiously scruple to be engaged in wars as soldiers, to follow after enemies, to take away lives, etc., adhering to the very same sentiments we have professed before the British parliament, when we obtained an act securing us against being forced to bear arms, or go to war, etc. Yet in the last troublesome time, when we were in danger of being fallen upon by the murdering Indians, we have kept strict watch, and have secured several of our settlements with stocadoes [sic], etc., which has been hitherto so successful for us and our neighbours, as to prevent a surprise and bloodshedding on both sides.[22]

This must surely be the most pacifistic petition ever drawn up by a home guard unit—or perhaps, more accurately, the most militaristic petition ever composed in the name of a pacifist church!

For the Pennsylvania Moravians the period of danger was over by 1758. We must now turn to the story of the little colony of Moravians who in 1753 had begun the first settlement in North Carolina. Several

---

[20] Reichel, "Friedensthal and Its Stockaded Mill," *TMHS*, II (1886), 30.

[21] *Pa. Archives*, 1st ser., III, 243, 244. John Hill Martin (*Historical Sketch of Bethlehem in Pennsylvania*, p. 22) speaks of this as a government report, and, although the exact provenance of the document is not completely clear, this identification would seem to be correct.

[22] Hamilton, *John Ettwein*, p. 219. The petition is printed in *Pa. Col. Records*, VIII, 459, 460. The actual signatories were Matthew Shropp and John Bechtel, but undoubtedly the wording was Spangenberg's.

communities were already in existence there when war broke out. However, it was not until the summer of 1756 that a danger threatened there similar to that which had arisen in the Pennsylvania settlements. At the beginning of July, so the diary of the Bethabara church records, news reached the brethren that the Cherokee Indians, hitherto friendly, had gone over to the side of the French, that the area stood in imminent danger of attack, and that already people were beginning to flee in panic to the more protected districts of the province. The brethren knew from correspondence of the defensive measures that their sister settlements in Pennsylvania had taken in a like situation. Extracts from letters describing these measures were now read out at a meeting of the unmarried brethren who formed this community. "The matter was discussed pro and con, but no conclusion reached." The brethren were therefore dismissed by their leader, Brother Christian Heinrich (who was, in fact, in favor of imitating Bethlehem's example), with the recommendation "that each Brother think the matter over quietly, and lay it before the Lord, and then state his view to the head of his room." "For himself," he added, "he had no fear, he was chiefly considering the others, but foresight was seemly for the Children of God." On the next day, 5 July, the single brethren gave a unanimous verdict. "All work," they agreed, "should be dropped until a palisade had been built around the houses, making them safe before the first incursion of the Indians should take place. Duties were assigned each man,—felling trees, digging the trench, continuing the harvest."

A week later two of the brethren were detailed to visit the local justice of the peace, who might well have been puzzled to know where the community now stood in regard to military preparations. The two brethren explained that their people still felt bound to take no part officially in "military affairs," claiming the benefit of exemption granted by Parliament; on the other hand, they were anxious to contribute generously in money to the defense of the country, which they hoped—which, indeed, they were sure—the governor would now undertake. "Justice Hughes," the church diary records, "was entirely satisfied with this explanation, which he accepted without argument; and the Brethren, having dined with the Justice, returned home."[23]

The other Moravian villages followed Bethabara in taking similar measures—establishing armed watches, constructing forts and stockades, and digging ditches.[24] A new settlement, which was named Bethania, arose to accommodate refugees from the outlying farms. The

[23] *Records of the Moravians in North Carolina,* I, 170.
[24] See, e.g., John Henry Clewell, *History of Wachovia in North Carolina,* pp. 35ff.

301

North Carolina communities, too, adopted the wording of Bishop Spangenberg's petition of March 1757, quoted above, for a statement of their position, which they presented to Governor Arthur Dobbs of North Carolina.[25] The statement, as in Pennsylvania, was composed as part of a request for official confirmation of the command exercised by the officer of the Moravian watch. This Governor Dobbs proved very ready to grant, appointing Brother Jacob Loesch both "captain of an independent company" for defense against the French and Indians and a justice of the peace. Thus the brethren avoided entanglement with the militia organization of the province and were able to maintain their claim—at least to their own satisfaction—to statutory exemption from military conscription.

"We hear that none of our Society Brethren or friends have been drawn for service against the Cherokees, for which we thank the Saviour," the Bethabara church diary noted for 19 November 1759.[26] They were ready, then, to defend their own villages against enemy attack with weapons in their hands—although they hoped that it might not be necessary to make lethal use of them. But they drew back in quite genuine alarm from involvement in the military machine, in hireling armies and conscript militias. Participation there would only give rise to temptations for the unwary and would in the end result in grievous sin. The church should remain a people apart, eschewing an aggressive spirit and following in the path of love toward all men.

They would stand guard over their own communities; at the same time, they said, they must insist on their legal right to stand aside from soldiering in the armies of this world. Yet they felt it their duty to assist the powers that be in their endeavors to protect the country from attack. In 1760, for instance, when at Eastertime fighting with hostile Indians was taking place not far from their settlements and a company of some sixty militiamen arrived in Bethabara, "at their request Brother Spangenberg [who was visiting from Pennsylvania] preached for them [in English] in the afternoon, one of the Brethren standing guard over the arms they left outside the Saal." The brethren gladly supplied the provincial forces with consignments of food, too: feeding the hungry, they could reflect with Mennonites and Brethren, was after all a gospel commandment. Thus we read in the Bethabara diary an entry of this

---

[25] This petition (printed in *Records of the Moravians in North Carolina*, I, 182, 183) appears to be dated around the same time. Nevertheless, it seems almost certain that the document originated with Bishop Spangenberg in Bethlehem, which acted as a center for American Moravianism during this period. It is probable that the draft was composed by Spangenberg a little earlier and similar versions then presented to the respective provincial authorities independently, but at roughly the same dates.

[26] *Records of the Moravians in North Carolina*, I, 214.

kind: "On the 24th [June 1761] about thirty horses, loaded with flour, started from our mill for the soldiers on New River. Other shipments were made from time to time, both of flour and corn."[27]

This attitude was confirmed by the count himself. In a letter dated 8 April 1759, Zinzendorf wrote:

Should we wish to occupy ourselves with an investigation into the justice of wars, we would have a real task cut out for us; and it would be thankless labor in the end. Our Saviour has said: wars are no concern of ours; nation shall arise against nation, but we are to remain quiet and attend to our work. If we concern ourselves with soldiery at all, it must simply be because they need our help as human beings; in that case we shall not fail in performing our humanitarian and Christian duty![28]

The passing of the invasion scare and the eventual return of peace brought a return, too, to a vigorous assertion of the church's noncombatant status, which had been so rudely shaken by the action of the brethren themselves. In Pennsylvania, of course, there was still no militia conscription, even though the Quakers were no longer in power. In North Carolina the provincial authorities continued to recognize the Moravians' exemption, apparently stipulating only that those members who were not actually communicants should pay a modest fine of a shilling for failure to muster. Communicants got off scot-free.[29]

II

The outbreak of the Revolutionary War reopened the old problem of the limits of Moravian pacifism that had been raised so acutely two decades earlier. Even though the issue of personal self-defense did not come up now except in one or two isolated instances (for law and order were maintained on the whole throughout the country despite the prevailing war conditions), a new complication presented itself to the Moravians, as it did to the other German peace sects and to the Quakers as well, in deciding whether it was to the established monarchy or to the Revolutionary authorities that they owed their allegiance. A historian who has examined the Moravians' record during the Revolution has rightly asserted that throughout "they sympathized with the American cause more than the other pacifist sects."[30] Yet a strong loyalist element existed within the church, especially among the

---

[27] Ibid., pp. 231, 237.

[28] Hamilton, John Ettwein, p. 255.

[29] See Records of the Moravians in North Carolina, II, 680, 681.

[30] Russell Howard Seibert, "The Treatment of Conscientious Objectors in War Time, 1775-1920," Ph.D. diss., Ohio State U. (1936), p. 16.

more elderly, who were often in positions of influence and trust. Accusations of "Toryism" made by the enemies of the church were undoubtedly (as in the case of the Quakers) much exaggerated, but at first, at any rate, the majority did apparently remain loyal to the British. Thus, divided political sympathies existed alongside contradictory views on the subject of war to create a highly complex pattern of behavior among the membership throughout the war years.

Fortunately, as in the case of the earlier war, the Moravian records relating to the American Revolution, both printed sources and those still in manuscript form (the latter barely touched in compiling the present account), still exist today in great abundance. This wealth of documentary material, which is matched among the peace sects only in the case of the Quakers, makes it possible to gain a fairly clear picture of the state of opinion within the church at this time.

In place of Bishop Spangenberg, who had returned to Germany in 1763, we now find the figure of John Ettwein (1721-1802) in a position of virtual leadership of the American church, although he was not actually consecrated bishop until 1784. Like Spangenberg, Ettwein was an immigrant from Germany, where Pietist contacts had eventually led him to join the Moravian church. He arrived on this continent in 1754 and settled in Bethlehem. A man of considerable intelligence but scant formal education, he interpreted the Moravian position on war in a spirit much more akin to the Quaker view than did Spangenberg. Yet, as Ettwein's biographer observes, even after Spangenberg's departure "his [i.e., Spangenberg's] influence was still too strong among American Moravians in the 'seventies for them to condemn the bearing of arms indiscriminately or unanimously."[31]

Ettwein's sympathies in the conflict definitely inclined toward "Toryism." He feared a renunciation of allegiance to the British on several counts. In the first place, renunciation would, he felt, lead to a deterioration of relations, hitherto excellent, between the American and English Moravian communities. The flourishing missionary activities conducted by the American church in British territories would most likely be seriously impeded by a break with the mother country. Again, he feared that this break would also make it much more difficult to bring Moravian immigrants out of Europe, since Britain had hitherto acted as a clearinghouse in the process. Most important of all, he felt strongly that renunciation of allegiance to the government that had

---

[31] Hamilton, *John Ettwein*, p. 219. Ettwein's "A Short Account of the Disturbances in America and of the Brethren's Conduct and Suffering in This Connection," which he composed in German (and which K. G. Hamilton has printed in translation), is a major source for Moravian history during the Revolutionary War.

granted the American church both religious toleration and exemption from military service and oaths would be not only an act of ingratitude but a demonstration of disloyalty to the powers that be, something that was clearly forbidden by scripture. Thus, his reluctance to acknowledge a change in the *status quo*, like that of the Quakers, derived both from considerations of a practical nature and from deep-seated religious principle.

But Ettwein's negative stand vis-à-vis the colonial cause—again, like that of the Quakers—went further than this. It embraced a conscientious opposition to war as a denial of Christian ethics and as an activity in which, therefore, Christians were forbidden to participate. "We live in the faith of what we preach," he wrote to a fellow pastor, "consequently we are all men's friends and lovers, even of those that hate and persecute us, according to the rule and example of our dear Lord." Ever since his Herrnhut days, he said, "I have been firmly opposed to the bearing of arms." Unlike some of the Moravian pastors at this time who still took a pacifist position, Ettwein also regarded the hiring of a substitute to fight in one's place as inadmissible for a person who held a conscientious objection to fighting himself, although he did make an exception in the case of a "lord of the manor or proprietor of an estate" who, like Zinzendorf back in Europe, was legally obligated to provide recruits as a condition of his landownership. "I do not consider [this] to be contrary to freedom of conscience." As for ordinary conscripts contemplating the hiring of a substitute as a way out of service, he writes:

I emphatically [consider] going to war in person or providing a substitute to be one and the same wrong . . . only, in the one case, one's own life and ease are better safeguarded than in the other. . . . My scruples are not caused by the fact that I might bring about their misfortune and death, should I by my money encourage them to fight, but by the fact that I am to reward someone, whether by my wish or contrary to my wish, to destroy people or to do them other violence and wrong in my name, and in my stead. And in the case before us there is this additional consideration: "Shall I defend myself per proxy by force of arms against the king and the parliament who have granted me one of the most glorious exemptions?" For a Brother that would be the greatest ingratitude and an infamy.

Although Ettwein did not equate killing in battle with murder, nevertheless in his opinion "a soldier and a manslaughterer are one and the same." True, not all soldiers actually by themselves perform the act of killing, but "it is not in a soldier's power to avoid shedding blood." "Yet," he adds with a touch of irony, "I will gladly yield as regards this phrase, too, and allow soldiers to be classed with executioners."

The brethren, he insisted, if they agreed with his viewpoint on the inadmissibility of soldiering for a Christian, must refuse to fight, trusting in the Lord for deliverance and ready to suffer persecution if that were His will. Only in this way would they prove that their scruples were genuine. "I consider the exemptions granted the Brethren in our day to be a great reward for the small degree of faithfulness shown by the Brethren from the beginning in this matter. . . . If we now endure some suffering for the sake of our principles and freedom," he exhorted the fainthearted,

we shall approve ourselves in the sight of God and man; if we permit ourselves to be frightened and unmanned by threats, we must continue a shameful existence; and our adversaries will be encouraged to force us to renounce our faith and place ourselves on the level of this world. . . . I would rather permit myself to be hacked to pieces than go to war, butcher people, rob people of their property or burn it down, swear that I owe no obedience to K[ing] G[eorge], that I desire to help maintain the independence of Pennsylvania, until and before time and circumstances make it clear and incontestable that God has severed America from England. . . . The conditions which prevail in the country at present have made the wisdom and importance of this particular article of the Brethren's-Church so significant and invaluable, that I cannot describe the matter. Surely it is worth suffering somewhat for it. I only regret that one might answer me: "It is easy for you to say this; you are exempted from this temptation as a result of your position and age."[32]

Utterances of this kind, obviously the outcome of a genuine and deeply held repugnance for war as it was then waged by so-called Christian nations back in Europe or on the frontiers of the New World, have an uncompromising ring. Nevertheless, even for a radical antimilitarist like Ettwein, Moravian pacifism was cast in a less rigorous mold than either the Quaker variety or the nonresistance of the Mennonites or Dunkers. The peace views of Ettwein differed from those of his fellow pacifist sectaries in Pennsylvania in two important respects. In the first place, he fully endorsed the legitimacy of permitting

[32] *Ibid.*, pp. 219-24, 286, 322-26. See also A. Gertrude Ward, "John Ettwein and the Moravians in the Revolution," *Pennsylvania History*, I, no. 4 (Oct. 1934), 194.

a diversity of opinion on the subject of war to exist within the church. "A soldier," he told Alexander Hamilton during the latter's visit to Bethlehem in 1791, "could become and remain a member." And he himself, during the Revolutionary War, permitted Moravian militia-men to take communion in his church.[33] Secondly, Ettwein's views on the use of force were perhaps not so far removed from those of Spang-enberg as one might at first suppose. For Ettwein, too, seems to have granted a limited right to employ armed force in cases of self-defense, differing thus from the nonresistant position of the other German peace sectaries who denied the legitimacy of using weapons even when the machinery of law and order had broken down. Ettwein writes:

> I have heard sensible Brethren make a distinction between self-defence against robbers and murderers, Indians and wild animals, since none of these recognize or are subject to any regulation or authority, and self-defence against lawful power, where constituted authority exists. And should anyone, on the basis of such a distinction, not scruple to shoot an individual who intends to commit murder—be he black, brown, or white—while cherishing scruples to go to war, far be it from me to judge his conscience. Let him rather yield life and person, than act against his conscience. Our brethren in the land of Labrador have built a kind of fort and are provided with arms. And they might use them, were they attacked by the Eskimos. But that does not prove that they do not have scruples against military service. No constituted authority exists to protect them; and the preparations for self-defence will suffice, perhaps, to cause the savages to respect them. I do not believe they would defend themselves against a Christian power.[34]

It is not completely clear from the passage quoted, however, whether Ettwein personally endorsed the position of the Labrador missionaries or whether he merely acknowledged it to be one of several legiti-

---

[33] Hamilton, *John Ettwein*, p. 216. This tolerance of nonpacifist views won the approval of the saintly Quaker Anthony Benezet. In a letter dated 17 May 1765 to the Quaker historian Samuel Smith (printed in George S. Brookes, *Friend Anthony Benezet*, p. 265), Benezet discussed the views of the various peace sects in Pennsylvania on war, mentioning that "a great part of ye Moravians" also objected to participation in war. But, he went on, "in that part they are wiser than we, in allowing some of their members to dissent in ye article of defensive war from those, who are better established, without casting them from under their religious care and example, which, one day or other, when wisdom and honesty prevail more amongst us, we will make one of the articles of our Christian union." Benezet was well acquainted with the Pennsylvania Moravians since a number of his closest relations, including his Huguenot-born father, his sister, and his brother-in-law, belonged to that church.

[34] Hamilton, *John Ettwein*, pp. 220, 221.

mate standpoints within the church. At any rate, this view was one that must have been held by many Moravians conscientiously opposed to organized war. Although, as we have noted, it diverges markedly from the Christian nonresistance of the Anabaptist-Mennonite tradition, it does have something in common with that Quaker pacifism which, while maintaining a testimony against warfare between nations, is prepared to support a limited degree of coercion used in upholding law and order, as well as with some varieties of modern nonreligious pacifism, which object to war as a social institution while reserving the right to use armed force in certain situations.

On the eve of war the provincial conference meeting at Bethlehem issued on 6 May 1775 a declaration in which the church once again asserted its legal right to exemption from military service, exhorting its members to uphold its noncombatant stand during "the present turbulent conditions prevailing in the land." The statement expressly recommended acceptance of either a commutation fee or some form of alternative service as a way of repaying their obligation to the state, should conscription be introduced. The brethren must be ready to alleviate distress wherever found. Finally, great emphasis was placed upon their separateness from the world as being the source from which their unwillingness to participate directly in military matters flowed. They were "a peculiar people of the Lord, set by Him for blessing and for the performance of His purposes of peace wherever He has gathered them together."[35]

Ettwein's influence led his own congregation from Bethlehem and the neighboring Moravian townships to take up a fairly consistent pacifist stand throughout the war (although elsewhere the minority who did not share such scruples was evidently freely tolerated). The church there stressed its submissiveness to the powers that be "in all things, where we can keep a good conscience" and its desire not to avoid the burdens of citizenship.[36] The reputation for disloyalty to the colonial cause and for covert pro-British sentiments which the sect had acquired at the beginning of the struggle was, in fact, gradually overcome, despite Ettwein's own inner convictions concerning the legitimacy of the old regime; so that, for instance, when William Ellery, of Rhode Island, stopped in at Bethlehem in early November 1777 on his way to take his seat in the Congress then being convened in York (Pa.), he felt able to grant the Moravians, in contrast to the Quakers, to be of good character, remarking in his diary:

[35] *Ibid.*, pp. 234-36; Preston A. Barba, *They Came to Emmaus*, pp. 107, 108.
[36] Hamilton, *John Ettwein*, pp. 236, 237; J. W. Jordan (ed.), "Bethlehem during the Revolution," pt. I, *PMHB*, XII, no. 4 (1888), 387.

This people like the Quakers are principled against bearing arms; but are unlike them in this respect, they are not against paying such taxes as government may order them to pay towards carrying on war, and do not, I believe, in a sly underhand way aid and assist the enemy while they cry Peace, Peace, as the manner of some Quakers is, not to impeach the whole body of them.[37]

On the whole, the Pennsylvania Moravians did indeed enjoy good relations with the new authorities. Ettwein himself was a personal friend of Henry Laurens, who was president of Congress from November 1777 until December 1778, and he was able to appeal for his intervention when the need arose. Another useful contact, though perhaps not quite so creditable a one for an antiwar church, was "Brother Billy," as the versatile William Henry (1729-1786) was known to his fellow church members. A former Episcopalian and a gunsmith by trade, Henry had joined the Moravians in 1765. But being a Moravian did not prevent him from becoming an ardent patriot a decade later. During the war he became a colonel in the Revolutionary army and an influential member of the Pennsylvania assembly, where he was able to be of service particularly to the Lititz Moravians in respect to various political problems they had to face during this period.[38] Henry's military activities apparently did not meet at any time with censure from the church authorities. Occasionally, however, the church's somewhat ambiguous attitude during the French and Indian War seems to have aroused suspicions regarding the sincerity of its antiwar stand. According to one Pennsylvania assemblyman in an interview with Ettwein in 1778, some persons were saying that the Moravians' opposition to war was based only on self-interest. "We just wanted to secure our estates in case the opposite party should win," was these people's opinion; "we had proved in the Indian war that we were not opposed to self-defence, etc."[39]

Since they dutifully paid their taxes to the state and found the alternatives to military service laid down by the authorities acceptable, the Pennsylvania Moravians were troubled in their war stand by only two issues. The first stemmed from their reluctance—which, as we have seen, they shared with both the Quakers and the German peace sects of the state—to make an affirmation of allegiance to the new re-

[37] "Diary of the Hon. William Ellery, of Rhode Island.—October 20 to November 15, 1777," *PMHB*, XI, no. 3 (1887), 326.

[38] Herbert H. Beck, "William Henry: Patriot, Master Gunsmith, Progenitor of the Steamboat," *TMHS*, XVI, pt. II (1955), esp. 81-83.

[39] "Three Letters written at Bethlehem, Pennsylvania, in 1778," *PMHB*, XXXVI, no. 3 (1912), 301.

gime, that was required for the first time in 1777. For refusing, they were fined and imprisoned, and so we find them petitioning the legislature and lobbying influential legislators to obtain relief from the legal penalties for their disobedience. Their attitude on this matter derived both from the feeling that it was God's concern, and not man's, to pull down an unrighteous ruler and from a realization of the benefits received by their church in the past from the British monarchy which they were now being asked to abjure.

The second issue, which occasioned frequent complaint, concerned the hardship inflicted by the heavy fines imposed on church members not only for their refusal of the test but for their noncompliance with conscription for the militia. As mentioned in an earlier chapter, these fines had risen, for each offense, from 50s. in the fall of 1775 to much larger sums in the subsequent years of the war, when inflation, too, caused a general rise in prices. Church funds were sometimes used for the purpose of helping the more indigent brethren with their fines; money was even forwarded from the churches in Germany for this purpose.[40] Reporting on the situation at Bethlehem, Ettwein wrote: "It was repeatedly proposed to treat all fines in lieu of drilling and assessments for substitutes, as a common concern, to raise them through a committee and pay them as a ransom or other charge of war. This did not meet with general approval, though subscriptions were taken to help those Brethren out of their trouble who had no property, and the single Brethren really did make a common concern out of this among themselves."[41] Even so, some of the brethren evidently were unable to find the wherewithal to meet the repeated demands for service or money. A "petition and humble representation" to the Pennsylvania assembly, signed by Ettwein and other leading bishops and elders and dated Bethlehem, 28 April 1778, states:

> They were fined and fined again, for not exercising in the use of arms; they have been enrolled, drafted with the several classes, and in Northampton County [i.e., where the main communities were located] exorbitant fines exacted from them, and no plea of disability of estate accepted; the justices of the peace signed warrants to commit their bodies to the common gaol, if they did not pay the fines; their houses, workshops and other property was invaded, and they to their great loss and damage turned out of their trades.[42]

[40] Henry A. Jacobson, "Revolutionary Notes concerning Nazareth, Friedensthal and Christian's Spring," *TMHS*, II (1886), 47.
[41] Hamilton, *John Ettwein*, p. 247.
[42] Printed in Barba, *They Came to Emmaus*, pp. 370-72.

310

Although most of the Moravians who found themselves in jail for short periods were sent there in connection with refusal of the test, a few were apparently imprisoned on account of their inability to pay militia fines. Ettwein notes concerning Northampton County, in which his own Bethlehem was situated, that, owing to the arbitrariness of local officers—"these little tyrants," he calls them angrily—Moravian conscientious objectors were being required, by repeated fining, to pay sums that would eventually add up to as much as from £100 to £200 a year. This, he adds, "is as much as to raise and keep 3 or 4 men all the year in the field." And if a brother had recourse in his distress to hiring a substitute (a course of action that was, in fact, now officially frowned upon by the church), he was again faced with the excessive charges that the militia officers imposed. "They did not consider justice and equity in getting substitutes," Ettwein writes, "but exacted ten times the sum of an equivalent of personal service."[43] They were, indeed, demanding for substitutes large sums which, if less than the total continued fining would reach, were still a heavy burden for poor men to carry. "In Bucks-County the officers immediately put the pay at £15 for 2 months, and in Conshohocken they have paid £25. How can a poor Brother pay such sums, even if he felt free in his conscience to hire such a [substitute]?" asked Ettwein indignantly. But the harassment continued, with threats that the recalcitrant would "be carried by force into the camp," while, as Ettwein relates,

The Lieutenants of the County did regard no plea of our single men, on account of inability of estate. Pay! or go to prison was all the comfort. Yea when the constable with the warrant came to carry them to prison if they did not pay, the steward of the single men and another of our Brethren engaged to pay for them . . . we must either pay £40 for every one noted down . . . or must let them go 4 months to prison, to which every one will rather submit, than go with the militia. . . . We don't like to let our Brethren lie idle in a prison, but how can we help it? We have saved some for a while by charity and may save others by contracting debts and at last they must submit to it nevertheless if they do not make an escape, to our loss and sorrow; and what gains the country by it, if a number of sober industrious young men lie in prison 4-8 months in a year or try to get out of the reach of their oppressors? There is not one of the Brethren, that I know, who does not do something for the service of others; yea, our shoemakers, bakers, the several smiths, tanners, stocking-weavers and farmers have been these 4 months chiefly em-

[43] Ettwein Papers, Moravian Archives, Bethlehem (Pa.), 1297. See also 1299.

ployed for the use of the soldiers and others belonging to the continental service.[44]

This account of the Moravians' difficulties was sent by Ettwein to Henry Laurens early in 1778. Perhaps it was because of Laurens' intervention that stringent measures of this kind were soon afterward lifted. Or, possibly, the local authorities themselves relented, seeing that their efforts to make the brethren conform were none too successful and that, in fact, the war effort was thereby losing the labors of these hardworking craftsmen and farmers. The fact that Pennsylvania was to cease soon to be a theater of war, thus easing the tense situation in the state, undoubtedly contributed toward relaxing the measures against the Moravian objectors, too. At any rate, in 1781 Ettwein, in looking back over the previous two years, could record: "Even with regard to the militia things were quite bearable. And whoever desired, might have observed the war, or heard about it, with all the detachment of a person living in France."[45]

Nevertheless, support for Ettwein's policy of refusing to participate in the armed forces had by no means been unanimous even in Bethlehem and the neighboring congregations. We read, for instance, of a group of single brethren who stole off secretly from the Brethren's House in Nazareth and enrolled in the militia at the nearby town of Easton. When discovered, they were severely reprimanded for contravening the discipline and were suspended from membership.[46] In the Emmaus congregation about half the young men of military age appear to have accepted service with the militia rather than pay fines in commutation. Although it is evident that their action did not receive official approval from the church, the men were apparently not disciplined in any way for such behavior.[47] In Ettwein's own Bethlehem there was a strong undercurrent of opposition to continuing to oppose military service in face of the heavy fines inflicted for refusal. "There . . . were those among us," he reports, "who would have preferred to have permitted the young men to drill, rather than pay such heavy fines." Against this view it was argued by Ettwein and those who thought like him that to conform now would be to betray the church's heritage, that for the ministry to yield to threats and persecution and to sanction the performance of military service would constitute "an unjustifiable

[44] Hamilton, *John Ettwein*, pp. 265-67, 325. See also pp. 281, 282.
[45] *Ibid.*, p. 309.
[46] Jacobson, "Revolutionary Notes," p. 47; Taylor Hamilton, *A History of the Moravian Church*, p. 253.
[47] Barba, *They Came to Emmaus*, pp. 128-33.

breach of trust." "This matter was a fundamental part of the Unity of the Brethren and . . . no settlement congregation could be established, where they were not granted freedom to be friends of all men."[48]

Another church center which also adhered fairly consistently to the traditional Moravian noncombatancy was Lititz. This position it owed in large part to the influence of its pastor, Brother Matthew Hehl, who saw to it that the young men of his congregation cleaved to the official line. While declaring that its members "would personally have nothing to do with the war," that they would neither serve in a military capacity nor take the political oath, the community from the outset of the struggle at the same time made clear that it was ready to contribute liberally to the colonial cause in money and kind and to pay such monetary or other alternatives to actual service as the state should demand. (In 1778, for instance, they were to do yeoman service devotedly nursing the sick and wounded soldiers of the American army, who were quartered in their settlement.) The young men of the church, however, seem to have had little personal attachment to a religious pacifism, agreeing to become conscientious objectors mainly out of loyalty to the tradition of their sect. Their attitude is revealed clearly in the entry in the church diary (kept by Brother Hehl) for 27 June 1775:

> The most of our young brethren would rather drill than pay so much money. They were therefore, June 27, spoken with singly by Brother Mattheus and Bro. Dreyspring who affectionately and earnestly pointed out to them that it was not the province of the Brethren's Unity to take part in these affairs; for, by an act of parliament we have been made exempt therefrom; therefore, it would be better for us to free ourselves with money from these obligations, which might result in injury to our souls. This was well received and fully understood.

Yet, even after receiving this advice, many of the younger brethren still remained restive, and we find Brother Hehl during the next few years expending considerable effort in keeping them from straying from the church's policy. On 24 July 1777, for instance, he complained that the young folk "take too much interest in the war and the state of the country." A few actually did do military service and were therefore disfellowshipped, but most of the congregation resisted all

---

[48] Hamilton, *John Ettwein*, p. 247.

attempts, by browbeating or severe fines, to get them to attend drillings. A few men were arrested, all had to pay heavily for the privilege of exemption.[49] Still, this uniformity in witnessing against war service, maintained in often trying circumstances, is more a tribute to the intensity of devotion in the younger generation (as among their elders) to the church of their fathers—as well as to the hold Brother Hehl possessed over his parishioners—than to any deeply held convictions about the wrongness of war itself and of participation therein.

In the bigger centers, where the young bachelors still lived a community life under semi-monastic discipline which made it easier for their leaders to impose uniformity of conduct, the influence of men like Ettwein and Hehl was for the most part successful in getting the young Moravians to refuse military service. On the other hand, in the congregations in the rural areas where the members usually lived on scattered farms, a cleavage of opinion appeared within the church. Even Ettwein had to admit: "Many Brethren belonging to the country congregations drilled and campaigned with the militia."[50] And this opinion is confirmed by the records.

Let us take as an example the Moravians of York County, which was situated not far from the frontier. There all the brethren of military age were eventually drafted into the militia, in spite of the efforts of pastor George Neisser (1715-1784), who, for all his decided sympathy with the American side, nevertheless attempted to maintain the neutrality of his congregation. Although most, it is true, were enrolled compulsorily as the war emergency led to increasingly stringent measures, some did enlist voluntarily. As early as August 1775, in fact, we find Brother Neisser recording: "A few of our number have consented to take part in the military drills; if only more will not be required of them. Several of our young men, in spite of remonstrances, enlisted as minute men." A year later he reported that all the young Moravian bachelors had had to go off with the Continental army, and apparently the able-bodied married men were also called out for short periods of duty with the troops around this time. In July, according to his description, the town of York was almost deserted except for women and children and the aged and infirm. In 1778, to give two further examples, the church diary's entry for 24 June states that "the militia guard, to which several of our brethren are attached, has been

[49] "Extracts from the Diaries of the Moravian Church at Lititz, Pa., relating to the Revolutionary War," *The Penn-Germania*, I (XIII), nos. 11-12 (Nov.-Dec. 1912), 849-53, 860; H. A. Brickenstein, "Sketch of the Early History of Lititz, 1742-75," *TMHS*, II (1886), 372, 373.

[50] Hamilton, *John Ettwein*, p. 247.

314

ordered out," and the entry for 20 July tells us that "Christian Hecke-dorn, with officers of his company, start for Philadelphia tomorrow, as a guard to protect the continental wagons."[51]

Equally revealing are the records of the country congregation at Hebron near Lebanon. In the entry for 8 August 1776 the church diary notes: "Today the last company from this town marched for the army. Numbers of our members called to take leave—Adam Orth and his son John; Baltzer Orth; Guenther; Gottlieb Kucker; Michael Uhrich; Michael Koch; George Volk and Henry Buehler. Our evening service was not held in the chapel, owing to so many of the members being in the army."[52]

Thus we see that in regard to the war issue there was no uniformity of thought and practice among the Moravian congregations of Pennsylvania during the years of the Revolution. In contrast to the situation two decades earlier, however, the question of personal self-defense did not now constitute a problem of immediate importance—though the atrocious massacre at Gnadenhütten in the spring of 1782 of a group of the Moravians' Indian converts, whom the local American militia wrongly suspected of connivance with the enemy, provided, it is true, an example of Christian nonviolence in practice that was probably inspired by the teachings of the Indians' preceptors.

The change in political sovereignty, which the Continental authorities were striving to effect by means of war, did indeed introduce a complicating factor, for many among the more weighty Moravian brothers were conscientiously opposed to a shift in allegiance brought about in this way. Still, this objection did not effectually blur the fact that the main point at issue was the justifiability of participation by church members in military service, either voluntarily or as conscripts. From the evidence available, three different viewpoints seem to have been present among the membership in Pennsylvania. In the first place, we have the opinion of the church leaders, men like Ettwein or Hehl, that direct military service was wrong in principle, contrary to the Christian gospel of love as expressed in the New Testament. Those who took up this position mostly sympathized to some extent with the British government, although a few looked with more favor on the colonial cause. In either case, this view may, broadly speaking, be described as a pacifist one, akin to the peace testimony of the Quakers, except that it might reserve the possibility of a legitimate use of armed

[51] J. W. Jordan (ed.), *Fragments of History and Biography relating to the Moravians in York County, 1744-1782*, pp. 15-18, 30-33. See also S. C. Albright, *The Story of the Moravian Congregation at York, Pennsylvania*, pp. 140-45.

[52] "Extracts from the Records of the Moravian Congregation at Hebron, Pennsylvania," *PMHB*, XVIII, no. 4 (1894), 450.

force in cases of individual self-defense. Alongside, and partly overlapping with, this pacifism on principle comes what we may call a purely traditional noncombatancy. This attitude resulted in large part from the fact that the leaders were able to insist on the maintenance of the peace testimony as official church policy, a policy that was accepted by large numbers of the laity (and some of the pastors) out of loyalty to the church rather than from any positive emotional or intellectual assent to its principles. A peace testimony based on such a shaky foundation, however, was unlikely either to persist for much longer in the future or to provide an effectual witness in the present, unless efforts were made to ground it more securely. Lastly, there were those who actively sided with the Revolutionary cause—at least to the point of being unwilling to refuse the call to military service when it came. Among the younger men, and among some who only joined the church during the war period, there was great enthusiasm for the struggle against Britain. As a Nazareth elder exclaimed in alarm about the young men of the congregation: "Sie reden von Freiheit" ("They are talking about freedom").[53] For such men as these, calls from the senior members of the church to stand by its legal right to have its members exempted from bearing arms fell on deaf ears. Many signed up as "associates" at the beginning, and they performed their military service or served the new regime in other capacities without complaint.[54] In most cases, as we have seen, they were not disciplined in any way for their failure to follow their church's instructions.

The same divisions of opinion appeared among the small Moravian congregation in the city of New York, which remained under British control from September 1776 until near the end of the war,[55] as well as in the much larger settlement in North Carolina.[56] However, although the church leaders in this province did indeed—in the wake of the Pennsylvania church—endeavor to maintain an official noncombatancy and, at least at first, a neutral stance between the two sides, pro-American sentiment seems to have predominated among the rank and file.

We meet with the following curious minute, passed at the outset of the struggle by the supervising board (*Aufseher Collegium*) of the Salem congregation on 9 August 1775:

[53] James Henry, "Nazareth and the Revolution," *TMHS*, II (1886), 41.

[54] Hamilton, *John Ettwein*, pp. 230, 244, 264.

[55] See Henry Emilius Stocker, *A History of the Moravian Church in New York City*, pp. 122-24.

[56] See Ruth Blackwelder, "The Attitude of the North Carolina Moravians toward the American Revolution," *North Carolina Historical Review*, IX, no. 1 (Jan. 1932), esp. 9-21.

The small amount of powder which we are reserving for our own defence (should that be necessary) shall be hidden by two Brethren, so that we do not get into trouble because of it. The guns which are in town should also not hang in sight, since we have conscientious scruples against bearing arms. The Brethren who have guns in their houses shall be asked to keep them hidden.[57]

In the same month the provincial church drew up a petition to the local authorities, reiterating their loyalty to the powers that be and asking, among other things, for continued respect for their scruples against bearing arms, which—they pointed out—were observed both by governments on the European continent and in the province of Pennsylvania.[58] Though unwilling to officially endorse armed support of the colonial cause, the North Carolina Moravians frequently expressed their sympathies with it by willingly supplying the Revolutionary armies with grain and other food supplies, clothing, and even powder for their cannon! After the Declaration of Independence had been signed, the church dropped its prayers for George III in its services and acknowledged the Continental Congress as the supreme authority in the country.

At first, the penalty for refusing to muster with the militia was a fine of 40s. on each occasion. No unanimity seems to have existed among church members liable for service concerning the course to be pursued. Most communicant members probably followed the church's instructions and paid their fines; among the youngest liable age group, however, there were many who did not refuse service. And, as in Pennsylvania, this was especially true of the country congregations. In 1776 the Rev. Lorenz Bagge, pastor of Bethabara, noted in his diary about these young members of the community:

Some of their parents had no real convictions as to military service, but when things got serious they came to the Brethren in Salem asking for advice and help for their children. Some of our young men came to Salem for a while, till the storm passed, for their fathers did not want to tell the officers plainly that they were opposed to bearing of arms, and were taking no part in the controversy, which would perhaps not have been true . . . there were some cases in which young men from our families voluntarily enlisted, and went into the war, though not from Salem or Bethabara.[59]

In the Friedberg congregation some among those ordered to muster, instead of paying the fine, "decided to go, but to explain that they

---

[57] *Records of the Moravians in North Carolina*, vol. II, p. 898.
[58] *Ibid.*, p. 944.   [59] *Ibid.*, III, 1024, 1025.

could not take part in the drill." One of the congregation's younger members who thought that this was a poor way of acting was Adam Spach, who told his pastor: "I will not attend muster, and will bear whatever they may bring upon me. I wish . . . that they all thought as I do, then one day in the week we could meet in the schoolhouse, and unitedly lay the difficult circumstances upon the heart of the Saviour, instead of going to muster once a month." Evidently, few of his fellow Moravian conscripts agreed with his stand. Later, however, in the summer of 1776, when it appeared likely that the county militia would be called out to march against the pro-British Indians, the young men of the community hid in the woods until the scare was over. A search was made to find them, but without success.[60]

In the Bethania community most of the brethren of military age attended the militia drillings, and some were called out for active service against the Indians. Such conduct, though it was apparently not penalized, drew down the disapproval of the church authorities. In a letter to Bethlehem, Brother Graff of Salem wrote: "They seem to have more desire for this [i.e., military service] than to be Brethren."[61] And in the following year pastor Bagge recorded: "Most of those in Bethania embraced the cause of Liberty, and from the latter village many residents, including older Brethren, went to muster and to drill." Bethania, it should be said, consisted in large part of persons who had only fairly recently joined the church, and their children: these new members did not have the same loyalty to the traditional opposition to participation in war that was felt in the longer settled communities, whose older members, at least, could recall the long struggle to gain recognition for their noncombatant status.[62]

If the behavior of the North Carolina Moravians lacked the uniformity that the Society of Friends or the other German peace sects imposed on their members, so, too, the actions of the authorities in the province in enforcing the militia law varied from place to place and from officer to officer. Usually, fines were imposed regularly. But in some instances, perhaps where the officer was particularly well disposed toward the Moravians, the fines were remitted. Sometimes,

---

[60] *Ibid.*, pp. 1112, 1113, 1116-18. The dilemma in which in similar circumstances a small isolated group of Moravians found themselves is described in a letter sent by Brother Johann Georg Wagner, then working with the Moravian mission for Negroes at Knoxborough in Georgia, to Brother Graff of Salem. He writes (*ibid.*, p. 1406, letter dated 2 July 1776): "Here all is most warlike, everybody is going to fight. For this reason my dear Brother Broesing is going to you for advice as to what we shall do. Congress has told us that we may take our choice of three ways,—help fight, pay, or go to jail,—all hard ways for us."

[61] *Ibid.*, p. 1087, letter dated 15 Aug. 1776.

[62] *Ibid.*, pp. 1129, 1197.

browbeating and threats were employed in an attempt to get the brethren to attend drill. As in Pennsylvania, the hiring of substitutes to avoid the expense of repeated fining encountered strong disapproval from the church authorities: voluntary collections were made among the congregations to help the poorer brethren with the payment of fines.

In 1778 the General Assembly of North Carolina passed a new law replacing the commutation fee of £10 previously demanded of conscientious objectors by a requirement either to furnish a substitute (which was, of course, contrary now to Moravian principles) or to pay a property levy to the value of £25. The church therefore hastened to draw up a petition to the assembly in which they pointed out that the Moravians had settled in the province on the understanding that their exemption from bearing arms and from taking oaths,[63] guaranteed by the British act of 1749, would be safeguarded. Their only desire, they reiterated, was to live peaceably and be good subjects of the land in which they dwelt.[64] This petition had its effect, for in the following year the assembly formally exempted the Moravians from militia duties on payment of a sum three times the amount of the ordinary provincial tax and freed them in effect from the obligation of oathtaking too.

The church authorities were required to issue certificates of membership in good standing to prospective conscientious objectors. This duty gave them an opportunity to weed out those who had not shown any marked enthusiasm for noncombatancy or had yielded in the matter of the oath; potentially, it was a weapon in the hands of the powers that be in the church to enforce uniformity of conduct and obedience to authority, too. At the end of March 1779, shortly after the new act had been passed, we find the Grosse Helfe Conference at Salem discussing

. . . the giving of certificates to men who had not signed our last petition to the Assembly. It was decided that we dared not extend the freedom from military service which we gained through our petition to those who did not sign. Some men from the English settlement and from near Friedberg weakened our position and took the Test, but now that another draft is to be made they would like to be included with us.

---

[63] Like their brethren in Pennsylvania, the Moravians in North Carolina refused to take the "test," even in the form of an affirmation, and were fined heavily as a result.

[64] *Ibid.*, pp. 1373-76.

The men were therefore refused their certificates and, presumably, either had to serve or buy their way out at great cost. Another settlement which was punished for its lukewarmness was Friedland. At the end of July 1779 the Salem diary reports:

The Friedlanders are in a state of confusion; in spring, when we secured the resolution from the Assembly, they wanted to join us and pay a three-fold tax, then when no more drafts were being made they changed their minds, on account of the high taxes, and now they again wish to be treated as Brethren.[65]

Finally, in the summer of 1781 the church decided to regularize the conditions under which certificates were to be issued—a matter of vital importance indeed to the young men who were affected by the draft. First, certificates were to be given only if the military absolutely insisted on receiving them. Secondly, the reception of new members into the church was to be suspended for the duration of the war. "To receive many persons into our Societies," it was explained, "would look as though we were depriving the land of able soldiers." Now that exemption had been made easier, there evidently existed some fear that an influx of persons with loyalist sympathies into the church would take place: we find one applicant being told peremptorily that he could not be accepted "until he is cured of his affection for the Tory cause." (How much basis there was for these apprehensions it is difficult to say.) In the third place, it was laid down that only those whose behavior conformed to that expected of a brother were to be supported in their applications for exemption.

This final provision was obviously the most telling point in the resolutions that were then passed. Considerable care seems to have been taken to enforce this regulation and to exclude anyone from benefiting from the act who was not fully conformed to the discipline of the church. In the following November, to cite only one instance, we are told that a certain James Wilson, a young man who had been living at Bethabara, "would like to settle among the Brethren and be freed from liability of draft." "The best way," he was sternly told by the elders' conference, "would be for him to behave as a Brother, and then have himself bound to someone" who was a practising member of the brotherhood.[66]

Thus, the North Carolina Moravians were eventually able to maintain a fairly consistent noncombatant witness within a narrow circle

---

[65] *Ibid.*, pp. 1297, 1310.

[66] *Ibid.*, IV, 1729, 1730, 1736, 1737, 1782; Blackwelder, "The Attitude of the North Carolina Moravians," p. 14.

of members who kept strictly to the church's discipline. In Pennsylvania this uniformity had been possible only in the church settlements like Bethlehem, where a semi-communal life still prevailed; in North Carolina the discipline seems to have been imposed more widely. But in neither state, in wartime at least, was there any serious attempt, as there was among the Quakers, Mennonites, and Dunkers, to force noncombatancy on all by rigorously excluding deviants from fellowship within the church. In North Carolina, as in Pennsylvania, those who did not feel impelled, where an emergency arose, to refuse to bear arms—either from belief in the incompatibility of war with the Christian faith or from desire to uphold a tenet which tradition and leadership in their church, if not their own convictions, combined to tell them needed preserving—usually continued to exercise the rights of membership. During the war the fighting Moravian took his place beside the Moravian conscientious objector in the church community: admission of error was seldom required of those who had failed to abide by its official requirements.

III

We have now traced the history of this somewhat ambiguous peace witness among the Moravians down to the end of the Revolution. Something must be said in conclusion concerning its final phase, even though this will take us beyond the chronological limits of this section.

The Moravian ministers and elders for several decades remained intent on preserving their church's noncombatancy. The young people, on the other hand, who had already been stirred by the Revolutionary struggle against Britain and who were provided with no clear guidance on the fundamentals of their refusal to render military service, evidently felt increasing reluctance to make a stand on this issue which isolated them from the rest of their age group. And their parents, at least in the Pennsylvania settlements where quite heavy militia fines were the price of conscientious objection, saw less and less point in undergoing repeated financial loss in support of their sons' witness to a testimony which had long ceased to be a vital element in their faith. Moreover, toward the end of the eighteenth century the Moravians had begun to drop their nonconformity to the world and to cease to be a sect apart living in isolation from the political and social life of their English-speaking fellow countrymen. Now they were taking an increasing part in this life, accepting office as justices of the peace, judges, and representatives and participating in elections on the various levels. The process of assimilation, however, took many decades to complete. It was nearly a half century after the Revolution had ended before the last remnants of Moravian pacifism were abandoned.

We can follow quite closely in the published church records this struggle between the traditionalism of the elders and ministers, who were bound, on largely pragmatic grounds, to support the church's objection to military service, and the impatience of the rank and file, and especially of the younger generation, at what they regarded as an outworn convention. The discipline of the church eventually proved powerless to bring the recalcitrant into line.

The chief concern of the church authorities was to keep the young people off the musterfield. In April 1786, for instance, we learn of the alarm of the Nazareth (Pa.) elders at the news that the military had arranged for the militia to exercise near the inn in the very center of the village. They feared the effect that this display would have on the single brethren, and reliable persons were therefore appointed to watch these young men to see that none were drawn to take part in the exercises.[67] The records of another Pennsylvania community show that there, too, difficulties in keeping their young men in line were being encountered. On May 2 it was reported: "This evening the brethren who last week, without permission, took part in the drill, were spoken to. It was represented that we scarcely could take it amiss of them, because of the continuous heavy fines laid upon them; and, especially, as they were not obliged to appear with arms; at the same time, because of the evil effect it might have upon the congregation, as well as upon the Brethren's Unity, it could not be permitted." However, the lecture given the boys did not prove sufficient in every case, for within a few days "two of the brethren went, secretly, . . . to drill." Therefore, they had to be warned by the elders "that if they persisted in doing as they pleased, to the disadvantage of the Saviour's cause, they could stay with us no longer. They promised with tears, not to do it again."[68]

From this report taken from the records of the Lititz church, it does seem as if a clearly pacifist element remained in the Moravian objection to military service—alongside the feeling, which by now was probably uppermost in the minds of those who still clung to this testimony, that such service tended to undermine separateness from the world; for it was pleaded in defense of the young men's action that "they were not

[67] Henry A. Jacobson, "Revolutionary Notes concerning Nazareth," *TMHS*, II (1886), 47.

[68] "Extracts from the . . . Diaries of the Moravian Church at Lititz, Pa.," *The Penn-Germania*, I (XIII), nos. 11-12, Nov.-Dec. 1912, 860.

obliged to appear with arms," that is, that they had not entirely thrown aside their pacifist stand.

Although already in the colonial period large sections of the Moravian church, including leading ministers, had abandoned personal nonresistance, a small number continued to take an absolute pacifist position, or one that was very near to it. Such a man, as we have seen, was Bishop John Ettwein. He was almost certainly responsible for the petition drawn up by the Pennsylvania Moravians on 1 September 1786 for presentation to the assembly. In it the church pleaded for a relaxation of the heavy fines that members were required to pay for being excused from militia service. They were not opposed in principle to "contributing . . . towards the defence of this commonwealth and the support of a militia in the same" by means of such fines, provided they were not so oppressive as at present. They had originally settled in Pennsylvania on the understanding that their scruples concerning bearing arms would be respected by the state. Now their situation in this respect contrasted unfavorably with that prevailing back in Europe.

> The penal laws for regulating the militia of this commonwealth, now in force, are rather forbidding than encouraging such foreigners, as conscientiously scruple to bear arms, to come over and settle in this country. These foreigners will at their homes consider, that in our days, most everywhere in Europe for new settlers an exemption from military duty may be obtained gratis, or purchased at a low price; when so heavy a penalty, as the militia fines amount to, awaits them in Pennsylvania, for no other cause than for following the dictates of their own conscience.[69]

Here the stress perhaps is more on pragmatic grounds, as befitted an appeal to hardheaded legislators. The existence of lingering pacifist scruples (as distinct from the desire to preserve the church's separateness from the world) is attested in a letter written by Bishop Ettwein four years later. On 8 July 1790 we find him addressing an influential friend of his church, the politician and former president of Congress during part of the Revolutionary period, Henry Laurens, Sr., concerning the proposed exemption for religious objectors in the new Pennsylvania Militia Act: "Tho' we cannot say that all our Brethren are scrupulous in that point . . . yet as there are many of our church members who really scruple about it and think to have good reason in the

[69] Petition in the Moravian Archives at Bethlehem.

Word of our Saviour for it, we think it our duty to provide for them and not to offend such Brethren by a contrary mind or action."[70]

However, the attitude of most of the church authorities who endeavored to maintain the traditional noncombatancy appears to have been compounded of a strange mixture of half-digested pacifism and semi-religious expediency. It is not surprising, then, not only that many ordinary members failed to follow the church's directions wholeheartedly but that the general populace sometimes looked askance at the exemption from military obligations of those whose scruples did not appear to have a quite genuine ring. On 16 October 1786 we read in the diary of the Bethabara congregation in North Carolina "that at the last general muster a petition against the Brethren was circulated for signatures. The chief complaint was our privilege in regard to drills."[71]

The attempt at this time was unsuccessful. But the Moravians in that state became more careful than ever to try to present a united front and to avoid any action that might give a handle for their enemies to grasp. In 1787 the Congregation Council of the Salem (N.C.) settlement rebuked those members who had been indulging in the popular pastime of shooting at a mark. "This does not become us," states the minute, "for we claim to be a quiet, peaceful people. If many see that we like to go about with guns they will wonder still more why we will not go to drill; they have already questioned it when they saw worldly actions on the part of persons who belong to us."[72]

Militia exercises, with their fine uniforms and panoply providing a welcome relief from the drabness of village or small town life, had an air of glamor and adventure for many of the Moravian young people. So we find the diary of the Friedberg (N.C.) congregation recording the following for 20 October 1805: "The house-fathers were asked to make clear to their grown sons how detrimental it is for them to attend muster as spectators, which brings scorn and hatred upon the Unity and may endanger our precious freedom from militia service."[73] Where Moravians were liable to some kind of commutation—either a fine or buying a substitute—for the privilege of exemption from military duties (in peacetime they were unconditionally exempt, as we

---

[70] "Fragments from the Papers of Bishop John Ettwein," *TMHS*, IV (1895), 209.

[71] *Records of the Moravians in North Carolina*, V, 2153. See also p. 2143.

[72] *Ibid.*, p. 2189. The guns mentioned as being in the possession of the Moravians were presumably used for hunting.

[73] *Ibid.*, VI, 2835. As late as 1822 we read in the diary of the Bethania congregation that the young men were to be requested "not to go to the muster grounds to look on, as being seen there would give offence and bring shame to the church." See VII, 3526, 3551.

have seen, according to the laws of North Carolina),[74] the church authorities arranged for the poorer brethren to receive financial assistance in obtaining exemption.[75]

The final sanction employed during this period by Mennonites, Brethren, and Quakers alike to preserve the purity of their peace witness was the weapon of disownment. Disownment had sometimes been carried out among the Moravians, too, especially when the pressure toward accepting service was relaxed at the end of the war. The North Carolina congregations continued the practice at least until the War of 1812. A case of this kind occurring as late as December 1811 can be found in a minute of the Salem Board of Elders, which reads: "The single Brother Heinrich Meyer, of Bethania, has of his own free will attended muster. He must be considered as having cut himself off from the congregation."[76] But the Pennsylvania communities had long ago become less rigid, and by this date disfellowshipping, in peacetime, for taking part in the militia had apparently ceased there entirely. Perhaps the financial burden that conscientious objection entailed in this state made it difficult for a ministry which had largely abandoned its faith in theoretical pacifism to compel church members, whose scruples in respect to service in the militia were even more pallid, to undergo considerable hardship on this account. The break had already come in the 1790's. Although the ban was still being enforced in the settled congregations,[77] some latitude appears to have been granted to members living in isolation away from the main Moravian settlements; and it was officially recognized that the consciences of some members could lead them to do military service, even though they were expected to abstain in practice on account of the general policy of the church.[78]

In North Carolina, it is interesting to note, the unconditional exemption which membership in the Moravian church carried with it seems to have been used by the church authorities on occasion as a stick with which to discipline unruly members. The church had, once the war was over, at first refused all requests from the military to provide its

[74] A North Carolina brother wrote on 28 October 1805 concerning their favored situation: "In this respect we have enjoyed more freedom than our Brethren in Pennsylvania, who must pay a heavy fine for each absence; on the other hand during the Revolutionary War we paid a three-fold land tax."

[75] Two Centuries of Nazareth 1740-1940, pp. 75-77; Records of the Moravians in North Carolina, VI, 2511, 2593.

[76] Records of the Moravians in North Carolina, VII, 3153.

[77] For instance, on the occasion of the outbreak of the Whiskey Rebellion in western Pennsylvania in 1794, those answering the call to service were threatened with disfellowshipping.

[78] Hamilton, John Ettwein, pp. 308, 309; Two Centuries of Nazareth, pp. 75-77.

members with certificates to prove their *bona fides*—on the grounds that this sort of request was unconstitutional since it was not demanded by state law, rather than from any pacifist-absolutist scruples. Furthermore, they felt that so long as the conduct of a member was in line with his religious profession, it should be clear that he was in good standing with the church. Later, however, they became willing to give the militia captain a list of their members in each congregation who were of military age, that is, between 18 and 45.[79] Those who had not been behaving as the church authorities thought proper might be refused support if called upon for drilling. For instance, a minute of the Salem Board of Elders for 1 August 1787 states: "S. S. has taken part in an affair which is contrary to our customs. If he is enrolled for militia service we cannot help his father, whose duty it was to keep his son in better order."[80]

The War of 1812 revealed the degree to which the Moravian peace testimony had declined among its members.[81] It had clearly ceased to be a living article of faith and in almost all cases was now accepted— if, indeed, it was accepted at all—merely as part of the ancestral furniture. Most of those who were liable for service no longer felt any scruples; some wished actively to conform to what they regarded as the call of duty.

In Pennsylvania the men chafed at having to pay the fines for refusal to drill or for the more costly substitutes, which were now being demanded, and many now participated in the musters. On 24 October 1814 the Nazareth church diary reports: "Today our Brethren attended military practice for the first time." And on the following 25 November the entry states: "The married Brother, Frederich Miksch, returned from the army in fairly good health."[82] There is, moreover, a record of several members being called out for active service with the troops. At the provincial conference of elders the question was discussed whether in these circumstances it was right—or even possible— to enforce the old ban on mustering. The decision was somewhat am-

[79] *Records of the Moravians in North Carolina*, V, 2146, 2348, 2379, 2477, 2478; VII, 3092, 3093, 3237, 3527.

[80] *Ibid.*, V, 2187. See also pp. 2181, 2238.

[81] It was at this time too, during the German War of Liberation when many Moravians, carried away on the wave of patriotic enthusiasm, joined in the armed struggle against the French, that the church in Saxony and Prussia officially abandoned its stand in favor of military exemption. In 1815 the Prussian government, under whose rule most of the Saxon congregations were now placed, withdrew its grant of exemption, and no protest was registered by the church. See G. Burkhardt, *Die Brüdergemeine*, 2nd edn., I, 136-38. The pacifist element in their objection to bearing arms had always been less, it would seem, in the case of the Moravians on the European continent than among their brethren in America.

[82] *Two Centuries of Nazareth*, p. 77.

biguous, but it was agreed that mustering need not necessarily entail disownment by the church. The subordinate General Helpers' Conference went even further and proclaimed that military service was not, in fact, contrary to Biblical teaching and that it would be positively wrong to try to discipline men for following the state's commands and their own consciences in accepting such service. There was only one dissenting voice, that of the Rev. John Gebhard Cunow (a newcomer from Europe in 1796), who argued in favor of maintaining the ban imposed by previous synods.

Meanwhile, the elders' conferences of the three church communities of Pennsylvania, which had been asked to give their opinions, sent in their replies. Bethlehem and Nazareth both agreed that it was impossible any longer to try to undertake disciplinary action against those who attended drills. It would lead to an open rebellion of the young people, who saw no reason for incurring the expenses of a substitute in order to uphold an out-of-date point of view that no longer won acceptance within the church. Let the matter be left to the conscience of the individual, they decided. The third congregation, the one at Lititz, however, gave a different answer. Service in the militia, it claimed, was not consistent with the church's tenets, and church members should continue to seek exemption, even at some financial sacrifice, and be disciplined if they were unwilling to abide by the rule. Behind this decision can be detected the influence of the pastor of Lititz, the Rev. Andrew Benade, who was Cunow's friend and, like him, a traditionalist of the old school.[83]

"The wartime relaxation of the regulations against participation in military drill now had its not illogical result. In mid-summer of 1815, in the midst of the military drill, in which quite a number of Brethren [at Nazareth] had been participating, an attempt was actually made to form a free uniformed company among the younger Brethren, quite against the tenets of the church, which promptly and successfully thwarted the move. The incipient militia company had procured a small cannon, which the younger element . . . wished to use at the Fourth of July celebration."[84] In Pennsylvania the final stage came in 1818 when its synod officially withdrew the ban on members performing military service. Whether to bear arms or to take the conscientious objector position was now left to the individual conscience. In fact, apart from a few old men, pacifism was dead within the ranks of the Pennsylvanian Moravians.[85]

[83] Levering, A History of Bethlehem, pp. 612, 613.
[84] Two Centuries of Nazareth, pp. 78, 79.
[85] Levering, A History of Bethlehem, p. 613.

327

The position of the North Carolina branch of the church was more conservative, and the old noncombatancy was not finally abandoned until more than a decade after the Pennsylvania congregations had made their decision. On 16 February 1813 we read in the minutes of the Salem Board of Elders: "As small parties of soldiers have marched through our town the single Brethren and some of the married Brethren have demonstrated their friendship by giving them food and drink. We will encourage and favor this, partly out of human kindness, and partly to show our appreciation of our personal freedom from militia duty, at least for the present." A little later in the same month, however, the elders discussed the possibility of federal conscription being imposed if the war continued, which would necessitate the provision of substitutes for those balloted for such service. Eventually, in February 1815, the North Carolina church reached a collective decision in the matter. In no event should the younger brethren be permitted to set aside the ban on military service. Those liable should pool their resources by forming a kind of mutual aid society to help pay for substitutes. Any brother who was unwilling to join would be ineligible for financial help toward costs.[86]

With the coming of peace the congregations of North Carolina again became entirely free from the obligation of military service. But the situation was causing increasing dissatisfaction both within the church and outside. In 1825 it was reported in a discussion of the subject: "It cannot be denied that some among us show by their conduct that they are not *regular* members of the Unity of Brethren; others in the country congregations belong to us because they wish to be exempt from drill, and there have been cases in which such persons, who have been treated with patience, have left us when they reached the age of forty-five."[87] Growing opposition was also apparent among the general populace to the continued exemption of a group that had long shed any real pacifist scruples and that continued to cling to its privileged position, not, it is true, out of cowardice or a deficiency of patriotism, but from a misplaced (so it must have seemed to outsiders) loyalty to tradition.

This agitation finally led the assembly to withdraw the Moravians' exemption. Beginning on Independence Day of 1831, their young men were to become liable for service. There were apparently no protests from the church's side, but, as a concession to Moravian nonconformity to the world, they were to be permitted to form "a Free Company"

[86] *Records of the Moravians in North Carolina*, VII, 3202, 3203, 3548-51. The attempt among the Pennsylvania Moravians to organize a similar pool during the war apparently broke down.
[87] *Ibid.*, VIII, 3747.

with its own officers drawn from church members. "When men are mustered," explains a report from the Salem congregation, "this company may remain intact, not mingled with others, except at the annual muster at which they must appear in like uniforms with the others, the uniforms to be furnished by themselves. Guns are furnished by the state." On this memorable Fourth of July, the writer goes on, "the whole company appeared in the early morning and again in the afternoon in their uniforms, and went through their military drills accompanied by martial music. Everything was conducted in good order, according to the constitution they had drawn up. We only wish that this change will not have any detrimental effect on the congregation." In the morning Brother Bechler, at the invitation of the company, had delivered "an appropriate address, basing his remarks on Proverbs 14:34" ("Righteousness exalteth a nation: but sin is a reproach to any people"). The transition from noncombatancy to participation in military service had been accomplished without a hitch. In the same year we find the company taking part alongside the regular militia in emergency measures against the possibility of a Negro insurrection (the Moravians in the South were slaveholders both individually and as a church).[88] In May 1832 we read of Brother Emanuel Schober, the captain in command of the Salem company, leaving for West Point to qualify himself for his new role.

So, with the sound of the martial music provided by the Moravian militiamen in our ears and the departure of Brother Schober for West Point, we may finally take our leave of Moravian pacifism.

[88] *Ibid.*, pp. 3960, 3969, 3972, 3990, 4017.

329

Part Two

*The Peace Sects from the American
Revolution to the Civil War*

"Placed in the midst of this world and its commotions, we shall know our situation to be as a garden enclosed."

—Samuel Fothergill, as quoted in R. Hingston Fox, *Dr. John Fothergill and His Friends.*

Chapter 8

The Quaker Peace Testimony, 1783-1861

Seventy-eight years passed between the end of the Revolutionary War and the outbreak of the war between the states. These years saw immense changes in every aspect of the new nation's affairs. Economic life was revolutionized; political institutions and parties were molded and remolded; social customs were transformed; new and vital intellectual trends sprang up among the educated; the religion of all classes was swept by the fires of revival and the cold winds of skepticism. Inside the three major American peace sects important developments were taking place, too. Some were beneficial to the health and well-being of these groups; others were harmful and represented a retrogression.

Whatever gains and losses the records of these sects (or "historic peace churches," as they are collectively known today) may show for this period of over three quarters of a century, their peace witness was marked on the whole by a decline in vitality. These years were for the most part years of peace. True, war was being waged in Europe almost continuously from 1792 to 1815, but only during its last few years—the War of 1812—was the United States involved directly. Thereafter, if we exclude trouble with the Indians and occasional abortive war crises, peace was punctuated only by the limited Mexican War of 1846-1848 until, nearly a decade and a half later, the rising tide of sectional conflict flooded over into open war. During these years separations stemming from disputed theology, or even from personality conflicts, occupied far more of the peace sects' attention than the maintenance of their historic testimonies against war.

I

The story of their continuing, if somewhat pallid, peace witness is to some extent fragmentary. The most coherent picture comes from the Society of Friends—as might be expected, both on account of the careful keeping and preservation of Quaker records and because of the higher educational level maintained within the Society. Quakers of both town and country were more articulate, more given to self-expression, more introspective than the German dialect speakers of the

333

Mennonite and Dunker faiths, whether back in their Pennsylvania home state or pushing out westward into the ever retreating wilderness. Quakers, not unlike the German sects, had grown increasingly isolated as a community from the surrounding world. They had come to pursue their advocacy of peace like their other activities as in "a garden enclos'd" (to use the words of the eighteenth-century English Friend, Samuel Fothergill). But the Quaker enclosure, for all its stifling narrowness in many respects, was still broader than the sectarian world of the pious Mennonite and Dunker farmer and backwoodsman.

Early in the second half of the eighteenth century, as we have seen, a movement originating in Philadelphia Yearly Meeting had begun in the American branch of the Society, aimed at the regeneration of the peace testimony as well as of the other aspects of the Quaker witness. To restore the purity of their faith and practice, the movement's leaders had insisted on the Society's separation from the world. Purged of its worldliness, the Society could then act—so it was hoped—as an agent of regeneration within the wider society of America. A reinvigorated Quaker pacifism, along with other humanitarian concerns, was thus part and parcel of this renewal of the Society of Friends as a whole. Yet, "in spite of being pacifists," Friends strove to be "essentially good Americans"[1] by holding up the Quaker enclosure as an example for the whole American nation.

In this period the Quaker as pacifist was concerned with a number of issues both in their direct impact on his personal life and in their theoretical implications for the religious life of the Society. What response should he make if called upon to muster with the state militia? Should taxes be paid if, wholly or in part, they were destined for military purposes? Might Revolutionary veterans who had become convinced Friends go on drawing their pensions? Where should the conscience of the Quaker merchant draw the line between peaceful trade and the profits of war? And, as Friends followed the frontier and thereby came into contact with the lawlessness of such regions, how would they meet the challenges this brought to their philosophy of nonviolence? These questions, and others like them, were practical matters which required individual decision. They were mostly questions which had had to be met in earlier periods—indeed, ever since Friends had come together in England around the middle of the seventeenth century. Friends also continued to concern themselves with the theoretical problems of war and peace. They composed treatises

---

[1] Sydney V. James, "The Impact of the American Revolution on Quakers' Ideas about Their Sect," *William and Mary Quarterly*, 3rd ser., XIX, no. 3 (July 1962), 375.

334

or drew up shorter statements expounding Christian pacifism in general or as it related to some particular situation. They did not neglect altogether the thorny old question of the relationship between pacifism and civil government. Finally, we may mention their reaction to the new focus of pacifism which developed outside the historic peace churches from 1815 on in the nondenominational peace societies, and to the radical philosophy of nonresistance in particular.

The conclusion of peace in 1783, though it greatly diminished the sufferings of Friends for their faithful maintenance of the peace testimony, did not end conscription for the state militias. In almost all states the law continued to require all able-bodied men to muster under arms for several days of training each year, with fines for nonattendance and distraints on property or short periods of imprisonment for failure to pay such fines. The law was not enforced with equal regularity or efficiency in all areas and, as time passed, the training period tended, except during national emergencies, to become more and more an occasion merely for junketing rather than for a serious military operation. Exemption might always be purchased by paying enough money to hire a substitute to train in one's stead. Quakers and the other peace sects were sometimes specifically granted exemption in a state's militia law—provided they were ready to pay a small sum in exchange. This, of course, the Quakers as a body refused to do, regarding it still—as they had done hitherto—as an infringement of the rights of conscience and freedom of religion. And, as before, distraints on property and occasional imprisonments ensued whenever and wherever the militia officers took their jobs seriously. More often, of course, neighborly friendliness, mixed with the unmilitary disposition of the majority of the American people, inhibited a harsh enforcement of the law on otherwise law-abiding citizens whose consciences had in this instance converted them into temporary law violators.

When in 1790 and again in 1795 proposals were put forward in Congress, then deliberating in Philadelphia, to exempt Quakers from the obligation of mustering with the militia provided they paid a sum of £2 to be used for nonmilitary purposes, protest came from Friends both individually and collectively. In 1790 a committee of twelve, including such weighty members of Philadelphia Yearly Meeting as James Pemberton, William Savery, and Warner Mifflin, drew up on behalf of the meeting an "Address and Memorial," which was duly presented to President and Congress.[2] In it they judiciously mixed in appreciation of the concern shown by the legislators for tender con-

---

[2] Quoted in full in Hilda Justice, *Life and Ancestry of Warner Mifflin*, pp. 178-82. See also Ezra Michener, *A Retrospect of Early Quakerism*, p. 306.

sciences with a warning that the conditional exemption proposed would not, in fact, be sufficient to allay Friends' scruples. In addition to refusing direct military service, they stated, Friends "have also considered themselves conscientiously bound to refuse the payment of any sum required in lieu of such personal service or in consideration of an exemption from any military employment, however laudable the purposes are to which the money is intended to be applied, as it manifestly infringes on the right of conscience."

Five years later, when the question was still being discussed in the legislature, an anonymous Friend attempted to argue the case for unconditional exemption in more detail. His views were originally expressed in private correspondence and published, apparently without permission, by the non-Friend sympathizer to whom they were addressed. The writer, naturally, recognized the religious foundation of the Society's pacifism and the importance of early training in inculcating its precepts. "The ardor of youth, ambition, and other powerful springs, which exist in the human breast," he explained, "are common to the members of our, as well as to those of every other society; but it is the early and assiduous care, which is bestowed upon the formation of our minds, and the direction of our ideas, which first initiates us into the habit of restraining our ambition, and other passions; and finally deters us from engaging in the field of battle." However, he based his case primarily on the liberties of the freeborn American, on "the ground of unrestrained freedom of opinions, which is the birthright—the constitutional right—of every citizen of these states, whether in religious or other concerns." If a man's conscience, his religion, forbids him to do military service, then it is an infringement of his freedom to require him to pay a "tax" for permission to follow his conscience, which is in itself an inalienable right. The objection that granting complete exemption to members of the Society would open the doors to a flood of slackers unwilling either to drill themselves or to pay a monetary equivalent was groundless. The exactitude with which the Society kept its membership records would prevent its being used as a cover for militia dodgers.[3]

After the bill became law in 1795, it remained, as before, the official policy of the Society that members should, if necessary, suffer the penalties of the law rather than buy their exemption at the cost of principle, however seemingly innocuous were the ends to which their exemption money might be put by the authorities. "Where deviations in this respect occur," states a minute of Philadelphia Yearly Meeting

[3] A Letter from One of the Society of Friends, Relative to the Conscientious Scrupulousness of its Members to Bear Arms, pp. 2-5, 10-12, 17.

of 1805 which expresses the practice then current among Friends, "tender dealing and advice should be extended to the party, in order to their convincement and restoration; and where they continue so regardless of the sense and judgment of the body, that the labor of their Friends proves ineffectual, Monthly Meetings should proceed to testify against them."[4] Thus Quaker absolutism, the refusal of all conditional exemption to military service, continued to be officially endorsed by the Society and enforced with the threat of disownment.

Lobbying state legislatures on behalf of their conscientious objectors became a frequent practice with the various yearly meetings, particularly when new militia legislation, or an amendment to the old, was being discussed. We find Philadelphia Yearly Meeting, for instance, doing this—not for the first or last time—in 1808. A delegation complete with a memorial drawn up by the Meeting for Sufferings was dispatched to the state capital, then situated at Lancaster. Its four members, so it is told, entered the legislative chamber just at the moment a representative, Michael Leib, was denouncing Friends as instigators of the attempt to insert into the militia bill then under consideration a clause giving religious objectors complete exemption. Looking up and recognizing among the delegates his old friend and neighbor, the prominent Quaker minister Thomas Scattergood, Leib immediately changed his tack and now began to praise the Society as warmly as he had only a few minutes before condemned it—much to the amusement of his fellow assemblymen.[5]

Perhaps the most cogent example of memorializing in favor of complete exemption was provided by the documents drawn up toward the end of 1810 by the talented clerk of Virginia Yearly Meeting, Benjamin Bates, and presented to the state legislature in the meeting's name. Both the "Memorial and Petition" and Bates's accompanying letter were subsequently reprinted several times and used by other yearly meetings even as late as the Civil War to support their claims to exemption. These documents do, indeed, argue the Quaker case with skill and clarity and show the author to be a man of education and culture, well versed in the political philosophy of his day.

The rights of religious conscience, the "Memorial" states, do not need to be proved. They should be "self-evident . . . in this enlightened age and country," and, besides, they had been guaranteed in federal and state constitutions. To confine freedom of conscience to the realm of mere thought and not to extend it also to action flowing from thought

---

[4] *Yearly Extracts for 1805* (folder issued by Philadelphia Y. M. in F.H.L.S.C.), pp. 2, 3. See also Michener, *A Retrospect of Early Quakerism*, p. 307.

[5] W. W. Cadbury in *Friend*, vol. 119, no. 10 (8 Nov. 1945), pp. 150, 151.

would be an injustice. Friends, following what they believed to be the example of the early church and many other good Christians, and also of their own society since its beginning, had always held it to be wrong for Christians to bear arms. "To require it under legal penalties, is to reduce them to the alternative of refusing a compliance with the laws of their country, or of violating what they most solemnly believe is, to *them*, a law of God, clothed with the most awful sanctions." Their conscientious scruples in this respect had been recognized as genuine by the Virginia Legislature immediately after the Revolution, but recent changes in the law had withdrawn this liberal exemption. Friends were now required to pay commutation money for their unwillingness to train, and the amount of these fines was fixed arbitrarily "at the discretion of the courts martial, and become in numerous instances, extremely oppressive." "The voluntary payment of a fine imposed for adhering to religious duty, or the receiving of surplus money arising from the sale of their property seized for the satisfying of these demands, would be to acknowledge a delinquency, which they cannot admit, and to become parties in a traffic or commutation of their principles."[6]

In his supplementary remarks, Bates stressed that Friends had no wish to escape from their civil obligations under the cloak of religion or to contest the right of the state to conscript, if such were the people's will, those of its citizens whose consciences were not opposed to militia training. At the same time, he explained in further detail why Friends felt unable to pay commutation money ("a muster-fine in disguise," he called it), even when, as in the present instance, it was to be put to some good use like the upkeep of schools.

> I am paying [he told the legislators] what is considered by the government as a debt—and for what consideration? Plainly for being allowed to enjoy the liberty of conscience. But I do not derive the liberty of conscience from the government; I hold it from a tenure antecedent to the institutions of civil society. It was secured to me in the social compact, and it was never submitted to the legislature at all. They have therefore no such privilege to grant or withhold, at their pleasure; and certainly no pretence or authority to sell it for a price.

Absolute exemption for religious objectors, then, was a natural, inborn right which their nonpacifist fellow citizens were powerless to barter away. "If the powers they surrender for themselves," Bates wrote of the

---

[6] *Memorial and Petition of the Society of Friends, to the Legislature of Virginia: with a Letter of Benjamin Bates, on the Subject of Militia Fines*, pp. 2-4.

338

latter, "involve the constitutional rights of others, they are binding only on those who have consented to them." The Quaker absolutist, in following his conscience and his God in refusing to obey a man-made law and in patiently suffering the consequences, was in fact defending at the same time the civil rights and the constitutional liberties of all free Americans.[7]

Benjamin Bates and his fellow memorialists were acting during a period of peace when the continental war had not as yet involved the United States in direct military conflict. The year 1812, however, saw the outbreak of hostilities between the United States and Great Britain. Although North America was only briefly and intermittently the scene of actual battle, so that the devastation and loss of life nowhere equalled that suffered back in Europe and the day-to-day existence of the majority of the country's citizens went on unchanged, the war years brought new and more acute problems to the Society of Friends. The edge of their peace witness, always liable to become blunted in periods of protracted peace, was sharpened, too.

The yearly meetings exhorted their members to maintain a consistent testimony against war in the face of increased pressures to conform. In 1813 Baltimore Yearly Meeting—to give just one instance—urged Friends to avoid any conduct that might "violate in any way this most precious testimony." History had shown the disastrous character of war and the fair fruits of peace, and it was incumbent on them to be prepared to face trials and sacrifices on its behalf.[8] Early in 1815 its Meeting for Sufferings warned members against even an "indirect payment of fines or other military demands."[9] As the Quakers had found in the past, it was not always easy to know just where to draw the line in defining action inconsistent with their peace witness. For example, a minute dated 14 August 1813, from a Pennsylvania rural community, the monthly meeting at Center, runs as follows: "This meeting requests the judgment of the quarterly meeting on that part of the discipline relating to military service whether the voluntary or involuntary furnishing of waggons, where compensation may be received for the owners, for the use thereof will bear a testimony."[10]

The main trials faced by Friends during the war years were naturally those connected with service in the militia. The rigor with which the military enforced its requirements was increased as the demand for men became greater. Again the practice differed even from county to

[7] *Ibid.*, pp. 10-12.
[8] Kenneth S.P. Morse, *Baltimore Yearly Meeting*, p. 34.
[9] Minute dated 4 Feb. 1815, copy in the Janney MSS, F.H.L.S.C.
[10] From Thomas Jenkins Papers, F.H.L.S.C., R G 5.

county within the same state. In Virginia before the outbreak of war, we are told, the "sheriffs of the counties to the southwest of Richmond were unrelenting in their collection of fines for failure to muster, whereas in other counties at the same period the county officials were either indifferent or purposely lenient with the Quakers." The harassment in the former area reached a climax in 1813. Eleven young men from Upper Monthly Meeting were arrested and taken off to prison in Norfolk or Petersburg.[11] Elsewhere in the same state Friends fared no better. The records of Western Branch Monthly Meeting show that funds were raised early in 1813 among members of the meeting to assist the families of those who "are carried off in the militia," as well as Friends who were suffering severely from distraints for nonpayment of militia fines. "On the 17th of the 3rd," it was reported, "three young men were taken and carried off into the army in or near Portsmouth and for refusing to bear arms they were by orders of Colonel Francis B. Boykin confined in the dungeon about 48 hours and are still detained in the army."[12] These were not isolated cases. But Friends in Virginia, a small minority group whose popularity was not increased by their outspoken opposition to slavery in this slaveholding state, often seem to have fared worse vis-à-vis the military than was usually the case with their brethren farther north and west.

True, poorer Friends anywhere who did not own enough property on which distraint could be levied might find themselves cast into the local jail until such time as the military or public opinion relented. This contrast in treatment comes out clearly in the narrative of an Indiana Quaker (later converted to Methodism), Henry Hoover, whose family was among the first to settle in the upper Whitewater Valley. Friends' views were not as well known there as in the older settled areas, and frontier mores were in any case intolerant of pacifist inclinations; thus, even before the outbreak of war, public opinion had forced the territorial legislature to withdraw the exemption they had granted Quaker objectors in 1810.[13] When war came, young Hoover was or-

[11] Hinshaw, *Encyclopedia of American Quaker Genealogy*, VI, 127. In the editor's opinion, the severity with which the militia regulations were enforced over the years—along with the unpopularity and embarrassments connected with Friends' testimony against slavery—were the chief reasons for the westward migration of most Quaker families from this and neighboring meetings in the course of a couple of decades after the war.

[12] *Ibid.*, pp. 48, 292.

[13] In August 1811 Indiana Friends had written to the governor, General William H. Harrison, and to the general assembly to thank them for the generous exemption given them in the previous year. "If," they say, "we may be useful in harmonizing our fellow citizens, or civilizing our Indian neighbors, we will with unreserved alacrity contribute thereto; as we hope ever to participate in the peaceful

dered out for eight days' service with the military. "A compliance would have ejected me from the Church," he writes, "and moreover brought trouble on the minds of my parents, who had taught me that all wars were antichristian." And so, upon refusing to serve, he was fined $16 by the court, and soldiers were sent to seize his sheep to cover the fine which, as a loyal Friend, he could not pay himself. "Others were used more severe," he adds, "not having property on which to levy, their bodies were seized and cast into the jail in Salisbury, in the dead of winter. . . . The jail had neither chimney, stove or bed. . . . They were for weeks confined in jail, but were ultimately discharged, but not until public opinion had begun to do its work of mercy."[14]

In the North, however, Quakers in many areas enjoyed considerable social prestige. In New England, New York, and Pennsylvania the Society included many prosperous merchants and traders in its membership. There, especially in Pennsylvania, arrest and imprisonment for refusing military service occurred only rarely, though fines were often heavy and, as usual, the value of the property distrained was frequently in excess of the amount of the fine.[15] This latter fact would seem to invalidate the stories told at that time (and later) of conversions to Quakerism in order to evade military service,[16] especially in view of the strict requirements laid down for membership. Sometimes, however, Friends were treated with remarkable sympathy and understanding—presumably because the Quaker peace testimony and the individual's membership in the Society were well known in the community. The experience of William Evans (1787-1867), then a young

---

improvement of our country's welfare." This letter and Friends' memorial of 1810 asking for complete exemption from militia service are printed in Rufus M. Jones, *The Later Periods of Quakerism*, II, 720, 721.

[14] Bernhard Knollenberg, *Pioneer Sketches of the Upper Whitewater Valley*, pp. 29, 41.

[15] See *Pennsylvania Colonial Records: Minutes of the Supreme Executive Council of Pennsylvania*, XV, 418, for an early example in a protest, dated March 1788, from Friends in Chester Co., whose goods were being made by the collectors liable to repeated distraint for the same fine.

[16] Samuel H. Cox, *Quakerism not Christianity*, p. 235: "In the last war [1812] some became sudden converts to Quakerism; growing quite conscientious in the time of danger against such profane exposures of life—and either joined the Society, or pleaded a kindred exemption from responsibilities." Dr. Cox was a convert from Quakerism to Presbyterianism. Pp. 234-56 of his bulky refutation of Quakerism are devoted to a discussion of the peace testimony. A more plausible, though equally partisan, criticism is that contained in a short political pamphlet published in 1808, *A Serious Expostulation with the Society of Friends in Pennsylvania, and Parts Adjacent*, where "Pacificus" comments (pp. 5, 6) on the lack of a genuinely pacific spirit among even many weighty Quakers where "their mercantile interest" is involved. See also *To Pacificus, in Reply to his Essay*.

man of 27 and a birthright Friend, is a case in point. He relates in his journal how in 1814 he was summoned "before a court-martial" in Philadelphia to answer for his failure to muster with the militia. The court gave him a respectful hearing, listening patiently to his explanation that, as a Friend, he would suffer the penalty of the law rather than comply with an order that went against his conscience. Evans heard nothing more from the military authorities, who evidently decided to leave the young Quaker in peace and not to proceed against him further.[17]

Thus, as earlier, in the Revolutionary War, the sufferings of Friends on account of their pacifist witness during the War of 1812 stemmed mainly from the heavy distraints on their property which refusal to pay the fines imposed by the military entailed. As usual, careful record was kept by most meetings of the losses endured. An example of the scrupulousness with which this accounting was carried on is shown in the case of Baltimore Yearly Meeting. In February 1815, Meeting for Sufferings admonished monthly meetings, when gathering information concerning "military" sufferings,

> . . . not to admit of any case as a suffering which may not appear to have been faithfully borne. We believe also that when goods are distrained, an advantage would arise from obtaining as far as practicable consistently with our peaceable profession from the officer making the distraint a certificate containing the articles taken, and the amount and nature of the claim they were taken to satisfy.[18]

In 1815 an era of external peace and of domestic "good feelings" came to the United States. In the internal affairs of the Society of Friends, however, the spirit of schism was growing, until finally it spilled over into the great separation of 1827, dividing the Society into Orthodox and Hicksite branches, each of which excommunicated the other. The deplorable discord within a religious denomination collectively dedicated to the gospel of peace did not, it is true, directly affect the maintenance of its historic testimony against war. This testimony continued as part of the heritage claimed by both branches. Nevertheless, energy and thought were channeled off into the problems generated by the factional conflict. One of the Friends' activities that suffered—but, of course, by no means the only one—was their peace witness.

For many decades the problem of militia service continued to occupy the main place in Friends' concern for the peace testimony. The

---

[17] *Journal of William Evans*, p. 32.
[18] Minute dated 4 Feb. 1815, copy in the Janney MSS, F.H.L.S.C.

pattern did not change very much. The heaviest burden still arose from the imposition of fines on the younger men for failure to appear for training at the annual musters and the subsequent distraints levied for their conscientious refusal to pay. It was calculated that during the single decade of the 1820's property amounting to the total value of $16,021.85 was taken from members of Philadelphia Yearly Meeting (which of course included, in addition to the Pennsylvania meetings, Friends living in western New Jersey as well as some in Delaware and Maryland).[19] The accuracy with which monthly meetings kept records of militia "sufferings" vouches for the reliability of these figures. There was frequent complaint about the rapacity of the collectors, usually shady characters who seized from their victims goods much in excess of the value of the original fine. "The office is so disagreeable," complained an Ohio Quaker, "it is seldom undertaken by a man of generous feeling." Self-respecting citizens were usually unwilling to undertake the task of confiscating the clothing, bedclothes, furniture, and household utensils of neighbors whose religious scruples they respected, even if they did not share them. Consequently, either the law was ignored or its execution was placed in the hands of the unscrupulous.[20] A writer in the Orthodox *Friend* provides several examples of these extortions. "For a fine of four dollars," we are told, "one of these deputies came into a store, took up the shears, and cut himself off two yards of the finest broadcloth, then selling at nine dollars per yard." "Another of these abandoned fellows actually seized a man's account books, and took them to a neighbour's to sell."[21]

We have a detailed description of how the system worked where the law enforcement officers were reasonably honest in the account left by Benjamin Hallowell (1799-1877), the Quaker schoolmaster (one of whose pupils was to be Robert E. Lee!). In 1824 he was teaching in Alexandria (then within the limits of the District of Columbia), and at the end of his first year there he was presented with a bill for $15 for failing to attend the statutory militia trainings. The militia captain, who in this case had the task of levying distraint on Hallowell's property when the latter persisted in his refusal to pay the fine, was obviously somewhat embarrassed at his assignment and asked the young man to point out to him what objects he could spare most easily. His Quaker conscience, however, restrained Hallowell from collaborating with the military even to this extent. So, in the end, the captain

[19] *Friend; or, Advocate of Truth*, N.S., I, no. 2 (Feb. 1832), 35.

[20] "Extract from an Address to the People of Belmont, Ohio, by Charles Hammond" in *Extracts from Several Writers on Militia Fines and War*, pp. 3, 4.

[21] *Friend* (Phila.), 29 Dec. 1832, p. 96.

took away a number of pieces of "our parlor furniture" to be sold by special auction where, however, because no respectable people attended "from a reluctance to make a profit from their neighbours' religious scruples," the goods went for a ridiculously low figure. The following year Congress exempted all teachers within the District from the obligation of militia service, and thus Hallowell's trials came to an end.[22]

The militia laws, in peacetime as in wartime, touched not only the purses of the Friends but upon occasion their persons as well, and, hence, we find that young Quaker conscientious objectors were sometimes dragged off to spend short periods in prison for nonpayment of their fines. Usually, as we have seen, it was the poorer brethren who suffered in this way, but not always. In the early 1820's, for instance, young James Mott (1788-1868), a fairly well-to-do Philadelphia merchant newly wed to the famous Lucretia, found himself in the city jail on Arch Street until, without his knowledge or consent, an unknown sympathizer paid his fine for him.[23] As late as 1845 the Hicksite New York Yearly Meeting could record: "Beside the loss of property taken from our members by distraint, three of our young men have suffered imprisonment for different periods rather than submit to military requisitions."[24] Constant distraints on property and occasional imprisonment continued—though with decreasing intensity—to be the lot of many Friends of militia age into the 1850's.

That most young Friends followed the Society's official line and refused to pay the fines imposed on them seems clear from the surviving evidence. That many did so more or less reluctantly appears equally certain, and, it seems, too, that, at least by the thirties, a few did pay and escaped the disciplining by their meetings that would almost inevitably have been their lot earlier. The issue, after all, was not as clearcut as the original refusal of service from which it had resulted. The penalties—whether in the form of distraints on property or brief imprisonments—were more inconvenient than harsh or cruel, and the whole position had a slightly ridiculous aspect. The sympathies of the community were often with the lawbreaker rather than with the law. The very mildness of this law, indeed, offered a temptation to relax opposition to its enforcement. So we find that even a man like Hallowell, who "cheerfully" suffered his furniture to be removed and auctioned for a song, had his inner doubts about the wisdom of his Society's uncompromising stand and its right to impose it on members

22 *Autobiography of Benjamin Hallowell,* pp. 210-12.
23 A. D. Hallowell, *James and Lucretia Mott,* p. 8.
24 From Thomas Jenkins Papers, F.H.L.S.C., R G 5.

344

who had different views, feeling that the payment of a fine was a legitimate submission to the penalty for noncompliance with the law. "But," he went on, "estimating very highly the privileges my birthright membership in the Society of Friends has given me . . . I will not pay such fines while the Discipline of the Society requires its members not to do so."[25]

Not all members who failed to go along with the discipline, which regarded the payment of fines as compromising their conscientious objection to war, were so loyal or so scrupulous as Hallowell. Thus, in an article which an anonymous writer contributed to the *Friend* in 1835 under the pseudonym of "Pacificus,"[26] we discover that not only the special efforts of "the present collector of militia fines in the city of Philadelphia" to enforce payment, but the evidence of "the very small number of cases sent up to our late quarterly meeting" of persons refusing payment, indicated (in the writer's opinion) that this testimony was growing lukewarm among the present generation. There were undoubtedly some who did not hesitate to pay outright; more often, there was resort to subterfuge through connivance at payment, usually by some non-Quaker friend. " 'Have you no friend to pay it for you?' is the enquiry of the collector; 'Friend so-and-so always *has his paid.*' 'Mr. S—— is a Friend and he pays me his fine; so does Mr. T——; they never make a disturbance about it.' " "Pacificus" goes on to point out what he regards as the insidious effects of this disobedience on the Society's discipline and brands the willingness to pay on the part of non-Friends as "mistaken kindness." It helps, he says, to bolster up "the onerous militia system," and it makes it more difficult for consistent Friends to maintain a clear testimony for peace.

By the fifties the pressure had been largely relaxed. Distrainment became infrequent, and imprisonment for nonpayment of fines ceased almost entirely. But for Pennsylvania Friends a new danger arose: they might inadvertently pay their militia fine along with their general state tax bill. An extra 50¢ (which by this time was the total exacted for militia delinquency) might not easily be noticed, and the whole amount might be paid willingly by the unsuspecting Friend. The state was probably not aiming at conscious deception when it sanctioned tacking militia fines onto the general tax bill in this way but, rather, was out to save on the costs of collecting at a time when, for most citizens of the state, this small fine had taken the place of the obligation to attend musters. For the militia system had fallen into decay, and delinquency had become almost universal among those

[25] *Autobiography*, p. 212.   [26] *Friend*, 14 Feb. 1835, p. 151.

who did not entertain any conscientious objections. The Quaker conscience, however, was distressed at the thought of giving even unwitting support to the war system, and throughout the decade the Quaker weeklies, all published in Philadelphia during that period, continued to sound the alarm from time to time lest Friends relax their vigilance.

> I was on the point of paying my militia fine to the tax collector a day or two since [runs a letter in the *Friend* of 6 July 1850], and that without thinking at all on the subject. No open reference is made to it in the tax bill, but the item of State *Personal* tax is 50 cents higher than usual. Some little occurrence excited my suspicion, but it was not until I had repeatedly and pointedly questioned the collector, that I learned from him, that the additional 50 cents was for my militia fine. As the time when our taxes are to be paid is now at hand, would it not be well to put Friends on their guard, lest they be led in this manner to support the militia system, without being aware of it?[27]

In the 1850's the war clouds were already mounting, and the testing period of the early sixties would make a storm over the 50¢ look small indeed. Nevertheless, a question of principle, the pinch of incense, was at stake here for Friends, and ultimately this, not the size of the stake, is what is important.

We have briefly surveyed the history of Quaker conscientious objection during the decades following the conclusion of the Napoleonic Wars. Friends collectively or individually, were active in upholding their conscientious objectors in various ways, too. As we have seen, they addressed state legislatures in favor of exemption, placed the case for such exemption before the public, and attempted, more generally, to prove not only the moral harm but also the practical uselessness of the militia system.

Among the most active in encouraging conscientious objectors was Elisha Bates (ca. 1780-1861), who was one of the leaders of Ohio Quakerism until his fervent evangelicalism led him in 1835 to leave Friends for the Methodist Episcopal Church. In the *Moral Advocate*, which he edited in Mt. Pleasant from 1821-1824, he included, along with material on "duelling, capital punishments and prison discipline," a number of articles—mostly from his own pen—protesting against the imposition of fines and other penalties on Friends for refusing militia service and explaining the grounds of the Quaker objec-

---

[27] *Ibid.*, 6 July 1850. See also *Friends' Review*, 30 April 1853, p. 521; *Friends' Intelligencer*, 12 March 1859, p. 822; *Journal of William Evans*, p. 661.

tion to war. Not much of this writing was original, but, in a time when no regular Quaker periodical press had yet appeared, it served a valuable function in freshening the traditional teaching on peace learned at home, school, and meeting. The paper closed at the end of 1824, and in the last number Bates gave the place of honor to his "Address to Young Men who believe in the Unlawfulness of War."[28] In it he explained to them the importance of Friends' peace testimony, "this noble testimony," to the Society to which they belonged. They must be prepared in their turn to make sacrifices for it, to face unpopularity as their forefathers had done, and the opportunity to do so they should welcome as a privilege rather than as a burden. They must see that gentle behavior and blameless conduct match their words of peace: this is the best means of disarming hostility. They should try to direct their thoughts to the source of Friends' peace testimony and not accept pacifism passively as merely an inherited belief. On this point he gave some sound advice to those who might have to take their stand as conscientious objectors:

> In declining to render to the laws, that active obedience they require, you should recur to principle, rather than rest on the example of your elder friends. In giving to those who inquire, the reasons for your conduct, still recur to the principle in your minds, rather than to any train of reasoning which you may have learned from others, or formed to yourselves by mere speculative reflection.

Bates had grasped one of the main weaknesses of an inherited religious testimony, whether it be against all wars or in any other sphere: that it would come to be accepted merely as a part of this inheritance and cease to have vital meaning, or any meaning at all perhaps, apart from the desire to maintain the traditions of the group as they had been handed down from the forefathers.

Friends' collective statements on militia service during our period tended to concentrate on the practical disabilities faced by members of military age. Often, however, they dwelt, too, on the general principles which lay behind the peace testimony. In protesting against a new act passed by the Delaware legislature requiring commutation money from religious objectors, we find Wilmington Monthly Meeting in 1827 explaining that their peace testimony was based not only on religious conviction but also on "right reason and the dictates of experience." Christian love coupled with a readiness to suffer without retaliation "would if collectively practised, be found equally effectual

---

[28] *Moral Advocate*, III, no. 12 (Dec. 1824), 192-94. For Bates's pacifism, see the M.A. thesis on Bates by Robert J. Leach, pp. 76-86.

in the preservation of *nations*" as it was for individuals.[29] Three years later, in 1830, when New York Friends faced similar revisions in the militia laws of their state, they appealed to the good feelings of the lawmakers. They were sure, they said, that imprisonment for following conscience, to which members of their Society had recently been subjected, was repugnant to the legislators.[30] Again, in 1833, Philadelphia Yearly Meeting (Orthodox) issued on behalf of its members living in New Jersey a memorial discussing proposals in that state to relieve conscientious objectors by allowing them to pay a special tax, that would go to the school funds, in place of the straight militia fine. Although the memorial recognized that the idea was well meant, "yet it is due to ourselves," it went on, "to state that so far as *we* are concerned, the proposed change in the law will not afford us the intended relief." Commutation money in any form was a tax on conscience, an infringement of religious freedom. The attempt to exact it at the cost of distrainment and imprisonment would prove as useless as it was costly.[31]

The convention, which met at Harrisburg in 1837 to frame a revised constitution for the state of Pennsylvania, aroused deep interest among Friends. The Orthodox Yearly Meeting drew up a "Memorial and Petition" to the convention, pleading for unconditional exemption for all religious objectors. It also reprinted a non-Quaker pamphlet published in Boston nineteen years earlier—*A Dialogue between Telemachus and Mentor on the Rights of Conscience and Military Requisitions*—which stated the case for all types of militia conscientious objectors. (The *Dialogue* will be discussed in the next section of this book.) The "Memorial" was presented to the convention by a Quaker member, Thomas P. Cope (1768-1864). After telling his fellow members that, "in this land of Penn, the Quaker has been deprived of his conscientious privileges," Cope went on to compare the provisions now made for Quaker conscientious objectors in the commonwealth of Massachusetts, Friends' fiercest persecutor in the seventeenth century, with those at present existing in the Quaker state—to the disadvantage of the latter.[32] The "Memorial" itself emphasized the civil liberties aspect of the Quaker case. Friends hoped "that the Society of Friends will not, in the nineteenth century, be deprived of those rights, which their predecessors, on the same soil, in the beginning of the eighteenth,

---

[29] *Address of the Wilmington Monthly Meeting . . . on the Subject of the Militia Law*, pp. 3, 4.

[30] *Memorial . . . on the Subject of Imprisonment, for Non-Compliance with Military Requisitions*, p. 4.

[31] *Friend*, 27 July 1833.   [32] *Ibid.*, 5 Aug. 1837, pp. 347, 348.

348

extended to every class of natives and emigrants." The right to the free exercise of religious conscience was the birthright of every American citizen; therefore, those who had genuine scruples concerning the bearing of arms, whether Quaker or non-Quaker, should be relieved of all obligation under the militia laws.[33] "It is the payment of an equivalent, as the purchase of a religious right; not the purpose to which it may be applied, to which we conscientiously object." Friends, by their sufferings for conscience in the past and their readiness to pay taxes and contribute to the public welfare, had shown that they were not actuated by a desire to contract out of their social obligations or to escape persecution or the hardships of battle. Moreover, by the very fact of firmly maintaining their pacifist ideals, they were making a contribution to the welfare of the whole, since "the diffusion of opinions, such as Friends have always held, must operate in favour of peace."[34]

One of those delegated to present the "Memorial" was Enoch Lewis (1776-1856), who was also responsible for drawing it up.[35] Lewis was by profession a lawyer, by inclination a scholar, in his religious views close to the evangelical party within the Society of Friends, and in the next decade was to become editor of its organ—the *Friends' Review*. In 1831 he had compiled a 35-page pamphlet entitled *Some Observations on the Militia System*, some of whose arguments were repeated in the "Memorial" six years later. Lewis's *Observations* were addressed to a broader audience than the Society of Friends, and it seems to have been quite widely read, since by 1846 it had gone through three editions. The author states his intention at the outset not to discuss the question of absolute pacifism (though he makes his own sentiments clear throughout and at times strays off into arguing about the merits of a peaceful over a warlike policy for a nation); his avowed object was to plead for the scrapping of a compulsory peacetime militia such as existed in all states at that date.

The first objection raised—and it was perhaps the most important one for Lewis—concerned the compulsory character of militia service.

[33] Friends always contended for the inclusion of all genuine objectors within the scope of any legal exemption, although state legislators were rarely as liberal, limiting the right to Quakers alone or to members of other specified peace churches. For instance, when the Maine constitution was being framed, the small group of Friends there attempted to get the rights of all C.O.'s written into it. Only "when we found that to urge so general an exemption was of no avail, we then confined ourselves to the narrow limits of our society." See Rufus M. Jones, *The Society of Friends in Kennebec County, Maine*, pp. 11, 12.

[34] *Memorial and Address of Friends on Military Exactions*, pp. 2, 3, 5, 6, 8.

[35] See Joseph L. Lewis, *A Memoir of Enoch Lewis*. Pp. 25-28 relate Enoch Lewis's personal witness as a young man against seeking security in armed defense when in the 1790's he was employed in surveying the frontier wilderness of western Pennsylvania.

How ironic it was that in the province founded by the peaceful William Penn, where religious freedom had been guaranteed from the beginning, men should be required to pay money to exercise a right which belonged to all, whether Quaker or not. "To presume that a plea of conscientious scruple is insincere, and upon that assumption to found a right to impose a penalty, is to reverse an established principle of law, which always presumes innocence where guilt is not proved." Therefore, all who desire exemption by reason of conscience should have this guaranteed them by law.[36] Lewis went on to present, in the second place, a series of utilitarian arguments against the militia system. Many Friends had attacked the institution on these grounds. A decade before, Elisha Bates had described it as "futile and contemptible in the estimation of military men: demoralizing to those who conform to it, and oppressive to those who conscientiously cannot."[37] In many states during this period, also, a widespread feeling existed, outside the peace movement, that the militia system had become outmoded and that it was merely burdensome to the citizen, fulfilling no useful function to offset the time and money expended on it. And so Lewis could write: "Scarcely any person acquainted with the subject pretends to believe that militia trainings, as practised in this state, are anything better than a ridiculous farce." He quotes from a number of statements by high-ranking military officers, showing that even they shared this opinion. Militia musters had become scenes of drunkenness and vice rather than exhibitions of the martial virtues. Lewis cites extensively from recent reports of the auditor-general of Pennsylvania, in order to show the large sums the state was lavishing on its militia. And it was for their refusal to participate in all this display that the conscientious continued to be fined and imprisoned. Let us disband the militia, Lewis pleads, and spend the money on some more useful purpose such as the education of deprived children.[38] Lewis's tone here is distinctly secular, his argument antimilitarist rather than pacifist, his appeal to persons outside the Quaker enclosure.

What of those Friends who overstepped the Quaker discipline and participated in military service in one or another capacity? Our period saw no change in the rigid enforcement of the discipline in regard to delinquents on this score. The procedure remained unaltered: the member was first "labored with" in an effort to bring him to acknowl-

[36] Enoch Lewis, *Some Observations on the Militia System, Addressed to the Serious Consideration of the Citizens of Pennsylvania*, pp. 4, 8-23.

[37] *Moral Advocate*, II, no. 2 (Aug. 1822), 22.

[38] Lewis, *Some Observations*, pp. 24-34.

edge his fault, but, where he remained adamant, the final step of disownment followed sooner or later. The records of local monthly meetings are filled with minutes to this effect.[39] The scions of aristocratic Quaker families were dealt with impartially along with the sons of humble rural farmers. When Dr. George Logan (1753-1821), son of a Quaker councillor, nephew by marriage of a Quaker speaker of the Pennsylvania assembly, and grandson of Penn's secretary and confidant, joined the militia, he too did not escape. "Friends were hesitant to take action against a Logan of Stenton, whose family history was so closely entwined with William Penn's 'holy experiment.'" He was visited by a series of weighty Philadelphia Friends who tried in vain to persuade him to withdraw. Although Logan was no militarist and believed "all war unlawful to a Christian except that which was strictly of a defensive kind" (a view that was held, in fact, by some who remained all their lives within the Society), he refused to change his course. In January 1791 came the final breach, and Logan was disowned.[40]

Usually, a decision by some young Friend to attend militia musters (the form infringing the peace testimony most often took) was, as has been shown earlier, part and parcel of a more general drifting on his part away from his Quaker moorings, one more step toward loosening the ties with his home environment. In these circumstances the elders were unlikely to reclaim the prodigal. We can see this clearly in a case like the following one, which is taken from the minutes of Cedar Creek Monthly Meeting (Va.) for 1807:

> Whereas, Micajah Crew, Jr., son of Nicholas Crew, of Hanover County, has so far deviated from our known rules as to use spirituous liquors to excess, also has engaged in military services, for which conduct he had been dealt without the desired effect, and has subsequently entered into marriage contrary to the rules of our Discipline, we do, therefore, disown him from being any longer a member, until he shall make satisfaction for his conduct.[41]

Sometimes, however, a young man might be led by local pressure, by desire not to seem different, or might be influenced perhaps by the glamor of the military to assume only temporarily a role in conflict with his family, to which he still remained closely bound by ties not only of sentiment but of genuine devotion. On other occasions, it might

[39] Several examples from this period are cited in Jones, *The Later Periods of Quakerism*, II, 721; Edward Needles Wright, *Conscientious Objectors in the Civil War*, p. 12.

[40] Frederick B. Tolles, *George Logan of Philadelphia*, pp. 106-8.

[41] *Our Quaker Friends of Ye Olden Time*, p. 146.

be a wish to escape the material inconvenience involved in a persistent refusal to train which led to action frowned upon by the Society. "Dear Friends," wrote one William Betts, a Virginia Friend, on 15 January 1798, "I hereby condemn my conduct in having been active in procuring a substitute to serve in the Militia, although by indirect means. . . . Hoping my future conduct may be more consistent, I desire Friends may accept this my acknowledgment and continue me under their care."[42] In cases of these kinds, meetings would have some chance of reclaiming the erring member and then, as with William Betts, proceedings would be closed by an acknowledgment of error.

Friends, as we have seen from the previous period, regarded all forms of noncombatant service in the armed forces as incompatible with the Society's peace testimony. And this held even for work which might be regarded by many as humanitarian, whose object was to save life (but, of course, within the framework of an institution, Friends maintained, whose aims were the exact opposite). In 1806 we find Birmingham Monthly Meeting disowning their member Dr. William Darlington, one of the leading Friends in Chester County, for accepting the post of surgeon to the militia.[43] However, the question of noncombatant service for the conscientious objector as an alternative to military service really does not arise before the Civil War.

In North Carolina, where Friends were for most of our period completely exempt from service in the militia, a requirement came into force in the early 1830's that conscientious objectors make an affirmation before the military authorities that they were unwilling to bear arms. Yearly Meeting thereupon advised members against compliance with the regulation: "it would be best for Friends to remain quietly at home."[44] In this advice, as we know, they were merely echoing decisions of the previous century.

The problem of war taxes had been one of the most trying ones for Friends during the Revolutionary War, and no satisfactory solution was reached at that time. It did not cease to be a problem with the coming of peace, for the previous conflict had still to be paid for and, after that, the long period of the European war which involved the United States itself in 1812 meant continued armaments and the need for money to finance them. Although the Society was united in its opposition to the payment of commutation money, a tax in lieu of personal military service, unanimity still did not exist—especially now

[42] *Ibid.*, p. 164.
[43] *Two Hundred Fifty Years of Quakerism at Birmingham 1690-1940*, pp. 25, 26.
[44] M. P. Littrell, M. E. Outland, J. O. Sams, *A History of Rich Square Monthly Meeting of Friends*, p. 23.

that hostilities had ceased—on the matter of general war taxes, and even less on those "in the mixture." Some members paid both, but many —especially among the more concerned—continued to regard doing so as a serious compromise of the peace testimony. They were prepared to go to prison rather than pay, even if their attitude was not shared by the whole Society. The following entry in the journal of a New Jersey farmer and craftsman, John Hunt (ca. 1740-1824), though taken from the beginning of the period covered by this chapter, reveals the spirit in which many Friends continued to act:

10th mo. 24th [1787]. This evening the constable took our son, Samuel, off to jail for refusing, to pay his tax. He went in a composed, commendable disposition, having, I believe, well considered the matter. I went to see him in prison, and he appeared to bear the trial in a proper manner, in thus suffering for his refusal to pay a tax for defraying the expenses of war. On the 29th, he returned home, being discharged by the sheriff; and we suppose somebody paid the constable his demand, while we had no desire should be done. It was a favoured time with us while he was in prison, which made it easy to us and to him; and I never was more fully and clearly confirmed that the Truth owned this testimony against war.[45]

Sometimes a war tax might be concealed under the guise of an import duty whose purpose it was less easy to distinguish. But here, too, the consciences of some Friends were aroused. An example of such scrupulousness is to be found in the pages of another Quaker journal, that of the New Jersey Friend and minister, Joshua Evans (1731-1798), who throughout his life bore a steadfast witness against slavery, war, and social injustice. Evans had regularly refused to pay taxes which, he considered, went mainly to the support of war and military preparations: "my refusal was from a tender conscientious care to keep clear in my testimony against all warlike proceedings." Early in the 1790's a duty was laid on imported goods, which he had good reason to believe was being substituted for a tax to raise money for military expenditure. "When the matter was brought under my weighty consideration," he writes, "I could see no material difference between paying the expenses relating to war, in taxes, or in duties." It is true that for some time now he had refrained from buying imported articles "because of the corruption attending the trade in these things." As a traveling minister, however, he had partaken of imported salt when it was used in cooking by his hosts—"people generally used it in almost every kind of food," he explains. But now not merely corrupt trading practices

[45] *Friends' Miscellany*, X, 247.

353

but support of war were involved; new scruples were aroused in Evans, and he prayed for guidance. As a result, he writes,

> I was made sensible, that it would be better for me to live on bread and water than to balk my testimony. . . . I therefore thought it right for me to make a full stand against the use of all things upon which duties of that kind were laid. Since which, I have to acknowledge, my way has been made easier than I looked for.[46]

During the War of 1812 we find the apothecary Isaac Martin (1758-1828) taking the same stand that Joshua Evans had earlier taken and reaching the same peace of mind after arriving at the decision that Evans had found. If it had involved the traveling minister in occasional embarrassments with the lady of the house where he was staying, it brought considerable financial loss to Martin the shopkeeper. "Scarcely a day passed," he relates, "that I had not to turn customers away who applied for articles which I had on hand, but could not sell" on account of the duty imposed for war purposes.[47]

The most trying problem, perhaps, arose in connection with taxes "in the mixture." Friends had been grappling with this problem for a century and more. Although, as we have seen, the general opinion among Friends was that such taxes might be paid without compromising the peace testimony, the issue still recurred from time to time as some more sensitive conscience was troubled about the implications of conformity.

Once again, it is to a Quaker journal that we are indebted for insight into how the issue developed in a typical country meeting. Rufus Hall (1744-1818) relates how in June 1800, while his meeting (Northampton, Montgomery County, Pa.) was drawing up answers to the queries, discussion arose on the question of how far members might contribute money to the government by way of taxation which they knew was largely to be expended for military purposes—to construct fortifications and build ships of war, etc. "But this tax," says Hall, "being so blended with other taxes and duties, made it difficult; some Friends not being free to pay it, as believing it inconsistent with their religious principles and testimony against war; while others had paid it." Friends now hoped some decision could be reached so that they would be able to present on this issue a consistent witness for peace. Two views were represented among members of the meeting. The more

---

[46] A Journal of . . . Joshua Evans, pp. 40, 41. Cf. the rather less uncompromising stand on this question taken by another Quaker tax radical, Warner Mifflin, at the time of the Revolutionary War. See p. 228.

[47] A Journal of . . . Isaac Martin, pp. 113, 114.

traditionally minded claimed that before the Revolution Friends had always paid such mixed taxes to the king, that New York Friends, among others, paid them to Congress today, and that this example should be followed. Others, however, felt that it should be individual conscience and not precedent or the conduct of other Friends, however respected, that should be decisive. "Friends would not do well," they said, "to look to New York or London, nor even to former customs, for direction; seeing we had to go forward and not backward, nor yet to stand still with the work of reformation." The discussions, Hall notes, were conducted in a spirit of unity and friendliness; there was no ill feeling nor heated tempers—"which is too often the case in such matters"—and in the end Friends agreed to differ. Most members, it was found, were against paying this kind of mixed tax, "but as the subject was new to some, and others were not altogether clear, by reason of long custom, so as to see the inconsistency of paying it,—it was thought best to let every Friend act according to their freedom therein."[48]

Calls for personal military service or for the payment of taxes and duties connected with war did not exhaust the areas in which Friends, especially the more concerned members, felt obliged to keep a vigilant witness for peace. The numerous disownments for infringing the peace testimony in one or another way, by means of which the Society had enforced the discipline during the Revolutionary War, had probably removed most of those who did not share, or were lukewarm toward, Friends' views on war, and the widespread unpopularity and sporadic persecution of the war years served to reinforce this process. Nevertheless, the coming of peace brought new temptations: in 1791, for instance, Philadelphia Yearly Meeting was compelled to threaten with disownment all found dealing "in public certificates issued as a compensation for expenses accrued and services performed in the late war."[49] Sometimes a veteran of the Revolution would join Friends, and the problem then arose (as it was to do again after the Civil War) whether he might be permitted to go on drawing his war pension. It was decided that this should be forbidden on pain of disownment, and the ban soon became incorporated in the disciplines of the yearly meetings.[50] The disciplines took a firm line, too, against Friends mak-

---

[48] A Journal of . . . Rufus Hall, pp. 112, 113.

[49] Rules of Discipline and Christian Advices (1797), p. 135.

[50] In areas where Quakerism had only spread among the inhabitants after the Revolution was over, the problem of pensions could become quite important. This was the case in Maine, for instance, where many who became Friends had fought in the recent war. Several were subsequently disowned for unwillingness to forego their pensions. See Jones, The Society of Friends in Kennebec County, pp. 22, 29.

ing profits out of war—a special temptation to a group of which many members, and among them some of the most influential, belonged to the merchant class. "Let all be careful not to seek or accept profit by any concern in preparation for war," Philadelphia Yearly Meeting warned its members, "for how reproachfully inconsistent would it be, to refuse an active compliance with warlike measures, and at the same time, not hesitate to enrich ourselves by the commerce and other circumstances dependent on war."[51] And we do, indeed, find a man like the Quaker millionaire, Nathan Trotter (1787-1853), who dealt in a large range of businesses from metals to real estate and stocks and securities, carefully refraining in the years after 1815 from the purchase of government bonds ("except when he purchased to make payments abroad," his biographer qualified) because of their association with the financing of the War of 1812 and, later, of the Mexican War.[52]

This sensitivity to the wider implications of one's actions—mingled, of course, with a strong sense of loyalty to the Society's collective decisions—was felt not only by the big merchant, whose wide business interests could absorb some losses without too much difficulty, but also by the small man for whom losses were less easy to take. Consider the case of a simple New Jersey smallholder, a Negro who had become a Quaker by convincement. He had made a living chiefly by selling the produce of his holding for the use of workers in a nearby iron foundry. In the War of 1812 the foundry began to make cannon for the army; so he now became "very uneasy at the thought that he was supplying that establishment with articles of produce, whilst they were principally employed in the manufacture of arms." The decision he reached to stop supplying the foundry and to try to find some other outlet for his produce unconnected with war meant temporarily endangering his livelihood.[53] The Society of Friends, despite its conservatism during this period and its failure to reach out with its message of peace to circles beyond the influence of the meeting, remained unique among the peace groups in its quest to relate its peace testimony to the widest ramifications of the war spirit.

We have dealt so far with the negative aspect of Friends' personal

[51] *Christian Advices* (1808), p. 108.

[52] Elva Tooker, *Nathan Trotter*, p. 176. Another example among the well-to-do merchant class of the conscientious Quaker pacifist is Elias Hicks's cousin, Isaac, of New York City. Isaac Hicks consistently refused to handle goods if he was aware that the transaction was in any way connected with military activities. "With regard to the Quaker testimony on war," writes his biographer, Robert A. Davison (*Isaac Hicks, New York Merchant and Quaker 1767-1820*, pp. 161, 162), "Hicks is a better Quaker than he is a businessman." See also pp. 114, 205.

[53] *Proceedings of the First General Peace Convention . . . in London . . . 1843*, p. 30.

witness for peace. This witness was, indeed, expressed mainly in the form of protest: refusal to serve in the militia, to purchase an exemption by one of the several means then open, to pay war taxes, to buy goods on which duty was levied to finance war preparations, to draw a war pension, or to accept financial profit tainted by its connection with war. In this way Friends attempted to preserve the integrity of their own individual consciences and the collective testimony of their Society to the Christian spirit of love in a warlike world.

After the Revolution, Friends in the old settled areas in the Eastern states seldom had the opportunity to test their pacifism in any direct encounter with the spirit of violence. One reason was that, except for occasional outbreaks of mob violence which occurred throughout most of the nineteenth century, law and order were firmly established in these areas. The frontier had retreated beyond the mountains, and the Indian peril had long since disappeared. Again, even in places where we might expect Quakers to have been the victims of rough treatment, they rarely encountered it during this period. They were a peculiar people—and a peculiarly respectable people, who could be permitted the indulgence of some peculiar ideas. Although, as we have seen, they were subjected to various minor hardships for their objections to fighting and in the Southern states endured considerable unpopularity for their abolitionist stand, these views were not usually regarded as too serious a threat to the institutions of either war or slavery; for the message was directed primarily to those inside the Society, and few outside it were ready to enter into the closely guarded Quaker enclosure. The chances that any wide area would be tainted by their obnoxious views were thus much reduced. This did not at all mean, of course, that Quakers tended to play down their views on war or on any other unpopular subject in their dealings with the outside world. Many were fearlessly outspoken, and the itinerant ministers, in particular, bore testimony not only within the confines of the Quaker meeting but, on occasion, outside among the general populace as well.

The case of Joseph Hoag during the War of 1812 is not an isolated example. In the autumn of that year he set out to visit Quaker communities in the South, and there at public meetings, although "it was thought dangerous," he spoke out against both war and slavery. In Washington, D.C., where by 1813 pro-war feeling ran high, he encountered strong opposition in his exposition of Quaker peace views.[54]

[54] Another Quaker visitor to Washington during the war was the rural Friend, Jesse Kersey of Chester Co. (Pa.), who succeeded in gaining access to both President Madison (whose wife was of Quaker stock) and his secretary of state, James Monroe. At these interviews Kersey urged the statesmen to conclude peace as soon as possible. See *A Narrative of . . . Jesse Kersey*, p. 195.

"When I mentioned that," he relates, "a number of them straightened themselves up and stared me full in the face with all the defiance of confident-countenance that they were able." However, after some hesitation he persevered and in the end succeeded in winning the respect, if not the agreement, of his hearers.[55]

Although the Society of the first half of the nineteenth century may not have produced a Woolman, it did contain many devoted souls willing and able to present Friends' views on war to an unsympathetic public when occasion required. Yet the withdrawal from society which marked the development of Quakerism as a whole during the half-century and more after the Revolution affected its peace witness, too, preventing any widespread missionary outreach in this area. And this withdrawal, along with the long period of external peace and internal security (the War of 1812 and the Mexican War, as we have seen, did not seriously affect the rhythm of life in the country), shielded Quaker pacifism in the East, at least from any serious trials.

For the practice of nonviolence in Quaker experience during this period we must turn, therefore, to the Western territories which were only then being opened up for European settlement. There, on the frontiers of civilization, the organs of orderly government functioned only with difficulty, or not at all, and the arm of the strongest laid down the law in many communities. In some areas, too, trouble broke out from time to time with the Indians, who were now being gradually forced out of their remaining hunting grounds by the advance of land-hungry white men. The danger from this source, which had ceased altogether in the Eastern states, continued to present, along with the disordered conditions of life, a challenge to the Quaker settlers coming to these territories in the great tide of western migration, which from toward the end of the eighteenth century, progressively enveloped the areas that eventually became the states of Ohio, Indiana, Illinois, Iowa,[56] Kansas, etc.

[55] *Journal of . . . Joseph Hoag*, p. 190. See pp. 199-204 for an account of his conversations on the subject of the Quaker peace testimony with the general in command of troops at Knoxville (Tenn.) in the summer of 1813. It was a time of alarm, owing to the possibility of an Indian invasion, and the general expressed his disgust to Hoag at local Quakers for not obeying the order given for a general muster of the able-bodied, attributing their disobedience to shirking and cowardice. In the end, after listening to Hoag, the general, though still a little puzzled, was ready to admit their sincerity and expressed his willingness to help get them exempted. A bystander who had listened attentively to the whole exchange of views between the Quaker and the general turned to Hoag and said: "Well stranger, if all the world were of your mind, I would turn in and follow after"— to which Hoag at once replied: "Then thou hast a mind to be the last man in the world to be good. I have a mind to be one of the first, and set the rest an example."
[56] Iowa contained a small group of Norwegian Quaker immigrants who, begin-

These Quaker farmers, some of them escaping from the unfriendly atmosphere of the slave states and others from Pennsylvania, New York, or New England seeking a more promising future than their home environment seemed to offer, were mostly simple men whose struggle with the wilderness left little time or inclination for recording their experiences and impressions. Friends' meetings, which as conditions became more stabilized were established wherever Quakers settled, continued to keep careful records just as they had done back in the East, but, of course, these records do not usually provide evidence for the practice of nonviolence on the part of these frontier Friends.

The conditions of frontier lawlessness and disorder, as we have said before, presented a lively challenge to those trying faithfully to uphold the Quaker peace testimony. Back in the home states the enforcement of the discipline had served to buttress the influence of Quaker home and school and the promptings of individual conscience in keeping the Friends a defenseless people. The carrying of weapons in an emergency was, of course, forbidden, and those who infringed the discipline on this point were brought to account. A single example will suffice. A Virginian Friend, one Enoch Robarts, sent the following declaration, dated 20 June 1789, to his meeting: "Dear Friends: Having so far deviated from the peaceable principles professed by us as to suffer the spirit of anger and resentment so to prevail as to procure firearms for my safety, all which conduct I condemn, hoping at the same time that my future conduct will evince the sincerity of this my acknowledgment."[57] Suppose now that this same Enoch Robarts were to migrate to the West, as so many Virginian Friends soon did, in families or as individuals. There, with wife and children as an added responsibility, he would be alone, isolated perhaps by many miles of virgin wilderness from the nearest Quaker family and therefore thrown on his own inner resources to face the menace of hostile Indians or equally dangerous white-skinned marauders. In such circumstances the temptation to seize a hunting rifle or knife in self-defense—or to flee for safety to some larger settlement or to an area where other Friends, who shared Quaker principles of peace, were more thickly settled—must sometimes have been almost overwhelming.

---

ning in the 1840's, left their native land—in part to escape the severe penalties imposed there on conscientious objectors to military conscription. They retained the Norwegian language in their meetings until near the end of the century. See H. F. Swansen, "The Norwegian Quakers of Marshall County, Iowa," *Norwegian-American Studies and Records*, X (1938), 127-34.

[57] *Our Quaker Friends of Ye Olden Time*, p. 163.

We can see something of all this, and of how in this instance the dilemma was successfully resolved, in the story of William Hobbs (1780-1854), who, along with a few other Quaker families, had come from North Carolina early in 1812 to settle in what was then the Indiana Territory. After war broke out in June between the United States and Britain, the Indians in the territory began to grow restless. As near as sixteen miles away some white families were killed, and the scattered group of new Quaker settlers grew alarmed.

> To quiet our families [Hobbs relates], we built little huts and lived together, that is, Friends, and those that held that way. Altho' I made no preparation to defend myself and family, having no gun, I did not feel peace of mind in so living. . . . After living so a few weeks, my wife and I felt the most peace of mind to move home. After we returned to our habitation, I do not remember of ever feeling the least alarmed, though the Indians killed a man about seven miles from us.[58]

In the middle of the nineteenth century, when already conditions over large parts of the "old" West had become more settled and the framework of law and order was more firmly established, the territory of Kansas became the scene, with the passing of the Kansas-Nebraska Act of 1854, of endemic civil war between pro and antislavery forces that added ideological hatred to the other ingredients of frontier lawlessness. Settlement was only just beginning. Quakers began to arrive just after the passing of the notorious act. "Bleeding Kansas" of the second half of the 1850's did, indeed, prove to be a testing ground for Quaker peace principles. Friends' sympathies were naturally with the antislavery elements: the ancestors of many of those settling had originally left the South because of the difficulties of living in a slaveowning environment. Their relatives back East were frequently engaged in helping the Negroes—as participants in the "Underground Railway" or in numerous philanthropic activities on behalf of colored freemen or runaway slaves. In fact, one of the reasons that Friends settled in this territory, apart from the lure of cheap and abundant land, was the desire to preserve it from becoming open to slavery. Friends in Kansas, therefore, placed their votes as well as their moral influence behind the free-soil movement. At the same time, Quakers as a whole could not sanction the attempt to maintain Kansas as free territory by the use of armed force against the aggression of Southerners mainly from across the Missouri border; still less, of course, did they approve the moral and material aid given by northern Chris-

[58] *Autobiography of William Hobbs*, pp. 7, 8.

360

tians, including many ministers even (Theodore Parker, for example), to the antislavery guerrillas. "Who can tell what scenes of blood may be chargeable to their counsels?" asked the evangelical *Friends' Review*, and the paper went on to recommend "resistance by suffering" as the Christian way to confront evil. This had been the method used by seventeenth-century Friends in their struggle for religious and civil liberty; nothing, the editor believed, had occurred since to disprove "that the same peaceable resistance to aggression and outrage would have been equally availing in Kansas."[59]

This advice might have been all right for peaceful Philadelphia, but it could easily have seemed oversimplified to the small communities of Quakers out in Kansas caught in the midst of a fierce struggle for predominance between two equally determined groups, both convinced of the rightness of their objectives. Friends, in fact, lived in the very area that was swept by sporadic border fighting. Quaker farms were raided, horses or cattle were seized, and occasionally a Friend was roughly handled.[60] A mission school founded by the Society back in 1836 among the Shawnee Indians was forced to close down temporarily. No lives were lost—but perhaps more because of luck than anything else. However, it is true that Friends did have a champion in the person of a former Quaker, Joel Hiatt, who moved in proslavery circles and spoke up there on behalf of his former coreligionists. "Stock men, peaceable, wouldn't fight," was Hiatt's description of them, "obedient to the laws no matter how things were settled"—antislavery, certainly, and in favor of a free state, but unwilling to impose a solution by force or to stir up rebellion among the slaves. His Quaker nephew later commented as follows on renegade "Uncle" Joel's unrequested, but not unuseful, intercession with the slavers: "We did not take much interest in this kind of talk; but it was our best policy at this time to keep still, and act when we had the opportunity to effect anything, which I believe we all bravely did."

So Quakers voted for the antislavery candidates at the polls but steered clear of active politics as much as possible. One young Friend,

[59] *Friends Review*, 8 March 1856. I have found occasional references to Quaker abolitionists carrying arms in order to defend fugitive slaves from recapture. The stories are not well documented but may well be true. However, such cases were not typical and probably occurred infrequently. If conduct of this kind were known to his meeting, a member would almost certainly have been disciplined.

[60] See Cecil B. Currey, "Quaker Pacifism in Kansas 1833-1945" (M.Sc. thesis, Fort Hays State College), p. 27, for an instance of this kind. On p. 24 the author relates a story concerning this period of a Quaker farmer who had purchased two expensive horses. One was seized later by a proslavery marauder. The Quaker, to counterbalance the advantage given thereby to the slavery side, then presented the remaining horse to the captain of a free-soil band—and thereafter traveled himself by mule!

however, was almost beaten to death for his official activities in connection with the elections of mid-January 1856. And it is at the time of these elections, too, that we find one of the most interesting examples of the workings of the Quaker spirit of nonviolence. Shortly before polling day a gang of proslavery marauders from over the Missouri border, which went by the name of the "Kickapoo Rangers," swept through the area where the Quakers were settled in widely scattered homesteads. On one such lonely farm lived young William Coffin (who was, incidentally, Joel Hiatt's nephew and also cousin of Levi Coffin of "Underground Railway" fame). He was alone, except for his wife and children, when he received warning that the Kickapoo Rangers, along with other marauding gangs from Missouri, were moving his way and that they were spreading terror in the whole neighborhood in an attempt to intimidate the antislavery vote in the forthcoming elections. Let us hear the story in William Coffin's own words:

> We could expect no favor from such a body of men, composed, as they were, of the worst description of border men, of the Jesse James type. . . . I do not think that I was afraid at that time, being young and excitable; but my education was such that I could not, with conscience, kill a man; but when I got to reasoning with myself about my duty in the protection of my family, my faith gave way. I had an excellent double-barreled gun, and I took it outdoors and loaded it heavily with buckshot. It was near bed time; my wife and children soon went to sleep, and I barred the door and set my gun handy, and made up my mind I would shoot any man or set of men that undertook to break in. A cabin, built as they were, of logs at that time, made a pretty good fort; but I could get no sleep, having laid down with my clothes on. Finally, towards midnight I got up, wife and children peacefully sleeping, drew the loads from my gun and put it away; and then, on my knees, I told the Lord all about it and asked His protection; and so casting all my care upon Him, I felt easy, went to bed, was soon asleep, and slept until sun-up the next morning.[61]

The Kickapoo Rangers, as it turned out, had followed another route, and to Coffin it seemed that his simple faith was justified. For us, the story illustrates the firm foundation which Quaker training and educa-

[61] William H. Coffin, "Settlement of the Friends in Kansas," *Transactions of the Kansas State Historical Society, 1901-1902*, pp. 332, 334, 335, 341, 343. See also Cecil Currey, "Quakers in 'Bleeding Kansas,'" *BFHA*, vol. 50, no. 2 (Autumn 1961), pp. 96-101.

tion were able to build for the Society's peace testimony in many of its members.

From mid-century, however, "fear of war over slavery continually oppressed Friends' minds." Opposed to both war and slavery, Quakers were faced with a difficult choice. A few Friends, even before the fighting broke out, decided in favor of a violent solution if this could win freedom for the oppressed.[62] We see here the struggle, especially in the minds of the young, between two seemingly irreconcilable loyalties: antislavery and pacifism. It was this conflict, for instance, that led the two young Quakers from Iowa, the brothers Edwin and Barclay Coppoc,[63] in 1859 to join John Brown in his famous and ill-fated raid on Harpers Ferry. Brown, after taking part in the guerrilla warfare in Kansas, had spent the winter of 1857-1858 in the Coppocs' home community of Springdale where he made many friends among the largely Quaker population. Most disapproved, of course, of his resort to arms; the young Coppocs, however, were fired by the image of the old warrior to abandon the nonviolent way in which they had been reared.

II

If we turn now from the practical implementation of Friends' peace principles to the contribution of American Quakers to the theory of pacifism during our period, we are struck at once by the paucity of material and the lack of creative thinking in most of what was written. British Quakerism produced Dymond (1796-1828), and "the masterly and altogether irrefutable arguments of Jonathan Dymond,"[64] contained in his writings on war, were to provide a staple source for American pacifists of the nineteenth century, both Quaker and non-Quaker. Although the Society in the United States produced some half-dozen pacifist tracts, occasional discussions in wider expository works, sporadic pronouncements on the subject of the peace testimony by various yearly meetings, and—with the rise of a Quaker periodical press from the end of the 1820's on—a number of articles discussing the implications of pacifism from the Quaker point of view, it cannot be said that any of this writing was of major significance. During this pe-

[62] Thomas E. Drake, *Quakers and Slavery in America*, pp. 190, 194-97.

[63] Edwin, however, had been disowned in 1857 for dancing; Barclay was not disowned until January 1860. See *The Palimpsest*, XLI, no. 1 (Jan. 1960), 22-30. This number is entitled "John Brown among the Quakers" and is edited by William J. Petersen.

[64] From the lecture by William J. Allinson (1810-1874), quoted in *Friends' Review*, 20 Sept. 1862.

riod the main contribution of the Society to religious and social thought was being made elsewhere. However, this Quaker writing on peace is worth reviewing briefly insofar as it may throw light on the condition of the peace testimony against war existing at the time.

The Society, as we know, exercised a considerable degree of censorship over the writings of its members, as much in regard to the subject of peace as in regard to other topics. The discipline printed by New York Yearly Meeting in 1810, for instance, threatened with ultimate disownment those who persisted "in promoting the publication of writings which tend to excite the spirit of war."[65] The Society thus found it easier to guard against the public expression of heterodox opinion than to promote vital thinking on peace. However, most of the peace tracts which Friends wrote, if hardly original, are competent pieces of work which succeed in giving a fairly adequate presentation of the traditional Quaker view.

The first tract on peace to appear from a Quaker pen after the end of the Revolution was the 52-page *Essay on War*, which John I. Wells (ca. 1769-1832) published in 1808. Wells himself had recently refused, when called on, to serve in the militia of his native Connecticut. As he wrote in the preface to his pamphlet: "Not long since, I was called upon as a delinquent on the military account." The author's object in publishing his booklet was to provide a reasoned case for refusal of such service on religious grounds, a necessary task in view of the overwhelming weight of opinion hitherto in favor of the legitimacy of war in certain circumstances. There is little that is especially striking in most of the arguments put forward; they are derived—as might be expected—mainly from the appropriate texts of the New Testament. In Wells's words, the Christian alternative to war is to trust in God for protection in all adversity. Calamities like war are usually the result of transgression of God's commandments, though Christians may have to suffer persecution for righteousness' sake. More interesting is his treatment of Old Testament wars, always a ticklish problem for pacifist writers before the development of Biblical criticism. Where success was granted, he claims these wars were waged "for the glory of God, and the punishment of sinners." "Under the Mosaic dispensation it was consistent that this most favoured nation should war and fight; the plan of the divine government at that time admitted of it. But . . . in the Jewish wars, it was only when they were commissioned, or authorized by express orders from the Lord, that they were prosperous." Christ's new dispensation, however, "forecloses all liberty to

[65] *Discipline*, p. 46.

364

engage in war."[66] Wells's tract was used as peace propaganda at that time by the American Quakers.[67]

The War of 1812 naturally turned the minds of Quakers, as it did the minds of such non-Friends as Dodge or Worcester who would later become leading advocates of peace, toward a reconsideration of the whole problem of war and peace and toward the need to put the Christian case against all war once again before the general public. There was a risk of misunderstanding here, of course, a danger that the pacifism of the Society would be misinterpreted as a purely political objection to the war at hand. This difficulty was not new; Friends had encountered it during the Revolution and were to meet with it again in subsequent wars. Answering charges of this nature which had been laid against its pacifist stand, Philadelphia Yearly Meeting felt bound to issue a statement in October 1814 that "subjects of a political nature make no part of the deliberations of our religious assemblies."[68] The yearly meetings in their pronouncements confined themselves chiefly to defending the sincerity of their conscientious objectors.

Some Friends, though, were thinking more deeply on their own— and not necessarily with publication in mind. We find William Evans, a future Quaker minister, for instance, wrestling at this time with the problem of what would happen if a nation accepted Friends' views on war and abandoned its arms. They were likely to be unmolested, he reasoned, not only because God would protect them against the aggression of their neighbors, but because other nations would no longer fear attack or interference and would be ashamed to start unprovoked aggression of their own against a defenseless people. His reasoning is superficial, his approach unduly optimistic, the problem oversimplified; yet it does show at least one Friend's mind reaching out beyond the traditional concern with scriptural interpretation and moral objection and with the problem of individual self-defense to the implications of Quaker pacifism if adopted on a nationwide scale. Evans's thoughts, however, were not intended for publication and were confided to the intimacy of his journal.[69]

The only substantial Quaker tract on the subject of pacifism that was directly inspired by the war came from the pen of James Mott, Sr. (1742-1823), Lucretia Mott's father-in-law. In 1814 he published a 33-page pamphlet entitled *The Lawfulness of War for Christians, ex-*

[66] J. I. Wells, *An Essay on War*, pp. 11, 25. See also Robert H. Morgan's article on Wells in the *Friend*, vol. 114 (1940), no. 6, pp. 89-91.
[67] Merle E. Curti, *Peace or War*, p. 35.
[68] *To our Fellow Citizens of the United States*, broadsheet dated 21 Oct. 1814.
[69] *Journal of . . . William Evans*, p. 35.

amined. His object in writing it, he tells us, was "to remove the prejudices of those who, through the influence of education, custom, or public opinion, have been induced to conclude that war is allowable for christians." Mott frankly acknowledged his debt to his predecessors in the peace movement, in particular to Erasmus, and to Mott's own contemporary, the Anglican Clarkson, whose studies of the attitude of the early Christian church to war were often used by nineteenth-century pacifists, and he did not himself bring anything new to the discussion. But it is interesting (though Mott here, like Wells, was only voicing the general view of the Society at this time) to note his qualified acceptance of Old Testament warfare. "The Jews," he writes, "went to war at the command of God, and against nations, whom for their wickedness he, in his inscrutable wisdom, had determined to extirpate from the earth. But it was only at his immediate command that they were to do it." We shall see a little later how his daughter-in-law Lucretia was to be regarded by conservative elements in the Society as something of a heretic (a reputation she had already acquired on many other counts) for contesting, in the name of Christ's teachings, the belief that God could ever have approved war at any time. It was, of course, on the gospels that the elder Mott rested his case for Quaker pacifism, and he calls the contemporary argument for war on the basis of the Old Testament "but a fig-leaf covering."[70]

In the years that followed the war, one of the most prolific exponents of the Quaker peace testimony was the Ohio publisher and publicist, Elisha Bates, whose fervid evangelicalism, as we have seen, eventually led him to abandon even Quaker Orthodoxy and to break completely with the Society of Friends. However, his exposition of the *Doctrines of Friends*, which first came out in 1825, long remained a standard work on the subject. In it he devotes a chapter of 30 pages (chapter XVI) to the subject of war, where he briefly reviews the evidence for the "non-resistance" of the gospels and the early church and urges the need for Christians to follow the example of their church's apostolic age. Though a useful summary of Friends' views, his argument yet brought nothing fresh to the development of the Quaker peace testimony.[71]

A regular Quaker weekly press did not come into existence until the founding in October 1827 of the Philadelphia *Friend*, which became

[70] Mott, *The Lawfulness of War . . . examined*, pp. 3, 14.

[71] Elisha Bates was also largely responsible for the drawing up in 1829 of a *Testimony of the Society of Friends on the Continent of America*, which was published in the following year in the name of eight Orthodox yearly meetings. It contains a brief section on war (pp. 27, 28), which is mostly taken up by citations from the Bible or from past Quakers' statements on the subject.

the organ of the Orthodox branch of the Society. The Hicksites did not establish a permanent paper of their own until the appearance of the *Friends' Weekly Intelligencer* in 1844, and it was not until three years later, in 1847, that the evangelical wing within the Orthodox branch began to produce the *Friends' Review*. Yet now that these journals (all of which were published in Philadelphia) had emerged, in the second quarter of the century, opportunity opened for a wider, more public discussion of the peace question among Friends, in which rank-and-file members could participate without the necessity of going to the expense of publishing a pamphlet of their own. They could get to know the views of other members more easily than before, and also, since the new papers reprinted from time to time articles from the press of the non-Quaker peace movement, they could become familiar with the thinking on peace being carried on outside the Society. Most of the material presenting the utilitarian case against war and attacking its economic waste, the failure of the war method to produce a lasting settlement, the horrors of battle, and the moral depravity of army life was reprinted from the publications of the American or British Peace Societies. Excerpts from the peace classics were also presented to readers from time to time. The contributions of Friends were confined mainly to discussion of the religious aspects of pacifism. In general, we may say that, although in the period before mid-century the Quaker periodicals devoted quite a lot of attention to the problems of peace (the two Orthodox papers rather more, perhaps, than the Hicksite *Intelligencer*), the amount of space given to this issue was indeed small compared to the total amount available. This fact seems to indicate that the peace testimony was not then one of the primary interests either of the leaders of the Society or of the rank-and-file members, whether Hicksite or Orthodox.

The original articles in these papers did not on the whole make any very original contribution to the debate on pacifism. But, occasionally, a Friend came out with some interesting suggestion or thought. A case in point can be found in the two articles contributed in 1837 to the Orthodox *Friend* by "L.S." under the title "Observations on War." In them the anonymous author, almost certainly influenced by the ideas of the peace societies, advocated the establishment of international courts of arbitration acting under an agreed international law to settle disputes between the nations. The power of world opinion, as well as some form of economic sanctions (the writer does not go into the details), would usually, in his view, be enough to bring about compliance with the court's decision. In rare cases, however, these factors might not be sufficient. "L.S." writes:

It may be imagined that wars would arise out of this system; as nations might refuse to comply with the award of referees, and thus nullify the whole procedure unless they were compelled by military force. Even supposing this effect to follow, the plan would still be an improvement upon the present barbarous mode of settling national disputes. For a government which should refuse to submit to the award of the national arbiters, would be placed in hostility, not merely to its original opponent, but to the civilized world. The object on the side of the national confederacy would be, not to redress a particular grievance, but to support the supremacy of the law of nations. Such a contest would probably be soon decided.[72]

This argument strikes a note that was only infrequently heard in the Society in those years. Yet it represents one strand, and an important one, in the tradition of Quaker pacifism running from William Penn's scheme for European federation to the Quaker supporters of the League of Nations and the United Nations. "L.S." believed as firmly as any of his brethren in the incompatibility of war with the Christian dispensation and supported the Quaker refusal to participate in it; at the same time, however, he sanctioned on the sub-Christian level measures which fall short of this Quaker ideal, provided they are directed toward the same goal of establishing peace on earth.

The outbreak of the Mexican War presented a twofold challenge to Friends. On the one hand, their pacifism made them reject resort to arms; while, on the other, a consideration that had not been present, at least to the same degree, in the War of 1812—the aggressive foreign policy and the threatened extension of the Southern slave system which lay behind the opening of hostilities—offended their antislavery feelings and their sense of political justice. These factors account for the outspokenness of their condemnation of the war. The evangelical *Friends' Review*, in particular, took a strong line against the government's policy and branded the war as one of aggression by the United States; even the more conservative *Friend* took a decided antiwar stand, reprinting the speeches of members of Congress against the war and increasing the space it devoted to antiwar material. Not untypical, probably, are the reactions of an anonymous woman Quaker, who, after reading accounts of military action in the press, wrote as follows to the *Friend*: "Is not this a time to proclaim more earnestly than ever to the world our Christian testimony against all war, and the spirit of war, now that our country is actually engaged in a

[72] *Friend*, 27 May and 15 July 1837.

368

barbarous contest with a neighbouring nation?" She was especially disgusted by the prayers being offered up in the churches for the success of the United States' arms. In her eyes, the war was "iniquitous," a reversion to savagery on the part of a civilized nation and not a subject for national pride. "We earnestly desire," she concluded, "that our young Friends may beware of catching the infection of the war-spirit, even so far as to feel any degree of exultation on account of this *gallantry* and *valour* of the American soldiers which is so loudly extolled."[73] This kind of antiwar protest, of course, was shared not only by Quaker and other pacifists but, in the North, by wide circles within the churches and outside them. Quaker pacifism had temporarily overlapped with a political movement against an imperialist war.

During the years of war the various Quaker yearly meetings of both branches issued a series of statements on the peace testimony, urging members to testify faithfully to principle in thought and deed and including at the same time undertones of political protest.[74] For Ohio Yearly Meeting (Orthodox) in its "Address on War" of September 1846, the conflict was "not surpassed, perhaps, in atrocity by any previous contest to which this nation has been a party . . . [a] horrid affair." What practical steps could Friends take, the "Address" asked, to express their aversion to it? Let them refrain from supporting military men or those in favor of the war at the polls. Let them boycott where possible imported products when they knew duty had been levied on them to provide income for the war. "Friends are also advised against performing any labor on the public roads in lieu of paying a military fine, or in any way give a sanction to military laws."[75] Baltimore Yearly Meeting in a small pamphlet issued on 19 December 1846, while urging Friends "to be separated from the spirit and the policy of this world," recommended arbitration to settle disputes between the two combatants.[76] The Hicksite Yearly Meeting of Philadelphia in its statement of 15 January 1847 concentrated on the need for young Friends not to compromise their pacifism by conniving at the payment of their militia fines.[77] We find their Orthodox brethren on the same day memorializing Congress on the subject of the war and taking a more political stand (while at the same time stressing, of course, that Friends' opposition was religious in principle and not motivated by any party considerations). The United States was especially favored

[73] *Ibid.*, 21 Nov. 1846, p. 71.
[74] Clayton Sumner Ellsworth, "The American Churches and the Mexican War," *AHR*, XLV, no. 2 (Jan. 1940), 317.
[75] *Friends' Weekly Intelligencer*, 19 Dec. 1846.
[76] *The Unlawfulness of All Wars and Fightings under the Gospel*, p. 7.
[77] Extracts from Minutes 1847 (printed folder in F.H.L.S.C., S G 2).

369

by Providence, they pleaded, and it was the country's duty to provide an example to the world of peace and international morality.[78] New York Friends, too, issued declarations in support of the peace testimony on 4 January 1848; the statement of the Orthodox branch, like that of its Philadelphia Yearly Meeting, was in the form of a memorial to Congress, while the Hicksites published a pamphlet addressed to the Christian churches throughout the country which summarized Quaker doctrine on the subject of war.[79] The Orthodox memorial, perhaps because it was destined for a political body, dwelt more on the unjustifiability of the present conflict, deploring the fact "that our citizens now compose an invading army within the acknowledged territory of a neighbouring nation, towards whom this country has heretofore been on terms of amity and peace" and calling for a speedy conclusion of peace. The Society's testimony was, indeed, against all wars, but some conflicts (including the present war, it was implied) might be more calamitous than others. The Philadelphia *Friends' Review* called the document a "strong memorial."[80]

The Mexican crisis inspired one Friend to compose a more detailed defense of Quaker pacifism than could be done within the limits of the kind of statement that we have been reviewing. In 1846 John Jackson (d. 1855), a respected minister of the Hicksite Yearly Meeting in Philadelphia, set down his *Reflections on Peace and War* in a booklet which he evidently hoped would find readers outside as well as inside the Society. There was nothing startling in most of what he had to say; once again, we find the familiar arguments for pacifism drawn from the New Testament, and expatiation on the horrors and waste of modern war in particular. But when (in chapter IV) Jackson came to discuss the question of the wars waged by the Jews in the Old Testament, he introduced an unfamiliar note in the literature of American Quaker pacifism by denying categorically that God had ever sanctioned such conflicts, even within the framework of the old dispensation. "Once take the ground that men have been divinely commissioned to fight," he said, "and there is no war for which this authority will not be claimed." The Jewish chroniclers of that time had been mistaken in believing that their warfare was divinely inspired. "These authors, whoever they were, were fallible men like ourselves, liable to mistaken views of the divine character and will." His reasons for doubting their claims Jackson drew from his understanding of God's love

---

[78] *Friend*, 6 Feb. 1847.
[79] *Considerations respecting the Lawfulness of War under the Gospel Dispensation.*
[80] *Friends' Review*, 19 Feb. 1848.

370

as revealed by Christ in the New Testament. How, he asked, could the barbarous policy of extermination pursued by the ancient Jews against the Canaanites and other tribes be reconciled with the spirit of Christian forgiveness? The Old Testament was an excellent historical source, but it must be judged primarily as history.[81]

Jackson's little book caused quite a flutter in the Quaker dovecote. In a short while it had gone through two editions. But the author's liberalism was regarded by most Friends, even in the more liberal Hicksite branch to which he belonged, as sheer heresy. To doubt the literal veracity of everything in the Old Testament was, in the view of many Friends, to undermine religious belief. This Biblical literalism entailed, as we have seen, the acceptance of the view that for his inscrutable purposes God had on occasion commanded his Jewish people to wage wars of atrocity against their neighbors, while later through his son Jesus Christ he enjoined an undeviating pacifism.[82] One of those who shared Jackson's rejection of this view was the redoubtable Lucretia Mott (1793-1880). Early in 1847, Mrs. Mott reported to an Irish Quaker concerning the reaction of Friends to Jackson's arguments: "This has brought up a new issue among our Friends, and many of us are now charged with unsound doctrine."[83] In the following summer, while out in Indiana attending Western Yearly Meeting, she took occasion to recommend Jackson's tract as suitable reading for young people. "This," her companion reported in her diary, "immediately brought out a spirited reply from a minister of this meeting . . . in which she expressed her 'astonishment' that such a thing should be recommended, as to read a book 'that despises the Bible.'" The same writer goes on to describe the strong feelings aroused in many members against Jackson's tract: "many would be afraid to suffer it in their houses, much less *read* it."[84]

Lucretia Mott was, in fact, mistaken in thinking that the literal inspiration of the Old Testament and the divine sanction for the Jewish wars chronicled there constituted a new issue for American Friends. The problem had been keenly debated at the beginning of the century in the case of a young woman Quaker from New York Yearly Meeting, Hannah Barnard (*née* Jenkins). It is, therefore, worthwhile at this point to review briefly the facts in the Hannah Barnard affair.

[81] John Jackson, *Reflections on Peace and War*, chap. IV.

[82] In the very same year that Jackson was writing, we find Baltimore Y. M. in the pamphlet cited above (n. 76) conditionally justifying wars "under a former dispensation." These, it stated, the Jews had waged with God's approval.

[83] Letter to Richard D. Webb dated 21 Feb. 1847, quoted in Hallowell, *Motts*, p. 283.

[84] *Ibid.*, pp. 290, 291.

Hannah had been born in a family of Baptists in 1754 but, at the age of 18, had become a convinced Friend. After marrying a fellow Quaker and becoming the mother of a family, Hannah was chosen a minister by her local meeting, which apparently regarded her highly on account of her character, intelligence, and gifts as a speaker. Her departure in July 1798 for a pastoral visit to the British Isles, in the company of another woman minister from Rhode Island, had the full approval of New York Friends. No suspicion of unorthodox views appears to have been felt at this time. Yet already, it seems, her espousal of the peace testimony had led her to have strong doubts whether a beneficent deity could really ever have sanctioned war under the old dispensation. If he had, so she reasoned, did not this constitute "an impeachment of the divine attributes" of love and goodwill toward the creation? Surely, Old Testament wars, like modern ones, stemmed wholly from men's passions and lust. Opinions of this kind had, indeed, been held by American Friends like Anthony Benezet or Job Scott in that century: Hannah did not think she was uttering any very novel views.

Now, while visiting Ireland, she came into contact with a group of liberal Friends, led by Abraham Shackleton of Ballitore and John Hancock of Lisburn, who at that very moment were pressing similar views on the British Society. Suspected of deism and influenced undoubtedly by the ideas of the Enlightenment in trying to bring their Quaker Christianity into line with the findings of reason, these Friends were soon either to be disowned by their fellow members or to resign themselves in protest at their Friends' illiberality.

Of course, the same suspicions fell on their young American disciple who, during her travels, could not contain herself from expressing her opinions on the subject. Like the Irish dissidents, Hannah not only denied that there had been any divine sanction of the Old Testament wars against the Canaanites but quite logically contested the infallibility of the scriptures as a whole and cast doubt on some of the miraculous stories contained within their pages. British Friends, among whom the evangelical trend was increasing in weight and importance, were shocked at their American visitor's impiety and were fearful of the effect it might exercise over weaker minds—feelings that were supported vigorously by another American visitor, the strongly evangelical Friends' minister, David Sands, who was in Britain at this time.

In May 1800, in the course of the annual gathering of London Yearly Meeting, an Irish Friend accused Hannah of "holding erroneous opinions concerning war." To this charge she replied that she believed

372

war was always and in all circumstances wrong, "a moral evil" resulting from man's abuse of the free will granted him by God. That she also asserted disbelief in (among other miraculous incidents in the Old Testament) any heavenly command to Abraham to sacrifice his son served only to further incriminate the intrepid young woman in the minds of a majority of her hearers. At the end of June, London Yearly Meeting forbade her to travel any longer in the capacity of a Quaker minister and requested that she return forthwith to the United States. Hannah lingered on for another year hoping, perhaps, to vindicate her orthodoxy in the eyes of her British Friends. "As to war," she once again told them her view "that in no age of the world [had] the great and merciful Creator ever commissioned any nation or person to destroy another; but that they were formerly, as at present, only permitted so to do."

On returning home her case was dealt with by her monthly meeting (Hudson), which, after lengthy deliberation, in June 1802 gave sentence of disownment. Her appeals to quarterly meeting and then to New York Yearly Meeting were rejected. Hannah Barnard certainly enjoyed some support in her views from her fellow members. However, the rising tide of evangelicalism, which was already apparent in the American branch of the Society as it was on the other side of the ocean, swept aside her protest against the avenging God of the old dispensation. A Quaker disowned for refusing to give support to war is a curious—and somewhat disturbing—incident in the history of Friends' peace testimony.[85]

The Hannah Barnard affair created quite a stir at the time among both British and American Friends. It was many years before another remonstrance of this kind was heard on this side of the Atlantic—even among the Hicksite opponents of Quaker evangelicalism in the Orthodox camp. Jackson's little effort, therefore, appears to be the first work to contest once again the compatibility of the concept of an all-loving God with his alleged approval of the bloodthirsty contests in which the ancient Hebrews had engaged. Again, the matter caused somewhat of a flutter in Quaker circles. But Jackson's Hicksites, although his ideas were as yet too radical for most of them, were not inclined to proceed against him as their fathers had been willing to

[85] [Thomas Foster], *A Narrative of the Proceedings in America of the Society called Quakers, in the Case of Hannah Barnard. With a Brief Review of the Previous Transactions in Great Britain and Ireland*, pp. x-xiv, 5, 6, 9, 50, 53, 120-24; *An Appeal to the Society of Friends, on the Primitive Simplicity of their Christian Principles and Church Discipline*, pp. 43-79, 115-17, 120, 158-63, 168, 169, 177, 184, 185, 193, 195, 207-10. See also Jones, *The Later Periods of Quakerism*, I, 292-307.

do in regard to poor Hannah Barnard. And so, after none too long a time, the excitement over Jackson's booklet died away, and, with the Mexican War ended, the issue of peace again retreated from the forefront of Friends' interests.

The period of the 1850's in America was one of mounting war clouds, but the tension between the sections as yet impinged only indirectly on the Quaker peace testimony. None of the Quaker periodicals at the time devoted much space to the testimony, and this neglect was reinforced by the fact that, in comparison with previous decades, Friends in the fifties came only infrequently into conflict with the law over the matter of militia service. Yearly meetings occasionally issued statements on peace,[86] but they lacked the urgent note of those of the Mexican War period.

We have noted already the absence of a missionary spirit in the Quaker pacifism of our period. The peace testimony was still cultivated assiduously, but on the whole only within the confines of the Quaker enclosure.

Aggressive championship of the peace position—taking its message outside the circle of Friends' meetings in an effort to bring it to non-Quakers instead of merely striving to strengthen the adherence of members of the Society to its principles—was unusual. A rare example of this militant spirit is to be found in the action of a mid-Pennsylvania woman minister of the 1830's, Ellen McCarty. A contemporary journal relates of her: "Hearing of a militia muster about three miles from her residence, she felt drawn to go there, and by her faithful dealing with some of the young men there assembled, she convinced two of them of the unlawfulness of war; and they afterwards joined the Society of Friends."[87]

More often than not, it was the very peculiarities of Friends, the distinguishing characteristics that marked Quakers off from the rest of society, that were also regarded as the surest means of preserving their peace testimony intact. Pacifism without the plain dress seemed almost a contradiction in terms to many nineteenth-century Quakers, young and old; so we find Maine Friends, for instance, heartily agreeing with the view voiced by outside critics that Quaker applicants for

---

[86] An example is the 8-page *Address on Peace*, which New England Y. M. issued in 1854 in connection with the outbreak of the Crimean War. In it Friends exhorted parents to bring up their children in the spirit of the peace testimony. "The exhibitions of military show and preparation should be set before them in their true light, and they early taught that they are parts of the antichristian system of war, and should be considered in that light, and not as attractive displays for recreation and amusement" (p. 7).

[87] *Journal of . . . William Evans*, p. 202.

exemption from military service "ought to certify by their appearance to whom they belong."[88] We can see the same attitude, the feeling that there was a vital connection between the Society's objection to bearing arms and to the whole method of war, on the one hand, and the peculiarities of garb and speech which it had retained from an earlier century, on the other, expressed even more clearly in an article by "Pacificus" published a decade and a half later in the columns of the Orthodox *Friend*:

> One weakness begets another. The laying waste of one part of the enclosure of the Society, enfeebles and makes way for the prostration of another portion of the hedge. When called upon to pay militia fines, some of our members who have already departed from plainness of dress and address, are *ashamed*—yea, *ashamed*—to acknowledge the motive which should induce them to refuse compliance with these demands, from a consciousness *that they do not look like Quakers*, that if they are sheep, they are not in their clothing, and, through weakness begotten of this very cause, they fancy themselves compelled to act in accordance with their appearance.[89]

III

Although a sectarian attitude toward peace may have had considerable psychological justification in earlier periods, it became less understandable in the decade after 1815, when an organized peace movement began to develop outside and independent of any of the peace denominations. This movement, and its absolute pacifist wing in particular, will be discussed in succeeding chapters. Something should be said now, however, concerning the relationship between the Society of Friends and the burgeoning non-Quaker pacifism, which was finding expression in such organizations as the American Peace Society, its affiliates and forerunners representing the right wing of the movement, and the later and more radical New England Non-Resistance Society on the left.[90]

By temperament and outlook Friends might be expected to have felt close sympathy with the more conservative wing of the peace movement. The gradualism of these peace societies had something in common with the long-term range of the Quaker objectives. The societies frankly acknowledged their debt to the peace witness which the Quak-

---

[88] R. M. Jones, *The Society of Friends in Kennebec County*, p. 12.

[89] *Friend*, 14 Feb. 1835, p. 151.

[90] See Peter Brock, "The Peace Testimony in 'a Garden Enclosed,'" *Quaker History*, 54, no. 2 (Autumn 1965), 67-80.

ers had upheld for almost two centuries. They quoted in their publications from Fox and Penn and from many of the Quaker journals. The Quaker experiment in the government of Pennsylvania (pictured in rather an idealized fashion, it is true) provided them with one of their most frequently used examples of the safety of peaceable principles; and they also drew for illustrative material upon the experiences of Irish Quakers during the rebellion of 1798, as described in the book by Dr. Thomas Hancock. The essay on war of the contemporary English Quaker Jonathan Dymond was, as we have said, immensely influential on the thinking of American pacifists throughout the whole nineteenth century. As a Delaware Friend wrote: "Many of the important testimonies which were maintained by Friends and were almost peculiar to them as a people are now picked up and become matter of deep interest to those very people, who reviled and persecuted Friends on account thereof—Peace Societies, Temperance Societies, Abolition Societies."[91]

True, the membership of the moderate peace societies was never confined to absolute pacifists. This was considered by many Friends a stumbling block in the way of collaboration. Others, however, joined with non-Friends on a common platform, agreeing, despite their different approaches, to labor together in the interests of international peace. Such a man was the venerable Moses Brown, a leading figure among New England Quakers. Around the time of the War of 1812, Brown became a friend of the two founding fathers of the American peace movement, David Low Dodge and the Rev. Noah Worcester, and in 1818 was himself instrumental, along with several other local Quakers, in getting a peace society started in his native Rhode Island, which he continued to support with his time and money.[92] Members of the Rhode Island Peace Society, in which Quakers were influential, were no more obliged to pledge themselves to complete pacifism than those of the other groups which eventually merged into the American Peace Society. On the whole, however, we do not find many Quakers among the leading figures of the early American peace movement. The initiative came from outside the Society, from Unitarians and Presbyterians, Congregationalists and Baptists, rather than from any of the peace sects. In some places, for instance in the small Pennsylvania Peace Society, Friends predominated, but its influence was confined to Philadelphia and its environs; in the movement as a whole Friends played a subordinate role.

This fact surprised—and disappointed—many non-Quaker peace

---

[91] Quoted in James A. Munroe, *Federalist Delaware*, p. 49.
[92] Mack Thompson, *Moses Brown*, p. 282.

workers. "Why it is thus, we of course do not know," remarked William Ladd, and he pointed out that, in England, Friends' participation in the London Peace Society was both larger and more effective.[93] Indeed, even though its support was to come mainly from non-Quaker sympathizers, a large part of the initiative in founding the British body had come from Quaker sources. It is not too difficult, perhaps, to resolve the enigma which puzzled William Ladd. Friends in America were slower in emerging from the social isolation into which the Society on both continents had retreated during the previous century. The reaction against the active participation of Pennsylvania Friends in political and social life, which had set in at the middle of the eighteenth century, had been felt more strongly, of course, on this side of the ocean, and other factors, such as the separations and the westward expansion, served to delay the return of the Society to a more active role in national life. For the bulk of American Quakers, then, the activities of the peace societies were worldly, creaturely. Friends were not, of course, actually hostile: they did give the societies a certain slightly condescending approval. Moreover, Friends' periodicals drew extensively on the literature of these societies, American and British, for their peace material, reprinting in their columns extracts from the British *Herald of Peace* and the American *Advocate of Peace* and other papers and drawing, too, on the declarations issued by the respective societies. But a narrowly conceived separatism prevented most Friends from throwing their energies into organized peace work, and as a result the whole cause of peace suffered. A representative example of the thinking of the Society in this respect is found in an article published in the Philadelphia *Friend* in the mid-thirties. Its author declared:

These societies, in their collective capacity, do not fully come up to the Christian standard according to our estimate of . . . the New Testament doctrine bearing upon this subject; and it therefore may not be expedient that our members should be found in their ranks. The Society of Friends as a body, . . . has emphatically been a Peace Society from its foundation, declaring to the world . . . that war in all its forms, offensive and defensive, is utterly at variance with the glorious gospel dispensation of "peace on earth, goodwill to men." And it is safer, at least in the present state of the world, that we keep much to ourselves, and not act as a body in reference to this important testimony, lest by joining with others we should unawares be led into a compromise or evasion of any of its requisitions.[94]

[93] *Calumet*, I, no. 15 (Sept.-Oct. 1833), 450.
[94] *Friend*, 30 Aug. 1834.

377

If Friends tended to assume a cautious attitude toward such bodies as the American Peace Society for, among other reasons, falling short of an uncompromising testimony against all wars, their reaction to the New England Non-Resistance Society, which came into being in September 1838 as a result of the efforts of William Lloyd Garrison and his abolutionist disciples, was more often than not one of downright hostility. To understand the reasons for this reaction, we must recall once more the principles governing the Quaker attitude toward civil government, since one of the key points in the platform of the New England nonresistants was their belief in the incompatibility between Christian pacifism and participation in any of the activities of government as then constituted.

The experience of the final years of Quaker rule in Pennsylvania, reinforced by the quietist trend which was a powerful influence at that time on Friends on both continents, had left American Quakers profoundly disillusioned with the world of politics and determined to keep themselves as far as possible separate from its corrupting influence. The strife engendered by party struggles and the lust for office were contrary, Friends now argued, to the spirit of Christian love that had led them to abandon reliance on armed force.[95] Yet the withdrawal was never complete. A few Friends continued to sit in the Pennsylvania legislature right up through the nineteenth century and to act as magistrates and hold various other offices, provided they did not conflict directly with the peace testimony. Above all, Friends went on voting in large numbers at elections, on both state and federal levels. "The peaceable exercise of the right of suffrage, Friends have always left to the private judgment of the members," states an epistle issued by the Meeting for Sufferings of the Philadelphia Yearly Meeting (Orthodox) in 1834.[96] Belief in the possibility of so organizing the protection of society that armed force would be eliminated altogether or reduced to an absolute minimum was still widely held. As an Ohio Friend wrote at the time of the Mexican War: "The civil power has, perhaps in ninety-nine cases out of a hundred been sufficient to bring criminals to punishment."[97] The same thought was developed further by the Hicksite leader Benjamin Ferris (1780-1867), who wrote: "The Society

[95] See, e.g., the *Christian Advices* issued by Philadelphia Y. M. (1808), pp. 9, 109.

[96] *Friend*, 13 Sept. 1834.

[97] *Remarks by a Member of the Society of Friends on the Subject of War*, p. 2. Its author "E.C." (probably Elijah Coffin) wrote the pamphlet in answer to a Roman Catholic who had published a pro-war "Address to the Society of Friends on the Subject of War" in the *Eaton Register* on 3 June 1847.

never set up the doctrines of *nonresistance*."[98] Approval of the positive aspects of government was expressed frequently in the official statements of yearly meetings, and participation rarely led to disownment where a connection with the military was not clearly apparent.[99]

Thus we see that opinion regarding the practical application of Quaker pacifism in the realm of government was by no means uniform within the Society. The majority, though as yet remaining somewhat on the fringe of political life, maintained basically the positive view of the state that had held sway throughout most of the period of the "Holy Experiment."[100] Nevertheless, a minority, whose exact strength it is very difficult to estimate, had veered over to a position that was not far removed from the Anabaptist-Mennonite view, rejecting participation in civil government even where questions of military force or war taxation were not involved. This antistate attitude, a kind of Christian anarchism, had been strongest perhaps in the last

[98] Ferris Collection (R G 5), ser. 4, box 12, MSS in F.H.L.S.C. Ferris had been a militia C.O. in the War of 1812.

[99] A more unbending attitude, however, was exhibited by some yearly meetings during the Revolution and the years immediately succeeding it toward members who held any kind of office. See, e.g., F. C. Anscombe, *I have called you Friends: The Story of Quakerism in North Carolina*, p. 156. But the question of the use of armed compulsion was only one contributory factor here along with such matters as the enforcement of a test and the question of slavery.

[100] It is interesting to note that the viewpoint of the "political" Quakers of the period of the "Holy Experiment," that compulsion backed by armed force might be dispensed with in individual relations but must be retained by Friends who acted in a public capacity, still had adherents a half century later. (Very similar considerations had led some Friends to advocate a complete withdrawal from political life.) We see opinions of this sort expressed in a letter Israel Foulke wrote to his brother on 22 Sept. 1793 (misc. MSS F.H.L.S.C.): "I . . . must confess I see no way to avoid giving my assent to thy conclusion, that civil government, and defensive war, is [sic] indivisibly connected for (under the present situation of mankind) it seems morally impossible that the former should be at all times supported, without the aid of the latter." He goes on, however, to say: "I think the doctrine of nonresistance may be of considerable use to mankind notwithstanding the above conclusion; especially in private citizens and religious societies for two reasons, 1st as being conducive to the internal peace and tranquillity of the state and secondly, as I look upon it to be a very delicate point to keep to the exact bounds between defensive and offensive war, which has [sic] perhaps never been clearly ascertained . . . so I conceive that the doctrine of nonresistance may be of use in the present state of things as a counterpoise even to defensive war. Thus as a private citizen or subject I think it my duty to encourage the doctrine of peace on earth and goodwill to men universally. But were I a legislator I should look upon myself entrusted as a guardian of the state, and should I apprehend an invasion intended, I should think it my duty to use every means in my power to prevent it, first by putting the state in a posture of defence, and at the same time preparing just and reasonable terms of peace, and if that proved ineffectual, to exert every power to repel force by force."

quarter of the eighteenth century, when the crisis of 1756 and the hard years of the Revolutionary War had still been fresh in the minds of Friends. But we find many individuals sharing it in the period up to and beyond the Civil War.

Perhaps the best known exemplar of this way of thinking among Friends during the first half of the nineteenth century is the Pennsylvania Hicksite minister, Jesse Kersey (1767-1845), whose zeal for nonresistance led him to condemn all existing governments and to advocate total Quaker abstention from politics. "My fears have been," we find him writing in 1815 in his often reprinted *Treatise* on the fundamentals of Quaker belief, a volume that was published with the *imprimatur* of Philadelphia Yearly Meeting, "that many are in danger of departing from the true ground of this testimony." He goes on to propose a boycott of political activity that in many ways foreshadows—although in more moderate language—the later theories of the Garrisonian nonresistants:

> I know of no constitution or government in the world that, at this day, agrees with Christianity: they all make provision for war, they all complete their ends by force. And therefore, it becomes a people who cannot act upon opposite principles, to be on their guard how they connect themselves with the measures of government. The Christian may live in the world, he may comply with all the commands of government, either actively or passively, and there is nothing to fear from him, if he be a Christian. And if all men were Christians, the principles of civil government would be changed from compulsion to consent, the subjects from force to submission without it.[101]

In 1847 we find the Hicksite *Friends' Weekly Intelligencer* complaining that the antipolitical current within the Society was on the increase: "The number of those who adopt this view is, we think, large and increasing; and we are informed, that in the neighboring Yearly Meeting

---

[101] Jesse Kersey, *A Treatise on Fundamental Doctrines of the Christian Religion*, pp. 93-101. Later Kersey had contacts with Garrison's New England Non-Resistance Society. We find him writing to the *Non-Resistant* (vol. II, no. 2, 22 Jan. 1840): "There is no doctrine, in my view, which can be embraced, more important to mankind than this." He went even further than most nonresistants in advocating that they refrain from petitioning Congress on behalf of oppressed minorities like the slaves—on the grounds that, however great our sympathies with the latter, such action was inconsistent with "no-government" principles. This statement brought a rejoinder from the paper's editor, Edmund Quincy, who explained to his readers: "We cannot pray Congress to make slaveholding a penal offence, but we think that we may ask for the abrogation of all the slave laws, so as to leave the slave system, unsustained by legislation, to the force of public sentiment."

of New York, so general is the feeling against voting, in many places, that a prominent Friend is rarely seen at the polls."[102] This was probably an exaggeration. But the activities of the non-Quaker nonresistants from around 1838 on seems to have made a certain impact on the Society of Friends, even though few of its members were to be found actually enrolled in the New England Non-Resistance Society.

John Jackson, the Hicksite minister whom we have met as the author of a tract expressing doubts about the justifiability of Old Testament wars, had come out six years earlier with a small pamphlet, which well illustrates this influence. Jackson did not swallow the whole nonresistant doctrine, but his approach is very similar to theirs. Although Friends might legitimately take part in government where it was carried on without the use of armed force, "it is our duty," he went on, "to abstain from a participation in the administration of such governments as are conducted upon anti-christian principles." Friends should exercise the suffrage only when a pacifist was standing for office. Since in Jackson's view (and in that of the nonresistants) the positions of President or Congressman under the existing constitution were inextricably involved in military affairs and the upholding of slavery, and a consistent pacifist who believed this could scarcely stand for office, Jackson was in fact advocating a total withdrawal from the political arena, to the point of complete abstention from voting.[103]

Jackson was an educated man and a representative of the upper ranks of Quaker society. But the same kind of view was expressed by many rural Friends. Take, for example, Edward Hicks (1780-1849), painter of the "Peaceable Kingdom" and a village coachmaker. In the mid-forties he had felt a concern to address the youth of the Society, and he therefore composed "A Word of Exhortation to Young Friends: presented to them without money and without price. By a poor illiterate Minister." In it he instructed the younger generation in regard to the peace testimony as follows:

His kingdom being a blessed state, arrived at by the redeemed soul, where there is no qualification for either war or politics, our young Friends could neither elect others, nor receive any office of honor or profit in the governments of this world, that are set up by the sword, and defended by the sword; but would feel conscientiously

---

[102] *Friends' Weekly Intelligencer*, 21 Aug. 1847.

[103] John Jackson, *Considerations on the Impropriety of Friends participating in the Administration of Political Governments*, esp. pp. 3-6, 11, 12. Cf. the similar views of Ezra Michener, who wrote around 1860 in regard to the upper governmental echelons: "We cannot consistently give our suffrage to others to fill any office, the duties of which we could not conscientiously discharge" (*A Retrospect of Early Quakerism*, p. 276).

381

bound, in justice, to leave these offices to such as are better qualified to fill them.[104]

A small number of Friends did join the New England Non-Resistance Society and collaborated wholeheartedly in its work, thereby sometimes risking disciplinary action if their meetings (as was quite likely) were unsympathetic. The nonresistants' first president was a highly respected New England Quaker, Effingham L. Capron; but he does not appear to have come into collision with his meeting. However, some of the lesser lights among Massachusetts' Friends who were active among the nonresistant abolitionists, men like William Bassett of Lynn, Joseph S. Wall of Worcester, and Clothier Gifford of Fairhaven, found themselves in trouble.[105]

Since the Non-Resistance Society's activities did not reach out much beyond the Northeast, a direct clash of this kind mainly affected New England Friends. However, mention should be made of Lucretia Mott's interest in the work of the Non-Resistance Society. Mrs. Mott, at least during the early years, attended its annual meetings in Boston as regularly as her domestic and philanthropic duties in Philadelphia permitted and took an active part in its proceedings. The militancy of the movement, the lack of compromise on vital issues like war or slavery, attracted a rebel spirit like Lucretia Mott. When a memorial meeting was held in Philadelphia after John Brown's execution, Mrs. Mott was one of the speakers. She expressed her admiration for him as a martyr for liberty, though at the same time making clear her disapproval of the methods he employed for its attainment. Afterward, a friend told her that she was "the most belligerent Non-Resistant he ever saw." Mrs. Mott was immensely pleased. "I have no idea, because I am a Non-Resistant, of submitting tamely to injustice inflicted either on me or the slave. I will oppose it with all the moral powers with which I am endowed." And she went on to expound her interpretation of Quaker pacifism. "Quakerism, as I understand it, does not mean quietism. The early Friends were agitators; disturbers of the peace; and were more obnoxious in their day to charges which are now so freely made than we are."[106]

Views of this kind had long before aroused strong resentment against Mrs. Mott inside her own Hicksite society; many of the more respectable felt that she was setting a dangerous example and that something

[104] *Memoirs of . . . Edward Hicks*, p. 346.
[105] *Non-Resistant*, vol. II, no. 21, 11 Nov. 1840.
[106] Otelia Cromwell, *Lucretia Mott*, pp. 61-63, 170. Mrs. Mott was also a warm (though not altogether uncritical) admirer of Kossuth and the cause of Hungarian independence.

should be done to prevent further harm. So in September 1842 when she was passing through New York on her way back home from the Non-Resistance Society's annual meeting in Boston, attempts were made to bring her to book. "The elders and others there," she wrote, "have been quite desirous to make me an offender for joining with those not in membership with us and accepting offices in these Societies. But our Friends here [i.e., in Philadelphia where Mrs. Mott held her membership] know full well that such a position is neither contrary to our Discipline, to Scripture, to reason, nor sense."[107]

Behind the action attempted against Lucretia Mott undoubtedly stood the figure of George F. White (1789-1847), minister and elder in the Hicksite meeting of New York. White may be taken as typical of the extreme conservative and sectarian element which dominated many meetings at this time—as much in the Orthodox branch as among the Hicksites, it should be added.[108] Only the previous year White's meeting had disowned the saintly Quaker bookseller, Isaac T. Hopper (1771-1852), for his abolitionist activities. For White and his fellow conservatives, those Friends who had thrown their energies behind the various reform movements of the day, whether peace or abolition or even temperance, and were prepared to work there alongside non-Friends were betraying the peculiar mission of the Society and by their creaturely activities helping to lay waste the fences so arduously erected around the Quaker enclosure. "Hireling lecturers," "hireling book-agents," "emissaries of Satan," White called the abolitionists. "I had a thousand times rather be a slave, and spend my days with slave-holders, than to dwell in companionship with abolitionists."[109] Despite a genuine devotion to the Quaker peace testimony, which was part and parcel of the heritage of the Society, White and his kind took

[107] Ibid., p. 111. Despite her "no-government" views, Mrs. Mott supported women's right to the franchise, even though she felt they should refrain from exercising it until the existing political system was reformed. In a Discourse on Woman which she delivered in December 1849 (quoted ibid., p. 150), she had the following to say on this subject: "Would that man, too, would have no participation in a government recognizing the life-taking principle—retaliation and the sword. It is unworthy of a Christian nation. But when . . . a convention shall be called to make regulations for self-government on Christian principles, I can see no good reasons why women should not participate in such an assemblage, taking part equally with man."

[108] See, e.g., the Orthodox Friend for 15 Oct. 1842: "The editor is aware that a class of people,—a sort of hair-brained sciolists,—has of late risen up in several of the eastern states, who, under the specious guise of reformers, and of superior degrees of enlightenment, propagate opinions, the tendency of which, if permitted to be carried out, would be to break up the foundations of all order in society, civil and religious." These were "abominable doctrines" of which no Friend could possibly approve.

[109] John Cox, Quakerism in the City of New York, p. 100.

up from the outset a position of implacable hostility toward the radical nonresistant movement, tainted as it was with the stigma of abolitionism, and did everything they could to counter its influence, particularly on the younger generation of Friends.

On one occasion, after White had blasted the nonresistants while on a pastoral visit to Philadelphia, a young Friend from Philadelphia Yearly Meeting's western quarter wrote to Lucretia Mott: "The attack upon non-resistants was most unexpected. I almost shuddered as he heaped his denunciations upon them . . . and my spirit sank with despondency, and yet with something of indignation, when I recollected that he was an accredited Minister of the Society of Friends."[110] Another young man, Oliver Johnson (1809-1889), who was one of Garrison's close collaborators in his work for abolition and nonresistance, had been led by his pacifist and abolitionist sympathies not merely to change his intention of becoming a clergyman in one of the orthodox churches but to withdraw from it altogether and seriously contemplate joining Friends. "My own experience," he says, "was similar to that of many others" (in much the same way, we may note, as many conscientious objectors in both the World Wars were later to become Quakers in no small part as a result of their common antiwar sympathies). The violent attacks of White and the social conservatives on the Non-Resistance Society came as an unpleasant shock to a man like Johnson (if we may trust his account, which he obviously wrote in a state of considerable emotion). "How surprising . . . that a minister of the Society of Friends can utter the language of scorn and reproach toward an institution based upon the identical principles" of his own church.[111] Johnson finally threw in his lot with the antislavery rebel spirits who formed the Progressive Society of Friends.

White told Johnson in a lengthy correspondence they had around 1840 that the Non-Resistance Society was a body framed "in the will of man."[112] The unorthodox religious opinions of many of its members, combined with their militant opposition against "human governments," was enough, indeed, to arouse conservative Friends against it. The obstructionist tactics and strong language adopted by the Non-Resistance Society's members in their campaigning, especially in their role as abolitionists, offended many Friends who had long favored quiet and unassuming methods of forwarding their aims. This emotional incompatibility made it extremely difficult for Quakers of this kind to find common ground with radical nonresistants, despite the similarity

[110] Hallowell, Motts, pp. 207, 208.
[111] Correspondence between Oliver Johnson and George F. White, pp. 21, 38.
[112] Ibid., p. 5. White's side of the correspondence is characterized by a rancorous and sarcastic tone.

384

of their ultimate objectives. Thus in 1840, for instance, the Orthodox yearly meetings in New England and New York in official pronouncements castigated the nonresistants roundly and dissociated themselves from "the views of those who deny the necessity of human government." The Hicksite *Friends' Weekly Intelligencer* was still fulminating some years later against the nonresistants, "whose souls were not baptized into the Spirit of the Lamb. . . . While they are preaching up forgiveness of injuries, and love towards enemies, they indulge in denunciations towards those who differ from them."[113]

Conservatively minded Friends in both branches clearly underestimated the earnestness and sincerity of the men and women who threw in their lot with the Non-Resistance Society. Differences regarding means and the debate on civil government were genuine sources of disagreement. But, as we have seen, they were issues which at this date divided Friends themselves. When Sarah Pugh (1800-1884), a Philadelphia school teacher who was a close friend of Lucretia Mott and her collaborator in many reform causes, first attended an annual meeting of the Non-Resistance Society, she was agreeably surprised by what she saw there. As she wrote with a tinge of surprise: "Here was a large body of people zealous and earnest for the right, dressed as the worldly dress."[114] Sarah Pugh, of course, was something of a rebel, and in fact only a handful of Friends ever came directly in contact with the nonresistant movement.

How did the latter react to Quaker attacks? At first, many nonresistants seem to have expected considerable support from Friends, and they stressed the similarities between their two viewpoints. However, as it became apparent that such support was not forthcoming, that, instead, downright hostility was all that they could expect from the Society as a whole, a note of anger appeared; the differences in approach were now emphasized, and Friends' official stand was sub-

---

[113] *Friends' Weekly Intelligencer*, 21 Aug. 1847. Cf. the "Admonitory Address" of the Hicksite Y. M. in Indiana (quoted in the *Practical Christian*, vol. IX, no. 19, 20 Jan. 1849): "But who are these that are running to and fro in the earth, in their own time, and will, and strength, babbling of temperance and non-resistance, and slavery and benevolence, and communities and the Scriptures, and the sabbath and woman's rights. These are the thieves that cannot abide the way of humility and the cross, but climb up some other way, and steal the testimony of Jesus, and are lifted up in their self-sufficiency."

[114] *Memorial of Sarah Pugh*, pp. 30, 31. The Rev. W. H. Furness, minister of the First Unitarian Church in Philadelphia, suggested that possibly his fellow nonresistant abolitionists "should wear Quaker hats as a method of telling the world that they abhor all *forcible* measures" (*Non-Resistant*, vol. I, no. 21, 2 Nov. 1839). Perhaps the sight of Garrison in a Quaker broadbrim burning his copy of the Constitution of the United States might have led to a speedier abandonment of Quaker peculiarities in dress on the part of the traditionalists!

mitted to critical analysis.[115] Nonresistant criticism of the Quaker position of giving a large degree of support to government measures for internal security, and to a police force in particular, as inconsistent with their pacifism comes at times extremely close both to that of Mennonite writers and of many nonpacifists.[116] That ardent nonresistant, Henry C. Wright, concluded that it was a realization that police duties under the present system were incompatible with their peace testimony that really kept Friends from entering this branch of government service.[117]

Responsibility for the use of armed force by a government rested in part on those who had voted that government into power, the nonresistants told their Quaker critics. One could not contract out of the unpleasant aspects of government, they argued, and say that one cast his vote for the President only in a civil capacity and not as commander-in-chief as well, or that one would act as magistrate or legislator only where armed force was not involved. In all law enforcement as practised at present "the bayonets are none the less present because unseen," wrote Edmund Quincy, editor of the *Non-Resistant*, in answer to a Quaker correspondent. Granted that a country might be run on Christian, pacifist lines—"*we* know that such a government is possible, and our object is to establish it in the land by first changing the hearts of the people"—these were still not the guiding principles "in *existing* government, which Friends support." Since, then, all present-day governments were based on the "life-taking principle," Quincy went on, "we pronounce the Society of Friends, as a body, false to their own principles, in taking part in such governments."[118]

How far the influence of liberal-minded Friends was able to counteract that of the conservatives it is hard to say. After a decade of inter-

[115] See, e.g., *Selections from the Writings and Speeches of William Lloyd Garrison*, p. 94.

[116] See the remarks of a nonpacifist critic of Quaker views on war, William Logan Fisher, *A Review of the Doctrines and Discipline of the Society of Friends*, 1854 edn., p. 61: "The Society of Friends have never been a non-resistant society. All their property is held by the power of the sword; their deeds and title papers are acknowledged before a magistrate, in order to place them under the protection of the law, sustained by the military force of the country, and yet they disown a man for paying a militia fine. They use the magistrate's sword to preserve order; others use their own; there may be a material difference in results, but they rest on the same foundation." Fisher was of Quaker ancestry and later associated with the Progressive Friends.

[117] Wright, *Six Months at Graeffenberg*, pp. 164-66. See also pp. 155-57, 161, 162.

[118] *Non-Resistant*, vol. III, no. 3, 10 Feb. 1841.

mittent scrapping between nonresistants and radical abolitionists, on the one hand, and their conservative opponents who dominated most Quaker meetings, on the other, H. C. Wright wrote of the latter: "Their sole business now seems to be to administer their Discipline to keep their members 'out of the mixture.' "[119] And, undoubtedly, many Friends who might have given the radical pacifists a more sympathetic hearing were led by the denunciations of White and his sort to close their minds to an impartial consideration of nonresistant doctrines. But it is very uncertain if at that date the majority of Friends in either branch were ready to throw down the walls which separated them from society and, while maintaining intact their own specific peace witness, to place their energies at the disposal of the common pacifist effort. For this situation, of course, the extremism and fanaticism displayed by many of the nonresistants were not altogether without responsibility. In any case, there was perhaps something inherently incompatible between the militant "immediatism" and perfectionism of the non-Quaker nonresistants and the "harmless" pacifism of nineteenth-century Friends, which, in the words of one of its advocates, "carries no enmity in its bosom; and leaves the rest of the world in the quiet possession of their own principles."[120]

The story of the Society of Friends' relations with the radical nonresistants illustrates both the strength and the weakness of the Quaker peace testimony during our period. The sober, traditional character of its witness against war prevented it from swallowing the extravagancies and eccentricities which, as we shall see, were associated with the Non-Resistance Society. Friends continued on their way (we cannot quite say unruffled, since some of the utterances and actions of meetings and their leading members were marked by considerable heat and acrimony), bearing a personal testimony against military service when called upon, considering carefully and prayerfully the implications of their pacifism in such matters as paying taxes and carrying on business, and occasionally demonstrating the depth of their pacifist principles in a situation of violence. Yet this witness, so carefully nurtured and so rigorously guarded, only too often lacked the vital spark. There was little creativity in Friends' thinking on peace, especially if we compare it with the contribution of the radical nonresistants. As pacifists, Friends now made little impact on society. The organized peace movement, both its left and its right wings, though drawing immense in-

[119] *Non-Resistant and Practical Christian*, vol. IX, no. 12, 14 Oct. 1848.
[120] From Elisha Bates's "Letter to a Military Officer of Distinguished Rank," in the *Moral Advocate*, I, no. 6 (Dec. 1821), 84.

spiration from Friends' witness in the past, gained little assistance or backing from the Society in the present. This was, indeed, a misfortune for the cause of peace, which needed to rally all the support it could get in its uphill struggle with widespread indifference on the part of many and actual hostility from a militarist minority in the nation.

Chapter 9

The Witness of the Non-Quaker
Peace Sects, 1783-1861

I

Quakers, as we noted in previous chapters, have always been assiduous record keepers. Their archives, from the local monthly meetings right up to the various yearly meetings, present to the researcher an almost frightening mass of material (even though there was, of course, considerable uniformity of conduct over the decades). However, official documents of different types by no means exhaust the sources available to writers on Quaker history. Equally, and sometimes more, revealing are the various personal records which Friends, simple and highly cultured alike, have left in the form of journals and memoirs. These were produced in large numbers in the eighteenth and nineteenth centuries by Quakers on both sides of the Atlantic. Correspondence of private Friends, especially during the nineteenth century, has survived in large quantities, too, and this frequently throws light on the thinking of the Society as well as on its day-to-day activities. The growth during the last three decades of our period of a periodical press within the Society adds yet another important mine of information for the historian. Finally, Friends produced a considerable amount of expository writing, though in the nineteenth century, it is true, the peace testimony was not well represented in it.

For our period, at least, these sources are almost nonexistent when we come to consider the history of the other two major American peace sects. Until after the Civil War the Mennonites and the Dunkers were poor record keepers, and, on the whole, surviving church archives are fragmentary and small in bulk. There are scarcely any autobiographical writings, certainly none that can compare with the Quaker type of journal, and even the leaders of the German-speaking sectaries during this period did not leave much personal correspondence for posterity. The periodical press of these denominations was still only in its infancy in the 1850's, nor was much being written on peace in the form of pamphlets or books. Yet in actual numbers Mennonites and Dunkers were beginning to overtake the Quakers; and throughout the period they continued to bear as faithful a witness to peace as the Society of Friends did, though a witness conceived in somewhat different terms.

Just as the crisis of 1756 and their experiences in the American Revolution had led many Pennsylvania Friends—indeed, Friends throughout the continent—to retire from the world of politics and high culture into the solitude of their gardens, so, too, the Revolutionary years had driven large numbers of Mennonites and Dunkers out into the frontier wilderness. The westward movement was, of course, one that was shared by the whole American populace. But its effect on these "Dutch" sectaries was to accentuate the cultural isolation from which their immigrant forefathers in the pre-Revolutionary days had been unable to escape. As German-speaking farmers in an English-speaking environment, with a long tradition in Europe of hostility toward a state and society from which they had suffered prolonged persecution, they had stood apart from those social and cultural currents whose influence urban Friends especially felt so powerfully. Even so, men like the younger Christopher Saur, a devoted member of the Brethren church, or his older contemporary, the Mennonite schoolmaster Christopher Dock, took a not inconsiderable part in the cultural life of colonial Pennsylvania. Perhaps the walls which divided the German-speaking peace sectaries from the rest of society would have begun to break down a century or more earlier than they did if events had not intervened to slow down the process of acculturation. However, the walls remained standing until after the middle of the nineteenth century, and this social and cultural isolationism was reflected in most spheres of their intellectual and spiritual life. Their inability to realize the need for preserving a historical record of their church life and their failure to enrich their peace witness by new insights into a traditionally held testimony were only a few of the many facets of this isolationism.

The Mennonites, like their Quaker brethren, were liable to service in the militia if sound in body and of military age. Yet, in contrast to what we know concerning Friends, we have scarcely any references during our period to Mennonite conscientious objectors. It is not difficult to discover why. Mennonites seem to have been granted legal exemption from military duties (at least in peacetime) in all states where they resided, provided that they paid a commutation fee. Traditionally, Mennonites had condemned the hiring of substitutes, since the guilt of blood shed by the substitute would rest on the head of him who had sent another to soldier in his place. But paying commutation money to the government they regarded, as we have seen, as submission to the legitimate demands of Caesar, which Christ had enjoined on his followers. Sometimes these fines may have weighed heavily on the poorer members of the church; on the other hand, it is doubtful whether their collection was always enforced with the full rigor of the law. Neighborly feelings or local slackness and indifference undoubtedly intervened at times in the direction of leniency. The scanty surviving records of the Mennonite communities throw little light on the subject. All we know for certain is that compulsory militia service did not present a serious problem for the Mennonites at this time. Even less were there difficulties over paying taxes which went for war, since Mennonites had always paid these cheerfully in the belief that responsibility for their use rested with the government. This, as we have seen, was an issue continually nagging at the Quakers. City Friends had also at times been concerned lest the profits of their trade and commerce should contribute to furthering war; Mennonite farmers in their rural seclusion did not have to worry about such problems.

The prolonged toleration of Mennonite pacifism (for the brief periods in which the United States was involved in external war, first in 1812 and again in 1846, did not materially alter the situation) was naturally welcome after the hardships of the Revolutionary War and the bitter persecution which their ancestors had at times had to endure back in Europe, where even now their brethren in many places were being more and more closely circumscribed in the practice of their nonresistant faith. But this toleration from outside, when combined with a growing sectarian intolerance within the community which led to a long series of schisms—as in the Society of Friends—and with a general intellectual and spiritual moribundity, the signs of which were recognized by many Mennonites themselves, did not have a healthy influence on the church's thinking on the subject of peace and war. The stimulus was lacking; all available intellectual energies appear to have been occupied with factional squabbles—sometimes doctrinal, though frequently of a mainly personal nature. Renewal eventually came, but only its first faint beginnings lie within our period. True, it was not merely a conservative clinging to tradition or the absence of outside pressure that kept the Mennonite communities loyal to their nonresistant principles. It was a genuinely and deeply held faith. But the fires of this faith had begun to burn low.

Among the Mennonites the ceremony of baptism had always been the symbol of acceptance of the young adult into the full community of the faithful. On such an occasion the candidate was reminded of the basic tenets of his church and had to affirm his own personal allegiance to them. He had to pledge himself to follow the path of nonresistance which Christ had taught the followers of his peaceable kingdom in place of the way of war permitted to the Jews of old.[1] No doubt this was sometimes an empty promise, an only half-understood episode in the course of a purely formal, external ceremony. But for many it must have been a genuine and deeply felt experience, which the shared life of the church and later reading and meditation on the devotional books of their ancestors, with their stories of meekly endured suffering for the faith, helped to broaden and confirm. Yet, in the absence of such accounts of spiritual development as are provided in many of the Quakers' journals, this kind of experience does not normally find outward expression in the few surviving records.

The farming folk who made up the membership of the Mennonite churches of the pre-Civil War period, and from whom its unpaid and untrained pastorate was drawn, had neither the inclination nor the time to draw up treatises on such subjects as nonresistance. They relied on the literature they had inherited from their forefathers for arguments to buttress their nonresistant beliefs, while drawing inspiration directly from their reading of the gospels. Occasionally, one of their leaders felt called upon to restate their Biblical nonresistance, usually either because of the threat to the solidarity of the church presented by the missionary activities of an outside denomination or because of a schism, when the founder of a new group felt bound to defend the orthodoxy of his own position against his former brethren.

In the 1790's, for instance, when the Methodists and the followers of Jacob Albright were beginning to make converts in the ranks of the Pennsylvania Germans, Christian Burkholder (1746-1809), a leading Mennonite bishop in Lancaster County, felt the need to protect the youth of his church from such bad influences and to exhort them to remain loyal to the faith of their ancestors. In 1792, therefore, he prepared a series of addresses—*Nützliche und erbauliche Anrede an die Jugend*, he styled them—which later, in 1804, he had published. The little book was subsequently reprinted a number of times in the United States and in Canada, in both German and English editions, and it exerted a considerable influence on nineteenth-century Mennonite thought.[2] The second half of the second address Burkholder devoted to the subject of "love of our neighbor." Love and charity, he told the young people, were of the essence of Christ's teaching, and they must be practised at whatever cost, toward enemies as well as friends. "The doctrine and deportment of Christ," he went on, "do not allow us to go to war, or to use violence towards our enemies. . . . no true Chris-

---

[1] Christian Burkholder, "Addresses to Youth," reprinted as an appendix to *Conversation on Saving Faith for the Young*, pp. 235-37.
[2] Robert Friedmann, *Mennonite Piety through the Centuries*, p. 239.

tian can be engaged in military service, not being allowed to 'do violence' to any one." He reminded them that Mennonites belonged to Christ's kingdom of peace and not to any of this world's realms, whose servants were ready to kill thousands, even of their own co-religionists, at the state's behest.[3] Burkholder followed the usual practice of confirming every statement with copious Biblical citations and references. His aim, of course, was to follow the words of scripture as closely as possible and not to stray off into creaturely notions of his own.

A couple of years earlier, in 1790, another Mennonite writer, Francis Herr (1748-1810), who was later to belong to a small group which drifted away from the main body of the church, published a short work on the subject of baptism, defending the Mennonite position against that of the Quakers. To this he appended a brief account of nonresistant doctrine, at the same attacking the Quakers for inconsistency in their practice of pacifism. Quaker writings asserted "that all revenge was forbidden under the new covenant." Herr agreed, but went on in his rather quaint English, "I must put this question to you, where war, is more and earnestly forbidden as going to law, resist force by force and to be elected into offices; and if we for the gospel and Christ's sake, cannot hold any office, how should we be capable, to elect others into offices." Friends rejected the war method, "but make use of going to law, by resisting force by force, almost as much and more as people of other denominations. I must ask you once more, where the one is more forbidden than the other," he concluded.[4] Polemical writing of this nature directed against another peace church is unusual at this period. In fact, during the last quarter of the eighteenth century when Herr was writing, the Society of Friends in America had come quite close to the antistate interpretation given to pacifism by the Mennonite tradition.

The European wars of the French Revolution and the Napoleonic epoch affected Mennonites in the United States scarcely at all. There was little change even when, in 1812, the country became directly involved in the continental war. In material terms, of course, war brought the Mennonite farming communities greater prosperity, owing to the increased demand for foodstuffs and the consequent rise in price of farm products. But, although a few Mennonite boys enlisted on their own (and thereby lost their good standing in the church until such time as they showed contrition for breaking their church's discipline), the menfolk were not called up—provided they paid their

[3] Burkholder, "Addresses to Youth," pp. 197-210.
[4] Francis Herr, A Short Explication of the Written Word of God, pp. 40, 41.

393

commutation money when required to do their turn of service with the state militia.[5] This was scarcely a burden financially, and, as we have seen, Mennonites did not object to rendering such tribute to Caesar. Many, indeed, voiced their gratitude to God and the powers that be for showing such tenderness to the claims of conscience. This feeling emerges in the correspondence of a leading Lancaster County Mennonite, Martin Mellinger (1763-1842), with his relatives back in the Rhenish Palatinate, where their conscientious scruples did not meet with the same respect from the authorities. In the middle of the war, in November 1813, Mellinger wrote to his sister and brother-in-law: "We have reason to thank God, since thus far none of us has been called to the militia, and since we have not had to furnish any money except the regular taxes." A little later in the same letter Mellinger wrote:

> Most Americans have not yet experienced anything of the war. But those who live on the borders and in Canada, where the real occasion for the war is as well as the fighting, have unfortunately experienced much, and have learned to know how precious peace is. For a number of years very many of our acquaintances among our people have been moving to Canada in English or royal territory. So far we have not heard that any of those who confess the nonresistant faith have been compelled by the king to take up arms, but . . . each one is compelled to pay . . . each year, . . . on condition of which they are not to be disturbed. . . . We do not know what may yet come but we hope for the best.[6]

The first Mennonites to settle in Upper Canada (as the later province of Ontario was soon to be called) had arrived there a few years after the Revolutionary War. As in the case of the Quaker groups, a number of factors led them to emigrate from their native Pennsylvania to the forest wilderness of the north: attachment to their former sovereign that was not too different, perhaps, from Tory loyalism,[7] fear that the new Revolutionary authorities would not heed their objections to mili-

[5] L. J. Heatwole, *Mennonite Handbook of Information*, chap. XVII.

[6] "The Correspondence of Martin Mellinger," *MQR*, V, no. 1 (Jan. 1931), 47, 48.

[7] In 1865 the Mennonite minister, David Sherk, whose father had emigrated to Canada in 1799, wrote: "When the time came that the colonies revolted against their government they [i.e., Mennonites] in general were very much grieved about it but according to their principles they kept still and had the hopes the colonies would not succeed but at length their hope was gone." Therefore, after the war they welcomed the offer of freedom of conscience made by Governor Simcoe to attract settlers to Canada. See "An Ontario Mennonite Petition," *MHB*, XXIII, no. 4 (Oct. 1962), 6.

tary service which British rule had respected, and doubtless, too, the lure of new lands to open up. Before 1800 the settlements had been small and confined to the area around the Niagara River; in the early decades of the new century Mennonites came in larger numbers and began to occupy land in the area of present-day Waterloo County as well as in the area north of Toronto (then called York). In the Militia Act which was passed in 1793 a couple of years after the creation of a separate province of Upper Canada, Mennonites (along with the Quakers and River Brethren, or Tunkers) had been granted exemption from service in the militia, to which all able-bodied men between the ages of 16 and 50 were liable, provided they could produce a certificate of membership from their church and were willing to pay an annual sum of 20s. in peacetime and £5 in time of war or insurrection.[8] In this way the colonial authorities hoped to attract members of the frugal and hard-working peace sect to come up and pioneer in the sparsely populated new province. Such settlers were highly desirable, and even the military could excuse their peculiar scruples in regard to bearing arms.

A further concession was granted them in 1810. In the Mennonite church there is no birthright membership, and admission comes only with adult baptism on confession of faith. A boy who had been reared in a Mennonite home and had there imbibed its teachings on nonresistance might receive the summons to perform military duties before he felt ripe for the call to accept baptism. For that reason, under the existing law of Upper Canada, many a young Mennonite conscript was not technically eligible for exemption from the militia. No doubt the authorities usually took a reasonable line and did not attempt to force them to muster against their will. But difficulties might arise from time to time: the position was anomalous. So early in 1810 Mennonites, along with the "Tunkers" (to be discussed later in this chapter) whose church regulations were similar, petitioned the provincial House of Commons for an amendment of the law.

Whereas [they told the legislators] many of our sons now under age and incapable of judging in matters of conscience, are not as yet actually considered as church members, and cannot of course secure the necessary certificates, we therefore humbly pray the same indulgence may be extended to them that is granted to ourselves, their parents, that is, that they may be exempted from serving in the

[8] An "Affidavit" for a Mennonite C. O., George Histand, dated 1869, is printed in "More Source Material for Ontario Mennonite History," *MQR*, V, no. 3 (July 1931), 222.

Militia by paying the commutation money until they arrive at the age of twenty-one or until they be admitted as church members.[9]

The petition was successful, and the young folk were confirmed in the privileges granted their elders. Of course, for some of the poorer members of the church, those "with large families . . . in new settlements," for instance, the commutation fees presented quite a financial burden,[10] and we find Mennonites from the beginning of the century seeking to get the size of the fees reduced. Yet, henceforth, the status of the Mennonite conscientious objectors in Canada satisfied their religious scruples.[11]

In the autumn of 1813 war came to the Canadian Mennonites of Waterloo County, and they discovered (as, indeed, they had always half feared) that in times of emergency the exigencies of the military situation might override legal status. The British, admittedly, made no serious attempt to force them to become combatants in the army. In the words of a later Mennonite petition: "The promise from the Crown was held good for there was no one of those people troubled to take up arms although the country was new and men very scarce."[12] Nevertheless, when, with the approach of two American armies from the direction of Detroit in the west and across Lake Erie to the south, the battle line drew near the Mennonite settlements, the British military authorities, hard-pressed by the Americans, began to impress the local inhabitants into service as teamsters. Mennonite farmers had to supply their own wagons and horses, and their sons went off with the army to drive them.[13] On 5 October the British forces were routed by the Americans in a battle near Moraviantown on the river Thames and forced to beat a hasty retreat. As a result, the Mennonites lost their horses to the fleeing British and their horseless wagons to the American invaders.[14]

[9] J. Boyd Cressman, "History of the First Mennonite Church of Kitchener, Ontario," pt. I, MQR, XIII, no. 3 (July 1939), 168.

[10] Ibid.

[11] See L. J. Burkholder, A Brief History of the Mennonites in Ontario, pp. 260-62, 349-54, for information on Canadian legislation concerning the military exemption of the Mennonites (as well as the Quakers and Tunkers) down to the First World War.

[12] "An Ontario Mennonite Petition" (1865), MHB, ibid.

[13] A story is told of one farmer who got a neighbor to remove the wheels from his wagon in order to keep it from being seized. The army, however, harnessed his horses to a neighbor's wagon and took his son along with them as driver! See H. S. Bender (ed.), "New Source Material for the History of the Mennonites in Ontario," MQR, III, no. 1 (Jan. 1929), 42

[14] Ibid., pp. 42-46. See also the account by Dr. Aaron Eby reprinted in Daniel K. Cassel, History of the Mennonites, pp. 322, 323. Bender in his article prints the detailed statements of losses, which Mennonites submitted in November 1813

This experience was more an annoyance than anything approaching persecution. It served, perhaps, to strengthen the Mennonites' feeling that in this world no guarantee could secure them against the possibility of having to suffer for their beliefs. Yet, as it turned out, Canadian Mennonites remained in some ways securer in the exercise of their pacifist scruples than their brethren across the border, and this undoubtedly was a factor in continued emigration from the United States. We may illustrate this point by quoting again from the correspondence carried on by the Lancaster County deacon, Martin Mellinger, with his relatives in Germany. On 1 December 1822 he wrote: "Under the king the nonresistant people have full freedom of conscience, so that they do not need to take up arms in time of war. . . . In a sense they are better off than we are. But one who knows his Bible can read there as well as experience in our day, that . . . everything is uncertain and transient."[15] In fact, Deacon Mellinger was being overpessimistic in regard to the future of his Canadian brethren, who continued to enjoy exemption from any kind of military service right up to, and even after, the outbreak of the First World War. By an act of 1849 (12 Vic. c. 88), even the necessity of purchasing such exemption by paying a small fine was abolished,[16] and henceforth all religious objectors continued to enjoy complete freedom of conscience.

Mennonites and Amish were emigrating from the United States to Canada during the first half of the nineteenth century. They continued to come over from Europe during this period, too, though, of course, not in such large numbers as in the previous century. The journey from Europe, like the migration to Canada, might be undertaken for a number of reasons. In the early decades of the century the economic motive probably predominated. But around mid-century we find a number of families crossing the ocean to escape the increasing pressure of military conscription on the European continent. This was true, for instance, of some of the Alsatian Amish and also of the Bernese Anabaptists of the Jura Mountains of Switzerland.[17] The same situation

---

to the British authorities to substantiate their claims for compensation. The sums claimed varied from £6 up to £128.

[15] *MQR*, V, no. 1, 58.

[16] In Canada, as in the United States, the militia system was becoming more and more a formality.

[17] Delbert L. Gratz, *Bernese Anabaptists and their American Descendants*, pp. 105-7, 128-29, 182. In 1815 Mennonites had been exempted from military service on payment of a special tax. This exemption was withdrawn in 1850, though it was not until the enactment of a new federal constitution in 1874 that the Swiss Mennonites were forced to do noncombatant service in the army. Each of these

397

prompted some German Mennonites to emigrate around this time, too. The family of Christian Krehbiel, who later became an outstanding figure in the General Conference of Mennonites in America, is a case in point. His father had settled in the Kingdom of Bavaria where Mennonite conscripts were permitted by law to buy substitutes to do the six years' military service in their place. But the cost was around 1,000 gulden. Christian's father bought his eldest son out of military service in this way, but even a prosperous Mennonite farmer could not afford to do this for all of his remaining five sons. "He did not want his sons to be soldiers because of his convictions on nonresistance," and so, after receiving satisfactory news of conditions from relatives who had already emigrated, the father sold his farm—at a loss—and in the spring of 1851 the whole family started for America.[18]

Most of the nineteenth-century Mennonite immigrants who arrived in America before the great "Russian" migration of the seventies originated from Central Europe. There the Mennonites were gradually abandoning their strict adherence to their traditional belief in nonresistance as a result both of pressure from without in the form of the nation in arms, where every able-bodied man was liable to the law of universal conscription, and from within their own community, which was slowly putting aside its nonconformity to the world and accommodating itself to the society around it. Many of those who chose to cross the ocean came, like the Krehbiel family, just because of their continued loyalty to Mennonite pacifism, and their departure meant a further weakening of the hold of the nonresistant testimony on European Mennonitism.

Among the Dutch Mennonites, or *Doopsgezinden* as they now called themselves, this process had taken place in the previous century. Pacifism had been almost completely given up by the beginning of the nineteenth century, and, since in Holland there had never been much economic incentive toward emigration, American Mennonitism was never reinforced—at least directly—by infusions from the culturally advanced stream of Dutch Mennonite life. An interesting exception to this generalization was the emigration of over half—fifty-two persons in all, if we include those not yet baptized—of the congregation of the Balk Mennonite Church in Friesland. It was, however, an exception that serves to illustrate the rule. For the Balk church was an isolated community adhering to the Old Frisian branch, which had re-

---

changes brought about a considerable emigration from the small Mennonite communities in Switzerland.

[18] Christian Krehbiel, *Prairie Pioneer*, pp. 21, 67.

tained much of the sixteenth-century simplicity in organization, dress, and beliefs. Almost alone among the *Doopsgezinden* of this period, the church remained loyal to its founder's nonresistant teachings. This stance brought difficulties with the state authorities. Until mid-century trouble had been warded off, even during the war with the new Belgium in the 1830's, by the payment of commutation money; but it was not clear how long this relative immunity would last. The immediate causes of the emigration, which took place between May 1853 and April 1854, remain obscure, but undoubtedly the problem of military service lay at its roots. The new immigrants settled to the southwest of Goshen (Ind.); however, the new community did not prosper, and eventually it disintegrated.[19]

Even though many of the fresh immigrants from Europe had come to America on account of their opposition to military service in the home country, they did not prove a large or a vital enough element to reinvigorate Mennonite pacifism in the United States. When the Civil War came, the Mennonite communities across the country—now split, like the Quakers, into several separate denominations—found themselves, as we shall see, unprepared to face the test of war fever and military conscription. One of the church's leaders, John F. Funk (1835-1930), who was to do more than any other man to help revive its nonresistant faith, wrote as follows of this situation: "In as much as there had been no war for a long period of time, the doctrine of non-resistance had almost been forgotten, at least in a sense of it being taught and impressed on the minds of the young men who were subject to military duties. The matter had to a large extent been lost sight of."[20] Doubtless, nonresistance was sometimes preached from the pulpit or taught in the schoolroom or the home. The older literature was there for those who wished to read. But of new material expounding the church's peace doctrines there was scarcely anything of importance during the period between the appearance, at the beginning of the century, of Bishop Christian Burkholder's "Addresses to the Youth," mentioned earlier, and the outbreak of the Civil War.

We may begin a brief review of these scanty materials on peace with Francis Herr's son John, the founder of the Reformed Mennonite Church which had in 1812 broken away from the main body because it had fallen into a moribund state. The younger Herr (1782-1850) was a prolific writer. Most of his works deal with strictly theological prob-

[19] Carl F. Brusewitz, "The Mennonites of Balk, Friesland," *MQR*, XXX, no. 1 (Jan. 1956), esp. 25-27, 30, 31.

[20] MS Notebook, p. 66, in John F. Funk Collection, Archives of the Mennonite Church, Goshen (Ind.).

lems, but in his *Illustrating Mirror,* a book-length commentary on the Sermon on the Mount which he published in German in 1827 and in an English version in 1834, he expounds the traditional nonresistant creed. The work is an artless compilation of Biblical texts strung together by means of the author's comments. The Sermon on the Mount, says Herr, should teach us readiness to lose all rather than retaliate against injury. "O that all men possessed this love! then the lawyer and the judge, the king and the magistrate would be needed no more, but Christ would be all in all." Later, he assails those who refuse to go to war "professing to be defenseless men" and yet are willing when their property is threatened to resort to the laws in its defense. "Now the one cannot be excused any more than the other. . . . Christians are also as dearly and explicitly forbidden by Christ to sue or go to law . . . as they are forbidden to employ the literal sword."[21] Herr was probably referring here to the Quakers, whose views on law and magistracy his father had sought to confute earlier. His work is unlikely to have exerted much influence outside the small circle of his Reformed Mennonite Church.

More interesting and more influential was the *Confession of Faith,* which the Virginia Mennonites issued ten years later in 1837. This volume is usually known as the Burkholder *Confession,* after Peter Burkholder (1783-1846), a prominent Virginia Mennonite who was partly responsible for its compilation and was himself the author of "Nine Reflections" and other items included in it. The book appeared in English, showing that by this time English had replaced German as the mother tongue of the old Mennonite community in this state. The translation from German (Peter Burkholder had written in German) was carried out by the well-known Mennonite printer and publisher, Joseph Funk (1778-1862), who was also mainly responsible for editing the volume. Some of the "Thirty-Three Articles" written by the Dutch Mennonite, Pieter Jansz Twisck, early in the seventeenth century, which Funk included, deal with the question of nonresistance. In addition, Peter Burkholder devoted his "Third Reflection" to this subject in the form of a commentary on Matt. 5:9 ("Blessed are the peacemakers," etc.). In it he defended his coreligionists from the charge of disloyalty to the state for their refusal to bear arms. Burkholder claimed that, on the contrary, government had no more loyal citizens than the peaceable Mennonites, who believed that the state is ordained of God and must be obeyed in all things that are not against conscience.[22]

[21] *John Herr's Complete Works,* pp. 241-48, 327-32.
[22] *The Confession of Faith,* pp. 142, 143, 218-25, 295-313.

Burkholder's *Confession* soon became a treasured possession of almost all Virginia Mennonite homes and remained one of their chief sources of belief for several generations. As we shall see, it was to prove a godsend in the trying situation of the Civil War that the church could produce in the English language (which made it accessible to government and legislators) this document of its faith in nonresistance and in passive obedience to the powers that be.[23] The *Confession*, it is true, contained nothing new or original on the subject of Mennonite peace doctrine. Its importance lies solely in its influence in maintaining interest in this doctrine among the Virginia communities during a period of ebbing faith in the church at large.

Shortly before the Civil War we find one last work, originating this time among the Lancaster County Amish, which touches on the question of nonresistance. The author of *Das Wahre Christenthum* (*The True Christianity*) was David Beiler (1786-1871), an Amish bishop from the Conestoga valley area, who composed the book in 1857 at the age of 71. It was written for the instruction of the younger generation of his church. Although it undoubtedly first circulated among the Amish in manuscript, it did not appear in print until 1888 after Beiler's death. "It is a remarkable piece of work in its austerity and simplicity," writes a historian of Mennonite religious literature, "and it permits better than any other source known a living insight into the way of thinking and feeling of the Amish in this country, reflecting also to a certain extent the spiritual climate of the Swiss Brethren in the old days of Europe."[24] It remained an important spiritual influence in the Amish communities right up into this century.

Beiler's object is to show that the doctrine expounded is the true Christian one, and he therefore marshals a wide array of Biblical citations on which to rest his argument. Nonresistance is discussed in the fourth chapter entitled: "Concerning Vengeance or Resistance." This chapter consists of a rather diffuse exposition of a series of Biblical texts along with illustrative stories also drawn from scripture. He does not touch directly on the question of war or civil government; nonresistance is, however, implicit in his emphasis on the Christian virtues of love and goodwill toward all men, even enemies and those who have done evil to us, and on the need to forgive injuries. This, he says, is part of "the calling of the true disciple of Christ."[25] Thus we find at the source of the pacifism of this rural Pennsylvania bishop of the mid-nineteenth century the same doctrine of "discipleship" that we see

[23] Harry A. Brunk, *History of Mennonites in Virginia*, I, 161, 163.
[24] See Robert Friedmann, *Mennonite Piety through the Centuries*, pp. 245-47.
[25] David Beiler, *Das Wahre Christenthum*, p. 133.

in the case of the Central European Anabaptists of the Reformation era.

The Amish, since the time they separated back in Europe at the end of the seventeenth century, have remained a somewhat peripheral group, a conservative backwater, in relation to the mainstream of Mennonitism. Another and later offshoot was formed by the River Brethren (now known as Brethren in Christ), who arose in the late 1770's and early 1780's among the Pennsylvania Germans of the Susquehanna valley. Their founder was a Mennonite farmer of Swiss extraction, Jacob Engle (1753-1833), who had been brought to Pennsylvania by his father in 1754. The new group was the outcome of one of those revival movements which swept different parts of the country at various times during the late eighteenth and early nineteenth centuries. Its first adherents were drawn very largely from members of the German peace sects, Mennonites especially but also Dunkers, who had grown discontented with the formalism and rigid piety of their traditional churches. We know very little of the new sect's history during the early decades of its existence, for scarcely any records from this period have survived. The small brotherhoods of earnest seekers were only very loosely associated with each other. They practised trine immersion and feet washing. Their ministers were unsalaried working farmers, who devoted their spare hours to their pastoral office. Strict nonconformity to the world entailed not merely the plain dress and plain customs but also an objection to swearing oaths or to having recourse to the law, an avoidance of all political activities, and a belief in nonresistance which would lead them to refuse to bear arms if called upon to do so. The derivation of these beliefs from the Mennonite and Dunker milieu out of which the sect crystallized is clear.

"There is not much actual history concerning the Church's attitude on non-resistance," writes the historian of the Brethren in Christ.[26]

---

[26] A. W. Climenhaga, *History of the Brethren in Christ Church*, p. 303. Climenhaga prints in full a translation of a German document found in Canada entitled "Articles of Faith of the Church of the Brethren," which he claims is an early confession of the River Brethren dating from the latter years of the eighteenth century. The "Articles" originated in Pennsylvania, and among the signatories was Jacob Engle. They treat, among other subjects, the doctrine of nonresistance: "The sword, revenge and self-defence are also entirely forbidden" (p. 102). However, another version of these "Articles" is known to have existed with the date 1770, i.e., before the formation of the River Brethren, and with a different signature. Unfortunately, neither version is extant today. It seems likely, however, that Jacob Engle and his fellow River Brethren had put their signatures to an older document, possibly slightly altering the wording in the process. See Carlton O. Wittlinger, "Was there an Eighteenth Century River Brethren Confession of Faith?" *Notes and Queries in Brethren in Christ History*, vol. II, no. 1 (Jan. 1961).

Owing to more recent research,[27] however, we are a little better informed on the pacifist record of the River Brethren in Canada. There they were known as "Tunkers" or "Dippers." The first Tunker settlers began to arrive from Pennsylvania in 1788 under the leadership of John Winger, who became their first bishop in Upper Canada. They did not come as Empire loyalists, but quite possibly, as in the case of their Mennonite cousins, their nonresistant faith was a contributing factor in making them exchange prosperous Lancaster County for the northern wilderness, since the same broad and generous exemption from military service was extended to this small group as to the larger settlements of Quakers and Mennonites. We have already, in telling the story of the early Canadian Quakers and Mennonites, traced the more important changes in the legislative provisions for religious objectors. Little needs to be added here. We may note, though, the activities of Bishop John Winger, the revered Tunker leader, in getting the military exemption extended in 1810 to young unbaptized members of the Mennonite and Tunker communities, a measure that has been mentioned above in connection with the Mennonites. He was especially diligent in interviewing government officials, explaining to them that in these churches young people were not accepted as members until they had experienced conversion. Tradition in his church relates that, in reply, the officials told Winger: "If they [i.e., the young people] would also comply with the same rules and conditions, that is, to be a peculiar people, practice nonconformity to the world, and have nothing to do with political matters they shall also be free."[28]

There is no direct mention of Tunkers being forced in the War of 1812 to serve as teamsters with the army, as we know happened in the case of the Mennonites of Waterloo County—although, as E. M. Sider remarks, "it is not illogical to assume that such service was required of some members." They would probably have had even less compunction in performing such service—to judge, at least, by the record of one of the earliest Tunker immigrants, John Troyer. For we find Troyer in 1795, while petitioning the Crown for land, including the following: "Your petitioner prays that your Excellency and the Honourable Council will please to have compassion on him, and if it is against the tenets of his profession to bear arms, he has no objection to employ his team in any service of the government either civil or military."[29]

[27] See E. Morris Sider, "Nonresistance in the Early Brethren in Christ Church in Ontario," MQR, XXXI, no. 4 (Oct. 1957), 278-85.

[28] Ibid., p. 281.

[29] Ibid., p. 285. The identification of Troyer as a Tunker is not beyond dispute. He may possibly have been a Mennonite.

403

On the whole, then, the Tunkers were left in peace since, like the Mennonites, they felt no scruples about paying the commutation money to satisfy the legal requirement, which was finally abolished in 1849. Militia fines, in fact, were not usually very onerous. "Sometimes," writes Sider, "the designated officer neglected to collect the fine, either through sympathy or indifference; but when such cases were discovered the delinquent officer was required to collect not only the immediate fine but all back payments as well."[30] For the small Tunker church, as for the larger Mennonite communities, Canada became a haven where they could enjoy almost unlimited freedom from the burden of military exactions.

The church of the German Baptist Brethren, whom we must consider next, had grown slowly. At the time of the Revolution it probably numbered around a thousand baptized members, most of whom lived in rural Pennsylvania.[31] The period in the church's history between the Revolution and the middle of the nineteenth century a Brethren historian has described as one of both "eclipse" and at the same time "expansion."[32] The activities of men like the younger Christopher Saur had brought the Dunkers of the colonial era, though a predominantly farming people, within the mainstream of German-American culture. Their experiences during the Revolutionary years and the subsequent trek of large numbers into the frontier wildernesses, to which these experiences were, indeed, a contributing factor, put a stop to this development. Culturally, the Brethren retrogressed. Their tight, compact communities became cultural backwaters; most of their rank-and-file members were almost illiterate backwoodsmen, their leaders semiliterate rustic preachers. Education, even Sunday schools, came to be opposed as a worldly influence; the church, it was felt, must remain separate from all worldly activities, whether in the social or in the political sphere. A rigid legalism, a narrow sectarianism, more and more replaced the creedless faith of the early Brethren, who sought nothing but to follow in the footsteps of the loving Savior.

But this was only one side of the coin. Over against this drying up of the cultural springs of the church's life we may set a physical expansion of the membership that by mid-century had brought the Brethren to the Pacific coast, dotting the whole Midwest and the states of the upper South with church communities, an expansion that au-

[30] *Ibid.*, p. 284.
[31] Floyd E. Mallott, *Studies in Brethren History*, p. 112.
[32] Rufus D. Bowman, *The Church of the Brethren and War*, p. 101.

404

gured well for the future once the tide of renewal had begun to flow in the spiritual life of the church.

We may obtain some insight into the thinking of the Brethren by perusing the minutes of their annual conferences, which began to be reported (rather meagerly at first, it is true, and with gaps) from 1778 on, though these meetings may date back as early as 1742. The record, therefore, is rather more complete in this respect than it is for the Mennonites during this period. On the other hand, the Brethren produced no literature dealing even incidentally with the subject of their peace testimony before the middle of the nineteenth century. We are dependent almost exclusively upon the evidence provided by these annual conference minutes.

The first official pronouncement by the church on the subject of war came in 1785. The absolute condemnation of war, which it passed at that time, was, of course, a confirmation of the stand the Brethren had taken even before their departure from Europe. The annual conference of that year, held at Big Conewago (Pa.), had to consider a letter sent in by one Valentine Power, a leading member of the church in Virginia. Valentine and his brother Martin, both ministers, were in disagreement with their congregation—the South Branch Church in what is now West Virginia, which they had helped to set up in the early seventies. The two brothers were evidently unwilling to accept the pacifist position which had been traditional in their church. Did not the words in Peter's First Epistle (2:13-14) require Christian participation in war, the brothers inquired, and the taking of an oath (to which the Brethren had also objected), if the magistrate so ordered? Because their fellow Brethren in the South Branch disagreed with their position, Valentine Power had written an appeal to the whole church assembled in annual conference. The delegates rejected Power's arguments, however, and in their place recommended the path of suffering and nonresistance which Christ had trodden. Jesus had rebuked Peter when he drew the sword to defend him and had told him to put it back in its place.

Here, indeed, was the greatest necessity (for self-defense), but all this time the Savior resisted not; but he suffered patiently, and even healed the one whose ear was smote off. . . . Thus our Savior had said before, "That we resist not evil"; for so he believed and thus he spake, and thus he did. . . . So we hope the dear Brethren [i.e., the Power brothers] will not take it amiss when we, from all these passages of Scripture, and especially from the words of Peter, can not see or find any liberty to use any (carnal) sword, but only the sword of the Spirit, which is the word of God. . . . But that the higher powers bear the sword of justice, punishing the evil and promoting the good, in this we acknowledge them from the heart as the ministers of God. But the sword belongeth to the kingdom of the world, and Christ says to his disciples: "I have chosen you from the world," etc. Thus we understand the beloved Peter, that we are to submit ourselves in all things that are not contrary to the will or command of God, and no further.[33]

Evidently, the Power brothers were not convinced either by the authority or the arguments of the annual conference, for they continued to advocate the admissibility for Brethren of bearing arms and taking oaths. In 1790 we find the assembly (meeting this time at Coventry, Pa.) again taking up the case of the two brothers. Valentine seems to have been the more active, since it is to him that the conference on each occasion addressed its injunctions. The meeting of 1790 asked "the beloved brother, Valentine Power" to "desist from this strange notion, because . . . we believe and confess that Christ has forbidden to his followers the swearing of oaths and partaking of war." Those among the Brethren who supported "swearing and war" would be shunned by the church. "It is impossible for us to break the bread of communion with such a brother, who pretends the higher powers were requiring such of him." At the present time, "thanks to God, we have . . . a government that will not require of us what is against our conscience. But should there be any among us having such a conscience as to be able to fight and swear oaths such a one would not be of us." This decision was considered of enough importance to be repeated again in the same year "at a (large and) numerous meeting of brethren on the Schuylkill, at (the place of Bro. John Bach)."[34]

The persistent policy of the church at this time had been to disfellowship members who, like the Powers,[35] either participated in warlike activities themselves or advocated a nonpacifist position inside the church. Yet there must have been some diversity of belief, if only among a small minority, and probably a greater laxity of practice within a larger circle. The same article passed at the conference of 1785 rejecting Valentine Power's interpretation of Peter also con-

[33] *MAM*, pp. 9, 10. See also Bowman, *Church of the Brethren and War*, pp. 43, 44, 47.

[34] *MAM*, p. 14.

[35] The Power brothers apparently joined the Methodists in the early 1790's. See F. M. Bittinger, *A History of the Church of the Brethren in the First District of West Virginia*, pp. 31, 32.

tained a significant tailpiece. Let no member of the church, it added, appear on the exercise field for militia musters or allow his sons to muster either, if he could prevent it.[36] This injunction, however, does not appear to have had everywhere the desired effect; for at a "Great Meeting" held at Pipe Creek (Md.) two years later, in May 1787, we learn that "there was a tearful complaint that some brethren, of their own free will, would allow their young folks to go to the drill-ground and parade-ground." The delegates "resolved that there could be no holy communion with such brethren as have been admonished and yet do not keep their young people off such places."[37]

The question of the church's peace testimony and its enforcement on members does not crop up again in the minutes which have come down to us until after the outbreak of the War of 1812. In 1813 the annual conference at Coventry (Pa.) passed a resolution against Brethren participation in elections. Already, from the period of the Revolution on, as part and parcel of the general withdrawal of the church from close contact with the world, there had been a movement among the Brethren toward complete nonparticipation in political life, though it does not appear to have been by any means universal throughout the brotherhood. Unwillingness to exercise the franchise was also, in part, connected with the Dunker objection to war, their feeling that voting for candidates who were not pacifists (as all were likely to be in districts where the Brethren lived) was somehow tantamount to giving approval to war measures which such candidates might later support. This connection comes out clearly in the decision of 1813. In view of the war situation (as well as of the rise of party spirit in the country), it states, the assembled Brethren consider "that it would be much better if no votes were given in at elections." They believed that those who sincerely desired "to be defenseless" would recognize the correctness of this policy. Certainly, they might pray to God on behalf of their country's government, but they should refrain from using the ballot-box, "else we might, perhaps, assist in electing such that would afterward oppress us with war."[38]

Probably complete uniformity in respect to not voting was never achieved among the Brethren; at least it would not have been too easy to enforce. But nonparticipation remained the official policy, as well as the practice, of almost all church members until at least the middle of the nineteenth century. Thereafter there was a slow change

[36] *MAM*, p. 10.
[37] Quoted in H. Austin Cooper, *Two Centuries of the Brothersvalley Church of the Brethren*, p. 128. The original minutes of this meeting have not survived. Cooper quotes from notes made by one of the participants, Elder Martin Urner II.
[38] *MAM*, p. 32.

toward greater participation in political life, which was, however, delayed during the Civil War years. Likewise, Brethren in the period we are discussing here continued to follow the Mennonite pattern in their opposition to officeholding wherever there was a chance of being involved by virtue of office not only in military measures but in law enforcement or the administration of oaths. For instance, a conference resolution of 1857 states the established position as follows: "We consider it wrong for brethren to accept of any office, which requires them to administer an oath, or to use physical force, in performing the duties of that office."[39]

A second peace issue which crops up in the minutes of the War of 1812 period is that of the payment of commutation money in lieu of military service. More men were liable for military service now that the country was involved in war, and the burden of payment rested heavily on some of the poorer Brethren. Moreover, many of the Brethren settlements were in or near the line of advance of the British troops who reached Washington in August 1814, and calls for the service of the able-bodied reached a peak at this time. After discussion the conference of 1815 resolved, therefore, that where Brethren of good standing in the church or their as yet unbaptized sons "shall be hard oppressed with the payment of fines they shall be assisted by the Brethren according to the teaching of the apostle—let one bear the burden of another, thus you will fulfill the law of Jesus Christ."[40]

The problem of militia service continued sporadically to be a subject of discussion at the annual conferences in the years following the war. Queries were presented in 1817 and again in 1822, 1835, and 1840, on the issue of whether Brethren, or their sons who were not yet members, might attend militia musters if called upon to do so. Evidently, some in the brotherhood wishing to avoid the financial losses incurred by repeated fines had failed to see that such attendance would seriously damage their church's peace witness. In an era of peace, to put in an occasional appearance at the none-too-serious militia exercises did not, perhaps, appear to the more thoughtless to be a very warlike activity. But, naturally, the practice met with stern disapproval from the Brethren assembled in conference. In 1817 they threatened those who continued to attend with disfellowshipping. The conference of 1835 explained that a compromise of this kind "is contrary to our baptismal vow, contrary to the word of God, and contrary to the professed

[39] Ibid., p. 167. See also Bowman, Church of the Brethren and War, pp. 107, 108.

[40] MAM, p. 40. See also Martin Grove Brumbaugh, A History of the German Baptist Brethren in Europe and America (1910 edn.), p. 492.

principle of the church, and can by no means be permitted or tolerated." And in 1840 the delegates further elucidated the reasons why Brethren should abstain from the parade ground. "The training or mustering," they said, "is a preparation for war, and since we are inclined to peace and a defenseless state, it would in no wise be proper nor allowable for brethren to learn war."[41]

The issue was not always as clear-cut as this, however. We have seen how, around mid-century, the militia system had fallen into a state of decay. In some states comparatively high militia fines, which were paid by all who for one reason or another were unwilling to appear at the annual musters, by the non-conscientious many as well as by the handful of religious objectors, were "the only means whereby the military musters are kept up." Therefore, asked a query of 1859, "would it not be better for brethren to muster a few times and thereby cause the military system to be abolished, than to pay an oppressive fine and thereby keep up the regimental muster?" The question, indeed, has a slightly casuistical tone; one cannot quite repress the thought that the questioners were more concerned with the high militia fines than the antiwar stand to which they professed attachment. The reply of the annual conference was, in fact, an implied rebuke. The teaching of our Savior, it stated, was that of nonresistance. "And when we go to musters we there learn the art of war, and the most appropriate method of shedding our fellow-creatures' blood."[42] Strangely enough, it seems to have occurred neither to those who framed the query nor to conference delegates that there was a third alternative: refusal to pay fines that went to the upkeep of a military institution and willingness to suffer the consequences of such refusal in confiscation of property or imprisonment. The Quakers had chosen this path. But, like the Mennonites, the Brethren regarded the fulfillment of the state's demands for money, even where the tax or fine was devoted to war purposes, as an obligation incumbent on the followers of a Christ who urged them to render unto Caesar his due.

Consideration of the militia question does not quite exhaust the peace matters which came before the annual conference during these years. In 1822 the resolution, mentioned above, forbidding Brethren to be present at the muster ground also banned attendance at Independence Day celebrations—obviously (though this is not stated explicitly) on the grounds that it was the celebration of a military vic-

[41] *MAM*, pp. 40, 41, 47, 48, 59, 70. See also Bowman, *Church of the Brethren and War*, pp. 104, 105.

[42] *MAM*, pp. 186, 187; Bowman, *Church of the Brethren and War*, pp. 105, 106.

tory. In 1836 a query was presented enquiring if Brethren who had served in the wars before joining the church might continue to draw government pensions. The answer was the same as that given later after the Civil War, when the question again became an urgent one: "Considered in union, that it can not be [right], according to the doctrine of Jesus." The annual conference of 1845, meeting as the war clouds grew darker with the approach of the Mexican conflict, felt obliged to reassert briefly the nonresistant position of the church.[43]

Finally, we may note the query sent to the conference of 1855: "Has a brother a right to defend himself with a deadly weapon at the appearance of being in danger?" This was not merely a theoretical question. Brethren were already beginning to move out into areas like the new Kansas Territory, where law and order were often in abeyance and the rule of the strongest prevailed. We can see the kind of background out of which such a query sprang by glancing at a letter written in 1853 to the editor of the new church paper, the Gospel-Visitor, by "your lonely brother," one Jacob Wigle pioneering out in Oregon Territory along with a handful of other Brethren. In the spring of 1852, he wrote, "I and two of my brothers set out for Oregon Territory. I was told before I started by [my uncle], that our crossing the plains was a denial of the faith, because we would have to travel under military form. Which we did not do; for we found no need of it, but the Indians were no hindrance to us, and rather entirely friendly to us."[44] Wigle and his brethren passed the test, but others might have to face more formidable enemies among the white desperadoes who roamed vast areas on the frontiers than the friendly Indians described in his letter. The temptation must, indeed, have been strong for the isolated pioneer to temporarily abandon his traditional pacifism and resort to the gun in defense of himself and his family. We cannot trace the struggles that must have occurred between the desire to ward off immediate danger to life and property and the loyalty to the teachings of peace learned in church and home. The conference delegates sent the questioners back to the gospel for an answer, to the words of Christ to his disciple Peter who had raised the sword in his defense. "Put up again thy sword into his place: for all they that take the sword shall perish with the sword" (Matt. 26:52).[45]

We do know, however, of one man from the Brethren milieu who actively preached peace in the frontier wilds. Adam Paine (ca. 1780-1832) had gone as a missionary to the Indians of what is today northern Illinois and southern Wisconsin. Whether he was actually a mem-

[43] MAM, pp. 47, 48, 85, 106; Bowman, Church of the Brethren and War, p. 105.
[44] Quoted in Mallott, Studies, p. 131.
[45] MAM, p. 145; Bowman, Church of the Brethren and War, pp. 105, 106.

ber of the Brethren church is not quite certain; he may possibly have been affiliated with the Evangelical Church, which Jacob Albright had founded in Pennsylvania in 1800. But, at any rate, he had come strongly under Dunker influence and accepted their faith in nonresistance. In July 1830 we find him preaching Christian pacifism at an intertribal meeting of the Indians, who had come together to hear the famous chief Black Hawk urge the formation of a great war federation against the whites. Paine spoke out against Black Hawk, telling the assembled braves of Christ as a man of peace who forbade his followers to shed blood and fight with earthly weapons. Paine won the day—but only temporarily, for soon afterward, in 1832, the Black Hawk War broke out; Paine himself, who did not cease to preach pacifism to white and Indian alike, was one of its early victims.[46]

This Indian war also tested the peace principles of the pioneer Brethren who had settled in Adams County (Ill.), not too distant from the scene of these troubles. Their leader, Elder George Wolfe, Jr., and other members of the congregation were drafted for service against the Indians. The pacifist principles of the Dunker church were not known in this new area as they were back in their home state of Pennsylvania, where they had lived for over a century; the local people were unsympathetic to a group which seemed unwilling to bear their share of danger at a time when life and property were threatened by the incursions of the redskin. Elder Wolfe, therefore, journeyed to the state capital to put their case before the governor, who received him in a friendly spirit. Wolfe emphasized the sterling pioneer qualities of the farmer Brethren and outlined the basis of their religious objection to war. If they could not enjoy freedom of conscience in their new home, he concluded, they would be forced to go back East where their objection was recognized by the state. The governor reassured him: "We need people like you to produce supplies for those who engage in the service." Thereupon he wrote out an exemption certificate on the spot for the elder and all the able-bodied members of his congregation. Unperturbed, evidently, by the implications of the governor's relegation of Brethren conscientious objectors to the role of food producers for the fighting men, Elder Wolfe returned home joyfully to his people.[47]

In most settled areas, at any rate, the Brethren appear to have encountered little difficulty from state or community in the exercise of their objection to military service. Like the Mennonites, they paid their

---

[46] J. H. Moore, *Some Brethren Pathfinders*, pp. 167-75.

[47] *Ibid.*, pp. 103, 104. Wolfe's congregation formed part of the so-called Far Western Brethren, who differed slightly in ritual from the rest of the church but did not quite form a separate sect.

411

militia fines dutifully, and their conscientious scruples were respected, if not always properly understood, in a society that by now had on the whole little use for an institution like the militia, which was rapidly falling into decay. The teaching of the church, as we have seen above, remained strictly nonresistant and cleaved to a Bible-centered pacifism deriving from the urge to follow the Christian way as nearly as sinful man was able. Periodically, from 1848 on, the annual conferences passed resolutions requiring those who underwent baptism—the symbol of the young adult's reception into the church community— to make a public declaration of their agreement with its principles of nonconformity to the world, which included nonresistance and the rejection of oaths.[48] Actually, this had probably been the practice of the church for many years before it was incorporated in a conference minute. Nevertheless, by the middle of the nineteenth century the church's peace witness had become formal, traditional, lacking the vital urge of the early years. As the historian of Brethren pacifism writes: "The Brethren during this period had no peace committee and no vigorous peace education program. There were no united efforts of the church to prevent the coming of war. War was wrong for them because Christ taught against it."[49] But little had been done to try to understand the full implications of a Christian rejection of war or to see that each generation renewed inwardly its church's traditional allegiance to absolute pacifism.

From the 1850's on, however, the German Baptist Brethren began to undergo a process of renovation. Progress was slow, especially at first. But several trends indicated that a turning point had been reached by the middle of the nineteenth century: the founding in 1851 of the first Brethren newspaper since the days of Christopher Saur by the former Lutheran immigrant minister and convert to Dunkerism, Henry Kurtz (1796-1874); the first shy recognition that within certain limits participation in political activities and public life might not be totally inconsistent with the vocation of a brother; the beginning in 1857 of the Sunday school movement within the church and a subsequent expansion of educational work on all levels from the 1860's on; and, finally, the inauguration of missionary activities a little later. The old rural isolation was just beginning to break down; gradually the Brethren were transformed from a sect of German-speaking farmers and frontiersmen into an English language bourgeois denomination

[48] *MAM*, pp. 97, 176, 227, 451. It is interesting to note that the old-time ban on wearing a moustache unless accompanied by a beard, which was a part of this nonconformity to the world, had seemingly arisen from the moustache's association with the army officer class: its adoption would have appeared as a concession to militarism. See Mallott, *Studies*, p. 250.

[49] Bowman, *Church of the Brethren and War*, p. 106.

412

(a process which has lasted into our own day). This change brought renewed life to the church and, also, new dangers to its spiritual vitality.[50] The church was slow in giving fresh forms to its traditional peace testimony, slower than in rejuvenating some other aspects of its witness. The experiences of the Civil War failed to move it more than temporarily, and, as we shall see in a later chapter, the first faint signs of renewal of Brethren pacifism appeared only in the years immediately prior to the outbreak of the European war.

We have spoken, in regard to the pacifism of the Brethren church, of eventual renewal which came late, indeed came fully only in our own day, but which finally arrived to work its effect. A similar renewal of a moribund witness, likewise slow in coming, has been observed in the case of both Quakers and Mennonites. We have now to consider a different phenomenon: the expiring pacifism of the Schwenkfelders, the smallest German-speaking peace sect of colonial times. (Its peace testimony in the post-Revolutionary era was, however, stronger than that of the very much larger and otherwise more vigorous Moravian church, the decline of whose pacifism has been discussed in chapter 7.)

The Schwenkfelders produced no literature on peace during the period following the Revolutionary War, but they still strictly maintained their traditional objection to participation in war and warlike preparations and enforced it on members with the threat of disownment. The teaching of the church, states article 8 of its constitution (published in German in 1851), has been that no one may take part in war or military matters "if he wishes to be a member of this church." The statement, drawing upon an earlier and undated minute, gives two reasons for the church's pacifism. In the first place, according to scripture, the warfare of the Christian may only be carried on in the realm of the spirit; secondly, we must obey the sixth commandment, which says: "Thou shalt not kill." It is interesting to note that, even though oathtaking is also forbidden them on Biblical grounds, members of the church are expressly permitted to hold public office on the grounds that such revered personages as Samuel, David, and Solomon had done so.[51] The pacifism of the Schwenkfelders is, indeed, more akin to the Quaker position than to that of the Anabaptist-Mennonite tradition, with which the group had been closely affiliated back in Europe.

There was probably little formal instruction of the younger generation of Schwenkfelders in the church's peace principles. That it some-

[50] *Ibid.*, pp. 102, 107. See also Mallott, *Studies, passim.*
[51] *Constitution of the Schwenkfelder Society,* p. 35.

times encountered difficulties in transmitting what had become to some extent a merely traditional belief is shown, for instance, in church conference minutes of 1828. In May there was brought forward the case of "some of our young people" ("der bedenkliche Zustand einiger unserer jungen Leute") who frequented the musterfield. Fathers of families and church elders were told that it was their obligation to remind the youth that all that had to do with war was contrary to the teachings of Christ and, consequently, to those of their own church. The following October, at a special meeting of heads of families, a resolution was passed that young men who mustered with the militia should be informed in future that, if they continued to do so, they would be considered as having thereby placed themselves outside the church community.[52] However, the pacifism of the Schwenkfelders seems by then to have lost much of its vitality; it was to be abandoned almost wholly by the beginning of the twentieth century.

II

The German-speaking groups that we have been considering hitherto in this chapter were almost exclusively rural people, who felt ill at ease in the more cosmopolitan and cultured milieu of the towns and cities where the English language held sway. On the other hand, the most important pacifist sect among the English-speaking inhabitants of the country, the Society of Friends, though it did contain a strong rural element which made its weight felt from time to time in the counsels of the Society, had drawn much of its support and its inspiration from urban members. Although the golden age of urban Quaker culture, which was exemplified by the Philadelphia grandees of the first half of the eighteenth century, had passed without hope of return, Friends remained to some extent a city-oriented community. We have now, however, to consider two small pacifist groups which arose among the English-speaking population of the countryside yet never succeeded in spreading to the towns. We have already said something about the Rogerenes of Connecticut, who date back to the late seventeenth century; and we must now look, too, at the Osgoodites of New Hampshire, who sprang up only after the American Revolution. Both remained extremely small in numbers and died out within the last century.

By the end of the eighteenth century the Rogerenes were confined almost exclusively to the area around New London. The persecution

[52] Minutes of the General Conference 1782-1890, MS, Schwenkfelder Library, Pennsburg, pp. 101-3.

414

they had endured during their early years had been prolonged for a century or so but by now had become a thing of the past; the farmers and small craftsmen and traders who made up the Rogerene church community were respected by their neighbors as good solid citizens. The middle years of the nineteenth century saw the departure of a number of the sect's members for the West during the widespread exodus in which most farming areas of New England shared. No new churches were set up by the emigrants, and those who remained began to dwindle in numbers.

The Rogerenes, though keen pamphleteers, were poor record keepers. But we do know something of their resistance to compulsory militia service during the first half of the nineteenth century. "We are not found in uniform," states an early nineteenth-century Rogerene tract, "for we were not trained to war . . . those who come under the new covenant are taken from protecting themselves or property by the law; and from making any corporal resistance."[53]

Their conscientious scruples, however, were not officially recognized by the laws of the state of Connecticut; they were, like the Quakers with whom they shared many beliefs and attitudes, unwilling to purchase exemption by the payment of the statutory fine. In January 1810, Alexander Rogers, a descendant of the sect's founder, published a leaflet entitled "The Subscriber's Petition to His Countrymen for His Rights and Privileges," in which he recorded the reasons why Rogerenes objected to the payment of commutation money. Rogers was by then a very old man—in his eighty-third year, he tells us. His protest was evoked by the summoning of his under-age son to appear for militia service. Evidently, in his younger days the old man, whose memories extended back to the days of persecution, had himself refused to serve or to pay the subsequent fine. He writes: "I am once more called to suffer for conscience's sake, in defence of the gospel of Christ; on the account of my son . . . in that it is against my conscience to send him into the train-band." As a consequence of his refusal, the authorities had seized and sold "my only cow that gave milk for my family . . . which circumstance, together with the infirmity of old age, has prevented my making my usual defence at such occasion." Instead, he had decided to publish this petition in defense of his rights and to warn "his fellow countrymen" that God would not allow in-

---

[53] *The Battle-Axe*, pp. 11, 18. The authors of this curious tract, an attack on the conventional denominations of New England and on the connection existing there between church and state, were three members of the Waterous family: Timothy, Sr. (who was chiefly responsible), Timothy, Jr., and Zachariah. It was first published in 1811 and printed on a small press operated by the family.

justice to be committed with impunity.[54] The document breathes an atmosphere quite different from the otherworldly spirit of passive disobedience that we find in the statements of the German peace sects. The old man is a stickler for his freeman's rights, and among these he obviously numbers the right of conscientious objection.

The main source for nineteenth-century Rogerene antimilitarism is to be found in the unpublished autobiography of Jonathan Whipple (1794-1875), of Mystic (Conn.). Stonemason and builder by profession, and teacher of the deaf by avocation, Whipple earned a high reputation among his neighbors for probity in business dealings and among reformers for his wide interest in the philanthropies of the day. The Rogerenes, indeed, did not practise secluded nonconformity to the world but, so far as their scanty numbers permitted, entered wholeheartedly into such causes as temperance, abolition, and the peace movement.[55] Whipple was only 18 when he first received the summons to serve in the militia. "From childhood," he tells us, "I knew it to be wicked to kill human beings. I had been taught that by my parents. And after I became of suitable age to read, and understand what I read, I found that the New Testament scriptures taught the same." It was the period of the War of 1812, and the military authorities, especially in the seaboard areas, were alert to the dangers of enemy attack. For Whipple, however, "the Britons seemed as much like my brothers as my own countrymen did. . . . And . . . I had no more right to kill them." In 1814 recruiting in the district was active, and a serious effort was made to force all to serve in the militia who had previously escaped the net. Among a number whose scruples were not so conscientious, the Rogerene young men were called to account. So we find Whipple and the others, accompanied by their fathers, "who felt a great interest in the cause . . . and spoke in our behalf," appearing before what was, in effect, an informal military tribunal and stating to the officers the grounds of Rogerene pacifism. "After hearing our excuse, said the authority, 'Friends, your excuse is quite different from any we have heard today.'" Their cases were therefore deferred, and, in fact, they heard nothing further. Later, says Whipple, they learned that one of their neighbors, a major in the militia, had advised his fellow officers: "You can do nothing with them, but make trouble for yourselves, and for them. They never will do military duty. They are friendly good people. Let them alone."[56] So, once again, neighbor-

---

[54] John R. Bolles and Anna B. Williams, *The Rogerenes*, pp. 386, 387.
[55] Ellen Starr Brinton, "The Rogerenes," *NEQ*, XVI, no. 1 (March 1943), 16.
[56] Whipple, "Autobiography," microfilm of MS in S.C.P.C., pp. 32, 36, 66-69. See also the *Voice of Peace*, 1st ser., II, no. 6 (June 1873), 11.

ly friendliness and common sense triumphed over the letter of the law —a tribute to the unmilitary spirit displayed by countryfolk in nineteenth-century America.

We have seen that the Rogerenes took the Quaker position of refusing to contribute money in lieu of military service, regarding compliance as inconsistent with upholding religious freedom, which in the eyes of both groups included the right to complete exemption. (Whipple, like many Quakers, also refused to pay military taxes.[57]) And each generation right up to, and even beyond, the Civil War had to face anew the problem of compulsory militia service.[58]

It is a long cry from the reform-minded Rogerenes ready to join with the world in promoting the kingdom of righteousness to the isolationist Osgoodites in the not too distant hills of southern New Hampshire. The sect derived its name from its founder Jacob Osgood (1777-1844), a semi-literate farmer; its adherents were mostly "simple, honest folk with little education."[59] Throughout its existence it remained confined to the area around the state capital at Concord. There in the township of Warner lived Osgood himself, and the one or two hundred families that he gathered around him were drawn from neighboring farms. Osgood was a seeker, whose consciousness of sin during a poverty-stricken boyhood and early strivings after a purer life had led him to pass unsatisfied from one religious group to another, from Baptists to Calvinists and on to Universalists, in order to find final rest and spiritual content in his own brand of creedless Christianity, founded on the gospel of love and the priesthood of all believers. Refusal to attend worship in an approved church and the holding of their own services in private homes led Osgood and his followers into conflict with church and state. Their leader's claim to powers of faith healing brought with it increased suspicion from the community (as well as added sanctity within the narrow circle of his own believers). Finally, eccentricities of dress—the plain dress of the women and the long unkempt hair of the menfolk—served to accentuate still further the sect's strangeness.

In the course of his spiritual pilgrimage Osgood came to adopt the

---

[57] Brinton, "The Rogerenes," *ibid.*

[58] E.g., we read in the *Non-Resistant and Practical Christian*, 13 May 1848, of Whipple's son, also called Jonathan, being ordered to report for "military service" and of his intention to refuse such service, or the payment of a fine, and to accept the consequences. His son-in-law, a merchant seaman, had also recently become a Rogerene. He had, therefore, resigned from the navy, intimating that he was ready to take a stand similar to young Jonathan's.

[59] See Kenneth Scott, "The Osgoodites of New Hampshire," *NEQ*, XVI, no. 1 (March 1943), 20-40.

pacifist viewpoint. "At length," he wrote, "God led me out of town meetings and trainings, but the churches were all in them, believing in politic religion, fighting and killing one another." Again, "after the brethren had forsaken all to follow Christ, they thought it wrong to train or to learn war, for they felt love to the children of men, and wanted to see them saved and not destroyed. . . . But they suffered under the yoke awhile, not knowing how they might be free." It is possible that his new-found pacifism derived from contacts with the Shakers, who had settled nearby at Canterbury. The inspiration for it was obviously drawn, too, from readings of the New Testament story. Whatever its origins, this pacifist stand involved the group in further trouble with the authorities whenever they were summoned to perform their annual service.

In the early 1820's, we learn, Osgood and his brethren were frequently imprisoned as conscientious objectors and their property, including valuable cattle, distrained for their refusal to pay militia fines when they were imposed. On one occasion, when their leader and several of his followers were haled before a local magistrate, Osgood informed the latter: "Christ has commanded me not to learn war, and beside I am a gospel preacher, and your law clears gospel preachers." When these pleas failed, Osgood (a little inconsistently, in view of the brethren's rigorous peace testimony, but perhaps merely as a practical move) claimed partial blindness in one eye as an excuse for not drilling, but the magistrate would not accept this excuse either unless Osgood's complaint were certified by the official doctor. "Brother Osgood then said, if I can't go to heaven without going through Dr. Lyman, I shan't go." A signed statement from the surgeon of the regiment in which Osgood had served before his conversion stating his incapacity for service for the rest of his life was likewise unsuccessful in moving the magistrate, who proceeded to sentence the men to fines and costs or jail. Although two chose to pay (evidently, there was no ruling on this matter among the Osgoodites, each acting according to his own conscience), Osgood and the rest went to jail for several months. "If one cent would clear him," Osgood had asserted, "he would not pay it, for he was not his own, he was bought with a price, and what they did to him they did to Christ and would have to answer to God for it."[60]

Osgood, it must be said, was distinctly unpacifistic in the readiness with which he prophesied the destruction of his oppressors and in the

[60] *The Life and Christian Experience of Jacob Osgood, with Hymns and Spiritual Songs*, pp. 9, 27-30. The book includes Osgood's unfinished autobiography, which was completed after his death by a disciple, Charles H. Colby.

joy he took when some natural calamity came to fulfill his threat. The misfortunes of himself and his followers were a frequent subject of the crude jingling verses he composed. Concerning his arrest and imprisonment on the occasion just described, he wrote:

> An officer and captain come,
> With letters took us from our farms;
> Nothing could lay unto our charge
> Except the law now of our God. . . .
>
> Three holy prophets of the Lord
> Were put in jail for serving God;
> Our confidence was firm and strong
> Because we knew we'd done no wrong.[61]

Osgood died in 1844. It seems as if he and his followers enjoyed a period of peace from their militia sufferings during the latter years of his life. His sect lingered on for a number of decades with his successor, Nehemiah Ordway, inheriting his bard's mantle. The songs and hymns composed by the two men, though they have no value whatsoever as poetry, are of interest insofar as they reveal the strong animus which these back-country farmers felt against the rich, against townsmen and the educated classes and politicians, and against all lawyers and representatives of officialdom. From the city came taxes and oppressive militarism. In the Civil War these feelings not only reinforced the religious pacifism of the Osgoodites but led them to oppose abolitionism and the Lincoln administration as forces from outside, forces they did not properly understand, which threatened to disturb their rural peace.

> The Lincoln party now should fight alone,
> And with their own brave hands the South put down.
> > They made the war, we know,
> > And for it let them go,
> > And to the people show
> > What they can do.[62]

Their rural radicalism was indeed unharnessed; it was a movement of inchoate protest which threw up no leadership capable of expanding it into a vigorous force. These uneducated farmers felt instinctively the wrongness of war and suspected—not without reason—that social injustice and the spirit of war were rooted in the existing governmental structure. But they could only express their feelings groping-

---

[61] *Ibid.*, p. 95. [62] *Ibid.*, p. 123.

ly and often with misdirected zeal against the wrong objects. The sect had no future (as it had little past), but its challenge, upheld with some courage, deserves at least brief mention in a history of American pacifism.

The Disciples of Christ were never a peace church—at least not in the same sense as the Quakers or the German sectaries considered in the preceding pages were. But the consistent, though limited, pacifism of their founder, Alexander Campbell (1788-1866), and of some of his closest collaborators in the work of the church, make it appropriate to deal with their peace views in this chapter.

The Disciples had gradually crystallized as a separate group under Campbell's leadership in the late 1820's and during the thirties when they united with the majority of the loosely organized "Christian" churches, which had been formed under the inspiration of Barton W. Stone. The new church laid great emphasis upon the New Testament as the source of all that was necessary for the Christian life and endeavored to create a community of believers modeled strictly on the pattern of the apostolic church. Their pacifism, indeed, formed part of their "restitutionism." This creedless Biblicist faith, together with the emotionalism and lack of a learned ministry which were also hallmarks of the early Disciples, was especially well adapted to become a religion of the frontier; in turn, the conditions of life on the frontier, where the Disciples won numerous converts, helped to shape the tenets of the young church.

Campbell began to concern himself early in his career with the problem of war. There was little in his Ulster Presbyterian background, or in the Baptist associations which he contracted after his arrival in America in 1809, that was likely to lead him to the espousal of the pacifist position. But from the time he began to edit the *Christian Baptist* in 1823, we find him taking a clear, if still only vaguely formulated, antiwar line. The chief source of his pacifism during this period was his reading of the New Testament, and of the Sermon on the Mount in particular. Indeed, there was something in Campbell's very temperament, peaceful and conciliatory even to the point of compromise, that was naturally drawn to the nonresistant gospel. One of his early biographers relates that he never carried a weapon on his numerous missionary journeys, which often took him through parts of the country infested by robbers and marauders. "It is the carrying of arms that creates the idea of the possession of money and invites attack," said Campbell in explanation, "but the being without arms has the directly contrary effect, and I am persuaded that many persons lose their lives simply from carrying arms."[63] In addition to the New Testament influence and this natural sympathy for the way of peace, a recent writer on Campbell has detected elements of eighteenth-century rationalism in his pacifism, the feeling that war is an irrational and stupid method of settling conflicts that might be solved by peaceful means such as international arbitration.[64]

In the mid-1830's a new influence made itself felt in Campbell's thinking on the subject of war: that of the organized peace movement. Campbell read the antiwar tracts of Thomas S. Grimké and Jonathan Dymond and other publications of the British and American Peace Societies (some of which will be discussed in the next section of this book), and his ideas became more well-rounded and took on clearer shape. Henceforth, in his writings and preaching "he used the arguments and literature of the peace crusade freely" when broaching the problems of war and peace.[65] Yet there remained serious defects in Campbell's position as a pacifist that in part (though not wholly) explain why he failed to carry the church he had founded along with him.

First of all, there was his attitude in regard to two issues intimately linked with the problem of peace. Campbell, despite his rejection of defensive wars, approved the application of the death penalty in a Christian society, and he also gave qualified approval to—or, perhaps it would be fairer to say, he only very mildly dissented from— the institution of slavery as it existed in his day. Always a supporter of colonization and an opponent of abolitionism, he wobbled between a personal disapproval of slaveholding—partly on grounds of its inexpediency—and the view that the "peculiar institution" was not, even in modern America, a contradiction of the Christian religion. In the 1850's he was to defend compliance with the Fugitive Slave Law.[66]

The issue of capital punishment is perhaps even more directly bound up with the problem of war and peace. Campbell's position here is similar to the view (to be discussed later) of the right wing of the American Peace Society, or to that of Francis Wayland, for instance, whose *Elements of Moral Science* Campbell used as a textbook in his classes at Bethany College.[67] In 1846 Campbell published a long article in his *Millennial Harbinger* entitled "Is Capital Punishment sanctioned by Divine Authority?," later reprinting it in pamphlet form.

[63] Robert Richardson, *Memoirs of Alexander Campbell*, II, 662, 663.
[64] Harold L. Lunger, *The Political Ethics of Alexander Campbell*, pp. 262, 263.
[65] *Ibid.*, pp. 242-46, 257.
[66] Lunger, *Political Ethics*, chap. XIII; Richardson, *Memoirs*, II, 189, 531-33.
[67] Lunger, *Political Ethics*, p. 289.

In it he took issue with the majority of his fellow pacifists, who believed God could never sanction the taking of human life under any circumstances. "Wars might cease and universal peace spread its halcyon wings over the earth," he told them, "and still the murderer be rightfully, and by the supreme authority in the state, put to death." The punishment of the most heinous crimes by execution was not incompatible with "the argument of settling national controversies by another way than by war." Reformation was not the sole object of punishment; in front of it Campbell placed the protection of the state and its citizens. "A sentence of perpetual confinement is not an adequate security against a murderer, in any view that can be taken of it. Society demands a higher pledge of safety—a more satisfactory guarantee. It demands the life of the murderer." To support his claim that the scriptures nowhere prohibit the taking of life for the crime of murder, Campbell resorted, as in his discussion on slavery, to the Old Testament rather than to the New, from which at the same time he drew inspiration for his international pacifism. "By the simple device of interpreting an Old Testament command as part of the immutable moral law," writes Lunger, "he was able to justify the use of Old Testament norms under the Christian dispensation."[68] Campbell concluded his article almost defiantly with an appeal to philanthropic and Christian opinion to support the efforts of state governments "to exterminate the crime of murder by a firm, persevering execution of the murderer according to the Divine precept."[69]

A second weakness in Campbell's peace position, in addition to his ambivalent attitude toward slavery and capital punishment—ambivalent, that is, in view of his decided advocacy of absolute pacifism—lay in his failure to integrate this pacifism with the main body of the teachings which he left as a legacy to his church. His pacifism remained a very personal faith, as it did with those other early Disciple leaders who shared it, and they failed to transmit it to the mass of the membership. This would have been difficult anyhow in view of the very loose congregational organization given to the new denomination, whereby within certain limits each church was, as it were, master in its own house. It would have been difficult, too, for Campbell and his pacifist colleagues to have imposed their position on the whole body when, in the 1840's and 1850's, the Disciples were already attracting an increasing number of substantial middle-class people, prominent men in their local communities who would look askance

[68] *Ibid.*, p. 241. See also all of chap. XIV.
[69] Alexander Campbell, *Popular Lectures and Addresses*, pp. 314-18, 333, 334, 340.

at such an unpopular minority opinion. When we further consider that the Disciples had quite a strong following in the South and that the church's main strength lay in the states along each side of the Mason-Dixon line, it becomes clear that it would in any case have been beyond its leaders' powers to have created a peace sect out of the burgeoning new bourgeois denomination.

In the same year that he had defended capital punishment, Campbell issued his first uncompromising statement in support of Christian pacifism. The Mexican War was already on, and he evidently felt a need to clarify his position to the readers of his journal, the *Millennial Harbinger*.[70] It was not that he wished to discuss the rights and wrongs of the existing conflict; rather, he would confine himself, he told his readers, to the abstract question of Christian pacifism. Curiously, in view of his use of arguments drawn from the Old Testament to defend contemporary slaveholders and the death penalty, Campbell rejects outright using them in the case of war. "We can justify many of the Old Testament wars," he writes, "on as good and relevant grounds as we justify polygamy, divorce, and certain forms of slavery, because there was no separate and spiritual community erected on earth from Adam to the last Pentecost."[71] As we might expect, the positive case against participation in war, wars of defense as well as wars of aggression, was based primarily on the Sermon on the Mount, which Campbell describes as "an exponent of the Savior's mind and will on the subject of war." However, although in one place he states it to be "the inevitable conclusion" of Christ's words that his servants should not fight, "even in a defensive war," yet toward the end of his article he appears to falter. Answering the objection that, even if as Christians we are perhaps called upon to be nonresistant in our personal relations, duty to the state nevertheless requires us to defend it by arms from attack, he remarks merely that this is "a grave question, and must be carefully considered."[72]

It was not until the war was over, however, that Campbell, in his "Address on War" delivered at the Lyceum at Wheeling (Va.) in the middle of 1848, made his principal contribution to the literature of

[70] From the outset Campbell had included brief items in his *Millennial Harbinger* expressing a pacifist viewpoint. E.g., in 1st ser., V, no. 7 (July 1834), 306-9, he had reprinted an article from the *Moral Lyceum* based on Dymond and Clarkson which outlined the case for Christian pacifism and for the refusal of the early church to fight. Campbell adds the comment: "To this we say, Amen!"

[71] Later, in his Wheeling "Address" of 1848, he was to use a telling phrase to describe the role of the ancient Jewish warmakers: they acted, he says, as "God's sheriff to punish nations" (*Millennial Harbinger*, 3rd ser., V, no. 7 [July 1848], 383). This commission no longer held for the followers of Christ.

[72] *Millennial Harbinger*, 3rd ser., III, no. 11 (Nov. 1846), 638-42.

pacifism. The speech, which was printed first in his *Millennial Harbinger* and subsequently reprinted many times, was at least until quite recently "still used by peace propagandists";[73] for it is, indeed, an effective piece of work woven together into a convincing argument, though decidedly too verbose to suit today's taste. It opens with the question: "Has one Christian nation a right to wage war against another Christian nation?" Since, in fact, no country at present is properly Christian, Campbell goes on, the query must be rephrased more exactly: "May a Christian community, or the members of it, in their individual capacities, take up arms at all, whether aggressively or defensively, in any national conflict?" This, we see, is the question to which he had avoided giving an unequivocal answer a couple of years earlier. Now he replies with a decided negative.

In the first place, it is impossible to distinguish properly between an aggressive and a defensive war, since "a mere grammatical, logical, or legal quibble, will make any war either aggressive or defensive, just as the whim, caprice, or interest of an individual pleases." Secondly, being expressly forbidden to fight in his own defense, the Christian must, if he is to be consistent, likewise refrain from killing in defense of sovereign or country. "How could such a one enlist to fight the battles of a Caesar, a Hannibal, a Tamerlane, a Napoleon, or even a Victoria?" (We must note, however, that Campbell is careful to state more than once his view that taking human life is not forbidden by the scriptures in all circumstances.) Much of the above argument was obviously derived from the literature of the peace movement, as was a great deal that Campbell had to say in his "Address" on war's folly and irrationality and the horrors, physical and moral, of the battlefield ("these all say to the Christian, how can you become a soldier?"), as well as on the need for providing an alternative to the war method in the shape of international arbitration and universal disarmament. Sometimes, the utilitarian in Campbell, measuring war by the happiness of the greatest number and finding it wanting, seems to take precedence over the simple follower of the Sermon on the Mount, as when he writes: "The right to take away the life of the murderer does not of itself warrant war, inasmuch as in that case none but the guilty suffer; whereas in war the innocent suffer not only with, but often without the guilty. The guilty generally make war and the innocent suffer its consequences." On other occasions, however, his viewpoint is rigidly New Testament in its insistence on a literal adherence to Christ's injunctions in regard to nonresistance.[74]

73 W. E. Garrison and A. T. DeGroot, *The Disciples of Christ*, p. 335.
74 *Millennial Harbinger*, 3rd ser., V, no. 7 (July 1848), 361, 362, 364-72, 374-

Campbell's "Address" is a forthright declaration, but it came a little late. As Lunger has written: "He deferred discussion of war when the issue was a live one, and returned to it only when the crisis was past."[75] Campbell himself appears to have had some misgivings on this score, and he expressed them toward the end of his "Address,"[76] regretting that a word spoken earlier might not have saved a few lives by keeping some from volunteering who were later to be killed. In extenuation, however, for having remained virtually silent throughout most of the war period in regard to pacifism's political implications, he pleaded reluctance to get involved in party issues (Campbell's general attitude toward political life varied between the lukewarm and the positively hostile); between the lines we may surely read his only half-submerged sympathies with the Southern viewpoint which had brought the war on.

After the Wheeling "Address" Campbell again remained silent on the problems of peace until after the outbreak of the Civil War, when he and his pacifist and near-pacifist colleagues were to take a firm stand against the war tide. During the Mexican War one other Disciples leader had ranged himself squarely alongside Campbell in defense of the pacifist position. This was Benjamin Franklin (1812-1878), who was long active in the Midwest as a preacher and a religious editor. Early in 1847 in the midst of the Mexican War, Franklin, prompted perhaps by the lead given by Campbell, opened the columns of his monthly *Western Reformer*, which he was then editing in Milton (Iowa), to a discussion of pacifism. "The great question," he wrote, "is whether *all war* is not at variance with the teachings of Jesus Christ. Can Christians in any case engage in what is called 'civil war,' righteously?" After thoroughly examining the question, he went on, "we are compelled to say, that our strongest impression is that they *may not.*" He shared Campbell's diffidence about broaching such a con-

---

79, 383-85. The whole "Address" is reprinted in Campbell's *Popular Lectures and Addresses*, pp. 342-66.

[75] Lunger, *Political Ethics*, p. 250. See pp. 247-58 for a discussion of Campbell's attitude during the Mexican War and immediately thereafter. See also David Edwin Harrell, Jr., *Quest for a Christian America*, pp. 140-44. Roland H. Bainton (*Christian Unity and Religion in New England*, p. 163) has described Campbell's pacifism as blending "a strict New Testament literalism resting on the Sermon on the Mount and the rationalism of the Enlightenment, which deemed it more prudent to obtain peace by purchase than to have recourse to war." Except for the apolitical utterances of a few individuals like Campbell and a protest against the war by some 150 members in New England, "the Disciples of Christ," writes Clayton Sumner Ellsworth, "were silent as a church" ("The American Churches and the Mexican War," *AHR*, XLV, no. 2 [Jan. 1940], 311).

[76] *Millennial Harbinger, ibid.*, p. 385.

troversial issue in time of war and, like him, stressed that his approach was exclusively on the theoretical level. His views, which indeed add little to what Campbell was saying, except perhaps for a greater emphasis on readiness to suffer as the Christian alternative to violent resistance on a national as well as an individual level, Franklin had expressed in a couple of brief articles.[77] Thereafter, he confined himself to printing the opinions of his readers for and against nonresistance.[78]

III

The founders of those communitarian experiments in America which included pacifism among their tenets—our next topic—were all (with the exception of Adin Ballou of Hopedale) European-born. While Campbell's church of the Disciples soon shed its sectarian features and expanded into one of the bigger religious denominations in the country, the communitarians remained very small in numbers and continued to a greater or lesser degree to be cut off from the society around them by the peculiarities of their beliefs and practice, and frequently by their hostility toward the "world" and by barriers of language as well. This isolation, however, assisted the preservation of the pacifism of their first leaders as much as the rapid growth and looseness of organization had hindered its adoption in the case of the Disciples.

The largest and most stable of the American communitarian groups was the United Society of Believers, commonly known as the Shakers. At its height around the second quarter of the nineteenth century, this group numbered about 6,000 members in eighteen societies situated in the states of Maine, New Hampshire, Massachusetts, Connecticut, New York, Ohio, and Kentucky.

The conclusion of the American Revolution had coincided with the end of the first epoch of Shaker history, for in 1784 their founder, "Mother" Ann Lee, had died. Three years later, in 1787, the first Shaker commune was founded at New Lebanon (N.Y.) under the inspiration of the sect's leader, "Father" Joseph Meacham (d. 1796), who had

---

[77] Western Reformer, V (1847), no. 4 (Feb.), 222-24; no. 5 (March), 310-13.

[78] Ibid., V (1847), no. 7 (May), 421, 422; no. 8 (June), 485-88; no. 10 (Aug.), 612-15; no. 11 (Sept.), 667, 668; VI (1848), no. 3 (Jan.), 163-67. The war generated quite an extensive discussion of the pacifist issue among the membership. Harrell (Quest for a Christian America, p. 144) cites the debate between two Disciples, which was carried on in the Gospel Proclamation, published at St. Clairsville (Ohio), in a series of articles beginning in December 1847 and continuing well into 1849. Arguments on each side were based primarily on the New Testament, with special attention given to the question whether there were Christian soldiers in apostolic times.

426

followed the Englishman James Whittaker, "Mother" Ann's immediate successor in the leadership. Now in a few years the whole society was "gathered into Society Order": that is to say, a communitarian economic organization was set up wherever there were adherents, and the familiar pattern of Shaker communalism was established for good. If Mother Ann had given the original spiritual impetus and enthusiasm to set the sect going, it is to the American-born "Father" Joseph that the credit is due for giving the United Society a firm organizational structure. From the beginning the Shakers, as we have seen, had professed pacifism among their religious beliefs, and this view had been among the causes of their early sufferings. Now, as part of his work of organizing the new church, Father Joseph drew up a statement briefly summarizing the Shaker peace testimony, probably the first they made on the subject. It is worth quoting:

> As we have received the grace of God in Christ, by the gospel, and are called to follow peace with all men, we cannot, consistent with our faith and conscience, bear the arms of war, for the purpose of shedding the blood of any, or to do anything to justify or encourage it in others. But if they require, by fines or taxes of us, on that account, according to their laws, we may, for peace sake, answer their demands in that respect, and be innocent so far as we know at present. . . . We believe we are free by the gospel, and that the time is near when others will be so far enlightened that they will be willing to exempt us.[79]

And so in this early period we find Shakers of military age dutifully paying their militia fines when required to attend the muster. On 10 September 1778—to give just one example—a manuscript Shaker journal records the meeting of two of the New Lebanon elders with a group of militia officers to hand over the sum of £10. 8s. in cash "for fines of 26 men for non-appearance Muster Day."[80] There was, therefore, as yet no clash with the law in states like New York where Shakers were not granted complete exemption.

Although at the beginning Shakers saw no objection to paying commutation money in lieu of military service, they always regarded it as incompatible with their peace principles for any member to accept a pension from the government which had been earned by military service before joining the United Society. Many of the early Shakers were veterans of the Revolutionary War, and thereafter from time to time a

---

[79] Edward Deming Andrews, *The People called Shakers*, p. 212.
[80] Daryl Chase, "The Early Shakers: An Experiment in Religious Communism," Ph.D. diss. (1936), U. of Chicago, pp. 188, 189.

former soldier threw in his lot with them. To continue to draw a pension (which presumably would have gone into the common fund) was tantamount, in the Shakers' view, to taking blood money.

The matter first came up in 1792 when one Amos Butrick, a member of the Shirley (Mass.) community, returned his pension allowance after consulting with Father Joseph about how he should proceed. Butrick's conduct aroused the amazement of the state treasury officials in Boston, who were only with difficulty prevailed upon to take the money back.[81] Later, when pleading with state legislatures for legal exemption, the Shakers were to point to this self-denial as proof of the consistency of their pacifism, and they presented at various times calculations of the amount of money saved the government by their conscientious scruples, a sum running to many thousands of dollars. The argument, directed as it was to the taxpayers' economic interests, was certainly a shrewd one.[82]

There is not much to record of the Shaker peace witness until we come to the War of 1812. The Eastern societies were little troubled with the problem of military service during the war years; they paid their fines as before, where they were not expressly exempted from doing so by state law. But in the new communities in the West, which had emerged only recently as a result of Shaker proselytizing in areas affected by the Kentucky revival at the beginning of the century, the war brought renewed trials. The new Shaker settlements in Kentucky, Ohio, and Indiana, had already had to face the same kind of hostility from the local populace that their Eastern brethren had suffered in Mother Ann's day. Luckily, the group was ably led by men of outstanding caliber like the former Presbyterian minister, Richard McNemar (1770-1839), who had been won over to Shakerism in the course of the revival. But widespread ignorance of the new group's beliefs on the part of authorities and populace alike, along with the threat of Indian attack, presented the Shakers with serious problems in living out their pacifism.

The community at Busro (Ind.), which had only been started in 1810, suffered the most. It was situated on the very edge of white settlement and was exposed to Indian attack when hostilities broke out toward the end of 1811 between the Americans and the Indian chief Tecumseh. However, an Indian occupation of their village proved to

[81] John Whiteley (ed.), "Letters & Documents respecting the Conscription, Arrest & Suffering of Horace S. Taber, A Member of the United Society, Shirley, Mass.," MS in Western Reserve Historical Society Library (Cleveland, Ohio), pp. 100-103.

[82] Anna White and Leila S. Taylor, *Shakerism, Its Meaning and Message*, pp. 175-78.

be a much less unpleasant experience for the Shakers than the depredations inflicted when troops commanded by the governor of the Indiana territory and future U.S. President, General William Henry Harrison, were subsequently quartered with them. The Indians had respected the peaceful demeanor and friendly attitude of the Shakers and were reported to have later told an inquirer why they had done them no harm: "We—we noble warriors! think we go fight people that hurt nobody? No. We too noble nation for that."[83] But the seizure of livestock and supplies by the American troops who moved in after the uncivilized Indians and the attempts to impress Shaker menfolk into the fighting forces (stopped finally by General Harrison who, instead, arranged for them to act as medical orderlies for the troops stationed in their village)—along with the hostility of the local people who, because Shakers had been treated well by the Indians, now suspected them of connivance with the enemy and the danger, too, of further trouble with the Indians—all contributed to the community's decision to abandon the settlement and to retire as soon as they could to the comparative safety of their brethren in Ohio and Kentucky.

One of their number perhaps expressed the confused feelings of his brothers and sisters when he wrote around this time:

War—with the British and Indians—was the general talk in the country. To which our faith and practice was entirely opposed. And of course we need not build forts, unless we intend to defend them. And our settlement was almost the very frontier. All these circumstances (and a great many more) had their bearing to our general center—which was that we had better abandon the ground in peace than to stay and fight for it, or even to run the risk of being insulted and abused by militia troops—or of being massacred by the Indians.[84]

The withdrawal, however, meant "a journey of several 100 miles thru' the wilderness, under great sufferings and difficulty," and it entailed, too, considerable financial loss.[85] The Shakers returned to Busro after the war was over, but, owing to an unhealthy climate, the settlement never prospered and was finally closed in 1827—the first Shaker community to be dissolved.

[83] Quoted in the *Calumet*, I, no. 2 (July-Aug. 1831), 47. The source is Shaker. The story was used as an illustration in the literature of the peace movement. See, e.g., Cyrus Yale's address to the Hartford Peace Society in 1832, *War Unreasonable and Unscriptural*, p. 18.

[84] Quoted in J. P. MacLean, *Shakers of Ohio*, p. 289.

[85] *A Declaration of the Society of People, (commonly called Shakers,)* (Albany, 1815), p. 13; Charles Edson Robinson, *A Concise History of the United Society of Believers*, pp. 74-76.

We know that some of the Shakers in the other Western communities of Kentucky and Ohio were called up for military service during the course of the war and that they refused. Most of them, however, were either left alone or fined; a few were briefly imprisoned for objecting to pay the fine. The practice probably varied according to the understanding of the local military authorities.[86]

Toward the end of the War of 1812 a significant shift became apparent in the Shaker attitude toward contracting out of militia service by means of a fine. The causes of this change, which may have been some years in the making, are not altogether clear. The approval given by "Father" Joseph Meacham to payment of militia fines in the statement quoted above implies that the decision was not a final one, that the church was still striving for light on the subject. The influx of American citizens into the Society—some of whom, like the influential Issachar Bates, had taken part in the Revolutionary struggle (though they had renounced the way of force when becoming Shakers) and were firm believers in the rights of free-born Americans—may have inclined the Society as a whole to extend its concept of religious liberty to include the right to complete exemption from military service. The war years certainly strengthened the Shakers' desire to be free of all possibility of contributing even indirectly to the work of killing; this is the reason the New York Shakers give in their *Declaration* of 1815 for their change of attitude. Finally, we can perhaps detect Quaker influence in the adoption by the Shakers of a similar objection to accepting fining as a way out of military requirements.

In some states, indeed, the Shakers had been explicitly exempted both from service in the militia and from the payment of commutation money. Such was the case in Massachusetts, which as early as 1793 had freed "those of the religious denominations of Quakers and Shakers" from all such obligations; a similar law had been enacted in 1808 in New Hampshire, too.[87] In the other states where there were Shaker communities fines, as we have noted, were paid in the case of those called up for muster; since their first settlement New York Shakers calculated that they had paid about $4,000 in militia fines.[88] On 2 February 1815 the two New York societies at New Lebanon and Watervliet, however, combined in issuing a joint *Declaration* addressed to the state legislature in Albany, setting forth the general grounds of

---

[86] Robinson, *A Concise History*, p. 103; Caroline B. Piercy, *The Valley of God's Pleasure*, pp. 73, 229.

[87] *A Declaration of the Society of People, (commonly called Shakers,)* (Hartford, 1815), pp. 21, 22.

[88] *Ibid.* (Albany, 1815), p. 15.

their conscientious objection and, in addition, stating their unwillingness now to accept any alternative to military service, whether in the form of fines or buying substitutes or in any other way. This document inaugurated the campaign the Shakers were to carry on for several decades in an effort to get legal recognition of their new found absolutist position in the states where it had not yet been given. The New York Shakers' *Declaration* of 1815 was also issued in a slightly different version in Hartford (Conn.), since the Connecticut brethren were in a similar situation in regard to militia service.[89]

The document is worth some consideration, for it contains the most eloquent and the best formulated statement of Shaker pacifism that was put out by the United Society. "Our objections," they stated, "are founded on a sense of duty to God, to ourselves and to our fellow creatures." In the first place, then, they believed that "divine revelation," the words and example of Christ and the early church, forbade the taking of human life. As for the fighting described in the Old Testament, "those wars, authorized under the dispensation of types and shadows, were figurative of the spiritual warfare of God's people against the corrupt and contentious passions of human nature, which must be subdued by and in every true follower of Christ." Christ had set up a new covenant for his people, abolishing at the same time "the law of types and shadows." This spiritualization of ancient Jewish history is, indeed, typical of the Shakers' mystical approach to religion.

Secondly, they devoted much space to upholding their claims to complete exemption from military service on the basis of "the Constitution and fundamental laws of our country," which secured religious liberty and freedom of conscience. These in turn were derived from "the natural rights of man." By a written covenant those who joined the Shaker community had pledged their lives and property to God's service; they never interfered in political affairs, abstaining altogether from voting or officeholding. Therefore, they appealed now to the state legislators to be allowed to pursue their way of life in peace.[90] Lastly, the *Declaration* dwelt on the positive contribution made to society by the Shakers' communitarianism.

By following Christ's injunctions to use no violence against their fellow men, they were in fact, they maintained, rendering good service to their country, proving themselves more useful citizens than they would be if they had pitched their lives on a lower key. For not only were they attempting to live as virtuously as possible, but they were

[89] The Hartford version was dated 8 May 1815 and issued in the name of the elders and deacons of the society at Enfield.

[90] *A Declaration* (Albany, 1815), pp. 3-5, 8-20.

also helping to bring nearer the era of universal peace foretold in prophecy, when wars would cease altogether among men. "We believe, beyond all controversy, that God has called us to this very work; and that it is required of us to set the example of peace, and to maintain it at all hazards." They might appear in the eyes of the world a small and inconsiderable group to be making such lofty claims; "yet it ought to be remembered that every important dispensation of the work of God, always had a small beginning."[91]

The Shakers had remained a separated people, who kept themselves apart from the world. Coercive laws were necessary to govern "those who will not be governed by the law of Christ," though "a real conscientious man will render all the services he can to government, consistent with his duty to God, without the compulsion of human laws." It might be necessary, too, to defend a country from foreign invasion (though the Shakers were careful not to commit themselves too far here: a pacifist nation would find protection in God from internal or external enemies). However, the *Declaration* goes on,

As we are the subjects of the Kingdom of Christ, who have separated ourselves from the politics of earthly governments; we have therefore nothing to do with their protection and defence against foreign invasion. The only benefit we claim of the government is, protection against the abuses of those lawless members of society who violate its internal regulations. For this we pay liberally; and what more can justly be required of us? We are the friends of our country and its government; but we are also the friends of man: and the principles of true Christianity inculcate universal benevolence and good will to all the human family; therefore we cannot by a partial connection with one community, assist in the destruction of another.

Much of this argument is reminiscent of the Anabaptist-Mennonite position toward the state. Yet, in their civil rights arguments and in their respect for the American political system," founded on the most benign and liberal principles ever established on earth," the Shakers showed themselves more akin to the Quakers, taking in some ways an even more positive attitude toward the established government than the Society of Friends always did during this period.[92]

The parallel with the Quakers comes out even more forcefully when we look at the explanations which the Shakers gave of why they were now asking for complete exemption. They were against military conscription on principle, they said—even for those who were not con-

[91] *Ibid.*, pp. 6, 7.   [92] *Ibid.*, pp. 14, 15, 19.

scientiously opposed to war. No government had the right to force a man to learn to kill against his will.[93] If, moreover, the conscientious at least should certainly be given legal exemption, this right could not be bought for money. They had always been ready to give of their substance when this did not conflict with their duty to God and with their own consciences. They paid their taxes regularly and provided both money and labor to keep up the bridges and highways. They maintained their own poor even while contributing to the general poor rate. They had given generously to the relief of others in time of calamity. They related these matters, they added, not in order to boast, but because "we believe these things are not generally known and considered."

Into their argument they introduced, in addition, the concept of Shaker property being "consecrated property," dedicated exclusively to the service of the Lord. This claim differentiated them from the other peace sects, some of whom, they admitted, might be willing to purchase exemption by paying commutation money. Shakers, on the other hand, had "solemnly and conscientiously dedicated both themselves and all their property to God for religious and pious uses, and . . . take no part in the government and affairs of the world." Thus, the other peace sects "can never be justly said to stand in the same peculiar situation with us; as to the righteousness of their paying fines, it is not for us to decide; but while they possess each one his own private property and are laying up riches to bequeath to their natural posterity, . . . they fully demonstrate that they were never yet broken off from that order, and differ as widely from us as any other people in the world." This passage reflects clearly the otherworldly sectarian character of Shakerism, its almost vocational approach to pacifism, which the rationalist and humanitarian elements in its beliefs—its consistent toleration of other opinions and its staunch advocacy of civil rights for all—tend to obscure.

Shaker pleas for exemption, we have seen, were founded on both a New Testament nonresistance and a modern-sounding belief in the natural rights of man and the constitutional rights of the American citizen. The recent war in which their country had become involved now brought home to them the implications of their previous practice when called up for service.

We have heretofore paid muster fines in time of peace, for peace' sake, being unwilling to make difficulty; altho' we have always remonstrated against it. But the war has materially altered our situa-

[93] *Ibid.*, p. 19.

433

tion in this respect. We cannot now do any thing of this nature, without directly supporting the cause of war and bloodshed; consequently we cannot proceed any further in this manner: for it is as decidedly against our consciences to procure a substitute, or pay an equivalent, as to render our personal services; since they equally promote the same cause.[94]

No immediate change in state law resulted from the *Declaration*. Early in the following year, therefore, the Watervliet society supplemented it with a further set of *Observations on the National and Constitutional Rights of Conscience, In Relation to Military Requisitions.* This document repeats for the most part the arguments used in the earlier pamphlet and endeavors as well to answer various objections, raised in the meantime, to fulfilling the Shakers' demands; but it is poorly arranged and repetitious, lacking the fluency and cogency of the *Declaration*.

The Shakers were by this time able to add Kentucky, "altho' particularly distinguished as a warlike state," to Massachusetts and New Hampshire as examples of states granting them complete exemption.[95] At last, in March 1816, the New York legislature passed a law freeing Shakers from all obligations under the militia law. The Shakers' good fortune did not last long, however, for two years later payment of commutation money was reimposed. This unfavorable development may have been the result, at least in part, of the hostility which a recent lawsuit (the Eunice Chapman case) involving the custodianship of some children in the Watervliet society had engendered against the Shakers in the minds of the general public. So the struggle was on again and was to continue without success through many decades. In 1824, after the introduction of new legislation confirming their liability to payments in lieu of service, with the money going now to help maintain the poor, the church leadership decided henceforth to transfer the young men of the New York societies to the Massachusetts communities as soon as they became liable for the militia.[96] In this way, a clash with the law on the subject of military service appears to have been once again avoided.

The New York Shakers, however, did not easily give up the fight. We find them again memorializing the state legislature at the beginning of 1826, reaffirming in general "our conscientious objections to the militia system" and protesting in particular the imposition of a

[94] *Ibid.*, pp. 12, 13, 15-17. The Shakers were mistaken, however, in thinking that the Society of Friends was in favor of paying militia fines.

[95] *Observations*, p. 16.

[96] Andrews, *The People called Shakers*, pp. 210, 212, 214.

fine for following their conscience. "Is it then reasonable that the whole society should be harassed and oppressed, year after year, for this pittance?" The new poor tax which conscientious objectors were required to pay was nothing "but muster fines in disguise," "a legal infliction of penalties as the forfeit or punishment for the exercise of conscience." What was the difference between their treatment of the conscientious objector and their treatment of the unconscientious evader when both alike were made to pay? Finally, the memorial called attention to the exodus of their young men from the state. "Their removal was a painful and afflicting event to the Society," but there was no other way "to avoid the oppression of the militia laws."[97]

The commonwealth of Massachusetts was the most consistently generous in its treatment of Shaker objectors. The new state of Maine, too, followed in the footsteps of its mother state in granting them the complete exemption which they sought. Connecticut had already done the same. In New Hampshire, where the Shaker position had seemed assured, a campaign was begun by hostile elements in 1816 and carried on for several years with the object of persuading the state legislature to withdraw its previous grant of complete exemption. The two Shaker communities in the state, at Canterbury and Enfield, composed a *Memorial* for presentation to the lawmakers, in which they outlined their case. They stated in it their conviction that their previous conduct had provided "a full proof of sincerity," which should be sufficient to convince the house of the indefensibility of restricting their rights.[98] A recent historian of the Shakers has called this *Memorial*, which was in fact based fairly closely on the New York *Declaration* of 1815, "an able and convincing presentation of the . . . Shaker views: . . . a strikingly logical statement of the futility of war."[99] It evidently convinced the New Hampshire legislators, for the law remained unchanged. Here, as in several other states, "the Shakers found good friends among the lawyers and lawmakers," who helped them to win support for their case.[100]

In Ohio the Shakers' old friend, General Harrison, who was then a member of the state legislature, was instrumental in getting that body to exempt Shakers from the statutory service in the militia in exchange for an equivalent amount of time to be put in on work on the public highways.[101] This concession, however, was no longer acceptable to

[97] *In Senate*, pp. 1-4, 6.
[98] *The Memorial of the Society of People of Canterbury, . . . and Enfield*, p. 2.
[99] Marguerite Fellows Melcher, *The Shaker Adventure* (1960 edn.), pp. 170, 171.
[100] *Ibid.*, p. 146.
[101] Robinson, *A Concise History*, p. 76.

the Shaker absolutists, and soon their crops and livestock began to be distrained for their failure to perform their obligations under the law. In 1818 the state legislature made the officers of the Shaker Communities responsible for collecting their members' militia fines and made the communal property liable to distraint for nonpayment. The group reacted at once with a sharply worded protest. This clause, which they attributed to the artifices of a clique of "military officers," they dubbed "evidently unscriptural, unreasonable, unjust and oppressive, and also directly opposed to the fundamental articles of the constitution of the United States and of this state." Moreover, it was aimed, they believed, at destroying their communal way of life.[102] These frontier Shakers, as one might expect, were no less insistent on their citizen rights than their Eastern brethren. In 1830, even, "the Shakers [in Ohio] prosecuted the constable and captain in action for trespass and damages"—but the judge dismissed the case.[103]

It is difficult, without combing through the voluminous manuscript records left by the various societies, to piece together the story of Shaker conscientious objection in the period between the War of 1812 and the Civil War. In the couple of states where Shakers were required to pay for the privilege of exemption—New York and Ohio—some kind of modus vivendi eventually seems to have been worked out. The United Society was entering the period of its greatest prosperity. Shakers were becoming economically affluent, even if their spiritual impetus was beginning to slow down. In some ways, as we have noted, their pacifism appears from the beginning as an outcome of their semi-monastic isolation from society at large. Celibacy and pacifism and community of goods hung together. "We oppose wars of households, and wars of nations," stated one of their sermons. "All wars are the results of lusts for land and for women. Those who marry will fight."[104] War was permissible in theory for those who had not made the great renunciation, who therefore remained on a lower plane than that of the full Christian dispensation.[105] Yet this sectarian attitude, more rigorous even than the Mennonite withdrawal from the life of the state, was mitigated in practice by increasing concern for the world which had been renounced. It is greatly to the credit of these native Americans, who had withdrawn into the security of their village communes, that they felt it incumbent upon themselves—and increasingly so, as the century developed and the earlier hostility between

102 *An Address, to the State of Ohio, Protesting against a certain clause of the Militia law, enacted by the Legislature, at their last session,* esp. pp. 3-7.
103 MacLean, *Shakers of Ohio,* p. 241.
104 Quoted in Mary Webb Gibson, *Shakerism in Kentucky,* p. 35.
105 William Alfred Hinds, *American Communities* (1961 edn.), p. 89.

436

sect and society diminished—to enter into the work of reforming that world from which they had fled, often in near despair of the possibility of its redemption. Thus, in striking contrast to the Mennonite and Brethren attitude of complete dissociation and to the aloofness of the Quakers during that period, we find Shakers actually participating in the work of the American peace movement from the 1820's on—as long, in fact, as the Shaker church still remained a vigorous organization. The Shakers' contribution was a small one because they were, after all, a small society; yet it witnessed to the outreaching spirit of their pacifist faith.

A specially significant contribution came in 1831 from the pen of the New Lebanon herbalist, Garret Lawrence, who in that year contributed anonymously to the American Peace Society's official journal, *Calumet*, an article under the title "Remarks on the Militia System by A Poor Man's Son." In it Lawrence made a forceful plea for the abolition of the militia system and for pacifism as ultimately the best guarantee of a nation's security. The article is marked by a vigorous social radicalism: the rich man's sons buy exemption so that the burden of militia service falls most heavily on the poor, who are least able to spare the time from their daily tasks.[106]

The same year also saw the publication of a much more ambitious work: *A Brief Illustration of the Principles of War and Peace*. The pseudonym "Philanthropos" hid the identity of the Watervliet elder, Seth Youngs Wells (d. 1847), a man of considerable education who had been a school principal in Albany before joining the Shakers— and not, as is sometimes stated, the authorship of William Ladd, who frequently used the same pseudonym.[107] The work runs to 112 pages and shows that Wells was well acquainted with the literature of both the British and American peace movements. The book attempts to prove the thesis that war not only is incompatible with Christianity but, even on the material level, does not profit a nation as much as a pacific policy. In drawing on the past for arguments to prove his case, the author shows himself master of much historical erudition. The fate of the empires of old, from Egypt and Assyria onward, illustrate, for him, the vanity of relying on military power, while instances where pacific, if not necessarily completely pacifist, policies have been adopted on a national scale prove the power of the peaceful way. Wells pleads for absolute pacifism only by implication: his views were aimed at a wider audience, at the people outside the small circle of

[106] *Calumet*, I, no. 2 (July-Aug. 1831), 45-51.
[107] See MS letter written in 1904 by a New York Shaker, A. G. Hollister, which has been sewn into copy 2 of the book in the New York Public Library.

convinced nonresistants. The book won the approval of the leaders of the American Peace Society and proved effective propaganda in their peace campaign.[108]

Shaker pacifism, then, although in theory it was based on an extreme sectarian position, found ways and means in practice of meeting the wider peace movement halfway. Of the other contemporary American communities which required adherence to Christian nonresistance from their members, only Adin Ballou's Hopedale experiment similarly took part in the work of noncommunitarian pacifists.

Before we come to discuss Ballou and his group, a few words should be said about those pacifist communities which remained within the closed orbit of their group life. Their members were drawn almost entirely from recent immigrants from Europe; their everyday tongue was German, and, especially at first, most were altogether unacquainted with the English language. They had within recent memory suffered in many cases severe persecution from the countries of their origin; the world remained alien even in their new and more tolerant environment. They did not belong to it in the same way as the native-born Shakers and the denizens of Hopedale, despite their conscious renunciation of this world, still did.

There is nothing on record to indicate that any specifically pacifist stand was taken before the Civil War either by the Separatists of Zoar, who had been assisted by the Quakers to emigrate from South Germany in 1817 and who eventually settled in Ohio under the leadership of Joseph Baumeler, or by the Bethel community founded in Missouri in 1844 by the German immigrant "Dr." Keil (1812-1879), a former milliner and self-styled physician, whose followers likewise came mainly from Germany, though with a sprinkling of Pennsylvania "Dutch." That they were opposed to participation in war is clear, however, from their behavior during the Civil War (which will be described in a later chapter). Neither the Separatists nor the more vocal Inspirationists of Amana, who had come together in Germany as a separate group within the radical Pietist movement early in the eighteenth century, had adopted communism of goods until faced with frontier conditions in America. The Inspirationists had already witnessed staunchly to their pacifist convictions back in Germany where they suffered imprisonment, confiscation of property, and severe ill-treatment for refusing to serve in the army. "We cannot," they said, "serve the state as soldiers, because a Christian cannot murder his enemy, much less his friend."[109] The strength of their peace wit-

---

[108] See Andrews, *The People called Shakers*, p. 216.
[109] Quoted in Bertha M.H. Shambaugh, *Amana*, p. 28.

ness had fluctuated during the century and more of their existence in Germany, as did the harshness of their persecutors. Driven from state to state in search of milder conditions, they finally decided in 1843-1844 to emigrate as a group to the New World after feeling themselves the recipients of a special direction from the spirit world to do so. On this side of the ocean their ultimate resting place was to be Iowa, where they succeeded in building a flourishing community life.[110]

Whenever these immigrants were required to do militia service in the decades of peace following their arrival in this country, the payment of a small fine undoubtedly satisfied their consciences,[111] for these German peasants asked nothing further of the state than to be left in peace that they might follow austerely the teachings of their master. What did they know of the natural rights of man or of the constitutional liberties of the American citizen? The state as they knew it in Europe was an oppressor; the small Christian flock must build the perfect community so far as possible outside the world, where wars and violence would continue to rage. The maturing of a new, an American-born generation and the transformation, with increasing prosperity, of their peasant into a middle-class culture would eventually break down the barriers between the community and the world and in the process go far toward disintegrating the communities themselves. But this change took place only after the Civil War.

Of the many English-speaking communities which sprang up in the thirties and forties, most dissolved within a few years, for they usually lacked the strict discipline and clear-cut religious basis that gave stability, if not originality, to the German-speaking groups. Ballou's Hopedale was in many ways one of the more successful of the English communities, though its heyday lasted only a decade and a half. It was certainly the most clearly pacifist. True, it was not so creative in the realm of social ideas, nor so enduring or financially self-sufficient, as John Humphrey Noyes's famous Oneida community. Noyes (1811-1886), we shall find, exercised considerable influence in the late 1830's on William Lloyd Garrison's perfectionist views, which led to his es-

---

[110] W. R. Perkins and B. L. Wick, *History of the Amana Society*, pp. 25, 41, 42, 43ff.

[111] We know, for instance, that members of the Harmony Society, sometimes called Rappites after their founder George Rapp (1757-1847), who had brought them to America in 1804, paid their fines promptly, if required to perform militia service. As the Rappites stated in 1830 in answer to some criticism: "We are ignorant of the fact that a county or militia tax collector has ever called twice for the amount we had to pay." This communitarian group had originated in Württemberg, where they had been associated with the pacifist-inclined religious separatists in that area. See Karl J. R. Arndt, *George Rapp's Harmony Society*, pp. 128-30, 167, 413.

pousal of Christian nonresistance and to the founding of the New England Non-Resistance Society in 1838. But Noyes's community was in no way a pacifist one, and Noyes's own concept of nonresistance was more akin to the antiwar stand of present-day Jehovah's Witnesses or of some medieval sectaries than to the mild and loving creed of most American nonresistants. It was fiercely chiliastic in tone. "The non-resistance which was inculcated on the primitive church by the apostles [Noyes wrote in 1847] was constantly mingled with promises of the speedy advent of a kingdom in which 'every man should be rewarded according to his works'—the wicked with destruction, as well as the righteous with eternal life." Henceforth, authority belonged only to a divine, "a theocratic government" to which all men were subject. This government required "total abstinence from war, either individual or national, offensive or defensive"—unless, that is, a specific command were issued to act as God's agent of punishment. Noyes, therefore, saw no incompatibility in spirit between Christ's teaching of nonresistance to his disciples and Joshua's leading the hosts of Israel against the Canaanites.

> We justify that war therefore, in perfect consistency with the peace principles of the New Testament, and without resorting to any obscure theory of change of dispensation, or leaving any ground of imputing mutable morality or policy to the divine government. The legitimacy of that war stands on the same basis as the legitimacy of the war which God will make on the wicked at the final judgment. It was a war carried on by the supreme government, in which men were authorized agents. . . . With these views, we have no occasion to make the distinction which is sometimes made between offensive and defensive wars. The supreme authority of the universe has as good right to make offensive as defensive war; and men have as good right to serve him in the one as in the others. . . . And on the other hand, men have no more right to make defensive than offensive war, without divine authority. The peace precepts of the New Testament are specially and almost exclusively directed against defensive war.

Noyes's objection to the wars fought between the nations since Christ's coming, then, was not that they were waged with carnal weapons but that they were carried on without the permission of God, the earth's theocratic ruler. Such conflicts he dubbed "lawless and murderous private brawls." The goals of the American Revolution, for instance, were good. "Neither do we object to its physical nature. The fault we find with it is, that it was an illegitimate war, undertaken on human responsibility, unauthorized by any provable order of the divine government."

Noyes's conclusions concerning the best methods to achieve a peaceful world indicate the gulf between him and both the left and right wings of the contemporary peace movement, even though they show a quite close affinity with the views of the German peace churches or even those of the Shakers. He writes:

We are to look for the termination of the wars of the world, not to a voluntary congress and agreement of nations, nor to the labors of Quakers, peace societies, and non-resistants,—so long as their efforts are directed mainly to the object of proclaiming the horrors of war and the immorality of using carnal weapons,—but to the promulgation of that gospel which brings man nigh to God, and lifts him out of the anarchy of unbelief into the light and order of the eternal government.

God alone might judge and punish. But man might sometimes be required to act as his executioner on this earth.[112]

Ballou, liberal Christian and former Universalist, was remote in his thinking from the millennial visions of his contemporary communitarian. Although his inspiration was religious and his temperament idealistic almost to the point of being starry-eyed, Ballou firmly rooted his utopian ideas in this world (though Noyes, it is true, proved himself in practice a more efficient organizer and business manager than Ballou). He strove to bring into existence a fellowship of men and women who would put into practice in their everyday lives the moral teachings of Jesus, without at the same time turning their backs entirely on the unregenerate world outside the community and on those working toward its redemption.

The Hopedale community was set up by Ballou in 1841 at Milford (Mass.). At its height it had about 200 members. On the economic side the group was not completely communistic; it resembled more the Fourierist joint-stock community with shares purchasable by members. Many of those who joined were educated and well-to-do people "belonging," as Ballou wrote, "to the more substantial, self-respecting middle class of American society": ministers, teachers, writers, and other professional men, as well as a number of farmers and skilled craftsmen.[113] Its constitution included a brief declaration of principles to which all who joined had to give their assent. Belief in the Christian religion as set forth in the New Testament and readi-

[112] J. H. Noyes, *The Berean*, pp. 446-51.
[113] Ballou, *History of the Hopedale Community*, p. 339.

441

ness to follow "all its moral obligations" were its basic provisions. Teetotalism and a renunciation of oaths, betting, and lotteries were included alongside an unequivocal nonresistant pledge. "I hold myself bound," it ran, "never, under any pretext whatsoever, to kill, assault, beat, torture, rob, oppress, persecute, defraud, corrupt, slander, revile, injure, envy, or hate any human being—*even my worst enemy;* . . . never to serve in the army, navy or militia of any nation, state or chieftain; never to bring an action at law, hold office, vote, join a legal posse, petition a legislature, or ask governmental interposition in any case involving a final authorized resort to physical violence."[114] The community organ, the *Practical Christian,* throughout the two decades of its existence was a steady exponent of pacifist ideas, and almost every number contained something on the subject of nonresistance.

Adin Ballou (1803-1890), who was originally a Universalist minister like his more famous cousin Hosea, had made contact with the left wing of the peace movement toward the end of the 1830's, around the time Garrison and his friends were bringing the New England Non-Resistance Society into being. He was soon convinced of the case against war and all violence. "I could not preach the brotherhood of man and all moral agents, and then teach them to kill, oppress, wrong, and trample one another under foot, as if only beasts," he writes of his conversion to radical pacifism. Ballou, therefore, sympathized from the beginning with the aims of the New England Non-Resistance Society and participated in its conferences and in its general work, though he did not at once become an actual member of the Society. He was especially active with his pen in defense of radical pacifism, becoming one of the leading theorists of nonresistance. And with his Hopedale followers Ballou, who became the Society's president in 1843, helped to keep it from completely disintegrating as the forties wore on. On two occasions, in 1845 and again in 1848, he revived the Society's defunct organ, the *Non-Resistant,* when it appeared under his editorship at the Hopedale press. His efforts, however, proved too great a strain on his scanty resources, and he had to give up after a few issues for lack of sufficient outside support.[115] After the Society itself finally faded out around 1850, Ballou's *Practical Christian* and his Hopedale community became the one active focus of New England nonresistance, which had seemed in such a flourishing state a decade or so earlier. This aspect of his work will be discussed in the next

[114] *Autobiography of Adin Ballou,* pp. 327, 328. See also Ballou, *History,* pp. 28, 40, 399.
[115] Ballou, *History,* p. 131; *Autobiography,* pp. 380, 381.

section of the book when we come to speak of the rise and development of the New England Non-Resistance Society.

Meanwhile, all was not going well inside Hopedale itself. The spirit of worldly materialism had somehow begun to seep in. As Ballou wrote later: "We sought to be all-sided saints,—bound to obey the law of divine righteousness as individuals, in social life, and in all governmental concerns. This was right, even though it should serve on trial to expose our frailties and imperfections."[116] In 1856 the crisis finally came with the withdrawal from membership of the two Draper brothers, who held around three-quarters of the entire joint stock of the community. As a result, the community had to dissolve a few years later, though Hopedale continued to exist for several decades as a religious society under Ballou's leadership. After the economic disaster something of the old missionary zeal for the Christian socialist and pacifist causes disappeared, too.[117] Once again the world had seemingly triumphed.

The failure of Hopedale to fulfill Ballou's high hopes that it might act as a center for the regeneration of the world left him a saddened, though not a disillusioned, man. His flock became scattered. He had wished to rear within the shelter of the community a generation that would naturally cleave to the paths of peace, eschewing violence and war as contrary to their nurture, if not their nature. The young, he wrote in 1854, should be brought up in an atmosphere of love and nonviolence and taught by precept and example that "enemies" and criminals were not to be hated, that with God's help even the most depraved evildoer might be won to goodness. Parents and educators

[116] Ballou, *Autobiography*, p. 340.

[117] Ballou, *History*, pp. 330-36, 352-61. Declining numbers, however, do not seem to have dampened the enthusiasm of two of the more exotic characters associated with Ballou's community: Brian J. Butts and Harriet N. Greene—his wife, although she refused on principle to surrender her maiden name—who in May 1859 started a reform journal entitled the *Radical Spiritualist*. The paper, according to its editors, was destined "for the outcast, the degraded, the prostitute, and the enslaved" (I, no. 2 [June 1859], 12). It advocated "Spiritualism, Socialism, Anti-Slavery, Non-Resistance, Woman's Rights, Anti-Oath-taking and Office-holding, Temperance, Vegetarianism, Anti-Tobacco (Tea, Coffee) and every other Reform which requires the practice of a higher life." The price was "fifty cents per annum to the able and willing: free to the oppressed and outcast." Beginning in 1860 it bore the slogan on its masthead: "No Union with Warriors." Its tone was militantly antiwar: "the *Radical Spiritualist* is NOW and FOR ALL TIME opposed to war in every case, offensive and defensive" (I, no. 5 [Sept. 1859], 38). Even the spirit guides were reproved on occasion for lack of consistency in their exposition of nonresistant doctrine: it was her right, states Harriet Greene, to criticize "all teachers whether in the body or out" (II, no. 9 [Jan. 1860], 69). With the issue of May 1860 the paper appeared under the title *Spiritual Reformer*. In both journals a special phonetic alphabet was employed to print some of the articles.

must struggle to overcome in their children and pupils "the animal instincts and impulses, which are developed in human nature before the spiritual sentiments can be rendered commanding."[118]

Two years before writing these words Ballou suffered a great personal loss in the death of his 18-year-old son, Adin Augustus, one of the most hopeful products of the community's educational theories. After his death Ballou composed a memoir of his son, a stilted and lachrymose document which successfully hides from modern readers the genuine grief that undoubtedly lay behind its compilation. It does, however, give us some interesting insights into the methods of a pacifist educator in mid-nineteenth-century America.

In one place Ballou reproduces the substance of a dialogue which had taken place some years before when his son was 10. The boy had asked his father's permission to go along with his friends to watch a local militia muster, pleading that he only wanted to see the fine uniforms and listen to the music of the bands. The father proceeds to explain to the boy the true meaning of the exercises being held, and the following dialogue takes place:

> *Father* . . . Now you must think whether it is *right* for you to be an admirer of these soldiers. You say you would not wish to go, if they were intending to fight, because that would be wicked. Is it not wicked for you to go and see them *learn how* to fight and kill men? Do you not encourage them in learning a wicked art? If you should see a man grinding a large knife to kill some one, and he should brandish it one way and the other to show how he meant to stab and destroy when the time came . . . would you stay by and hang round such a man, even if he had a red coat on, a plume in his cap, or a band of music to play for him? . . .
>
> *Augustus* O no, I would not do that. . . . But I cannot make the *muster* seem like a man grinding and flourishing his murderous knife. . . . I cannot tell how much I want to see them march and hear their music!
>
> *Father* . . . I will leave you to settle the matter in your own mind. You must answer to God and your conscience. Go, if you think it right. I will not hinder you.

Finally, of course, Augustus decides not to go and his father is happy.[119] The tone in which the dialogue is conducted is irritatingly moralistic and priggish. Ballou's pedagogical methods succeeded, how-

---

[118] Ballou, *Practical Christian Socialism*, pp. 322, 323.
[119] *Memoir of A. A. Ballou*, pp. 21-26.

ever, so far as we can see, in making an enthusiastic and loyal non-resistant out of the boy.[120]

Ballou the communitarian was inseparable from Ballou the reformer who participated in the humanitarian movements of the day. He bridged the gap—as did the Shakers also to some extent—between the otherworldly withdrawn pacifism of the sects and communities and the peace societies of varying degrees of radicalism, which sprang up after 1815 in America and Europe unaffiliated to any one particular religious group or social philosophy. This development will occupy us in the next section of the book.

The pacifist witness of the groups described in this chapter varied greatly in character. In their attitude toward militia service they ranged from the absolutist standpoint of the Shakers from 1815 on to the more accommodating one of the German peace sectaries, who believed it incumbent upon themselves as followers of Christ to "go the second mile." For all, indeed, the primary source of their pacifism was the New Testament, but their interpretation of its meaning differed greatly. Whereas the Mennonites and allied groups felt themselves called to practice a thoroughgoing and consistent nonresistance, the communitarians viewed pacifism as integrally linked with a communistic way of living. If we exclude the Disciples, whose leaders never succeeded in injecting their pacifism into the church as a whole, pacifism was an essential part of these groups' credo, and those who infringed the discipline on this point might ultimately have to face being disfellowshipped. All the groups (again, with the partial exception of the Disciples) were opposed, also, to participation in the political life of the state, which they regarded as hopelessly entangled with the apparatus of violence: there were differences of degree in their withdrawal from the affairs of the world, but this element was present in all. They found no need to devise a blueprint for a success-

---

[120] Ballou in his *Memoir* (p. 78) quotes the following from the journal his son kept while a student at the normal school: "A. had quite a talk with me on Non-Resistance. He is anxious to get a Midshipman's birth in the Navy. I asked him if that was his highest end in life—to kill or murder people? He said he didn't know anything about that, but should like to be a Middy, and go to Naples, and cruise round the world. One thing led on to another, and we went over nearly the whole ground of Non-Resistance. He says it is worse than nonsense. If a man would kill *you*, kill *him*. The same story this, from one end of the world to the other. People have no idea that there is a principle involved; that if they would kill one man, by the same rule they might kill a thousand, a million, or the whole race, just to save their own lives. *No*: human life is inviolable. Better die than shed human blood. The end never sanctifies the means. *Right ends* by *right* means, shall be my motto, and I will try to live to it."

445

ful pacifist policy. Wars and violence, in their view, were probably inevitable in this world: a conditional justification of the coercive power of the state may be read in many Mennonite statements, for instance. Theirs was the witness of suffering love, a testimony to a higher way which, however, only a handful would find the strength to follow. Their pacifism, in short, was a sectarian pacifism—as was also true, to a large degree, of the Quaker peace testimony during this period—which made little attempt to reach out to the world with the message of peace and nonviolence. This it was, above all, that differentiated them from the pacifists (even when, like Garrison, they called themselves "nonresistants"), who worked in the new American peace movement in the era following the end of the Napoleonic wars.

Part Three

Pacifism in the American Peace Movement
before the Civil War

"We have reason for pious gratitude, that we live to see a day more auspicious to the cause of peace than any since the apostolic times."

—From the Annual Report of the Maine Peace Society printed in the *Christian Mirror*, 19 May 1826

Chapter 10

The Pioneers: Dodge and Worcester

I

An organized peace movement on the American continent dates from the conclusion of the Napoleonic wars.[1] Before 1815 the pacifist position had been almost entirely confined to the peace sects: Quakers, Mennonites, Dunkers, and several smaller bodies. Outside these groups, it is true, an isolated individual in one of the other churches would very occasionally raise his voice in protest against all Christian participation in war; during the Revolutionary War, too, as shown in an earlier chapter, there have come to light cases involving conscientious objectors against militia service who had no affiliation with any of the pacifist sects. But it is not really until the early decades of the nineteenth century, a period of continuous war back in Europe, that we discover other pacifist stirrings alongside the peace testimony of the sects. Indeed, a growing number among the clergy, though still only a handful, had now begun to attack the institution of war in general terms on both Christian and humanitarian grounds; and to this censure was added, after the outbreak in 1812 of hostilities between the United States and Britain, a wave of political opposition to the war throughout the New England states, although it derived more from the injury the conflict threatened to the economic interests of the area than from a moral repugnance to the waging of war itself.

In the War of 1812 conscientious objection was still confined almost exclusively to the peace sects. However, the recorded cases of Baalis Bullard of Uxbridge (Mass.) and of Joshua P. Blanchard (1782-1868), who was later to become a veteran member of the peace movement, are not likely to have been the only ones involving men who did not share this sectarian background. Bullard (described in his obituary as "a real Puritan, inflexible in his adherence to what he deemed

---

[1] The most important studies of the subject are Merle E. Curti, *The American Peace Crusade*, and W. Freeman Galpin, *Pioneering for Peace*. See also Christina Phelps, *The Anglo-American Peace Movement in the Mid-Nineteenth Century*, *passim*; A.C.F. Beales, *The History of Peace, passim*; Alice Felt Tyler, *Freedom's Ferment*, pt. III, chap. 15; Frank Thistlethwaite, *America and the Atlantic Community: Anglo-American Aspects 1790-1850*, pp. 96-102.

right"),[2] whose decision to refuse military service stemmed "from his solitary study of the Gospel," petitioned the Massachusetts legislature for exemption "on the ground of conscientious scruples," and presumably it was given to him. He was later to become a deacon and a pillar of his local Congregational church.

More significant for the future than these isolated witnesses for peace was the conversion to pacifism in the latter years of the Napoleonic struggle of a prosperous New York merchant, David Low Dodge (1774-1852),[3] with whose activities the organized peace movement in America really begins. Dodge was a largely self-taught and self-made man, who had worked his way up from a humble Connecticut farmstead to considerable affluence as a result of his successful business activities. An elder of the Presbyterian church, rigidly Calvinist in his theology, and a respectable member of middle-class society, he was deeply imbued with the evangelical and philanthropic spirit of his time, and this spirit provided the main source from which his pacifism sprang. For many years, however, he had not questioned the conventional Christian acceptance of war, had exercised with the militia, and had been ready to carry firearms on his business journeys when an outbreak of highway robberies seemed to make this precaution necessary. An incident at an inn where he was spending the night, when he nearly shot the landlord in mistaking him for a robber, led him for the first time to question the compatibility of carrying arms with the profession of a Christian. "I pondered on the event," he writes, "and tried to realize what would have been my situation and feelings had I taken his life; but especially in what light God would have viewed the transaction? I then resolved, by the help of God, to examine the question by the light of revelation, as to the duty of Christians arming themselves with deadly weapons for self-defence."

Over the next three years Dodge studied the question more deeply, finding to his surprise that, whereas the letter and spirit of the gospels seemed to him to rule out armed defense and the prosecution of war by Christians, the theologians and moralists down through the centuries had almost unanimously upheld the right to use force in self-defense or for a just cause. The contradiction worried him. "I struggled hard to satisfy myself that defensive war, in extreme cases, might be tolerated by the Gospel; otherwise, the American revolution could

---

[2] *Advocate of Peace*, XII (1857), 382.

[3] The source for Dodge's life on which all subsequent accounts are based is his "Autobiography," printed in the *Memorial of Mr. David L. Dodge*. See also Edwin D. Mead, "David Low Dodge: Founder of the First Peace Society," *World Unity* (N.Y.), 1933, XI, no. 6, 365-72; XII, no. 1, 29-36.

not be justified."[4] He was puzzled, too, to find that, when he took his doubts to those friends whom he esteemed most highly, they all avoided discussion of the scriptural basis for an opinion on the subject and justified war primarily on grounds of expediency. "In this inquiring state of mind," he writes, "no one circumstance led me so much to doubt the soundness of the sentiments of my opponents as their general want of faith in the promises and providential protection of God; and when I laid aside my pistols, exchanging them for the protection of the Lord God of Hosts, I was no more tormented with the fear of robbers."

In 1808 came his final conversion to the full nonresistant position, the consequence of what appears to have been an almost mystical experience during a nearly fatal attack of spotted fever. The whole question became quite clear to him. "From this period, my war spirit appeared to be crucified and slain." He only regretted that hitherto he had failed to take a public stand against all war; he resolved, therefore, if he recovered, to devote himself henceforward to furthering the cause of peace.[5]

The result appeared the next year in the publication in New York of a small tract entitled *The Mediator's Kingdom not of this World but Spiritual, Heavenly and Divine.* This was Dodge's first literary effort; it appeared anonymously as the work of "an inquirer." The pamphlet made quite a stir at the time, and the first edition of 1,000 copies was sold out within a fortnight. "Three literary gentlemen" replied, also anonymously, to Dodge's arguments, and the latter published a brief answer to their objections. "These publications," writes Dodge, "gave the first impulse in America (if we except the uniform influence of the Friends) to inquiry into the lawfulness of war by Christians."[6]

In his pamphlet[7] Dodge uncompromisingly condemns defensive wars as well as personal self-defense: "that all kinds of war, revenge, and fighting were utterly prohibited under the gospel dispensation we think appears evident not only from the life of our glorious Mediator but from his express precepts." A host of texts from the New Testament, as well as the example of the early Christians, is summoned in support of the thesis that love and forgiveness and prayer can be the Christian's only answer to enmity and hatred. The horrors of the battlefield provoke him to inquire: "Who amongst our fellowmen would

[4] Later, Dodge testified (*Memorial*, pp. 90, 101), "my greatest impediment in advocating the doctrines of peace in the United States" lay in "the example of our fathers in the American Revolution."

[5] *Memorial*, pp. 77-81.   [6] *Ibid.*, p. 89.

[7] I have used Mead's edition of 1905, where it is printed on pp. 123-68, along with the later and longer *War Inconsistent with the Religion of Jesus Christ.*

451

receive the thrust of a sword as an act of kindness?" Existing governments which uphold warfare are pagan, "under Satan's dominion" (on principle, Dodge would neither vote nor hold office),[8] to be obeyed, certainly, but only insofar as they did not require any act—like fighting, for instance, which he dubs "spiritual whoredom" in a Christian—repugnant to a Christian's conscience.

This modest little pamphlet is, indeed, a pioneering work, yet it suffers from several defects. In the first place, the style, overloaded as it is with Biblical quotations and farfetched interpretations of prophetic passages along with its almost apocalyptic tone, makes the work difficult reading—at least for later generations. Secondly, the argument is mainly negative: Dodge nowhere alludes to any alternative to the violent method of resisting evil, beyond a somewhat naive reliance on God's protection. Indeed, it was to be several decades before any of the early pacifists were to come to grips with this problem.

His three critics had in their pamphlet charged Dodge with a willingness in fact, if not in intention, to hand over the law-abiding to the mercies of the wicked.[9] While stating his belief that "peaceable men are not more liable to be assaulted than the retaliating," Dodge in his reply relies mainly on the moral imperative: under the new dispensation, in contrast to the Mosaic, God has commanded Christians to forgive, not to destroy, their enemies. "Until it is proved, from the Scriptures, that destroying an enemy is consistent with forgiving him, we cannot admit the principle of war as a gospel doctrine.[10]

Dodge had refrained from answering his critics in the sarcastic and ironic tone they had employed against him. Courteous and charitable in all his dealings, this respectable New York citizen patiently explained that he had not taken up an unpopular position simply in order to be different; it had, in fact, been a trial for him to have to disagree with so many of his most respected friends, and only a strong sense of duty had driven him to persist in his course.[11] Some of these friends soon began to gain interest in his ideas,[12] and by 1812 the

---

[8] *Memorial*, p. vii. A twentieth-century Mennonite historian, Guy F. Hershberger, has called Dodge "a nonresistant biblicist who rejected the state and the social order of this world as fully as the nonresistant sects ever did" ("Some Religious Pacifists of the Nineteenth Century," MQR, X, no. 1 [Jan. 1936], 80).

[9] *The Duty of a Christian in a Trying Situation*, pp. 25, 26, 29, 30.

[10] Dodge, *Remarks upon an Anonymous Letter*, pp. 24, 31, 32, 36, 37.

[11] *Ibid.*, pp. 5, 6.

[12] An echo of Dodge's ideas is to be found in the letters written home from Bombay in India by the Rev. Gordon Hall (1784-1826), one of the first missionaries sent out to that country by the American Board of Commissioners for Foreign Missions. Hall, a New Englander by birth and education, writes: "As to war, you may mark me for a thorough Quaker. . . . I wish everybody could read Barclay,

project of forming a peace society in New York had taken shape in the minds of Dodge and these associates. The outbreak of hostilities with Britain, however, caused them to postpone its realization in order to avoid possible confusion of their movement with a purely political opposition to the war. Instead, his friends urged him to prepare a longer essay on the relationship of Christianity and war, which he completed by the end of the year.[13] The publication of his book, which he called *War Inconsistent with the Religion of Jesus Christ*, was held up by its author until the conclusion of the war in 1815 for the same reason that had caused the postponement of the projected peace society.

Dodge had been surprised that, in an age when so many good Christians had had their consciences aroused against institutions such as the slave trade or intemperance, they still remained silent, on the whole, concerning the much greater evil of war. The reason for this indifference, he concluded, lay in the propensity of human nature to accept without questioning time-hallowed institutions and customs— unless aroused by some vigorous and sudden challenge to the evils involved in their continuance.[14] His book was intended as just such a challenge.

His argument against giving any kind of sanction to war or violence is carried on here on several different planes. Fundamentally, of course, its core is religious, but economic and political factors, as well as general humanitarian considerations, are blended in to form a well-knit whole, with the Biblical text taking a subordinate place in the general pattern.

First, there is the economic case against war, as Dodge saw it. War entails both the destruction of property, thus damaging the material interests of the well-to-do classes, and the infliction of great hardship on the poor, who do most of the actual fighting and on whose shoulders finally the cost of war usually rests. "The calamities of war necessarily fall more on the poor than on the rich, because the poor of a country are generally a large majority of its inhabitants." But, even so, Dodge argued in anticipation of Norman Angell in the next century,

---

Clarkson, and Dodge, on this subject." Hall succeeded in converting two evangelically inclined young British officers to his views, and they thereupon resigned from the army. "You must leave the army, or do violence to your conscience," Hall had told them. The correspondence, dated August to October 1813, is reprinted in an 11-page pamphlet, *The Military Profession Unlawful for a Christian* from the 1834 Glasgow edition of Horatio Bardwell, *Memoir of Rev. Gordon Hall, A.M.* For the correspondence, see also the Andover 1834 edition, pp. 80-91.

[13] *Memorial*, p. 95.

[14] Dodge, *War Inconsistent with the Religion of Jesus Christ*, pp. 75-77.

no one really gains from war, not even the wealthy, because war is a waste of man's resources, of God's gifts. "Notwithstanding an avaricious individual or nation may occasionally in war acquire by plunder from their brethren a little wealth, yet they usually lose on the whole more than they gain." Think of the prosperity which would have come, if all the money expended on the destruction of war over the last two decades had gone into peaceful enterprises.[15] Curti has suggested that the losses Dodge's firm had incurred during this period as a result of the seizure of merchandise by the European belligerents led him to consider the economic as well as the strictly religious and moral arguments against war.[16] Such losses at least may have sharpened his pen.

War, in Dodge's view, is not merely economically unprofitable in the long run; it is unsound biologically, too. It kills off the young and healthy, the flower of the human race, who are attracted to enlist because of the false glamor of military life. "To be active in any measure which has a natural tendency to wantonly multiply widows and orphans in a land," pleads Dodge, "is the height of inhumanity as well as daring impiety," for Christian philanthropy must strive to provide for the widowed and fatherless and destitute. Moreover, in addition to corrupting the morals of those who enlist, war leads to a decline in morality in the population at large. Desecration of the Sabbath and spiritual pride, stealing and financial scandals, drunkenness and brawling and gambling, profanity and licentiousness are all concomitants of war. War, too, Dodge holds, is politically absurd, self-defeating, because it is incapable of securing what it sets out to achieve: protection against attack and personal liberty. Above all, military preparations conjure up counter-preparations. Each state wishes to be stronger than the others, an arms race ensues, and the resulting war tends to engulf nation after nation. Because of the hatreds engendered by war and the desire for revenge among the defeated, peace when it comes fails to break the accursed circle. Defense by means of arms proves an illusion. "The pretended distinction between offensive and defensive war," Dodge concludes, "is but a name." Likewise, war and militarism are destructive of civil liberty within a nation, while violent revolution to overthrow despotism usually leads to the imposition of a worse tyranny in its place (a fact which "ought well to be considered by every one of a revolutionary spirit"). History shows that warlike nations have usually lost their liberties. Civic free-

[15] *Ibid.*, pp. 8-11, 28-30.
[16] Curti, *American Peace Crusade*, p. 7.

dom flourishes only in time of peace.[17] The course of recent events in France provided ample proof of this point for the worthy New York merchant.

On the servile condition and moral depravity of that unhappy being, the enlisted man, Dodge also grows eloquent. He is ready to concede that some soldiers may be naturally kind and humane, but their occupation, he claims, forces them to inflict injury and pain on others, hardening their hearts and making them insensitive to human suffering, when Christianity enjoins love and forgiveness of injuries and tenderness toward others. They must risk the likelihood of dying in a state of sin for the sake of the things of this world, which should count for nothing in comparison with the glories of eternal bliss. The life of at least the private soldier, too, is a miserable one, especially in wartime. But this disadvantage is nothing compared to the bondage in which the conscience of the fighting man is kept by the governments of the world. He must always kill when ordered, so that, even if it were possible (which it is not, Dodge again reminds us) to distinguish between defensive wars and wars of aggression, it would still not be practicable for governments, democracies as well as despotisms, to allow the soldier to decide according to his conscience. For this indulgence would undermine military discipline and the country's fighting potential. Moreover, even if an individual soldier might be found here and there ready to risk being shot rather than execute an unjust command, such action would involve him in breaking his previous oath of obedience taken upon entry into the service—which is also a sin in the eyes of God. Thus, Dodge concludes:

> Soldiers actually resign up their consciences to their commanders, without reserving any right to obey only in such cases as they may judge not contrary to the laws of God. Were they at liberty to judge whether commands were morally right or not, before they yielded obedience, it would be totally impracticable for nations to prosecute war.[18]

Dodge, having dealt with the inhumanity of war and its folly, goes on to discuss its "criminality . . . when judged on the principles of the gospels." This charge, of course, constitutes the core of his objection to war and the use of armed force. But his previous utilitarian arguments, it is interesting to observe, are not kept in isolation; instead, they are fused with the purely religious objections to form an integral

[17] Dodge, *War Inconsistent* . . . , pp. 16-20, 23-28, 31-33, 36-42, 44-47.
[18] *Ibid.*, pp. 2-6, 14, 15, 42-44, 49-55.

whole. Since war is inhumane and "very unwise" even from a worldly point of view, how much more must it "be wrong for Christians to do anything to promote it, and right to do all in their power to prevent it." But there are, of course, particular reasons grounded in the scriptures why men of religion should renounce war. Here Dodge elaborates many of the arguments used in his pamphlet of 1809, dwelling now more on the spirit of the gospels than on the importance of any one text. Christ taught men to show mercy, to forgive enemies, to put up patiently with oppression, returning only good for evil and love for hatred. All these precepts are completely contrary to the prosecution of war: "the whole trade of war is returning evil for evil: this is a fundamental principle of the system of self-defence." Therefore, if Christ's injunctions were fulfilled in earnest, it would mean an end to the institution of war, which at best aims to accomplish good by evil means. "Christ taught his disciples the doctrines of peace, and commanded them to take up the cross and follow him; to live in peace and follow peace with all men."[19] Repeatedly, Dodge underlines the conclusion to be drawn from this argument, an inference before which many previous writers condemning war on humanitarian and Christian grounds—Erasmus, for instance—had stopped short: that Christians should take no part in war, should refuse to participate in it in any way.

Dodge had expressed his surprise, as we have seen, that so many good Christians who had been aroused to protest against the evils of the slave trade or of intemperance had failed to see the total incompatibility of war and the carrying of arms with the Christian message.[20] To help resolve their doubts he attempts toward the end of his book to answer possible objections that may have been aroused in the minds of his readers.

First come difficulties connected with personal nonresistance and the so-called right of self-defense. In fact, Dodge is careful to point out, this problem, however important it is in itself, has little relevance to the problem of war. "War between nations is a business of calculation and debate, affording so much time for reflection that men need not act from sudden and violent impulse." This might not be the case with an armed attack on one's person, such as was envisaged by the non-pacifist objector. Yet even in this case, in Dodge's view, we must not look to consequences and refuse on that account to follow the Christian way. God is ruler of the universe, and there cannot be two contradictory rules of conduct; both originate from the same source, so

19 *Ibid.*, pp. 47-49, 56-75.   20 *Ibid.*, pp. 75-77.

that natural law and the gospels can never conflict. Let the non-resistant trust in God's protection and in the power of love, such as had been exemplified in the history of the Society of Friends, and he would in all likelihood survive.[21]

Dodge goes on to wrestle with a second possible objection. Could not the lawfulness of war be grounded on the books of the Old Testament? Dodge concedes the lawfulness of the wars of Old Testament times, which were approved by God for the Jews under the old dispensation. (Indeed, what good Presbyterian of the early nineteenth century could fail to concede this!) Yet, although it is quite true, he writes, that

> the essence of religion is the same under the present as under the former dispensation, . . . the laws for external conduct under the two dispensations differ widely, and the practice of war involves much of the external conduct of men. It was never right for men to indulge unholy feelings in the act of war, but the external act was required as a means of executing the divine vengeance; the gospel does not command, but seems plainly to forbid, the external act of war. . . . It is perfectly plain that if God should positively command Christians to take the weapons of war and not only repel invasion but actually exterminate nations, it would be their duty to obey, and a refusal would be open rebellion against God. The Old Testament saints received such commands, but Christians have no such authority, which makes a material difference in the circumstances.[22]

The reasoning here seems to belong to an earlier age. More telling for us today is Dodge's further contention that both wars of aggression and slavery, already widely condemned by Christians of his time, might also be justified by an appeal to the Old Testament.

A third line of defense in the armory of his opponents lay in the overwhelming support given to war by the Christian churches down through the centuries. But this, says Dodge, is in fact no proof that they were not in error. Let us look to the gospels and to the example of the early church for the touchstone of conduct. This suggestion leads him, of course, into the familiar discussion of the New Testament texts on the subject. For the pacifism of the early church he draws upon the writings of the church fathers, as well upon Erasmus and the recent work of Thomas Clarkson.[23]

Finally, having disposed of the nonpacifist's objections based on

21 *Ibid.*, pp. 24, 77-87.   22 *Ibid.*, pp. 22, 87-99.
23 *Ibid.*, pp. 99-102, 112, 113, 116-19.

the Old and the New Testaments, Dodge goes on to consider the relationship between the claims of the individual Christian conscience and those of the magistrate. It is not true, he urges, that nonresistance applies only in private life and not in national and international affairs. War and the use of force cannot in this way be brought in through the back door. The teachings of the gospels are universally valid, "so that whatever is morally wrong for every individual must be equally wrong for a collective body." A nation is not an abstraction: "a nation is only a large number of individuals united so as to act collectively as one person." Pacifism does not mean anarchy, the undermining of the authority of the magistrate. For, truly, the powers that be are ordained of God. They are, indeed, serving God—sometimes in spite of their wickedness; so that, for instance, if commanded to go to war, Christians must refuse and suffer the consequences.[24]

Dodge's book remained the most effective American statement of Christian pacifism for some decades, and much of it still remains relevant today. As has been pointed out, many sections are devoted to presenting what is, for all its outmoded theology, essentially a rationalist and humanitarian case against war. The tract is immensely more readable than his effort of 1809. The style is clear and pungent, the argument usually convincing and always buttressed with a wide array of facts, which henceforth became the stock-in-trade of antiwar writers. Above all, his sincerity and moral integrity and his concern for the welfare of his fellowmen shine clearly from its pages. His condemnation of all war was uncompromising. With this slim volume of Dodge's, pacifism takes its place among the reform movements of the age along with antislavery, penal reform, temperance, education, and the many other contemporary manifestations of the spirit of philanthropy.

The coming of peace in 1815 had opened the way for the publication of Dodge's plea for pacifism; the same year also saw the maturing of Dodge's second long delayed project—the creation of an instrument through which to propagate the doctrines of peace. In August 1815 the New York Peace Society came into being with Dodge as its first president. It was probably the first peace society in the world. The idea had been Dodge's (he tells us in his autobiography that he had no knowledge of the efforts along the same lines that were being made

[24] *Ibid.*, pp. 102-12. Among several unpublished works Dodge left at his death in 1852 was an essay on "The Relation of the Church to the World" (see *Memorial*, p. vii). The allegiance of the Christian, he pleads, is solely to Jesus Christ and not to any earthly government, "whose ultimate reliance is the sword." Perhaps he may have come later under the influence of Garrisonian "no-government" ideas.

simultaneously in Massachusetts and back in England), and the driving force behind the Society's work over the next decade and more was to be his, too. At the beginning it numbered between thirty and forty members, mostly solid New York citizens with a sprinkling of well-to-do Quakers and "respectable clergymen" in the city. Within a couple of years membership had doubled, but thereafter it began to decline. "Our object," writes Dodge, "was not to form a popular society," to pursue "a popular course." Instead, by means of discussion in small groups and the circulation of peace literature, the good word was to be disseminated gradually.[25] The small band was to act as a leaven within American society.

What was the program of this first modern peace society? Mead[26] and Curti[27] agree that it came out on a full-fledged nonresistant platform, that it specifically condemned defensive wars along with wars of aggression. Galpin, on the other hand, believes that, if not at first, at least by the time its constitution was published in 1818 its stand was more moderate.[28] Dodge himself writes in his autobiography: "Our articles of association were of the strict kind, against all carnal warfare, whether offensive or defensive, as being wholly opposed to the example of Christ, and the spirit and precepts of the gospel."[29] This was, admittedly, written some years later, but it is unlikely that Dodge's memory would have been completely astray on such an important issue. A careful reading of the Society's first annual report containing its constitution may help to elucidate the matter. There it is stated that the executive committee should be open only to persons "decided in the belief that war is inconsistent with Christianity and the true interests of mankind," only, that is, to Christian nonresistants of Dodge's own stamp. On the other hand, all persons "disposed to aid in the promotion of peace on earth and goodwill to men" (one may be surprised that this category appeared only to embrace three score of the citizens of the city of New York) might, on paying the necessary fee, become ordinary members of the Society.[30] Thus, it would seem that the controlling elements in the Society were all convinced pacifists but that it also attempted to enroll other sincere peace lovers behind its banners. That those among the rank and file who did

[25] *Memorial*, pp. 95, 99, 100.
[26] Introduction to *War Inconsistent* . . . , pp. xx-xxii.
[27] *American Peace Crusade*, p. 8.
[28] Galpin, *Pioneering for Peace*, p. 16. However, Galpin quotes a letter written by William Ladd in 1836 to Henry Wright, stating that the New York Peace Society took a stand against all war (p. 108).
[29] *Memorial*, p. 99.
[30] *Report of the New York Peace Society* . . . *1818*, p. 7.

not feel strong enough to accept the whole of the absolutist doc-trine grew impatient with the line dictated by Dodge from above is made clear in the following passage in his autobiography:

The lax doctrines advocated in [the *Friend of Peace*, edited by Noah Worcester: see below] decreased the zeal of some of our members. The investigation of the question upon secular principles turned away the thoughts of some of the members from the divine prohibi-tion of war, to the mere question of its expediency and utility. Doubts began to arise whether, under the light of the gospel, its precepts were equally binding on nations as on individuals. On the other hand it was urged, that all under the light of the gospel were morally bound by its precepts; and if these are binding on every one individually, they must of course be binding on the whole com-munity, or nation. It was further urged against the lax sentiments of the "Friend of Peace," which permitted in extreme cases defen-sive war, that the gospel made no such distinction, but on the contrary, its most pointed precepts were directly against the prin-ciples of defensive war with carnal weapons. So, if it was morally wrong for individuals to quarrel and fight, instead of returning good for evil, it was much more criminal for communities and nations to return evil for evil, and not strive to overcome evil with good.[31]

The membership of the little Society was eminently respectable, de-cidedly bourgeois, with its Wall Street brokers, merchants and busi-nessmen, clergymen and philanthropic gentlemen active "in the most benevolent enterprises of that day." That Dodge was able to shape it so uncompromisingly in his radical mold is perhaps a tribute to his patent sincerity and the force of his personality. His high hopes at first that "these sentiments would become universal on the fulfilment of the prophecies concerning the prevalence of Christianity" were not to come about within the lifetime of the Society—or his own.[32] The report of 1818 remarks optimistically: "The number of decided friends of Peace upon the basis of Christian principles, and in oppo-sition to all war, is by no means inconsiderable; and of those dis-posed to inquire into the subject, there are many in almost every town and village." But numbers in the Society did not increase, despite all the efforts of Dodge and his friends with their publication and circulation of tracts on peace, including Dodge's own *Observations on the Kingdom of Peace, under the Benign Reign of Messiah* (1816) in 1,000 copies and those of the Massachusetts and London Peace So-

[31] *Memorial*, p. 101.　　　　[32] *Ibid.*, p. 100.

460

cieties.[33] The resourceful Dodge is said to have packed boxes of the Society's literature along with his own merchandise to help spread the word of peace.[34] In 1828, after more than a decade of a somewhat vegetating existence, the New York group decided to fuse with the newly founded American Peace Society (see below), thus becoming merely one of its branches. Its impact on society at large had been minimal, its influence barely perceptible outside the confines of New York City, its membership restricted to a handful of the well-to-do, at whom its propaganda seems to have been mainly directed. Nonetheless, as Galpin writes, "the mere fact . . . that the body held together and kept the peace flag flying was vital and significant."[35]

Within Dodge's circle of friends there arose several expositions of Christian pacifism that do not, perhaps, have quite the qualities that give special value to the city merchant's treatise on war and are now quite forgotten. But they still have considerable interest as pioneer works in the history of the peace movement.

We may mention first Dodge's own father-in-law, the Rev. Aaron Cleveland (1744-1815), of Norwich (Conn.), well known as an opponent of slavery. Early in the second decade of the century, out of some twenty evangelical clergymen with whom Dodge had been in correspondence—including that militant Calvinist, the Rev. Lyman Beecher—Cleveland alone had come round to Dodge's nonresistant

[33] Among the tracts circulated by the New York Peace Society at this time must have been Dodge's own *Observations on the Kingdom of Peace, under the Benign Reign of Messiah*, an 11-page reprint of an address given to the Society in 1816. In it (p. 9) Dodge prophesies: "We, my brethren, live in the last days, under the mediatorial reign of Messiah, when all these glorious events [i.e., the second coming of the Prince of Peace] are to be fulfilled." Another, and slightly less millennial, production of the same year emanating almost certainly from Dodge's circle was Eleazar Lord's *Thoughts on the Practical Advantages of those who hold the Doctrines of Peace, over those who vindicate War*. On p. 20, Lord, who may be described as a forerunner here of modern war resistance, tells his fellow radical pacifists: "Wars . . . will never cease, unless your sentiments and practice are generally complied with . . . it were absurd to hope for such an event, unless the spirit and principles, and practices of war, are first renounced by individuals. War will become unpopular, and fail of support, in proportion as the number of individuals, who embrace the doctrines and habits of peace, is enlarged." The same emphasis on personal renunciation of war is found in the Society's Tract Number III issued in 1818 with the title *The Question of War Reviewed*. Should a "sober," "humane," "conscientious" Christian wait until all have abjured the barbarity of war before doing so himself, the tract's anonymous author asks (p. 13)? "Even should war continue for ever to be perpetrated by the lowest and worst of the species, will that recommend it to such a man . . . ?" War, then, like drink, it is implied, is a sin that must be given up regardless of the consequences.

[34] Curti, *American Peace Crusade*, p. 9.

[35] *Pioneering for Peace*, p. 18. See also Curti, *American Peace Crusade*, pp. 30, 31, and *Peace or War*, pp. 36, 37.

461

position, though "for two years [he] disputed every inch of ground."[36] In March 1815, Cleveland preached two sermons on the text "Thou shalt not kill." The spirit and the reasoning are very similar to Dodge's. The Mosaic dispensation, which permitted war at God's behest, has been replaced by the new Christian gospel. Henceforth, the sixth commandment admitted of no exception; Cleveland speaks of "the anti-gospel law of self-preservation." Christ's teaching and practice, and that of the apostles and early church (how useful Clarkson was to be to pacifist-minded divines!), forbade taking life even in self-defense. And this prohibition held for communities and nations, not merely for individuals—more so perhaps, because who in practice could distinguish in the international arena between the attacker and the attacked?

All this was, of course, to become familiar stuff in later pacifist literature, but in 1815 it was novel, daring indeed for a Connecticut Congregationalist minister. Cleveland is perhaps a little more subtle than his son-in-law in his discussion of the limits of pacifism. Here, in fact, he brings to mind the arguments of the sixteenth-century Antitrinitarian, Faustus Socinus (whom he had certainly not read). He is ready, specifically, to give sanction to the coercive power of the state. Moreover, he approves the necessity of "confinements and constraints" on the wicked for the sake of the well-being of society, provided this does not entail the taking of life. Certainly, "the Christian principle of non-resistance" means a readiness for martyrdom such as the apostles and early church had shown. Therefore, even if attacked by an armed man intending to kill—the traditional test case of the anti-pacifist debater—the Christian nonresistant must refrain from taking, or threatening to take, life. "But should you maim him for the purpose of disarming him," Cleveland goes on, "this would not be rendering evil for evil. . . . Thus you may bind, or maim, or disarm an enemy, and at the same time, act not inconsistently with his best good." To kill a man is always wrong, even in the name of the law or in self-defense. But to kill in repelling an unprovoked attack by some individual or nation is less heinous a sin than to kill where no such excuse exists. But these were borderline cases of mainly theoretical interest. What was important for Cleveland, as for Dodge and most of the early peace advocates, was international war as it existed in practice in their own day, an evil that admitted of no excuse or palliation, a crime of utmost magnitude that was at the same time unfortunately accepted with resignation by the overwhelming majority of their

[36] *Memorial*, pp. 90-92. See also Devere Allen, *The Fight for Peace*, p. 8.

fellow Christians. "Surely, blood-shedding is the crying sin of the world," Cleveland exclaims. He goes on: "Christians by abetting wars, delay the millennium. . . . We may never expect the world to reform in matters of war and blood-shedding, so long as Christians hold swords, and countenance it in others."[37] Here lay the most important sphere of activity for the Christian pacifist.

Dodge and his new Peace Society had another keen supporter in the prominent New York minister, the Rev. Samuel Whelpley (1766-1817)—like Dodge, a devout Presbyterian. In 1815 Whelpley began a series of open letters to Governor Caleb Strong of Massachusetts, "showing war to be inconsistent with the laws of Christ and the good of mankind" (clearly an echo of the title of Dodge's pamphlet). These he later published in book form under the pseudonym "Philadelphus," dedicating the volume to Governor De Witt Clinton of New York. The treatise ran into several editions, being published as late as 1870 by the Peace Association of Friends in America. It is, indeed, an effective propaganda piece for the pacifist cause.

"The question has been agitated of late," Whelpley tells Governor Clinton, "whether Christians have a right to engage in war." He had himself been led to study the matter as a result of the impact of the recent series of bloody revolutions and wars in Europe. "I have been much gratified," he remarks optimistically, "to hear that several societies are already formed for the promotion of the principles of peace. The effects of union and concentration are well known and were never more necessary than in this grand concern. I trust that measures will not be delayed to let the remote and solitary friends of peace, in various parts of the country, know that the subject is under consideration, and that they do not stand alone."[38] In the course of his letters the author presents the results of his own investigations into the problem of war and the Christian. His conclusion, after consideration of the Biblical evidence and the witness of the early church, is a conviction of the complete incompatibility of war "in every form" and of capital punishment, too, with the profession of a Christian. As civilization and knowledge extend, the peace movement would grow. And he appeals to his fellow churchmen to speed the work on: "The change of times, of manners and customs, and of the established religion of nations, seems to lay Christians now under incomparably stronger obligations than ever before, to be pacific, and renounce war and resistance. Surely, if the primitive Christians did not fight, when they had

---

[37] Aaron Cleveland, *The Life of Man Inviolable by the Laws of Christ*, pp. 3-9, 19, 20, 22, 31, 32, 36-39.
[38] Samuel Whelpley, *Letters addressed to Caleb Strong*, pp. iii, 125.

no other way to save their lives, why should Christians resist and shed blood now, when their religion is established by law, and persecution has ceased through Christendom."[39] Perhaps Whelpley had forgotten here what he had written earlier about the early church falling away from its nonresistant principles, not on account of "her sufferings, but by her prosperity"[40]—or possibly he was just more optimistic, more imbued with current notions of human progress, than his fellow pacifist, the Rev. Cleveland, with his talk of the "dark and depraved world."[41]

The epistolary form used by Whelpley as a vehicle for his ideas deprives his work of the easy sequence into which the arguments in Dodge's treatise fit. It lacks the wealth of illustrative material drawn from the social and economic field that Dodge marshals behind his case against war. The theme of individual conscientious objection is kept in the background. Whelpley, however, is clearer than Dodge (who evidently had difficulty in imagining a government that would be truly Christian) in envisaging the consequences of the adoption of pacifism not only on the individual but also at the national level.

While not excluding the possibility that God might work miracles to protect from injury those following out Christ's example of love and nonresistance, Whelpley cites in support of his case the Quakers' policy of nonbelligerency, which had frequently permitted them to go peaceably about their business unharmed amidst the turmoil of war and rival armies. The results of personal nonviolence in the case of "an individual, refusing from principle to fight or take life on any account" he depicts as follows:

> Let that man go through the world, among all nations, both civilized and savage, and his person will be considered as sacred. This is a known fact, which no one will controvert. He may meet with ignorant savages, who will mistake him for a spy, or an enemy in disguise, and may take his life. But let them once understand that he is perfectly harmless, and they will not hurt him, but treat him with kindness. It must be allowed that they may sometimes lay hands on his property by stealth, or by violence, and may on that account take his life; but this is not common. A man known to be a son of peace, in China, India, Persia, Turkey, Tartary, and among the rudest savages of Africa and America, as well as through all Europe,

[39] *Ibid.*, pp. v, 10-25, 42, 56, 104-12, 122.
[40] *Ibid.*, p. iv.
[41] Cleveland, *The Life of Man Inviolable* . . . , p. 24.

is generally speaking, considered inviolable, both in his person and property.[42]

Not that Whelpley is overly concerned, it should be noted, about the defense of property. Elsewhere he points out the close connection between the pursuit of wealth and the way of violence. Wars (unless they are being waged for that chimera, so-called national honor) turn out more often than not to be sordid businesses of profit and monetary gain.[43] How rarely are they truly wars to protect the life and liberty of the state's citizens. "In fine, if there were no wars but such as are strictly defensive, and none were to kill, but such as have a right to do it on the principle of justice, there would be few wars, and few men would fall in battle."[44]

Never wage an "unjust" war, then, and, in Whelpley's view, one would have gone the better part of the way toward abolishing international war altogether. He does not, however, avoid the issue of what would result for a nation adopting a policy of unilateral disarmament. The common view—that such a nation "would be liable to insult, degradation, oppression and subjugation"—was plausible, certainly; yet it would not stand up, he believed, under close examination. For himself and his family he would opt—"all other circumstances being equal"—to live in a pacifist state rather than in one that was militarily strong and powerful.

Let us suppose, to take a concrete case, that Great Britain disarmed and announced to the world that she had abandoned the use of armed force. What, asks Whelpley, would happen to her? First of all, before embarking on such a course, the government would certainly have taken steps to rectify all outstanding grievances with other nations and thus have removed the main causes of a future war. But more important would be the vast moral influence that such a renunciation of force would exert throughout the civilized world. This, Whelpley believed, would suffice to ward off invasion. "The whole world would say, 'These people make no war: they even refuse to shed blood in their own defence; their dealings are just and honourable; they live in peace; they injure nobody; and shall we invade and seek to destroy them? God forbid!' . . . Should Great Britain declare for peace and non-resistance, it is not probable she would long remain alone, on that ground." True Christians, all the friends of peace, would rally round her. Governments would adopt international arbitration, would set up

[42] Whelpley, *Letters*, pp. iii, 30, 31, 89, 90, 121-23.
[43] *Ibid.*, pp. 117-21.　　　　　　　　[44] *Ibid.*, pp. 76, 103.

a supernational tribunal to administer the law of nations, and would use this as a means of settling disputes instead of appealing to the arbitrament of war. Finally, even if in some rare instance a pacifist nation might be invaded by a power-lusting adversary and subjugated, had not this frequently been the fate of nations armed to the teeth? Putting on one side for the moment consideration of the Christian basis of pacifism, Whelpley draws up the balance sheet between a policy of unilateral disarmament and the pursuit of security through armaments. Over against the remote possibility (in his opinion) of invasion of a disarmed nation, we must mark up against war (the inevitable outcome, he thought, of preparation for war) the destruction of life in battle and among the civilian population, the moral wickedness accompanying all armed conflicts and their vast expense, and—not least—the aftermath of human suffering lasting many decades. "War is, therefore, incompatible with the best interests of nations." A nonresistant people would enjoy God's special protection and favor, since only a virtuous nation would be ready to take the first step in renouncing war in this radical way. On grounds of both expediency and Christianity, therefore, unilateral disarmament is the best policy.[45]

A third work on pacifism emanating from Dodge's group came from the pen of Adna Heaton (ca. 1786-1858), who was also a member of the Society of Friends. His *War and Christianity Contrasted*, published in 1816, was a plea to the Protestant churches to complete the Reformation by abandoning their support of war.[46] As a member of the New York Peace Society, Heaton had evidently seen the need, if the Society was to expand, of drawing upon the vast resources represented by church membership. The work is scarcely original—unless it be in the prominence given to Old Testament prophecies of the coming of Christ's kingdom as an argument for pacifism. It draws heavily on the previous writings of Clarkson and Dodge. At the same time, it is simply and clearly written and not excessively weighed down with Biblical citations, which figure so prominently in the writings of many of the early peace advocates. Judged by the membership roll of his Peace Society, however, Heaton's small book can have made little impression.

Among those drawn very largely by their reading of Dodge to espouse complete pacifism may probably also be numbered a young Baptist minister from New England, Daniel Chessman (1787-1839). Chessman's first doubts about the legitimacy of war were aroused in

---

[45] *Ibid.*, pp. 88-103.

[46] For Heaton's tract, see the article by Robert H. Morgan in *Friend*, vol. 114 (1940), no. 6, pp. 91-93.

1815, soon after the return of peace, when he came upon a small tract against war (very possibly Dodge's effort published around that time) which prompted him to begin a careful examination of the Bible to see what it really said on the question and to discuss the whole matter with his friends. "The more I read, and conversed, and reflected," he relates, "the more my doubts prevailed, the more my mind was shaken," until, finally, he started to put his thoughts down on paper in an effort to clarify his own beliefs. "The result was a complete conviction, that war in all its forms, is contrary to the gospel." "An Essay on Self Defence designed to show that War is inconsistent with Scripture and Reason," a work of some 20,000 words, was finished on 8 June 1816.[47] Its author's attempts to find a publisher were, however, unsuccessful—the time was still premature for the pacifist case to find an easy hearing in America—and so "the Chessman manuscript . . . browning at the edges, the ink fading on the passionate pages" remained undiscovered until a couple of decades ago.[48]

Chessman was quite an able writer, a man of some education—he held degrees from Brown University—and one, too, who obviously felt keenly on the subject of war. Not political considerations, he stressed, but deep religious conviction had led him to compose the essay. "I . . . feel it my duty," he wrote, "to avow my sentiments, and use all my influence to spread the light of the gospel of the Prince of Peace."

In his discussion of the New Testament basis of pacifism and in his pleading of the humanitarian case against war, Chessman has little to say that was not to be said with greater or less eloquence by the other publicists of the contemporary Anglo-American peace movement. On the other hand, he shows greater awareness than some among the latter of the fact that war is not simply the outcome of human sin but is a more complex phenomenon—the result, too, of social maladjustment. While believing that a truly peaceable nation would most likely be secure from attack. Chessman has a vague notion of the need to devise a nonviolent strategy of defense, although he puts forward no concrete proposals. Unlike Dodge, he does not consider that government is incompatible with nonresistance. He conceives of a noninjurious use of force in dealing with the "enemies" of the community. In this case, he sees no parallel between law enforcement and the bringing of serious offenders to justice and the unchristian arbitrament of war. The death penalty and harsh punishments are certainly wrong. But "for incorrigible offenders, confinement to

---

[47] The manuscript is now in the S.C.P.C. See esp. pp. 4-18, 26, 27, 73-76.
[48] See Devere Allen, "Daniel Chessman: An Unheard Voice for Peace." *Friend* (Phila.), 10 July 1952.

labor for a period, or for life, would effectually preserve the peace of society" in a pacifist state, provided it was understood that the prevention of crime, and not revenge, was the object.

In several passages Chessman deals with the position of the conscientious objector. He is opposed to any refusal to pay taxes on the grounds that "they may be appropriated to improper uses," that is, to the support of war. He believes, too, that a pacifist, if called upon to serve in a military capacity, might disengage himself, where possible, by the payment of a fine, "which is the same as a tax." But under no circumstances should a Christian objector agree to perform any kind of military service. In wartime, Chessman advises, "it might be prudent for Christians to retire as far as possible from the bustle of war" to avoid any temptation to abandon the way of nonviolence; for, although he advocated personal nonresistance in case of attack, he realized that there might be situations when it would be extremely difficult for a man, in the heat of the moment, to resist resort to armed defense.

II

While Dodge and his associates were preaching nonresistance down in New York, a second center of peace activities was forming in Boston around the person of the Unitarian minister, the Rev. Noah Worcester (1758-1837). Dodge and Worcester were, indeed, the real founders of the American peace movement, each at the beginning working independently without knowledge of the other's efforts and never wholly united on the means to be pursued toward their common goal of universal peace.

Worcester, like Dodge, had been raised on a small New England farm, and he spent most of his early life in his native New Hampshire. In his childhood he had listened to Quaker views on war, but, whatever fruit they may later have borne, they made little impression on the lad at the time. He had blithely enlisted in the Revolutionary army and felt little or no scruples at that time about participating in war. According to his own account (set down by him in 1822), his conversion to an antiwar stand came only gradually, in stages. The first impulse to serious reflection on the consistency of war with the Christian religion was given him by the minister of the country parish to which he came at the end of the Revolutionary War. The Rev. E. Estabrook, whose antiwar stand has been mentioned earlier in the section dealing with the American Revolution, was not the missionary type of pacifist, but he gave Worcester a book examining the arguments both for and against war from a Christian point of view that profoundly affected the young man. Though far from being a pacifist yet, Worcester says of himself: "I could no longer take pleasure in anything of a military nature." Ordained as a Congregational minister (Worcester was later to go over to Unitarianism) and soon Estabrook's successor, Worcester came more and more to feel that all war was a horrible business and that preparation for it, too, was incompatible with Christianity. He began to doubt the propriety of the military chaplain's office. But still, as he wrote later, "my ideas on the subject were dark, perplexed and confused. . . . I did not then understand that all wars are conducted in an offensive as well as defensive manner, nor that the spirit of war is repugnant to the spirit required by the gospel, and exemplified by the Prince of Peace."[49] When Dodge published his little peace tract in 1809 Worcester thought the New Yorker had gone too far in his uncompromising condemnation of all wars.[50] It was the War of 1812, he tells us, that "was the occasion of perfecting the revolution in my mind in regard to the lawfulness of war." He believed the war to be unnecessary for either side, to be "unjust." He preached in favor of peace and felt unable to offer up prayers in church for the success of the republic's arms, becoming, as the struggle progressed, increasingly convinced of the barbarous and unchristian nature of the whole war method as a means of settling disputes.

Out of this conviction of the wrongness of war arose a short treatise to which he gave the title *A Solemn Review of the Custom of War*. It appeared in print in Boston on Christmas Day 1814 just as the Treaty of Ghent bringing the war to an end was being signed in Europe. In the course of writing the little work, says Worcester,

I became thoroughly convinced that war is the effect of delusion, totally repugnant to the Christian religion and wholly unnecessary except as it becomes necessary from delusion and the basest passions of human nature; that when it is waged for a redress of wrongs, its tendency is to multiply wrongs a hundredfold; and that in principle, the best we can make of it, is doing evil that good may come.[51]

Curti has described the *Solemn Review* as "an epoch-making classic in the history of peace literature." It was to be many times republished and has exerted a very considerable influence on the peace movement since Worcester's day. However, at the time, with the war

[49] Henry Ware, Jr., *Memoirs of the Reverend Noah Worcester*, pp. 60-63.
[50] *Memorial*, p. 89.
[51] Ware, *Memoirs of . . . Worcester*, pp. 64, 66, 67.

still on and no organized peace groups in existence to serve as sponsors, it had been impossible to find a publisher for it, and the author paid for its printing himself out of his very modest resources.[52]

Worcester's overriding theme in the pamphlet is the inhumanity and unchristian character of international war and the possibility of its abolition, which was as feasible, he argues, as had been the abolition of the slave trade by the British. He reviews in turn, and refutes, the arguments urged in favor of war: that it has been sanctioned by God through the Old Testament or that it is necessary to redress national wrongs, to defend national honor, and to resist aggression. The Messiah's kingdom, he replies, which has replaced the law of the old dispensation, should be a reign of peace. For the righting of grievances not war, which usually only aggravates the evil, but the formation of "a confederacy of nations" and of "a high court of equity to decide national controversies" is the answer. And as for the danger of aggression and of national humiliation, which it is alleged would result from "a spirit of forbearance on the part of a national government," Worcester points to the experience of two pacifist sects, the Quakers (especially Penn's experiment in Pennsylvania) and the Shakers (whom he must have known in his own New Hampshire), for proof that a policy of peace was most likely to evoke a like spirit in the other party.

War and preparation for war, then, must be "abolished," "banished," from the intercourse of civilized nations. For this end Worcester goes on to plead two further reasons. There is, in the first place, the difficulty in a quarrel between two or more governments of distinguishing which among them is truly the aggressor: a vital point, since wars of aggression by this date were pretty generally condemned among Christians. Secondly, the involvement in war of guilty along with the innocent, which is almost inevitable under modern conditions, makes it ineffective as a moral agent. In most cases, the people actually responsible for an evil national policy escape scot-free in war, while those who had nothing to do with the framing of policy suffer and die for the sins of the rulers. "A mode of revenge or redress which makes no distinction between the innocent and the guilty ought to be discountenanced by every friend to justice and humanity."[53]

Immediate action was necessary if war was ever to be abolished. As a first step, Worcester proposes the organization of peace societies throughout Christendom to put pressure on the governments to pur-

---

[52] Curti, *American Peace Crusade*, p. 10.

[53] Worcester, *A Solemn Review of the Custom of War* (1904 edn.), pp. 3, 4, 6-12, 14-16.

sue a conciliatory foreign policy and at the same time to spread peace literature among the peoples of the world. Education in peace had a vital role to play in this work and so did organized religion. Worcester pleads for ministers of religion and Bible and missionary societies to join in the crusade alongside the Quakers and Shakers and peace sects.[54]

Worcester, unlike Dodge, was always a gradualist in this question of war. He aimed, by the slow dissemination of the word of peace through societies and convinced individuals, to eliminate war from the civilized world. Dodge always had at the back of his mind—and we can see this train of thought between the lines of all that he wrote —a personal refusal by the Christian man of peace to have anything to do with the work of war. When he read the Solemn Review, he regretted what he considered Worcester's prevarication, regarding him as a man of merely half measures. But he adds of Worcester: "He took an intermediate course, as a matter of expediency, rather than his own private sentiments."[55] That, as Dodge hints here,[56] Worcester even as early as this was more radical in his peace views than most writers have thought seems to be true. His message was directed primarily at his fellow Christians; the inconsistency of armed conflict with the gospel teachings was at the heart of his objection to war. It is extremely probable that privately, in the recesses of his heart, he had already come to accept the radical position; at least, if not, he was on the brink of doing so. In his Solemn Review Worcester puts forward no plea for "defensive" wars, never urges that in some—however unlikely—circumstances the waging of war is compatible with Christianity. He simply does not come down on either side; he ignores the whole question of the relationship between the Christian witness and the state's demand of military service from the individual citizen. But he does speak glowingly of the peace testimonies of Quakers and Shakers and does not attempt to soften their absolutism. It is the institution of international war, however, that is the real enemy for him; there is no need to cloud the issue by considering the question of individual conscientious objection. The "custom of war" (one of his favorite phrases) must be brought into disrepute and finally eliminated altogether, with arbitration and a world court substituted as a means

---

[54] Ibid., pp. 5, 18-20.　　　　　[55] Memorial, pp. 89, 90.

[56] Dodge's associate, the Rev. Samuel Whelpley, writing in 1815 in his Letters (p. 9), also regards Worcester as then opposed to all war. Joshua Blanchard, on the other hand, who was associated with the Massachusetts Peace Society from 1816 on, writing much later implies that at the time of his joining the Society Worcester still balked at condemning defensive wars as unchristian. See his statement in S. E. Coues's "Peace Album," Harvard University Library, MS Am.635*.

471

of settling international disputes. This was the most pressing task as the war drew to a close, and the coming era of peace gave promise of the fulfillment of his hopes.

On 28 December 1815—almost exactly a year after the publication of his *Solemn Review*—Worcester, together with a few intimate friends, brought into existence the Massachusetts Peace Society at a meeting held in Boston.[57] The membership list of the new Society was eminently respectable, more august, indeed, than Dodge's New York Peace Society, for it included, in addition to an imposing array of ministers of religion and substantial Boston merchants, "the names of the governor, the lieutenant governor, two respectable judges, the president and several professors of Harvard University." Clearly, from the outset, it accepted persons who did not hold the full pacifist position. Indeed, at first, the nonpacifists easily predominated. Its object was simply to unite all those who wished to exclude the war method as both unchristian and inhumane from the community of civilized nations. As the constitution passed at the opening meeting and designed—as it said—"to embrace the friends of peace of every name, . . . men of different sentiments, both as to politics and religion" expressed it:

> We intend that this society shall be established on principles so broad, as to embrace the friends of peace who differ on this as well as on other subjects. We wish to promote the cause of peace by methods which all Christians must approve,—by exhibiting with all clearness and distinctness the pacific nature of the gospel and by turning the attention of the community to the nature, spirit and causes and effects of war. We hope that by the concurrence of the friends of peace in all nations, and by the gradual illumination of the Christian world, a pacific spirit may be communicated to governments,—and that, in this way, the occasions of war, and the belief of its necessity, will be constantly diminished, till it shall be regarded by all Christians with the same horror with which we now look back on the exploded and barbarous customs of former ages.[58]

There was nothing revolutionary or antipatriotic or subversive, therefore, about Worcester's Society; it was much less uncompromising in its stand than either the New York Peace Society or the London Peace Society set up in the following year. Its main work was to en-

---

[57] See esp. Curti, *American Peace Crusade*, pp. 11ff.; Galpin, *Pioneering for Peace*, pp. 25ff.

[58] *A Circular Letter from the Massachusetts Peace Society*, pp. 4, 11, 14-16.

lighten public opinion through tracts and articles on the moral iniquity, the economic waste, and the unchristian character of international war. It strove to influence those in high places.[59] It hoped to work through governments (even the Holy Alliance won the Society's praise until the Society became disillusioned with its reactionary policies). At first, the Society appeared to be making fairly good, if slow, progress. In 1818 it had about 1,000 members, including those in local branches outside Boston. But during the twenties numbers began to drop off; with only wavering support now from the branches, the parent Society began to wither. In 1828, like the New York Society, it merged with the newly founded American Peace Society.

It was, indeed, quite a diversified group that Worcester had gathered under the umbrella of his Peace Society. For, in addition to prominent figures in politics and law, education and the ministry, who gave the Society its respectability, there were also a few radicals in it who insisted on condemning all wars, defensive as well as aggressive, and on identifying Christianity with a Quakerlike pacifism. Worcester, as we have seen, was himself sympathetic to this viewpoint. Then there were such men as Joshua P. Blanchard who, despite his well-to-do Boston mercantile background, had consistently refused to serve in the militia and, as we have seen, had been a conscientious objector during the recent war. It may have been their influence that led the Society in 1816 to petition the state legislature against compulsory militia service for those conscientiously opposed to it. (The militia, it is true, was also none too popular in wide circles that had no connection with pacifism.) It asked for the exemption not only of Quaker objectors, "but of all that believe with them that war is inconsistent with Christianity," regardless of which church they belonged to.[60]

The Society was probably responsible, too (though not, perhaps, officially), for an interesting little pamphlet published two years later, which in dialogue form pleads the case for widening the exemption granted hitherto only to Quakers. "Other Christians may have consciences and rights," Mentor argues. What advantage can be derived

[59] But it did not meet with approval everywhere. Ex-President John Adams in 1816, on receiving an invitation from Worcester to become a member of the Society, wrote: "Experience has convinced me, that wars are as necessary, and as inevitable, in our system, as hurricanes, earthquakes and volcanoes. . . . Instead of discouraging a martial spirit, in my opinion it ought to be excited. We have not enough of it to defend us by sea or land. Universal and perpetual peace, appears to me, no more nor less than everlastingly passive obedience and non-resistance. The human flock would soon be fleeced and butchered by one or a few. I cannot therefore, Sir, be a subscriber or a member of your society." (Quoted in Allen, *The Fight for Peace*, pp. 208, 209.)

[60] Curti, *American Peace Crusade*, pp. 21, 30.

473

by the state from forcing men to serve against their consciences? Furthermore, he asks the skeptical Telemachus, supposing it "to be one article of your religious faith, that public war[61] is absolutely murderous, and perfectly repugnant to the precepts and the spirit of the Messiah, thru' whom you hope to be saved," in this case do you think it fair to be required to pay a fine—like a criminal—in exchange for exemption (as in peacetime was usually done in cases of conscience, instead of putting the objector in prison)? Is not this penalizing a man for doing what he considers right, for following his religious convictions; in fact, is it not an infraction of our constitutional rights? He points out to Telemachus that in their own state of Massachusetts fines and imprisonment had in fact been meted out to a number of young men for refusal to train with the militia; and Mentor reckoned the total number of persons throughout the country holding Quaker views on war to run into many thousands. Finally, of course, the doubting Telemachus is won over by his opponent's arguments in favor of granting complete exemption to objectors from the nonpacifist denominations.[62] The lawmakers of the commonwealth, however, remained unconvinced, and prosecutions for dereliction in regard to militia duties, as we shall see, cropped up from time to time well on into the century.

The same pattern we have observed in the case of the Massachusetts Peace Society, of including radical pacifist and conservative peace worker within one organization, can also be seen in a whole host of small (and mostly short-lived) peace groups that sprang up in various other parts of the country from Georgia in the South to Indiana in the West and Maine in the North, spilling over even into Upper Canada and Nova Scotia.[63] In several of these societies Quaker influence

---

[61] This term—"public war"—is frequently used by peace advocates like Worcester and Ladd to denote war between states, as distinct from civil war or, of course, self-defense or the use of armed force to maintain the law. Mentor seems to be pleading here for a right to refuse military service, not only for full Christian pacifists outside as well as inside the peace churches but also for men whose objection (naturally, on religious grounds, too) is to international war and not necessarily to all uses of armed force. Such objection is, in fact, what in the twentieth century would be called a political, a selective one. Mentor's plea was, therefore, in harmony with the policy of the Massachusetts Peace Society in not touching the question of personal nonresistance.

[62] A Dialogue, between Telemachus and Mentor, on the Rights of Conscience, and Military Requisitions, pp. 2-7, 10.

[63] In the first half of the nineteenth century, seemingly the only known instance from the area that was to become the Dominion of Canada of a person converting to a completely pacifist position (i.e., outside the three peace denominations: Quakers, Mennonites and Amish, and Brethren in Christ) is that involving the Rev. Nathaniel Paul, Baptist minister at Wilberforce Settlement in Upper Canada. His acceptance of pacifism stemmed from a lecture that he had heard given in

was strong—in the Warren County (Ohio) Society, for instance, which antedated Worcester's Society by a few weeks, or in Rhode Island where that doughty (and wealthy) Friend, Moses Brown, was the *spiritus movens*. The fifty or so societies that came into existence during this period appear to have contributed little, if anything, directly to the evolution of pacifist thought. But at least they helped lay the foundations for the development of radical pacifism in the thirties and forties by being the first to plant the seed of peace in the hearts of many a later nonresistant radical.

They proved, also, to be useful fields of activity for those who had already embraced pacifism before becoming connected with any peace society. Take, for instance, the case of the Rev. Henry Holcombe, D.D. (1760-1824), for many years pastor of the First Baptist Church in Philadelphia. The doctor as a young man had served as a soldier in the Revolutionary War. The War of 1812 prompted him to examine the problem of pacifism, but he had concluded then that, if all peaceful means of defending independence and liberty against aggression and tyranny failed, the use of armed force was not in fact contrary to the profession of the Christian.[64] Further reading and meditation, and some knowledge, perhaps, of the Quakers, Mennonites, and Dunkers of his own Pennsylvania, however, caused him to reverse his opinion. At the beginning of the 1820's, as a leading member of the Pennsylvania Peace Society, which he had been instrumental, along with some Quakers, in bringing into being at the end of 1822,[65] he preached radical pacifism from his pulpit and censured communicants in the church and his fellow ministers for giving support, whether active or passive, to the war system. He had no desire, he wrote, to

> . . . diminish a particle from the merited eulogy bestowed on thousands for their patriotism and bravery in the revolutionary war. I, implicitly, like many others, held their sentiments, until, at the pressing instance of a learned friend, I was recently led to examine them

London in 1835 by the pacifist apostle, George Pilkington, late captain in the Royal Engineers. See Pilkington, *Testimonies of Ministers, of Various Denominations, showing the Unlawfulness to Christians of All Wars*, pp. 35, 36. The only other testimony printed by Pilkington from the New World was from the Quaker evangelical, Elisha Bates.

[64] Holcombe, *The First Fruits, in a Series of Letters*, pp. 135-44.

[65] In 1829, after Holcombe's death, the Pennsylvania Peace Society was responsible for issuing a radical pacifist organ, the *Advocate of Peace and Christian Patriot*. The journal had to close after a few months, however, for lack of funds. In its last issue (vol. I, nos. 10-12 [June 1829]) we find the following typical comment: "As to *defensive* war, it is altogether a vague and indeterminate term; each nation claims to justify itself under this specious pretence" (p. 75).

in the light of the gospel: the result was my cordial renunciation of the principles of war "in its fairest form," as by no means congenial with the religion of our common Lord. I now see, as war is respected, in a new light, his precepts, life, and whole ministry.[66]

It was not enough to renounce only offensive wars; for who in the Christian churches admits to supporting them? Condemnation of wars of aggression alone would leave the door open for the justification of every war that had ever taken place. "After, and above all, where does any inspired writer say, 'Thou shalt not kill,' *except in self-defence?* . . . Is not, let me die, rather than kill my brother, the language of every consistent Christian?" Let those who think like him have the courage to come out into the open, to risk being dubbed "a maniac or a Quaker," or losing employment or customers, or offending friends and relatives. He called on all the churches in turn, from Roman Catholic to Congregationalist, to come forth boldly with a similar condemnation of all war as contrary to their Christian religion.[67] The summons of course—it was a century or more too early—remained without response.

Returning now to the dominant figure in the early peace movement —if such a phrase may be used of the mild and sweet-tempered Dr. Worcester—we can detect in the course of the decade following the end of the war a certain radicalization in his public utterances on the peace question. Later historians have usually considered that Worcester throughout his career sanctioned wars of defense in certain circumstances, or at least left the question open. Devere Allen, for instance, describes him as merely "a near-pacifist."[68] On the other hand, his contemporary, the famous Unitarian minister, William Ellery Channing (1780-1842), wrote of this last period in Worcester's life: "On the subject of war, Dr. Worcester adopted opinions which are thought by some to be extreme. He interpreted literally the precept, Resist not evil; and he believed that nations as well as individuals would find safety as well as 'fulfil righteousness' in yielding it literal obedience."[69] And who was in a better position to know the exact state of Worcester's

---

[66] Holcombe, *The Martial Christian's Manual*, p. 15.

[67] *Ibid.*, pp. 13-20.

[68] Allen, *The Fight for Peace*, pp. 365-69.

[69] Ware, *Memoirs of . . . Worcester*, p. 141. George Beckwith, Ladd's successor as secretary of the A.P.S. and, hence, third in line from Worcester, wrote later of the gradual evolution in the thinking of his two predecessors from a limited justification of some wars to belief in the incompatibility of all warfare with Christian principles. William Ladd himself, on the basis of conversations later with Worcester on the subject, dated the latter's conversion to the complete pacifist position to the mid-1820's. See his *Obstacles and Objections to the Cause of Permanent and Universal Peace*, pp. 4, 5.

thinking on the subject than Channing, who, though not himself a pacifist ("Brother Farley, sometimes we *must* fight!"),[70] was Worcester's close associate from the beginning in the work of the Massachusetts Peace Society? As his whole career would lead one to expect, Worcester never denied that men might be good Christians (many of them better Christians, he said, than himself) and yet believe in the necessity of what they considered purely defensive wars.[71] But an examination of the files of the *Friend of Peace*, the journal which Worcester edited between 1815 and 1828 under the pseudonym "Philo Pacificus" and for which he wrote most of the columns himself, confirms the impression that he had by this time reached the full pacifist position, although—not wishing to create dissension in the ranks of the peace movement—he was careful to avoid pressing his views on those who could not yet follow him so far along the road.

Take, for instance, the imaginary dialogue on the "Duty of Self-Preservation"[72] between "Beza" (the nonpacifist interested in the problem of peace) and "Erasmus" (the supporter of the work of the peace societies), which was published in the third volume of the *Friend of Peace*. It almost certainly comes from Worcester's own pen. Beza begins by asking Erasmus his opinion on the justifiability of defensive wars. He has been worried by the fact that the *Friend of Peace* has printed little or nothing in their favor. Erasmus answers that history cannot show a single example of such a war, that, moreover, the first to start a war is not necessarily the guiltier party. "Every public war," he goes on, "is on both sides a war of aggression. . . . Hence as wars are generally conducted, the pretended distinction between offensive and defensive war is worse than useless." To justify the latter is, in fact, to justify all wars; to condemn wars of aggression is tantamount to condemning all wars. International conflict should be treated in the same way as the practice of fighting duels. We do not ask who is the aggressor and who the aggrieved; instead, we forbid the practice altogether. In the end, of course, Beza is won over by Erasmus to "the principle that all wars and fightings are antichristian." Nations, like individuals, may do everything to protect themselves and their property from attack—everything, that is, consistent with Christian love and peaceableness, of which war is the complete antithesis. "The precepts of the gospel are the best laws of self-defence and self-preservation, both to individuals and nations." They cannot guarantee, it is true, any more than the war method, absolute immunity from at-

---

[70] Allen, *The Fight for Peace*, p. 368.
[71] Ware, *Memoirs of . . . Worcester*, pp. 68-70.
[72] *Friend of Peace*, III (1824), no. 6, 169-72.

tack and even loss of life. They are more likely, however, to bring security, and they are, besides, morally binding on the followers of Christ.

In 1828 Worcester retired from active work, though he was to live on, a respected figure, for another nine years. Worcester's withdrawal from the scene, which coincided with the creation of a united American Peace Society, gathering together into one fold the scattered peace groups up and down the country, marks the end of the first chapter in the history of the organized peace movement in America.

The movement which, as we have seen, had sprung up spontaneously around 1815 in more than one part of the world ("the world in 1815 had particular reason to be weary of war," writes Curti),[73] had in America grown only very slowly, especially if we compare its progress with the overoptimistic hopes of its leaders and with the exaggerated claims put forward in its publications. It made as yet little headway outside New England. The movement, especially the faith of the radical minority, was widely held to be unpatriotic, directed against the security of the state and the safety of its citizens.[74] Witness, as an illustration of this attitude, the use of pseudonyms by writers like Dodge or Whelpley or Worcester to put forward what they rightly feared would be unpopular views. Not that these men lacked courage or willingness to make sacrifices for the cause; their whole careers show that they were prepared to risk opprobrium and to give freely of their time and money to further what they considered right. But they were a mere handful (despite the weight given by a few dignitaries who supported the work of the Massachusetts Peace Society) pitted against the combined forces of tradition and inertia. They lacked men; they lacked money. They had only boundless enthusiasm and limitless optimism.

Most of these pioneer peace men, the rank and file as well as the leaders, were recruited from members of the larger churches. There were Unitarians, Presbyterians, Congregationalists, Baptists, and Methodists. Episcopalians and Roman Catholics were scarcely, if at all, represented. Officially, of course, the Protestant churches held aloof. Strangely enough, the Society of Friends in America, though their historic peace testimony was a constant inspiration for early pacifist writers—conservatives as well as radicals—contributed, as we have

---

[73] *American Peace Crusade*, p. 4.

[74] The case for defensive war is argued, e.g., by the Rev. Sylvanus Haynes, a Baptist minister from upstate New York, in *A Brief Reply to the Friend of Peace, or A Concise Vindication of Defensive War*, published in 1824. Unlike the authors of some other similar efforts, Haynes is never vituperative in his arguments against the peace men, whose sincerity and goodwill he recognizes.

shown, very little directly to the work of the peace groups. A few Quakers, though none were among the most prominent peace leaders, joined the new societies, and some were active in their work. But there was little collaboration between the peace societies and any of the Quaker yearly or quarterly meetings. Dodge, according to Curti,[75] "had a peculiar prejudice against the Quakers"; in New England, on the other hand, many Friends were suspicious of Worcester's group because of its refusal to condemn all war.

The peace societies were predominantly middle-class in composition (though men like Dodge and Worcester had worked their way up from the humble farmhouse), with clergy and teachers and professional men most largely represented. It was at this class of persons that their tracts and pamphlets were primarily directed.[76]

As we read the pacifist literature of this period, we are frequently struck by the naive optimism and the oversimplifications, the kind of thing we meet in the works of the utopian socialists which began to appear around this time. But this is understandable. The pacifists' appeal was primarily, of course, to the scriptures interpreted in a fundamentalist, literalist spirit, as might be expected before the era of Biblical criticism. (The liberal Unitarian, Worcester, was an exception here.) The familiar distinction was made between the old Mosaic dispensation, when the Jews waged righteous wars at God's express command, and the new dispensation ushered in by Christ. Texts, naturally enough, were bandied about by all the writers: the Sermon on the Mount, as it must be with all pacifist exegetes, was the favorite. However, it was the gospel spirit, Christ's law of love that suffuses the whole New Testament, that they exalted rather than the letter of the text. The radicals concluded from the example of the first Christians, as portrayed in the pages of Clarkson's work on the early church, that the performance of military service is incompatible with the profession of a Christian. And nearly all peace writers agreed with the Rev. Whelpley[77] in castigating the professional soldier as little better than a murderer. Many of the pioneers were already elderly before they reached the full pacifist position, or else their clerical profession exempted them from military service. (The office of military chaplain, it should be noted, was regarded with nearly as much disfavor by the conservatives of the movement as by the radicals.) Some young men, however, were to be found outside the peace sects who refused, when called upon, to serve in militia or army.

[75] Curti, *American Peace Crusade*, pp. 16, 17.
[76] See Curti, *Peace or War*, pp. 13, 36, 37; Galpin, *Pioneering for Peace*, pp. 66-71, 210, 211.
[77] *Letters*, pp. 61-63.

The religious objections to war in the writings of these pioneers were buttressed by more secular arguments. Not only the cautious Worcester but the nonresistant Dodge attacked war for its inhumanity[78] and its economic waste; they held it up as an enemy of liberty and morality. Even those who conceded the theoretical possibility of a defensive war were prepared to admit its unlikelihood in practice. The absolute pacifists, on the other hand, were ready to demonstrate that, in fact, a ban on all wars but the "just" would be equivalent to the condemnation of warfare altogether. The radical Whelpley joined with the conservative Worcester in pleading for international arbitration and the establishment of a world court.

This concentration on the evils of war as an institution may explain in part the absence of any serious attempt on the part of the absolute pacifists of this period (with the exception of Whelpley) either to envisage the consequences of a nation adopting a policy of unilateral disarmament or to provide a nonviolent alternative to the war method. We are in most cases told to trust in God and to pray for his protection. If the abandonment of arms is the gospel method, it is binding on all Christians, who must follow it regardless of consequences. True, one could point to the experience of the Quakers, especially with the Indians in Pennsylvania or their story during the Irish rebellion of 1798 as told by Dr. Hancock, to show that pacifism was also a practical policy, that it had proved to be as secure as, perhaps even more secure than, the pursuit of armed might. But the main task of these writers, as they conceived it, was to measure war and the way of arms by the gospel standard, and by humane and civilized values, and to show by how much they fell short. Theirs were thin voices crying in the wilderness. Their aim was to rouse men to the monstrous evils of war and armed force, not to think through the consequences of their abandonment. In view of the thick crust of indifference and downright hostility they had to hew their way through, this latter task might be left to later generations.

From the outset, indeed, the peace movement was divided, as we have seen, over the limits of pacifism. Did it apply only to relations between states and to wars of aggression? Were defensive wars ("so-called," the radicals were careful to qualify) and armed police action consistent with the peace principles of a Christian? Might one plead a genuine conscientious objection to military service for "public war" and yet not oppose the use of arms in self-defense or for the enforcement of the law? How far must the radical pacifist go in refusing

[78] He also condemns it for its cruelty to the innocent animals, who are slaughtered in its battles. See his *War Inconsistent* . . . pp. 6-8.

480

to collaborate with a state, which depends upon the use of armed force and exacts the penalty of death from its malefactors? Was a pacifist state, indeed, possible at all? Again, must the radical pacifist be a non-resistant; were there even subtle differences of opinion within this last category? All these questions were raised during this early period, and answers attempted according to the beliefs of the different writers. They did not yet, however, threaten to split the movement, which, in any case, was only very loosely organized. Nonresistants and radical pacifists of various shades worked fairly harmoniously alongside the more conservative peace men: in Dodge's New York Peace Society under radical leadership, and with the conservatives in command in the Massachusetts Peace Society and the groups that had arisen under its inspiration. To turn men's minds toward the way of peace, to challenge age-old beliefs in military glory—these tasks were more than enough to occupy the meager forces of the peace societies in those early days. Soon, however, as the radicals grew in strength and influence within the movement and the divergencies in thinking became clearer, the time arrived for a more thorough examination of the principles underlying the practical activities of the peace societies.

Chapter 11

The American Peace Society:
The First Decade

The foundation in 1828 of an American Peace Society uniting in some form of loose association the diverse groups which had been active over the last decade and a half marks a new stage in the development of the peace movement. It coincides, too, with a change in the leading figures that directed its work. Worcester retired in the same year, and Dodge had already made his important contribution by that date. The regional societies that they had founded now became merely sections of the national organization—national, however, mainly in name, for New England continued to be the center of the peace movement's activities for some decades to come. Growth, indeed, only came slowly; at the beginning, the new national Society had only about 300 members.[1]

It was on the stalwart former sea captain, William Ladd (1778-1841), that Worcester's mantle had fallen.[2] Ladd became the new Society's acting secretary and the editor of its journal, *Harbinger of Peace*, which started publication in May 1828. The son of a well-to-do merchant, Ladd had exhibited no interest in scholarly studies during his years at Harvard; instead, shortly after graduating, he had gone to sea for a number of years. Forced out of business by the War of 1812, he had settled in Maine on a large farm owned by his family. Ladd loved rural life and country pursuits, and the farm remained his headquarters even later during his hectic years as a peace propagandist. For many years merely lukewarm toward religion, around the year 1818 Ladd experienced within himself a renewal of religious feeling and became an active member of the Congregational church. His interest in peace dated only from the early 1820's when he read Worcester's *Solemn Review*, joined the Maine Peace Society, and became associated, too, with the larger Massachusetts Peace Society. Peace, therefore, was a latecomer among the good causes to which Ladd gave enthusiastic support. But temperance, Sunday schools, home and foreign missions, the welfare of seamen, as well as of the American Indians, and antislavery were in the end all to take second

[1] Curti, *American Peace Crusade*, p. 43.
[2] See John Hemmenway, *The Apostle of Peace: Memoir of William Ladd*; Curti, *American Peace Crusade*, pp. 34-36.

482

place behind the overriding demands of the peace movement. To it Ladd was soon devoting much of his time and energy, writing to the papers and traveling around giving lectures. The captain had a fluent pen and was an excellent speaker.[3] This work was to grow immensely after he took over the helm from Worcester. His influence on the peace movement, writes one of its earliest historians,[4] "was correlative to that of Noah Worcester. He gave it popularity among the people such as Worcester had won for it among thoughtful clergymen. He carried the doctrine among the mass which before had been confined to the study, or despised as the harmless heresy of a few retired minds." He was un-tiring in his devotion to the cause of peace; as the leading figure in the American Peace Society, he traveled constantly up and down New England and the middle states. "I would impress it on every friend of peace," he had written in 1827, "that he must act as though the peace of the world depended on him alone."[5]

Ladd would only reach the full pacifist position slowly and after much soul-searching; like Worcester, he always remained a moderate. "He was a conservative reformer," writes his successor as secretary of the Society, George Beckwith (1800-1870), who knew him well. Beck-with goes on: "Not William Penn himself was more thorough on peace, yet he preached no crusade against church or state, nor allowed him-self to weaken the foundations of either. . . . He did not expect men to come, at a single leap, the whole length of any reform."[6] This sen-sible, kindly, and tolerant man, who was at the same time practical, not given much to abstract speculations, yet genuinely idealistic and deeply religious, is one of the most attractive figures in the early peace movement. As we watch him making gallant, though not always suc-cessful, attempts to curb his own hasty temper after his conversion to the cause of peace, or applying his gift for conciliation and his bluff good humor to a situation threatened by the strife of colleagues, we are struck by his transparent sincerity and his capacity for leading a movement that was already experiencing the growing pains of early manhood. That he was not successful in preventing it from splitting proved only that the underlying differences of approach had outgrown the possibility of keeping all the peace forces within one organization.

---

[3] According to Dr. Potter of Union College: "The students would hear him for hours, and never grow weary of his anecdotes and illustrations" (letter from Aaron Foster, 7 Feb. 1845, in S. E. Coues's "Peace Album," Harvard University Library, MS Am.635*).

[4] Frederick W. Holland, "The History of the Peace-Cause," B.P.L., MS *5577.98, p. 40.

[5] Quoted in Curti, *American Peace Crusade*, p. 36.

[6] George C. Beckwith, *Eulogy on William Ladd*, pp. 18, 19.

The American Peace Society had come into existence in New York on 8 May 1828. As might be expected from the fact that Worcester himself had drawn up its constitution, which was adopted with only small changes,[7] it continued the policies and principles of its predecessor, the Massachusetts Peace Society. It opposed, in Ladd's words, "the custom of war" as unchristian, "subversive of the liberty of mankind, and destructive to their happiness." Its object was to enlighten men's minds concerning war's iniquity and to bring about its eventual abolition. In respect to the troubled question of the legitimacy of so-called wars of defense, Ladd has this to say on the new Society's position in the first issue of its periodical:

> We do not, as a society, agitate the question, whether *defensive* war can be carried on on Christian principles. We receive into our communion all who seek the abolition of war, whether they hold to the lawfulness of defensive war, or condemn all war in every shape —whether they allow a latitude of construction to the injunctions of our Saviour, or take the exact and strict letter of them. We endeavour to avoid all "doubtful disputation," and to walk peaceably with all who will walk with us, whether they go further, or not so far, as the majority of the society.

Ladd adds, however (following Worcester's line of argument mentioned earlier), that the abolition of wars of aggression would, in fact, mean that an end would be put to war as a whole. "Tamerlane and Napoleon called their wars defensive; and all conquerors, from the one to the other, have done the same. *Such* defensive wars we condemn." The whole controversy, he implies, is a bit academic, irrelevant to the real task awaiting them.[8] But, in fact, as Ladd himself remarks in a later issue, the overwhelming majority in the movement were not pacifists.[9] It might include within its active membership men like Blanchard and Dodge and the Quakers, George Benson of Connecticut and Moses Brown of Rhode Island, but at the other extreme it also numbered in its ranks an array of military officers[10] and state officials.

At the outset, in his first issue, Ladd had opened the columns of the *Harbinger of Peace* to discussion of the limits of pacifism. Contributions to the subject would be welcome, he stated. In his capacity as editor, however, he would be strictly neutral between the two parties:

---

[7] Curti, *American Peace Crusade*, p. 43.
[8] *Harbinger of Peace*, I, no. 1 (May 1828), 6, 7, 17.
[9] *Ibid.*, I, no. 4 (Aug. 1828), 91.
[10] Galpin, *Pioneering for Peace*, p. 215.

the absolute pacifists and the protagonists of the admissibility of defensive wars. "We shall lay no such restraints on our correspondents," he goes on, "and will receive with pleasure, any well written essays on the great cause, should the writer take either side of the question for granted. We have no Procrustean measure by which to gauge our correspondents."[11]

The commonsense, middle-of-the-road attitude which comes out in these remarks is typical of Ladd. Mention a little later of "our own private views" leads one to ask what position Ladd himself had arrived at by this period. The sources do not provide a completely clear answer: at least we cannot exactly date the various stages in the evolution of his views on peace and war. From a perusal of Ladd's signed contributions to the *Harbinger of Peace* during the two years of its existence, as well as the unsigned editorials which presumably were his, also, it seems that he was not far from, if he had not already accepted completely, the full pacifist position. In April 1830, for instance, we find him writing: "We hesitate not to say that from the advent of our Saviour to the present day, there *never has been* a war, in which both sides have not broken his commands. Nor is it at all probable, that there ever will be a war, in which this will not be the case."[12] There is still the element of hesitation that we have noticed with Worcester at a similar stage in his development, an unwillingness to commit himself unreservedly to what many considered an extreme standpoint. But that he had gone far beyond the neutral position which he believed incumbent upon himself to take up officially on this question seems quite clear. Some of his pacifist friends, like Samuel J. May (1797-1871), who as Unitarian minister at Brooklyn (Conn.) was active in his local peace society in Windham County, thought Ladd far too cautious, too slow, too much concerned with the danger of alienating the conservative wing of the peace movement. "We differed only upon one point," writes young May, "the expediency of pressing the highest truth first. No non-resistant believed more sincerely than Mr. Ladd did, that the most strictly defensive war could not be justified upon Christian principles. But he forbore, as I thought too long to press the faith upon others—saying, 'it is never wise to drive a wedge butt-end foremost.' "[13]

From the early thirties on, at any rate, Ladd was openly stating his belief that no Christian should participate in war, that all warfare was —in the current expression—"unlawful for a Christian," and that it was

[11] *Harbinger of Peace*, I, no. 1, 21, 22.
[12] *Ibid.*, vol. II, no. 12. See also II, no. 10, 217, 218.
[13] Letter from Samuel J. May, 4 Jan. 1845, in Coues's "Peace Album."

wrong to take human life under any circumstances, even in self-defense or to protect others. "I am not afraid" in case of attack, he writes, "to trust to moral weapons and the providence of God, and to do as I suppose Christ or Stephen, or any of the apostles would have done in like circumstances, and leave the consequences to God."[14] He supported the stand of the conscientious objector to service in the state militia.[15] He continued, however, like Worcester, to speak in respectful terms of his fellow Christians, who believed in the necessity of sometimes using the sword, trusting that they might eventually be enlightened as to the full truth; and he was always careful to point out that this position was not *ipso facto* incompatible with opposition to every form of international war.[16] He strove, in fact, to keep the issues of "public war" and personal pacifism completely separate. It was the entanglement of these two questions that was soon to cause so much trouble within the peace movement.

The story of his gradual conversion to pacifism is set forth most vividly in an autobiographical passage from an article he contributed to the *Christian Mirror* in 1837. He wrote there as follows of the inner road he had traversed:

When I first began to act in the cause, I saw only "men as trees walking." I saw in war an iron colossus stalking over the earth and trampling down the inhabitants, impoverishing the nations, the father of every crime. But I paid but little attention to the immortal souls which war was sweeping into eternity "with all their sins on their heads." Nor was I aware of the full extent of the law of love. I thought all which was expected of a follower of Christ was, that he would live peaceably with those who would live peaceably with him. Like the first temperance societies, which were established on the principle that it was right to drink a little, but not to drink too much; so I thought it right for Christians to fight a little, pro-

---

[14] Hemmenway, *The Apostle of Peace*, pp. 71, 72.

[15] "Are you past the age of boyhood?" he wrote in one article. "You may soon be called upon to decide, whether you will give your testimony in favour of the horrid and demoralizing custom of war, or not: for you may be called on to do militia duty. . . . On your decision may hang your eternal destiny. As you value your immortal soul, I conjure you to keep away from such scenes. *Now* is the time for *you* to decide. If you once submit, it will be difficult for you to refuse hereafter. Make up your mind, and plead the liberty of conscience guaranteed to you by the constitution, and to which you have as good a right as a Quaker, a Shaker, or a Moravian. You may suffer for it; but if you suffer for conscience sake, you will not lose your reward." (William Ladd, *Obstacles and Objections to the Cause of Permanent and Universal Peace considered by a Layman*, p. 37.)

[16] Hemmenway, *The Apostle of Peace*, pp. 13, 58, 59; *Advocate of Peace*, IV, no. 12 (Dec. 1842), 268.

vided they did not fight too much. It was more than seven years before I could so far divest myself of the prejudices of education, as to see clearly, that *all* war is absolutely forbidden in the Gospel. . . . I cannot distinctly mark the time when my mind changed; . . . I have read almost everything written on this subject, which I have ever heard of, and I have retreated before the light of truth, step by step, until I have at length, as I think, got on gospel ground.[17]

Ladd's public witness, then, was against the institution of international war; privately, however, he had reached the Quaker, indeed almost the full-blown nonresistant testimony against all use of armed force. His position was more radical than Worcester's had been; at the same time, all his influence was used in favor of moderation, of a united front of all shades of peace opinion against their common enemy—war between nations. And, indeed, one of Ladd's favorite peace concerns was the congress of nations: the projected establishment of an international parliament drawn from the representatives of all civilized governments with a tribunal attached for the peaceful arbitration of international disputes. The idea, which has a long history stretching back at least to the fifteenth century, if not to the ancient Greeks, was one which could be supported by those who asserted the right of national self-defense, not to speak of personal resistance to attack. Ladd, along with other publicists of the American peace movement, had been writing on behalf of the project from at least the beginning of the thirties; his work for this cause reached its climax in the publication in 1840 of his famous essay on a congress of nations. Providing "a cheap and sure mode of redress" in the case of national grievances and designed "to moderate the severity of war" should it nonetheless break out,[18] the congress, in Ladd's view, was a desirable step on the road toward a peaceful world. No sanctions were envisaged in Ladd's plan to enforce the decisions of congress or international

[17] Quoted in Hemmenway, *The Apostle of Peace*, p. 64. In 1826, for instance, we find him telling the selectmen of Exeter (N.H.): "I detest all war (for measures purely defensive I do not call war)" (*Christian Mirror*, 28 July 1826). His conversion to personal pacifism must have come sometime before the end of that decade or very shortly thereafter.

[18] William Ladd, *An Essay on a Congress of Nations for the Adjustment of International Disputes without Resort to Arms*, 1916 edn., pp. 17, 96. Ladd's essay was originally published in 1840, along with those of the five winners in the prize essay competition on the subject sponsored by the American Peace Society. Ladd's work was meant as a summary of the most significant points in the rejected essays, but, in fact, it constitutes an original contribution. See also Sylvester John Hemleben, *Plans for World Peace through Six Centuries*, pp. 104-13. See A.C.F. Beales, *The History of Peace*, pp. 56-64, for American and British support for a congress of nations during this period.

court, apart from the moral force of international opinion. On the other hand, the scheme fell short of complete pacifism. And, as critics have pointed out, it ignored both the question of national oppression and the problem of social injustice within the state—two subjects of acute interest to the nineteenth and twentieth centuries. Ladd's interest in the scheme does witness, however, to the catholicity of his concern for peace.

The first couple of years of the American Peace Society and of Ladd's leadership in the movement saw the growth—timid as yet and confined, as we have noted, to only a handful—of the radical pacifist position. Several members or associates of the Society, unfettered by the official responsibilities of a Ladd or perhaps not so fearful of offending the susceptibilities of their less enlightened brethren, now gave open expression in address or pamphlet to their views on the disputed questions of defensive wars and personal nonresistance. Indeed, as we have seen, Ladd himself had encouraged such discussion in the columns of the journal he was editing for the Society. Let us briefly take a look at some of these writings; though they contain little that had not been said before, they will help to show the stage which pacifist thought had reached at this time.

"Thus saith the Lord" is their keynote. Even though the Old Testament warfare was permissible under the Mosaic dispensation, Christ's law of love has precluded the waging of national wars since his coming. What he has laid down for the individual is binding also on the group, the nation. All this is familiar stuff. The Rev. Henry Grew, addressing the Hartford Peace Society in September 1828, impressed on his hearers that the war method was ruled out for Christians as a means by which to defend liberty or property (rank heresy this, in the America of the 1820's!) or to obtain redress for personal or national injuries. Even if we are invaded, we are not justified in killing enemy soldiers—unless, possibly (he leaves the contingency vague), as a last resort in case of an actual attempt on our lives. If we do not resist the invaders by force, Grew believes, they will not actually try to kill us. He reminds his listeners that renunciation of war does not mean opposition to government. "Surely a right to punish those who *do evil*, implies no right to inflict evil on thousands who *do well*."[19]

Two months after Grew's discourse, the Rev. Elijah Jones in his address on 5 November to the peace society in Ladd's own township of Minot in Maine, while acknowledging that "peace societies in this country have not generally denied the right of absolute self-defence, when actually invaded" and asserting his disinclination on this occasion

[19] Grew, *Address delivered before the Peace Society of Hartford*, pp. 8-11, 15.

to discuss the pros and cons of personal nonresistance, stated it as his own opinion, based on the experience of the past, that an unarmed people could survive. The Jews of old had been "God's executioners" in the wars they waged. "At his command they cut off nations whom he thought proper to destroy." But the gospel principle meant non-violence: the early Christians had preferred death to service in the Roman army. In any case, he concluded, the civilized world must outlaw war as a method of settling international disputes. Although he admitted his idea of a nation modeling its foreign policy on Christian love might appear visionary, Jones was certain that international war could be abolished in the present.[20]

In 1829 a young Massachusetts clergyman, the Rev. Thomas T. Stone (1801-1895), produced a small volume of *Sermons on War*. In these sermons Stone runs over the usual arguments of the contemporary peace movement against war, based on scripture, morals, and practical utility. It might, he continues, seem "expedient" sometimes to wage war for the sake of "national preservation"—though on no other grounds. In all other instances, negotiations and concessions are preferable to a resort to war, even on the practical plane. Hinting at, though never explicitly owning to, a personal faith in nonresistance, Stone does, however, advocate national renunciation of the use of force, pleading that his own United States should provide an example here to the world by undertaking unilateral disarmament. This, he admits, would entail risk in the world as constituted in his day. But we must "act as Christians." We must adopt a peaceful stance if we wish others to take the way of peace. And he believed the other nations would ultimately follow in his own country's footsteps, if it disarmed completely.[21]

In the same year that Stone published his peace sermons, we find that ardent pacifist, Joshua Blanchard, addressing the Massachusetts Peace Society (now an affiliate of the American Peace Society) on the occasion of its thirteenth anniversary and expatiating on the nature of true patriotism. He looked forward, he said, to the day when the United States—"to which I owe my dearest political affection"— would abandon the use of arms, even for defense, and devote itself, instead, entirely to the pursuits of peace, "to the diffusion of its own comforts and improvements, and liberty, and religion, through a suffering and darkened world." "What brighter vision could Patriotism unfold?" The example of such disinterested concern for humanity

[20] Elijah Jones, *Address delivered at the Fifth Anniversary of the Peace Society of Minot*, pp. 3, 4, 8-11, 17-21.
[21] Thomas T. Stone, *Sermons on War*, pp. 85-87.

would be a surer bulwark against attack than all the country's armaments on land and sea. People might call this utopia, he added, but the gospels promise the coming of peace on earth, which it is the duty of Christian peoples to strive to bring about.[22]

More specific than Blanchard in his advocacy of the nonviolent way, and more radical than Grew or Stone in the matter of personal nonresistance, was the Rev. Samuel W. Whelpley, a namesake of the pacifist author of the *Letters to Caleb Strong* (see earlier). In 1830 we find him addressing a meeting of the Hartford County Peace Society on the question whether "in any case" a man has the right to take the life of his fellowman. His answer is a decided negative. He does not avoid (as Ladd, for instance, did) the term "nonresistance." "Our Saviour," he says, "expressly, constantly and very strongly inculcated the doctrine of passive obedience and non-resistance in opposition to the principle of retaliation and war." For the state to exact the death penalty was an unmitigated evil. Instead, he suggests that "perpetual confinement with hard labour" would be a more effective deterrent than death—and it would also give the criminal ample time for repentance.[23] Whelpley does not touch upon the question of the refusal of military service by the individual Christian convinced of the wrongness of war: he seems to presume that wars are waged on the voluntarist principle.

In the same year, however, another clergyman—this time, it is interesting to note, an Episcopalian, the Rev. Ezra B. Kellogg—asserted the duty of conscientious objection in forthright fashion in a sermon preached before the Windham County Peace Society. God must be obeyed rather than human governments in cases where the two conflicted, he told his audience. The question to be asked was: "Has God given Christians a right to fight and war?" If they believed (as he did) that this was expressly forbidden them, it was then the responsibility of each individual to see that he did not break God's law. Kellogg made good use of the researches of his fellow Anglican, Clarkson, into the attitude taken up by the primitive church in regard to war, quoting with approval the examples of early Christian conscientious objectors to service in the Roman army. He also cites the Quaker, Hancock, on the pacifist stand of the Society of Friends during the Irish rebellion of 1798 and the often quoted Pennsylvania experiment

[22] Blanchard, *Address delivered at the Thirteenth Anniversary of the Massachusetts Peace Society*, pp. 13-15.
[23] S. W. Whelpley, *An Address delivered before the Peace Society of Hartford County*, pp. 5-9, 12, 13.

in order to buttress his case against the participation of churchmen in war.[24]

Finally, let us consider the 28-page pamphlet written under the pseudonym of "Pacificus" and published in 1830 by the executive committee of the American Peace Society under the title *Appeal to American Christians on the Practice of War*. The little work deals mainly with a couple of subjects, which had become by now standard themes in the literature of the peace movement: the horrors and moral evils of war and military life in general and, secondly, "the Christian testimony against war" as reflected in the books of the New Testament and the history of the early church. It condemns the terrible record of Christianity in bringing war and desolation, the sword along with the Bible, to the heathen continents of Asia, Africa, and South America, and in its final pages it calls on the churches to unite in a condemnation of all war.[25] What is interesting about the pamphlet is not the general arguments, which are similar to those we have been discussing, but the fact that here a radical position is taken up in a publication issued officially in the name of the Society.

In its pages "Pacificus" contests in the strongest terms the permissibility of defensive wars for the followers of Christ.[26] He does not, it is true, go on to condemn, as Whelpley had done, the retention of capital punishment by the state. This question, in his view, is entirely separate from that of war between nations. "I can understand," he writes, "how the punishment of death for capital offences may be inflicted, as to promote rather than sacrifice the future happiness of the criminal."[27] On the positive side of his general argument, the author recommends the establishment of an international tribunal for settling disputes between governments. This, combined with a national policy of goodwill toward all the world's peoples, should suffice to assure peace to the country.

But what, it might be asked, if no government were yet ready to try this way? What should the peace-loving Christian citizen do in the meantime if his nation was involved in war? "Pacificus" replies: "The time was, (and it may again arrive, after so many ages of moral darkness), when the declaration, 'I am a Christian,' was equivalent to a renunciation of military service. . . . The course then which Christians may pursue, is an extremely obvious one. It may be self-denying and hazardous." He is ready to

[24] Kellogg, *War Contrary to the Gospel*, esp. pp. 24, 25, 27, 28.
[25] *Appeal*, pp. 26-28.
[26] *Ibid.*, p. 28. See Allen, *The Fight for Peace*, p. 380.
[27] *Appeal*, p. 19.

. . . admit the right of individuals, in circumstances where little time is left for reflection, and where no alternative is presented but that of killing or being killed, to follow the first impulse of nature and protect themselves at every expense, without justifying the practice even of defensive war. [However,] there is no such alternative, as the one supposed, presented to a nation, by its most insulting and ambitious enemies. A declaration of war is a subject of cool deliberation, and may usually be prevented by a comparatively trivial sacrifice. . . . Do not, because Providence has placed you at a distance from the scene of blood, or your profession, or any other cause, protects you against the summons to arm and prepare yourself for actual combat, imagine that you have nothing to do with the subject of war. You may hereafter have a more painful connexion with its calamities than you now anticipate.[28]

While prepared for the sake of argument—as we have just seen—to concede to the individual the right of self-defense in the case of armed attack on his person, "Pacificus" hastens to explain that he himself is far from convinced of its permissibility. Against the use of arms for self-defense he urges three considerations. We must put our trust in God's protection alone. We should draw back before the awful prospect of sending a fellowman, the murderer, to his death unprepared and with the certainty of eternal damnation awaiting him on the other side (a curious argument, perhaps, to us today but one quite frequently urged by pacifist writers of the evangelical age). And, thirdly, should we shrink from the privilege of suffering martyrdom for obedience to Christ's commands?[29]

"Pacificus" was obviously an absolute pacifist, albeit a conservative one, and it is, therefore, a little surprising that his pamphlet came out under the official imprint of the American Peace Society at this time, when the nonpacifist element within the Society was still in control and Ladd in his *Harbinger of Peace* was pursuing a neutral line in the debate over defensive wars and personal nonresistance. We know from the *Christian Mirror* (3 February 1831) that the author was a New York clergyman and that his tract was distributed free by the Society. The circumstances of its appearance, therefore, and the voices in favor of absolute pacifism being raised from time to time in the Society's local branches indicate that a fresh wind was blowing in the Society's ranks.

The most sensational statement of the pacifist case, and from a most unexpected quarter, came in 1832. In that year a respected South

[28] *Ibid.*, pp. 22-24, 26. [29] *Ibid.*, pp. 24, 25.

Carolina lawyer, Thomas S. Grimké (1786-1834),[30] was invited by the Connecticut Peace Society, an affiliate of the American Peace Society, to speak in New Haven at their first anniversary meeting on Sunday evening, 6 May. The state legislature was then in session, and, therefore, many of its members, together with state dignitaries, attended Grimké's *Address on the Truth, Dignity, Power and Beauty of the Principles of Peace, and on the Unchristian Character and Influence of War and the Warrior.* "For sheer audacity coupled with cogent pacifist apologetics," writes Devere Allen,[31] "its equal is almost non-existent. Dehydrate it by removing the sanctimonious verbiage and the rhetorical flourishes *au fait* of the period, and the effort is extraordinarily powerful."

Since his undergraduate days at Yale, Grimké had been distinguished for his evangelical piety (he was an Episcopalian) and for the excellence of his classical scholarship. He had had a successful career in law in his native South Carolina; a brilliant orator, he had sat in the state senate for four years. Like so many evangelicals of the period, he had striven to express his faith in works and had given enthusiastic support to a number of "causes," from Sunday schools to the defense of the rights of the Cherokee Indians. "One of the most famous rulers in the benevolent empire" is how a recent historian has described him.[32] Grimké had become interested in the subject of peace toward the end of the 1820's. It was then that he had begun to correspond with Ladd and Samuel J. May, and around 1830 he read—and was greatly influenced by—Hancock's account of the Irish Quakers during the rebellion of 1798 and, a little later, Jonathan Dymond's treatises on peace. He was to have copies of Hancock's book distributed in large numbers among Sunday school children in the South.[33] It was his known interest in peace that prompted the Connecticut group to invite the distinguished Southerner, and Yale graduate, to address their public meeting. His whole career, as well as his family background, was conservative (and he was himself a slaveowner of considerable affluence!); he had not so far openly displayed any particular sympathy with the radical peace position. It was not, in fact, until 1832,

---

[30] See the *Calumet*, vol. II, no. 5, Jan.-Feb. 1835; Catherine H. Birney, *The Grimké Sisters*, pp. 102, 103; Allen, *The Fight for Peace*, pp. 375-80.

[31] *The Fight for Peace*, p. 377.

[32] Gilbert Hobbs Barnes, *The Antislavery Impulse*, p. 153.

[33] "Do you want any of Hancock on Peace?" Grimké wrote to Ladd early in 1833. "I have already distributed upward of seventy or eighty of the precious seed, and I doubt not it has made many a one think who never thought before, and has made many a one acknowledge the true courage of the peace principle" (*Calumet*, I, no. 12 [March-April 1833], 364).

in the course of preparing his *Address,* that he became fully convinced of the incompatibility of war with Christianity and the obligation laid on the Christian to refuse war service.[34] This fact explains the sensation his *Address* made within peace circles, as well as with the general public.

The underlying message, which runs like a thread through the whole *Address,* is the contrast between "the law of violence" exemplified in war and "the law of love" exemplified in peace. It is the spiritual, the moral damage done by war rather than the physical destruction, the losses in lives and property, that is emphasized by Grimké. He does not spare even his beloved classics but condemns them for their dangerous cult of militarism, which inspired youth with a false sense of the glories of war. "Why," he asks, "should the children of a *Christian peaceful* people, be forever under the influence of men, so entirely *the reverse* of what *they* ought to be?" Ancient history's chief value (indeed, the value of all human history) was to show the futility and destructiveness of war. That "the mysterious providence of God" tolerated "the law of violence and retaliation" in Old Testament times, and even used it for his own ends in governing the world, must not lead us to glorify war in the same spirit as the classical historians, because Christ came to institute a new war, the war for peace.[35]

So far, perhaps, Grimké was not likely to have caused offense, at least to anyone ready to attend a meeting of a peace society. Sentiments little different from these had been heard for centuries from countless pulpits. It was the conclusions he was to draw that aroused a storm of criticism.

"War," he goes on to say, "in any shape, from any motive, and carried on in any mode, is utterly indefensible on Christian principles and utterly irreconciliable with a Christian spirit." "There was a time," he reminds his audience, "when the distinguishing mark of Christians was, that they would not bear arms. . . . O! that Christians had persevered in the primitive spirit, which regarded the character of a soldier as pagan, not Christian! O! that they had abided inflexibly by the rule, never to bear arms!" Instead, the Christian church had succumbed first to the martial spirit of the Roman Empire and then to the barbarism of the northern invaders, when its followers should have refused to take up arms to resist the barbarians and have suffered the consequences. They should have answered the call to service by saying: "We will love them that hate, and pray for such as persecute and oppress us. Thus

[34] *Calumet,* II, no. 5, Jan.-Feb. 1835, 136.
[35] Grimké, *Address,* pp. 3-6, 10, 26.

and thus only will we conquer our enemies, and convert the heathen to Christianity."[36]

Finally, Grimké brings up as a test case the American Revolution. Here, at least, for almost all Americans of his day, was an example of a war, the justice of which only enemies of liberty or the pusillanimous would deny. Yes, says Grimké, its aims were unimpeachable, but the means used were wholly wrong and unchristian. After exhausting all possible channels for negotiation, placing their case squarely before the British government and public, the Americans should have told them: "Our purpose is irrevocably taken: we will be free: we will have the precious rights of British freemen; but, never shall violence and bloodshed be our arms." Grimké was convinced (like Whelpley before him) that by pursuing a policy of nonviolent resistance against Britain, "in such an age and such a country, with such a government and such a religion," the American people (had they not, moreover, been endowed with a divine mission, did they not enjoy the special favor of God?) would have ultimately won through to freedom.[37]

Grimké's oration was greeted with shocked ridicule by the general public. It did not by any means win the approval, either, of the whole peace movement, small as it then was. The Connecticut Peace Society, which published the *Address* in pamphlet form, was careful to point out that Grimké alone was responsible for his sentiments on the American Revolution: "On this subject, various opinions exist in the minds of members of peace societies and of others eminent for talent and piety."[38] However, Ladd, while reserving the American Peace Society's neutral position in relation to the legitimacy of defensive wars, commented favorably in the Society's official journal on Grimké's presentation of the radical viewpoint. "To object to war," he writes, "is so contrary to the whole course of our education, that there is a very strong reluctance, in the mind, against thinking of it as unlawful. To one, however, who will take the pains to examine defensive war by the light of the Gospel, it will appear that the opposers of it have much better ground to stand upon than he at first imagined. The subject undergoes an entire change in the examination; and one is astonished at his former opinions."[39]

Other correspondents wrote in to controvert the views of the *Address*. One writer, for instance, while agreeing that nonviolent resistance was fine in theory, thought that in practice it would mean the subjection of civilized nations to ruthless barbarians. What of the fate

[36] *Ibid.*, pp. 29, 30.   [37] *Ibid.*, pp. 42-48.   [38] *Ibid.*, p. 42.
[39] *Calumet*, I, no. 8 (July-Aug. 1832), 232.

495

of the peaceful Peruvians at the hands of the Spaniards? Was not the most effective policy for peace to try to restrict warfare to the strictly defensive and to humanize its conduct when it became unavoidable? In reply Grimké urged the necessity of obedience to Christ's commands (his adversary agreed that this seemed to imply pacifism), of trust in God's protection (which the latter seemed to feel less certain about), and of a readiness, like that of the early Christians, to suffer martyrdom. As for the Peruvians, did not the warlike Aztecs of Mexico also suffer the same fate? And, in any event, the former were scarcely Quakers "without arms or fortifications or military instruments, but the reverse"; the parallel, therefore, did not apply.[40] The argument is interesting, since it is one that was frequently to crop up between pacifists and their opponents. The latter would often cite some instance of the subjugation or extermination of a people who, while not fully pacifist perhaps, were said to be peace-loving and nonresistant; the pacifist, like Grimké, would reply that, in fact, the case did not fit, since the moral force of a nation abandoning arms from conscientious scruples and relying on the power of reconciliation was absent.

Having on account of his *Address* stirred up plenty of opposition in New England both within and without peace circles, Grimké had then to face fresh trouble on his return to South Carolina when he attempted to measure up to his principles in his native state, which was at that time in a condition of acute political crisis. In 1832 a state convention duly elected at the call of the legislature had declared that recent commercial tariffs introduced by the federal administration were contrary to the Constitution and thereby null and void, and that, furthermore, the state had a right to secede from the Union rather than be forced to submit to measures which were deemed a deadly menace to Southern agriculture. President Andrew Jackson reacted strongly to this policy of "nullification" in its most extreme form, and for a time war seemed to threaten between South Carolina and the federal forces, until finally a compromise on the issue was reached. Meanwhile, Grimké, one of the most prominent citizens of the state, felt it incumbent upon himself to make his position perfectly clear in case the impending conflict should come to a head. "For myself," he addressed the people of South Carolina and their leader, John C. Calhoun, in an open letter,[41] "I trust, that I hold with an inflexible conviction the sentiment, that the character of the Warrior, in any point of view is UNCHRISTIAN, and

---

[40] *Ibid.*, I, no. 13 (May-June 1833), 402-8. See also Grimké, *Correspondence on the Principles of Peace, Manual Labor Schools,&.*, pp. 3-7. "Mine is the *Christian*, yours the *heathen* theory," he told one correspondent who disagreed with his nonresistant position.

[41] Grimké, *A Letter to the People of South Carolina*, p. 15.

in CIVIL contest, is absolutely and unchangeably ANTI-REPUBLI-CAN." Moreover, whatever the wrongs his beloved state might have suffered, fratricidal conflict should be avoided at all costs. Let "the law of love" be substituted for "the law of violence," "the law of the sword," he now told his own people, as he had told his New Haven audience a little earlier.

With civil war threatening, the state legislature had proceeded to raise the age limit for those liable for service in the state militia. Grimké, aged 47, came within its net—at least in theory, for it is scarcely probable that he would in fact have been called upon. The conscientious lawyer nevertheless felt obliged to petition the state senate for exemption—or perhaps he welcomed the opportunity to make a public protest in favor of Christian pacifism and against the political policy of "nullification." He pleaded his case solely on the grounds of religious objection to all war, a position he had reached—he states—only about a year previously as a result of a careful investigation of the New Testament. "For the sincerity of these opinions, your petitioner can only refer to the best testimony which man can offer to his fellow-man, the uniform tenor of his public and private life." He believed he could truthfully say now that, unless he completely lost command over himself, he would never wittingly take a human life or even answer blow with blow. He was confident that "to grant his petition will be an act of magnanimity, and of justice to the rights of conscience: and can be no disadvantage to the public; as your petitioner knows of no other person in the State who is of the same opinion." This might, it is true, be regarded as "a strong argument to prove that he is in error; but is it not a still stronger one to establish the strength of his conviction and the sincerity of his scruples? . . . he thus exposes himself in the cause of conscience to . . . ridicule and contempt."

The petition[42] was rejected, Grimké's political opponents representing it to the legislators—it was reported—"as a violent and inflammatory production." Grimké's failure to gain exemption (which apparently did not have any practical ill consequences for him) was undoubtedly the result of political considerations, anger at his determined stand against the dominant majority's policy of "nullification," rather than by the religious pacifism which underlay his objection to military service. His house had been threatened with attack, and he became one of the most hated men in the state.[43]

[42] It is printed in full in the *Calumet*, I, no. 14 (July-Aug. 1833), 432, 433. See also vol. II, no. 6 (March-April 1835).

[43] For Grimké as a many-sided reformer in state politics, see William F. Freehling, *Prelude to Civil War*, pp. 180-82.

Within the somewhat narrow limits of the peace movement, Grimké's challenging stand on behalf of absolute pacifism made a big impact. As we have seen, there had already been some discussion of the problem in the columns of the American Peace Society's monthly organ, the *Harbinger of Peace*, and occasionally in the local societies, too. The debate continued in the Society's new journal, a bimonthly which appeared in succession to the *Harbinger* from 1831 on under the title *Calumet*, the name given to the symbolic peace pipe of the American Indians. Ladd was still in charge, although he did not act officially as editor now on account of the difficulties encountered in running a paper published in New York or Boston from his farm at Minot up in Maine. Soon a lively controversy inspired by Grimké's utterances was being waged in the pages of the *Calumet*.

Meanwhile, the peace groups of Connecticut, emboldened by Grimké's stand in his May *Address*, had temporarily become a center of the more radical pacifist opinion. The Windham Peace Society, in fact, had been responsible in the previous March for printing the first American edition of the famous pacifist tract by the English Quaker, Jonathan Dymond. It was published at Brooklyn (Conn.) in 1,000 copies under the title *On the Applicability of the Pacific Principles of the New Testament to the Conduct of States: and on the Limitations which those Principles impose on the Rights of Self-Defence.* We have seen what an influence its brief 19 pages was to have on the receptive mind of Thomas S. Grimké.

The Windham County Society during this period had as its corresponding secretary the young Unitarian pastor at Brooklyn, Samuel J. May, with whom we shall be concerned later in his role as a devoted Garrisonian abolitionist and nonresistant and as a close friend of the master. In 1832 we find the young minister already grappling with a problem that was to haunt him all his life: the dilemma of how to reconcile Christian nonviolence with the struggle for human freedom. In his review of the Society's activities over the past year, May had mourned the failure of Poland's recent fight against Tsarist oppression. "We deprecated that catastrophe as fervently as any could have done," he wrote, "although that ill-fated nation sought her deliverance by an appeal to arms. While the issue of her contest was undetermined, we cordially united in the wish that she might throw off the yoke of her oppressor." In retrospect, however, the main lesson of the Polish uprising appeared to May to illustrate the futility of a resort to arms in however just a cause. "War is not the means appointed by our heavenly Father for the redress of any of our grievances." And he lamented the fact that the Poles, for all the righteousness of their aims, had not realized this in time, "had not learnt the more excellent way of overcoming evil." On the whole, however, he assessed most positively the stirrings of liberty on the European continent, which had begun to shake the reactionary obscurantist forces that hitherto had almost everywhere been in control. The people were awakening—and this was all to the good in May's view, for the growth of self-awareness among the masses meant indirectly an increase of the sentiment for peace. "We therefore hail every indication of increasing knowledge among the people (however it may be attended by temporary commotions) as auspicious to the cause of peace." That cause, he believed, too, meant pacifism and the refusal of military service in the name of Christ.[44] Not all Christian pacifists, it is true, then or later, looked with such favor on the revolutionary political and social movements of their time. We need not be surprised, then, that May soon found himself on the left wing of the peace movement.

In November 1832 the Rev. Cyrus Yale (1786-1854) spoke—in a more conservative strain than May's remarks just quoted—to a meeting organized by the neighboring Hartford County Peace Society on the theme *War Unreasonable and Unscriptural.* His talk was confined mainly to a discussion of the religious and moral objections to the institution of international war, for, as he said,

> The society which I have the honor to address, stops not to settle the question of defensive war. At this point, the members agree to differ. To those who ask, what shall we do in case of invasion and rebellion? This society would simply say; let us do all we can to persuade other nations not to invade us—to persuade our own countrymen to "leave off contention before it be meddled with."[45]

When the address was printed, however, Yale added a few pages at the end[46] urging some nation—preferably his own United States— to try the experiment of abandoning reliance on the method of armed defense, in the expectation that its courage would find favor in God's sight and its example be followed gradually by the other governments of the world. "There must be a *beginning* somewhere," he wrote. It would entail risks, of course, but not more than the war method which he had shown to be wanting. He cites the examples of the un-

---

[44] May's remarks summarized here are found in extracts from the sixth annual report of the Windham County Peace Society, which was published as an appendix (pp. 13-16) to a pamphlet by the Rev. Richard P. Cleveland: *Abstract of an Address before the Peace Society of Windham County, at its Annual Meeting in Brooklyn, August 22, 1832.* Cleveland's address contains nothing of particular interest.

[45] Yale, *War Unreasonable and Unscriptural,* p. 1.

[46] *Ibid.,* pp. 17-24.

armed Quakers and Shakers, and he points out that the partitioning of Poland, for instance, was not inflicted on a nation that had renounced the use of arms. Was not the experiment of unilateral disarmament worth trying out at least once? "In case of failure, it will be easy to resume the sword."

Of interest, too, are the reasons urged by Yale for the United States to become the first country to adopt what he calls "the principle of entire abstinence from war." The country was, as he says, somewhat removed from the center of militarism in Europe, and its people were not yet inured to the continuous warfare to which the European nations had been subjected over the centuries. Moreover, it had more than enough territory to satisfy the needs of its population for a long time to come; it was unlikely, therefore, to have any inclination to embark on a war of conquest. It was prosperous; there was no lack of employment; there was no economic motive for the people to desire war. A democratic government, the absence of a power-lusting monarchy or aristocracy, was a further guarantee of peaceful intentions. (Yale does admit, though, that the country was perhaps more subject to internal dissension than some European lands.) Finally, on the moral side, he paints a picture of a nation more susceptible than others to philanthropic appeals, strong in the faith of Biblical Christianity, and ready in its youthful vigor to respond to new ideas. Thus we see even America's pacifists at that time sharing in some way in the general feeling of their country's manifest destiny—a destiny, as they saw it, to lead the peoples of the world into an era of universal peace.

In the following year, this time to celebrate the second anniversary of its founding, the Connecticut Peace Society invited a local clergyman, the Rev. Laurens P. Hickok (1798-1888), later to achieve some renown as a professor of philosophy, to address it. More circumspect than his predecessor Grimké, Hickok was careful to remind his audience that the Society itself did not presume to take sides on the question whether any wars were ever justified by Christian standards, that its members agreed to differ on this question, uniting in the desire to bring about the abolition of war and the establishment of universal peace. But he, too, in the course of his lecture declared himself personally a pacifist. "I have no hesitation," he said, "in declaring it as *my own* solemn conviction, that, even to the full extent of non-resistance in all cases of aggression, the danger would be far less than seems generally to be apprehended." He himself believed that the view common among the peace groups that renunciation of defense by arms must await the moment when all had agreed to disarm was an illusion, regrettable in that many potential recruits to the movement were kept away on this account.[47]

In 1834 the Connecticut group even went so far as to publish as its Tract No. I a small pamphlet entitled *War Unchristian; or the Custom of War Compared with the Standard of Christian Duty*, which came out strongly against the whole concept of defensive wars and in favor of nonresistance. The distinction so often made by peace advocates between wars of aggression and just wars of defense was, it claimed, "specious," "a mere delusion," invented by the protagonists of militarism to obscure the issue. Until this fact is realized by the peace movement, it said, the movement will make no progress. The early Christians had preferred death to bearing arms for any cause. Every conflict ever fought, moreover, had been justified as a righteous war. Neutrality was not enough.

It is frequently said by those who attempt to advocate the cause of peace, that they do not intend to say any thing on the subject of *defensive* war. Plainly, then, they had better be silent. For if this false distinction is to be kept up, and if what is called defensive war is justified, or even tolerated, then the cause of Peace has already triumphed; and there is probably not another convert to be made to it in Christendom. For it may be doubted whether any one can be found with the slightest knowledge of the Bible, who will pretend for a moment to justify what is generally called offensive war.[48]

The pacifist current within the movement was not by any means confined to Connecticut. Even as far west as Circleville, Ohio, for instance, we find the Rev. R. V. Rogers—an Episcopalian, too—putting the "argument from Scripture against defensive war" in a sermon to his congregation.[49] Many of the younger men, new recruits to the cause, were strongly influenced by the trend toward radicalism. Take as an example the case of the young banker, Amasa Walker (1798-1873), then in his early thirties.[50] Usually on the side of moderation, he was later to become a leading figure in the American Peace Society and a

[47] Hickok, *The Sources of Military Delusion*, pp. 8-10, 12.

[48] *War Unchristian*, pp. 5-10.

[49] Printed in the *Calumet*, vol. I, nos. 14-15 (July-Oct. 1833). Galpin (*Pioneering for Peace*, p. 98) mentions a synod representing various Protestant denominations held at Adrian, Michigan, where on 1 October 1835 a resolution was passed declaring war an unmitigated evil and urging that Christians "decline military service on conscientious grounds."

[50] See his letter, dated 23 Jan. 1845, in Coues's "Peace Album." See also Curti, *American Peace Crusade*, p. 45.

prominent Massachusetts politician. He had been introduced by a friend to Ladd's *Calumet* shortly after it started publication, and he became a subscriber to the paper. Reading its articles, he soon became convinced that war was not only the greatest calamity that could befall man but, as he wrote later, "that it was under all circumstances, and in every degree and form sinful." Total abstinence from war and preparation for war was a Christian's duty, as much as total abstinence from intoxicating liquor. He brought the question up at a meeting of the Massachusetts Peace Society, which he had recently joined, seeking to persuade its members to come out "openly and boldly" against all war and to abandon the temporizing policy which, he believed, would get it nowhere. He was not successful, of course; despite the rising strength of radical peace views in the constituent societies of the movement and the growing impatience of some of the more active elements in it, the rank and file were as yet unready to follow so far.

Equally interesting is the story of the conversion to pacifism of the young Unitarian minister, the Rev. Andrew P. Peabody (1811-1893), later to become a professor of theology at Harvard.[51] It was not until 1834, when he had to give a series of discourses on the Sermon on the Mount, that he came to think seriously about the relationship of Christianity and war. "I had taken for granted," he writes, "the current opinions of the Church and the world in general, supposing the Quakers to be labouring under a hallucination of mind as to those matters." When he came to prepare his sermon and read through the relevant chapters of scripture, he was surprised to find his old views on the legitimacy of wars of defense giving way to a conviction of the indefensibility of war in general. He astonished his congregation the following Sunday when he preached to this effect; at that date, he records, he found only two male members of his parish who expressed agreement with his sentiments. "I at that time supposed myself to stand entirely alone. I knew of no Christian, out of the sect of Quakers, who maintained the views, at which I had arrived, though I convinced myself that primitive Christian antiquity was on my side." However, he soon afterward became a member of the American Peace Society, another recruit to the band of those who were striving to bring the Society openly to the higher ground of opposition to all wars.

It was Grimké who had given them courage and confidence. This high-minded Southern lawyer, for all the overblown and artificial rhetoric of his style, had spoken to the condition of many earnest enthusi-

---

[51] See his letter, dated 28 Oct. 1845, in Coues's "Peace Album."

asts for peace up and down New England. He had shocked and shaken some of the more conservative members of the peace movement, as well as the outside public, who saw in his doctrines a threat to the security and stability of the state. The limits of pacifism had become a live issue, a subject of animated discussion, in peace circles —as was shown, above all, in the large amount of space now being devoted to it in the columns of the *Calumet*. It was more than eighteen months, however, before an effective counter-blast to Grimké appeared in the form of an article entitled "Defensive War Vindicated" by the redoubtable Dr. William Allen (1784-1868), president of Bowdoin College and a vice-president of the American Peace Society. It was published in the *Calumet* at the beginning of 1834.[52]

Allen prefaced what he had to say by stating that he regretted that the question of defensive wars had been raised within the Society at all. Since it was being discussed, however, he said he wanted to set forth the Christian case for the rightness of such wars. This case he based mainly on the comparison of defensive war with the enforcement of justice. Killing in such conflicts was equivalent, not to murder, but to the execution of a murderer after due process of law. He was not convinced, either, by Clarkson's evidence for the pacifist stand of the early church. And anyhow, he asked, what would Grimké, learned as he was in the law, actually do if he were the chief magistrate of a city attacked by pirates? "What is there in Christianity to discountenance such a defensive war, any more than there is to prohibit the killing of a mad bull or a hungry wolf?"

Allen's article was a serious challenge to the pacifists, not only because of the cogency of many of its arguments but, equally, because of the authority its author enjoyed as a leading educationalist and one of the foremost figures in the peace movement. The first to rush into the breach was Ladd himself.[53] "It is the most forcible defence of the right of defensive war I have ever seen," he readily admitted. "In short, it reasons in the same manner as I myself reasoned, though much more forcibly, for many years after I was an advocate for peace." Explaining that his present comments would be brief, a stopgap only until Grimké had had time to compose a considered reply, Ladd stated his objection, in the first place, to Allen's comparison between international war as it had existed hitherto and the judicial process. A closer parallel, in Ladd's opinion, would have been with the medieval institution of trial by combat or with the custom of dueling. If a congress of nations and an international court of justice administering an inter-

[52] *Calumet*, I, no. 17 (Jan.-Feb. 1834), 324-32.
[53] *Ibid.*, I, no. 18, 553-56.

national code of law were established, then, he said, he would be prepared to concede some validity in Allen's reasoning here. "The argument will have some force to prove the necessity of physical power to carry into effect the sentiments of the court"—if, however, as was indeed most likely, the nations had not by that time outgrown the need for using physical force. Secondly, Ladd accused Allen of ignoring the injunctions of the New Testament which, if followed, seemed to him clearly to debar Christians from ever resorting to war. "The great error [in Allen's presentation] is, putting the doctrine of expediency in place of the precepts of the gospel." Abandoning the higher ground of scripture for the quagmire of expediency, the doctor made far too much play of the argument from supposition. "If such and such happened, what would . . . ?" seemed to Ladd of only secondary importance beside the gospel imperative.

In the following issue,[54] Allen reiterated his belief that the early church had not, in fact, been pacifist. And Ladd retorted with the comment that the attitude of the Christians of those times, especially in view of the uncertain nature of the evidence, should not, indeed, be made the touchstone of conduct for contemporary Christians, who were as able as the early fathers themselves to reach their own conclusions—a line of reasoning that could, of course, be turned as much against pacifist writers as against their opponents.

The *Calumet*'s editor, however, was still merely marking time while he waited for the busy Grimké to complete his authoritative reply to Dr. Allen's onslaught. It was never to be finished, for in October 1834 Grimké died suddenly and unexpectedly in the course of a lecture tour in the West. His death at the comparatively early age of 48 was a big loss for the pacifist cause and, indeed, for the whole reform movement. Still at the time of his death an owner of slaves, he was just beginning to give the whole question of slavery his serious consideration, and his reforming friends were almost certainly right in believing that, if he had lived, he would eventually have come around—as his two sisters, Sarah and Angelina, were soon to do—to the full abolitionist position.[55] In the nineteenth century, at any rate, absolute pacifism and slaveholding could surely not lie long together in a man so conscientious as Thomas Grimké.

Ladd was able to print some 25 pages of the manuscript which Grimké had left unfinished. They appeared in the *Calumet* in the first half of 1835,[56] reproduced at the latter's special request in his own re-

---

[54] *Ibid.*, II, no. 1 (May-June 1834), 12-23.
[55] See, e.g., May's letter cited above in Coues's "Peace Album."
[56] II, no. 5 (Jan.-Feb. 1835), 140-51; no. 6 (March-April 1835), 165-80.

formed system of spelling. Grimké is mainly concerned here with the relationship between civil government, the office of the magistrate which he recognized as one worthy of the Christian citizen, and the armed defense of the community against external attack. It was at this point that Allen had made his most pertinent sallies against the pacifists' position, and Grimké began by pointing out the opposing concepts the two men held of the functions of the magistrate. Allen took it almost for granted that the magistrate, the ruling authority, had a right to take life. Grimké was inexorably opposed even to capital punishment: "the *first* duty of the Magistrate is *the reformation of the offender.*" How would this be possible if the offender was to be punished by death? Certainly, St. Paul had said of the magistrate: "He beareth not the sword in vain" (Rom. 13:4); but this Grimké interpreted as a metaphor for the general right of government to punish citizens for breaking the law, and not as a sanction for the infliction of the death penalty. In any case, he went on, a parallel could not fairly be drawn between the legitimate functions of civil government and the waging of even a defensive war, since no supranational community, no international code of law, was then in existence.

Finally, Grimké took up Allen's challenge to explain what course he would pursue if in the position of chief magistrate of a city attacked by pirates. If the people were unwilling to follow him, he said, he would resign. If they were ready to give him their confidence and support, on the other hand,

I should make proclamation, that all the churches be opened, and that prayer be offered by the clergy, and all the pious, that God would be pleased to change the hearts of our invaders, and to manifest his power and mercy in our deliverance. That done, I should throw open the gate that fronted the enemy. Thence would I issue forth . . . with all the clergy, and a long line of Sunday School Teachers and Scholars, dressed in the white robes of peace, and chanting . . . the hymn of Christian faith and hope.

They would either die as Christian martyrs or, with God's grace, melt the hearts of the invaders. If they put up armed resistance, however, they might still have suffered defeat and all its horrors or, as victors, have conjured up a train of revenge and retaliation on the part of their enemies. For all its air of fantasy, Grimké's reply had made some telling points in refuting the analogy between international war and the police functions of national government.

This discussion of the limits of pacifism in the pages of the *Calumet* had not been confined to Grimké, Ladd, and Allen. Many readers joined in, and almost all supported the opposition to defensive wars. While still backing the Society's officially neutral stand, with freedom of discussion of the issue among its journal's readers, Ladd now felt "that articles in favour of war in any shape, should not" be "published, without . . . answer."[57] Most of the Society's leaders, he was able to claim, had taken "the high ground" of opposition to all forms of war as contrary to Christianity.[58] The majority of members, however, obviously less vocal than the energetic group of radical pacifists who were writing to the *Calumet* and making their influence felt in the counsels of the Society, still continued to cling to a belief in the legitimacy of war in certain circumstances.

In the mid-thirties the absolute pacifists had gained powerful allies in the persons of two prominent academic philosophers: Dr. Francis Wayland, D.D. (1796-1865), president of Brown University and a Baptist minister, and the young Bowdoin professor, Thomas C. Upham (1799-1872). Dr. Wayland's support, it is true, was somewhat hesitant, and he was never very closely associated with the work of the peace movement. He was, in fact, no more sound in his views (in the eyes of the strict reformers) on the question of capital punishment, for instance, which he regarded as appropriate for at least the crime of murder,[59] than he was on the issue of slavery when asked whether slaveholding was not incompatible with Christianity. Nevertheless, his explicit defense of nonresistance in the pages of his very popular textbook of moral philosophy, *The Elements of Moral Science*, first published in 1835 and repeatedly reprinted for many decades to come (though today it appears to us a turgid production), gave the doctrine respectability in circles where it would otherwise have been looked at askance and brought it to the attention of young men who might otherwise have passed it by.

The doctor deals with the problem of war and its relation to morals (Christian, of course) in half a dozen pages of his chapter on "Benevolence toward the Injurious."[60] Here Wayland posits a "law of benevolence" deriving from the precepts of the gospels, whereby not only individuals but nations, too, must return good for evil. "Hence it would seem," he goes on, "that all wars are contrary to the revealed will of God, and that the individual has no right to commit to society, nor society to commit to government, the power to declare

---

[57] *Calumet*, II, no. 6, 163.   [58] *Ibid.*, II, no. 5, 138.

[59] Francis Wayland, *The Elements of Moral Science*, 1835 edn., p. 440.

[60] *Ibid.*, 1835 edn., pp. 441-46. See also the introduction by Joseph L. Blau to the 1963 edn. of Wayland's tome, pp. xlviii-xlix, for the latter's views on war. Blau also reviews the previous editions published.

war." So much may be generally admitted. But how must a nation act until the day when all governments are ready to accept the benevolent principle? Answer: a Christian nation must not wait until all are agreed. Abandoning all weapons of defense, as well as of offense, and relying solely on "the justice of its own conduct, and the moral effect which such a course of conduct would produce upon the consciences of men," such a nation would most likely emerge unscathed from the aggressive designs of its neighbors. "There is not a nation in Europe that could be led on to war against a harmless, just, forgiving and defenceless people." "But suppose this method to fail. Why, then, let us suffer the injury. This is the preferable evil of the two. . . . I answer, suffer injury with forgiveness and love, looking up to God, who, in his holy habitation, is the Judge of the whole earth." He will not try us beyond our powers of endurance, because He could never demand of us the impossible. If we have to suffer aggression, it will come as a punishment and an object lesson for departing from "the law of benevolence," as a result of our nonloving actions in the past.[61] Such were the lessons which Wayland in his textbook placed before several generations of students of philosophy.

Thomas Upham was never the figure that Wayland was in the world of American learning. His textbook of pacifism, however, is of much greater importance in the history of the peace movement than the few pages which Wayland devoted to peace in his textbook of moral philosophy. Upham's *Manual of Peace*, which he published in 1836 (and which sold out in a few months), was a kind of encyclopedia of peace, a century before Aldous Huxley's attempt at something similar in the 1930's and on a much more ambitious scale. (It runs to more than 400 pages.) It is, in fact, one of the first attempts to give a full-scale exposition of pacifist ideology. In this aim it is not altogether successful, but it is as a pioneer work that it must be judged and its defects assessed. As Devere Allen aptly remarks of Upham: "He, too, was subject to the inadequate critical knowledge of his time, yet his vocabulary seems less

[61] In 1865 Wayland, then retired, published in Boston a "revised and improved edition" of his *Elements of Moral Science*. While still maintaining the duty of Christians, even in a collective capacity, to return good for evil and still condemning war as a method of settling disputes, the doctor made certain small but significant changes. The use of armed force, he now asserts, may be necessary against a nation which fails to respond to a policy of benevolence and enters on a course of aggression. "Force must be repelled by force, just as far as it is necessary to resist their evil design" (p. 394). Thereafter, with the defeat of the aggressor, love and friendship should again prevail toward the former enemy. For an account of Wayland's fervent, though reluctant, support of the Northern cause in the Civil War, see Francis Wayland and H. L. Wayland, *A Memoir of Francis Wayland*, vol. II, chap. XI. His antislavery feelings had increased during the antebellum years.

507

colored with theological phantasms than that of some pacifists who were contemporaneous."[62]

Upham conducts his argument on two planes. On the lower one, he confines himself to an indictment of the institution of international war, familiar to us from the writings of Worcester and the orthodox peace men, depicting its wastefulness, futility, and moral evil. To the general case against war he devotes his first seven chapters. In the last two parts of the book, a little over a third of the whole, he returns to this theme and suggests ways of mitigating the horrors of war, if it should unfortunately break out, and of eventually eliminating it altogether from the intercourse of nations. The reforms he proposes in international law in regard to the right of blockade, the confiscation of enemy and neutral property on the high seas and the like, and the establishment of a congress of nations as the nucleus of a world organization are not put forward as alternatives to "the doctrine of nonresistance," which he regards as the core of the peace idea but rather as necessary concessions to the fact that, as he has to admit, the overwhelming majority of even the civilized peoples of the world are as yet far from accepting this doctrine. International law will disallow war altogether only when mankind is further advanced on the road to peace.[63]

In the central portions of his *Manual*, therefore, he concerns himself with the relationship between Christianity and war on both the national and the personal levels. Here he occupies the higher ground. Here "the doctrine is, that human life, both in its individual and corporate state, as one and as many, is INVIOLABLE; that it cannot be taken away for any purpose whatever, except by explicit divine permission; and that war, in every shape and for every purpose, is *wrong*, absolutely *wrong*, wholly *wrong*." Any position which stops short of this will be ineffective in ultimately removing the curse of war from mankind. "The principles of the gospels [to the discussion of which he devotes a couple of chapters] are binding upon men in their social capacity."

Where Upham grapples with the problems connected with the practical application of noninjurious force, we see clearly the influence of Dymond and especially of Grimké. Missionaries, unarmed travelers, Quakers and other peace sectaries, even Switzerland and San Marino, are cited as examples of successful nonviolence, nonviolence in practice. He is careful to explain that the nonviolent method does not threaten "the existence of civil government" and "the exercise of its authority to control and to punish" within the limits of the inviola-

[62] *The Fight for Peace*, p. 381.   [63] Upham, *Manual of Peace*, p. 267.

508

bility of human life. "There are some extreme cases, (very few indeed, but still some *extreme* cases,) where resistance and the use of force, so far as is necessary to disarm and confine the assailant, are justifiable and a duty." He recommends, in addition, what he calls "the practice of Non-Intercourse," in effect, a cross between boycott and economic sanctions, as a nonviolent method for enforcing treaties, trade agreements, repayment of debts, and even on the level of personal relations (rather on the model of the Mennonite "avoidance").[64]

What, the professor asks, can we do for peace now? At this stage of the peace movement's evolution, his suggestions are of considerable interest. Let us set up peace societies, he proposes, in each of the Protestant denominations on the basis of complete pacifism, of a renunciation, that is, of all defensive as well as offensive wars. Members would pledge themselves (in the manner of the teetotal pledge, says Upham) not to participate either by personal service[65] or in any other manner in a military organization. The problem of paying a sum of money in lieu of service—which, as we have seen, was the traditional solution used by many state legislatures to relieve the conscience of the occasional objectors to the militia, the "Pacific Exempts," as Upham calls them— was a complicated one. Should such fines be paid? "Certainly not," replies Upham, "if the fines, as is generally the case, are exacted and are applied for military purposes." But should the authorities in granting exemption "at the same time impose on the Pacific Exempts, in consideration of their exemption, a tax, which should be expended on roads, schools, the poor, civil officers, hospitals and the like, it might be a question, whether it would not be a duty to pay it." This must be something for each to decide for himself according to conscience.

[64] *Ibid.*, pp. 80, 81, 96-125, 146-60, 211, 217.

[65] Upham recommends the refusal by pacifist ministers of chaplaincies in any of the armed services, since the office only helps to give the cloak of religion to an essentially antichristian activity. Cf. Allen, *The Fight for Peace*, p. 19, who quotes from a letter of the Rev. Stephen Thurston (of Maine) published in the *Christian Mirror* (19 March 1835), explaining why he would not accept the offer of a chaplaincy for the local militia. "If it is right for me to act as chaplain to the militia at home," Thurston wrote, "it would be right for me to join the army in that capacity in time of war. . . . If I were to join the army in this capacity, I should be expected to impart, on all suitable occasions, moral and religious instructions to the soldiers. Suppose that on the eve of some important battle, I should preach from the well-known words of our Saviour, 'Put up thy sword in its place; for all they that take the sword shall perish by the sword'; or the words 'Love your enemies'; . . . should I be considered as acting the part of a good chaplain? Would it be a suitable preparation for a work of slaughter upon which they were soon to enter? But would not such preaching be in perfect accordance with my duty as a minister of the gospel of peace? And is it not evident that my duty as chaplain to an army would be quite inconsistent with my duty as a minister of Christ?"

He himself was inclined to favor payment. "It would probably tend to satisfy public feeling, and to hush complaints; it would be an evidence of our sincerity; and would discourage those, (for undoubtedly some such would be found), who might for the sake of saving their time and money, hypocritically pretend conscientious scruples in regard to war." But, torn between the fear of strengthening the military spirit and a desire to fulfill so far as was consistent with conscience the duties of a loyal citizen, he still retained doubts about the rightness and feasibility of payment.

> If by paying any tax whatever, on the principle of commutation, (that is to say, on the principle of *purchasing* an exemption from military duty,) we find that we are promoting, even in the least degree, the cause of war, we cannot rightfully do it. And if we are forced to pay such a tax, then there is a violation of religious right. Going on Gospel principles, no military service is to be performed; no military fine is to be paid; nor is there to be a payment of any commutation tax, imposed for exemption from military services, so long as such payment is in any degree subservient to the purposes of war.

Talk of conscientious objection and nonresistance, Upham fully realized, might frighten the majority of people away. A peace movement grounded on such principles would long remain small. But it must persist in them, since they alone accorded with the precepts of Christianity.[66]

Upham contributed nothing original to the theology of Christian pacifism. He was content to repeat, and elaborate, the thoughts of his predecessors. He wrote within the rigid framework of the fundamentalist, literalist viewpoint. The historical approach to Biblical studies was alien to his outlook. His work is important, however, for the systematic way in which he presents, from the complete pacifist position, many of the ideas which had been the stock in trade of peace advocates for at least two decades. It represents, too, a significant landmark in the history of the peace movement in the case it presents for a transformation of the movement from one uniting all varieties of peace sympathizers to one based on a pledge of personal war resistance and active conscientious objection. Upham, like Ladd and even Grimké,[67] was es-

---

[66] Upham, *Manual of Peace*, pp. 167-69.

[67] In the interesting notes he appended to his edition of Jonathan Dymond's *Inquiry into the Accordance of War with the Principles of Christianity* (published posthumously in 1834 just after his death), Grimké stressed (pp. 158-61) that in his view condemnation of all war did not undermine and was not in any way opposed to civil government—except insofar as government might involve the

sentially a moderate; he had little liking for the anarchistic hostility to the state that was shortly to make such headway in the movement's ranks. Like the Quakers, he found a place for the use of some degree of coercive force by government, if not for the sword of the magistrate; like them, he, too, did not deny the usefulness, so long as world opinion had not opened to the truth of the Christian law of love, of wider schemes of international order from which armed force would not be entirely excluded. But—and this was important—he had broken with the practice of the peace societies hitherto by advocating a new (and, some might think, a narrower) basis for their activities. As we shall see, the idea was welcomed enthusiastically by some peace workers, especially among the younger men and women; for other, and many of them older, heads however, it remained unacceptable. The seeds of schism latent in the movement from the beginning had now ripened.

We shall now see how, with little groups based on the absolutist position (and undoubtedly influenced in part by Upham's work) coming into existence in different parts of the country, the more radical ideas were fermenting among the rank and file of the peace movement. Not surprisingly, Upham's own Brunswick, Maine, produced two societies which took up this position, one in the town and the other among the students at Bowdoin College. The student pacifists, having adopted "the most thorough principles," reported that they were "resolved to carry out their principles, in their intercourse with their fellow-men, so far as to decline all military service, or the payment of military fines." The resolution, of course, rejoiced the heart of their philosophy professor. "When *young men* of character and station," he wrote, "occupying places of influence in the community, and enjoying the confidence and respect of the Christian public, come boldly forward to advance and maintain, in the face of contumely and reproach, the grand principle of *total abstinence from all war*," then surely the success of their cause must be approaching.[68]

Down in Boston we meet with similar developments. After heated debate lasting three evenings, the newly established Boston Free Church Peace Society had included in its constitution an article asserting its opposition to "all wars, both offensive and defensive, and all preparations for war," as "sinful and inconsistent with the spirit and

---

taking of human life. The Christian pacifists, he asserted, must always be ready to obey the decrees of the government, except where the act—whether military service or the payment of war taxes or the undertaking of work connected with war—went against conscience.

[68] Rufus P. Stebbins, *Address on the Subject of Peace*, p. 32.

precepts of the gospel." Members expressed, too, their determination to fight the inculcation of "a military spirit and education" among the youth of the city. "It will be noticed," wrote a commentator on the Society's constitution, "that it is one step in advance of any movement which has yet been made. All *preparations* for war are subject to the pledge; consequently no member can do military duty." After the adoption of this constitution, "a committee of three was appointed to draft and circulate a petition to the legislature, praying to be exempted from military duty, as such duty is inconsistent with a Christian profession."[69]

In February 1835 another Boston peace society had been formed—the Bowdoin Street Young Men's Peace Society—and a ladies' branch had been added in March. The young Boston pacifists were perhaps more plebeian than the Bowdoin College boys, but the roster of members included such future stalwarts of American pacifism as the well-connected Amasa Walker, who was elected chairman, Charles K. Whipple, William S. Heywood, Isaac Knapp the publisher, and that stormy petrel of the movement, the Rev. Henry C. Wright. All these young men will figure in our story shortly. The Society was affiliated to the American Peace Society, and it seems to have been in the forefront of the struggle to get the parent organization to come out squarely against all war. To give its first anniversary address, the Bowdoin Street Society had invited the Rev. Rufus P. Stebbins (1810-1885) from the Harvard Divinity School, and he had proceeded to deliver a frontal attack on the concept of defensive wars. "Go to the head of an army," he told the young men, "and read to them Christ's sermon on the mount. . . . Our religion forbids fighting."

The Bowdoin Street group proposed, among other activities, to distribute peace tracts among the pupils of Boston's 62 Sunday schools as soon as suitable literature was available.[70] We do not know if this plan

[69] *Ibid.*, p. 31.

[70] *Ibid.*, pp. 14, 15, 25, 27, 28, 30. Information concerning these peace societies is taken from the appendices to Stebbins's *Address on the Subject of Peace.* On 4 July 1838 we find Stebbins delivering, on this anniversary of independence, another strongly antimilitarist *Address,* this time before the peace society at Amherst College, of which he was an alumnus. "To prevent war," he told the college boys, "be unprepared for it; so when the passions are up they will have time to subside, ere we can act" (p. 8). In the course of his talk he gave support to Upham's proposals for "non-intercourse" with any country refusing to abide by the decisions of an international tribunal. A little earlier Stebbins had written of himself that he had come to his new parish at Leominster (Mass.) "all ablaze," to use his own words, "with enthusiasm, flaming with zeal to correct all evils and perfect all good in a day . . . restless, dissatisfied, aggressive, belligerent" (quoted in *Dictionary of American Biography,* XVII [ed. Dumas Malone], N.Y., 1935, 550, 551).

was actually carried out. But the group did publish in pamphlet form a couple of years later a fascinating little dialogue between two brothers; in it the older, William, instructs young Frank in "the Principles of Peace." The work had originally appeared anonymously in a juvenile paper, *Youth's Cabinet* and it was now reprinted with supplementary material. The avowed object of the pamphlet was said to be to help mothers to train their offspring to follow the ways of peace. Even the best behaved children, states the author, may show bad temper and bellicosity at times (though it is perhaps hard to believe this could ever have been the case with the pious, sanctimonious William, who appears to us a terrible prig). Therefore, by means of the dialogue between the two boys and for the edification of parents as well as children, the writer outlines the nonresistant doctrine: the law of love and its scriptural foundation, the need to practice nonretaliation in respect to injury done us, and the consequent renunciation of all recourse to violence and war or preparation for it.

This long-forgotten pamphlet is seemingly the first attempt at peace education of youth in a consciously pacifist spirit. As propaganda, it is really not particularly good, with its stilted and didactic style. But it deserves some attention as a pioneer work in a field where in our century there were to be many successors. Let us concentrate on its treatment of two topics of special interest to our theme: the problem of law enforcement, of civil government, and the problem of conscientious objection.

As the law now stands, William explains to Frank, a magistrate, at least in his official capacity, cannot act in a spirit of Christian love and forgiveness. Justice demands the imposition of harsh penalties, including death itself for some crimes. A Christian should, therefore, refuse to accept office until the penal system is changed—and this it can be, William goes on, in a country like theirs if enough people desire it. We must do all in our power to persuade public opinion and the legislature to bring into effect much needed reforms in the laws. "How would you have them changed?" asks Frank. William replies: "I would have them always designed and suited to promote the interest, reformation, and permanent welfare of the criminal; and if an offender cannot be seized and punished without violating this principle, I think it is better that he should escape for the time." Next, Frank asks his brother what should be the attitude, in case of an armed invasion of his country, of a Christian pacifist magistrate (who, presumably, before accepting office had first satisfied himself that he would not have to act against his conscience in the exercise of his authority). William's answer follows closely, indeed is obviously copied from, Grimké's

513

reply to Dr. Allen in their recent controversy. "We are never released from the obligation to obey God's rules. We have no more right to render evil for evil to an army than to individuals," William says in summing up his standpoint here.[71] But obviously government, some measure of restraint and degree of force, is not incompatible with the profession of Christian pacifism.

A little further on, we find William explaining to Frank that training to fight is as wrong, as unchristian, as the act of fighting itself. Their discussion of this topic is worth quoting in full:

Frank   ... But I thought they could compel you to train, whether you wanted to or not.

William That would be a difficult matter. How would they go to work to compel me to buy a gun and cartridge box to-morrow morning, and to go to the common, instead of going to my store as usual?

F. I thought they could prosecute you if you did not go.

W. Very well. Then according to your own account, I can choose which I please, either to train or to be prosecuted. I prefer the latter.

F. But they will put you in prison.

W. Very well. Still I have the choice of training or going to prison, just which I like best. This is not compulsion; and I had much rather go to prison than train.

F. Oh, William! Go to prison?

W. Certainly, Frank. And I hope *you* would go to prison, if necessary, rather than deliberately do something you knew to be wrong. I see you are shocked at the idea of a prison, because you think that none but bad men are put there. But men have sometimes been sent to prison for being good, and when that is the case, it is no shame, but rather an honor.

F. But do men ever go to prison rather than train?

W. Yes. A friend of mine was put in Leverett Street jail last year for that very reason. I went to see him there two or three times. He was confined in the prison about a week.

F. Was he not very dull and miserable?

W. On the contrary, he was remarkably cheerful. He carried his books and papers there, and occupied himself pleasantly in reading and writing. And above all, he carried with him a good conscience, which can make even a jail pleasant.

F. But is everybody put in jail that refuses to train?

[71] *Dialogue between Frank and William*, pp. 36-38.

W. No. Many people escape by paying a fine.

F. Why then should you not pay the fine?

W. I do not think it would be right. These fines are paid to the companies, and go to support the military system. I must not escape doing a wicked thing by paying other people to do it for me.

Here Frank inquires if it is not true that Quakers are granted exemption from militia duties. Yes, William replies, and goes on to explain that they had won this right only after having long and patiently borne persecution on account of their refusal to fight.

F. But if you have the same scruples, why should not you be excused too?

W. There is no good reason why I and all who think thus should not have the same exemption.[72]

Finally, we may mention the peace group formed in the summer of 1836 by some of the students at the Oneida Institute in upstate New York. They too, like the student pacifists at Bowdoin College, adopted Upham's idea of a peace pledge, a pledge to renounce war and military service in any form, including the hiring of substitutes or the payment of fines in lieu of service. "We cannot," they state, "in these days of violence, keep silence on this great question without incurring the guilt of shedding the blood of men." A novel feature of the Oneida group's constitution was the article it contained allowing for the expulsion, on a two-thirds vote, of any member who continued to violate its provisions after visitation and kindly admonishment to repent.[73]

The groups we have been discussing were small and ephemeral. The mainstream of pacifist effort still ran within the confines of the American Peace Society, and here radical ideas were gaining increasing support among the more active members. Ladd in his "Farewell" as editor of the *Calumet* had declared: "I am myself opposed to all war in every form, as utterly inconsistent with the spirit of the Gospel."[74] Despite his continued desire to accommodate all shades of peace opinion under the Society's umbrella, he looked with a sympathetic eye on the aspirations of the young enthusiasts—some would call them firebrands—who were beginning to speak out in favor of getting the Society

[72] *Ibid.*, pp. 41-43.

[73] William Lloyd Garrison, Scrap-book, B.P.L., *4261.64, p. 1, cutting from the *Friend of Man*.

[74] *Advocate of Peace*, II, no. 6 (March-April 1835), 163. See also *The Duty of Women to Promote the Cause of Peace* (1836), pp. 8-11.

to take a more unequivocal stand against all varieties of war and violence.

There was, for instance, young Henry Clarke Wright (1797-1870), a Congregational minister (about whom more will be said in the next chapter). In 1836 he was employed by the Society as one of its agents. An early convert to absolute pacifism, he had been agitating within the Society for several years now for its adoption as the Society's platform. Intensely idealistic and religious, Wright found it impossible to compromise on any issue; a certain rigidity in his character also made it difficult for him to understand sympathetically the motives of those unable to "go the second mile." He has been called a "persistent trouble-maker," "a conceited, mischief-making incompetent."[75] Disliked intensely by his political adversaries, he was, nevertheless, always highly respected by a small circle of admirers. He soon came to feel that the doctrine of complete nonresistance and "no-government" was the only consistent position for a practising Christian. "I made up my mind when I embraced the peace principle some years ago," he wrote in 1836, "that in this cause I might be called to lay down my life; and in endeavoring to gain converts to this cause, I have uniformly impressed on men the necessity of making up their minds to die, unresisting and unprotected, except by the arm of that God who is almighty to save."[76] It was to the American Peace Society's shilly-shallying on the question of defensive war that he, along with a number of others, as we have seen, attributed the slow progress the movement had been making up to that time.

Ladd certainly followed Wright a good part of the way and was probably to some extent influenced toward radicalism by his young colleague, but he drew back at the thought of the eventual alienation of conservative opinion within the ranks of the movement, which might result from too startling a change in the Society's platform. "I am myself what they would call an ultra," he admitted to Wright in a letter of 20 September 1836. "The members of our Executive Committee are very moderate peace men and are very much afraid of ultraism."[77] He warned Wright against the probable consequences of being too outspoken in this question in another letter written about this time. In it Ladd told his younger colleague: "You should preach against war generally and not . . . specify *defensive* war unless you are asked— but let your arguments go against all war offensive and defensive

---

[75] Barnes, *The Antislavery Impulse*, p. 252.

[76] Scrap-books of Henry C. Wright, I, 2-4, 9, quoting from the *New England Spectator* (1836).

[77] Galpin, *Pioneering for Peace*, p. 109.

without specifying either." And he warned Wright not "to mix up with your public exercises the subject of capital punishment. . . . If you are asked your own private opinion give it, but do not implicate the American Peace Society as though they commissioned you to preach against capital punishment or any other punishment." And he added that he much doubted "the *expediency* of declaring it to be a sin against God for a man or nation to defend itself as the case may be, when attacked. This is your opinion and mine also but neither of us adopted it at once and the world is not prepared for such a leap."[78]

Ladd had, indeed, been alarmed by reports of Wright's activities during the summer months of 1836, when the indefatigable agent had traveled nearly 2,000 miles through the northern parts of New York state and in New England lecturing on peace and preaching non-resistant doctrines to all and sundry, to adult and child, indeed, to all who would listen. "I have much discussion on the subject of peace," Wright wrote in September, "in the stage, in the cars, in the boats, in the house, by the way-side, and in hotels."[79] Included in his itinerary, for instance, was a visit to the Springfield arsenal, where he addressed the munition workers on peace and the duties of Christian nonresistance, telling them "that they ought to engrave on every lock, barrel, and bayonet of every musket, 'love your enemies,' 'overcome evil with good,' 'thou shalt not kill.' " They listened to him attentively and courteously, he reported.[80] Elsewhere, however, he met with a less friendly reception. In one church where he was preaching, two members of the congregation, a general and an elder, walked out angrily.[81] The usual reaction seems to have been puzzlement rather than anger; the chief objection urged against his views was that they were not applicable in the world as it then existed. But the danger was obvious that the Society might be credited with the extreme opinions of its agent.

"Notwithstanding this difference of views," wrote Ladd at this time in reference to the divergence that had arisen in the Society between the protagonists of defensive war and the absolute pacifists of the Wright variety, "the friends of peace move harmoniously along together."[82] Nevertheless, that some change in its platform was called for, if the Society was not to lose the support of the radical wing, and that a more outspoken condemnation of war in general was necessary before new life could be pumped into the already somewhat mori-

[78] *Ibid.*, pp. 107, 108.   [79] Scrap-books, I, 62ff.
[80] *Ibid.*, I, 61, quoting from the *New England Spectator* (July 1836).
[81] Curti, *American Peace Crusade*, p. 74.
[82] Ladd, "History of Peace Societies," in *Scientific Tracts for the Diffusion of Useful Knowledge*, p. 190.

bund organization was readily admitted by many members, even though they looked at Wright's activities with some misgivings and were not very sympathetic to his suggestions that the peace society should be transformed into a nonresistant association. At the Society's annual meeting of 1836 a committee (with Ladd as one of its members) had been set up to revise the constitution. After weighing the pros and cons, this committee—undoubtedly under the guidance of Ladd, who felt strongly that the time had come for some fairly drastic step if the Society was not to decline in influence and numbers[83]—had concluded not only that sentiment within the Society, at least among the leadership and active workers, favored a total condemnation of international war in all its forms, but that this position was in fact the truly scriptural one. At the next annual meeting, therefore, it recommended that changes be made in the Society's constitution to this effect.

As Ladd wrote around this time:

> It ought not . . . to be suppressed, that most of the leaders in the peace cause are in favour of total abstinence [i.e., from war]; and that almost all of those who have looked into the subject by the light of the gospel, have been brought, often reluctantly and to their own surprise, to adopt the total abstinence principle as the only safe one for a Christian. Let any one who has any doubts on this subject take the gospel, and study it prayerfully and diligently in reference to peace and war, and let him improve what light he has by *acting* in the cause of Peace, and he will have more light, and will find that his dreaded difficulties were but bugbears, and that it is safest to follow the precepts of Christ, wherever they may lead us.[84]

Taken by surprise perhaps, the members present showed no opposition to the committee's proposals, which were accepted unanimously.[85] Article II of the newly adopted constitution now read as follows: "This society, being founded on the principle that all war is contrary to the spirit of the gospel, shall have for its object to illustrate the inconsistency of war with Christianity, to show its baleful influence on all the great interests of mankind, and to devise means for insuring universal and permanent peace." Article III, however, went on to add: "Persons of every denomination, desirous of promoting peace on earth, and good-will towards men, may become members of this society."[86] Thus, although the Society had now taken its stand publicly against de-

---

[83] Hemmenway, *The Apostle of Peace*, p. 63.
[84] Ladd, *Obstacles and Objections*, p. 4.
[85] *Advocate of Peace*, I, no. 3 (Dec. 1837), 120.
[86] *Ibid.*, I, no. 1 (June 1837), 30.

fensive wars as well as against wars of aggression, although it had denied the possibility from the Christian point of view of such a thing as a just war, the nonpacifists were still welcome to join its ranks. In fact, almost all those nonpacifists holding office within the Society continued on in their positions.

In its first issue the Society's new periodical, the *Advocate of Peace*, hastened to explain that *plus se change, plus c'est la même chose.* "This step is less a change than a distinct avowal of sentiments long cherished. The society has never taken any ground at variance with this position; it has merely left the point for its members to settle, each for himself in the light of revelation; while the tone of its appeals, the drift of its measures, and the deep-seated convictions of its leading friends, have always been against every species of war as repugnant to the Sermon on the Mount." Those members who now accepted the full pacifist position had "been brought upon this high ground, not by the ultraism of the age, nor yet by the impulses of a blind or visionary enthusiasm, but by a calm, prayerful examination of the gospel."[87]

As later issues reiterated,[88] all who strove for universal and permanent peace—as in the London Peace Society, which had taken the "high-ground" as its official position from the outset—would continue to be welcome within the Society's ranks, whatever their views on such subjects as defensive wars, capital punishment, the proper limits of the use of force in government, or the inviolability of human life. The change had become necessary it was explained, owing to the idea becoming current outside the Society that it positively approved of defensive wars. This state of affairs, in turn, had begun to alarm the absolute pacifists, those, in fact, who were most active in the promotion of the Society's activities, and voices had more and more been raised in favor of having the Society take a clear stand against war in all its forms. "The demand appeared so reasonable, that the revised constitution gave such a pledge, by recognizing for its basis the contrariety of *all* war to the *spirit* of the gospel." This statement was not intended as a test of membership, as an instrument by which to measure the purity of the principles of its followers. "We merely give it as a guarantee, that our influence as a society shall never go to countenance *any* form of war. Our *general* course is still the same." There must still be unity between the two wings of the movement united together under the Society's banner. No good would come, either, from denouncing the absolute pacifists as "ultraists" or abusing those who clung to the need for some measure of defense as "time-servers."

[87] *Ibid.*, p. 8.
[88] See, e.g., *ibid.*, vol. I, no. 3 (Dec. 1837).

One man, at least, remained unconvinced by such arguments. In August 1837, soon after the changes had been introduced, Dr. Allen, president of that center of radical student pacifism, Bowdoin College, a vice-president of the American Peace Society, and Grimké's doughty opponent in the recent controversy, wrote Ladd an angry letter of resignation.[89] "I am not," he wrote, "a believer in the Quaker principle of the criminality of defensive war. I ought not, therefore, to lend even the poor support of my name to a principle which I think not founded upon the gospel, not true, and blasting to the prospects of usefulness of a society . . . which I hoped would tend to correct the public opinion concerning war." With its present constitution, he continued, the American Peace Society set itself in effect, if not in intent, against all civil government. This stance would prevent it from spreading further among sound Christian ministers and laymen, its best source of support, and would damage its reputation with the public at large.

Ladd replied mildly in his usual conciliatory style, at the same time not concealing where his own sympathies lay.[90] "A peace society," he told Allen, "which should allow its members to fight when they thought it necessary . . . would have no more effect in banishing war from the world, than a temperance society which should allow its members to drink rum when they thought it necessary, would have in banishing intemperance." While answering Allen's arguments point by point, he was, however, ready to concede that the pacifist position had its problems, too. "In the transition state of society from war to peace, there are difficulties to be encountered similar to temperance." But, in any event, there was no need at all, in Ladd's view, for Allen to have resigned because the leaders of the Society had declared themselves in favor of total abstinence from war. Diversities of opinion would still be tolerated within its ranks, and there was more than enough work for persons of varying peace views to do in helping to bring about a warless world.

Although Dr. Allen had withdrawn altogether, it is clear that most of the nonpacifists in the Society had not followed his lead. At the annual meeting of 1838, held as usual in Boston in May, an attempt was made to water down the declaration against all war taken in the previous year. Its leader was the Rev. George C. Beckwith, a Congregational minister whom Ladd himself had selected to take over his own duties as secretary of the Society and to edit the *Advocate of Peace*. In fact, Beckwith, who was to play a very important role in the Society

---

[89] *Ibid.*, I, no. 3 (Dec. 1837), 111-19.   [90] *Ibid.*, pp. 119-25.

for several decades to come, far outdid Ladd in his conservatism and caution and in his anxiety to appease the moderate elements within the movement. He now came forward with a resolution to amend the wording of Article II of the new constitution to read as follows: "The object of this society shall be to illustrate the inconsistency of war with Christianity, to show its baneful influence on all the great interests of man and to devise means for insuring universal and permanent peace." Thus, by omitting the offensive clause—"all war is contrary to the spirit of the gospel"—the sting would be removed from the article and the Society would return to its position prior to the revisions of 1837. A majority, however, rejected the motion; even Beckwith's mentor, Ladd, voted against it, and it was finally agreed to leave the existing constitution as it was. But, not unnaturally, the radicals were disturbed at the rapid resurgence of conservatism within the Society, and, after the annual meeting had adjourned, a further and informal meeting of members was held on the following day. At this time, a motion proposed by Henry C. Wright was carried, calling for a peace convention later in the year to thresh out some of the pressing problems which were besetting the peace movement. Attendance was not to be confined to members of the American Peace Society: all interested in peace might come. An arrangements committee was also appointed. But, since both Ladd and Beckwith refused to serve on it—ostensibly, on the grounds that the Society should not be connected officially with such a convention, more likely in reality out of well-grounded fears that such an assembly would be far to the left of the existing Society leadership—members of this committee were chosen entirely from the radical camp.[91]

A new crisis was now approaching. Hitherto, moderates and radicals had been kept in uneasy partnership within the framework of the American Peace Society. Credit for this achievement was largely due to William Ladd, who had succeeded in maintaining the respect and allegiance of the moderates even after declaring himself in favor of radical pacifism. The constitution as reframed in 1837 made concessions to both camps, but it did not succeed in satisfying either the left or the right wing. The more extreme among the radicals were the least contented, and their discontent was fanned by intellectual influences and by personalities standing apart from, and even outside, the organized movement, who wished to broaden the range of discussion from its center hitherto in the problem of war between nations so as to embrace also the whole issue of the use of force in the do-

[91] Galpin, *Pioneering for Peace*, pp. 109-13, 121-23; Curti, *American Peace Crusade*, pp. 75-79; Allen, *The Fight for Peace*, pp. 383, 384.

mestic arena by either government or individual citizen. Nonresistance and "no-government" were now being propounded as the slogans of a radical peace movement, in place of the narrower (and less inflammatory) principle of the incompatibility of international war with Christianity. This new battle of the peace men would lead shortly to a split in the movement; then some of the more fervent among the radical pacifists would break with the old Society and create their own organization, the New England Non-Resistance Society.

Chapter 12

The Genesis of the Garrisonian Formula: No-Government and Nonresistance

The first generation of American peace men, the absolute pacifists as much as the relativists, were on the whole a socially respectable group of people. This did not mean that they did not come in for their fair share of abuse, that they were not accused of subversion and of lack of patriotism and did not have to suffer a certain amount of inconvenience on this account. But they were, as we have seen, almost to a man solid citizens, upholders of the existing political and social order, protagonists of civil government insofar as it did not infringe upon the rights of private conscience. They did not deny a rightful place in God's order to the magistrate. In the tradition of Quaker pacifism, law and order, with perhaps some degree of coercive force, were not deemed irreconcilable with the Christian law of love. This opinion was held equally as much by those who called themselves nonresistants as by their moderate and conservative brethren who balked at the implications of full pacifism. The prosperous, well-to-do middle-class from which the peace movement drew the overwhelming majority of its members gave it also its most prominent absolutists: Ladd the wealthy farmer, Grimké the successful lawyer, Blanchard the substantial merchant, Amasa Walker the banker, Upham the college professor, the sprinkling of worthy Quakers (too few, it is true, to reflect much credit on the foremost peace church in the land), and the numerous clergymen drawn from all denominations, from Episcopalians to Unitarians. However, none of these men, for all their renunciation of defensive wars and the use of armed force in the protection of person and property, ever went so far as to contest the necessity of government or the moral rightness of political action, when directed toward desirable ends and if carried on by proper means.

Perhaps old David Dodge (still active in New York but no longer in the forefront of the peace movement) had come nearest, with his refusal to vote in elections, to doubting the compatibility of a belief in nonresistance with collaboration in even the beneficial aspects of government as then constituted. It is true, however, that this problem of government had been at the back of all these men's minds as they wrestled with the implications of their peace beliefs. (They were, for instance, opposed almost to a man to the state's imposition of the

523

death penalty for the most serious crimes.) And even if they had not already been aware of the problem themselves, their opponents, like President Allen of Bowdoin, hastened to bring it to their attention. Briefly stated, the problem amounted to this: could a man who had renounced the use of armed force in international affairs and in his own personal relations approve or, indeed, voluntarily collaborate in any way with the machinery of state, so long as this was connected with violence and the military? And, conversely, could national governments ever be so ordered as to dispense with the use of armed force; were not, perhaps, Christian pacifism and Christian government mutually contradictory concepts? We have seen that the answer that they were, that no true Christian might participate in the work of the state, had been the traditional attitude of members of the pacifist sects before the Quakers made their attempt to reconcile pacifism and the political order, and that it had remained the belief of those of the sects' descendants who still clung to their forefathers' pacifist faith. Therefore, "no-government," to use the phrase current at this time, was not something new in the history of pacifism. What was novel was the effort now to extend the doctrine outside the narrow limits of the more conservative peace sects, the attempt to spread it among the clergy and laity of the Christian church at large.

By 1838 these ideas were acting as a ferment within the American Peace Society. We can see their effect, for instance, in the case of the famous essayist and poet, Ralph Waldo Emerson, who, though never intimately associated with any peace group or committed unreservedly to either moderate pacifism or radical nonresistance, was yet strongly attracted to pacifist and nonresistant ideas during the thirties and forties. For the transcendentalist, love was the cement that would bind all human souls in a oneness of spirit. On 3 October 1831 the young Unitarian minister (as he then was) had entered in his journal:

> I wish the Christian principle, the *ultra* principle of nonresistance and returning good for ill might be tried fairly. William Penn made one trial. The world was not ripe and yet it did well. An angel stands a poor chance among wild beasts; a better chance among men; but among angels best of all. And so I admit of this system that it is like the Free Trade, fit for one nation only on condition that all adopt it. Still a man may try it in his own person and even his sufferings by reason of it shall be its triumphs. . . . Love is the adamantean shield that makes blows ridiculous . . . it is said that it strips the good man bare and leaves him to the whip and license of fools and pirates and butchers. But I suppose the exaltation of the general mind by

the influence of the principle will be a counteraction of the increased license. Not any influence acts upon the highest man but a proportion of the same gets down to the lowest man.[1]

In 1838 we find Emerson lecturing on the topic of "War," the last in a series of addresses sponsored by the American Peace Society.[2] As before and later in his life, he did not deny that warlike instincts were deeply embedded in man and that war's heroic qualities had value at a certain level in mankind's development. It was, however, "a juvenile and temporary state," which the human race must outgrow. He spoke appreciatively, though not without some ambiguity, of those who advocated both the repudiation of war, even of a defensive kind, and personal nonresistance. Should one be ready, then, to stand by and see his family slaughtered by thugs? To such inquiries Emerson, who avoided recourse to specifically Christian arguments, gave a twofold answer. In the first place, such a formulation of the question tended to ignore the positive aspect of absolute pacifism while concentrating on "the passive side of the friend of peace." "If you have a nation of men who have risen to that height of moral cultivation that they will not declare war or carry arms, for they have not so much madness left in their brains, you have a nation of lovers, of benefactors, of true, great and able men." Such men would generate an all-conquering moral force. Secondly, in regard to individual nonresistance, "the good and just man" who adopted this position would, Emerson thought, only very rarely be subject to attack. However, such a man, if he was also wise, would not "decide beforehand what he shall do in a given extreme event. Nature and God will instruct him in that hour." Finally, Emerson declared in his address his disbelief that universal peace would come merely through organizing societies, for, if in the meantime war should break out, most members would be swept up in the martial enthusiasm of the conflict—a prophetic vision of what did, indeed, take place in the case of the peace society he was then addressing. Instead, what was needed, in his view, was individual conversion to the concept of peace: "private, dear and earnest love."

Among those who were most impressed by Emerson's stand was Garrison himself, who was soon to become the chief apostle of radical nonresistance. To friends Garrison "expressed . . . his hopes in

[1] *The Journals and Miscellaneous Notebooks of Ralph Waldo Emerson,* III (1963), 295, 296.

[2] The address on "War" is printed in XI (*Miscellanies*) of Emerson's *Complete Works,* 1904 edn., 149-76.

[Emerson] as a man of the new age."[3] True, Emerson had dealt only with the question of war and personal self-defense, and not with the problem of organized government: he had said kind things about the Quakerlike brand of pacifism while refraining from discussion of its relation to the institution of the state. Yet, by implication, at least, Emerson had appeared to commend the "no-government" perfectionism that was being broached now by Garrison and his friends.[4]

These ideas had indeed begun to attract many of the most vigorous and capable of the younger peace men, who had come more and more to feel that the middle-of-the-road policy represented by Ladd and his associates was, despite the more radical constitution adopted by the American Peace Society in 1837, in general stultifying to the Society's growth and that the attempt to conciliate the nonpacifists would lead to its speedy decay. These dissenters within the peace ranks were not all of one mind on the limits and obligations of radical pacifism. Some were well advanced along the road to thoroughgoing nonresistance and the renunciation of all association with the state; others went little beyond Ladd himself in their position on the duties of absolute pacifism. That their strivings and searchings crystallized to form an independent peace society dedicated to the twin principles of no-government and nonresistance, and divided from the older Society by its attitude toward the state, was attributable in particular to the efforts

---

[3] *Ibid.*, XI, 578 (quoted from A. Bronson Alcott's diary).

[4] Emerson's conversation with Carlyle and some English acquaintances in 1847 on the subject of nonresistance was recorded in his essay "Stonehenge" (in V [*English Traits*] of the *Complete Works*, 1903 edn., 286, 287). Upon the Englishmen's inquiring if he knew of any Americans "with an American idea—any theory of the right future of that country," Emerson thought at once of his friends in the New England Non-Resistance Society: "the simplest and purest minds," he called them. Many might think them fanatics, regard their theories as visionary or ridiculous. Nevertheless, he goes on, "I opened the dogma of no-government and non-resistance, and anticipated the objections and the fun, and procured a kind of hearing for it. I said, it is true that I have never seen in any country a man of sufficient valor to stand for the truth, and yet it is plain to me that no less valor than this can command my respect. I can easily see the bankruptcy of the vulgar musket-worship,—though great men be musket-worshippers;—and 't is certain as God liveth, the gun that does not need another gun, the law of love and justice alone, can effect a clean revolution." By the 1850's, however, Emerson's sympathies with nonresistance had almost ebbed away. We find him supporting the purchase of "Sharp's rifles" for Kansas; in the Civil War he was enthusiastically and unqualifiedly in favor of the Unionist cause. "The brute noise of cannon," he told the students at Tufts College in July 1861 in words that might, indeed, have been spoken by Carlyle himself, "has a most poetic echo in these days, as instrument of the primal sentiments of humanity" (*Complete Works*, XI, 579). For Emerson's attitude toward the Civil War, see William Allen Huggard, *Emerson and the Problem of War and Peace*, chap. IV; Merle E. Curti, "Poets of Peace and the Civil War," *World Unity*, X, no. 3 (June 1932), 154, 155.

of a handful of men led by that stormy petrel of mid-century reform, William Lloyd Garrison (1805-1879). It is to their story that we must now turn.

Garrison's role was central in the history of New England non-resistance. He dominated it by his moral conviction as well as by the strength of his personality, his gift for leadership, and his ability to inspire unswerving confidence in his disciples. Garrison, it has been aptly remarked, was essentially "a man of action, . . . a man to whom ideas were revealed in relation to passing events, and who saw in ideas the levers and weapons with which he might act upon the world."[5] He contributed little to the formulation of the ideology of nonresistance; yet he gave it its shape and its drive, and his energy made of it for a brief while a force that attracted many of the best minds and finest spirits in the New England of that day. Although we cannot at all ignore the other figures in its history, we would not be wrong in calling this radical peace movement "Garrisonian" pacifism, just as the same epithet is applied to one branch of the radical abolitionism of the period.

In his very background and early upbringing we find a striking difference between Garrison and the peace leaders we have been studying until now. The grinding poverty of his home, the small boy's weary hours first as a cobbler's and then as a cabinetmaker's apprentice, and later the possibility for self-education and self-improvement that employment in the printing trade afforded him contrast sharply with the middle-class affluence and the educational opportunities of the older generation of peace leaders. Even when in his early twenties Garrison was able to exchange the printer's shop for the editor's office, he still remained desperately poor, a struggling young journalist without money or social connections or educational qualifications. Much of the later Garrison, of Garrison the pacifist as much as of Garrison the abolitionist (for it is, of course, in the history of the antislavery movement that his major claim to fame lies), can be traced back to these early years. His mother, who brought him up by herself, was a Baptist, and his early church ties were with the Baptists; from the religious upbringing in his home derive that rigidity and inflexibility, that uncompromising mark, that rests on his whole character and on all his manifold activities. Next, let us note his intense Biblicism, the profound knowledge of the scriptures that he constantly drew upon —and with such effect—in his speeches and writings, continuing to do so, indeed, long after he had abandoned his early fundamentalist views

---

[5] John Jay Chapman, *William Lloyd Garrison*, 2nd edn., p. 162.

527

and had broken finally with organized Christianity. "The source of Garrison's power," to quote John Jay Chapman again, "was the Bible. . . . From his boyhood upward Garrison's mind was soaked in the Bible and in no other book."[6] It was his reading of the New Testament, and perhaps some contact with Quakers in his neighborhood, that brought Garrison as a very young man, even before he left his native Newburyport for good at the beginning of 1827, to the conviction that all connection with war was a sin, as sinful, indeed, as indulgence in alcohol. His pacifist convictions, therefore, predate his allegiance to the abolitionist cause.[7]

When, at the age of 23, he was appointed editor of a small and vegetating temperance sheet in Boston, the *National Philanthropist*, its publisher generously permitted him, in addition to pushing his main theme of the evils of strong drink, to use its columns as a platform from which to launch vigorous attacks on war as well as on a multitude of other iniquities: smoking, Sunday postal deliveries, and immorality in general. It was in 1828, while he was engaged in editing the *National Philanthropist*, that Garrison first met the gentle Quaker, Benjamin Lundy (1787-1839), who roomed for a short while in the same house as Garrison. Contact with Lundy led to a radical change in the young man's views on the slavery question. Soon he had developed from an advocate of colonization to become the fiery apostle of immediate emancipation. Probably, too, conversations with Lundy led to a strengthening of Garrison's burgeoning pacifist convictions. Both his abolitionism and his pacifism, in fact, flowed from the same source: his belief in the freedom and dignity of man, all men, as the necessary outcome of his religious faith.

During the winter months of 1828-1829, Garrison spent a six months' period as editor of a short-lived paper, the *Journal of the Times*, which had been started up in Bennington (Vt.) to support the candidacy of John Quincy Adams, who was then running for the presidency against Andrew Jackson. Garrison, whose journalistic talents were beginning to attract notice—and whose political sentiments were then Federalist—accepted the invitation to Bennington on condition that he could continue as before his advocacy of his favorite reform causes. His object as editor, he wrote in the first number, would be to promote "the suppression of intemperance and its associate vices,

---

[6] *Ibid.*, pp. 164, 165.

[7] Garrison's first known contact with the peace movement was in the summer of 1826, when William Ladd visited Newburyport and the young journalist wrote approvingly of Ladd's views on war in the local *Free Press* he was then editing. See John L. Thomas, *The Liberator*, pp. 49-51.

the gradual emancipation of every slave in the Republic, and the perpetuity of national peace"—in addition, of course, to the support of Adams' candidacy.[8] Antislavery and peace had already become the dominant themes in Garrison's life.

Since his first arrival at Boston, the young man had been receiving repeated summonses to serve in the state militia. These he had always refused, but until the summer of 1829 (a witness, indeed, to the laxity with which militia regulations were then enforced) he had not been called upon either to pay the customary fine which exempted from actual service or to provide any explanation of his nonattendance at drill. In 1829, however, the authorities caught up with him, and he received a visit from the clerk of his militia company back home, who was the local blacksmith ("a saucy, smutty faced son of Vulcan, as well as an ambitious follower of Mars" and "a poor, worthless scamp" are Garrison's descriptions of him). After pleading both nonresidence and his nearsightedness to no effect, Garrison submitted to the payment of the small fine. As he wrote of himself shortly afterward:

I am not professedly a Quaker; but I heartily, entirely and practically embrace the doctrine of non-resistance, and am conscientiously opposed to all military exhibitions. I now solemnly declare that I will never obey any order to bear arms, but rather cheerfully suffer imprisonment and persecution. What is the design of militia musters? *To make men skilful murderers.* I cannot consent to become a pupil in this sanguinary school.[9]

Six months after penning these words, Garrison was, indeed, to find himself in a prison cell—not, however, as a result of his conscientious objection to military service, but on account of the fiery campaign he had commenced for the immediate abolition of Negro slavery. The story of his prosecution in the spring of 1830 by a Massachusetts slave-trader for alleged calumniation of character in the columns of the *Genius of Universal Emancipation*, the antislavery paper which Lundy had invited Garrison to help him edit in Baltimore, and of his conviction and subsequent imprisonment in the Baltimore city jail is well known, and it need not be retold here. In prison he penciled on his cell walls a sonnet entitled "The Guiltless Prisoner," not very good poetry perhaps, but often quoted in later years:

[8] Russel B. Nye, *William Lloyd Garrison and the Humanitarian Reformers,* pp. 13, 21, 22.
[9] *Genius of Universal Emancipation,* N.S., IV, no. 2 (16 Sept. 1829), 14, quoted in part in *W.L.G.: Story of His Life told by his Children,* I, 124, 125.

Perchance thy fault was love to all mankind;
Thou didst oppose some vile, oppressive law;
Or strive all human fetters to unbind;
Or wouldst not bear the implements of war. . . .

Soon after his release, Garrison parted company amicably with Lundy, whose Quaker mildness made it hard for him to stomach the violent tone that Garrison was giving to his attacks on slavery and the slaveholders. Now Garrison began on the great venture of his life. Returning to Boston, he started up, with scarcely any funds but with unbounded faith in his cause and confidence in himself, a paper devoted primarily to the policy of immediate emancipation. The first issue of the *Liberator* appeared on 1 January 1831; in the following year an obscure group of enthusiasts inspired by Garrison formed an antislavery society in New England to support the work of the *Liberator*, and the end of 1833 saw the foundation at a conference in Philadelphia of a national organization dedicated to the policy of immediate abolition. The abolitionists, though still a handful, were slowly beginning to make their influence felt, and Garrison's name, especially after the slave revolt led by Nat Turner in Virginia in 1831 (with which, of course, the pacifist Garrison had not had the slightest connection) had alarmed the South into creating a bogey out of the *Liberator's* editor, soon became known up and down the country.[10] For most, he was just a professional troublemaker, the epitome of reckless extremism, if not of downright incendiarism; for a few, he became the acknowledged leader of reform. These Garrisonian abolitionists were to form the nucleus of the New England nonresistance movement.[11]

The delegates assembled at the Philadelphia conference of December 1833 adopted for the newly founded American Anti-Slavery Society a "Declaration of Sentiments." Although the initiative for the conference had come more from the abolitionist group centered in New York led by the Tappan brothers than from the New England (later Massachusetts) Anti-Slavery Society that Garrison had founded

---

[10] It is true, however, that now, as later, Garrison the nonresistant asserted that, *if* "white men" were justified in revolting against oppression, black men were equally entitled morally to rise in arms against those who held them in slavery. See Thomas, *The Liberator*, p. 136; Walter M. Merrill, *Against Wind and Tide*, pp. 50-52.

[11] "It was by no means a mere coincidence," writes John R. Bodo, "that the leadership of the abolitionist societies and of the peace societies overlapped to a considerable extent: the fiercest abolitionists . . . were also the champions of the most uncompromising antiwar platform" (*The Protestant Clergy and Public Issues*, p. 229).

530

at the beginning of the previous year, the Declaration itself emanated almost entirely from Garrison's pen. It has quite a lot to say that bears on the use of nonviolent methods in combating evil, passages that were later to be the subject of controversy within abolitionist ranks. Stressing the efficacy of propaganda by the written and spoken word for promoting the cause, the Declaration compares the methods of the patriots of the American Revolution with their own today as they struggled against the infinitely greater evils of the slave power. Referring to the men of the Revolution, it declared:

> Their principles led them to wage war against their oppressors, and to spill human blood like water, in order to be free. Ours forbid the doing of evil that good may come, and lead us to reject, and to entreat the oppressed to reject, the use of all carnal weapons for deliverance from bondage; relying solely upon those which are spiritual, and mighty through God to the pulling down of strongholds. Their measures were physical resistance—the marshalling in arms— the hostile army—the mortal encounter. Ours shall be such only as the opposition of moral purity to moral corruption—the destruction of error by the potency of truth—the overthrow of prejudice by the power of love—and the abolition of slavery by the spirit of repentance.[12]

Was this disavowal of the use of force in fact a declaration in favor of nonresistance? Though admittedly it says nothing either of international war or of civil government (both these subjects were, indeed, only indirectly related to the matter at hand), the implication seems to be against the use of force for even righteous ends. Most of the Garrisonians, Samuel J. May and David Lee Child, for instance, understood it thus. The numerous Quaker delegates, who made up a considerable proportion of the conference's membership, must have interpreted it thus, too. However, Garrison himself, the virtual author of the Declaration, while conceding that the doctrine of nonresistance might not unfairly be read into it, admitted at the same time that it would not be correct to consider it as a purely pacifist document.[13] And it is fairly certain that it was not understood in this way by some influential members of the new Society, those in particular, like the wealthy Tappan brothers, who were to be most active in the Society's New York headquarters and were always to remain critical of Garrison's policies and his Bostonian group.

The issue of nonresistance, however, was not to stir the abolitionist

---

[12] Garrisons, *W.L.G.*, I, 409, 412.
[13] *Ibid.*, II, 303, 304. See also *Liberator*, 5 Jan. 1838.

movement for several years after the founding of the American Anti-Slavery Society. Before discussing the Lovejoy case of 1837, which brought out into the open the deep differences of opinion that divided the movement on this subject, let us turn our attention to the small band of men and women gathered around Garrison and the Boston *Liberator.*

Nearest to Garrison himself in spirit, in the intensity of his hatred for both war and slavery, was the Rev. Henry Clarke Wright.[14] Originally a hatmaker from Connecticut, Wright, after being ordained a Congregationalist minister, had worked for the American Sunday School Union and, as we have seen, for the American Peace Society. His pacifism stemmed directly from his sternly Puritan and Bible-centered religion, from his study of—and reflections on—the books of the New Testament. He had been greatly impressed, too, by the arguments put forward by Grimké in his 1832 *Address* in favor of thoroughgoing nonresistance. We have already watched Wright causing alarm and embarrassment in the summer of 1836 to the officers of the American Peace Society by the vehemence with which he propounded radical nonresistant views while acting as the Society's traveling agent. In debate with moderate peace men like Wayland and Beckwith (the Society's secretary since 1837), he ridiculed the idea of opposing all forms of international war while maintaining the validity in the last resort of the magistrate's use of the sword in domestic relations. "A glaring absurdity" he called such views. Wright early became associated with Garrison in his campaign for immediate abolition. For him, as for Garrison, antislavery and pacifism were but facets of the same underlying principle: "How can anyone," he wrote in April 1837 in an article in *Zion's Watchman,* "plead the cause of the slave, on *Christian* principles, and not oppose the law of violence, the basis of all war? And, what is slavery but the carrying out of the war principle and spirit to the end."[15] Thus, in the second half of the thirties, Wright took his place alongside Garrison in combining militant abolitionism with extreme nonresistant views and in giving direction and meaning to the efforts of those within the orthodox peace movement who had become discontented, even after the changes in 1837, with the conservative inclinations of the American Peace Society's leadership.

A very different character from the belligerent Wright, but also one of the shaping influences on New England nonresistance, was the saint-

[14] See M. E. Curti, "Non-Resistance in New England," *NEQ*, II, no. 1 (Jan. 1929), esp. 35-39, for Wright's early pacifism.
[15] Scrap-books of Henry C. Wright, I, 9, 54.

ly Unitarian minister, the Rev. Samuel J. May.[16] "One of heaven's own," the Quaker Lucretia Mott called him;[17] he was more successful in embodying nonviolence in the practice of everyday life than some of the other, and more militant, contemporary nonresistants.[18] Unlike Wright—or, for that matter, Garrison—May came from a distinguished Massachusetts family related to many of the other clans of the social elite, and he moved with ease in society circles, even while prepared to make himself unpopular by his advocacy of radical views. Already an absolute pacifist by the late 1820's, May had been converted by Garrison to abolition early in the next decade. May, writes Chapman, "had not Garrison's strategic understanding of the fight, nor Garrison's gift of becoming the central whirlpool of idea and persecution. But he was the diviner spirit of the two."[19] With the ardent espousal of peace and antislavery May united the advocacy of temperance, penal reform, and women's rights, and, in fact, the cause of all the oppressed, from native Indians to immigrant Irish. In the 1830's, under the influence of Garrison and Wright, though without following them all the way in their arguments concerning "no-government," he more and more became the spokesman within the American Peace Society of those elements who believed the Society should come out unequivocally on a fully pacifist platform.

All these men, then—Wright and May and a number of lesser figures, mostly from within the Massachusetts Anti-Slavery Society, always the most important stronghold of Garrisonism, or in the ranks of the American Peace Society—had begun to look more deeply into the bases of pacifism and to see to what conclusions peace principles might lead. From Garrison they drew much of their inspiration, and along with him they eventually came to accept, to a greater or lesser degree, an extension of nonresistance to include the renunciation of civil government altogether. Political anarchism, in other words, was to appear to most of them the only logical outcome of Christian pacifism.

Many writers have emphasized the influence on Garrison's thinking from around 1836 of John Humphrey Noyes, Christian perfectionist, Utopian socialist, and founder of the famous Oneida Community,[20]

---

[16] See W. Freeman Galpin's MS life of May: "God's Chore Boy"; Joseph May, *Samuel Joseph May: A Memorial Study.*

[17] Otelia Cromwell, *Lucretia Mott*, p. 101.

[18] See *Memoir of Samuel Joseph May*, pp. 254-56, for the story of how May courageously consented to sleep beside a lunatic with homicidal tendencies in order to calm him.

[19] Chapman, *Garrison*, p. 81.

[20] See Nye, *William Lloyd Garrison*, p. 105; Galpin, *Pioneering for Peace*, pp. 114-16; Thomas, *The Liberator*, pp. 227-35.

whose views on war were touched upon in an earlier chapter. Though unwilling to accept Noyes's later communitarian views (or his ideas on sex), Garrison did at this time imbibe much of his thinking on the problem of government. In particular, Noyes's rejection of all man-made laws and civil government as superfluous, as a hindrance for all who strove perfectly to follow the law of God as set forth in the Bible, appealed to Garrison. Let man only be guided by the voice of God within him and all the paraphernalia of church and state would be revealed as an encumbrance, which must be thrown aside as soon as possible. For Garrison now, the position he had already reached concerning the validity of Christian nonresistance seemed to lead logically to the fuller perfectionism of the "no-government" doctrine. Christians, he wrote to Henry Wright early in 1837, "are not authorized to combine together in order to lacerate, sue, imprison, or hang their enemies, nor even as individuals to resort to physical force to break down the heart of an adversary. And, surely, if they cannot do these things as a body, or in their private capacity, they have no right to join with the ungodly in doing them." They must peacefully await the inauguration of "the Kingdom of God's dear Son." "It has no swords, for they are beaten into ploughshares—no spears, for they are changed into pruning-hooks—no military academy, for the saints cannot learn war any more—no gibbet, for life is regarded as inviolate—no chains, for all are free. And that kingdom," Garrison concludes, "is to be established upon the earth—for the time is predicted when the kingdoms of this world will have become the kingdoms of our Lord and of his Christ."[21] It was several years, however, before Garrison and his friends sought to create an institutional framework for propagating their ideas.

Among the most enthusiastic converts to Garrisonian views were the two Grimké sisters, Sarah (1792-1873) and Angelina (1805-1879). No doubt, before his premature death, their brother Thomas had been influential in their spiritual quest, which took them from the family plantation in South Carolina into the ranks of Philadelphia Quakerism and the abolitionist movement. Their appearance on antislavery platforms did indeed cause a sensation at a time when such conduct was considered unbecoming in a member of the weaker sex. Soon the two sisters had been won over by Henry Wright to the full nonresistant gospel as well.[22] And we see them in their voluminous correspondence seeking, with all the zeal of the newly converted, to bring over other abolitionist leaders to nonresistance and "no-government."

Their letters are revealing of the crusading spirit which made a

[21] Garrisons, W.L.G., II, 148, 149.
[22] Benjamin P. Thomas, *Theodore Weld: Crusader for Freedom*, pp. 142-46.

vital force of Garrison and his circle during this period. To Gerrit Smith (1797-1874), a wealthy and influential abolitionist and reformer of New York state, Sarah writes in April 1837 deploring the lack of trust in God among abolitionists "on the great subject of self-defense." For her, to yield to the desire to resist by physical force is similar to the impulse to drink with the drunkard. "This doctrine of non-resistance is the greatest test of our faith." In a further epistle she describes to Gerrit Smith the liberating effect which "the sublime doctrine of acknowledging no government but God's" has had upon her. It has made her feel free with Christ. "I cannot describe to thee the blessed influence which my ultra Peace Principles have had upon my mind." Slavery is the outcome of war, the war spirit lodged within the domestic life of the nation. "It does appear to me," she writes in a letter to Henry Wright, "that if the simple precept 'resist not evil' were once entrenched in the hearts and consciences of men, slavery and war and oppression and domestic tyranny and the usurping of authority over one another must wholly cease."[23]

For the Grimké sisters, then, as for men like Garrison and Wright and many of their friends, the fight against oppression was one. A person could not oppose war, or renounce violence for himself and urge its rejection by his community, without opposing slavery and working actively for its abolition. That was common ground with the older generation of pacifists. Now, the state, the instrument and incarnation of violence, must go, too; it had failed to pass the test when the principles of the gospels were rigorously applied to its actions.

The Grimké sisters seem to have received a sympathetic hearing from Gerrit Smith—though ultimately, as we shall see, he was not won over to nonresistance. With another leading figure among the abolitionists they had to acknowledge defeat. While stating his belief in returning good for evil on the personal level, Theodore Weld (1803-1895) told them bluntly his opinion of the "no-government" idea as thoroughly unsound from a Christian point of view. "*That* doctrine fills me with shuddering and I pray for you and all who are bewildered in its mazes and stumbling on its dark mountains."[24] Moreover, Weld finally succeeded in winning the younger Grimké sister, Angelina, for his wife, a marriage that led to the disownment of both sisters from the Society of Friends—Angelina for "marrying out" and Sarah for attending the wedding—and to their eventual withdrawal from active interest in the peace movement.

[23] *Letters of Theodore Dwight Weld, Angelina Grimké Weld and Sarah Grimké,* I, 377, 407-9; II, 614.
[24] *Ibid.,* II, 513, 706, 707, 856.

Meanwhile, however, late in 1837 the question of the relationship between abolitionism and nonresistance, and of the validity of the latter for the Christian citizen, was brought to the forefront by events cut in frontier Illinois. The murder of the Rev. Elijah P. Lovejoy (1802-1837) at Alton in November 1837 constitutes a landmark in the history of the freedom of the press, as well as in the history of abolitionism. It also led to repercussions in the development of the pacifist movement in America. His death marked a climax in the long series of violent acts directed against the protagonists of abolition by mobs and individual supporters of slavery, who felt increasingly menaced by the rise in antislavery feeling. In October 1835 Garrison himself had barely escaped death at the hands of an enraged crowd in the city of Boston. He had refused to defend himself by arms, though urged to do so. "I will perish sooner than raise my hand against any man, even in self-defence," he had said, "and let none of my friends resort to violence for my protection."[25] He was finally rescued by the somewhat dilatory police force headed by the mayor. Henry C. Wright, on another occasion, had refused to strike back when attacked in a Philadelphia hotel, telling his assailant: "I feel no unkindness toward you, and hope to see you at my house," whereby he succeeded in winning the man over.[26] In many parts of the country nameless abolitionist speakers had acted in the same way. But none had been tested to the same degree as Lovejoy, whose attempts to publish an abolitionist paper, first at St. Louis (Mo.) and then across the state border at Alton (Ill.), were frustrated by repeated mob attacks on his press and even on the persons of himself and his family.

In Lovejoy's case two new factors were present: the absence in the area of an effective police force along with the connivance of the authorities and most of the community at mob violence and, secondly, the effect of the continuous threats on Lovejoy's own family, especially on the health and even sanity of his ailing wife. Lovejoy had started out as a convinced Garrisonian nonresistant but had finally abandoned his pacifism and, with the sanction of the mayor of the town, had armed himself and his family and friends. It was in repelling an attack by the mob on his printing press that Lovejoy met his death.[27] Not long before the end, Lovejoy wrote to a friend:

It is now Tuesday night. I am writing by the bedside of Mrs. L., whose excitement and fears have measurably returned with the dark-

[25] Fanny Garrison Villard, *William Lloyd Garrison on Non-Resistance*, p. x.
[26] Curti, "Non-Resistance in New England," p. 37.
[27] John Gill, *Tide Without Turning*, pp. 108, 137, 142, 143, 167; Merton L. Dillon, *Elijah P. Lovejoy, Abolitionist Editor*, pp. 114, 115, 123, 124, 153.

ness. She is constantly starting at every sound, while her mind is full of the horrible scenes through which she has so lately passed. . . . A loaded musket is standing at my bedside, while my two brothers, in an adjoining room, have three others, together with pistols, cartridges, etc. And this is the way we live in the city of Alton! I have had inexpressible reluctance to resort to this method of defence. But dear-bought experience has taught me that there is at present no safety for me, and no defence in this place, either in the law or the protecting aegis of public sentiment. I feel that I do not walk the streets in safety, and every night when I lie down, it is with the deep settled conviction, that there are those near me and around me, who seek my life. I have resisted this conviction as long as I could but it has been forced upon me. Even were I safe from my enemies in Alton, my proximity to Missouri, exposes me to attack from that state. And now that it is known that I am to receive no protection here, the way is open for them to do with me what they please.[28]

Thus Lovejoy stated the agonizing dilemma in which he had been placed as a result of his stubborn refusal to retreat before mob rule.

The reaction of the antislavery movement (and of many other fair-minded men outside its ranks) was unanimous on one point: that Lovejoy had died a martyr to the cause of liberty and of the freedom of the press. They united in their abhorrence of the murderers and in their admiration for Lovejoy's courage. But was he justified as an abolitionist in abandoning the weapon of moral suasion for armed defense of the cause? And, moreover, how should a professed nonresistant react to this abandonment of nonviolence?

The executive committee of the American Anti-Slavery Society, representing the New York group in particular, took the view that abolitionists in general were not pledged to the nonresistant way. For once, Garrison himself went a long way in agreement with them. Abolitionists—unless they happened also to be "no-government" men like himself—had not, in his view, renounced the use of force in support of the law. "I wish it were otherwise," he wrote; "I wish all in our ranks could be led to see, that civil government—a government upheld by military power—is not justified *among Christians*."[29] But his followers continued to press the point—though with some hesitation, for fear that any criticism of Lovejoy's conduct might be construed as justi-

[28] Joseph C. and Owen Lovejoy, *Memoir of the Rev. Elijah P. Lovejoy*, pp. 257, 258.

[29] W. L. Garrison to S. J. May, 30 Dec. 1837, Garrison Papers, B.P.L., MS A.1.1., vol. 2, no. 74. See also the *Liberator*, 5 Jan. 1838.

fying his enemies—that Lovejoy, though a martyr, had not died "a *Christian* martyr." The board of managers of the Massachusetts Anti-Slavery Society (followed a little later by the Rhode Island abolitionists) declared:

> That while it is not the province of their Board to determine for the friends of universal emancipation, how far and under what circumstances it is right to use arms in self-defence; . . . yet, as abolitionists, we are constrained to believe, that if the doctrine of non-resistance had been practically carried out by our brethren in Alton . . . victory would, in the providence of God, have been the result; or, if not, that the spilling of the blood of defenceless men would have produced a more thrilling and abiding effect.[30]

Even Dr. Channing, who was far from being an absolute pacifist, took much the same view, and so did William Ladd of the American Peace Society.[31] The *Liberator*, whose columns Garrison opened to discussion of the issue,[32] showed the distress and pain which Lovejoy's defection had caused his fellow nonresistants, torn between admiration for his bravery in the face of overwhelming opposition and regret that he had not been willing to crown it with a nonresisting martyr's death. "I think I never received so great a shock to my feelings as in the intelligence of the death of Elijah P. Lovejoy," wrote Angelina Grimké. "It was not because an abolitionist had fallen. . . . Oh no! . . . it was because he did not fall the unresisting victim of that fury." Her sister, Sarah, in a private letter of lamentation to a friend, wrote: "How appalling the spectacle! a minister of Jesus Christ engaging in the work of killing his brother man, of sending to the bar of judgment beings who were mad with fury."[33] Even the mild Samuel J. May expressed his regret at "the unchristian spirit which he [Lovejoy] manifested."

Although the lines of demarcation were by no means clear-cut, the

---

[30] *Liberator*, 24 Nov. 1837.

[31] *Ibid.*, 22 Dec. 1837; John Hemmenway, *The Apostle of Peace*, pp. 66-69. The Rev. Leonard Worcester, brother of the late Noah Worcester and himself a near pacifist, who roundly condemned Lovejoy's assailants as well as the whole institution of slavery, considered that "it was no . . . sudden and unavoidable peril in which the victim of the Alton mob was placed. The evil which he resisted had long been threatened and foreseen." His death was, therefore, avoidable. Lovejoy, in his view, had died, not in strict self-defense, which was permissible even in a follower of Christ, but "in defence of his rights, and of his property." This action, although legally justifiable, was contrary to Christ's precepts, which urged nonresistance in such circumstances. See L. Worcester's *A Discourse on the Alton Outrage*, pp. 6-9.

[32] *Liberator*, esp. 1 Dec. 1837; 8 Dec. 1837; 22 Dec. 1837; 5 Jan. 1838; 16 Feb. 1838.

[33] *Weld-Grimké Letters*, I, 481.

538

discussion on Lovejoy's death which ensued made it plain that large sections of the abolitionist movement rejected nonviolence, not merely as a principle but also as a practical tactic. Nor were all of Garrison's followers, for that matter, supporters of no-government and non-resistants in the strict meaning of the word, although all eventually came to reject political means for bringing about abolition. Henceforth these doctrines were more or less confined to the Garrisonian division of the movement.

Protagonists of nonresistance and no-government had so far not formed an organization of their own. Belief in the inviolability of human life and the unchristian nature of all human government had begun to make headway among reforming circles in New England, even outside Garrison's group of personal followers. We have noted in the previous chapter the restlessness among the more radical members of the American Peace Society at what they considered the unduly circumspect policy of Ladd and the leadership. It was this feeling that gave the impulse to prepare a grand peace convention in the autumn of 1838 to thresh out a new and, it was hoped, nonresistant policy for the peace movement. We have mentioned that the committee in charge of preparations was manned by nonresistants and their sympathizers, Henry C. Wright and Samuel J. May among them. "A number of deeply interesting radical questions will be presented for debate," stated the committee in outlining the forthcoming convention's program. Its main task was to be a searching examination into the question whether, according to the Christian gospel, defensive war—or even war for some holy cause—was not totally excluded and nonresistance commanded in its place. "We propose," they concluded, "not to evade any question that may be found incidental to the decision of this one, namely; how is the evil that is in the world to be overcome? By violence, or sacrifice?"[34] Wright, in particular, was busy all the summer in organizing meetings in Boston and the surrounding country at which the radical case was presented and fresh converts made to the cause.[35]

Garrison, meanwhile, was backing Wright's efforts in the field by devoting a considerable amount of space in his *Liberator* to nonresistance and no-government, alongside news of the abolition movement, which had been the main concern of the paper hitherto. He had by now become as stern a critic of the conservative elements which still continued to dominate policy in the American Peace Society as the ebullient Wright. Despite mutual respect for each other, which they succeeded in maintaining to the end, Garrison and Ladd were poles apart in

[34] *Ibid.*, II, 685-88.
[35] Curti, "Non-Resistance in New England," pp. 42, 43.

temperament. For Garrison (and even more so for Wright, of course) moderate reform was a contradiction in terms. It was almost worse than useless to write absolute pacifism into a peace society's platform if one still admitted nonpacifists into the membership, for the effect was to water down the testimony for truth. "Be assured," he once told Ladd, "that until . . . your cause is honored with lynch law, a coat of tar and feathers, brickbats and rotten eggs—no radical *reform* can take place." This was as true for the peace cause as it was for antislavery. In the *Liberator*, early in September 1837, Garrison drew a comparison between the American Peace Society and the American Colonization Society, which he had done so much to discredit in the eyes of antislavery opinion both in America and back in Britain. Such bodies, he said bluntly, "are mischievous, instead of being beneficial, because they occupy the ground without being able to effect the object. What a farce it is to see a Peace Society enrolling upon its list of members, not converted, but belligerent commanders-in-chief, generals, colonels, majors, corporals, and all! What a wonderful reform may be expected where there are none to be reformed!" He concluded his attack with the following threat: "I hope to be more deeply engaged in the cause of Peace by and by, than I can at present; and unless they alter their present course, the first thing I shall do will be to serve our Peace Societies, as I have done the Colonization Societies."[36] No wonder then that, within a few months, the hapless Beckwith was complaining publicly of Garrison's and Wright's pugnacity as a serious obstacle to the success of the peace cause![37]

And so, as September approached, the radicals went ahead with high hopes of winning over to their platform the most active sections of the peace movement, the only ones that really mattered in their view. Opinion was not unanimous, however, even among the members of the preparative committee. We find Samuel J. May, for instance, writing to Garrison in July: "You and brother Wright have startled me, but I am determined to follow wherever *truth* may guide. I look forward to the Convention with high expectation. If we do not drive off the timid ones by broaching our ultra doctrines in the beginning, but lead them along through the preliminaries,—getting them to concede certain fundamental truths,—we may at last surprise many into the acknowledgment of a faith from which at first they would revolt." May him-

[36] *Liberator*, 8 Sept. 1837. Cf. *Advocate of Peace*, I, no. 4 (March 1838), 189, where Garrison is described charitably as "a devoted friend of peace," although it is pointed out that nonresistance and no-government are "political reforms," with which matters the A.P.S. has no concern officially.

[37] Scrap-books of H. C. Wright, vol. I, quoting from the *Morning Star* (Feb. 1838).

self seems to have been hesitant about whether Garrison and Wright were in fact correct in their belief that the infliction of imprisonment on the criminal was not consistent with the Christian gospel of love.[38] And even Garrison agreed that, while many who came to the convention might be prepared to accept the validity of nonresistance (especially since, as one of his colleagues reported, they might expect "the attendance of only pretty thorough men"),[39] it might be harder to get them to oppose the whole institution of civil government. As he confided to May: "We shall probably find no difficulty in bringing a large majority of the Convention to set their seal of condemnation upon the present militia system, and its ridiculous and pernicious accompaniments. They will also, I presume, reprobate all wars, defensive as well as offensive. . . . But few, I think, will be ready to concede, that Christianity forbids the use of physical force in the punishment of evildoers; yet nothing is plainer to my understanding, or more congenial to the feelings of my heart."[40]

The peace convention opened on 18 September in Marlboro Chapel in Boston.[41] Between 150 and 200 persons attended, almost all New Englanders, and of these the greater number were from Massachusetts. The delegates included a contingent of moderates from the American Peace Society led by Beckwith, who had met the previous day in conclave to decide on the tactics to be pursued at the convention. It seems that they had some hopes, despite the radical initiative, of being able to secure a majority for their point of view and thus protect "the cause . . . from the extravagance of the ultra men."[42] However, their hopes were disappointed, and they withdrew after a few hours, using as a pretext (though they were undoubtedly also genuinely shocked by) the admission of women to full membership in the convention and its committees.

The "women's rights" question, indeed, was already beginning to split the abolitionist movement, though the final schism was not to come until 1840. Garrisonian nonresistance had won the enthusiastic support of a number of capable and energetic women who did much to further its spread. We have already mentioned the Grimké sisters (who were unable to be at the convention). The well-known novelist,

---

[38] Garrisons, W.L.G., II, 223. [39] Ibid., II, 223, 224.
[40] Ibid., II, 225.
[41] See Proceedings of the Peace Convention and the Liberator, 26 Sept. 1838, for the official account. See also Garrisons, W.L.G., II, 222-42; Curti, American Peace Crusade, pp. 81, 82; "Non-Resistance in New England," pp. 43-50; Galpin, Pioneering for Peace, pp. 124-131.
[42] Garrisons, W.L.G., II, 226.

Lydia Maria Child (1802-1880), one of the most popular writers of her day, the stalwart abolitionist Mrs. Maria Chapman (*née* Weston; 1806-1885), the two unmarried Weston sisters, scions of patrician Boston, and the fiery Quakeress and advocate of women's rights, Abby Kelley (1810-1887), were all to do the new movement yeoman service over the next few years. New England nonresistance owed much to its women devotees.

The convention lasted three full days, and, even after the withdrawal of Beckwith and his associates (mostly clerics), there was no lack of animated and sometimes heated discussion. Aside from the presence of a few nonpacifists, like Wendell Phillips (1811-1884), attracted to the meetings through their association with Garrison in one or another of his other causes, and in spite of the predominance of Garrisonian abolitionists among the delegates, there was still much diversity of opinion in the ranks of the pacifists present. The main debate was over the resolution introduced by the banker Amasa Walker, who was later prominent in Massachusetts politics. It ran as follows: "Resolved that human life is inviolable, and can never be taken by individuals or nations without committing sin against God."[43] Eventually the motion was carried, and the convention passed on next to set up a society based on the principles of nonresistance. A committee of nine headed by Garrison was chosen to draft a Constitution and a Declaration of Sentiments for the new organization, which was given the name of the New England Non-Resistance Society. Before concluding its business, the convention accepted the reports of the committees appointed to examine, among other matters, the rights of conscience in relation to the existing militia laws in Massachusetts and to inquire into the practical results of the adoption of a nonviolent policy. Orders were given for the Declaration of Sentiments to be "engrossed upon parchment" —those in sympathy with its aims were to append their signatures—and for the proceedings of the convention to be published. Thereupon the delegates dispersed to spread the good word throughout the limits of New England and beyond.

The key document produced at the convention was undoubtedly the Declaration of Sentiments. There is some evidence that the Declaration, and the Constitution as well, had been prepared in outline by Garrison and his friends before the convention opened.[44] It certainly

---

[43] *Proceedings*, pp. 4, 5.

[44] On 10 August 1838 Edmund Quincy wrote to Garrison (Garrisons, *W.L.G.*, II, 223, 224) as follows: "Brother Wright was in town yesterday, and we talked over together the approaching Peace Convention and its probable results. . . . The result of the Convention will probably be a new organization on the principle of

goes a good way beyond the mere faith in the inviolability of human life, for it takes up a negative position toward the whole apparatus of government along with the armed forces and police. Garrison, who was most responsible for its style and contents, wrote proudly to his wife at the conclusion of the convention:

> Never was a more "fanatical" or "disorganizing" instrument penned by man. It swept the whole surface of society, and upturned almost every existing institution on earth. Of course it produced a deep and lively sensation, and a very long and critical debate; and, to my astonishment was adopted by a vote of more than five to one.[45] . . . It will make a tremendous stir, not only in this country, but, in time, throughout the world. All who voted for it were abolitionists.

The tempo of persecution, he added in a letter to his sister-in-law, was likely to increase when its message became known, and they would have to face afresh the fury of the mob. "But my soul is in perfect peace, for my trust is in the living God."[46]

"We cannot acknowledge allegiance to any human government," states the Declaration at the outset.[47] Christ is our only ruler and law-giver, and we must obey him and his laws rather than any earthly king or government. We can make no distinction among ourselves according to rank or sex or national origin. "Our country is the world, our countrymen are all mankind" (the now familiar words that Garrison had adapted from Tom Paine to use in black-letter type as the masthead in his *Liberator* were repeated here). Nonresistants do indeed love their native land, but neither more nor less than the other coun-

---

the Inviolability of Human Life. Now, as it will be well to be prepared for such a result, I write you, at his request, to ask you and your brother [-in-law], G. W. Benson, to lay your heads together and concoct a Declaration of Sentiments and Constitution, or a Constitution, including the emphatic annunciation of this great principle. Especially try to fix upon a *name* for the association—something that shall convey the idea of the principle of the movement: the anti-man-killing principle. This last has puzzled us a good deal. Brother Wright is going to Scituate to spend a week with Bro. May, with whom he is to attempt what we ask of you. I shall apply to Amasa Walker here to assist me in concocting something of the kind; so that when we come together at the time of the Convention, we shall be tolerably well prepared for the emergency. Please do not neglect this."

[45] The Declaration was carried toward the end of the third day by a vote of 27 to 5, while the Constitution had been passed on the second day 28 to 5. Though voting for the former took place fairly late in the proceedings, the small numbers of those who took part is still surprising.

[46] Garrisons, *W.L.G.*, II, 228, 229; W. L. Garrison to Mary Benson, 22 Sept. 1838, Garrison Papers, B.P.L., MS A.1.1., vol. 3, no. 19.

[47] Printed in *Principles of the Non-Resistance Society*, pp. 3-9. The Declaration has been reprinted in full by Devere Allen, *The Fight for Peace*, pp. 694-97.

tries of the world and their inhabitants, who are all God's children. For that reason,

> We register our testimony, not only against all war, whether offensive or defensive, but all preparations for war; against every naval ship, every arsenal, every fortification; against the militia system and a standing army; against all military chieftains and soldiers; against all monuments commemorative of victory over a foreign foe, all trophies won in battle, all celebrations in honor of military or naval exploits; against all appropriations for the defence of a nation by force and arms, on the part of any legislative body; against every edict of government requiring of its subjects military service. Hence, we deem it unlawful to bear arms, or to hold a military office.

But this protest alone was not sufficient. To deny the use of physical force by national states to ward off attack by external enemies while retaining its use within the country to deal with domestic evildoers was a contradiction that must not be allowed. "The unit cannot be of greater importance than the aggregate." No domestic government was to be found at present ready to renounce its trust in armed might to enforce the law. It was therefore incumbent upon nonresistants to voluntarily dissociate themselves from government so far as possible. Refuse all public offices, the Declaration goes on, and refrain from voting or sitting in any legislative body or acting in any judicial capacity. Eschew politics altogether. Otherwise, the guilt of blood shed will be upon you, too. "It follows, that we cannot sue any man at law to compel him by force to restore anything which he may have wrongfully taken from us or others; but, if he had seized our coat, we shall surrender up our cloak rather than subject him to punishment." Prisons and punishments could form no part of Christ's order; this was not the way to the moral regeneration of mankind. By meekness and love and long suffering alone would evil be overcome in the end. "We advocate no jacobinical doctrine. The spirit of jacobinism is the spirit of retaliation, violence and murder." They were ready to suffer for their opinions, while fearlessly putting their ideas before their fellowmen. The Declaration ended on a note of confidence, with the belief that time and God were on their side. "Having withdrawn from human protection, what can sustain us but that faith which overcomes the world?"

The document has vigor and considerable rhetorical force; it is not mere verbiage covering empty sentiments but has an authentic ring about it. It does not so much argue as state what it believes to be moral truth. It has its fair share of the sententiousness current at the time, its tone is too often priggish and moralistic, and it has little or nothing to say about the relationship of nonresistance and no-government to the social order. Its Christian anarchism is of the individualist variety. In relation to the state the Declaration takes an extremist view that has not usually been shared by the modern pacifist movement. But here, indeed, there is some ambiguity as to its exact position. Was the state as such condemned root and branch? Or was it to be regarded as unchristian only so long as it was tied up with the instruments of oppression and war and punishment? If—to paraphrase its wording —the state ceased to be upheld by physical strength, or its laws enforced by the bayonet, would the way then be open for the genuine nonresistant to participate in the work of human government?

In fact, while stating the obligation incumbent upon its members to refrain from violence and from all attempts to punish the wrongdoer, a matter to be left to God's judgment, the synopsis of the new Society's principles goes on to say: "All human governments *at present existing* are based on the principles of violence and retaliation. Therefore I cannot approve or maintain any of them."[48] Was a constitution, an administration, a legislature and judiciary that would in the future have shed the trappings of military might and coercive power and have thereby become acceptable to a simon-pure nonresistant really conceivable? Perhaps, as for the earlier peace sects, such questions were not quite relevant since, in the eyes of men like Garrison, such a state of affairs was not likely to come to pass until "the kingdoms of this world will have become the kingdoms of our LORD and of his CHRIST, and he shall reign forever."[49] Without reference to the perfectionist and millenarian ferment of that time, in which Garrison and his friends fully participated, a proper understanding of the document is impossible. For all its exaggeration, it has remained a landmark in the evolution of pacifist thought. Tolstoy was greatly influenced by it (and so, through him, was Gandhi, too); Tolstoy reprints lengthy extracts from it in his famous treatise *The Kingdom of God is within you* (1893).[50] "On the face of it erratic, contradictory, ill-considered," writes Devere Allen of the Declaration, "yet a study of it will induce only respect,

[48] *Proceedings*, p. 29. My italics.   [49] *Principles*, p. 7.
[50] See Leo Tolstoy, *The Kingdom of God and Peace Essays*, pp. 5-11, 22, 575-82, for details concerning Garrison's impact on Tolstoy. The Russian learned of the writings and activities of Garrison and other American nonresistants only after the publication in 1884 of his *What I Believe*, the first public statement of his own nonresistant faith. In the introduction he wrote in 1904 to the condensation of the four-volume life of Garrison by his sons, which was undertaken by Vladimir Chertkov and Florence Holah, Tolstoy (*The Kingdom of God*, p. 575) speaks of "the spiritual joy" he experienced at his first encounter with the New England nonresistants.

if not agreement. . . . It is a great historic paper."[51] It is important rather for the striking challenge to accepted ideas on war and society that it threw into the arena than for logical thought or original argument.

Let us now turn for a moment to a second document emanating from the convention, which is of considerable interest to our study. In July, Samuel May had written to Garrison that Edmund Quincy (1808-1877), a young Boston patrician and a recent convert to abolition and nonresistance, would prepare a report for presentation at the forthcoming convention "on the right of others, as well as members of the Society of Friends to have their conscientious scruples respecting military training, etc., duly regarded."[52] On the second day of the convention Quincy was elected to lead a committee to consider this subject, and the committee's report, or rather Quincy's, was accepted by the convention.

The payment of a small monetary fine in lieu of militia service, which was then the penalty for nonattendance at musters, was not a trifling question, Quincy stated in his report.[53] It was one that raised important matters of principle. What purpose did the proclamation of religious liberty serve if a man were not free to put his religious beliefs into practice in a matter like military service? He recommended that the various state legislatures be petitioned on behalf of liberty of conscience; a number of nonpacifists, he thought, would probably be glad to sign, since the matter concerned the principle of religious freedom as fully as it did the narrower one of nonresistance. Four additional considerations, he said, should be urged on the state lawmakers in support of the petitions. In the first place, the existing law penalized the genuine conscientious objector who was unwilling to submit to a fine, while the shirker got off with paying a few dollars. Secondly, it was unlikely that an exemption clause would be abused by the unconscientious, for (and here we meet again the same argument used by Thomas Grimké in his unsuccessful petition to the South Carolina legislature, discussed earlier) "it is not probable that the profession of peace principles will be for some time to come so popular, that many worldly-minded persons will be willing to incur, the odium of being of that sect everywhere spoken against, for the sake of saving a few dollars." Next, Quincy pleaded the exemption already granted Quakers in Massachusetts and several other states.

[51] *The Fight for Peace*, p. 395.

[52] Garrisons, *W.L.G.*, II, 223. In his diary Quincy wrote enthusiastically of the acceptance of "that immortal instrument," the nonresistants' Declaration of Sentiments (Merrill, *Against Wind and Tide*, p. 146).

[53] *Report on the Injustice and Inequality of the Militia Law* . . . , esp. pp. 6-11.

Were not the grounds of objection and the right to consideration of their conscientious scruples the same in the case of those Christians in other churches who rejected war? Lastly, he pointed out that exemption on conscientious grounds from the taking of oaths had been extended, at least in Massachusetts, to non-Quakers.

Quincy and his colleagues thought that petitions of this kind, if properly organized, would in the end bring the desired exemption. But what should objectors do before this is achieved? They must "firmly, though meekly . . . refuse to comply with the requisitions of the military laws." Some in the movement would consider that it was enough to make their protest by refusing to drill and would then voluntarily pay the fine laid down by law. Others—and among them "some of the most consistent and honored of the friends of peace"—would feel bound to go further and would, as part of their peace witness, refuse to pay the fine and either have their property distrained by law or go to prison for a time. Quincy and his committee, while feeling that at present the payment of the fine could not be regarded as a compromise of principles, stated their belief that the more radical witness would become, as time passed, increasingly effective as a protest against war.

Another report which the convention approved was one on "the tendency and effects of the pacific principle." It was prepared and presented by a committee of three otherwise obscure members of the convention.[54] It is interesting as an attempt to investigate the practical effects of the adoption of a nonresistant policy. The convention had already passed a resolution that "to doubt its safety and expediency is to deny the wisdom and goodness of Jehovah."[55] But it was evidently felt that more tangible proofs of the efficacy of nonresistance would be helpful. "Has this principle," the authors of the report inquire, "when carried out agreeably to the precepts and example of Christ, a natural tendency to secure, and would it result in the general safety and happiness of mankind?" That is, was nonresistance expedient as well as moral? On the positive side, the report pointed to instances, most of them extracted from Biblical history, where love, kindness, and forbearance toward evilly inclined persons had finally succeeded in winning them from their course. "These examples on divine record, being the natural and legitimate effect of the pacific and kind course, afford a strong and conclusive argument in favor of the utility and expediency of perfectly following the precepts and example of Christ in respect to non-resistance, and overcoming evil with good." It was

---

[54] *Report on the Tendency and Effects of the Pacific Principle* . . . , pp. 3-20.
[55] *Proceedings*, p. 9.

argued, too, that the "pacific principle" was capable of evoking feelings of shame on the part of an aggressor and leading him to make amends for wrong done. Or, again, when followed fearlessly, nonviolence had been known to win the respect and love of savages: this was shown in the relations of Penn and the Quakers with the American Indians, who, on the other hand, reacted with hatred and deadly enmity to attempts to molest them. On the negative side, it was urged that the risks of living according to this pacific principle were far less than those incurred by following the way of self-defense in violence and war. There would be martyrs for peace: indeed, defense by means of arms did not always succeed—as the case of Lovejoy clearly showed. "Almost all the wars which have . . . desolated the earth, have owed their existence to some kind of bloody self-defence, in returning evil for evil, and would have been avoided in returning good for evil." Let a beginning be made somewhere, the report concluded: violence and wars will only cease if men refrain from sanctioning them.

Like every self-respecting society of that day, the New England Non-Resistance Society was furnished not only with a Declaration of Sentiments, embodying the leading principles which were to guide its action, but also with a Constitution, which concerned itself mainly with organization. The author of this document was once again Garrison himself. "I first wrote the Constitution, radical in all things, and presented it without delay," he reported to his wife at the convention's conclusion.[56] According to its provisions, a majority of the executive committee was, for practical reasons, to be drawn from the Boston area. But membership and full voting rights in the Society were to be open to all, irrespective of color or sex or creed, who were prepared to assent to Article II of the Constitution, which ran as follows:

> The members of this society agree in opinion, that no man, or body of men, however constituted, or by whatever name called, have the right to take the life of man as a penalty for transgression; that no one, who professes to have the spirit of Christ, can consistently sue a man at law for redress of injuries, or thrust any evil-doer into prison, or fill any office in which he would come under obligation to execute penal enactments—or take any part in the military service— or acknowledge allegiance to any human government—or justify any man in fighting in defence of property, liberty, life or religion; that he cannot engage in or countenance any plot or effort to revolutionize, or change, by physical violence, any government, however corrupt or oppressive; that he will obey "the powers that be,"

[56] Garrisons, W.L.G., II, 228.

except in those cases in which they violate his conscience—and then, rather than to resist, he will meekly submit to the penalty of disobedience; and that, while he will cheerfully endure all things for Christ's sake, without cherishing even the desire to inflict injury upon his persecutors, yet he will be bold and uncompromising for God, in bearing his testimony against sin, in high places and in low places. . . .[57]

For the honorary position of president of their Society, the nonresistants chose Effingham L. Capron, "a Friend," it was said, "of the straitest kind,"[58] who had been converted early in the decade to abolitionism by reading the *Liberator*. Several other Quakers served as officers, including Garrison's brother-in-law, George W. Benson of Brooklyn (Conn.), though—as we know—official Quakerism was extremely cool, in some cases downright hostile, to the Non-Resistance Society. Garrison and Henry C. Wright, the most energetic and dynamic of the Society's leaders, were chosen as corresponding secretary and vice-president, respectively. Among its other officers, the names of Mrs. Maria Chapman (who acted as recording secretary), Charles K. Whipple (the treasurer), Oliver Johnson (who eventually became Garrison's biographer), Edmund Quincy, and Miss Anne W. Weston are worth recording for the part they played in the Society's counsels in its early days.

Garrison, at least, had felt very satisfied with the outcome of the convention. The immediate preparations for it he had left mainly to Henry C. Wright and others, owing in part to his continuing preoccupation with the antislavery question and, also, to illness in his own family, which had taken up much of his time. However, as it turned out, he writes, "I took a much more active part [in the sessions of the convention] than I thought of doing."[59] "The three days of the past week in Boston," he prophesied after its conclusion, "are destined to become more memorable in history, than the famous 'three days in Paris.' They will constitute an important chapter in the annals of Christianity. Mankind shall hail the TWENTIETH OF SEPTEMBER with more exaltation and gratitude, than Americans now do the FOURTH OF JULY."[60] He had good reason to be pleased with what had been achieved. From the strange assortment of saints and fanatics, selfless reformers and professional agitators, who had made up the convention's membership, a majority had been found to vote into existence an organization dedicated to Garrison's program and based on the sentiments and constitu-

[57] *Principles*, pp. 11, 12.   [58] Garrisons, *W.L.G.*, I, 398.
[59] Garrison Papers, B.P.L., MS A.1.1., vol. 3, nos. 17 and 19.
[60] *Liberator*, 26 Sept. 1838.

tion which he had himself drawn up for it. His disciples had shown themselves ready to follow him, and not only in his crusade to emancipate the slave; they were willing, moreover, to outdistance the ordinary run of Christian nonresistants and challenge the right of the mighty state power itself to exercise coercive authority over men.

It was hardly surprising, then—even though a few voices of sympathy were heard[61]— that almost the whole press of New England and beyond, especially the church journals, raised a hue and cry against Garrison and his Society. "The most fanatical ultraist in New England," "ultra beyond ultra," "truly, Jack Cade is come again"[62] were typical of the reactions among the educated classes at large.

There was considerable hesitation, even in the ranks of the radical pacifists, at accepting the full nonresistant creed as presented, in particular, in the Declaration of Sentiments. It was certainly too strong a medicine for some to swallow at a gulp; others came to accept it only after lengthy consideration and much soul-searching. It is interesting to note, for instance, that the Hon. Sidney Willard (1780-1856), a prominent Harvard scholar and provincial politician who had been elected to act as president of the convention, took no further part in the movement. We know quite a lot, from their correspondence and other writings, of the tussle that was going on in the minds of several leading pacifists, who had hesitated to sign the Declaration when the invitation came at the conclusion of the proceedings. This inner debate is extremely revealing of some of the problems which faced the radical section of the pacifist movement at this time.[63]

Let us take first the case of the Rev. Samuel J. May.[64] We have already seen him actively participating in the preparations for the convention and in its sessions. He had long been a nonresistant. But the relation between pacifism and politics did not present itself to him in the simple, black-and-white terms in which men like Garrison or Wright viewed it. May, as contemporaries witnessed, was more than half a

[61] Orestes Brownson's *Boston Quarterly Review*, for instance, in its March 1839 issue (quoted in *Principles*, p. 14), considered that the nonresistants were quite correct in regarding no-government as the logical outcome of Quaker pacifism. Garrison, it is interesting to note, had disciples in the editors of the *Vermont Telegraph* (the Rev. Orson S. Murray) and the *Herald of Freedom* (Nathaniel P. Rogers). For the nonresistant movement in Vermont from 1837 into the early forties, see David M. Ludlum, *Social Ferment in Vermont 1791-1850*, pp. 169-75. Murray was eventually disfellowshipped by the Baptists in 1841 for his unorthodox utterances.

[62] *Greenfield Gazette, Concord Baptist Register*, and *Christian Statesman*, respectively, as quoted in the *Liberator*, 18 Oct. 1838; 16 Nov. 1838. See also Galpin, *Pioneering for Peace*, pp. 131, 132.

[63] See Galpin, *Pioneering for Peace*, pp. 129, 130.

[64] See Galpin, "God's Chore Boy," chap. V.

saint, a man overflowing with charity toward his fellow creatures, who was often irked—despite his genuine admiration for the man—by Garrison's bitter personal attacks on those he believed to be in the wrong. Now, toward the end of the convention, May came forward with a resolution, as circumlocutory in diction as it was tolerant in spirit, which was adopted by the delegates: "That, while our perceptions of the truth as it is in Jesus impel us to announce other principles and pursue other measures than those pursued by other friends of peace, we feel no hostility to them, but cordially wish them success in all their endeavors to promote the cause of our Lord and Savior Jesus Christ."[65] Shortly afterward, when a vote was taken on the Declaration of Sentiments, May abstained along with a few others. "Though almost ready to swallow it entire . . . Bro. May acted very inconsistently, got frightened, confused and did some harm." Thus writes Garrison.[66] But this judgment fails to appreciate May's dilemma. May felt profoundly at one with the thoroughgoing rejection of violence, which was at the basis of the principles enunciated in the Declaration. But that this rejection necessarily entailed for the nonresistant a withdrawal from the whole political order, and not merely from those sectors of it clearly connected with violence, was not so obvious to May. Nor did he feel satisfied that the apparatus of justice was inevitably only a synonym for oppression and coercion. He was, indeed, apprehensive of the farfetched conclusions that might be derived by some from such premises. And lastly, he may have drawn back, sensitive and modest as he always was, from a sense of personal inadequacy. He was to write a few years later: "Non-Resistance is the gospel of the Cross. . . . I do not therefore presume to call myself a non-resistant. I am sure Jesus was one. I acknowledge that I ought to be one; and pray for faith and love and courage enough to make me one."[67]

Garrison was most anxious to gain May's adherence, and perhaps this explains the note of irritation Garrison displayed at May's behavior at the convention. Let him only give his agreement, Garrison pleaded a short time later, to the general principle of nonviolence that is the kernel of the Declaration of Sentiments—and, assuredly, he assented to this—and that would be enough in all conscience to justify his adding his signature to the document. "This instrument contemplates nothing, repudiates nothing, but the spirit of violence in thought, word and deed. Whatever, therefore, may be done without

[65] *Proceedings*, p. 12.   [66] Garrisons, *W.L.G.*, II, 229.
[67] Letter from May, 4 Jan. 1845, in S. E. Coues's "Peace Album," Harvard University Library, MS Am. 635*.

provoking that spirit, and in accordance with the spirit of disinterested benevolence, is not touched or alluded to in the instrument." The argument is a little disingenuous, and Garrison himself seems skeptical about the effect it would have on Brother May.[68] Finally, however, while not wholly abandoning his belief in the legitimacy of political action (as will be seen later in this story), and while also remaining unwilling to sever his connections completely with the American Peace Society May by the summer of 1839 had yielded to Garrison's entreaties and over the next few years was to give lavishly of his time and energy to the work of the Non-Resistance Society.

Instrumental, along with Garrison, in bringing May into the fold was his friend, Edmund Quincy,[69] who, like May, had himself had serious reservations about some of the sentiments in the Declaration, despite his active part in planning and carrying through the convention. Quincy is an interesting figure, typical perhaps of the aristocrat in reform. Born in 1808, the second son of President Josiah Quincy of Harvard, and related to most of the "best" families in Boston, Quincy had studied law, though he was never to practice it, and then had entered for a time on the life of a young man about town. The murder of Lovejoy had led to his conversion to abolition, and association with the Garrisonians soon brought his enlistment in a number of other humanitarian causes: women's suffrage, temperance and, by no means least, nonresistance. A wit, a man of elegant and cultivated taste who showed distinct talent as a writer, he now threw himself without reserve into the public arena alongside Garrison and Wendell Phillips and the others of their circle. "Every letter of his in the Garrison life," writes John Jay Chapman, "casts as much light as a bush-burner on the queer crowd of enthusiasts he spent his life with." With an ample private fortune he remained throughout his life to some extent a dilettante, one who devoted himself, in the words of the poet James Russell Lowell, "deliberately to the somewhat arduous profession of gentleman." But this profession he interpreted as demanding service and sacrifice for the welfare of the oppressed and in support of unpopular reforms. A Boston Brahmin by birth, he was, like Phillips, not afraid to risk the abuse and obloquy of his caste.

At the convention Quincy's legal training had been useful in drawing up the recommendations for amending the militia law in favor of conscientious objectors who did not belong to any of the peace

---

[68] Garrisons, *W.L.G.*, II, 237.

[69] See J. P. Quincy, "Memoir of Edmund Quincy," *Proceedings of the Massachusetts Historical Society*, 2nd ser., XVIII (1905), 401-16; M. A. DeWolfe Howe, "Biographer's Bait: A Reminder of Edmund Quincy," *ibid.*, LXVIII (1952), esp. 377, 378.

churches. But for a lawyer, even if he did not have a legal mind, parts of the Declaration of Sentiments were indeed difficult to accept as they stood. Therefore, Quincy, like May, had not signed. He repudiated utterly all powers of government based on bloodshed and force, he explained to Garrison in a letter of 21 September; he trusted in the power of nonresistance. However, he went on, "there are certain things originating in Government, and sanctioned by it, which I think are innocent, and may be innocently used": the use of banknotes and coinage, for instance, and of legal contracts—life could not be carried on in a state of civilization without them. Garrison was apparently willing to meet some of Quincy's objections by making slight alterations in the text of the Declaration as it appeared in the *Liberator*.[70] It was not very long before Quincy, putting aside his reservations, took the decision to join the Society, and by the spring of 1839 he felt able to inform May: "I have been much happier since I have attained to the high and sound ground of Non-Resistance."[71]

In the following September, Quincy consummated his attachment to nonresistance by resigning his commission as a justice of the peace. In his letter to Governor Everett he wrote of his conviction of the incompatibility of officeholding with belief in the inviolability of human life. "I do, therefore," he stated, "in the presence of Almighty God, and before you, as Chief Magistrate of this Commonwealth, hereby abjure and renounce all allegiance which I may at any time have acknowledged myself to owe to any government of man's institution. And I call upon Him and you to witness that I have put away from myself this iniquity forever!"[72]

Quincy was to be extremely active in the work of the Non-Resistance Society and to do it yeoman service through his editorship of its paper, the *Non-Resistant*. Surprisingly enough, the two Grimké sisters, whose ardent advocacy of the nonresistant cause we have discussed a few pages back, were to take little part in the movement from now on. Perhaps the influence of Angelina's husband, Theodore Weld was partly responsible. Wrote Abby Kelley: "As for Theodore he is unsparingly severe upon us. Says all that Garrison, [Lucretia] Mott, Chapman and all others who have adopted the will o'wisp delusions of non-resistance, can do for the emancipation of the slave will be undermined and counteracted by these idle notions on this subject. He thinks however that there is to be no permanent harm apprehended, as they have been caught up by us without thought—and that we shall

---

[70] Garrisons, *W.L.G.*, II, 234-37.
[71] Quoted in Galpin, *Pioneering for Peace*, p. 129.
[72] *The Non-Resistant*, 7 Dec. 1839.

soon abandon them—fact of our having embraced them is full evidence that we have not considered them with any *depth* of thought." However, he respected their sincerity, telling them, Abby reports, that "we should be untrue to our own souls did we not proceed in their dissemination. Indeed it seems to me that he looks upon the whole matter with deep contempt mingled with pity."[73]

In any case, we find Sarah Grimké in the middle of October informing her tutor in nonresistance, Henry C. Wright, that she did not believe that she would have felt herself able to sign either the Declaration of Sentiments or the Constitution had she been present at the convention in September. "Perhaps thou mayest be surprised at this, and query what change has taken place in my views." She was not herself conscious of any alteration, she goes on—unless it be a realization that the matter demanded *deep searching of my own heart* and a fuller insight into the mysteries of God's kingdom, than I have yet attained." In particular, she was troubled—and what she writes here is interesting in view of similar difficulties experienced by the whole evangelical generation of pacifists—by the seeming discrepancy between the God of love as revealed in the New Testament and the God of battles as portrayed in the pages of the Old. "I have labored in vain hitherto to reconcile the Mosaic and Christian dispensations, yet I am persuaded they must be *reconcilable* in principle, however various in practice." And so, "until this stumbling block is removed out of my way," however much her private sentiments might draw her toward absolute nonresistance, she felt unwilling to commit herself by endorsing these documents "to the principle that one of Jehovah's dispensations is contrary to the other in those principles of fundamental morality on which they are based." She wished Godspeed to those who had fully accepted the nonresistant covenant. And with womanly commonsense and some experience, perhaps, of the belligerence sometimes shown by pacifists in their private lives, she adds: "May they remember that home is the first place to exhibit the meekness and lowliness of Him whom they have called master."[74] Already, if but faintly, we can read in this letter from Sarah Grimké the dilemma that was increasingly to face the nonresistant abolitionists over the next two decades and right up to the outbreak of the Civil War. Were they to be the followers of the Lord God of Hosts ready to do battle with the unrighteous on behalf of the oppressed, or were they to be the long-

[73] Abby Kelley to A. W. Weston, 29 May 1839, Weston Papers, B.P.L., MS A.9.2, vol. 11, no. 112.
[74] *Weld-Grimké Letters*, II, 705-7.

suffering disciples of the meek and humble Jesus willing to wait for the righting of injustice until God's good time?

But this conflict of conscience lay in the future. The main focus of contention now centered in the belief of those, like Garrison and Wright, that nonresistant pacifism, if it was to be consistent with itself, necessarily involved a form of spiritual anarchism, a belief that proved unacceptable to many who shared these men's rejection of force in international and political life. As we have just seen, some who dissented were sooner or later led to throw in their lot with the Non-Resistance Society, considering that agreement on essentials was more important than their private reservations concerning the full implications of the "no-government" idea. Still others, on the other hand—among them some of the most dedicated of the absolute pacifists—saw in this idea an insuperable object to their collaborating with the new Society. As Ladd remarked: "There is such a thing as going beyond the Millennium."[75]

Take Amasa Walker, for instance, a sensible, practical man certainly, but one sensitive to the humanitarian call on conscience, who had at the September convention proposed the resolution in favor of the inviolability of human life. "For myself," he wrote to Garrison at the end of the year in a letter which the latter described as "catholic and gentlemanly in its spirit—just what we should expect from its author," "for myself I regard your Society with entire good will." But, he added, "I could not subscribe to the doctrines of the Non-Resistance Society, because I would not see my way clear to do so; I could not see that they were sound and correct." Was it reasonable on their part, as citizens of the state, to refuse to exercise their privilege of voting or to stand aside from all responsibility for the administration of the country even where coercive methods were not being used?[76]

It was, of course, William Ladd who, more than any other man then living, represented the peace cause in the public mind. We have watched the evolution of his views on the peace question from a qualified acceptance of defensive wars to the open avowal of absolute pacifism. Even Garrison, despite impatience at what he considered his appeasement of the nonpacifist element in the American Peace Society, treated Ladd with respect and tolerant affection. His role at the peace convention Garrison described amusingly in the following words: "The deep solemnity of the occasion was somewhat disturbed by the broad and irresistible humor of William Ladd. He is a

[75] Quoted in Hemmenway, *The Apostle of Peace*, p. 77.
[76] *Liberator*, 11 Jan. 1839; letter from Amasa Walker, 23 Jan. 1845, in Coues's "Peace Album."

huge and strange compound of fat, good nature, and benevolence. He went with us nineteen-twentieths of the way, and said he expected to 'go the whole' next year!"[77] In fact, however, Ladd was never to tread the remainder of the road, and the real extent of his difference with the Garrisonians was greater than perhaps either side realized at the outset.

Although Ladd had voted against the Constitution and had refrained from signing the Declaration of Sentiments and had, moreover, been somewhat shocked by the participation of women in the debate at a mixed gathering,[78] he wrote to a friend, not unenthusiastically, about the sessions of the convention, which had just ended the day before:

> If the American Peace Society are called ultra for adopting the principle that *all* war is contrary to the gospel, the new society must be called ultra beyond ultra. . . . I fully agree with many of their sentiments, and I bid them Godspeed so far as they follow Christ. . . . I consider the new society as ultra high; but almost the whole world are ultra low on this subject, and, if I must choose between the two ultras, give me the ultra high one; for I have always found it more easy to come down to the truth, than to come up to it.[79]

He spoke appreciatively of the ability and energy the nonresistants had shown, and he surmised that soon their Society would in all likelihood eclipse the American Peace Society as the mainspring of the peace movement. "I have no doubt that they mean well, and perhaps have more light on the subject than I have. I dare not say positively that they are wrong." His failure to accept their position wholeheartedly, he went on, was possibly due to an old man's caution, his failure to perceive a new truth. "If they are of God, they will prevail, if not they will come to naught. If the new society do [*sic*] anything, they will turn the world upside down! but the world has been wrong side up these six thousand years."[80]

After a few weeks, however, Ladd was to give a more detailed exposé of the serious misgivings that some of the "no-government" ideas had aroused in him. In a letter to the *Liberator* early in November, he expressed his disappointment at the withdrawal of his colleague Beckwith's contingent from the convention. If they had stood their ground, they would very likely have succeeded in giving a more moderate tone

---

[77] Garrison to Sarah Benson, 24 Sept. 1838 in *W.L.G.*, II, 229.

[78] Cf. Sarah Grimké's comment to Henry C. Wright: "I rejoice that you organized the Convention on the basis of humanity; it is one step, a great step towards the redemption of woman" (*Weld-Grimké Letters*, II, 707).

[79] Quoted in Hemmenway, *The Apostle of Peace*, pp. 73, 74.

[80] *Christian Mirror*, 22 Sept. 1838, quoted in the *Liberator*, 18 Oct. 1838.

to the declarations which were issued in the convention's name. (It seems probable that Ladd himself would have welcomed the coming into being, alongside his own somewhat unadventurous American Peace Society, of a spirited group embodying the radical pacifist idea, but without the admixture of antigovernment notions which Garrison and Wright had grafted on to it.) Turning now to the points at issue between himself and the Non-Resistance Society, Ladd declared his disapproval of capital punishment along with war, yet the question of its abolition, he felt, should not be attached to the peace question any more than abolitionism or the temperance cause, both of which he also supported, should. Again, the nonresistants were right in believing that lawsuits were symptoms of evil. They must be avoided by Christian people wherever possible. But Ladd did not believe that appeal to the law was forbidden in every instance; he could not feel that in all cases there was a contravention of gospel love. And as for the imprisonment of offenders, here again he had to register his dissent from the Garrisonian view. "I believe that . . . culprits may be seized and condemned without a necessary violation of that principle of love; consequently, that civil and criminal jurisprudence ought to be supported by Christians, to a certain extent. . . . I also believe that physical force may sometimes be used in the spirit of love, as in family government, and restraint of drunkards, lunatics, and criminals." Lastly, Ladd, even more forthrightly than May, took issue with the Society on the question of the franchise. To vote for the best man in an election, he felt, even where the choice lay between candidates not connected in any way with the peace movement, was not a surrender to war and militarism.[81] In other words, active citizenship and Christian pacifism were not mutually exclusive in his view.

The founders of the New England Non-Resistance Society, therefore, had failed to bring into existence an organization which would unite under its umbrella all absolute pacifists. The American Peace Society still retained the loyalty of a number of its more radical members. The new body was predominantly, as its name indicated, a New England group. In reality, at the outset at any rate, membership was confined mainly to the eastern districts of Massachusetts. In respect to both the leaders and the rank and file, it was essentially an organ of the Garrisonian abolitionists; the life and vigor of the new group came from the members of the Massachusetts Anti-Slavery Society. As we shall see, this was in some ways to have an unfortunate influence on the Non-Resistance Society's development.

[81] Letter of 7 Nov. 1838, reprinted in Hemmenway, *The Apostle of Peace*, pp. 75, 76.

Even more fatal in the long run to its chances of expansion than the narrow geographical base from which the Society operated at first was what we may call the anarchist slant given to the traditional non-resistant view by Garrison and his colleagues. Their idea had boldness, and it excited and attracted reformers of the time, including some of the best intellects of New England, by the moral force and the thoroughness of its attack on power, "THE POWERS THAT BE," the state power that sanctioned slavery and war and domestic coercion. Nearly fourteen years before Garrison's celebrated act, on the Fourth of July 1854, of burning a copy of the United States Constitution, he had in penning the Declaration of Sentiments of the New England Non-Resistance Society virtually renounced allegiance to that "covenant with death . . . and agreement with hell." Yet the Declaration was mainly a negative document. It remained to be seen whether the New England nonresistants could supplement it with a positive program of action such as the older generation of peace workers had endeavored to forge for the American Peace Society, whether they could develop a cohesive body of doctrine, which would offset to some degree the sectarian narrowness of the "no-government" view.

Chapter 13

The New England Non-Resistance Society

The founding of the New England Non-Resistance Society in September 1838 marked a dividing line in the history of the American peace movement. The radicals now had their own organization and the possibility of developing their ideas free from interference from the more conservative sections of the movement. The Society flourished for several years, attracting the allegiance of some of the most talented intellects of New England and a number of the most devoted spirits in its reform circles. Soon, however, the movement began to lose momentum, and by mid-century the Society had ceased to function altogether. Yet, during the brief years of its existence, it had showed considerable creativity and at first, at any rate, a many-sided activity.

Among the most immediate tasks facing the new Society was to define its relationship to the organizations with whose work its founders were most closely associated. With the American Peace Society, in which hitherto pacifists had worked with greater or less harmony alongside nonpacifists, as we have seen, relations were bad from the beginning, despite Ladd's attempts to bridge the gap. Ladd sincerely desired to reach a modus vivendi with the new Society. Both shared the same enthusiasm for the work of peace, and Ladd, though not quite a nonresistant, considered himself as much an absolute pacifist as the radicals. His attendance and conduct at the foundation convention and at subsequent annual meetings of the new Society testify to his genuine desire for good relations; at the same time, he did not ignore differences in outlook or conceal his own feeling that the nonresistants, though sincere, were carrying their principles to unwarranted extremes. Nevertheless, some members of the American Peace Society soon began to express doubts whether Ladd had not gone too far in trying to understand the nonresistant point of view.[1] And from the other side, too, it was not long before strong criticism of the American Peace Society was being voiced by the new Society's leaders.

Late in the summer of 1839 an editorial in the recently established *Non-Resistant* stated: "As to the services of the American Peace Society in the cause of Peace, we are not disposed to undervalue them. It has done much in the preparation of materials for a more scorching

[1] *Advocate of Peace*, III, no. 10 (Dec. 1840), 232-35.

559

reform. We cannot perceive, however, that it has made much impression on the martial spirit of the nation. We believe that it has accomplished its mission, and will ere long be no more."[2] In particular, the American Peace Society's panacea for universal peace, the establishment of a congress of nations to arbitrate international peace, in which Ladd was, as we have seen, particularly interested, met with no support from the nonresistants. "Impracticable" their organ called it. The editorial doubted whether the world's governments would be ready to honestly adopt the scheme and make it work: in any case, it would need military sanctions and not merely the backing of public opinion, if its decisions were not to be "but so much empty breath." Peace workers, the article concluded, must begin by working a revolution in the human conscience; to commence at the top with governments was to start at the wrong end.[3] The debate brings to mind the controversy on the question of sanctions inside the peace movement in our own day. A curious similarity, too, may be detected between the arguments used by the nonresistants and those of the American Peace Society's military-minded critics, who likewise maintained that the world was not yet ripe for such a scheme and that, anyhow, it would fail unless backed by armed force.

By the 1840's relations between the two peace bodies had deteriorated to the point where there was little, if any, contact between them—except for an occasional outburst of polemics. Personal friendships between many of the pacifists in each camp, of course, continued, and they worked together harmoniously on other reform platforms. Beckwith, however, correctly summed up the situation (from the American Peace Society's point of view) when he wrote toward the end of the decade: "There is a class of radical men whom we have never reached as a body; men who would never work harmoniously with our sort of peace men, even tho' we agreed with them in sentiment; a class of men who have seldom come near us, and when they did, were always sure to embroil us in difficulty."[4]

A second problem facing the nonresistants at the outset of their Society's existence was to sort out its relationship with the various other reform movements, besides the peace movement, in which both leaders and rank and file were actively involved. Most important of these, of course, was abolitionism. In the minds of most nonresistants, the two causes were expressions of a single principle: the brotherhood of man. As the novelist Mrs. Lydia M. Child wrote: "Abolition principles and nonresistance seem to me identical; . . . the former is a

---

2 *Non-Resistant*, 7 Sept. 1839.   3 *Ibid.*, 12 Feb. 1840.
4 *Advocate of Peace*, VII, no. 2 (Feb.-March 1847), 34.

mere unit of the latter. I never saw any truth more clearly, insomuch that it seems strange to me that any comprehensive mind can embrace one and not the other."[5] Garrison, who shared this belief, was yet at the same time always careful to point out that the activities of the non-resistants in no way committed the abolitionist movement. It was, however, not so easy for him in practice to keep his two concerns separate. As editor of the *Liberator*, he had given over a considerable amount of space to discussion of nonresistance after his conversion to the radical position and, especially, after the founding of the Non-Resistance Society. His statement that the peace question was "merely incidental"[6] in the paper's policy began to look a little disingenuous. Some of his antislavery followers, even among those who were also convinced nonresistants, began to fear that the abolition cause would suffer from too close an identification with the still more unpopular nonresistance; for many others, Garrison's "non-combatism and his perfectionism" were "downright fanaticism." For them—to use the words of the abolitionist Elizur Wright—"the wind of perfectionism" had "blown off the roof of his judgment."[7] Indeed, the "no-government" views of Garrison and his associates became one of the factors, along with their advocacy of woman's rights and other reform causes, contributing to the split in the abolitionist movement finally consummated in 1840, which left it divided between the Garrisonian apolitical wing centered in Boston and the supporters of political action with headquarters in New York.

Discontent at the prominent place given to nonresistance in the columns of the *Liberator* was felt, as we have said, not merely among Garrison's opponents among the reformers but inside his own circle, too. Part of the trouble lay in the fact that in the early months of its existence the Non-Resistance Society as yet lacked a journal of its own. It was natural, therefore, for Garrison not only to include in the *Liberator* his own pleas on behalf of the new faith but to open the

---

[5] *Letters of Lydia Maria Child*, p. 44. Letter written on 27 May 1841.

[6] *Liberator*, 26 Sept. 1838.

[7] W. Freeman Galpin, *Pioneering for Peace*, p. 116. See John Demos, "The Antislavery Movement and the Problem of Violent 'Means,' " *NEQ*, XXXVII, no. 4 (Dec. 1964), 502, 515-19, and John L. Thomas, *The Liberator*, pp. 266-71, for the nonresistant issue in the relations between the two wings that eventually emerged within the abolitionist movement. Among those who became Garrison's opponents there were antislavery men like the Rev. William Goodell (1792-1878), editor of the abolitionist *Friend of Man* published at Utica (N.Y.), and the Quaker poet, John Greenleaf Whittier (1807-1892), who held pacifist—though not, of course, thoroughgoing nonresistant—views, just as there were a number of fervent Garrisonians who, like Wendell Phillips, were never pacifists. For Goodell's belief in "the peace principle as generally held by the Society of Friends," see the *Liberator*, 14 Aug. 1840; *Non-Resistant*, 22 July 1840; 12 Aug. 1840.

columns of the paper to other devotees of "the non-enforcing principle," like the prolific Henry C. Wright, and to publish news there of the Non-Resistance Society's activities.

The position was obviously unsatisfactory. We find dissatisfaction expressed, for instance, in a letter written to Garrison by one of the Weston sisters, who were all enthusiasts for both nonresistance and antislavery. Mixing the two causes in the *Liberator*, Anne Weston now told Garrison, was fair neither to the abolitionists who were not nonresistants nor to the nonresistants who felt that, nevertheless, their cause was not being given the attention it deserved. Both were discontented. She went on to suggest that henceforth the *Liberator* be devoted solely to antislavery matters and that at the same time steps be taken to start a new paper devoted exclusively to promoting nonresistance—with Garrison as editor, if he still felt able to combine this task with running the *Liberator*. "The idea has originated wholly with myself," Miss Weston concluded.[8]

Probably others, too, had been thinking along the same lines, for in January 1839 the first number of the *Non-Resistant* appeared.[9] It was published as the official organ of the Society: the words "Resist not Evil—Jesus Christ" stood underneath the title in each issue. Evidently, Garrison felt that the work of running two papers would exceed even his capacities, for Edmund Quincy was chosen as editor instead. The paper was to appear twice monthly from January 1839 until June 1842, with each issue consisting of four pages. It was printed for convenience' sake from the same type that was used for the *Liberator*. Unlike Garrison's paper, which long remained a byword for antislavery radicalism, the *Non-Resistant* was soon forgotten after being either ignored by contemporaries or subjected to ill-informed abuse and ridicule. Yet it was in many ways a lively little paper, and in its columns were aired many of the problems which have occupied the peace movement since that time. It was not until after the outbreak of the First World War that we find another American paper carried on in the spirit of absolute pacifism. The relationship of pacifism to government, penal reform, and capital punishment were discussed, along with articles on the more familiar themes in the arsenal of the antiwar movement. Most of the prominent nonresistants contributed to its pages, including Garrison himself and the indefatigable Henry C. Wright, who sent in periodic and detailed reports of his journeys up and down New England and beyond as the Society's general agent. It also print-

---

[8] Garrisons, W.L.G., II, 240-42 (letter dated 11 Nov. 1838).

[9] See Fanny Garrison Villard, *William Lloyd Garrison on Non-Resistance*, pp. 42-45.

ed countless letters and a good number of articles from ordinary members and sympathizers—quite a few of whom, it would appear, had reached the nonresistant stand independently many years before coming into contact with the peace movement—and it served to keep them in touch with the activities of the Society and the thinking that was going on in its ranks. The editor did not hesitate to print hostile comment at length (though from the nature of most of these attacks it would seem that printing them may well have served rather to discredit the critics than to injure the Society).

"The warrior, as well as the man of peace, shall be entitled to a respectful hearing," Quincy wrote in the first number. Earlier in the same editorial he had defined the object of the new paper in the following words: "Such a periodical, in this seditious, warring, anarchical age, is greatly needed; . . . it cannot fail to exert a most salutary influence upon individuals, communities, governments, restraining what it may not wholly reform, and making that which is rigorous or despotic in power lenient and tolerable."[10] Even such a modest, almost reformist aim was not in fact to be realized. For the failure of the *Non-Resistant* to weather more than a brief three and a half years, both personal and financial factors were responsible. Although in the very early days the paper almost seemed to prosper, with the rabid attacks and ridicule meted out to it by opponents proving less effectual than had been feared, it soon ran into financial difficulties. The nonresistants certainly made up in enthusiasm (some would say fanaticism) what they lacked in numerical strength. But in 1840 the paper had only about 1,000 subscribers.[11] Since the nonresistants were not a wealthy group and since the paper failed to attract a large number of subscribers, it had to rely more and more on its few well-to-do backers. Ultimately, the breaking point was reached. But there was a second factor which contributed as much, if not more, to the eventual closing of the paper: the increasing absorption of its chief sponsors and of many rank-and-file members, from the beginning of the forties on, in the antislavery struggle, a shifting of emphasis that was particularly true of Garrison. We find him telling his friend H. C. Wright: "Our time, our means, our labors are so absorbed in seeking the emancipation of our enslaved countrymen, that we cannot do as much specifically and directly for non-resistance as it would otherwise be in our power to perform."[12] This was written late in the winter of 1843, but already, several years earlier, Garrison's main interests had again begun to center in his antislavery crusade.

[10] *Non-Resistant*, 1 Jan. 1839.   [11] *Ibid.*, 14 Oct. 1840.
[12] Garrisons, *W.L.G.*, III, 80.

Wright himself continued to put the energies of several men into his work for the Non-Resistance Society, and, as we shall see, it was partly due to him that its life was protracted until the end of the decade. The efforts of one man, however, were insufficient to keep the paper solvent; Quincy was finding it an increasingly trying task to battle with financial deficits and the reluctance of his most prominent supporters to take time off from their other reform interests to help the paper. In August 1841 we find him writing to Mrs. Maria W. Chapman to ask her to supply an editorial later that month, as well as further contributions at a subsequent date: "The truth is," he confided, "the N.R. is getting [to be] a dead loss to me, and sometimes I am almost disposed wickedly to wish that it might fall through. But with an occasional article from you and the other friends, I will try to keep it along for the present." When no article was forthcoming, he wrote in a tone of reproachful banter to Mrs. Chapman at the beginning of the next month: "It was indeed enough to make a perfectionist swear after he had attained a sinless state."[13] Though both the editor and the editorial board served without pay, the paper was running with a steady deficit, which was made up by voluntary contributions from members. Appeals for help were published in each number, and for a time financial disaster was staved off by this means. Since the editorial board's policy was rather to close the paper than to carry on at the price of running into debt, its position was indeed precarious. At last, a notice appeared in the number of 29 June 1842: "The treasury of the Society is entirely empty. No other paper can be issued until the means are supplied by the friends of the cause." Thus expired the first, and for many decades the only, pacifist journal in America.

Once again, the New England nonresistants were without a press organ of their own. The *Liberator* had still continued to give prominence to the subject of nonresistance for a year or two after the appearance of the *Non-Resistant*. But at the time the latter ceased publication, articles on pacifism had become rare in Garrison's journal, and he did not choose to reverse this trend. Although meetings of the Non-Resistance Society were still reported fully and regularly and its editor remained an ardent nonresistant, the *Liberator* had returned to being primarily an antislavery organ. Adin Ballou twice attempted to revive the *Non-Resistant*, carrying on the editorial work from his Hopedale community, but without success. By this time enthusiasm had ebbed, the number of active sympathizers had dwindled, and the nonresistant movement was on the decline.

Even at the outset the Society had had to rely rather on the high

[13] Weston Papers, B.P.L., MS A.9.2, vol. 15, nos. 54 and 59.

intellectual quality of its leadership and the fiery enthusiasm of many rank-and-file members than on numerical strength, which was clearly lacking. On 29 September 1838, Garrison wrote to his brother-in-law, George W. Benson, the Quaker nonresistant: "We shall not have a *great* and *sudden* rush into our ranks! There are very few in this land, in this world, who will be able to abide by the principles we have enunciated; though there may be many whose consciences must assent to their correctness."[14] Indeed, even a conscientious Quaker sympathizer like Elizabeth Buffum Chace (1806-1899) hesitated to accept all the conclusions to which the nonresistants pushed their doctrine. "I am ready to join the Non-Resistance Society as far as entire belief in the doctrines goes," she wrote to Mrs. Chapman on 26 October 1839, "but I feel that I am not ready to promise to obey them always in spirit as well as in letter." Though she finally joined the Society, the decision came only after many months of hesitation stemming, as she expressed it, from "a solemn sense of the responsibility" such a step entailed.[15]

[14] Garrisons, *W.L.G.*, II, 237. For the conversion to full "no-government" nonresistance of one who had taken the C.O. stand as early as the War of 1812, see Thomas Haskell's account in the *Voice of Peace*, 1st ser., vol. II, no. 8 (Aug. 1873), printed on the unpaginated inside end cover. Haskell was a Massachusetts man from West Gloucester and a farmer by calling. During the war he had been introduced to pacifism by his brother. After two years of thought and study of the New Testament, he felt compelled to refuse both militia service and the fine. "I practiced giving to the different commanding officers my reasons for not training. They said the laws must be obeyed, but after a number of years they became ashamed and left off warning me, thus I was delivered of this burden." However, it was only with the advent of the Non-Resistance Society that he became convinced that pacifism entailed rigorous nonparticipation in government. Within a year we find him refusing to serve as a juror. "I then saw," he goes on, "that I could not apply to government for protection, nor voluntarily give it any support. Thus I have lived an outlaw for thirty five years, and am now fully convinced that moral power is the only sure protection." Haskell also became (like Garrison) a spiritualist and a worker in a multitude of reform causes. In his old age he was elected a vice-president of Alfred H. Love's Universal Peace Union (see later). See the *Voice of Peace*, 1st ser., II, nos. 11-12 (Nov.-Dec. 1873), 12. It is also interesting to note the accession to the nonresistance movement of several army veterans, who had earlier renounced the sword for the ploughshare. This, indeed, was almost literally the case with Samuel Ledyard of Pultneyville (N.Y.), son of a Revolutionary War hero and, as a young man, himself a keen militarist. On conversion to pacifism in the early 1820's, he had taken the sword to the local blacksmith and himself converted the weapon into a pruning hook. "His minister and his family called him crazy." See the *Non-Resistant*, 28 Oct. 1840. A parallel case is that of the two brothers, Elisha and Joseph Bradley of Williston (Vt.), both Revolutionary War veterans, who since about 1808—to quote the *Practical Christian* (20 Jan. 1849)—"were so conscientious in their peace doctrines that they strenuously opposed all attempts to gain for them their pensions," maintaining that for them to accept would be tantamount to receiving "the price of blood."

[15] Weston Papers, B.P.L., MS A.9.2, vol. 12, no. 63; vol. 13, no. 32.

Another earnest Christian who, though of a very different temperament from Mrs. Chace, long toyed with the idea of linking up with the nonresistants but finally decided against doing so was the New York landowner and philanthropist, Gerrit Smith, whose interest in the peace movement dated back several years. His influence and affluence would have made his adherence to their Society an important asset to the nonresistants. Garrison, Wright, and Quincy did all they could to attract him into their orbit.[16] In March 1839, Smith sent $100 for their paper, the *Non-Resistant*—the largest donation ever received by the Society[17]—expressing at the same time his keen interest in its work. A couple of months later he wrote to Wright of "the unsettled state of my peace views." "I was not alarmed at the organization of the New England Non-Resistance Society," he went on. "I had a strong impression at the time, that its principles were right. The impression has become stronger." Yet at the end of the letter we still find him hesitating to embrace the full doctrine.

Not long afterward, Wright during one of his propaganda tours as the Society's agent visited the Smiths at their home at Peterboro in upstate New York. He found Smith's wife Nancy already a convinced nonresistant, and he had lengthy discussions with them on the subject during his stay. "We took up the Constitution [of the Non-Resistance Society], paragraph by paragraph, and compared it with the Divine Will" as shown in the Bible, which lay open before them the whole time. Agreement seemed to have been reached; Smith soon afterward even went so far as to display the nonresistants' "Declaration of Sentiments" prominently in one of his rooms. "Brother Smith says," Wright reported, "no man can become in heart and life a non-resistant, till the lust of *dominion over man is eradicated*." Realizing the close connection between the abolition of slavery and the abolition of war, Smith, it appeared to Wright, had come to accept the nonresistant arguments with his heart and not merely with his head.[18]

But Smith's doubts seem to have increased rather than diminished over the ensuing months, and by September 1839 he felt unwilling to attend the Society's first annual meeting. His state of mind at that

[16] On 25 February 1839, Anne W. Weston wrote to her sister, Deborah, that she had learned confidentially "that G. Smith is very friendly to non-resistance. We really feel alarmed lest there should not a single fighting man be left to us, for Collins is a non-resistant" (*ibid.*, MS A.9.2., vol. 11, no. 46). John A. Collins (ca. 1810-1879), a man of a militant temperament, was one of the few agnostics who attached themselves to the Non-Resistant Society. He later became a communitarian.

[17] Galpin, *Pioneering for Peace*, pp. 137-39.

[18] *Non-Resistant*, 6 April; 4 May; 18 May 1839; *Practical Christian*, vol. V, no. 9, 14 Sept. 1844.

566

time distressed Edmund Quincy, who wrote him: "I regard the position in which you stand, . . . as one of imminent moral peril. I tremble for your soul. . . . May God give you the victory, the greatest of victories, the victory over yourself."[19] Smith in the end did not throw in his lot with the nonresistants. Instead, in the very next year he accepted, somewhat reluctantly it is true, nomination for the governorship of New York on the new Liberty Party ticket. Wright made one last effort to prevent Lucifer's fall, begging him to issue a categorical statement that, if elected, he would refuse to act in the capacity of commander-in-chief of the state militia. Smith parried by replying that, as he had in fact no chance of election, the gesture would be pointless.[20]

Despite Smith's renunciation of nonresistance in his actions, his unwillingness to abdicate from the political road to moral reform, and his inability to quell his doubts about the efficacy of nonviolent means for overcoming internal disorder or foreign aggression, his heart continued to hanker after the certainties of radical nonresistance. "If my mind should supply me with any arguments, my heart would be too much on your side to let me utter them," he wrote.[21] Smith continued to support the activities of the peace movement and to respect the radical nonresistants as persons, but his flirtation with their ideas was only a short interlude in a career which finally led him to back unequivocally the militancy of the free-soil guerrillas in Kansas and of John Brown at Harpers Ferry.

Gerrit Smith may be taken as typical of the reforming intellectual, who supported the nonresistant impulse with his heart but drew back because his head refused to give its allegiance. Smith had also been attracted to the Non-Resistant Society by his strong evangelical faith; indeed, for all the opposition of the churches and their cry of "infidelity," the Society drew some of its staunchest members from the theologically orthodox. On the other hand, paradoxically, it also attracted some of the most vocal religious rebels of that religiously ebullient generation. Edmund Quincy summed up the kaleidoscope of religious belief that went to make up the Society well when he wrote: "The number of professing non-resistants is not large—but is large enough to embrace almost every shade of belief from the highest Calvinism to the simplest rationalism. The great majority, however, hold the sentiments of the stricter 'evangelical' denominations."[22] Although

---

[19] Quoted in Galpin, *Pioneering*, p. 142.
[20] Ralph Volney Harlow, *Gerrit Smith*, p. 150. See also pp. 108, 109.
[21] Quoted in Galpin, *Pioneering*, pp. 142, 143.
[22] *Non-Resistant*, 28 April 1841. As will be shown in the next section, the non-resistant cause even found supporters among the millennial second Adventists, who

some of these evangelical nonresistants remained lifelong members of their churches, coldness and sometimes downright hostility drove others, like Garrison himself, to leave. Even the Society of Friends, as we have seen, remained at best extremely cool toward what they considered the extremism of the New England nonresistants. Several stalwarts of the nonresistant cause of the caliber of Samuel J. May came from the Unitarian fold, which had contributed many prominent workers, beginning with Noah Worcester, to the more conservative wing of the peace movement. But the liberal religious groups, Unitarians and Universalists, whose stronghold was in New England, remained on the whole indifferent to the persuasions of the nonresistants. The Universalists in particular, despite their broad humanitarian faith and opposition to capital punishment, were tardy in taking up a radical stand against war. One of the very few Universalist nonresistants expressed his surprise at the attitude of his church. The doctrine of nonresistance, he told the Vermont Universalist convention in 1846, "lies at the foundation of practical Universalism, . . . no man can be a true genuine Universalist, who is not a non-resistant in theory and practice. Why should it be deemed any more out of order for a Quaker to fight than for a Universalist? Judge ye."[23] But his plea seems to have evoked no response.[24]

Most typical of the nonresistants in the public mind were the radical "come-outers," those militants who had withdrawn from one or another of the churches in symbolic protest against their failure to condemn the institutions of slavery or war as sins against God and who spent much of their time subsequently in denouncing what they regarded as the treason of the clerics. Not all the "come-outers" were pacifists, and many who were abandoned their belief in nonviolence in

---

had succeeded in weathering the debacle of 1844 when Christ's second coming, foretold by their leader, William Miller, had failed to come about.

[23] John Gregory, Anti-War, pp. 8, 69, 94-96, 98. Gregory might have found support for his assumptions in an unexpected quarter. A decade earlier Dr. Samuel Hanson Cox, a former Quaker turned Presbyterian minister, had written in his book Quakerism not Christianity (p. 240): "It comes to pass observably that many opposers of the plainly revealed doctrine of eternal punishment (as universalists, unitarians, infidels, pseudo-philanthropists of every description) grow very specially tender in their clemency on the topics of capital punishment, war, . . . and the superlative excellence of the ethics or creed of passive endurance!"

[24] Gregory also made the interesting suggestion (Anti-War, p. 49) that pacifists should adopt the "white feather" as a badge, "showing to the world that we cannot and will not war against any portion of our fellow men—that we cannot be induced by any consideration to take up arms against our brother man." The adoption of a distinctive emblem is common to most twentieth-century pacifist organizations; this appears to be the first time such a proposal was put forward.

the stormy fifties. But in the previous decade we find them prominent among the Garrisonian nonresistants: men like farm-bred Parker Pillsbury (1809-1898), who was (in Emerson's words) "a tough oak stick of a man not to be silenced or intimidated by a mob, because he is more mob than they; he mobs the mob";[25] or Stephen S. Foster (1809-1881), "the modern 'steeple-house' troubler," as a contemporary aptly dubbed him,[26] who had been put in prison as a conscientious objector against militia service while a student at Dartmouth College and in jail both had won the confidence of the debtors, thieves, and other felons sharing his incarceration and had succeeded in exposing the bad conditions to which they were subjected while serving their sentences;[27] or Nathaniel P. Rogers (1794-1846), who made his Concord (N.H.) paper, the *Herald of Freedom*, a bastion of abolitionism and non-resistance—and, indeed, of a multitude of other reforms—until his premature death in 1846;[28] or—to mention yet another—the redoubtable Austin Bearse, New England sea captain and owner of the *Moby Dick* which carried out a number of armed rescues of fugitive slaves during the fifties, who had acted as one of the *Non-Resistant's* agents in the previous decade. These were fighting men even when they were preaching nonresistance, men who did not hesitate to disturb church services, including Quaker meetings, in an attempt to show up what they believed was the church's apostasy. And in due course they were forcibly ejected from these churches by infuriated parishioners (and even, on occasion, by angry Quakers).[29] At the same time, they

[25] From Emerson's *Journal* for 1846, quoted in Louis Filler, "Parker Pillsbury," *NEQ*, XIX, no. 3 (Sept. 1946), 315.

[26] *Practical Christian*, 29 Oct. 1842, p. 47.

[27] Parker Pillsbury, "Stephen Symonds Foster," *The Granite Monthly*, Aug. 1882, p. 370.

[28] Pillsbury, *Acts of the Anti-Slavery Apostles*, pp. 33, 43, 44. Rogers helped to found the New Hampshire Non-Resistance Society in 1841. See Robert Adams, "Nathaniel Peabody Rogers," *NEQ*, XX, no. 3 (Sept. 1947), 365-76. "I would quit the ballot box, as I would the militia," Rogers wrote (p. 374). "It is as immoral to vote or be voted for, for political office, as to train or enlist in the army. . . . The spirit of them is the same. . . . The weapons of both are violence, and the instrumentalities of both, bloodshed and murder." Rogers eventually split with Garrison on account of his own extreme aversion to all kinds of organizational activity, even in the cause of nonresistance or antislavery.

[29] Instances of this are given by Pillsbury in his *Acts*, pp. 303, 305, 312-15. One of those who ended with three months in jail for disturbing the Quaker meeting at Lynn (Mass.) was the Garrisonian nonresistant and former Congregational minister, Thomas P. Beach. For such men as this, the Society of Friends was indeed a "wicked body" in its failure to support the abolitionist movement. And Beach himself wrote as follows of the Lynn Friends (quoted in *Acts*, p. 318): "Those quiet, meek, peaceable, persecuting followers of Jesus have marched up and bowed their joints at the door of the court house and begged the state to stretch out the bayonets, load up the big guns and rifles, and drive this blood-

were men of courage, who put nonviolent resistance into practice when they faced angry mobs alone and without arms (despite Lovejoy's example a few years back) and who took a beating and countless man-handlings without attempting to retaliate. "We never doubted that our non-resistance principles saved our lives in many a desperate encounter," wrote Parker Pillsbury.[30] For their abolitionist militancy, too, they were assaulted by irate mobs and jailed by the authorities. Their reply was to practice the techniques of Gandhian *satyagraha*. Of Stephen S. Foster, for instance, it was said that, when physical force was being used against him, he always put himself "into a perfectly passive state,"[31] a state, that is, of complete physical passivity such as we find being used in the contemporary practice of direct nonviolent action.

These advocates of direct action, however much they may have figured in the public mind as typical of the Garrisonian radical non-resistant, were not, in fact, representative of the Society's membership. Rather was it the grave, respectable churchman, conventional in behavior if not in outlook, a man like the Unitarian minister, Samuel J. May, who gave the tone to the Non-Resistance Society. It was the direct actionists, however, who brought the Society publicity and tended to form in the public mind, and among many conservative peace workers, too, an image of the nonresistant as a wild fanatic intent on disrupting society.[32]

---

thirsty Beach to prison *sine die*, or till he pays a fine of a hundred dollars, which he has no means of paying, and could not pay conscientiously if he had. . . . I am not astonished that . . . Baptist majors and captains should fly to the courts and the forts, but that meek, loving, forgiving Quakers, who cannot *bear arms*, which are the only possible support of human governments, can step forward and say to the state, 'Please imprison Thomas Beach. . . .' Spirits of George Fox and Edward Burroughs, awake! awake!" The situation was, of course, more complicated than Beach could perceive. See chap. 8 for a discussion of the differences between Quakers and the New England nonresistants.

[30] *Acts*, p. 194.   [31] *Acts*, pp. 310, 311.

[32] That the Society's leaders cannot be acquitted altogether of overindulgence of the less balanced section of the movement is clear, for instance, from a letter Edmund Quincy wrote Anne Weston in 1839, supporting the candidacy of one James Boyle, ex-clergyman, faith healer, and general eccentric, for the post of agent for the Society. Boyle might not be quite the man they were looking for, Quincy admitted, but "we cannot afford to be too particular as to the entire eligibility of our agents," provided they show evidence of a nonresistant spirit in their thought and conduct. "What we want," Quincy went on, "is a man or men who will startle the community, now dead in trespasses and sins, from their living death. . . . And I am mistaken in the man if James Boyle will not sound a blast that will break the fat slumbers of the church and the iron sleep of the world . . . be assured, my dear sister, that the most hateful and odious man, hated and feared for his fearless denunciation of sin and exposure of iniquity, is the very man to give an impulse to our holy enterprise. He will doubtless bring down upon us all

How far this attitude was mistaken when applied to nonresistants without distinction comes out clearly in the case of that cultured and refined Boston gentleman, Edmund Quincy, whom we have already met as the editor of the *Non-Resistant*. At the end of February 1839 we find Miss Anne W. Weston writing to her Aunt Mary: "Edmund Quincy took tea here and we had much interesting conversation. Edmund has written a letter, begging for money for the N.R. Society. It is a beautiful letter, as I think you will say when you see it. I think very highly of Edmund as a good man."[33]

The letter referred to here came out in lithographed form on 1 March;[34] in addition to the appeal for funds ("our efforts, hitherto, have been cramped by the narrowness of our resources"), it exhorted the followers of nonviolence to stand firm against the unfair and often untrammelled criticism that had been unleashed against the Society. Lack of money to carry out necessary tasks ("we have materials for a mighty array of tracts," the letter stated), recognition that they formed a tiny band pitted against a hostile world, and consciousness at the same time of being crusaders called to fight a "holy warfare," all emphasized in this early address, continued to be characteristic of the Society throughout its existence.[35]

At the end of September 1839 the Society held its first annual convention under the chairmanship of its president, the Quaker Effingham L. Capron, and with the charming Mrs. Maria W. Chapman as its recording secretary. Almost all those attending came from Massachusetts; but Lucretia Mott was there from Philadelphia, risking the displeasure of her conservative Hicksite brethren, and the Midwest was represented in the person of the Rev. Amos Dresser, whose ill-treatment in the South four years earlier had made him something of a public figure outside antislavery circles.[36] Naturally, the interminably

---

manner of calumnies and slanderous misrepresentations, perhaps persecution, and make us more and more hateful for a season to the world; but is not this the baptism with which our Lord was baptized, and which He ordained for the proof of his disciples in all ages?" Quoted in J. P. Quincy, "Memoir of Edmund Quincy," *Proceedings of the Massachusetts Historical Society*, 2nd ser., XVIII, 405. For Boyle's "ultraism," see Whitney R. Cross, *The Burned-over District*, 1965 edn., pp. 189, 190. On p. 236, Cross draws attention to the influence of religious "ultraism" in the "Burned-over District" of upper New York state in producing pacifists and nonresistants, although its Biblicism might also have had an opposite effect.

[33] Letter of 27 Feb. 1839, Weston Papers, B.P.L., MS A.9.2, vol. 11, no. 48. See also A. W. to D. Weston, 25 Feb. 1839, *ibid.*, no. 46.

[34] Garrison Papers, B.P.L., MS A.1.2, vol. 8, nos. 12, 13.

[35] These features are evident in almost every number of the *Non-Resistant*.

[36] For Dresser's pacifism, see below, chap. 15. In a letter published in the *Non-Resistant*, 16 March 1839, Dresser declared his support for the aims of the Society,

loquacious Abigail Folsom, the bane of every reform meeting in Boston (until, finally, one day patience was lost and she was carried bodily out of the hall by two stout nonresistants), was in attendance; among a number of well-known figures in Boston reform circles present we may mention the name of Amos Bronson Alcott (1799-1888) of "Fruitlands" fame, who took an active part in the debates at this and subsequent annual meetings. The main resolution—"that human life is inviolable; and that no man can rightfully take, threaten, or endanger life"—was moved by Henry C. Wright, who in addition debated the subject of nonresistance in open session on two successive evenings with the Rev. Nathaniel Colver, a Baptist minister well known as an abolitionist and reformer. Although the meeting showed little evidence of any considerable increase in the strength of the nonresistant cause, Garrison at any rate felt able to pronounce it a success. "Our Non-Resistance Convention is over," he wrote to his brother-in-law, George W. Benson, "and the peace and blessing of heaven have attended our deliberations. Such a mass of free mind [sic] as was brought together I have never seen before in any one assembly . . . there was much talent, and a great deal of soul. Not a single set speech was made by any one, but every one spoke in a familiar manner, just as though we constituted but a mere social party." "The resolutions that were adopted," he added, "were of the most radical and 'ultra' stamp, and will create, I think, no little agitation in [the] community."[37]

The winter of 1839-1840 marks perhaps the peak of Garrison's enthusiasm for the cause of nonresistance. In June 1840, on the high seas en route for England to attend the international antislavery convention in London, we find him writing to Edmund Quincy on the subject in exalted tones:

My mind has been greatly exercised on the subject of non-resistance since I left New York. It magnifies itself wonderfully as I reflect upon it. It is full of grandeur, sublimity, glory. It is a mine, the riches of which are inexhaustible, an ocean of disinterested benevolence, at once shoreless and fathomless. Aside from it there is no such thing as our being "crucified unto the world, and the world unto us." It is the consummation of the gospel of peace, for it is that perfect reconciliation which the Messiah died to make between God and

---

describing, too, his efforts to spread nonresistant ideas in his part of the world. "There is another little church," he wrote, "with whom I have labored some the winter past, most of whom come fully into the peace principles of the ultra stamp."

[37] Letter dated 30 Sept. 1839 in W.L.G., II, 328. The convention was reported in the Non-Resistant, vol. I, nos. 19-23.

man, and among the whole human race. It makes babes and fools more sagacious and intelligent than the wisest statesmen, the deepest philosophers, and the most acute political economists. Its principles and doctrines receive the cordial detestation of all that is selfish, ambitious, violent and lustful on earth.[38]

Contacts with sympathizers like Dresser in the Midwest (noted above) were bearing fruit around this time in the establishment in these still pioneer areas of a small number of local groups. On 18 June 1840, for instance, we find a nonresistance society being formed at Oberlin, which became quite a center of nonresistant sentiment. Its constitution was based on that of the parent Society, and it accepted, too, the latter's Declaration of Sentiments. Its members, about thirty in all, were mostly students from the college with a sprinkling of faculty; a few local clergy and church people, some of whom, we learn, had held pacifist sentiments for several decades without being in any sort of contact with those of like views, also supported the work. According to the secretary, the overwhelming majority of students and faculty, however, were either indifferent or actually hostile to the idea of nonresistance, and, evidently, some heated arguments took place on the subject both on the campus and at meetings in the town. The group felt obliged to disclaim the "unchristian spirit manifested by some who sustain our views in part," protesting that its members were not "anarchists" or "disorganizers" as their opponents were trying to prove. Perhaps because of their isolation (or was it a means of quenching the excessive fervency of some of their young recruits?), the Oberlin nonresistants took a milder stand than many of their New England brethren who, like Garrison himself at times, gloried in the task of —nonviolently—"disorganizing" a corrupt society.[39]

We hear, too, of other small groups being formed in Ohio as well as in Michigan.[40] At Greenfield, in Lagrange County (Ind.), those who shared nonresistant views had banded together to form a pacifist church, accepting the nonresistant Declaration of Sentiments as their covenant. Their leader was one Samuel Bradford, according to Garrison "a self taught, uneducated man," who had, however, "an excellent simplicity of character, and a naturally rigorous and philosophical cast of mind." Although Garrison was unable to agree with what he con-

[38] Letter dated 13 June 1840 in the Garrison Collection, Sophia Smith Collection, Smith College, Northampton (Mass.).

[39] Non-Resistant, 9 Sept. 1840. The Oberlin society also reprinted its foundation documents as a separate pamphlet.

[40] See the Non-Resistant, 6 July 1839; 11 March 1840; 12 Aug. 1840; 27 April 1842.

sidered the sectarian spirit of the little group, its emphasis on outward observances such as baptism by immersion or breaking of bread each Sunday, he did admire their courageous stand for peace. "Though they reside in a frontier state, where they are continually exposed to outrage and danger, the Lord has protected them from all harm."[41]

These Midwestern nonresistants, small in numbers and scattered over a vast area, had to contend with spiritual isolation and the hostility or indifference of their environment to a larger degree than their brethren in New England.[42] We do not hear much, however, of their suffering disabilities on account of any refusal of service in the militia. Even in the East, cases of conscientious objection were seemingly rare among nonresistants. Certainly, the comparatively small size of the movement would preclude its producing as many conscientious objectors against militia service as the Quaker communities did. Some nonresistants undoubtedly were prepared to pay the commutation fine—as the young Garrison had been a decade earlier. Others must have been exempt on account of age or occupation (there were not a few clergymen, as we have seen, among the Society's supporters). Still others, known to have held peculiar views on the subject of war, may just have been left alone by sympathetic neighbors who understood to some extent the grounds of their objection, even though they did not share their views. Nevertheless, it is puzzling that—if we may judge by the columns of the movement's organ, the *Non-Resistant*, or of Garrison's *Liberator*—so few when called upon by the authorities for military service took the absolutist stand of preferring prison to all alternatives in the way of fines, etc. The Non-Resistance Society, indeed, left it up to the conscience of each of its members to determine how far he might rightly go along with the requirements of the state, while demanding, as we have seen, the same right to complete exemption for non-Quaker conscientious objectors as the commonwealth of Massachusetts had already granted to those of its citizens affiliated to the Quakers and Shakers.

Some absolutists were to be found among nonresistants of military age (most of the cases reported in the *Non-Resistant* or *Liberator* come from the late 1830's or early 1840's). To begin with, let us take the case of David Cambell, an ardent health reformer and publisher of

[41] Garrison to S. J. May, 22 June 1839, Garrison Papers, B.P.L., MS A.1.1., vol. 3, no. 35. Bradford was living in an area shortly to be settled by Amish and Mennonites, but they did not begin to move in until 1841.

[42] Some attempt seems to have been made during the forties to organize Midwestern nonresistants into a Western Peace Society. See *Non-Resistant and Practical Christian*, 9 Dec. 1848, where the former Lane seminarist Marius R. Robinson is mentioned as president.

the *Graham Journal of Health and Longevity*. Cambell first found himself behind the bars of the Leverett Street jail in Boston in the 1830's; in 1840 we still find him undergoing his annual term of six days in the city prison. In 1838 he had written to Garrison that he was not concerned about any hardship he might be suffering, "but I feel a solicitude for the young men who are just entering our ranks. To them the trial may be somewhat severe, not having been so thoroughly disciplined as those soldiers who enlisted [in] the service fifteen or twenty years ago"[43]—a reference to the thin trickle of men who had taken an absolutist stand in the past and been subjected to a mild form of "cat-and-mouse" treatment. The penalty was light; more difficult to face perhaps was the lack of understanding from associates and friends. Amos Wood, a Congregational deacon, for instance, was sent to the Hopkinton jail in Merrimack County (N.H.) by a justice who was a member of his own church.[44] Again, the situation was complicated, as we have seen, by the fact that exemption might be obtained by merely paying the fine laid down by law. In January 1840 we find young Charles Stearns, a clerk in the local Anti-Slavery Depository, writing to Garrison from the Hartford County jail (to which he had been committed for an undefined term, as was then possible under Connecticut state law) to ask his advice "not only for my own sake, but for that of others, who may be placed in the same circumstances." "Since I have been here," he explained, "some of my friends have tried to persuade me, that I am in the wrong concerning this matter; that by paying the fine, I do *not* countenance the military system, as I do it unwillingly; I as much countenanced it by coming to jail as by paying the fine." While admitting that it was "something of a gloomy prospect for a young man just commencing life, to think of spending it in prison," Stearns nevertheless disagreed with his friends' arguments. He felt strongly that some clear-cut witness for peace was needed in the circumstances. Those with no scruples concerning war could gain exemption by way of a fine, so that in reality no testimony was being borne to peace principles by paying it.[45] Although he stuck to his absolutist position, Stearns did not, however, have to spend the rest of his young adult life in jail, and we shall meet him again later in the fifties out in "bleeding Kansas," where he was to undergo a change of heart in respect to his pacifist views.

Although few had to witness to their faith by going to jail like Cambell or Stearns, the nonresistants were busy during these early years,

---

[43] *Liberator*, 27 April 1838; 14 Feb. 1840.
[44] *Non-Resistant*, 23 Dec. 1840.
[45] *Liberator*, 14 Feb. 1840; *Non-Resistant*, 12 Feb. 1840, 11 March 1840.

when enthusiasm was still high and the effects of a dwindling treasury not yet fully apparent, in putting their case over to the public as best they could by means of public meetings or the distribution of literature. Each year, at the end of September, they gathered for a few days in Boston for their annual convention, coming up for the occasion from the towns and villages of Massachusetts and some from further afield in New England. William Ladd has left us with an amusing description of the 1840 convention. In April, H. C. Wright had written in his journal: "William Ladd does not differ from me at all in principles,"[46] and Ladd, as we have seen, was indeed ready to pay tribute to the devotion of the Society's adherents and to their good intentions. But the waywardness, amounting sometimes to fanaticism, of some of the convention's participants aroused his wry sense of humor. On the debate on that perennial issue—the inviolability of human life— for instance, he had this to say: "The discussion took a wide range, . . . far from the resolution . . . Arminianism, Transcendentalism, and all kinds of radicalism were drawn into the debate." At another session he described how "one speaker denounced all governments, ministers, churches, Sabbaths and ordinances, and pretended to be as much inspired as any man ever was." Of a woman orator he wrote: "There was a breathless silence while she soared away into the regions of transcendentalism, far, far beyond my ken. She seemed to rejoice in the approaching abolition of all orders, days and ceremonies, and fully accorded with the brother who had preceded her, in his transcendental notions of pantheism." Ladd, in fact, had earlier shown his hesitations concerning the active participation of women in public assemblies; as full equality between the sexes was among the most cherished principles of the Society, he was not an entirely impartial witness here. However, on this occasion he noted that the ladies rarely spoke ("Miss Folsom twice, in all not exceeding five minutes"), "but employed themselves with knitting, sewing, embroidery, etc."[47]

[46] M. E. Curti, "Non-Resistance in New England," NEQ, II, no. 1 (Jan. 1929), 48.

[47] Non-Resistant, 28 Oct. 1840 (reprinted from the Christian Mirror). Cf. the somewhat similar tone of the report on the Society's annual meeting of 1842 in the Practical Christian, 29 Oct. 1842. Its author, a member of the Hopedale Community and therefore, like Ladd, an absolute pacifist, was disturbed by the extremism manifest during the sessions. The Society he dubbed "a mere agitation club." "It breathes out such a spirit of antagonism and defiance; it speaks a language of such burning damnation against all who in any way uphold the prevailing institutions of government and religion; it rides on such a whirlwind of disorganizing radicalisms, and puts on so forbidding an aspect to the great mass of gentle and tender minds, that the genuine non-resistance of Christ will in our opinion gain little more by its movements than the mere excitement of public attention to the general subject."

Next year the *Non-Resistant* reported the annual convention as being "on the whole a very well attended, well conducted, profitable meeting," the most successful of the three held thus far. Ballou, who wrote the report, expressed the hope that the Society would be able to maintain its specifically Christian character and not go over to "a deistical or pantheistical philosophy, however sublimated and refined."[48] Bronson Alcott, on the other hand, left the convention "with the conviction deepened that a few years will bring changes in the opinions and institutions of our time of which few now dream. All things are coming to judgment, and there is nothing deemed true and sacred now that shall pass this time unharmed. All things are doomed. . . . A band of valiant souls is gathering for conflict with the hosts of ancient and honorable errors and sins. . . . I would be of and with them in their work."[49] At any rate, for the time being the Non-Resistance Society could provide a meeting ground for Christian communalist and communalistic transcendentalist.

The presence of a "lunatic fringe" on the periphery of the Society, which was especially vocal on the occasion of public meetings and conventions, was perhaps inevitable. Almost all radical reform movements have suffered from this burden. As will be seen, the primary causes of the Society's decline lay elsewhere however. That its life was prolonged until the end of the decade was due largely to the efforts of two men: Henry C. Wright and Adin Ballou. Wright was indefatigable as the Society's traveling agent, facing hostile audiences and exhausting journeys in all types of weather, ready to engage all and sundry in conversation on the subject of peace and ready to take any platform at a moment's notice if it gave him the opportunity to plead the cause. His extremism offended many of his contemporaries,[50] and later writers are divided as to the value of his contribution to the reform movement. But there can be little doubt that his vigor injected new energy into the flagging Non-Resistance Society, to the extent that, when he departed for a prolonged visit to Europe in 1843, the Society began to show increasing signs of inertia. Garrison was in a good position to observe the situation. In December 1843 he confided

[48] *Practical Christian*, vol. II, no. 13, 30 Oct. 1841.

[49] Quoted in Odell Shepard, *Pedlar's Progress*, p. 279, where it is dated ca. Oct. 1839. Extracts from a different draft of this letter are given in F. B. Sanborn and William T. Harris, *A. Bronson Alcott*, I, 324, 325, with the date 28 Sept. 1841. This appears to be the correct one.

[50] In his *Autobiography* (p. 381) the moderate nonresistant Ballou gives the following verdict on Wright: "His zeal and activity were preeminent, his devotion to the cause unquestionable, his pen prolific, but his discrimination and soundness of exposition did not always command my admiration or satisfy my judgment."

in a letter to Wright, then on a speaking tour in Great Britain: "Little has been done, directly, to promote the heaven-born cause of non-resistance since you left. No agent has been found to take the field, and the Executive Committee of our little Non-Resistance Society are so occupied with their antislavery labors and responsibilities, that they have neither the time nor the means to put any efficient machinery into motion."[51] A year later he was writing in the same strain: "The Society, I regret to say, has had only a nominal existence during the past year —and, indeed, ever since your departure. It is without an organ, without funds, without publications."[52] Another year passed, and Garrison was still sounding the same note: no replacement for Wright in the field, most of the stalwarts like Abby Kelley, Stephen S. Foster, and Parker Pillsbury (and, of course, Garrison himself) almost completely absorbed in the work of abolitionism.[53]

In England, Wright had closest contacts with radical antimilitarists like John Scoble or antislavery men like George Thompson or the Quaker Joseph Sturge, who were also pacifists. Although his lecture tours on peace understandably did not do much to bridge the gap between the New England nonresistants and the somewhat conservative London Peace Society, which had taken the side of the American Peace Society in its dispute with the nonresistants, they do appear to have made a considerable impact on the burgeoning antimilitarist movement in Great Britain.[54] On the European continent, where the military spirit was everywhere in the ascendant and the peace societies, where they existed, did not renounce the possibility of defensive war, Wright's message was less effective. We do find him, however, arguing the nonresistant case assiduously with his fellow patients while spending six months in 1844 taking the water cure at Graeffenberg in Silesia.[55] "They were astonished to find," wrote Garrison, "that they could not excite in him any *American* feeling of exultation or exclusiveness; that he truly embraced all mankind as his countrymen."[56]

Wright was, indeed, almost indispensable to the Non-Resistance Society—at least in view of the absorption of its other capable leaders in antislavery activities. In part, however, his place was filled during

[51] Garrison to Wright, 16 Dec. 1843, Garrison Papers, B.P.L., MS A.1.1., vol. 3, no. 114.

[52] Garrison to Wright, 1 Oct. 1844, quoted in *W.L.G.*, III, 80.

[53] Garrison to Wright, 1 Nov. 1845, Garrison Papers, vol. 4, no. 17.

[54] See, e.g., the Manchester Peace Society's quarterly report to the London Peace Society for the spring of 1843 (B.P.L., MS G. 31.26.).

[55] See H. C. Wright, *Six Months at Graeffenberg*, for an account of his sojourn in Europe generally.

[56] *Practical Christian*, 7 Dec. 1844.

the years of his absence by Adin Ballou, who succeeded Quincy as the Society's president in the autumn of 1843 and was responsible for the two short-lived revivals of the *Non-Resistant* in 1845 and 1848. Yet, for all his greater intellectual depth, deeper spiritual resources, more stable temperament, and more balanced outlook, Ballou lacked the drive Wright had, which alone might have served to inject renewed energy into an already moribund organization. In addition, a considerable part of Ballou's attention had to be given to overseeing his Hopedale experiment. The communitarian leader was much less of an individualist, much less of an iconoclast, than either Wright or Garrison or many of their followers, even though his contribution to framing a coherent philosophy of nonresistance was unequalled (an aspect of his work that will be discussed in the next chapter). As chief organizer in the absence of Wright, Ballou was not, however, particularly effective.

"On your return," wrote Garrison to Wright toward the end of 1845, "we shall endeavor to give a new impulse to the cause of nonresistance. Its converts are steadily multiplying, and it has ceased to be assailed so wantonly and abusively as formerly."[57] That there was any increase in the number of adherents, however, was wishful thinking on Garrison's part, and the dying down of criticism and hostility was probably due more to lack of interest than to the growth of a greater understanding of nonresistance on the part of its opponents.[58]

Even the excitement of the Mexican War did little to reinvigorate the expiring Society. Garrison and his friends were, of course, among the most vehement opponents of the war and the administration's policy that had preceded it. Garrison himself, hoping for "success to the injured Mexicans and overwhelming defeat to the United States,"[59] for a moment almost appeared to grant, in the case of the former, that there could be a legitimate war of defense. And Thoreau (1817-1862) in 1845 had taken the step of offering passive resistance to the collection of taxes that might be used in the impending prosecution of what he regarded as an unjust war, "a peaceable revolution"[60] that landed

[57] Garrison to Wright, 1 Nov. 1845, Garrison Papers, vol. 4, no. 17.
[58] Cf., though, *Practical Christian*, 20 March 1847: "The cause [of nonresistance] is an unpopular and despised one, every where spoken against and treated with more or less contempt by the leaders of the people."
[59] Quoted in John L. Thomas, *The Liberator*, p. 343. See also Walter M. Merrill, *Against Wind and Tide*, pp. 209-11.
[60] "Civil Disobedience" in X (*Miscellanies*) of *The Writings of Henry David Thoreau*, 1893 edn., 150. This essay was first published in 1849. Thoreau's objection to the tax for which he was briefly jailed in 1845, on the eve of the war, however, stemmed more from his opposition to slavery than from his repugnance to war. We discover this, for instance, in a passage in *Walden* (1854) at the end

him for one night in the Concord jail. Thoreau, of course, was not a member of the Non-Resistance Society or of any other peace society, but the essayist's famous attempt to withdraw his collaboration from a warmaking, slaveowning state was certainly influenced to some extent by the example of the New England nonresistants.[61]

Wright, when at last he returned to the United States, was unable to turn the tide back in his capacity as "a voluntary, unhired lecturing agent of the Non-Resistance Society."[62] But he was able to achieve something, as we see from his account of his tour of Ohio in the late summer and early fall of 1848, in an area where, as he wrote in his journal, "war-making priests and churches have but little influence over the people."[63] Wright undoubtedly put new courage into the scattered handful of nonresistants in the state[64] and aroused considerable interest

---

of the chapter entitled "The Village," where he writes as follows of the motives of his refusal: "I did not pay a tax to, or recognize the authority of, the state which buys and sells men, women, and children, like cattle at the door of its senate-house." For the pacifist movement in this century, the essay on civil disobedience has served as a kind of brief manual of nonviolence. For Thoreau's impact on Gandhi and his philosophy and practice of *satyagraha*, see George Hendrick, "The Influence of Thoreau's 'Civil Disobedience' on Gandhi's *Satyagraha*," *NEQ*, XXIX, no. 4 (Dec. 1956), 462-71. Gandhi came upon the writings of Thoreau in the first decade of this century during his residence in South Africa.

[61] In 1843 Bronson Alcott, who was closely associated at this date with the Non-Resistance Society, had refused to pay his poll tax on grounds similar to Thoreau's. Another leading New England literary figure influenced by, though perhaps not entirely sharing the views of, the nonresistants was the poet James Russell Lowell (1819-1891), at that time a strong supporter of radical abolition. In his *Biglow Papers*, published in 1846, he makes Hosea Biglow say: "Ez fer war, I call it murder/ . . . I don't want to go no furder/ Than my testyment fer that." On 16 August 1845 we find Lowell writing Charles Sumner shortly after the latter had given his famous pro-peace Fourth of July oration (discussed in a subsequent chapter): "I only regret that you should have deemed it necessary to disavow any opposition to the use of force in supporting human governments. But I am willing to leave you entirely to the principle you yourself have advocated which will inevitably lead you to a different conclusion. *All* force is weak and barbarian, whether it sheds blood, or locks the doors of prisons and watch-houses" (Worthington Chauncey Ford [ed.], "Sumner's Oration on the 'True Grandeur of Nations,'" *Massachusetts Historical Society Proceedings*, L [1917], 266). Both Thoreau and Lowell, under the influence of their intense antislavery feelings, abandoned their pacifistic views in the next decade and in the Civil War became enthusiastic supporters of the Northern cause.

[62] *Non-Resistant and Practical Christian*, 22 Jan. 1848.

[63] *Ibid.*, 16 Sept. 1848.

[64] In his journal (reprinted *ibid.*, 16 Sept. 1848) Wright mentions meeting one such person, Valentine Nicholson, "a man who is striving for a purer and higher order of the social state." Nicholson had placed boxes outside his house and filled them with pacifist and abolitionist literature, including copies of the *Liberator* and Wright's antiwar tracts. Notices were nailed on posts supporting the boxes with the following inscription in large letters: "Whatever tends to injure

in the communities he visited. "We have been in session nearly four hours," he reported from New Salem, "and the people seem unwearied and indisposed to leave. War is a terribly absorbing question."[65] In addition, he was to prove once again a thorn in the flesh of many Quakers and moderate peace men, whose support for government he constantly proclaimed as tantamount to approval of the war system and of human exploitation.

Wright also toured New England and the middle states around this time. And in the former area, the heartland of the nonresistance movement, the Mexican War does seem to have led to some slight revival of activity. From around the spring of 1847 until at least the summer of 1848, we find quarterly meetings of the Society being reported in the columns of Ballou's *Practical Christian*—apparently a new development; these were held successively at various centers in Massachusetts and Rhode Island. But after the first few years, the annual reports of the Society tell the same story. Each year there is the same lament over diminishing numbers attending the conventions. True, those who came might be "the most active and efficient spirits in the various reforms of the age," as the *Liberator* reported of the 1844 meeting;[66] they might very well be persons "of the true stamp whose interest in the cause of non-resistance is deep and abiding" (it was now 1845), indeed "highly intelligent, embracing some of the best reformatory spirits of the age" (as was said of the participants in 1847).[67] Yet all this could scarcely cloak the sense of frustration at the failure of the movement, so bold only a few years back in depicting the confusion that would ensue among the forces of violence and governmental oppression at the onset of the power of nonresistance. Repeatedly, too, these annual reports tell a story of dwindling funds, finances insufficient to accomplish more than an iota of what had originally been planned. The pamphlet series outlining the principles of nonresistance, the extra agent to carry the word about the country where assuredly many must only be awaiting his arrival to become recruits in the crusade against war and violence, the expansion of the Society's program of meetings in Massachusetts and beyond, the steady appearance of a nonresistant journal to knit the membership together and provide regular am-

---

any portion of the human race should claim the attention of all mankind. Hence this effort to circulate information on the subjects of War, Slavery and Intemperance. If there are any books or papers remaining in this box, *travellers* are invited each to take one and circulate it."

[65] *Ibid.*, 28 Oct. 1848.

[66] Reprinted in *Non-Resistant*, 7 Dec. 1844.

[67] *Non-Resistant*, 9 Jan. 1847; *Non-Resistant and Practical Christian*, 22 Jan. 1848.

munition in the campaign for peace—all these hopes had to be abandoned one by one. The melancholy refrain—"the Society has not been able to carry on its operations the past year with much efficiency" (the words appear in the report for 1844)[68]—sums up the history of the nonresistance movement during these years.

If we look at accounts of the discussions at the successive annual meetings, we are struck by the repetition of the same themes year after year, a sterility of thought which could not find release in action. The affirmation of the power of nonresistance, the pros and cons of the ballot, and the iniquity of the war-supporting Constitution crop up year after year, and the same old arguments are gone over by much the same roster of speakers. Among a number of symptoms of decayed vitality was Ballou's failure to attract more than 280 subscribers for the Non-Resistant, which he resuscitated for a brief while in 1845 before merging it with his communitarian organ the Practical Christian. Admittedly, the paper under Ballou's editorship, with its highly moralistic tone, makes rather dull reading in comparison with its predecessor, which had ranged over a wide array of philosophical and political discussion: it was not likely now to make much appeal to the intellectuals of the movement. In any case, his failure to arouse sufficient interest among nonresistants and peace sympathizers was disappointing.

The last regular annual meeting of the Non-Resistance Society appears to have taken place in December 1849. According to most sources, this year also saw the final dissolution of the Society itself. However, it seems to have maintained some sort of shadowy existence at least into the middle of the next decade, for we find meetings being organized in Worcester in the name of the Society in March 1855 and again in November 1856.[69] Possibly, the organization was revived for the sole purpose of holding these meetings. At least it appears to have been completely inactive during the intervening years. Ballou and his Hopedale communitarians were mainly responsible for this short-lived renewal of activities. Some of the nonresistant "old guard" —"a precious few," Ballou had to admit[70]—including Garrison, H. C. Wright, and the Society's former Quaker president, Effingham L. Capron, participated. Prominent in the discussions was the loquacious Stephen S. Foster, who with his wife Abby (Kelley) was now living in Worcester.[71]

[68] Non-Resistant, N.S., 1 Jan. 1845.
[69] See the detailed reports printed in the Practical Christian, 7 April 1855; 21 April 1855; and 13 Dec. 1856.
[70] Practical Christian, 13 Jan. 1855.
[71] It was Foster who at both conventions raised the question of the relationship

582

At the end of 1849 Ballou had printed a letter from a rank-and-file sympathizer, one H. O. Stone from Concord (N.H.), which expressed with much feeling the dilemma that was to face the movement in the next decade. "When I consider the progress of the *Anti-Slavery* sentiment," wrote Stone, "and compare it with the progress of genuine *Peace* principles, I confess that I rejoice with fear and trembling. I rejoice unfeignedly in the appreciation of the rights of three millions of enslaved human beings. I *fear* lest those rights will be demanded or defended at the point of the bayonet, by an appeal to injurious force, through the destruction of human life." "Some," he continued, "who have agitated the anti-slavery question upon the broad basis of human brotherhood, and acknowledge the abstract truth of non-resistance have so far forgotten their brotherly love and so greatly outraged truth as to declare themselves ready to sweep slavery from the land, without regard to the requirements of absolute peace principles as soon as the people were ready to do it."[72]

Was the choice now: peace or brotherhood? Could nonresistants approve the broadening of human liberty by violent means if the mass of men stubbornly refused to follow along paths of peace? Some found themselves quite unable to resolve the question. Others, like Sam J. May, while holding on to their personal pacifism, were to abandon altogether the "no-government" views of Garrisonian nonresistance and collaborate in the not always pacific activities of the political wing of the antislavery movement.[73] A few, like Ballou, remained adamant in their refusal to countenance violent measures, even at secondhand, as it were. The passing of the Fugitive Slave Law in 1850 was to increase these difficulties immeasurably.

It had, indeed, been the issue of slavery that, first, by siphoning off the energies of many of the most capable nonresistants and, then, by challenging the validity of the nonresistant faith as an instrument for bringing about God's justice on earth had fatally weakened the movement.

The failure of the Society to develop after the first few years had, however, a second cause. Its extreme views on government, its philosophical anarchism, kept many out of its ranks whose pacifist sympathies would otherwise have brought them into the Society.[74] We have

---

between nonresistant love and the demand for social justice, as presented in the case of the slave (see chap. 16). The difficulties in reconciling the two were among the most potent causes of the dissolution of the nonresistant fellowship.

[72] *Practical Christian*, 8 Dec. 1849.

[73] See Galpin, "God's Chore Boy," chaps. VII and X.

[74] See Curti, "Non-Resistance in New England," pp. 54, 55; Galpin, *Pioneering for Peace*, p. 151.

seen this happen in the case of William Ladd and other moderate pacifists, who refused to leave the American Peace Society even after it had veered away again from absolute pacifism. Boldness of thought (at least at the outset), high intellectual quality, and unbounded enthusiasm (though mingled, it is true, with a good measure of eccentricity in some of its supporters) could not compensate for the paucity of the Society's numbers, its failure to expand beyond a very limited circle and a very confined area. In fact, after the first shock on public opinion had worn off, the Society made little impact on its environment. An intellectual elite soon became a closed coterie.

As an episode in the organizational history of reform movements in nineteenth-century America, the New England Non-Resistance Society deserves perhaps only a small niche. But as the first organized expression of radical pacifism in the country, it is certainly of much greater importance. We must now turn, therefore, to a consideration of its ideology.

Chapter 14

The Ideology of the New England Non-Resistance Society

The Declaration of Sentiments, which Garrison wrote for the new Society at the Boston Peace Convention of September 1838, had been a foundation manifesto rather than a systematic apologia for the creed of nonresistance as conceived by its New England adherents. It was, like so much that came from Garrison's pen, highly charged with emotion and written to meet the needs of the moment. Although he composed a number of articles in behalf of nonresistance, Garrison in fact added little to the development of its ideology. For this aspect of the movement we must turn to the works of several of his colleagues.

Most important from this point of view was Adin Ballou, whose treatise on *Christian Non-Resistance in all its Important Bearings* was published in Philadelphia in 1846[1] and reprinted several times subsequently. In addition, Ballou wrote two shorter pieces which deal with specific aspects of nonresistance: *Non-Resistance in Relation to Human Governments*, published in Boston in 1839 before he had formally joined the New England Non-Resistance Society, and *A Discourse on Christian Non-Resistance in Extreme Cases*, which came out twenty-one years later and was published by the community press in Hopedale. Next, we should mention the pamphlets of the less well-known theorist, Charles K. Whipple (1808-1900). In 1839 his *Evils of the Revolutionary War* was issued in Boston by the Society (and in 1846 a second edition appeared, this time a product of the Hopedale community press). Two years later, in 1841, Whipple published, again in Boston, a brief exposition of the Pauline text *The Powers that be are ordained of God* and of its relation to modern nonresistance. Then, as with Ballou, we have a long gap until 1860 when Whipple composed two further short works, the first entitled *The Non-Resistance Principle: With Particular Application to the Help of Slaves by Abolitionists*, and the second, *Non-Resistance applied to the Internal Defense of a Community*. Finally, we may mention the writings of the inordinately prolific Henry C. Wright. In his voluminous unpublished

[1] Lucretia Mott's son-in-law, Edmund M. Davis, suggested to Ballou that he undertake the work and shouldered the expense of publishing the first edition. See A. D. Hallowell, *James and Lucretia Mott*, p. 277. Davis, though a Quaker and former nonresistant, took part in the Civil War as an officer in the Union army. This metamorphosis he owed to his strong antislavery feelings.

journals and in the countless articles and letters he published in various papers, chiefly in the *Liberator* and the *Non-Resistant*, he dealt with various aspects of nonresistance which arose in connection with his work as chief propagandist for the nonresistance cause. In addition, he published in the forties a number of tracts on nonresistance, ranging from pamphlets of a few pages to treatises of book length. Several of these works came out in Britain, and they appear to have circulated in fairly large quantities on both sides of the Atlantic. In the 1850's the slavery issue seems to have dominated Wright's interests to the virtual exclusion of nonresistance. The polemical and propagandist element is very strong in everything that Wright wrote; yet some of it is useful in helping us to piece together a coherent picture of the ideology of the New England nonresistants.

Such a picture of their beliefs is, indeed, possible. But at this point we must set down several provisos. In the first place, even among the four writers mentioned hitherto, there were differences in emphasis and sometimes even disagreements on at least minor issues. Ballou, for instance, stressed the Christian basis of nonresistance more rigorously than the others, but he was less implacable in his opposition to government and was more ready perhaps than they were to stretch the limits of the allowable in noninjurious force. Secondly, we must not forget that nonresistant pacifism, even if we restrict its meaning to the ideology held by members of the New England Non-Resistance Society, was always a fluid doctrine and never formed a well-defined and completely rounded creed. It was constantly being argued out among members at public and private gatherings and in the press. The columns of the *Non-Resistant* (so long as it was in existence) and, to a lesser extent, Garrison's *Liberator* and Ballou's communitarian organ, *The Practical Christian*, are filled with discussions of one or another aspect of nonresistance, of its relation to current issues and to the problems of history and Biblical exegesis. Rank-and-file members of the movement wrote in to express their views, ask questions, and thresh out problems among themselves. This process of continual reexamination, of course, was kept up particularly during the first half dozen years when the nonresistance movement was still a vigorous element in the fermentation of New England's intellectual life. Later, as it became increasingly moribund and the interests and energies of its members were siphoned off into other channels, the argument grew less lively. Although little was contributed to the debate during the 1850's, there was at the beginning of the next decade a slight revival of interest in the theoretical side of nonresistance, owing perhaps to problems generated by the imminent clash between the claims of pacifism and those of the militant antislavery movement in the minds and hearts of the nonresistant abolitionists. Thus, if we bear in mind these limitations in generalizing on the subject and remember those subtler shadings in emphasis that existed between person and person and from one year to another and if we realize that a perfectly rounded philosophy of nonresistance never actually existed, we should be able to form a reasonably accurate, yet at the same time cohesive, impression of the body of doctrine held by the men and women who gave their allegiance to the New England Non-Resistance Society.

Ballou in opening his large-scale treatise on Christian nonresistance attempts to define the various types of belief on which nonresistance can be based. One category he dismisses somewhat perfunctorily: the "necessitous," that is, the adoption of nonresistance, not on principle, but simply from expediency, from the inability to resist by force of arms—a policy that might be pursued, for instance, by the subjects of an oppressive and all-powerful tyrant. The three remaining types he groups together. But, whereas "philosophical" nonresistance, based purely on rational considerations, such as the futility of war and violence and its moral impropriety as human action, and "sentimental" nonresistance, which draws its inspiration from a belief in man's higher nature progressively improving itself on the way to perfection, take no account of religion or revelation, Christian nonresistance flows directly from a desire to follow in their entirety the teachings and example of Christ as portrayed in the New Testament.[2]

Ballou thereafter concerns himself solely with the Christian variety of the nonresistant creed—and undoubtedly, with one or two exceptions,[3] the New England nonresistants, however unorthodox in some cases they may have been from the theological viewpoint,[4] were nonetheless professing Christians. Still, it is interesting to find Ballou referring here to what we would call today rationalist and humanitarian types of pacifism. This is perhaps the first mention of the possibility of the existence of an absolute pacifism not stemming from religious (that is, Christian) considerations.

The appeal of the nonresistants (as of some of the earlier exponents of pacifism) was to the spirit of Christ's teachings as much as, if not

[2] Ballou, Christian Non-Resistance, pp. 1, 2.

[3] For instance, nonresistant views were held by John Collins, the associationist and a Garrisonian abolitionist, who was openly a Freethinker and gained some notoriety for expression of "infidel" views.

[4] Many had become "come-outers" from the orthodox churches because of the latter's refusal to renounce war and slavery without qualification. For one of the many examples of this hostility to the churches, see H. C. Wright, Christian Church; Anti-Slavery and Non-Resistance applied to Church Organizations (1841), passim.

more than, to particular texts in the New Testament. They were convinced that this spirit spoke against war: war in fact is sin, and not only war but the whole exercise of coercion by the state. It is quite wrong, wrote Henry C. Wright, for the Christian to search through the scriptures trying to extract some justification for killing or harming, bodily or mentally, fellow creatures created, as they were, by God. "He must sit at the feet of Jesus, and ask, 'Lord, what wouldst thou have me to do?' And having learned this, he should do it without further consultation with flesh and blood." The kind of actions which would thereby be learned (in Wright's opinion) are: love to enemies as well as to friends, forgiveness of injuries, returning good for evil, readiness for sacrifice of self rather than doing the least harm to others, the full implementation of human brotherhood.[5] In one of his short tracts Wright lists thirty reasons for the incompatibility of the armed forces with such teachings of Christ and concludes: "Thus the existence of the army and navy is a *practical* abolition of Christianity and of human brotherhood—a practical dethronement of God, and the deadliest enemy of human life and human liberty."[6] As Wright explained: "The business of the army and navy is not to forgive, but to kill enemies. A soldier is merely a human butcher, hired by the month, to butcher his brethren, should he be called on to do so."[7]

Garrison, in particular, strove to liberate belief in nonresistance from

[5] Wright, *Defensive War proved to be a Denial of Christianity*, pp. 24-105. In his book of cautionary tales for small children that he published in 1843 under the title *A Kiss for a Blow: or, A Collection of Stories for Children; showing them how to prevent Quarrelling*, Wright attempted to inculcate his pupils with the nonviolent way of life, to instruct them "how much more pleasantly they could live together without fighting" (p. v). "Children fighting for a toy," he adds, "afford an illustration, in miniature, of nations contending for empire" (p. vii). The little volume, whose tone to a modern reader appears too often mawkishly sentimental, became a kind of primer of nonresistance and went through many editions in both the United States and the British Isles (including a Welsh translation printed as late as 1908). Wright was extremely fond of children, and they of him, and his own nonresistant philosophy was basically a childlike faith in the goodness of his fellow humans. "Of one thing," he wrote in 1839, "I am more and more convinced; i.e. that metaphysics and philosophy, *falsely* so called, have much less to do with non-resistance than the simple, subdued, childlike spirit of the heart" (*Non-Resistant*, 18 May 1839). Perhaps his growing vehemence during the antebellum decades against the slaveholding class in the South represented an unconscious reaction against men who had not responded as they should have done to the moral suasion of Northern abolitionists.

[6] Wright, *The Immediate Abolition of the Army and Navy* (Peace Tract, No. 3).

[7] Wright, *Forgiveness in a Bullet!* (Peace Tract, No. 2). In his antimilitarist writings, Wright (like most contemporary peace advocates) always had in mind the voluntarist principle by which the armed forces of Britain and the United States were then recruited, and not an army raised by conscription. A representative example of this view is to be found in the conclusion of his Peace Tract, No. 1: *The Heroic Boy.*

a stifling dependence on Biblical authority. Steeped in the Bible since childhood and familiar with its every page as few men have been, he came over the years to feel increasingly that it, too, could exercise a tyranny over the mind, could prevent the growth of a living religion in men's hearts, as effectually as the domination of the orthodox churches, which he so fiercely denounced for their loss of a truly Christian outlook. His Christianity remained Bible-centered but not Bible-bound. His nonresistance still rested on his interpretation of the Christian gospel to mankind; but the letter of the scriptures, even the words of Christ himself, no longer held authority with him unless confirmed by the assent of the human conscience. In 1848, for instance, we find him telling the annual meeting of the Non-Resistance Society: "We must appeal to reason, conscience, facts. Why should we go to a book to settle the character of war, when we could judge of it by its fruits? If war promoted peace, safety, and holiness, it was good; let us welcome it with joy and exultation. If, on the contrary, its fruits were evil, let it be condemned."[8] Echoing the words of scripture, he pleaded for an empirical pacifism which was justified by its consistence with reason and conscience, and not because of any divine mandate empowered to overrule these sources. Wright, too, adopted much the same view. The Bible was a record of the past spiritual experiences of the Jews and not an infallible guide to present conduct. Its precepts must be tested by the inner light within each human being; it was because they accorded with this that Christ's teachings should find acceptance.[9]

Garrison eventually went so far as to maintain that the nonresistant ethic was in no way necessarily connected with the teaching and example of Jesus, that its source was solely within each individual human soul and might be held independently of Christian belief. God could never, in his view, command any action that was contrary to morality. The act of war, like the institution of slavery, was "a *malum in se*" which no book, Jewish or Christian, could cleanse: they were both "essentially wrong." If a sacred book sought to justify them, the book must be put on one side and the promptings of conscience followed instead.[10] Garrison's pacifism, then, was basically an ethical impulse, an impulse—he would have said—that was implanted in all men and not a peculiar revelation to those within the Judaeo-Christian tradition.

[8] *Practical Christian*, vol. IX, no. 19, 20 Jan. 1849. Garrison himself attributed his emancipation from Biblical fundamentalism in large part to the influence of the liberal-minded Hicksite Quaker couple, Lucretia and James Mott, and especially to the forthright Lucretia. See Hallowell, *James and Lucretia Mott*, pp. 296, 297.

[9] Wright, *Anthropology*, Letter III.

[10] *Selections from the Writings and Speeches of William Lloyd Garrison*, pp. 89, 90.

589

To this Ballou, indeed, took exception. "True Non-resistance," he told Garrison, "Christian Non-resistance . . . came down from Heaven." It was exemplified in the life and teaching of Christ, and to him we must look primarily for its authority.[11] And, in fact, all the leading nonresistants made plentiful appeal at least to the New Testament to buttress their arguments. Their aim was a restitution of primitive Christianity; Ballou entitles a chapter in one of his books "On the primitive Christian virtue of non-resistance."[12] The name they had taken for themselves was derived, of course, from Christ's words: "Resist not evil" (Matt. 5:39). The Sermon on the Mount was for them the center of Christian doctrine. "The term," wrote Ballou of nonresistance, "is considered more strikingly significant than any other of the principle involved, and the duty enjoined in our Saviour's precept. Hence its adoption and established use." By evil Christ had meant the infliction of personal injury by one human being on another. What deductions should we draw from this, asked Ballou, for use in everyday life? "Consider the context; consider parallel texts; . . . consider the known spirit of Christianity"; and then see how far this carries you. Briefly, Ballou's view was that a Christian nonresistant could neither kill nor maim in self-defense or in defense of others, nor willingly collaborate in any way with those engaged in such action. Further, he was precluded from any kind of participation in administration, either by voting in elections or holding office, however seemingly innocuous, since all governments as then constituted were ready to wage war and to exact the death penalty for certain offenses.[13]

In his *Christian Non-Resistance* Ballou devotes two full chapters[14] to arguing his case on scriptural grounds. He arrays his proof texts and gives his interpretation of them;[15] he then goes on to deal in considerable detail with possible objections that might be raised by nonpacifists or by pacifists who stopped short of the "no-government" position; and to this he adds further evidence for his case, culled from the writings of the apostles and from the history of the early church. On

[11] *Autobiography of Adin Ballou*, pp. 439, 447-49.
[12] *Primitive Christianity and its Corruptions*, vol. II, Discourse XIII.
[13] Ballou, *Christian Non-Resistance*, pp. 12-20.
[14] Chap. II, "Scriptural Proof," and chap. III, "Scriptural Objections Answered."
[15] For another New England nonresistant who made much of the textual argument for and against pacifism, see the *Remarks offered in a Non-Resistance Convention . . . 1841* (pp. 4ff) by the Universalist minister, the Rev. John Murray Spear. His conclusion (p. 22), so different from Garrison's more broadly ethical Christianity, was: "I am ready to engage in human butchery when God requires it by my hand," but in no other circumstances. (Spear later became a spiritualist and in the 1850's founded a community on the borders of Pennsylvania and northern New York state, which was commonly known as the "Spiritual Springs.")

the positive side, the argument was summed up in the assertion that Christ's law of love as revealed both in the letter and spirit of his teachings involves the inviolability of human life under all circumstances. As Henry C. Wright expressed it: "The position taken by *armed resistants* is, that man's right to live as man depends on his guilt or innocence. . . . Non-resistants hold that *human* government never did and never can have the right to say how much and what kind of guilt renders a man worthy of death. God alone has power to decide this."[16] On the negative side, the argument counseled a withdrawal from society, a dissociation from governments that contravened the sacredness of the human personality.

Wright defined the essence of Christian nonresistance as submission to injuries, "non-resisting and non-resenting submission to affront and wrong," along with a belief in the power of love to ultimately transform human relationships. Without the spirit of nonresistance Christianity was dead. To the question "To what extent are we required to submit?" Wright answered that there were indeed "no limitations— no exceptions in favor of extreme cases or of nations." In all instances "Christianity says—submit. Jesus suffered death without resentment or resistance; but committed himself to Him that judgeth righteously. And in this thing we are commanded to walk in his steps."[17]

In presenting the case for nonresistant pacifism, its advocates soon came upon two major stumbling blocks in the minds of the unconvinced regarding its theoretical validity. The first has been met with already in our discussion of the earlier stages of the pacifist movement in America. How could God's apparent approval of the wars waged by the Jews in the Old Testament and their repressive penal code be brought into line with Christ's prohibition of all forms of violence in the New? To this we find two different answers in the writings of the New England nonresistants. Ballou gave the conservative one pleaded by earlier pacifists: that the old dispensation has been replaced by the new, that the prophets of the Old Testament were in a sense forerunners only of the more perfect revelation given by Christ. "The New Testament," says Ballou, "supersedes the Old on all questions of divine truth and human duty."[18] This answer left pretty well unshaken the idea of the general, if not the literal, inspiration of the whole body of the scriptures and still assigned a certain relative justification to the

---

[16] Wright, *Man-Killing by Individuals and Nations, Wrong-Dangerous in All Cases*, p. 8. In 1850 he wrote (*Anthropology*, p. 11): "To inspire man with affectionate respect for the person of man, to rescue him from individual and governmental violence and to throw around his life and liberty the sanctions of absolute inviolability, has been the object of my life for twenty years."

[17] Wright, *Man-Killing*, p. 18.   [18] *Christian Non-Resistance*, p. 66.

591

wars of Old Testament times. But men like Garrison and Wright, far more radical than Ballou in their whole outlook and temperament, were prepared to cast such ideas completely aside and to brand the Jewish patriarchs as warmongers along with the military leaders of more recent times.

Listen to Garrison again at the New England Non-Resistance Society's annual meeting of 1848 presenting a resolution "that God, as a just, beneficent and unchangeable being, never did and never can authorize one portion of his children to kill and exterminate another portion, any scriptures (whether styled sacred or profane) to the contrary notwithstanding." Wright, who was present at the meeting, supported Garrison's view. Indeed, we find Wright in his public addresses up and down the country during this period occupied with this very question. For Wright, the wars of Old Testament times seemed particularly bloody, cruel, and barbaric—impossible to square with the loving Father of mankind presented in the gospels. If all use of injurious force was wrong (as the nonresistants believed), how much the less could these primitive feudings have found pleasure in God's sight? Were it true that under the so-called old dispensation Moses and Joshua had waged war at God's behest against the Canaanites and that God had inspired the Jews to enforce a penal code of exceptional harshness, then, indeed, this God acted contrary to the law of love and all morality. "The God who could sanction such an atrocity," Wright cried out, "was a demon, not the God of Love and Justice!" Or, rather, it all showed that the morality of the Old Testament books was only too fallibly human.[19]

The nonresistants not only attempted to prove their case on scriptural grounds but, in the second place, sought to answer their opponents who argued empirically that nonresistance was contrary to nature. Let it be admitted, these men said, that it is ideally the perfect Christian conduct, but in practice it goes against the natural law of self-preservation. True, Ballou replied, fighting is the usual method of self-defense among animals and men. But is there not a better way for the latter? How effective in fact has the use of injurious force been in the history of mankind? "The whole world is in arms, after nearly six thousand years' close adherence to this method of self-preservation."[20] Ballou enunciated a new law to be derived from nature, that of reciprocation: "that like must beget its like—physical, mental, moral, spiritual." According to this principle, the way of noninjury, always

[19] *Practical Christian*, 20 Jan. 1849. See also Wright, *Anthropology*, Letter IV; *Man-Killing*, pp. 9-41, 51-57.
[20] Ballou, *Christian Non-Resistance*, p. 104.

returning good for evil, will eventually evoke an answering note in an enemy, will finally bring around the evildoer from his ways. "Though the injuries we do them are done only in resistance of aggression, still they follow the same law. . . . They breed a fresh brood of injuries. If this be not strictly true in each individual case, it is true on the great whole."[21] Ballou believed that, even though the practice of nonresistance could never guarantee the security of any one individual or group from attack or even death, still it was by and large a safer, as well as a more moral, line of approach than that of using injurious force of one kind or another.[22]

In his book on *Christian Non-Resistance* he devotes a chapter entitled "The Safety of Non-Resistance" to this point, and both here and elsewhere in the book he produces a number of illustrations of the successful practice of nonresistance. "Behold," he exclaims, "robbers looked out of countenance and actually converted; ferocious banditti rendered harmless; wild savages inspired with permanent kindness; and all manner of evil overcome with good."[23] The stories tell of unarmed travelers journeying unharmed through brigand-infested lands or successfully extricating themselves from the clutches of highwaymen and robbers in more civilized countries, of Quakers and Shakers living peaceably with American Indians, of Christian missionaries preaching the gospel of peace in darkest Africa or among the cannibal-infested South Seas. "Who can contemplate such practical exemplifications of Christian non-resistance as these," Ballou writes, "and not be ravished with the excellence and loveliness of the sublime doctrine."[24] Although some of the stories do not appear to be very well authenticated, doubtless most were true.

The weakest element in the use of such illustrative material in arguing the case for pacifism (a weakness true not only of Ballou but of Henry C. Wright, whose writings are crammed with stories of this kind, as well as a host of other pacifist writers of this period) would seem to be the lack of examples of collective pacifist action. Quaker government in Pennsylvania and the experience of the Irish Quakers in the troubles of 1798 are almost the only cases cited which approximate to this kind of action. They had become, as we have seen, part of the stock-in-trade of every peace propagandist, and the New England nonresistants were able to do little to advance the argument

---

[21] *Ibid.*, pp. 115-21.

[22] This theme is developed at length in his *Discourse on Christian Non-Resistance in Extreme Cases.* "I might fall from my principles," he writes (p. 16), "and be driven to distraction. But I should pray that it might be otherwise."

[23] *Christian Non-Resistance*, p. 182.   [24] *Ibid.*, p. 206.

at this point. However, although it is true that they were hard put to discover instances of the adoption of nonviolence by nations or large groups, they do appear to have felt that it was personal nonresistance that was proving more of a stumbling block to the acceptance of their pacifist position rather than the adoption of pacifism on a nationwide scale. Adoption by a whole nation, it was supposed, would inspire group cohesiveness and a firmness of collective purpose, which could steel a man's will up to the point of martyrdom.

Moreover, the practical case against international war—a realization of the horrors of the battlefield, of war's economic wastefulness, and of its frequent failure to bring lasting security (an aspect of the pacifist argument, incidentally, that the New England nonresistants stressed almost as much as the religious and moral objections)—had already made some headway, in reform circles at least, if not with the public at large. The idea of unilateral disarmament—as expounded, for instance, by the American Peace Society—had even found assent in circles which were not committed to absolute pacifism. A renunciation of all forms of injurious force at the personal level, on the other hand, seemed more unfamiliar to many people at that date. This unfamiliarity, therefore, in part explains the emphasis given by Ballou and the other nonresistants to proving the efficacy of nonviolence in individual relations rather in the sphere of international politics.

The New England nonresistants were above all "immediatists," in their pacifism as much as in their abolitionism. Let us not wait to practice our Christianity until the millennium when everyone will be perfect, cries Ballou. Let us grant that nonresistance may be impractical in the present state of society, says Wright, but our object is to alter society by preaching and living out our ideals until a change comes about.[25] Let a beginning be made now. Let the vicious circle once be broken and the redeeming influence of love will eventually eradicate violence from society. For individuals as for nations, "defensive violence as surely begets offensive, as offensive violence begets defence. Nothing but the all conquering power of Christian love can subdue this spirit of resistance and attack."[26]

But what of love and justice in the relations between the members of society? It was in their attitude toward government that the New England nonresistants parted company not only with all nonpacifists but with many who shared their radical opposition to war. Those great examplars of American pacifism, the Quakers, as well as the

[25] *Ibid.*, chap. VI; Wright, *Man-Killing*, pp. 54-57. Wright (e.g., in his *Six Months at Graeffenberg*, pp. 83, 90) makes use of the well-worn analogy between teetotalism and the nonresistant pledge.
[26] Wright, *Man-Killing*, p. 46.

founding fathers of the American peace movement like Worcester and Ladd—even after they had moved over to absolute pacifism—had all found participation in the offices and activities of the state compatible with their peace principles, so long as it had no clear connection with war or the taking of life. Many of the functions of contemporary government appeared to them of positive benefit to mankind, and they felt it a duty to join with their fellow citizens in getting the best men into office. Indeed, although they differed from nonpacifists regarding the best methods to be employed in its execution, they considered civil government as essential to the very existence of a civilized, Christian society. It was hardly surprising, then, that the frontal attack made by the New England nonresistants on the very concept of "human government" in a Christian society shocked or dazed the overwhelming majority of persons who came into contact with them, and that they were subjected on all sides to virulent abuse and to ridicule for holding such opinions.

Their views on government were actually very similar to those of the pacifist sects of the Anabaptist-Mennonite tradition (though the latter probably had no direct influence on the thinking of the New England nonresistants). Both gave qualified recognition to government within God's order, while both denied that government could have any place in a Christian society. The Anabaptist-Mennonite groups were pessimistic about the possibility of achieving a nationwide, let alone a worldwide, acceptance of Christian nonresistance: the small flock of those who followed Christ's teaching would remain alone and isolated in a hostile world until the latter days. The New England nonresistants on the other hand, comprising for the most part men and women of education and culture who shared the optimistic philosophy of progress then current and were influenced, too, by the religious wave of perfectionism that had spread far and wide throughout the American populace, were not content—not even Ballou in his Hopedale community—to withdraw themselves effectively from contact with political life. One might almost say that their protest against government had to be made within government. We can see in Ballou's writings, for example, that, somewhat like his contemporary John Humphrey Noyes, he conceived of the millennium, not so much as a future event in time and space, but rather as a complete transformation of a moral and religious nature taking place within an individual. The millennium is, as it were, here already. Millennial, perfectionist rules of conduct could be carried out in the actual world as increasing numbers of individuals were caught up in the process of inner renewal. As this transformation led to the adoption of nonresistance and the un-

595

limited acting out of the Christian gospel on an ever widening scale, the millennium within the individual soul would evolve into the coming of Christ's kingdom on earth.[27]

For all Garrison's pride in the "disorganizing" principles of his new Society, the New England nonresistants deeply resented—and with considerable justification, it should be said—the accusations of anarchy and subversion hurled against them from press and pulpit, until a curtain of silence was brought down around them that proved more effective against them than oceans of clerical and journalistic verbiage.[28] "We are no Jacobins, Revolutionists, Anarchists; though often slanderously so denominated," Ballou protested in 1839. They were not out to reform government or to purify it or to rebel against it. Theirs was a revolution of the inner man, their appeal was to the individual. Until they had succeeded in effecting an inner moral revolution in a sufficient number of such individuals so as "to supersede" human government by the laws of Christ's kingdom, laws enforced by the promptings of human conscience alone, human government would have to continue.

So if men will not be governed by God, it is their doom to be enslaved one by another. And in this view, human government—defective as it is, bad as it is—is a *necessary evil* to those who will not be in willing subjection to the *divine*. Its *restraints* are better than *no* restraints at all—and its *evils* are preventives of greater. For thus it is that selfishness is made to thwart selfishness, pride to humble pride, revenge to check revenge, cruelty to deter cruelty, and wrath to punish wrath; that the vile lusts of men, overruled by infinite wisdom, may counterwork and destroy each other. In this way *human* government grows out of rebellious moral natures, and will *continue*, by inevitable consequence, in some form or other among men, till HE whose right it is to reign "shall be all in all."[29]

Such sentiments, indeed, would not have been out of place on the lips of a fifteenth-century Czech Brethren or a sixteenth-century German Anabaptist. Although Ballou belonged in some respects to what we might call the right wing of New England nonresistance, even the

---

[27] See esp. Ballou, *Non-Resistance in Relation to Human Governments*, pp. 15, 24.

[28] See—to cite just one example—the anti-nonresistant lecture entitled *A Vindication of the Right of Civil Government and Self-Defence* by a member of the Massachusetts legislature, Jeremiah Spofford. "I am for peace," wrote Spofford (p. 15), "but the way to secure it is to cause all men to do justice," even if war were the only means available.

[29] Ballou, *Non-Resistance in Relation to Human Governments*, pp. 8-11.

more thoroughgoing Garrison took essentially the same position. "The abrogation of existing laws and governmental regulations for the punishment of evil-doers," he writes, "would be calamitous, without a moral and spiritual regeneration of the people." The burden of human government was a species of punishment laid upon society for failure to live up to the full Christian ethic. For those who genuinely strove to realize this ethic in their lives, to live out the kingdom of Christ already on earth, active collaboration with government was ruled out. "Prisons, swords, muskets and soldiers are necessary to uphold governments which punish evil-doers by fines, imprisonment, and death. But these are prohibited by Christ; therefore, governments of force are prohibited to his followers."[30] Christian anarchism, not anarchy, was their ideal.

Nonresistant writers, like other exponents of Christian pacifism, were forced to give special attention to St. Paul's views on civil government in Romans 13 on account of the use made of them in the arguments of nonpacifist opponents. According to Garrison, these verses had become, as it were, "a frowning Gibraltar, inaccessible by sea and land, filled with troops and all warlike instruments, and able to vanquish every assailing force."[31] Against such a threat, "by far the most plausible and seductive objection, now urged against Christian non-resistance,"[32] the latter's defenders marshaled all their forces. The text, they declared, urged submission to, not participation in, worldly governments which have not renounced the use of the sword. Christians of St. Paul's time, while renouncing all thought of armed revolt, kept themselves apart from the powers that be, giving them only a conditional recognition within the framework of God's order. In this sense, Pharaoh and Nebuchadnezzar and Caesar were all God's instruments; yet no Christian could associate himself with the administration of such rulers.[33]

Garrison's colleague, C. K. Whipple, wrote a little tract on the subject, which he entitled simply *The Powers that be are Ordained of God.* It begins: "This proposition is fully admitted by non-resistants." But, Whipple went on, when man enacts laws and constitutions that are contrary to "God's laws," as had been the case throughout history with all rulers, whether in despotisms or democracies, then those who wish to obey God rather than man must withdraw from active collaboration in the work of government. They are forbidden the use of violence against injustice and must be submissive, meekly suffering the penalty for refusal if ordered to do wrong. Thus, as God may be said

[30] *Selections from . . . Garrison*, pp. 91, 92, 95, 97.   [31] *Ibid.*, pp. 95, 96.
[32] Ballou, *Christian Non-Resistance*, pp. 77.   [33] *Ibid.*, pp. 76-96.

to have ordained slavery, since the slave, too, along with all other men, is forbidden by the Christian gospel to use violence to right wrongs done him and must be guided in all his action by the law of love, in the same sense even the worst government may be called a divine institution.[34] In fact, in the hands of the nonresistants—as to a certain degree with some of their pacifist predecessors—St. Paul's injunctions were transformed into a proof text for the pacifist and "no-government" positions.

The New England nonresistants did, of course, recognize that man was a social being. Theirs was far from being the extreme individualistic variety of anarchism exemplified, for instance, by their contemporary in Germany, Max Stirner. If only the existing system of government with its armies and armed police force, with its capital punishment and repressive prisons, with its support of slavery and denial in practice of the brotherhood of man, and with all the pomp and panoply of power were transformed into a voluntary association of citizens living as best they could according to the ethical code of the gospels and controlling deviants from this ethic by moral suasion alone, then government would have no more enthusiastic supporters than the nonresistants. As Ballou expressed it: "If human government be understood to imply only divine government clothed in human forms and administered by human organizations, with merely incidental imperfections, non-resistance is for it *per se*. It has no necessary opposition to it whatever."

Why, then, did the nonresistants not wish to act by all legal means open to citizens in a democratic state in order to reform and remold the machinery of government according to their desires? Here all the nonresistant writers gave the same answer: the existing system was not reformable. A clear break, a clean sweep, must come before government could be christianized. The war-making power, capital punishment and a harsh penal system, slavery—these were all basic constituents of the American governmental machine; and the situation was essentially no different in other so-called Christian lands. These institutions were not merely external accretions which might be sloughed off by the judicious exercise of the franchise, leaving the system as nearly perfect as could be hoped for in this imperfect world. Instead, as Ballou maintained, "military and injurious penal power is their very life blood—the stamina of their existence." They formed a fundamental part of every constitution. To participate voluntarily in the working of government, even in the seemingly innocuous functions of voting or holding civil

[34] C. K. Whipple, *The Powers that be are ordained of God, passim.* See also H. C. Wright, *Six Months at Graeffenberg*, pp. 333-44.

598

office, was to be a party to an unholy compact, a betrayal of the principle of Christian nonviolence. First let us remove all those evils "with which all that is good in existing governments is inseparably interwoven," and then, perhaps, it would be proper for a nonresistant to associate himself with the world of politics.[35] Meanwhile—and here H. C. Wright was expressing the united opinion of the nonresistant movement—"It is wrong to hold an office in which we must consent to be vested with life-taking or war-making power, or to come under an obligation to use it. . . . It is wrong to VOTE for others to offices which it is wrong for us to hold. . . . Here, then, all who reject military, or man-killing power as wrong, must take their stand."[36]

The suffrage brought responsibility: the voters, in the opinion of most nonresistants, were ultimately responsible both for the total platform of the man for whom they cast their ballot and for all the functions he might possibly have to perform in the way of duty. Under the Constitution of the United States "the war-making power" was indissolubly linked with the functions of both President and Congressman, as well as with those of most other federal and state officials. The guilt of blood shed in war or law enforcement rested also on all who had elected the administration into office. "The American nation is a MURDERER. . . . The blood of murdered millions cries out against all existing national organizations."[37] President and administration in a democratic state like America are merely agents of the people. H. C. Wright, in particular, assailed voting pacifists like the Quakers or the supporters of the American Peace Society. "They say war is wrong, yet vote for it. The report of such peace-men is not believed." It was no use pleading, said Wright, that we have an obligation to elect the best man into office. We must first look to the character of the office itself and not to the candidate and the measures he proposes, however good these may be. To exercise the franchise even to effect the abolition of slavery would be wrong, would be to "vote for MURDER to prevent THEFT." "No man can love the slaves who will violate a known and acknowledged rule of right to free them," H. C. Wright explained

[35] Ballou, *Christian Non-Resistance*, pp. 210-17; Wright, *Anthropology*, pp. 68, 69.

[36] Wright, *Man-Killing*, pp. 50-51.

[37] Quoted from one of the Non-Resistance Society's tracts entitled "National Organizations," reprinted in the *Liberator*, 11 Jan. 1839. "Let all soldiers and all advocates of war be told," wrote H. C. Wright in 1848, "that they are murderers, and let this truth be brought home to them on all occasions, till they feel its force; and then, and not till then, will men learn and advocate war no more" (*Dick Crowninshield, the Assassin, and Zachary Taylor, the Soldier*, p. 12). See also his *The Employers of Dick Crowninshield, the Assassin, and the Employers of Zachary Taylor, the Soldier: The Difference*, for a continuation of this argument.

599

somewhat smugly. It was Wright, too, who gave us one of the clearest expositions of the nonresistant objection to the exercise of the franchise:

All preparations for war, in this nation, are begun at the ballot-box. Voting is the first step; . . . a *bullet* is in every ballot; and when the ballot is cast into the box, the bullet goes in with it. They are inseparable, as the government is now constituted. Every voter, as he casts in his vote, says—"This is my will—if you resist it, I will kill you." Every ballot contains a threat of death; and he, who casts it, pledges himself to aid the government to execute it. The ballot-box is the first step—the gallows or battlefield the last; and whoever takes the first, must take the last. There is no consistent or honest stopping place between them.[38]

This uncompromising approach to the question of voting and office-holding was not matched, however, by an equally forthright stand in the matter of paying taxes to what all good nonresistants considered a warlike government. Here, at least in the past, many American Quakers had adopted a more thoroughgoing position by withholding taxes in time of war. For the nonresistants, all governments as at present constituted were in a state of perpetual warmindedness; so we might expect that they would have refused on principle to give them the financial support represented by the payment of taxes. Yet this was not the case. All the New England nonresistants, from Garrison on down, complied with Caesar's demands. They could point, of course, to Christ's words in reply to the agents sent by the chief priests and scribes. But they even went further, arguing that the submission enjoined by Christ on his followers justified a passive acceptance of the demands of government for money. "Voting is an act of government," wrote Ballou, "and assumes all the responsibility of injurious compulsion. Tax paying is submission to compulsion assumed by others. Therefore tax-paying is *non-resistance*, and *voting* is the assumption of a power to aggress and resist by deadly force."[39] Thus, a clash was avoided on this issue between the New England nonresistants—most of them law-abiders by nature and nurture, if not by conviction—and the state. On this point the movement was not called upon either to produce its Thoreaus to spend their night of lonely protest in the local jail or to endure the prolonged distraints suffered earlier by the Quakers during the Revolutionary War.

We have seen that the nonresistants' objection to civil government

[38] Wright, *Ballot Box and Battle Field*, pp. 1, 4-20.
[39] *Practical Christian*, vol. V, no. 6, 3 Aug. 1844.

was qualified by their readiness to give positive approval if all reliance on international war and internal coercion were abandoned. Was such a radical purging of the violent element in statecraft possible in this world? Was a renewal of society attainable in the foreseeable future? Or would the uncompromising followers of the peaceable kingdom always remain a minority in the kingdoms of this world? On this question the nonresistants, unlike the exponents of the Anabaptist-Mennonite tradition whose opinions on many points they shared, gave an optimistic answer. With many of their contemporaries among the purely religious revivalists, they saw the millennium at hand, when nonresistance would sweep first the American continent and then the world. "Let us all adopt it, that we may be saved," the New Hampshire editor and abolitionist, Nathaniel P. Rogers, wrote enthusiastically.[40] Ballou believed that the conversion of only two-thirds of the population to nonresistance, "with even a large share of imperfection lingering about them," would be sufficient to warrant a total abandonment of "injurious force" and the inauguration of government based on the laws of God alone. "If here and there a disorderly individual broke over the bounds of decency, the whole force of renovated public sentiment would surround and press in upon him like the waters of the ocean, and slight *uninjurious* force would prevent personal outrage in the most extreme cases." The example of the United States' conversion to nonresistance would sooner or later be emulated by the other nations of the world.[41]

Even after "the great work of revolutionizing public opinion"[42] had been completed and nonresistant pacifism was spreading to the rest of the world, its practical application would still continue to pose several difficult problems. The question of attempted conquest of a nonresistant nation by an aggressive outsider does not, however, seem to have greatly exercised the theorists of nonresistance: pacifism as a policy, they believed, would soon take root throughout the civilized world, once an example had been given. It was to the problem of maintaining public order within a nonresistant society, and of protecting it against

---

[40] *Non-Resistant*, vol. IV, no. 2, 26 Jan. 1842.

[41] Ballou, *Christian Non-Resistance*, pp. 226-29.

[42] *Practical Christian*, vol. V, no. 9, 14 Sept. 1844. The phrase is Ballou's. Toward the end of his life he appears to have become less optimistic about the chances of a speedy mass conversion to Christian nonresistance and, at the same time, more tolerant of the existing governmental system as a makeshift for the millennium. Perhaps his disappointment and dillusionment at the slow progress and setbacks inside his Hopedale community and its final dissolution made him less sanguine about any widespread appeal that nonresistant ideas might have, even within the ranks of reform. See his *Primitive Christianity and its Corruptions*, vol. II, Discourses XIII and XIV, given at the beginning of the seventies.

unprovoked attack on the part of antisocial elements, that they turned their thoughts first.

In their attitude toward the treatment of crime, the nonresistants displayed the most positive side of their faith. Here was an aspect of their creed that even friendly critics tended to ignore;[43] while, on the whole, the general public looked on the group as a bunch of wild incendiaries bent only on promoting general disorder. In fact, their views on this question were in line with the trend of modern penological theory. Ballou, for instance, saw the source of crime in bad social conditions. He castigated the self-righteous attitude of the affluent of his day, who called for the gallows and penal servitude for those who fell foul of the law. "Let them spare their maledictions against the punishable class of their fellow creatures," he wrote, and ask if they would not themselves be standing in the prisoner's dock had they been born to the poverty and material and moral misery that was the lot of the vast majority of the criminal class. What was needed was loving care and a good example, not deterrence by severity. "Therefore," he concluded, "Christian non-resistance protests against the wickedness of the *punishing* as well as the *punished* classes."[44] The principle of retaliation that underlay the existing legal and penal systems was inconsistent with the Christian spirit of love that put the redemption of the sinner in the forefront. To substitute reform for punishment as society's answer to crime: this was the stated aim of nonresistant theory.[45]

Much might be done by removing the occasion for crime. C. K. Whipple called for the "suppression" by a nonresistant community of such breeding grounds of delinquency as grog shops, gambling dens, and brothels.[46] But it was clear, of course, that this would not be sufficient to eliminate crime altogether. Here the nonresistants came up with their concept of "noninjurious physical force" (the phrase is Ballou's), a species of forceful action directed against the offender that aimed both at restraining him from doing harm to others and at helping him to become a useful member of society. Its use would also be necessary sometimes against all who were not wholly responsible for their actions, against dangerous lunatics, inebriates, the temporarily delirious as well as against minors not yet able to make moral judgments on their own. An essential condition of its remaining non-violent was the spirit of love that must transfuse it. And, above all, the physical force used should not be so great as to risk the infliction of

[43] Whipple, *Non-Resistance applied to the Internal Defence of a Community*, p. 3.
[44] Ballou, *Christian Non-Resistance*, pp. 229-33.
[45] Whipple, *Non-Resistance applied*, pp. 5-10, 12, 13.
[46] *Ibid.*, p. 25.

injury, still less of death, on the person being restrained. Ballou, for instance, was particularly insistent on this point. "The principle of non-injury must be inviolable," he writes. "It is worth worlds and must be preserved at all hazards. What cannot be done uninjuriously must be left undone."[47]

In most instances, it was believed, the use even of such noninjurious force would be unnecessary in coping with the criminal. It would be enough just to tap him on the shoulder and lead him away—especially in view of the new principles that were to motivate the whole system of law enforcement. "Without use of deadly weapons," even the most desperate of men might be induced to submit. Perhaps, on some rare occasion, one or more policemen (who were to be recruited, Whipple suggests, from tried nonresistants and men of known humaneness, like the benevolent Quaker Isaac T. Hopper, for instance) might be killed before the criminal could finally be overwhelmed by the combined efforts—kept always within the bounds demanded by a nonviolent ethic—of the police and other members of the community whom they had called to their aid. Mob violence, too, would be dealt with by the same method. Many of the New England nonresistants, rank-and-file agitators as well as leaders like Garrison himself or Henry C. Wright, had had to face angry mobs out for their blood, especially in connection with their abolitionist activities. They had succeeded in giving personal demonstrations of the efficacy of a nonviolent stand. Although they had at times suffered severe manhandling, no life—they pointed out—had so far been lost. Their determination not to resort to arms in self-defense might, perhaps with some justification, be considered a factor in having prevented the mob in its fury from shedding blood.[48] In his discussion of the ways and means to be adopted by a society dedicated to nonviolence in dealing with mobs, Whipple, therefore, called for "a fearless and prompt interposition of the physical strength and the moral power of the police," acting without weapons but able to call upon the community for support.

Let us suppose that the lawbreaker is now in custody. What did the nonresistant writers propose to do with him next? They agreed that society had the right to impose restraints on the offender by depriving him of his liberty—with the object of training him to become a good

[47] Ballou, *Christian Non-Resistance*, pp. 3-12. See also, e.g., Whipple, *Non-Resistance applied*, p. 4; *Practical Christian*, vol. 5, nos. 6 and 9 (1844).

[48] This was H. C. Wright's view. "I have often been exposed to danger from mob violence," he wrote in his *Six Months at Graeffenberg* (p. 245), "and all my experience has resulted in the conviction of the safety of nonresistance."

citizen again. "This course," writes Whipple, "must not be the abandonment of patience and love, but a prolongation of them under a new form." Prisons were to be transformed into "reform schools" (or "safe moral hospitals," as Ballou called them),[49] staffed by men and women ready to work in the spirit of nonviolence. The work of reforming criminals was comparable to caring for children or the insane, persons unable to look after themselves and needing the care of loving guardians, who might sometimes have to protect them from harming either themselves or others. And, in addition, special care would be taken of the children of the criminal class, who should be brought up as wards of the state away from the demoralizing influence of their parental background.

After a suitable term, most inmates of the adult reformatories would, it was hoped, emerge cured of their social ailments and ready then to be returned to society. A handful, however, might prove less amenable to treatment. Therefore, wrote Whipple,

> A Non-Resistance government, having put under restraint a man who was dangerous to the community, . . . would keep him under restraint until he had ceased to be dangerous . . . the laws must be altered, to allow either the detention of a prisoner until he is reformed, or his discharge as soon as he is reformed . . . the convicts who remain unreformed will remain in custody, with no power any further, or in any manner, to injure the community.

Whipple contrasted these proposals with the existing state of affairs, where a genuinely penitent murderer would still be put to death while unreformed criminals (often having become even more depraved through the demoralizing atmosphere of prison life) were let loose on society at the termination of their sentences, to menace once again the security of society.[50]

From Whipple's argument, however, it was not clear what psychological criteria could be employed to ascertain when the work of reformation had been completed. We may question, too, his view that perpetual incarceration was more in line with Christian nonviolence than the employment of more obviously injurious force, the resort to which he roundly condemned. The whole atmosphere of the discussion which Whipple and the others conducted on the subject was, like so

[49] Ballou, *A Discourse on Christian Non-Resistance in Extreme Cases*, p. 23.
[50] Whipple, *Non-Resistance applied*, pp. 8, 13-30. Cf. H. C. Wright's reactions to his visit to the Connecticut state prison at Wethersfield (*Non-Resistant*, vol. II, no. 4, 26 Feb. 1840): "Did the spirit of Christ, of love to enemies, build this prison and supply these deadly weapons to win these erring men to God?"

much other reformist writing of the period, naively optimistic as to the immediate efficacy of the power of love in dealing with the anti-social elements in human society. The pedagogical theories of Whipple and the other nonresistants left many questions unanswered; they were, after all, amateurs, and such problems were not at the center of their social concern. Nevertheless, they pointed toward a new and more enlightened view of crime.

The moral validity of the use of violence to achieve freedom, to bring about national or social liberation, was a problem which occupied the New England nonresistants as much as, if not more than, that of its use within the community. For above all else they were crusaders, crusaders for righteousness in all its aspects—fanatics, if you will, but fanatics for the right as they conceived it. Peace was only one of the causes to which they gave their allegiance. They were universal reformers, libertarians who strove to break man's shackles to the evil past. They felt a kind of instinctive sympathy toward all who fought, even with weapons in their hand, in the name of freedom: freedom from the tyranny of absolute government, freedom from the arbitrariness of colonial rule, freedom from the worst oppression of them all—the limitless despotism of the slavemaster. Were nonresistants to condemn those who took up arms to further the causes both had at heart? Could they offer any alternative way to achieve the same goals, or was the rule of evil inevitable in this world and all efforts to better it in vain—the doctrine the German nonresistant sectaries of this continent had brought over with them from Europe?

Such complete nonconformity to the world the radical nonresistants found hard to accept. Instead, they groped for some technique, some formula which would satisfy both their pacifist impulse and their search for human freedom.

From the end of the previous century, Europe had been rocked by a series of upheavals, the result in no small part of the liberal and nationalist ferment generated by the French Revolution. By the middle of the nineteenth century, Italians and Germans, Poles and Hungarians, Serbs and Greeks, as well as Britain's Irish, had all made a bid for freedom against oppression, which usually appeared in the guise of an alien ruler. The defeat of bourgeois nationalism and liberalism had followed quickly on the heels of the premature successes of early 1848. The exiled liberals and nationalists now preached war and revolution to liberate their silenced and suppressed peoples, and their friends and sympathizers abroad underlined their pleas for support.

The New England nonresistants (along with the more conservative wing of the peace movement) welcomed the aims for which these

605

revolutionaries were struggling. Garrison chides a critic who accused him and his friends of passivity. "Our correspondent is greatly in error," he says, "in speaking of non-resistance as a state of 'passivity.' On the contrary it is a state of activity, ever foremost to assail unjust power, ever struggling for 'liberty, equality, fraternity.'" Their disagreement with national leaders like the Magyar Kossuth, who visited the United States in the early fifties, was more one of means than of goals. True, the nonresistants deplored the European's narrow nationalism: their own definition of freedom was conceived "in no national sense, but in a world-wide sense."[51] Their chief objection, however, related of course to method. Garrison, in an article written in 1849, contrasted the "patriotism" of Kossuth with the "christianity" of Jesus and his followers.[52] The first was exclusive: Kossuth sought primarily the good of his own countrymen. Jesus's teachings, on the other hand, embraced the whole world, and he included in the orbit of his love even the oppressors of his own people. "The land of his birth was in bondage to the Roman power, but he exhibited no 'patriotic' indignation, and made no appeal to Jewish pride or revenge." He wished to overcome the enemy "by a moral regeneration, not by a physical struggle." Therefore, he refrained from inciting his oppressed fellow nationals to deeds of patriotic violence against the occupiers, while urging them at the same time to stand up to power and to refuse obedience where wrongdoing would result—"though a cruel martyrdom should be their lot."

To Garrison, Ballou, and the rest, then, nonviolent resistance seemed the only possible Christian reaction on the part of the oppressed. Garrison apostrophized the Hungarian as follows: "Oh Kossuth! not of thy abhorrence of Austrian oppression do I complain, but join with thee in execrating it. But the lessons of vengeance which thou art teaching thy countrymen are such as degrade and brutalize humanity. Tell the Hungarians, that a bloody warfare to maintain their nationality is incompatible with moral greatness and Christian love, and for an object which is low and selfish"[53]—low and selfish, however, only in comparison with the higher goal of human freedom, for Garrison gave conditional approval to the movements of national independence and meted out unqualified condemnation to their foreign oppressors.[54]

[51] *Selections . . . from Garrison*, p. 88.   [52] *Ibid.*, pp. 78-86.

[53] *Ibid.*, pp. 84-85. In the early fifties Kossuth excited Garrison's wrath for having failed to condemn Southern slavery during his visit to the United States.

[54] See, e.g., *ibid.*, pp. 86-87, where Garrison writes: "We grant that every successful struggle for freedom on the part of the oppressed, even with the aid of cannon and bomb-shells, is to be hailed with rejoicing; but simply in reference to

606

The New England nonresistants, while registering their dissent from the methods of violence the European nationalists employed, did not attempt (perhaps they did not presume) to instruct them in the details of a nonviolent struggle. In some ways, indeed, this vagueness constitutes a serious weakness in the nonresistants' presentation of their position. But Europe at that time was still far away for the average American, and in the country's own present and past there were conflicts of principle and power more immediate to their concerns. We must turn again to that rather obscure member of the movement, Charles K. Whipple, for the best exposition of the nonresistant response to the issues presented by the War of Independence of the previous century and the long drawn out contemporary antislavery struggle, whose bloody conclusion was already beginning to shape itself in the minds of men.

The very title of Whipple's 16-page pamphlet, *Evils of the Revolutionary War* (1839), appeared almost as a challenge and was in all probability intended as such. We have seen from earlier chapters that the aura surrounding the Revolutionary legend in the minds of most Americans constituted a serious handicap in getting the pacifist message across to the public. If all war is wrong, if it is a sin, many people asked, what about our own Revolutionary struggle which made us an independent nation? It was natural, therefore, that at the outset the Non-Resistance Society should welcome a tract by one of its members which attempted to answer objections on this score.

Whipple accepts without argument the rightness of the aims of the Revolutionary leaders. His thesis is simply that "we should have attained independence as effectually, as speedily, as honorably, and under very much more favorable circumstances, if we had not resorted to arms." To have achieved this, he goes on, three things would have been necessary: a determined refusal to carry out unjustified demands, an efficient system of making the colonial case widely known, and a Quakerly readiness to endure without retaliation all violent measures taken by the home government in order to cow the colonists into submission. The boycott of imported tea and other articles arbitrarily taxed and the refusal of taxes unjustly demanded would eventually have had their effect. The patriots would, indeed, have suffered much hardship and distress, but "the evils thus endured are infinitely less than the calamities of war."[55]

We must go on the assumption, says Whipple, that "governments

---

its object, and not to the mode of its accomplishment. . . . Our correspondent burns with indignation in view of Austrian tyranny; so do we. He rejoices to see its victims rising against it; so do we."

[55] Whipple, *Evils of the Revolutionary War*, pp. 3-5.

are composed of men and not of brutes" (a proposition, incidentally, that many nonresistants, among them Whipple, found some difficulty in maintaining later in face of the enduring intransigence of the slave power). Therefore, in order that measures of passive resistance might work a moral change in the camp of the opponent, before the publicity given to the colonists' demands and their posture in support of them could win them wide support in the home country, they might have been forced to provide a clearer expression of their determination not to give in by taking the further step of declaring their independence of the mother country. Whipple continues:

> This movement excites new and more violent demonstrations of hostility on the part of the British functionaries. The signers of the Declaration of Independence, and the officers of the new government, are seized and sent to England to take their trial for high treason. . . . They are tried by the constituted authorities of England, and calmly avow and defend their revolutionary measures. They are found guilty, sentenced to death, and (for we will suppose the worst) actually executed as traitors. But their defence, their bold and clear explanation of the principles of liberty, their new view of the relative rights and duties of a government and its subjects, are in the mean time eagerly read and pondered by all the British nation.

Despite the seizure of their leaders, the American people persist in their campaign of civil disobedience, continuing to keep it within the limits of nonviolence. New leaders emerge. The prisons are filled to overflowing. The military carry out executions of selected civilians in an attempt to terrorize the rest. This only serves to strengthen the determination of the Americans to resist—"for I take it for granted that they [the British] would not attempt to put to death the great mass of the population." Meanwhile, sympathy for their cause increases throughout Europe and in Britain, too. "Can it be imagined," Whipple asks, "is it consistent with the attributes of human nature to suppose, that such a persevering and undaunted defence of principles so just would fail of working conviction in the hearts of a people like the English?" The pressure of world opinion, combined with that of domestic opposition and the resolute stand of the American people, would eventually force king and parliament ("governors and legislators are never destitute of the feelings and sympathies of men") to recognize colonial independence.[56]

[56] *Ibid.*, pp. 5-7.

608

Whipple saw a fourfold gain in such a substitution of nonviolent methods of gaining liberty for the arbitrament of arms. In the first place, there would have been a tremendous saving in human lives. Even if we were to calculate a loss of some ten thousand civilians, either executed by British authorities as traitors or killed by exasperated British soldiers (a figure which Whipple considered almost certainly an exaggeration), this would still have been a substantial improvement. Secondly, there was the economic argument. Material losses there would inevitably have been: losses to commerce and industry owing to the boycott, as well as those resulting from wanton destruction by the British army in its efforts to break the passive resistance campaign. But these would have been nothing compared to what the country had had to suffer in fact as a result of warlike operations. "We should have been more prosperous . . . had there been no revolutionary war." Of equal importance, on Whipple's balance sheet, with any material advantages which the nonviolent way possessed—perhaps even more important than these advantages—was the gain it would have brought to morality and religion by avoiding, at least on the American side, those inevitable concomitants of war: intemperance and Sabbath-breaking, licentiousness and profanity, and lust for killing and destruction. Finally, the nonviolent accomplishment of independence would have prevented the incorporation into the law and practice of the new state of policies inconsistent with the nonresistant creed. Thus slavery, child of war, would have had to go; the treatment of the Indian would have undergone a revolution; the spirit of revenge would have been banished from the penal system and excluded from the external relations of the country; and the death penalty, harsh prisons, and the corporal punishment of adult offenders would have become things of the past.[57]

The Gandhian strategy of nonviolent action, so influential in our century, was already foreshadowed in Whipple's pamphlet. His inspiration derived from the Christian ethic, but his presentation was almost entirely pragmatic. The moral and religious aspects, which usually predominated in contemporary expositions of pacifism, were kept in the background. Whipple's object was to show that, at least in the case under discussion, passive resistance would have *worked*. It was an attempt, and—crude as it is in parts—a not altogether unsuccessful one, to draw up a blueprint for achieving national liberation by means of this technique. For convenience' sake, the author projected the discussion into the past. Two objects were thus attained: a pillar in the

[57] *Ibid.*, pp. 8-11.

609

case against nonviolence—the Revolutionary legend—was shaken and, at the same time, nonresistant strategy for the future had been outlined.

The limits of the discussion, however, were of course fixed by the historical circumstances. The "enemy" was the British government, and the Whig constitutionalists who ruled eighteenth-century England were, like the parliamentary democrats of twentieth-century Britain, amenable to pressure, at least insofar as it was exerted by the political nation. The rule of law and the sovereignty of Parliament were still maintained in principle, whatever the lapses from them in practice. Gandhi and the colonial movements of our time against British imperialism used nonviolence against a power that did not prevent their case from being heard and from influencing opinion in the home country. Although democracy often looked threadbare on the peripheries, it was a real force at the center, in the places where final decisions were made. Something of this sort, *mutatis mutandis*, was implicit in Whipple's reasoning, in the importance he placed on making the colonists' case known in Britain and in his emphasis on the essential reasonableness and humanity of even the rulers—or, at least, the rulers' sensitivity to their expression in others.

The question of slavery in the American South, like that of resistance to totalitarian regimes in our own day, was in many ways less amenable to any easy solution, even on paper; it presented more agonizing dilemmas to the nonresistant than the resolution of differences between colony and mother country in the past. At first, abolitionists almost to a man eschewed all thought of the use of armed force in the task of liberating the slave—except for a half-suppressed premonition among some of inevitable violence to come, confided usually to the privacy of correspondence or diary. If not from pacifist scruples, at least from expediency and a desire to explore all ways of effecting emancipation peacefully and by due process of law, the antislavery movement—nonpacifists as much as the most convinced nonresistant— had, as we have seen in an earlier chapter, assented to the propositions incorporated by Garrison into the Declaration of Sentiments he had penned for the American Antislavery Convention of 1833. Our principles, he had written there, contrasting them with the appeal of the Revolutionary fathers to arms for the righting of wrong, "forbid the doing of evil that good may come." They relied instead on "the abolition of slavery by the spirit of repentance."[58]

But, far from repenting, the slave power had passed from almost

---

[58] *Selections . . . from Garrison*, pp. 66, 67.

apologetic defense to attack, presenting slavery now as a positive good and suppressing within its orbit all voices raised in protest. During the forties and fifties the antislavery crusade was slowly, but seemingly inevitably, transformed into a sectional conflict. Large portions of the abolitionist movement now looked to the ordeal of battle as the final solution. In the fifties the rising tide of violence on each side carried along some who had only just in the previous decade pledged allegiance to the nonresistant cause. The time seemed ripe, therefore, for someone among their diminishing band to review the position nonresistants should adopt in face of the increasingly bellicose stance of so many of their co-workers in the abolition movement. Again it was C. K. Whipple who undertook the task, and it was John Brown's raid in 1859 that prompted him to write his short work on *The Non-Resistance Principle: With Particular Application to the Help of Slaves by Abolitionists*, which was published in Boston in the following year.

The author praises Brown for his heroism and for the nobility of his aims; then, entering upon a discussion of the hoary old ethical problem of ends and means, he restates the nonresistant position that only the use of "noninjurious force" is consistent with Christ's teachings. All else is the casting out of Satan by Satan. By adopting a policy of nonviolence carried out in the spirit of love, we would have a good chance of winning over the adversary, for "God's arrangement for mankind is, that wrong-doing should breed self-reproach, and that this should tend to confession and amendment."[59] True, slaveowners possess no rights to their slaves' labor and are "robbers" insofar as they seize the fruits of this labor without due recompense; nonetheless, the law of love applies to them as much as to other men. In this situation the obligation of the slave, who is also a Christian, is to stand up for his rights as a human being without at the same time losing hold of the principle of love for all men. "His first duty of good-will to the slaveholder is utterly to refuse any longer to be a slave. . . . Quiet, continuous submission to enslavement is complicity with the slaveholder."

The nonresistant, whose free status precludes him from being able to take such direct action in defense of liberty, must assist in other ways. Best of all would be the achievement of emancipation legally and by general agreement. This, Whipple is forced to concede, is well nigh impossible, owing to the wicked intransigence of the slaveholders. Yet, even so, "the thing could be accomplished which John Brown sought to do, *without the resort to violent and bloody means*

---

[59] Whipple, *The Non-Resistance Principle*, pp. 3-11.

by which he proposed to maintain it against the resistance of the slave-holders." The slaves for the most part are too ignorant and down-trodden to make any effective collective resistance (a consideration that, indeed, seriously impaired the efficacy, though not the moral validity, of the nonviolence Whipple had been urging on them); there-fore—and this is Whipple's main proposal—the free must help the op-pressed through a vast extension of the underground railway. Hideouts must be set up in the mountains of the South where runaways could "hold themselves safely entrenched" until the loss in manpower forced the slaveowners to capitulate. If the movement failed to materialize on a large enough scale, then as many of the fugitives as possible should be helped to escape to the North.

> If also it be necessary in accomplishing such a movement, to seize and put under restraint, by uninjurious means, the persons of any slaveholders, until the departure of the slaves is safely effected, this would be perfectly right, for it is only what the government ought long since to have done. A slaveholder is a public nuisance; a per-son eminently dangerous to the community; and if the government does not do its duty in restraining him, any person who has the power may properly use all uninjurious means to do it.[60]

Whipple had come very near that undefined, perhaps undefinable, borderland between injurious and noninjurious force. Many of his fel-low nonresistants, in fact, were having to grapple in earnest with this very problem in the course of their activities as members of the radical abolitionist camp.

Differences of opinion had existed from the beginning over the limits of nonviolence, not only between the Garrisonian nonresistants and the pacifists who remained within the American Peace Society, but also within the Non-Resistance Society itself. Some extremists, like Charles Stearns (who was to renounce his pacifism in the fifties in "bleeding Kansas"), disapproved of the employment of even noninjurious physical force in the restraint of the criminal and the antisocial; Stearns called it "a mere shame, unworthy of the name" of nonresistance, though he did not object to its application to the insane and the intoxicated, who were not in full possession of their reasoning faculties.[61] The use of physical compulsion in bringing up children was debated at length in the pages of the *Non-Resistant*. Although corporal punishment whether in school or within the family, was condemned by most,[62] nonresist-

---

[60] *Ibid.*, pp. 16-24.
[61] *Practical Christian*, vol. VIII, no. 16, 11 Dec. 1847; no. 18, 8 Jan. 1848.
[62] A lady freshly converted to nonresistance wrote to Maria Chapman: "But I

ants like Ballou considered it right to use some degree of force to restrain a child from hurting other children or itself, just as they approved of its use, as we have seen, in dealing with crime.

The discussion, maintained sporadically during the forties and fifties, died away as Garrisonian nonresistance finally dissolved in the fires of the Civil War. Shortly before Ballou's death at the ripe age of 87, the question reappeared in a fascinating correspondence which sprang up between the aged patriarch of nonresistance and its greatest apostle in modern times, the Russian Count Leo Tolstoy. Ballou had read a translation of Tolstoy's book *What I Believe*, which had first appeared in Russia in 1884. His feelings about it were mixed. "Found many good things in it on ethics," he confided to his journal in February 1886, "with here and there an indiscriminating extremism in the application of Christ's precepts against resisting evil with evil. . . . But on theology found him wild, crude, and mystically absurd. . . . So it seems to me in this first perusal. But I will read further and think him out more thoroughly." However, he continued to be puzzled by the extreme literalism with which Tolstoy interpreted the saying "Resist not evil," "making it inculcate complete passivity not only toward wrong-doers but toward persons rendered insane and dangerous by bad habits, inflamed passions, or unbalanced minds, to the exclusion of non-injurious and beneficent force under any and every circumstance of life."

Four years later, in June 1889, Ballou's friend and follower, the Rev. Lewis G. Wilson, who was then pastor of the Hopedale Unitarian parish, sent Tolstoy several of Ballou's writings on peace and sociopolitical problems. It was not long before the two old men struck up a lively correspondence, only to be cut short by Ballou's death in the following year. Tolstoy, who was previously unaware of the pioneering work of his American forerunner, was extremely gratified to find many of his own unorthodox opinions on these matters presented here in such compelling detail. "Two of your tracts," he wrote Ballou in March 1890, "are translated into Russian and propagated among believers and richly appreciated by them."[63] He himself agreed with much that Ballou had written; at the same time, he had to express dissent on several points, in particular with Ballou's liberal delimitation of the area of strictly nonviolent action by including within it some measure of physical force. "The Master made no concessions and we

---

must confess . . . I cannot see how our common schools could be managed by Non-Resistants. I do not say but if the children were rightly dealt with the first two years of their lives they would not need punishment but who has ever done this or will do it?" (21 Jan. 1841, Weston Papers, B.P.L. MS A.G.2, vol. 13, no. 14).

[63] *Autobiography of Adin Ballou*, pp. 508-11.

can make none," Tolstoy asserted. "A true Christian will always prefer to be killed by a madman, rather than to deprive him of his liberty."

This was a little too much for Ballou to swallow. He denied the charge that he was sanctioning a line of action that was not "dictated by the law of pure good will" and consonant with Christ's teachings, one that the person being restrained would not approve when he regained his reason. "And to construe his precept, 'Resist not evil,'" he went on, "as meaning absolute passivity to all manner of evil, because he made no specific qualifications, is to ignore the context and make him the author of self-evident absurdity." Christ never intended his injunction to mean that we must stand by and see someone out of his senses kill our nearest and dearest "rather than restrain or help restrain him by uninjurious physical force of his insane liberty."[64]

The exchange of views continued a little longer. Ballou had been perplexed by Tolstoy's earlier admission that, although we must be unyielding in upholding the theoretical absolute, compromise on an issue such as nonresistance was inevitable in practice. He suspected that the principle of nonviolence itself was being adulterated by such concessions from the man who at the same time had reproached Ballou with a lack of consistency. Tolstoy hastened to reassure him:

> What I mean is this: Man never attains perfection, but only approaches it. As it is impossible to trace in reality a mathematically straight line, and as every such line is only an approach to the latter, so is every degree of perfection attainable by man only an approach to the perfection of the Father, which Christ showed us the way to emulate. Therefore, in reality, . . . such a compromise in practice is not a sin, but a necessary condition of every Christian life. The great sin is the compromise in *theory*, is the plan to lower the ideal of Christ in view to make it attainable. And I consider the admission of force (be it even benevolent) over a madman (the great difficulty is to give a strict definition of a madman) to be such a theoretical compromise.[65]

Even if Ballou's death had not cut short the dialogue, it is doubtful whether the New Englander would ever have become a convinced Tolstoyan. The gap between theory and practice that is typical not only of Tolstoy but of much of Russian revolutionary thought was alien to the American nonresistant communalist, who, for all the utopian-

[64] Correspondence published in Lewis G. Wilson (ed.), "The Christian Doctrine of Non-Resistance," *The Arena*, III, no. 13 (Dec. 1890), 4-7.
[65] *Ibid.*, p. 10.

ism he and his fellows exhibited, had at least one foot firmly grounded on the rocky New England soil.

The New England nonresistants, both by their writings and by their example, had, as we know, helped to confirm Tolstoy in his faith in nonviolence.[66] And, ironically enough, their legacy was transmitted to twentieth-century America by way of the Russian seer (and his Hindu disciple, the mystic Gandhi) rather than through a native American line of intellectual descent. The ideological testament of these New England precursors of the contemporary nonviolent movement was only fragmentary, their reasoning often naive, and their solutions unrealistic. Yet they strove mightily in their day to win release for mankind from the wheel of violence by some other method than that of renewed conflict and governmental tyranny.[67]

[66] See *The Kingdom of God and Peace Essays*, pp. 11-22, for Tolstoy's acknowledgement of his debt to Ballou.

[67] The Society's ideology is also discussed in E. M. Schuster, *Native American Anarchism*, pp. 58-81.

Chapter 15

The Moderate Pacifists
and the League of
Universal Brotherhood

I

The adoption by the American Peace Society in 1837 of a pacifistic platform in respect to international war had not prevented the pacifists from dividing on the issue of the use of physical force in the domestic arena. The dissidents, who refused to recognize the validity of state and civil government so long as they had the slightest connection with coercive power, had broken away to form their New England Non-Resistance Society. This left wing within the peace movement had succeeded in attracting, as we have seen, some of the most energetic and single-minded, some of the most saintly, and some of the most intellectually gifted among the reformers of the day—as well as a generous share of the cranks and the cantankerous. By the second half of the 1840's the vigor of the nonresistant group had begun to ebb, though it was not to fade away finally until the Civil War days.

Less intellectually challenging perhaps, certainly less exotic, but no less interesting is the story of those pacifists who did not affiliate with the Non-Resistance Society, remaining—at least for the time being—within the framework of the older and more conservative organization. My purpose here is not to give a detailed account of the history of the American Peace Society but to isolate for special consideration the stream of absolute pacifism which still continued to exist within it. This element continued to be important and influential for some eight years at least after the break with the Garrisonian nonresistants; until 1846 the revised constitution of 1837 with its avowedly pacifist stand remained the official program of the Society. We have seen how men like William Ladd and Amasa Walker (not to mention that stalwart pacifist, Joshua P. Blanchard, who had withdrawn near the beginning from the Boston Peace Convention of 1838 along with George C. Beckwith and his group) had, in spite of their sympathies with some aspects of the nonresistant creed, been repelled by the "no-government" overtones of the program as shaped by Garrison and Wright. It was not merely that they were unwilling to cut their ties with the nonpacifist section of the peace movement, to end the collaboration of peace workers of various shades of opinion within one organization that had continued to exist after, as before, the changes in the American Peace Society constitution in 1837; for they disagreed as well with the basic political philosophy of the Garrisonian nonresistants. The latter, for all their disavowal of Jacobinism and their disregard of social issues, were, especially on account of their anarchistic denial of government, essentially revolutionary pacifists; while Ladd and those who thought like him were the reformists of nineteenth-century pacifism.

The two prominent members of the American Peace Society who had not withdrawn with Beckwith but remained to take part in the Boston Peace Convention, Ladd and Amasa Walker, had been impressed with the seriousness of purpose and sincerity of most of its participants. Though unwilling to join the new Non-Resistance Society, they regarded its formation—at first, at any rate—as a positive step. Ladd wrote after the convention was over that he could see no reason for antagonism between the old and the new organization—or at least, he adds, "I am determined that, so far as I am concerned, the fighting shall be all on one side."[1] At the end of the year Walker, too, was to write to Garrison that he hoped "we shall labor together *peacefully* and affectionately in the cause of universal peace."[2] But already the first shots had been fired in the battle for peace. Perhaps, as Galpin suggests,[3] fear on the part of the American Peace Society's executive committee that their policy was being confused in the public mind with that of the Non-Resistance Society was largely responsible for the pains which the American Peace Society now took to dissociate itself entirely from the new body.

In November 1838 it had issued a statement disclaiming all responsibility for the recent peace convention. Only a handful of its members had joined the new Society, whose principles and aims were "entirely foreign from the cause of peace." "It is quite another enterprise, entirely distinct from what *we* have ever taken the cause of peace to be." In fact, it really had no claim to be regarded as a distinctly peace society at all.[4] Misunderstandings concerning the American Peace Society's position continued, however, especially in view of the pacifist Article II of its existing constitution, which branded all war, including the so-called defensive war, as unchristian. In 1838 and again in 1839, therefore, the executive committee issued a detailed statement in an effort to clarify what was and was not meant by this article.

---

[1] *Liberator*, 18 Oct. 1838. [2] *Ibid.*, 11 Jan. 1839.
[3] W. Freeman Galpin, *Pioneering for Peace*, p. 157.
[4] *Advocate of Peace*, II, no. 6 (Nov. 1838), 143, 144.

These "Explanatory Resolves," five in number, though declaring Article II "as designed to assert that all national wars are inconsistent with Christianity, including those supposed or alleged to be defensive," nevertheless went on to state categorically that "the article has no reference to the right of private or individual self-defence, to a denial of which the society is not committed." No pledge, "expressed or implied," was being required from members to uphold a completely pacifist, let alone a "no government," position. As in the past, so now "we invite the cooperation of all persons who seriously desire the extinction of war, whether they agree with the principle of the article as thus explained, or not."[5]

This was certainly a watering down of the pacifist witness—at least so it must have seemed to the more ardent nonresistants. They had not, from their side, shown a very conciliatory spirit toward the older organization, which they regarded, in effect, as useless in promoting true peace because of its concessions to those who had not abandoned belief in organized violence. In particular, the American Peace Society's advocacy of a congress of nations as a substitute for the war method of settling international disputes (an idea that Ladd was particularly active in promoting) was regarded as a waste of time by the nonresistants of the Garrisonian variety. Indeed, it is easy to understand why those who regarded all state organisms then existing as incarnations of violence, oppression, and the war spirit—as negations of the Christian way to a better life—should have had scant hope of founding a peaceful world order on a gathering of these very nation-states whose "overthrow," according to the Declaration of Sentiments of the Non-Resistance Society, "by a spiritual regeneration of their subjects is inevitable."[6] It was, in their view, an infinitely more useful and ultimately much surer way to work for this spiritual regeneration by means of a radical transformation of society and the elimination of all forms of violence in its midst. As Sarah Grimké had written to Henry C. Wright in the spring of 1838: "I agree entirely in your views of a Congress of Nations, it is entirely playing the fool with the public mind, fixing its attention on an igneous future which will continually flee be-

---

[5] *The Tenth Annual Report of the American Peace Society* (1838), p. 2; *Advocate of Peace*, III, no. 1, 2, quoted in Galpin, *Pioneering for Peace*, pp. 157, 158. The American Peace Society still continued to stress that it was solely with international war, and not with such matters as capital punishment and penology, the maintenance of internal order within each society, or individual defense of person and property, that the Society was concerned. "We restrict ourselves to the intercourse of states," wrote the author of the Tenth Annual Report (p. 7), who was presumably Beckwith.

[6] *Principles of the Non-Resistance Society*, p. 5.

fore it. I shall rejoice to see it exposed."[7] Garrison, too, was to denounce the scheme as a chimera: he had already launched out into a diatribe against "the moderate fighters—those who believe in blowing out a man's brains in self-defence, occasionally, or who are partial to hanging criminals, or who can think of nothing but a congress of nations."[8] After the first year the two Societies on the whole simply ignored each other, devoting most of their attention to the uphill work of winning new adherents to their cause among a sometimes hostile, or more often simply indifferent, populace.[9]

The question of the correct attitude for the peace movement to adopt toward the use of physical force within the national community was to continue to trouble the American Peace Society, however, especially so long as the moderate pacifists were to be well represented in its counsels. The latter would all have agreed (as probably not a few, like Samuel May, who were working with the Non-Resistance Society would have also) with Ladd's opinion "that a peace-man did not compromise his principles, and acknowledge the right of nations to go to war, by voting for rulers who had the power to involve the country in war."[10] Even Garrison himself did not urge a refusal to pay taxes (unless specifically for military purposes, of course). But there were further problems on which agreement was not so easily reached.

It was perhaps to help overcome the doubts of some members, as well as to clarify the American Peace Society's position for the general public, that Beckwith wrote for the Society a small tract under the title "Peace and Government."[11] What is remarkable about this production is its decided assertion of the nonresistant position in international affairs, which was, of course, the position of the Society of which Beckwith was the secretary, along with an official rejection of the principle of the inviolability of human life in domestic affairs.[12] Beckwith's views recall those of his predecessor, Noah Worcester, during his latter years.

"All war must be utterly unchristian," states Beckwith, "unless the New Testament permits it as an *exception*"; and of such permissive-

---

[7] Galpin, *Pioneering for Peace*, p. 121.   [8] *Liberator*, 26 Sept. 1838.

[9] In a debate between Amasa Walker defending the moderate pacifist position and three advocates of the inevitability of war in the existing state of the world, which took place in the Boston Odeon on 3 January 1839 before an audience numbering some three thousand persons, the voting went heavily against pacifism. "And the audience claims to be enlightened and christianized! It manifested a tiger-spirit" was Garrison's comment in a letter to S. J. May (dated 4 Jan. 1839 in Garrison Papers, B.P.L., MS A.1.1., vol. 3, no. 26).

[10] *Advocate of Peace*, III, no. 10 (Dec. 1840), 233.

[11] Reprinted in George C. Beckwith, *The Book of Peace*, pp. 425-32.

[12] Most of the Society's pacifists, like Ladd or Walker or Blanchard, did assent to this principle, however.

ness he could find no trace in the gospels themselves. Until the defenders of the admissibility of war in certain circumstances can produce better evidence on this point, "we have no more right to kill an army of invaders in self-defence, than we have to renounce our religion." But it is quite a different matter with law enforcement within the community. "I regard civil government," writes Beckwith, "as lawful, expedient and necessary," and as in no way incompatible with the renunciation of force between nations. Civil government has been ordained by God, and as the instrument of his justice it must be endowed with the means of enforcing its will upon the refractory. It must have the power to punish the evildoer, otherwise it will be ineffective. It is permissible for it to inflict even death itself. True, capital punishment conflicts with the Biblical injunctions to love our enemies, to resist not evil, and to refrain from killing. The New Testament, however, Beckwith goes on, makes an exception here, an exception which is not to be discovered in the case of international war: "the theory of exceptions is indispensable to the vindication of civil government as an ordinance of God." "I plead, then," he says, "both for peace and for government, nor deem them at all incompatible. I believe all war contrary to the gospel, yet regard government as an institution divinely appointed for the good of mankind, and authorized at discretion to punish and coerce its subjects."

At this point Beckwith seems to have realized that his argument might not carry conviction even with his own executive committee. Had not William Ladd stated his opposition to capital punishment and Amasa Walker pleaded publicly for the inviolability of human life? And there were critics, too, from the other, the nonpacifist wing of the movement, who believed that to deprive a nation of the right to wage what it considered a defensive war on the grounds that all war was unchristian could be justified only from the standpoint of complete nonresistance. Speaking to the students of Amherst College in 1839, the Rev. John Lord (1810-1894), who had very recently resigned as agent of the American Peace Society because he could no longer agree with its new official policy, argued this view with some cogency. "When does protection begin and end," he asked, "and how many men does it take to make a mob, and where is the difference on the grand principle, between a foreign and domestic body of robbers and murderers? Do we not enforce the same principle in regard to a multitude of foreign enemies that we do of domestic ones? . . . The doctrine that *all* war is opposed to the gospel *does* run into nonresistance. It is vain and trifling to deny it."[13]

[13] John Lord, *An Address . . . before the Peace Society of Amherst College*, p. 9.

It was admittedly a difficult problem, the same that Pennsylvania's Quaker rulers had had to face a century or so earlier. If government in a Christian country might punish a score of pirates or half a dozen murderers with death, or, again, if it might suppress a mob or a riot or an insurrection by armed force if necessary (all which instances Beckwith had cited), why, indeed, was it wrong for it to repel by arms an invading army intent upon robbing and killing? After posing this question to himself, Beckwith answered by asserting: "*God permits the taking of life in one case, but not in the other.* He authorizes rulers to govern, but not to fight; to punish, but not to quarrel. Such acts, even if they were physically the same, would be morally different; and hence one *may* be permitted, while the other is forbidden." Even if we cannot comprehend why God has made such a distinction, still we must abide by it.[14] Moreover, civil government aimed at establishing justice among men. The outcome of war was quite different from punishment as a result of judicial process in a court of law. War was "no more than a rencounter [*sic*] between tigers." The soldiers who did the fighting and were killed were usually innocent of any crime; "if taken as prisoners, not one of them could be tried for murder."

Beckwith expressed his belief that there were other ways besides war whereby governments could protect their citizens from invasion from without. Although he does not state what he thought these ways were, it is probable that he was thinking of the avoidance of war by means of universal disarmament, conciliatory national policies, and the development of international arbitration for settling disputes, rather than of any form of nonviolent resistance such as had been tentatively outlined by several contemporary peace writers.

Beckwith undoubtedly believed that he did in fact adhere to what he called "the strictest principles of peace";[15] it is not hard, however, to discover in his discussion of peace and government in the early 1840's the outlines of his justification of the use of armed force against the Southern "rebellion" of the early 1860's. The fact is that Beckwith, like many peace workers of that day, was reasoning on the assumption that all wars (between civilized nations, at least) were, with a little patience and goodwill, avoidable and that, therefore, they were unnecessary in the long run. This assumption may have been largely true. But the deeper implications raised by wars of national liberation or by ideological conflict or the will toward aggression, not

---

[14] As Beckwith wrote elsewhere: "The same God that proclaimed . . . thou shalt not kill, bade Abraham slay Isaac" (quoted in Galpin, *Pioneering for Peace*, p. 157).

[15] Quoted in *ibid.*

to speak of the economic causes of international war, were on the whole either ignored or put to one side as irrelevant to the peace issue. "We are concerned solely with the intercourse of one government with another,"[16] Beckwith writes of the American Peace Society. And it is this dichotomy in his thinking that led him into difficulties in the admittedly extremely complex and, for the pacifist, baffling problem of reconciling abandonment of the use of force in international relations with its retention in some measure in the internal affairs of the nation.

This ambivalence in the views of the secretary of the Society (which were considerably less radical, we see, than the views of his immediate predecessor Ladd or those of most of the other members of the executive committee) is not reflected on the whole in the multitude of propaganda tracts and leaflets put out by the Society during these years—understandably so, since in line with previous policy, which the new pacifist course of 1837 had not altered, the main line of attack continued to be against the institution of international war.

War was ethically wrong, economically unsound, politically ineffective in the long run, and contrary to Christian morality. Permanent and universal peace was practicable, as well as desirable, even in the world as it then existed. This, broadly, was the theme of most of the tracts which Beckwith was to gather together from the Society's publications (many of them reprints from the peace classics and from other earlier writings on the subject) and issue in book form in 1845 under the title *The Book of Peace: A Collection of Essays on War and Peace.* Out of 64 items printed, 10 condemned war *in toto.* The writings of the Quakers, Dymond and Gurney, appear here as well as Clarkson's exposition of the pacifism of the early church and Thomas Grimké's fervid plea for the adoption of nonviolent resistance by the nations. A well-known Baptist divine, Dr. Howard Malcolm (1799-1879), then president of a college in Kentucky, who was long to be a pillar of the American Peace Society and a stout upholder of the Beckwithian, conservative trend within it, contributed two pamphlets denouncing the participation of Christians in war of any sort and imploring them to withdraw from all association with military preparations. It is interesting to note that an anonymous piece entitled "Safety of Pacific Principles" argued the case for the method of love and reconciliation in dealing with evil and aggression and with the insane. The writer drew heavily for his illustrative material, as usual, on the Quaker experience in Pennsylvania and on the Irish rebellion of 1798. This method might not

[16] *Advocate of Peace*, II, no. 9 (Feb. 1839), 201.

622

work in all instances, he concluded, but it would do as well, if not better, than the "war-principle."

Propaganda by the written and the spoken word was, of course, only one weapon in the American Peace Society's armory. It also petitioned governments, especially in periods of international tension or war crisis; it organized public meetings and framed resolutions in favor of peace; it developed and strengthened ties between peace workers in America and those back in Europe; and it attempted to influence politicians toward pacific policies wherever possible.[17] But, as Curti has shown,[18] these efforts met on the whole with indifference; even the stimulus of a violently hostile reaction, such as the abolitionists met with from the public at first, was not vouchsafed America's early pacifists. They remained small in numbers, a chosen band, perhaps, and certainly of importance for the future, but a factor of little weight in the existing political and international scene.

The clergy, who should at least, one might think, have had a professional interest in peace, for the most part held themselves aloof. However, some progress could be recorded here, and we see an increasing number of ministers of religion adopting the Society's pacifist platform, though not necessarily endorsing the moderate nonresistance of a Ladd or an Amasa Walker. Evidence of this trend is to be found in the writings of contemporary peace workers. Ladd, for instance, reports from Portsmouth (N.H.) in March 1840: "A paper, pledging the signers to the principle that *all* war is contrary to the spirit of the gospel, has been signed by all the ministers in town except the Universalist, who is absent, and it is expected that the signatures of 300 male professors of religion will be obtained to it."[19] Again, in the middle of the 1840's, the Rev. A. P. Peabody, who has recorded his sense of almost complete isolation when a mere decade before he had reached unaided a full pacifist position (see chap. 11), could write of the present situation: "I am acquainted with very few clergymen, who do not think and feel as I do."[20] This was certainly an exaggeration, but it is indicative of the fact that peace propaganda had by this time succeeded in making considerable inroads within the ranks of the professional ministry.

The literature of pacifism continued to grow in the late thirties and during the forties. We have seen in the previous chapter the significant

[17] See Curti, *American Peace Crusade*, pp. 106ff; Christina Phelps, *The Anglo-American Peace Movement in the Mid-Nineteenth Century*, chap. II.

[18] Curti, *American Peace Crusade*, pp. 104, 105.

[19] Quoted in John Hemmenway, *The Apostle of Peace*, p. 85.

[20] Letter of A. P. Peabody, 28 Oct. 1844, in S. E. Coues's "Peace Album," Harvard University Library, MS Am.635*.

contribution to pacifist ideology made by the nonresistant group. A number of pamphlets and addresses were also produced by pacifists outside the orbit of the Non-Resistance Society, usually by clergymen and usually by persons connected more or less closely with the American Peace Society, which—aside from some small societies confined to a comparatively small locality—remained the only substantial organization devoted to the peace cause until Elihu Burritt formed his League of Universal Brotherhood in 1846.

Although the peace movement had also made some progress outside New England in the middle states and in the Midwest, it had scarcely penetrated at all into the South. Perhaps Thomas Grimké, if he had lived, would have acted as its pioneer in this area; more likely, however, he would have imitated his two sisters in migrating north. The usual combination of peace views with antislavery and strongly abolitionist opinions debarred the peace movement, from at least the 1830's on, from making any headway in the South. Indeed, the regimentation of opinion behind the proslavery ideology and the ruthless suppression of opposition views, which became more marked as the years went by, created a climate of opinion extremely hostile to the peace movement in even its more conservative guise. If we disregard the not very numerous members of the historic peace sects, pacifism after Grimké's death had, it would appear, only one vocal advocate in the deep South.

John Jacobus Flournoy (d. 1879)[21] was certainly an eccentric, both in his physical appearance and personal habits as well as in many of his views on life and politics, and he should probably be described as a fanatic, too. But he was an individualist, a man who thought independently, if inconsistently, and one who had the courage to maintain his viewpoint over the years in the face of continuous hostility from the community. An opponent of the institution of slavery (though he owned a small plantation with some dozen slaves himself) who at the same time was filled with a deep hatred of Negroes, whom he wished to see deported en masse from the country, an upholder of the Union even during the Civil War days who regarded Lincoln as a tyrant, a temperance advocate who himself was a heavy drinker, a good member of the Presbyterian church who wrote in favor of a form of polygamy which he called "trigamy" (he did, however, base his case on Biblical grounds), an outspoken pacifist who engaged in innumerable

---

[21] See E. Moulton Coulter, *John Jacobus Flournoy: Champion of the Common Man in the Antebellum South.* Coulter regards Flournoy as a spokesman for the grievances of the class of poor Southern whites, who hated both slavery and the Negro and resented the political and economic dominance of the planter aristocracy.

lawsuits resulting from a species of persecution mania and who did not hesitate to physically assault a man with whom he had quarrelled, this citizen of Athens, Georgia, was regarded by his neighbors—and no wonder!—as a crank, as a local joke, indeed as a man whose foibles might be tolerated because they were completely harmless. It was this seemingly harmless eccentricity, combined perhaps with the obscurity of his style which makes him almost unreadable, that gave him immunity to publish his unorthodox views on political matters freely.

Flournoy's interest in peace led him to become a member of the American Peace Society. He tried unsuccessfully to raise money for it and to find new subscribers for its publications. The same lack of success, despite his repudiation of any connection with Northern radicalism, accompanied his efforts in the late thirties to start up peace groups in the South: by these means—he tells us—he hoped to help restrain the bellicose impetuosity of young Southerners by demonstrating to them that real courage lay in the readiness, as he wrote, "to endure insults and forgive injuries." His attendance at compulsory militia musters he turned into a demonstration against militarism (though he could have gained exemption on account of his serious deafness) by supplying himself with a cotton umbrella instead of a gun. "Christ Jesus utterly, entirely prohibited warfare," he wrote to a friend. In 1838, in order to bring his peace views to the attention of the public, Flournoy published at his own expense a small pamphlet of 19 pages entitled *An Earnest Appeal for Peace to all Christians.* It sold for the modest sum of 10¢, but only one copy was bought. When its author offered to give the remainder away free, "the people of Athens," he relates, *"had the meanness to accept them."*[22]

The booklet, which is interesting as a curiosity, if for no other reason, is a passionate plea for the renunciation of all war on religious grounds. "The single expression, 'Love thy neighbour as thyself,'" he writes, "forever precludes all admission of warlike ideas and martial feelings into any part of the human economy." War has been forbidden by "that incomparable effort of Divine benevolence, the Sermon on the Mount." He reproves the clergy for not preaching in favor of peace and holds up to his fellow Christians for imitation the example of the Quakers—"the very best and finest spirited Christians," he calls them— and of their steady refusal to fight under any circumstances. "For a forbearance of man to man—a refusal to molest for molestation, and a returning of 'good for evil,' will . . . certainly disarm the most virulent oppressors," such behavior is "an injunction from Heaven."[23] (Six

[22] *Ibid.*, pp. 67-72.
[23] *An Earnest Appeal for Peace*, pp. 3, 4, 6, 12, 17-19.

years later he was to write: "Some christian country must set an example of forbearance by enduring wrong—with long patience.")[24] A refusal to participate in wars on the part of Christians would deprive the rulers of the world, whom Flournoy held primarily responsible for stirring up conflicts between nations, of the means to wage them. With war banished from the world and the Negroes—slave and free—expelled from the country ("to have them gone is my object," he writes),[25] a new era would begin for mankind.

In the antebellum South, outside the traditional sanctuary of the uninfluential historic peace sects, pacifism might normally be preached openly only where its advocate was protected by the label of harmless crank. In the North, on the other hand, the apathy, rather than the active hostility of the public, was the main barrier to a rapid and widespread dissemination of peace doctrines, whether of conservative or radical hue. As the editor of the *Christian Mirror* (22 June 1837) wrote concerning Ladd: "He has sometimes wished that his doctrines might, at least, attract notice enough to be opposed." Yet, as we have seen, there was one issue in the peace repertoire where strong feelings were immediately aroused and the peace man who touched upon it had to be ready to face abuse and unpopularity in good measure. This issue was the justifiability of the American Revolution or— as it was usually called then—the Revolutionary War against Britain. The Revolution and the Revolutionary fathers had become part of the national mythology; to question any aspect of the myth was to risk accusations of lack of patriotism. But could an absolute pacifist accept its necessity? That he could not do so had been recognized ever since the days of Dodge (though Beckwith might, indeed, have succeeded again in reconciling the irreconcilable), and, as we have seen in previous chapters, some peace writers had spoken their opinion boldly on the subject. Others had handled it with kid gloves, and still others ignored it altogether; even Ladd felt it would be wiser to avoid the topic where possible, so as not to arouse unnecessary antagonism against the peace movement.

But now, in 1842, there came along "an interesting, earnest, devoted young clergyman of the Unitarian faith," by name the Rev. Sylvester Judd (1813-1853), who was willing, eager even, to state the full pacifist case againt the American use of arms to win freedom from their British rulers. "Mr. Judd," writes a contemporary, "had no dread of public opinion: he rather enjoyed braving it: he saw the advantage

---

[24] Coulter, *J. J. Flournoy*, p. 69, quoting from the *Southern Whig* (1844).
[25] *An Earnest Appeal*, p. 11.

to the peace cause of a hearty opposition."[26] Judd's hatred of war and militarism apparently went back to his school days. Anyhow, by the beginning of the 1840's the young pastor had become a convinced, and even militant, pacifist. On 8 November 1841 we find him writing as follows to his brother: "I am sorry you must train. The militia is a horrible system; barbarous as ten heathenisms; utterly antichristian. So I view it. Can a Christian be a fighter, a killer of his own flesh and blood? What think you of that?"[27] In the following year he made public his protest against war, choosing to do so in what was perhaps a somewhat provocative manner.

In a sermon preached to his own congregation of the Unitarian church in Augusta (Me.) on 13 March 1842, Judd presented "a moral review of the Revolutionary War," an address that frankly revealed "some of the evils of that event" as considered from the viewpoint of a Christian pacifist. Perhaps his sermon came as no great surprise to his listeners, for Judd had made no secret of his antiwar views, his belief "that if Christ himself were now on the earth he would never, for any pretext, reason or motive whatever engage in war." The young men of his parish he had advised to "wholly abjure *all war*"; in season and out he had urged—"not as a politician, but simply as a moralist and a Christian"—that the way of peace was ultimately a surer road to freedom and security than the war method.[28]

As he began his sermon, however, there was as yet no reason for alarm among his listeners. First he recorded his view of the Revolution as "the holiest war on record" and then went on to pay tribute to the nobility of purpose and fine character of the Revolutionary fathers. But as he started to develop his theme, we cannot doubt that looks of apprehension and disapproval were seen creeping into the faces of some of the congregation. Briefly put, his thesis, while not questioning the necessity in the circumstances for the colonies to separate from the mother country, condemned the validity of the means used to gain independence. A policy of peace, not recourse to arms, was the course which a Christian people should have adopted to achieve what admittedly were legitimate ends. Judd's critique of the war was mainly political. In his opinion, the causes, ostensible and real, were not sufficient to justify starting a war. The violence used by the colonists provoked the British government to send over more troops, and so the war

[26] Frederick West Holland, "The History of the Peace-Cause," B.P.L., MS *5577.98, pp. 47-49.
[27] Arethusa Hall, *Life and Character of the Rev. Sylvester Judd*, pp. 28, 190.
[28] Sylvester Judd, *A Moral Review of the Revolutionary War*, pp. 3, 5, 47, 48.

spread—despite the fact that a number of influential people on each side had been opposed to the outbreak of hostilities. Judd strongly criticized the many instances of bad conduct on the part of the Revolutionary army and corruption among many civilian officials. He deplored what he called the "military dictatorship" imposed by Washington and the disastrous consequences of the French alliance. The war, he thought, could have been ended much earlier if its continuation had not been in the interests of highly placed American officials. "The separation from England," he concluded, "was unavoidable, and necessary, and certainly involved in the course of things; but . . . it might have been made peaceably, without the spilling of a drop of blood."[29]

Judd, unlike his contemporary, the nonresistant Whipple, did not put forward any nonviolent alternative to winning independence by armed rebellion. He implies that the force of events, together with the existence in England of a powerful group sympathetic to the colonists, would have sufficed to achieve this goal by peaceful means. His approach to the problem of responsibility for the war is reminiscent of the "revisionist" school of historians after the First World War: in both cases there is considerable exaggeration in the effort to redress the balance. His narrative is replete with footnote references and bibliography. His intention, however, is clearly didactic. "He looks upon war in the abstract," he writes of himself, "upon all war, as antichristian and demoralising. . . . It is war, war as practically exhibited in our own country, and among our own citizens, that he desires to exhibit in its true light."[30] If once this holiest of wars, in the eyes of the American citizen, could be shown to have been both unnecessary in its origins and, regarding the manner in which it was waged on the American side as much as on the British, scarcely consistent with Christian morality, then, indeed, one of the main obstacles in the country in the way of pacifist propaganda would be removed. This clearly was Judd's aim, and not simply the scholar's search for objective historical truth.

The sermon certainly succeeded in shocking conservative minds, and, as a result, Judd was dismissed from the honorary post of chaplain to the Maine legislature, which happened to be in session at that time. Many of its members had attended the sermon, some walking out angrily in the course of its delivery. At the next meeting of the state House of Representatives, a Mr. Otis put forward a resolution that Judd in his sermon had "evinced total disregard of the feelings of every American citizen." His dismissal was accepted by a vote of 127 to 5. On the other hand, the pacifist camp was jubilant. The Boston *Non-*

---

29 *Ibid.*, pp. 3, 6ff., 42, 43.   30 *Ibid.*, pp. 43, 47.

Resistant reprinted the sermon in installments, while "at the Anniversary of 1842, the [American] Peace Society passed a vote of sympathy with the persecuted lecturer."[31]

At this same anniversary meeting, held in Boston on 23 May, the Society heard an address from its new president, Samuel E. Coues (1787-1867). The address is revealing as an example of a certain ambiguity frequently displayed in the thinking of the American Peace Society leadership. Coues was an active exponent of the pacifist position within the Society. In the light of Christianity, he now stated, "war is either right or it is wrong. It is either permitted or forbidden" —by which he meant war under all circumstances. He took pains to prove that, in fact, armaments had never given the nations security, that they were, indeed, positively harmful, a heavy burden laid upon the peoples of the world, while, on the other hand, international disarmament would bring peace and prosperity. His ultimate appeal, however, was to the moral imperative, the Christian standard of right and wrong, which must be followed even to our material disadvantage. Come what may, we must look to principles, and not to consequences, in shaping our conduct on the national as well as the personal level. "Even if life would not be altogether safe from the abandonment of the sword, if our principles expose the nations to loss, let the loss come. If blood must flow as the price of safety to others, let it flow." At the same time, Coues was careful in his lecture to deny that his conclusions, as many critics of the American Peace Society maintained, led logically "to ultra ground, to radicalism, to non-resistance," although we know that privately he upheld the inviolability of human life as the Christian way. Why this reticence on Coues's part? It was, of course, because—to quote his own words— "we do not, as a Society, concern ourselves with the question of the right of private or personal self-defence, nor do we advocate any change of the penal code."[32]

An even more conservative stand than Coues's, but one based on somewhat similar thinking, was taken by the speaker at the Society's next anniversary meeting in 1843, the Rev. A. P. Peabody, then pastor of the Unitarian South Church in Portsmouth (N.H.). Peabody con-

---

[31] Holland, "The History of the Peace-Cause," p. 49; *Non-Resistant*, vol. IV, no. 9 (11 May 1842); Hall, *Judd*, pp. 191, 199, 211, 212, 294, 297-303. Judd was supported by his own congregation and was later reinstated as chaplain by the legislature. He continued to preach, lecture, and write on behalf of pacifism (as well as an array of other humanitarian reforms) until his death. He publicly denounced the Mexican War and around that time became a keen supporter of Burritt's League of Universal Brotherhood.

[32] S. E. Coues, *War and Christianity*, pp. 1, 5, 9-14, 16-18, 21, 22.

ceded (although what he says here is not altogether in consonance with other statements of his on the subject[33]—perhaps because he now wished to conciliate the nonpacifist element in the Society) that "violent measures in self-defence" were justified "in extreme cases,— in cases of immediate and intense danger, where the alternative is forcible resistance, or submission to severe personal injury." But he denied any parallel between such a situation and the incidence of international war. "In order to justify war on the ground of self-defence, a nation, in an unarmed condition, and in perfect quietness, must be the subject of an unprovoked attack from some other nation. Now, it is, in the very nature of things, impossible that a nation, occupying such a position, should be assailed. It is the aggressive posture—the armed truce, so to speak,—in which nations professedly at peace stand towards each other, that invites assault." Therefore, in regard to the possibility of waging defensive war, he answers: "There are no such wars." The New Testament gives war no sanction under any circumstances, and the early Christians were conscientious objectors. For a just war to exist, says Peabody (had he perhaps some acquaintance with Catholic writings on the subject?), in the first place all blame for aggression must be on one side alone—and to discover where the blame lay would necessitate the prior existence of an international court of justice to judge the case impartially, the setting up of a supranational tribunal such as the American Peace Society had, indeed, advocated for some years. Secondly, "the retribution taken must bear a just proportion to the injury received, must affect directly the authors of the injury alone, and must affect others, if at all, only indirectly and incidentally." And war, of course, could not possibly conform to these conditions.[34]

The moderate pacifists in the American Peace Society, it should be said, had considerable justification for their refusal to officially raise questions pertaining to the use of force in a country's internal government and for centering their efforts instead on international war, thereby gaining the support of peace workers who could not go quite as far as themselves in taking what they called "the high ground." They were fond of pointing out that mutual toleration existed among members on the question of civil government. But though the Society gained in numbers by this width of view, it lost in cohesiveness by the somewhat unsatisfactory compromise between the two philosophies of peace. The moderate pacifists' approval of the positive aspects of civil government, despite the continued reliance of the nations on armed

[33] E.g., his *The Triumphs of War* (1847), p. 12.
[34] Peabody, *The Nature and Influence of War*, pp. 4-7, 10.

force, made it natural that they should wish to dissociate themselves from the more extreme exponents of nonresistance. However, the moderates cannot be acquitted of the charge of failing to give an entirely consistent witness for their Christian pacifist ideal.

Some of the confusion arising from this artificial separation into entirely different categories of the issues of armed force in the international arena and in domestic policy (a confusion, be it noted, that was not present, for all its faults, in the thinking of the Non-Resistance Society) was overcome in another address given by a member of the American Peace Society. At the twenty-seventh annual meeting of the Rhode Island Peace Society on 30 June 1844, the Rev. Edward B. Hall (1800-1866), pastor of the First Congregational Church in Providence (Roger Williams's church, incidentally) spoke on the topic "Christians forbidden to fight."[35]

Like Coues, Hall bases his case primarily on a pacifist interpretation of the Sermon on the Mount. Its meaning admits of no doubt for him: "the direct word is, that we must not *return* aggression." Better "our own death" than "the violation of conscience." He believed, despite the assertions of many churchmen to the contrary, that its precepts were capable of being carried out in practice in the present. At least, he pleads, let us go as far as we humanly can in trying to do so. The early Christians and in our time the Quakers and the Moravians have made the attempt, with some measure of success, rightly believing that the same standards of Christian conduct applied in the collective affairs of the state and the nation as in personal relationships. "If it be inhuman and unchristian, in one man to kill another, it is inhuman and unchristian for one hundred men to attempt to kill a hundred men." "Christianity forbids war, without qualification."[36]

When he comes to consider the application of the teachings of the

[35] Although this local peace society was very small, Hall was not the only pacifist among the ministers of Providence. In August 1842, for instance, his colleague, the Rev. James A. M'Kenzie from the Free-will Baptists had preached a forthright *Discourse against Life-Taking*. To the question, Do the gospels ever sanction the taking of human life?, he gave a decided no. (See James A. M'Kenzie, *A Discourse, against Life-Taking*, esp. pp. 3, 9-11, 17-22.) Although M'Kenzie did not deny divine sanction for the Jewish wars of the Old Testament (pp. 3-11), he argued in favor of the efficacy of nonresistance as a defensive technique to be employed under the new dispensation (pp. 11-13). In December of the same year, M'Kenzie had inspired the members of his congregation to pass unanimously a resolution "that war, arms-bearing, learning the art of war, and the intentional taking of human life in any case or under any circumstances, are each and all contrary to the gospel" and to pledge themselves to work for peace in the spirit of the resolution they had approved. See *The Proceedings of the First General Peace Convention* . . . , London, 1843, pp. 108-12.

[36] E. B. Hall, *Christians forbidden to fight*, pp. 6-13, 23.

Sermon on the Mount to the problem of civil government, his step indeed falters; yet his argument makes a valiant attempt to grapple with some of the problems involved. It is perhaps worthwhile to illustrate this attempt by quoting Hall at some length here.

It is objected that an argument against all war, which yet allows and defends government, defeats itself. Why? Has government never been sustained on peace principles? Did not the first Christians admit and uphold government? Were they guilty of treason and rebellion, when they refused to fight? . . . Had William Penn no government, or were seventy years no test of its strength? . . . Our government does require us to yield up a slave who flies to us for protection, and surrender him to bondage. Can you do it? I cannot, neither can I fight. I will rather suffer the consequences of refusing, whatever they may be. . . . But, it is still urged, government cannot be *sustained* without arms, nor its commands enforced. That has not been proved. It appears so in theory, I admit; and I may not see, or be able to show, in every case, how the obvious difficulties are to be overcome. But that does not destroy the principle. It does not disturb my faith in the principle. Though all theory were against it, as men reason, and all experience, as men are, I should still believe in the practicability of a thoroughly Christian government, on thorough peace principles, because I believe in the Christian religion, and in Christ's knowledge of man. But experience is not against it. Just so far as the trial has been made, the result has been favorable. Even if it could be proved, as it cannot, that a spirit of unarmed peace and uniform justice would fail to conquer an invading force, or suppress an actual insurrection, it would not follow that this spirit might not *prevent* both.

By making concessions in time, England might have avoided the American Revolution, or the French government its revolution and all the bloody consequences that ensued for all Europe.[37] Insurrections and internal disorders—he appears to be saying—are usually the results of faults in government. Effect a timely removal of abuses, and, quite in-

[37] *Ibid.*, pp. 21, 22. Hall's approval of certain forms of mildly injurious, but nonlethal force, if used in defense, met with stern disapproval from the nonresistant Ballou. See the controversy between the two in the *Practical Christian*, vol. V (1844), nos. 10, 12-15. Hall summed up his position on the government question as follows (*ibid.*, p. 55): "No power on earth can compel me to violate a Christian law . . . I will not fight. I will not sentence a man to death. I will do no wrong. But I will support a government which guards our rights, and, with some great evils, is an instrument of incalculable good. I will vote for the best men that are proposed to administer the government. I will do all I can to expose its errors and bring it to Christian principles."

dependently of the moral validity of using physical force within the community, need for the exercise of armed repression will also have been removed.

The approaching conflict with Mexico brought the immediate policies of the American Peace Society at least, if not the more radical nonresistants, into line with a larger segment of New England society than that which usually supported the peace cause. In that part of the country the administration's handling of the issue of Texas and its relations with Mexico were widely unpopular. Among its most vehement opponents were the "Young Whigs" (or "Conscience Whigs," as they were later known), one of whose leading spokesmen, the rising young Boston lawyer, Charles Sumner (1811-1874), had also been connected with the American Peace Society since the beginning of the decade. It was William Ellery Channing who had brought Sumner to espouse actively both peace and antislavery. (In religion Sumner inclined toward Unitarianism, though he was never a member of any church.) On both issues, however, Sumner had soon advanced further than his teacher. In regard to peace, we find Sumner early in the 1840's confiding to a friend: "I hold all wars unjust and unChristian."[38]

In 1845 the city of Boston invited Sumner to give its annual Fourth of July oration. It was a considerable honor for a man of his comparative youth: the occasion was a solemn one, with dignitaries of church and state attending the delivery of the oration, which took place in Tremont Temple. Among those present were military and naval officers. The celebration of the country's Declaration of Independence during its war with Britain was usually the opportunity for voicing patriotic and martial sentiments. Imagine, then, the surprise of Sumner's audience when, instead, they were treated to a discourse on the iniquity of war and to a lesson on universal peace as constituting, in the words of the oration's title, "the true grandeur of nations." "In our age there can be no peace that is not honorable," Sumner proclaimed, "there can be no war that is not dishonorable." Arbitration and a congress of nations must replace the old method of settling disputes through "trial by battle." Therefore, war now between civilized nations was in all circumstances no better than "organized murder: it in truth constituted civil war." Above all, international conflict is unchristian. "Christianity not only teaches the superiority of Love over Force; it positively enjoins the practice of the one, and the rejection of the other." It calls for peaceful suffering of wrong, for forgiveness and love

---

[38] David Donald, *Charles Sumner and the Coming of the Civil War*, p. 107. Sumner's near pacifism is discussed on pp. 106-20 of Donald's biography.

of enemies—in the case of nations as well as for individual men and women. Sumner praised Quaker defenselessness as a road to true security and urged its adoption by the Christian governments of his day. He called for the disbanding of a standing army and a regular navy and of the state militias. Let the United States dismantle all its fortifications, too, he added, for armaments tend to provoke war, even if they were not originally intended for aggression. Let a new patriotism, which sought its victories in the furthering of peace, be substituted for one that saw glory in its country's wars.[39]

The compelling eloquence of Sumner's delivery, the orator's obvious sincerity and his imposing presence, and the wealth of classical and historical learning displayed in the course of his arguments impressed, if they did not convince, all his hearers. True, his allusions are sometimes rather bookish, and there is a somewhat cloistered air about his discussion of the issues of peace and war. But it was not these defects that worried those among his auditors who objected to his line of reasoning (if we exclude the military, who could scarcely be expected to approve). It was rather the seeming transformation of the young hope of progressive Bostonian society into a peace extremist, if not quite an extreme nonresistant, that made many anxious who heard him on that Fourth of July or read his speech not long afterward.[40]

Yet their anxiety was scarcely justified. During his oration Sumner had expressed his wish to see armed naval forces preserved for the suppression of piracy or slavetrading.[41] Clearly, he was not a "no-government" man. For all his references to the Sermon on the Mount and his citing of Clarkson and others on the early Christian conscientious objectors, he can scarcely even be classified as a pacifist of the Quaker type. And for all his oblique allusions to the Christian obligation of personal nonresistance, his attacks, like the policy of the American Peace Society, were directed essentially against war as an institution, which he defines as "a public, armed, contest between na-

[39] Charles Sumner, *The True Grandeur of Nations* (1845 edn.), esp. pp. 4, 26, 27, 31-36, 46, 67, 72, 73, 78, 79. In subsequent editions Sumner toned down the asperity of his attacks on war. For the oration, see also the article on Sumner by R. Elaine Pagel and Carl Dallinger in William Norwood Brigance (ed.), *A History and Criticism of American Public Address*, II, 752, 753, 755-57, 760-63, 775.

[40] E.g., Professor Francis Bowen, of Harvard, wrote Sumner: "Hating all ultra-isms, I only wished you to disclaim utter stark *non-resistance* principles in their widest latitude" (quoted in Worthington Chauncey Ford [ed.], "Sumner's Oration on the 'True Grandeur of Nations,'" *Massachusetts Historical Society Proceedings*, L [1917], 250). W. C. Ford has printed (pp. 249-307) a number of letters giving the reactions of some prominent New Englanders to the oration immediately following its delivery.

[41] Sumner, *The True Grandeur of Nations*, p. 60.

tions, in order to establish justice between them."[42] In a letter to the city administration six days later, Sumner disclaimed the notion "that force may not be employed under the sanction of justice in the conservation of the laws and of domestic quiet," even though at the time he hesitated to assert that armed coercion behind the law could easily be squared with the precepts of the gospel. "It does not seem to be in harmony with the views of Dymond," he admitted. "Still, it seems to me sufficiently clear," he went on, that a valid distinction might be drawn between the two uses of force.[43]

Sumner claimed—not without justification—that his case against war rested on arguments that were independent of religion, on arguments that were utilitarian, economic, or humanitarian in character. Still, it was the Sermon on the Mount that gave Sumner his moral inspiration and provided the prophetic fervor for many of his utterances.[44] His oration became a *cause célèbre*, for many of his critics overlooked the reservations he had inserted into his apologia for pacifism; and the fact that the occasion was a military celebration and not the gathering of a peace society highlighted the boldness of his antimilitarist views. The mid-forties, in fact, mark the peak of Sumner's enthusiasm for the peace cause.[45] In the next decade, when in 1851 he became a member of the United States Senate, his energies became increas-

[42] *Ibid.*, p. 7.

[43] Edward L. Pierce, *Memoir and Letters of Charles Sumner*, II, 377, 379. In the appendices to the printed version of the oration (note A, p. 90) Sumner wrote: "I think that human life may be defended at the cost of human life; in the weakness of my nature, I cannot ascend to the requirements of the gospel." These, he reiterates in the next sentence, forbid the taking of human life under any circumstances. See also note D, pp. 97-99.

[44] Sumner was well read in the literature of both the American and the British peace movement. Wayland's *Elements of Moral Science*, however, he only came upon after delivering the oration.

[45] In his anniversary address to the American Peace Society in May 1849, which he entitled *The War System of the Commonwealth of Nations*, Sumner repeated most of the arguments against international war that he had used in his 1845 oration. His repudiation of nonresistance, which was elaborated extremely hesitantly and not without some ambiguity at the earlier date, is now rather more forthright, though still tinged with a certain reluctance. "If," he writes, "sorrowfully, necessarily, cautiously—in a yet barbarous age—the sword, in the hand of an assaulted individual, may become the instrument of sincere self-defence—if, under the sanctions of a judicial tribunal, it may become the instrument of justice also—*surely it can never be the Arbiter of Justice.* Here is a distinction vital to our cause, and never to be forgotten in presenting its Christian claims. The sword of the magistrate is unlike—oh! how unlike—the flaming sword of War" (p. 24). Sumner, undoubtedly influenced in this view by the revolutionary events of the previous year, was now prepared, also, to grant the right of armed revolt in cases of terrible oppression (pp. 9-11).

ingly absorbed in the antislavery struggle. In the Civil War the Unionist war effort had no more ardent supporter than Charles Sumner.

With the outbreak of the Mexican War in April 1846, the steady trickle of pamphlets attacking war, either from the absolute pacifist standpoint[46] or on a lower ground, was joined by a stream of antiwar publications as various opponents of the war rushed into print to express their sentiments against it. As in the case of the War of 1812, the antiwar literature was mostly directed specifically against the conflict then being waged, though argument was based on moral and religious grounds as well as on purely political and economic reasoning. Opposition to the policy of "Manifest Destiny" from large sections of the North (a feeling that was by no means confined only to the so-called Conscience Whigs but was widespread, especially in New England), and their fears of an eventual domination of the whole country by the Southern sector if its schemes of expansion in the vast areas to the southwest were realized and a new life given to the hard-pressed slave system, made the war unpopular in circles unconnected hitherto with the peace movement. The American Peace Society, of course, was active in agitating against the war and the policies which led up to it, and here both the pacifist and nonpacifist wings of the movement collaborated harmoniously. Theodore Parker (1810-1860), for instance, whose opinion of war, a just war—"I hate it, I deplore it, but yet see its necessity"—epitomizes his militant crusading zeal for righteousness, opposed the Mexican War on political grounds and urged all who thought like him to refuse participation in it.[47]

Nearer to the pacifist position (though prepared to grant to governments "the right of self-protection" against actual invasion) was the

---

[46] Two pieces written from the complete pacifist position may be noted from 1845, the year of the annexation of Texas and near the climax of the Oregon Crisis between the United States and Britain. The first is a series of discourses by the Disciple, A. C. Comings, on *The Reign of Peace*, which was published in book form in Boston. Acknowledging his debt to the English Quaker pacifist Dymond ("His argument . . . appears to me to be incontrovertible," p. 77), Comings calls on Christians not to participate in war. The same message was contained in the sermon preached in Boston at the end of December by the Episcopalian minister, the Rev. Frederic Daniel Huntington (1819-1904), which was published early the following year under the title *Peace, the Demand of Christianity*. For Huntington, "Resist not evil" formed the core of Christ's gospel. "Indirectly, as well as directly, in a thousand ways, he forbids all violence. . . . The gospel proclaims the brotherhood of men; and whoever believes in the brotherhood of men must conclude not to believe in fighting." Although he avoided equating soldiers of the past with "murderers and highwaymen," Huntington nonetheless denied that either romance or honor could be connected with modern war. Let men, he said, substitute international arbitration and mutual negotiations for the outmoded method of war. See pp. 9-11, 21, 24.

[47] Henry Steele Commager, *Theodore Parker*, 1960 edn., pp. 192, 193.

learned Dr. Francis Wayland, whose textbook on moral philosophy has been discussed in an earlier chapter. His wartime sermons on *The Duty of Obedience to the Civil Magistrate* were preached in the chapel of Brown University. Wayland laid it down as a citizen's duty to refuse the command of the magistrate if this ran contrary to his own conscience—as in the case of fighting in an unjust war like the present one. In other words, refusal of the draft, it was implied, was the proper reaction of the conscientious American to a war of aggression.[48]

Some of the more ardent pacifists, however, felt dissatisfied with attacks on the conflict in progress which denounced it for its unchristian character but at the same time failed to condemn war as such. "I have no faith," writes one of these critics in a Thanksgiving address in November 1847, "that such opposition to war will ever accomplish much in its removal from the earth. It is no repudiation of war itself, but only of *this* war."[49]

This kind of censure of the moderate antiwar men could not fairly be leveled at the author of one of the most complete and devastating examinations published of the Mexican War and its origins, which, however, did not come out in book form until 1849. Its author, the Rev. Philip Berry, was a Southerner, an Episcopalian clergyman with a parish in Maryland, who was connected with the American Peace Society. His *Review of the Mexican War on Christian Principles*, to which he later appended "An Essay on the Means of Preventing War," was first issued in the *Southern Presbyterian Review* and then published in Columbia (S.C.) as a book. The publication in the Southern sector of a critical discussion of U.S. policy toward Mexico during and previous to the recent war, and the accusation of a lack of a conciliatory spirit on the American side, showed an independent spirit on Berry's part. Although he did not touch directly on the question of the validity of defensive wars, Berry in his examination of ways of preventing

---

[48] For Wayland's opposition to the annexation of Texas and the subsequent Mexican War, see Francis Wayland and H. L. Wayland, *A Memoir of Francis Wayland*, II, 54, 55. I have only been able to discover one Mexican War C.O. who was apparently unconnected previously with either a peace church or the pacifist movement. In its issue of 9 Oct. 1847 (XXI, no. 3, 24) the Orthodox Quaker *Friend* of Philadelphia reports the case of one James Thompson, a private in the second regiment of artillery, on whose behalf a clergyman and another gentleman wrote to General Winfield Scott asking for his discharge. In reply the general admitted: "It is alleged that he has imbibed conscientious scruples against performing military duty." If his refusal of service were due simply to cowardice, Scott went on, he would receive continued punishment until he agreed to fight; if, on the other hand, it was a case of insanity, the man would be discharged on a doctor's certificate. Thompson's scruples appear to have been based on religious belief rather than on an objection to a particular war.

[49] The Rev. W. P. Tilden, *All War forbidden by Christianity*, p. 4.

637

war goes so far as to advocate unilateral disarmament by one country, preferably the United States, as the most promising first step toward a more peaceful world.

In one passage Berry makes the very interesting suggestion of creating a kind of international peace army, a nonviolent world police force such as was to be envisaged by some pacifists in the next century, which at the threat of hostilities would interpose itself between the prospective combatants. Intervention by such a force, Berry believed, might have averted the recent war. To quote his own words, what he proposed was:

> . . . that a body of peacemakers from different countries, and especially from the two recently at war on this continent, might with some effect have stood in the breach, at the commencement of the war. At the peril of their lives, if necessary (though the adventure would probably not have involved great peril) they might have shewn what it is to be soldiers of peace, whose business it is to die, if required as a testimony, equally as the soldiers of any other cause. Had this been fanaticism, then, for once, there had been good in fanaticism. The enterprise of a world-police (so to speak) however few, armed with the olive-branch alone, to arrest the collision of two armies, or to perish between them, would never have been lost on mankind, particularly the nations through whose encounter they were rendered martyrs. . . . [But] why might not the parties succeed in preventing the fray and yet live? . . . Why then may there not be hope, that nations professing to be *already christianised*, should be converted rapidly from mutual slaughter! The day may yet arrive, when opposed armies may adopt a new method of "conquering a peace," and, rejecting the sword, be baptized into reconciliation at the waters of strife.

Berry, it is true, puts forward these suggestions very tentatively, fearing perhaps that he would be ridiculed as a fantastic visionary, a dreamer of absurd dreams.[50] In the meantime, until a more propitious age dawned for the realization of such schemes, he fell back on the familiar American Peace Society policy of advocating the organization of peace conventions and congresses of nations, furthering free trade, etc., as the best methods of bringing universal peace nearer.[51]

In the same year that Berry's antiwar tract appeared in print, another and equally outspoken plea in favor of complete pacifism was published by a 37-year-old antislavery veteran, the Rev. Amos

---

[50] Berry, *A Review of the Mexican War*, pp. 53-55.
[51] *Ibid.*, pp. 55ff.

638

Dresser. In 1835 Dresser, while a student at Lane Seminary, had been sentenced in Nashville, Tennessee, to receive twenty lashes on his bare back for acting as a colporteur of abolitionist literature in that state. A staunch pacifist, as we have seen (p. 571), Dresser in the next decade worked for Elihu Burritt's League of Universal Brotherhood, settling in the fifties as a pastor at Farmington, Ohio. His *The Bible against War* forms a small volume—"printed for the author" in Oberlin, Ohio— of just over 250 pages. It won high praise from Amasa Walker, who described it as "one of the best works yet published, perhaps, on the religious aspects of the war question. . . . It is a work which gives evidence of great ingenuity and research, and an excellent book of reference for any one who would examine the Bible argument against war."[52]

In fact, the book does not quite equal the earlier efforts of such writers as Dodge, Worcester, or Upham: it is rambling and discursive in many places, none too well organized, and peppered with overcopious quotations from scripture, though obviously the result of a careful, and even critical, examination of both Old and New Testaments for their bearing on war. Dresser consulted the original Hebrew or Greek where he believed the Authorized Version to be inaccurate. On the question of the divine inspiration of the Jews in their Old Testament wars, he was a wholehearted modernist. "The wars which the Bible is said to sustain," he writes, "*were aggressive*. Such as no one now thinks of justifying." Echoing the sentiments of the Quaker Hannah Barnard earlier, Dresser asserts that "wars and fightings come from men's lusts as self-inflicted judgments for sin. . . . We find that even with the faint light that the Jews possessed, they had no war while they walked in that light." In modern times, the American Revolution was another example of bloodshed resulting from the sins of a people—the American people in this case having been punished for their ill-treatment of slaves and Indians. As for the problem of civil government, which had split the peace movement at the end of the previous decade, Dresser supported the moderates and refused to repudiate public office and the ballot box as essentially unchristian.[53]

The coming of the war with Mexico, if it had united all shades of opinion within the peace movement at least on the point of opposition to the war, saw the American Peace Society once again divided on the issue of its basic philosophy of peace. How deep the controversy penetrated into the rank and file of the Society it is difficult to say. At any rate, it caused a serious upheaval on the leadership level, the with-

[52] Amasa Walker, *Memoir of Rev. Amos Dresser*, p. 8.
[53] Amos Dresser, *The Bible against War*, pp. 59ff., 116, 137, 145-54.

639

drawal of the pacifist element from positions of influence within the Society, and a reorientation of its policy in a conservative direction.

In the late thirties and early forties, complete renunciation of war, international war, of every kind appeared to be firmly established as a basic tenet of the Society's program. True, the Garrisonian nonresistants on the left questioned the thoroughness of its opposition to violence, on account of its neutrality on the subject in other spheres of human activity than war. It was true, too, that the Society did not exclude from membership those peace men who could not in good conscience accept its full pacifist platform. But the controlling voice in the Society's policy was that of the moderate pacifists led by the *doyen* of the peace movement, William Ladd. Ladd's death in 1842, however, had removed the hand that was able to hold together—by the gift of conciliation rather than by the imposition of his own will—the divergent viewpoints that existed within the Society concerning its basic principles.

The confidence of the absolute pacifists that their position had now finally become the established view of the organization is shown in the words of the Rev. A. P. Peabody. In 1843 we find him writing: "When this Society was first formed, there was perhaps, out of the sect of Quakers, not an individual in the country, who stood upon the ground on which our Society now stands, namely, that of the entire and irreconcilable discrepancy between war and the gospel. Even the fathers of our Society were not then prepared to occupy this position in its full length and breadth."[54] Today, he went on, owing to the sound stand of the Society on the matter of defensive war and its quiet but not ineffective work in bringing a number of people over to this view, its position was more firmly rooted than in the past.

But Peabody was reckoning without Beckwith, who had virtually succeeded Ladd in the leadership of the movement. While giving lip service, as we have seen, to the Society's official pacifist stand, Beckwith was out of sympathy with a position which he considered an obstacle to the successful expansion of the Society's work. It tended, he believed, to scare away potential recruits from among the influential sections of society; and it gave a handle to the movement's enemies to identify it with the extremist views of the Non-Resistance Society. If the pacifist plank were removed from the Society's platform, the pacifists would not thereby be prevented from continuing to collaborate as before in the work of the Society, and, at the same time, the broader position would throw the doors wide open for the entry into

[54] Peabody, *The Nature and Influence of War*, p. 22.

640

the Society of all those interested in promoting peace who were yet unwilling to subscribe to an indiscriminate renunciation of all wars. Beckwith, therefore, commenced to mobilize the conservative forces in the Society in an attempt to bring about this change.

These efforts brought Beckwith up against the man on whom to some degree the mantle (though not the authority) of Ladd had fallen, Elihu Burritt (1810-1879), the "Learned Blacksmith." Burritt now came to represent those elements within the American Peace Society which strongly opposed the movement to water down its pacifist testimony.

Burritt is one of the most remarkable among those rugged self-taught individualists in which nineteenth-century Britain and America abounded.[55] Born in 1810, the son of a poverty-stricken cobbler, he was inured to poverty from his childhood on. Self-help was the only ladder available to him for climbing upward. All outward circumstances were against him. His strength of character, steady determination and native intelligence, however, proved enough to carry him to world fame in his day. Having had scarcely any formal schooling and apprenticed as a young boy to a village blacksmith, Burritt succeeded by his unaided efforts over the following years in acquiring a formidable stock of general knowledge and a prodigious mastery of foreign languages, ranging through Latin, Greek, and all the better-known European and Near Eastern tongues to such exotic items as Amharic and Breton. The exact number of languages of which he had at least a working acquaintance is disputed, but it certainly ran into several score. If knowledge of foreign languages is one of the paths to world peace, never was a peace advocate so well endowed as Burritt. His capacity for acquiring foreign languages was matched only by the enthusiasm with which he devoted himself to a large range of humanitarian causes. Abolition, temperance, the moral and material betterment of the working classes, as well as peace and internationalism, all had Burritt's ardent support. Modest and unassuming, and with a distinct dislike of publicity, he continued to work at the forge long after his learned accomplishments and his philanthropic labors had begun to win him a fair measure of local renown. Eventually, lecturing and writing in support of his good causes (Burritt, indeed, was never interested in learning for learning's sake apart from the utilitarian purposes which it could be made to serve) came to occupy all

---

[55] See Merle Curti, *The Learned Blacksmith: The Letters and Journals of Elihu Burritt.* In this volume Curti gives a brief biography of Burritt, followed by extensive extracts from the enormous bulk of his correspondence and journals.

his time and energies, but he still retained the way of life of the artisan and continued to consider himself a man of the laboring class.

The learned blacksmith first began to take an interest in the peace cause around 1843 when he was already in his early thirties. His conversion to pacifism (for he was to pledge himself to the idea of nonviolence for the remainder of his life) appears to have been a sudden one. In the course of his scientific studies, which he pursued with the same avid interest as his linguistic education, he was struck as if by a revelation with a realization of the oneness of the whole universe and all its phenomena, including man himself. Burritt's pacifism was always to be centered on this vision of the unity of all things, which expressed itself in terms of the Christian faith—for him a creed of optimism that contrasted with the New England Congregationalism to which he was nominally affiliated. His pacifism found an outlet in countless works of practical peacemaking but was essentially akin to the universal experience of the mystics of all the great religions of the world. It was, however, modern "infidel" science which had given Burritt this vision, this concept of the harmony of the universe from the smallest atom to the outermost reaches of space. That war and violence ran contrary to this "perfect symmetry" of God's work, that they contravened the law of love, "the force of gravity in the moral world" equivalent to the law of gravity in the physical world holding all the material creation in right ordering, was what had awakened Burritt to take part in the struggle for peace and for a moral nonviolent alternative to warfare.

In an essay written a few years later we can sense something of Burritt's passionate feeling for this oneness of all things gathered up in the Godhead. In lyrical and ecstatic language—too flowery, it is true, to altogether please us today—Burritt expatiated on the text, God "hath made of one blood all nations of men" [Acts 18: 26]:

> Christians, hear it! hear it in the harmonies of the universe and the voices of visionless things, that commune like whispering angels with the human soul. Hear it in the music of the birds, that never lose a note to settle any disputed territory in mid air. Hear it! the night winds sigh, that have fainted beneath the burdens they have borne from the battle-fields and scenes of human butchery. Hear it! whisper the summer breezes, that go out by moonlight a wooing the blushing flowers of every zone, and sing the same song of love over boundaries that alone make enemies of nations. Bend your ear to the lily and the rose, and hear it there. . . . Read it! for it is the autograph of every sunbeam, written at dawn and dewy

642

eve on every inch of the firmament above. Every rain-drop distilled from the ocean, that patters against your window or glitters on the rose beneath, is sent to you with this special message of love.[56]

The purple passage, for all its color, is not necessarily an indication of insincerity: Burritt's whole career was a living illustration of his dedication to the cause of peace.

Burritt spoke for the first time on the subject of peace at a meeting in Boston in June 1843. He does not appear ever to have been a very impressive speaker, but his moral earnestness and the care he took in preparing what he had to say ("Read Arabic and wrote a page on my Peace lecture" is his diary entry, a typical one, for 23 May 1843)[57] went a long way to compensate for his other inadequacies as an orator. At any rate, the leaders of the American Peace Society welcomed this new and promising recruit to their movement with open arms, and he was soon elected to its executive committee. Here he worked closely with the moderate pacifist group, supporting its policies and developing a close friendship with such men as Coues, Blanchard, and Amasa Walker. With Beckwith, Burritt never found it easy to work; "he . . . felt hampered by Mr. Beckwith's narrowness of scope and dictatorial spirit," wrote a contemporary.[58] Beckwith disliked Burritt's radical pacifist ideas, while his own conservatism was looked at askance by the latter. In particular, Burritt and his associates began to feel increasingly unhappy at the spirit in which Beckwith was editing the Society's organ, the *Advocate of Peace*. They wanted to give it a more decided slant against every kind of war and in favor of nonviolent methods of dealing with situations of conflict than Beckwith was prepared to do.

On New Year's Day 1845, Burritt had confided these thoughts to the pages of his journal: "I find my mind is setting with all its sympathies toward the subject of Peace. I am persuaded that it is reserved to crown the destiny of America, that she shall be the great peacemaker in the brotherhood of nations.[59] And I think that I cannot better employ the

---

[56] Elihu Burritt, *Thoughts and Things at Home and Abroad*, pp. 78, 79. See also pp. 114-17, 129, 130.

[57] Quoted in Curti, *The Learned Blacksmith*, p. 20.

[58] Holland, "The History of the Peace-Cause," p. 51.

[59] Another example of this identification by a radical pacifist of America's destiny with the consummation of world peace, and also a manuscript source penned only a month later, is to be found in the letter of Aaron Foster, 7 Feb. 1845, in S. E. Coues's "Peace Album." There Foster predicts that in the not too distant future "the United States will inform the civilized nations that we have resolved to make the experiment of living on principles of confidence and peace with nations, and of ceasing from military preparations, and invite the civilized

talents and time that God may give me, than to devote a year or two to this cause."[60] The opportunity for this work came in August of the same year, when the pacifists succeeded in replacing Beckwith with Burritt himself as editor of the Society's organ. As a symbol of the new and more radical policy, the paper at the end of the year became the *Advocate* not only of *Peace* but also of *Universal Brotherhood*.

Beckwith, however, was clearly unwilling to acquiesce in the new direction being given to the Society's program. He was to write a little later, rather vaguely, of efforts made "during the last two years to *radicalize* its policy, and introduce such changes as would exclude under reproach the very class of peace men who have for the most part made our Society what it is."[61] At the next annual meeting, in May 1846, he succeeded in mobilizing conservative opinion within the membership behind him for an attack on the positions of the more radical peace men. First, he charged the latter with mingling in their administration of the Society "other reforms with the cause of peace," in particular with agitating against the institution of capital punishment; and, secondly, he declared his own aim to be to place "the cause of peace aright before the christian public." Beckwith failed to gain all his points,[62] but he did succeed in carrying, by an overwhelming majority, a resolution considerably modifying the forthright stand against all war taken up by the Society since 1837. Great stress was now put upon concentrating solely on the abolition of international war, while avoiding any suspicion of dabbling with "extraneous subjects" such as capital punishment. No action was to be taken which might make it difficult for nonpacifists to collaborate in the work of the Society. This work must "be conducted in a way to render such co-operation practicable, consistent, and cordial, by not conflicting in its operations with principles, institutions or interests which the Christian community hold dear and sacred."[63] The resolution was passed over the protests of the pacifist members of the executive committee. True, Article II of the 1837 constitution had not been withdrawn, but the tenor of the new resolution was so clearly in contradiction with its spirit, if not its letter, that the Society had in effect been placed on a new basis. Next month, therefore, the pacifist members on the executive committee, among them such leading figures as the Society's president Coues,

and Christian world to cooperate in carrying these sublime principles into harmonious success."

[60] Quoted in Curti, *The Learned Blacksmith*, p. 42.

[61] *Advocate of Peace*, VII, no. 2 (Feb.-March 1847), 32.

[62] Quoted in Allen, *The Fight for Peace*, pp. 418, 419.

[63] *Advocate of Peace and Universal Brotherhood*, June 1846, quoted in Allen, *The Fight for Peace*, p. 415.

J. P. Blanchard, Burritt, Dr. Walter Channing (1786-1876),[64] and Amasa Walker, handed in their resignations.

Attempts were made to heal the breach. The voting had shown that the bulk of the Society's membership, though perhaps not the majority of its most active workers, were out of sympathy with the official pacifist platform and felt its elimination would further the Society's growth. The dissident members abided loyally by the decision of the majority. They remained on in the Society, but they were unwilling to withdraw their resignations, holding it incompatible with their principles to continue in office while profoundly disagreeing with the new policy. The split was only made public, however, in December. On 17 December Burritt, who had departed shortly before the annual meeting on a peace mission to the British Isles which resulted in the formation of his famous League of Universal Brotherhood, wrote in his journal: "The division of the American Peace Society is almost consummated."[65] The last number of the *Advocate* to appear under his direction had come out with the dissidents' lengthy letter of resignation published in full in its columns.[66]

This document is both an apologia for their past policies and a manifesto in favor of radical Christian pacifism. They record their dissent from the argument used by their opponents that the pacifist platform, "the fundamental principles of our society," had proved an obstacle in the struggle for peace. "It is said by those desirous of the change, that the radical position of the society narrows its influence, closes pulpits to its lectures, and prevents the hearty cooperation of 'the moderate friends of peace.'" "We believe," they go on, "that no increase of members can compensate for the loss of the high Christian principle which alone can give real and permanent strength." After all, even governments and their military advisers normally advocate war only as a last resort. What is the point of a peace society, whose standards of right and wrong are no higher than the standards of those they are trying to educate in the way of peace? They pointed to the recent success of Burritt in winning thousands of recruits within a few

---

[64] The brother of the famous Unitarian minister, William Ellery Channing, he writes of his conversion to pacifism: "I came into the service of Peace most simply and naturally. It was in the latest period of my labors after a religious life, that I became convinced that peace was its ground-principle,—the object of the coming of Christ, the leading doctrine of his religion,—the ruling practice of his life. Without the spirit of peace I felt that man could be none of His" (letter of Walter Channing, 2 Nov. 1844, in Coues's "Peace Album").

[65] Quoted in Curti, *American Peace Crusade*, p. 94.

[66] *Advocate of Peace and Universal Brotherhood*, Dec. 1846, quoted in Allen, *The Fight for Peace*, pp. 417-19. After receiving back the paper, Beckwith dropped Burritt's addition of "Universal Brotherhood" from the title.

months in both Britain and the United States to the absolutist pledge of his League of Universal Brotherhood (see below). Surely this showed that "the common sentiment of the most active friends of peace throughout the world" in fact responded more readily to the radical message than to any attempt to place the peace issue "on lower ground." "The day of doubt and fear to the friends of peace has passed away. . . . Our minds are clear on the subject, and we cannot in justice to our own views of duty, retain office in a society which abandons the principle that *all* war is forbidden by christianity."

What they write in their statement reveals that the division between the radical and the more conservative members of the executive committee centered ostensibly on a matter of tactics rather than on a disagreement as to the extent of their repudiation of international war, which of course remained the fundamental cause of the rift. "The question between us and our former associates of the Executive Committee," the dissidents said, "is not whether christianity, under any circumstances, tolerates international war, but whether the *Society* can be most efficient with or without asserting the radical principle." For the pacifists, this principle implicitly entailed a renunciation of violence in society as well as in international relations, an assertion of the sanctity of human life in all circumstances. To refuse to kill one's fellowmen in battle and to partake, if only indirectly, in taking life by the hand of the executioner, while not strictly contrary to the regulations of the Society, appeared a monstrous inconsistency in the eyes of Burritt and his associates. True, they had been careful to maintain (and this had been recognized at the last annual meeting) that this was a private view, the testimony of individual conscience. "But," they write, "it is still asserted, and perhaps with truth, that the position of some of us individuals, in regard to capital punishment, injures the society; that men will not separate individual acts from official conduct. By retiring from office, we remove this obstacle to the hearty cooperation in the American Peace Society of those in favor of capital punishment."

Without a clear mandate from the Society the pacifist members of the executive committee felt unable to carry on in the spirit of a commitment against all wars. "It is not a question for a majority to decide, leaving a dissatisfied minority in the executive board. The society should be organized definitely and distinctly on the one ground or on the other." The annual meeting had shown on which side the majority inclined; no other alternative remained to the minority but to withdraw from active direction of the Society, at the same time wishing the new leadership "under the more lax constitution" every suc-

646

cess in their endeavors for peace. "We form no new organization to contend with the old," they concluded. "We . . . raise our voices against all war, against all preparations for war, and against every manifestation of the military spirit; yet we would not reject the aid of those who do not fully coincide with us in this belief; the cause of peace requires the efforts of all those who profess themselves her friends; but we have no faith in any principle or policy which tolerates for any purpose whatever that which is opposed to the spirit of christianity." Feeling that opinion in the Society was against them, nothing remained for them to do except to retire with dignity.

Burritt, in particular, was adamant in his refusal to sanction any position short of a total renunciation of war. "We could not retain any official relation to that Society for a moment after one jot or tittle of this vital principle had been abated," he wrote in December 1846 in the *Advocate*, as he prepared to place the paper back into Beckwith's hands. "*Peace advocates of defensive wars*" he derisively called his opponents, whom he criticized in the strongest terms for their readiness to attract new members "by cutting down the constitution of the society to their low level of faith." Where was the Society's distinctive testimony for peace now? "We can see no disqualifying reason why the Mexican and American soldiers who stabbed at each others' hearts in the streets of Monterey, might not alternatively subscribe to the highest article of faith remaining in the Society's creed, and that too, with the points of their bayonets newly dipped in human blood."[67]

At this point, however, Burritt had let his feelings of disappointment and frustration at the new policy of the American Peace Society overcome his sense of fairness. Although there had not yet in fact been any formal changes in the Society's constitution of 1837 (alterations were, however, being prepared by the new executive committee) and although the controversial Article II condemning all wars as incompatible with Christianity still remained, therefore, officially in force, Burritt was of course right in his view that the new interpretation given, with its implied criticism of the Society's pacifist-minded late executive, represented a repudiation of the absolute pacifist principle. But peace-minded nonpacifists, if not perhaps the soldiers of Monterey, had always been welcome to join and to participate fully in the Society's work. The Society had never required its members to take a pacifist pledge (such as Burritt had now devised for his newly formed League), and, of course, nonresistance had never constituted a part of its platform. Although before 1837 the pacifists had been a tolerated

[67] *Advocate of Peace and Universal Brotherhood*, I, no. 12 (Dec. 1846), 275.

minority, with the Society officially adopting a broad antiwar platform, from 1837 onward the situation was reversed, with pacifism the official policy and toleration given to the nonpacifists within it. The events of the summer of 1846 had simply represented, at least on the surface, a return to the pre-1837 era in the history of the Society.

The American Peace Society was now reconstructed by Beckwith on the basis of a general opposition to the institution of international war. The secretary was quick to point out that the changes were in fact aimed rather at clarifying the existing position than introducing any entirely new principles. He maintained that there had been a danger that the Society under the old management would have developed into a nonresistant society. "From these views we of course dissented," Beckwith wrote early in 1847, "but, if any article of our constitution was *liable* to such a construction, it was very naturally thought proper to let the Society have an opportunity of making such alteration in its phraseology as they might deem best." This was the reason for the new draft constitution which was being drawn up for the Society by the new executive along the lines indicated at the last annual meeting.[68] "Most of our late associates in office," wrote Beckwith a little later, "were not at home with us; and at length it became evident to themselves, as to others, that, with their views, and habits, and modes of management, they could not be comfortable as leaders in such a society as ours, and that the class of men hitherto united with us in this cause, would not work cheerfully and harmoniously under their auspices. So they wisely concluded to retire; and our best wishes go with them."[69] And so, with expressions of mutual esteem on each side, but naturally with a feeling of sadness and disappointment on the part of the ousted leaders, the division in the Society had finally been consummated.[70]

In fact, no amendments were made in the Society's constitution when the subject came up for discussion at the next annual meeting in May 1847. For this situation three reasons appear to have been responsible. In the first place, with the Mexican War still being waged, such action might have been interpreted by outsiders as intended to give the Society's support to the war. Respect, too, for the memory of the late William Ladd, who had been largely responsible for the offending Article II of the 1837 constitution, impelled the new executive to

[68] *Advocate of Peace*, VII, no. 1 (Jan.-Feb. 1847), 2-4.
[69] *Ibid.*, VII, no. 2 (Feb.-March 1847), 33.
[70] See Curti, *American Peace Crusade*, pp. 94, 95; Allen, *The Fight for Peace*, pp. 403, 404, 412-15; Galpin, *Pioneering for Peace*, pp. 163-67; Edson L. Whitney, *The American Peace Society*, pp. 81, 82.

use caution in the matter. And lastly, there existed a fear that too rapid a change in the Society's basic principles might cause further dissension among the radical wing, who had retained their membership though their influence was gone, and bring about new schisms. The resolutions interpreting the constitution in a latitudinarian spirit, which had been adopted the previous year, were reaffirmed as the Society's policy, and there the matter was allowed to rest. Beckwith, with the executive committee manned by his followers, mostly respectable Congregational clergy, was henceforth in complete control of the Society. Though the radicals renewed their attacks on his policies during the subsequent years, controversy degenerated after a time into a clash of personalities rather than of principles, and bitterness and heated tempers were generated on both sides. Beckwith's position within the Society remained on the whole unshaken. The reputation of the American Peace Society, however, was undoubtedly impaired as a result of these prolonged wranglings.[71]

The new era in the Society's history, which began with the withdrawal of more radical pacifists from the leadership, saw the gradual withering of its original vigor and inspiration. The process actually can already be detected earlier when the most vital peace impulse was channeled off into the Non-Resistance Society.[72] Now the organization was to become increasingly respectable in the eyes of society. It was to continue to do good work in fostering a general interest in peace, in pressing for the adoption of international arbitration, and in keeping the ideal of a congress of nations before the public. But it lacked a wider vision; it became overcautious for fear of offending public opinion and of acquiring the label of "ultraism"; creative thought on the subject of peace was banished along with the vagaries of a more radical pacifism. A hostile critic, who was a member of the moderate pacifist opposition of this period, writes of "the Jesuitical manoeuvres of Rev. George C. Beckwith, D.D."[73] Beckwith was certainly a skilled politician in organizational matters: he was in a way the *apparatchik* of the mid-nineteenth-century peace movement. But it is not fair to saddle him with conscious duplicity in furthering his own interests, as this writer goes on to imply. The latter is on firmer

[71] Curti, *American Peace Crusade*, pp. 96-102.
[72] Burritt's relations with the Garrisonian nonresistants were not always good. In particular, his support of the Liberty party riled them. In Edmund Quincy's view, Burritt was lacking in "moral courage." He had "never heard of any warrior or slaveholder, or proslavery or fighting parson that was offended by anything he has said." (Quoted in Peter Tolis, "Elihu Burritt: Crusader for Brotherhood," Ph.D. diss., Columbia U. [1965], pp. 170, 171, 187, 192, 193.)
[73] Holland, "The History of the Peace Cause," p. 45.

649

ground, however, when he characterizes Beckwith's activities after he had gained control of the Society in the following terms: "He, monopolizing nearly all the offices of the American [Peace] Society, wedded to a monstrous routine of money-collecting, editing the Advocate and arranging an annual meeting, with an occasional petition to Congress, seemed neither willing to move himself nor to let others move."[74] The American Peace Society soon became fossilized.

After his victory Beckwith in 1847 had published a small volume of some 250 pages, which summarized the new official Society position. Most of its pages are devoted to the indictment of the institution of war on both economic, humanitarian, moral, and religious grounds, such as is familiar to us now from our study of earlier writings of the peace movement. Remedies for war are found in a system of arbitration and the setting up of international congresses for settling disputes. Beckwith calls his book *The Peace Manual*; it would serve to counteract some dangerous notions to be found in the earlier *Manual of Peace* from the pen of Professor Thomas Upham (himself no fiery radical but an upholder during this period of the moderate pacifist position), which was still popular as propaganda in peace circles.

> The cause of peace [Beckwith wrote in the preface to his book] aims solely to do away [with] the custom of international war; and I trust there will be found in this book nothing that does not bear on this object, nor anything that interferes with the legitimate authority of government. As a friend of peace, I am of course a supporter of civil government, with all the powers requisite for the condign punishment of wrong-doers, the enforcement of law, and the preservation of social order. I deem government, in spite of its worst abuses, an ordinance of God for the good of mankind; nor can I, as a peace man, hold any doctrines incompatible in my view with its just and necessary powers over its own subjects. I condemn *only* THE GREAT DUEL OF NATIONS.

That took care of the nonresistants—and also of the absolutists within the ranks of the American Peace Society, who could scarcely uphold Beckwith in the support he gave to "*all* the powers requisite for the condign punishment of wrong-doers" (my italics), for the executioner and the application of troops to suppress mobs and rebellion were assuredly included in this array of authority, as was the use of deadly weapons in personal self-defense, too.[75] "This view of peace," con-

---

[74] *Ibid.*, p. 85.

[75] Cf. Francis Wayland, *The Duty of Obedience to the Civil Magistrate* (1847), esp. pp. 11, 19-23, 26, 30-32. Writing in the same year, Wayland was even more

tinued Beckwith later, "relieves it from a variety of extraneous questions." Let there be tolerance among members on such issues: "all these are grave questions, but come not within our province." He makes it clear, however, where his own stand, and that of the Society, lay on these issues.

In his attitude toward international war, it must be pointed out, Beckwith still seems to have maintained the pacifist stand against all war—including those claimed as purely defensive, which, we have seen from his pamphlet discussed above, was his position earlier. Beckwith's own words, however, are not altogether clear. In one place, while discussing the platform of the international peace convention held in London in 1843 ("that war is inconsistent with Christianity, and the true interests of mankind"), on which the American Peace Society had modeled itself when it adopted the controversial resolution of 1846, Beckwith says: "We grant that this language is indefinite, allowing a pretty free play of the pendulum. . . . We can *make* it express the belief of *all* war unchristian; but it *pledges* us only to a condemnation of the custom." Certainly, we know he wished to attract into the Society in greater numbers peace men who were unwilling to renounce the possibility of a nation waging a just war: that, indeed, had been one of the chief reasons for his forcing through the recent changes. But what were his personal views on the subject? And did the Society officially take a stand on the subject aside from proclaiming tolerance for divergent views?

Both Beckwith's writings and the official pronouncements issued by the American Peace Society under his direction show that the witness was still, on the whole, against all war between nations. Asks Beckwith after quoting from the Sermon on the Mount: "Now, do not such passages convey a most unequivocal condemnation of war in all its forms?" "If war is right for us," he writes a little later, "it must have been equally so for our Saviour; but can you conceive the Prince of Peace, or one of his apostles leading forth an army to their work of plunder, blood and devastation?" The moral precepts of the Bible, he says, apply as much to governments as to individuals—unless God

---

explicit than Beckwith in sanctioning the right of individuals and governments to use the sword in self-defense (provided its use was confined strictly to warding off attacks on person and liberties), while at the same time denying the legitimacy of its use in wars between the nations. "The one is a righteous and the other an unrighteous employment of force," he writes, "and to concede the necessity of one, is by no means to admit the rectitude of the other . . . the right of self-defence in no manner involves the right to wage war as it is commonly waged between nations. The objects pursued in the two cases are entirely unlike, and the means of attaining them are widely dissimilar."

specifically exempts the former from them. The alleged contradiction between the use of armed force to maintain legitimate government *within* the state and the injunctions of the gospels has, indeed, nothing in common with the Christian ban on war *between* states. "The former is the *government* question, the latter the *peace* question; points that are entirely distinct, and ought never to be confounded." Against war the early Christians, if called upon to fight, took up the stand of the conscientious objector, an attitude which was conditioned, Beckwith points out, as much by a realization of war's incompatibility with Christianity as by the fear of becoming involved in idolatry. His manual, from which these quotations have been taken,[76] was issued in the name of the American Peace Society and may properly be considered an official exposition of its position.

In fact, as we have shown, the American Peace Society had ceased to be a pacifist society despite remnants of "ultraism" in the philosophy of its director. It devoted itself henceforward almost exclusively to institutional aspects of peace and war, and the individual protest against war as the incarnation of violence, which is at the root of pacifist philosophy, was more and more relegated to the sphere of private conscience. With this the Society was no more concerned now than with, let us say, the creed of vegetarianism to which a few of its members adhered. Once the controversy over the changes accomplished in 1846 had died down, the transformation was achieved by silence and not by any overt statements repudiating formerly held positions. A body inscribing on its banners the renunciation on religious grounds of all forms of war yet composed, in fact, on both higher and lower echelons of men who regarded national wars of "defense" of the past or in the future as not inconsistent with Christianity was not likely to remain a focal point for rallying those who saw in the peace movement primarily an expression of a philosophy of nonviolence.

II

For a time, Burritt's League of Universal Brotherhood was to provide the moderate pacifists with an organization through which they could work satisfactorily for their concept of peace. As we have seen, Burritt departed for England in May 1846 on a peace mission connected with the oganization of his "Friendly International Addresses," the exchanging of which between British and American towns Burritt had arranged as a gesture of solidarity at a period of war crisis in the relations of the two countries. As Burritt was departing from the shores of

[76] Beckwith, *The Peace Manual*, pp. 7, 11, 147-66.

America, the two governments reached a solution of the Oregon Crisis, and tension between them relaxed. The original idea for the inter-city addresses Burritt owed to the Manchester Quaker, Joseph Crosfield, and after his arrival on British soil the American pacifist was to repay the debt by setting up in England the first international pacifist organization in the world, with a platform which pledged members to refuse participation in wars of any kind. Burritt, who had at first planned to stay in Britain for only three months, in fact remained in Europe, apart from several brief visits back home, until the middle of the next decade. Burritt's activities during these years belong, therefore, in part to the story of the British and continental peace movement. But the man himself and his approach (with all his genuine internationalism) were nineteenth-century American through and through, and the proper place for their consideration would seem to be with American pacifism, out of which, indeed, the League of Universal Brotherhood had sprung.

The idea of founding such a brotherhood had come to Burritt before he set out on his visit to England. The brotherhood, in fact, appears to have had a prototype in the little Worcester County Peace Society, which Burritt and Amasa Walker had founded in the previous February on the platform of opposition to all war and as a center of opposition, too, to the policies of Beckwith and his party within the peace movement.[77]

"We had conceived," Burritt writes, "that in travelling from village to village through England, we might find many by the wayside and fireside, especially among the poorer classes, who would be willing to subscribe their names to the pledge and principles of such an organization." Soon after his arrival in Britain, he set out on his projected missionary journey in the cause of peace. At the end of July, as he approached the village of Pershore near Worcester (England), he sat down and sketched out the wording of a pledge, which he felt should be taken by all who wished to become members of his brotherhood in order to stress the need for individual responsibility that had been lacking, in his view, in the older peace societies. Burritt would have none of the compromise with so-called defensive war so dear to the hearts of the conservative element in the American Peace Society. Instead, their exclusive concentration on the issue of international war for fear of offending someone's susceptibilities, a policy of which Burritt strongly disapproved, would be replaced by a program which de-

[77] Tolis, "Burritt," pp. 146, 171. Tolis attributes the genesis of the idea of a new international organization to Walker as much as—if not more than—to Burritt himself.

clared war on every obstacle obstructing the brotherhood of man in the belief that all humanitarian reforms were but different aspects of one cause, the welfare of all God's children.

Burritt's pledge ran as follows:

Believing all war to be inconsistent with the spirit of Christianity, and destructive to the best interests of mankind, I do hereby pledge myself never to enlist or enter into any army or navy, or to yield any voluntary support or sanction to the preparation for or prosecution of any war, by whomsoever, for whatsoever proposed, declared, or waged. And I do hereby associate myself with all persons, of whatever country, condition, or colour, who have signed, or shall hereafter sign this pledge, in a "League of Universal Brotherhood"; whose object shall be to employ all legitimate and moral means for the abolition of all war, and all spirit, and all the manifestation of war, throughout the world; for the abolition of all restrictions upon international correspondence and friendly intercourse, and of whatever else tends to make enemies of nations, or prevents their fusion into one peaceful brotherhood; for the abolition of all institutions and customs which do not recognize the image of God and a human brother in every man of whatever clime, colour, or condition of humanity.

That very evening Burritt attended a small gathering of some twenty people, all simple folk who had come in after their day's labors in the field or at the shop counter to hear the famous American speak. Burritt lectured for some three hours on the purpose of his mission to Britain and on the implications of his peace pledge and membership in the proposed League. He produced copies of the pledge that he had written, one of which he had first signed himself, and succeeded in getting as many as nineteen further signatures from his audience. From these humble beginnings sprang an organization which was to gather in members from half a dozen countries.

After coming to England, he had found that he had, indeed, underestimated the response to his proposals and that, in addition to those in humble stations of life, many among the middle ranks of society would give them a favorable reception. In particular, the Birmingham Quaker and social reformer, Joseph Sturge (1793-1859), was active in helping the stranger to popularize the idea in England. At a soirée given on 5 August for the delegates attending the World's Temperance Convention in London, Burritt seconded Sturge in expounding the objectives of the proposed League and the nature of the pledge which its members would sign. The place chosen for announcing the idea to

654

the public was an appropriate one, for his idea of a peace pledge—a "teetotal peace pledge," as he called it[78]—Burritt had, indeed, borrowed from the temperance movement. "We had but a few of the printed Pledges with us," Burritt relates, "but these were filled up on the spot with names that stand high in the estimation of the public, on both sides of the Atlantic." Among about sixty persons who then signed the pledge were Sturge himself, the secretary of the London Peace Society, the Rev. Joseph John Jefferson, and the well-known radical politician and reformer, James Silk Buckingham.[79]

Burritt continued to tour England, gathering in signatures for his pledge and speaking in private homes and in Quaker meetinghouses—in fact, wherever he could find a hearing. Nearly a thousand pledges came in during the first few months of the campaign. In the United States, too, Burritt's associates were busy in the work, and his weekly paper, the *Christian Citizen*, which was published in Worcester (Mass.), printed the names of the peace pledgers in both countries as they came in. Burritt's *Citizen*, together with the *Bond of Brotherhood*, a popular monthly which he had started up in the same town at the time of the Oregon Crisis and soon after transferred to England, acted as organs of the new movement.[80] The British Quakers in particular, who were less averse to action of this kind than their brethren in the United States, gave warm support to Burritt's efforts. Among them was Edmund Fry (the son of the famous prison reformer, Elizabeth Fry), who was to become one of Burritt's closest collaborators on the English side in the work of the League. "My right hand co-partners in this glorious enterprise," he calls his Quaker colleagues.[81] Many of the non-Quaker free-traders were sympathetic, too. Their economic internationalism often sprang, as in the case of John Bright, from religious roots.

How busy Burritt was at this time and how bright his hopes were for the work ahead come out in his correspondence. In October he

[78] "Lecture of Elihu Burritt" (1847), MS American Antiquarian Society, Worcester (Mass.), p. 16.

[79] Curti, *American Peace Crusade*, pp. 144-46; Burritt, *Ten-Minute Talks on All Sorts of Topics with Autobiography of the Author*, pp. 20, 21; *Christian Citizen*, vol. III, no. 38, 19 Sept. 1846.

[80] Curti, *American Peace Crusade*, pp. 146, 147, 156. The paper was edited in Burritt's absence by Thomas Drew. It campaigned for a number of causes besides peace. According to the statement of its principles (obviously Burritt's work), which was inserted in frequent numbers: "It will speak against all War in the spirit of Peace. It will speak for the Slave, as for a brother bound. It will speak for the Universal Brotherhood of mankind. The Gospel it shall preach from, will be the Gospel of the Millennium."

[81] Quoted in Curti, *The Learned Blacksmith*, p. 46.

655

wrote to a friend in the United States: "I have been absorbed to the whole capacity of my heart and hands in getting the 'League of Universal Brotherhood' under way. . . . I hope that 5000 in Great Britain and 5000 in the United States will have joined the covenant of peace before the close of the present year; thus constituting not only an international society for the abolition of war, but also for the abolition of slavery, restrictions on commerce and correspondence. You see that the platform of the League is large enough for all the organizations that need be formed for the elevation of mankind."[82] A couple of months later we find him writing in the same strain to a Quaker schoolmaster friend active in recruiting for the pledge: "What say you to a Peace Establishment in 1847, of 100,000 pledged *brethren* on each side of the Atlantic? Let us try for it. . . . We must try to establish a League branch in every town." Another month and he was writing: "We must say 200,000 for the year in both countries."[83]

These hopes were, of course, vastly exaggerated. Nevertheless, the new organization grew rapidly both in Britain and in the United States and even recruited a few scattered members on the continent in France, Germany, and Holland. The pledge to refuse participation in the armed forces, however, proved an obstacle in these lands, where military conscription was being enforced. The figures of signatories, fairly equally divided between Britain and the United States, went up from over 10,000 at the end of 1846 to well over 30,000 in 1847 and over 50,000 by 1850. On paper, at least, the numbers were impressive; they certainly witness to the energy and zeal of Burritt and his co-workers on both sides of the Atlantic. "A young lad of 13 years," Burritt reported, "has obtained 500 signatures to the Pledge in Worcester [England], within two months."[84] As Curti has pointed out,[85] the strength of the League on both continents lay in the simple artisans and farmers who constituted the vast majority of its membership and, encouraged by Burritt and his colleagues, made the League a flourishing concern for several years at least.[86]

[82] Letter dated 9 Oct. 1846, S.C.P.C. Archives—Elihu Burritt.

[83] Burritt to Elias Lane, letters dated 4 Dec. 1846 and 6 Jan. 1847, S.C.P.C. Archives—Burritt.

[84] *Ibid.*, 6 Jan. 1847.

[85] Curti, *The Learned Blacksmith*, p. 32.

[86] Here are two illustrations, taken from the American branch, of the way the League spoke to the condition of ordinary men and women with a concern for peace. At its first general meeting in Boston in May 1847, Thomas Haskell (see earlier) took the floor. "He was an unlearned man," he said, "and sometimes he felt glad of it when he saw men of learning and talent twisting and perverting the plainest commandments of the Almighty, to suit them to man's narrow ideas of rectitude. He had been a peace man nearly all his life; the inconsistency of

It was not until May 1847 that a formal organization was set up in both the United States and Britain; even thereafter, however, informality was its keynote, in contrast to the increasing bureaucratization of the American Peace Society under Beckwith. "Mr. Burritt's idea," writes an American colleague, "was to have as little organization as possible, employ no hired secretary, concentrate all the funds upon publications—whose sale and circulation would of course furnish fresh aid and impulse."[87]

The founding of the League had received a mixed reception from other branches of the peace movement. The London Peace Society was outwardly friendly but held itself rather aloof. In America the Garrisonian nonresistants for the most part would have nothing to do with it. "Humbug" was how Edmund Quincy dubbed it in the *Liberator*.[88] True, the Rev. Samuel J. May welcomed its appearance, but he was never too sound on the "no-government" issue anyway. Beckwith for the American Peace Society (of which, incidentally, Burritt remained a member, though he was extremely critical of its new policy) damned the League with the faintest of praise. "It is a fine conception," Beckwith wrote patronizingly, "but altogether too vague and broad for any specific purpose. It covers everything in general, but fixes necessarily on nothing in particular. . . . It is one of those vague, magnificent generalities, which for a time enrapture persons of a sanguine, excitable temperament."[89] Outside peace circles the League, where it was noticed (and it was noticed considerably more often than the older established peace organizations were now), received a not altogether unfriendly reception, although the pledge idea was usually considered too far in advance of the times.

At the meeting in Boston at the end of May 1847, when the American branch of the League was formally set up, Burritt was elected pres-

---

war and all the spirit of war with Christianity had appeared to him more than thirty years ago, as he was reading his Bible. He had always refused to do military duty, and striven to live up to the true peace principle all his life." (*Burritt's Christian Citizen*, vol. IV, no. 23 [5 June 1847].) A shoemaker from Oberlin (Ohio), where the League was particularly strong both in the college and in the town, wrote to Burritt: "I carry on a cobbler's shop here, but my mind refuses to be contained in it. It will fly away and perch itself upon the Peace Cause. I am willing to be a hewer of wood and a drawer of water to promote it. We have a few more than 700 signers of the pledge in Oberlin. I have not collected quite all, but most of them, and that in the face of the leading influences. I concluded, if I caught the sheep, the shepherds would be likely to follow" (*Bond of Brotherhood*, Dec. 1847, quoted in Allen, *The Fight for Peace*, p. 427).

[87] Holland, "The History of the Peace Cause," p. 58.

[88] Quoted in Curti, *American Peace Crusade*, p. 153.

[89] *Advocate of Peace* (May-June 1847), quoted in Allen, *The Fight for Peace*, p. 426.

ident even though lengthy absences in Europe made his office more or less nominal for the time being, and Amasa Walker became one of the corresponding secretaries. The radical pacifist group in the American Peace Society acted as the core of the new organization.

A spirited debate soon arose over the exact implications of signing the pledge. Did it savor of infidelity, as some of the clergy were alleging? At the inaugural meeting we find a Mr. Jewett, of Providence, answering such accusations. "He was," he said, "one of the most rigid of Calvinists, but he could see nothing in his faith to prevent him from signing the Pledge; and if it was incumbent upon any man on earth more than on any other to give in his adhesion to the Pledge, the true believer in the atonement, the genuine orthodox Christian was the man."[90] Did it deprive a man of the right to defend himself from attack by physical force? Was it a declaration of belief in complete nonresistance? "Many were of opinion (and some of the good peace men) that the pledge traverses the right of self defence," reports E. W. Jackson, a lay member of the Methodist Episcopal Church and one of the radical pacifists who had resigned along with Burritt from the American Peace Society leadership the previous year; "I fear that not so much good will be accomplished by the pledge in this country as would be if we had a simple pledge against the institution of war and nothing else, a simple Peace Pledge pledging ourselves never to enter any army or navy etc. etc. Such a pledge would unite nearly all." Charles Sumner, for instance, had refused to sign on this account, and some of the clergy pleaded the same reason for refusal.[91] But others were of a different opinion—the Rev. Joshua Leavitt (1794-1873), for example, who as a leader of the political anti-Garrisonian wing of abolitionism was very far from being a nonresistant. "It was a protest against war," he said of the pledge, "and every form of oppression. It was proper and necessary that those who signed it should interpret it for themselves. He signed it, as he understood it, and it was absurd to insist that he must take any other man's interpretation of it."[92] Although, it is true, "no-government" advocates were sometimes to make themselves heard at gatherings of the League, as a whole the organization—in the spirit of Burritt[93] and its other sponsors—supported the positive

[90] *Burritt's Christian Citizen*, vol. IV, no. 23, 5 June 1847.

[91] E. W. Jackson to Elias Lane, 29 May 1847, S.C.P.C. Archives—Elihu Burritt. The nonpacifist Theodore Parker, however, signed the pledge. See Tolis, "Burritt," p. 204.

[92] *Burritt's Christian Citizen*, 5 June 1847.

[93] See, e.g., Burritt's essay on "The Policeman and the Soldier" in *Thoughts and Things at Home and Abroad*, pp. 290-94. How he must have shocked Garrisonian nonresistants when he wrote, for instance (p. 290): "The State Prison has become, perhaps, the best barometer of the philanthropy of the country. It has

aspects of civil authority. Moreover, a large number of the signatories were clearly interpreting the pledge in as "broad" a fashion as the conservatives in the American Peace Society were doing in respect to the pacifist plank in its program. The New England Conference of Wesleyan Methodists, for instance, perhaps in reaction against the Mexican War which was still in progress and unpopular in some church circles, had expressed its collective approval of the pledge and advised all church members to sign it individually.[94] This was not necessarily a triumph for absolute pacifism, but more probably merely a registering of dislike for American involvement in foreign wars.

In the United States the League enjoyed an initial period of success: membership expanded rapidly, especially in the hinterland area of New England and in the Midwest; local groups sprang up; its activities received favorable publicity at first in sections of the press; the churches in many cases gave it some support. But, in comparison with its progress in England, the League failed to develop after the first few years. Undoubtedly, the increasingly tense situation inside the country from the Compromise of 1850 on, which affected the Midwest regions in particular, made peace work more difficult. Among convinced supporters of the peace movement, some, as we have seen, felt the pledge was too radical;[95] others, on the other hand, considered it too mild to be effective. But Curti points to what was the most cogent reason for the League's rapid decline in the early fifties when he writes: "Chiefly it failed in America because it possessed no outstanding leader."[96] The League, for all the dedicated service given it by men like Edmund Fry (son of the famous Elizabeth Fry) in England or Amasa Walker in the United States and by a number of devoted

---

become even now an institution of merciful and beneficent ministry to thousands —the very gate of salvation to souls arrested from the steep broad road to ruin." Of the police in contrast to the soldier he remarks (p. 291): "Their cardinal function or duty is to save life, not to destroy it; to elevate, not to degrade public morals."

[94] Allen, *The Fight for Peace*, p. 427.

[95] Burritt on a brief visit to America in the spring of 1847 devised two alternative "Declarations" to meet the requirements of some prominent peace workers in the United States who felt conscientiously unable to sign the absolutist pledge yet desired to be associated in the work of the League. The wording of the Declarations was slightly different in each case, but, while omitting the C.O. pledge, both committed signatories to a general condemnation of war, to working for its abolition, and to an assertion of the brotherhood of man. See letter from J. P. Blanchard in *Boston Daily News*, 11 April 1863. One of the Declarations is to be found printed, along with the full pledge, in a leaflet in Harvard University Library, Int.6809 (box). Here it is stated that the original suggestion to allow a looser form of association came from Charles Sumner. This may well be true.

[96] Curti, *American Peace Crusade*, pp. 155, 156.

agents working for it in both countries, was essentially a one-man organization in the sense that it was the inspiration and driving force of a single man that kept it in motion. Burritt during these years had back in Europe more work than even his hands could properly manage. Thus the League in America suffered through the prolonged absence of its founder.

At the end of 1846 Burritt had written: "Peace is a spirit, and not an intellectual abstraction; it is a life, not a theory."[97] The words are an excellent summing up of his basic philosophy of peace. But peace for Burritt was not merely a philosophy of action. We have seen that he regarded peace as but a single manifestation of the oneness of all being, of the unity of God's creation. In all the varied endeavors to improve mankind morally or spiritually he saw "a oneness or identity of spirit, aim and end, whatever may be their respective departments of labour in the great field of humanity." It would be wrong therefore —and this in particular was what riled him about Beckwith's careful paring down of the peace issue to the institution of international war alone—to isolate one reform from another, to keep each in a watertight compartment as if one issue had no close bearing on another. Burritt saw only "one broad highway of humanity" along which all who strove to help their fellowmen must go. "True philanthropy," he told his peace pledgers, "is one and the same spirit, here, now, everywhere, and forever. It comes from one source; it tends to but one end. It comes from the love of God dwelling in human hearts, and shed abroad from those human hearts upon all the immortal beings within their neighborhood; and their neighborhood is the world."[98] Thus what to some was the League's weakness, its tendency to dissipate its energies on a variety of separate causes and to divide instead of unite on a single aim, was an essential ingredient for Burritt, if not its very purpose. He was against war and all preparations for war. But a pacifist who was not also prepared to pledge himself against racial and religious prejudice, political and social injustice, and all forms of inhumanity of man against man was a pretty poor kind of pacifist in Burritt's view.

Peace was not merely negative either; it must be a leaven working in a positive fashion within society and between nations. In November 1846 he wrote in the *Bond of Brotherhood* of the objectives of the League:

Its operations and influence will not be confined to the work of mere *abolition* [i.e., of war]; as if nothing more were requisite for the

[97] Quoted in Allen, *The Fight for Peace*, p. 420.
[98] "Lecture of Elihu Burritt" (1847), pp. 1-5, 8-11.

660

symmetrical development of society, or the universal growth of human happiness, than the axe to be laid to the root of existing evils. It will seek to build up, as well as to pull down. . . . It contemplates something more than a mere Peace Society, or the object of inducing nations merely to abstain from war, or to leave each other alone. It will not only aim at the mutual pacification of enemies, but at their conversion into brethren . . . being based on the whole compass of the principle, that every man is bound to be as much a brother, as God is a father, to every human being, however deep may be the moral darkness and degradation of that being; however fallen or low in the estimation of the world he may be by crime or color, or any condition of humanity within or beyond his control. Long after nations shall have been taught to war no more, long after the mere iron fetters shall have been stricken from the limbs of the last slave, and every visible yoke shall have been broken, and every formal bastille of oppression levelled with the ground, there will be a work for the League.[99]

In fact, the life of the League was cut short even before it could witness the approaching end of American slavery. The task which its founder had set for it far outstripped its capacity and outran the enthusiasm of the rank and file, even when spurred on by the indefatigable Burritt.

The decline in the activities of the League's American branch was followed within a few years by that of the British section where, as has been remarked, Quakers had formed "by far the strongest supporters of the League."[100] (On the European continent, despite Burritt's close contacts and fruitful collaboration with the leaders of the peace movement there, the League had never flourished.) The outbreak of the Crimean War in 1855 and Burritt's departure for America in the same year seriously affected its growth. Two years later its formal existence came to an end with the fusion of the British organization with the old London Peace Society and of the organization in the United States with the American Peace Society.

What had Burritt and his peace pledgers accomplished? "A work of no mean proportions" is how Curti sums up their practical achievements. For reasons we have discussed above, more was done in Britain than in the United States, but aims and methods were the same in both countries. The scheme for exchanging "Friendly Addresses" between American and British cities, which Burritt had originated at the

[99] Quoted in Allen, *The Fight for Peace*, p. 426.
[100] Tolis, "Burritt," p. 182.

661

time of the Oregon Crisis, was continued now in the form of interchanges between French and British towns during the periodic crises occurring during this period in the relations between the two countries. In 1849 Burritt initiated his series of "Olive Leaves," short statements on some important issue relevant to peace, which the League published and circulated in the press on both sides of the Atlantic and which evidence shows to have been read by many tens of thousands of people in various stations of life. "War must cease if Christians will not fight" and "A Word to American Christians about War"[101] were typical of the titles devised by Burritt to head such statements. Now, too, Burritt, supported by the League, began to agitate for such reforms as Ocean Penny Postage ("if the League should effect this one object alone," wrote Burritt, "it would be well worth its existence to the world")[102] and assisted emigration to America, which he believed would be a step, though an indirect one, toward a more peaceful world.[103]

Most important of all, however, was the series of international peace congresses, which were held every year in one of the great European capitals from 1848 to 1851. Here, too, the initiative and driving force behind their organization was Burritt's, though he was backed by a much larger cross section of the peace movement than his own comparatively small League and the idea itself he had derived from the earlier international peace convention held in London in 1843. The composition of the congresses reflected all shades of opinion within the peace movement, pacifist and nonpacifist, the religiously inclined and the nonreligious peace workers, with only the American nonresistants staying away. The organization of the congresses represented a visible protest against the increasing militarism and reliance on physical power that were making themselves felt, especially in Europe. Even though its immediate effect on international relations was small, it symbolized a growing unity among the forces that were working for a peaceful world order.[104]

[101] *Ibid.*, p. 160.   [102] "Lecture of Elihu Burritt," p. 26.
[103] Curti, *American Peace Crusade*, pp. 157-64.
[104] See *ibid.*, chap. VIII; A.C.F. Beales, The History of Peace, chap. IV. It is interesting to note that, after the international peace convention of 1843, Beckwith had proposed to the London Peace Society in 1844 the formation of an international peace organization to link up peace workers of all shades of opinion, from radical nonresistants to the opponents solely of aggressive war who, he realized, predominated on the European continent. "We should spread our sails," he wrote in defense of this broad platform, "for every breeze that may waft us sooner into the port of universal and permanent peace" (*A Universal Peace Society*, p. 9). For the reaction of the American peace movement to the "Springtime of the Peoples" in Europe, see Curti, "The Peace Movement and the Mid-Century Revo-

In the few years of its active existence the League, then, had been very busy. As Curti writes: "The older peace societies had never begun to carry the word of peace so effectively and on such a scale into the heart of Europe. The enthusiasm and activity of the League was comparable to that of Methodism. . . . Whereas the older peace societies sought in general to convert dignified and influential clergymen and government officials, the League aimed" at reaching the people directly.[105] For the first time a peace organization, instead of being confined to a single country or even only one limited area of a country, had flourishing sections on both continents. This was an almost unique achievement in the nineteenth century.

Although it allowed (somewhat inconsistently, perhaps) a form of associate membership for those sympathizers definitely unwilling to commit themselves to the absolutist position, the League had, as we have seen, a fully pacifist pledge. Its signatories had taken a stand against all war. Burritt was particularly firm on this point. "Until you take this ground," he had written, "claim not to be an advocate of peace. O that weak and weakening reservation in favour of *defensive* wars! So long as it is made by the Christian, of Christendom, so long will that happy epoch be deferred, when nations shall learn war no more."[106]

To sign was not difficult; but to commit oneself wholeheartedly to what one may have lightly undertaken was another matter. That old pacifist stalwart, Joshua P. Blanchard, deplored the fact that many persons attracted to the League by vaguely humanitarian sentiments had signed up without fully comprehending "the extent of its obligations" or "the sacrifices which may be required to maintain their resolution." A thoroughgoing pacifist and himself a peace pledger, he still doubted the general value of such undertakings. In the case of temperance, the pledge would steel the weakening will at the moment of temptation through fear at the breaking of a vow once taken. "But in the case of abstinence from war and military service," he argued, "the restrictive resolution is in perfect coincidence with the disposition of the mind; for such service is an object of dread, and not of desire; and a man must have come to an abhorrence of war and all preparations

---

lutions," *Advocate of Peace through Justice*, vol. 90, no. 5 (May 1928), pp. 305-10. Burritt on the whole welcomed these liberal revolutions as a step toward a peaceful world, while of course deploring the violence involved in their outbreak and maintenance (see Tolis, "Burritt," pp. 211-14). See also Curti, *American Peace Crusade*, pp. 128, 129; Galpin, *Pioneering for Peace*, pp. 196, 197.

[105] Curti, *American Peace Crusade*, p. 163.
[106] Burritt, *Voice from the Forge*, p. 44.

for it, before he will consent to give his pledge against it; and that abhorrence affords him all the resolution of abstinence he requires, to which a pledge cannot add a particle of power, for he has no opposing propensity to overcome."[107] In other words, the mere signing of a pledge to become a conscientious objector in wartime or if required to serve was no guarantee that the pledger would in fact be ready to do so when the time came; on the other hand, those who took this stand really had no need for a previously taken pledge to support the promptings of their conscience. However, this argument, though largely true, neglects the genuine influence which a mass organization of such a character might have both in guiding public opinion toward pacifism and in acting as a pressure group to counter warlike measures on the part of a government.

A second weakness of the League as an international pacifist organization lay in the difficulty of implementing the full peace pledge position on the European continent. Burritt seems to have conceived of a kind of balance in League membership among the world's leading countries, by which means the pledge would pressure the respective governments in about equal measure toward policies of peace. In this way, no one country would be exposed, as critics objected, to more than their share of potential conscientious objection. As he explained: "If the League movement were confined to one country, it might be objected with some appearance of reason, that it would be impairing the relative strength of that country, to bind a large number of its citizens by a pledge of total abstinence from all war, without reference to the attitude or disposition of other nations." This, however, was the exact opposite of the League's intention. "We intend to present the pledge to the people of every nation, whose laws will permit them to sign it, and thus to detach an equal number of persons from any participation in the custom of war, if possible, in every country. This must meet the objection of those who depend upon a balance of brute force between different nations. . . . Surely such a Peace Establishment could not endanger the safety of the countries over which it might be extended."[108]

Calculations of this sort proved quite unrealistic, of course. If membership was about equally divided between Britain and America, there were probably few on the European continent, even among the small

---

[107] *Christian Examiner* (May 1848), quoted in J. P. Blanchard's Scrap-book, S.C.P.C. Archives. See his *Communications on Peace* (1848) for Blanchard's views on peace and war during this period and his belief in the efficacy of "the non-resistant, non-coercive principle" (p. 10) at the national as well as the personal level.

[108] "Lecture of Elihu Burritt," pp. 14, 15.

numbers there who signed the full peace pledge and would have been willing to carry it out in practice to the extent of personally resisting their country's conscription laws. As Blanchard aptly remarked, "unhappily in despotic countries, the people dare not venture on such an opposition,"[109] while under constitutional or even revolutionary governments the situation was little better. Burritt himself was careful always to point out that on principle the League would always work through open, legal channels. "We would not seek," he writes, "to distribute any publications in France, Italy or Germany, which would not receive the approbation of the severest censorship of the press existing in these countries; nor would we desire to hold any public or private meetings which their laws would not permit and protect."[110] In fact, however, if we put on one side the fairly favorable reaction among West European peace workers to his idea of international organization for peace, the response to Burritt's basic antimilitarist and anticonscriptionist ideas was so weak in these areas that no clash with the powers that be threatened.

Ultimately indeed, as an alternative to defense by arms, Burritt was a believer in the power of nonviolence. He devoted four essays[111] written in the early fifties to different aspects of a policy of "passive resistance": its power, its dignity, its patriotism, and its economy. For all their inadequacy, these short pieces remind one of the post-Gandhian attempts to grapple with the problems associated with the adoption of nonviolence on a national scale. For Burritt, of course, there could at that date have been very little documentation of previous successful uses of nonviolent techniques in resisting oppression and invasion. The few cases he cites are not very convincingly developed: their adoption in each instance had been due to expediency, to the weakness of the force at the disposal of one side, and not to a conscious rejection of violence as such. However, of passive resistance he writes: "Necessity does not make it a virtue in any case; but . . . its inherent virtue always makes it a necessity." It was faith in its efficacy and a conviction of its moral superiority, then, rather than study of its functioning in practice that provided Burritt's impulse here. He speaks of "the irresistible power of *passive resistance*, when opposed to oppression, either from home or from abroad, by any population or people, great or small . . . [as] a force, which any community or country might employ successfully in repelling and disarming despotism, whatever amount of bayonet power it might have at its command."

[109] *Christian Examiner* as above in n. 107.
[110] "Lecture of Elihu Burritt," pp. 11-14.
[111] *Thoughts and Things at Home and Abroad*, pp. 269-86.

665

And of a people resolutely adopting this nonviolent way he writes: "How is this people to be subjugated? It cannot be hung, put in prison, or transported, entire, or by sections. A dozen or two, in every considerable town, might be hung, hundreds imprisoned, and hundreds exiled. Thousands might be spoiled of their goods. But all this loss of life and treasure, and calamity of another species, would not equal the bloody casualties of a single battle." Burritt, of course, is being naively optimistic, unaware apparently of the many problems involved in any nonviolent alternative to war and internal oppression. But these essays do show that he, unlike many of his contemporaries in the peace movement, was at least aware of the need for an organization like the League to develop a positive philosophy of peace action in addition to pressing the negative case against war.

For all its shortcomings, the League of Universal Brotherhood had been a grand concept, a product of vision and insight on the part of its founder. Its practical achievement, though modest, was not inconsiderable, particularly in view of the powerful forces of tradition and apathy arrayed against it. It was truly international in design and, to some extent, in practice also. It appealed to a far greater range of social classes than the older peace societies did; its propaganda campaigns, too, covered a wider variety of interests and went down deeper into the populace. Moreover, however superficial had been the assimilation in practice of his peace radicalism among the majority of those who flocked to sign the pledge in all its austerity, Burritt did not flinch from placing his organization on the "higher ground" of opposition to all war and refusal to participate therein. And on this principle he maintained the League during the eleven years of its independent existence. His efforts, indeed, represent the crowning point of the endeavors of the moderate pacifists in America over nearly two decades to combine in an effective symbiosis radical pacifism in the international field and a positive attitude toward government in the domestic arena. While upholding the need for the exercise of civil authority, they at the same time believed that this might be achieved according to principles not inconsistent with their nonviolent beliefs. Within the peace movement itself, they were assailed both by left-wing nonresistants embattled against all government and by the more conservative elements who justified armed violence under some circumstances between the nations or in their internal affairs. Nonetheless, the moderate pacifist philosophy of peace with its roots in the Christian tradition, yet more and more reaching out to grasp the modern scientific case against war, remained a positive force in the movement for the future.

Chapter 16

The Ebbing of the Pacifist Impulse

The Compromise of 1850, not the firing at Fort Sumter, finally brought down the old-time pacifist movement in the United States. Not only did the decade which followed the Compromise witness a rising tide of militancy in the North (for, if the people as a whole were very far from wishing civil war, yet feeling in the North was slowly swinging over in favor of antislavery and against the South); but the conflict which we have observed already existing within the pacifist movement itself between the demands of the abolitionist cause and the promotion of peace and conciliation also became increasingly acute. This held for both wings of the movement: the radical Garrisonian nonresistants and the moderate pacifists within and outside the American Peace Society. Garrison and his followers might preach both disunion—the peaceful separation of North and South, which, somewhat illogically, they expected would bring nearer the emancipation of the slaves—and the renunciation of a federal constitution that upheld slavery along with war and police action; Burritt, together with many Quakers, might patronize the free labor movement and advocate schemes of compensated emancipation; increasing numbers were coming to favor political action and the ballot box as the most promising path toward the desired goal. But in one way or another the apostles of nonviolence became caught up in the dynamic of the sectional struggle, which was eventually to transform itself into an irrepressible conflict between North and South and find solution on the battlefield. In their reactions to the Fugitive Slave Act of 1850, the Kansas-Nebraska Act of 1854, and John Brown's famous raid on Virginia of 1859 which ended at Harpers Ferry, we can watch the working of the pacifist dilemma, the agonizing choice which presented itself to men who prized both liberty and peace at a time when the demands of the two appeared to conflict.

We have seen, however, that the strength of pacifism had already begun to decline before mid-century and that the causes of this decline lay in certain weaknesses inherent in the movement itself. The New England Non-Resistance Society, after vegetating for half a decade, had virtually ceased to function by 1850. The American Peace Society had before this date already purged itself officially of pacifist abso-

667

lutism, if not entirely of its absolute pacifist members.[1] Burritt's League of Universal Brotherhood was to wither rapidly in the course of the early fifties and to disappear altogether in 1857. Thus, by the second half of this decade (if we exclude, of course, the peace sects and such sectarian communities as Adin Ballou's Hopedale), pacifism was without organizational expression. Few new recruits were gathered in now for the cause. What we are left with is a handful of individuals, formerly active in peace organizations and now increasingly absorbed in one or other branches of the abolition movement. Aside from Burritt's League, with which we have already dealt, the history of the nonsectarian variety of pacifism in the 1850's is, therefore, fragmentary. We can, however, observe the interaction and conflict between loyalty to peace and devotion to abolition as it revealed itself in the words and actions of a number of leading individual pacifists.

The dilemma was most acute among the Garrisonian nonresistants. Their protest against all forms of violence had been an extremely emotional one, expressed in particularly dramatic form. For them, international war and civil government and Negro slavery had all three been merely different facets of one underlying evil. An army, a prison, and a slave plantation were alike crimes against God and man— crimes against God just because of their inhumanity. No wonder, then, that the passing of the Fugitive Slave Act, a measure which attempted to reinforce the recovery of runaway slaves by their former masters, in particular by making it the responsibility of the federal government, aroused the anger and dismay of the Garrisonian pacifists and filled them with as much a feeling of shame as it did the nonpacifist abolitionists. They were equally determined that this man-made law, which, they believed, directly contravened the higher law, must be resisted. That this should be done without violence was also their wish. But where was one to draw the line when it became a question of common action with the vast majority of the abolitionist faith, who entertained no such scruples concerning the use of violence, at least where it was likely to be immediately effective? Even among Garrison's followers, the nonpolitical wing of the abolitionist movement grouped in the American Anti-Slavery Society, and its New England

---

[1] Curti writes (*American Peace Crusade*, p. 228): "Its meetings were not always dull gatherings of up-in-the-air idealists who merely talked vague and agreeable platitudes. Who could ask for a livelier meeting than the annual one of 1851, when the radicals packed the house and tried by strategy to gain their points; when the old guard led by the faithful Beckwith tried to outwit them by an unannounced meeting; and when finally such pandemonium reigned that the gathering had to be dispersed? The secession of the nonresistance group and its activities show how high the feeling ran."

668

affiliate, which he still dominated, absolute pacifists were probably by now a small minority. The dilemma presented by this situation led, in effect, to a far-reaching revision in at least the tactics of New England nonresistance, if not in the theory itself.

At the end of October 1850 an English peace worker wrote one of the Weston sisters: "We are much amused at the very qualified advocacy of ultra peace principles of the non-resistant abolitionists at this political juncture. Their argument is certainly most sound and unanswerable, that all should now use whatever weapons they would themselves use in behalf of the fugitive, but the doctrine from the lips of Mr. Garrison, H. C. Wright, S. S. Foster seems very strange."[2] We may agree about the strangeness of the picture, but the position of Garrison and his friends was not without its own compelling logic, as, indeed, the above citation recognizes: in essence, it was but the application of principles long held and enunciated.

As far back even as 1831, during the *Liberator's* first year, Garrison had maintained that those who sanctioned the use of arms against despotism and domestic oppression, all who approved of its use in the American Revolution or in the struggles of Greeks or Poles or Latin Americans for their independence, must approve too—if they were not to be guilty of inconsistency—of armed violence when directed by the Negro slaves of the American South against their white masters.[3] One of Garrison's biographers has suggested that his adoption of nonresistance stemmed in part from a desire to avoid approval of slave revolts.[4] This seems improbable, especially since his pacifism predated his interest in antislavery. Nonresistance and abolition, as we have seen, were both, with Garrison, the outcome of the humanitarian urge, the great reform impulse. Be true to your concept of the right, he told his fellow citizens, employ armed force to help the slave where necessary if you would use it in defense of yourself and what you hold dear. It is better, of course, to use nonviolent means, to eschew the way of force to promote righteousness, if such are your convictions. (Ironically, Garrison considered "Uncle Tom" as a practical exemplar of nonresistance.)[5] But do not apply a double standard to your own and the slave's interests, preaching nonviolence to the Negro where you would advocate armed resistance or assistance to the white man in a similar situation.

[2] M. A. Estlin to Caroline Weston, 30 Oct. 1850, Weston Papers, B.P.L., MS A.9.2., vol. 25, no. 35 A.
[3] *Liberator*, 9 July 1831.
[4] Ralph Korngold, *Two Friends of Man*, p. 141.
[5] Walter M. Merrill, *Against Wind and Tide*, p. 266.

Garrison's position here is strikingly similar to that of Gandhi in the twentieth century, especially to the latter's actions during the First World War. In both cases, it was misunderstood by enemies and friends alike. Essentially, it was not a compromise on principle, a concession to the way of force in human affairs, and certainly not a renunciation of a nonviolent philosophy. But it was a path fraught with difficulties when followed in practice, needing a delicate sense of the appropriate in word and action. And it must be admitted that Garrison and his nonresistant disciples were for the most part much less successful than Gandhi later in finding and maintaining a balance between outright approval of violence or incitement to violence (if perhaps with a conscience clause for oneself), on the one hand, and a doctrinaire endeavor to impose nonviolent methods in a setting where they were not acceptable, on the other.

The 1850's, especially the early part of the decade, witnessed a series of attempts at carrying out the Fugitive Slave Law. However, the return of fugitive slaves encountered throughout the North the opposition, not only of convinced abolitionists, but of many who had not before given much thought perhaps to the problem of slavery yet now resented the new law as a threat to civil liberty and a manifestation of hostility to Northern interests on the part of the Southern section. The law did much to awaken sympathy among the general population in the North for the hitherto unpopular abolitionists and was an important step in widening the breach between the sections, which eventually led to war.

Resistance to the law was rapidly organized by the abolitionists, nonpolitical Garrisonians being active in this work along with their opponents of the political wing of the movement. Vigilance committees sprang up in many places to prevent the capture and extradition of fugitives, to organize their rescue or escape where their arrest could not be prevented, and also to bring strong and even rough pressure on slaveholders and their agents seeking to recover fugitives to desist from the attempt and return back south. The abolitionists were, of course, leaders in proclaiming the need, indeed the duty, of resistance to an unjust law and obedience to the "higher law" which it contravened, although many outside the movement came more and more to sympathize and even cooperate with them in preventing the return of fugitives to their masters. Most abolitionists, including many close to Garrison himself, like his friend Wendell Phillips, were quite willing —many, indeed, were eager—to use arms in defense of the fugitive, if occasion demanded, and in resistance to what they deemed tyranny and injustice.

670

Where, then, did the nonresistant abolitionists stand in this situation? Let us take as our first example the case of the mild and almost saintlike Samuel J. May, whom we have met already as a close colleague of Garrison in the work of the New England Non-Resistance Society. True, May had parted company with Garrison on the issue of exercising the franchise, and his position by this time was much closer to the political abolitionists than it had been a decade earlier. Nevertheless, he remained a convinced nonresistant and was also, like Garrison, a strong disunionist, and the two men continued to be close friends. May was now Unitarian minister at Syracuse in upstate New York and a man of some influence in his local community. How did he react to the passing of the Fugitive Slave Act?

Resistance to "this diabolical law" was what he called for in the situation. In a sermon preached soon after the bill had become law, he told his congregation: "Every man and women among you is bound, as I am, to do for the protection or rescue of a fugitive from slavery what, in your hearts before God, you believe it would be right for you to do in behalf of your own life or liberty, or that of a member of your family. If you are fully persuaded that it would be right for you to maim or kill the kidnapper who had laid hands upon your wife, son, or daughter, or should be attempting to drag yourself away to be enslaved, I see not how you can excuse yourself, from helping, by the same degree of violence, to rescue the fugitive slave from the like outrage. . . ." May urged that all men of good will were "under the highest obligation to destroy this law," to prevent its execution under any circumstances. "If you know of no better way to do this than by force and arms, then are you bound to use force and arms to prevent a fellow-being from being enslaved." Their cause was just: "there cannot be, a more righteous cause for revolution than the demands made upon us by this law." Although, he went on, he had long been known as "a preacher of the doctrine of non-resistance" as an essential tenet of Christianity, "I shall go to the rescue of anyone I may hear is in danger, not intending to harm the cruel men who may be attempting to kidnap him. I shall take no weapon of violence along with me, not even the cane that I usually wear. I shall go, praying that I may say and do what will smite the hearts rather than the bodies of the impious claimants of property in human beings, pierce their consciences rather than their flesh." And he concluded his address with an impassioned appeal to action: "Fellow-citizens, fellow-men, fellow-Christians! the hour is come! A stand must be taken against the ruthless oppressors of our country. Resistants and non-resistants have now a work to do that may task to the utmost the energies of their souls."[6]

Such sentiments voiced in another climate of opinion than that of the North in the early 1850's might have brought the speaker into serious trouble with the government, whose laws he had urged be disobeyed. In fact, it was to prove extremely difficult, even hazardous, for the federal authorities to enforce the law or to bring to book those who defied it in action as well as in speech or on paper.

May's most recent biographer rightly remarks on the "modification" in May's views on nonresistance which the passage of the Fugitive Slave Law had brought about. "He had altered his concept of nonresistance in respect to the conduct of others. At Boston, Brooklyn, South Scituate, Lexington and even during the early years at Syracuse, he had faithfully taught that man under no circumstances had the moral right to use arms to protect life or property."[7] Now he seemed to falter. While reserving his own nonresistant position, he positively urged nonpacifists, "resistants" as he calls them, to take up an aggressive stand in face of the threat to liberty and human values which he saw in the new law. Only the thinnest of dividing lines separated him from fully sanctioning the employment of armed force, such as most of his abolitionist friends wanted to see used in defense of runaway slaves.

In the following year, 1851, the test came. A fugitive, Jerry McHenry, was actually arrested in Syracuse. The situation in the town was tense. Now May was faced with the decision of either holding aloof from any active attempt to save the unhappy man from return to slavery or cooperating with other antislavery people in forcible resistance to the enforcement of the law. The dilemma was a real one. His friend, Gerrit Smith, was particularly pressing; along with May himself, Smith was probably most responsible for organizing the famous "Jerry Rescue," which succeeded in delivering the man out of the hands of the law and smuggling him eventually to freedom over the Canadian border.[8] The rescue force was able to capture the police station and overpower the officers. In planning the sortie, May had insisted that no intentional injuries should be done to the policemen. "If any one is to be hurt in this fray," he said, "I hope it may be one of our own party."[9] Undoubtedly, his influence prevented the use of firearms in the affair and reduced the incidence of physical violence to

[6] S. J. May, *Some Recollections of Our Antislavery Conflict*, pp. 361, 362.
[7] W. Freeman Gilpin, "God's Chore Boy," chap. X.
[8] See R. V. Harlow, *Gerrit Smith*, pp. 297-304.
[9] *Memoir of Samuel Joseph May*, p. 220.

672

a minimum. The action may have been consistent with maintaining a pacifist stand at large. But it was scarcely an act of nonresistance: "When I saw poor Jerry in the hands of the official kidnappers," May confessed to Garrison, "I could not preach non-resistance very earnestly to the crowd who were clamoring for his release."[10] All this might well seem strange in a man who still continued to consider himself a nonresistant, and May's attempts at reconciling the discrepancies between his ideas and his actions are not quite convincing. Wrote May to Garrison at this time: "I have seen that it was necessary to bring the people into direct conflict with the Government—that the Government may be made to understand that it has transcended its limits—and must recede."[11] But it was not so much the act of defying authority, as the method of defiance, that seemed out of place now in May.[12]

The prosecution of May, Smith, and their accomplices for their attack on the agents of government was not in the end proceeded with, despite a full and public avowal of responsibility on the part of the accused. Similar leniency—imposed, it is true, by the state of public opinion and the weakness of the law-enforcing machinery—was shown in other cases where the existing law was set at nought by the abolitionists in obedience to what they considered the higher law of helping the fugitive slave. Eastern Massachusetts, in particular the Boston area, was the center of such civil disobedience. And this, too, was where Garrisonian nonresistance had been strongest, where its adherents were still to be found scattered among the ranks of the abolition movement. Not unexpectedly, Garrison, the leader of nonresistance and still perhaps the most formidable, if no longer the most influential, leader of nonpolitical abolitionism, did not attempt to hold back from the use of violence those who had no scruples against it. He went on stressing that the Negro slave had as much right to defend life, liberty, and property by force of arms as any other man. Implicitly, as well as explicitly, he declared the obligation of those who had not arrived at the nonviolent way for themselves to defend the rights of the slave by the best means they could.[13] Nevertheless, Garrison does not seem to have been in the confidence of those among his friends

[10] John L. Thomas, *The Liberator*, p. 381.

[11] Quoted in Harlow, *Gerrit Smith*, p. 299.

[12] The same might be said, for example, of the equally courageous participation of May's brother-in-law, the transcendentalist philosopher and quondam nonresistant, Bronson Alcott, in the Anthony Burns rescue in Boston in 1854. "To my astonishment," wrote a friend (Frederick L.H. Willis, *Alcott Memoirs*, pp. 72-76), "I saw the serene, gentle, non-resistant Alcott transformed into a warlike belligerent."

[13] See Korngold, *Two Friends of Man*, pp. 221, 224-25.

and colleagues who now organized a series of armed rescues and intimidations of prospective "kidnappers," successful and unsuccessful, over the following years. He could not very well have unreservedly approved their policies, and his presence at their counsels might have been an embarrassment.

"It was . . . not expected," wrote one of the nonresistants many years later, "that action of this sort would be taken by those abolitionists who were also nonresistants." He goes on to relate, however, how at an informal gathering of pacifists the question of the propriety of accepting an invitation to take part in such a rescue came up. Could there be some sort of aid and assistance that a believer in nonviolence could give on such an occasion (Samuel May, we have seen, believed that there was) without completely abjuring his belief in nonresistance? "A significant silence—a silence which did not imply consent— was broken by Stephen S. Foster, who said: 'I am ready to go.' 'But,' someone remonstrated, 'in expeditions of this sort active conflict is expected and is always probable, and the opponents will be armed men.' 'I have arms,' said Foster, holding them out. And the impression he made was that his share of the work in hand would be no less effective than that of any associate who put his trust in deadly weapons." Nonetheless, the writer goes on, his fellow nonresistants, who may well have doubted such claims, at any rate "agreed in thinking Foster's attitude one of doubtful propriety."[14]

The passing by Congress of the Kansas-Nebraska Act in 1854 presented no less striking, if not so direct, a challenge to American pacifists than the Fugitive Slave Act had done. The probable extension of slavery to these vast territories, which the Act had made possible, was viewed, of course, with the gravest alarm, not only by the whole abolitionist movement but by wide sections of the Northern population who feared an impending dominance of the Southern section within the Union. In addition, land speculators and the expanding railroad interests were anxious to win the area for Northern economic expansion. A struggle, therefore, ensued to forestall the South by settling the territories with Northerners wedded to a policy of free soil in such overwhelming numbers as to preclude the possibility, when the time came for granting these territories statehood, of their entering the Union as slave states. Thereby, too, they would become part of the Northern economy and political system. Kansas, the southernmost of the two territories, became the main focus of a bloody struggle, an endemic civil war between "free soilers" from the North and supporters of the

---

[14] C. K. Whipple, "An Armed Non-Resistant," in the *Boston Commonwealth*, 7 Nov. 1885.

slave interests coming in from the South. The former were reinforced morally and with money and arms from back east; and in the campaign to lend them support the abolitionists took the lead. Events in "bleeding Kansas" in the second half of the fifties became an important link in the chain leading up finally to civil war between North and South.

Some members of the peace movement, faced with the alternative (as they saw it) of peace and the extension of slavery or the maintenance of freedom by armed force, chose the latter. Among them was Gerrit Smith, who, we have seen, had been extremely sympathetic to the idea of nonresistance some fifteen years earlier (though he had never, it is true, been won over completely) and who continued active in the moderate wing of the peace movement, figuring for instance, as vice-president of the American branch of Burritt's League of Universal Brotherhood. Smith, now a member of Congress, as late as the summer of 1855 could write in answer to a request for money to buy muskets for a boy's brigade in Washington: "I am so afraid of war and patriotism, that I dare not help buy one musket—not even a boy's little musket." But a brief six months later we find him donating $250 to the New England Emigrant Aid Society, on the express understanding that it would be used to buy rifles for the free-soil settlers that the Society was helping to send out to Kansas. "Much as I abhor war," wrote Smith on this occasion, "I nevertheless believe, that there are instances in which the shedding of blood is unavoidable." He was soon to become one of the most active sponsors of the Kansas aid movement.[15]

Strangely enough, at least at first sight, at the very time he was vigorously promoting armed action on the Kansas borderland and when his faith in a peaceful solution of the slavery question was fast ebbing away, Smith delivered before the American Peace Society an eloquent plea for international pacifism and unilateral disarmament. The thesis of his address at the Society's thirteenth anniversary meeting in May 1858 was "that war can be avoided always and everywhere, and that no nation, known to refuse to engage in it, need fear it. She need not fear it at the hands of a heathen nation, nor at the hands of either a truly Christian nation or nominally Christian nation." "Such a refusal" to fight, he went on, "must be open and unambiguous. Fully and un-

---

[15] Harlow, *Gerrit Smith*, p. 345. See chap. XV: "Gerrit Smith and the Kansas Aid Movement." Cf. the reaction of the nonresistant enthusiast of the late 1830's, Mrs. Angela Weld (*née* Grimké): "We are compelled to choose between two evils, and all that we can do is to take the *least*, and baptize liberty in blood, if it must be so" (quoted in John Demos, "The Antislavery Movement and the Problem of Violent 'Means,'" *NEQ*, XXXVII, no. 4 [Dec. 1964], 522, from the *Liberator*, 7 July 1854, p. 106).

equivocally must she express her confidence that war will not be made upon her. To this end she must disband her armies, and dismantle her forts and vessels of war. Thus will she give ample proof of her trust in the power of her professed principles to protect her, as shall lead other nations to study and respect the principles which have accomplished in her effects so great and novel." A disarmed nation, therefore, "an unresisting people" disarmed not from weakness but from a principled objection to war, would not suffer from thus exposing itself to attack; rather would the other civilized, Christian nations combine (by armed intervention if necessary, Smith hints) to prevent its being molested by some predatory "heathen" invader, and sooner or later they would disarm themselves. It was useless, he told his listeners, to preach peace and prepare for war by piling up armaments; it was, in fact, as effectual "as would be a temperance lecturer who should persist in carrying a bottle in his pocket for the occasional gratification of his yet unconquered appetite."

Smith might be considered obtuse or hypocritical in uttering these words when he himself was busy at this time in arming the Kansan borderers in a situation which verged on war. But this judgment would be unjust, for he himself clarifies his position in later sections of his address.[16] He was not a nonresistant, he said. "I am slow to speak against non-resistance; for in the first place I love the pure-minded men and women who have embraced the doctrine; and in the second place I have often been deeply impressed by the ingenious and strong arguments made in its favor." But, after reflection, he had come to the conclusion that it was neither enjoined by scripture (Christ, it is true, practised it during his earthly ministry, but rather from "expediency" than as a matter of absolute principle for either himself or his followers) nor consistent with the welfare of society. Armed force was essential for effective police action, though it should, of course, be used with as much restraint as possible. Nonresistance, however, was not simply an impractical doctrine; it was, he believed, positively "pernicious." "It places on the same level the taking of life in the unnecessary and wicked strife of war, and the taking of it in the necessary and righteous work of breaking up a nest of pirates"; in this way, many who can-

[16] His plea for unilateral disarmament on the international level seems to have given rise to some misunderstanding as to his real position in regard to absolute pacifism. We find him, for instance, in 1861, after civil war had broken out in his own country, writing in reference to his proposals of 1858 that his speech, it is true, "argues that the other nations would not suffer a nation to make war upon an unresisting nation. But it does not argue that they would interpose to save a nation which refused to arm herself against traitors in her own bosom" (*Sermons and Speeches*, pp. 193, 194).

676

not conscientiously assent to the rejection of all force in society will feel —unnecessarily, Smith thought—that they must also reject a total repudiation of international war. In fact, after disarming unilaterally, a government would still need to keep an armed police force (let it be recruited, though, from the best, not the worst, elements in society) to maintain law and order throughout the country. (He spoke, too, of the need to suppress frontier violence, to back "the irregular but righteous government" set up on Kansas territory with arms, to deliver the slave "at whatever harm to the slaveholder," and to restrain the slaveowners "from enslaving their fellow men by whatever terrors it is necessary to hold over them.") He believed, indeed, that no nation would be persuaded to disarm unless it were at the same time permitted to maintain an armed police force within the country. "Such a police would, it is true, be a brute force; but it would be a moral force also."[17]

Smith's address surprises us, not by the content of either of the two separate arguments against external war and in favor of armed force to maintain internal order, which are presented with considerable cogency in each case, but by the juxtaposition of his advocacy of an "unresisting" nation in the international sphere alongside the militancy of his stand in the intersectional conflict within the nation. The lawabiding American Peace Society secretary, George C. Beckwith, had not approved of Smith's references to dispatching arms to Kansas and the intervention of private individuals to defend the slave where the state was remiss; yet he had had the speech printed and distributed in both a full and a condensed version in several hundred thousand copies.[18] More forcibly than any earlier utterance perhaps, Smith's address foreshadowed the dilemma that was soon to face the old peace organization: what if the use of armed force in internal law enforcement, of which the Society did not disapprove, should eventually spill over into full-fledged war, not, it is true, of nation against nation but of sectional government against sectional government—still, war which the Society had seemed officially and explicitly to repudiate?

Only slightly less militant than Gerrit Smith's stance was the attitude of some Garrisonian nonresistants, who not so very long ago had been among the most ardent proponents of nonviolence. "Even our devoted indomitable reformers, S. S. Foster and H. C. Wright," Ballou had

[17] Gerrit Smith, *Peace better than War*, pp. 5-10, 12-15, 18-21. Cf. his "Speech on War, Jan. 18, 1854" in *Speeches of Gerrit Smith in Congress*, pp. 45-67, where he voiced very similar ideas on peace and war without, however, directly broaching the question of unilateral disarmament.

[18] Smith, *Peace better than War*, p. 31. See also Harlow, *Gerrit Smith*, p. 401; Curti, *American Peace Crusade*, p. 221.

written in 1850, "though affirming that they themselves are Non-Resistants, declare it to be the duty of such as hold it right to fight and kill their fellow-men . . . to arm and fight to the death for the poor slave."[19] Now, at the Worcester conventions in the middle of the decade, which were organized by the almost defunct New England Non-Resistance Society,[20] it was Foster ("an unequalled intellectual gladiator on any platform," as the Rev. Thomas W. Higginson, then Unitarian minister in Worcester, described him) who expressed with considerable force the perplexed views of these nonresistants hovering uneasily on the brink of commitment to the use of violence in the cause of righteousness.[21]

Foster no longer based his pacifism on the Christian imperative or a belief in the inviolability of human life, so he told his audience. "He . . . advocated it because it is useful . . . and renders life, liberty and property safe." It was not, then, on the authority of any man, however wise—indeed, "he did not think Christ perfect, and left at liberty to criticize him"—that he still believed in practising nonviolence in his own life. "It is no violation of principle, or of justice," he went on (in the words of the convention report), "to take life; but it is not expedient for him to do so. Nor is it expedient for all others to rely on non-resistance. Brutes cannot defend themselves by moral means; no more can brutish or uncultivated men." Should a kidnapper come to Worcester searching for some fugitive slave, "he [Foster] would call all the people to the rescue; and he would tell them to bring with them such weapons as they believe in using, and give the slave such protection as they would give to their own families." "The liberty of the slave," in his view, was far more valuable than "the life of the kidnapper." "He would rather a hundred lives should be sacrificed, than that one fugitive should be carried back to bondage." If Foster still felt impelled to refuse to use violence against a fellow man to defend his own life and thus to point to a higher road to the welfare of

[19] *Practical Christian*, 21 Dec. 1850.

[20] See *ibid.*, 7 April 1855; 21 April 1855; and 13 Dec. 1856. Citations from speeches at these conventions given below are taken from these numbers.

[21] Back in the mid-forties, at the time of the Samuel Hoar case, the ebullient Foster was already displaying his militant spirit. According to Anne W. Weston (letter of 23 Jan. 1845, Weston Papers, B.P.L., MS A.9.2., vol. 21, no. 7), Foster at a meeting "introduced a resolution saying it was the duty of Mass. to apply to the General Gov. for a military force to sustain our agent in the port of Charleston and if that be refused instruct the senators and representatives to come home. Dr. [Walter] Channing, Mr. May, and others opposed this on the ground of Non-Resistance." Foster, however, supported by the nonpacifist Wendell Phillips "sustained it on the ground of the propriety of holding up Mass. to her duty, to her own standard which was one of violence."

mankind, expediency, on the other hand, could equally cause a man to take up the sword. As Foster reached the final peroration of his speech at the 1855 convention, telling his audience that "he rejoiced in the death of the kidnapper, and prayed he might never go away from Worcester with his victim," he was greeted by a wave of applause.

Foster was always to be "ultra beyond ultra" (and his substitution of a broadly humanitarian and rationalist ethos as grounds for his pacifism in place of strictly religious ones was probably not shared by most nonresistants), yet his feelings were not far removed from those of Garrison or Wright during these years. Clearly, the tablets of the Mosaic law had come to replace the Sermon on the Mount in the hearts of many of the more ardent nonresistants.

As a final pendant to the story of the New England Non-Resistance Society, which may serve as a melancholy epitaph to the buried hopes and dreams of earlier years, we may cite here the letter which Charles Stearns wrote from Lawrence, Kansas, from the very center of that strife-torn territory, early in December 1855. It was published in the *Anti-Slavery Standard*. We last took leave of Stearns some fifteen years before as he sat disconsolately in a prison cell in the Hartford County jail, with the prospect of an indefinite period of incarceration for his refusal of service in the state militia before him. His fears were not, in fact, realized, and he soon returned to an active life of anti-slavery activities and reform journalism. His abolitionist fervor ultimately began to outpace his nonresistant enthusiasm. And now we find him addressing the editors of the *Standard* as follows:

> When I came to Kansas, little did I dream of ever becoming a soldier, but stern fate has driven me into the ranks of the Non-Resistant *corps de reserve*, who are to fight at the last extremity. Not until the war had existed for ten days did I arm myself, and then only in consequence of becoming convinced that we had not human beings to contend with. I always believed it was right to kill a tiger, and our invaders are nothing but tigers. Christ says, "If a *man* smite thee on the one cheek, turn to him the other also." These Missourians are not men. I have always considered that, bad as they were, they had in infinitesimal spark of divinity in them; but . . . our invaders were wild beasts. . . . When I live with men made in God's image, I will never shoot them; but these pro-slavery Missourians are demons from the bottomless pit, and may be shot with impunity.

Not men, but beasts. Ballou, who reprinted the letter, devoted an

679

indignant editorial to it under the title "Diabolical Non-Resistance." After pointing out that Stearns only a decade or so earlier had argued against Ballou's advocacy of the use of uninjurious force against drunkards or the insane as incompatible with thorough nonresistance, the latter inquired why Stearns had gone out to Kansas. "That is not the place for Non-Resistants any more than New Orleans or Charleston is for Abolitionists."[22]

At the 1856 convention Abby Foster had said: "Kansas was the great argument against us." The dilemma was a reality for all nonresistants, who were both radical pacifists and at the same time radical antislavery men. Stephen Foster and Charles Stearns, however, represented extreme reactions.[23] Their views were not shared, at least as yet, by most of their fellow nonresistants. In 1856, in the columns of the *Liberator*, Garrison had roundly condemned the action of such prominent clergymen as the Unitarian Theodore Parker and the Presbyterian Henry Ward Beecher in sending "Sharp's rifles" out to the Kansas settlers. He could find nothing in Christ's life or teaching which could justify this action.[24] An article he wrote for his paper a couple of years later gives a good presentation of his position in face of the rising tide of reliance on violence, which was encompassing the whole antislavery movement. In it he told his readers: "Do not get impatient; do not become exasperated; . . . do not make yourselves familiar with the idea that blood must flow. Perhaps blood will flow—God knows, I do not; but it shall not flow through any counsel of mine." "The Southern slaveholder," he went on, "is a man, sacred before me. He is a man, not to be harmed by my hand nor with my consent. . . . He is a sinner before God—a great sinner; yet, while I will not cease reprobating his horrible injustice, I will let him see that in my heart there is no desire to do him harm."[25]

So far, so good. But was there not some disingenuousness in the attitude of Garrison, May, and the other radical nonresistants during

[22] Letter of 9 Dec. 1855, reprinted in the *Practical Christian*, 26 Jan. 1856. See also the *Liberator*, 13 March 1863.

[23] Equally extreme was the attitude a few years later of the former nonresistant "come-outer" Parker Pillsbury, who, according to the *Liberator*, 4 Feb. 1859, p. 19 (quoted in Demos, "The Antislavery Movement and the Problem of Violent 'Means,'" p. 523), declared that, as a result of the mounting conflict in the country over slavery, he now "longed to see the time when Boston should run with blood from Beacon Hill to the foot of Broad Street."

[24] *W.L.G.: Story of His life told by His Children*, III, 437, 438. How far, one might ask, was the action of an S. J. May, who raised funds to settle immigrants from the North in Kansas, knowing presumably that these men went all ready and armed for the struggle, consistent with the Garrisonian concept of nonresistance?

[25] Quoted in *ibid.*, III, 473, 474.

this period? It was logical, indeed highly commendable, that they should urge on each loyalty to their highest principles: the "resistants" to seek justice in their fashion and the nonresistants to abide by their belief in a nonviolent way. It showed a Christian spirit when Garrison, as we have seen, called on them to see in a slaveowner a man with a personality as sacred in God's eyes as that of his slave. (Did Garrison recall perhaps that one of the founding fathers of radical nonresistance had been a South Carolina slaveowner?)[26] But when, in season and out, he and his fellow abolition pacifists preached no compromise, no concessions, no union with slaveholders, it is difficult—even after taking into consideration both the evils of slavery and the intransigence of the South, and for all the Garrisonians' theoretical advocacy of non-resistance—to acquit them altogether of responsibility for bringing war a shade nearer. Said Samuel May: "Oppressors have no right to be what they are."[27] Men of this way of thought could show little elasticity in a concrete situation; they were doctrinaires, and for this reason alone they were scarcely able to exercise a ministry of reconciliation in a situation of desperate conflict.

At the beginning of 1857, Garrison had met for the first and only time the man who, more than any other, symbolized the fanatical spirit of the antislavery struggle in the Kansas borderland. Among other topics Garrison discussed that of nonresistance with John Brown. The debate was fruitless. The two men found no common ground, with Brown quoting copiously from the Old Testament and Garrison drawing upon the New in defense of his pacifism.[28] Two years later, in October 1859, Brown led the famous raid on Harpers Ferry which ended in his capture and execution. The character and methods of Brown and those of the Garrisonian nonresistants appeared to be diametrically opposed to each other: Old Testament ruthlessness—one may almost say—over against the gospel doctrine of love in its extremist interpretation. Garrison and his nonresistant group were not told of the plans which Brown and his abolitionist sympathizers had been

---

[26] It is, of course, not at all unlikely that Thomas S. Grimké would before long have followed his two sisters into the antislavery movement, if death had not intervened. On 9 Feb. 1833 we find him writing to another sister: "With regard to . . . slavery, I should have no difficulty on the score of interest, in parting with all I own. I keep them because I have them. I do not free them, because the law will not let me, and I am not disposed to do indirectly, and by secret trusts and concealment, what I cannot do openly" (quoted in *Letters of Theodore Dwight Weld, Angelina Grimké Weld and Sarah Grimké*, II, 518). Nevertheless, their beloved brother's attitude was a source of some embarrassment afterward to his two abolitionist sisters.

[27] May, *Liberty or Slavery, the Only Question* (1856), p. 25.
[28] W.L.G., III, 487, 488.

681

concocting, and the raid came as a surprise to them.[29] How, in fact, did New England nonresistance react?

We cannot expect its followers to have been properly informed concerning the brutal murders Brown had carried out a few years earlier at Pottawatomie. They accepted without question the view that pictured him as a spotless and selfless fighter for liberty, and commendably, like many other Northerners who in 1859 did not necessarily approve of the adventure, they at least honored his courage and spirit of initiative. They approved of the goal for which he was sacrificing his life, and they condemned his opponents and captors for the real responsibility for blood shed. All this, within the framework of the group's thinking, is understandable. Mrs. Lydia Child, for instance, was ready to go immediately to nurse old Brown in his Virginia prison; her offer, of course, was ignored by Governor Wise. "Believing in peace principles," she wrote to Brown, "I cannot sympathize with the method you chose to advance the cause of freedom. But I honor your generous intentions—I admire your courage, moral and physical. I reverence you for the humanity which tempered your zeal. I sympathize with you in your cruel bereavement, your sufferings, and your wrongs. In brief, I love you and I bless you."[30] This statement, if somewhat high-flown, has a genuine ring.

It is not easy, however, to acquit at least some of the Garrisonian nonresistants of inconsistency when we consider their reactions to the methods chosen by Brown and his party. If we compare, for instance, their present attitude in discussing the Harpers Ferry raid with that adopted by them some twenty-two years earlier in commenting on Lovejoy's resort to arms, we notice a significant change. It is not so much the outward content of their message: there is the same formal condemnation of violence. But the tone is different; the protest is so much weaker; the qualified approval of a solution by the sword (deplored by Garrison barely a year before) is so much more emphatic.

Listen to Garrison (contrary to general opinion, probably the most consistent of the nonresistant group in his pacifism) speaking at the protest meeting organized in Boston by the American Anti-Slavery Society on 2 December 1859, the day on which Brown was to be hanged. In the course of his address at this gathering, Garrison was to call, "as a non-resistant," for a revival of the spirit of Bunker Hill, Lexington, and Concord to oppose submission to the slave power.

[29] For Gerrit Smith's complicity in Brown's schemes, see Harlow, *Gerrit Smith*, chap. XVII.
[30] *Correspondence between Lydia Maria Child and Gov. Wise and Mrs. Mason, of Virginia*, p. 14.

Earlier in his speech he had clarified his position as a pacifist in the following words, which deserve to be quoted in full:

> I am a non-resistant—a believer in the inviolability of human life, under all circumstances; I, therefore, in the name of God, disarm John Brown, and every slave at the South. But I do not stop there; if I did, I should be a monster. I also disarm, in the name of God, every slaveholder and tyrant in the world. . . . How many agree with me in regard to the doctrine of the inviolability of human life? (A single voice—"I.") There is *one*! Well, then, you who are otherwise, are not the men to point the finger at John Brown and cry "traitor" —judging you by your own standard. Nevertheless, I am a non-resistant, and I not only desire, but have labored unremittingly to effect, the peaceful abolition of slavery . . . yet, as a peace man—an "ultra" peace man—I am prepared to say: "Success to every slave insurrection at the South, and in every slave country." I do not see how I compromise or stain my peace profession in making that declaration. Whenever there is a contest between the oppressed and the oppressor . . . God knows that my heart must be with the oppressed, and always against the oppressor . . . I thank God when men who believe in the right and duty of wielding carnal weapons are so far advanced that they will take those weapons out of the scale of despotism, and throw them into the scale of freedom. It is an indication of progress, and a positive moral growth; it is one way to get up to the sublime platform of non-resistance; and it is God's method of dealing retribution upon the head of the tyrant.[31]

Even more passionate were the exhortations to civil war and insurrection issuing from the pen of another leading nonresistant, Henry C. Wright, whom we have seen as the New England Non-Resistance Society's leading propagandist in the forties and one of those chiefly responsible for elaborating its intellectual platform. Again, we have with Wright the same theoretical adherence to pacifism ("as to *armed* or *military* resistance to slaveholders, or to ANY evil-doers, my soul has ever resisted it, and ever must, as inexpedient, unjust and inhuman"),[32] to the most extreme "no-government" doctrines, coupled with an attitude of extreme intransigence and inflexibility in the existing situation, a refusal to explore possibilities of a peaceful solution, ex-

---

[31] Quoted *ibid.*, III, 491, 492. For Garrison's attitude toward John Brown, see also Thomas, *The Liberator*, pp. 396, 397; Merrill, *Against Wind and Tide*, pp. 271-73.

[32] Henry C. Wright, *The Natick Resolution*, p. 27. See also p. 18.

cept on the plane of a universal conversion to complete nonresistance. We have here doctrinaire pacifism without practical peacemaking.

For Wright, at any other level except that of absolute pacifism, Brown had been correct and had shown an example to be emulated "in resolving . . . to shoot down all who should oppose him in his God-appointed work." Let Northerners who were not convinced nonresistants, he wrote Garrison, strain their utmost to arouse the slaves to rebellion. Insurrection, "the torch and sabre," were holy for such an end, a duty in those who had not already on religious principle renounced their use. "Let the North cut loose from their bloody alliance with slaveholders, imitate John Brown, and form a league of offence and defence with the slaves against their enslavers."[33] A few months after Brown's execution, in a pamphlet published in Boston, Wright gives a further exposition of his views on the impending struggle. The thesis he presents is simple. Slaves have no obligations at all to their masters, who, good or bad, deserve no more respect or consideration than a gang of pirates or kidnappers. Freedom must be won by the slaves themselves in alliance with their sympathizers among white freemen—by all and every means that the latter would feel justified in using "against burglars, incendiaries and highway robbers" who might threaten them. "It is the duty of the people and States of the North," wrote Wright, "to invade slaveholding States to free the slaves, and annihilate the power that enslaves them." This was their obligation under the existing constitution, since that document had called for armed defense against aggression, the aggression in this case being that of the Southern slaveholders. "There are but two sides in this conflict to break up those kidnapping, piratical hordes of the South, called States. . . . You must fight for liberty or slavery—for the pirates or their victims. You must be wholly for one or the other."[34] Wright, then, saw the impending conflict, which he hoped would soon become actual, in terms of unrelieved black and white. That by speech and writing he had helped, in however small a way, to make the conflict inevitable is hard to deny. Probably Wright himself would not have wished to deny it.

Garrison and Wright were the most vocal among the nonresistant remnant at the time of Harpers Ferry. The reaction of others in the group, if lacking Wright's vehemence and Garrison's grandiloquence, was essentially of the same pattern.[35] There was at least one veteran

[33] Ibid., pp. 28-30.
[34] Wright, No Rights, No Duties, esp. pp. 17, 24.
[35] For May's reaction, see Galpin, "God's Chore Boy," chap. XIII; S. J. May, An Address Delivered Before the American Peace Society (1860), pp. 18, 19. For

of the old Non-Resistance Society, however, who strongly dissented. Adin Ballou from his Hopedale community had, as we have seen, been chiefly responsible for prolonging the Society's existence during the second half of the forties. Perhaps his communitarian way of life allowed him, for all his abolitionist sympathies, to stand somewhat apart from the struggle, to view it in a larger perspective, and to give deeper consideration to the issues of principle involved. The attitude of Garrison and the other nonresistants toward Brown surprised and profoundly shocked Ballou. That the nonpacifist abolitionists should rejoice in Brown's exploits seemed understandable to him, but he was pained by the degree of approval given by opponents of all violence who had been for many years his colleagues in the work of the New England Non-Resistance Society. The spectacle of nonresistants, he writes, vying "with avowed pro-war men in paying homage to one whom I could regard only as a well-meaning, misguided, unfortunate zealot," was saddening. "As for me, I remained unmoved, except by sorrow for such a deplorable exhibition of mistaken ambition to promote a good end by evil means, and pity for the sufferer who had rashly plunged into a lion's den." Ballou's criticisms, which he published in his community journal, the *Practical Christian*, had no effect, however, in moderating the standpoint of Garrison and his friends.[36] The stance they had taken up in the late fifties did not change substantially after the conflict had blown up into the storm of war.

Sarah Grimké, see Benjamin P. Thomas, *Theodore Weld*, p. 237. Stephen S. Foster, who still claimed to be a nonresistant—"but not . . . a fool" (*Autobiography of Adin Ballou*, p. 419)—considered that "Brown has shown himself *a man* in comparison with the Non-Resistants," because the latter had "never been baptized into the sufferings of the slave" (*Practical Christian*, vol. XX, no. 16, 26 Nov. 1859).

[36] *Autobiography of Adin Ballou*, pp. 416-22; *Practical Christian*, vol. XX, nos. 16, 17. "We . . . appeal from the William Lloyd Garrison of to-day, to the William Lloyd Garrison of former years," wrote Ballou.

Part IV

Pacifism in the
American Civil War

"While we mourn the destruction of human life, and the sad consequences ever attendant upon a state of war, and while we cannot regard carnal warfare as pertaining to the Kingdom of Christ, we desire to impart to you our heartfelt rejoicing that millions of our fellow-beings have, by the power of Him who overrules the purposes of men, been released from cruel bondage."

—From an address sent to President Andrew Johnson by Philadelphia Yearly Meeting (Hicksite), 19 May 1865.

Chapter 17

The Civil War and the Antebellum Pacifists

The outbreak of hostilities between North and South in April 1861 faced the older peace movement with a crisis of conscience of the first magnitude. The friends of peace supporting a war—this seemed to make a mockery of what they had been preaching year in, year out over the previous half century. And yet for many reasons, quite apart from the pressure of public opinion on a small minority in the direction of conformity, peace workers of varying views were drawn toward a full or at least qualified endorsement of the Unionist war effort.

In the first place, the organized peace movement was confined entirely to the North; as we have seen, its efforts to gain entry into the South had been short-lived and ineffectual. It therefore shared, however much its members might differ in their views on peace and war with the majority of the population, in the general ethos of the North, in its social attitudes, its prejudices, preconceptions, and enthusiasms. It was part of the North; the South was an alien land. Secondly, most peace workers, not only the Garrisonian nonresistants and the more moderate pacifists but the middle-of-the-road and the conservative nonpacifists among them, sympathized to a greater or less degree with the abolitionist cause. Antislavery had become for them the most important aspect of that general humanitarian urge of early nineteenth-century America, from which both abolition and pacifism had originated. Thus, even Henry C. Wright's theorem—"MAN-KILLING is the basis of MAN-STEALING"; therefore, as an abolitionist I must be a nonresistant[1]—might easily be reversed to run: man-stealing is the basis of man-killing; therefore, the destruction of slavery, by whatever means, must precede the establishment of peace.[2] By 1861 the antislavery argument would certainly act as simply and quickly in favor of war with those peace men who did not hold to the inviolability of human life as with the nonresistants—and probably more quickly. Thirdly, there was no longer—in fact, there had not really been for almost a decade—an effective focus for radical pacifism. The American Peace Society, whatever the exact wording of its constitu-

[1] Henry C. Wright, *The Natick Resolution*, p. 27.

[2] Cf. Gerrit Smith: "When slavery is gone from the whole world, the whole world will then be freed not only from a source of war, but from the most cruel and horrid form of war. For slavery is war as well as the source of war" (quoted in Merle E. Curti, *Peace or War*, p. 54).

689

tion might be, had abandoned its stand against all war, and the pacifists were by now a small and powerless minority among its members. The whole peace movement, indeed, had lost its vitality. It had ceased to attract the young and the enthusiastic (few new names appear, for instance, either on the roster of the active Garrisonian nonresistants or among the more moderate peace men during this period). It had, of course, no sympathy with the political antiwar movement, which was to spring up as a result of war weariness or from latent sympathy with the Confederate cause. On the other hand, it proved itself incapable of generating a genuine and effective protest movement of its own, directed not against the ends for which the war was ostensibly being fought but against war as such.

Although the American Peace Society had publicly deplored the use of force on the occasion of Brown's attack on Harpers Ferry[3] and had continued to plead for a peaceful solution of the crisis right up to the outbreak of hostilities in 1861, it rallied to the support of the Northern war effort as soon as fighting began.[4] One member of the small pacifist group still left within the Society, Joshua P. Blanchard, now in his eighties, has given us an eyewitness account of the debates at its annual meeting in May 1861.[5] Participants could be grouped under three headings, he says: nonmembers who came in large numbers to observe the reaction of a peace society to the coming of war; a majority (as it turned out, perhaps not surprisingly) of members who had abandoned their opposition to war; and a handful who still hoped that the Society, whatever personal differences of opinion might exist within it concerning the justifiability of the present conflict, would confirm its stand, hitherto official, against all war. "The course of the Society, on that occasion," Blanchard relates, "was a surprise to all: a stranger, unapprised of the purpose of the meeting, would have supposed it for the vindication of war, rather than that of peace." The argument of the pro-war majority was simply that the conflict, which had broken out between the government and the Southern states ("the domestic traitors and pirates who are at work to overthrow it," Gerrit Smith called their leaders),[6] did not come under the heading of war and that, therefore, it did not come under the ban of the Society. It was a rebellion, and the suppression of rebellion was a legitimate task of government

[3] Curti (*American Peace Crusade*, p. 222) suggests that the statement issued to this effect by the American Peace Society was the result of the temporary influence of the pacifist J. P. Blanchard during a serious illness of the secretary, George C. Beckwith.

[4] See Curti, *Peace or War*, pp. 52-55.

[5] *Liberator*, 25 Sept. 1861.

[6] *Sermons and Speeches of Gerrit Smith*, p. 192.

and should have the full backing of the Society.[7] If the use of armed force to put down the rebels were contrary to Christianity, wrote the *Advocate of Peace*,[8] "then all real, effective government is wrong, and society must be abandoned to a remediless, everlasting anarchy."

Throughout the war and on into the peace years, Beckwith and the leadership of the Society continued to maintain that it had not in fact abandoned the stand taken by Article II of the 1837 constitution against all war (that is, they added, all international war) and that absolute pacifists, along with believers in defensive war, might still find a niche in an organization which officially stood about midway between these two positions. War is war between nations: civil war is not war but police action.[9] There is, one cannot help feeling, nevertheless something sophistical in such reasoning. In such a situation, the rejection of pacifism ("the anti-war and anti-army principles of our Society," in the words of Gerrit Smith)[10] would have commanded respect: to support war and pacifism showed neither clear thinking nor intellectual integrity. The Society undoubtedly lost the esteem of many outside peace circles for its lack of consistency in the hour of crisis. It would, indeed, have been better if the Society had modified its official stand to match its actual performance. As Blanchard noted: "'All war' includes civil war as well as foreign war, and, most certainly, civil war is as inconsistent as foreign with Christianity and exerts as baleful an influence." The present fighting was, he added, "a war of regions, rather than parties, like any foreign war."[11] War fever had swamped the American Peace Society to such an extent that its leaders were no longer able to discern the occurrence of war, the social evil which it was their whole reason for existence to fight, when it finally came to the American nation.

The coming of war, indeed, witnessed a flight from the peace camp of a large number of the stalwarts of the old peace movement and hesitations and doubts on the part of others, who eventually decided, for all their sympathy for many of the Northern war aims, to maintain their pacifist witness. When, for instance, old Blanchard wrote to all surviving signatories of the declarations of associate membership of Burritt's League of Universal Brotherhood (see p. 659, n. 95), inquiring whether they considered that the pledge against war given then ap-

[7] However, calling on both sides to avoid the arbitrament of arms and its attendant miseries, the *Advocate of Peace* in its March-April 1861 issue (vol. XIII) had used the significant phrase "civil war" (p. 201). It was not to appear again in its columns—at least with the editor's endorsement.

[8] Sept.-Oct. 1861, XIII, 298.

[9] See Edson L. Whitney, *The American Peace Society*, chap. XIV.

[10] *Sermons and Speeches*, p. 194.

[11] *Liberator*, 25 Sept. 1861.

plied to the present situation, only two answered in the affirmative.[12]

The argument that the fighting was not really war, but simply police action, appears to have made the transition from pacifism to belligerency easier for many in the peace movement. Listen, for example, to the Rev. A. P. Peabody, now Professor of Christian Morals at Harvard, whose conversion as a young and unknown Unitarian minister to absolute pacifism in the mid-thirties we have described earlier. For him now, the conflict "had none of the moral characteristics of a war. It was rather a vast police-movement for the suppression and punishment of multitudinous crime, justified by the same law of self-preservation which would arm the ministers of the State against a body of brigands. It was a sad necessity." He admits that it had all the forms of war, "all its horrors and sufferings; it must bear that name in history." But it was unavoidable, and, whatever the deeper causes of conflict, "those who are forced into it are blameless."[13]

Let us take one further example, one of the most striking, in fact, but not untypical—again from the Unitarian camp. The Rev. W. H. Furness (1802-1896) was the respected minister of the First Unitarian Church in Philadelphia and, on the very eve of war, a convinced non-resistant. Preaching in Boston in March 1860, not long after Harpers Ferry and in the pulpit of John Brown's militant supporter, Theodore Parker, he took as his text, "Put up thy sword into the sheath" [John 18:11]. He compared the nonviolent way of Christ and his apostles even unto death with the method of Brown and his followers in meeting the terrible crime of slavery. True, Brown was a man of courage, and a Christian could not be neutral or wash his hands of evil. What, therefore, were Christians in the North to do in face of the wrongs done to the slave? We must rely on the effectiveness of truth alone, Furness answers; it will finally conquer. To take this path may require more courage than armed resistance. But if we take up the sword in defense of liberty, we may soon find it impossible to draw a line between defense and aggression. A surer, even if perhaps slower, method of overcoming evil was the Christian way of nonresistance carried out in a spirit of love and readiness to sacrifice even life itself in the cause of peace.[14]

The outbreak of war led seemingly to a complete transformation in Furness's thinking. "This war plays the deuce with peace principles," he confided to his fellow Unitarian, Moncure D. Conway, early in

---

[12] Letter in *Boston Daily Courier*, 11 April 1863. See Curti, *Peace or War*, pp. 59, 60.

[13] A. P. Peabody, *Lessons from Our Late Rebellion*, pp. 2, 3.

[14] W. H. Furness, *Put up Thy Sword, passim*.

May 1861.[15] In a discourse given in September 1862 to console the kindred of those who had fallen in battle, he raises a paean in praise of the Northern war cause. The tone of exaltation, the chiliastic note that pervades the whole discourse, is perhaps more reminiscent of a late medieval sectary than a nineteenth-century Unitarian. "Words cannot tell," he says, "the benefits that are to accrue from these generous self-sacrifices. . . . The blood of these Northern freemen is the blood of a new covenant which our country is making with Liberty, with Righteousness, with God." God is binding the North together in ever closer ties of Christian love and fraternal fellowship. The war is ushering in a wonderful new age, a golden age of freedom for all mankind.[16]

As Curti has aptly said: "By its very nature a civil war is a severer test of pacifism than a foreign war, particularly when it is associated with purposes or alleged purposes demanding from idealists some measure of loyalty."[17] Maintenance of the Union and the freeing of the slave were purposes which (if we except the extreme nonresistants' advocacy of disunion) most pacifists held dear. The reaction of men like Peabody and Furness showed that, when faced—as in the present crisis—with the necessity of choosing, their pacifism took second place.

An interesting example of the other sort, where loyalty to the peace cause over three decades finally won out against devotion to abolition and the Union, is the case of Amasa Walker. We have met Walker in the forties as one of the leaders of the absolute pacifist wing of the American Peace Society and later as a close collaborator with Burritt in the American branch of the League of Universal Brotherhood.

In 1859 Walker had published an interesting little satire on war preparations as a method of national defense entitled *Le Monde; or In Time of Peace Prepare for War*, which put succinctly, in the form of an allegory, the pacifist case against armaments. In his story, the peace and harmony of a group of families shipwrecked on an uninhabited island is spoiled when one family begins to arm itself with swords "in self-defence." It is followed by the other families on the island, and from swords they proceed to rifles and then to cannon. The arms race is at last halted by the doubts of one young man who asks: "Is not

---

[15] Letter dated 7 May 1861, quoted in James M. McPherson, *The Struggle for Equality*, p. 52. This study throws considerable light on the wartime and postwar activities and attitudes not only of Garrison himself but of a number of other leading nonresistants: Maria W. Chapman, Lydia M. Child, Stephen and Abby Foster, Oliver Johnson, Samuel J. May, Parker Pillsbury, Edmund Quincy, Charles Stearns, Angelina Weld, Charles K. Whipple, and Henry C. Wright.

[16] Furness, *A Word of Consolation*, esp. pp. 5-7, 12.

[17] Curti, "Poets of Peace and the Civil War," *World Unity*, X, no. 3 (June 1932), 150.

the whole system of arming against each other an absurdity, father?" And he succeeds in persuading the islanders to throw away their weapons and to use the method of conference instead in cases of dispute: "Wonderful, truly, are the results of this abandonment of preparations for self-defence," admits in the end the man who had begun the whole process of arming.[18] The pamphlet was published in both England and America by the respective peace societies and proved an effective piece of propaganda for the peace cause.

A solid citizen, a well-to-do banker, and a prominent figure in the public life of Massachusetts, a man averse to the extremism of non-resistance, Walker at the opening of the war had been caught up in the tide of war enthusiasm and brought to doubt the validity of pacifism in the existing situation, if it meant compromise with slavery as the only alternative to war. His wavering alarmed Elihu Burritt, whose own firmly anchored peace witness apparently remained unshaken throughout the struggle. "He is my dearest friend on this side of the water," wrote Burritt on 26 May 1861 to the secretary of the London Peace Society, the Rev. Henry Richard (1812-1888). He went on to speak of "the insidious drifting that has carried nearly all our peace friends into the wake of this war. It has indeed been a sifting time here. I have been saddened and amazed at the spectacle. Men who we thought stood strong and firm upon the rock, have been washed away. I have almost trembled for dear Walker. His nature is warm and impulsive, and all his sympathies run out so exuberantly for a struggle for freedom versus Slavery. His son is an adjutant general in the army, and every influence works to wash him into the rushing current of popular sentiment."[19] Nevertheless, despite a strong emotional pull initially toward support of the war, Walker decided not to abandon his pacifism, and on several occasions during the course of hostilities he spoke out fearlessly in its behalf.

In this same letter to Henry Richard we can feel Burritt's sense of disillusionment with the orthodox peace movement and his frustration at being unable to make an effective protest against the prosecution of the war.

The great trouble with professed friends of peace here, is the habit of working up fictitious premises, then building an argument and a policy upon them. Mr. Beckwith in the Advocate, has done a great deal to commit the Peace Society to this quicksand footing. He has assumed from the beginning that this terrible conflict, in which each party is arraying 500,000 armed men against the other, is not

[18] Amasa Walker, *Le Monde*, pp. 10, 23, and *passim*.
[19] Quoted in Curti, *The Learned Blacksmith*, pp. 138, 139. See also Curti, *Peace or War*, pp. 50, 51.

694

war but quelling a mob on the part of the Federal Government, that the Northern army of half a million is only a sheriff's *posse* called out to put down an organisation of riotous individuals. I feel that this sophistry and position have shorn the locks of the Society of all the strength of principle; and I have been saddened to silence. I fear that 49 in a hundred of all the *Quakers* in America have drifted from their moorings in this storm of passion or indignation. This is truly a *trial hour*. All the ministers of the gospel, the religious press, all classes of the community have been swept into the current. I have felt distressed at my inability to put forth a feather's weight of influence against the war spirit. . . . The position taken by the Advocate of Peace completely nullifies that as an exponent of our fundamental principles, and there is no possibility of getting a hearing of a public audience for views adverse to the war. . . . I feel I have gone as far as I could, without exposing myself to arrest, in opposing the war; I feel powerless and almost alone. Dear old Father *Blanchard* stands strong as a mountain of iron, and I hope there are a few scattered through the country who hold steadfastly to our principles.[20]

If the maintenance of the Union and the desire to back the government to the hilt in its struggle with the Southern secessionists had ranged the American Peace Society officially behind the Northern war effort and had rallied to it almost all former peace men associated with the Society in some way (apart from a few scattered individuals powerless now to express their dissent in any effective way), then what of the radical nonresistants? With all their passionate (some would say mistaken) zeal for the cause of the Southern slave, had they not called for "disunion" long before the South had seriously meant secession? Could "no-government" men, who had renounced the United States Constitution and denounced all its works, be overly concerned with upholding the authority of the state against disrupters?

On 16 July 1861 an Irish Quaker wrote to one of the original founding members of the New England Non-Resistance Society: "I own that the outbreak of this war in America has caused me many surprises. I wonder greatly at the unreserved exultation on the part of many out and out friends of nonresistance among the abolitionists at the opening of a long and bloody struggle. I don't wonder that they should be glad at the prospect of the overthrow of slavery at almost any price; but I am surprised that it is such unqualified gratification."[21] Some of the

[20] *Ibid.*, pp. 139, 140. See also Curti, *Peace or War*, p. 50.
[21] Richard D. Webb to Anne W. Weston, 16 July 1861, Weston Papers, B.P.L., MS A.9.2., vol. 30, no. 70.

New England nonresistants had by this time already abandoned their pacifism; others, though not formally abandoning nonresistance, now put it aside for the duration. This seems to have been more or less the position of Henry C. Wright, whose peregrinations we have watched from the most fervid apostleship for nonviolence to the most rabid incitement to slave revolt and civil war, while all the time he still maintained, however uneasily, his personal pacifism. The Grimké sisters went further and gave the war unlimited support without any reservations of conscience. "You see how warlike I have become," wrote Angelina (now Mrs. Theodore Weld, of course) to Gerrit Smith toward the end of 1862, "O, yes—war is better than slavery."[22] A couple of years later her sister Sarah in a letter to Garrison grew almost lyrical in describing the benefits the war would bring to both white and black: "This blessed war is working out the salvation of the Anglo-Saxon as well as of the African race. The eyes of the nation are being anointed with the eye-salve of the King of heaven. . . . This war, the holiest ever waged, is emphatically God's war."[23] The Grimké sisters' old colleague in both the abolitionist and the nonresistant causes, Mrs. Lydia M. Child, was almost as militant. "I abhor war," she wrote to the abolitionist Congressman George W. Julian in June 1862, "and

[22] Quoted in Benjamin P. Thomas, *Theodore Weld*, p. 245. However, the Welds' son, Charles Stuart Faucherand Weld (1839-1901), then a student at Harvard, chose to take the stand of a C.O.—obviously to the distress of his father, who had hoped "a sense of duty" would lead his son at least to allow him to hire a substitute to fight for freedom in Charles's place. "All I have to say on the point is this," Charles answered indignantly (letter dated 2 June 1862, Weld-Grimké Papers, William L. Clements Library, University of Michigan). "I must request you if the conscription takes place to let the law take its course. . . . I should much regret that I was even the *indirect* means of sending one more man to fight in what I regard as an unjust cause and very possibly to be thanklessly and mercilessly slaughtered." He contested his father's legal right to make payment without his own prior agreement; he stressed his unwillingness to escape arrest if that were the consequence of his refusal to fight. If his father paid, Charles went on, "I shall feel in duty bound to see the U.S. officers and tell them *how the case stands*. I should feel mean if I did not. They shall know that I am not such a coward that though supporting the war I refuse to fight or that condemning the war as I do I can for an instant consent to escape the penalty of a refusal." In the fall of the same year, when it was rumored that Harvard was to introduce compulsory drilling for the students, Charles wrote to his father (letter dated 25 Sept. 1862): "I hope on your account the whole matter may fall through so that at all events there will be no requisition about it. I confess father I am astonished that you do not regard my view respecting this matter as correct." To comply would be equivalent to approval of the war and a seeming readiness to fight if called upon to do so. "This would be a deception, a false promise, a lie, and I can have nothing to do with it." (See also Thomas, *Weld*, p. 239.) The correspondence is tantalizingly fragmentary. One would like to know the precise grounds for Charles's pacifism (seemingly a selective objection), how far it was the fruit of his mother's former nonresistant faith, and what her reactions to her son's stand were now.
[23] *Liberator*, 15 Jan. 1864.

696

have the greatest dread of military supremacy; yet I have become so desperate with hope—deferred, that a hurra goes up from my heart, when the army rises to carry out God's laws. . . . I am convinced that this is the great battle of Armageddon between the Angels of Freedom and the Demons of Despotism."[24] Other former nonresistants were carried along, too, like the Grimké sisters and Mrs. Child, into full approval of the war method.[25]

What of Garrison himself and his closest associates among the nonresistants? It would lead us too far afield to enter into a discussion of Garrison's attitude toward the Lincoln administration and of the increasing differences between him and his fellow radical abolitionist, Wendell Phillips—Garrison advocating restraint and understanding and trust in Lincoln's good intentions in regard to the slave and Phillips distrustful of the President's half-measures and his procrastination in proclaiming full emancipation and suspicious, also, of his earnestness in opposing the Confederate power.[26] We do, indeed, see in his late fifties a somewhat mellowed Garrison ready, unlike the young editor of the *Liberator* three decades or so earlier, at least to consider in some instances the subtle shadings in opinion, which make it difficult to divide good and bad into categories of unrelieved black and white. In his hatred of slavery and the slave power he remained inflexible. But war and government he had now ceased to see as totally evil. There was a plane on which they might be considered as the lesser evil, if not quite a positive good. The slaughter was a judgment of God on both sides for so long tolerating such a monstrous evil in its midst, for so long withstanding all attempts to abolish slavery by peaceful means. War for the maintenance of the Union certainly held little

[24] James A. Barnes (ed.), "Letters of a Massachusetts Woman Reformer to an Indiana Radical," *Indiana Magazine of History*, XXVI, no. 1 (March 1930), 53. After the war had come to an end, she was to call for life imprisonment for the former Confederate president. Explaining that she was, indeed, opposed on principle to capital punishment, she confided to Julian that otherwise she would have felt that only death was commensurate retribution for Davis's terrible crimes. In any case, she concluded, "as long as *any*body is hung, I can see no good reason why Jeff Davis should be exempted from the penalty" (p. 58).

[25] See *Liberator*, 13 March 1863, letter from Seward Mitchell of Maine, for an example of a rank-and-file nonresister who had been converted to the Garrisonian position seventeen years earlier and now, after two years of war and increasing doubts about the relevance of pacifism, had become convinced that only armed force was possible in dealing with the South. "All our appeals to tyrants, on the ground that their acts are wrong, are despised . . . I now see the use of war. I see its *absolute necessity.*" See also Devere Allen, *The Fight for Peace*, pp. 449-60, for other examples of pro-war or near pro-war attitudes on the part of former pacifists.

[26] See Russel B. Nye, *William Lloyd Garrison and the Humanitarian Reformers*, pp. 169-77, 180-87.

697

attraction for him (had he not earlier been ready to let the recreant South go sooner than see the North linked any longer with the upholders of Negro slavery?); but he welcomed the opportunity war gave the administration to effect the liberation of the slaves (for he believed, as we see, in the reality of Lincoln's antislavery principles). So much for the lower level, the plane on which ninety-nine percent, or more, of the American nation moved. Garrison's recognition of its legitimate existence—people being what they were—did not mean, he still claimed, that in his opinion the nonviolent way was not preferable if adopted from conviction, or that, even though as yet only a handful, pacifists must abandon their belief in the higher ground of nonresistance. But he had no sympathy whatsoever with the political opposition of the "copperheads" to the Northern war effort.

Let us allow Garrison to speak for himself and show the substance of his thinking on these problems as it reveals itself in two letters he wrote to friends in the second half of April 1861, just as hostilities were beginning.

Now that civil war has begun [he told Oliver Johnson] and a whirlwind of violence and excitement is to sweep through the country, every day increasing in intensity until its bloodiest culmination, it is . . . no time for minute criticism of Lincoln, Republicanism, or even the other parties, now that they are fusing for a death-grapple with the Southern slave oligarchy; for they are instruments in the hands of God to carry forward and help achieve the great object of emancipation, for which we have so long been striving. The war is fearfully to scourge the nation, but . . . grand results are to follow, should no dividing root of bitterness rise up at the North. All our sympathies and wishes must be with the governmemt, as against the Southern desperadoes and buccaneers; yet, of course, without any compromise of principle on our part.[27]

A few days later, writing to another friend, he continues in the same strain concerning the struggle:

I see the hand of God in it for judgement long withheld, but not unmixed with mercy. All my sympathies and wishes are with the government, because it is entirely in the right, and acting strictly in self-defence and for self-preservation. This I can say, without any compromise of my peace-principles. The struggle is necessarily geo-

---

[27] Garrison to Oliver Johnson, 19 April 1861, in *W.L.G.*, IV, 21, 22. For a good summary of Garrison's pacifist position in time of war, see Johnson, *William Lloyd Garrison and His Times*, pp. 347, 348. See also John L. Thomas, *The Liberator*, pp. 413, 422, 423, 480, 481.

graphical—between the North and the South—between freemen and a desperate slave oligarchy—and on either side of the line, a unity of purpose prevails to conquer or die, which is prophetic of one of the fiercest and bloodiest appeals to arms that the world has ever seen. The whole land is to be severely scourged—there will be desolation and death on a frightful scale, weeping, and mourning, and lamentation for the slain and wounded in thousands of families—but if it shall end in the speedy and total abolition of slavery . . . it will bring with it inconceivable blessings, and the land will have rest, and the old waste places be restored. But if it shall terminate in new compromises, whereby the traffic in human flesh shall be indefinitely prolonged, then our condition as a nation will be awful indeed, and the next outpouring of divine retribution will be for the extinction of the republic. It seems to me that the day has gone by for any compromises to be made, and that either freedom or slavery is to obtain universal supremacy. God grant it may be the former![28]

Throughout the war Garrison kept the columns of his *Liberator* open for discussion of nonresistance (it was almost the only forum left to pacifists outside the press of the peace sects), and contributions for and against are to be found scattered among its pages. Of course, the question of emancipation and the progress of the conflict occupy most of the space. The paper supported vigorous prosecution of the war and opposed concessions to the South, attacking in particular any movement for a negotiated peace before victory had completely routed the slave power and the efforts of the so-called peace democrats to terminate hostilities. The bellicosity and irreconcilable tone of the paper contrasted strangely with Garrison's theoretical pacifism. It is clear that Garrison failed to see any incompatibility between theory and practice in his conduct. "Although non-resistance holds human life in all cases inviolable," he argued with Adin Ballou and his Hopedale communitarians, who deplored what they regarded as his lapse from the spirit, if not the letter, of nonviolence, "yet it is perfectly consistent for those professing it to petition, advise, and strenuously urge a prowar government to abolish slavery solely by the war-power."[29] In fact, although his "moral line of measurement" might still be "the Golden Rule" and the Sermon on the Mount,[30] his political line differed in no essential from that of the war's most ardent supporters.

[28] Garrison to T. B. Drew, 25 April 1861, Garrison Papers, B.P.L., MS A.1.1., vol. 6, no. 7.
[29] Adin Ballou, *Autobiography*, p. 439. The exact wording of the quotation is Ballou's, but its substance is undoubtedly accurate.
[30] Garrison, *The Abolitionists and their Relations to the War*, p. 31.

Most of the Garrisonian nonresistants were already middle-aged by the time the Civil War broke out. Their heyday had been in the thirties and forties. As we have seen, by the fifties few young people could be attracted into a movement that had virtually disintegrated. The pulse had slowed down, the vital spirit had departed. The nonresistant creed, once so vigorous, had become an empty formula devoid of real meaning in the very situation it had been designed to meet. All that was left was a handful of aging men and women straining to preserve in theory a way of thinking whose spirit they had long since abandoned in practice. Militant abolitionism had almost wholly overlaid the pacifist vein in their philosophy.

The imposition of federal conscription, therefore, scarcely affected the nonresistant group in any personal way. In an editorial in the *Liberator* published anonymously in October 1862 under the title "Drafting—The Time of Trial," Garrison pleaded for equal consideration of the claims of nonresistant conscripts as conscientious objectors under the Federal Militia Act of the previous July. They had as much right, he thought, to complete exemption as members of the Society of Friends and should not be required to find a substitute or pay a fine in lieu of personal service, a way out of active military service still remaining open to all who were ready to provide the necessary money. The law had in fact confined the right to plead conscientious objection to members of the peace sects. Garrison, somewhat intolerantly, but obviously in an effort to buttress the claims of any "no-government" nonresistants who might appear, went on to suggest that the administration would be perfectly entitled to exclude from exemption as conscientious objectors all claimants who had exercised the suffrage, an act that he continued, as earlier, to consider as tantamount to approval of the state's military machine. Since they were excluded from the Act's exemption clause, Garrison foresaw that nonresistant conscientious objectors would probably have to face imprisonment for their convictions, if drafted. He ended his article, therefore, by giving some advice as to how they should conduct themselves in the hour of trial. Let them at the outset, he says, make it quite clear to the authorities that they abominate the attitude of the South. In all cases they should refuse to hire a substitute or voluntarily pay the military fine. This was not like a general tax (Garrison never pushed his "no-government" views so far as to refuse to pay taxes to Caesar); it was clearly designed to assist military operations. It was, he said, really equivalent to fighting oneself. However, if the only alternative to payment was imprisonment or worse, then he would not himself think it wrong to pay up. Anyhow, decision to pay or not must be left to the individual conscience of each objector.[31]

Later conscription acts stiffened the provisions for conscientious objection and went far to close the loopholes for those who were unwilling, for whatever reason, to serve. But the *Liberator* does not seem to have taken the matter up again. Early in 1864, however, Garrison was concerned in a personal way with the problem of conscientious objection when it seemed likely that his young son Frank, then at the Boston Latin School, would be required to undergo military drill along with the other boys in the top classes. He wrote, therefore, to the headmaster to get his son excused. "This I do," he wrote, "on the ground of conscientious scruples on my part, as well as in accordance with his own wishes."[32]

In fact, all Garrison's children, when they grew up, came to accept their father's nonresistant beliefs[33]—except the eldest son, George.[34] In the summer of 1863 George decided to volunteer for active service and received a lieutenant's commission in a newly formed Negro regiment, the 55th Massachusetts Regiment. "Though I could have wished," wrote Garrison to his son, on 11 June, shortly before his departure for the battle area with his regiment, "that you had been able understandingly and truly to adopt those principles of peace which are so sacred and divine to my own soul, yet you will bear me witness that I have not laid a straw in your way to prevent your acting up to your own highest convictions of duty; for nothing would be gained, but much lost, to have you violate these."[35]

[31] *Liberator*, 19 Sept. 1862.

[32] Garrison to Francis Gardner, 13 Jan. 1864, Garrison Papers, B.P.L., MS A.1.1., vol. 6, no. 70.

[33] Fanny Garrison Villard, *William Lloyd Garrison on Non-Resistance*, p. 19.

[34] In August 1862 Garrison wrote to Mrs. Elizabeth Buffum Chace (L.B.C. and A. C. Wyman, *Elizabeth Buffum Chace*, I, 241): "I have three sons of the requisite age—George, William and Wendell. Wendell is in principle opposed to all fighting with carnal weapons. So is William. In any case, they will not go to the tented field but will abide the consequences. George is inclined to think he shall go if drafted, as he does not claim to be a non-resistant." Garrison himself at this time hoped George and other nonpacifist abolitionists would refuse to be conscripted so long as "entire emancipation" was not proclaimed by the administration and would "take the penalties of disobedience as the friend and representative of the slave" (p. 242). Lincoln's first Emancipation Proclamation of 22 Sept. 1862 put an end to Garrison's advocacy of this type of political objection to military service.

[35] W.L.G., IV, 80. In a farewell to a young friend departing for the war, Garrison had wished him Godspeed without, however, making the slightest mention of his disapproval of war in general (see Ernest Crosby, *Garrison the Non-Resistant*, p. 85). A military camp for Negro troops was named after Garrison (see Korngold, *Two Friends of Man*, p. 333), apparently without any protest on Garrison's part. At the conclusion of the war, too, the famous nonresistant took a foremost and honored part in the victory celebrations.

We have seen how Garrison's own boys reacted to the impact of war. But what of the wider family of Garrisonian nonresistants? Did not some of them have to face the challenge of conscription and the trials which Garrison had envisaged at its introduction? We know, it is true, of a small number of individual cases during the Civil War, where men apparently unconnected with any of the peace churches took the conscientious objector stand on religious grounds when called up. But they did not emerge from the Garrisonian milieu—with the exception, seemingly, of only two instances.

There is, first, the case of the Philadelphian, Alfred H. Love, with whose peace activities we shall be concerned in later chapters. Love, though not a member of the Society, had been reared among Friends and was himself a lifelong attender at Quaker meeting. His pacifist inspiration, therefore, was not exclusively Garrisonian.[36] The second case is that of a young man from Quincy (Mass.) named John Wesley Pratt. Pratt at the outset of the war had for a short time wavered in his allegiance to pacifism. "The excitement consequent on the firing on Sumter," he relates, "carried me away in its almost irresistible might, until I found myself advocating the carrying on a war more cruel and relentless than any yet recorded in history." Later, however, he returned to his previous position. Therefore, when called up in the autumn of 1863, Pratt declared himself a pacifist of the Garrisonian variety, who on principle had never voted in his life and who objected as a Christian nonresistant both to bearing arms for any cause whatever and to buying his way out of service. He stood for complete exemption, though prepared to do hospital duties while under detention. The rough treatment he received at the hands of the military, which was probably aggravated by the fact that he did not belong to any church ("Non-Resistant? Nonsense!" an irate commanding officer told him on his arrival at the army depot), continued until his release came by order of higher authorities after several months spent in the army. Later, Garrison gave Pratt's experiences as a conscientious objector under military command considerable publicity in the *Liberator*.[37]

[36] *Liberator*, 12 Feb. 1864 (letter from A. H. Love). For Love's pacifist stand, see below, p. 720.

[37] *Ibid.*, 12 Feb. 1864; 1 April 1863. Pratt's long letter to the editor in the latter issue is given the heading: "Experiences of a Non-Resistant Conscript." After being taken by sea to Virginia, Pratt, who now became an unwilling member of the Army of the Potomac never far from the front line, among his other trials suffered at times near starvation—along with the other military prisoners. "I picked here and there an acorn, that the squirrels had not seen," he later wrote; "I gathered the kernels of corn that the horses had left before us; I picked up bones all covered with dirt, and gnawed them, until weak with hunger and exhaustion, and sick from exposure, I reached Kelly's Ford." Pratt's release in January 1864 was

The remnant of New England nonresistance, then, contributed little to the story of conscientious objection in the Civil War. We have seen its leader, Garrison, absorbed almost completely in the struggle to make the war for the Union a war for the emancipation of the slave. What of some of the other older nonresidents who, though not liable for active service, still, like Garrison, maintained a clear, if qualified, personal pacifist faith, juxtaposed somewhat uneasily perhaps alongside their antislavery crusading zeal? Take, first, Samuel J. May at Syracuse. He had greeted Harpers Ferry, indeed, with some enthusiasm and showed a genuine regard for John Brown, though his admiration was mingled with disapproval of the method Brown had chosen to forward the cause of the oppressed. In the following year, just a year before the outbreak of civil war, while addressing the American Peace Society, May had given a very forthright criticism of the idea of defensive war and had pleaded instead for a nonviolent alternative to war. Neither the American Revolution, he said, nor the Polish uprising of 1830, whatever the provocation, had been proper ways for a Christian people to obtain redress for wrongs done or the maintenance of liberties threatened. "How wicked, how impious then, is it for any man to become a soldier. He ought to refuse to submit to the degradation, as did the primitive Christians. He ought to refuse, though it should cost him his life. Better to die at the stake as a martyr to principle, than to be a soldier."[38]

Yet, when shortly afterward May was confronted with the seeming alternatives of either sanctioning the war method and thereby bringing about the victory of the cause he had so much at heart or maintaining a consistent pacifist witness and appearing indifferent to the speedy emancipation of the Southern slave, he began to waver. "The conduct of the rebels," he wrote, "and the impending fate of our country has shaken my confidence in the *extreme* principles of the nonresistants." All the same, he added, "I cannot find it in my heart to urge men to enlist." He left this decision to the consciences of those who believed in the war method. Instead, he busied himself with the spiritual and material welfare of the troops, visiting army camps to find out where he could be of use and assisting the families of those in the service.[39]

---

the result of intervention with the authorities by several leading New England pacifists. One of those who had shared at the beginning Pratt's detention in the camp on Long Island in Boston Harbor was the Shaker C.O., Horace S. Taber (see chap. 20). The MS Letters & Documents, edited by John Whiteley, contain some interesting sidelights on Pratt's experiences at that time, as well as later with the army near the front (see pp. 50, 53, 78-87).

[38] S. J. May, *An Address . . . before the A.P.S.*, pp. 11, 12.
[39] *Memoir of S. J. May*, pp. 226-29.

Like Garrison, he strongly urged that no compromise be reached to end the war until slavery was rooted out completely, and he was fierce in his denunciations of the Southern leaders. On news of the capture of President Davis at the end of the war he wrote: "Jeff Davis of course ought to be hanged if any man should." Even though he adds as an afterthought, "what good can it do to hang even him?" his whole attitude appears tantamount to urging the hanging of the Southern leader by those who were not conscientiously opposed to capital punishment. A sympathetic biographer writes of May's attitude in the latter years of the war: "His . . . views in 1864 and 1865 were far from being generous or humane. Indeed, it stands as the only blot upon the career of a man who always had championed truth, honor and justice."[40] May's dilemma was a real one. Even less satisfactorily perhaps than Garrison, however, had he succeeded in the difficult task of reconciling radical pacifism with militant abolitionism, when the latter cause was submitted finally to the arbitrament of war.

We can watch this curious admixture of theoretical pacifism and practical belligerence in the case of a second member of the original New England nonresistant group, who in the late fifties had become Garrison's editorial assistant on the *Liberator*. Charles K. Whipple was not one of its most outstanding members intellectually, but he was very active on its behalf and, as we have seen in an earlier chapter, had written several pamphlets in defense of nonresistance. In 1863 Whipple took issue with the English pacifist leader, Henry Richard of the London Peace Society, who had criticized in his Society's journal, the *Herald of Peace*, the bellicosity (as he considered it) of Northern abolitionists and the increasing ferocity with which the war was being waged, especially on the part of the North. Attempts by the London Peace Society at fostering negotiations between the two sides, and earlier criticisms of the belligerence of Northern peace men, had already aroused the resentment of the American Peace Society, temporarily ruffling the good relations which had hitherto existed between the peace societies of the two countries.[41]

Now Whipple entered the fray against Richard, and their correspondence was published in the columns of the *Liberator*.[42] "This is strictly a war of self-preservation," the American told Richard; "the inevitable alternative before us is to conquer or to be conquered; . . . compromise between non-slaveholders and slaveholders is precisely equivalent to a defeat of liberty; and . . . defeat for us, means the

[40] W. Freeman Galpin, "God's Chore Boy," chap. XIII; A. C. F. Beales, *The History of Peace*, pp. 106-9.
[41] See Curti, *Peace or War*, pp. 55, 56.
[42] *Liberator*, 28 Aug. 1863.

704

forcible establishment of the slave code North as well as South. So that there is absolutely no resource for us but to fight." He called for "extermination" of the Southern secessionists and slaveholders, if this were needed to prevent the legal reestablishment of slavery throughout the country and of the overseas slave trade, and not for any softening in the forceful prosecution of the war. Not independence but slavery was what the South was fighting for; "we can escape war with such a neighbor only by one possible means, complicity in the enforcement of slavery and suppression of anti-slavery." "Are you prepared to advise that *this* price be paid for peace?" he asked the English pacifist. And then, as if recollecting that, after all, both he and Richard still stood for the same ideal of peace and nonviolence, Whipple attempts to knit together two seemingly irreconcilable strands, an effort which soon develops into a declaration of practical impotence in making an effective peace witness. "You and I, Mr. Editor," he tells Henry Richard, "are Peace men. As we understand Christianity, it never allows fighting; and *we* propose *not* to fight, under any circumstances. But surely these ideas of ours do not prevent our recognizing the fact that most men (and some worthy and excellent men) are of the opposite persuasion; still less do our peace principles prevent us from recognizing the grounds of difference between two parties who are fighting, and distinguishing one party to be right and the other wrong in the matter about which they began to quarrel." The pacifists in America, "always an insignificant minority" of the population, had now become more impotent than ever. The abolitionist cause, on the other hand, was in the ascendant; all its advocates rejoiced that the end of slavery approached. It was slavery's Northern supporters who were raising the cry of peace with the rebels. Therefore, Whipple told Richard, "recognizing this fact . . . I, a peace man, say without hesitation that I have no desire to see an end to this contest until slavery is utterly extirpated. Call this paradoxical or self-contradictory, if you will; but I do not see the least abandonment of my principles." Can you not distinguish, he asks Richard, between the relative justice of two causes? Do you equate, for example, the Poles' cause with that of their Russian masters, the Italians' with that of their Austrian overlords? "Does no thought enter your mind but the official and technical one—'How wicked they both are to be fighting?' . . . Is Peace the *one* thing needful when it leaves one party established as tyrant and the other as slave?"

Whipple, indeed, protests too much. His remarks touching the need for pacifists to evaluate the relative merits of the contestants in any armed struggle, a point made much of by Garrison also, are certainly apt. But there is little of the healing oil of reconciliation in what Whipple has to say. It is the whole spirit of his argument that is so much in contradiction with the pacifist ethos and that makes his protestations of continued loyalty to it ring hollow.

Whipple, when pressed by Richard whether he had now abandoned the view he had held steadily since publishing some twenty years earlier his pamphlet on the *Evils of the Revolutionary War*—that passive resistance, if entered on wholeheartedly, was capable of achieving liberty and justice, the best objectives of war, but without war's bloodshed and wasted resources—gives a rather unsatisfactory answer:

> I still hold in regard to the unjustifiableness of war, precisely the ideas which I then held. But I recognize the fact that our present conflict in this country (a Revolutionary war not less than the other) is materially different from that other in regard to the attainment of its object by means other than war. Resolutely determined not to fight, myself, and continuing firm in the position of advising no one else to fight, I yet recognize the fact that, if *somebody* does not fight to prevent the success of the slaveholders, they will succeed, and will bring the whole nation under the operation of the slave system.

He still believed, he continued, as firmly as ever in "the . . . power of Christian love": that was why he would not himself fight in this war, which was being waged by the North to prevent the spread of the slave system. Love had worked with the civilized and the savage and often, too, with the criminal and the depraved. But as for its efficacy with Southern slaveholders, he was not so sure. "You speak of these people as 'our fellow-Christians.' I pray you not to do Christianity so great an unjustice. Slaveholders are *not* Christians." "God of course can, and will accomplish some good purpose with them, in some one of his days of a thousand year." But "in all *human* probability, there is not the remotest chance of succeeding with these men by the use of kindness or forbearance." That was why he could not expect American statesmen or the people of the North to adopt the personal philosophy of the nonresistants.

Whipple's arguments, growing more and more angry as the correspondence proceeded, failed to convince Richard, who was profoundly distressed by the American pacifist's belligerence. "A long plea in favour of war from the pen of an old Peace man," a "grievous apostasy among our friends" was how he described them. "It seems painfully

706

clear," the Britisher went on, "that you are all breathing such an atmosphere of passion as to have become far too feverish to listen with any temper to what appear to you the cold-blooded counsels of unprejudiced observers." To Richard it seemed that, if Whipple were right, if pacifism and the way of Christian love had no relevance in the existing situation, then the whole crusade for peace, which their movement had been carrying on for nearly half a century, was a mistake built on false premises. The moral grandeur of the objectives which the American abolitionists hoped to see accomplished as a result of the fighting he saw as itself a source of danger to the advocate of peace. "When I see a war waged in the name of religion or of philanthropy," he wrote, "I look upon it as the worst of all wars, because it tends to consecrate an evil system, in the estimation of mankind, by associating with it a great and sacred cause, while this cause is, itself, in reality, degraded and dishonoured by the association." The two men failed completely to understand each other. To Whipple (along with almost all the other Garrisonian nonresistants at this time, as we have seen), the evil of slavery, and what appeared to be the wickedness of those who upheld it, overshadowed all other considerations. Pacifism seemed to provide no answer which could be presented to those fighting for liberty as a practical alternative to the war method.[43] It could only remain a personal philosophy for those ready themselves to endure the burden of suffering that its adoption would bring with it. For Richard, on the other hand, standing, as it were, above the battle and perhaps underestimating, because of his distance from the conflict, the strength and resilience of the slave power, the way of love and its application to each individual Southerner were all-important. Pacifism, if it were to be meaningful, must speak to the man in the slaveowner, must recognize a brother in the enemy.

If the American Peace Society leadership and the overwhelming majority of rank-and-file members had capitulated completely to the war spirit and if most of the Garrisonian nonresistants had put their pacifism into cold storage and their energies into the struggle to achieve the final victory of the abolitionist cause, a scattered handful of the pacifist old guard continued to maintain a radical peace testimony in wartime, alongside that of the peace sects. It was actually the moderate pacifists, who had opposed the "no-government" views of the Gar-

[43] Two decades after the conclusion of the Civil War, Whipple, then an old man, published a virtual recantation of his earlier views. The nonresistants of the antebellum era, he now wrote, had failed to realize that Christ's injunctions such as "Resist not evil," etc., were given in expectation of an imminent end of the world. They could not be applied literally in later times. See *Boston Commonwealth*, 7 Nov. 1885.

707

risonian nonresistants, who now in wartime proved the more consistent in their advocacy of peace views.[44]

Amasa Walker, for instance, spoke up manfully for the absolutist position at the American Peace Society's annual gatherings in 1862[45] and 1863. True, he did not contest the position we have seen the Society had taken at the outset, that the Civil War, "the rebellion," was a matter of internal order and therefore outside its cognizance; nor did he feel that, once passions had been aroused to fever pitch on each side, appeals for a just termination of the war on grounds of reason or religion would have much chance of success. But he stated his own pacifist convictions quite frankly. "I have no faith in war," he said. "I had none at the commencement of our own contest, and if it were possible, I have less now. I expect nothing good from this or any war, that might not be obtained in a better way. My confidence in the principle on which our movement is founded, and the feasibility of it, are entirely unshaken. The consummation may be further off than it seemed ten years ago, but not the less certain."[46]

Elihu Burritt, too, whom we have watched at the opening of the struggle apprehensive at signs of wavering in his old friend Amasa Walker, spoke out publicly against the war, urging as a solution what he called "a plan of adjustment, involving a partial separation of the Southern and Northern States."[47] "I have from the beginning," he wrote to Henry Richard on 27 October 1862, "been opposed to this war not only on principle but on policy. . . . I condemn it here up to almost the prison door."[48] However, it is interesting to note that his open antiwar attitude did not prevent the Northern administration

---

[44] But see, e.g., the small work by H. H. Brigham, *A Voice from Nazareth* (1865), for a New England nonresistant's wartime defense of Christian pacifism. Brigham, a lay Baptist, had withdrawn in 1841 from his church in South Abington (Mass.) because of its refusal to come out squarely in favor of abolition, but he now opposed war as a means of bringing about emancipation. (See esp. pp. 7, 19, 33.) Another little-known product of New England pacifism during the war period is the 32-page pamphlet which T. F. Tukesbury published in Boston in 1864 under the title *The Taking of Human Life Incompatible with Christianity*. There is little that is original in the work, which bases its appeal for nonparticipation in war and for the application of noninjurious methods of overcoming evils, even of the magnitude of slavery, on the injunctions of the New Testament and the gospel spirit of love. "The Word is full of proofs," Tukesbury wrote, "that the doctrine of physical . . . resistance is wrong, and that peace is right, and always right; and that it is the duty of an individual to act upon this principle whether others do or not." (See pp. 21, 27, 28, 30.) It is very unlikely that the author made an impression on more than a handful of his contemporaries.

[45] Walker, *Iron-clad War-ships*, esp. pp. 9-11.

[46] Walker, *The Suicidal Folly of the War System* (1863), pp. 5, 6, 18-20.

[47] Quoted in Curti, *Learned Blacksmith*, p. 140.

[48] Quoted *ibid.*, p. 146.

708

from recognizing his talents (and the importance of the contacts he had with influential circles in England) by appointing him American consul in Birmingham early in 1865—a credit, indeed, to its tolerant spirit.[49]

Most vigorous and determined in its opposition to war was the little pacifist circle that had formed around such men as the now aged Joshua P. Blanchard and the younger Ezra H. Heywood (1829-1893), who was to be active throughout his life in radical reform. The British pacifist, Henry Richard, described Heywood as "this brave man who dares to be faithful among the faithless," "the bravest man in the federal states."[50] From 1862 onward the group used to meet together privately in Boston (the times were not yet ripe, they considered, and their resources too meager for any widespread public agitation). They were in touch with a few scattered sympathizers in other parts of the country, and from time to time Garrison, although he disagreed, if not with their basic viewpoint, at least with their stand on current politics, tolerantly allowed them space to express their opinions in the columns of the *Liberator*.[51]

The group regarded the attitude of the peace movement as a whole as little less than a betrayal of the truth entrusted to it. "The American Peace Society and the nonresistants generally," wrote Heywood after the war was over, "were so recreant to their principles in 1861 and thereafter, that the faith delivered to peace saints was kept only by 'copperhead' sinners. Opposed to all wars except the present one, at the very time when their ideas were of practical importance, and should have given law and unity to distracted States, in violation of all the kindly and mutual interests of the common people North and South, they joined the reprehensible pro-slavery and anti-slavery leaders in merciless advocacy of violence and blood."[52] Heywood and Blanchard, like Burritt, believed strongly that their pacifism had practical relevance even in the context of war. It was not only right from

[49] Devere Allen, *The Struggle for Peace*, p. 400.

[50] Quoted in Curti, *Peace or War*, p. 58. In 1863 Heywood wrote of the Quaker absolutists: "They are quite right in refusing to bear arms or pay the fine in obedience to this despotic, wicked conscription" (Wymans, *Chace*, I, 253).

[51] Robert W. Doherty, "Alfred H. Love and the Universal Peace Union," Ph.D. diss., U. of Pennsylvania, p. 39.

[52] Letter by Heywood to the *New York World*, 3 June 1868, cutting in J. P. Blanchard's Scrapbook, the second volume of which, containing *inter alia* a number of Blanchard's pacifist articles from the Civil War period, is deposited in the S.C.P.C. The first volume is presumably lost. It is interesting to note in connection with Heywood's attitude to the "copperheads" expressed here that his associate Blanchard contributed pro-peace articles to the *Boston Daily Courier*, the leading Democratic paper in that city and one that was opposed on political grounds to the Union war effort.

the standpoint of Christian morality; it was expedient, they thought, on the political level as well.

In the early months of the war Blanchard had pleaded for a negotiated peace on the basis of an agreement between the two sides to separate. Like the prewar advocates of "disunion," he believed that the institution of slavery would wither away in the South if no longer given the tacit consent of the Northern section. He felt, too, that in the circumstances secession was the only possible solution compatible with the American tradition of democracy, of government derived from the consent of the governed. The shame of the Fugitive Slave Law would be done away with, and the impending loss in life and property in the course of a long and bloody war would be avoided. He called his plan "the speediest and most peaceable one of abolishing slavery that can be devised."[53] If the war were continued, he felt certain that it could not be carried on in a spirit of Christian charity—as some prowar clerics maintained was possible—and that hatred would grow into a consuming fire that would destroy love in their hearts and all desire for reconciliation.[54] Even after Lincoln had announced his preliminary Emancipation Proclamation in September 1862, Blanchard continued to speak up against the war and in favor of—to use his own words at this time—"the law of benevolent persuasion in opposition to the malignant law of force."[55] A year later we find him writing in the English *Herald of Peace*: "Christianity does not permit physical force for any but benevolent purposes. Its principle is government, not by fear, but by love"; this rules out the way of war, either civil or international, since there the object is the destruction, not the reformation, of the so-called enemy.[56] The argument is a familiar one in pacifist literature but one not often heard, even from peace advocates, in those years of fratricidal struggle.

As the war went on and each side seemed determined to fight to a finish, Blanchard, having failed to make the least impact on government, came more and more to feel that a new tactic was needed, that, in fact, the technique of the peace movement itself had been at fault over the years, since governments clung as tenaciously as ever to their powers of making war. "Some other means must . . . be found for the abolition of this enormous and mischievous power," he concluded after reviewing briefly the movement's history since its beginnings in 1815. Let the peace message be brought more directly to the

[53] See J. P. Blanchard, *Plan for Terminating the War* (single-sided broadsheet); *The War of Succession*, pp. 4ff.

[54] *The War of Succession*, pp. 2-4.

[55] In the *Bond of Brotherhood*, 1 Oct. 1862, p. 156, cutting in his Scrapbook.

[56] In the *Herald of Peace*, Oct. 1863, cutting in his Scrapbook.

people and in its most radical form. "Let us cease our hopeless attempts to influence interested rulers and statesmen in favour of peace and humanity. Let us turn to the masses of the depressed and martially-enslaved with the animating and reforming doctrine of individual independence." He did not advocate resistance to properly constituted authority in all things lawful; disobedience to the law where it infringed God's commandments, however, was another matter. If large sections of the populace were to refuse to fight out of a genuine conviction of the wrongness of all war, if a mass movement of potential conscientious objection could be generated in case of war or the threat of war, then the rulers would be forced to cease from conflict.[57] Thus, finally, in his old age this solid Boston merchant, long the pillar of the conservative wing of absolute pacifism in the American peace movement, was led to advocate a form of radical antimilitarism.

While the war lasted, Blanchard and his friends remained an obscure, isolated group powerless to influence public opinion in any substantial way. They are not without importance, however, as a link between prewar pacifism and the postwar movement which was at first centered in the Universal Peace Union (see the next section). They alone (if, again, we exclude the activities of the peace sects) attempted to give, within however confined a compass, something more than a purely personal witness to their pacifist faith.

Pacifism in America from the mid-thirties on, especially in its most radical form of nonresistance, had been the twin of abolitionism. War and slavery, though not by any means the only scourges besetting mankind, were perhaps, to that reforming generation at least, the most glaring denials of Christian love and brotherhood then existing. Freedom from war and violence and the liberation of the slave were but facets of one struggle, one movement to bring about the kingdom of God on earth. At least so it seemed until around mid-century the possibility grew that it would not be peaceful persuasion, but force of arms, that would in fact bring an end to slavery in the South. The dilemma was posed. What a modern historian has aptly said of abolitionists in general during this period applies with even greater cogency in the case of the nonresistant abolitionists: "Abolitionists might argue," he writes, "that they believed in the methods of peace but they could not indulge in wild talk about a bloody end of slavery without arousing a reciprocal madness in the South. . . . The slave owners were men capable of losing their tempers; when the time came for them to lose their temper completely, the abolitionists would no longer have in their

---

[57] From an article entitled "Unresisting Disobedience" in the *Herald of Peace*, March 1864, cutting in his Scrapbook.

711

own hands the choice between peace and war."[58] In a way, it is not untrue to say that Garrison and Wright and the other abolitionist non-resistants, as well as some of the pacifists outside their ranks, even if they did finally renounce their pacifism as war approached, had helped to bring the war nearer by their extreme belligerence. In their zeal for moral righteousness, which sometimes, indeed, became a species of self-righteousness but at best stemmed from a very genuine hatred of oppression, and in their efforts to avoid that common failing of peace men at all times, crying "peace, peace; when there is no peace," they had forgotten that peace is a spirit and not merely a personal credo, and that, without the spirit of peace that works reconciliation, pacifism is indeed a barren faith.

There were, as we have seen, only a few scattered individuals from the remnant of the pacifist crusade of earlier decades, men like Blanchard and Heywood, Ballou and Burritt, who succeeded in maintaining a consistent peace stand throughout the war years. The pacifist witness was borne most fully at this time of stress and testing by the young men, mostly from the peace sects, who became conscientious objectors on either side of the battle lines. To their story we must now turn.

[58] R. V. Harlow, *Gerrit Smith*, p. 305.

Chapter 18

The Quakers in the Civil War

The story of the Quakers during the Civil War period has been told on more than one occasion. Edward Needles Wright, for instance, devoted the greater part of his study on *Conscientious Objectors in the Civil War* (1931)[1] to the stand of the Society of Friends, while back at the end of the last century the Quaker minister, Fernando G. Cartland, compiled an artless yet moving account of the trials and tribulations of Friends under the Confederacy with the title *Southern Heroes* (1895). That there were many Friends who took the traditional conscientious objector position of their Society and that there were also others who in the North broke with tradition and joined actively in the struggle against slavery and secession are facts known to all who are at all acquainted with Quaker history. In truth, the pattern of conduct among Friends in the war period was more complex than this simple dichotomy implies, and it caused some confusion at times in the minds of the authorities. Even among those who upheld the Society's peace testimony, there was by no means always unanimity as to what reaction to the various demands of a war situation this testimony required of members.

The peace testimony of the Society of Friends, as we know, was not in its essence a literalist belief, a dogma based on any one, or any number, of Biblical texts. It sprang from the spirit that underlay the scriptures and that might be revealed to the perceptive soul directly in the present, as it had been revealed nearly two thousand years before. The spirit of peace might speak to the Indian untutored in the Christian scriptures. The evangelical trend that had come to predominate in many meetings of the Orthodox branch did not succeed in altogether obliterating this spiritualism in the pacifism of the Friends. The peace testimony at bottom resulted from an outpouring of the Inner Light, a discipleship of the spirit, and not merely from the keeping of the letter of the gospel. We find an excellent illustration of this attitude in one of the wartime epistles of the Orthodox Yearly Meeting of Philadelphia. "Our testimony against all war and fighting," it states, "is founded on the precious precepts contained in the New Testament,

[1] As the author points out (p. 1), the term "conscientious objector" was not yet in use at the time of the Civil War. The men were described as "non-resistants," "non-combatants," "those scrupulous against bearing arms," etc.

713

and the immediate openings made on the mind by the same Spirit which dictated it."[2] It was a loving spirit that was needed to conquer the forces driving toward war; it was this that must provide the impulse toward asserting the primacy of peace. As an address of the Meeting for Sufferings of Baltimore Yearly Meeting (Hicksite this time), which was published early in the war, put it: "Let us keep ever in mind, that the practical ground-work of our profession . . . is love, universal love—love to God, and love to all men."[3]

It was, nevertheless, this very principle of universal love, when Friends tried to apply it in practice, that from the outset of the war created one of the most trying dilemmas that beset them. In spite of the fact that the first Emancipation Proclamation was not promulgated by the Lincoln administration until September 1862, for most Quakers, as for many millions of their fellow citizens then and since, the war seemed from the first to be fought with the slavery issue in the foreground. The *Friend*, organ of the Philadelphia Orthodox Yearly Meeting, for instance, describing the war as "a wanton and unjustifiable attack on the Union" by the South seldom paralleled in the whole course of history, went on to affirm "the real causes of their treasonable and murderous proceedings, to be the maintenance and extension of the abominable system of human slavery."[4] How in these circumstances was universal love to be reconciled with universal peace? How was a desire to see our fellow men freed as soon as possible to be squared with an abhorrence of shedding the blood of human beings, even in order to free the oppressed? It is true that this was not a new dilemma for Friends, but the war presented it to them with a new urgency and in new ways that demanded in many cases some immediate and decisive action.

Their long held testimony against slavery had been so conceived as not to conflict with their viewpoint on peace. They advocated gradualism in getting rid of the peculiar institution, the use of persuasion

[2] *Friend* (Phila.), 16 May 1863.
[3] *Friends' Intelligencer*, 19 Oct. 1861.
[4] *Friend*, 23 Aug. 1862. A postwar pacifist, the Rev. John M. Washburn, in his book *Reason vs. the Sword* (1873), pp. 374, 375, criticizes this kind of attitude even on the part of those Friends who upheld their Society's pacifism throughout the war. He writes: "Their testimony had become traditional and shadowy, and existed rather as a dogma than as an active principle; but the question of slavery, constantly agitated, was vivid in their minds, and so led them very generally to sympathize with the work of the sword . . . so, too, the Quakers were seduced into the common but erroneous belief that *the act of the South in seceding was in itself a wrong and sin*, apart from violence and war." Washburn, though antislavery and pro-Union, maintained that the Confederacy had possessed the same right to a separate existence as Ireland or Italy. His remarks on the Quakers, penetrating in some ways, lack understanding of the issues involved.

and example. Yet Friends were not slow to recognize that difficulties must persist among members in reconciling these two separate expressions of what was fundamentally one organic faith. The position was aptly described by a contributor to the Hicksite *Friends' Intelligencer,* writing after Lincoln's final Emancipation Proclamation of 1 January 1863 had made the question more acute:

There is danger, under present circumstances, of allowing our testimony against war to be modified or lessened, from the fact that this war will certainly be the means of putting down slavery. This war having been begun by slaveholders more firmly to secure themselves in their authority over slaves, we cannot be sorry to see that authority overthrown; yet it is done by a means that we, as Christians, cannot recommend or uphold.[5]

This general sympathy with the Unionist cause on the part of most Friends may be illustrated by an incident told of old Thomas Garrett (1783-1871), a Wilmington (Del.) Friend, who had devoted many years to the cause of the slave, helping the "Underground Railway" in smuggling runaways up north. Garrett remained loyal to Quaker pacifism during the war. He did not hesitate, however, to encourage a former slave, whom he was assisting, to join up with the Union army. "Am I naughty, being a professed non-resistant, to advise this poor fellow to serve Father Abraham?" he inquired of a friend.[6]

I

Friends of all branches of the Society in the Union states, to whose wartime experiences we turn first, continually stressed their loyalty to the administration, their lack of all sympathy with the Confederate cause, and their willingness to undergo all the burdens of citizenship except where these infringed on their conscientious scruples. As opposition grew within the Northern states to a continuation of hostilities—an antiwar trend not based on any abstract pacifism but on indifference or hostility to the war aims of the Union administration, combined usually with some degree of sympathy for the South—and as the party of "peace democrats" or "copperheads" (as they were derisively dubbed by their opponents) gradually consolidated in the country, the Quakers carefully pointed out the clear-cut distinction between their own stand and that of the political antiwar party. In a document drawn up in September 1863 (the year of the antidraft

[5] *Friends' Intelligencer,* XX, no. 30 (3 Oct. 1863), 474.
[6] Thomas E. Drake, "Thomas Garrett, Quaker Abolitionist," in *Friends in Wilmington, 1738-1938,* pp. 85, 86.

rioting in New York City) by their Meeting for Sufferings for transmission to its counterpart in London, the Orthodox Yearly Meeting of New York stated:

Although our religious Society is known as the unfeigned advocate of peace, it is cause of embarrassment to us at this time, that unscrupulous men, assuming the name of peace makers, are doing all they can to further the objects of those who seek to destroy our general Government, and to rivet the chains of slavery in this land. And while we find it our duty to refrain from all connection with war, both in spirit and in practice, we cannot do or say anything calculated, even remotely, to identify our members with these men.[7]

We shall find in the course of the story that the authorities in the North, particularly Lincoln and some members of his administration in Washington, showed on many occasions both consideration and a large measure of understanding for the Quaker position on the war. Wright has commented on the astonishing freedom in which Friends were allowed to spread peace propaganda. Tracts expounding Quaker pacifism were sometimes distributed even among the military. A major-general, on being presented with one such document by an Indiana Friend, is reported to have remarked: "That tract is true, and the doctrine right, but we must wait to put it in practice, until after the war closes."[8] We read again, to give a second illustration, of the woman minister, Ann Branson (1808-1891), an Orthodox Friend from Ohio, who felt a concern to visit two recruiting officers and inform them of Friends' testimony against war and of the wrongness of oppressing those whose consciences led them to refuse to bear arms. Despite a recent law threatening imprisonment for any who tried to discourage men from enlisting, she determined to regard "the law of the Lord more than the law of man, and paramount to the laws of the land." "I used great plainness of speech," she tells us, "in regard to the inconsistency of war with the gospel dispensation." Nevertheless, the officers listened courteously to what she had to say, and no bad consequences resulted from her outspokenness.[9] A fairly widespread recognition of the fact that Quaker opposition to war stemmed from opposition to it as a method, rather than from any hidden sympathy with the enemy, and that, therefore, it did not constitute a subversive influence in the land, seems to have existed in the American community at that date.

[7] Quoted in E. N. Wright, *Conscientious Objectors in the Civil War*, p. 2.
[8] *Ibid.*, pp. 166, 167.
[9] Martha H. Bishop, "Ann Branson" in *Quaker Biographies*, 2nd ser., II, 84, 85.

The militant antimilitarist propaganda of Ann Branson was perhaps less usual than the quieter form of nonpolitical lobbying in favor of peace that is exemplified in the activities of Eliza P. Gurney (1800-1881), the American-born widow of the famous English evangelical Friend, Joseph John Gurney. In October 1862 Mrs. Gurney, accompanied by three other Quakers, felt called upon to make "a religious visit" to the President. Her message to Lincoln was one of peace. She told him of her own and the whole Society's sympathy for him in his responsible position, of her people's oneness with him in his aim to free the oppressed, and of their need to trust in God. Lincoln was deeply moved and wept; they all knelt in prayer together. She did not dwell particularly on the Quaker peace testimony, either during this interview or in the subsequent correspondence with Lincoln in which she engaged at the President's request, though this was obviously in the thoughts of both. On 4 September 1864 Lincoln wrote to her: "Your people, the Friends, have had and are having a great trial. On principle and faith opposed to both war and oppression, they can only practically oppose oppression by war. In this hard dilemma some have chosen one horn and some the other." He assured Mrs. Gurney that he would do all in his power, consistent with the law and the obligations of his office, to help any Quaker conscientious objectors in difficulties, whose cases became known to him.[10]

Ann Branson exhorting the recruiting officers and Eliza Gurney praying beside Lincoln were both seeking to give expression to the Quaker peace testimony, each in the manner which most suited their individual temperaments. Collectively Friends were active, too, in spreading the same message during the years of war. The various yearly meetings of the Orthodox and Hicksite branches, as well as the smaller Wilburite Conservative one, all contributed a steady flow of petitions, addresses, and memorials. These were usually drawn up for presentation to the state or federal legislatures; sometimes they were addressed to some other body or to the general public. Very often they were occasioned by one or another piece of draft legislation and had as their object to expound the reasons for Friends' refusal to comply. They appeared quite frequently as pamphlets or leaflets, and many of them were printed in a Quaker periodical—either the Orthodox *Friend*, the *Friends' Review* (belonging to the same branch but more evangelical in tone), or the Hicksite *Friends' Intelligencer*. The con-

[10] *Memoir and Correspondence of Eliza P. Gurney*, pp. 307-22. In her last letter to Lincoln written on 8 Sept. 1864, one that he is known to have valued highly, Mrs. Gurney, agreeing with the President that "Friends have been placed . . . in a peculiar and somewhat anomalous position," went on to give him a straightforward exposition of the grounds of Friends' objection to war.

tents of these documents followed traditional lines: innovation on such an issue was, indeed, alien to the thinking of most sections of the Society at that time, even if conservatism was not so deeply ingrained as among the German peace sects. Friends brought out their love of country and loyalty to its authorities, their recognition of the need for civil government, and their abhorrence of "the wicked rebellion"; they pointed out, too, that obedience must be limited by conscience and that Friends had shown by their former sufferings the sincerity of their devotion to pacifist views, which they believed were the only ones compatible with the message of the gospels. They often mentioned the peaceable nature of Quaker government in Pennsylvania as an indication of the practicability of their principles. And, finally, they frequently stressed the view that liberty of religious conscience, which was their constitutional right as American citizens, included the right to unconditional exemption from military service, that the government was not entitled to demand any alternative service or payment in exchange for the free exercise of conscience.[11]

The Quaker press also printed a large amount of material on the pacifist issue in the form of editorials and articles contributed by individual Friends. The discussion centered on the implications of Christianity in regard to war; the political and economic aspects of war were only occasionally touched on. The Philadelphia *Friend* devoted most space to the subject, but its style tended to be duller than the contributions of the other two Quaker papers.

The presentation of war news presented a special problem to Quaker editors. Some Friends considered that such news might have an inflammatory effect on those who read it. A typical illustration of this viewpoint is to be found in an epistle issued by the men's meeting of New York (Hicksite) Yearly Meeting: "Might not the inquiry be made of us individually," they ask, "whether the perusal of the war news of the day, unless guarded against, is not calculated to excite and foster those passions in our breasts, which are in direct opposition to the blessed precepts of our Saviour, as expressed in his most excellent Sermon on the Mount?"[12] And so we find some Friends in all branches

---

[11] A typical example of this kind of memorializing is to be found in the address of the Ohio (Wilburite) Y. M. sent to the governor of Ohio on 30 August 1862. "The Governor," it stated, "may rest assured that as a religious body we are loyal to the government and deeply regret the difficulty which has beset it. But acting on the ground of our religious principles we can neither engage in military service nor hire substitutes. Nevertheless it has always been the practice of the consistent members of our religious society, in cases where they cannot comply actively with the requisitions of the law, passively to submit to the penalty if not released therefrom." (Quoted in Charles P. Morlan, *A Brief History of Ohio Yearly Meeting of the Religious Society of Friends [Conservative]*, p. 82.)

[12] *Friend*, 22 June 1861.

of the Society uniting in their disapproval of either reading or printing news on the progress of the war. But there existed a second, and less narrow, attitude which held it to be desirable for Friends to keep informed on the momentous events of the day. They regarded it as an advantage that this news should be presented "in the least objectionable manner" by journals which were edited in the spirit of Quaker pacifism. "Many take no newspaper," it was reported, "being unwilling to admit within their family circle, the contaminating literature they so frequently contain." For such Quakers, for instance, the "Summary of Events," which the *Friend* printed weekly (until pressure from those who disapproved led the editor to suspend this item for a time), was welcome. On the whole, the bulk of Friends, including the editorial staffs of their papers, saw no inconsistency between an interest in the news of the day, even if this were mainly concerned with battles, and a strict adherence to the peace testimony.[13]

Quaker papers were read by few outside the ranks of the Society, while the statements on their peace witness, which we have seen them issuing from time to time as the need arose, were *ad hoc* affairs not intended as full-length expositions of their peace testimony. We have seen that a not inconsiderable literature on peace had been produced by Friends on both sides of the Atlantic, and some of these works continued to be used effectively during the Civil War period. But the war years were singularly lacking in any original contributions to the pacifist debate. An example of the conservative, traditional nature of Quaker peace propaganda is the continued use made of even such a minor piece as Benjamin Bates's letter and memorial to the Virginia legislature of 1810 (discussed earlier), which was not only given a prominent place in several Quaker papers but was also presented by Ohio (Orthodox) Yearly Meeting to their state legislature on the occasion of its discussion of the exemption of conscientious objectors to the wartime militia. That new literature on the peace testimony was so meager can be explained in large part by the absorption of Friends in the immediate exigencies of the war situation and, in particular, in the defense of Quaker conscientious objectors.

The first summer of the war saw the composition of two small pamphlets on war from the Quaker point of view. In September 1861 a Rhode Island Friend, John W. Foster, disappointed at the failure of the New York *Tribune* to print a letter he had written defending Christian nonresistance against attacks made on it in that paper, sat down to compile a pamphlet, which he entitled *War and Christianity Irreconcilable: An Address to Christians.* It was printed privately at

[13] *Ibid.*, 28 Dec. 1861. See also Wright, pp. 45, 46.

719

the author's expense. The work consists largely of extracts from other pacifist writers, including Dymond on war and a couple of pieces from local Providence nonresistants outside the Quaker fold, and contains little that need detain us here.

At about the same time, in Philadelphia, a young man by the name of Alfred H. Love (1830-1913), who was to make his mark on the postwar peace movement, had also taken up his pen to defend pacifism, this time against attack from a former nonresistant and onetime treasurer of the Pennsylvania Peace Society, a Baptist minister who had left the peace ranks on the outbreak of war to become a regimental chaplain. As we mentioned in the previous chapter, Love, although not an actual member, was very close to the Society of Friends and had been reared in a Quaker home. He therefore felt keenly disappointed when this man, the Rev. William J. Mullen, had urged his fellow Christians to support the struggle as "a defensive war," "an honorable resistance in the cause of justice." It was the effect that Mullen's utterances would have among the little band of Philadelphia peace workers that chiefly prompted Love to compose his *Appeal in Vindication of Peace Principles*. Love did not attempt to prove that pacifism presented a practicable political alternative in the existing situation. He appealed instead to the central teaching of the Christian gospel and contrasted this with the essential nature of war, even for the best of causes. "Think of it," he went on, "each section appealing to the same Father for directly opposite ends! There is but one God, he is not a 'God of Battles.' He cannot answer both prayers—is it likely he will hear or answer either?" Christians must work quietly for peace between the two sides, acting in the faith that would move mountains and not being carried away by the folly of believing that one side was perfect and the other wholly evil. Slaveholders, though thoroughly misguided, were still people.[14] Love's pamphlet, it is true, went through two editions, yet the circulation was very small and this quiet voice of reason was barely audible above the battle.

In 1862 three further pamphlets on war of a general nature appeared from Quaker authors. Ezra Michener (1794-1887), self-educated scholar, scientist, and medical practitioner, and throughout his long life a keen pacifist, published under the imprint of the Book Association of Friends a 34-page piece entitled *A Brief Exposition of the Testimony to Peace, as exemplified by the Life and Precepts of Jesus Christ, and the Early Christians, and held by the Religious Society of*

[14] Love, *An Appeal in Vindication of Peace Principles*, pp. 2-6, 7, 9-11, 13, 14, 16, 17.

720

Friends. His object was to answer compendiously the questions being asked by many both within and outside the Society concerning Friends' peace testimony; he had found out himself, he tells us in the preface, how difficult it was to refer questioners to suitable literature, "which would afford them a ready answer, without cost, or laborious research." The treatment is rather disorderly, but the author covers the ground fairly adequately, ranging from the pacifism of the New Testament and the early church through a number of later Christian advocates of peace, including the Quakers and their Pennsylvania experiment (in which Michener was particularly interested). For further reading he recommended Barclay's *Apology*, Clarkson's *Portraiture of Quakerism*, Dymond's *Essays on Morality*, and Adin Ballou's works on Christian nonresistance.

In the same year that Michener produced his little book, two thin pamphlets were published by Friends in New York state, both named Cornell. W. T. Cornell's effort was entitled *On the Incompatibility of War with the Spirit of Christianity* and was aimed, in the words of the preface, to give "proof that should forever shame and put to silence the professor of Christianity who is an advocate of war." Follow Christ and do not look to the consequences was its simple message. John J. Cornell (1826-1909) was clerk of Genesee Yearly Meeting in upstate New York at the time war broke out. The *Address* on the peace testimony, which he published in 1862 with the approval of his fellow members, was meant primarily for internal consumption, to strengthen Friends in his yearly meeting in upholding the Society's opposition to all war by bringing them back to the sources of Quaker pacifism in the Sermon on the Mount and the other teachings of the gospels. He had been led to write it, he stated, by observing that

> There are some amongst us who, either from inattention to the unfoldings of Divine Light, or by intermingling with the strivings and contentions of political life, or from inexperience in the school of Christ, are yet either hesitating to carry out this noble testimony, or have suffered their feelings to become so enlisted in favor of what they deem to be the right in the present contest, that they have given their allegiance to the doctrine that a war conducted for self-defense, or to put down rebellion, is admissible and even right.[15]

After 1862, members of the Society of Friends published little or nothing new relating to the peace testimony for the rest of the war (apart from the official pronouncements of the various meetings and contributions to the Quaker periodicals). Yet the Society included in

[15] J. J. Cornell, *An Address*, pp. 1, 2.

721

its membership at least one concerned Friend with outstanding literary gifts, a figure of note in the world of letters who, moreover, felt a deep obligation to place his pen at the service of humanitarian causes. Was John Greenleaf Whittier, then, ardent abolitionist as he had shown himself in the prewar years and with his passionate temperament, one of those Quakers who had been carried away by their hatred of slavery to put their allegiance to the peace testimony into cold storage for the duration of the war? We find that his patriotic verse written in the early years of the conflict and published in book form under the title *In War Time and Other Poems* (Boston, 1863) did, indeed, act as a great boost to Northern morale. They gained the poet an invitation in 1864 to visit the Army of the Potomac and the eulogy there of a brigadier-general: "Your loyal verse has made us all your friends, lightening the wearisomeness of our march, brightening our lonely campfires, and cheering our hearts in battle."[16] Yet Whittier never relinquished his personal adherence to the peace testimony and rejected the appellation of war poet. "I have never written a poem in favor or in praise of war," he remarked many years later.[17] He always admitted to feeling profound sympathy with the better aspects of the Unionist cause and deep admiration for those who had selflessly given their service, and sometimes their lives, to the struggle. But, as he wrote to the Newburyport *Herald* at the beginning of the war when that paper published a report that he had contributed toward raising volunteers, "as a settled believer in the principles of the Society of Friends, I can do nothing at a time like this beyond mitigating, to the extent of my power, the calamities and suffering attendant upon war, and accepting cheerfully my allotted share of the privation and trials growing out of it."[18] And, after he had watched the youthful Colonel Shaw marching off at the head of his Negro regiment, the 55th, to the battlefront from which he was not to return, Whittier, deeply moved, wrote to Mrs. Lydia Maria Child, an old friend who shared his brand of nonresistant abolitionism: "I have longed to speak the emotions of that hour, but I dared not, lest I should indirectly give a new impulse to war."[19] With the two impulses

[16] Samuel T. Pickard, *Life and Letters of John Greenleaf Whittier*, II, 476.

[17] Letter to John J. Pratt, 7 Dec. 1878, quoted in *Bulletin of Friends' Historical Society of Philadelphia*, vol. 9, no. 1 (1919), p. 43.

[18] Letter dated 15 May 1861, quoted in *Friends' Review*, 1 June 1861. A month later, on 18 June, Whittier addressed an open letter to members of the Society of Friends, urging them to give their utmost to relieving the suffering of war, whether on the battle front or back at home, as an essential part of their peace testimony. "Let the Quaker bonnet," he wrote, "be seen by the side of the black hood of the Catholic Sisters of Charity in the hospital ward." See Pickard, *Whittier*, II, 441.

[19] Quoted in A. T. Murray, "Whittier's Attitude toward War," *Present Day Papers*, II, no. 7 (July 1915), 216.

of peace and antislavery warring in his heart, it is not surprising, therefore, that we do not find Whittier an active protagonist of the Quaker peace testimony. He felt it his task rather to urge his fellow Quakers to acts of mercy for suffering humanity than to expound nonresistance to a people fighting oppression.[20]

The same deep commitment to the purposes of the war (or what were thought ought to be its purposes), combined with a purely personal pacifism, is to be found in a small group of intellectuals and radicals on the fringe of the Quaker world. The Progressive or Congregational Friends of Pennsylvania, because of the high moral and intellectual caliber of many of the members and the fact that both leadership and rank and file were leavened with a goodly number of militant nonresistants, might perhaps have been expected (at least by one not acquainted with the wartime attitudes of other survivors of the nonresistant movement of previous decades) to make some contribution to the ideology of Quaker pacifism. The reverse rather was the case.

The group, which dated from 1853, belonged to an offshoot of the Hicksite branch of the Society, which had arisen in the late forties and early fifties. Its activities were centered in the Philadelphia area, with smaller groups in New York state and in the Midwest. The movement represented a protest against Quaker sectarianism and theological intolerance, as well as against the predominance of conservative authority in the Society in general. Its main interest lay in the promotion of humanitarian reforms, and in antislavery work in particular. There was no formal membership and no set discipline—and, therefore, no disownments. Its theology was liberal: all were welcome who believed in God and in the brotherhood of man. There was, indeed,

[20] Merle E. Curti ("Poets of Peace and the Civil War," *World Unity*, X, no. 3 [June 1932], 151) has suggested that, if Whittier had not felt bound by his loyalty to his Society's peace testimony, he would probably have given unqualified support to the war. As it is, "one looks in vain in Whittier's war poetry for anything like a condemnation of the War; he does not see fit to observe that even so holy a cause as freedom might be ill-served by bloodshed." (It may be noted, too, that the militant revolutionary nationalist, Garibaldi, had always been one of the poet's heroes.) A certain ambiguity remained in Whittier's attitude toward peace in the postwar years. Witness his admiration and praise for what he considered the heroic Christian spirit of General Gordon ("a providential man") at the time of his death in the Sudan in 1885, an attitude which brought down on him the censure of John Bright. (See Murray, *Present Day Papers*, II, no. 7, 217, 218.) As an old man he reaffirmed his basic agreement with the peace testimony of the Society to which he belonged in a letter to Hannah J. Bailey on 1 January 1890. "The cause of Peace," he wrote there, "lies very near to my heart. War seems to me now to be the great evil to be abolished. While it exists there are no *Christian* nations. I am glad to see thee so earnestly devoted to the cause of Peace. It is the great mission of our Society." From MS letter in the Whittier Collection, F.H.L.S.C.

723

within this framework a wide diversity of opinion. It included within its ranks those who retained membership in the old established Hicksite meetings, like Lucretia Mott and her husband or Thomas Garrett, former members of the Society who had been drummed out of one or another of its branches for transgressing the discipline, and also a number of sympathizers from other churches or of no defined religious affiliation, ranging from the near-Quaker Alfred H. Love to religious liberals like Samuel J. May, William Lloyd Garrison, Cyrus M. Burleigh, and a number of others.

Although nonpacifist associates participated in its activities, its prewar stand had been strongly pacifist, and the influence of radical nonresistance of the Garrisonian variety on its pronouncements on war was marked. However, after war had broken out, enthusiasm for overthrowing slavery led the Progressive Friends into denunciations of the opposite side that were rarely outdone in the most warlike sections of the popular press. Take, for instance, this extract, dealing with the Confederate authorities, from the published proceedings of their yearly meeting held at Longwood (Pa.) in June 1862:

> Of the crimes and barbarities these conspirators have committed since they madly commenced the war—outraging all the claims of humanity and civilization—it is needless to speak at length. They will make such a volume of horrors as can scarcely be paralleled by the most savage warfare in the darkest ages of the world. Scalping, poisoning, and assassinating the living—mangling the bodies of the dead—making the skulls of Northern soldiers into drinking cups, and their bones into ornaments for barbarous display—repeatedly and persistently hoisting the white flag of truce, only to betray and slaughter those to whom they thus professed to surrender—carrying desolation and war everywhere in their train—these are but specimens of the almost numberless deeds of treachery and ferocity that have marked their bloody career.

Curiously enough, the passage is taken from the meeting's "testimony" for peace! In the same document the government is denounced—for not carrying on the war with enough vigor and for "dealing with the rebels as misguided brethren rather than as enemies of mankind." Yet the "testimony" also goes on to state its opinion that "in thus expressing our [general] sympathy with the government, we do not conceive that we repudiate or invalidate even the most radical peace principles that may be cherished by any of our Society."[21]

21 *Proceedings of the Pennsylvania Yearly Meeting of Progressive Friends . . . 1862*, pp. 11, 12. This "testimony" and several other documents issued by the

In 1864 its yearly meeting proceedings contain alongside a "testimony" on "the evils of war," which "was adopted without discussion," exhortations to the administration not to weaken its efforts to crush the "slave oligarchy" completely. They saw no reason why "scrupulous non-resistants" should hesitate in collaborating (so far as conscience permitted) in their government's efforts "in suppressing the rebellion." Although it should respect the scruples of religious objectors, the administration had both "the right and the duty" to impose federal conscription on the country.[22]

If avowed nonresistants of long standing felt this way, what wonder that many young men who had been reared in Quaker homes and in the teachings of the peace testimony, ignoring the subtle distinction between conscious support of the war and a purely personal pacifism such as Garrison and the Progressive Friends nursed throughout the war years, decided—some only after long hesitation—to go against the discipline and traditional behavior of their church and participate actively in the struggle. Comments from both the major branches of the Society[23] indicate that many young Friends had been insufficiently grounded in the meaning of the peace testimony by the education they received at home and in school and that they were easily swept off their feet by patriotic fervor and enthusiasm for the cause of the oppressed slave—Friends' other great testimony which seemed to conflict in the moment of crisis with their pacifism.

A few days after the shelling of Fort Sumter, the poet, Bayard Taylor, himself of Quaker stock, wrote of his home town of Kennett Place (Pa.): "All the young Quakers have enlisted. The excitement and anxiety is really terrible. We are so near the frontier." Two days later he reported in another letter: "The women are heroes. Old Quaker women see their sons go, without a tear."[24] Early the following month we find Sarah M. Palmer, daughter of the Quaker abolitionist, Isaac

---

assembly were drawn up by Garrison, who was present at its sessions. See Garrisons, W.L.G., IV, 52. In his Liberator, Garrison retailed equally gruesome and gory stories of Southern barbarities in battle. (See John L. Thomas, The Liberator, p. 413.) Garrison's associate, Oliver Johnson, was clerk of their yearly meeting for many years. The yearly meeting for 1861, scheduled for June, had not in fact been called, ostensibly on account of the tense war situation but perhaps principally because of the inflamed feelings of many associates of the group, and not only the nonpacifist minority. The movement declined after the war and eventually disappeared altogether.

[22] Proceedings . . . 1864, pp. 11, 14-16.

[23] See, e.g., Friends' Review, 11 May 1861; Friends' Intelligencer, 30 Nov. 1861, 20 Dec. 1862.

[24] Life and Letters of Bayard Taylor (5th edn.), I, 375-77: letters of 21 and 23 April 1861.

T. Hopper, whose antislavery activities had eventually earned him disownment from the Society, describing the situation in Philadelphia in the following words: "Quakers are drilling, contrary to all the peace principles of the sect; indeed from all appearances we may suppose their hopes are based on war. I'm opposed to war—to cutting down men like grass—but if ever war was holy, this one, in favor of the most oppressed, most forbearing, most afflicted, downtrodden, insulted part of humanity, is a holy war."[25] In July 1862 the English-born Friend, Mrs. Elizabeth L. Comstock (1815-1891), who was active in the ministry and in various Quaker philanthropies, wrote to a friend: "We hear of many young Friends taking up arms for the North." She went on to relate the story of three young Union soldiers previously unacquainted with each other who fell into a casual conversation. Soon it transpired that all three were birthright Quakers: one the son of Dr. Samuel Boyd Tobey, clerk of New England Yearly Meeting, another the son of Sybil and Eli Jones, well known as Quaker ministers in Maine, and the third the son of a leading Friend, William Henry Chase.[26] On the whole, however, the rural meetings contributed "very few volunteers"; more came from Quaker communities in urban areas.[27]

Garrison's words, spoken to his Quaker friends to comfort them in their distress at seeing so many of their young men abandon the traditional position on war, probably to a large extent coincided with the feelings of Friends themselves at this time:

> I told them [he wrote in the autumn of 1861] that however much they might regret that their sons could not meet the test when it was applied they should at least rejoice that the boys were true to their real convictions when the shot at Sumter revealed to them that they were simply birthright Quakers, and had not fully comprehended and absorbed the principles of their fathers. They had imagined they were on the plane of the Sermon on the Mount, and they found they were only up to the level of Lexington and Bunker Hill; but they should be honored none the less for their loyalty to truth and freedom.[28]

Owing to the regular record keeping of the Society of Friends and the preservation in good condition of almost all of the materials dat-

[25] *Life of Abby Hopper Gibbons told chiefly through her Correspondence*, I, 292: letter from Sarah H. Palmer, dated 5 May 1861.
[26] *Life and Letters of Elizabeth L. Comstock*, p. 109.
[27] Rufus M. Jones, *The Later Periods of Quakerism*, II, 729. Jones reached this conclusion after examining a number of monthly meeting records.
[28] Garrisons, *W.L.G.*, IV, 37.

ing from the Civil War at least, a systematic examination of these records would probably yield a reasonably accurate figure of the number of Friends who entered the Union army and the proportion this figure bears to the total number of Friends drafted. But in the absence of a study of this nature generalizations have to be based to some extent on probabilities and surmise rather than on statistical fact. Assertions have been made that the number of Friends serving with the forces was higher in proportion to total numbers than was the case with any other religious group.[29] But, as Rufus Jones correctly remarks, there appears to be "no historical evidence whatever to justify such a statement." The "deviations" from pacifism, he goes on, "were more numerous than one would have expected in a conservative body which made the testimony an absolutely essential feature of its faith." However, in view of the strong pressures exerted on the young in the direction of active participation in the war, "the total number appears small."[30]

According to the minutes of the Meeting for Sufferings of Philadelphia (Orthodox) Yearly Meeting, to take one example, 150 men were drafted. Although some were rejected on grounds of health or for some other disability, only 4 actually accepted military service.[31] On the other hand, if we take a small Orthodox preparative meeting, that of Jericho (Randolph County, Ind.), out in the Midwest near the frontier where the weight of traditional authority would have been less than in metropolitan Philadelphia and its environs, we find a rather different pattern. There 16 young men connected with the meeting served in the Northern army, and only 9 appear to have become conscientious objectors.[32] And on another frontier, the borderland area between North and South, it is possible that in the Baltimore (Hicksite) Yearly Meeting fewer men of military age abided by the traditional peace testimony than were drawn by loyalty to the union and devotion to the antislavery cause to join the ranks of the army. In September 1861 the address issued by the yearly meeting lamented concerning members' attitude toward war: "There are few among us who have fully realized the evils connected with this anti-christian practice."[33] Two years later one of its monthly meetings had this to say on the way its members were upholding the peace testimony:

[29] This was stated, for instance, in regard to the Hicksite branch by Albert G. Thatcher, "The Quakers' Attitude to War," *Advocate of Peace*, LXXIX, no. 8 (Aug. 1917), 238.
[30] Jones, *The Later Periods of Quakerism*, II, 736-40. See also Wright, pp. 184-86, 188, 189.
[31] Wright, p. 183. [32] *Jericho Friends' Meeting and Its Community*, pp. 53, 54.
[33] *Friends' Intelligencer*, 19 Oct. 1861.

Our testimony against a hireling ministry, oaths, clandestine trade, prize goods, and lotteries appears to have been generally maintained, but we have mournfully to acknowledge a wide departure on the part of most of our members from our Christian testimony against war. Many of our young men have taken up arms, and are actively engaged in the unhappy contest now desolating the country. Whilst many also of more mature years and even among the elder class have openly advocated war, and countenanced, encouraged and assisted those performing military [service]; nevertheless we believe there remains a remnant who are concerned for the preservation of our members and humbly desire to adhere faithfully to this ancient testimony against war.[34]

This situation, where only "a remnant" of the meeting continued to uphold Quaker pacifism, was surely exceptional if we consider the Society in the Northern states as a whole. But it is true that the considerable number of deviations from the peace testimony, especially among the younger members, indicated that in large sections of the Society this part of Quaker belief lacked the vitality and living reality it had possessed at times in the past among American and British Friends.

What happened to those Friends who contravened the Society's discipline and took up arms? How did meetings react to what in a few cases amounted to almost a mass desertion of Quaker pacifism and in almost every instance presented a problem for the Society? Again, no overall statistical data have been collected, and we are dependent here, too, on only partial evidence.

The act of becoming a soldier constituted an infringement of the Quaker discipline similar to marrying outside the Society, taking an oath,[35] or committing some offense against the Society's moral code. Disownment was the usual penalty for such infringement, unless due contrition was expressed.

Sometimes, disownment may have been carried out while the war was still in progress and the delinquent members on active service. We read of this happening soon after Gettysburg, for instance, to several young Quakers belonging to an Ohio country meeting, who had taken part in the battle. One of them was Benjamin Butterworth, (1837-1898), later to become a prominent figure in the Republican

[34] Report of an unnamed monthly meeting, dated 15 Aug. 1863, from Thomas Jenkins Papers, F.H.L.S.C.

[35] Curiously enough, Friends who had contravened their Society's testimony against war by entering the army were usually reluctant to break a minor commandment by taking the oath of allegiance and, in most cases, were permitted on request to substitute an affirmation. See the article by Thaddeus S. Kinderdine in the *Friends' Intelligencer*, LXVII, no. 25 (24 June 1911), 395.

Party in Ohio, whose own father on this occasion was responsible for proposing that proceedings should be commenced against the young men. "His father had not heard from him since the great battle and did not then know whether he was asking for the disownment of a dead son, or a live soldier."[36] But such almost Roman severity was rare. In most cases where a Friend had joined up, final action was postponed until the conclusion of hostilities.[37] Generally, postponement of a decision stemmed from a desire not to deal too harshly with their young people, who had been carried away by the enthusiasm of the hour to uphold, by un-Quakerly methods it was true, a cause with which most Friends sympathized. A minute of Genesee (Hicksite) Yearly Meeting passed at the end of the war summed up feelings that were widespread throughout the Society when it expressed the hope concerning "delinquent" members that

> . . . now, as the conflict has ceased, and as they return to their peaceful homes, they may become so convinced of the superiority of the principle of love to that of force, and that it is better to suffer wrong for a season than to do wrong, that they may so live in the future as not only to give satisfaction to their friends, and thus be continued in the bosom of Society, but by being convinced by experience . . . of this divine principle become its devoted advocates.

The returning soldiers were to be dealt with in a spirit of "sympathy and affectionate solicitude" (to use the words of Philadelphia [Hicksite] Yearly Meeting), brought to a renewed trust in the principles which underlie the Quaker peace testimony, and then received back lovingly into the religious community of their friends.[38]

There were some, of course, whose wartime experiences caused them to drift away from Quakerism altogether; some among these, even before the war, may have been only nominally attached to the faith of their ancestors. Others, although unwilling to break their association with the religion in which they had been reared, were yet not ready to condemn their conduct in taking up arms. "Those friends who entered the military forces and later justified their actions on patriotic or other grounds," as Wright says, "were generally 'disowned'

[36] H. E. Smith, *The Quakers, Their Migration to the Upper Ohio, Their Customs and Discipline*, p. 53. Yet Butterworth was listed later as a member of the Society, a fact which seems to cast some doubt on the accuracy of Smith's account.

[37] Wright is mistaken in asserting (p. 153) that General Henry W. Halleck retained membership in the Society throughout the war. In fact, General Halleck was never associated with Friends, and hence there could be no question of disciplinary action by the Quakers against him.

[38] *Friends' Intelligencer*, 8 July 1865. For a similar attitude on the part of Philadelphia (Hicksite) Y. M., see *ibid.*, 10 June 1865.

by their local Meeting."[39] Proceedings were not taken, however, or were stopped if already begun, when the returned soldier presented "an acknowledgment of error." Many examples of these acknowledgments have been preserved in the records of monthly meetings. They differ considerably in their exact wording, but their purport and content are remarkably similar. Here is one, a collective acknowledgment taken from the records of Westbury Monthly Meeting, a country meeting in New Jersey:

> Dear Friends, Having so far departed from the discipline and testimonies of Society, as, under an impression of duty, in view of the peculiar circumstances by which we were surrounded, to take up arms in defence of the government, sensible of our deviation from the principles of our education, yet desirous of retaining our rights in membership we hope that this with our future conduct may reconcile us to our Friends again.[40]

How genuine such repentances actually were it is difficult to say. Many who joined up continued to regard the peace testimony as a lofty ideal. Although they themselves had felt unable to live up to it in the existing circumstances, they were glad that the Society still remained loyal to its principles. Others, while finding it hard to comprehend how they could have acted otherwise than they did when their country seemed in danger and while continuing to hold inner reservations on the subject of Quaker pacifism, were yet willing to make concessions to the weight of opinion within the religious Society to which they were attached by so many bonds of affection.

We find, on the one hand, a young Quaker like Cyrus W. Harvey (1843-1916), who later became a weighty Friend out in Kansas and a keen pacifist, not being satisfied with the formal acknowledgment of error that he had presented to his home meeting in Indiana, along with several other boys who had served like him with the Union forces. Therefore, several months later, in fear "that he had not done his full duty in the matter," he stood up in meeting to make "a clear confession of his wrong-doing, and of his sorrow on account of it, condemning all carnal warfare as being un-Christian."[41] The sensitive conscience of the veteran, now turned pacifist, is matched on the other side by those who, anxious to return as soon as possible to full communion with their fellow members and prepared to recognize the Society's pacifist position as a whole, still did not feel it in their

---

[39] Wright, pp. 209, 210, where several examples of testimonies of disownment in such cases are given in full.

[40] MS in F.H.L.S.C.   [41] *Memorial of Cyrus W. Harvey*, pp. 8, 9.

hearts to condemn their wartime conduct. An example of this attitude is to be found in the dignified statement presented by Wilmer Atkinson (1840-1920), who later founded the *Farm Journal*, and a number of other young men and accepted by Horsham Monthly Meeting (Hicksite). They wrote:

> We, the undersigned members of Horsham Monthly Meeting, having been engaged in the service of our country in her peril and need . . . individually acknowledge we have departed from the injunctions of the discipline of the Society of Friends. In extenuation of this deviation we plead the regard and love of our common country, her laws and civil institutions, endangered . . . by a wicked and causeless rebellion involving us all in one common desire to maintain and perpetuate them. Feeling desirous that the testimonies of our Society may be maintained as founded in truth we present this declaration as an acknowledgement which we request to be placed on the minutes of the Monthly Meeting with our names appended and renew our desires of continued membership and ask that any proceedings had on account of our deviation may from henceforth cease.[42]

Most meetings, in fact, took great pains in trying to reclaim the strayed member. We can see the extent of such efforts in an example taken from the records of Kansas Friends. One of their members, Samuel Worthington, enlisted early in 1863, and his preparative meeting appointed a committee to speak with him. It was reported that "he manifests love for Society, but is not yet willing to acknowledge his deviation, whereupon after full consideration, the meeting comes to the judgment to continue the case." The matter dragged on for nearly three years; only at the end of 1865, when, perhaps, Worthington's term of service was finished, did he express the necessary sorrow for his "error."[43]

The general feeling in the Society at that time seems to have been in favor of enforcing the discipline at least against those who had participated in warmaking so far as to bear arms. Opinion, however, was by no means unanimous, especially among Eastern meetings of the Hicksite branch and also in some communities of Orthodox Friends in the Midwest.[44] As might be expected, such reservations were strong-

[42] Dated 28 Dec. 1866, in Thomas Jenkins Papers, F.H.L.S.C., cf. Wright, pp. 212, 213.

[43] Cecil B. Currey, "Quaker Pacifism in Kansas, 1833-1945," M.Sc. thesis, Fort Hays Kansas State College, pp. 32, 33.

[44] Thaddeus S. Kinderdine, *op. cit.*; Jones, *The Later Periods of Quakerism*, II, 738.

est among those rebel spirits, many of whom, like Lucretia Mott, were associated with the Progressive Friends. The New York *Friend*, which was connected with this group of religious liberals, commenting in June 1866 on the disownment by the Hicksite monthly meeting in New York City of a young Quaker soldier who maintained the rightness of his action in enlisting, wrote: "We have serious objection to any clause of discipline which requires a Friend to be disowned for acting up to his highest conviction of duty. Warfare is horrible in the flesh—but it is heaven-born innocence by the side of a war upon conscience."[45]

In some meetings, however, it does not seem to have been primarily a theoretical stand in favor of liberty of religious conscience so much as a very deep-seated division of opinion among even weighty Friends in the meeting as to the validity of the peace testimony, at least in relation to the circumstances of the recent war, that led to opposition to the disownment of the unrepentant Quaker fighters. In the Hicksite Yearly Meeting in Indiana, feelings were so divided that in the autumn of 1867 the yearly meeting appointed a committee of twenty to investigate the question. In its report the committee recommended that, since those who had deviated from the peace testimony had done so "from motives of conceived duty and patriotism" and, therefore, were "unable truthfully to say they are convinced of the error of their course," "the spirit of our discipline" and "the best welfare of our Society" did not require the disownment of those former soldiers who wished to continue in membership, were in unity with Friends' other testimonies, and yet felt that they could not in good conscience denounce their military activities.[46]

It was the Baltimore (Hicksite) Yearly Meeting that included some of the most deeply divided Quaker communities. At its yearly meeting in 1865, "the Committee appointed to consider the question" of deviations from the peace testimony recommended that "a lenient course should be pursued." Where possible, "voluntary acknowledgements" of error should be obtained verbally; when such endeavors proved ineffectual, "the names of the delinquents shall be reported to the Monthly Meeting."[47] What further action, if any, should be taken

[45] *Friend* (N.Y.), I, no. 6 (June 1866), 85. See pp. 87, 99, 119, 147 of the same volume for letters from readers pro and con allowing freedom in the matter to the individual conscience.

[46] From Thomas Jenkins Papers, F.H.L.S.C. The author of a recent study of one of the meetings in Indiana, which produced a goodly number of Quaker soldiers, comments: "On the whole, however, the minutes of the White River Monthly Meeting are singularly free from condemnation of the boys who had borne arms" (*Jericho Friends' Meeting*, p. 54).

[47] Quoted in Wright, p. 211.

732

was not specified: this, presumably, was the individual responsibility of each monthly meeting. In country meetings, always strongholds of Quaker traditionalism, disownment seems to have followed fairly regularly on the failure of a returned soldier to express contrition. But among urban Friends within this yearly meeting, and especially in the case of Baltimore Monthly Meeting, no action seems to have been taken against deviants from the peace testimony. The minutes of the latter meeting record for 8 March 1866: "There has been a general deviation on the part of our membership." A half century later Joseph J. Janney, a highly respected member of the meeting in Baltimore (he had himself volunteered for the Union army but was never called to account for his conduct), wrote: "There were not enough members who were entirely innocent to pronounce judgment on the alleged violators." He relates how, when the question of taking disciplinary action against the returned veterans came up, an aged Friend, "a much beloved minister . . . who sat at the head of the Meeting," arose and said: "If the discipline is to be applied in these cases commence with me. Although I did not enlist in the army I am not innocent, in some ways I am as guilty as those who did."[48] In this meeting, at any rate, no attempt was made to exclude the delinquent members.

An interesting case where an unrepentant veteran was permitted to retain membership is that of William J. Palmer (1836-1909) of Race Street (Hicksite) Monthly Meeting in Philadelphia. After volunteering at the outset of the war, Palmer achieved the rank of brigadier-general before he was finally demobilized in 1867. The young man viewed his wartime service quite unapologetically. He wrote to another young Friend on 19 April 1867 after being approached by a committee of his home meeting:

> I have every desire to retain my connection, and hope they will look upon my case with that liberal and charitable spirit which I think distinguishes them from most other sects and which is one of the strongest incentives in my mind towards remaining a member of the Society. I think my views on the subject of Peace can hardly differ in essential points, from those of our Meeting, or at least of a majority of the members as I have incidentally learned them through their conversation and actions during and since the war. Of course under the same circumstances as existed in the summer of '61 I would act precisely as I did then and I do not understand that Friends desire me to think or say otherwise—as they would be the last to believe that principle should be compromised for the sake

[48] From Thomas Jenkins Papers, F.H.L.S.C.

of avoiding troubles ... one of the most essential principles of Friends is obedience to conscience—much more essential than a belief in non-resistance. I do not ask more than that my case should be treated in that light. I think that Peace is holy and should be encouraged constantly—and that an unjust war is only legalized murder. But the inner light made it very plain to me in the summer of '61 that I should enter the army.[49]

Palmer was correct in his assumption that his meeting would accept his statement without requiring any expression of regret for his past actions.[50] A pacifist church (as the Society of Friends might still be considered at that date) may be congratulated for its liberalism in retaining a brigadier-general on its roll of members, but it is clear that the war had wrought a profound change in the position the traditional peace testimony held within the framework of the Quaker ethos.

II

The fighting Quaker, a seeming contradiction in terms, might catch the public eye by the very incongruity of his action. The Quaker who, though of military age, remained in one way or another a noncombatant was a less unfamiliar figure. He was following the traditional pattern of the Society and, although a nonconformist in relation to the general behavior of a community at war, was, as we have seen, a conservative in relation to his own background and home environment. Nevertheless, the pattern of behavior of the Quaker pacifist in wartime was a complex one, whether it was a case of a young man facing the challenge of conscription or of an older Friend who had to decide how he would meet the various demands of the authorities connected with the prosecution of the war. We must now turn, therefore, to consider how this group, which undoubtedly constituted the majority of Friends taken as a whole, and especially those of more mature years, fared under wartime conditions.

In the early months of the war Friends, along with the other peace sects, had hoped that enough recruits would be raised for the armies of the North by the voluntary method. But this optimism slowly faded

[49] *Letters 1853-1868: Gen'l. Wm. J. Palmer*, pp. 87, 88. It appears that the Philadelphia Y. M. of the Hicksite branch was laxer than most other sections of the Society is disowning its ex-soldiers who failed to make acknowledgment of error. See T. S. Kinderdine in *Friends' Intelligencer*, LXX, no. 27 (5 July 1913), 420-22.

[50] See his obituary in *Friends' Intelligencer*, vol. LXVI, no. 5 (10 April 1909). General Palmer remained a Friend until his death.

during the first half of 1862. On 17 July of that year Congress passed the Federal Militia Act, which, although it left enrollment of men between the ages of 18 and 45 in the hands of the state authorities, provided for the intervention of the President in case the latter were unable to execute the law properly. And, in fact, in the following month, by his General Order of 9 August, the President summoned 300,000 men to the colors for a period of nine months. Since the position of those who had religious scruples against bearing arms was far from clear under the new legislation, Friends busied themselves with trying to obtain satisfactory assurances from the state authorities that such scruples would actually be respected. To some extent, as we have seen in an earlier chapter, conscientious objection had been recognized in the prewar militia legislation of many of the states at least, and this fact was frequently alluded to in the discussions over wartime conscription which now ensued. "Before the end of the year 1862 Friends and other noncombatants realized the seriousness of the military situation, and braced themselves for the struggle ahead." It became obvious that the Act of the previous July was proving inadequate for providing the men necessary to carry on the struggle and that the introduction of full federal conscription was not far away. Friends, therefore, now turned their attention to the Federal administration, and a series of memorials setting out the Quaker position on war and asking for adequate provision to be made in forthcoming legislation for the rights of conscience were presented to President and Congress by a number of yearly meetings. The final draft of the Conscription Act as it passed Congress on 3 March 1863 proved extremely unsatisfactory to all sections of the Society of Friends. Those drafted and unwilling to serve were permitted to furnish a substitute to take their place in the ranks, or, if they preferred, they might pay the sum of $300 in commutation money to procure such a substitute. No mention was made of conscientious objection.

E. N. Wright comments as follows on the reaction of Friends to the contents of the Act:

The provision for the payment of commutation money in lieu of personal service was satisfactory to many noncombatants, but not to those who were most conscientious in their attitude toward military requirements. Quakers, especially, rightly surmised that the commutation money would be used for the purchase of substitutes and that payment of the fee was therefore a direct aid to the military authorities and virtually an equivalent to personal service . . . throughout 1863 and the years which followed, the attitude of the

735

Society of Friends as a whole remained consistently opposed to the payment of commutation money or the procuration of substitutes.[51]

Yet, as Wright goes on to point out, although the official attitude of the various yearly meetings remained set—at least at first—against any compromise on this issue, considerable variations in opinion and practice existed among individual Friends.

Throughout the war Quaker meetings attempted to provide counsel and care for those younger members who faced the ordeal of the draft. There was at times something a little condescending, a certain patriarchal note, in the way advice was dispensed. We find the *Friend*, for instance, early in the war, while summoning older Friends to show "patience and forbearance" in guiding the Society's sometimes faltering, bewildered, and brash young people of draft age, making it plain that, in return, the latter should properly "appreciate the privilege of being under the care and partaking of the sympathy and Christian regard of those of riper experience, more mature judgment, and greater stability in the Truth than themselves."[52] Those young folk whose youthful exuberance had led them to deviate from the sober behavior that was thought to befit a Friend, either by abandoning the plain attire or by attending dances or participating in one or another of the world's amusements, were sternly rebuked in another issue of the same paper. "In the present trials consequent on drafting for the army," it was pointed out with obvious satisfaction, "many of our gay young members have found how much harder it has been for them to appear before the commissioners to claim exemption on the ground of conscientious scruples, than it would have been had their conduct, conversation and clothing, all borne witness for them that they were bearing the cross of Christ."[53]

But if on occasion there was a note of priggishness in the manner in which Friends expressed their sympathy for the young people on whose inexperienced shoulders rested the main burden of upholding the Society's testimony against war, the records do show a widespread and genuine concern at this time of crisis to help "our precious young Friends," who were struggling to reach a decision on the conscription issue, and to strengthen those of them whom conscientious conviction brought into conflict with the authorities. Many meetings at various levels appointed special committees entrusted with the task of overseeing their conscientious objectors, and from time to time these committees issued reports of their activities. They show older Friends not

[51] Wright, pp. 39, 40, 49-65.
[52] *Friend*, 23 Aug. 1862.
[53] *Ibid.*, 8 Nov. 1862.

only in the role of advisers but active in accompanying Quaker conscripts to the boards of enrollment and helping them state their case to the authorities, in keeping in regular contact with those who had been arrested for noncompliance and placed in military camps, and in negotiating on their behalf with, and lobbying, the whole gamut of civilian and military authorities concerned, from the lowest rung right up to the President in Washington.[54] Some of the more fiery spirits in the Society occasionally complained of the timidity of elders and of their lack of sympathy for those drafted Friends who refused all compromise with the making of war.[55] But on the whole, and despite considerable difference of opinion among Friends who upheld the peace testimony on a number of points of behavior in connection with the war, the Quaker conscientious objector was well supported by his Society.

We spoke a little earlier about the complexity of the pattern of behavior among Quaker pacifists during the Civil War. Let us take first the question of hiring substitutes. Opinion was fairly unanimous here that a Quaker who paid another man to fight in his place was offending against the spirit of the peace testimony as much as, perhaps even more than, if he had taken up arms himself. The editor of the Orthodox *Friend* of Philadelphia was speaking for all branches of the Society when he wrote: "If it is wrong for me to fight and kill my fellow-creatures, it must be wrong to pay my money to hire another to do it; just as it would be to pay my money to hire a man to steal or murder." How do we know, he added, that the substitute may not be a brutal fellow who will commit various atrocities, when given the occasion, in addition to the routine killing of a soldier's career.[56] In the past, as shown earlier in this history, the penalty of disownment was regularly meted out to Friends who resorted to this practice when called upon for military service. Yet in the Civil War some Friends when drafted did undoubtedly furnish substitutes, and their meetings in many instances failed to take action against them. The Thomas Jenkins Papers (F.H.L.S.C.) contain several examples of such cases. Henry Dillingham of Granville Monthly Meeting (N.Y.) was drafted for service "but found a man who was going any way, and so he paid him the amount required to buy a substitute. As he was a poor man he was glad to get the money." Another Dillingham, Reuben by name, escaped the draft because his aunt hired a substitute for him. The fact that in this meeting members who had volunteered for the army were

[54] Wright, pp. 70, 190-98.

[55] For an example of such criticism, see the letter from Gideon Frost in the *Friend*, 22 Oct. 1864.

[56] *Friend*, 1 Aug. 1863.

737

not dealt with perhaps explains why no action was taken, either, against the two Dillinghams. In Brooklyn Monthly Meeting, too, some members paid for substitutes when drafted. These examples are all drawn from Eastern Hicksite meetings where, as we have seen earlier in this chapter, enforcement of the discipline for infringements of the peace testimony was laxer than in other parts of the Society. Disownment for hiring substitutes was certainly practised during the war.

When we come to the question of paying commutation money, the right course to follow was not quite so clear even to concerned Friends. Under the act of March 1863 the problem was in a way simplified by the probability that the money paid in this manner would be used for the purchase of recruits and was thus very little, if at all, distinguishable from straight hiring of a substitute. This objection, however, was removed by the clause in the subsequent act of 24 February 1864 (see below), whereby religious objectors would pay their commutation fine into a fund for the benefit of sick and wounded soldiers (a provision, however, that still might not be acceptable in itself to strict pacifists). It still left unchanged, of course, the major reason why Friends as a body now, as before the war, considered it wrong to pay commutation money: that no government was entitled to exact any penalty, or demand any service, in exchange for permission to follow the dictates of conscience. This absolutist point of view, the claim that it implied for unconditional exemption from military service, was well summed up in a minute, dated 13 April 1865, of the Meeting for Sufferings of Philadelphia (Orthodox) Yearly Meeting. "Believing," it stated, "that liberty of conscience is the gift of the Creator to man, Friends have ever refused to purchase the free exercise of it, by the payment of any pecuniary or other commutation, to any human authority."[57] That the state's demand was for something otherwise quite innocuous, perhaps highly commendable, could make no difference to the principle involved, which was one that, in fact, concerned not so much pacifism as the inborn rights of man.

An interesting discussion of the problem was carried on during the second half of 1863 in the columns of the Hicksite *Friends' Intelligencer*. The exchange of views started at the end of June with the publication of the first of three articles on the subject of "Friends and Government Requisitions" by a Byberry (Pa.) Friend, who signed himself "N.R." In his articles "N.R.," using arguments reminiscent of Mennonite or Dunker writers, urged that there was nothing inconsistent with Quaker pacifism in paying a fine in exchange for exemp-

[57] Quoted in Wright, p. 217. See also pp. 48, 49, 65-70.

738

tion: it should be regarded as a form of tribute paid to Caesar in the spirit of Christ's injunction. True, government had no right to control conscience, but it might dispose of our property within certain limits; the use that government then made of it, the writer implied, was not our responsibility. Even if, as some correspondents pointed out, payment was forbidden by the Society's discipline, surely the books of discipline were not so sacrosanct that they might not be a subject of discussion and changed, if not found to be sound on some point. Advice on how to respond to the small militia fines of prewar days might not be the appropriate answer to demands of the magnitude of $300 and to the exigencies of a war situation.

On the whole, the other contributions published by the editor disagreed strongly with "N.R.'s" views. Some writers feared their effect in undermining trust in the discipline and doubted the editor's wisdom in giving them publicity and, in particular, in stating that the matter was "a disputed point" among Friends. A Long Island Quaker gave expression to the predominant opinion when he wrote: "If Friends cannot themselves fight, it is wholly inconsistent for them to pay a fine, or tax in lieu of it, as that would be an acknowledgment that the demand is just, and that liberty of conscience is not due." "He is already a conscript in the Lamb's peaceable warfare," wrote another correspondent rather quaintly, and, therefore, no further demand for service in connection with terrestial warfare could rightly be made of him.[58]

The consensus of opinion on the pages of the *Intelligencer* went against "N.R.," but undoubtedly many among both the Hicksites and the Orthodox resorted—whether willingly or perhaps with an uneasy conscience, it is not often easy to say—to the method of paying commutation in exchange for exemption from service. We know that in the Philadelphia (Orthodox) Yearly Meeting, which kept more strictly to the discipline in such matters than its Hicksite brethren, 24 members were listed as paying their $300, with 7 hiring substitutes, in comparison with only 19 who rejected all forms of alternative service. (And, it should be added, 34 men had been discharged as a result of others paying their fines, usually without their consent, and in a further 5 cases the county officers, and not the men themselves, had hired substitutes.)[59] The same story is repeated in other sections of the So-

[58] *Friends' Intelligencer*, 27 June, 11 July, 18 July, 1 Aug., 8 Aug., 15 Aug., 29 Aug., 5 Sept., 12 Sept., 3 Oct., 5 Dec., 26 Dec. 1863; 9 Jan. 1864.

[59] Wright, p. 183. See pp. 164, 165, for details concerning two young Friends whose relatives paid their fines without their knowledge and contrary to their wishes.

ciety.[60] Official expressions of regret were certainly expressed frequently in meeting minutes or reports of committees. "They have been pained to find," the members of a committee of Philadelphia (Orthodox) Yearly Meeting "to assist Friends who are drafted" wrote at the conclusion of the war, "that some of our members have compromised our peace principles by paying the penalty imposed: thus lowering our profession of religious scruple in the estimation of those in authority, and greatly adding to the embarrassment and difficulty of such members as could not for conscience sake comply with the demand." But these offenders against the discipline—for such, indeed, were those who paid fines—rarely appear to have been penalized. Therefore, no schism such as had taken place within the Society at the time of the American Revolution, when the group led by Timothy Davis was disfellowshipped for supporting the payment of fines, resulted from the even more considerable falling away from the letter of the discipline during the Civil War period.

When new and more stringent draft legislation was under preparation in Washington toward the end of 1863, Edwin M. Stanton, the secretary of war, wishing to make some concessions to the position of the Society of Friends although not feeling empowered to press for the unconditional exemption that the Quakers hoped for, proposed the creation of "a special fund for the benefit of the Freedmen" into which the Quaker conscripts would pay their $300. To two delegates from Baltimore (Orthodox) Yearly Meeting "he expressed deep interest in organized, and individual efforts of Friends to elevate the moral, and physical condition of the manumitted Slaves"—a field of philanthropic endeavor in which the Society had long enjoyed a deserved reputation. However, Friends as a body were unwilling to accept this form of alternative, regarding its compulsory nature as an infringement of religious liberty. Such scruples, when communicated to him, Secretary Stanton found hard to comprehend.

> He said he could understand no such abstraction as that—that it was a work of mercy, and in accordance with the commands of Christ, and that if our members did not choose to accept so liberal

---

[60] See Louis Thomas Jones, *The Quakers of Iowa*, pp. 333, 334, for the case of a monthly meeting borrowing in order to pay the fines of members unable to raise the money themselves. Meetings of the evangelically minded Western Y. M. seem to have done the same thing (see Wright, p. 195; *Semi-Centennial Anniversary Western Yearly Meeting of Friends' Church 1858-1908*, p. 198). But these instances probably occurred after the February 1864 act, when the use to which commutation fines were being put was less objectionable to Friends than under the earlier act.

an offer, he could do no more for them, and the law would have to take its effect.[61]

Despite the rejection by Friends of all forms of alternative service and despite a steady stream of memorials and petitions to this effect from their various meetings and a number of delegations dispatched by them to Washington to explain Friends' absolutist views, the new act, which came into force on 24 February 1864, did (in Section 17) provide specific alternatives to army service for all genuine members of the pacifist denominations. They might choose either to "be assigned by the Secretary of War to duty in the hospitals, or to the care of freedmen" or to pay the same commutation fine of $300 as before, but with the guarantee that it would "be applied to the benefit of the sick and wounded soldiers" and not to hiring further recruits or some other military purpose. Although minor amendments were made subsequently in the federal conscription law, the provision for conscientious objectors remained unaltered.[62]

The reaction of Friends to the considerable concessions which the February act made toward satisfying the scruples of religious pacifists was mixed. These concessions did not, as we have seen, remove the fundamental objections held by many Quakers who were most active and concerned about peace: indeed, nothing short of unconditional exemption could satisfy the most scrupulous. The Quaker papers stressed the appreciation which Friends felt for the good motives of the administration in trying to meet their case. But, as an editorial in the Orthodox *Friend* once more made clear,

> We do not see how it can relieve our members, or they consistently avail themselves of any of its provisions; inasmuch as to be sent into the hospitals or serve as nurses, &c., or to be assigned to the care of freedmen, is just as much a penalty imposed for obeying the requisition of our religion in not performing military service, as is the fine of three hundred dollars. It matters not whether the commutation for military service is money or personal service in some other department; in either case it is an assumption on the part of the government of a right to oblige the subject to violate his conscience, or to exact a penalty if he elects to obey God rather than man.[63]

A further argument urged by the same paper against accepting such work of national importance as was being offered conscientious objec-

---

[61] Quoted in Wright, p. 75. See also p. 218.
[62] *Ibid.*, pp. 71-86.
[63] Quoted *ibid.*, pp. 83, 84. See also p. 217.

tors was that such employment, whether in military hospitals or even in the camps for freedmen which were under army control, was in fact aiding the prosecution of the war. "None of us would hesitate to relieve the sufferings of a sick and wounded fellow-being because he was a soldier; but this is wholly different from connecting ourselves with a military establishment got up expressly as a part of the machinery for . . . maiming and destroying our fellow creatures." The aim of the army medical service was to get the men fit again to return to the battle front. Additional arguments against accepting such service were provided by another editorial in a later issue of the *Friend*. It brought up the undesirability of Friends' wearing military uniform, which they would probably be required to do in army medical work, and the fact that any relaxation of the Society's official support of unconditional exemption hitherto would only serve to make things more difficult with the authorities for those young Friends who continued to take an unconditionalist line.[64] In the opinion of the *Friend* and that of many other Quakers, not only was the principle of requiring from genuine conscientious objectors civilian service in place of military service untenable, but the actual alternatives offered were to a greater or lesser degree unacceptable in themselves.

This view was, however, contested by some influential circles within the Society of both the major branches. Samuel Rhoads in an editorial in the *Friends' Review*, a periodical evangelical in tone but belonging like the Philadelphia *Friend* to the Orthodox camp, spoke out in favor of accepting the work provided by the government. "We presume," he wrote, "few of our members can be found who are unwilling to aid in the care of the freed-people, or, to a certain extent, in the relief of the sick and wounded. . . . We cannot but regard it as a mistaken view, to look upon the service substituted for arms-bearing, as a *penalty* or as a *purchase* of religious liberty." Friends had never refused to make an affirmation in place of an oath because the former was required as an alternative. We should rejoice that the government, in the midst of a bitter and prolonged struggle, had devised this scheme for alleviating Friends' conscientious scruples. A similar positive position was taken up by the Hicksite yearly meetings of New York and Ohio.

In a later issue the *Friends' Review*, while conceding that differences of opinion as to the consistency of Quakers' working as nurses or doctors in military hospitals might exist, maintained that absolutely no objection could properly be raised against rehabilitation work with freedmen. Do not let us make crosses for ourselves, the paper ad-

[64] *Friend*, 27 Aug., 29 Oct. 1864.

742

vised.[65] For the most part, the various yearly meetings left it up to the consciences of individual Friends to determine whether they felt able, if drafted, to participate in one or other of the forms of alternative service offered by the government. In this spirit the Meeting for Sufferings of Indiana (Orthodox) Yearly Meeting urged members to display "a large measure of Christian charity" toward those who were faced with the difficult choice of accepting the government's terms or disobeying the law.[66]

But even if on the whole meetings were tolerant of differing responses to the call for military service on the part of their conscientious objectors, it was undoubtedly the absolutists—those rejecting the alternatives provided by the government in the name of a higher law of spiritual liberty—who at this point in the Society's history most nearly expressed its peculiar testimony as found in the requirements of the books of discipline and in the thinking of its most concerned members.

By no means all such objectors had to suffer for their radical stand, in spite of the fact that the law made no provision for unconditional exemption. In many areas, and among the civilian authorities at least, the Quakers' uncompromising objection to fighting was well known and often respected, if not fully understood. Refusal to pay the commutation fee was usually punished by distraint of the property of the delinquent Friend, as we have seen in previous chapters had been the practice since colonial times.[67] But now, as earlier, the rigor of the law was often tempered by neighborly kindness and administrative good feeling. In one such case, Allen Jay (1881-1910), a young Quaker minister in Indiana who later became prominent in the evangelical movement leading to the setting up of Five Years' Meeting, was drafted but refused either to serve or pay commutation, which at that time was still being used to purchase recruits. "I would prefer to go myself," he told the officer, quoting to him antiwar utterances from the early church fathers, "rather than to hire someone else to be shot in my place." Later, an inventory of the livestock on Jay's farm was made in preparation for distraint, but, apparently on orders from Governor Morton, the sale was indefinitely postponed. Jay heard later that his non-Quaker neighbors, reluctant to see a man penalized because of sincerely held religious principles, had determined, when the sale took

[65] *Friends' Review*, 30 July, 20 Aug. 1864; *Friends' Intelligencer*, 24 Sept. 1864. Cf., e.g., *Friend*, 29 Oct. 1864; *Friends' Intelligencer*, 22 Oct. 1864.

[66] Wright, p. 84.

[67] *Ibid.*, pp. 183-87. Wright (p. 185) quotes the figure of $2,217.76 for the value of property distrained from members of the two New York yearly meetings for nonpayment of commutation fines during the period of the war.

743

place, to buy up his goods and return them to him as a gift.[68] Or take the case of another future evangelical leader of the postwar period, Samuel A. Purdie (1843-1897). Although of military age and in good health, he was left by the authorities to work on the family farm; for his continued absence from local militia musters, he received nothing worse than a mere $5 fine on one occasion (which presumably had to be distrained).[69]

A number of Friends, however, were drafted into the army as a result of their refusal to accept the alternatives offered by the government and thereby came under the control of the military authorities and were subject to all the rigors of military law. That the fate of such men was not worse than it was resulted in large part from the sympathetic stand of the highest authorities in the land, to whom Friends made direct appeal from time to time on behalf of their conscripted brethren. "Religious objectors to military service," says E. N. Wright, "were particularly fortunate in having President Lincoln and Secretary Stanton show a friendly attitude at all times." Lincoln's understanding and appreciation of the Quaker peace testimony emerges clearly in Wright's book, as does his desire to prevent anything in the nature of a persecution of religious conscience.[70] After his assassination many tributes to his efforts to relieve Quaker objectors came in from Quaker meetings. "We hold in grateful remembrance," wrote Friends of Green Street (Hicksite) Monthly Meeting in Germantown (Pa.), for instance, "the consideration with which he regarded our conscientious scruples in relation to military enactments, and believe he did for us in this respect all that his position allowed."[71] The method that the administration devised to deal with the Quaker unconditionalists, whose scruples were not met by the existing law, was that of paroling or furloughing them for an indefinite period: in fact, in such cases the men were not called up again before federal conscription was ended. The practice, while used earlier as a way of gaining release for objectors who had been caught up in the army, was employed fairly regularly from the end of 1863, on the orders of Secretary Stanton, to prevent such men from being taken into the army at all.[72]

The entanglement of Quaker objectors in the army machine occurred in most cases, therefore, in the years 1862 and 1863, though a

[68] Autobiography of Allen Jay, chap. X.
[69] James Purdie Knowles, Samuel A. Purdie, pp. 35, 36.
[70] Wright, pp. 121-30.
[71] F. B. Tolles (ed.), "Two Quaker Memorials for Abraham Lincoln," BFHA, vol. 46, no. 1 (1957), p. 42. See also Wright, pp. 90, 125, 126; Memoir and Correspondence of Eliza P. Gurney, p. 321.
[72] Wright, pp. 86-88, 124-26, 192-95.

few instances are to be found in the last year and a half of the war. No overall figures of the number of men involved have been compiled; in a few meetings records are defective. The most complete account kept by Friends in the North appears to be that compiled by the Philadelphia (Orthodox) Yearly Meeting soon after the end of the war from reports sent in by its constituent quarterly and monthly meetings. Of its absolutists it records:

Two of those who refused on conscientious grounds to serve in the army, or to pay a commutation, or to hire a substitute, were arrested as deserters, but prompt application to those in authority, procured a speedy release on parole. Five were arrested, forced into military clothing, and sent some to Barracks, and some to a Camp in Philadelphia. On application to the Secretary of War, they were all released after periods of confinement, varying from a few days to 5 weeks. Three were drafted and sent to Camp Curtin, near Harrisburg, but on application for them to those in authority by Friends of Philadelphia, they were in a few days released. One was sent to the army, but after two months of trial and suffering, his release was obtained by application to the Secretary of War. Four of those who appeared before different Provost Marshals and stated their conscientious scruples were heard with kindly consideration and were not afterwards molested.[73]

This bare factual statement shows among other things the interplay between, on the one hand, Quakerly intercession for the release of the impressed men and, on the other, willingness on the part of many authorities, both locally and at the top in Washington, to relieve genuine conscience, if they could, within the framework of the existing law.

Those young Friends whose refusal to pay what Caesar considered his due led to their arrest and incarceration in one or another of the military camps that dotted the country met on the whole with courteous treatment. Sometimes they had to face threats of punishment and even the firing squad from senior, or more often, junior officers, but here, too, a more tolerant attitude frequently resulted from the objector's steady purpose and a somewhat closer acquaintance with, if not always much greater comprehension of, sincerely held opinions on the rightness of fighting. E. N. Wright in his book on the conscientious objectors of the Civil War relates several experiences of this kind on the part of young Quakers forcibly inducted into the army, and they seem, on the basis of admittedly rather scanty evidence, to

[73] Quoted in *ibid.*, p. 183.

745

have been more typical than instances of severe brutality toward the unwilling soldier.

Take the case of A. M. Jenkins, a country lad from around Dayton (Ohio). After he had been brought to camp, the "Captain of the Day" refused to place him in the guardhouse, saying that "it was a shame to put a decent man" there, as it "was full of the worst characters in the camp." (A couple of years later two other Ohio Quaker conscripts, who found themselves in the guardhouse of Todd Barracks in Columbus for refusing to drill, found a sympathetic guard there who told them: "Men, I do pity you, as it is such a filthy place and such hard cases to be your company but I do like to see men live up to their principles.") Despite the expressed wish of the colonel of the camp to which Jenkins and another Quaker boy were eventually transferred "to see how Quakers would look drilling," they received good treatment there, too; when they were permitted to return home not long afterward, the colonel told them good-humoredly "that he could give us an 'honorable discharge,' as we had maintained our 'conscious [sic] principles.'"

The story of another Ohio Quaker, Barclay Stratton, who was drafted in the autumn of 1864, two years after Jenkins's release, provides us with a further example of respect shown in the army to "conscious [sic] principles." Ordered to put on military uniform, Stratton quietly explained his reasons for refusing to exchange his Quaker garb for army blue, and, instead of the harshness he had expected to follow, the major in charge patted him on the shoulders and said: "My friend, I admire your candor." They soon came to an understanding whereby the uniform was put on the unresisting Quaker by one of the army clerks, without Stratton having to give actual consent. The major told him that "he did not blame me in the least for not doing it myself." Although Stratton and another young Quaker from his home area, who had been drafted to the same camp, were eventually sent south to Richmond (Va.) and although the two men steadily refused to accept offers of hospital work which were made to them by the military authorities, they continued to receive mostly kindness and consideration from both officers and rank and file, until at last they were sent home on indefinite parole.

Wright points out that sometimes hostile treatment was replaced by a more friendly attitude on the part of the military when it was realized that the recalcitrant soldier was in fact a member of the Society of Friends, whose peculiar views on the subject of war were fairly well known in the community. He cites the case of Joseph G. Miller, a Hicksite Quaker from Brooklyn, who, after being taken to a camp on

746

Rikers Island, had been forced into uniform and harshly treated there by the officers.

But when it became known that he was a Friend [relates a minute, dated 6 April 1864, of New York Monthly Meeting, to which Miller belonged] and was actuated by conscientious scruples their manner towards him underwent an entire change. After a detention of about three weeks on this Island he was on the 23d of 10th month removed to Governors Island, where he was furnished with a comfortable bed in the hospital, was permitted to resume his own clothes, and was required to do nothing contrary to his feelings, on the 11th of Eleventh Month he was liberated under parole.

In the summer of 1863 some yearly meetings—the Orthodox of Philadelphia and New York are examples[74]—prepared special statements for presentation by drafted members to the provost marshal and other military officials concerned with the draft. The statements mentioned the draftee's membership in the Society of Friends and his objection, as a Friend, to all forms of conditional exemption as an infringement of "the free exercise of his natural right to liberty" of conscience, while at the same time stressing the Quaker's entire loyalty to the Union government and its laws, "so far as these things are not inconsistent with his religious obligations." In this way, it was hoped that, however the fate of the objector was decided, the authorities from the outset would be left in no doubt as to the position he took and the fact that it had the backing of his church.

In some cases, a statement of this kind must have contributed toward a decision by the authorities to send the drafted man home without further ado or release him after a few days. But it did not always prove effective, as was shown in the case of the Smedley cousins, William and Edward, from Delaware County (Pa.). Although they had provided themselves with such a paper, as their Friends had advised them to do, they soon found themselves en route for Philadelphia under military escort. The lieutenant in charge was an old schoolmate of Edward's who, disliking his enforced task, treated the cousins with as much consideration as he could. But, when on arrival in the Quaker city, Edward relates,

... the officers ... were informed of the circumstances of our declining from conscientious motives to participate in any warlike measures, they utterly repudiated such notions, commanded our immediate compliance with their orders, and when we quietly declined,

[74] See *ibid.*, pp. 69, 70.

747

manifested great resentment by wordy abuse and threatenings of punishment. After their passions were pretty well spent, we were sent to the third floor of the building, turned in with some hundreds of drafted men and substitutes, and left to make the best we could of the situation till morning.

During their subsequent sojourn in the Philadelphia barracks the Smedleys were well treated, although there was a danger that they might be sent south. Meanwhile, Friends outside were busy trying to obtain their release; after seventeen days they were so far successful that the boys were given their liberty on condition that they reported daily to the barracks until further notice. A month or so later, on Secretary Stanton's orders, the two Quakers were "honorably" discharged from the United States Army.[75]

Some uncompromising unconditionalists at times fared better than this, however, since they never found themselves under military control at all. Take the case of Benjamin P. Moore, a Hicksite Quaker who kept a general store in a small Maryland village. When war came, writes this staunch antisecessionist, "and the military spirit broke out among my associates (chiefly on the 'rebel' side) . . . I emptied the powder I had left into the street, refused to sell ammunition to anyone, or to pay a state tax in aid of the war, for which some of my goods were levied and sold." Upon receiving notice that he had been drafted, in the late fall of 1863, he hurried to Washington to put his case before the President. That this obscure country shopkeeper succeeded in gaining a personal interview with Lincoln, who listened patiently to him before sending him on to the Secretary of War, bears witness to the surprising accessibility of the President even during the crowded years of war. Stanton told Moore that he would be assigned to work in a military hospital. "Now I had no objection to nursing the sick and the wounded," the Quaker wrote later, citing the fact of his volunteering for such work in the emergency after the battle of Antietam in September 1862, but he was not willing to do so as an alternative to military service. In the end, he received an indefinite parole before he could actually be inducted into service.[76]

In contrast to the mild experiences of a man like Moore, already in his thirties and with his mind made up as to the course he should pursue in face of the draft, we may instance those of 22-year-old Jesse Macy (1842-1919), a birthright Quaker from Iowa who much later,

[75] The above paragraphs are based on the accounts given in Wright, pp. 153-63. Jones (*The Later Periods of Quakerism*, II, 731, 732) prints young Miller's story as told in the minutes of Westbury M. M.
[76] *Friend*, vol. 114, no. 17 (20 Feb. 1941), pp. 297-99.

after he had left the Friends for the Congregationalists, was to gain a considerable reputation as a political scientist and historian. At the outset of the war, the antislavery enthusiasm of this son of free-soil pioneers led him almost to the point of volunteering. Loyalty to the faith of his fathers held him back. (Macy already seemed marked by his exceptional intelligence and obvious moral earnestness for leadership in the Quaker community in Iowa, and he had already begun, young as he was, to play a significant role in it.) In addition, until after Lincoln had proclaimed emancipation, the war to a fervid emancipationist like young Macy was scarcely one for the liberation of the slave: this also was a factor in dissuading him from joining up in the early days. In September 1864 Macy, then a student at Grinnell College where he was later to spend much of his life as a teacher, was at last drafted. His parents would willingly have seen him pay his $300 commutation and come back to work on the farm. But their son was anxious to seize this opportunity to do something positive to help the oppressed, now that the administration had given them their freedom, and so he decided to report for service, with the determination to accept only hospital duty or work with freedmen that the law had granted his people.

In spite of being furnished with a certificate of Quaker membership, however, he was told on arrival in camp that his exemption would not be recognized and that he would be required to serve as an ordinary soldier. His regiment, the 10th Iowa, was soon sent south to join the army there. Macy refused to draw a gun, feeling quite correctly that, if he once did so, even with the intention of never using it to kill, it might be difficult for him to prove his noncombatancy when they arrived in the battle zone. Then, and in the days following, all his former doubts and hesitations about what it was right for him to do, the inner conflict between his pacifist heritage and the militant antislavery feelings that were both his inheritance and his own heartfelt convictions as well, came again to the fore. His was, indeed, a "perplexing and intolerable situation," as he described it later.

I had endured and was still enduring a good deal of mental agony with reference to my own personal duties in respect to the war. My role as representative of a church was not in harmony with my convictions as a man. . . . I had believed that I could enter the army and fight for liberty while still remaining worthy of the Christian's name; but such action *now* I felt would be a betrayal of trust reposed in me, a sacrifice of loyalty and truth and so of true manly integrity.

Therefore, he decided that his policy should be only to obey orders

749

relating to the care of the sick and wounded and to regard all others as essentially illegal, since they ignored the noncombatant status that the law had granted him. He does not appear to have been in contact with any others of similar views: spiritual loneliness and his isolation must have compounded his difficulties. Nevertheless, he stuck to his resolution throughout the period when, with his regiment, he participated in Sherman's march to the sea; his fellow soldiers showed him sympathy, and the officers on the whole left him alone. In March 1865, on orders from the Secretary of War, he was sent to Springfield (Ill.) to work as a camp medical orderly; several months later he received his discharge from the army.

Macy's reflections on his wartime stand, as written down some years later, may serve as an example of the inner conflict set up by divided allegiances in the minds of many young men reared in the Quaker community, even among some of those who, like Macy, preserved an outward adherence to the Society's peace testimony. He writes:

> At the close of the war I felt a lasting regret that my peculiar position in the army had been a source of annoyance to military officers whose work I regarded with sympathy and approval. I would have been willing to sacrifice my life to further the great work of saving the Union and abolishing the iniquity of slavery; but I was not clear in my mind as to the proper attitude of the Society of Friends. Each individual Quaker in North and South prayed daily for the success of the Union Army. . . . I felt that I had done practically nothing. Many [i.e., young Friends] had accepted full military service, others, like myself, had passed through the momentous period in a troubled state of mind, uncertain what was the path of duty. One of my cousins, Elwood Macy, believing when it was too late, that his own failure of duty to his country was due in large measure to the attitude of the Friends' Church, in which he had been educated, abandoned the Society and joined the Methodist Church.[77]

[77] *Jesse Macy: An Autobiography*, pp. 36, 41-46, 48ff., 63, 69, 75-77. Cf. an interesting correspondence relating to this subject carried on between Garrison and Elizabeth B. Chace in the summer of 1862, which is printed in L.B.C. and A. C. Wyman, *Elizabeth Buffum Chace 1806-1899: Her Life and Environment*, I, 241, 242. Mrs. Chace, daughter of the Rhode Island Quaker hatter and abolitionist, Arnold Buffum, was an ardent Garrisonian nonresistant who had resigned her membership in the Society of Friends in 1843 because of its hostility to abolitionism and had then slowly drifted away from organized religion during the subsequent years. From her Quaker heritage, however, she retained her pacifism, and this, together with her strong maternal instincts, led her to use all her influence on her two sons, Samuel (b. 1843) and Arnold (b. 1845), to dissuade them from enlisting in the army—despite the strong desire of the elder one, at least, to do so. Their father, Samuel B. Chace, had remained a Quaker, joining the Wilburite

When we turn from the torn and divided hearts of birthright Quakers like Jesse and Elwood Macy to the single-minded devotion to Quaker pacifism of a convinced Friend like Cyrus Guernsey Pringle (1838-1911), we breathe another atmosphere. Sincerity and high-minded idealism and loyalty to a cause there was aplenty in men like the Macys, but they were directed toward a different object. For them, some of the traditional testimonies of their Society had grown cold and formal, lacking the vital spark of a personally felt faith. Pringle was a convert who had joined the Friends only in 1862. For him, the peace testimony formed a living cell of his new found belief. This devotion shines clearly from every page of the diary that he kept of his draft experience, the manuscript of which was only uncovered a short time after his death. Although it has since been published and twice reprinted, this minor classic of conscientious objection deserves more than a bare mention in these pages. Its most recent editor, Professor Henry J. Cadbury, rightly calls it "a vivid, intimate human document," a simple record of the "timeless problem of a sensitive conscience."[78] Pringle in later life made a reputation for himself as a botanist, but he was mainly self-educated and during the Civil War was working on the small family farm in northern Vermont. On 13 July 1863 he received notice that he had been drafted. His reaction to the news, as he recorded it in the opening page of his diary, was typical of the man. "With ardent zeal for our Faith and the cause of our peaceable principles, and almost disgusted at the lukewarmness and unfaithfulness of very many who profess these, and considering how heavily

---

Conservative group when it was formed. Parental pressure, therefore, weighed heavily on the boys. On one occasion the mother told Samuel, Jr.: "I think the time will come in which thee will be very glad thee did not go into the army"; to which her son replied: "No, I shall never be glad that I did not help to save the Union." In her distress Mrs. Chace wrote to Garrison for advice. "Conjure them to act as duty may seem to require" was the essence of Garrison's answer, and he warned her that, if the boys were drafted eventually, they could not plead their parents' veto in extenuation of their unwillingness to serve. Nevertheless, the Chace boys, as was undoubtedly the case in a number of other Quaker households, seem to have yielded to family influence in holding back from service rather than following the light of personal conviction into active participation in the war. See also *ibid.*, pp. 216, 219, 220.

[78] *The Civil War Diary of Cyrus Pringle* (1962 edn.), p. 4. In his foreword, Professor Cadbury remarks (p. 6): "The almost naive approach of a single individual a century ago has relevance today among nations that toy under various pretexts with the possible guilt of mass extermination. The ultimate preventive against the commitment of such evil is the human conscience. It is the moral deterrent. For that reason the simple modest testimony of Cyrus Pringle may have more lasting meaning than appears on the surface. Human moral progress has often depended on the spontaneous response of one or two sensitive persons to quite unexpected situations, when that response became convincing and contagious."

slight crosses bore upon their shoulders, I felt [able] to say, 'Here am I, Father, for thy service. As thou will.'"

Friends and acquaintances, during a short period of grace granted him by the enrollment board to think matters over, urged the young man to pay the commutation, which would have extricated him from the clutches of the military. This, however, Pringle would not do from "a higher duty than that to country." He asked, he said, for "no military protection of our government and [was] grateful for none, [denying] any obligation to support so unlawful a system, as we hold war to be even when waged in opposition to an evil and oppressive power." There followed a final appearance before the provost marshal and involuntary induction into the army. Sent first to Brattleboro (Vt.) and then on to Boston, Pringle, who was joined by two other Quaker boys, shared the discomforts of the first days of army life along with a miscellaneous selection of conscripts and substitutes from country and town. Their final destination was the military camp on Long Island in Boston Harbor. We find Pringle recording in his diary for 28 August: "All is war here. We are surrounded by the pomp and circumstance of war, and enveloped in the cloud thereof. The cloud settles down over the minds and souls of all; they cannot see beyond nor do they try; but with the clearer eye of Christian faith I try to look beyond all this error into Truth and Holiness immaculate: and thanks to the Father, I am favored with glimpses that are sweet consolation amid this darkness." A consolation, too, was the sympathy and kindliness displayed by the ordinary soldiers in the camp, who showed no signs of resentment at the fact that the Quakers did not partake in all the drills and fatigues that were their own portion. Some of the officers, however, were hostile, and refusal to obey orders soon brought confinement in the guardhouse and threats of worse treatment and even of shooting.

Pringle's diary brings out the continual alertness of himself and his companions in maintaining an undefiled witness to the truth as they believed it to be expressed in the Quaker peace testimony. Back at the beginning of their army days there had been the problem of uniforms: they agreed to wear them but were unwilling to sign for them since they felt that would imply an acceptance of military service. Finally, they certified merely that the clothes were "with us." Later, after arriving in camp, they were confronted with the choice of performing, when ordered, certain seemingly quite innocuous chores or facing the consequences of disobedience. On one occasion they were required to help in cleaning the camp and in fetching water. "We wished to be obliging," Pringle recorded, "to appear willing to bear a hand toward that which would promote our own and our fellows' health and convenience; but as we worked we did not feel easy." It seemed too great an acquiescence in the military service, and, when a command from the sergeant bidding them "Police the streets" followed their fears were confirmed. And this time disobedience brought punishment. But most distressing of all the decisions they had to make, not least because compromise was recommended by respected members of their own Quaker community (Friends in both New England and New York Yearly Meetings were active on behalf of their conscientious objectors who were facing the trials of the army camp),[79] was the resolve to turn down the offer the authorities now made. This offer, put forward with the best intentions, proposed that they be transferred to work in the camp hospitals, a privilege that as yet was not formally guaranteed to objectors by law. They wrote to Henry Dickinson, a leading member of the Representative Meeting in New York: "We cannot purchase life at cost of peace of soul." Their situation now looked serious indeed, for, if they maintained their unwillingness to serve in the hospital, the alternative would be shipment south with one or another of the contingents that left the island at frequent intervals bound eventually for the scene of battle.

And so at last, in the middle of September, we find Pringle embarked for the final and hardest part of his adventure. After its arrival in Virginia, the regiment was sent on to a camp near Culpeper. Pringle and two companions refused to handle the gun which was issued to each of them for the march, "even though we did not intend to use it"; "in the hurry and bustle of equipping a detachment of soldiers," it was not easy for them to explain satisfactorily the reasons for disobeying orders. As they marched through the war-devastated Virginia countryside, with their rifles and equipment strapped onto them by order of the officers, Pringle found confirmation in the scene of the rightness of their stand. "When one contrasts the face of this country with the smiling hillsides and vales of New England," wrote the Vermonter in his diary, "he sees stamped upon it in characters so marked, none but a blind man can fail to read, the great irrefutable arguments against slavery and against war." In the days following their arrival at Camp Culpeper, there ensued the most trying period for the three Quakers. Harsh treatment and threats of court-martial and shooting were followed by attempts on the part of the colonel in command of the 4th Vermont regiment, to which they were now assigned, to get them to accept work with the medical service. "He urged us to go

[79] For further details in regard to New England Friends who were drafted into the army and of the efforts made to gain their release, see Ethan Foster, *The Conscript Quakers*; Wright, pp. 124, 125, 192-95; Jones, *The Later Periods of Quakerism*, II, 735.

into the hospital, stating this course was advised by Friends about New York. We were too well aware of such a fact to make any denial, though it was a subject of surprise to us that he should be informed of it." Once more they were faced with the same dilemma. If they refused his offer contrary to the advice of older and more experienced Friends, they would seem fanatics, irresponsible and deaf to the needs of the unfortunate around them. Active service on behalf of those urgently needing help—"we saw around us a rich field for usefulness in which there were scarce any laborers"—appeared so much more satisfying than a passive and perhaps sterile witness for an abstract principle. "At last," writes Pringle, "we consented to a trial, . . . reserving the privilege of returning to our former position."

But inner peace of mind did not follow. "At first a great load seemed rolled away from us; we rejoiced in the prospect of life again. But soon there prevailed a feeling of condemnation, as though we had sold our Master. And that first day was one of the bitterest I ever experienced. It was a time of stern conflict of soul." So eventually they returned to the colonel and told him that they were unwilling any longer to set aside their previous position: a clear testimony against war could only be borne by refusing to accept any alternatives to combatant service. The colonel, angry at what he considered their unreasonableness, now lost patience with them. Pringle's diary records the story of the punishments which followed their declaration of defiance. "I dreaded torture," he writes, "and desired strength of flesh and spirit." The climax came as a result of refusing an order to clean his gun, which was already becoming yellow with rust. What followed must be told in his own words, written down shortly afterward:

Two sergeants soon called for me, and taking me a little aside, bid me lie down on my back, and stretching my limbs apart tied cords to my wrists and ankles, and these to four stakes driven in the ground somewhat in the form of an x. I was very quiet in my mind as I lay there on the ground [soaked] with the rain of the previous day, exposed to the heat of the sun and suffering keenly from the cords binding my wrists and straining my muscles. And, if I dared the presumption, I should say that I caught a glimpse of heavenly pity. I wept, not so much from my own suffering as from sorrow that such things should be in our own country. . . . And I was sad, that one endeavoring to follow our dear Master should be so generally regarded as a despicable and stubborn culprit.

Evidently, this represented a last attempt to cow Pringle into submission, for—unknown to him—an order had already been sent from

Washington, as a result of Quaker intervention there, to bring to the capital not only Pringle and his two companions but several other Quaker objectors who had ended up in the military camps of Virginia, as a preliminary to their eventual release from the service. On 7 November they received their paroles, and at last Pringle was able to return home—to quote the concluding words in his diary—"through the mercy and favor of Him, who in all this trial had been our guide and strength and comfort."

It was Friends of military age, of course, who had had to bear the main burden of war resistance. But the dilemma of conscience also presented itself in one form or another during these war years to many Quakers who were not challenged directly by the state's demand for military service. The Civil War took place before the coming of the age of total war, yet even then the threads of warmaking were subtly interwoven with the whole social fabric. To detach oneself from activities which helped, albeit indirectly, in the prosecution of the war was becoming increasingly difficult. The Society of Friends, more wary of rendering Caesar more than his due than were the American peace sects of German origin, had always striven to guard against a peace testimony which refused participation in war while at the same time acquiescing in activities which made the waging of war possible. We have seen this scrupulousness exemplified in their refusal to accept exemption from combatant duties through any form of alternative service, even where this was otherwise of an unobjectionable nature. But every activity, so their most concerned members constantly urged, must be carefully scrutinized to see if it did not contain hidden within itself the seeds of war.

This is the message of many of their wartime utterances, both those for public consumption and those intended primarily for the edification of members, documents that often appear platitudinous in their repeated exhortations to eschew evil and smugly moralistic in their style and whole approach. Yet in this very fastidiousness in the search for righteousness, despite the danger (by no means always avoided) that it would slide over into priggishness and a moral pharisaism, lay one of the sources of strength in the Society's peace testimony that has never entirely disappeared.

Consider, for instance, two documents drawn up in the first year of war by meetings from the two main branches of the Society. In an address of 23 April 1861 we find a special Representative Meeting of the New York (Orthodox) Yearly Meeting calling on members to "guard most watchfully against every temptation in any manner or degree to foster or encourage the spirit of war and strife" and "to be very careful in conversation upon passing events, both among themselves and with others—that nothing be allowed to escape their lips that may promote or countenance an appeal to arms or reliance upon them."[80] The same care to see that Friends should make their actions conform to the spirit as well as to the letter of their pacifism is shown in the minutes of the Western Quarterly Meeting of Philadelphia (Hicksite) Yearly Meeting. There the monthly meetings were urged to diligently exercise "a more watchful Christian care over the conduct of their members, especially in regard to the support of our testimony against War, and all warlike preparations; in order that they may be preserved within the pale of our Religious Society."[81] True, such pastoral care was often needed and not always exerted. Nevertheless, the Society's history during the period of the Civil War provides plenty of evidence that the thoughts and prayers of a considerable number of Quakers were directed toward the steady perfecting of their witness for peace.

The relationship between the exercise of civil government and the waging of war had occupied the minds of more thoughtful Friends ever since the days of the Quaker experiment in Pennsylvania. The coming of war had served to sharpen the issue, and it seemed to some that it was just here that the Quaker peace testimony of the day was weakest. Friends in large numbers had helped to vote the war administration into office. Was this (for all the admirable qualities of the President and his colleagues and Friends' sympathies with them in their task) a proper outcome of Quaker principles in politics? And then there was the knotty problem of the nature of the conflict: whether it was properly speaking a war between two states or a rebellion within the framework of civil government. In the latter case, and if its suppression were a legitimate function of the United States government, was not perhaps a complete and unequivocal withdrawal from political life, as a handful of Friends had been advocating for many decades, the only consistent policy for members of the Society to adopt?

These issues probably troubled only a minority of Friends. For most of those who remained according to their lights loyal to the peace testimony, upholding law and government—insofar as this did not entail a directly warlike function—and voting in elections did not appear to be un-Quakerly activities. The *Weltanschauung* of their fellow pacifists of the Mennonite and Dunker persuasions was fairly remote from the frame of mind of most American Quakers of that day.

[80] *Friend*, 22 June 1861. See also Wright, pp. 43, 44.
[81] *Friends' Intelligencer*, 16 Nov. 1861.

756

A keen pacifist like the clerk of Genesee (Hicksite) Yearly Meeting in upstate New York, John J. Cornell (whose peace pamphlet has been discussed earlier in this chapter), felt able to answer affirmatively the query whether a Quaker could properly claim "protection" from a government like their own, which relied ultimately on the sanction of the sword, provided such protection did not involve the use of armed force. The example of Quaker Pennsylvania, he believed, had shown that government need not necessarily involve injurious force and might be based on Christian principles of redeeming the wrongdoer, and not on retributive punishment. Meanwhile, until such government were established again, since some form of decent administration was essential for human well-being, the individual might give it his general support without being personally responsible for those of its actions of which he could not approve.[82]

Cornell's views were probably fairly typical of the main trend of opinion within the Society at this time. They were contested both from within the Society and from outside. Of outside criticism we may take as an example the views of the *Advocate of Peace*, the organ of the pro-war peace men who now controlled the rather conservative American Peace Society. The *Advocate*, as one might expect, was by no means unsympathetic to Quaker and other religious objectors. It stressed on several occasions that these men, for all their refusal to take part in the war, were staunchly antislavery and antisecessionist. But, asked an article published in the spring of 1864, how far could their form of pacifism in fact be squared with civil government? "If a Quaker were mayor of Philadelphia, . . . how would he deal with a gang of burglars, incendiaries or murderers infesting the city?" It went on to cite the actual case of a mayor of a city in New England who belonged to the Society of Friends. "Would you censure him for the use of such force as he would find necessary in executing the laws?" And what if he had been, instead, mayor of New York during the previous summer's "copperhead" riots in that city. "Ought he on Christian principles to let the rioters have their way in their work of robbery, murder, and conflagration?" Finally, and inevitably, the article raised the question: what if a Quaker were President of the United States? Would he permit the rebels to flout the law of the Union with impunity and not take active measures to prevent it? "We regret to find Friends . . . treating such an enforcement of law as the same thing in principle with an ordinary war between nations."[83]

[82] Letter dated 8 Feb. 1862 in *Autobiography of John J. Cornell*, pp. 124-26.
[83] *Advocate of Peace*, XV, March-April 1864, 46, 47.

For the members of the American Peace Society and the millions of their more belligerent fellow citizens who also supported the war, the Quaker position appeared equivocal on account of its failure to endorse the full extent of governmental authority. In the eyes of its critics within the Society, on the other hand, its inadequacy lay in the degree of approval it was prepared to give government. It was in particular the question of voting at elections, when, as in wartime, most candidates were likely to be in favor of prosecuting the war (except those who had a secret partiality with the enemy cause), that aroused serious reservations among some Friends. The conservative Wilburite, Joshua Maule, for instance, had exercised the franchise before hostilities, but the coming of war led him to the conclusion that a consistent Friend must practice total abstinence in the realm of politics.[84] A contributor to the Hicksite *Intelligencer* on one occasion raised a problem that may have bothered many Friends of military age when he wrote:

> The President we have aided to elect, in the fulfillment of his official duty, calls upon us, through his subordinate, to do our share of military service. We unhesitatingly object, and proceed, forthwith, to state the grounds of the objection—that we are Christians, therefore cannot fight. . . . Our demanding officer is struck with surprise, and inquiries where our christianity and conscientious scruples were at the time we voted for the President, whose official duties, in part, we knew to be of a military character, and were now only in proper progress of fulfillment; and further urging that they who place a man in office, pledge themselves to the observance of all such requisitions upon them as the duties of that office in its execution may require.[85]

The approach of the presidential election of 1864 again faced the Quakers with a difficult choice. Many Friends were enthusiastic supporters of Lincoln; few wished to give their votes to his rival, McClellan. But some had serious doubts whether they could consistently vote for a war leader, however unquestionable his integrity. No ruling was ever issued by any of the branches of the Society: the discipline remained silent, and the matter was left for decision to the individual conscience of each Friend.[86]

If there was some difference among the Quakers concerning the degree to which they might properly become engaged in politics—especially in time of war—opinion in the Society was also divided to

[84] Joshua Maule, *Transactions and Changes in the Society of Friends*, p. 267.
[85] Quoted in Wright, p. 41.   [86] Wright, pp. 87, 88.

some extent as to how far certain civilian activities, otherwise unobjectionable, were permissible when their beneficiaries were soldiers. Naturally, if personal profit was involved, as in selling horses or grain for the use of the army, at least the stricter Friends registered strong disapproval. And there was an even more general reprobation of any business that had become associated directly with the waging of war. Thus, we hear of Benjamin Tatham, Jr., a New York Friend who had emigrated from England in 1841, turning over his firm from its pre-war business of making shot to the manufacture of lead piping, which even in wartime did not offend against his Society's peace testimony.[87] As an epistle of Philadelphia (Orthodox) Yearly Meeting of 9 January 1864 put it:

> Keep clear of business of any kind, which depends for its emoluments on its connection with war. Sorrowful indeed will it be, if any of the professed advocates of peace are found engaged in business which, in the eyes of a quick-sighted world, may cause the sincerity of our testimony to the peaceable principles of the gospel to be doubted, and give occasion for the charge of inconsistency, if not of hypocrisy, to be made against our religious profession.[88]

But it was not so easy to make a hard and fast ruling (and still more difficult to persuade Friends to keep to one) when it was a question of humanitarian aid to the army's soldiers. We have seen that all branches of the Society officially, and many Friends individually, refused such work if it was offered as an alternative to direct combatant service. But what if it were undertaken voluntarily, as an expression of the humanitarian impulse that led the best elements in nineteenth-century Quakerism out into the highways and byways of philanthropy? Was it to fall under a ban just because the recipients of Quaker relief happened to wear a soldier's uniform? Quaker women, in particular, felt the urge to join in the work of providing various comforts for the men in the army and of thus helping, if only indirectly in their homes, the sick and wounded especially. The young Mitchell sisters, for instance, children of a respected Nantucket Quaker, were engaged in such work, striving in this way to give expression both to the Quaker message of goodwill to all men and to their emotional attachment to the Northern cause, when a member of their meeting raised the question with them whether as good Quakers they should participate in such "war" work. They referred the matter to

[87] John Cox, Jr., *Quakerism in the City of New York*, p. 129. Tatham was offered the post of Commissioner for Indian Affairs by Lincoln, but he refused it on the grounds that it was too much of a worldly honor.
[88] *Friend*, 9 Jan. 1864.

their father, whose strict adherence to the discipline was well known among New England Friends. "I think the Good Samaritan would not have asked [what was] the cause of suffering where suffering existed," he told them, and the sisters now felt able to continue their work with an easy conscience.[89] We find, indeed, no less a person than the English-born Mrs. Elizabeth L. Comstock, wife of a Midwest Friend and herself a minister influential in the counsels of the Orthodox Quakers of that region, extremely active in humanitarian work on behalf of sick and wounded soldiers in military hospitals and camps. Her labors gained high praise from Lincoln himself and other government officials.[90] It should be pointed out, however, that this work was part of her general concern for all sufferers—prisoners, the insane, as well as the freedmen and Southern prisoners of war—and in this way harmonized with the Quaker concept of service.

Nevertheless, strong sentiment existed, at least in regard to donations of clothing and other gifts for the troops, that this was a mistaken form of expressing the Quaker concern to relieve suffering. Although its mainspring was not any selfish motive, as it was for those whose businesses led them to deal in articles which promoted the war effort, still it contributed to the support of war, if in a more subtle way. In the eyes of such critics, it represented a compromising of the peace testimony and would easily be misinterpreted by outsiders as tacit support for the war. The Philadelphia *Friend*, in an editorial condemning such relief efforts as misplaced, reported the following remarks of a high-ranking officer in Washington spoken in the writer's hearing: "I understand your testimony against war, but the Friends at ——— have sent several barrels of articles for the soldiers; they must certainly believe in war."[91]

This issue, the problem of deciding where to draw the line so that what was intended as labor on behalf of suffering humanity should not prove an unwitting abetment of the act of destruction, was to present itself again to the Society of Friends during the two world wars of our century.

From the eighteenth to the twentieth century American Friends have, as we have already seen, had to face another and perhaps more difficult question: the relationship of their peace testimony to the tax demands of a war-making government. The call for service, whether a compulsory requirement of state or federal law or a voluntary outgrowth of the inner conscience, affected the individual person who

---

[89] *Recollections of Lydia S. (Mitchell) Hinchman*, pp. 45, 46.
[90] See *Life and Letters of Elizabeth L. Comstock*, chaps. VIII-XIII.
[91] *Friend*, 29 Oct. 1864. See also *Friends' Review*, 9 Nov. 1861.

must bear responsibility for his own actions. But taxes affected property on which state and society had legitimate claims irrespective of use, which the majority of Quakers as well as the more quietist Mennonites and Dunkers acknowledged as ordained by God. During the Civil War the general sentiment among Friends, not only the Orthodox but Hicksites and Wilburites as well, remained that state and federal taxes "in the mixture," that is, those taxes that were not *in toto* allocated specifically for the purposes of war, should be paid without further questioning. "We feel," stated the Western Yearly Meeting of Friends in September 1861, "that we escape condemnation when the Magistrate and not the tax payer assumes the responsibility of its specific appropriations." And New England Yearly Meeting, a year later, was even more emphatic, urging members to continue to pay their taxes "cheerfully . . . without attempting to make any impracticable distinctions respecting such taxes as may be imposed upon them for the support of our Government."[92] This was, in fact, the traditional standpoint, although from time to time some sensitive spirit had arisen to challenge it; a period of war brought the whole issue more forcibly before Friends. While most, therefore, paid their ordinary taxes willingly, there was no attempt to bring into line the minority who refused by any kind of disciplinary action. Mutual toleration was to be observed in regard to honest differences of opinion between the moderates, who believed that a prompt and full rendering of tribute was essential in the present state of the world for good governance, and the more radical, who felt payment of such taxes meant a watering down of their peace testimony.[93]

Of these radicals an excellent example is to be found in the person of the Ohio Quaker, Joshua Maule, whose protest against voting has been mentioned above. Maule, who was already middle-aged when war broke out, had been an active member of the Conservative or Wilburite branch of the Society, which had begun to separate in the 1840's and 1850's. In 1861 he sided with a small splinter group within the Conservative Yearly Meeting of Ohio, which took the name of Ohio Primitive General Meeting. From these few details of his career we can see that Maule was a man who cleaved to the old ways and wished to see at least his branch of the Society maintain the letter as well as the spirit of the discipline in regard to Quaker peace principles. Wilburite Friends in Ohio, he tells us, when the test came, "flinched and failed" to bear a consistent testimony in this matter of paying taxes in wartime. He would have liked to see them

---

[92] Quoted in Wright, p. 48. See also, e.g., *Friend*, 1 Aug. 1863.
[93] See, e.g., *Friends' Intelligencer*, 26 Oct. 1861.

adopt the stand of eighteenth-century Friends like John Churchman or Job Scott or John Woolman (his belief that their view was the same as that of all early Friends was, of course, mistaken).

Throughout the period of the war Maule was considerably troubled by what he regarded as a general apostasy on the part of Friends, who for the most part consented to paying general taxes as in peacetime. They had failed, in his view, to think through consistently the full implications of their pacifism; he attributed this failure in large part to the influence of certain weighty Friends, who had advised compliance. A highly respected Wilburite elder told Maule: "I have not yet felt at liberty to withhold the just dues of government on account of a portion being woven in with it that I do not approve of." But it was just this view that Maule contested; he tried to disentangle in the case of his own tax returns the portion that was destined for war purposes. He did not, it is true, feel that he could hold back the money which he gave the government in the form of various trading licenses and purchase taxes levied in connection with his business, since it was impossible to determine what percentage of the whole was allocated to war. But at the end of 1861 we do find Maule going down to the county treasurer's office and, when handing in his total tax payment, deducting from it the 8½%, "which was the part expressly named in the tax list as for the war," and explaining at the same time the reasons for his somewhat unusual behavior. A few weeks later some pieces of his property were distrained in lieu of the unpaid amount. "And so what appeared at the first like a mountain of difficulty has passed comfortably away," Maule recorded.

In the following year he followed the same procedure; this time the county treasurer accepted Maule's explanations, telling him, "I have known you well; you are a consistent man: I will take your tax as you desire." True, in the remaining years of war Maule did not get off quite so easily, since he notes that distraint was made on his goods on these occasions. But his standpoint appears to have found more understanding among the tax-gatherers than in the circle of his own brethren, who may, indeed, have found his accusations of complicity in bloodshed a little trying. A few Quakers in Maule's area followed the same policy of not paying taxes "in the mixture," and there were others elsewhere; but the overwhelming majority saw no inconsistency between pacifism and payment.[94]

It was quite a different matter, however, with the special war taxes

[94] Maule, *Transactions and Changes in the Society of Friends*, pp. 220-24, 233-46, 251, 261-65, 271, 282-85, 299, 315. See Wright, pp. 46, 47.

of the period and the semi-voluntary contributions to the county fund for subsidizing recruits, where in each case the object was solely the more efficacious prosecution of hostilities, which was therefore objectionable to the spirit, if not also to the letter, of the Quaker discipline. As a Hicksite Friend from Duchess County (N.Y.) wrote of county taxes: "What a man does by the hand of another, he does himself."[95] Bounty money appeared in the eyes of Friends as being more tainted with blood than other special war taxes, since it was used to hire men for war rather than to provide only the indirect means for waging war. Although there were differences in practice (once again Baltimore [Hicksite] Yearly Meeting proved more accommodating to variation in opinion then did some other yearly meetings), the records show many Friends undergoing distraint of their property for nonpayment of such levies. "The object of refusing to pay a specific war tax," stated a special committee set up by the New York (Orthodox) Yearly Meeting to consider the whole question, "is to bear our testimony against war, and not to embarrass government, nor to avoid our share of the public burdens which can be paid without violating our religious principles."[96] Those Friends whose high regard for the rights of government ("the best civil government, as we believe, that has ever been established among men," in the words of Baltimore [Hicksite] Yearly Meeting)—or, perhaps, whose disinclination to face the economic disadvantages of defying the law—overrode their religious scruples against payment do not appear to have been called to account in any way by their meetings. This situation led to complaints in some quarters about the unfairness of penalizing, even to the point of disownment, young and inexperienced members who had risked their lives as soldiers in their country's service, while older and more mature Friends who had likewise transgressed, by complying with the state's demands in the way of bounties and special war taxation and sometimes also, as we know, by purchasing government bonds whose only object was the financing of the war, continued to sit unscathed on the elders' benches.

It is interesting to note that the question of paper currency, which had played so large a role at the time of the American Revolution in Friends' thinking on the wartime implications of their pacifism and had stirred up so much dissension within the Society, did not become an issue during the Civil War. Even a tax radical like the Conservative Joshua Maule did not see anything wrong in handling paper money, although apparently some of his Quaker opponents, in their efforts to show that Maule himself was not altogether consistent in his testi-

---

[95] *Friends' Intelligencer*, 17 June 1865.
[96] Wright, pp. 44, 183, 184, 186, 196, 197, 211.

mony for peace, did urge that notes were in part utilized by the government to finance the war.[97] Both Maule and his adversaries were obviously acquainted with the earlier controversy among Friends on the question, but paper money had by this date become firmly entrenched in public life. And, most important of all, the legitimacy of the issuing government was in no way in doubt now among Quakers, as it had been in the case of the Revolutionary authorities.

The Quaker civilian in the Northern states, if he aimed at giving consistent expression to his Society's stand against war, confronted some difficult problems of inner conscience. But his life on the whole continued in its accustomed way. His material prosperity was untouched, apart possibly from some losses from the distraint of goods taken for nonpayment of war taxes. He belonged to a religious denomination which, if it was still considered by some to be rather eccentric, yet enjoyed widespread respect among all sections of the population, from the administration in Washington downward. The loyalty of Quakers to the Union and their long and devoted antislavery record protected them on the whole from suspicion of sympathy with the enemy. They were not subject to the bitter hostility and even violence that some pacifist groups have experienced in time of war, before and since. And even those young men, like Cyrus Pringle, who had to witness to their pacifism in army camps and barracks often met with unexpected consideration and courtesy from officers and men alike. Some of them did, of course, become the victims of harsh and cruel treatment, but this was of short duration and was the result, not of official policy, but of the actions of some local military bully.

III

We must now turn our attention to the wartime experience of the considerably smaller group of Quakers whose homes were in the Confederate states. Friends were still to be found in Virginia, although the Virginia yearly meeting had been "laid down" in 1844 as a result of the large-scale migration of members to the West: only five monthly meetings now remained within the borders of the Old Commonwealth. Most Southern Quakers were to be found in North Carolina, which had its own yearly meeting of about 2,000 members,[98] where Friends were concentrated in the central and northwestern parts of the state and in a few small meetings in the east. The Quaker groups in Georgia

[97] Maule, *Transactions and Changes*, p. 250.
[98] *An Account of the Sufferings of Friends of North Carolina Yearly Meeting,* . . . *1861-1865,* p. 6. This Y. M. had also diminished greatly in numbers over the preceding decades as a result of emigration of its members to the West.

were extinct by this date, but three monthly meetings continued to exist in eastern Tennessee. Southern Quakers, like their Northern brethren, were opposed to slavery and strongly attached to the Union—yet in a land that was fighting to maintain its peculiar institution of slavery in independence of the Union. These circumstances, added to the fact that the Society here was numerically weak and comparatively little known in the community at large, account for the harsher treatment meted out to many Southern Quakers who refused to bear arms for the Confederacy and for the hardships suffered by a number of Friends who were not liable themselves for military service.

The contrast between the situation created by the antisecessionist, antislavery, and pacifist sentiments of Southern Friends and the mild hostility with which, at worst, Quakers in the North were sometimes confronted was brought out very well by North Carolina Yearly Meeting when Quakers there wrote in their records: "Unlike our Friends in the Northern States, it was not on the few that the trial came, but on the many, and in another more important respect our position differed widely from them. In our own case, the existing government and the officers were far from having sympathy with us."[99]

During the first year of war, however, Southern Friends received comparatively mild treatment despite their declared opposition to the war. On 1 July 1861 the Meeting for Sufferings of North Carolina Yearly Meeting approved a statement drawn up by a subcommittee specially appointed for that purpose, setting forth the Quaker position; "it was directed that each of the monthly meetings be furnished with a copy." Petitions were also prepared for dispatch to the two contending governments, earnestly begging them to make peace. The yearly meeting, when it assembled in the fall, followed the earlier example of Virginia Half-Year's Meeting in reiterating its old objection to paying commutation fines in lieu of military service, while at the same time expressing willingness to pay ordinary taxes and to do all possible to relieve war sufferers "(soldiers as well as others)." Several monthly meetings in Virginia likewise drew up declarations of their pacifist faith for the information of outsiders and the edification of their own members. The Goose Creek Monthly Meeting stated: "In as much as a state of war, now unhappily exists in this country, we deem it our religious duty to take no part in it; and to abstain from every act that would give aid in its prosecution." If members of the meeting were ordered to perform any duty that ran contrary to their conscience, "our principles and clear sense of religious duty would forbid our active compliance, even though there was connected therewith the

[99] Quoted in Fernando G. Cartland, *Southern Heroes*, pp. 125, 126.

heaviest penalty." They would, however, suffer the consequences of disobeying the law passively and would under no circumstances attempt any kind of active opposition to the government, for that would be entirely repugnant to their conscience.[100]

Half-Year's Meeting in Virginia, as a result of hostile comments in some local papers to the effect that the record of Quakers in the North proved all Friends to be radical abolitionists in their sympathies, also felt it incumbent upon themselves to publicly disclaim such insinuations. They pointed out, first, that Quakers wherever they were to be found were noncombatants on principle. If some young Friends had joined the Union army—just as a few had joined the Confederate forces —they had thereby separated themselves from the rest of the Society. In the second place, referring to the militant abolitionist group known as Antislavery Friends, they stated: "We here take occasion to say that several years ago some of our members in the West withdrew from their connection with us because the body of the Society *would not* unite with them in taking an active part in the Abolition movements of that day." They had no connection with this group, they said, and could not be held responsible for its actions.[101]

While making sure so far as they could by means of public statements that the religious basis of their opposition to war was rendered clear, Friends at the same time busied themselves with lobbying the state legislatures of North Carolina and Virginia, both of which were known to be preparing new military laws. North Carolina passed hers in September 1861, but Virginia not until March 1862, on the eve of the introduction of Confederate conscription. In each case, religious objectors were exempted on payment of a commutation fee, which was not, of course, acceptable to many Friends. North Carolina did not at first specify the sum required but eventually, in the early summer of 1862, set it at $100. Virginia demanded the much higher figure of $500 plus 2% of the value of the applicant's taxable property.[102]

[100] Wright, pp. 92-93, 97.

[101] *Encyclopedia of American Quaker Genealogy*, VI: *Virginia*, W. W. Hinshaw *et al.* (eds.), 48.

[102] Wright, pp. 93-99. An attempt made in December 1861 to push an act through the North Carolina legislature making it obligatory on every free male over the age of 16 to renounce his allegiance to the United States government and to assert his readiness to defend the Confederate States—on pain of banishment in case of refusal—was unsuccessful. Friends were active in lobbying against the bill. And the state governor, William Graham, himself opposed its passage, declaring in the course of his speech (cited in Wright, p. 146): "This ordinance wholly disregards their [the Quakers'] peculiar belief, and converts every man of them into a warrior or an exile. . . . This ordinance, therefore, is nothing less than a decree of banishment to them. . . . From the expulsion from among us of such a people, the civilized world would cry, shame!"

Some Friends were drafted during this early period of the war, but their release from service was obtained without too much difficulty. A number of Quakers of military age decided to escape across the lines to the Union side. A few were captured and brought back; others were successful in the attempt. Thus, we find an entry dated 7 March 1866, in the Minute Book of Hopewell Monthly Meeting near Winchester (Va.), recording: "The first summer of the war a few of our young men were forced out in the Militia, and placed to work on fortifications, but through the favor of a kind Providence were soon enabled to obtain their enlargement and escaped as refugees into the loyal states."[103]

The coming of Confederate conscription in 1862 made the situation considerably more serious for the Quakers. Now, in addition to their own state legislatures, to many of whose members their pacifist principles were fairly well known,[104] they had to deal with the Confederate Congress and administration, made up for the most part of men for whom the word "Quaker," if known at all, was a symbol of disloyalty to all that the South stood for. There were exceptions, of course: Friends were lucky to find a sympathetic ear and genuine understanding in no less a person, for instance, than the assistant secretary of war, Judge John A. Campbell. After the war was over, while Judge Campbell was in prison for his association with the defeated government, the Meeting for Sufferings of North Carolina Yearly Meeting petitioned the Federal government on his behalf, citing as part of the evidence in his favor the kindness and help the Quakers had received from him during the war.[105]

The first measure of Confederate conscription was passed on 16 April 1862. Although substitutes might be furnished in place of personal service in the army, conscientious objection was not provided for, and the position of Friends and the other peace sects seemed precarious. After some preparatory work, including the presentation of a memorial to the Confederate Congress asking for unconditional exemption for Friends, a delegation consisting of four leading members of North Carolina Yearly Meeting and John B. Crenshaw from Virginia was appointed in August to intervene personally in the Confederate capital of Rich-

[103] *Ibid.*, p. 173. Hopewell M. M. belonged directly to Baltimore Y. M. and did not form part of the Half-Year's Meeting of Virginia. See also *An Account of the Sufferings*, p. 7.

[104] E.g., Jonathan Worth, state senator, later treasurer, and then governor of North Carolina, was of Nantucket Quaker ancestry and genuinely anxious to avoid anything in the nature of a persecution of Friends on account of their pacifism. We frequently find him interceding on their behalf. See Wright, pp. 100, 146-48; Cartland, *Southern Heroes*, pp. 144-46.

[105] Wright, pp. 138-42.

mond. Jefferson Davis, whom they succeeded in seeing, was courteous but noncommittal. They also stated their case before the military committee of Congress, prefacing the presentation of their evidence by several minutes of silence after the manner of an informal Quaker meeting—much to the astonishment of the congressmen present. One of them later in the proceedings asked the Quaker minister, Isham Cox: "Doubtless your people are in the Northern army fighting us, and why should you not join us in fighting them?" To which Cox at once replied: "I am not afraid to agree to fight, single handed, every true Friend in the Northern army."[106] As a result of such efforts, as well as those of the Mennonites and Brethren (see below) with whom Southern Quakers cooperated fairly closely in working for exemption, the draft law of 11 October 1862 contained a clause excusing all who were at that date members of these three peace sects (or of the Nazarenes, a group whose identity has never been unravelled) from the performance of military duties on payment of the sum of $500.

The exemption granted in the act proved satisfactory to the Mennonites and Dunkers, but it fell short of the unconditional status that the Quakers had requested. At their yearly meeting held at the beginning of November, North Carolina Friends expressed in the following minute a mixture both of disappointment and of gratitude for goodwill shown:

> We have had the subject under serious consideration, and while in accordance with our last yearly meeting we do pay all taxes imposed on us as citizens and property-holders in common with other citizens, remembering the injunction, "tribute to whom tribute is due, custom to whom custom," yet we cannot conscientiously pay the specified tax, it being imposed upon us on account of our principles, as the price exacted of us for religious liberty. Yet we do appreciate the good intentions of those members of Congress who had it in their hearts to do something for our relief; and we recommend that those parents who, moved by sympathy, or those young men, who dreading the evils of a military camp, have availed themselves of this law, shall be treated in a tender manner by their monthly meetings.

Nevertheless, despite the fact that Friends had once again come out publicly against paying commutation, many Quakers—as had been envisaged—did, in fact, avail themselves of their statutory right to exemption set down in the act of October 1862, a privilege which remained in force until the end of the war. (By that time, wartime inflation had so depreciated the real value of the Confederate currency

[106] *Ibid.*, pp. 100-102; Cartland, *Southern Heroes*, pp. 125-28.

768

that the commutation fine of $500 had ceased to be much of a financial burden.) North Carolina Yearly Meeting instructed the clerks of its constituent monthly meetings, in conjunction with committees specially appointed for that purpose, to provide applicants for exemption with the certificates of membership that the authorities required. "By this action," says Wright, "the Yearly Meeting definitely allowed its members to avail themselves of the exemption privilege if they could conscientiously do so."[107] A similar position, if anything a little more compliant, was taken up by Half-Year's Meeting in Virginia. In a memorial, dated 5 October 1863 and addressed to the state legislature, they stated that, since in wartime no legal machinery existed for distraint on the property of those who refused commutation, Friends were paying the fines "under protest," regarding this as in line with Christ's injunction when he "directed the tribute money to be paid—'That we offend them not.' "[108] The explanation is a little disingenuous: undoubtedly, the very considerable pressure to which Southern Friends were subjected made it much harder for them than for Quakers in the North to take up an uncompromisingly absolutist stand. The more yielding attitude of Virginia Friends perhaps explains why their sufferings were less than those of their brethren in North Carolina.

The position of the Quakers and the other peace sects in the South remained uncertain right up to the day when the surrender of Appomattox brought the conflict to a close. Not merely were there periodic threats to abolish the exemption granted conscientious objectors, but, with the widening of the age of those liable for the federal draft, the net of conscription encompassed an ever larger number of men. In mid-1862 the age limits were set at 18 to 35, but the upper limit was raised in 1863 to 45. In 1864 all men between 17 and 50 became liable, and in the last few weeks of the war a further extension of the age limits was about to come into force. Friends, therefore, lived in a continual state of crisis, and it often became necessary for their representative bodies to petition or memorialize either the Confederate Congress or the state legislatures of North Carolina and Virginia in defense of their pacifist position.

Leading Friends were active, too, in visiting prominent government and state officials. The name of John Bacon Crenshaw (1820-1889), a Quaker minister in Richmond (Va.), constantly occurs in this connection in the documents of the time. He was on friendly terms with Judge John A. Campbell, and his residence in the Confederate capital made

---

[107] Wright, pp. 104-10.
[108] *Memorial to Legislature of Virginia*, p. 2. The *Memorial* was reprinted in part in S. F. Sanger and D. Hays, *The Olive Branch*, pp. 229-31.

it easier for him to maintain contacts in government circles than it was for the more distant meetings in North Carolina. Crenshaw was immensely energetic—not only in lobbying government and legislature but in working for the release of drafted conscientious objectors, both Quaker and non-Quakers, from prisons and army camps and in raising money to pay the fines of those willing to accept commutation. He helped, too, in the relief of sick and wounded soldiers of both sides and in work for Northern prisoners of war. And, finally, he was able to promote a fair degree of cooperation between his own Friends and the Mennonites and Dunkers (not so simple an undertaking as it might sound).[109] Among the North Carolina Quakers the most outstanding personality at this time was the well-known educationalist, Nereus Mendenhall. Of Mendenhall's fearless advocacy of Quaker pacifism it has been said: "He did not hesitate to maintain the principles which it professed, on the street, in the railway trains, anywhere and everywhere he would show the incompatibility of all war with the spirit and teaching of Christ."[110]

We must now turn to the experiences of those Friends who were drafted after the introduction of Confederate conscription in 1862. A few young men from the meetings had volunteered for service, but a considerably smaller proportion than in the North since, quite apart from the question of pacifism, the Confederate cause had little appeal for those reared in the staunchly antislavery atmosphere of the Society. We read, too, of one Friend—Isaac Harvey of New Garden Monthly Meeting in North Carolina—who, upon being drafted and after resisting service for several weeks, yielded and agreed to bear arms. As soon as his meeting heard what he had done, it took steps to disown him.[111] All those who served voluntarily in a combatant capacity were naturally disowned by their meetings, also.[112] A number of young men of military age continued to escape to the North in order to avoid conscription. Others hid for a time in the forests; sometimes, local home guards hunting for the escapees would torture their parents in an effort to get them to reveal their sons' whereabouts. These draft dodgers for conscience' sake were, of course, but a small proportion of those potential conscripts who, either by hiding in the woods or by fleeing

[109] Margaret E. Crenshaw, "John Bacon Crenshaw" in *Quaker Biographies*, 2nd ser., III, 173-85. See also Wright, pp. 199-202.

[110] Quoted in Wright, p. 203.

[111] Cartland, *Southern Heroes*, p. 223.

[112] Wright, pp. 187, 188. Disciplinary action was also taken against any who furnished a substitute. We hear in 1865 of a Friend being "eldered" for hiring an armed guard to watch his property; after being dealt with, he acknowledged his conduct "to be inconsistent" with Quaker principles.

westward or northward, were attempting to escape fighting in a cause which, for one reason or another, they did not feel to be theirs.

Some who tried to escape were captured before they succeeded in crossing into Northern territory, like the Quaker brothers from North Carolina, Mahlon and Joshua Kemp. They were placed in the army and were present in December 1862 at the battle of Fredericksburg, where they consented to look after the wounded, helping to remove them from the battlefield at the risk of their lives. Perhaps as a result of the courage they displayed in action, the Kemps were released shortly afterward on paying the $500 commutation. We read of another young Quaker from the same state, William Woody, entering the army when called up, accepting a gun (although with the firm intention of never using it), and then taking the first opportunity to desert to the enemy. After arriving in Union territory, he made his way to Indiana without further mishap.[113]

Among those Quaker conscientious objectors who successfully made the journey across the lines was 18-year-old A. Marshall Elliott (1846-1910), who was later to become a professor of Romance languages at Johns Hopkins University and a prominent scholar in that field. Elliott's father was a Quaker farmer in North Carolina. In the summer of 1862, finding that the authorities would not recognize the conscientious objection to fighting which he had learned in his home and suffering from bad health, which made his position additionally precarious, the boy decided to escape to the North. Quaker neighbors helped conceal him and smuggle him across the boundary. "Once over it," he wrote later, "my next object was to make all possible speed for the headquarters of the Federal Army stationed then at Suffolk, Va. General Mansfield was at this time in command of the department of East Virginia, and through his kindness I was furnished with an escort of two soldiers to Baltimore and with a free passport to Philadelphia." The remainder of the war he spent as a student at Haverford College.[114]

Among the small group of Friends still remaining in the eastern part of Tennessee, those who were unwilling or unable to pay the commutation fine hid themselves in a large cave, the entrance to which was concealed from sight by thick undergrowth. Leading members of the local Quaker community, who were not liable themselves to military service, acted as contacts with the outer world and helped keep the men supplied with food and drink.[115] Most Friends, however, remained

[113] Cartland, *Southern Heroes*, pp. 225-27.
[114] George C. Keidel, *The Early Life of Professor Elliott*.
[115] Cartland, *Southern Heroes*, chap. XV.

at home and awaited whatever might befall them at the hands of the authorities. In North Carolina some accepted employment in a reserved occupation, such as the state salt works; "not a few" of these, however, records the official account of North Carolina Friends' wartime experiences, "finding their work too closely connected with war, relinquished it."[116]

As mentioned above, many Friends were prepared to pay the commutation fine of $500, which was acceptable to the meetings. After the Confederate Congress had passed this exemption, there remained three groups of Friends (or near Friends) who found themselves in difficulties with the military authorities and in many cases suffered severe hardship, sometimes becoming the victims of considerable brutality.

There were, in the first place, some Quakers who were drafted into the army "under irregular proceedings" (to use the phrase in North Carolina Yearly Meeting's official account).[117] These were men who were legally entitled to exemption and willing to take advantage of it but who had been refused their rights by the local military authorities. Usually the matter was corrected in a fairly short time: both John B. Crenshaw and leading Friends in North Carolina were active in intervening on behalf of such men. Wright cites the case of three Quakers—Nere and Seth Cox and Eli Macon—who appealed to the sympathetic and influential non-Quaker Jonathan Worth for help, writing to him rather quaintly as follows: "There is three in Camp Holmes members of the society of Friends and we want thee to come over immediately on receiving these lines in order to pay our exemption tax and let us go home. If thee cannot furnish us with the money we want thee to come and see us any how."[118]

More serious was the position of the second group: those who had joined the Society only after 11 October 1862, thereby being excluded from the provisions of the act's exemption clause, and sympathizers with Quakerism who were not actual members of the Society. Many of those who eventually escaped from the Confederate states belonged to this category. About 600 persons (including the womenfolk and children) were admitted into membership during the course of the war. The pacifism of the Quakers was undoubtedly one of the tenets which attracted many of the new members (as it was in the wars of this century); for the suspicions of some government officials that the So-

---

[116] *An Account of the Sufferings*, p. 9. The state authorities were favorably inclined toward employment in the salt works as a recognized form of alternative service for Quaker objectors. But the yearly meeting rejected the idea when it was proposed. See Wright, p. 100.

[117] *An Account of the Sufferings*, p. 8.

[118] Wright, p. 146.

ciety was gaining recruits from political malcontents or physical cowards, however, there was no evidence. The hardships that some of these men had to bear as a result of their antiwar stand indicates rather the reverse. In addition, some in this group had been brought up in a Quaker environment; for one reason or another, however, usually because only one parent had been a Friend, they had not become birthright members of the Society and were therefore in the position of the much larger group of young Mennonites and Brethren, whose churches only accepted their young people into membership after reaching adult life. Most of these men were willing to pay the commutation fine if given the opportunity to do so.

Cartland in his *Southern Heroes* gives many instances of harsh and repeated punishment being meted out to these men while under military command.[119] Prolonged periods of "bucking down" were frequently imposed in the attempt to subdue their spirit (as it was with other recalcitrant soldiers) and to force them to accept combatant service. Cartland describes this punishment as follows:

> The man who is condemned to this trying ordeal is made to sit down on the ground; his wrists are firmly bound together by strong cord or withes; drawing up the knees his arms are pressed over them until a stout stick can be thrust over the elbows, under the knees, and thus the man's feet and hands are rendered useless for the time being.

Other cruelties inflicted included piercing repeatedly with a bayonet, hanging up by the thumbs, beatings and kickings, gagging with an open bayonet, deprivation of sleep, long periods on a bread and water diet, incarceration in filthy cells, and deprivation of means of washing. Frequently, the men were threatened with shooting or hanging. (Gideon Macon was about to be strung up on a tree when the regiment to which he had been assigned was forced to beat a hasty retreat by the advancing Northern army, and Seth Loflin would have been shot, following a court-martial sentence, had not the twelve men in the firing squad, overcome by his calm courage, refused to carry out the sentence and thus given time for it to be reconsidered.) In many cases, with their rifles forcibly strapped to their backs, they were compelled to accompany the army on active service, their position becoming increasingly precarious as they were brought into contact with the actual fighting.

Yet none were in fact executed (although several died from illness

[119] See, e.g., pp. 181-94, 201-11, 222, 376-79. See also Wright, pp. 116-20; *An Account of the Sufferings*, pp. 10-18.

773

induced by their previous sufferings). Moreover, ill-treatment was usually the result of excessive zeal on the part of junior officers and not of orders from the higher command. There were sometimes abuse and rough usage at first from the ordinary soldiers; many, however, showed sympathy and appreciation of the men's courage and endurance and a growing awareness of the depths of conviction from which their resistance derived. "Taking all things into consideration," Wright remarks judiciously, "it is apparent that the cases of excessive severity in the South were the exception rather than the rule."[120]

Those who remained adamant in rejecting commutation were sometimes kept in army camp or army prison for several years, being released only as a result of the final collapse of the Confederate war effort. The refusal of these absolutists to compromise by undertaking any, even seemingly unobjectionable, duties done under military orders—cooking or orderly chores or carrying officers' baggage, for instance—brought added punishment. "We are in the entrenchments near Petersburg, in Company F. 27th regiment," Seth W. Loflin and J. A. Hill wrote home in September 1864 on behalf of nearly a dozen young men from Marlboro and Springfield Monthly Meetings in Randolph County (N.C.). "We have thus far refused to take any part in military duty, for which we are receiving severe punishment. . . . They say we must suffer until we drill. We still expect, by the Grace of God, and the help of your prayers, to be faithful to our profession." One of those who maintained a rigidly unconditionalist stand after being forced into the army was the 18-year-old potter's apprentice, Tilghman Ross Vestal, from near Columbia, Tennessee. A high-ranking Confederate officer, who knew him in camp, wrote later of this "remarkable boy": "He refused . . . to do the least thing that could be tortured or construed into military duty." When Vestal, who was not yet himself a member of the Society but whose mother, a Quaker, had brought him up in that persuasion, learned that the North Carolina Yearly Meeting, to which his mother belonged, did not disapprove of those in his situation taking advantage of the legal exemption, he agreed to allow Friends to petition President Davis on his behalf for permission to pay the commutation tax. As a result of their intervention, the boy was finally released from prison, after enduring many months of almost continuous ill-treatment.[121]

---

[120] Wright, p. 179.

[121] Ibid., pp. 142-44; Cartland, Southern Heroes, chap. XVI. After attempting to prove Vestal wrong on the basis of the New Testament in his refusal to fight, former Governor Henry S. Foote of Mississippi was forced to admit: "I believe he knows more about that than I do."

In some instances, the military authorities even allowed unconditionalists to return home eventually. And if a "new" Quaker was willing
to gain his release by paying his commutation fee, the Confederate
government was usually willing (as in Vestal's case) to stretch a point
and grant him in the end the exemption to which he was not entitled
according to the exact letter of the law. The same accommodating
spirit, as in the cases of men who were brought up in the Quaker environment but were not themselves members or who had recently
joined the Society, was not infrequently shown by the Confederate
authorities in dealing with those who held Quaker views but were not
as closely connected with the Society. We read in John B. Crenshaw's
diary, for instance, the following entry for 18 October 1862: "Put in a
petition for Jesse Gordon, who professes to be a Friend in principle.
The Secretary of War agreed to pass him as a Friend, much to our
relief." Or again, for 7 February 1863: "Interceded for M. H. Brad-
shaw, not a Friend. Secretary of War agreed to pass him as a Friend.
I paid the tax and brought him home with me."[122] Another case that
may be cited at this point is that of "J. G.," a North Carolina man,
who was a Methodist when fighting broke out, although he held
Quaker views on war. Not eligible for exemption, he attempted to
escape to the West when threatened with the draft in the autumn
of 1862 but was arrested and put in an army camp. "Just put away
your Quaker notions" if you wish to escape the firing squad, the officers told him when he refused to accept military orders or wear a uniform. Somehow his plight reached the ears of North Carolina Friends,
who succeeded in obtaining exemption for him from the authorities in
Richmond. Not long after his release, "J. G." was formally accepted
into membership of the Society of Friends.[123]

Others in this class, however, had a harder road to travel. Take the
story of Jesse Buckner of Chatham County (N.C.), a Baptist and colonel in the local militia at the time of the outbreak of the war. Puzzled
to find that no members of the Society of Friends, which he held in
respect although he had only a very passing acquaintance with its doctrines, had joined up, he was led on from discovering that they objected
to war on principle to ponder the matter more deeply in his own
mind. By the autumn of 1861 he had become convinced of the incompatibility of war with the Christian religion, and he resigned his
commission in the militia. His troubles began when he was drafted
in the following March and only ended with the Confederate surrender. Although he finally joined Friends in the spring of 1863, he still

---

[122] Cartland, *Southern Heroes*, pp. 353, 355.
[123] *Ibid.*, pp. 150-52.

775

had to face several lengthy spells in army camps, where he was subjected to almost continuous ridicule, threats, and harsh treatment in an attempt to break his spirit.[124]

Perhaps the strangest story of all is that of Rufus P. King (1843-1923), an illiterate North Carolina country boy, who was conscripted into the Confederate army early in 1862. His natural religious bent, strengthened by the experience of "conversion" which he underwent at a Methodist revivalist meeting during a furlough, had produced in him a strong repugnance to the idea of shedding blood. He had had no contact with Quakers, nor was he in touch, apparently, with any others holding pacifist views. Yet he determined, whatever the consequences, not to be instrumental in taking life. A seemingly chance assignment to work with the ambulance corps King saw as an answer to his prayers. Later he was present at the battle of Gettysburg, acting as a stretcher-bearer; during the subsequent retreat he was taken prisoner by the Union forces. After a year in Point Lookout prison, he was returned to the South as a result of an exchange of prisoners between the two sides. Called back into the army, King succeeded in deserting to the North and was able to make his way finally to Indiana. Here it was that he first became acquainted with Friends, who helped him get an education. He joined the Society in 1865 and returned thirteen years later to North Carolina, where his natural gifts brought him leadership in the Society's work and counsels.[125]

The third group of Quaker conscripts in the South who had to suffer severe hardship on account of their conscientious objector stand—probably the least numerous of the three, although no exact figures are available—were the men who, although members of the Society prior to the passing of the act of 11 October 1862 and, therefore, fully eligible for the exemption then granted, refused to avail themselves of this on the grounds of the traditional Quaker objection to accepting any alternative in exchange for permission to do what they believed was right. We have seen that at least the higher civil and military authorities were not anxious, if some way out could be devised, to add to their problems by having on their hands men who, it became increasingly obvious, would never make fighting material. We have seen, too, that Friends in both North Carolina and Virginia, while acknowledging it to be to some extent a compromise of their principles, were prepared *faute de mieux* to sanction the payment of commutation money by drafted members, if they were conscientiously able to pay.

---

[124] *Ibid.*, pp. 146-50; Wright, pp. 175, 176.
[125] Emma King, "Rufus P. King" in *Quaker Biographies*, 2nd ser., II, esp. 177-82; Cartland, *Southern Heroes*, pp. 290-98.

There were still, however, not a few who felt called to testify to the full Quaker witness for peace. For them, the position was hard indeed, for there was no legal machinery through which they could be released from liability for military service. In theory, therefore, they might find themselves under army command and driven from army camp to army camp, and even into the battle zone, until defeat brought about the dissolution of the Confederate armies. In practice, however, this situation rarely occurred: more often, means were found in the end to furlough an individual of this kind, if no other opportunity of ridding the army of him had occurred earlier.

The best known instance among the Southern Friends of this type of Quaker absolutist is that of the three Hockett brothers from Center Meeting near Greensboro in Guilford County (N.C.): William, Himelius, and Jesse. Himelius and Jesse were called up first, in April 1862. The provost marshal used the fact that a fellow Quaker, who had been drafted with them, had consented to pay the commutation tax, in order to persuade the two brothers to follow his example. They could, however, point to their yearly meeting's minutes of the previous year, a copy of which Himelius had luckily brought with him, to show that their own position was the official one of the Society. There ensued for the brothers over six months of continuous pressure to get them to obey military orders, including hanging by the thumbs, pricking with a bayonet, and nearly five days without food or drink, which they stubbornly resisted. Himelius was confined for a while in a military fortress with a heavy ball and chain attached to his legs. Of his prison he wrote in the journal he kept: "Notwithstanding its gloomy appearance, it seemed to me as a secret hiding-place, and my chains as jewels, for they were taken as an evidence of my suffering for Christ's sake." Their release, when it came, was the work of another Quaker, who paid the commutation on their behalf, but without their knowledge or consent.

Their brother William had had his call-up deferred by the military authorities from the fall of 1862 until June of the following year. Refusing to pay commutation, he was placed with the 21st North Carolina regiment and sent to join it near the battle front in northern Virginia. The nearness of the front line made his position extremely dangerous, since he refused both to wear army uniform and to drill or perform any tasks when ordered. As he wrote in the journal which he kept, comparing his present position with that of Shadrach, Meschach, and Abednego in the fiery furnace or Daniel's in the lions' den: "The army is a very trying place for a Christian to be in, because there are so many things that we cannot for conscience' sake do that must be

777

done if the war goes on. So we are constantly beset on every side." During his sojourn in the army William experienced both kindness and sympathy from the ordinary soldiers and considerable cruelty from some of the officers, who were angered by his refusal to carry out orders and to perform any kind of work. With his gun forcibly strapped on to his back, he spent what leisure time was allowed him reading his Bible. In July 1863 William was taken prisoner by the Union forces, and, freed eventually from captivity by the ending of hostilities, he made his way back to his home in North Carolina.[126]

The Quaker absolutists of the South and the new and near Quakers were the ones who had had to bear the most heavy burden in witnessing to Quaker pacifism in time of war. All Friends in that sector who were of military age had had to face difficult decisions, if not actual suffering. As in the North the war had brought its special problems, too, for those Southern Quakers who on account of age, sex, or sickness were not liable for military service; in addition, many suffered considerable material losses, which their Northern brethren were spared. The question of whether Friends should pay special war taxes bothered Friends in the Confederate as well as in the Union states. In the summer of 1863, for instance, when a "tax in kind" was imposed to help subsidize the war effort, the North Carolina Meeting for Sufferings reported that, in the past,

> Friends have not felt at liberty to pay such taxes. Such we think should be the case with the demand for the tenth part of the produce of our lands. We believe that this is designed for the direct support of the army. It is strictly a *war measure.* Hence believing as we do that all wars are contrary to the Spirit of the Gospel of our Lord and Savior Jesus Christ, and that by the payment of this tithe, we are directly aiding to prolong these evils; it is the sense and judgment of this meeting that we cannot consistently pay said tithe.[127]

That all Friends were prepared to incur the heavy losses through distraint of their property which would probably have resulted from not paying the tithe is unlikely. But some undoubtedly there were who chose this way of bearing a clear witness to the Quaker peace testimony.

The Quaker communities, along with the rest of the civilian population, suffered severe damage to their property from the depredations of occupying Northern troops whenever they visited the area. Their treatment by the Confederate military was often just as bad, and some-

---

[126] Cartland, *Southern Heroes,* chaps. XII, XIII; *An Account of the Sufferings,* pp. 19-22; Wright, pp. 177-79.
[127] Wright, pp. 110, 111.

778

times even worse.[128] Some older Friends were arrested on suspicion (not unfounded, though hardly deserving such treatment) of being pro-Unionist in sympathies and were kept in confinement for periods from a few days to two years and over. A number of Friends were active in helping men of military age, whether pacifists or non-pacifist opponents of the Confederate war effort, to escape over the lines into Northern territory. If caught aiding such runaways, they were liable to be severely punished.

Thus the war years were in many ways even more of a testing time for Southern Friends than for those living in the Northern states. Nevertheless, if the physical hardships Quakers in the South had to endure were considerably more severe than in the North, the refusal to fight on behalf of a government that had implanted the maintenance of slavery and the destruction of the Union in the center of its war aims, on the other hand, caused less soul-searching and mental stress. The main dilemma faced by Friends in the North had been to reconcile their peace testimony with their equally strong desire to see the whole country rid of slavery. A few years after Appomattox, a Northern Quaker minister then traveling in the South, who was later to become the first historian of the Southern Quakers' wartime experiences, felt a sudden surge of emotion when he saw the Stars and Stripes flying in a small North Carolina town. His feelings would have been shared by most Friends on both sides of the former battle lines. The sight of the national flag, he wrote,

. . . filled his soul with feelings of patriotism such as a peace-loving Friend might safely indulge. There, in the heart of the land which had been so recently under the Confederate government and so long the land of slavery, the writer bowed before the God of all grace and thanked Him that the struggle was ended; that slavery . . . was a thing of the past; and that the dear old flag could once more be unfurled in . . . the Southland, and be recognized as the flag of "Our Country."[129]

[128] See *An Account of the Sufferings*, p. 25, for details on the material losses suffered during the war by Friends in North Carolina.
[129] Cartland, *Southern Heroes*, pp. 176, 177.

779

Chapter 19

Mennonites and Brethren
in the Civil War

I

In the Civil War the Quaker peace testimony had continued to follow the traditional pattern. It stressed as before not merely the duty of a Christian conscience to suffer for the faith but also the rights of that conscience over against the state. It represented in its most considered form an assertion as much of civil rights as of religious obligation. The peace sects of German origin, on the other hand, remained loyal to their concept of pacifism with its careful demarcation between the world and its ways and the community of Christ's followers. Defense of the rights of man born to be free was not their concern; they strove rather to preserve a way of life in conformity with the teachings of the suffering Savior of man. After the failure of the Holy Experiment and the trials of the Revolutionary War, the Quakers had partly withdrawn from the world, had drawn nearer in their outlook to the political position of the German peace sectaries. Yet the gap had not been completely bridged. Stemming from the same source in the teachings of the New Testament, the pacifism of Quakers and German peace sectaries continued to find expression in rather different forms.

The Mennonites—if we ignore the various schisms which had already, in the decades before the outbreak of war, begun to fragment the church—were still the most numerous body among the German peace sects. From Pennsylvania and Virginia they had spread out with the great westward movement of population, so that by the Civil War we find Mennonite communities in most of the states of the Midwest: Ohio, Indiana, Michigan, Illinois, Iowa, and Missouri. However, the decades of geographical expansion had not coincided, as we have seen, with any expansion of intellectual or spiritual horizons. On the contrary, in the words of a Mennonite historian, "the period prior to the Civil War was a period of spiritual decline in the Mennonite Church," and this decline resulted in "the intellectual and spiritual immaturity of the church in the Civil War period."[1] In some frontier areas the physical isolation seems to have exercised a harmful influence

[1] Guy F. Hershberger, *War, Peace and Nonresistance*, pp. 100, 111.

780

on the church's spiritual life. In all branches of the denomination we find a serious deficiency in the instruction of the youth in the teachings of the church, including its peace testimony; the Sunday school was frowned upon as an instrument of the world, so that the religious education of the future church member depended largely upon his family and the general influence of the community.

It is hardly surprising then that, at least in some areas, we find among the younger generation a falling away from their church's traditional pacifist stand when the time of testing came. "To judge from the records, many men from Mennonite and Amish homes must have entered the ranks of the Union armies."[2] In the South among the small community of Virginia Mennonites, an oasis of antislavery feeling set down in a hostile environment, opinion was more united in opposition to war, which in effect meant, of course, the Confederate war effort. (The wartime tribulations of these Southern Mennonites and their almost unanimous witness for peace will be dealt with later in this chapter.) In the Union states the official church attitude also remained unalterably set against all participation in direct military activities. In most cases, members who joined the forces either voluntarily or, later, as conscripts were disfellowshipped—and reinstated after the war only if they were prepared to make public confession of error. This was the practice, for instance, in the Franconia Conference of the Mennonite Church. There, indeed, according to the Conference's historian, "very few Mennonites accepted military service."[3] But such strictness, especially perhaps in communities where the backsliding had been greater, does not appear to have been a universal rule, if we may judge by the minutes of the Eastern District Conference of the General Conference branch. At a meeting held at Springfield (Pa.) in early October 1863, it was recommended "that when members of congregations bear arms each congregation is to handle such brother according to circumstances, but in a way that the Council is respected."[4] This somewhat ambiguous wording would seem to indicate that expulsion from the church community was not always and everywhere meted out to Mennonite soldiers.

Of course, many of these boys, at the time they joined up, had not yet become full members of the church, for admittance was usually postponed until manhood and, in many communities, until after marriage. It was just this age group, immature and usually (as we have just

[2] Edward Yoder, "Peace Principles from a Spiritual Viewpoint," *Gospel Herald*, XXXIII, no. 3 (18 April 1940), 78.
[3] John C. Wenger, *History of the Mennonites of the Franconia Conference*, p. 64.
[4] Minutes of the Eastern District Conference (1847-1902), tr. (anon.) from the German.

781

seen) without proper grounding in the doctrines of the church, that was most susceptible to the mass enthusiasm for the Union cause which was sweeping so many of their contemporaries into the ranks of the army. These circumstances, too, would make it easier for them to find acceptance again in their home community after the war. Of those who did not return, the following obituary inserted toward the end of the war in the leading Mennonite paper bears moving testimony: "Died in the hospital, in the State of Texas, Andrew Weaver, aged 18 years and 9 months. He had volunteered and joined the army, contrary to the wishes of his parents, and his time of service had almost expired, when he was called from this to another world by Him who doeth all things well."[5]

It was not until the coming of federal conscription in March 1863 that military service became a pressing issue among the Mennonites in the North. In the early months of the war, since they gladly continued to accept the conditional exemption granted to them by state law in exchange for paying commutation money, their position was in principle the same as in the prewar period. True, military service was no longer only for brief yearly exercises in the moribund and often unpopular state militia and in a country in a state of peace; it was now in defense of the Union and free institutions against the Southern enemy. Many a Mennonite farm saw one or more of its younger men leave to volunteer for service with the Union army. But group pressures toward joining up were naturally less in communities where the majority belonged to a peace church. Until the coming of the federal draft, the ranks of the army continued to be filled by the volunteer system, while exemption from personal service in the state militias could be obtained for a small sum on certification of membership. The federal act of 3 March 1863 permitted any man drafted either to hire a substitute or to pay $300 to the authorities for that purpose. A subsequent act of 24 February 1864 restricted the exemption of able-bodied men who were unable or unwilling to obtain a substitute to those who belonged to a peace church and pleaded conscientious objection on that account; the objector was then required either to pay $300 in commutation money, which would be devoted to the care of sick and wounded soldiers, or to serve personally by working in military hospitals or looking after freedmen.

This legislation, especially the act of February 1864 with its explicit recognition of the rights of conscience, was welcomed by Mennonite leaders. In an editorial published in the *Herald of Truth* and entitled "The Draft," John F. Funk (1835-1930), after summarizing the pro-

[5] *Herald of Truth*, vol. II, no. 2 (Feb. 1865).

vision made for conscientious objectors in the recent act, commented: "We cannot feel too grateful for the kindness our Rulers have manifested in regard to us."[6] Such feelings of relief and gratitude to the government stemmed from the traditional Mennonite loyalty to the powers that be as God-ordained instruments of his will; as a wartime minute of the Eastern District Conference says, "loyal support of our civil authorities was stressed."[7] Although Funk's seeming approval of noncombatant status in the medical service under army control is somewhat ambiguous, Hershberger is probably right in interpreting this as merely a general approbation of humanitarian service to relieve suffering wherever found. Anyhow, this issue was in fact never brought into the open, since such service was not demanded of religious objectors who, like the Mennonites, were willing and able to pay the commutation fee.[8]

Most young Mennonites in the North, therefore, stayed on their family farms, paying their $300 and praising God for his mercy in delivering them from the tribulations which their ancestors had so often had to face in upholding their faith. After receiving notice that he was to be drafted, the objector's first step to gain exemption was to file a petition, accompanied by a supporting letter from the authorities of his church, solemnly affirming that he was not only opposed to bearing arms himself but was a member in good standing of a church which held to nonresistance as one of its tenets. The petition was then certified as correct by a local justice of the peace, and, on payment of the required sum of $300, the conscientious objector received from his board of enrollment, along with a receipt, a "Certificate of Non-Liability," which he could show if an attempt were made in the future to conscript him.[9]

The problem of exemption, however, was not always so simple. Although, unlike the Quakers, the Mennonites, consonant with their whole tradition and outlook, do not seem ever to have held out for unconditional exemption, there were at least two issues in connection with the draft that they had to grapple with. The first, and easier, question concerned the poorer members of the church, who could not afford to pay the full $300. The Mennonites by that date were on the whole a fairly prosperous community; but the amount required might be be-

[6] *Ibid.*, vol. I, no. 8 (Aug. 1864).   [7] Minute dated early Oct. 1863.

[8] Hershberger, *War, Peace and Nonresistance*, pp. 104, 105.

[9] This account is based on the draft documents of an Amish Mennonite, Samuel D. Guengerich (1836-1929), of Somerset Co. (Pa.), who was drafted in March 1865 at the age of 29. They are now in the Archives of the Mennonite Church at Goshen and have been published by Melvin Gingerich in "The Military Draft during the American Civil War," *MHB*, vol. XII, no. 3 (July 1951).

yond the capacity of some members, especially if the family contained several sons of draft age. Sometimes the money could be borrowed,[10] for the honest and thrifty Mennonite enjoyed good credit among his neighbors. But the congregations were urged to come to the help of their impecunious brethren, too, as we see from a minute of the Eastern District Conference: "All such members who have not been called out by the draft owe it as a duty and not a charity to render assistance to the full extent of their ability to those who have been called."[11] It is most improbable that a Mennonite congregation would have permitted any of its members to miss the legal exemption for lack of funds.

The permissibility of hiring substitutes presented Mennonite communities with a second and more difficult question. In the period of almost a year between the acts of March 1863 and February 1864, the only possibility of gaining exemption, if a man were caught in the draft, was to hire a substitute or pay money so that the authorities could hire one. But was this a practice that the Christian principle of rendering unto Caesar the things that were Caesar's covered? Or was it not perhaps, on the contrary, a sinful act not only to hire another to fight in one's place but even to provide the authorities with money, knowing that it was destined to pay a man to fight, an act which might bring with it the blood of others, that of the man who had substituted perhaps and of those whom he slew in battle? We know of at least one Mennonite who answered the latter question in the affirmative. Wenger mentions the case of Jacob S. Overholt, who, according to his son's account, feared that innocent blood might rest on his head and therefore refused to seek exemption on these terms, was drafted into the army, but finally released from camp on grounds of poor health.[12]

In principle, the hiring of a substitute to fight in a drafted man's place was undoubtedly condemned by the church authorities, but it appears from the evidence available[13] that the payment of money, which would ultimately be used by the authorities to hire soldiers, was not viewed in the same light. In this instance, it could be argued, the responsibility for the use made of the fine, as for the use made of

[10] A case of this kind is reported in the *Herald of Truth*, vol. II, no. 2 (Feb. 1865).

[11] Minute dated early Oct. 1863. See also the earlier and briefer minute dated 7-8 May 1863, passed at the Eastern District Conference's meeting at West Swamp (Pa.) soon after the first federal draft legislation.

[12] Wenger, *History of the Franconia Conference*, pp. 63, 64.

[13] See, e.g., the minutes of the Eastern District Conference for 1863, quoted above. See also the Goshen College Biblical Seminary paper by Richard B. Yoder, "Nonresistance among the Peace Churches of Southern Somerset County, Pennsylvania, during the Civil War," for the practice in that area.

ordinary taxation, was the government's.[14] But direct hiring of substitutes, too, was in fact resorted to not infrequently both by individuals and by whole Mennonite communities, even after the more liberal provisions of the federal conscription act of February 1864 had come into force, and apparently this practice usually escaped censure by the church.

Take the case of Christian Krehbiel (see chapter 9), who later became a leading figure among the General Conference Mennonites out in Kansas. At the time of his drafting in the late summer of 1864, Krehbiel, a devout young man of 32, who was chosen to be a minister two months later, was farming at Summerfield (Ill.). He had emigrated as a boy in 1851 from South Germany along with his family, who had found the strain of buying exemption from military service in their homeland too heavy for their financial resources. His Mennonite upbringing in Germany, where this method was traditional in his church, along with his desire as a recent immigrant to show his loyalty to the country where he had found refuge, accounts perhaps for the readiness of this convinced nonresistant to purchase exemption by means of a substitute. "After I had been drafted," he relates in his autobiography, "I had to settle this question with my conscience. It became clear to me that I was called to be a fighter, but not as a soldier. Several of us had agreed to pool our money ($2,000) to secure substitutes for those drafted." Krehbiel's substitute was a young German from the Black Forest, who soon after being inducted into the army in Krehbiel's place was sent to the front where he participated in battle. After the war was over, the Krehbiel family remained on excellent terms with him, and the whole transaction does not appear to have had any adverse effect on young Krehbiel's standing in the church.[15]

For one group within the Mennonite community, the buying of a substitute was often in fact the only alternative to forcible induction into the army. Since formal acceptance into membership of the church, symbolized in the rite of baptism, came late, as we have seen, a young man might already be drafted while still technically outside the Men-

[14] See letter by "J.M.C." in *Herald of Truth*, vol. II, no. 3 (March 1865). See also vol. II, no. 9 (Sept. 1865) and vol. III, no. 9 (Sept. 1866).

[15] Christian Krehbiel, *Prairie Pioneer*, pp. 43, 44, 146. Earlier in the war some of the young Mennonites in Krehbiel's General Conference branch church, of the same recent south German origin as himself, had joined an unofficial home guard organized to resist any attempt at invasion by the South. Devotion to the Union cause was evidently strong among this section of the Mennonite community. On the other hand, among the "Sonnenbergers" of Wayne Co. (Ohio), who had emigrated from Switzerland in the 1820's and still remained largely ignorant of the English language, we find pacifism strongly entrenched and Lincoln unpopular because of his war leadership. See S. H. Baumgartner, *Brief Sketches of Eight Generations*, pp. 238, 239.

785

nonite church. No certificate of membership in good standing would then be available, and, if the military authorities insisted on the letter of the law (as they were not unlikely to do where war feelings ran high and as the demand for manpower grew more urgent), the plea of conscience could not be maintained. In this situation the only course of escape open to the young unbaptized Mennonite was to hire a substitute. And we find sums as high as $1,000 being paid for this purpose.[16]

We read of four young Mennonites of the Bower congregation in South Indiana, unable or perhaps unwilling to engage a substitute, being drafted into the army in the fall of 1864 on the grounds that they had been baptized only after the draft had been proclaimed. In the army they were assigned hospital duties, "which we believe," wrote the deacon of their home congregation to the *Herald of Truth*, "is not contrary to the dictates of our conscience, and no violation of the Gospel or the principles of our church."[17]

We can easily appreciate the dilemma of these young men, who had been reared in the tradition of Christian nonresistance yet, because of their age, had been deprived of the legal recognition granted to membership in a peace sect. But it is more difficult to reconcile with the peace principles of the church the payment of bounty money, a semi-compulsory levy raised to provide volunteers for the armed forces, by a great many of the adult members—apparently without much protest.[18]

Yet, on the whole, even if the peace witness of the Mennonites in the Northern states was an unspectacular one, it did provide a quiet testimony to the faith of their ancestors. At the outset of hostilities, however, the spiritual life of the church was at a low ebb: it had seemed to some that, among the younger generation at least, there was a danger of widespread abandonment of the traditional Mennonite doctrine of nonresistance. Like the Quakers and the other peace sects, the Mennonites had long been opposed to the institution of slavery; loyalty to the Union, patriotic feeling, too, had grown steadily but was almost unheeded beneath the protective covering of Mennonite apolitical otherworldliness. Above all, there was an almost complete failure either to rethink the traditionally accepted pacifist doctrine or to produce an adequate peace literature, which could help the membership in gaining a more thorough understanding of their church's stand. "Not until the draft question actually faced the Church was there an effort made to teach nonresistance through special literature."[19]

[16] Wenger, *History of the Franconia Conference*, p. 63.
[17] Wenger, *The Mennonites in Indiana and Michigan*, p. 23.
[18] Wenger, *History of the Franconia Conference*, p. 62.
[19] Edward Yoder, "Peace Principles," *loc.cit.*

786

One of those most concerned to reinvigorate the Mennonite peace testimony, indeed to bring new life into all aspects of church life, was John F. Funk, who, significantly enough, was a convert to Mennonitism, having only joined the church in the late fifties. At that time he was engaged in the lumber business, but he was subsequently to become Mennonitism's foremost publisher and editor. Funk was deeply distressed by the fact that during the first two years of war, as he writes, "so many of our Mennonite boys had already and were still enlisting." In order to help the younger men of the church who had to face a personal decision in the matter, Funk began work early in 1863 on a pamphlet expounding the Mennonite doctrine on war and explaining the grounds for taking the conscientious objector stand. "During my writing of this booklet," Funk relates, "I was wearied with work and discouraged with the idea of advocating this unusual doctrine, meeting the opposition that it would bring up besides the work and expense it would cause, and with these discouragements I laid it aside and gave up the idea of publishing it." Soon afterward, however, Funk made the acquaintance of a Mennonite minister from Ohio, John M. Brenneman (1816-1895), a man with scarcely any formal education but of considerable ability who had a lively concern for the renewal of the church. He then discovered that Brenneman, too, was acutely aware of the inadequacy of their church's peace testimony and of the urgent need for new literature on the subject and had been thinking of getting down to work on a peace pamphlet himself. From their meeting and the exchange of views that ensued, both men derived renewed inspiration to complete their task. Funk, the younger man and a bolder spirit than Brenneman, went ahead first. "I got my unfinished booklet," he writes, "and completed the work and at once gave it over to the printer and made [it] into a little booklet. I had 1000 copies printed and distributed them among the churches and ministers. The people in Canada were evidently pleased with the work and had the booklet reprinted in Canada and circulated there."

The reception of Funk's pamphlet, which he entitled *Warfare, Its Evils, Our Duty,* not only among the Mennonite communities of the war-torn states but in the Canadian congregations in a country still at peace, showed clearly that such a work was badly needed. The more timid Brenneman, whom Funk describes as "one of those who was not willing to cause disturbance or trouble anywhere," "fearing the opposition of politicians and war-men," was now encouraged to continue with his project.

When he saw what I had written and circulated [Funk goes on] and [that] I had been left in peace and that [I] met with no trouble or

787

violence in any way he took courage and wrote the little booklet. . . . He sent it to me and I read it over, gave it the proper punctuation and added such other corrections as I considered necessary and proper and then had it printed and sold and circulated a number of thousands of copies and the Mennonite people were awakened again to the fact that there was in the gospel of Jesus Christ and in the Mennonite Church and in the Dunker Church and in the River Brethren Church and in the Quaker Church the maintenance of a doctrine that did not permit the members to engage in warfare.[20]

Funk's little pamphlet of 16 pages appears to have been the first American Mennonite publication devoted solely to the issue of war. It had been composed, as the author states in his preface, with the express purpose of encouraging adherence to the old Mennonite peace principles. That it fulfilled this task adequately seems clear, but in content it is rather thin to the reader of today. In it Funk contrasts the hatred and destruction arising out of war with the loving spirit of Jesus and finds the two totally irreconcilable. He expresses forcibly his sense of desolation at the carnage and devastation in his country, which had been so recently the home of peace and law. The lukewarm he exhorts to remain firm in their unwillingness to shed human blood.

With its 64 pages, Brenneman's tract on *Christianity and War*, which the author cast in the form of a sermon, was a more elaborate production than Funk's. It was written not merely for use within the church but as an exposition of Mennonite pacifism for the general Christian reader. The treatment, as one might expect from Brenneman's lack of formal schooling, is rather chaotic, and the text is burdened with an overabundance of Biblical citations. The traditional Mennonite insistence on discipleship is at the center of Brenneman's argument: the example of Christ and the apostles must be followed even at the cost of life itself, for scripture and the history of the church show "that God's people have always been a suffering people."[21] To follow the word and spirit of the gospels, with their many injunctions to return good for evil, is to enter into a way of life which precludes the bearing of arms in however good a cause. Toward the end of the pamphlet, in "An Address to the Mennonite Brethren," Brenneman expresses his church's loyalty to the government, despite their refusal to fight, and their gratitude to it for allowing them, instead, "to pay an equivalent in money." "In reason we could ask no more."[22]

---

[20] From MS Notebook in John F. Funk Collection, Archives of the Mennonite Church, Goshen (Ind.), pp. 66-71. See also Aaron C. Kolb, "John Fretz Funk," pt. I, *MQR*, VI, no. 3 (July 1932), 150, 151.
[21] Brenneman, *Christianity and War*, p. 9.   [22] *Ibid.*, p. 53.

Funk had published the first edition of Brenneman's tract anonymously—a further example of its author's extreme caution. It was eagerly read by church members, who had little other literature to turn to in order to help them resolve their doubts and queries, the many problems of a peace people in a land at war; it subsequently ran through several editions in both English and German.

Funk was also responsible for producing at the beginning of the following year the first number of a new Mennonite journal under his own editorship, which appeared monthly in English under the title *Herald of Truth* and in a slightly different German edition as the *Herold der Wahrheit*. The new paper soon proved a leading factor in the process of renewal, which was slowly to infuse new life into the Mennonite denomination over the coming decades. During the remaining years of the Civil War, Funk devoted a considerable amount of space in his paper to discussion of nonresistant principles, printing extracts, for instance, from the writings of the English Quaker Jonathan Dymond. In the prospectus for 1865 he wrote: "We shall spare no effort to make the Herald . . . a true exponent of . . . a non-resistant Christianity, such as we believe the gospel teaches."[23] Along with his and Brenneman's pamphlets, Funk's *Herald of Truth* helped the Mennonites to clarify for themselves the grounds of their objection to war.

It was not, however, from either of the two main branches of the Mennonite Church that the most systematic and effective restatement of Mennonite pacifism came. Daniel Musser, whose tract *Non-Resistance Asserted* later earned praise from Leo Tolstoy,[24] was a member of the small Reformed Mennonite Church centered in Lancaster (Pa.). The impulse which led Musser to write in defense of nonresistance, as in the case of Funk and Brenneman, was the impending draft; his aim was to explain these views both to his fellow Mennonites and to the outside world, which might be expected to look with envy and disfavor on the seemingly privileged position of the nonresistant sects. His position was uncompromisingly Biblical—or, rather, evangelical since, as he wrote, "no one will pretend to deny" that under the old dispensation war had sometimes been permissible.[25]

In Musser's view, the truth of the nonresistant position must become

---

[23] *Herald of Truth*, vol. I, no. 12 (Dec. 1864).

[24] Tolstoy devotes several pages of *The Kingdom of God is Within You* (1893) to a discussion of Musser's tract. See *The Kingdom of God and Peace Essays*, pp. 27, 29-32. Tolstoy does not mention that Musser was a Mennonite, but, since he was acquainted with the pacifism of the Mennonites in Russia, he was probably aware of the fact. See Gingerich, "Leo Tolstoy and the Mennonite Author Daniel Musser," *MQR*, XXXII, no. 3 (July 1958), 234-35.

[25] Musser, *Non-Resistance Asserted*, pp. 5, 6, 10-23, 27, 45, 46.

apparent to anyone who begins to examine the gospels with an impartial spirit. The essence of their teaching is the gospel of love. In any war, including the present conflict, there were likely to be well-meaning people on both sides, and it was extremely difficult to discover where right and wrong lay in the dispute which had led to hostilities; no such problems existed in espousing the nonresistant cause, for its validity should be clear to "the poorest, most illiterate, or least-informed disciple of Jesus." "Theirs not to reason why" the conflict had broken out: their only concern should be to watch that they trod in their Master's footsteps. "Their hope and prospects are in the world to come. They are well contented that the dead may bury their dead, if they are only permitted to follow Christ."[26]

Musser's rigid nonconformity to the world comes out most clearly in his discussion of the relationship between nonresistance and civil government. The refusal to participate in war, a total renunciation of the use of violence, is only admissible in one who has also renounced a world in which violence is an essential element. "A pilgrim or stranger" in this world, the Christian nonresistant is in the position of a resident, if friendly, alien in the land of his birth.

No government can exist without the sword, and occasionally having war and the idea of having government without it is an absurdity. Therefore, if we will not use the sword, we must separate ourselves from the kingdom of this world, otherwise we are inconsistent, and liable to censure and suspicion. Foreigners who would claim exemption from military duty, and would yet criticise the acts of those in authority, seek to control elections, shape the laws of the country or influence the policy of the government and nation, would be looked upon with a great deal of suspicion.[27]

Musser, unlike his predecessor, John Herr (see earlier), does not mention the Quakers explicitly in his polemic with those Christian pacifists who saw no inconsistency between voting in elections for candidates supporting the war effort (for very rarely, if ever, did they have the opportunity to support a pacifist candidate) and at the same time taking the stand of a conscientious objector when drafted. But he seems to have had them in mind, along with those of his own Mennonite faith who ignored the numerous official warnings at this time against exercising the franchise.[28] The assumption behind Musser's

---

[26] Ibid., pp. 26, 34, 35, 46.

[27] Ibid., pp. 7-10, 32, 33, 40-42.

[28] For an example of such an injunction, see Minutes of the Indiana-Michigan Mennonite Conference 1864-1929, p. 8, where we read that the Council of the Indiana Conference of the Mennonite Church, meeting at Yellow Creek on 14

reasoning here is that every vote cast was tantamount to a vote for a policy based in the last resort on force; to draw back later from enforcing this policy with the sword was to be guilty of inconsistency. "Whenever a person seeks to influence or control the kingdom of this world," he writes, "or mould it according to his interests or fancy, and then, in the hour of its need, refuses it his support, it is no wonder he should be looked upon with suspicion and disgust." Such persons were only pseudo-nonresistants, who had refused by their conduct to dissociate themselves from "the great Babylonian structure" of the war state. It was not necessarily wrong for the "unconverted," who form the overwhelming majority of mankind (many of them, indeed, "moral, just, humane and honorable" men), to fight, like the Jews of old, in a good cause, since it was not to them that Christ's commandments were given. "They still stand where man did before the Gospel was promulgated, and are under the same influence. This is the reason why Government is still recognized in the New Testament." The regenerate, however, have dwelt henceforth under a new dispensation which precludes all participation in government as well as in war.[29]

Musser's tract is mainly a theoretical exposition of Christian nonresistance. But he does discuss briefly the immediate problems of a pacifist in wartime, especially those connected with the enforcement of the draft. Engaging a substitute, he tells his readers, was in no circumstances permissible (it seems from his account that, on occasion, hiring a substitute might have cost less than the statutory commutation fee of $300); nor was the voluntary payment of bounty money or any voluntary contribution toward equipping soldiers. On the other hand, there was no inconsistency involved in seeking exemption from compulsory military service in exchange for the $300 laid down by law. "The money belongs to the kingdom of this world," explains Musser, "and they had a right to demand it as their own." The Christian objector thus had the obligation to pay Caesar his due. War taxes, too, might freely be paid, even if it were known that they would be used for military purposes, since once again the money really belonged to the state, which might demand its return at any time, taking the responsibility on itself for the use it made of the contribution.[30]

October 1864, resolved: "Since we are a nonresistant people . . . therefore we acknowledge that it is inconsistent for us to vote for worldly officers, inasmuch as by so doing we would make ourselves liable also even by force to defend and sustain those whom we elect." From the rest of the minute it appears that such participation was not infrequent among church members. Disfellowshipping does not appear, however, to have been laid down as a penalty for disregarding this prohibition.

[29] Musser, *Non-Resistance Asserted*, pp. 9, 10, 27, 42, 74.
[30] *Ibid.*, pp. 31, 42-45.

The tract as a whole betrays a rather narrow and sectarian mind. No concessions are made to any pacifist position which falls short of complete nonconformity to the world. The treatment of the New Testament basis of Christian nonresistance is oversimplified: the author, like almost all the church leaders of the German-speaking peace sects of that day, was a simple man without any special training in theology or church history. But at least in the final and more important of its two parts, the style is clear, the argument sensible, and the text fairly free from the avalanche of Biblical quotations that tended to overwhelm so many of the religious compositions of that day. The treatment is more detailed than in the contemporary works on the same subject by Funk and Brenneman; furthermore, Musser's tract could have been usefully studied by non-Mennonites interested in gaining insight into that church's position on peace and war, although there is no evidence to show how wide the audience it actually succeeded in reaching was. It is perhaps the best statement of Mennonite pacifism produced by a member of any of the church's branches in the New World in the period before 1914.

The pattern of wartime action among the main branches of the Mennonites was mirrored to a large degree in the conduct and thought of the church's most conservative wing, the Amish. The second half of the nineteenth century was "a period of great transition among the Amish. It was a period of inner struggle, adjustments, and of new birth."[31] The impact of modern ways of transportation, of new methods of agriculture, and of other forms of modern conveniences was making itself felt among the Amish as among all the rural sects of America. By the outbreak of the Civil War, the Amish had spread from Pennsylvania into Ohio, Indiana, Illinois, and even as far as Iowa. The continuing rural isolation, combined with different conditions of settlement in the various areas, had resulted in divergencies in customs, religious practice, and general outlook between the various settlements. The complete autonomy enjoyed by the Amish congregations tended to emphasize this trend even more strongly than among the rest of the Mennonites or among the Dunkers. And, in addition, the immigration of Amish from South Germany and Switzerland earlier in the century had introduced a new element, which before emigration had virtually lost touch with the American branch.[32] After

[31] John A. Hostetler, "Amish Problems at the *Diener-Versammlungen*," *Mennonite Life*, IV, no. 4 (Oct. 1949), 34. I am indebted to this article for information used in this paragraph.

[32] Even in the Civil War there were instances of Amishmen of draft age being crossed off the roll of those eligible for service on the grounds that they were not United States citizens. See Gingerich, *The Mennonites in Iowa*, p. 64.

the Civil War a growing split between the conservative and the more progressive Amish, who eventually fused with the Mennonite church, revealed itself.

Like the Mennonites proper, the Amish communities at the outbreak of war were in a state of spiritual decline. Among the latter there had been even less cultivation of the peace testimony. We know that many of their young men, especially in Pennsylvania, which had been the original home of the American Amish, entered the army either as volunteers or later as conscripts. This act, of course, was contrary to the sect's discipline, but in most cases the men were apparently not disfellowshipped. A study of the Civil War experiences of the peace sects of southern Somerset County (Pa.) has shown that, although several of the Amish bishops refused to accept former soldiers at the communion if they had not first expressed penitence for their conduct, the Amishman veteran might easily transfer his membership to another congregation where he would encounter no such difficulties. In some communities, indeed, it seems that the overwhelming majority of those liable to the draft did in fact serve in the army, so that a serious drop in membership might have resulted if the discipline had been rigidly enforced.[33] Perhaps some of the men served in a noncombatant capacity (though there does not appear to be clear evidence that any did); even so, service of this kind was also contrary to the teaching of the church. At a conference (*Diener-Versammlung*) in May 1863 of representatives from a wide number of congregations from Pennsylvania to Iowa, it was laid down "that no member should be permitted to go into military service as a teamster."[34] This resolution probably referred to occasional service with horse and wagon which might be required of farmers when one of the armies was quartered in their vicinity. How much more reprehensible in the official view would be the more intimate connection with the military which any form of more permanent noncombatant service in the army entailed!

The accepted course for the Amishman who had been drafted, as for his Mennonite cousin, was to pay the exemption fee. Although, at

[33] R. B. Yoder, "Nonresistance." See also Gingerich, *Mennonites in Iowa*, p. 130.
[34] *Verhandlungen der zweiten jährlichen Diener-Versammlungen der Deutschen Täufer oder Amischen Mennoniten*, p. 16. These conferences were held between 1862 and 1874 in barns, with a number of ministers from widely scattered congregations as well as some local laity attending. The conference minutes show that the meetings discussed the most pressing problems which had arisen within the church; their resolutions, however, though they obviously bore great weight with members, had no binding force on the congregations. The conferences were discontinued after 1874, owing to growing divergencies between the more conservative and more progressive elements, which eventually ended in schism. See Hostetler, *Mennonite Life*, IV, no. 4 (Oct. 1949), 34-38.

first, payment was regarded as the responsibility of the individual family, soon, as conscription widened its net, the local congregation (at least in Pennsylvania) became aware that it had a collective obligation for those who were called to witness for the common faith, especially in cases where the sum required would have overtaxed the resources of a single family.[35] There is evidence that in some cases Amishmen resorted to engaging a substitute when drafted. In Davis County (Iowa), for instance, we read of Christian Baughman having to sell his farm of eighty acres in order to raise enough cash for this purpose, so high was the price of a substitute in this area.[36] But this practice, as with the Mennonites, was frowned on by the church. It was denounced in no uncertain terms, for example, by Bishop Jacob Schwarzendruber (1800-1868) of Johnson County (Iowa), "an outstanding Amish leader in his day, better informed and more widely read than most Amish bishops" and a stern upholder of his church's discipline, who had emigrated from Germany as a young man of 26. In his conference epistle of 1865, parts of which had been composed during the previous couple of years, he told his fellow Amish:

> Concerning the draft, or buying volunteer substitutes or paying volunteers to send them out to fight, I hold that it is wrong according to God's Word and the teaching of Jesus and the apostles, as it has been in our congregations. And I hold that it is a guilt upon us ministers and the church. . . . The Saviour's teaching is not as we have done, that we should be permitted to buy substitutes or help to pay for people and let them go to kill others. . . . Do I then pay someone to do injustice?

It was fear of material loss, according to the bishop, that had prompted many Amishmen of his own and other congregations to resort to this practice despite the legal exemption granted conscientious objectors by the government. "If it is true as I have heard tell about the Dunkards [and Quakers] in regard to nonresistance, we are behind them and could well take them for a pattern."[37]

Disapproval of two further practices stemming from the sect's pacifism is to be found in the (extremely scanty) records. One of the members of the 1863 conference raised the question: "Should the congregation allow a brother to make a list (*einzuschreiben*) of names of the militiamen [i.e., of those members liable to militia service]?" The

---

[35] J. B. Miller, "Some Reminiscences of the Civil War," *Family Almanac for . . . 1918*, p. 12.

[36] Gingerich, *Mennonites in Iowa*, p. 64.

[37] "An Amish Bishop's Conference Epistle of 1865," *MQR*, XX, no. 3 (July 1946), 222-25. See also Gingerich, *Mennonites in Iowa*, p. 127.

resolution against permitting any brother to make such a list was passed unanimously.[38] On the question whether it was permissible for a nonresistant people to exercise the franchise, which came up for discussion in 1864, members of the conference took a less decided stand. Most favored total abstinence from voting, but opinion was divided as to the advisability of doing more than issuing a warning against the practice. One delegate, J. R. Yoder, considered that enacting a total prohibition would lead to a schism—an indication, incidentally, that voting was by no means infrequent among the Amish of this period. In the end, no action seems to have been taken.[39]

Bishop Schwarzendruber was certainly a severe critic of his fellow Amish. Looking back over the four years of war, he castigated them for wanting "to stay at home and have a vain and easy life," to "live well" while thousands of their fellow countrymen were suffering and dying on the battlefields. "Do we think that God will let this go unpunished?" he asked.[40] But perhaps the sins which had incurred the bishop's wrath were not a great deal more serious than the sumptuous wedding feasts of the period or the old custom of "bundling" among courting couples. For the most part, the Amish continued to lead frugal, hardworking lives on the family farm, carefully guarding, along with their German language and oldtime customs, a strict, if narrow, morality. Their shortcoming as pacifists in wartime lay not so much in any relaxation of their traditional moral code as in their inability to instill fresh life into the nonresistant faith of their forefathers and to incorporate this faith into the fabric of their daily thinking and being. The lack of peace education, rather than any supposed moral shortcomings, accounts for the failure of so many young Amishmen to uphold their church's position on war.

Not so closely related as the Amish to the main trunk of the Mennonite family, yet affiliated to it both genetically and on many points of church doctrine and practice, were two other small sects whose members took the conscientious objector stand in the Civil War. The older denomination was that of the River Brethren, who had come into existence in Pennsylvania toward the end of the eighteenth century. In the nineteenth century doctrinal wrangling resulting, it would seem, from attempts to give the church a slightly more tightly knit organization and from some relaxation in strict practice, which the passing of the years had brought about, had led to the formation of two small offshoots. Thus, in 1843 some members of the sect centered in York County (Pa.) had broken away to found the Old Order or

[38] *Verhandlungen*, 1863, p. 16.   [39] *Verhandlungen*, 1864, p. 11.
[40] "An Amish Bishop's Epistle," p. 229.

795

"Yorker" Brethren, and a decade later a second schism, led by Matthias Brinser, gave birth to the United Zion's Children. Both these groups remained very small and in regard to nonresistance maintained, if anything, an even stricter adherence than the main body of River Brethren did.

The extreme congregationalism of the River Brethren posed a serious problem for the sect after the outbreak of war, for it led the federal authorities to express doubt whether the Brethren in fact formed a religious denomination and whether, therefore, they were legally entitled to the exemption granted by law to members of nonresistant churches. In order to remove this difficulty, leaders of the Brethren came together in council at Lancaster (Pa.) in 1862. After drawing up a statement of their belief in nonresistance for presentation in Washington, the delegates took steps to form a legally recognized church under the name of "Brethren in Christ."[41]

Since almost no records have been preserved for the history of the Brethren in Christ until after the Civil War, we know next to nothing about their experiences as conscientious objectors during the war years. One incident has been handed down, however, concerning Isaac Trump, well known later as an evangelist and bishop, who was drafted as a young man for service in the Union army.[42] Accompanied by another conscientious objector, "a Baptist student-preacher," he reported to the army authorities and asked for exemption on grounds of conscience. Trump was only asked one question by the board: "Have you ever exercised your franchise?" His negative reply resulted in his receiving exemption without further ado, while on the other hand the Baptist was turned down for his admission that he had always voted. "What would you do if everybody was like Trump?" the latter asked indignantly; to which the chairman of the board was alleged to have replied: "I would to God that we had a hundred thousand men in our fair Union such as Trump and this trouble might have been averted. Then we wouldn't need an army."[43]

[41] A. W. Climenhaga, *History of the Brethren in Christ Church*, p. 303; *Census of Religious Bodies 1936: River Brethren*, pp. 7, 10, 12. A similar case, where fear that the federal authorities would refuse to recognize their legal right to military exemption led early in the war to formal organization into a church, is to be found among the Amish of Davis Co. (Iowa). Here, however, failure to organize earlier had been due less to dislike of all organization than to the complete lack in this pioneer community of anyone qualified to act as minister. See Gingerich, *Mennonites in Iowa*, p. 59.

[42] E. J. Swalm, *Nonresistance under Test*, p. 22. Swalm's intention in relating the story is clearly to bring home his church's traditional objection to voting as connivance with the military machine. It would have been interesting to know more about the Baptist C.O.

[43] We read of a member of the "Yorker Brethren," Noah Nissly of Mount Joy

Although the connection of the Apostolic Christian Church with the Mennonites was more tenuous than that of the River Brethren, it likewise held many similar doctrines, including adult baptism, nonresistance, objection to swearing oaths, and a general nonconformity to the world. The church had originated as a movement of church renewal in Switzerland in the 1830's and 1840's; its founder was a former minister of the state Protestant Reformed Church, Samuel Heinrich Froehlich (1803-1857), and some, though by no means all, of his earliest adherents came from the Swiss Mennonites. The sect spread from Switzerland into Central and Eastern Europe; it was brought over to America by immigrants who sought to escape from the persecution frequently meted out to Froehlich's followers in Europe. The newcomers, who already numbered several hundred by the outbreak of the Civil War, settled mainly in the Midwest.[44] Federal conscription does not seem to have affected them; perhaps, as recent immigrants, they had not yet acquired citizenship and did not, therefore, come within the compass of the draft.

Along with the Mennonites, the Brethren or Dunkers formed the other major peace sect of German origin, and the wartime outlook and experiences of the two denominations offer many parallels. Whereas there was close collaboration between the two in the South, as we shall see, especially in defense of the rights of their conscientious objectors, in the states of the Union, where their main strength lay, each acted for the most part independently. Here they were not tiny and isolated groups, whose pacifist views usually found scant understanding or sympathy from the authorities and whose opposition to slavery and secession made them suspect of treason; on the contrary, in many areas they formed substantial and respected communities, whose peculiar beliefs, along with their distinctive garb and German language, had become almost as familiar as the landscape to their neighbors and fellow citizens. Here in the North, too, the federal authorities showed much greater familiarity and friendliness toward the wartime attitudes of the peace sects, whose general loyalty and devotion to the Union was realized. The pressure to come together in the face of threatened persecution was not present to nearly the same extent and could not overcome the centrifugal tendency of long-standing, if seemingly minor, doctrinal differences.

Township in Lancaster Co. (Pa.), serving with the Union army as a "bridge builder." See F. K. Ivie, "The Quest for Peace," *Annals of Iowa*, 3rd ser., XX, no. 4 (April 1936), 246. From this account it is not clear what the precise character of Nissly's noncombatant service or his exact status as a church member was.

[44] See *Census of Religious Bodies 1936: Evangelistic Associations*, pp. 6, 9.

The vitality of church life among the Brethren, as among the Mennonites and Quakers, had declined in the course of the first half of the nineteenth century. The first signs of revival showed themselves around mid-century, a little earlier than with the Mennonites. The man who was chiefly responsible for infusing new life into what had become a half-fossilized piety was Henry Kurtz (see chapter 9), who, like John F. Funk, was not a birthright member of the church community but a convert in early adult life from the Lutheran church, of which he had been an ordained minister. In April 1851 he brought out at Columbiana (Ohio) the first number of the *Gospel-Visitor*, with himself and another Brethren, James Quinter, as co-editors. The *Visitor* soon became an effective rallying point for what we may call the conservative reformers, who wished to see changes gradually introduced into the thought and practice of the by now rather moribund church.

Adherence to nonresistance had been a requisite for membership in the church. But in the decade before the outbreak of war the *Visitor* paid little attention to the subject. Extracts from the English Quaker Dymond were printed, as well as some articles of a general character outlining the New Testament basis for pacifism. Evidently, however, Kurtz and his associates did not feel any great urge to attempt to revitalize the church's peace testimony, and outside their paper there was scarcely anything recent on it for Brethren to read. Curiously enough, the annual conference minutes for 1861 and 1862 do not mention nonresistance, but this was probably because the problem of the draft had not yet become a pressing one. Officially the church never wavered in its nonresistant position, while at the same time it attempted to make clear that its pacifism flowed from a purely religious source and that it was in no way opposed to the policies of the lawful government, even if Brethren themselves might not participate in worldly affairs. "Lest the position we have taken upon . . . war," says an annual conference minute of 1864, "should seem to make us, as a body, appear to be indifferent to our government, or in opposition thereto, in its efforts to suppress the rebellion, we hereby declare that it has our sympathies and our prayers, and that it shall have our aid in any way which does not conflict with the principles of the gospel of Christ."[45]

[45] *MAM*, p. 232 (quoted in Rufus D. Bowman, *The Church of the Brethren and War*, p. 119). The assurance of the church's sympathies and prayers for the Union government in its armed struggle with the South seems, as Bowman points out (pp. 120, 121), scarcely consistent with a strict pacifism; it does, however, reveal how strongly the peace sects were emotionally behind the Northern cause. Witness the remark of one of the church's most outstanding leaders, elder D. P. Sayler of Frederick Co. (Md.), at the annual conference of 1865: "I have often

The problems, occasional hesitancies, and basic steadfastness of the Brethren in their pacifist faith, in what had from the beginning been "a prominent doctrine of our fraternity,"[46] are mirrored in the minutes of annual meeting, a source for opinion within the church which is unfortunately absent in the case of the Mennonites. There is no clear evidence concerning the number of Brethren who became soldiers. A minute of the annual meeting of 1863, held at a time when federal conscription was impending, indeed, betrays some confusion as to what attitude the church should adopt toward those members who had rejected its peace position. To the question "How are we to deal with our brethren who have enlisted and gone to the army as soldiers or teamsters, or those who have been drafted, and are gone to the army?" the rather ambiguous reply was given: "We think it not expedient to consider (or discuss) these questions at this time. Still it is believed, and was expressed, the gospel gave sufficient instruction."[47] This response would appear to conceal some difference of opinion among the delegates on the proper policy to pursue in such cases. Yet, in fact, the practice of the church favored a fairly rigorous disownment of those who joined the army in any capacity, either voluntarily or as a result of the draft. This was the policy upheld by church leaders like Henry Kurtz[48] and carried out by most, though not all, of the local congregations throughout the war period. At Lewistown (Pa.), for instance, the council records of this country church for the summer and autumn of 1862 state that "some young brethren . . . had gone to war" and that it had been "agreed that they should be considered out of the church according to the Gospel." Acceptance at communion could only be allowed after "an open confession of their fault before the church."[49] That such strictness was not confined to country congregations or to participation only in combatant service is shown in the case of Dr. Henry Geiger, a prominent member and minister of the First Church of Philadelphia, who resigned his membership prior to enlisting in the army medical service. "Being about to engage in the service of our country," he wrote to the elders, "and thus violate the rules of our church, I respectfully beg leave to offer my

---

prayed God that what he cannot do otherwise, he will do at the mouth of the cannon."

[46] *MAM*, pp. 231, 232 (quoted in Bowman, pp. 118, 119).

[47] *MAM*, p. 218.

[48] See the petition for military exemption drawn up in February 1863 by Kurtz and other elders for presentation to the General Assembly of Ohio, *Gospel-Visitor*, XIII, no. 9 (Sept. 1863), 277.

[49] *A History of the Church of the Brethren in the Middle District of Pennsylvania*, p. 32.

resignation as a member." After discussion by the congregation, his resignation was accepted.[50]

As with the Mennonites, young men born and reared in the Dunker community but not yet received into membership by the rite of baptism presented a special problem. This was the group that would be most susceptible to the call of military service. And it was probably. this group, rather than any converts made in the ranks of the armed forces, that the annual meeting of 1864 had in mind when it gave the following answer to the query whether serving soldiers might receive baptism before obtaining their discharge from the army: "We cannot encourage such proceedings: but in case of extreme sickness, and when there is a promise to shed no more blood, we will let the churches applied to, decide what shall be done; but let the principles of the church be acceded to by all candidates."[51] Thus it was left open to the local churches to temper the full severity of the discipline where a Dunker boy in service was in danger of dying outside the church.

Even in this case, however, the soldier was to promise to withdraw from military service and return to the paths of peace. In the final year of war the annual conference again reiterated its position. The question was raised: "Can a brother be held as a member of the church who will, when put into the army, take up arms and aim to shed the blood of his fellowmen?" "He cannot," was the conference's succinct answer. Earlier in the proceedings it had been stressed that bearing arms "in order to sustain the civil government," which the church believed to be of divine origin even though it relied on the sword for enforcing the law, was still an infringement of church discipline, which required exclusion of the guilty member.[52] The War of the Rebellion was still a war.[53] That the question of the fighting Dunker could be raised this late in the war does seem to indicate, however, that among some Brethren there was still uncertainty, still reluctance, to exclude from communion with the congregation those who had sincerely interpreted their duty to God and country in a fashion different from the traditional standpoint of their church.

Something of the difficulties which the young men of the Brethren communities faced can be learned from the experience of D. L. Miller

[50] Bowman, pp. 116, 117.
[51] *MAM*, p. 230 (quoted in Bowman, p. 117).
[52] *MAM*, pp. 235, 237 (quoted in part in Bowman, p. 117).
[53] The conference of 1865 threatened all church members, whether ministers or laymen, with exclusion from the church (unless they expressed repentance) if they had given support, either in word or deed, to the Confederate cause—"the rebels in this bloody rebellion." See *MAM*, pp. 238, 239, 242. It does not appear, at least in regard to ministers, that any were in fact disfellowshipped for pro-Confederate activities.

(1841-1921), who later became a prominent minister and leader of the church. A young man of 20 when war broke out, he was then working on his uncle's farm out in Illinois, where many of his family had emigrated from Maryland. Like most Dunker bachelors of his age, he had not yet received baptism. His natural impulse at this time was to enlist with the Union forces, despite the pleas of his relatives. Still uncertain as to the right course to follow, young Miller had occasion both to visit one of the battlefields soon after the carnage and to view the aftermath of fighting in the military hospitals. These experiences proved decisive in convincing him of the unchristian nature of war, and he determined to stand by the church's peace testimony.[54]

Another case, concerning "Uncle" John Trackler, a highly respected old Dunker, is mentioned by Mallott, who had known him in his childhood.[55] Trackler had been reared in a Brethren family but, unlike Miller, was one of those who finally decided to break with tradition and join the army, where he served for three years. The teachings of his childhood, however, were too strongly ingrained in him to be entirely eradicated by military training and the experience of battle. "Later in his old age he found consolation in the fact that he had always aimed his musket low and thus had never killed anyone in his soldier days."

The church had, indeed, condemned not merely combatant service, the bearing of arms, but all service which entailed the wearing of military uniform. "It is considered not advisable," ran an annual conference minute of 1864, "for any brother, whether a minister or a private member, to wear any military clothing, and if he is admonished, and still persists in being disobedient, he should be dealt with according to Matthew 18."[56] The acceptable alternative to military service for the Brethren, as for the Mennonites, was to pay the commutation fee set out in the various draft laws. Thus, Brethren were not usually required to suffer hardship for their stand. "The Brethren located in the North," writes Bowman, "paid the $300 and remained on their farms."[57]

In the various statements prepared by one or another group of church leaders in support of their right to conscientious objection, their readiness to pay a monetary equivalent is always stressed. For instance, in the petition of the Upper Conewago Church (Adams County, Pa.) to the state governor, dated 29 August 1862, the "elders

---

[54] Bess Royer Bates, *Life of D. L. Miller*, p. 26.
[55] Floyd E. Mallott, *Studies in Brethren History*, p. 271.
[56] *MAM*, p. 227 (quoted in Bowman, p. 117).
[57] Bowman, p. 127. On pp. 127-129, he prints examples of certificates given by Dunker elders in support of members applying for military exemption.

and teachers" declare that, although in obedience to the teachings of the gospels they "do not find freedom of conscience to take up arms," they are prepared, "according to Christ's command to Peter, to pay tribute and to render unto Caesar those things that are Caesar's, and to God those things that are God's, although we think ourselves very weak to give God his due honour, he being a spirit and life and we only dust and ashes."[58] Henry Kurtz and his fellow church elders in Ohio, petitioning the general assembly in February 1863 for the privilege of conscientious objection for their Brethren, explicitly mention that they thought it only fair for them—"in order to perfectly equalize us with our fellow-citizens"—to pay "an extra-tax" such as was required in Canada and in some countries in Europe also.[59] In line with their thinking in the antebellum era, the Brethren of the war period regarded commutation fees as in the same category as taxes. As one writer expressed it: "All the estate or property we own we hold only by the tolerance and authority of the powers that be [who] . . . have [a] right to demand so much of it as they have need of . . . I have no right to withhold the payment of that money any more than I have a sum of money that I have borrowed."[60] One might disapprove of the use the state made of its property, as when it assigned commutation fees to military purposes, but the responsibility for this allocation lay with the government.

The hiring of substitutes, however, was another matter. The practice was officially condemned by the church, as it had been by the Mennonites, although undoubtedly some Brethren likewise resorted to this method of escaping the draft and the terms in which the church's disapproval was expressed were not as forthright as might be expected. The query was raised at the annual conference of 1865: "How is it considered if a brother who is drafted hires a substitute to perform military service, and afterward removes to another district— shall the church grant him a certificate of membership?" The comparatively mild answer probably mirrored existing sentiment in the church: "Since the law has exempted brethren from military duty, by paying a tax in lieu of service, we consider that Brethren do wrong to resort to other means, unless they are ignorant of the provision of the law."[61]

[58] From photostat of MS in the Pennsylvania State Library and Museum, Harrisburg, deposited in the S.C.P.C. (U.S. Peace Materials, Misc.). The petition refers to the exemption already granted by the state constitution of 1838 to C.O.'s on payment of a monetary equivalent for service.

[59] Gospel-Visitor, XIII, no. 9 (Sept. 1863), 278.

[60] Ibid., XV, no. 5 (May 1865), 142. From an article entitled "Non-Resistance Defended" by "H.D."

[61] MAM, p. 237 (quoted in Bowman, p. 118).

Feeling would certainly have been against penalizing those as yet unbaptized members of the community, for whom hiring a substitute might have provided the only alternative to being taken into the army. But the practice of pooling resources in order to distribute the burden of the commutation fees among all full members of the church (often including those who were not themselves liable to military service) made it possible for all such draftees to avail themselves of the legal exemption. In the autumn of 1862, for instance, many Brethren churches in the West had adopted a system whereby every man liable for the draft paid $25 into a special "commutation fund." If he was in fact to be called up, he was to pay an additional $75. The remainder due would be apportioned "among all the tax-paying members according to last year's tax receipt."[62] After federal conscription was enacted in March 1863, the annual conference of that year, following (as we see) the initiative of some of the local churches, urged Brethren to contribute toward paying the fines of those drafted "according to the true avails of their property."[63] In April of that year we find the Lewistown (Pa.) Church, to give one example, resolving that a draftee "should pay $75.00 and have his assets taxed with the rest of the members to make up the balance."[64] Evidently, all were considered capable of finding at least $75 in an emergency.

On 22 July of the same year, with the new federal conscription likely to affect one or more members of most Dunker homes, Henry Kurtz sat down to compose a letter in which he tried to work out how the resolution of the recent annual conference could best be implemented among the congregations. Take as an example, he wrote, the case of a church of 150 adult members, of whom 20 were liable for the draft. The latter, or their families, would have to provide between them a sum of $6,000, an amount that would in fact be likely to prove a crippling burden on most of those concerned. But let it be distributed among all 150, with the young men drafted paying "a reasonable share" according to their resources, and it would come to an average of merely $50 per person. He emphasized in his letter the moral obligation that the church had as a collective body in the matter.[65]

A few days earlier Kurtz in a letter to Ephraim Bee, a delegate to the West Virginia legislature who was favorably disposed toward religious

---

[62] Gospel-Visitor, XIII, no. 9 (Sept. 1863), 281.

[63] MAM, p. 221.

[64] History of Brethren in Middle District of Pennsylvania, p. 32.

[65] Gospel-Visitor, XIII, no. 9 (Sept. 1863), 280. See ibid., XV, no. 3, 91 (March 1865), for a variant scheme adopted by the Pipe Creek Church (near Windsor, Md.), whereby those liable for the draft were to pay at least $50 into the commutation fund, if able to do so, and those Brethren who were not liable were to cover the money due from those who could not afford to pay.

objectors, discussed the possibility that in the new state of West Virginia, and elsewhere in new areas, the example of old Virginia on the Confederate side would be imitated and as much as $500 required as commutation fee. To provide this sum would not, Kurtz stated, impose an impossible burden on old established communities, where there were enough well-to-do to help share the cost. But it was a quite different story on the frontier, "where people have had scarcely time to open a farm in the wilderness, and make an honest living. If these cannot be exempted on such terms that they possibly can fulfil, we see no other way but they must emigrate to some other country, where they will be permitted to enjoy liberty of conscience to the full extent of the word."[66] Kurtz's fears were not realized; his remarks, however, do shed light on the growing differences in wealth within the church of the Brethren.

A money payment in lieu of military service was, then, an acceptable compromise between the demands of the government and the scruples of the Brethren. It was on a level with paying taxes and came within the legitimate exercise of authority to which a God-fearing Christian should willingly submit. To make a voluntary contribution for the prosecution of the war, on the other hand, was classed along with the hiring of a substitute as an illegitimate connivance with the warmaking power, even where the pressure of public opinion made refusal difficult—as was usually the case, for instance, with the bounty fund, the purpose of which was to raise money to cover the cost of additional troops. That many Brethren paid into this fund when asked to do so is clear from the very mild form in which the prohibition was couched in official resolutions. The annual conference of 1865 provides an example. "We think it more in accordance with our principles," the delegates concluded, "that instead of paying bounty-money, to await the demands of the government, whether general, state, or local, and pay the taxes and fines required of us, as the gospel permits, and, indeed, requires. Matt. 22:21; Rom. 13:7."[67]

Exercise of the franchise was considered by leading Brethren to be almost more of a dereliction of the duty of a nonresistant than hiring a substitute or paying bounty money. In the eighteenth century in Quaker Pennsylvania the Brethren, as we know, had voted regularly under the leadership of the Saurs. But after government had passed out of the hands of the pacifist Quakers, the Brethren, along with the Mennonites and many in the Society of Friends itself, had come to regard

[66] Ibid., XIII, no. 9 (Sept. 1863), 279.

[67] MAM, pp. 231, 232 (quoted in Bowman, p. 119). Cf. the minutes of meetings of the newly formed Middle District of Pennsylvania for 28-29 March and Oct. 17 1864, History of Brethren in Middle District of Penna., pp. 289, 290. See also Gospel-Visitor, XV, no. 5 (May 1865), 142.

voting as part and parcel of the military establishment. It was wrong to help to put a man into an office, the duties of which we consider it wrong to perform ourselves. This feeling became embedded in Dunker tradition over the next century and was naturally intensified after the outbreak of war in 1861. Although even then opinion was by no means unanimous, Henry Kurtz's *Gospel-Visitor* was certainly expressing the dominant view when it stated: "The war principle is inherent in all political governments." The legislatures supported war, while the President and the state governors were at the same time commanders-in-chief of the armed forces: a vote for any of them was tantamount to a vote for war.[68] In the course of the Civil War both the *Gospel-Visitor* and the *Christian Family Companion*, which H. R. Holsinger (1833-1905) started to publish at the beginning of 1865, printed not a few articles expounding the church's opposition to voting, and the annual conferences of 1863 and 1864 strongly advised members to abstain altogether from politics or electioneering. Participation in the political life of a state at war, even in the passive function of casting a vote, it was felt, might compromise their nonresistant stand.[69] The conference resolutions did not amount to a formal ban, but voices were heard advocating the disownment of Brethren who ignored the feeling of the church and continued to vote.[70] The Lewistown (Pa.) congregation, for instance, put pressure on its younger men in this direction by resolving at the beginning of 1864 that the church was not obliged to cover the commutation fines of "members . . . voting or electioneering and afterwards drafted."[71] There is not enough evidence to judge with any certainty how widespread this kind of disciplinary action was, but one may safely say that there could have been very few voters among conscientious objectors who came from the ranks of the Dunkers.

II

Wartime attitudes among the small communities of Mennonites and Dunkers in the South were basically the same as among the much larger groups in the North. In their pattern of experience, however, there were obvious differences, owing largely to the fact that the Southern congregations were radically out of harmony with the political philosophy of the government and people of the Confederate states. Antislavery and antisecessionist, the German peace sectaries could not expect the same understanding that they were to meet with in the

---

[68] *Gospel-Visitor*, XIII, no. 12 (Dec. 1863), 377, 378.
[69] Bowman, p. 122.
[70] E.g., *Christian Family Companion*, I, no. 12 (21 March 1865), 90, 91.
[71] *History of Brethren in Middle District of Penna.*, p. 32. See also p. 289.

North. As the breach between the two sides widened, John Kline, the leading minister among the Virginia Dunkers, with a premonition of what was in store for his people, confided to his diary on 1 January 1861: "A move is clearly on hand for holding a convention at Richmond, Virginia; and while its advocates publicly deny the charge, I, for one, feel sure that it signals the separation of our beloved old State from the family in which she has long lived and been happy." "Secession," he went on, "means war and war means tears and ashes and blood. It means bonds and imprisonments, and perhaps even death to many in our beloved Brotherhood, who, I have the confidence to believe, will die, rather than disobey God by taking up arms."[72]

The struggle that divided the nation, however, led Southern Mennonites and Brethren, whom a pacifist stand and the same general outlook on affairs brought under a similar suspicion of disloyalty to the new state, to cooperate closely in making their views known to the government. This degree of unity the two churches had only rarely achieved earlier in their history, nor were they even in the present crisis able to reach it in the North.

The Virginia Conference of Mennonites located in the valley of the Shenandoah numbered at the outbreak of the Civil War probably no more than about 350 baptized members. In the early months of the war, before the introduction of Confederate conscription, their young men were placed in a most precarious situation. In the spring and summer of 1861 the state militia was called out for active service with the Southern army, and the way of escape which had existed in peacetime in the payment of a small sum (50¢) for nonappearance at muster no longer existed. There was confusion among the congregations as to the attitude to be adopted by those who were drafted. In the absence of any legal provision for exemption from military service in wartime, the alternative which faced these country boys, unprepared by proper education in the nonresistant principles of their faith, might be court-martial and execution. In these circumstances, and with little guidance at this time from their church elders, most of the young men who were now drafted (apart, that is, from a handful with sympathies for the Confederate cause, whose voluntarily accepted military service would inevitably lead to their disownment unless they were prepared to make confession of error) appear to have gone into the army with the silent resolution to maintain their church's peace testimony, even in the ranks, by never in fact using their weapons to kill. "At least one of this group informed the officer of his pledge,"

[72] *Life and Labors of Elder John Kline*, p. 438 (quoted in Bowman, pp. 114, 115).

writes a historian of the Virginia Mennonites.[73] "When Jacob Wenger," it is related, "entered the Confederate Army and shouldered the musket, he remarked that by compulsion he would be obedient so far but assured the officer that he would harm no one." Some of the men actually participated in encounters fought at Winchester and Harpers Ferry. Refusal to shoot when ordered to fire brought threats of court-martial, but, perhaps because of the strong solidarity existing among these Mennonite conscripts (they were often able to gather together when off duty to sing their familiar hymns) and probably some understanding of their religious scruples on the part of local officers, none appear to have been punished. Soon it became the practice to detail them for work in a noncombatant capacity—as cooks or teamsters or medical orderlies. When the Confederate army entered into winter quarters at Winchester in the fall, where it remained until the following spring, the Mennonite soldiers were mostly furloughed, or else they just left for home on their own; they would, indeed, have been more useful to the country in helping to bring in the harvest at home than in being confined unwillingly in camp. A few returned when their leave expired, others just remained on the farm, and still more probably joined those who had already gone into hiding in the nearby forest and mountains when the draft began.[74] The army authorities, after having had to deal for several months with the problem of conscience in the ranks, were probably not altogether sorry to see the men go. And General T. J. ("Stonewall") Jackson is reported to have said about them:

There lives a people in the Valley of Virginia, that are not hard to bring to the army. While there they are obedient to their officers. Nor is it difficult to have them take aim, but it is impossible to get them to take correct aim. I, therefore, think it better to leave them at their homes that they may produce supplies for the army.[75]

Jackson's remarks about these peace-loving "people" almost certainly

[73] Harry A. Brunk, *History of the Mennonites in Virginia*, I, 158. The most recent study of the Civil War pacifism of the Southern Mennonites is Samuel Horst's *Mennonites in the Confederacy* (1967). See chap. III, "Reluctant Cooperation," for the earliest period in their Civil War witness.

[74] J. S. Hartzler and Daniel Kauffman, *Mennonite Church History*, pp. 207, 208.

[75] Quoted in E. N. Wright, *Conscientious Objectors in the Civil War*, p. 167. Another example of General "Stonewall" Jackson's sympathetic attitude toward the pacifism of the Virginia Mennonites and Brethren is cited in Elmer Lewis Smith, John G. Stewart, M. Ellsworth Kyger, *The Pennsylvania Germans of the Shenandoah Valley*, p. 78. "I am authorized to say to the Tunkers and Mennonites, that Gen. Jackson believes them to be sincere in their opposition to engaging in war, and will detail them as teamsters, etc. They can serve their State as well in such a capacity as if bearing arms," states one of Jackson's officers in an order, dated 31 March 1862, mobilizing the militia in Rockingham Co.

apply to the Brethren of the Valley as well as to the Mennonites, for, although there were small groups of the former in Tennessee and the Carolinas, their main strength in the South lay in Virginia, where their reaction to the state draft during this period followed that of the Mennonites. The sources for the Brethren are even more exiguous than they are for the Mennonites.

The little volume entitled *The Olive Branch*, whose compilers collected information around the turn of the century from surviving Virginia Brethren concerning their Civil War experiences, tells the story of 29-year-old John A. Showalter, a teacher of singing, who was drafted in June 1861. Despite pleas of both ill-health and conscientious objection, Showalter was forced to enter camp. Furloughed twice on account of illness, he continued stubbornly to refuse to bear arms; his recalcitrance led to a court-martial and threats of dire punishment. "Finally," Showalter relates, "I was asked if I would assist in cooking for the company. To this I consented, and I was not punished."

The farmer William Peters was also a Brethren, but a recent convert to the church, who lived in an isolated little valley where there were very few other Dunkers. As a pro-Union man, he received threats on his life from local "patriots." Four times a military escort came to take him off to the army (he refused all advice to flee or hide), and each time he reasoned with them, explaining his religious scruples and pleading that, "if they would leave me at home, I would feed the hungry that came to me as long as I had anything."[76] Evidently, the soldiers were of the same opinion as General Jackson, for they finally left him alone.

The Virginia Mennonites possessed a capable and dedicated leader in the person of Bishop Samuel Coffman (1822-1894).[77] But it was the Brethren who produced a man with outstanding talent, which he displayed not only in ticklish negotiations with government officials but also both in keeping his own people loyal in time of war to their traditional pacifist stand and in forging links of cooperation between the three historic peace churches of the South. The Dunker elder, John Kline,[78] was born in 1797 of Brethren parents. Virginia was his native state and the Valley of Virginia remained his home throughout his life, although he was to travel widely as a preacher and minister. A self-educated man, he nevertheless acquired enough knowledge of

---

[76] S. F. Sanger and D. Hays, *The Olive Branch*, pp. 105, 106. For community pressures behind recruiting at this date, see p. 78, based on Sanger's recollections of his boyhood.

[77] Hershberger, *War, Peace and Nonresistance*, p. 111.

[78] For Kline's wartime activities, see Roger E. Sappington, *Courageous Prophet*, pp. 82-112.

medicine to practice as a physician in his neighborhood. The diary he kept for many decades shows him as a man of broad religious views, who was able to rise above the narrow sectarianism of his denomination. He always had a warm affection for the Quakers, for instance, on account of both their simplicity of manner and dress and their peace testimony.[79] His breadth of vision showed itself again in his enlightened patriotism, a love of country that was, nevertheless, subordinated to his concern for the welfare of "the whole human family." "Were this love universal," he wrote on the occasion of the Washington birthday celebrations in 1849, "the word *patriotism*, in its specific sense, meaning such a love for one's country as makes its possessors ready and willing to take up arms in its defense, might be appropriately expunged from every national vocabulary."[80] Kline was always forthright in his abhorrence of the institution of slavery, and, as war approached, he made clear his opposition to secession; he helped, too, to keep his fellow Brethren in Virginia antislavery and antisecessionist during the years of civil conflict.

It was natural, therefore, that it was Kline, ably assisted by another elder of the Virginia church, B. F. Moomaw (1814-1901), who presented the case for exempting members of the two peace churches of the Valley from military service before both the state and, later, the Confederate authorities. Kline proved himself a skilled lobbyist. A pacifism that inculcated obedience to the powers that be insofar as conscience permitted—this kind of apolitical nonresistance as presented by Kline in numerous letters to, and interviews with, government officials usually found a sympathetic response, in contrast to the hostility which these Southern pacifists sometimes met in their home communities or at the hands of junior officers in the army. Looking back on his experiences, Kline's associate, Brother B. F. Moomaw, wrote: "We are much safer in the hands of *great* men, than in the power of the lower class."[81]

An example of Kline's method of argument, compounded in this instance of Christian principle, constitutional precedent, and a shrewd

[79] *Life of John Kline*, pp. 199, 200.

[80] *Ibid.*, p. 246 (quoted in Bowman, p. 110).

[81] Sanger and Hays, *The Olive Branch*, pp. 58, 151. Cf. pp. 83, 84, for a more favorable light on the relations between Brethren and the lower ranks of the army. There S. F. Sanger tells of a friendly debate on the topic "Has a Christian the right to use carnal weapons?" which took place between his father and a non-commissioned officer of the troop of Confederate soldiers temporarily encamped on his farm. The son writes: "The discussion took place in the open yard, with a dozen or more soldiers as spectators. Father was slow of speech but well versed in the Scriptures. . . . The discussion was earnest, but pleasant, and at its conclusion the soldiers said, 'Well, sergeant, the Dutchman beat you,' and they dispersed."

appeal to the Confederacy not to lag behind Northern practice, is to be found in a letter he wrote on 16 December 1861 to a prominent officer of the Confederate army on behalf of the men who had been forced into the ranks despite conscientious scruples in regard to military service. In it he told "My dear friend Col. Lewis":

We German Baptists (called Tunkers) do most solemnly believe that the bearing of carnal weapons in order to destroy life, is in direct opposition to the Gospel of Christ, which we accept as the rule of our faith and practice. To this we have most solemnly vowed to be true until death. Hence we stand pledged to our God to carry out that which we believe to be his commandment. . . . We feel bound to pay our taxes, fines, and to do whatever is in our power which does not conflict with our obligation to God. . . . But in this unholy contest, both law and all former precedents of making drafts have been set aside. The privilege usually granted Christian people to pay a fine has been overruled and set aside, and they are compelled to take up weapons of carnal warfare. This is not only revolting to them, but a positive violation to their solemn vow to their God. This is without precedent in a land of Christian liberty. Who the prosecutor of this outrage on our constitutional rights is I know not, but that it is so is clear. . . . This state of things the much abused Abe Lincoln would have much deplored. For I am credibly informed that he issued a proclamation that no conscientious Christian should be forced to war or to take up arms. Thus it should be in a land of Christian liberty. None but those who have a disposition or desire to rear up a hierarchy or despotic government could feel otherwise. None that have the spirit of Washington or Jefferson in their hearts would desire to compel their fellow countrymen to take up arms against their conscience, and to force them to kill their fellow man . . . a great breach of the constitution has been practiced on us for we have been enforced, restrained and molested because of our religious belief and opinion. Please give this matter your earnest attention and tell it or read it to your fellow officers, and if expedient, to Gen. Jackson.[82]

Yet during the early months of 1862 the position of the young Brethren and Mennonites who had been conscripted or were liable to be called up remained uncertain. Would those already drafted and then

---

[82] D. H. Zigler, *History of the Brethren in Virginia*, 2nd edn., pp. 99-101 (quoted in Bowman, pp. 132, 133). See also Bowman, pp. 114-16, 121, 131, 134ff., and the chapter on "Military Service and War-Time Activities" in a book on the Brethren in Virginia being prepared by Professor Roger E. Sappington of Bridgewater College (Va.), for Kline's negotiations with the civil and military authorities.

furloughed in the fall be recalled to the colors? And would attempts now be made, with the coming of spring and the renewal of active campaigning, to drag more men unwillingly into the army? A few lucky ones might still be able to buy their way out by securing substitutes at exorbitant prices running from $600 up to $1,500. But, as John Kline wrote in a letter to the Northern *Gospel-Visitor*, this was a financial imposition which was well beyond the means of all but a handful of families.[83] There was a general uneasiness in regard to the future in many Mennonite and Dunker homes: parents and wives became increasingly apprehensive about what was in store for their menfolk at the hands of the military. There were rumors that "all the men subject to military duty would be called to arms in a very few days."[84] Prompted by such fears, two successive groups, numbering 18 and 74, respectively, and consisting of both Brethren and Mennonites (along with a few unattached who wished to escape military service with the Confederate forces but who probably did not share their pacifist convictions), set out early in March to make their way across the Allegheny Mountains into West Virginia, parts of which were then in Union hands. Before they were able to leave Confederate territory, however, the men were captured and taken as prisoners, the 18 to Harrisonburg and the 74 to the capital, Richmond, where they were incarcerated in "Castle Thunder," a former tobacco warehouse which had been converted into a jail. At Harrisonburg the men received some harsh treatment and worse was threatened, but at Richmond the authorities handled them with consideration.[85]

The morale of the prisoners, both Mennonite and Dunker, remained high. "During the whole time they were all together like one," wrote one of them afterward.[86] The men at Richmond were examined by a member of the War Department, Sidney S. Baxter, whose courtesy and helpfulness were gratefully remembered by them in later years. Baxter composed a sympathetic report of his findings,[87] recognizing

---

[83] Quoted in Bowman, p. 133.

[84] Quoted in Sanger and Hays, *The Olive Branch*, p. 66.

[85] Zigler, *Brethren in Virginia*, pp. 103-8; Hartzler and Kauffman, *Mennonite Church History*, p. 209. Accounts by two later Brethren ministers who had participated in the escape in their youth are printed by Sanger and Hays, *The Olive Branch*, pp. 62-73. See also Peter S. Hartman, *Reminiscences of the Civil War*, pp. 12-19; Horst, *Mennonites in the Confederacy*, chap. V. Horst points out (on p. 50) that there were around this time other parties of Mennonite and Brethren escapees from the draft who attempted to cross over into Union territory.

[86] The Mennonite Simeon Heatwole, quoted in Sanger and Hays, *The Olive Branch*, p. 108. The patriarch Gabriel Heatwole, who had emigrated in his youth from Lancaster Co. to Virginia, had five sons, two sons-in-law, two grandsons, and a grandson-in-law in the jail at Richmond, as well as a son-in-law in the guardhouse at Harrisonburg (see pp. 108, 109).

[87] Quoted in Bowman, p. 136.

that the attempt to escape was not the result of cowardice or hostility to the government but flowed instead from deep religious conviction, and recommending the men's release from captivity:

> As all of these persons are members in good standing in these churches [i.e., Dunker and Mennonite] and bear good characters as citizens and Christians I cannot doubt the sincerity of their declaration that they left home to avoid the draft of the militia and under the belief that by the draft they would be placed in a situation in which they would be compelled to violate their consciences. They all declared that they had no intention to go to the enemy or to remain with them. They all intended to return home as soon as the draft was over. Some of them had made exertions to procure substitutes. . . . Others had done much to support the families of volunteers. Some had furnished horses to the cavalry. All of them are friendly to the South.

Baxter went on to mention that he had heard that a law was about to be passed by the Virginia legislature to exempt religious objectors on payment of a commutation fee, as had been possible in the case of the peacetime militia. Such a law was, indeed, enacted on 29 March, giving conscientious objectors the alternative of either contributing $500 plus 2% of the value of their taxable property or, if they could not afford to pay this sum, undertaking teamster or other noncombatant duties in the army. In addition, a declaration of allegiance was required.[88] The terms were indeed stiff, especially when compared to the insignificant sum paid before the war for exemption from mustering, but they were acceptable on the whole to both Mennonites and Brethren.

The imprisoned men were all eventually released during April. Meanwhile, however, the uncovering of the attempted escapes had brought further suspicion of disloyalty on the two churches; Elder Kline's endeavors on behalf of the men were looked at askance by the local authorities, and they finally landed him in jail in Harrisonburg where he was confined in the guardhouse for thirteen days.

[88] *Ibid.*, p. 137. According to Baxter's report, he was told by the imprisoned men that "those who are unable to make the payment will cheerfully go into service as teamsters or in any employment in which they are not required to shed blood." The official teaching of both churches opposed teamster service, but, as was the case with the hiring of substitutes or contributing toward the recruiting of volunteers, the practice of some church members sometimes fell short of the ideal. However, according to a former Dunker prisoner (quoted in Sanger and Hays, *The Olive Branch*, p. 71), the men at Richmond held out against attempts on the part of the authorities to get them to act as teamsters with the army. Baxter may have misunderstood their position on this point.

The granting of exemption by the state proved for young Mennonites and Dunkers a very short-lived release from the threat of being forced into the ranks. With the enactment of Confederate conscription on 16 April began the struggle of Kline and the Mennonite bishop Coffman, whose clear stand now against accepting any kind of army service eventually forced him to leave Virginia for a time because of the threats he had received, and of their associates among leading Brethren and Mennonites in the South to obtain a similar exemption from the impending Confederate draft. This was in many ways a more difficult task, for no longer were they dealing only with legislators from their native state, some of whom would be acquainted with the churches' position on war; now they had to convince a majority in the Confederate Congress, to whom their tenets were mostly quite unknown and their scruples smacked of treason. That the churches' leaders (in collaboration with Southern Quakers, as we have seen) were eventually successful on 11 October 1862 in winning the exemption they sought was attributable largely to two factors: first, the friendliness shown to them by certain highly placed officials, of whom their fellow Virginian and representative in Congress, Colonel John B. Baldwin, was among the most helpful; and, next, the use they were able to make of literature setting forth their traditional nonresistant faith to substantiate the validity of their claims to exemption.

Colonel Baldwin advised Kline to draw up a petition on behalf of both Dunkers and Mennonites for presentation to the Confederate Congress. This Kline proceeded to do, urging in it that the same consideration be given in Confederate legislation to their conscientious scruples as had already been granted by the law of the Old Dominion. "Under the excitement of the hour," stated the petition, "indiscreet and inconsiderate persons have preferred the charge of disloyalty against our Churches. This charge has not the semblance of truth, in fact, and has doubtless originated from our faith against bearing arms." Signatures were also obtained for the petition from nonmembers, and then it was forwarded to Colonel Baldwin, who introduced it in the Congress on 1 September.[89]

During their detention at Richmond in "Castle Thunder" the Mennonites had been able to refer to Peter Burkholder's *Confession*, a home-grown product of the Virginian branch, in confirmation of their claims that their people had always been noncombatants. The Brethren in Virginia, on the other hand, had produced no literature on peace, so that their men could only say that their community, too, held to the beliefs that were expounded in the Burkholder *Confession* and point

[89] Bowman, pp. 138-43.

to the fact that successive generations of their people had refused to muster with the militia and had been permitted to pay the commutation fee in lieu of service.[90]

When, in April, Colonel Baldwin had written to a Brethren leader, Samuel Cline, to ask him for some work that would be useful in the efforts he was then making to obtain exemption for the peace sects from the Confederate Congress, Cline sent him a copy of a recently published pamphlet by William C. Thurman entitled *Non-Resistance, or the Spirit of Christianity Restored*. Its author had joined the Brethren shortly after writing the tract. This work, he states, he had originally composed less with the object of justifying Christian pacifism to the government and people of the South than of straightening out his own thoughts on the subject of war resistance and leaving a testament of nonresistance for posterity, in case he were called upon to suffer death as a result of his conscientious objection to military service. He had held pacifist views, he tells us too, for some ten years before the outbreak of war, although he had not been affiliated to any peace church. The pamphlet appears to have been circulated fairly extensively among the congressmen at Richmond, and Colonel Baldwin acknowledged later that he had found it helpful in establishing the claims of the peace sects to military exemption.[91]

Thurman was, indeed, a stormy petrel whose sojourn with the Brethren was to be fairly brief. One of their historians has written of him: "He was a dreamer, an idealist, and was prone to follow vague theories and fancies . . . a ready talker, an ardent student of the Bible, in his way an interesting and intelligent man; and so he impressed himself favorably upon the Brethren." The Virginia Dunkers were in need of someone who could wield a ready and able pen in their defense, who, whether on paper or in the pulpit, could give convinc-

[90] Daniel K. Cassel, *History of the Mennonites*, p. 138; Sanger and Hays, *The Olive Branch*, p. 83.

[91] Sanger and Hays, pp. 164, 165. Thurman was apparently granted C.O. status. See Wright, *Conscientious Objectors in the Civil War*, p. 105, where his name is given incorrectly as Thurber. According to the *World's Crisis and Second Advent Messenger*, XX, no. 7 (1 Nov. 1864), 26, Thurman, on being drafted earlier, had been taken to Richmond (Va.) where he refused to handle a gun, saying he would rather be killed than fight. The authorities released him and allowed him to return home. When he tried to get his pamphlet on nonresistance printed, "he had to give security to the whole amount of the worth of the publication to the publication office, before he could get it published in Charlottesville." Its appearance brought him fresh trouble, but "his relations being loyal and influential, succeeded in getting him off." Before the conclusion of hostilities he went across the lines and visited the West, where he gained popularity as a preacher. When, however, he began to advocate pacifism in his sermons there, "he had the Union flag hoisted over his head several times . . . and was met once with drums."

814

ing expression to their deeply held beliefs. Men like John Kline or B. F. Moomaw inspired confidence in opponents through their simple faith and obvious sincerity and were persons of intelligence well fitted to carry on negotiations with officials. But they lacked the ready tongue and fluent pen of Thurman. So the latter, shortly after joining the Brethren, was elected a minister and soon became active among them as a preacher and evangelist. Around the end of the war, however, he began to propagate unorthodox opinions, practising the "single mode" of feetwashing and expounding millenarian views— activities that brought down on him the censure of the church. This reaction soon led him to break with the Brethren, and some of his disciples among them left with him.[92]

Thurman's tract did not contribute anything new to the literature of pacifism. Its author was evidently well acquainted with the antiwar writings of Clarkson and Dymond, as well as with the Dutch Mennonite *Martyrs' Mirror*, historians like Gibbon and Millman, and the lawyer Grotius. The bulk of the book is entitled: "An inquiry as to whether the Christian may use the sword." Thurman uses his authorities quite skillfully, in addition to copious scriptural citations, to bring in a negative verdict. Twenty pages of appendices deal with the question of war resistance in the early church. At the end he prints a model peace pledge to be taken by contemporary Christian war resisters:

> We, whose names are hereto affixed, do hereby promise and solemnly pledge ourselves that, yielding a lamblike, passive submission to the powers that be, we will neither, by proxy, nor the use of the sword ourselves, nor by casting a vote for those who are thus placed in authority, nor in any other way, save that of paying a legal tribute, give any support whatever to any of the hostile powers under the canopy of heaven.[93]

Despite, or perhaps because of, this challenging conclusion, the first edition of Thurman's booklet was soon exhausted, and it had to be reprinted.

The Confederate law of 11 October 1862 giving members of the peace sects the alternative of either furnishing a substitute or paying a commutation fee of $500, a provision which was probably due in some measure to the influence of Thurman's tract, helped to ease the situation of Mennonites and Dunkers in the Valley. They did not share, as we know, the absolutist scruples of the Quakers and so were able

---

[92] John S. Flory, *Flashlights from History*, pp. 59-61; Thurman, *Non-Resistance*, Preface and Introduction, also p. 5.
[93] Thurman, *Non-Resistance*, p. 70.

to pay their $500 into the treasury with an untroubled conscience. Their reaction to the new legislation was one of profound relief and of gratitude both to God and to Caesar for delivery from imminent danger. The Brethren, therefore, set aside New Year's Day of 1863 as a day of thanksgiving, celebrating it with church services and special prayers. Urging his fellow members to give liberally to all who had suffered through the war, John Kline told them: "We must look upon our exemption from army service as one proof of those interpositions in behalf of his children which our heavenly Father has promised, and which he is constantly fulfilling." The Mennonites followed the example of the Dunkers by making 28 January their day of thanksgiving. And there were to be subsequent celebrations of this kind as renewed threats to impose military conscription on these people came to naught.[94]

Yet some problems still remained for solution after the enactment of exemption. In particular, there was the question here in the South, as in the North, of the as yet unbaptized members of the communities, who were not covered by the act.[95] Some of these men continued in hiding or escaped to the North; occasionally, arrests were made among Brethren or Mennonites for aiding the fugitives.[96] Those who were taken were kept in prison or forced into the army, where most of them, given the opportunity, either deserted to the Union side or just went back home. A few of these unwilling conscripts are known to have died during army service. Sometimes the boys' parents were well enough off to afford eventually to buy substitutes.[97] (We hear of one case involving a Mennonite, possibly not a full member, who escaped

[94] Bowman, p. 145; *Life of John Kline*, p. 460; Sappington's unpublished book; Brunk, *History of the Mennonites in Virginia*, I, 165, 166.

[95] Hartzler and Kauffman, *Mennonite Church History*, p. 211.

[96] Sanger and Hays, p. 85. Cf. R. J. Heatwole, "Reminiscences of War Days," *Gospel Herald*, IV, no. 28 (12 Oct. 1911), 444, 445: "Our people [i.e., Mennonite conscripts] . . . kept hid from the soldiers. One aged brother was asked where they were hidden. He replied, 'I can't say,' and he being German, they thought he meant he didn't know, so the soldiers went off." The spread of Mennonitism to West Virginia seems to have stemmed from seed sown by a wartime C.O., Peter John Heatwole, a potter by trade, who, pursued by the provost-marshal's men, had found refuge in the North Fork Valley. He told the people who had taken him in about the Mennonite faith, including its nonresistance, and showed them the copy of the Burkholder *Confession of Faith* which he had succeeded in bringing with him. Returning home after the war, he reported the receptivity of the people in this area to the Mennonite message, and missionary work was begun there, leading within a few years to the establishment of the first Mennonite church in that state. See Hartzler and Kauffman, pp. 214, 215; Brunk, *History of the Mennonites in Virginia*, I, 361, 362; Horst, *Mennonites in the Confederacy*, chap. IV and pp. 72-74.

[97] An example of such action on the part of a Dunker family is given in Sanger and Hays, pp. 76-78.

conscription by the purchase of a mailman's route for the considerable sum of $1,000, a transaction which was subsequently confirmed by the government.)[98] The status of the young men of this group in regard to the draft, owing to their failure to establish a claim to membership because of the omission of baptism, remained ambiguous throughout the period of the war. It was they who suffered the most hardship.

However, there were also problems—though not such difficult ones—in seeing that all those who were legally entitled to exemption were actually able to take advantage of it. There were attempts to retain the few conscientious objectors who were still with the army on the pretext that the act did not apply to them. In some cases, demands were made that those who had already paid their $500 commutation fee under the Virginia state law should pay again for Confederate exemption. Local officials sometimes continued to refuse exemption, hoping to intimidate these simple plowboys, who might be unaware of their exact rights, into accepting army service. These matters, however, were fairly soon cleared up, at least for the time being, in negotiations between the Brethren and Mennonite representatives and the secretary of war at Richmond.[99]

Payment of a commutation fee as high as $500 was no easy matter for many families, even though the peace people of the Valley were fairly well-to-do. Commenting on this situation early in July 1862, when conscription was still in practice under state control, Kline wrote: "Our brethren truly have much to pay, so much so, it will be a considerable burden for them to bear. . . . To pay the $500 fine falls heavy." And the old man added, in good Puritan strain, that, nevertheless, it might help them turn away from earthly cares.[100] At the end of the year we find Kline handing over on behalf of his brethren the sum of $9,000 to the receiver of fines.[101] A financial load of this nature might well be chastening to worldly inclinations, but it could have been paid only by a united effort of the congregations. The practice of pooling resources was put into effect among the Virginia Mennonites and Brethren both as a practical measure and on grounds of equity. No special system, such as was sometimes attempted in the North, seems to have been set up to allocate the amount each family should contribute, but we know that the richer members helped out with the expense in cases where the draftee came from a less well-to-do background.[102]

[98] Cassel, *History of the Mennonites*, pp. 135-37.
[99] Bowman, pp. 143, 145, 146; Sappington's unpublished book.
[100] Quoted in Bowman, pp. 134, 135.
[101] *Ibid.*, p. 144.
[102] *Ibid.*, p. 143; Sanger and Hays, p. 78.

As the months passed and calls for manpower on each side grew louder, rumors that the existing exemption would be withdrawn and replaced by harsher conditions, or that exemption would perhaps be withdrawn altogether, spread. After the capture of Vicksburg by the Union forces and the defeat at Gettysburg in July 1863, the governor of Virginia recommended to the legislature the creation of a home guard without provision for religious objectors. In alarm, Brother B. F. Moomaw wrote to John Kline on 2 September 1863:

> The question that I would ask is if the Legislature be so lost to every sense of Christianity as to require our brethren to go into the army, what is to be done? . . . We have in every case complied with the requirements of the government, because we could do so without a departure from our principles, but if they now require us to go into the army without any alleviation, what shall we do? What can we do? Shall we not unanimously petition for permission to leave the country with, or without our property?[103]

Although Moomaw's fears as to state action were not realized, it was known that something similar was also being contemplated by the Confederate government. This became clear after President Jefferson Davis's speech of 7 December 1863, when he called for a radical restriction of the categories of the exempt in order to make up manpower deficiences.[104] So, at the end of the year, plans were on foot to send Moomaw, who had been chiefly responsible from the side of the Brethren for working out with government officials the implementation of the Confederate exemption, and another Brethren to Richmond in order to try and prevent removal of the exemption clause for religious objectors in any new draft legislation. He intended, Moomaw wrote Kline on 27 December 1863, to bring to the attention of the authorities the church's loyalty to the state, their punctual payment of their taxes, including commutation fees, and "what we have done for the destitute and suffering soldiers and the quantity of produce that we are making." If these representations were unavailing (the reference to church members' importance to the country as food producers was, indeed, a shrewd one in the existing war situation) and exemption was withdrawn after all, they had been "authorized to request a peaceable passport out of the country, constantly averring that we cannot nor will we fight."[105] Once again, we find emigration being proposed if the situation should become unbearable—the classic solution of groups like the Brethren and Mennonites when faced with

[103] Zigler, *Brethren in Virginia*, pp. 134-36.
[104] Bowman, pp. 146, 147.   [105] Zigler, *Brethren in Virginia*, p. 139.

demands for military service which it did not seem possible to avoid short of martyrdom and the possible extinction of the church. Migration was also, of course, a familiar pattern of behavior among the American people.

In practice the exemption granted the peace sects in 1862 was never withdrawn, although in the last few weeks of the war an act was passed by the Confederate Congress cancelling the exemption of religious objectors (but was never put into effect during the brief period before the conclusion of hostilities). In the latter years of the war Brethren and Mennonite objectors did suffer hardship at the hands of overzealous local authorities on the lookout for able-bodied men to fill the increasingly depleted army ranks. "Those with scruples against war never knew whether their consciences would be respected," writes Bowman. There were suspicions on the part of the government that membership in the peace sects was augmented in wartime by converts whose primary object was to escape military service. Therefore, exemption was usually interpreted as applying only to those who had held membership before the passing of the act of 11 October 1862. We have seen the trials the young unbaptized men of these communities had to endure on this account; and as the war situation deteriorated, the manhunts for fugitive conscripts became more relentless. Difficulty in establishing any right to exemption was likewise often encountered by those who were drawn to join from outside, men whose motives were rarely those of the shirker, since the peace sects' antiwar and antislavery stand made them generally unpopular in the country and often the object of active hostility.[106]

On 15 June 1864 the Brethren leader, John Kline, was shot dead by unidentified assassins not far from his home. Even after the outbreak of war he had continued to attend the annual conferences of the Brethren and had had to cross the lines into the Northern states to do so. Each year he had been elected moderator by the delegates, who thus expressed their confidence in his leadership. But it undoubtedly also made him suspect in some quarters of disloyalty to the Confederacy and thus almost certainly contributed to his murder. Brethren and Mennonites, along with the other farmers of the Valley of Vir-

---

[106] Bowman, pp. 145-51; Hartzler and Kauffman, *Mennonite Church History*, p. 212. H. R. Holsinger (*History of the Tunkers and the Brethren Church*, pp. 800-802) relates the story of Addison Harper, an officer in the Confederate army whose wife was a member of the Brethren. As a result of his growing conviction of the unchristian nature of war, he eventually resigned his commission and went back home. He was baptized shortly after the war. Harper seems to have escaped the attentions of the military after he had left the army. This may have been because his resignation occurred late in the war (Holsinger does not give a date to the anecdote).

ginia, also suffered very considerable losses in property at the hands of the Union forces, when in October 1864 General Sheridan, carrying out Grant's orders to pursue a "scorched earth" policy in this fertile area, swept through the Valley setting fire to buildings, destroying crops, and killing or driving off the livestock. Many young Mennonites and Brethren, it is interesting to note, took the opportunity furnished by this brief visit of the Union army to escape Confederate conscription by accompanying the troops back North.[107]

This account has so far been confined to the churches of the Valley of Virginia. But the Brethren had some congregations in eastern Tennessee, too. There, in the summer of 1863, the local military authorities, because of the increasing shortage of men for the army, began to disregard the exemption granted by the law of the Confederacy and to arrest men of military age, even when they had paid their $500 fee. They were put "in prison or the stockades" in an effort to force them to agree to serve. The Brethren, therefore, held a council where they drew up a petition to the Congress at Richmond and entrusted it to a young minister, Peter R. Wrightman. According to his account,

> At the proper time I went to the House of the Confederate Congress, presented my petition and made my plea, stating among other things that our people were always a peace people; it is no use to take them to the army, for they will not fight. . . . They are mostly farmers, raise grain and your men come and take it. In this way we feed the hungry. Our people never molest your men, but are loyal and law-abiding citizens. If you will let us stay at home, we will be loyal citizens to the powers that are over us. We humbly plead for your acceptance of our petition.

Once again, the argument concerning the usefulness of these pacifist farmers for the war effort had its effect, and Brother Wrightman soon returned home with authorization to have the prisoners released.[108]

The Brethren and Mennonites of the South had been tested more severely than their peoples under Union rule. Even more difficult trials seemed to be in store for them in the early spring of 1865 as the Con-

---

[107] Bowman, pp. 152, 153; Hartzler and Kauffman, pp. 212, 213; Brunk, I, 168-71; Horst, *Mennonites in the Confederacy*, chap. VIII. See Brunk, I, 172-77, for an account, based on research in the National Archives at Washington, of the claims of the Valley Mennonites with the Southern Claims Commission for compensation for losses resulting from the war. Many were successful, since the conduct of the Mennonites during Sheridan's raid was accepted as proof that they had been not merely neutral but pro-Union in their attitude, a necessary precondition for compensation. The records also show the large-scale nature of the losses sustained.

[108] Sanger and Hays, pp. 89-92 (quoted in part in Bowman, pp. 144, 145).

federate Congress withdrew their military exemption. The end of the war saved them from this new ordeal. On the whole, at least after the hesitancies and confusion of the first months of the conflict, they had borne a consistent testimony according to their lights. Grateful for the opportunity to remain on their farms in exchange for the payment of the special commutation tax, they never felt called upon, as the Quakers had been, to contest the legitimacy of making such a contribution. Nothing in their past would have led them to make this challenge. Their peace testimony was above all a conservative one; it was aimed at preserving the testament of their forefathers intact. The pattern of war resistance among Brethren and Mennonites in the South, as in the North, had followed its familiar line.

Chapter 20

Religious Pacifism outside the Major Historic Peace Sects, 1861-1865

I

Conscientious objection and religious pacifism during the Civil War, especially in the Northern states, was by no means confined to Quakers, Mennonites, or Brethren, or a tiny remnant left over from the prewar nonsectarian pacifist movement. In addition to the three major historic peace sects, we find a number of other denominations at that time whose members as a whole, or most of whose leaders, took a pacifist position. Sharing a common war resistance, they yet differed widely in theology, organization, social composition, and general outlook on the world. There also existed a few isolated conscientious objectors unaffiliated to any peace group.[1] This chapter, therefore,

[1] Several objectors of this kind have been mentioned earlier in this section; among them should also be included Dwight L. Moody (1837-1899), the famous evangelist. A young man of 24 when war broke out, Moody, although not affiliated to any of the pacifist denominations, refused on grounds of conscience to participate in the struggle, despite strongly held abolitionist views. The provenance of his pacifist beliefs is not recorded; perhaps they came from previous contacts with the Quakers or Garrisonian nonresistants, or possibly they were reached as a result of a simple reading of the gospels by this exceptionally religion-filled personality. "The story of Dwight L. Moody as a non-resistant Christian," it has been said, "is almost unknown" (*Dwight L. Moody and War*, p. 1). It is a phase of his career that is sometimes ignored by his biographers. E.g., J. Wilbur Chapman, *The Life and Work of Dwight L. Moody*, has a chapter (XII) of 15 pages on "Mr. Moody in Two Wars." But nowhere does he mention his subject's pacifist stand in the Civil War, and he only briefly alludes (p. 189) to his opposition to the outbreak of the Spanish-American War. In 1861 Moody was engaged in evangelical work in Chicago; many of his converts had joined one or another of the volunteer companies that were forming in the city, and his friends and colleagues urged him to join up, too. He refrained from doing so, however, despite all his sympathies for the slave and the Union, explaining: "There has never been a time in my life when I felt I could take a gun and shoot down a fellow-being. In this respect I am a Quaker" (William R. Moody, *The Life of Dwight L. Moody*, p. 82). Moody's objection to bearing arms appears to have had its roots in a literalist interpretation of scripture. He does not ever seem to have considered the implications of his pacifism beyond a bare refusal to fight. He saw no reason to prevent him from carrying on evangelistic and welfare work among the Union troops; indeed, he was extremely eager to do so. He became a leading light in the "Christian Commission," a private organization which, with the sanction of the army authorities, took care of the soldiers' spiritual welfare. As the chairman of its devotional committee, he was welcome in army camps, military hospitals, and prisoner-of-war camps, where he comforted the wounded and dying, preached

must necessarily lack the cohesion of the previous ones on the war, for the inspiration for the pacifism discussed here, though still firmly anchored in the Christian tradition, was filtered through very diverse sources.

Many Quaker views, including their pacifism, were shared by the Rogerenes of Connecticut, with whom we may begin our discussion. Something has been said earlier about the dogged stand for peace that this small New England group took. Unfortunately, we know very little about their activities during the Civil War: they were by this date much reduced in number and not too far from final extinction. They did, however, produce several conscientious objectors from among their young men, at least one of whom was confined along with Quaker conscripts in military camp. Another, Ira Whipple of Ledyard, was more lucky. Appealing to the governor of the state, "with his bible in his hand, . . . he addressed him, reading passages from the New Testament. After he had finished the Governor said, 'Go home and do not worry for no soldier leaves the State against my wishes and you will not be required to do military duties.' "[2] The Rogerenes were a well-known and respected group in Connecticut, and this probably explains young Whipple's good fortune on this occasion.

---

revivalist sermons to big gatherings of soldiers, and distributed Bibles and religious tracts to them in large numbers. He even participated in patriotic rallies. Nowhere do we hear of his ever giving any verbal expression to his pacifist beliefs while ministering to the troops. His, indeed, was a very personal witness for peace that did not go beyond an unwillingness to be directly instrumental in the inhuman and unchristian work of destruction that was war. Yet, although it lacked the radical and militant antecedents of Garrison's wartime stand, Moody's position was not entirely dissimilar to that of the great abolitionist during the war period. See W. R. Moody, *Life*, chap. VIII, for Dwight Moody's activities in the Civil and Spanish-American Wars.

From several chance references it would seem as if some pacifists were to be found among Southern Baptists. For instance, the Quaker C.O., Himelius M. Hockett, during his imprisonment in 1863 along with his brother Jesse, records in his diary: "There was with us at that time a man named Blackmore, a Baptist, who refused to bear arms for the same reason as ourselves. He was soon after removed, and we understand that he died in camp." From the context it is clear that Blackmore was not a pacifist Dunker—or German Baptist—but a member of one of the regular Baptist churches, and that his objection was an objection to war itself, and not one based simply on sympathy with the Northern cause. Again, we hear of a Baptist minister called Thorne, who encouraged the Hockett brothers in their stand, telling them that he agreed entirely with their pacifism and stating his belief that his own church ought to have adopted the Quaker position on war. (See Fernando G. Cartland, *Southern Heroes*, pp. 262, 263, 270.) That there were others in the same denomination who shared the views of the layman Blackmore and pastor Thorne is not unlikely; that they formed a mere handful of isolated individuals is, however, certain.

[2] E. N. Wright, *Conscientious Objectors in the Civil War*, p. 136, quoting the *Peacemaker*, XXII, no. 9, 194.

Most akin to the Brethren and Mennonites were the German-speaking communitarians who had migrated to the United States in the first half of the nineteenth century. Not all of them held fully pacifist views: the noncombatancy of some groups resembled that of the early American Moravians, treated in a previous chapter of this book. We read, for instance, of the Harmonists (or Rappists) of Economy (Beaver County, Pa.) that during the Civil War they made liberal contributions "for the equipment of volunteers, for special bounties, for the support of the families of absent soldiers, and for the Christian, Sanitary and Subsistence Commissions, for the fortification of Pittsburgh, for the relief of the freedmen, for the support of soldiers' widows, and the education of their orphan children."[3] How far such contributions were made as an alternative to military service in the same way as they were made by Brethren or Mennonites, as a willing recognition of the conditional validity of the political order based on the sword, or whether they signified a rather fuller support of the Union war effort is not quite clear. The Harmonists, as we have seen earlier, steered clear of the army, but, again, this unwillingness to serve may have been due as much to the reluctance of a communitarian to become sullied by the world as to any theoretical belief in nonresistance.

The Harmonists had originally migrated to America in 1803-1804. In 1817 another group of German religious dissidents had followed them across the ocean from their native Württemberg in order to escape persecution in their homeland. The leader of these Separatists, Barbara Grübermann, had died before their departure, and her place was taken by Joseph Baumeler (d. 1853). Under his direction the sect adopted communism of goods, which they had not practiced back in Germany, in order to cope more adequately with the pioneer conditions of life encountered in their new home. The group was never large, numbering at its height in the 1830's only about 500 persons. Many of the tenets of the sect, including pacifism, bore considerable resemblance to those of the Quakers, who had been drawn by this resemblance to help them migrate to the United States. Eventually, the Separatists settled in Zoar in Ohio. By the outbreak of the Civil War the community was already on the decline. Hinds writes of their wartime activities:

In the civil war they took no part as a Society except to pay their share of the taxes required to secure volunteers; and they would

---

[3] W. A. Hinds, *American Communities*, 1961 edn., p. 21. The author was a journalist and a member of the Oneida Community. His book was originally published in 1878.

have been glad to have kept their young men at home at any cost; but fourteen of them were swept away with the current, to be killed, or die in hospitals, to absent themselves for ever from the communal home, or to return begging for re-admission.[4]

Hinds also notes that members of the Bethel community in Missouri (mentioned in an earlier chapter), which had been founded by an immigrant from Prussia, Dr. Keil, originally a milliner by trade, were "averse to war." The community was German-speaking and included some "Pennsylvania Dutch" among its members. In 1856 a subsidiary community had been set up out in the Far West at Aurora in Oregon; at their height the two communities together numbered about 650 persons. During the Civil War, when the largely native-born population of the Missouri settlement was liable to the draft, many of the younger men went out west to Aurora to avoid military service.[5]

Of the Inspirationists of Amana in Iowa we know somewhat more because they themselves published a considerable amount of their community records under the editorship of one of their members.[6] Whereas their communism, as we have seen earlier, was engendered by the situation they faced after their arrival in the United States in 1842, their pacifism and refusal to serve as soldiers dated back to their beginnings in Germany early in the eighteenth century. Thirteen years after the Civil War we find them a community of some 1,600 scattered among seven villages, by this period mainly middle-class folk leading a peaceful and prosperous existence.[7]

Strong aversion to both war and slavery faced the Inspirationists with the same dilemma as it did the Quakers and the German peace sects. Their sympathies were from the beginning wholeheartedly with the Northern cause. On 29 April 1861, Christian Metz (1794-1867), the community's outstanding leader, wrote to the brethren, who had remained behind in Ebenezer village in New York state, that they must all stand behind the Union. The "rebel states" were in the wrong; they had begun the war, and God would punish their wickedness.[8] At the same time, Metz was always careful to point out to his people that, for all their sympathy with the war aims of the Un-

[4] *Ibid.*, p. 34. See also pp. 24, 26, 33; George B. Landis, "The Society of Separatists of Zoar, Ohio" in *Annual Report of the American Historical Association for the Year 1898* (1899), p. 181.

[5] Hinds, p. 43.

[6] Gottlieb Scheuner, *Inspirations-Historie oder historischer Bericht* (1891).

[7] However, E. N. Wright (*Conscientious Objectors in the Civil War*, p. 208) states that in 1860 the community numbered about 1,200.

[8] Scheuner, *Inspirations-Historie*, pp. 719, 720.

ion, war and military service did not belong to "our calling and faith."[9] Nevertheless, they should be willing to contribute to the cause in ways that did not offend their conscience.[10] And thus we find the Inspirationists on a number of occasions providing food, clothing, and blankets for the use of the army and contributing money to the bounty fund for the recruiting of volunteers. Hinds states that the total value of their contributions amounted to nearly $20,000.[11] Although they waited before coming forward until a clear need for help became apparent, the money and supplies they gave were not regarded as an exaction extracted only by threat of worse. Metz reported in October 1861 that "nearly all were so willing in the matter that it was a joy."[12]

It was another question, however, when it came to demands for personal service in the army. Here there was no compromise, although it appears that they would not have been opposed to furnishing substitutes if there had been no other way out. In the summer of 1862, with the drying up of an adequate supply of volunteers for the Union army, federal conscription appeared likely to replace the less rigorous draft for the state militias, and the outlook for the Inspirationists grew increasingly uncertain. On 7 August, Metz wrote to the brethren at Ebenezer of the impending conscription: "Ach, I fear very much that we too will now be drawn into it." A petition was therefore drawn up for presentation to the governors of Iowa and New York—since the draft still remained for the time being under state control—both setting forth the gospel grounds of their pacifist faith and pointing out that it had been attempts to conscript them and to curtail their religious freedom that had originally led them to leave their native land for America. They stated, too, that their pro-Union sympathies were well known in government circles and that they had made substantial contributions in clothing and foodstuffs for the forces. The petition achieved its aim at least to the extent that the call-up of members was indefinitely postponed by the state authorities. During that winter the villages on more than one occasion gave sums ranging from $500 to $1,000 in support of the wounded and of war widows and orphans as a token of their willingness to make sacrifices for their country, even if they were not ready to fight themselves. This generosity, Scheuner comments, "awakened a good disposition towards the Community both with the authorities and in the imme-

[9] Quoted in Bertha M. H. Shambaugh, *Amana: The Community of True Inspiration*, p. 164.

[10] Scheuner, *Inspirations-Historie*, p. 721.

[11] Hinds, *American Communities*, p. 58. See also pp. 49, 50.

[12] Scheuner, *Inspirations-Historie*, p. 732.

diate neighbourhood, which, in view of the disturbed times, also had great value."[13]

The federal legislation of 3 March 1863 and 24 February 1864, which has been outlined earlier in this work, finally relieved to a large extent the apprehensions of the Inspirationists and their leader, Christian Metz. They gratefully paid the $300 commutation fee, and the fact that under the act of 3 March 1863 the money was allotted to the employment of substitutes does not appear to have aroused any reservations. Frequent entries in the community's records, as well as references in Metz's correspondence, illustrate the severe strain on the treasury which was caused now by the need to pay the commutation fees of members caught up in the draft, in addition to the other financial contributions to the war. In December 1863, for instance, Metz reports from Amana that sixteen men had been demanded from their township by the draft authorities; to gain exemption for them would mean that the community would have to contribute $4,800. The money was found, however, and turned over to the local recruiting officers, who went ahead with raising a number of volunteers. In 1864, Amana Township received several calls to furnish conscripts; under the new act of 24 February the commutation fine went toward the relief of sick and wounded soldiers, instead of toward furnishing new recruits. In July of that year new troubles for the community arose when attempts were made, with the growing manpower shortage, to revive the state militia and to claim that no law existed on the statute books to exempt the brethren of military age from attending its military exercises. The brethren determined to resist, whatever the penalties, but in the end they were again left in peace. "Everything, however, remained still," relates Scheuner; "no one enquired any further in the matter and so the Lord helped in a wonderful manner even out of this emergency."[14]

Despite their devotion to the Union, which they were so keen to stress, these German immigrants were in some ways even more strangers in the land than were the otherworldly Mennonites or Brethren. Not only were the German communitarians for the most part recent comers to the country, who betrayed in their speech and in their customs their foreign origin, but their communal and self-sufficient way of life alone would have made them wary of participating in war, even if they had not at the same time had sincere scruples of conscience. Their conscientious objection, however, was even more narrowly confined to the act of shedding blood than for most Brethren

[13] *Ibid.*, pp. 756-59, 767, 772, 773.
[14] *Ibid.*, pp. 797, 811-13, 820, 821, 836, 837.

827

or Mennonites, who, we have seen, officially banned hiring substitutes or voluntarily contributing to the prosecution of the war. The communitarians, on the other hand, gave enthusiastically of their substance to the warring state in gratitude for—or in some cases in hope of—being left in peace to pursue their communal way to salvation. It was an anxious time for them, as the records of the Inspirationists of Amana show, but they were spared the testing to which they had been subjected back in their homeland.

The first half of the nineteenth century was the golden age of the communitarian movement in the United States. By the outbreak of the Civil War this movement was already in decline, and of the English-speaking communities only two took up a pacifist stand in the war. The peace witness of the Shakers and of Adin Ballou's community at Hopedale, contrasting in its sturdy assertion of rights with the passive otherworldliness and apoliticism of the German communitarians, has already occupied our attention in the chapters on the antebellum period. By now both groups, and particularly Hopedale, had lost much of their earlier vigor. Of the two, the Shakers were by far the more numerous and the more active.

Conscription did not touch the United Society until March 1862. Then we find some of the young Shakers being called upon for military service. As in the past, the leadership of the Society continued to maintain an absolutist position. The men were told not only to refuse to hire a substitute or to serve in the army in any noncombatant capacity, such as teamster work, but to refuse to accept the alternative of the commutation fine of $300, which the federal law eventually provided as a way out of military service. They were instructed to "stand up in the integrity of free men" and bear the consequences manfully, "and never turn aside from conscientious duty for any power."[15] As a result, several arrests were made. From the North Union community (near Cleveland, Ohio), for instance, two men were called up. One inflicted injuries on himself in order to escape the draft; the other, George Ingels, was inducted into the army, where he consented to serve as a hospital orderly.[16]

From the community at Shirley (Mass.) we have an interesting manuscript concerning the conscription experiences of one of its young men, a simple country boy named Horace S. Taber.[17] Taber was one

[15] Daryl Chase, "The Early Shakers: An Experiment in Religious Communism," Ph.D. diss., U. of Chicago, p. 191; E. D. Andrews, *The People called Shakers*, p. 215.

[16] Caroline B. Piercy, *The Valley of God's Pleasure*, p. 229; M. F. Melcher, *The Shaker Adventure*, 1960 edn., p. 171.

[17] Letters & Documents respecting the Conscription, Arrest & Suffering of Horace

of three Shakers selected for service in August 1863 by the draft board at Concord. The other two were found medically unfit, but the board proceeded to induct young Horace—even though he was apparently nearly blind in one eye and suffered from severe bronchitis and neuralgia! Refusing, according to his Society's precepts, either to find a substitute or to pay the $300 fine, Taber continued to ignore his call-up notice until near the end of September, when the deputy sheriff was sent to arrest him. He was taken first to Concord, and then, chained to another military prisoner, he was sent on to the guardhouse in Boston, preparatory to being shipped over to the military camp on Long Island in Boston Harbor. In a letter to elder John Whiteley recounting his misfortunes, Taber wrote: "It makes me think of dear Mother Ann. I often pray to her for protection and deliverance." He also confided to the elder his doubts about the rightness of his having consented to wear army uniform (while making clear his intention not to bear arms): "I thought if I put it on it would not make me any less a Shaker at heart." As we have seen from the story of the Quaker Cyrus Pringle and his companions, the military authorities on the island had already had experience of conscientious objectors, and so, apart from a few threats from the officers during his first few days in camp, Taber does not seem to have met with any ill-treatment during his stay; he was assigned to cleaning duties and other chores around the camp and was never asked to carry arms. The brothers and sisters at Shirley sent him letters and verses, encouraging him to stand firm and transmitting warm greetings from the spirit world. "Good spirits are with you, though *we* are not near," sang Sister Lucy Mitchel. And the community nursing sister, Lucretia M. Godfrey, wrote in concern for the young man's well-being:

Dear Horace:-

We send you a bottle of "Sweet Linament" to take if you should catch cold. A teaspoonful at once is sufficient. Put some of it on your throat. We also send a box of pills with directions for them. A flannel shirt and drawers. One pair cotton flannel shirts—a jacket—a towel—some cloths to [wrap] your throat—some pins on a cushion with my best kind love and remembrances. Also the love of all the family.

Farewell. Lucretia.

A veteran of the War of 1812, Abraham Whitney, who had subsequently joined the Shirley Shakers, sent his certificate of renunciation of a pension, "thinking it might be of use to Horace."

S. Taber. See also Anna White and Leila S. Taylor, *Shakerism, Its Meaning and Message*, p. 181.

Meanwhile, John Whiteley and the other elders at Shirley had been making efforts to get Taber another and more thorough medical examination, and toward the end of October they did succeed in obtaining his release from the army on medical grounds. During his incarceration on the island Taber's main anxiety seems to have been that he would be shipped off south to the battlefront, as Pringle and his companions had been earlier. Upon his return home, he was welcomed by the Shirley Shakers with a joyful song:

> Welcome home, dear gospel friend,
> Joyfully we greet you.
> Your conscript troubles at an end,
> How we rejoice to meet you.
> We've prayed for you each night and day
> That you might be protected
> And left to walk within the way
> That Mother has directed.

Scattered among the various Shaker communities then under Union rule there were in all some seventy men liable for the draft. Soon after federal conscription was enacted, the Shaker leader, Frederick W. Evans (1808-1893), accompanied by another elder, Benjamin Gates, had gone down to Washington to interview Lincoln and Stanton on behalf of these men. They carried with them a memorial outlining the story of their stand against war in the past and asking that in this case, too, their conscientious scruples in regard to military service or any alternatives to it be respected. In conversation with the two delegates, Lincoln paid tribute to the sturdy spirit of the Shakers when he told them: "We need regiments of just such men as you."[18]

After the administration had in fact issued a blanket exemption furloughing Shaker draftees for an indefinite period, the President and secretary of war received in August a second Shaker petition, this time sent by the elders of the South Union Community in Kentucky, which had recently been under Confederate rule. Earlier in the year the men there had refused to make the declaration of allegiance which was required in territories regained from the Confederates, on the grounds that doing so might make them liable to military service; the general in command had not insisted. The petition also mentioned the fact that the Confederate government had not attempted to force them to act against their pacifist principles. "These young men, through us their leaders," the elders wrote of the roughly twenty-five potential conscripts in their community, "have pledged

---

[18] White and Taylor, *Shakerism*, pp. 182, 183.

themselves (we do not swear) not to fight against the Confederate government. Must we be compelled to violate this pledge?" They went on to stress the losses incurred by the community through the fighting in their area, to point out the depredations and requisitioning inflicted by troops from both sides, and to affirm their loyalty to the federal government. But "now that our young men are threatened with enrollment and draft," they "are only held (some of them) by their friends, from crossing the Tennessee line" back into Confederate territory[19]—thus in exactly the opposite direction, it may be pointed out, to that taken by the Quaker, Mennonite, and Brethren objectors of the South. Finally, they pleaded for exemption on grounds of the hardship that would be caused a settlement with so many women, old people, and invalids if the men on whom they depended for their existence were taken away. An entry in a Kentucky Shaker diary of this period records: "It is now thoroughly understood at Washington that Shakers are not going to serve in any capacity in the military department; it is also understood that they will not compromise their principles by paying money for substitutes or to commute for exemption from service."[20] In December 1863, Secretary Stanton issued instructions that the Kentucky Shakers should also be included in the general exemption granted the sect.

The Shaker peace witness in the Civil War reflected in some respects an unbending absolutism which, like the Quakers', rejected such alternatives as the payment of commutation money as a bargain with evil. But, at the same time, it displayed a certain spirit of compromise, which is rather surprising at first sight. The Ohio Shakers, at least, appear to have sometimes bought war bonds. Their elders more than once advised members to "give freely to the Sanitary Committee for the benefit of the suffering soldiers." "Such things as dried fruits, jellies etc., as were not provided by the army," were suggested as suitable gifts.[21] Here their libertarian views were bal-

[19] *Ibid.*, pp. 195-99. Elder John Rankin wrote to Lincoln: "We bind the conscience of no one, but those who have conscientious scruples we would preserve. If there ever was a time in the world's history that the shedding of human blood was justifiable, that time is now. For never were lines more clearly defined. The one for—the other *against, liberty* and the *rights* of *man.* The former *must,* the latter *cannot* succeed" (quoted in Julia Neal, *By Their Fruits,* p. 192). See chaps. XIII and XIV for the experiences of the South Union Community (Ky.) at the hands of the two armies. The Kentucky Shakers, though in a slave state, had risked great unpopularity by maintaining the Society's opposition to slavery; they did, however, make one compromise in hiring slaves to work as laborers with them. They paid them (or, rather, their masters) full wages, and it is recorded that they treated the slaves well.

[20] Quoted in Melcher, *The Shaker Adventure,* 1960 edn., p. 172.

[21] Quoted in Chase, "The Early Shakers," p. 191; Andrews, *The People called Shakers,* p. 215.

anced rather uneasily beside their humanitarian impulses, while in the case of purchasing war bonds the economic connection with the actual warmaking may not have been clearly recognized.

The process which eventually transformed the Shaker society into an ever shrinking community of aged men and women was already perceptible at the time of the Civil War, though the able direction given it by leaders of the caliber of Frederick W. Evans helped to slow down the onset of decay. The Hopedale community, on the other hand, as we have seen in a previous chapter, was already in a state of dissolution before the outbreak of war. In 1861 it numbered less than 50 persons.

Ballou had been extremely critical of his co-workers in the New England nonresistant movement who, in the excitement of the anti-slavery struggle, either had abandoned pacifism altogether or, while retaining it as a purely personal creed, had vied with the most fiery abolitionist militants in calling for resistance to the encroachments of the slave power. Yet Ballou, too, shared to some degree the feelings of a Garrison or an H. C. Wright that an armed conflict over slavery between Northern and Southern sections was irrepressible, given the intransigent attitude of the latter and the failure of more than a handful in the former to adopt a nonresistant position.[22]

The war fever carried away several members of the community at Hopedale. In June 1861 one influential brother resigned, feeling that he was "not in spirit or feeling or practice or purpose a Non-resistant" and that pacifism was "impracticable under existing circumstances."[23] The overwhelming majority of those who remained at Hopedale, however, in contrast to the uncloistered section of the New England nonresistant movement, continued in their rejection of all war—a reflection of the disciplined thought that community living usually produces.[24]

In the late summer of the first year of the conflict the members unanimously adopted seven resolutions expressing their position in regard to "the great and deplorable civil war." They were almost certainly drawn up by Ballou but were issued in pamphlet form in the name of the community. The South was roundly condemned for

---

[22] Ballou, *Autobiography*, pp. 421, 422; *History of the Hopedale Community*, pp. 310-21.

[23] Ballou, *Autobiography*, p. 429.

[24] "While there are many men (and women) of many minds, there is a strong non-resistant sentiment in the community," wrote a correspondent in 1862 (*Spiritual Reformer*, III, no. 12 [April 1862], 93). Ballou's *Practical Christian* ceased publication with the issue of 14 April 1860, after a life of twenty years; the *Spiritual Reformer* for a brief while became virtually the organ of the Hopedale Community.

initiating an "organized revolutionary insurrection against the constitutional government of the Federal Union." The community's familiar position of giving qualified assent to the need for human government —"societary institutions"—in order to curb human wickedness, while at the same time reserving the right of some to choose a higher, nonviolent way of life in line with Christ's teachings, was restated:

> Though we have no moral sympathy whatever with the insurrectionists, but much with the Federal government and its loyal adherents; and though we see that the loyalists, on their own worldly plane of moral action, must conquer the rebels by overwhelming deadly force, or ignominiously abandon their constitutional government, and falsify their solemn obligations of allegiance; yet we feel none the less bound to abide with Christ on his high plane of peaceful righteousness, and thereby endeavor, however gradually, to leaven the minds of mankind with those benignant principles which alone can put an end to all disorder and violence.

They were publishing their views, they said, in order that all should know that they were both good and loyal citizens and at the same time conscientiously opposed to all participation in the fighting.[25]

Later Ballou ruefully admitted that the community's statement had had practically no effect. "It served to appease the conscience of a few devotees of an ideal."[26] Next year the Hopedale press again appeared in defense of Christian pacifism when Ballou issued a reply to the attacks of the Rev. Henry Ward Beecher (1813-1887) published in the *Independent* of 14 March 1862. "I despise this whole idea of non-resistance," that fiery crusader had said in his sermon, dubbing it "Christian nonsense." Failure to use war in self-defense was cowardly and unchristian, Beecher maintained, and, if practised, would lead to the dissolution of society, exposing it to the depredations of bandits and evildoers. Ballou's answer took the line followed in his numerous books, pamphlets, and articles of the previous two decades by distinguishing between cowardice and the readiness to suffer even death passively and between the destruction of violence and war and the noninjurious force needed to maintain order, which alone befitted a follower of Christ. "Mr. Beecher," wrote Ballou, "gives us the ethics of a plucky pugilist. . . . If this be Christianity, we may as well have no Christianity!"[27]

In August 1863 Hopedale's first (and apparently only) conscien-

---

[25] *Declaratory Resolutions of the Hopedale Community* (8 pp.).
[26] Ballou, *History of the Hopedale Community*, pp. 316, 317.
[27] Ballou, *Christian Non-Resistance defended* (20 pp.).

tious objector received notice that he had been drafted. The young man in question was John Lowell Heywood, son of one of the community's leading members, William S. Heywood. No one advocated the purchase of a substitute. Opinion was divided among members, however, whether or not young Heywood should avail himself of the law and opt to pay the $300 commutation fee, which would, of course, have to be provided by the community. A good many thought that only an absolutist stand, readiness to face even death rather than accept the state's unjustified demand for an alternative to doing right, was compatible with pacifist principles. Ballou inclined toward this position, but, as he wrote afterward, "my personal sympathies for his family in their distress overruled my sterner convictions." "I advised the payment of the money," even though in that period the sum would be used toward procuring a substitute. As a kind of compromise—rather a device to save face, it would appear, than a genuine act of protest—young Heywood, when handing over his commutation fine to the military authorities, presented them with a memorial (undoubtedly from Ballou's pen) inveighing against payment. In later years Ballou regretted what he considered the half-hearted stand the community had made in the matter, "yielding to the unprecedented pressure of events."[28] The opinions of the young man himself seem to have gone unrecorded.

The religion of Ballou's Hopedale community was an ethical Christianity, a rational religion that in its theology had much in common with the Unitarianism with which it eventually merged. The small Bible Christian Church of Philadelphia,[29] although it did not share either the communitarianism or unitarianism of Hopedale, also expressed a somewhat similar attempt to incorporate New Testament ethics into daily living. The group had arisen in England at the beginning of the nineteenth century: the date of its formal establishment was 1809. A congregation was founded at Salford in Lancashire under the leadership of a former Anglican clergyman, the Rev. William Cowherd. In 1817 a party of these Bible Christians, as they became known, emigrated to the United States and settled in Philadelphia, where they set up a church. At the time of the Civil War they numbered about 100 members; thereafter they began to decline, and the group finally died out during the first quarter of the present century.

The central tenet of the church was its belief that vegetarianism is

[28] Ballou, *Autobiography*, pp. 449-52; *History of the Hopedale Community*, pp. 317-21.
[29] See *History of the Philadelphia Bible-Christian Church*, esp. pp. 33, 61, 62.

an essential part of the Christian religion, that Christ had forbidden the taking of animal life in any form for the purpose of providing food. The step from this dogma to an avowal of nonviolence in relation to human life was an obvious, though not necessarily an inevitable, one. And the Bible Christians do indeed seem, if not at the very outset, at least fairly soon in their history, to have become adherents of nonresistance and the "Universal Brotherhood of Man." "Justice never demands," stated their annual address of June 1846, drawn up at a time of national crisis, "nor Righteousness ever requires a sword to uphold it. Injustice and cruelty alone appeal to violence. A Christian nation, with a good cause relies upon the rectitude of its course, and would rather suffer injustice than inflict cruelty."[30]

Staunchly abolitionist, the Bible Christians were placed in the same dilemma by the outbreak of the Civil War as were the Garrisonian nonresistants: they were torn between their faith in the efficacy of nonviolent means for ultimately righting wrongs and their desire to see the iniquity of slavery expunged from the land as speedily as possible. Existing materials for the history of the Bible Christian Church during the Civil War, as for its history during other periods, are extremely scanty. Several of the menfolk joined the Union army, and the church's Ladies Aid Society helped the soldiers with gifts of money and articles. However, the church officially maintained its pacifist position. We can see something of the moral problem facing these Bible Christians in the story of the English-born Henry S. Clubb (1827-1921), who joined the church soon after emigrating from Britain in 1853, became minister in charge of the Philadelphia church in the latter part of the nineteenth and during the early twentieth century, and engaged as an active worker in the post-Civil War peace movement. In accordance with the precepts of his church, Clubb always maintained his personal objection to being directly instrumental in taking human life. Therefore, out in troubled Kansas in the 1850's he had refused to carry a weapon on principle, despite the ever present danger. When war came, he continued his private testimony to nonviolence. But his abolitionist sympathies led him to volunteer for the Union army—with a secret understanding with himself, however, that he would never actually bear arms and kill a fellowman—and he rose to be a captain and assistant quartermaster. In this last capacity he was even at one time in charge of an ammunition train! He participated in a number of actions and was wounded at the bat-

[30] *The Annual Address and Minutes of the Twenty-Eighth Annual General Assembly of the Bible-Christian Church*, p. 6.

835

tle of Corinth in May 1862.[31] Clubb's ambiguous witness reflected not so much a lack of conviction as a conflict between two strongly held convictions.

The same cannot quite be said of the Civil War position of the Disciples of Christ.[32] Here the dilemma was different: it lay in the opposed attitudes to war of, on the one hand, some of the leading figures in the church, including its venerable founder, Alexander Campbell, and of the overwhelming mass of members on the other. By 1860 the Disciples numbered around 200,000. The majority were in the North, but there was a considerable Southern following. The denomination was not at that time (indeed, it never had been) a peace church in the proper sense of the word, and some of its antiwar utterances in the course of the war did not spring from strictly pacifist sentiments. The authors of the standard work on the history of the Disciples are correct in pointing out that even the "Missouri Protest," issued in September 1861 over the signatures of fourteen ministers and preachers, did not advocate pure pacifism.[33] True, not only did its authors condemn the "fratricidal" conflict then being waged as one that could find no justification in the teachings of the New Testament, but they even stated their resolution, "whatever we may think of bearing arms in extreme emergencies," to follow in the footsteps of the early Christians in an "utter refusal to do military service," should they now be called upon. Still, their condemnation of war was a qualified one; it applied, not to all, but to "almost" all wars.[34] Several of the signatories were undoubtedly pacifists; the majority were expressing, not an abstract faith in Christian nonresistance, but the temper and feelings of the numerous Disciple congregations of the border states, who felt the fratricidal nature of the conflict more keenly perhaps than their brethren deeper south or further north. The anti-

[31] For Clubb's army career, see History of the Philadelphia Bible-Christian Church, pp. 79-81. On p. 89 the following quaint passage is quoted from an obituary notice in the West Suffolk Gazette (England): "An extraordinary feature of his military career, which was an extended one, was the fact that while he was in the thick of the battles (in the Civil War) and had many narrow escapes, he never carried arms even for self defence, being conscientiously opposed to their use as a means of protection even in periods of greatest danger. Perhaps as a soldier this renders his career unique in the history of the world." After the war Clubb served for a time as a state senator in Michigan.

[32] The most recent treatment of the Disciples' Civil War record is to be found in David Edwin Harrell, Jr., Quest for a Christian America, chap. V. See also Earl Irvin West, The Search for the Ancient Order, I, 333-38.

[33] W. E. Garrison and A. T. DeGroot, The Disciples of Christ: A History, pp. 335, 422.

[34] Millennial Harbinger, 5th ser., IV, no. 10 (Oct. 1861), 583, 584; H. O. Pritchard, "Militant Pacifists: A Study of the Militant Pacifists of the Restoration Movement," World Call, XVIII, no. 3 (March 1936), 13.

war stand of the Missouri Protest stemmed chiefly, therefore, from revulsion against civil war, from a reaction against rending the garment of a church that encompassed both slaveholders and abolitionists.

The loose organization of the Disciples, which allowed great latitude to local churches, helped preserve the unity that, despite the efforts of men like Campbell, might have been shattered, as had happened in many of the Protestant churches, if a rigid policy on a subject like slavery had been imposed from outside the local congregations. Disciple leadership on the whole stood up consistently for maintaining the unity of the church, and it refrained from sweeping condemnation of the position of the other side in the conflict, which the somewhat indeterminate stand of Campbell and his associates on the antislavery issue undoubtedly made easier. And, in fact, schism, which had eventually divided many of the Protestant denominations into separate Northern and Southern branches, was finally avoided. Disciples served in large numbers on both sides, quite a few ministers becoming army chaplains, mainly with the Union army. The denomination produced one general on the Union side in the person of James A. Garfield, a future United States president. It had its fire-eaters and its sectional haters, even among the ministry, who preached the conquest and extermination of the enemy. At the same time, however, it is true that "the patriotic temperature of the Disciples was reduced by the Christian pacifism of many of their leaders."[35] It is this strand of thought in their church that we must examine in further detail here.

Alexander Campbell still remained nominally in charge of the leading church paper, the *Millennial Harbinger*, until the beginning of 1864, although his writing lacked its old vigor and increasing signs of old age began to show in the years before his death in 1866. The active role in the direction of the paper was now taken by younger men: his brother A. W. Campbell, Isaac Errett, and W. K. Pendleton, who finally succeeded him as editor in January 1864. While Campbell and his brother contributed articles expounding an uncompromising pacifism based, as earlier, on a New Testament literalism,[36] Isaac Errett went over to a pro-war position and W. K. Pendleton somewhat qualified his initial nonresistance. In July 1861, in "A Plea for Peace," Pendleton had strongly attacked the idea of a fighting Christian, set-

---

[35] Garrison and DeGroot, *The Disciples of Christ*, pp. 327, 330, 333-37. See also C. H. Hamlin, "The Disciples of Christ and the War between the States," *The Scroll*, XLI, no. 4 (Dec. 1943), 106-19.

[36] A. W. Campbell, "The Spirit of War" in the *Millennial Harbinger*, 5th ser., IV, no. 6 (June 1861), 338, 339; "Wars and Rumors of War," *ibid.*, 344-48.

ting the gospel way over against the method of war. He wrote, addressing especially those who were contemplating enlistment:

When you shoulder your musket and equip yourself with all the instruments of death, ask yourself have you the right thus to take the life of your fellow? Who gave you the right? What has your brother done that you may shoot him? Has he stolen your property? can you murder him for that! Has he differed with you about political governments? can you not part in peace?[37]

But in the following October we find Pendleton confessing that, although he had given the question much thought, he was still unable to quite make up his mind whether he was a believer in nonresistance in the abstract. "I can *conceive* of a case in which I might think it right, and a sacred duty, to offer armed resistance." On the other hand, he might, even in these circumstances, come to the conclusion that the correct response was not to resist evil.

These remarks Pendleton published in connection with the discussion (reprinted mainly from Benjamin Franklin's Cincinnati *American Christian Review*) in the October and November issues of the *Harbinger* on the topic "Should Christians go to War?"[38] Most of those who contributed to the debate belonged to the nonpacifist wing of the church. But a professor at the College of Eureka, Walnut Grove (Ill.), wrote: "I cannot censure our non-resistant brethren for warning the brotherhood against what they regard as a dark and damning sin." And, in fact, the general antiwar line of the *Millennial Harbinger* appears to have received widespread approval from many of its readers, who certainly did not share the absolute pacifism of the Campbells and some of their associates in the leadership—an approval due not only to the personal prestige of the church's founder and the influence of his gospel-centered Christianity but to the still unsevered links which united Disciples on both sides of the battle line.[39]

In Cincinnati the Disciple leader, Benjamin Franklin, in his *American Christian Review* had pursued a policy similar to that of the editors of the *Millennial Harbinger* in refusing to allow discussion of the rights and wrongs of the existing conflict in order to thus avoid exacerbating the hatreds generated by the war. His columns were open, however, as we have just seen, to the expression of opinion on the theoretical issues of pacifism. In April 1861, Franklin published a letter from John W. McGarvey, one of the signatories of the "Missouri Pro-

---

[37] *Millennial Harbinger*, 5th ser., IV, no. 7, 410.
[38] *Ibid.*, no. 10, 583-90, 593-96; no. 11, 654, 655.
[39] Harold L. Lunger, *The Political Ethics of Alexander Campbell*, pp. 259-62.

test." Whatever the cost of such an unpopular stand, wrote the latter, "I would rather, ten thousand times, be killed for refusing to fight, than to fall in battle, or to come home victorious with the blood of my brethren on my hands."[40] Franklin endorsed his stand. In the following year, as the Confederate armies approached Cincinnati and all able-bodied adult males were called up for labor in fortifying the city, Franklin himself had to face the issue of conscription for military purposes. He drew his shovel and pick and answered the call: "he was willing to and did submit to the authorities in everything except in fighting."[41]

Not long after the conclusion of hostilities, another leading Disciple, Moses E. Lard (1818-1880), who had been active during the war in church work in Kentucky, published a lengthy article in the paper he was then editing entitled "Should Christians go to War?" A convinced pacifist himself, Lard regretted in particular that Campbell's views on the subject, which he had been putting forward for many decades before the outbreak of hostilities, had been ignored by the church in practice. He went on:

> That our brethren have generally . . . inclined to the view that a Christian can, in no case, go to war with the approbation of Christ may, I believe, be truthfully said. Still they have not so strongly so inclined as to control, in all cases, their action. And then not a few have boldly taken the ground, not merely that the Christian may go to war, but that he is bound, even by Christ, in certain cases, to do so. . . . Let us have it decided, yes or no; and then let us life-long abide by this decision.

Lard understates the degree of support members of his church on both sides had given to the war effort. That he did not realize that the pacifist viewpoint was much less firmly entrenched than he imagined was due perhaps to his own strong sympathies with it: for a Chris-

---

[40] Pritchard, *World Call*, XVIII, no. 3 (March 1936), 13.

[41] Joseph Franklin and J. A. Headington, *The Life and Times of Benjamin Franklin*, pp. 286-90. However, after the war was over, Franklin appears to have retreated to some degree from his wartime pacifism. In November 1866 we find him writing as follows: "We incline strongly to the opinion that when the authorities call out men to arrest a robber or murderer, then the men called out are not responsible even though an innocent man should be arrested, or though lives should be lost in making the arrest. It may be, in like manner, that when the civil authorities call out men in war, they are responsible for all that is done in war." (Quoted in E. I. West, *The Life and Times of David Lipscomb*, p. 105.) It is possible, however, that Franklin's intention here was not to repudiate an antiwar stand but to dissociate himself from the pacifist views of Southern Disciples, who were then under attack in the church for alleged pro-Confederate sympathies (see below).

tian to undergo war service, whether as a volunteer or a conscript, was still, for him, "a wrong act." "Hence," he continued, "on this conclusion we hold that every Christian man is bound to act; and that he has no discretion in the case. Consequently, if the State command him to go to war, let him mildly and gently, but firmly and unalterably, decline. If the State arrest him and punish him, be it so; if the State even shoot him, be it so; *never let him go to war*."[42] Lard's writings[43] represent the swan song of Disciple pacifism, at least in the Northern states. They seem to have remained without echo there.

The authors of the standard Disciples' history have complained at the omission of any mention of their church in works like those of E. N. Wright or Devere Allen dealing with conscientious objection and pacifism in the Civil War.[44] There does appear to be one reference in Wright's book, however, to a Disciple who became a conscientious objector to military service, though his church affiliation cannot be established beyond doubt. Wright relates the unsuccessful attempt of Levi M. Stringer, an Alabama man, to obtain discharge from a Confederate army camp on the grounds that his state's constitution granted exemption from personal service to those ready and able to pay a commutation fee. He stated that he was a member of a "Christian Church" and was conscientiously opposed to the bearing of arms.[45] Although Wright does not appear to have recognized this, it seems almost certain that Stringer was in fact a member of one of the Southern congregations of the Disciples (or, just possibly, a member of the closely related "Christian" denomination, founded by Barton W. Stone). Apparently, nothing further is known about Stringer's fate after the court had rejected his appeal, ruling that the Confederate act of 11 October 1862 overrode individual state law and that it granted exemption only to members of the denominations enumerated in it.

Although there do not, indeed, seem to have been any Disciple conscientious objectors in the North (at least I failed to discover any), we know of a number of such cases in one borderline state—Tennessee.[46] There, on the outbreak of war, were some 15,000 Disciples,

---

[42] *Lard's Quarterly*, III, no. 3 (April 1866), 225, 226, 232-41, 243, 244.

[43] In April 1868 Lard did publish a further article expounding his pacifist views entitled "Jewish Wars as Precedents for Modern Wars" (*ibid.*, V, no. 2, 113-26) in which he set out to refute the Old Testament basis for Christian militarism. The strongly New Testament-oriented Christianity of the Disciples made it easy for Lard to demonstrate the inapplicability of ancient Jewish practice to Christian times.

[44] Garrison and DeGroot, *The Disciples of Christ*, p. 337.

[45] Wright, *Conscientious Objectors in the Civil War*, pp. 108, 109.

[46] See D. E. Harrell, Jr., "Disciples of Christ Pacifism in Nineteenth Century

mostly living in the mid-Tennessee counties. The most outstanding among the church's leaders in the state was Tolbert Fanning (1810-1874), an eloquent preacher who was active as an educationalist. Fanning shared Alexander Campbell's views on war; indeed, he went beyond the master in totally condemning the infliction of capital punishment, exercise of the franchise, and Christian participation in civil government. Even if most of the mid-Tennessee Disciples probably did not follow him on all these points, by the outset of the war he had brought round to his point of view a number of young men who were to play an important role in the development of the Southern branch of the Disciples in the postwar period: David Lipscomb (1831-1917), Elisha G. Sewell (1830-1924), and several others. Under the guidance of these men, who also inherited Fanning's conservative theology, mid-Tennessee developed into a center of the movement which eventually split away from the more liberal Disciples and from 1906 became known as the "Churches of Christ."

Fanning had opposed the Mexican War—a most unusual, indeed courageous, position for a minister in a Southern church to take. He was even more forthright in his opposition to the Civil War. His dissent from slavery had been mild, milder than his dissent from abolitionism, and his pacifism was not rooted in any special sympathy for the Union cause. He certainly shared the views expressed in the "Missouri Protest." Yet his antiwar stand was based not merely, as in that document, on Christian expediency—the desire to be guiltless of a brother's blood and to escape from complicity in a fratricidal conflict—but on a belief in the unchristian character of all "carnal warfare." And there were evidently a number of pacifists among ordinary church members in Tennessee, as well as among the Disciples' leading preachers in that state.

"Very few at first took a decided stand" against military service, however, wrote E. G. Sewell nearly a half century later.[47] Thus in the early period of the war, while the state was still under Confederate control, young Disciples opposed to fighting found themselves in the Southern forces or threatened with induction into the Confederate army. Some fled from the clutches of the recruiting officer into a neighboring state.[48]

Tennessee," *Tennessee Historical Quarterly*, XXI, no. 3 (Sept. 1962), 264, 268, 269.

[47] "Reminiscences of the Civil War. Again," *Gospel Advocate*, 18 July 1907, p. 456. The mid-war conversion to pacifism of a prominent Missouri Disciple preacher, Jacob Creath, Jr. (1799-1886), is told in E. I. West, *The Search for the Ancient Order*, II, 213, 214.

[48] E. A. Elam, *Twenty-five Years of Trust: A Life Sketch of J. M. Kidwill*, p. 50.

On 13 November 1862, therefore, "elders and evangelists" from some ten to fifteen congregations met together at Beech Grove (Williamson County) and drafted a petition to Jefferson Davis. "A large number of the members of the Churches of Jesus Christ" in mid-Tennessee take the Bible as their supreme rule in life, they told the Confederate president. The scriptures call for quiet submission to government "except when compliance with the civil law would involve a violation of the law of God"; then God must be obeyed rather than man. Although they were ready to pay lawful "tribute" and to comply with "any demands on our property or time, modified only by the first and highest obligation to obey God," they held it wrong "in any manner [to] engage in, aid, foment, or countenance the strifes, animosities and bloody conflicts" of the governments of this world. Therefore, the petition went on, the Tennessee Disciples were asking for the same measure of exemption as the Confederate Congress had recently given other nonresistant denominations in the South who maintained a similar "position of Christian separation" from "the world" (see chapter 19). If this were not granted, great distress would be caused

> . . . to those members of our churches holding these convictions. Some of them will be driven as exiles from their homes, for no political preferences, but because they dare not disobey the commandments of God. Others may be thrown into seeming opposition to your government, suffering imprisonment and such punishment as may be inflicted on them. Others still, by the pressure of circumstances, may be driven to a deeply sadder fate, the violation of all their conscientious convictions of duty to their Maker and Master.

E. G. Sewell and another preacher were selected to carry the petition to Richmond (Va.). On their way the two Disciples stopped in at the local "Conscript Department" at McMinnville to talk to the officer in charge, Colonel Wright. The colonel, after reading the petition, remarked that he wished to "respect the conscience of every man that honestly believes it is wrong for him to fight," even though he disagreed with such views. He offered to take the document to Richmond himself and try to get relief from the Confederate officials there. "And besides," he went on, "I will release any of your brethren that can give satisfaction that such is their conviction, subject to the decision of the authorities at Richmond." The two delegates gladly accepted the colonel's offer: perhaps from previous dealings they had already got to know him as their friend. He was, in fact, as good as his word. Any objectors in his hands were released, and no further attempt was made in the province to force reluctant Disciples into the Confederate army.[49]

In any case, the menace of Confederate conscription was soon replaced by even greater fear of the Union draft as the state of Tennessee, frequently fought over by the contending armies, came more thoroughly under the control of the Northern administration. A delegation of leading Disciples, therefore, now approached the Washington-appointed military governor of the state, Andrew Johnson, in an effort to assure the exemption of the church's objectors from this threat, too. Governor Johnson seemed at first a little nonplussed by their request. "Gentlemen," he eventually told them, "I think you need not be uneasy. I do not think anybody will be hurt."[50] And, in fact, the pacifists among the Tennessee Disciples were never called upon for service in the Northern armies.

II

By the outbreak of the Civil War the Disciples, especially in the North, were largely a middle-class denomination, a socially respectable group drawing members from a variety of different callings. The Adventists, with whom we must now proceed to deal, were still a church of the proletariat, whose followers were mostly farmers or mechanics, simple men of little account in the eyes of the world. They represented the remnant which survived after the debacle of the Millerite movement of the mid-forties, when the coming of the millennium foretold by its leader, William Miller, for 22 October 1844 failed to materialize. At the time of the Civil War they numbered only a few thousand.[51]

That something had been saved from the wreck of their millenarian hopes was due in no small part to the efforts over the subsequent decades of a remarkable woman, Mrs. Ellen Gould White (née Harmon;

[49] David Lipscomb, *Civil Government*, 1957 edn., pp. 128-30; E. G. Sewell, "Reminiscences of the Civil War," *Gospel Advocate*, 18 July 1907, p. 456; E. I. West, *Lipscomb*, pp. 79, 87-89. A second petition of roughly similar content was subsequently dispatched to the Union authorities. The dating of these documents, as well as of other incidents in the story, is sometimes hard to place exactly.

[50] E. G. Sewell, "Reminiscences of Civil War Times. No. 3," *Gospel Advocate* 25 July 1907, p. 473; Lipscomb, *Civil Government*, p. 132.

[51] David Mitchell (*Seventh-day Adventists: Faith in Action*, p. 293) gives the number of Seventh-Day Adventists in 1863 as 3,500. Arthur Whitefield Spalding, *Origin and History of Seventh-day Adventists*, I, 314, gives the figure as nearly 4,000. In the twentieth century the Seventh-Day Adventists have gained in numbers, so that there are now almost 1,000,000 adherents scattered throughout the world.

1827-1915), who was comparable in many ways to those other two founders of native American churches, the English-born Shaker, Ann Lee, and the Christian Scientist, Mary Baker Eddy. Mrs. White remained the mother of her church until her death at a ripe old age in 1915. Remaining to some extent in the shadow of her dominating personality, James S. White (d. 1881), her husband and a former minister in the Christian Church, was the second important figure in this period of the Adventist movement. The two of them together were chiefly responsible for grafting on to it an element that had been absent at the beginning: sabbatarianism. The observance of Saturday, the seventh day of the week, as the Sabbath, which Mrs. White probably borrowed as a result of contacts with Seventh-Day Baptists up in Maine, eventually led to a split. The majority of Adventists followed the Whites in forming a separate Seventh-Day Adventist church; a few hundred stuck by Sunday observance and in 1861 formed a rival Advent Christian Association (later Church), whose members were known as Second Adventists. The gathering together, which resulted from the schism, of what had formerly been only loosely knit congregations took place early in the Civil War.

With the Adventists we enter a religious world very different in outlook from the simple discipleship of the German peace sects, or the rational Christianity of most of the New England nonresistants, or even the restrained mysticism of the later Quakers. With their apocalyptic visions of the imminent destruction of the world, which in many ways are more reminiscent of the fiery sectaries of the Reformation era than of the nineteenth century in its more sober aspects, the Adventists nevertheless represent a not uncommon aspect of American religion, which was also revealed in the great revival movements sweeping the country from time to time. It was a religion which contained a large element of latent violence and pent-up emotionalism. Yet the Adventists at the same time shared much of the pacifist creed of the quieter nonresistant sects, and in the Civil War, as in the world wars of our century, we find most Adventists taking the conscientious objector stand.

The source of Adventist pacifism (putting aside, of course, the direct influence of readings in the New Testament), its genetic roots, lay, curiously enough, in the Garrisonian nonresistant movement of New England. This somewhat unlikely offspring (though there was perhaps something distinctly apocalyptic, millenarian, in Garrison's vision of the peaceful kingdom) has not, it would seem, been observed hitherto by historians of the nineteenth-century peace movement. Joshua V. Himes (1805-1895), who, like James S. White, was originally ordained in the Christian Church and was at one time minister of the Chardon Street Chapel in Boston, then one of Miller's leading coadjutors and Adventist editor, and later leader of the Second Adventists, had been a friend of Garrison in the forties, sharing to some extent his nonresistant and abolitionist beliefs.[52] Another prominent figure in this Adventist group, Isaac C. Wellcome (1818-1895), had been a member of the New England Non-Resistance Society; among the group's sympathizers also was none other than William Ladd's biographer, friend, and fellow pacifist, J. Hemmenway. And James S. White, co-founder with his wife of the Seventh-Day Adventists, was connected with the Non-Resistance Society, too, having contributed articles advocating nonresistance not only to the Millerite *Advent Herald*[53] but also to Ballou's *Non-Resistant and Practical Christian.*[54] In transition, the pacifism of the Non-Resistance Society lost most of its intellectual ballast and was transformed in the hands of the Adventists into a literalist otherworldly code narrowly centering on selected Biblical texts.

It was the Adventist group gathered around the paper, the *World's Crisis*, published in Boston, that first raised the problem of pacifism after the outbreak of civil war. These people were not sabbatarians; here in New England the Garrisonian influence would naturally have been stronger than out West where, at Battle Creek (Mich.), the pro-

[52] Himes's connection with the peace movement dated back to the 1830's. In 1837, for instance, he is listed on a petition (printed as an appendix in the 1916 edn. of William Ladd, *An Essay on a Congress of Nations*, p. 120) as a member of the executive committee of the moderate Massachusetts Peace Society. Barton W. Stone's Christian denomination, like the allied Campbellite Disciples of Christ, was pacifistically inclined in its early days.

[53] In its issue of 15 July 1848 (N.S., I, no. 24, 190) White published a long letter headed "Can War be a Christian Duty?" In it he denied that the Mosaic law or Old Testament practice could justify Christian participation in war of any kind, even a defensive one. Christ's injunction was to turn the other cheek. Therefore, he goes on, "we are not to use injurious or carnal weapons, in defence of our *property*, or persons." In a second contribution with the same title published on 7 Oct. 1848 (N.S., II, no. 10, 78) White contended that in practice it was never possible to determine which side in a conflict was the real aggressor—an argument obviously borrowed from the armory of the peace movement. Brother White continued his advocacy of "Christian non-Resistance" in the issue of 18 Nov. 1848 (N.S., II, no. 16, 126), when the editor J. V. Himes put an end to the discussion, claiming that it was really irrelevant to the paper's main concern of preparing for the Second Advent. Himes, though not unsympathetic, does not appear at this date to have fully shared White's radical nonresistance. In this period pacifism was probably as yet a minority position among the Adventists, although the still inchoate movement was naturally drawn by its belief in the imminent end of the world to a noncombatant position vis-à-vis earthly conflicts. See also the *Advent Herald*, N.S., II, no. 18 (2 Dec. 1848), 142. In the Civil War, White, as we shall see, was less outspoken in his advocacy of nonresistance.

[54] See the *Non-Resistant and Political Christian*, vol. IX, no. 12 (14 Oct. 1848).

ponents of the seventh day were now centered in another Adventist periodical known for short as the *Review and Herald*. The Bostonians were a rather more sophisticated group than those at Battle Creek, and the issue of the Sabbath, of course, does not figure in their arguments for pacifism.

"War has begun," announced the *World's Crisis* in its issue of 17 April 1861. "All should keep in a continued state of readiness to welcome the coming King of kings and Lord of lords." "The end of all things is at hand."[55] Within the first few weeks of the conflict, a leading brother, P. B. Morgan, had devoted a Sunday morning discourse to the problem that war presented for Adventists. Adventists were strongly antislavery, he pointed out, and all their sympathies were with the North. They lived in daily expectation of the coming end of the world and the accompanying extirpation of the wicked. Yet this act of destruction, he went on, was not to be the work of the godly —"fifth-monarchy men," he called them: "after a diligent searching of the Scriptures, and especially the New Testament—the only rule of Christian conduct, we fail to find anything that sanctions the followers of Christ in engaging in carnal warfare; but on the contrary, much that forbids it." He appealed to the spirit of Christianity rather than to any isolated text as witness to its nonresistant message. Could one conceive of one of the apostles donning an army uniform? That "would certainly be rather a sorry picture for an imaginative mind." "My life I can lay down, but I cannot fight," should be the reaction of "a God-fearing, New Testament-reading Christian" to the call to arms. Let him pray to the powers that be; yet he must "stand aloof" from the violence around him.[56] The address, which was subsequently published in pamphlet form, is superior in its freedom from excessive Biblical literalism or fantastic interpretation to the bulk of Adventist writing on the subject of war and is one of the ablest statements of the Adventist position.

During the summer of 1861, from May into August, there was considerable debate on the nonresistant issue in the columns of the *World's Crisis*. Readers sent in articles, revealing differences of opinion on a subject to which only a few in the brotherhood had probably given much thought in days of peace. "Not having settled views on the subject," wrote even the editor, Miles Grant, "we welcome everything that affords us light." Their appeal must be to the meaning of the gospels: where the Old Testament conflicts with the New,

[55] *World's Crisis*, vol. XIII, no. 6.
[56] P. B. Morgan, *The Coming Conflict*, pp. 4, 15-18, 23. See also the *World's Crisis*, XIII, no. 10 (15 May 1861), 38.

it must be the latter that settles the question. Adventists were trying to feel their way along, and he asked for readers to display charity toward those who held different opinions on "the war question." There were a few rather hesitant voices in favor of direct participation in the conflict if the call came. But most contributors to the debate would have endorsed the views of a leading Adventist, H. F. Carpenter, when he wrote: "Carnal warfare is not our calling. . . . We cannot fight, or prepare fight, or talk fight. . . . Shall the Christian exchange the 'lamb' for the 'tiger'?" "We are a nationality of ourselves," wrote Carpenter a little later. Adventists were about to inherit their own supraterrestrial kingdom: what need did they have for an earthly sword? God might use one nation of this world to punish another, as in the present war, but true Christians were prevented by Christ's express commandment from fighting for the kingdoms of the earth. There was "no true analogy" between police action, which should be bloodless and unarmed, and the suppression of rebellion by the sword. The consensus among Adventists seemed to support also the familiar nonresistant view that exercise of the franchise amounted to support of war, that nonvoting was an essential part of Christian nonconformity to the world ("many Advent people habitually abstain from voting," stated a correspondent).[57]

By the middle of August, despite the pleas of I. C. Wellcome that it would "be difficult to keep the minds of christians from the spirit of war without frequent admonition" and with plenty of material on the subject from readers still unpublished, the editor decided that the discussion had gone on long enough and should be allowed to rest awhile.[58] The World's Crisis, by now the organ of the Second Adventist minority within the movement, did continue to print isolated articles expounding nonresistance in the remaining years of war. But there was no more discussion such as had taken place during the early summer of 1861. That ardent pacifist I. C. Wellcome, however, remained active in the cause of peace throughout the war period. In 1862 he had brought out a booklet entitled *Should Christians Fight?* The first edition of 1,000 copies, despite its being almost completely ignored by the religious and general press, sold out within two months of its publication. Further editions followed: by 1864 it had gone into its fourth thousand.[59]

[57] *World's Crisis*, XIII, no. 12 (29 May 1861), 48; no. 13 (5 June 1861), 49, 50; no. 15 (19 June 1861), 57; no. 16 (26 June 1861), 61, 62; no. 20 (24 July 1861), 77.

[58] *Ibid.*, no. 23 (14 July 1861), 86.

[59] See the *World's Crisis and Second Advent Messenger*, XVII, no. 24 (25 Aug. 1863), 94; XXI, no. 18 (18 July 1865), 72, for details about the pamphlet's

Of its author and his path to pacifism we know rather more than in the case of most of the other leading Adventists of the Civil War period. Wellcome was a native of Maine, born at Minot in 1818. His parents were both Universalists, but he left this denomination, after undergoing the experience of conversion in 1840, for a brief sojourn in the Methodist Episcopal Church, only to be swept two years later into the Millerite movement. The debacle of 1844 did not serve to disillusion him. In 1850 he was ordained an Adventist preacher and was active in the ministry up and down New England and out in the Midwest; he was active, too, with his pen and wrote a number of books and pamphlets in defense of Adventism.[60] It was to a time when he was still a Methodist, in 1841, that he later dated his first inclination toward pacifism. The ferment of conversion was perhaps still active in him, unsettling the sediment of long held opinions. Hitherto, he relates, "I had taken great delight in military exercises," was extremely patriotic, and had enlisted in the militia in order to defend the "New England boundary" against possible attack from the British in the north. One day, he goes on,

> . . . while on the muster field I was much troubled about my feelings being so changed from former days. I was gloomy, thoughtful, prayerful, distressed. When the chaplain rode on to the ground and made a prayer, I was awakened to consider what prayer and christianity had to do with training and fighting with carnal weapons. I was disgusted. It was the last day I ever wore a soldier's uniform. I entered upon a careful scriptural study of that matter.

Announcing his conversion to nonresistance (and thereby evidently fixing on himself the stigma of radicalism by association with dangerous Garrisonian ideas), he "received considerable persecution from the Methodist church of which I was a member." Dissatisfaction with the reaction of stuffy and conservative elders may, indeed, have also been a factor in pushing him into the Millerite movement. Deeper studies in the scriptures, he tells us, only confirmed his intuition on the musterfield. At the end of the Civil War, nearly a half century later, we find him writing: "If my views on this are radically wrong, I can say I was never converted to Christ, nor do I know what Christianity is."[61]

---

circulation. In the twentieth century it was still being reprinted by a Mennonite publishing house.

[60] See I. C. Wellcome, *History of the Second Advent Message*, pp. 567-72, for a brief autobiographical section.

[61] *World's Crisis and S.A. Messenger*, XXI, no. 18 (18 July 1865), 72.

Wellcome's "pamphlet on war" does not read so easily today as P. B. Morgan's briefer and slighter effort of the previous year. We are put off by its strict fundamentalism, its narrow sectarianism, and the often rather fantastic interpretations placed upon prophetic passages of scripture. Adin Ballou, when he read it, penciled in the margin of his copy: "It is good and able in the main . . . [but] I think the author is too servile to mere *verbalism* and pays too little heed to fundamental principles."[62] Undoubtedly, however, it was effective in its day—and with men and women for whom prophetic visions and the sound of Armageddon were little less real than the sights and sounds of everyday.[63] The pamphlet is written in the form of a dialogue between "Demi" and "Christian." Christian is prepared to grant that, if ever a war were justified, it was the present one, engendered by the wickedness of the "rebels." He approves humanitarian work to aid the wounded and war sufferers. But his main attention is devoted to showing, by means of a wearisome array of Biblical excerpts, the entire incompatibility of the old dispensation, of the kingdoms of this world with their governments and voting and fighting, on the one hand, with Christ's kingdom, on the other, whose subjects have been forbidden to use armed violence on any pretext. "If we die for refusing to fight we may 'save our lives unto life eternal.' "

Wellcome had written his little tract with the problems of members and sympathizers of the Adventist movement who were preparing to face the issue of conscription partly in mind.[64] "Should Christians Fight?" was a question occupying many of them at that time. At first, as was the case in the other pacifist sects, some had been optimistic that the government would not resort to compulsory service and would leave the Lord's people at home in peace. As H. F. Carpenter expressed it: "The devil has too many willing subjects to be dependent upon God's servants."[65] Nevertheless, the devil's supply did begin to run out sooner than was expected. The Federal Militia Act of 17 July 1862 registered a further stage in the growing shortage of manpower in the Northern states. And now, during these summer months, with the first tentative threat of a federal draft, the problem of conscientious objection was aired in the Adventist press of both the branches into which the movement had by then divided.

[62] Ballou's copy is in the S.C.P.C.

[63] In the *World's Crisis and S.A. Messenger*, vol. XX, no. 7 (1 Nov. 1864), a correspondent writes concerning a friend: "He was a member of the Freewill Baptist Church, but they preached so much war, that he withdrew from them. I gave him what tracts I had, and among them Bro. Wellcome's work on Christian fighting, which he prizes very highly, and desires every Christian to read."

[64] Wellcome, *Should Christians Fight?*, pp. 3-5, 21, 22, 30, 31, 35-40, 45.

[65] *World's Crisis*, XIII, no. 12 (29 May 1861), 48.

849

At this date, as we have seen, there was still no adequate provision for religious objectors in the law. Even the position of the established peace sects was ambiguous, and the Adventists were a comparatively new and little-known group. I. C. Wellcome urged his brethren to refuse all compromise: if called upon in the traditional fashion to pay a fine in lieu of service, they should refuse and choose jail instead. The government, he thought, would quickly tire of keeping them fed and clothed there and, recognizing that they were acting for conscience' sake and not from any sympathy with the rebel cause, would soon send them back home.[66] In August the Advent Christian Association addressed a petition to the President asking for exemption for their people on the same footing as the Quakers or Shakers. It stated their conscientious objection to military service, expressing at the same time their complete loyalty to the government and the Union.[67] At the end of September an editorial in the World's Crisis reported: "We hear of a few of the Lord's children who have been drafted." If called up, a brother should tell the magistrate that he refused on grounds of conscience to bear arms and should suffer the penalty, if necessary.[68] And in the next issue, as if to provide the future conscript with arguments with which to underpin his case, an article was printed entitled "Fighting Christians," giving extracts from patristic writers like Tertullian, Lactantius, and Justin Martyr, who supported the pacifist position, and also telling the story of the young conscientious objector of the early church, St. Maximilian. "Are there not some in our day," wrote the author, "who will stand as firmly for the principles of Christ as did this young man? We think there may yet be an opportunity."[69]

[66] World's Crisis and S.A. Messenger, XV, no. 20 (30 July 1862), 77. The paper also strongly condemned the office of war chaplain as inconsistent with Christianity. "We can see no correspondence," stated an article entitled "War Chaplains" in its issue of 7 May (XV, no. 8, 30), "between the spirit of such ministers and that of Christ, who taught his disciples to love their enemies." See also XV, no. 14 (18 May 1862), 54.

[67] Ibid., XV, no. 22 (13 Aug. 1862), 86. The editorial, commenting on the drawing up of this petition, relates the following incident: "A good brother in the ministry was in our office a few days since, and we asked him what he should do if he was drafted? He replied, 'I shall obey the orders of my Captain.' We remarked, 'Then you can't fight.' Said he, 'I will rot in jail first.'"

[68] Ibid., vol. XVI, no. 3 (30 Sept. 1862), editorial entitled "Drafting." The paper (ibid., XVII, no. 2 [23 Sept. 1862], 8) mentions the case of a Massachusetts Adventist, Alba Bellows, who had gone into the army for three months as a volunteer. Before the expiry of his term, he became a convinced pacifist, determined not to serve again in the army if called upon.

[69] Ibid., XVI, no. 4 (7 Oct. 1862), 14. Wellcome also devotes several pages of his booklet to the early Christian attitude toward war, and the subject is dealt with again in later issues of the World's Crisis. The source is probably Clarkson or Dymond.

Of the actual experiences of Second Adventist conscientious objectors we know very little. Letters from two such objectors (and the church must certainly have produced more) were printed in the *World's Crisis*.[70] They date from the summer and autumn of 1863, that is, after the Federal Act of 3 March 1863 had made it possible to buy exemption by a fine of $300 that went toward the purchase of a substitute, if the objector did not wish to hire one directly. These letters are, indeed, of some interest as revealing the workings of conscience in ordinary men.

G. W. Gillespie, a citizen of Hartford (Conn.), was conscripted in the early summer of 1862. He writes:

> I was drafted. What to do I hardly knew for awhile. I consulted the brethren, for I wished to do *right* in the matter; that is, I did not want to resist the government unscripturally. One said it was right to go; others said, "Go, but [do] not carry the gun; dig trenches, drive [a] team, etc."; and others said, "Take no part in it whatever, but suffer the penalties, if God wills it." My shop-mates decided to help me to get a substitute. To be *certain* about *doing right*, I appealed to the Lord for wisdom and direction. Soon my mind became calm and clear. I was the Lord's . . . I resolved to take *no* part in the war, . . . the idea of hiring a man to kill *for* me would implicate *me* in the crime; so I refused to give even five cents for a substitute.

In the last resort he would have been prepared to pay the $300 commutation money allowed by law, although some in his church advised against doing so on the grounds that it would be an unjustifiable compromise. He himself felt, however, that, even if the money would be used to provide a soldier in his place, paying it was only giving Caesar his due, as Christ had taught his followers to do. In the end, a small physical defect (and, possibly, a desire on the part of the authorities to be rid of a potential problem) caused him to be rejected as medically unfit for service.

The second account comes from a John H. Dadman, of Concord (N.H.), who had apparently already made up his mind about his position well before he received his draft notice. "I am a man who fears God . . . and escheweth evil . . . so much so that I could not bear arms under any circumstances whatever," he told the examining doctor, a Methodist, at his medical examination. To the draft board he explained that, although he would refuse to buy a substitute because doing so would be equivalent to fighting himself, he did not object

[70] *Ibid.*, XVII, no. 24 (25 Aug. 1863), 96; XVIII, no. 6 (27 Oct. 1863), 22.

to paying the $300 commutation money, which he regarded in the light of a tax. The provost marshal agreed to allow him to be furloughed for eight days in order to give him time to raise the money.

Under the act of 24 February 1864 giving conditional exemption to members of pacifist denominations, the Second Adventists finally gained a recognized status as a noncombatant church. Though ready in most cases to pay the $300 tribute to Caesar, they were now required only to produce a certificate signed by a properly ordained elder or preacher, stating that "the rules and articles of faith and practice" of their church forbade participation in carnal warfare, in order to obtain exemption along with the older peace churches.[71]

The sabbatarians of Battle Creek do not at first seem to have been so concerned as the New England Adventists were with their attitude toward the war. At least, if they were, it has not been reflected in the pages of their organ, the *Review and Herald*. In the early months of the war we find the name of the leading sabbatarian, James S. White, still appearing on the publishing committee, of the *World's Crisis*, which was controlled by the Boston group. It was not until after the two groups had finally split over the Sabbath issue, and after the same threat of conscription that we have seen the Second Adventist group grappling with during the summer of 1862 had presented itself likewise to the Seventh-Day Adventists, that we find the latter taking a public stand. As a result of the threat of conscription, "many of our brethren," wrote James S. White, then editor of the *Review and Herald*, "were greatly excited, and trembled over the prospect of a draft."[72]

Discussion began in August in the *Review and Herald* with a leading article entitled "The Nation," written by White.[73] The article drew attention to the seeming contradiction between their people's strongly antislavery position and the fact that until then they had stood aside from the war. But "the requirements of war" conflicted with both the fourth commandment ("Remember the Sabbath day, to keep it holy") and the sixth ("Thou shalt not kill"). Nevertheless, White went on, if a brother were drafted, "the government assumes the responsibility of the violation of the law of God, and it would be madness to resist." Refusal to obey might end in the resister being shot by the

---

[71] See the *Gospel-Visitor*, XV, no. 3 (March 1865), 90, 91, quoting from the *World's Crisis* and *S.A. Messenger*.

[72] *Advent Review and Sabbath Herald*, XX, no. 20 (14 Oct. 1862), 159.

[73] *Ibid.*, XX, no. 11 (12 Aug. 1862), 84. See also J. N. Loughborough, *Rise and Progress of the Seventh-Day Adventists*, pp. 243, 244; A. W. Spalding, *Origin and History of Seventh-day Adventists*, I, 322, 323.

military: this "goes too far, we think, in taking the responsibility of suicide."

Two points are worth pointing out in connection with White's arguments. In the first place, he gives prominence to the sabbatarian objection to military service that became of primary importance to the sect in the wars of the twentieth century. Once in the army, it was feared, the Seventh-Day Adventist would not be allowed to observe Saturday as his day of rest and prayer. (Were he permitted to do so, and were this to become the only grounds of his objection, the reasons for refusing to serve would naturally disappear.) Secondly, White implied not only that the disproportionately heavy cost of a refusal to fight, together with any guilt involved in breaking God's laws resting on the shoulders of the government, made it inexpedient to resist the draft but that the strength of the government's case in the midst of a struggle against "the most hellish rebellion since that of Satan and his angels" was a factor to be taken into consideration in reaching a decision on how to act.

From August until the end of October, week after week, the controversy over White's article filled many columns of the *Review and Herald*, and a large amount of further correspondence remained unpublished. Leading brethren wrote in their opinions. The immediacy of the issue facing brethren of draft age gave an added urgency to the discussion which White's advocacy of compromise had generated. His views aroused the opposition, in particular, of a group of pacifist militants: "those who have been most highly tinctured with the fanaticism growing out of extreme non-resistance," wrote White, "are generally the most clamorous against our article." He had never given any encouragement to voluntary enlistment, he explained to his readers: Seventh-Day Adventists "would make poor soldiers, unless they first lost the spirit of truth." His article was aimed primarily at checking the extreme antidraft position which had been growing among them.[74]

The general impression created by White's conclusions seems to have been one of confusion, and even of dismay among some brethren.[75] Brother White's views carried weight but, of course, did not

[74] *Review and Herald*, XX, no. 15 (9 Sept. 1862), 118. See also no. 16 (16 Sept. 1862), 124. Loughborough (*Rise and Progress of the Seventh-Day Adventists*, p. 244) states that the leaders of the radical pacifist group in the brotherhood, who spoke of "dying before they would be placed in the army where they would be obliged to break the Sabbath," abandoned the sabbatarian position a few years later.

[75] See, e.g., the *Review and Herald*, XX, no. 17 (23 Sept. 1862), 136, for comments on White's article sent in by readers. One puzzled Adventist, A. G. Carter of Rubicon (Wisc.), writes: "I acknowledge that I am a right-out-and-out coward

have final authority among them. Besides, it was not quite clear from his article precisely what course he did advise drafted Adventists to take, although those who interpreted him as recommending submission even to the point of bearing arms would appear to have been correct. Tempers at times began to get frayed, so that we find one writer, R. F. Cottrell, commencing his contribution on "Non-resistance" with the words: "There is no necessity for brethren to go to war with each other on *peace principles.*" For him, "the only question was whether it was [our] duty to decline serving in the army at all hazards, even of life itself. It is by no means certain that a man's life would be taken because he declined fighting for conscience sake." If death were the only alternative to submission, however, he thought that he, too, would opt with Brother White for the latter, at least until God should grant further guidance.[76] For Brother Henry E. Carver, on the other hand, such conduct smacked of apostasy: "untenable and dangerous ground," he called it. Despite his abomination of the Southern slaveholders' rebellion, he had "for years had a deeply-settled conviction (whether wrong or not) that under no circumstances was it justifiable in a follower of the Lamb to use carnal weapons to take the lives of his fellow-men." If an act was wrong, should it not be shunned at all cost, even that of martyrdom? Surely the individual was not entitled to transfer to the government responsibility before God for his own actions?[77] J. M. Waggoner, a leading minister in Burlington (Mich.), was another brother who, though respectful toward White's views (while confessing himself rather startled by them at first), nevertheless supported the pacifist position. He opposed the idea of paying commutation money in lieu of personal service, preferring to "trust in God for the consequences" of a refusal to fight. Exemption on such terms was "not only doubtful in principle, but inefficient as a practical measure of relief. Not over one in one hundred, if as many, could avail themselves of its provisions, while the poor, the great mass of our brethren, whose consciences are as tender and as valuable as those of the rich, stand precisely where they would stand

---

when I am required to go into the carnal war, and if the same law that was to be binding on us that was on the Jews, I would surely show my heels. See Deut. XX, 8. 'And the officers shall speak further unto the people and say, What man is there that is fearful and faint-hearted, let him go and return unto his house, lest his brethren's heart faint as well as his heart.' But let me have a place in that war whose weapons are not carnal, and I will stick as close as a brother."

[76] *Review and Herald*, XX, no. 20 (14 Oct. 1862), 158.

[77] *Ibid.*, no. 21 (21 Oct. 1862), 166, 167.

without it." Thus it would create a rift in the brotherhood between the well-to-do minority and the rest.[78]

Many contributors, however, expressed in varying degrees their approval of participation in the struggle that was being waged in their earthly homeland. There was the enthusiastic pro-war position of Joseph Clarke, who, pleading with the editor that Seventh-Day Adventists should be allowed to become combatants, contributed two articles with the titles "The War! The War!" and "The Sword vs. Fanaticism," and who wanted "to see treason receive its just deserts." "I have had my fancy full of Gideons and Jephthahs, and fighting Davids, and loyal Barzillais," he writes; "I have thought of brave Joshua, and the mighty men of war that arose to deliver the Israel of God, from time to time." He had dreamed, his mind full of heroes of Old Testament times, of the day "when a regiment of Sabbath-keepers would strike this rebellion a staggering blow." He itched to be able to get at the Southern traitors and had only scorn for those many brethren who were "whining lest they might be drafted." Were not "the military powers of earthly governments" instituted by God for our protection? Was not the time to refuse their summons when they were acting unrighteously, and not in the present crusade against Confederate wickedness?[79]

Several prominent ministers supported a pro-war position, though in more restrained terms than the excitable Clarke, who had evidently been deeply stirred by seeming parallels between the apocalyptic happenings related in scripture and the events of his own day. J. N. Loughborough (1832-1924), who had joined the Adventist movement back in the forties and was now among the most respected leaders of its sabbatarian wing, implied that even in an unjust cause the guilt lay with the state and not with the conscript, quoting as his authority John the Baptist's admonition to the Roman soldiers, instruments of an alien domination, to be content with their wages.[80] D. T. Bourdeau could not understand why "civilized warfare, or capital punishment, are against the sixth commandment," since God had clearly given his sanction to war in the Old Testament as well as to the extirpation of the wicked. Brethren, however, should avoid being drafted, if possible, he said, because of the obstacles to a strict observance of the Sabbath that existed in the army.[81] A brother from New York state, likewise an ardent believer in the righteousness of the Union cause who was unconvinced that Seventh-Day Adventists must become conscientious objectors from a belief that war as such

[78] Ibid., no. 17 (23 Sept. 1862), 132, 133.   [79] Ibid., no. 17, 134, 135.
[80] Ibid., no. 18 (30 Sept. 1862), 140.   [81] Ibid., no. 20, 154.

was incompatible with their calling as Christians, nevertheless went into considerable detail in describing the moral dangers for his people of life in an army camp. They would, he was convinced, be forced to work, drill, and fight on the Sabbath. Although it might be "rash and uncalled for" in the circumstances to resist the draft "to the last extremity," he felt it best to stand aside as long as possible, so that time might be given them to wait for God to reveal his will for them in the matter.[82] Brother B. F. Snook in an article on "The War and Our Duty," confessing his conversion from long-held nonresistant views ("an untenable extreme") to belief in the compatibility of a just war, such as the present one, with Christian principles, believed that God had already spoken. "Dear brethren," he wrote, "let us be united and not resist our government in its struggle for existence. Our neighbors and friends have nearly all gone; and if God allows the lot to fall upon us, let us go and fight in his name."

Toward the end of the discussion, after he had published selected opinions both pro and con from the correspondence and articles which flowed in to him, James S. White restated his views on the attitude his church should adopt toward the coming draft. This was, in fact, not merely a restatement but a slight modification of the position taken in his "Nation" article, although it was still not without considerable ambiguity. He reproved what he designated extreme points of view on either side: both those who wished to give unqualified support to the war effort and the brethren who called for unconditional nonresistance. "We cannot see how God can be glorified by his loyal people taking up arms" was, however, his final summing up. If the whole nation had followed God's will, some other path than war would have been found to resolve the country's problems. Seventh-Day Adventists he called upon to wage a war whose weapons were not carnal.

> We did say in case of a military draft, it would be madness to resist. And certainly, no true disciple of non-resistance would resist a military draft. . . . We have advised no man to go to war. We have struck at that fanaticism which grows out of extreme non-resistance, and have labored to lead our people to seek the Lord and trust in him for deliverance. How this can and will come, we have no light at present.[83]

And so the debate petered out in this way rather inconclusively. Behind the editorial desk of James White, however, we may detect

82 *Ibid.*, no. 21, 163. See also no. 22 (28 Aug. 1862), 173, 174.
83 *Ibid.*, no. 20, 159; no. 21, 167.

856

the figure of his wife, Mrs. Ellen G. White. She had not participated in the discussions in the *Review and Herald,* perhaps because it would not have appeared seemly to the Brethren for a woman to do so. More important was the fact of Ellen White's prophetic role in the sect: a prophetess does not confide her utterances to the columns of a newspaper even when it is edited by her husband. Several months before the attack on Fort Sumter, Mrs. White had had a vision of the coming bloody conflict between the states.[84] The war, when it came, she viewed as a judgment of God on wickedness on both sides; yet her intense hatred of slavery, offspring of the abolitionist connections of her circle in earlier days, aroused in her warm sympathy for the struggle being waged by the North. She was, then, no neutral. But, at the same time, she saw the end of the kingdoms of this world at hand. "Prophecy shows us that the great day of God is right upon us," she wrote in 1863. God's people, her people, must—in spite of their hatred of the satanic iniquity of slavery—hold themselves apart from the armed struggle and wait quietly and peacefully for the second coming.

After the indecisive debate in the *Review and Herald,* that we have dealt with above, and before conscription actually touched any of the brethren directly, Mrs. White, it seems, reached certainty on the stand that the brotherhood should collectively take in reply to the army's call whenever it should come. "I was shown," she wrote, "that God's people, who are His peculiar treasure, cannot engage in this perplexing war, for it is opposed to every principle of their faith." In the armed forces it would be impossible for them to follow the voice of conscience if, as would inevitably happen, the commands of the officers directed them otherwise. "There would be a continual violation of conscience." However, she went on to criticize those who had acted impetuously in proclaiming their willingness to suffer prison and death rather than submit to the draft. Instead, "those who feel that in the fear of God they cannot conscientiously engage in this war, will be very quiet, and when interrogated will simply state what they are obliged to say in order to answer the inquirer." They must make quite clear, too, their abhorrence of the rebellion.[85]

Thus the Seventh-Day Adventists, even those who at first appeared

[84] Spalding, *Origin and History of Seventh-day Adventists,* I, 315, 316.

[85] Mrs. E. G. White, *Testimonies for the Church,* 3rd edn., I, 356-58, 360-62. She notes: "There are a few in the ranks of Sabbath-keepers who sympathize with the slave-holder. When they embraced the truth, they did not leave behind them all the errors they should have left" (p. 358). The Seventh-Day Adventists were in fact confined almost exclusively at this time to the Northern states, although some adherents were to be found in the border regions.

857

to hesitate or rejected outright the nonresistant viewpoint, closed their ranks. Through a human agency God had spoken, dissipating their doubts. True, there was little likelihood of universal peace ever being established among the nations of this world; but in the short space before the establishment of a new dispensation on earth, God's children, it was now clear, must refrain from shedding human blood and desecrating the Sabbath. To court martyrdom was wrong. To avoid martyrdom, on the other hand, action was needed; the government must be informed of the reasons for their refusal to bear arms, and advantage taken of the legal provision for exemption provided by successive federal conscription acts.

Although membership in a peace church, as we have seen, was not a requirement of the act of March 1863, the act of February 1864 demanded such membership from applicants as a prerequisite for exemption as conscientious objectors. However, opting out of service still remained possible even after February for those prepared to pay, although only enrollment as a conscientious objector brought the privilege of having the money devoted to humanitarian purposes or of choosing, as an alternative, the army medical service or work with freedmen. Content that, simply by paying, their scruples concerning the taking of human life and work on their Sabbath were respected, Seventh-Day Adventists, with their eye more on the letter than on the spirit of the law, did not at first insist on their recognition as a noncombatant denomination within the meaning of the act. Poorer members were helped out with the necessary money by the church as a whole, while some evidently accepted induction into the army, when drafted, hoping nevertheless to be able to take advantage of the recent act and be assigned noncombatant duties.[86] But on 4 July Congress passed an amending act which, although it did not alter in any way the provisions made in February for conscientious objectors, did abolish the general privilege of escaping military service through commutation.

The brotherhood now became alarmed that their men, since they did not belong to a recognized nonresistant denomination, would be drafted into combatant service in the army, where they would find themselves forced to break both the fourth and the sixth commandments. As one of them wrote: "Not having had a long existence as a distinct people, and our organization having but recently been perfected, our sentiments are not yet extensively known." So it came about that on 2 August the three members of their general conference

---

[86] See, e.g., the *Review and Herald*, vol. XXIV, no. 6 (5 July 1864), for reference to a brother who had been drafted and was then with the Union forces in Virginia.

858

executive committee drew up a "Statement of Principles" for presentation to the government of Michigan, in whose state the church's headquarters at Battle Creek was located. There is no trace in the document, the first public statement of the group's noncombatancy, of any of the doubts or hesitations or divergencies in view that had revealed themselves only two years earlier in the debates in the *Review and Herald*. One of the three authors was, indeed, none other than J. N. Loughborough, who in those discussions had championed the case for full participation in the present contest. But now, according to the "Statement," the church was "unanimous in their views" that war is contrary to Christian teachings; in fact, "they have ever been conscientiously opposed to bearing arms." For the performance of military duties, the "Statement" went on, would prevent them from an exact observance of the fourth and the sixth commandments; neither would their Saturdays be free from labor nor their hands from the stain of blood. "Our practice," the authors continued, "has uniformly been consistent with these principles. Hence our people have not felt free to enlist into the service. In none of our denominational publications have we advocated or encouraged the practice of bearing arms."[87]

Similar statements were presented soon afterward to the governors of the other states where Seventh-Day Adventists were to be found in any numbers: Wisconsin, Illinois, and Pennsylvania. The object of these approaches to the state authorities was to gain confirmation at the highest level locally—that is, in their home states where their views and practices ought to have been best known—that they were, in truth, a people whose principles forbade them to fight, who were therefore entitled to the exemption granted several such denominations in the act of the previous February. All but the governor of Illinois, who does not appear to have given an answer, replied that they believed that members of the church were, indeed, covered by the recent legislation.[88] And even from Illinois a certain Colonel Thomas J. Turner could be quoted as having said that, in his view, the Seventh-Day Adventists were "as truly noncombatants as the Society of Friends."[89]

And so, armed with the "Statement of Principles" of 2 August and the supporting letter of the governor of Michigan, which had been printed as a pamphlet under the title of *The Draft* together with

[87] *The Views of Seventh-Day Adventists relative to bearing Arms, as brought before the Governors of Several States*, . . . (1865), pp. 6, 7 (quoted in Francis McLellan Wilcox, *Seventh-Day Adventists in Time of War*, p. 58).
[88] *The Views* . . . , pp. 8-14.
[89] Wilcox, *Seventh-Day Adventists*, p. 60.

several other documents,[90] a leading minister, John N. Andrews, was sent from Battle Creek to Washington around the end of August to plead his church's claims to noncombatant status. In the capital Andrews had a friendly talk with the provost marshal general, Brigadier-General James B. Fry, who assured him that the act intended exemption to apply not merely to Quakers or members of the older peace sects but to all denominations whose members were precluded from bearing arms, and that he would issue orders to that effect. Andrews was further advised that, in addition to producing confirmation of membership in good standing and, preferably, too, of consistency of conduct from neighbors, conscripted Adventists should present a copy of *The Draft* to the district marshal "as showing the position of our people."[91]

Andrews had succeeded in his mission. Henceforward, until conscription ended, there was no major conflict between Seventh-Day Adventists and the military authorities. Some continued to pay the commutation fee. But attempts to create a fund from which to pay the fines of poorer members broke down—perhaps because the sect at that time did not possess enough well-to-do members to make this a practicable plan. Anyhow, we find most of their draftees entering the army and opting there for hospital or freedmen work, according to the provisions of the February act. Trouble occasionally resulted, however, from unsympathetic officers attempting to make the men perform duties which went against their conscience.[92] At the very end of the war, at their third annual session in May 1865, the church once again confirmed its noncombatant stand. "While we . . . cheerfully render to Caesar the things which the Scriptures show to be his," the conference stated, "we are compelled to decline all participation in acts of war and bloodshed as being inconsistent with the duties enjoined upon us by our divine Master toward our enemies and toward all mankind."[93]

The noncombatancy which the Seventh-Day Adventists had achieved, not without much soul-searching and spiritual travail, was a doctrine of multiple roots. In the first place, these Adventists

[90] *The Draft*, which had the alternative title of *The Views of Seventh-Day Adventists relative to bearing Arms, together with the Opinion of the Governor of Michigan, and a Portion of the Enrollment Law*, was a 9-page pamphlet published at Battle Creek. It is reprinted verbatim on pp. 1-8 of *The Views* . . . (1865).

[91] *The Views* . . . , pp. 14-19; *Review and Herald*, XXIV, no. 16 (13 Sept. 1864), 124; Wilcox, *Seventh-Day Adventists*, pp. 62, 83, 84; Spalding, *Origin and History*, I, 323, 324, 407.

[92] Spalding, *Origin and History*, I, 324.

[93] Quoted in Wilcox, *Seventh-Day Adventists*, p. 24.

shared with the other pacifist groups we have been considering the belief that participation in war, the shedding of human blood for whatever cause, was contrary to the Christian faith. Loving one's enemies and killing them in battle seemed to them a contradiction impossible to resolve. The gospels forbade the use of any weapon but the sword of the spirit. Resist not evil, turn the other cheek—these were Christ's clear commands. "Could this scripture be obeyed on the battlefield?" asked a writer in the *Review and Herald*.[94] Even here, however, the Adventists put much greater emphasis on the Old Testament commandment, "Thou shalt not kill," than most of the other peace sects of that day did. Moreover, in general, their discussions of the war issue and the draft were heavily interlaced not only with Biblical citations but with fantastic interpretations of them based on prophecy. Secondly, refusal to bear arms stemmed in the case of these Adventists from a deeply ingrained otherworldliness, a desire for nonconformity to this world even more intensely felt than that which underlay, for instance, the pacifism of the Mennonites. What, indeed, had God's people to do with the fighting of this world that was about to be destroyed and replaced by another where they would come into their own? And, thirdly, we get the sabbatarian objection, an element that had basically nothing in common with pacifism. Unwillingness to risk the desecration of their Sabbath as a result of military orders was not, of course, their sole reason for refusing army service: Seventh-Day Adventist conscientious objectors insisted on their status as nonresistants even after induction into the army. Still, especially among some of their leaders, as we have seen, the question of Sabbath-keeping figured prominently in their thought.

There were also in existence at the time of the Civil War several smaller sects which, along with the Seventh-Day Adventists, represented the extreme fundamentalist and millenarian wing of the pacifist movement. The Christadelphians were one such group, a comparatively new and small denomination then numbering on this continent probably less than 1,000 members altogether. Their founder, Dr. John Thomas (1805-1871), had come from England to the United States in the 1840's and soon, breaking with orthodox Protestantism, had begun to organize small groups of followers in the United States, Canada, and Great Britain. An objection to bearing arms was among the tenets of the sect from its prewar days, one which it maintained rigorously throughout the war. It was not any belief in the possi-

---

[94] Quoted *ibid.*, p. 38 (from an article by George W. Amadon, one of the framers of the Statement of Principles of 2 August 1864, in the *Review and Herald*, 7 March 1865).

bility of achieving universal peace, however, that underlay their non-combatancy, for, like the Mennonites or the Adventists, they believed that wars were an essential ingredient of life in this sinful world, a necessary means for effecting God's judgments at a certain level of existence. Their pacifism stemmed rather from their wish to preserve themselves from the stain of sin during their life on earth. Their leader, Dr. Thomas, for instance, had proposed a resolution at a meeting of the London Peace Society, which he attended in February 1849, that, although "a Bible Christian must not fight in the absence of the captain of his salvation," war between nations was both essential to God's plan ("an institution of divine appointment for the bruising to death of the serpent power") and valuable as an instrument for defending liberty and truth against despotism and superstition. Since no existing nation was truly Christian, it was not merely "visionary, utopian and impracticable" to attempt to bring about international peace but actually harmful, since lack of military defense would expose the more democratic countries to conquest by tyrannical states like Russia. It is not surprising that in such a gathering as this the resolution was not passed.[95] Its conditional pacifism, with its hint of millenarian warrings in the future in the name of an avenging Savior, when Christ would call his followers to help destroy the wicked, is typical of the Christadelphian position.

The outbreak of war between the states seemingly caught some of the Christadelphian brethren unprepared as to the stand they should take if called upon to serve in an earthly army. In a letter dated 17 April 1861 which he sent to Dr. Thomas's paper, *Herald of the Kingdom and Age to Come*, a correspondent from Norfolk (Va.) asked as his state was about to secede from the Union: "Which of the two alternatives shall we accept,—take up arms in defence of our homes and firesides, or allow ourselves to be imprisoned by the state authorities during the contest?" He was clear about the wrongness of Christians fighting in wars of aggression, but concerning a war to protect home and hearth, as the present conflict evidently appeared to him, he was less certain.

Meanwhile, other letters came pouring in to the editor. A Massachusetts brother, for instance, was convinced that Christians could not fight under any circumstances. But what should the brethren do now: stay at home and wait to be put in jail probably, or move out of reach of any recruiting officer? In an article he entitled, somewhat ungrammatically, "Let Satan Fight their own Battles," which appeared in the June issue, Dr. Thomas attempted to answer his followers' questions

[95] Robert Roberts, *Dr. Thomas: His Life & Work*, 1884 edn., pp. 275-78.

862

and put their fears at rest. "Be not enrolled" was his advice to men of military age; "go to prison rather. The authorities will perhaps soon get tired of feeding men in prison at the public expense." It was useless to try to flee—unless possibly to Canada, if the situation should become unbearable. In the meantime, mindful that they were citizens of Christ's kingdom and not of any of the kingdoms of this world, they were still required to obey the commands of the latter wherever such laws did not conflict with Christ's laws. In September, Dr. Thomas gave much prominence in his journal to an article by a leading minister of his church, Dr. H. Grattan Guiness, which stressed that participation in earthly warfare had been decisively forbidden the Christian disciple in the gospels. In his article the author gave a clear exposition of the Christian nonresistant position, arguing that all governments of the world in that day were organized for war.[96]

In the South, where there were Christadelphians in Richmond, Lunenburg, and King William County, Virginia, and in Jefferson County, Mississippi, men of draft age in the church were granted exemption by the Confederate government—as a result of Dr. Thomas's intervention on their behalf. The journey that he undertook to Virginia for this purpose in the first summer of war attested to Thomas's bravery and initiative. Although he held British citizenship, his long residence in the North and his association with ideas unpopular in the Confederate states exposed him to possible arrest and imprisonment. During his stay in Virginia he did not hesitate to voice his religious opposition to the war effort of both sides and to urge the Southern brethren to refuse military service as their Northern coreligionists were going to do.

"All the states and their people," he told a Christadelphian meeting in the Confederate capital at Richmond, "are guilty, and all are under condemnation." At Zion in King William County he was asked pointblank whether, in his opinion, the call to service should be obeyed. Non-Christians—by which he meant, of course, those who did not belong to the Christadelphian church—should comply, he replied. "But those under law to Christ should not, and according to the law, need not go to the war. Let Satan do his own fighting; there is no obligation resting on the saints to lend a hand to help him in distress." On another occasion, he explained his position as follows:

> We do not say that Methodists, Presbyterians, Baptists, and such like should not bear arms. Of these, we say, carry as many arms as you please; blow out one another's brains to your hearts' content, and

[96] *Herald of the Kingdom and Age to Come*, XI, no. 6 (June 1861), 137-40; no. 9 (Sept. 1861), 193-201.

when you are exhausted you will cease. It is all the same whether they die thus, or in their beds; not being Christians they are a law to themselves, and heirs of capture and destruction every way.

Thomas's attitude, with its somewhat nonchalant disregard of the calamities that might befall non-Christadelphians as a result of the war, may appear unsympathetic. But there could be no doubt of the courage of this Englishman as he moved from congregation to congregation in what was virtually enemy territory, exhorting the brethren to remain firm in their resistance to any attempt at conscripting them.

In some places it was uphill work. He found that among the younger brethren there were even some who had volunteered for service in the Confederate army. "They feared being drafted," he reported, "and preferred to volunteer that they might select their company." "They were too easily scared," in his opinion, "for the draft did not ensue." They must resign from service forthwith, he told them. But his advice appears to have gone unheeded, for, he adds sadly, "they professed to wish to do so, but how is profession to be believed, when the means of redemption are disregarded?" Indeed, anti-Union feeling was strong in certain congregations: Thomas speaks of the "violence" against the North displayed by some among the "saints."

In August, while visiting Lunenburg (Va.) where he held consultations with the local brethren shortly before his return north, Thomas proposed that draftees from the church should claim exemption as licensed preachers of the gospel. "Convinced that this was correct reasoning, brother Ellis applied to the Court, and obtained exemption from all military duty"; the rest determined to follow his example when their turn came.[97]

Indeed, the consideration which continued to be shown Southern brethren by the Confederate authorities[98] was cited a few years later in a petition presented by Christadelphians to the Northern Con-

[97] *Ibid.*, XI, no. 10 (Oct. 1861), 229, 230, 234, 235, 237. Could the Christadelphians by any chance have been the mysterious "Nazarenes" mentioned in Southern conscription acts?

[98] In the 3rd edn. (1954) of Robert Roberts's life of Dr. Thomas, pp. 219-21, we find details of negotiations with the Confederate military authorities, conducted after Thomas's return in February 1863 from nearly a year in England, on behalf of ten of the brethren in Henderson Co. (Ky.) who had been drafted during Southern occupation of that area. The doctor claimed that all were in fact ministers of religion and therefore entitled by law to exemption. The commanding officer, on being told that they belonged to one congregation, exclaimed in surprise: "Ten ministers in one church? That's the most extraordinary church I ever heard of." Nevertheless, the men were excused from service—a tribute both to Dr. Thomas's powers of persuasion and to the tolerant spirit of the Confederate officer.

gress. The act of 4 July 1864 had seemed to jeopardize the concession, contained in previous legislation, that allowed them to avoid the draft by payment of commutation money (the same alarm, we have seen, had been displayed by the Seventh-Day Adventists). "They belong," said the author of the petition (who was certainly Dr. Thomas) of his coreligionists, "to 'a very small remnant' of that sect, which, in the days of the apostles, was 'everywhere spoken against,' because of its testimony" against wickedness in high places. "The brethren of Christ," the petition went on, "positively refuse, under any circumstances whatever, to shed the blood of their fellowmen in the service of any of the sin-powers of the world. The Divine Word teaches them, that wars and fightings come of men's lusts. The brethren of Christ have no sympathy with such conflicts; and ask of the world-rulers, to be kind enough to let them alone."

This petition seems to have originated in the anxiety concerning the draft shown by the brethren in Ogle County (Ill.), who appealed to Dr. Thomas to help them. They were determined to suffer death rather than fight, they told him, but were unsure how their resolve would fare if it came to a test and they were refused exemption. According to Dr. Thomas's account,

I told them that the Federal law exempted all who belonged to a denomination conscientiously opposed to bearing arms on condition of paying $300, finding a substitute or serving in the hospitals. . . . They feared that in the browbeating presence of a Provost-Marshal's Court they might not be able to stand successively against the taunts and ridicule which were sure to be brought against them. They wished, therefore, that I would write something that they could put into Court on the ground of their claim to exemption according to the law. It would be necessary to give the name a denominational appellative; that being so denominated, they might have wherewithal to answer the inquisitors. This seemed the most difficult part of the affair, though not altogether insurmountable.

His choice of the name "Brethren in Christ," however, he thought might seem too long for the authorities, who apparently preferred single-word nomenclature. And so he devised the title "Christadelphians" for this purpose. In addition, Dr. Thomas drew up a formula to be used as a certificate of membership for those drafted, stating his people's loyalty to the government, the religious nature of their scruples against bearing arms, and their right to exemption under the existing law. The Christadelphians, as a result, remained un-

865

touched by the draft for the remainder of the war.[99] Thus, as with the River Brethren of Pennsylvania a little earlier in the struggle, it was the threat of military conscription in the Civil War that led the Christadelphians to take an official name and organize more compactly.

The noncombatancy of religious groups like the Seventh-Day Adventists, the Christadelphians, or the even more minute group of Plymouth Brethren (for whose experiences in the Civil War there do not appear to be any surviving sources), may be described as forming an extreme "right-wing" element in the pacifist movement. It was an element that, with the appearance of new sects of a similar kind later in the nineteenth and in this century, was numerically well represented among American conscientious objectors of the two world wars. It contained a strong strain of violence, yet a violence that was projected into the near or more distant future. Its pacifism was absolute in this present age, but, not unlike the political pacifism of Marxists refusing to participate in a capitalist war, it was conditioned by the eventuality of the need to use armed force in order to bring in a new and higher order. These millenarian nonresistants when drafted have usually, though by no means always (as the case of the twentieth-century Jehovah's Witnesses has shown), been content with noncombatant duties within the army. Keeping strictly apart from politics and the affairs of this world, they yet represent a proletarian element—especially if we contrast them with the intellectual pacifists of the peace societies, the middle-class Quakers, or the solid farmers of the German peace sects and the communitarian groups. They have more in common perhaps with the German Anabaptists of the 1530's than have those who have come into the Anabaptist inheritance.

[99] Roberts, *Dr. Thomas*, 1884 edn., pp. 282-85; Wright, *Conscientious Objectors in the Civil War*, pp. 31, 32, 89, 90. See also *Bulletin No. 4* (July 1937) of the Christadelphian Military Affairs Committee.

866

Part V

Pacifism between the Civil War and the First World War

"The friends of peace are to be judged by something more than testimonies in Friends' meetings. It is their attitude towards the questions of the hour, which are of the hour because in the world's progress they are ripe."

—From an address by William Lloyd Garrison, Jr., to the 1895 annual meeting of the Universal Peace Union at Mystic (Conn.), printed as *The Things that Make for Peace*.

Chapter 21

The Quaker Peace Testimony, 1865-1914

Almost half a century elapsed between Appomattox and the firing of the guns of August 1914. Although the war in Europe appeared to have its roots in events remote from the North American continent, it involved the United States as an active combatant within three years of its outbreak. The First World War ultimately proved to be a landmark in American history, almost as much as it did in the history of the rest of the world. Within the narrower limits of the peace movement, too, we find that 1914 marked for both its pacifist and nonpacifist wings a turning point; the war years saw the creation of a new movement which was to evolve new ideas and new techniques of action in response to a vastly changed situation.

Yet the pacifism of the post-1914 period was, for all the differences that clearly existed between the two periods, embedded in the past. The half-century which preceded 1914 is particularly significant, because it was during these years that the changes that eventually produced these new ideas and new techniques were taking place within the whole movement. But when we actually come to relate the story of absolute pacifism (which is the particular theme of this book) during this period, it is difficult to avoid a certain sense of frustration. Pacifism appears to have been at a standstill: older groups, like the Society of Friends or the German-speaking sects (which were becoming increasingly English-speaking), seemed as a whole relatively unconcerned with the issue of peace, while new organizations based on a pacifist platform, such as the Universal Peace Union, were singularly ineffective. No outstanding leader—or even any person of middling stature—arose to challenge the surrounding apathy of an age of materialism.

The sources for many aspects of the story are meager—or submerged in a vast sea of reports and periodical literature dealing primarily with other topics. The most important elements, we begin to feel, are perhaps to be sought elsewhere: in the social transformation which was bringing Mennonites and Dunkers and their like out of their rural isolation, in the theological revolution within the American Society of Friends that was subtly undermining Quaker pacifism in large sections of the Society, in new ideologies that had as yet little or no contact

869

with religious pacifism, like international socialism with its ideal of the brotherhood of man or anarchism with its goal of maximum freedom for all human beings. These forces—and others—were at work beneath the surface, but their effect was not to show itself properly until after the events of August 1914 engulfed the nations in war.

During the preceding half-century the Society of Friends remained the most active and concerned element within the pacifist movement. The Society was divided theologically and organizationally, but, despite the inroads that the Civil War had made in the ranks of its younger members in particular, the overwhelming weight of opinion within it still stood solidly behind the traditional Quaker peace testimony. No detailed study has been made of this period in the history of Quaker pacifism, and generalizations based on examination of only part of the evidence can only be provisional.

The Quaker press at this time was for a small denomination fairly large. The Hicksites had their *Friends' Intelligencer*, and from 1873 to 1882 they published, also in Philadelphia, a second periodical entitled the *Journal*. The Orthodox branch was represented as earlier by the Philadelphia *Friend* and the more evangelical *Friends' Review*. This paper merged in 1894 with the *Christian Worker*, founded in 1871 as an organ of the pastoral element which was growing increasingly strong among Friends, to become the *American Friend* under the editorship of the young Rufus M. Jones (1863-1948). In addition, there were other ephemeral and less important periodicals published in the Quaker spirit.

From a perusal of the Quaker press it would seem that, after the turmoil of the Civil War years had begun to subside, the Society's interest in questions of peace and war declined considerably. True, articles on Christian pacifism, as well as interpretations of world events from a Quaker angle and support for the efforts on behalf of international peace being made by the wider peace movement, did appear from time to time. There is rather more space devoted to peace in the Orthodox *Friend* than in the other papers.

A distinct change is noticeable toward the end of the last century and in the early years of the present one—largely owing to the efforts of some outstanding figures in the new generation of Friends then coming to maturity, men like Rufus Jones, Dr. Richard H. Thomas (1854-1904), Elbert Russell (1871-1951), and others. It cannot be said that at this time the Quaker press reflected any striking innovations in the theoretical groundwork of pacifism. But its columns were devoted to peace issues more often than in the previous decades. The discussion was more intelligent, better informed, and, above all, wider in scope; it included more frequent articles on arbitration and the various economic and political aspects of pacifism (in addition to pacifism's strictly religious aspects), as well as protests against the growing militarism and expansionism displayed by the United States.

A second method by which the Quakers continued to express their pacifism was the time-honored one of issuing public statements giving their views on the subject. These were frequently styled "addresses," sometimes "appeals" or "testimonies" or some similar title, and were usually issued in the name of a yearly meeting, which published them in pamphlet or leaflet form. Their contents followed a fairly uniform pattern. In the first place, they restated briefly the Christian case for pacifism, quoting a cloud of witnesses from the history of early Christianity, drawn almost invariably from the writings of Jonathan Dymond. Secondly, these documents usually went on to discuss, from the Quaker viewpoint, a number of topics connected with current affairs. They pleaded both the desirability and the practicability of disarmament, including unilateral disarmament, and preached the folly, even on the material plane, of piling up armaments indefinitely. They called for the adoption by their government of the principle of international arbitration to replace the final arbitrament of war. They protested against various manifestations of the militarist spirit in national life: the activities of the veterans associated with the Grand Army of the Republic, the pomp connected with Memorial Day, the militarization of youth through boys' brigades, and drilling in schools and colleges, etc. During the last two decades or so before 1914, these arguments tended to increase in proportion to the space devoted to discussion of the principles of religious pacifism. However, although the yearly meetings of the various branches of the Society were considerably more busy than the other peace sects in producing peace literature of this kind, it does not appear to have figured with them as a primary concern in comparison with such activities as education, foreign missions and Sunday schools, Indian work, temperance, prison reform, and even, in some quarters, revivalism.

In the postbellum period the main product of organized Quaker activity for peace was the founding in 1867 of the Peace Association of Friends in America. This association resulted from the initiative of a number of Orthodox yearly meetings—Baltimore, Indiana, Ohio, and Western—which were among those that came together eventually to form the strongly evangelical Five Years' Meeting. They were joined a little later as sponsors of the Peace Association by other Orthodox yearly meetings with an evangelical bent, including Iowa, Kansas, New York, and North Carolina. Their war experiences had brought about a revival of Friends' active concern for peace in the immediate postwar period. A rather inward-looking testimony was given a new outreach.[1] That it was the Orthodox branch that took the lead now was understandable, not only because the Hicksites had been more deeply divided on the war issue but because the evangelical sympathies of the Orthodox prompted them to use the new techniques of publicity that had been evolved by the evangelical movement for the furtherance of both their religious and philanthropic aims. That later some of the evangelical yearly meetings of Orthodox origin in the West came very largely to abandon pacifism in actual fact—insofar, that is, as individual members were concerned, and not the official doctrine in the book of discipline—is due to the peculiar developments in religious life in this area. This matter will be dealt with a little later in this chapter.

The Peace Association grew out of two peace conferences initiated by Ohio Yearly Meeting and held at Baltimore in November 1866 and at Richmond (Ind.) in March 1867.[2] Only Orthodox yearly meetings were represented (the delegates formed *ad hoc* peace committees of their respective meetings), although one non-Quaker sympathizer attended the second gathering. At the first conference two problems in particular were wrestled with. The number of Friends, especially in the West, who had abandoned pacifism during the war was evidently worrying concerned members (even if some of the figures for such delinquency were much exaggerated). And so the sponsors of the conference asked delegates to consider in the first place: "In what manner can we promote with the greatest efficiency amongst our own members, a more enlightened understanding of the Gospel of Christ as a gospel of Peace?" For the time being, no more startling recommendation was adopted than the printing and circulation in 20,000 copies among members of the Society of an address on peace, which was drafted by a committee of the conference. The second problem discussed by the gathering centered on methods by which Quaker peace principles could be spread among other denominations, and among the clergy in particular.

The dissemination of Quaker pacifism among non-Quakers was also one of the chief subjects of discussion at the Richmond conference early in the next year. And the methods suggested to achieve that end included writing memorials to Congress urging that body to promote the settlement of international disputes by peaceful means (a congress of nations and an international court were favored by some dele-

---

[1] See the *Advocate of Peace*, 1867, p. 283, for comments in the American Peace Society's annual report on this renewed peace activity among Quakers.

[2] *American Friend*, I (1867), no. 1, 5-10; no. 4, 88-97.

gates), allocation of money by yearly meetings to finance permanent committees for peace, and collaboration in peace work with "other Christian Professors" (not excluding Unitarians, some delegates thought, while others strongly dissented). Several delegates, it was reported, "spoke of the necessity of being willing to labor and patiently wait the Lord's time for the result, of the slowness of the progress that peace principles could reasonably be expected to make in the world." And, indeed, the time proved premature for the setting up of standing peace committees, which were to be a vital element in twentieth-century Quaker work on behalf of peace. But Charles F. Coffin's remark that "we must keep up a *continuance* of effort" found general agreement among the assembled Friends. And even if all the conference's proposals for further activities did not bear immediate fruit, it was out of this widespread desire not to allow the enthusiasm generated by the two conferences to dissipate without result that the Peace Association of Friends in America was born.

The prime mover in getting the Association started was Daniel Hill of New Vienna (Ohio), who acted as its secretary until his death in 1899.[3] A 4-page explanatory leaflet which Hill issued, probably in the 1880's, had this to say on its origins: "After the close of the late terrible rebellion in this country, the horrors of war were so freshly and vividly brought to light that many Friends were led to believe that the time had fully come for more energetic and persistent efforts to be put forth to try to prevent wars in the future." It defined the Association's objective as the advocacy in a Christian spirit of "the brotherhood of mankind" and of the idea "that we can not injure another without injuring ourselves." The Association believed "that war is unchristian, inhuman and unnecessary" and that it could be banished from human society if men so wished.[4]

At first, at any rate, Hill and his fellow workers were able to achieve a considerable amount in the way of publishing books, pamphlets, and leaflets. But the Association aspired to be more than a tract society, and we find it also organizing a limited number of public meetings and lecture tours by its agents and setting up prizes for essays on peace topics. Beginning in October 1870 there appeared in New Vienna under Hill's editorship the Association's own monthly journal, the *Messenger of Peace*, which continued publication in one form or another until 1943, although in much reduced format during the last three decades

---

[3] His successor was Allen D. Hole, who remained secretary until 1927. Although the Association finally ceased activities only in the 1930's, it had long been superseded in importance by other Quaker bodies concerned with work for peace.

[4] The leaflet is undated and is in the S.C.P.C. The statement quoted appears also in some of the Association's publications.

and more of its existence.[5] Ohio remained the center of the Association's activities as long as Daniel Hill was alive.

Most of the classics of the peace movement of the first half of the century, British and American, were reprinted by the Association, often in abridged form. So we find in their list of publications such staples of the older peace movement as Dr. David Bogue's lecture *On Universal Peace*, Thomas Chalmers's *Thoughts on Universal Peace*, Whelpley's *Letters* to Governor Strong, Sumner's oration on *The True Grandeur of Nations*, Thomas Thrush's *Letter addressed to the King*, the works of Elihu Burritt, as well, of course as the essays of Jonathan Dymond on war and Joseph John Guerney's little tract on the same subject.[6] There were peace pamphlets for children—including stories from the pen of that stalwart of New England nonresistance, Henry C. Wright—and anthologies of writings exemplifying the horrors of war and commending the virtues of peace. There were biographies of leading pacifists and of other outstanding peace workers. By no means all the Association's publications were reprints of older works, though it is not without significance that the most important items were not new. We find Hill himself issuing an exposition of the scriptural testimony against war and compiling a slim booklet giving the evidence why Christians might not fight with carnal weapons. Among the more interesting of the Association's original publications was a small volume by Josiah W. Leeds (1841-1908) entitled *The Primitive Christians' Estimate of War and Self-Defense*, which consisted mainly of short biographies of the early church fathers with copious extracts from their writings against war and military service.

The Association's main effort, however, was concentrated on producing the *Messenger of Peace*. Until it temporarily ceased separate publication in 1894, the paper had a circulation of between three and four

---

[5] Hill remained editor until the end of 1894, transferring the paper in August 1887 from New Vienna to Richmond (Ind.). In January 1890 it began to appear under the title *Christian Arbitrator and Messenger of Peace* as the organ of the Christian Arbitration and Peace Society with its headquarters in Philadelphia. From Hill's resignation until April 1900, the paper was not published separately, appearing only as a section of the *American Friend*. From 1900 the *Messenger* was edited in succession by Anna Thomas (1900-1905), H. Lavinia Bailey (1905-1913), and Allen D. Hole (1913-1923). In 1869 the evangelical wing of Orthodox Quakerism had a second and short-lived peace organ in the Chicago *Herald of Peace*, edited by W. E. Hathaway and Willet Dorland.

[6] A personal link with antebellum pacifism was provided by the New England Congregationalist John Hemmenway, William Ladd's friend and biographer and his associate in the earlier peace movement. Hemmenway frequently contributed to the *Messenger of Peace*. As he wrote in its issue of July 1872 (II, no. 10, 146): "Though I am not of Quaker profession and religion, but a Puritan, yet, on *War*, I am, and for thirty years have been, a *Quaker of the Quakers*."

874

thousand; after its revival in 1900 the number was probably less. Copies were distributed free to the clergy, as well as to colleges and libraries expressing an interest in receiving them. The paper certainly dealt with a wide range of topics connected with peace, although there was little discussion on the economic aspects of war and little or no original thinking on pacifist theory. During the nineteenth century, at least, the paper was conducted in a strongly evangelical spirit with emphasis on the Quaker pacifist case against war. Articles printed were usually didactic in tone and were not perhaps on a very high level, but a fairly consistent degree of competence was maintained. The public declarations against war of both Friends and of non-Quaker peace groups were given prominence in the columns of the *Messenger*, as were reports of peace meetings held in different parts of the country. The historical heritage of Christian pacifism was emphasized, and stories and extracts illustrating this theme were frequently published. International arbitration was constantly advocated as a solution for disputes between countries, and we find the annual Lake Mohonk Conferences on International Arbitration, organized by the Quaker Albert K. Smiley (1828-1912), well reported in the *Messenger*. More space came to be devoted to news of the European peace movement and to comment on world affairs from a Quaker point of view. From 1900 onward protests against the increasingly militaristic spirit being displayed in the domestic life and foreign policy of the United States and against the nation's growing expenditure on armaments grew stronger. This last factor gave rise, too, to a revived interest in the problem of paying taxes to a government preparing for war.

The *Messenger of Peace*, at least if we compare its circulation with the number of Quakers in the country, appears to have enjoyed rather meager support within the Society, especially considering that some of its readers and subscribers were non-Friends. The activities of the Peace Association were in part subsidized, as we have seen, by a number of Orthodox yearly meetings. But the initiative and drive to carry on the work was supplied by a small group of enthusiastic pacifists, who, despite endeavors stretching over half a century, evidently failed to inspire the bulk of members with their ardor for peace. In the twentieth century the Association and its journal played only a minor role in the Quaker quest for peace. For some three decades after its foundation, however, the Association—in spite of its somewhat narrow approach to the problems of peace, stemming from the doctrinaire evangelicalism of its sponsors and its simplified view of affairs that often bordered on the naive—fulfilled a useful function in keeping the issue of pacifism before a Society whose attention was focused for the most part on other, and what then seemed to many Quakers more urgent, problems.

In the period between the Civil War and the coming of world war, their environment, indeed, presented the Quakers with much fewer direct challenges to their pacifist beliefs than the preceding centuries had done. Although in the immediate postwar period we hear of small distraints being levied on Friends in Pennsylvania and some other states for nonpayment of the militia taxes which had replaced the old annual muster, this matter was of only very minor and passing concern to Friends. Federal conscription had come to an end, and the state militias were a dead letter. Toward the end of the century the imposition of compulsory military drill in some schools and colleges and the militarization of youth implied in the training given in the boys' brigade aroused Friends' attention. Quakers were also busy early in the new century in seeing that provision for religious objectors was included in legislation for mobilization of a national militia in the event of war. But all this activity was of only peripheral importance. During this period the decision whether the Quaker testimony against participation in war was in fact meaningful enough for them personally to face some sacrifice on its behalf confronted few members of the Society of Friends.

Nevertheless, a personal and direct witness for peace was sometimes called for even at this time. There was once again, for instance, the old problem of war pensions in the case of Friends who had served in the armed forces during the Civil War. Some of these Quaker veterans may have been converts to the Society in the years succeeding the war; others were members who had joined the army and who had subsequently, for this infraction of the discipline, been received back into the Society only after confession of error or after remission of this penalty by an indulgent meeting. In some cases, these men drew their pension apparently without feeling that they were compromising their Society's peace testimony. In many other cases, however, they refused to do so, even though there may have been no formal ruling against it in the discipline. We read—to give only one example—of an Iowa Friend, a small farmer who had been severely crippled in action and was therefore eligible to draw an annual amount of $30, consistently refusing to accept the money over a period of some forty years, even though he was himself in straitened circumstances.[7]

Occasionally we hear of a Quaker manufacturer or businessman curtailing his profits in order to avoid involvement with war preparations. The Lukens Iron and Steel Company of Coatesville (Pa.), a Quaker

---

[7] *Friend* (London), XLV, no. 52 (29 Dec. 1905), 860.

876

firm, received toward the end of the last century a lucrative order from the United States Navy for 10,000 tons of "protective armor plate." Its president, Dr. Charles Huston, turned down this and subsequent government orders connected with armaments on the grounds that they clashed with his Quaker pacifism. "War," he explained, "only decides which of the combatants has the superior strength, and it is more expensive than arbitration, as well as destructive to life and property."[8] Scrupulous conduct in business had long been a characteristic of the Quaker commercial ethos; the same scrupulousness was manifested by many Friends then, as at other times in their history, in seeing that their day-to-day activities conformed to the Society's testimonies on peace and other related issues.

The Quaker of military age no longer had to face the issue of conscription, at least for the time being. But all male adult Friends had to come to a decision whether to exercise their democratic right to the franchise or whether to refrain on principle because of a possible connection with the warmaking power. They might have to decide, too, whether political office of any kind was compatible with Quaker pacifism. And considerations of this sort might lead on to reflections on the general character of civil government and its relation to the peace testimony of Friends. A not uncommon feeling continued among some Friends in the postbellum period that voting and officeholding were incompatible with a consistent pacifism. On the whole, however, a majority of Quakers of the period would probably have agreed with the opinion expressed in the New York *Friend*, an organ of the liberal Hicksites, that "the higher executive offices are the only ones in which direct participation in military matters cannot readily be avoided" and that, therefore, taking part in elections and acceptance of local office and of seats in state legislatures represented, at least in peacetime, a commendable outlet for Friends' energies.[9]

Increased participation in public life marks the history of the Society from this time onward. True, the element of coercion in all existing government continued to trouble many Friends, as it had done earlier. On the other hand, for a small—but growing—number it presented little difficulty since, while retaining membership in, and usually a warm regard for, the Society, they had come to disagree with its pacifism, considering this as a non-essential component in its beliefs. Thus, for them, entry into political life was hedged around by few reservations or doubts such as afflicted many other Friends who were also drawn to politics. For the latter, however, the positive good that

[8] Fernando G. Cartland, *Southern Heroes*, pp. 16, 17.
[9] *Friend* (New York), I, no. 4 (April 1866), 48, 49.

877

might result from public service outbalanced in the final analysis the possible risk of involvement in the use of coercive force—and this might be dealt with, when the problem arose directly, by a strategic withdrawal from association with the agents of coercion. Government, they believed, was capable of being purged of the element of injurious force, as it had been in Quaker Pennsylvania, if enough citizens in a democracy so wished; meanwhile, such government, even if it rested on a foundation of force, was essential for civilized life.

A committee of Philadelphia (Hicksite) Yearly Meeting in 1871 went further than many of its fellow members could go when it stated in a minute (which in fact was withdrawn on account of the opposition it met in the meeting):

> Bad as war is, it is not the worst of evils. Anarchy, riot and mob violence, in which innocent women and children indiscriminately suffer, are even worse. Hence the necessity in our large cities of a police, sustained by military force, to check these in their early stages, to which arrangement the inhabitants are indebted for their quiet and security.[10]

But views not far removed from this in their conditional justification of violent coercion in the work of government are to be found not infrequently among responsible Friends of this period. This may be seen, for instance, in the following rather involved entry under the heading "War," which appears in the book of discipline issued by the Illinois (Hicksite) Yearly Meeting in 1878. It states:

> While we recognize the need of law and order, which in the present condition of mankind can perhaps only be maintained by governments resting on human authority, we believe that in the degree that we come individually under the government of that principle of justice and unselfish regard for the welfare of others, that lies at the foundation of the Christian faith, we shall render governments sustained by force, unnecessary, and build up through self-restraint, the government of Righteousness in the earth.[11]

The degree of coercive action that was permissible within the framework of civil government, the amount of approval that might be given to the application of injurious force by properly appointed officers of the law, had always been a debatable question for Quakers, as for other pacifists and supporters of the peace movement.

---

[10] *Autobiography of Benjamin Hallowell*, p. 334.
[11] *Rules of Discipline and Advices of Illinois Yearly Meeting of Friends* (1878), p. 11.

But with the Quakers, at any rate, the problem of war had been more clear-cut. The discipline forbade members to participate in any activities connected with war, and, although it was not always easy to know where the line should be drawn, especially in actual wartime, the intent was clear. True, insofar as many of the younger men who had entered military service were never disciplined in some sections of the Society and other Friends not liable to the draft who had given support in one way or another to the war effort were also untouched, the Civil War may be said to have marked a relaxation of the discipline in regard to war. But, despite individual deviations, the general consensus of feeling in the Society still regarded the peace testimony as an essential element in the Quaker faith.

It was in the post-Civil War period that a very significant trend began, especially in certain yearly meetings, away from the traditional Quaker attitude toward war. Its stages are not at all easy to trace, however, since during these years the peace issue had retreated into the background of Friends' concerns: there was no conscription to test the strength of pacifism within the various branches of Quakerism. The factors that brought about this change were often only indirectly linked with Quaker thinking on peace and war, though their influence was no less effective for being remote.

It was in the more newly established Western yearly meetings of the Orthodox branch that we find the first large-scale retreat from Quaker pacifism, a transformation that occurred slowly and almost imperceptibly and without the conscious knowledge of those involved. The full dimensions of the change were only observable in this century, when the small numbers of conscientious objectors supplied by these meetings in the two world wars revealed the extent of the loss of ground which pacifism had suffered there.

Various factors were at work. The most important of these was the strong influence exercised by the religious revivals of the 1870's and 1880's on Friends in the West, bringing in a host of new recruits to the Society from other denominations. "The converts who joined Quakerism accepted it for other reasons than its peace views. In fact many of them never really accepted" Quaker pacifism, even if this still remained the official doctrine of their yearly meetings. And no issue presented itself before 1914 to force them to clarify their own individual stand. For this trend in Quakerism the most important object appeared to be to bring Christ to the people as their Savior, to win souls for salvation. Mission work, not pacifism, was their major concern. Not merely in their theology but also in their whole mode of worship these Quakers drew closer to Protestant fundamentalism and away from the more

879

traditional type of Quakerism, and even away from some groups that, like them, had adopted the pastoral system.

A second factor contributing to the decline of pacifism among large groups of Western Friends lay in the deepening suspicion with which some Friends in the West regarded Eastern Quakerism, a suspicion that had originated in the isolation, both physical and intellectual, of pioneer life (an isolation that had also been a prime factor leading to the adoption of the pastoral system). Now, for many Western Friends, Friends in the East appeared to have become increasingly tainted with theological liberalism, and the peace testimony, still maintained as a central concern in this area, suffered through guilt by association. In the twentieth century the fundamentalist majorities in the Orthodox yearly meetings of Ohio, Kansas, and Oregon withdrew from their association with other pastoral Friends in the Five Years' Meeting, and within these newly independent yearly meetings pacifism was to wither away almost entirely.[12]

A special study has been made by Cecil B. Currey of the development of the peace testimony among the Friends of Kansas Yearly Meeting, which was set up in 1872—in the period, that is, of strong revivalist influence. In the following year the meeting established a peace committee that under successive changes of name continued to lead a rather vegetating existence. In 1875 the committee reported: "The membership of this Yearly Meeting, as a mass—are not well informed in the Gospel matter of peace." But little seems to have been done at this time, beyond the printing and distribution of a small number of tracts and the preaching by pastors of an occasional peace sermon, to deepen members' understanding of Quaker peace principles. "Friends came to feel," Currey writes of the period from the late seventies on, "that the testimony of pacifism would develop in new converts without special instruction. . . . This doctrine did not seem to be considered an integral part of Quaker teaching. The exposition of pacifism was included in the Yearly Meeting *Discipline* and was available to all who wished to learn of it but the viewpoint was no longer stressed." There was some revival of interest in the subject of peace from the mid-1890's on. "Many of our ministers," it was remarked, "make the subject of Peace a prominent feature in their sermons." In 1911 we find Kansas Yearly Meeting petitioning President Taft in support of international arbitration. But, despite these signs of a growing concern with the practical implementation of Quaker pacifism on the

---

[12] See *Report of American Commissions of the Conference of All Friends* (1920): *Report of Commission V*, pp. 13-16; Cecil B. Currey, "Quaker Revivalism and the Peace Testimony," *Friends Journal*, vol. 8, no. 4 (15 Feb. 1962), pp. 75-77.

part of a small number of Kansas Friends, it is clear that on the membership as a whole the peace testimony had only a slight hold.[13]

Currey sums up well the position in which Quaker pacifism stood among the fundamentalist yearly meetings of the West during the early years of this century when he writes:

Proclamation of the peace testimony was acceptable only if directed toward those already accepting it. For those whose conscience dictated otherwise, pacifism was irrelevant. Closed circles of believers were created who could discuss the tenet among themselves but who were frowned upon when they advocated it for others. Growing numbers of Evangelicals regarded the doctrine as superfluous.[14]

The younger generation, when a major war eventually involved the country in 1917, were in many cases insufficiently grounded or largely unacquainted from their home and meeting background with the Quaker pacifist position. The proportion of young men who entered the army from these yearly meetings, though considerable in the First World War, reached an even higher figure in the Second. In this section of the Quaker community the tide had turned against pacifism, seemingly irrevocably.

But the tide was also on the turn in other and less extreme sections of the Society. The process was advanced farther perhaps among pastoral Friends of the former frontier areas, where the same factors were at work as we have seen in the case of the meetings captured by the fundamentalism of the revivals, but the same process was also taking place among more traditional Orthodox groups as well as in Hicksite meetings. The prime cause of this defection from pacifism seems to be twofold. In the first place, there was, as we have seen above, a lessening interest in the peace testimony during the long years of peace and of freedom from conscription, an absence of challenge in this area, a concentration of effort on other "causes." Secondly, the abandonment (except among Wilburite Conservatives) of disownment as a means of enforcing the discipline,[15] combined with increasing

[13] Currey, "Quaker Pacifism in Kansas, 1833-1945," M.Sc. thesis, Fort Hays Kansas State College, pp. 41-49; "Quakers in 'Bleeding' Kansas," *BFHA*, vol. 50, no. 2 (Autumn 1961), pp. 100, 101.

[14] Currey, *Friends Journal*, 15 Feb. 1962, p. 76.

[15] Among the Protestant churches as a whole, a decline in membership standards can be observed in the second half of the nineteenth century. This, as in the case of the Quakers, was part result, part cause of the influx of large numbers of new members who were not properly initiated into the beliefs and practices of the denomination they had joined. After small groups of conservative and rigorist old believers had broken away on one pretext or another, the churches emerged with

integration of rural as well as urban Quakers into the surrounding society (which was not, of course, pacifist), made it possible for members to reject pacifism as a personal faith while adhering to a denomination which still maintained pacifism as a tenet of its collective witness.

The extent of this change in the attitude of Friends to war must not, however, be exaggerated. Up to 1914 and beyond that date, pacifism still held the allegiance of a large number of the most active and concerned Quakers in the West[16] as in the East, if we except the fundamentalist yearly meetings dealt with above. Even here the remnant remained faithful, and we find in this section of the Quaker community a man like Cyrus W. Harvey, a birthright Friend from Indiana and a Civil War veteran turned pacifist (see earlier), becoming a leading figure among Kansas Friends and a fervent upholder of the peace testimony. His pacifism, as we see it set forth in a small tract which he published in 1901 under the title of *The Prince of Peace or the Bible on Non-Resistance and War*, represented the narrowly scriptural approach, which by this date was already being leavened among some Quaker groups in the East by a concern for wider issues connected with peace. Harvey might have been old-fashioned, but his approach was forthright. "How can a Bible reader," he asks, "read all this, in faith, believing his own Bible, and find a place in his own conscience for war or self-defense?"[17]

Nevertheless, as a more significant figure for the future than Harvey, we may take a Quaker of the type of Joseph Gurney ("Uncle Joe") Cannon (1836-1926), also a birthright Friend from the Midwest, who was elected to Congress in 1872 and eventually reached the position of Speaker of the House of Representatives, which he held for many years. Although he remained a loyal member of the Society of Friends until his death at the age of 90, Cannon was avowedly not a pacifist and in politics belonged to the more reactionary wing of the Republican Party.[18] Cannon has his successor in our day in Richard M. Nixon; there have been few from this section of the Society, however, who have followed in Harvey's footsteps.

If the peace testimony was beginning to wither in some parts of the

---

their discipline relaxed and the traditional dogmas diluted. In large sections of the Quaker community pacifism, along with the plain dress and the plain speech, was among the items eventually discarded.

[16] Indeed, pastoral meetings in the West have produced quite a few of the most able and devoted exponents of Quaker pacifism in the present century.

[17] Cyrus W. Harvey, *The Prince of Peace*, p. 15.

[18] See L. White Busbey (ed.), *Uncle Joe Cannon*.

Society of Friends, renewal was slowly coming about elsewhere among Quakers from the 1890's onward. This process was operative mainly, though by no means exclusively, in the Orthodox and Hicksite meetings of the East.[19] Its chief characteristic lay in an increased awareness of the need to extend the boundaries of the traditional peace witness from a simple exposition of New Testament nonresistance to consideration of possible causes of war in the economic and social order, as well as in the political sphere, and of methods for their eradication. Analysis had still not gone very deep: international arbitration continued to be generally put forward as a kind of cure-all,[20] and there was little consciousness as yet of the need for any radical changes in the existing social structure. Although the Quakers' work for peace remained firmly anchored in their total rejection of the war method and any kind of social revolutionary approach to peace was quite alien to even the more politically liberal Friends, the emphasis nevertheless was gradually changing.

We can see this—to give only a few examples—in the work of such Friends as Benjamin F. Trueblood (1847-1916), Hannah J. (Mrs. Moses) Bailey, or William I. Hull. All three were active in the peace movement from around the end of the last century, and all three, though convinced pacifists themselves, collaborated closely with individuals and organizations which were not based on an absolute pacifist platform—a contrast to the narrowly sectarian position which we have seen the Society taking up earlier in relation to peace societies outside the Quaker enclosure.

Trueblood was secretary of the American Peace Society from 1892 to 1915 and editor of its journal, the *Advocate of Peace*. An ardent proponent of international arbitration, he represented the older and more conservative school of peace men. Nevertheless, in his international politics he was a unilateralist, urging on his country that to lead the way in disarmament, though clearly entailing risks, was the

[19] The Conservative or Wilburite Friends, who were considerably fewer in numbers than the other two main groups, maintained strict adherence to the peace testimony as part of their general traditionalism. The conservative nature of this witness is illustrated by the persistence into the twentieth century in the sections on war of their books of disciplines of items which had long lost all relevance to the existing situation. In the *Discipline* of their Iowa Y. M. published in 1914 (pp. 87-90), for instance, we still find advices inserted against paying taxes to buy drums and military colors, against buying or selling prize goods or being concerned in any way with men-of-war, and against paying militia fines. These advices were long out of date, but style and content in several cases differed little, if at all, from the eighteenth-century wording.

[20] In the books of discipline of some Hicksite yearly meetings early in this century were included items urging Friends to support arbitration as a method of settling international disputes.

only moral policy, the only one worthy of a Christian nation and one that had (he believed) every chance of success. "No nation," we find him saying in an essay written in 1895, "would think of attacking us if we had not one single war-ship, not one coast-defense gun."[21] For all the shortcomings of his type of peace action, his attitude, with its attempt to investigate in association with other men of goodwill how "the Christian law of love" could be made effective short of the millennium, represented a definite advance on the ingrown witness of the previous generations—a return, in fact, to the American Quaker tradition that had been cut short as a result of the fall of Quaker rule in Pennsylvania.

Hannah J. Bailey (1887-1923) was another Quaker pacifist who went out from the closed Quaker circle, and from her home at Winthrop Center in Maine she carried on the work of the Peace and Arbitration Department of the National Women's Christian Temperance Union. Pacifism for her was but a part of what she called, in the first number of the periodical, the *Pacific Banner*, which she edited between 1889 and 1895, "the grand work of moral reform": it was one issue alongside prison reform and temperance and Sabbath observance. This approach was in the style of the great antebellum reform movement, but now Quakers like Mrs. Bailey, instead of being looked at askance by large numbers in the Society as their predecessors had been, gained widespread support among their fellow members.

The active life of William I. Hull (1868-1939), the well-known Quaker historian and educationalist, lasted well into the period after 1914. He may be taken here as a representative of a school of thought that would gain increased support in our time among Friends on both sides of the Atlantic: he is typical of those personal pacifists who were prepared to grant a conditional sanction to the use of armed force in support of international law. "Peace *and* Justice," Hull wrote in 1909, were the aims of the contemporary peace movement, in which he hoped Quakers would take their part alongside other peace workers who did not share their unconditional pacifism. The immediate goals of the movement he defined as "International Courts of Law, the Limitation of Armaments and their sole use as a genuine International Police Force." Hull rejected any analogy between an international police force and national armies. Not merely was the source of their authority completely different, but the police force would be controlled by a power above the contestants, while a national army was the instrument of one side only in the quarrel. An international force, moreover, would act only to carry out the verdict of an impartial court.

---

[21] Benjamin F. Trueblood, *The Development of the Peace Idea and Other Essays*, p. 92.

Soldiers, of course, are sometimes used in aid of the police to enforce law and order within the jurisdiction of the soldiers' own country. At such times, they form in no true sense of the word an *army*; but are an auxiliary of the *police* force, subject to the same sovereignty and law to which those who threaten violence are subject; and even when acting in this police capacity, they are rightfully ... carefully circumscribed by the civil authority.

Further proof to Hull of the fundamental difference in character between police action and the employment of national armies lay in the fact that in war guilty and innocent suffer alike and indiscriminately, in contrast to the punishment of the guilty party in proportion to his offense, which, along with the prevention of crime before it happens, was the object of force used in support of law. Moreover, whereas the aim of army training was to kill as many of the enemy as possible, a police force was either unarmed or only lightly armed for self-defense, being "made to feel that homicide is absolutely the last resort."

How fallacious [Hull writes] is the analogy drawn between armaments and a true police system, may be readily seen when one compares the present system of national armaments with a system under which all the world's armies and navies, vastly reduced in size, would form part of an international force, and would act against any member of the family of nations only when it received a warrant for so doing from an international court, before which the delinquent member had been legally and impartially tried and sentenced. Such an armament would indeed be a genuine police force both for the punishment and prevention of genuine international crime and for the enforcement of genuine international justice.[22]

Hull was a pioneer in the kind of internationalism that has since gained widespread support as a result of the experiences of two world wars. Some of his thinking proved unrealistic, particularly his failure to recognize that the imposition by an international authority of military sanctions against a delinquent nation, especially if it were a major power, might easily result in a situation that was in fact little, if at all, removed from a state of war. (In the interwar years Hull entertained strong misgivings about the League of Nations in connection with its powers of enforcing military sanctions.) The nature of an international sovereign body and the extent of its powers were problems which were inadequately dealt with, too, in his writings of this period.

[22] William I. Hull, *The New Peace Movement* (published as *Swarthmore College Bulletin*, VII, no. 9 [Sept. 1909], 6, 7, 12-24).

What is particularly interesting for our purposes, however, is the rather uneasy combination which he contrived of nonpacifist internationalism on a lower, with Quaker pacifism on a higher, plane of morality, his attempt—not altogether successful—to attain "an intermediate resting-place in the world's journey upward towards Christ's goal of Love thine enemy." He called on men to refuse "uncompromisingly and inevasively" to "take the lives of their fellow men under any pretext whatsoever." To maintain that war was not just murder on a large scale was, in his opinion, mere sophistry.[23] Yet international arbitration and Hague Conferences seem today an insufficient response, a somewhat ineffectual compromise between the way of radical nonviolence such as was being propounded contemporaneously by Tolstoy and Gandhi and their disciples, on the one hand, and the increasingly influential school of internationalist thought that wished to see effective force placed at the disposal of a supranational authority, on the other.

The opening of the twentieth century, then, found the Society of Friends less united than in past centuries on their attitude toward war. Some sections, especially the Western yearly meetings that had been strongly influenced by the late nineteenth-century revival movements, and individuals in all branches of the Society had moved away from pacifism. Elsewhere, on the other hand, there had been a revival of interest in the peace testimony and a desire to give it new life, both by exploring its relationship to the facts of international politics and by bringing it into touch with the efforts of the non-Quaker and nonpacifist peace movement, which was growing in strength and influence. Both Hicksite and Orthodox yearly meetings in the East began to establish permanent peace committees from the 1890's on and to show renewed interest on an official level in the problems of peace and war. Although Quakers, like other pacifists, were not affected directly by war, the Spanish-American War of 1898 and American imperialist designs in regard to Cuba and the Philippines gave an added impulse to Friends to reconsider the implications of their peace testimony.

In December 1901 a three-day peace conference was held in Philadelphia, to which Quakers of all branches of the Society on the North American continent were invited. Among those who played a leading role in its initiation and proceedings we find the names of most prominent Friends who were helping at this time to refurbish Quaker pacifism: Benjamin F. Trueblood, Rufus M. Jones, Hannah J. Bailey, Alexander C. Wood, Howard M. Jenkins (the editor at that time of the *Friends' Intelligencer*), Alfred K. Smiley (the organizer of the

---

23 *Ibid.*, pp. 26-28, 31, 33.

886

annual Lake Mohonk International Arbitration Conferences where in the previous year the idea of this gathering of all Friends was conceived), and many others. The conference itself, which its sponsors planned as both a public demonstration of Friends' continued concern as a body for the peace of the world and as a forthright protest against "the awful iniquities and crushing burdens of modern militarism," consisted mainly of a series of papers given by leading Friends on various aspects of the peace testimony. Many of them seem rather platitudinous today. The pacifist basis of Friends' concern for peace was stressed, but collaboration with nonpacifists was urged by many of the speakers. "The outcome of this Conference," said M. Carey Thomas (1857-1935), president of Bryn Mawr College, "should be an aggressive peace propaganda, not carried on separately by the Quaker Church, but in concerted effort with all believers in peace and arbitration." Friends, with their long pacifist tradition, she thought, "should become the backbone of such a propaganda." Rufus Jones suggested that it would help the cause if American Friends would imitate British Friends who, although much fewer in number, were well represented in the House of Commons, and send some ten to twenty of their members to Congress. "We must accomplish something with those who determine the destiny of nations," he added.[24]

The conference had little to say about the economic causation of war or about the clash of rival imperialisms and the search of finance capitalism for overseas markets, subjects to which the socialist and labor movements of the day were giving widespread publicity as being among the major causes of international conflict. But, at the same time, the gathering, in the way it put stress on the political aspects of pacifism and in its call for cooperation with the wider peace movement that had grown up outside the Society of Friends (although, of course, this call was made within the framework of the religious inspiration of the Quaker peace testimony), demonstrated that a new era was beginning in the history of Quaker pacifism. Men like Rufus Jones or Alexander C. Wood, who did much to shape the direction of Quaker peace efforts in the postwar period, were active, as we have seen, in the 1901 conference and during the next decade and a half. The full effects of the new spirit now beginning to reinvigorate Quaker pacifism were not to become completely apparent, however, until the United States' involvement in world war began a new epoch in American history.[25]

[24] *The American Friends' Peace Conference . . . 1901*, pp. 3, 4, 83, 104, 105. See pp. 30, 54, for evidence of nonpacifist feeling within the Society. This report on the conference was published in the following year as a volume of 236 pages.

[25] See LeRoy C. Ferguson, "The Quakers in Midwestern Politics," *Papers of the*

A fresh spirit was also making itself felt among the two other historic peace churches, the Mennonites and the Brethren. Only here new influences were more subdued, slower and less complete in accomplishing their work. Their peace testimony remained more traditional, more circumscribed by the centuries-old otherworldliness of these groups. The sectarian ethos was still uppermost in their witness for peace. We must now turn to consider developments among groups of this kind and see how far change had proceeded by the outbreak of war in 1914.

Michigan Academy of Science, Arts and Letters, XXXII (1946), 425, 426, for some peace activities among Ohio and Indiana Friends from the 1890's on.

888

Chapter 22

Non-Quaker Sectarian Pacifism in an Era of Peace, 1865-1914

Among the Mennonites of the postbellum era the old established communities of Pennsylvania and Virginia, along with their daughter colonies in the Midwest and the Canadian settlements in Ontario, continued to pursue their agrarian way of life as a people apart, separated from their fellow citizens not only by a different religious ethos but by the barriers of language and culture. Even so, new forces were at work: German began very slowly to give way before English; wealth accumulated over the years by these frugal farmers brought new demands for the amenities provided by the outside world; the younger generation—at first only a sprinkling of young men—began to seek the advantages of an education above the primary level, thereby eventually bringing new ideas and influences to bear on their home communities. The world impinged more and more on the separated life of the sect. This change led to problems of adjustment and to conflicts both between the generations and among the membership at large. The doctrine of nonresistance, a central part of the Mennonite nonconformity to the world, underwent a period of stress as a result of these increasing contacts between the church and the outside world. The full extent of the crisis in this area did not become apparent in the period before 1914, because after the Civil War the problem of peace was relegated to a level of secondary importance in the church's scale of interests. Yet, as in the case of the Quakers, the era between the close of the Civil War and the outbreak of war in Europe was of vital importance on account of the slow but effective transformation that was taking place in the intellectual and cultural life of the group.

A new and important element entered the story of the American and Canadian Mennonites in the 1870's with the large-scale immigration of their coreligionists from Russia, many of whom had left their homes in order to avoid the new conscription law introduced in June 1871 by the Tsarist government, which put an end to the complete exemption from service granted the Mennonites by Catherine II. The rising tide of Russian nationalism was largely responsible for the introduction of compulsory military service; moreover, special privileges granted

889

an alien group were regarded by the nationalists as inimical to the nation's welfare and cohesion. Of the 45,000 Mennonites then settled in Russia, about 18,000 came to America (roughly 10,000 to the United States, mainly to Kansas, and 8,000 to Manitoba in Canada). In addition a few hundred arrived in 1876 from the Mennonite communities in West Prussia where, by an order-in-council of March 1868 following upon the new conscription act passed by the diet of the North German Confederation in the previous year, noncombatant service in the army was now required of all Mennonites.

The Mennonites in Russia were given the alternatives of either submitting to the new law (which was originally planned to include no provision for conscientious objection but in fact contained the possibility of noncombatant service in the army) or emigrating within ten years. From the moment in 1870 when rumors of the impending changes in legislation began to circulate, those who were unwilling to conform began to turn their eyes to the New World, where they knew that their coreligionists lived in the enjoyment of religious freedom and material well-being. At first, the Mennonites attempted to persuade the Tsarist government not to withdraw their exemption, but without effect. In 1875, however, after emigration to America had got under way on a wide scale, the government, having become alarmed at the loss of so many frugal and hard-working farmers, somewhat relented and permitted Mennonite conscripts to choose forestry work as an alternative to service in the army. This concession satisfied some members, but the more conservative congregations in particular, that regarded alternative civilian service as a dereliction of the traditional faith, continued to emigrate until all were located in the New World.

Among those leaders who urged the Mennonites to emigrate rather than submit was Cornelius Jansen (1822-1894)—the Moses of the Mennonite migration, his biographer has called him[1]—a man of considerable initiative, talent, and education who, originating from the West Prussian Mennonite community, had migrated to Russia, where he became a grain merchant in Berdyansk and for a time acted as Prussian consul there. His zeal in urging migration and opposing acceptance of any compromise with the new conscription act—he got pamphlets printed in Danzig advocating this course, which he preceded to distribute among the Mennonites in Russia—earned him summary expulsion from that country early in 1873 as a hostile alien. He continued to work on behalf of the new Mennonite immigrants after moving to the United States.

[1] Gustav E. Reimer and G. R. Gaeddert, *Exiled by the Czar*, p. vi.

When it became known that at least a part of the Mennonites were contemplating immigration to the American continent, both the United States and the Canadian governments began to compete for these highly desirable settlers for their new territories opening up in the West. True, these immigrants held peculiar views on the subject of war, but such opinions were already familiar to the two governments from their experience with the indigenous Mennonite and Quaker communities.[2] Negotiations with the British consul at Berdyansk, which were conducted mainly by Cornelius Jansen, finally brought an assurance from Ottawa in September 1872 that, if they decided to choose Canada, they would be guaranteed the same exemption from military service, in war as in peacetime, that had already been granted to the three peace churches there. They were also promised assistance in defraying the cost of transportation and free land on which to settle after their arrival in Canada.[3]

Since the Russian government was proving adamant against all attempts to get it to restore the Mennonite immunity from service, in the spring of 1873 a delegation of twelve was chosen from the various colonies (including the Hutterites, who practised community of goods) to visit both Canada and the United States. In both countries the delegates were assisted in their fact-finding survey by government officials and by leading American Mennonites.[4] In the United States, western railroad agents, in particular Jay Cooke of the Northern Pacific Railroad, took the delegates under their wing. As Cooke wrote in a letter of introduction to President Grant: "These people, the Mennonites, are somewhat similar to our Quaker population. They do not believe in wars or fighting, are moral, sober, frugal and industrious people, and desirable as citizens of our country"[5]—and undoubt-

---

[2] E.g., Senator Thomas W. Tipton of Nebraska declared: "In God's name, have we not enough of the fighting element in America? . . . Our people are a peculiar people; and if there is any portion of the world that can send us a few advocates of peace, in God's name let us bid them welcome. We want settlers of that kind" (Ernest Correll [ed.], "The Congressional Debates on the Mennonite Immigration from Russia," *MQR*, XX, no. 3 [July 1946], 219, 220).

[3] See Correll, "Mennonite Immigration into Manitoba: Sources and Documents, 1872, 1873," *MQR*, XI (July and Oct. 1937), 210, 211, 225, 226, 268-70; "Sources on the Mennonite Immigration from Russia in the 1870's," *MQR*, XXIV, no. 4 (Oct. 1950), 335, 337-41. See also *Wichtige Dokumente betreffs der Wehrfreiheit der Mennoniten in Canada*, p. 10; *Das Klein-Geschichtsbuch der Hutterischen Brüder*, pp. 621, 622.

[4] Among them was John F. Funk, who used the columns of his *Herald of Truth* to bring the plight of their "Russian" brethren to the attention of American Mennonites. See Kempes Schnell, "John F. Funk and the Mennonite Migrations" in *From the Steppes to the Prairies* (ed. Cornelius Krahn), pp. 69-91.

[5] Correll, "President Grant and the Mennonite Immigration from Russia," *MQR*, IX, no. 3 (July 1935), 146.

edly desirable also, though Jay did not say so here, as potential users of his railroad.

The two Hutterite delegates, Paul and Lorenz Tschetter, who were especially disturbed by the fact that, unlike Canada, the United States government was apparently unwilling to guarantee exemption from military service should conscription be imposed in the future, sought out President Grant in his summer home on Long Island where on 8 August they presented him with a petition. In its first draft they stated among their requests: "For at least fifty years we want to be entirely free from all military obligation. After fifty years we are willing to pay the amount that all the rest of the Mennonites or peoples whose confessions of Faith are against their taking up arms pay." Asking for exemption, too, from officeholding and the taking of oaths, as well as for their own schools in the German language, they pledged their readiness to obey the laws of the land in every other respect and to pay all taxes demanded of them.[6] Grant received them in a very friendly spirit, promising to give their petition sympathetic consideration. After their return to Russia the secretary of state, Hamilton Fish, wrote to them on the President's behalf explaining that, although the President was not entitled by the Constitution to guarantee them exemption either from the state militia or from a future federal draft, he was sure that, if the country ever became involved in a war calling for nationwide conscription, "Congress would find justification in freeing them from duties which are asked of other citizens."[7]

Further attempts to get Congress to approve special privileges for the Mennonite settlers, including an implicit understanding concerning their military exemption, failed.[8] Kansas and the other states where they eventually settled did, however, pass legislation freeing them from any liability to serve with the militia, provided they registered annually a certificate of conscientious objection.[9] In Kansas the declaration ran as follows:

[6] Gertrude S. Young, "A Record concerning Mennonite Immigration, 1873," *AHR*, XXIX, no. 3 (April 1924), 521. See also *Das Klein-Geschichtsbuch*, pp. 603, 605, 606; "The Diary of Paul Tschetter," pt. II, *MQR*, V, no. 3 (July 1931), 214-17.

[7] C. Henry Smith, *The Coming of the Russian Mennonites*, pp. 71-74. Among an extensive literature this is the most comprehensive account of the "Russian" Mennonite immigration. I have drawn on it frequently in these pages.

[8] See Leland Harder, "The Russian Mennonites and American Democracy under Grant" in *From the Steppes to the Prairies*, pp. 54-67.

[9] Smith, *The Coming*, pp. 265-68. E.g., in 1877, Nebraska, fearing that the Mennonite immigrants might all go to Kansas or Manitoba, speedily passed legislation exempting them from any obligation to serve in the militia. The prime mover in this matter was the Burlington and Missouri River Railroad, which was then all-powerful in the state legislature. The railroad was interested in attracting

I do solemnly, sincerely and truly declare and affirm that I am a resident of ——— county, State of Kansas, and a member of the Religious Society or Church known and called by the name Mennonites, and that according to the creed and discipline of said Society, the bearing arms is forbidden, and this I do under the pains and penalties of perjury.[10]

The church officials urged members to comply with these regulations. A conference in 1888, for instance, argued that cooperation was necessary "that the authorities may know, when soldiers are needed, who have belonged to a non-resistant association, and thereby favor us so that we may be undisturbed."[11] But, in fact, probably because of the generally moribund condition of the state militia system at that time and the feeling that, in case of war, conscription would become a federal and not a state matter, only a small percentage of Mennonites required by law to register appear to have done so.[12]

The main body of Mennonite immigrants left Russia in 1874, but the migration continued in decreasing intensity until the mid-eighties. "The more progressive culturally, approximately two thirds of the total number remained in Russia. The most conservative Mennonites who had lived in the *Old Colony* and its daughter-colonies migrated to Canada because they were promised complete exemption from all compulsory military service by the Canadian government. . . . The third [group] came from the *Molotschna Colony* and settled in the United States. They were joined by the Hutterites."[13] Along with their desire to escape from the newly imposed conscription, which was the main force driving them toward emigration, the Mennonites

---

Mennonites to Nebraska and not leaving them to settle in areas where its line did not run! See John D. Unruh, Jr., "The Burlington and Missouri River Railroad brings the Mennonites to Nebraska 1873-1878," pt. I, *Nebraska History*, vol. 45, no. 1 (March 1964), pp. 13, 14.

[10] "Affirmation of Non-Resistant," printed copy in Bethel College Historical Library, signed by Peter A. Schmidt of Harvey Co., 28 April 1886, and countersigned by the county clerk.

[11] *Conference Record containing the Proceedings of the Kansas-Nebraska Mennonite Conference 1876-1914*, pp. 16, 17.

[12] Cornelius Cicero Janzen, "A Social Study of the Mennonite Settlement in the Counties of Marion, McPherson, Harvey, Reno, and Butler, Kansas," Ph.D. diss., U. of Chicago (1926), p. 62.

[13] Krahn in *From the Steppes to the Prairies*, p. 8. In 1899, as a result of the outbreak of the Spanish-American War, the Hutterites contemplated removal from South Dakota to Canada, whose government was ready to grant them complete military exemption. See *Das Klein-Geschichtsbuch*, pp. 468, 629-32. But, in fact, it was not until after the First World War, when they had to suffer severe hardships in the United States on account of their pacifism, that (with the exception of one Bruderhof) they all moved to the Canadian prairies.

also had reasons for leaving that were common to other German emigrants from Russia: the search for new land (most of the Mennonite newcomers came from the poorer and landless sections of the community) and fears for the fate of their German culture in face of the rising tide of Russianization.[14]

The majority of the "Russian" Mennonites linked up after their arrival with the General Conference branch. Although in the First World War most of their young men, if called up, accepted noncombatant service (a form of alternative service that their fathers had left Russia to escape), it appears that the Russian groups produced a higher percentage of conscientious objectors than the old established branches of the American Mennonite community.[15] To a limited degree, therefore, the immigration led to an infusion of new strength into the somewhat lethargic Mennonite peace testimony.

It had been in large part their pacifism, as we have seen, that had caused thousands of Mennonites to leave their homes in Russia or Prussia and face the hardships of frontier life in unknown surroundings in a new country whose language was unfamiliar to them and many of whose ways were strange. Those Mennonites who remained behind in Europe had, in Holland or Germany, largely abandoned their nonresistant ideas or, in Russia, been prepared to accommodate themselves to the demands of the state, provided these stopped short of an outright command to bear arms. In America the decades after the Civil War represented for the most part a period of stagnation in the history of Mennonite pacifism: renewal was not, at first, apparent either in the field of peace literature or pacifist activity. No challenge arose to shake the Mennonites out of a merely routine loyalty to a traditional article of faith into a living testimony for peace.

For John F. Funk, the Mennonite editor who had worked hard during the Civil War to inspire his church's nonresistance with new vigor, the period was one of marking time. Writing soon after the emigration from Russia, he summed up the situation as follows:

In America, while there has been a large falling away of the faithful, it is our opinion that the doctrine has not lost ground. The steady growth of the church, and the continual gain by new accessions both from the rising generation and emigration from foreign countries, gives us reason to believe that we have not lost, while at the same time we cannot claim any special gain.[16]

14 Smith, *The Coming*, pp. 34-36, 96, 97.
15 *Ibid.*, pp. 273-75.
16 *Herald of Truth*, XII, no. 8 (Aug. 1875), 131-32.

One of the most crying needs, if the church's nonresistant testimony was to be strengthened, still remained to be filled: the production of literature on peace to instruct the membership, young and old. It was all very well for a gathering of church leaders, like that which took place in Indiana in October 1867, to call not only for strict adherence to the doctrine of nonresistance among church members but for its propagation in the outside world. "There are very few among the great mass of mankind who know anything about the principles of nonresistance," they correctly added.[17] But the snag lay in the availability of sufficient peace literature to keep the issue constantly in the foreground of the church's concerns. In the mid-eighties, Funk's capable assistant as editor of the *Herald of Truth* and one of the most effective evangelists of his day, John S. Coffman (1848-1899), complained of this inadequacy. "We seldom, if ever, hear," he writes, "even among our peace professing people, a sermon that is wholly devoted to this subject; conversations in which peace is ably defended are rare. It is only occasionally that we have an article in our Church that speaks clearly for . . . peace." The young people were only too often ignorant of this aspect of Mennonite doctrine. He recommended the Quaker-run *Messenger of Peace* to Mennonite ministers, in particular: in most cases, sermons on peace in Mennonite churches had derived their arguments from the *Messenger's* pages. But this outside help, he concluded, was really no substitute for thorough discussions of the meaning of their peace principles in the church's own publications.[18]

Indeed, a perusal of the post-Civil War files of the *Herald of Truth*, the organ of the Mennonite Church which was managed by Funk himself, later with Coffman's help, confirms the latter's comments concerning the exiguousness of peace materials in the paper. After 1865 there were at first usually some half dozen articles a year on pacifism —with the space devoted to the subject slightly increasing from the beginning of the 1890's. Original contributions from Mennonite authors were usually simple and somewhat naive affairs: expositions of New Testament texts for nonresistance or exhortations to remain loyal to this tenet of the traditional faith. But most peace articles were extracted from non-Mennonite journals. Often it was the Quaker press or the organs of the British and American Peace Societies—the *Herald* and the *Advocate of Peace*—that the editors drew on; occasionally an article was taken from one of the Church of the Brethren papers. Passages from the pacifist classics—the early church fathers, Dymond and

[17] *Minutes of the Indiana-Michigan Mennonite Conference 1884-1929*, p. 12.
[18] *Herald of Truth*, XXI, no. 22 (15 Nov. 1884), 838. See also the supporting article by Daniel Shenk in vol. XXII, no. 6 (15 March 1885).

the Quaker apologists, Thomas Upham, and, of course, Menno Simons —were reprinted in the paper. The German version of the *Herald*—the *Herold der Wahrheit*—which Funk published from 1864 until 1901, although it differed slightly in content from the English, brought most of this peace material before the many church members who did not understand English. For those interested in reading further on the subject of peace, the *Herald* office was able to supply at a small cost copies of Dymond's treatise on war, Brenneman's little pamphlet on Christianity and war published during the Civil War (see earlier), the Adventist I. C. Wellcome's *Should Christians Fight?*, Beckwith's *Peace Manual*, and later publications of the Peace Association of Friends. In 1885 the General Conference Mennonites began to bring out an English-language paper, the *Mennonite*. Its pages, however, provide no evidence that at this date peace had become a vital issue in this section of the Mennonite community.[19]

It was, in fact, John Holdeman (1832-1900), the founder of the small and strongly evangelical group of the Church of God in Christ, Mennonite, that split off from the Mennonite Church in 1859, who produced the most elaborate exposition of Mennonite pacifism in this period. Holdeman had been a farmer before he became an evangelist and sectarian leader. Yet he was deeply versed in the Bible, had on his own acquired knowledge of several languages, including some Greek, and was a prolific writer on religious subjects.

His main work, *Ein Spiegel der Wahrheit* (*A Mirror of Truth*), appeared in 1878. The bulky volume ranges over a wide variety of theological topics. A lengthy chapter (reprinted in English in 1891 in slightly revised form as a separate booklet) is devoted to "Magistracy and War." Consistent with the Mennonite tradition, Holdeman, of course, rejects the holding of civil office by a nonresistant people. His discussion of war is both detailed and well organized.[20]

[19] German editions of Dymond and Brenneman were published by Funk. In 1899, J. G. Ewert (1874-1923) from the General Conference Mennonites published at Hillsboro (Kan.) a German translation of the correspondence between Ballou and Tolstoy, which the Rev. Lewis G. Wilson had printed in the *Arena* (see earlier). It appeared with the title *Die Christliche Lehre von der Wehrlosigkeit*. A small pamphlet giving the contents of an address at a Sunday school on the subject of nonresistance by another General Conference member, S. S. Haury (1847-1929), a former missionary, was published at Dayton (Ohio) in 1894 under the title *Die Wehrlosigkeit in der Sonntagschule*. Little else was published in German specifically on the pacifist issue by either of the two main branches of American Mennonitism.

[20] Its superiority in relation to a lot of other Mennonite peace literature of the period becomes immediately apparent if we compare Holdeman's work with a production like J. K. Zook's pamphlet, *War, its Evils and its Blessings* (n.d., n.p.p.), which is crude and naive both in its style and in its arguments.

896

Although in no way original, Holdeman's arguments are intelligently and plausibly presented; Biblical citations are numerous, but he does not by any means rely on them exclusively. He disagrees with those who took the commandment "Thou shalt not kill" as a text for non-resistance,[21] for killing evildoers was often enjoined by God in the Old Testament and to argue otherwise was to twist the meaning of scripture. The case for nonresistance he places squarely on the Christian law of love as revealed in the New Testament and on the necessity for Christ's followers to avoid complicity in the kingdoms of this world. In regard to the problem of military service that had agitated Mennonite communities only a decade and a half earlier, Holdeman condemns not merely the hiring of substitutes but all forms of non-combatant service in the army, including the care of the sick and wounded. "I cannot call it anything else but hypocrisy," he writes, "to wear the soldier's uniform and still claim to be a nonresistant." Our bodies are, indeed, God's alone; nevertheless, on our material possessions the state has legitimate claims. We must pay taxes to Caesar, even if some of the money goes to war purposes, and we may pay fines in lieu of personal military service where this alternative is permitted.[22]

Holdeman's exposition of Mennonite nonresistance was, indeed, almost unique at this time, for scarcely anything new on the subject had appeared in either German or English, apart from an occasional article in the church press.[23] Holdeman's pacifism had been exclusively Bible-centered. But from the 1880's on, and especially in the early years of the next century, there gradually appeared a novel element: the secular argument against war. We can see this change reflected in the pages of the *Herald of Peace*, where space began to be devoted to news of the American and international peace movements. Alongside the Biblical citations appeared protests against the horrors of war and its cost in lives and money, against the increasing militarization of North American life and especially of youth, and articles in favor of arbitration as a panacea for war's ills. A conference in 1898, for instance, stated: "Als wehrlose Christen befürworten wir internationale Arbitration zur Ausgleichung und Beilegung aller Differenzen zwischen Völkern und Nationen."[24] Canadian Mennonites a little later,

[21] A later example of a pacifist interpretation of this text is to be found in the volume published in 1914 by the Mennonite Church, *Bible Doctrine*, p. 542: "The Bible says, 'Thou shalt not kill.' This command put into practice would forever end all wars."

[22] John Holdeman, *A Mirror for Truth*, pp. 393-95.

[23] See, however, the Rev. Henry H. Ewert, *The Confession of Faith of the Mennonite Denomination and Its Mission*, pp. 21, 22.

[24] *Abdruck der Gesammt-Protokolle der Kansas und Westlichen Distrikt Conferenz der Mennoniten von Nord-Amerika, 1877-1909*, p. 264. The German pas-

in 1906, went even further, resolving: "That we recommend the organization of a Peace and Arbitration Association in each congregation, for the circulation of Peace Literature and for advancing the cause of non-resistance in every legitimate way."[25] In the following year and again in 1909, they drew up protests against "the spirit of militarism" that, in their view, was being inculcated by their government.[26]

All this witnesses to a new spirit at work among Mennonites in respect to the peace question. It was shown again—to give a further illustration—in the fact that the Intercollegiate Peace Association, which came into existence in 1906 as a nondenominational body to promote interest in peace among college students, owed its foundation in large part to Mennonite initiative. President Noah E. Byers of Goshen College and the young Mennonite historian C. Henry Smith were active here alongside the Quaker Elbert Russell from Earlham College. Outside the academic community but immensely influential in promoting a renewed interest in peace (as well as in revivifying Mennonite theology and historiography) was the immigrant from Germany, John Horsch (1867-1941), who had come to the United States in 1887 in order to escape military service. For Horsch, whom steadfast adherence to nonresistance had driven to leave family and fatherland, the doctrine was of primary importance in his faith and its reinvigoration a matter of urgency. He continued to champion it in a long series of writings on Anabaptist and Mennonite history and theology.

The protagonists of the nineteenth-century American peace movement, as well as most Quaker pacifists, were essentially optimistic in their estimation of human nature. Traditional Mennonite nonresistance, on the other hand, was basically pessimistic in its outlook and had long been grounded in the idea of an irredeemable world from which the righteous must separate. A quite novel optimism, however, can be detected in some Mennonite peace writings from the end of the nineteenth century. It can be seen, for instance, in the very title of a prize essay composed in 1894 for a Quaker competition on the subject of peace by a young theological student, H. P. Krehbiel (1862-1940): *War Inconsistent with the Spirit and Teaching of Christ and Hence Unwise and Unnecessary.* Although old school Mennonites could have

---

sage cited runs in English as follows: "As defenseless Christians we promote international arbitration [to achieve a] compromise and settlement of all differences between peoples and nations." (My translation.)

[25] *Conference Resolutions . . . 1906,* no. 11.

[26] *Conference Resolutions . . . 1907,* no. 7; *Resolutions . . . 1909,* no. 5.

found nothing with which to quarrel in Krehbiel's exposition of New Testament nonresistance, they might well have felt reservations about pronouncing war unnecessary in a sinful world. Krehbiel clearly hoped that eventually a whole nation might be led to adopt a pacifist policy (although only the contemporary United States appeared to him to be going in the right direction). "That mankind may learn to . . . become a perfect society" was Christ's design in enunciating his moral teachings. Although Krehbiel's essay was not published separately until much later, it was printed soon afterward in the pages of both the General Conference *Mennonite* and the Mennonite Church's *Herald of Truth.*

Krehbiel's essay was the expression of individual opinion; it represented the views of a young man who had as yet no official standing in his church. But this same optimistic outlook emerges even in an official compilation of the Mennonite Church like the 700-page tome on *Bible Doctrine,* which Daniel Kauffman (1865-1944) brought out in 1914. The brief chapter on nonresistance, of course, is largely a reworking of the traditional doctrine. But the influence of the outside non-Mennonite peace movement is very evident. We can see it in the author's denunciation of the barbarities of the war method, his elaboration of the thesis that in the long run war does not pay, and in the concept of a nonresistant nation.[27] The example of a truly nonresistant people, the author pleads, would give an immense impulse toward universal peace; God would protect such a nation if it were his will. The case of Quaker Pennsylvania was cited in support. Finally—and this, too, was something absent in earlier Mennonite literature on peace—a qualified approval was given to the activities of peace societies, provided they were grounded on Christian principles and uncompromising rejection of war.

A slow awakening of interest in the problems of peace and war was, then, apparent within the main branches of American Mennonitism toward the end of our period. It was the new generation of college-educated men, still a mere handful, who showed most awareness of the need to seek out new avenues of approach and to attempt more creative thinking on such issues. Nevertheless, it is clear that nonresistance still represented a weak element within the complex of Mennonite interests. During the long years of peace there were in practice only two points where the war issue impinged directly on the life of the community: first, the problem of war pensions (which only concerned a very small minority of members) and, secondly, the

[27] See *Bible Doctrine,* pp. 541, 543, 544, 547, 548.

proper relationship between nonresistance and peacetime citizenship.

The position of the army veteran in a peace church, as we know, gave rise to difficulties among Quakers, Amish, and Brethren, as well as in the Mennonite community. Although they would in many cases have given public expression in the past to their regret at not having followed their church's rejection of war, many peace church veterans were—not unnaturally—anxious, when eligible, to draw the war pensions to which their services had entitled them. In some cases, where a man had been incapacitated by wounds, renunciation might endanger his livelihood. There was, indeed, no unanimity in the attitude of the various Mennonite conferences, even within the same branch. In the Mennonite Church, for instance, the Franconia Conference in Pennsylvania and the Indiana-Michigan Conference out west permitted members to go on drawing war pensions.[28] The Missouri-Iowa Conference, however, forbade their acceptance, branding this in a minute passed in 1899 as inconsistent with a nonresistant faith. The minute stated: "(a). It is inconsistent for a man to accept a bounty for sin repented of. (b). Christians should depend upon the Lord rather than on questionable gifts for support. (c). Pensions for military services encourage war."[29]

On the question of the magistracy there was unanimity at this time throughout all the branches that participation in most civil offices was impermissible. But with regard to certain peripheral activities of a political nature, mainly exercise of the franchise and sitting in legislatures, there was uncertainty. The question of voting had been bothersome, as we have seen, during the Civil War, and conferences of the Mennonite Church in October 1864 and again, after the war was over, in May 1866 (without categorically forbidding participation in elections) had recommended abstention from the franchise and all involvement in politics. There was a widespread feeling that membership in Christ's kingdom, and the calling of the nonresistant that this entailed, precluded active citizenship in a worldly state. It would be shameful if the brethren got involved in party strife, campaigning and voting one against another. Would not the rulers reproach nonresistants when they refused to call to arms at a time of danger if the latter had helped to put them in power? It was argued that Christians must choose to which kingdom they wished to give their undivided allegiance. Therefore, as regards the franchise, "in my opin-

[28] J. C. Wenger, *History of the Mennonites of the Franconia Conference*, p. 64; *Minutes . . . Indiana-Michigan . . . Conference*, p. 12.

[29] Missouri-Iowa Mennonite Conference Minutes, 1883-1920 (MS in Archives of the Mennonite Church, Goshen), p. 97.

ion," wrote the influential John F. Funk in an editorial, "I consider it, at least, safe to abstain from it."[30]

Representative of a large section of opinion within the Mennonite community were the views of Tobias E. Moyer (1863-1933), a Lancaster County flour miller who in middle life had converted from the Reformed to the Mennonite Church:

> Bro. Moyer believed firmly that a Christian should not go to the polls to vote. He believed that voting belonged to the world and that as a Christian he should keep away from any such contacts with the world. He thought that if he voted, that is, if he helped someone into office, he would be obliged to render service to the country in the event of war.[31]

Sometimes this uncompromising standpoint found expression in decisions of representative bodies. A conference of the Mennonite Church in Illinois, in 1872, for instance, after stating that the faithful were forbidden by the Lord either to take up the sword or to swear oaths, went on:

> Sie sollen keine Aemter bedienen, ausgenommen solche, die bedient werden können ohne Gewalt anzuthun oder ein Eid abzulegen; sie sollen nicht als Jurymann sitzen wo, in Fall, der Verbrecher schuldig gefunden wird mit dem Tode bestraft zu werden. Sie sollen auch kein Theil nehmen an weltlichen Wahlen u.s.w.[32]

But in other cases a less rigid line was taken—and undoubtedly many Mennonites voted during this period without feeling that in doing so they were compromising their position as nonresistants. The first printed discipline issued by the Lancaster Conference of the Mennonite Church specifically permitted members not only to hold such public offices as "school director, road supervisor, poor director and postmaster" but to vote in elections, provided that they did not participate in any kind of electioneering. However, "it is for the best interests (of all) that the bishops, ministers and deacons will not vote at the polls."[33]

[30] *Herald of Truth*, vol. III, no. 11 (Nov. 1866). See also the anonymous article "The Non-Resistant and the Ballot-Box" in vol. V, no. 6 (June 1868).

[31] J. S. Umble, *Mennonite Pioneers*, p. 63.

[32] *Verhandlungen der ersten Zusammenkunft in Illinois*, printed leaflet in Historical Memorandums, John F. Funk Collection, Archives of the Mennonite Church, Goshen. The German passage cited runs in English as follows: "They shall not serve in any offices, except in those which can be held without having to do violence or to take an oath. They shall not sit as jurymen where the criminal, if found guilty, would be punished with death. They shall also take no part in worldly elections, etc." (My translation.)

[33] Ira D. Landis, "The First Lancaster Conference Printed Discipline," *Mennonite Research Journal*, I, no. 1 (April 1960), 7.

Among the newcomers from Europe, whose immigration to this continent has been discussed earlier in this chapter, interest in politics developed more rapidly than among the older communities of the East and Midwest. Participation in elections and in lower offices, where the use of armed force was not involved, began in the 1880's. The political views of the newcomers tended to be conservative; their allegiance went mainly to the rightward-tending Republican Party. It is from their midst that there came the first prominent Mennonite politician, Peter Jansen (1852-1923). Jansen, who became a prosperous rancher, was elected a justice of the peace in 1888, a Nebraska assemblyman in 1898, and a state senator in 1910. Although he belonged to the conservative wing of the Republican Party, he maintained the traditional Mennonite opposition to war. This led him to decline to run for the governorship of Nebraska and to support the rights of conscientious objectors in the First World War.[34]

Thus, at least in the ranks of the General Conference Mennonites, a more positive attitude toward the state was slowly evolving. Yet there still remained a great disparity between the otherworldly nonresistance of the Mennonites and the pacifism of the Quakers and the general peace movement which strove to purge the existing state and the international order of the element of armed violence. Whereas the latter were beginning slowly to attempt, as the early Pennsylvania Quakers or Garrisonian nonresistants had done, to devise techniques whereby crime and international disputes and outside aggression could be dealt with nonviolently, for the Mennonites these were areas where only the sword of the magistrate could suppress the evildoer.[35]

The Mennonites during this period were, in fact, little concerned with the practical implementation of their peace doctrines. The Spanish-American War made little impact on their life. Some Mennonites were not averse during the war to making "heavy overcoats and similar garments for the soldiers at a dollar per garment." When government bonds were issued after the war to help finance its cost, "the Franconia Mennonites bought freely," their historian tells us.[36] Among the "Russian" Mennonites of the West approval was given to members' participation in Red Cross work, if they felt called to volun-

[34] *Memoirs of Peter Jansen*, p. 127. See also C. C. Janzen, "A Social Study," pp. 53-58.

[35] Cf. article quoted above in *Herald of Truth* (June 1868): "I believe that a murderer would care but little for a civil officer whom he knew to be conscientiously opposed to taking up and using deadly weapons, and would not be likely to permit himself to be arrested by such officer."

[36] Wenger, *Franconia Conference*, p. 64.

902

teer for such service. "Sehen wir es doch also Christenpflicht an, Wunden heilen zu helfen" ["We thus regard it, then, as a Christian duty to help to heal wounds"], their conference held at Newton (Kan.) in May 1898 declared.[37] Since there was no federal conscription and the state militia system was virtually extinct, the war did not produce any significant developments in Mennonite pacifism.

The outbreak of war in Europe in 1914 found the Mennonite churches, for all the shortcomings that have been touched on in previous pages, on the whole better able to uphold their traditional pacifism than they had been on the eve of the Civil War. Despite the underlying changes serving to disintegrate the traditional way of life, new educational techniques such as Sunday schools, Bible conferences, the church press had helped—however imperfectly—to instill more understanding of the Mennonite stand on war. The church still practised its nonconformity to the world; renewal from outside thus helped to reinvigorate the basic tenets of this nonconformity, including nonresistance. For the Mennonites, as for the Society of Friends, the period between the Civil War and the First World War was a period of quiet, opening into one of renewed outreach.

This same post-Civil War period saw a split between the more progressive elements among the Amish, most of whom finally fused with the Mennonite Church, and the ultra-conservative Old Order Amish, who clung to their separate status and traditional way of life, preserved almost intact from the seventeenth century. The Amish have rarely given literary expression to their beliefs, whether on peace or on other subjects, even though their ministers were expected to teach nonresistance as one of God's commandments for his people as well as one of the church's requirements. It is clear, however, not merely because of the absence of any peace literature but from the other evidence, that peace was not among the Amish's primary concerns at this time.

We do from time to time catch an occasional glimpse in the printed minutes of conferences, such as the *Diener-Versammlungen* that were held between 1862 and 1878, of some problems arising then from their nonresistant position. The question of war pensions loomed largest. Many as yet unbaptized young men from Amish communities had, as we have seen in an earlier chapter, entered the Union army. At the conference of 1868 the query was raised: "Kann es als schriftmässig

---

[37] *Abdruck*, p. 264. This resolution witnesses to the growth of a feeling of American patriotism among the younger generation, at least of "Russian" Mennonites. Peter Jansen always supported the idea of army medical work as alternative service for young Mennonites, a policy which he was to advocate for C.O.'s in the First World War.

903

annerkannt werden, dass einer, der ein Brüder war und sich als Soldat anwerben liess um in Militär zu dienen, und dort werwundet wurde, und jetzt nach den Landesgesetzen eine Pension erhält, in die Gemeinde aufgenommen werden und die Pension fortziehen kann?" The matter was referred for settlement to a committee of five, which subsequently brought in a negative verdict. Since war service of any kind is "contrary to the gospels," all that is connected with it must be rejected. "Ferner, so es die Noth erfordert, ist es der Gemeinde Pflicht die Armen zu versorgen, anstatt Pensionen zu ziehen."[38] Similar declarations may be cited from the subsequent decades.[39] Yet such strictness was definitely not observed in all communities, especially where serious hardship might have ensued from the sacrifice of a pension. Among the Somerset County (Pa.) Amish we read of one Amishman, Christian Hostetler, who received his war pension until his death in 1904, when his widow was allowed by the government to draw it until she died in 1922. Uris Tressler—to take another case—continued to receive his pension until 1900, when his church put pressure on him to give it up by promising to pay him an equivalent sum ($12 per month) from church funds.[40]

Civil office was still firmly rejected, except (as with the Mennonites) in instances where there was no question of the use of physical coercion.[41] Abstention from voting in elections was sometimes demanded;[42] but this obviously was not the rule everywhere and at all times. In 1868, in the course of the *Diener-Versammlungen* of that year, there took place a lively but not wholly conclusive discussion of whether a Christian was justified in collaborating with the authorities in the apprehension and punishment of a thief. The first committee to whom the matter was referred failed to reach a unanimous conclusion. A second committee, however, resolved in the negative. "Wir erkennen es für unevangelisch einen Dieb der Obrigkeit zu

---

[38] *Verhandlungen der siebenten jährlichen Diener-Versammlungen der Amischen Mennoniten Brüderschaft*, pp. 5, 7. The passages cited run in English as follows: "Can it be acknowledged as according to scripture that a brother who allowed himself to be recruited to serve in the army and, having been wounded, is now, according to the law of the land, in receipt of a pension, should be taken back into the congregation and still continue to draw the pension?" "In addition, it is the congregation's duty to care for the poor in case of need, instead of drawing pensions." (My translations.)

[39] E.g., *Western District A. M. Conference: Record of Conference Proceedings* (1890), p. 10.

[40] Richard B. Yoder, "Nonresistance among the Peace Churches of Southern Somerset County, Pennsylvania, during the Civil War," pp. 15, 19.

[41] E.g., *Western District A. M. Conference* (1891), p. 11; *Report of the Eastern Amish Mennonite Conference* (1898), p. 11.

[42] *History of the Amish Mennonite Conference (Conservative)* (1912), p. 12.

überliessen um ihn gestraft zu haben, dieweil wir uns als wehrlos erkennen, und uns nach der Apostel Lehre, nicht rächen sollen." Nevertheless, this decision failed to satisfy some of the delegates, and discussion was reopened on the following day. Again there was no complete agreement. This lack of accord was reflected in the last committee appointed to deal with the issue which, while repeating the earlier resolution concerning the incompatibility between Christian nonresistance and the pursuit and punishment of crime, yet added a qualifying clause. "Wir halten es für pflichtmässig in solchen Fällen mit der Gemeinde Rath zu halten," it declared, thereby virtually placing the final decision on each congregation.[43]

Nonresistance was founded on the idea of the New Testament as a gospel of love. Yet both Amish and Mennonites as a whole clung to the idea of hell—a literal hell with fire, brimstone, and tormenting demons—as a fitting place of eternal punishment for the wicked.[44] It was an Illinois Amishman, Joseph Yoder, who in 1872 stirred up a hornet's nest by composing a poem, "Die frohe Botschaft," in which he expressed the belief that a loving and merciful God would never condemn even the worst sinner to eternal punishment. The *Diener-Versammlung* in that year condemned universalism of this kind as heresy, but Yoder's own bishop, Joseph Stuckey, supported him, refusing to excommunicate the rebel poet. This led to a rift between Stuckey's congregation and the more conservative Amish.[45] It was, indeed, not merely a conservative Biblical literalism that led these peace sects to cherish the doctrine of eternal punishment; there was almost certainly an unconscious desire for compensation against the worldly who on this earth, at least in the past, had inflicted savage persecution on the godly.

Of two small offshoots of the Mennonites, the eighteenth-century Brethren in Christ and the nineteenth-century Apostolic Christian Church, little need be said in regard to the post-Civil War period. The latter, as we have seen in a previous chapter, had originated in

---

[43] *Verhandlungen der siebenten jährlichen Diener-Versammlungen*, pp. 6-10. The German passages cited run in English as follows: "We consider it as contrary to the gospels to hand a thief over to the authorities to have him punished, since we regard ourselves as defenseless, and, according to the teaching of the apostle, we should avenge nothing." "We consider it as obligatory in such cases to take counsel with the congregation." (My translations.)

[44] See *Bible Doctrine*, pt. VIII, chap. II: "Hell." Kermit Eby (1903-1962) in his delightful *For Brethren Only* (Elgin, Ill., 1959) has a chapter entitled "Revival at Baugo" describing his boyhood memories of the visiting evangelists in the Church of the Brethren to which he belonged and the way they used to play up hellfire in their sermons in an effort to achieve conversions.

[45] John A. Hostetler, "Amish Problems at the Diener-Versammlungen," *Mennonite Life*, vol. IV, no. 4 (Oct. 1949).

Switzerland among the followers of a former Reformed Church minister, Samuel Heinrich Fröhlich, who came under Mennonite influence in the course of the religious awakening that he was leading. Because of their refusal to perform military service, members of Fröhlich's group (which later spread into Germany, Hungary, Yugoslavia, and Rumania where today they are known as Nazarenes) began to emigrate to the United States from the end of the 1840's on. In their new home they built up congregations, especially in the Midwest; newcomers from among the local people, including Mennonites and Amish, joined them. However, the church never numbered more than a few thousand adherents. Nonresistance became a tenet of the American congregations, just as it has remained a tenet for those back in Europe. Although originally opposed to the acceptance of hospital or sanitary work in the army,[46] most members accepted noncombatant status in the two world wars.

In regard to the pacifism of the older established Brethren in Christ during this period, there is the same lack of source materials as in the case of the newly imported Apostolic Christian Church. In 1874 in a Confession of Faith that may have been based on some earlier statement, the Brethren in Christ say of their attitude to war:

We believe that the Scriptures teach that Christians should not be conformed to this world, but that they are a separate people, and that it teaches the doctrine of non-resistance in a qualified sense; that it is not the Christian's privilege to take up the sword or fight with carnal weapons, yet it is his duty to be strictly loyal to the Government under which he lives, in all things that do not conflict with, or are not forbidden by the Word.[47]

[46] Cf. *Glaubensbekenntnisz, der Neuen Deutschen Baptisten Gemeinde in den Vereinigten Staaten* (1880): "Das Gleiche [i.e., that, like bearing arms, it is not consistent with Christianity] glauben wir vom Sanitäts—, oder Spitaldienste; weil von Denen, die in diesem Dienste sind, verlangt wird, Waffen zu tragen und Exerziren zu lernen, sowie auch, Militär-Uniform zu tragen, was nicht verträglich ist mit dem wehrlosen Zustande." In regard to civil office and voting, this Confession of Faith accepted the Mennonite standpoint.

[47] *Minutes of General Conferences of Brethren in Christ (River Brethren) from 1871-1904*, p. 298. See also Harry Bert, "Notes on Non-Resistance in the Brethren in Christ Church to the End of World War I," *Notes and Queries in Brethren in Christ History*, VI, no. 1 (Jan. 1965), 2-5, for pre-1914 references to nonresistance in the church's newspaper, the *Evangelical Visitor*, founded in 1887, as well as in the annual general conference minutes. In 1912 an interesting case arose when a serving soldier converted by the church's San Franciso Mission applied for baptism and membership. After lengthy consideration the general executive board of the church decided that the man, who did not possess sufficient means to buy his way out of the army, might be accepted into fellowship before the expiry of his term of service in ten months' time, on condition that he meanwhile make every effort to obtain an earlier release on conscientious grounds.

In Canada, where the sect continued to be exempt from military duties along with Mennonites and Quakers, the Boer War prompted them on several occasions to restate their objection to all war. At least one member was disowned for enlisting in the army.[48]

The Church of the Brethren, still known up to 1908 as German Baptist Brethren, which in numbers had begun to overtake the Mennonite community, underwent the same growing pains as the latter during our period. But it, too, still remained an overwhelmingly rural church. Members displayed only a desultory interest in the peace question. Inevitably, the matter of war pensions cropped up at the church's annual conferences. A decision was given approving acceptance of pensions by members entitled to draw them. During these years the old objection to voting died away, and by 1914 most Brethren were exercising the franchise. Reluctance to hold office was also less strongly felt than earlier, and in 1915, when war was already on the horizon, we find one of the church's most prominent ministers and its first historian, Martin G. Brumbaugh (1862-1930), accepting office as governor of Pennsylvania, in which capacity he would be responsible for the military forces of the state. Earlier, however, annual conferences in 1888 and 1890 had forbidden Brethren to join the Grand Army of the Republic and other veterans' organizations or to attend their gatherings. Even the justifiability of police protection at the church's daylong communion services, at which many nonmembers were present, had been debated by members. The annual conference in 1879 decided that "only in extreme cases," such as this, was it permissible "to employ a police force to keep order."

There was little sign of organized peace activities until the twentieth century. In 1875 the annual conference was asked to approve cooperation of the church in the work of the Peace Association of Friends in America. The somewhat smug reply ran: "Our church itself being a peace association we need not, as a body, co-operate with others, but we may as individuals give our influence in favor of peace." As Bowman points out, although there were evidently some members who realized the need for concerted interdenominational action on behalf of peace, the church as a whole was as yet unprepared to emerge from its enclosure. For a long time nonresistance took a very subordinate place in the gamut of church concerns: education and missions absorbed the interest and energies of the most active Brethren.

The faint beginnings of a new outreach in the matter of its pacifism

---

[48] E. Morris Sider, "Nonresistance in the Early Brethren in Christ Church in Ontario," *MQR*, XXXI, no. 4 (Oct. 1957), 285, 286.

may be detected in the records of the church from the beginning of the new century. In 1902, on the request of the small group of Brethren in Denmark (the result of an earlier missionary effort), the annual conference agreed to petition the king of Denmark on behalf of conscientious objectors in that country. In 1909, as a result of the initiative of one of the Virginia congregations, the annual conference drew up a memorial to Congress protesting "against the ever-increasing expenditures for the navy and the enlarging of the same." In the following year the annual conference exhorted "the entire membership to activity in the cause of peace," and, finally, in 1911, on the request of the congregation at Wichita (Kan.), a peace committee of three members was set up. Its purpose was to be threefold: to distribute literature expounding the Christian pacifist viewpoint, to help in the search for solutions to international disputes, and to keep members informed on the progress of "the peace movement." Yet little appears to have been accomplished before 1914, a fact which is scarcely surprising, since no funds seem to have been allocated to support its work.[49]

As far back as 1874, the following query and answer had appeared in the minutes of the annual conference, demonstrating an awareness on the part of some Brethren of the need for peace education if their peace testimony was to be nourished:

> Inasmuch as the public mind is awakened on the subject of peace, both among nations and societies, should not the church at large take notice of "the signs of the times," and teach more earnestly at this time this cardinal doctrine of Christ and the church?
>
> Answer: We think the church should do so.[50]

Indeed, the church covenant, which was accepted by each member on receiving baptism and thereby full membership in the church, should have served to keep pacifism a living faith. For, before baptism was bestowed on an applicant, he was required "to declare his agreement with us, in regard to the principles of being defenceless, nonswearing, and not conforming to the world."[51] Yet, in fact, this must have been for many Brethren little more than a formal acquiescence, a mechanical acceptance of a tenet because it formed part and parcel of the traditional way of life.

[49] Rufus D. Bowman, *The Church of the Brethren and War*, pp. 157-62; *MAM*, pp. 257, 284, 325, 358, 367, 432, 481, 521, 767, 768, 898; and separate reports for 1911 and 1914.

[50] *MAM*, p. 315.

[51] H. B. Brumbaugh, *The Brethren's Church Manual*, p. 15.

The extremely exiguous Brethren peace literature of the post-Civil War period is both an expression of this apathy toward the peace issue and a factor contributing toward the growth of such apathy. The church press of the period devoted little space to peace problems: the number of peace tracts originating during this era may be counted on the fingers of one hand.

In 1867 a Virginia Brethren, Benjamin F. Moomaw, whom we have already met as Bishop Kline's coadjutor in the Civil War, published a long dialogue on nonresistance as an appendix to a book devoted to (what he felt to be) the far more absorbing topic of trine immersion.[52] The need which he had experienced to defend the Brethren position on war had prompted the author to compose this piece, which took the form of an argument between "Friend" defending the idea of a just war against aggression and "Brother" upholding the Dunker position. The latter's standpoint is, of course, strictly Biblical —or, rather, New Testament, for he makes considerable play with the difference between the old dispensation and the new which replaced it. His emphasis is somewhat legalistic, a trait that was typical of Brethren (and Mennonite) pacifism at this time. Nonresistance is depicted as forming part of a covenant—or, as he calls it, a "constitution"— which is embodied in the Sermon on the Mount. "Whatever [God] commands is right, and whatever he forbids is wrong, however much these commands may differ under different dispensations or circumstances," "Brother" tells his "Friend," when the latter was unable to comprehend how God's commands could ever contradict each other. Wars in fact (here we may probably see the influence of the American peace movement on sectarian thinking) almost invariably stemmed from "interest or ambition, either acquisition of property, or political aggrandizement," whatever the ostensible reasons might be.[53]

Although its circulation probably did not extend much outside the Virginia congregations, Moomaw's dialogue is, within its limitations, well written, forcibly argued, and not overburdened with citations of Biblical texts. The long poem of over 100 printed pages entitled *Ecclesianthem, or A Song of the Brethren, embracing their History and Doctrine*, which a church member, James Y. Heckler, published in 1883, is a very different affair. Naive and artless to an extreme, it was nonetheless almost the only other work that touched—though only

---

[52] The dialogue, which is entitled "The Inconsistency of War, In all its Phases, when viewed in the Light of the Divine Code, as Delivered to us in the New Testament, or Christian Constitution," covers pp. 220-74. On pp. 275-82, there is added an "Address to the Reader," also dealing with the subject of war.

[53] Benjamin F. Moomaw, *Discussion on Trine Immersion . . .* , pp. 220, 223-26, 232, 252.

briefly—on the church's pacifism until shortly before the end of the century. Heckler saw in the church of his fathers, small in numbers though it was, the repository of divine wisdom. He writes:

> I sing of the Doctrine upheld by the Brethren,
> The doctrine delivered from heaven by Christ,
> A song that is founded on principals [sic] perfect,
> On principals such as the Savior advised.

Of their nonresistant faith he says:

> The Brethren are called a peculiar people
> They differ in many respects from the world; . . .
> They go not to law with the world, nor each other,
> They are a non-litigant people, you see;
> They go not to war nor engage in its service;
> They claim a non-combatant people to be.
> They fight but the battles of life in the Spirit:
> Their weapons are not of the carnal, whate'er,
> But mighty through God to discomfort the devil
> When he and his imps or his angels appear.[54]

The effusions of a crude backwoods versifier, though they may possibly have reached a wider audience than Moomaw's more solid exposition, were no substitute for a presentation of the traditional case for Brethren pacifism that would help to deepen the membership's understanding of this tenet of their faith. A couple of short tracts published toward the end of the century tried, none too successfully, to fill the gap. The pamphlet by Daniel Hays (1839-1916), "The Path of Life" attempted once again to expound the relationship within the divine order between a government wielding the sword against evildoers and the nonresistant handful of Christ's disciples following the higher law of love. "Christ and War" by Daniel Vaniman (1835-1903) was a mere leaflet (selling at 20¢ per 100 copies). It contrasted Christ's and St. Paul's words with the fruits of war and concluded that nonresistance was "the only true and successful law of self-defense. . . . It has always proved successful when properly tested."[55]

That the historian of the Brethren's attitude to war could describe Hays's and Vaniman's productions as "possibly the clearest expression of the Church of the Brethren's Biblical position on peace which had

---

[54] James Y. Heckler, *Ecclesianthem*, pp. 1, 46.

[55] These items were reprinted in the first volume of *The Brethren's Tracts and Pamphlets*, published by the Brethren's Book and Tract Work in Dayton (Ohio) in 1892 and again in a new edition in Elgin (Ill.) in 1900. Hays's tract deals with nonresistance on pp. 26-29.

been made up to this time"[56] is revealing, at least of the intellectual weakness of Brethren pacifism. Absorbed in extending its educational program at home and its missionary outreach overseas and unconcerned with any wider social or economic implications of its radical stand against war, "the denomination," Bowman concludes, "had taken its peace position for granted. . . . The character of the church had changed [i.e., since 1865] and it had not adjusted its teaching program to the new conditions. The Brethren were not prepared for World War I."[57]

The old separation from the world, in which nonresistance had been one of the agents of withdrawal from the community at large, was beginning to break down. The old plain dress—to give only one outward manifestation of inward separation—was disappearing, except among the small group of Old Order Brethren, who have preserved it to this day. Currents of religious thought like fundamentalism, which was basically inimical to pacifism (as those sections of the Society of Friends that came under its sway showed), were making inroads into the ranks of the Brethren.[58] Would the Brethren's nonresistant stand eventually go the way of their discarded bonnets and beards? On the eve of the First World War it may well have seemed as if this would be the case. Yet here, as with the Friends and with the Mennonites (though among the latter traditionalism was retreating more slowly), new forces were also working in the direction of a regeneration of the church's peace testimony, leading it into new and more creative channels. To quote Bowman again: "From a negative attitude towards state and society, from a largely inlooking pacifism, . . . the Brethren moved . . . toward the position of accepting responsibilities for citizenship."[59] This transition, however, belongs properly to developments after the close of our story.

Very similar to the antistate nonresistance of the Mennonites and Dunkers were (as we have seen in an earlier chapter) the convictions

---

[56] Bowman, *Brethren and War*, p. 160. A rather more interesting presentation of pacifism by a Brethren is to be found in the volume published in Elgin (Ill.) in 1910 by Jacob Funk: *War versus Peace*. Its arguments were drawn mainly from the literature of the peace societies and from Quaker writers. The book may, indeed, have been intended primarily for non-Brethren readers, for there is only bare mention of Funk's church and its stand against war.

[57] Bowman, pp. 163, 164, 167, 168, 320, 321, 323. See also Frederick Denton Dove, *Cultural Changes in the Church of the Brethren*, pp. 163, 164, and Bowman, chap. VIII, for the effect of this unpreparedness, especially in the younger generation, on the church's stand during the First World War.

[58] Among the Progressive Brethren, who in the early 1880's split off from the main body under the influence of fundamentalism, pacifism has slowly died away in the course of this century.

[59] Bowman, p. 329.

of many of the conservative, fundamentalist Disciples of Christ in mid-Tennessee, where these views continued to be held into the twentieth century. Their chief proponent, David Lipscomb, may possibly have derived his position—via his teacher, Tolbert Fanning—from the Anabaptist-Mennonite attitude toward the state. At least, this is more likely to have been the source than, for instance, any influence of Garrisonian nonresistance, which would have been suspect to men like Fanning and Lipscomb both for its theological liberalism and for its abolitionist taint. But, of course, the latter may have reached their conclusions by independent reading of the scriptures, or perhaps through the influence of Barton W. Stone, who had frowned on Christian participation in politics,[60] or even Alexander Campbell, whose views on the state were not, however, completely negative.

During the recent conflict Lipscomb had courageously stood up for his opinions on war, thereby incurring threats of lynching from war enthusiasts of both sides. Among both church leaders and the rank and file there were many in this section of Tennessee who took a stand similar to Lipscomb's. But there were also Disciples in the province who had taken a pro-war stand. Most would have been supporters of the Southern cause, although there were Unionist sympathizers among them, too. Some younger men, of course, had taken an active part in military service. And so voices were now raised demanding that "all church members, who were engaged on both sides in carnal warfare and wholesale destruction of life, should [publicly] confess their wrong." In the end, in order to avoid the dissension that such a measure would inevitably have caused, especially while war passions were still running high, no action was taken.[61]

In January 1866, with Lipscomb's assistance, Fanning restarted his paper, the Nashville *Gospel Advocate*, which he had closed down at the outbreak of war. Soon the aging Fanning handed over the direction of the paper to Lipscomb, who was assisted by Elisha G. Sewell. These two, along with a number of devoted collaborators, soon made the *Gospel Advocate* both a rallying point for the theologically con-

---

[60] David Edwin Harrell, Jr., *Quest for a Christian America*, p. 55.

[61] E. A. Elam, *Twenty-Five Years of Trust: A Life Sketch of J. M. Kidwill*, p. 51. Kidwill (1836-1892), who was to become prominent among Tennessee Disciples in the post-Civil War period as a leader of the church's conservative wing, opposed this kind of action when it was proposed in his congregation. A similar position was taken by David Lipscomb in 1875 when a Texas Disciple raised the matter of disfellowshipping combatants—as well as voters and officeholders—among the membership. Lipscomb advised "patient instruction . . . in the church, instead of withdrawal from the weak." Only in the last resort, and in cases of willful opposition to the truth, should expulsion be tried. See Earl Irvin West, *The Search for the Ancient Order*, II, 216, and *The Life and Times of David Lipscomb*, pp. 109, 110.

servative forces among Disciples in the South and a focus for the ebbing pacifism of the church. "Lipscomb was a southerner," his biographer has written, "his sympathies in the war lay with the South, and . . . as to slavery, Lipscomb had always said that it was neither right nor wrong in itself, [though] certainly he had never advocated it at all."[62] The church schism that ended by 1906 in the creation of two bodies, the fundamentalist Churches of Christ and the more liberal branch which retained the name of Disciples of Christ, was ostensibly caused by issues such as the latter's support for the use of organs in the church service. In fact, the separation stemmed in large part from the division between the poorer, more rural churches of the South, which shared the alienation from the postbellum political order felt by their whole section of the country and which retained their old conservative ways of thinking, and the Disciples in the North, who accepted the ethos and way of life of the Northern states. Some Northern Disciples regarded Lipscomb's pacifism as a product of crypto-Confederate sympathies rather than of a genuine Biblical nonresistance. This accusation was unjust, although his *Gospel Advocate*, it is true, did become to some extent the mouthpiece of the Southern point of view within the church.

Lipscomb was certainly a separatist, but he advocated separation from the world rather than merely disunion with the North. He did, indeed, attack Northern preachers because they had "supported the government in its war" and condemned General (later President) James A. Garfield both for his soldiering and his politics. And he found a ready response to his utterances on these subjects among his coreligionists in the South. But his pacifism was part of an entire *Weltanschauung* and not simply a piece of political expediency dressed up in the guise of religious principle.

Early in the postwar period Lipscomb outlined his position vis-à-vis the political order in a series of articles in the *Gospel Advocate* of 1866 and 1867. Subsequently, in 1889, he published them in book form under the title *Civil Government*.

For Lipscomb, as for the Anabaptists and their descendants (and for William Lloyd Garrison, too), God is the world's "only rightful law-maker and ruler." Thus, although human government—"this great Babylon," Lipscomb calls it—was necessary in present-day conditions and ought to be obeyed in all things lawful, it is nevertheless the realm of Satan, the outcome of man's sin and his turning away from God. "The chief occupation of human governments from the beginning has been war. Nine-tenths of the taxes paid by the human family have

[62] West, *Lipscomb*, pp. 107, 108.

913

gone to preparing for, carrying on, or paying the expenses of war." And war, of course, is totally incompatible with Christian discipleship. Consequently, not merely should the Christian refuse military service: he must also refrain from voting for, or holding office in, the governments that make war inevitable.[63]

These views Lipscomb and his friends on the *Gospel Advocate* continued to propagate in season and out for another half-century. This was a strictly sectarian nonresistance, pacifism of a kind with which, as we have seen, the Quakers and German-speaking peace churches were beginning to break during this period. In regard to nondenominational peace societies, we find Lipscomb writing in 1870: "A Christian is wasting time in seeking peace for the world in other institutions" than the true church. And in regard to the half-measure American Peace Society which had, as we know, given support to the Union war effort, Lipscomb wrote scornfully: "Some of the bitterest war men in the land are leaders of this peace association."

Yet Lipscomb's group maintained a staunch, if narrow, witness to the pacifist cause at a time when the traditional peace sects were largely inactive in the matter. The *Gospel Advocate* preached peace whenever war threatened and denounced bellicose policies on the part of the administration. When the Spanish-American War opened in 1898 and there was much enthusiasm among American Protestants (including the Northern Disciples) for a fight against Catholic Spain, Lipscomb called upon the readers of his *Gospel Advocate* to refuse military service if conscription should come again. He also republished the petition explaining their stand against being drafted that the Tennessee Disciples had sent the authorities of both sides during the Civil War. And we find one of the paper's contributors expressing himself vehemently on the subject of the war in the following words: "I would as soon risk my chance of heaven to die drunk in a bawdy house as to die on the battlefield, with murder in my heart, trying to kill my fellow man."[64]

It was assuredly Lipscomb's theological conservatism and his pro-Southern stance that gave him a position of leadership among the Disciple churches of the South rather than his pacifist views. These were tolerated rather than adopted with any degree of enthusiasm by most church members in Lipscomb's sector of the country. Nevertheless, the fact that in the First World War the Churches of Christ

[63] David Lipscomb, *Civil Government*, 1957 edn., pp. iii, iv, 10, 11, 57ff., 101, 132.

[64] D. E. Harrell, Jr., "Disciples of Christ Pacifism in Nineteenth Century Tennessee," *Tennessee Historical Quarterly*, XXI, no. 3 (Sept. 1962), 271-74.

(the denomination that Lipscomb had helped to bring into being) rank sixth on the list of religious sects producing the largest number of conscientious objectors,[65] must have been due, in some measure, to the influence of Lipscomb and the group that he had gathered around his paper, the Nashville *Gospel Advocate.*

In addition to the three larger historic peace churches and the Disciples of mid-Tennessee, there existed in the period under discussion several other small groups which collectively adhered to a pacifist interpretation of the Christian gospel. Of these the Rogerenes of Connecticut, who finally died out before 1914, were the oldest, dating back to the late seventeenth century. Although the sect was on the point of expiry, it showed more activity on behalf of peace than several larger pacifist groups, owing largely to the efforts of the vigorous Whipple family settled in and around the little seaport of Mystic. In the early seventies we still find several of their young Rogerenes spending a few weeks in jail for refusal to pay militia fines (a form of commutation that was fast disappearing, as the militia became increasingly moribund, in the various states where it had been enacted).[66] A number of the sect were active in the Universal Peace Union (discussed in the next chapter), and old Jonathan Whipple (d. 1875) and other members of his family were responsible for bringing out the Union's organ, the *Bond* (later the *Voice) of Peace,* from 1872 to 1874 and, along with some local Quakers, for organizing its Connecticut branch, which was known as the Connecticut Peace Society. It was also for many years the tradition in the Union to hold its annual meetings at Mystic, where the delegates could enjoy the hospitality of neighboring Rogerenes.

The Schwenkfelders of Pennsylvania reached this continent a half century or so after the Rogerenes had come into existence, and, though now reduced in numbers to a few thousand, they have persisted until today. They appear to have discarded their pacifism somewhere in the decades between the Civil War and 1917. At any rate, the church as a whole did not take a pacifist stand in either of the two world wars.[67] The shift in attitude is not easily traceable in the church's scanty print-

[65] See the table in E. N. Wright's *Conscientious Objectors in the Civil War,* p. 223.

[66] John R. Bolles and Anna B. Williams, *The Rogerenes,* pp. 315, 316; *The Voice of Peace,* 1st ser., I, no. 1 (June 1872), 7; no. 3 (Aug. 1872), 2, 3; no. 5 (Oct. 1872), 12; II, no. 6 (June 1873), 10, 11; no. 7 (July 1873), 8, 9. In Pennsylvania C.O.'s were exempted from the militia tax in 1872.

[67] "In the war with Germany, not only was no exemption asked [i.e., by the church as a body] on the ground of religious belief, but a considerable number of the young men entered the national service." See *Census of Religious Bodies 1936: Schwenkfelders,* p. 3.

ed literature of the period. The church *Constitution* mentioned earlier, which was published in German in 1851 and in an English translation in 1882, took a forthright stand against participation in war. And, in fact, Schwenkfelders during the Civil War, if drafted, appear to have refused at least combatant service. But their discipline of 1902 shows some uncertainty. "In view of the fact that war is an unmitigated evil," states the section on "Civil Government," "members are earnestly enjoined to discourage and discountenance whatever may be regarded as incitements to war, and to avoid, wherever possible, active participation in the same."[68] In the revised edition of this discipline published in 1912, all reference to war is omitted.

The Shakers—the final group that needs to be discussed in any detail here—had originated, as we have seen, at the time of the American Revolution. By the outbreak of the Civil War the Society had begun to show signs of decline in both numbers and energy. The old enthusiasm that had led Mother Ann Lee and her little band to face opprobrium and sometimes physical violence from the state and society undaunted was still present in some of the Shaker leaders of the postwar period. But the Society was beginning to withdraw into itself and was well on the way, with its increasing wealth and declining membership, to becoming the small closed circle of highly respectable and increasingly elderly persons that it has become in our day as it now nears final extinction.

Yet the leading figure in late nineteenth-century Shakerism, Elder Frederick W. Evans, was something of a radical, who battled throughout his long life on behalf of a number of causes, ranging from the fight against land monopoly to the war against war. The connection he saw between land reform and pacifism Evans once explained as follows:

> There would have been no Civil War if no chattel slavery. And no chattel slavery if no wage slavery. No wage slavery, if no land monopoly. If no land monopoly, no poor landless people. If no poor landless people, no soldiers and nothing to fight about. With an inalienable homestead, men can feed and shelter their families, if they will cease to kill. And if they cease to kill there will be no war. "Thou shalt not kill."[69]

Views of this kind seem to belong more to an agrarian age that was rapidly passing as a result of the impact of industrialization and mech-

---

[68] *Formula for the Government and Discipline of the Schwenkfelder Church*, chap. XIV, art. 4. The original draft was approved in 1898.

[69] Quoted in Anna White and Leila S. Taylor, *Shakerism, Its Meaning and Message*, p. 203.

anization than to late nineteenth-century America, just as did the group's self-sufficient economy which no longer answered the needs of the time.

Among Evans's varied activities was his support for the work of the Universal Peace Union. He and other Shakers participated in its annual gatherings. In 1899, for instance, we find one of the Shaker stalwarts, Eldress Anna White, telling her audience at the Union's Mystic meeting: "I agree with Tolstoy, that no compromise should be made with this monster of evil. If all refuse to take up arms, what then? Whoever heard of a fight without fighters?"[70] In the summer of 1905 the Society, as a result of the initiative of Eldress Leila Taylor in particular, held its own peace convention at Mount Lebanon, which was attended by a number of persons prominent in the peace movement. Resolutions sponsored by Eldress Taylor were passed, advocating a radical reduction in armaments throughout the world and unhampered exchange of goods as a first step toward international peace.[71]

In 1891, shortly before his death, Evans had entered into correspondence with the great Russian writer and nonresistant, Count Leo Tolstoy. After reading the Shaker tracts that Evans had sent him, Tolstoy expressed his pleasure in finding himself so much in agreement with these American communitarians. Yet certain points of difference remained. Tolstoy balked at the idea of property, even communally held property, in a group claiming to be followers of Christian nonresistance. "Do you acknowledge the possibility for a Christian, to defend property from usurpators?" he wrote Evans. "I ask this question because I think that the principle of non-resistance is the chief trait of true Christianity; and that the greatest difficulty in our time, is to be true to it: how do you manage to do so in your community?" Evans's reply is extremely revealing of the contrast between the Russian, whose pacifism was an expression of his alienation from society, and the American (by adoption, if not by birth), for whom the state was not so much the enemy as the framework within which nonresistance and community life might freely develop. So we find Evans telling Tolstoy that, although "in no case, or any circumstances" did the Shakers believe it right to injure a fellow human being, they saw nothing inconsistent with this belief in holding and defending their community property "under the civil laws." And he goes on:

You see that our civil government is the voice of the people, "*vox populi, vox Dei*"; and the people, who are the rulers, are more

[70] Anna White, *Voices from Lebanon*, p. 8.
[71] Edward Deming Andrews, *The People Called Shakers*, p. 217.

progressed [sic] than are the rulers of Russia, or of any church and state government on the face of the earth. Consequently, we [the Shakers] can, under the American secular government, carry out the abstract principles taught by the Christ-spirit's revelation, more perfectly than has, hitherto, ever been done by mortal men and women.[72]

Thus we find the superiority of the New World over the Old being proclaimed through the lips of the obscure communitarian nonresistant.

The Shakers, for all their English origins, are surely a typical expression of the optimism and boundless horizons of post-revolutionary America. Equally American in both origin and outlook are the various "holiness" and pentecostal churches that began to crystallize from around the turn of this century. We know that the Assemblies of God, which came into being on the eve of the First World War, and the Missionary Church Association, founded in 1898, urged members to refuse at least combatant service, if they actually did not forbid it outright. Their pacifism, like that of the older Adventist groups, who continued to maintain their previous noncombatant stand, and that of the Plymouth Brethren, who had originated in England, was based primarily on a Biblical literalism. The Mosaic commandment "Thou shalt not kill" was as relevant here as the injunctions of the Sermon on the Mount. On the other hand, the noncombatancy of the International Bible Students (later known as Jehovah's Witnesses), whose origins date back to the latter decades of the nineteenth century, was not based on strictly pacifist premises, but rather on a desire to keep the group separate from the world until the dawn of the fiery millennium.[73]

Before America's entry into war in 1917 brought home the issue of military service, however, these pentecostal and millenarian groups devoted little attention to the question of pacifism. Drawing adherents mainly from the educationally underprivileged and from the rural areas and their impetus from obscure social and religious impulses

---

[72] *Shaker-Russian Correspondence between Count Leo Tolstoi and Elder F. W. Evans*, a 7-page pamphlet.

[73] The nonresistance of the Dukhobors, who settled in Canada at the beginning of this century, still belongs at this time to the history of Russian sectarian pacifism more than to the history of North American pacifism. Their religious faith, centered in an ethical pantheism within a loosely Christian framework, had been greatly influenced by the teachings of Tolstoy. A few of the more independently minded Dukhobors moved early in this century from the Canadian prairies to California. See my article "Vasya Pozdnyakov's Dukhobor Narrative," *Slavonic and East European Review* (London), XLIII (1964-1965), no. 100, 152-76, and no. 101, 400-414, for literature on the subject of Dukhobor pacifism prior to 1914.

that were far removed from either the legalism of the Mennonites and Brethren, the mysticism of the Quakers, or the rationalism of the non-sectarian peace movement, sects of this kind have remained of only very peripheral importance to the history of American pacifist thought. Nonetheless, their comparatively large following and the often remarkable energy which they exert in the task of proselytizing have made them a phenomenon of considerable sociological importance in contemporary America.

Chapter 23

The Reemergence of Nonsectarian Pacifism

If the Civil War had found the traditional peace sects unprepared for the ordeal, pacifism outside the peace sects had virtually ceased to exist as an organized movement even before the firing started. The slavery issue had finally dealt it a fatal blow: only a few scattered individuals salvaged their private consciences from the movement's wreckage. Most peace workers, radicals and conservatives alike, had been swept along—some reluctantly, others eagerly—in the wave of war enthusiasm that had engulfed the Northern states, at least for a time. The bankruptcy of pacifism, indeed of the whole peace movement, at the moment of its trial demanded a radical reorientation, a deepening of its search into the sources of conflict and into the means of eradicating violence within both the domestic and the international orders. In fact, in subsequent decades a transformation of this kind was only effected in part and rather inadequately: the process, indeed, had not got very far before the outbreak of war in Europe shattered the peace, this time of the whole world. "All in all," writes Merle Curti, "the [Civil] war left an inheritance of fervent patriotism and widespread belief in the sacred efficacy of the appeal to arms."[1] The militant and self-confident imperialism that came to the fore toward the end of the century continued to make it difficult for any form of radical pacifism in America to achieve even the very modest successes that had been achieved in the 1830's and 1840's.

At the end of the Civil War some former peace men were still in a belligerent mood. Beckwith of the American Peace Society advocated strong measures against the defeated Confederates, including the death penalty for some of their leaders. Charles Sumner, along with the genuinely pacifist Amasa Walker and others from the peace camp, vehemently supported the program of "thorough" reconstruction that was being promoted by the radical Republicans. In the famous "Alabama" case in the late sixties that possibly might have ended in war between Britain and the United States—at least if Sumner and Walker's policies had been adopted by the administration—both these men took up an aggressive stance. "Sumner," says Curti, "the great champion of peace, whose pronouncements were at the very mo-

[1] Merle E. Curti, *Peace or War*, p. 73.

920

ment circulating as antiwar propaganda in two countries lamentably delayed the peaceful solution of a bitter controversy."[2]

Yet a handful of old-time peace radicals continued to stand by their prewar principles both during and after the termination of the armed struggle. Elihu Burritt was one of them. After the war, however, he was more active on behalf of peace as a writer than as an organizer. Shortly after the Franco-Prussian War of 1870, prompted by the rising arms race in Europe and the unlikelihood of any existing government summoning enough courage to disarm unilaterally, Burritt proposed a workers' strike against war and the war method. The threat of such a strike, he hoped, might pressure the powers into agreeing to at least a gradual and proportional reduction in their armaments. "This, then, is the alternative," he concluded, "either a Congress of Nations for simultaneous and proportionate disarmament, or an organized strike of the working-men of Christendom against war, root and branch."[3] The idea of direct action of the proletariat ("the great, honest, toiling masses of the world," in Burritt's words) against war, although not entirely novel even in Burritt's day, was one that was to play a considerable role in radical pacifist thought in the twentieth century.

But Burritt, despite his humble origins and his sympathy for the cause of labor, was not really a political radical (as the United States government perhaps realized when it appointed him U. S. consul in Liverpool in 1865). And on some aspects of international affairs his thinking lagged far behind Garrison's, for instance. Take the views he expressed on nationalism at this time. He showed no understanding of the aspirations and grievances of the smaller nationalities of Europe. Their aims, in his view, were both unnecessary and even harmful to general well-being, and he spoke disparagingly of their "pigmy stature," "their worthless being." The emergent nations of Eastern Europe were far better off, in his view, under Russia, Austria, or Turkey than they could ever be as independent states, with a "deceptive and fruitless independence." Let Ireland remain part of the United Kingdom, and Belgium return to her union with Holland, and Portugal throw in her lot with Spain, and so on.[4] Burritt's viewpoint, it is true, was one he shared with other leaders in the contemporary Anglo-American peace movement (Richard Cobden, for example). But, however unconsciously, it represented more a great-power mentality than a genuinely internationalist outlook.

[2] *Ibid.*, pp. 83, 91-94.
[3] "The World's Working-Men's Strike Against War," reprinted in his *Ten-Minute Talks on All Sorts of Topics*, pp. 259-66.
[4] "The Cost of Small Nationalities," *ibid.*, pp. 334-39.

William Lloyd Garrison, the other great figure in prewar pacifism, had virtually retired from active participation in the peace movement. If his position during the war had seemed ambiguous to some pacifists, his postwar advocacy of stern retribution against the South (he even wanted to impeach President Andrew Johnson for his failure to implement a program of radical reconstruction) brought expostulation from his friends. "You are exceedingly severe upon the South," wrote Gerrit Smith in March 1867 in an effort to convince Garrison of the expediency of a policy of mildness toward the defeated; to Smith, the guilt of slavery and war ultimately rested on both North and South alike, and repentance, therefore, had to be undertaken in common.[5] Garrison's present bellicosity, as well as his long and uncompromising antislavery record, probably contributed to the fact that in 1866 the appeal for a "National Testimonial" to be presented to him in the form of a gift in money was signed, among others, by the president of the U. S. Senate, the chief justice of the Supreme Court, and the governor, lieutenant-governor, and chief justice of the commonwealth of Massachusetts.[6] This recognition surely was not without a certain irony when bestowed on an enthusiastic "no-government" nonresistant such as Garrison had been in the prewar era. To an inquiry whether his qualified support of the recent conflict meant that he had abandoned nonresistance, however, he replied with some passion: "Whoever supposes or reports me to have gone back upon my pacific principles does me great, though probably unintentional injustice. Nothing has occurred to make me doubt their soundness. . . . That war, instead of confounding the radical advocates of peace, only strengthened their position—if, indeed, it needed any strengthening."[7]

Until his death in 1879 Garrison still remained in many ways the grand old man of the radical peace movement, as well as a living monument to the abolitionist impulse. Visitors to his home would sometimes come away inspired to dedicate themselves to the propagation of his nonresistant ideas.[8] Among his children, two—William Lloyd, Jr., and Fanny (Villard)—followed in his footsteps and became pacifist prop-

---

[5] *Gerrit Smith to Mr. Garrison*, a leaflet in the Houghton Library, Harvard University (*f A C 8. Sm574. B867g). Smith supported the efforts of the Universal Peace Union soon after the conclusion of the war to promote a conciliation with the South. See Ralph Volney Harlow, *Gerrit Smith*, p. 470.

[6] Ralph Korngold, *Two Friends of Man*, p. 358.

[7] *Voice of Peace*, 1st ser., I, no. 5 (Oct. 1872), 2.

[8] Ernest Crosby, *Garrison the Non-Resistant*, p. 51: "His conversation so impressed a young Japanese student who was preparing himself in America for the army of his country that on his return home he refused to serve for conscience' sake, and was duly cast into prison."

agandists.[9] Even more important, of course, was the continuing influence that his earlier writing and agitation on behalf of a radical pacifist program exerted on thinkers both within his own country and outside it. As we have seen, both Tolstoy and, later, Gandhi owed much to the American prophet of nonresistance.

The Universal Peace Union, which a young man of Quaker background, Alfred H. Love, founded in 1866 and which under his leadership remained until the First World War the sole organized expression of radical pacifism outside the peace sects, was, despite significant differences, in many senses the direct successor of earlier Garrisonian nonresistance.[10]

The old American Peace Society, it is true, continued alongside Love's organization as the center of the conservative peace movement, which aimed to embrace all who wished to work for the elimination of war. Its efforts were directed as before mainly toward campaigning for universal and compulsory arbitration between nations and for the setting up of an international court of justice. This campaign, the Society hoped, would be implemented abroad through international peace congresses and similar societies in other countries; at home it would be carried on by publishing literature on the subject as well as by lobbying Congress and government officials. The Society's supporters were predominantly middle-class: well-to-do businessmen figure prominently among its members during this period. It did good work in combating increasing manifestations of militarism and navalism in public life and in protesting against the Spanish-American War of 1898 and the aggressive policies of the early twentieth century. But, even though the Quaker Benjamin F. Trueblood, who became its secretary in 1892, succeeded in reinvigorating the by now rather moribund Society and under his direction won for it in the early years of this century considerable—and perhaps too easy—popularity, the American Peace Society failed to probe deeply into the roots of war, neglecting almost entirely its economic and social causes. Seeking above

[9] See, e.g., two pamphlets by W. L. Garrison, Jr.: *The Things that make for Peace*, an address delivered at the annual conference of the Universal Peace Union in 1895, and *Non-Resistance a Better Defence than Armies and Navies*, a talk given to the yearly meeting of Progressive Friends at Longwood in 1908. The younger Garrison (1838-1909) was an ardent single-taxer and free trader as well as a nonresistant in the style of his father.

[10] In the account of the Universal Peace Union given below, I have relied mainly on the valuable Ph.D. diss. (U. of Pennsylvania, 1962) by Robert W. Doherty, "Alfred H. Love and the Universal Peace Union." Doherty's main sources are Love's own "Journal" in 24 volumes and the files of the successive organs of the Union: the *Bond of Peace*, *Voice of Peace*, and *Peacemaker*, all in the S.C.P.C. See also Curti, *Peace or War*, pp. 76-80.

all to influence the well-to-do, the influential, and the highly placed, it mistook the dubious patronage of governments—as manifested, for example, in the two Hague Peace Conferences of 1899 and 1907—for a readiness to abandon the traditional war system in favor of a new world organization. Alfred Love's Universal Peace Union, on the other hand, though even at its height a much smaller and less well-connected organization than the American Peace Society, nevertheless succeeded in avoiding at least some of these shortcomings.

Love was born in 1830 into a well-to-do Quaker merchant family in Philadelphia, and he continued in the woolens business throughout his life. He had early become associated with the heretical Progressive Friends; his liberal religious views, however, later brought about the rejection of the application he eventually made for membership in the Hicksite branch of the Society of Friends, although he continued to attend their meetings until his death. We have seen him in the Civil War appearing in print as a defender of Quaker pacifism; he took his stand as an absolutist conscientious objector when called up for service, refusing, despite the opposition of his family, not merely to hire a substitute but to pay commutation money and even to plead the genuine physical disability of nearsightedness that eventually gained him his exemption.[11] During the war, too, he refused in his business to handle army orders, even though turning them down meant a considerable loss of income at a time of financial difficulties; moreover, he consistently refused to pay his militia tax for as long as he was required to do so. Yet in his attitude toward the authorities he shared the Quaker spirit of conciliation in which he had been reared. Ready to suffer for his principles if called upon, he "regretted being drafted," he writes, "for the single reason that I preferred not to add to the complications of the Government already painfully encompassed with trials, which I would gladly lessen rather than increase."[12] Throughout his life, in spite of his diffident and retiring nature, he was tireless in attempting to give positive expression to his nonviolent philosophy of life, not only in working for peace but in striving to remove injustice and hardship from society. Both before and after the war he was active, therefore, in a wide range of causes: race relations, penal reform, temperance, women's rights, and social rehabilitation, among others. Yet, as so often with "do-gooders" of the Love variety, there was some self-righteousness in his make-up as well as a stubbornly doctrinaire side to his character bordering on eccentricity, a

[11] See Alfred H. Love, *Address before the Peace Convention . . . 1866*, pp. 7-14, for an account of his experiences before the Board of Enrollment.

[12] *Ibid.*, p. 8.

924

rigidity and narrowness of view that often made him a colleague none too easy to work with.

The Universal Peace Union in its origins was a direct continuation of Garrisonian nonresistance. In the first place, there was the formative influence that Garrison exercised on its founder Love, who came into close contact with the older leader during the war (both were participants in the activities of the Progressive Friends, for instance). In his journal Love calls Garrison "my echo and answer to my spirit longings for peace principles." Love's whole approach to the problem of peace, with its stress on the moral iniquity of war, was essentially Garrisonian, even if he did not fully share Garrison's earlier repugnance to government[13] or, even less, the latter's lifelong lack of sympathy for the cause of labor. Love was a believer in the efficacy of nonviolence as a method of resolving disputes and practised it in his daily living, although he never worked out practical techniques for its implementation such as have been attempted in the twentieth century. His nonviolence flowed both from his interpretation of Christianity and from his concept of the whole universe as the harmonious creation of a loving God and of peace as the expression of God's working in it.

Secondly, the beginning steps to rally the nonresistants after the shock of war had finally disintegrated their ranks, efforts that eventually led to the emergence of the Universal Peace Union, came while the war was still being waged from a tiny group of Garrisonian nonresistants in Boston. Old Joshua P. Blanchard was one of them, but their most dynamic personality was Ezra H. Heywood (see earlier). At first, while the war continued, the group had no formal organization. The decision to set one up was taken at a conference in Boston in December 1865. Blanchard was in the chair; in addition to the remnants of New England nonresistance, Alfred Love was among the thirty-five or so delegates attending. A new note was struck when one of the delegates demanded that "a radical peace society" should inquire into the economic causes of war and work for "the emancipation of Labor" as a means toward peace.[14] Both Love and Heywood, indeed, favored such a broadening of the basis of war resistance. And the general disillusionment with the wartime stand of the American Peace Society underlined the need for a new and more forthright peace organization. Further conventions were held the following year,

[13] However, from 1864 on, Love, who had earlier supported the Republican party, refrained from voting on account of the tacit support that he believed this gave to the war method.

[14] Bryan J. Butts, *The Conditions of Peace*, pp. 7, 8. Butts, as mentioned earlier, was associated with Ballou's Hopedale experiment.

925

in March in Boston again and in May in Providence, when a formal decision to set up the Universal Peace Union (or Society, as it was at first called) was taken.[15] Delegates to the Providence meeting were drawn from a number of states, and among them were included, in addition to names already mentioned, such peace stalwarts as Adin Ballou and several of his Hopedalers, Lucretia Mott from Philadelphia, Henry C. Wright (once again in a militantly nonresistant mood),[16] Amasa Walker, and several former pacifists who had strayed away from the fold during the antislavery excitement, like Professor T. C. Upham and Abby and Stephen Foster. Love was elected president of the new society, and, with Heywood's assistance, he proceeded to draw up its constitution, which was published along with an address to "all persons, families, communities and nations."

The Universal Peace Union came out on a platform of complete pacifism: Christianity never "sanctions war under any circumstances whatever." "War is a sin against God and opposed to the best interests of mankind, and its immediate abandonment is alike a religious duty, the wisest expediency and an imperative necessity." The old American Peace Society was "good, as far as it goes, but it does not go as far as goodness," since it had continued to uphold defensive wars—and "all wars are construed to be defensive." The new society would work, through "popular conventions, lectures, tracts, petitions, the pulpit, the press," to impress on public opinion the obsoleteness of war and the necessity of solving international disputes by peaceful means. Finally, in consonance with the group's Garrisonian lineage, there was to be no involvement in politics, no "political complications with governments of force."[17]

There was, however, some difference of opinion among the new movement's supporters regarding the degree of noninvolvement that was incumbent on radical pacifists. Love, for instance, while agreeing that governments still needed to be purified "of all taint of blood," urged members to make use of the ballot to further the pursuit of peace whenever it was not against their conscience so to do. H. C. Wright, on the other hand, wished to make it the society's policy for members to refrain personally from all participation in political activity, both active and passive; but he lost a resolution to this effect that

[15] See *Proceedings of the Peace Conventions, held in Boston, March 14 & 15, 1866; and in Providence, May 16th, 1866.*

[16] See the *Declaration of Radical Peace Principles*, which Wright drew up on 4 July 1866 for signature by members of the recently founded organization.

[17] *Address of the Universal Peace Society to All Persons, Communities and Nations*, pp. 2, 9.

926

he introduced at the society's first annual meeting in 1867.[18] Love felt, too—and he was obviously influenced here by memories of the Civil War dilemma of the nonresistant abolitionists—that it would be wrong for the society to enter into detailed criticism of the war measures of a government that was felt to be acting for the best according to its own lights. Heywood, however, considered such Quaker mildness unjustified.

The Universal Peace Union throughout its existence supported the stand of the conscientious objector, although not quite all of its members—or, still less, all of its more loosely affiliated sympathizers—were absolute pacifists. In its early years, when the state militia tax for non-attendance at drillings was still being levied, Love himself and a number of others refused payment, suffering distraint of goods and, in a few cases, short imprisonment as a consequence. The Union pressed for legal recognition of the right of conscientious objection to both military service and its commutation, which it claimed had been guaranteed implicitly in the Declaration of Independence and the First Amendment to the U. S. Constitution. But H. C. Wright's proposal that members should subscribe to a pledge "never to enlist in the army or navy, to do what we can to prevent others enlisting, and to induce all to cease from studying the art and plying the trade of human slaughter" does not seem to have been implemented.[19]

Branches of the new society, at first sometimes describing themselves as "Radical Peace Societies," were soon established in Massachusetts, Rhode Island, Connecticut, and Pennsylvania, and in a few other places later. Its activities came more and more to be centered in Philadelphia, partly because this was Love's home town and also because it could rely there on the support of some Quakers from the Hicksite branch and of the small group of Progressive Friends. (Among some Hicksite and most Orthodox Friends, however, the Union was looked at askance for its failure to stress the divinity of Christ and the place of the Atonement in its Christian pacifism.) Love at times laid claims to over 10,000 supporters, but this figure is a gross exaggeration, unless—as Love evidently must have done—one includes the membership of the various European peace societies with which the Universal Peace Union was loosely affiliated. Around 400 active members, with between 3,000 and 4,000 sympathizers in the United States, would be a more accurate figure for its size during most of its existence. The Union got its most enthusiastic support from small pacifist

---

[18] *Proceedings of the First Anniversary of the Universal Peace Society, . . . 1867.*
[19] Henry C. Wright, *Declaration of Radical Peace Principles,* pp. 2, 3.

927

sects like the Shakers, Rogerenes, and Bible Christians. Some members belonged to the larger nonpacifist denominations; others were unaffiliated religious liberals. They were mostly located in New England or the middle states and were drawn almost exclusively from persons of British Protestant stock. Women made up about one-third of the total active membership. Such prominent advocates of women's rights as the Quakers Susan B. Anthony and Lucretia Mott, Belva Lockwood (the first woman to stand for the presidency), Lucy Stone, and Ernestine Rose took part in its proceedings;[20] and the vital role of women in bringing about a peaceful world was stressed in its propaganda.

The basic aim of the Universal Peace Union, as Love saw it, was to remold society in a spirit of Christian love and human brotherhood. War was the supreme expression of man's negation of this ideal; hence, the preservation of peace between the nations, along with the achievement of social justice within the nation, was the practical goal for which he felt the Union must work. Many of the Union's policies ran parallel with those being pressed by the older and more conservative American Peace Society: international arbitration and the setting up of an international court of justice; opposition to military appropriations in Congress, to imperialist policies abroad, and to the militarization of youth and the glorification of war in public life at home. Its publications stressed the economic waste of war, along with its inefficiency as a method of solving disputes and its basic immorality and inconsistency in a nation professing to be Christian. The Union, however, unlike the American Peace Society during this period, went on to plead that the United States give a lead to the world by adopting a policy of unilateral disarmament. It campaigned against capital punishment as a violation of the sacredness of all human life. (It did not, however, adopt vegetarianism as part of its program, even though some of its members were vegetarians and Love hesitated on the brink of becoming one.) Much attention was given in the publications of the Union to the problem of pacifist education. No corporal punishment in home or school, no military drill in school or college, no warlike playthings for the young were to be permitted; the war spirit was to be expunged from school textbooks, and even games like football were discouraged by the Union for being likely to foster violent habits in later life.

Conservative pacifism, as represented by the American Peace So-

[20] See *Proceedings of the Second Anniversary of the Universal Peace Society . . . 1868*, pp. 15, 33. Curti (*Peace or War*, p. 114) points out that it was not until 1871 that the American Peace Society permitted women to hold office.

ciety, concerned itself exclusively with the peace issue. The Universal Peace Union, like its Garrisonian predecessors and under the influence of men like Love and Heywood, held to a wider conception of what was involved in a nonviolent philosophy. It campaigned on behalf of underprivileged ethnic groups like the Negroes, the American Indians, and the newly arrived immigrants from Europe and Asia. Above all, it interested itself in the labor problem, which was growing in intensity with the country's rapid industrialization after the Civil War. A note of social radicalism was apparent in the organization from the outset. For instance, at a meeting in Providence in the spring of 1867 attended by Love, Heywood, and Wright, it was resolved that the public's attention be directed to the fact "that wars are usually inaugurated by the upper and governing classes for the purpose of personal or national ambition, preferment or pride, and the mutilation, torture and death of men from the lower and laboring classes is less an object of consideration than the money which is required for their equipment and support as soldiers."[21] Although the anarchistic socialism of a man like E. H. Heywood was not adopted by the Union, it recognized the connection between war and economic injustice and strove, if somewhat gropingly, to work for social reform along with international peace. Love advocated profit-sharing in industry and the arbitration of disputes between capital and labor; he condemned the use of force in suppressing strikes, while remaining suspicious of trade unionism for its connection with violent action and skeptical of socialism as a political panacea. The Universal Peace Union was in fact, like the more conservative sections of the peace movement, predominantly middle-class and had little contact with organized labor. Toward the end of the century enough members became adherents of Henry George's single-tax reforms to lead the Union to adopt them in its program, although Love himself was not completely convinced of their validity.

The written word remained the chief vehicle for reaching the general public. The Union published a number of tracts and booklets, some by its own members, others reprints of works by such authors as Ballou, Tolstoy, and the Baroness von Suttner. These booklets apparently did not sell very well. Moreover, the successive journals put out by the Union—the *Bond of Peace* (1868-1872), the *Voice of Peace* (1872-1882), and, finally, the *Peacemaker* (1882-1913)—led a vegetating existence. Poorly edited and poorly produced, always carrying a deficit covered by donations from wealthy members, they "were a failure

---

[21] *Radical Peace Resolutions*, p. 1.

as an agency of propaganda. They never attracted a wide audience and therefore did not become a positive force for pacifism."[22]

The time-honored methods of peace and other reform societies—the lecture and the occasional public meeting, lobbying in Washington, petitions, letters to the press and to politicians—were also employed by the Union. The yearly convention at Mystic, in particular, attended in the 1890's by up to 5,000 persons with sessions lasting up to four days, provided an occasion for displaying the rather bizarre methods of publicity that Love favored for making his cause known. Peace flags and banners inscribed with slogans, community singing (of special peace hymns), the releasing of symbolic doves of peace, peace tableaux at international exhibitions, were all employed—not with any great success, it must be admitted—to get the message across to a wide public. Old Elihu Burritt, in fact, thought that the peace plow and pruning hooks, forged from old swords belonging to former officers who had become pacifists, that were exhibited at the 1876 convention would only serve to bring ridicule on the peace movement, and this type of rather sensational gimmick with its forced symbolism met with disapproval from some peace workers. Indeed, "strive as he might, Alfred Love lacked the ability of social communication."[23] The influence of the Union never extended much beyond a small circle of convinced pacifists, despite Love's growing inclination toward the end of his career to include distinguished figures in public life among the honorary officers of his Union. The adornment of the rostrum of vice-presidents with the names of men like the dictatorial President Porfirio Díaz of Mexico, Cardinal James Gibbons, William H. Taft, Elihu Root, Andrew Carnegie, and a host of others in fact contributed very little of real value toward spreading the principles of the Union, for most of these men shared little in common with its radical concept of peace beyond a vague concern sometimes for international conciliation.

The Universal Peace Union, after vainly proposing arbitration as a solution of the conflict before the fighting broke out, put up a courageous, but of course quite ineffectual, opposition to the Spanish-American War of 1898. Love was burnt in effigy in Philadelphia; he and his Union were furiously attacked for their antiwar stand in press and pulpit. Thereafter, from the end of the century, the Union began to decline rapidly in numbers (which, as we have seen, were never

---

[22] Doherty, p. 78. The maximum number of subscribers reached was about 650; usually the number was considerably less. Love took over the job of editor in the mid-1890's.

[23] *Ibid.*, p. 70.

930

large) and in energy, as the old stalwarts of the movement died off and new recruits from the younger generation were not forthcoming. Love himself died in 1913, and the Union virtually expired with him. He and his policies had long been out of touch with the realities of the contemporary scene and were therefore incapable of galvanizing radical pacifism into renewed life. "Love," writes his biographer, "was isolated from the twentieth century. He continued to see and think as a Garrisonian."[24] More, indeed, was necessary before the essence of the pacifist message could have meaning for the new age; a refurbishing of the slogans of the 1830's and 1840's proved insufficient. Love and his band had nurtured radical pacifism through an arid period when increasing materialism and a rising spirit of imperialist jingoism held sway; by the early years of the new century, however, awareness of the need for international cooperation and for deepening the inquiry into the sources of war was growing. For all the good intentions and undeniable merits of the Universal Peace Union and its leader, they were able neither to combat effectively the currents making for war nor to make a significant contribution to the development of the factors in favor of peace.

Neither Love himself nor any member of his group had attempted to present a systematic elaboration of the pacifist position. The literature put out by the Union, insofar as it was original, consisted mainly of short tracts or articles in its journal. Apparently, only three books dealing specifically with the question of pacifism were published in the United States in the period under discussion; and none of the authors of these works appears to have been connected with the Universal Peace Union or prominent in other ways in the peace movement.

The Rev. John M. Washburn, who in 1873 published a bulky volume of 470 pages entitled *Reason vs. the Sword*, was a Presbyterian minister with a parish at that time in New York City. His conversion to pacifism, he tells us, had taken place in the course of the recent war when he had come to feel, despite his strong antislavery convictions, that all war was a crime and participation in it contrary to Christianity. After the war had ended, while occupying a living at Wabash (Ind.), he had contacted the evangelical Friends who were instrumental in organizing the peace conferences of 1866 and 1867 (described in an earlier chapter). He himself participated in the latter gathering held at Richmond (Ind.) and was the only non-Quaker delegate.[25]

The results of his thoughts on the subject of war Washburn em-

24 *Ibid.*, p. 155.
25 *American Friend*, I (1867), no. 1, 10; no. 4, 95.

931

bodied in his book, which—as even he had to confess—is excessively verbose, repetitive, and diffuse. Yet, on the whole, Washburn argues his case effectively and with obvious sincerity. Noteworthy is the fact that, contrary to most previous expositions of pacifism and despite the religious basis of the argument (indeed, Washburn is uncompromisingly fundamentalist in his outlook), he gives most prominence to rational objections to war. "Peace-doctrines," he writes, "are based on the idea that men are rational beings, and may hence be induced to pursue their worldly interests by motives presented to reason." His book is permeated, too, with a strong feeling of disillusionment with the outcome of the Civil War and subsequent reconstruction. Was the material waste and moral damage really necessary? Had the war not resulted merely in replacing one injustice by others equally serious? Could not some other, a peaceful, solution have been found—even if it had to include secession? "War can decide nothing," he exclaims, "save that one people have more brute force than another. It can not decide between right and wrong. Why, then, O *rational* man, fight?"

In one section Washburn inveighs against the evils of conscription. "Like Polycarp and the early Christians," he says, "the true peace-man cannot fight, though he is spoiled of his goods, thrown into noisome bastiles, or suffers death."[26] But he did not share the "no-government" views of some of the earlier nonresistants, even though he admitted the difficulty of the question of "how, on peace-principles, the officers of the law can enforce the sanctions of the law? how they are to arrest offenders who offer resistance?" He believed that Quaker Pennsylvania had pointed the way toward a solution of the problem; it would, however, take time, perhaps as much as a century, before coercion became entirely unnecessary as a result of the gradual permeation of pacifistic sentiments among the populace at large. In the meantime, "let a potent public opinion, firmly and constantly enforce the doctrines of peace; and, first, there will be few persons to be arrested; and secondly, such arrests as may be necessary, will be more easily made without force *than* they are with force *now*."[27] The question of nonviolent action against outside invasion Washburn does not deal with at all: the employment of armed violence in personal self-defense is, he claims, contrary to Christ's teachings, and "personal and national self-defence" are then simply equated as pertaining to the same category of moral action.[28]

[26] John M. Washburn, *Reason vs. the Sword*, pp. 215, 304, 376-80.
[27] *Ibid.*, pp. 253, 254.
[28] *Ibid.*, pt. III, chap. VI, sections 1 and 2.

Washburn, with both a Biblical literalism reminiscent of the outlook of his fellow Presbyterian, David Low Dodge, earlier in the century and a rationalist pacifism bringing to mind the Norman Angell school of antiwar thought in the following century, is a transitional figure in the history of American pacifism. James H. MacLaren, the author of *Put Up Thy Sword*, which, having been written during the Spanish-American War, appeared in print in 1900, on the other hand, stands squarely in the new century. He accepted the Christian nonresistant position. "Church-members," he says, "should refuse to do military service."[29] But he believed, too, that war has no justification even apart from its inconsistency with Christianity and must be rejected on rationalist and humanitarian grounds. And it is to the arguments proving war irrational, wasteful, and destructive of civilized values that the author's creation, "Brain," devotes his main attention in his exchange of letters with the puzzled supporter of war, "Brawn," a correspondence that makes up the little volume. MacLaren is sentimental and almost maudlin in his descriptions of the horrors of war and overoptimistic to the point of naivety in his belief in the efficacy of such devices as international arbitration and a world court for eliminating the institution of war and in the power of education for developing a universal sentiment for world peace. Although much that MacLaren wrote was eminently sane and sensible, he failed, like Washburn, to discuss either the implications of the unilateral disarmament that he urged on nations or the practicable nonviolent alternatives to the war method, should the machinery of international conciliation break down.

It was the Spanish-American War that inspired another writer, a civil servant by profession, to put pen to paper in defense of pacifism. Horace Everett Warner (1839-1930) at this time delivered before the Ethical Club in Washington a series of lectures on the subject, which were published in book form in 1905. "I am under no illusion that this book will have many readers or exert any remarkable influence," wrote the author, who had been a Civil War veteran on the Union side. Like MacLaren, Warner, who was a Congregationalist, came down squarely in favor of Christian pacifism: "the doctrine of non-resistance is as clearly and unmistakably set forth [in the gospels] as language can state it. . . . [Christ] did not allow the use of force even in self-defence."[30] Yet, again like MacLaren, his main concern was not to restate the religious case against war but to prove that warfare was now outmoded, economically wasteful, as a means of settling

[29] James H. MacLaren, *Put Up Thy Sword*, pp. 31, 164.
[30] H. E. Warner, *The Ethics of Force*, pp. iv, 65-81.

933

disputes between nations and would have to be abolished if mankind were to survive. He called for a new heroism in the service of peace to replace the old, merely physical courage of war and for loyalty to the wider international community to supersede the narrower patriotisms of past centuries. He did not foresee the elimination of all coercion, even some degree of mild physical force, in the state's dealings with the criminal elements of society, but he did hold persuasion to be preferable in most cases. Once again, however, the problems raised by the substitution in place of armed force of nonviolent techniques for coping with aggression and disorder were not treated at all adequately.

A deeper understanding of the roots of war within the social order and within man's own psyche was to be found in the teachings of the great Russian apostle of nonviolence, Count Leo Tolstoy. Tolstoy's rejection of violence, however, was carried to an unprecedented extreme: his attitude was itself a reaction to the coercive violence inherent in the political and social order of Tsarist Russia. The Tolstoyan variant of nonresistance also found adherents, who made up for their paucity of numbers by their intensity of belief, in most European countries from the Balkans to England and Scandinavia. Tolstoyism began to percolate through, too, to the United States in the second half of the 1880's. In 1889 a Tolstoy Club was founded in Boston; a decade later it had 100 members. Some prominent figures in the country's literary, political, and social life were influenced by Tolstoy's ideas. The international lawyer, Ernest Howard Crosby (1856-1906), was one of his most ardent disciples. Jane Addams (1860-1935) was influenced by Tolstoy in her approach to peace and social problems. But for a time perhaps the most famous American Tolstoyans were the politician William Jennings Bryan (1860-1925) and the lawyer Clarence Darrow (1857-1938).[31]

There was much that was ambivalent in Bryan's attitude toward peace. As Curti writes: "He loved peace, labored arduously for it, and dearly prized his achievements in its behalf; and yet he fought in one war, was responsible, with President McKinley, for fastening on the country a treaty which inaugurated our imperialism, . . . and, at his own request, was buried with military honors in the national cemetery at Arlington."[32] It was really only after the Spanish-American War, to which he had given somewhat reluctant support, that Bryan

[31] Curti, *Peace or War*, p. 112. For Tolstoy's influence on Jane Addams and for her humanitarian pacifism in the period before 1914, see John C. Farrell, *Beloved Lady*, pp. 141-47.

[32] Curti, *Bryan and World Peace* (Smith College Studies in History, vol. XVI, nos. 3-4), p. 113.

became a thoroughgoing antimilitarist and anti-imperialist. His attitude on these questions was an outgrowth of his deep Christian faith, which saw in violence a negation of the teachings of the Bible; Bryan, indeed, remained throughout his life a fundamentalist, opposed to any compromise with religious liberalism. His antimilitarism stemmed also from his passionate attachment to democratic individualism: war and expansionist policies he associated with plutocracy and the aristocratic principle in politics.

Bryan's encounter with Tolstoy's writings marked a further important influence in the development of his peace views. He became—with certain reservations with regard to Tolstoy's hostility to the state as antichristian, a viewpoint which he never accepted—an ardent admirer of the Russian's philosophy of nonviolence, sharing with Tolstoy his belief in the power of love as a protection against violence. During the winter of 1902-1903, Bryan, then a mature man of 42, visited Tolstoy at his home at Yasnaya Polyana, and during the next decade we find Bryan propounding Tolstoyan nonresistance as a way of life, not merely for the individual but also for states.[33] "There is no question—domestic or foreign," he told the World's Missionary Conference held in Edinburgh in 1910, "which can be permanently settled by any rule that is not in harmony" with the gospel of love, Christ's "law of life," whose strength was mightier than armies. He praised Tolstoy's vision of universal brotherhood, which was also "the Christian ideal." This forbade men to kill their fellows even if provoked: the forgiveness of wrong was "the test of love." It was the responsibility of Christians to do their utmost to see that their government's policies lived up to the Christian ideal.[34]

Yet Bryan never appears to have been an advocate of war resistance: this, in a democratic state, would have been contrary to his faith in the popular will. "The spirit of the conscientious objector he never entertained or even understood."[35] True, he advocated in the early years of the century that the people should be ready to accept nonviolence as national policy (his support for treaties of arbitration, which

[33] Bryan's reaction to Tolstoy's ideas was at the beginning still somewhat skeptical, but he thereafter became increasingly enthusiastic. See Paolo E. Coletta, *William Jennings Bryan*, I, 318.

[34] Bryan, *The Fruits of the Tree*, pp. 27-29, 31, 36-39, 46. Curti (*Bryan*, p. 138) quotes the following from another speech made in 1910: "I believe that this nation could stand before the world today and tell the world that it did not believe in war, that it did not believe that it was the right way to settle disputes, that it had no disputes that it was not willing to submit to the judgment of the world. If this nation did that, it not only would not be attacked by any other nation on earth, but it would become the supreme power in the world. I have no doubt of it, and I believe that the whole tendency is toward that policy."

[35] Curti, *Bryan*, p. 139.

would include even matters involving national honor and vital interests, was a practical reflection of his ideal and, in Curti's opinion, Bryan's chief concrete contribution to the peace movement). Yet, if the people were not prepared to go so far, he would shrink from any attempt to pit the individual conscience against the democratic state. After America's entry into the war, when he had already abandoned his campaign for neutrality and given his reluctant assent to the struggle, he publicly condemned the stand of the conscientious objector.

In March 1913 Bryan became secretary of state in the Wilson administration, the first person connected with the American peace movement to be responsible for the country's foreign policy; he held the post until his resignation in June 1915. This step resulted from his opposition to the U.S.'s involvement in the European war on the side of the Western allies, an involvement that was growing despite the country's formal neutrality. A Tolstoyan in government was, of course, a paradox, but, as we have seen, Bryan wore his Tolstoyism with a difference.[36] Despite all his undoubted good intentions, Bryan's tenure of office was not always consonant with even a moderate pacifism. Curti has written: "The line between violence and non-violence was for him a thin and shifting one; and if national honor were affected, he did not hesitate to move the line to permit the use of force. If he must choose between nationalism and pacifism, the choice was clear, however painful it may have been. . . . Bryan loved peace indeed, but he had other loyalties as well."[37] "The disciple of Tolstoy, confronted by a concrete problem [namely, whether to use warships in 1914 to carry out U.S. policy in the Caribbean area], did not hesitate to rely on force to effect an end which he had so often said could best be achieved by love, charity and the example of goodwill."[38]

Clarence Darrow likewise abandoned his Tolstoyan views on force after little more than a decade. In his case it was the German invasion of Belgium in August 1914 that brought this change of view about. Earlier he had embraced Tolstoyan nonresistance, he tells us in his autobiography,

> . . . not only because I never wanted to fight, but because I considered it a sound philosophical doctrine that should rule men and states. For many years I had been an ardent reader of Tolstoy, and regarded myself as one of his disciples. When Germany invaded Belgium I recovered from my pacifism in the twinkling of an eye.

[36] In British Labour governments after the two world wars several pacifist socialists held office and were faced with the same dilemmas of power that Bryan had faced in his time.

[37] Curti, *Bryan*, p. 183.   [38] *Ibid.*, p. 175.

It came to me through my emotions, and it left me the same way. I discovered that pacifism is probably a good doctrine in time of peace, but of no value in war time. The reasons became perfectly clear to me, and all my reading and thinking and observation since have thoroughly confirmed my view. The doctrine of pacifism involves a philosophy of the emotions that move men, and the relative importance and power of the emotions as against reason; and this, I am satisfied, hardly admits of argument.[39]

In reality, before 1914 Darrow had been less concerned with the implications of Tolstoy's nonviolence for international life than he had been with its application to the field of internal government—a fact that may account for his apparent failure to think through his position in regard to external aggression and the abruptness with which he threw over his nonresistant views.

As a practising lawyer Darrow had been vitally interested in the problems of law enforcement and penal reform. A Marxist opponent once said of him that he treated nonresistance "as if it were a department of modern criminology."[40] And this was, indeed, well put, for Darrow saw in a nonviolent philosophy primarily an instrument for transforming society. It would lead to the removal of the element of violence represented in the make-up of all contemporary states, including those claiming to be democracies, with their coercive institutions—army, police, and prisons. Crime was not due to wickedness but was a disease of the existing inequitable social order. Abolish poverty and social injustice, Darrow urged, and the need for so-called defense and punishment would disappear. Vestigial remnants of the old violent order could be cured by the application of a minimum of restraint exercised in a spirit of loving kindness. Darrow called, therefore, for "the abolition of all judgment of man by man, the complete destruction of all prisons and the treatment of all men as if each human being was the child of the one loving Father and a part and parcel of the same infinite and mysterious life."[41] Armies would have to be disbanded: their main purpose was not to ward off outside attack but to enforce the hegemony of the ruling class within the state.

[39] Clarence Darrow, *The Story of My Life*, p. 210. That Darrow's renunciation of pacifism was not perhaps quite so sudden as he depicted it in his autobiography, written nearly two decades later, appears evident from a sentence spoken during a debate with the Marxist Arthur M. Lewis in 1911, where he says: "I am not quite sure of this theory [i.e., of nonresistance], or of any other theory. I used to be a good deal more positive than I am today" (Darrow and Lewis, *Marx versus Tolstoy: A Debate*, p. 13).

[40] Darrow and Lewis, *Marx versus Tolstoy*, p. 37.

[41] Darrow, *Resist not Evil*, p. 76.

Nonviolence was a method of change; if it were not to be mere hypocrisy, it would have to provide an alternative whereby the oppressed classes could achieve social justice without resort to armed violence and the inevitable danger of thus replacing an old tyranny by a new. (Darrow failed, however, to elaborate on the techniques of applied nonviolence.) A nonviolent revolution, too, would be infinitely more likely to succeed against the established order than a violent one, whose chances of success Darrow estimated as very low. His, then, was a revolutionary creed in contrast to the static pacifism of the established peace movement. It was the existence of the state as at present constituted that seemed, to Darrow as to the Garrisonian nonresistants earlier, the main obstacle in the way of achieving a world without violence. "The non-resistant," he wrote, "ever appeals to the courageous and the manly. Without weapons of any kind, with the known determination to give no violence in return, it would be very rare that men would not be safe from disorganized violence. It is only the state that ever lays its hands in anger on the non-resistant."[42]

Unlike Garrison and the earlier peace radicals, or even Tolstoy himself, Darrow did not derive his pacifism from an exclusively Christian source; he himself was an agnostically minded humanist. "It has never been any substantial part of the Christian religion," he claimed, and he refused to agree "that non-resistance is a religious doctrine."[43] Or, rather, he saw it as implicit in all the great religions of the world, including Christianity, as well as in the nonreligious humanist philosophies, though it had been disavowed by most of the churches that were derived from their founders' teachings.

Thus with Darrow and his like[43] (though after 1914 Darrow himself was never to return to his earlier allegiance to nonviolence), a new type of pacifist absolutism appeared in America, as in Europe, that was to become a major component of the radical peace movement

[42] *Ibid.*, p. 174.
[43] *Marx versus Tolstoy*, pp. 104, 105. Another agnostic pacifist, active around the turn of the century, was the pioneer humanist, Moncure Daniel Conway (1832-1907). Conway's pacifism derived from early contacts with the Quakers. In the 1850's, first as a Methodist and then as a Unitarian minister, he had pleaded in favor of nonresistance. In 1861, however, he had reluctantly accepted the need for a Union victory. Later, toward the end of the century, he again became convinced that all war was wrong (though it is not quite clear if he advocated personal nonresistance at this time): his pacifism was now based on rationalist and humanitarian grounds, and not on Christian belief. Humanist ethics, not revealed religion, was its source. See his *Autobiography: Memories and Experiences*, I, 115; II, 67, 88, 89, 94, 450-54.
[43] See E. M. Schuster, *Native American Anarchism*, pp. 81-85.

in the period beginning with the First World War. This new absolutism was a creed intensely concerned with the struggle for social justice and thus closely associated with the political left. Historically, however, it derived in large part from the earlier Christian pacifism whose history we have outlined in this book. Some adherents of the new pacifism were to be members of the orthodox Christian churches (a few would be drawn from Quaker meetings and from Jewish congregations), but most were to be unaffiliated to any religious denomination. Their pacifism, like Darrow's, though often religious in tone, was based rather on rationalist and humanitarian considerations than on any formal religious creed. They accepted the ethic of the Sermon on the Mount as a rule of conduct for individual and society. But this acceptance did not stem from reliance on Jesus' supernatural authority or from a belief in a supreme being whose will this ethic expressed; instead, its doctrines appeared to them as the quintessence of their humanistic creed, of the religion of Man.

Conclusion

Conclusion

Pacifism in North America grew out of European roots. In the course of several centuries, however, it developed characteristics of its own. It acquired an autonomous existence, so that, although there continued to be some interconnection between the peace sectaries of the two continents and, even more, between nonsectarian peace workers on each side of the Atlantic from the first decade of the nineteenth century onward, pacifist thought and practice took on some of the coloring of its native American environment. It ceased to represent merely a reflection of, an overflow from, modes of thought and feeling that had matured in the Old World. Faced with fresh problems and with new demands on the part of a society that usually remained as firmly resistant as ever to the pacifist ethos, American pacifists—despite the traditionalism that was a major ingredient in the outlook of all the peace sectaries, at least—were eventually forced to rethink inherited positions and to devise new strategies and new arguments to meet situations that could not easily have been foreseen in their Old World environment.

We have seen this transformation happen within the first half century of the arrival on the American continent of the Quakers, the first group to implant there the lasting seed of a nonviolent ethic. In the first place, early American Friends—the original immigrants would, of course, have regarded themselves rather as English or Scottish, Irish or Welsh, German or Dutch Quakers, according to the place of their origin—were required to exemplify their belief in nonviolence personally in ways that had seldom been practised back in the old country.

An Indian on the warpath, inflamed to savagery by repeated acts of injustice and cruelty suffered at the hands of white settlers, was a novel phenomenon for those New England Quakers (the first, apparently, among Friends who had to cope with a situation of this kind) who were now caught up in the midst of interracial warfare. They, too, had in the beginning been persecuted, and then barely tolerated, by the Puritan regimes of Massachusetts and Connecticut; but they were of the same blood and color and origin as the Indians' enemies and were liable, therefore, to become victims of their rage. Might they not, living, as they did, dispersed among a non-Quaker white population, seek protection, if not in arms, at least in the fortified places provided by their fellow citizens?

A similar situation faced the isolated Quaker communities scattered throughout the islands of the British West Indies; only, in place of

943

angry redskins, there were the equally menacing pirates or privateers of varied European extraction and, in the seat of white government, not pious Puritans, but blustering colonial officials and tough-minded planters. Dissociation from the power structure, so far as possible, and reliance on the reconciling force of the spirit as manifested in calm behavior—this, broadly, was the strategy Quakers employed in conflict situations.

Yet power and pacifism could not so easily be dissociated in all circumstances attending the Quaker plantation in America. First in the colony of Rhode Island (where the Quaker response was ambiguous) and then more emphatically in the Quaker commonwealth of Pennsylvania, Friends attempted to mediate between reasons of state and the demands of the law of love. Just as American Indian warfare and West Indian piracy posed problems for the practical implementation of a nonviolent way of life that had not been presented by the occasional highwayman or marauder in Britain, so the establishment of a Holy Experiment in government faced Friends with dilemmas scarcely dreamed of back in Britain, where even the Glorious Revolution meant no relaxation in the will to exclude Quakers and other dissenters from any share of government. Quaker rule in Pennsylvania, therefore, constitutes a second area where, comparatively early, the Quaker peace testimony underwent subtle permutations in adapting itself to its American environment.

However, while the Quaker politicians of Pennsylvania (and Rhode Island) attempted, especially in the later phases of their rule, to pare down their Society's repudiation of war until it came to have scarcely any relevance on the political level, radicals within Pennsylvania Yearly Meeting, like John Woolman, strove to give their peace testimony new meaning by sensitizing Friends' minds to its implications and making them aware of the full significance of a religious community dedicated to the path of nonviolence. At the very moment when Quaker government petered out, Woolman and his associates were exploring new ways of making Quaker pacifism a more vital belief. Whether in their reexamination of the tax issue or in their struggle to free their Society from the taint of slaveholding (in which they rightly detected the hidden seeds of war) or in their first stumbling efforts to relate their views on war to inequalities in the social order, these Friends were pioneers. Their radicalism was a country radicalism, based mainly on the rural meetings of Pennsylvania and New Jersey rather than on the still influential city meetings of Philadelphia with their strongly ingrained politicism; the pacifist rigorism of the radicals, like many other of their sociopolitical beliefs, was homespun from the same cloth that produced the agrarian democracy of the early American republic.

In the Revolution, it is true, Quakers had obtained a reputation for "Toryism," for pro-British sympathies. And certainly, even in the country meetings, traditionalism of a kind long held sway as much as did social conservatism among the Quaker grandees of Philadelphia. The history of the Quaker peace testimony in America, indeed, presents, over the first two and a half centuries at least, the interplay of two major forces: inherited norms of social conduct alongside fresh approaches periodically undertaken.

If in early America Quaker rural radicalism and the urban Whig politics of Philadelphia Friends each served, though from opposing standpoints, to integrate the Society's peace testimony with American thought and society as these began gradually to take on shapes distinct from those of the mother country, the rural isolation and cultural ghetto in which most Mennonites and Dunkers and other German-speaking nonresistant sects lived after their arrival in America tended to freeze their thinking and practice on the issue of peace, as on other aspects of their creed, at the stage reached immediately prior to their departure for the New World. In one group, however, acculturation proceeded more rapidly and brought with it around the turn of the eighteenth century (if not earlier) the complete abandonment of their objections to military service. Still, the example of the Moravians is scarcely evidence that even a far-reaching integration of sect with society must inevitably entail the repudiation of a pacifist stance. It does show, though, that this is likely if no steps are taken to adapt items of the ancestral faith to meet the exigencies of a novel and changing environment.

The American frontier left its impact on the peace sectaries of this continent, changing their outlook on state and society. The changes were greatest when frontier conditions were experienced by groups migrating from the more cultivated societies of the eastern seaboard, where contact with the Old World was always fairly closely maintained, to the wilderness of the West. But the effect of this experience on the evolution of the peace testimony among the Quaker communities of the areas opened up by the westward migration differed radically from the response it brought out from the German-speaking nonresistant groups. These groups, on account of language, way of life, and rural habitat, had become largely closed societies. True, the evangelical and revival movements of the nineteenth century succeeded in breaking through in certain areas. But acculturation to American society on a wide scale was to come only in this century with the spread of urbanization to these communities. The contours of Mennonite and Dunker pacifism, therefore, were—at least externally—to remain much the same until near the very end of our story. And this stability was almost as typical of their churches in the eastern states as of those in the Midwest.

The Society of Friends, on the other hand, owing to its use of the English language and the closer assimilation of its members to the American milieu (and for all its distinctive and rigorously upheld peculiarities of speech and dress, conduct and thought, and religious practice) was a more open community. The Society's adaptability led much more easily to the infiltration of new modes of religious thought, not only in its old habitat but in the novel environment of the frontier areas. For this reason, too, the Society in the new communities received an inflow of fresh recruits, many of whom were unprepared to assimilate important aspects of Quaker belief, including its peace testimony. The effect these trends were to exert on Quaker pacifism has been discussed in previous pages. The Civil War witnessed a considerable falling away from the traditional Quaker attitude toward war, especially among the younger generation. But the full impact of this process did not appear until well into the present century, and Quaker meetings had long ceased to enforce adherence to pacifism by means of the Society's discipline.

At the same time, however, Friends (and the Brethren and the Mennonites to some degree as well) were reframing their approach to the problems of peace and war. The legalism that had been common among pacifists of all hues up to and beyond the middle of the nineteenth century—especially the idea that war was simply sin forbidden the Christian by the injunctions set out in the Sermon on the Mount and elsewhere in the New Testament—gradually receded in importance, as increasing emphasis came to be placed on searching out and eradicating the seeds of war and hatred within the individual and within national and international society.

The pacifism not only of the Quakers, Mennonites, and Dunkers but of the various smaller religious groups that we have discussed in this book was a sectarian pacifism. Adherence to it was conditioned by acceptance of the other tenets of the sect; its outreach, therefore, was limited by the missionary potentiality of the sect. The German-speaking peace sects, even before their departure for North America, and the Quakers, too, within a half century or so of their arrival, ceased for some time to be effective proselytizing agencies; even the militant Shakers fairly soon contracted their activities to await the millennium within the confines of their little communities. Thus the impact on

American society at large of a philosophy of nonviolence as formulated by these groups was necessarily limited. While the constitutional claims and practices of early eighteenth-century Pennsylvania Quakers found a ready response in wide circles of politically conscious Americans, the pacifism of the Society of Friends, since it was presented as an integral part of a sectarian ethic, had only a very limited influence, at least on contemporaries.

The conclusion of the War of 1812 and of the Napoleonic struggle in Europe saw the birth of a nonsectarian peace movement uniting—somewhat uneasily, it is true—both nonpacifist workers in the cause of permanent and universal peace and believers in one form or another in a nonviolent approach in national and international affairs. Although with both wings of the movement the primary inspiration remained religious, the peace issue was detached from its association with the discipline and theology of any one sect. A parallel movement had developed in Britain (and, less effectively, on the European continent). But the American peace societies of the nineteenth century arose independently and, for all their ideological roots in the Old World and the continuous interchange of ideas and personalities between America and Europe, remained an integral part of the great American reform movement that ranged from millennialism and utopian communitarianism to a motley variety of humanitarian crusades.

Nineteenth-century American pacifism, unlike the antistate ideology of the Anabaptist-Mennonite tradition, was essentially an optimistic creed which placed its faith in the eventual perfectibility of man. Some of its adherents strove for the immediate installation of the millennium. The New England nonresistants, for instance, pleaded for the abandonment of all instruments of coercion here and now. However, for all their bitter attacks on the American republic's power apparatus and on the Constitution of the United States, these men and women implicitly—and sometimes explicitly—believed with great fervency in the role of the New World in bringing about a peaceful international order. Their faith was firmly American.

Neither the more conservative wing of the peace movement nor the radical New England Non-Resistance Society was very successful in its efforts to enlist mass support for the peace cause. At their best these groups formed a small elite, at their worst they constituted a closed coterie. Yet, despite their naivety and their many other shortcomings, these groups did attempt to grapple with the major problems that have faced the twentieth-century peace movement. While the conservatives among them concentrated on investigating institutional means for eradicating war from human society, the radicals explored the possibilities of individual war resistance and of the application of noninjurious force on the domestic scene, and occasionally even sketched in outline collective techniques for nonviolent action in the international sphere as well. The grand dilemma that American pacifists of this period ultimately failed to resolve was the problem of squaring the quest for international peace with the attainment of justice and freedom within the national community (represented in this instance by the slavery issue). The old peace movement in the United States never really recovered from the impact of the Civil War; it was only the problems of global warfare in the twentieth century that eventually regalvanized the scattered peace forces.

The respectable middle-class men and women who made up the bulk of members of both the radical and conservative wings of the antebellum peace movement, it is true, found it difficult—despite manipulation of the political and economic case against war in their societies' propaganda—to comprehend the degree to which war was embedded in the socioeconomic conditions of their time. But they did at least go beyond the somewhat negative antimilitarism of the pacifist sectaries, who had hitherto often failed to carry effective opposition to the use of violence beyond a personal refusal to render military service.

In the two world wars of the twentieth century it has been the apocalyptic pacifism of such bodies as the Seventh-Day Adventists or Jehovah's Witnesses that has produced a high numerical proportion of conscientious objectors. Again, it is true that in our century the historic peace churches in America, liberal Quakerism in particular, have begun to display new insights into the issues of war and violence and a new humanitarian outreach in their relief work for war sufferers. Yet the world pacifist movement that sprang out of the turmoil of the First World War and its aftermath, in which American pacifism has formed an integral and important sector, has been interdenominational, indeed interfaith, in character and has embraced, too, those whose pacifism stems from ethical and humanitarian, rather than religious, considerations. However, the vision that has inspired its participants, both in the United States and in other countries, derives in large measure from the labors of their predecessors on the North American continent, who, with varying success in their day but with considerable determination and courage (along with occasional faltering and backsliding), pioneered for a peaceable world.

Bibliography

A. PRIMARY SOURCES

1. Archival Materials

American Antiquarian Society (Worcester, Mass.):
MS Lecture of Elihu Burritt.

Bethel College Historical Library (North Newton, Kan.):
Affirmation of Non-Resistant (printed).
"Minutes of the Eastern District Conference 1847 to 1902. Translated from the Original German Records" (typescript), tr. N. B. Grubb.

Boston Public Library:
Garrison Papers, MSS A.1.1. and A.1.2.
Wm. Ll. Garrison's Scrap-Book, MS *4261.64.
Holland, Frederick West, "The History of the Peace-Cause," MS *5577.98.
The Manchester Peace Society to the London Peace Society. Report for 1843 Spring Quarter, MS G.31.26.
Weston Papers, MS A.9.2.
Wright, Henry Clarke, Scrap-Books, 2 vols., *7573.15.

Harvard University Library:
Coues, Samuel E., Peace Album, MS Am. 635*.

Haverford College Quaker Collection:
Allinson, Samuel, "Reasons against War, and paying Taxes for its Support" (1780), MS.
New England Yearly Meeting MS Discipline [1781?], *BX 7617 N5C5 1781.

Mennonite Church, Archives of the (Goshen, Ind.):
Historical Memorandums [sic], John F. Funk Collection.
Missouri-Iowa Mennonite Conference Minutes, 1833-1920.
Notebook in John F. Funk Collection.

Michigan, University of, William L. Clements Library:
Weld-Grimké Papers.

Moravian Archives (Bethlehem, Pa.):
3 misc. items.

Philadelphia Yearly Meeting, Department of Records:
"Minutes of the Yearly Meeting of Friends at Philadelphia" for 1749-1779.

Public Record Office (London):
C.O. 5/639.

Schwenkfelder Library (Pennsburg, Pa.):
"Memorandum Das ist Ordentliche Verzeichnis derer bestimmten Haupt-Tagen der Schwenckfelder Gemeinde was von zeit zu zeit an Denselben verhandelt worden ist wegen gemeinschaftlicher Verfassung und Verordnung" (Minutes of the General Conference of the Schwenkfelder Church, 1782-1890, MS in German).

Smith College Library (Northampton, Mass.):
Garrison Letters in Sophia Smith Collection.

Swarthmore College, Friends Historical Library:
"A Collection of Christian and Brotherly Advices given forth from time to time by the Yearly Meeting of Friends for Pennsylvania and New Jersey . . . Alphabetically Digested under Proper Heads" (1762), MS.
"A General Testimony against all looseness and vanity or what else may tend to the hurt of the souls of youth or others" (1694), MS.
Thomas Jenkins Papers (R G 5).
Kennett Monthly Meeting Sufferings 1757-1791.
Mifflin, Warner, "Statement concerning his refusal to use and circulate Continental currency" (1779), misc. MSS.
New Garden Monthly Meeting Committee on Sufferings, Minutes 1777-1778.
Radnor Monthly Meeting, Minutes of Sufferings 1776-1779.
7 misc. items (incl. Ferris, Janney, and Whittier Collections).

Swarthmore College Peace Collection:
Blanchard, J. P., Scrapbook.
Chessman, Daniel, "An Essay on Self Defence designed to show that War is inconsistent with Scripture and Reason," MS.
Collective document groups: Elihu Burritt.
Whipple, Jonathan, "Autobiography," microfilm of MS.

Western Reserve Historical Society Library (Cleveland, Ohio):
Whiteley, John (ed.), Letters & Documents respecting the Conscription, Arrest & Suffering of Horace S. Taber, A Member of the United Society, Shirley, Mass. [including Statements of Amos Bulrick Concerning his Service in the Revolutionary War].

2. *Newspapers and Journals*

Advent Herald (Boston).
Advent Review and Sabbath Herald (Battle Creek, Mich.).
Advocate of Peace (Boston—later Washington, D.C.).
Advocate of Peace and Christian Patriot (Philadelphia).
Advocate of Peace and Universal Brotherhood (Worcester, Mass.).
American Friend (Richmond, Ind.).
Boston Commonwealth, 7 Nov. 1885.
Boston Daily Courier, 2 April 1863.
Calumet (New York).
Christian Citizen (Worcester, Mass.)—also known as *Burritt's Christian Citizen*.
Christian Family Companion (Tyrone City, Pa.).
Christian Mirror (Portland, Me.).
Friend (New York).
Friend (Philadelphia).
Friend; or, Advocate of Truth (Philadelphia).
Friend of Peace (Cambridge, Mass.).
Friends' Miscellany (Philadelphia).

950

Friends' Review (Philadelphia).
Friends' [Weekly] Intelligencer (Philadelphia).
Genius of Universal Emancipation (Baltimore).
Gospel-Visitor (Columbiana, Ohio).
Harbinger of Peace (New York).
Herald of the Kingdom and Age to Come (West Hoboken, N.J.).
Herald of Truth (Chicago and Elkhart, Ind.).
Lard's Quarterly, devoted to the Propagation and Defense of the Gospel (Lexington, Ky.).
Liberator (Boston).
Messenger of Peace (New Vienna, Ohio, and later Richmond, Ind. and still later Baltimore, Md.).
Millennial Harbinger (Bethany, Va.).
Moral Advocate, A Monthly Publication, on War, Duelling, Capital Punishments, and Prison Discipline (Mt. Pleasant, Ohio).
Non-Resistant (Boston).
Non-Resistant and Practical Christian, 1848 (Hopedale, Mass.).
Practical Christian (Hopedale, Mass.).
Radical Spiritualist (Hopedale, Mass.), later *Spiritual Reformer*.
Voice of Peace, 1st ser. (Philadelphia and Mystic, Conn.).
Western Reformer (Milton, Iowa).
World's Crisis (Boston).

3. Books and Pamphlets: Contemporary Printings

An Account of the Sufferings of Friends of North Carolina Yearly Meeting, in Support of their Testimony against War, from 1861 to 1865, Baltimore (Md.), 1868.
Acta Fratrum Unitatis in Anglia, London, 1749.
An Address on Peace. Issued by the Yearly Meeting of Friends for New England, n.p.p., 1854.
An Address, to the State of Ohio, Protesting against a certain clause of the Militia enacted by the Legislature, at their last session; and shewing the Inconsistency of Military power interfering with persons or property Consecrated to the pious and benevolent purposes of the Gospel, Lebanon (Ohio), 1818.
Address of the Universal Peace Society to All Persons, Families, Communities and Nations, n.p.p., 1866.
Address of the Wilmington Monthly Meeting of Friends, to Its Members, on the Subject of the Militia Law, enacted at the last Session of the Legislature of Delaware, Wilmington, 1827.
Allinson, William J., *Right in the Abstract*, Philadelphia, 1862.
The American Friends' Peace Conference held at Philadelphia Twelfth Month 12th, 13th and 14th 1901, Philadelphia, 1902.
The Ancient Testimony of the People called Quakers, reviv'd. By the Order and Approbation of the Yearly Meeting, held for the Provinces of Pennsylvania and New Jersey, 1722, Philadelphia, 1773 edn.
The Annual Address and Minutes of the Twenty-Eighth Annual General Assembly of the Bible-Christian Church, Philadelphia, 1846.
Appeal to American Christians on the Practice of War. By Pacificus, New York, 1830.

Ballou, Adin, *Christian Non-Resistance defended against Rev. Henry Ward Beecher*, Hopedale (Mass.), 1862.

———, *A Discourse on Christian Non-Resistance in Extreme Cases*, Hopedale, 1860.

———, *Memoir of Adin Augustus Ballou: Written and Compiled by His Father*, Hopedale, 1853.

———, *Non-Resistance in Relation to Human Governments*, Boston, 1839.

———, *Practical Christian Socialism: A Conversational Exposition of the True System of Human Society*, Hopedale and New York, 1854.

Bates, Elisha, *The Doctrines of Friends; or, Principles of the Christian Religion, as held by the Society of Friends, commonly called Quakers* (1825), 5th edn., Providence, 1843.

Beckwith, George C., *The Book of Peace: A Collection of Essays on War and Peace*, Boston, 1845.

———, *Eulogy on William Ladd, late President of the American Peace Society*, Boston, 1841.

———, *The Peace Manual: or War and its Remedies*, Boston, 1847.

———, *A Universal Peace Society, with the Basis of Co-operation in the Cause of Peace*, Boston, 1844.

Beiler, David, *Das Wahre Christenthum. Eine Christliche Betrachtung nach den Lehren der Heilingen Schrift*, Lancaster (Pa.), 1888.

Benezet, Anthony, *The Plainness and Innocent Simplicity of the Christian Religion with its Salutary Effects, compared to the Corrupting Nature and Dreadful Effects of War*, Philadelphia, 1782 edn.

———, *Serious Considerations on Several Important Subjects; . . . ,* Philadelphia, 1778.

Berry, Philip, *A Review of the Mexican War on Christian Principles: and an Essay on the Means of Preventing War*, Columbia (S.C.), 1849.

Besse, Joseph, *A Collection of the Sufferings of the People called Quakers for the Testimony of a Good Conscience*, vol. II, London, 1753.

Blanchard, J. P., *Address delivered at the Thirteenth Anniversary of the Massachusetts Peace Society, December 25, 1828*, Boston, 1829.

———, *Communications on Peace; Written for the Christian Citizen*, Boston, 1848.

———, *Plan for Terminating the War, by Division of the United States, without Concession of Principle or Right on the Part of the North*, n.p.p., [1861].

———, *The War of Secession*, Boston, 1861.

The Book of Discipline, Agreed on by the Yearly Meeting of Friends for New England . . . , Providence (R.I.), 1785.

Bownas, Samuel, *An Account of the Life, Travels, and Christian Experiences in the Work of the Ministry of Samuel Bownas*, London, 1756.

Brenneman, John M., *Christianity and War. A Sermon setting forth the Sufferings of Christians*, Chicago, 1863.

The Brethren's Tracts and Pamphlets, setting forth the Claims of Primitive Christianity, vol. I, Dayton (Ohio), n.d.

Brigham, H. H., *A Voice from Nazareth. A Letter addressed to the Rev. H. D. Walker, in reply to a War Sermon, preached by him in September 1864*, Plymouth (Mass.), 1865.

Brumbaugh, H. B., *The Brethren's Church Manual*, Huntingdon (Pa.) and Mt. Morris (Ill.), 1887.

Bryan, William Jennings, *The Fruits of the Tree*, London and Edinburgh, 1910.

Burkholder, Peter, *The Confession of Faith, of the Christians known by the name of Mennonites, in Thirty-three Articles; . . . also, Nine Reflections, from Different Passages of the Scriptures, illustrative of their Confession, Faith and Practice*, Winchester (Va.), 1837.

Burritt, Elihu, *Ten-Minute Talks on All Sorts of Topics, with Autobiography of the Author*, Boston, 1874.

———, *Thoughts and Things at Home and Abroad*, Boston, 1854.

———, *Voice From the Forge*, London, 1848.

Butts, Bryan J., *The Conditions of Peace*, Hopedale (Mass.), n.d.

Campbell, Alexander, *Popular Lectures and Addresses*, Philadelphia, 1863.

Chalkley, Thomas, *A Journal or, Historical Account, of the Life, Travels, and Christian Experiences, of that Antient, Faithful Servant of Jesus Christ, Thomas Chalkley*, Philadelphia, 1754 edn.

Chew, Samuel, *The Speech of Samuel Chew, Esq., Chief Justice of the Government of Newcastle, Kent and Sussex upon Delaware; Delivered from the Bench to the Grand-Jury of the County of New Castle, Nov. 21, 1741; and now published at their Request*, Philadelphia, 1741.

———, *The Speech of Samuel Chew, Esq., Chief Justice of the Government of Newcastle, Kent and Sussex upon Delaware: Delivered from the Bench to the Grand-Jury of the County of New-Castle, Aug.20.1742; and now published at their Request*, Philadelphia, 1742.

Child, Lydia Maria, *Correspondence between Lydia Maria Child and Gov. Wise and Mrs. Mason, of Virginia*, Boston, 1860.

———, *Letters of Lydia Maria Child*, Boston, 1883.

Christian Advices: published by the Yearly Meeting of Friends held in Philadelphia, Philadelphia, 1808.

Churchman, John, *An Account of the Gospel Labours, and Christian Experiences of a Faithful Minister of Christ, John Churchman, Late of Nottingham in Pennsylvania, deceased*, Philadelphia, 1779.

A Circular Letter from the Massachusetts Peace Society, respectfully addressed to the Various Associations, Presbyteries, Assemblies and Meetings of the Ministers of Religion in the United States, Cambridge (Mass.), 1816.

Cleveland, Aaron, *The Life of Man Inviolable by the Laws of Christ*, Colchester (Conn.), 1815.

Cleveland, Richard C., *Abstract of an Address before the Peace Society of Windham County, at its Annual Meeting in Brooklyn, August 22, 1832*, Brooklyn (Conn.), 1832.

Comings, A. G., *The Reign of Peace. A Series of Discourses*, Boston, 1845.

Conference Resolutions. At the Annual Conference of the Mennonite Church of Canada, . . . 1906, n.p.p.

Conference Resolutions. At the Semi-Annual Conference of the Mennonite Church of Waterloo County, held at the Berlin Meeting House, on Thursday April 11th, 1907, n.p.p.

Considerations respecting the Lawfulness of War under the Gospel Dispensation addressed to the Teachers and Professors of Christianity in the United States of America, New York, 1848.

Constitution of the Schwenkfelder Society . . . as also By-Laws, ed. Joshua Schultz, Skippack (Pa.), 1882.

953

Conway, Moncure David, *Autobiography: Memories and Experiences*, 2 vols., Cambridge (Mass.), 1904.

Cornell, John J., *An Address to the Members of Genesee Yearly Meeting of Friends, in Relation to a Testimony against War*, Rochester (N.Y.), 1862.

———, *Autobiography of John J. Cornell*, Baltimore (Md.), 1906.

Cornell, W. T., *On the Incompatibility of War with the Spirit of Christianity*, Catskill (N.Y.), 1862.

Correspondence between Oliver Johnson and George F. White, a Minister of the Society of Friends, New York, 1841.

Coues, Samuel E., *War and Christianity: An Address before the American Peace Society on the Fourteenth Anniversary in Boston, Mass., May 23, 1842*, Boston, 1842.

Cox, Samuel Hanson, *Quakerism not Christianity*, New York, 1833.

Darrow, Clarence S., *Resist not Evil*, Chicago, 1903.

———, *The Story of My Life*, New York, 1932.

———, and Arthur M. Lewis, *Marx versus Tolstoy: A Debate*, Chicago, 1911.

Davis, Timothy, *A Letter from a Friend to some of his Intimate Friends, on the Subject of paying Taxes, &c.*, Watertown (Mass.), 1776.

A Declaration of the Society of People, (commonly called Shakers,) shewing their Reasons for refusing to aid or abet the Cause of War and Bloodshed, by bearing Arms, paying Fines, hiring Substitutes, or rendering any Equivalent for Military Services, Albany, 1815.

Declaratory Resolutions of the Hopedale Community with reference to the Existing Civil War, reaffirming their Original Principles, Positions and Testimonies, unanimously adopted, Sept. 15th, 1861, Hopedale, [1861].

A Dialogue, between Telemachus and Mentor, on the Rights of Conscience, and Military Requisitions, Boston, 1818.

Dialogues between Frank and William, illustrating the Principles of Peace, Boston, 1838.

Dickinson, James, *A Journal of the Life, Travels, and Labours in the Work of the Ministry, of that Worthy Elder, and Faithful Servant of Jesus Christ, James Dickinson*, London, 1745.

The Discipline of Iowa Yearly Meeting of the Society of Friends revised and printed by Direction of the Meeting held at West Branch, Iowa, in the Year 1914, n.p.p.

Discipline of the Yearly Meeting of Friends, held in New York, for the State of New York, and parts adjacent, . . . , New York, 1810.

Dodge, David Low, *Observations on the Kingdom of Peace, under the Benign Reign of Messiah*, New York, 1816.

———, *Remarks upon an Anonymous Letter, styled, "The Duty of a Christian in a Trying Situation": addressed to the Author of a Pamphlet, entitled, "The Mediator's Kingdom Not of This World," Etc.*, New York, 1810.

Dresser, Amos, *The Bible Against War*, Oberlin, 1849.

Edmundson, William, *A Journal of the Life, Travels, Sufferings, and Labour of Love in the Work of the Ministry, of that Worthy Elder, and Faithful Servant of Jesus Christ, William Edmundson*, Dublin, 1715.

Evans, Joshua, *A Journal of the Life, Travels, Religious Exercises, and La-*

bours in the Work of the Ministry of Joshua Evans, late of Newton Township, Gloucester County, New Jersey, Byberry (Pa.), 1837.

Evans, William, *Journal of the Life and Religious Services of William Evans, a Minister of the Gospel in the Society of Friends,* Philadelphia, 1870.

Ewert, Henry H., *The Confession of Faith of the Mennonite Denomination and Its Mission,* Berne (Ind.), 1901.

Extracts from Several Writers on Militia Fines and War, n.p.p., n.d.

Fisher, William Logan, *A Review of the Doctrines and Discipline of the Society of Friends,* 2nd edn., Philadelphia, 1854.

Fitch, George, *The Duty of a Christian in a Trying Situation: A Letter to the Author of a Pamphlet, entitled, "The Mediator's Kingdom not of this World, but Spiritual, Heavenly, and Divine,"* New York, 1810.

Flournoy, John J., *An Earnest Appeal for Peace, to all Christians, who, in Heart and Soul, truly love the Lord Jesus Christ, and ardently wish for his Triumph,* Athens (Ga.) 1838.

Formula for the Government and Discipline of the Schwenkfelder Church, n.p.p., 1902.

Foster, John W., *War and Christianity Irreconcilable. An Address to Christians,* Providence (R.I.), 1861.

Foster, Thomas, *An Appeal to the Society of Friends, on the Primitive Simplicity of their Christian Principles and Church Discipline; and on some Recent Proceedings in the Said Society,* London, 1801.

————, *A Narrative of the Proceedings in America of the Society called Quakers, in the case of Hannah Barnard. With a Brief Review of the Previous Transactions in Great Britain and Ireland . . . ,* London, 1804.

Frantz, Michael, *Einfältige Lehr-Betrachtungen und Kurtz-gefasztes Glaubens-Bekantnisz,* Germantown (Pa.), 1770.

Funk, Christian, *A Mirror for All Mankind,* Norristown (Pa.), 1814.

Funk, Jacob, *War versus Peace,* Elgin (Ill.), 1910

Funk, John F., *The Mennonite Church and Her Accusers,* Elkhart (Ind.), 1878.

————, *Warfare: Its Evils, Our Duty,* Chicago, 1863.

Furness, W. H., *Put up Thy Sword: A Discourse delivered before Theodore Parker's Society, at the Music Hall, Boston, Sunday, March 11, 1860,* Boston, 1860.

————, *A Word of Consolation for the Kindred of those who have fallen in Battle. A Discourse delivered September 28, 1862,* Philadelphia, 1862.

Garrison, William Lloyd, *The Abolitionists, and their Relations to War,* n.p.p., 1862.

————, *Selections from the Writings and Speeches of William Lloyd Garrison,* Boston, 1852.

Garrison, William Lloyd, Jr., *Non-Resistance a Better Defence than Armies and Navies,* n.p.p., 1908.

————, *The Things that Make for Peace,* New York, 1895.

Glaubensbekenntnisz, der Neuen Deutschen Baptisten Gemeinde in den Vereinigten Staaten, Elkhart (Ind.), [1880].

Gregory, John, *Anti-War, Two Discourses, delivered at Williston and Burlington, July 1846. Likewise a Discourse, delivered at the Universalist*

955

State Convention, Montpelier, Aug. 26, 1846, Burlington (Vt.) and Boston, 1847.

Grew, Henry, *Address delivered before the Peace Society of Hartford and the Vicinity, Sept. 7, 1828*, Hartford, 1828.

Grey, Isaac, *A Serious Address to Such of the People called Quakers, on the Continent of North America, as profess Scruples relative to the Present Government: exhibiting the Ancient Real Testimony of that People, concerning Obedience to Civil Authority*, Philadelphia, 1778.

Grimké, Thomas S., *Address on the Truth, Dignity, Power and Beauty of the Principles of Peace, and on the Unchristian Character and Influence of War and the Warrior: delivered in the Centre Church at New Haven, during the Session of the Legislature of Connecticut, at the Request of the Connecticut Peace Society. On Sunday Evening, the 6th of May, 1832*, Hartford, 1832.

———, *Correspondence on the Principles of Peace, Manual Labor Schools, &c.*, Charleston (S.C.), 1833.

———, (ed.), J. Dymond's *Inquiry into the Accordance of War with Christianity etc. . . .* , Philadelphia, 1834.

———, *A Letter to the People of South-Carolina*, Charleston, 1832.

Hall, Edward B., *Christians Forbidden to Fight: An Address before the Rhode-Island Peace Society; at its Twenty-Seventh Annual Meeting, June 30, 1844*, Providence, 1844.

Hall, Rufus, *A Journal of the Life, Religious Exercises, and Travels in the Work of the Ministry of Rufus Hall*, Byberry, 1840.

Hallowell, Benjamin, *Autobiography of Benjamin Hallowell*, Philadelphia, 1883.

Harvey, Cyrus W., *The Prince of Peace or the Bible on Non-Resistance and War*, Galena (Kan.), 1901.

Haynes, Sylvanus, *A Brief Reply to the Friend of Peace, or A Concise Vindication of Defensive War*, Auburn (N.Y.), 1824.

Heaton, Adna, *War and Christianity Contrasted; with a Comparative View of their Nature and Effects. Recommended to the Serious and Impartial Consideration of the Professors of the Christian Religion*, New York, 1816.

Heckler, James Y., *Ecclesianthem, or A Song of the Brethren, embracing their History and Doctrine*, Lansdale (Pa.), 1883.

Herr, Francis, *A Short Explication of the Written Word of God; Likewise of the Christian Baptism, and the Peaceable Kingdom of Christ. Against the People called Quakers*, [Lancaster, Pa.], 1790.

Hickok, Laurens P., *The Sources of Military Delusion, and the Practicability of their Removal. An Address before the Connecticut Peace Society; delivered at their Second Anniversary, during the Session of the Legislature of Connecticut, Sunday Evening, May 5, 1833, in the Centre Church, Hartford*, Hartford, 1833.

Hicks, Edward, *Memoirs of the Life and Religious Labors of Edward Hicks, late of Newtown, Bucks County, Pennsylvania. Written by himself*, Philadelphia, 1851.

Hinchman, Lydia S., *Recollections of Lydia S. (Mitchell) Hinchman*, n.p.p., 1929.

Hoag, Joseph, *A Journal of the Life and Gospel Labors of that Devoted Servant and Minister of Christ, Joseph Hoag*, Sherwoods (N.Y.), 1860.

Holcombe, Henry, *The First Fruits, in a Series of Letters*, Philadelphia, 1812.

————, *The Martial Christian's Manual*, Philadelphia, 1823.

Hull, Henry, *Memoir of the Life and Religious Labours of Henry Hull*, Philadelphia, 1858.

Hull, William I., *The New Peace Movement*, Swarthmore (published as *Swarthmore College Bulletin*, vol. VII, no. 1, Sept. 1909).

Huntington, F. D., *Peace, the Demand of Christianity. A Sermon preached in the South Congregational Church, December 28, 1845*, Boston, 1846.

In Senate, January 10, 1826 . . . The Memorial of the United Society, (commonly called Shakers,) of New-Lebanon and Watervliet. To the Legislature of the State of New York, n.p.p.

Jackson, John, *Considerations on the Impropriety of Friends participating in the Administration of Political Governments*, Philadelphia, 1840.

————, *Reflections on Peace and War*, Philadelphia, 1846.

Janney, Samuel M., *Peace Principles exemplified in the Early History of Pennsylvania*, Philadelphia, 1876.

Jansen, Peter, *Memoirs of Peter Jansen: The Record of a Busy Life: An Autobiography*, Beatrice (Neb.), 1921.

Jay, Allen, *Autobiography of Allen Jay*, Philadelphia, 1910.

Jones, Elijah, *Address delivered at the Fifth Anniversary of the Peace Society of Minot, November 5, 1828*, Portland (Me.), 1828.

Judd, Sylvester, *A Moral Review of the Revolutionary War, or Some of the Evils of that Event Considered*, Hallowell (Me.), 1842.

Kauffman, Daniel (ed.), *Bible Doctrine: A Treatise on the Great Doctrines of the Bible*, Scottdale (Pa.), 1914.

Keith, George, et al., *An Appeal from the Twenty Eight Judges to the Spirit of Truth & true Judgement in all Faithful Friends . . .* , Philadelphia, 1692.

Kellogg, Ezra B., *War Contrary to the Gospel. A Sermon, preached before the Peace Society of Windham County, February 4, 1830*. Providence (R.I.), 1830.

Kersey, Jesse, *A Narrative of the Early Life, Travels and Gospel Labors of Jesse Kersey, late of Chester County, Pennsylvania*, Philadelphia, 1851.

————, *A Treatise on Fundamental Doctrines of the Christian Religion: in which are illustrated the Profession, Ministry, Worship, and Faith of the Society of Friends*, Philadelphia, 1815.

Krehbiel, H. P., *War Inconsistent with the Spirit and Teaching of Christ and hence Unwise and Unnecessary*, Newton (Kan.), 1934.

Ladd, William, *The Duty of Women to Promote the Cause of Peace*, Boston, 1840 edn.

————, "History of Peace Societies" in *Scientific Tracts, for the Diffusion of Useful Knowledge*, Boston, 1836.

————, *Obstacles and Objections to the Cause of Permanent and Universal Peace considered by a Layman*, Boston, 1837.

Leeds, Joseph W., *The Primitive Christians' Estimate of War and Self-Defense*, New Vienna (Ohio), 1876.

A Letter from One of the Society of Friends, Relative to the Conscientious Scrupulousness of Its Members to Bear Arms, n.p.p., 1795.

Lewis, Enoch, *Some Observations on the Militia System, Addressed to the Serious Consideration of the Citizens of Pennsylvania*, Philadelphia, 1831.

Lipscomb, David, *Civil Government: Its Origin, Mission, and Destiny, and the Christian's Relation to it*, Nashville (Tenn.), 1957 edn.

Lord, Eleazar, *Thoughts on the Practical Advantages of those who hold the Doctrines of Peace, over those who vindicate War. Addressed to those who "follow Peace with All Men,"* New York, 1816.

Lord, John, *An Address delivered before the Peace Society of Amherst College, July 4, 1839*, Amherst, 1839.

Love, Alfred H., *Address before the Peace Convention, held in Boston, March 14 & 15, 1866*, Hopedale (Mass.), 1866.

———, *An Appeal in Vindication of Peace Principles, and against Resistance by Force of Arms*, 2nd edn., Philadelphia, 1862.

Lovejoy, Joseph and Owen, *Memoir of the Rev. Elijah P. Lovejoy; who was murdered in Defence of the Liberty of the Press at Alton, Illinois, Nov. 7, 1837*, New York, 1838.

MacLaren, James H., *Put Up Thy Sword: A Study of War*, Chicago, 1900.

Martin, Isaac, *A Journal of the Life, Travels, Labours and Religious Exercises of Isaac Martin, Late of Rahway, in East Jersey, Deceased*, Philadelphia, 1834.

Maule, Joshua, *Transactions and Changes in the Society of Friends, and Incidents in the Life and Experience of Joshua Maule*, Philadelphia, 1886.

May, Samuel J., *An Address delivered before the American Peace Society, in Park Street Church, Boston, May 28, 1860*, Boston, 1860.

———, *Liberty or Slavery, the Only Question*, Syracuse, 1856.

———, *Some Recollections of our Antislavery Conflict*, Boston, 1869.

M'Kenzie, James A., *A Discourse, against Life-Taking, delivered by request, before the Rhode-Island Quarterly Meeting in Tiverton, August 24, 1842*, 2nd edn., Providence, 1842.

Memorial and Address of Friends on Military Exactions, [Philadelphia], 1837.

Memorial of Cyrus W. Harvey, Philadelphia, 1918.

Memorial to the Legislature of Virginia. Issued by the Religious Society of Friends, at their Half Yearly Meeting, held at Richmond 10th m. 5th, 1863, Richmond, 1863.

Memorial of Sarah Pugh. A Tribute of Respect from her Cousins, Philadelphia, 1888.

The Memorial of the Society of Friends, to the Legislature of the State of New York, on the Subject of Imprisonment, for Non-Compliance with Military Requisitions, New York, 1830.

The Memorial of the Society of People of Canterbury, in the County of Rockingham, and Enfield, in the County of Grafton, commonly called Shakers, n.p.p., [1818].

Michener, Ezra, *A Brief Exposition of the Testimony to Peace, as exemplified by the Life and Precepts of Jesus Christ, and the Early Christians, and held by the Religious Society of Friends*, Philadelphia, 1862.

958

Mifflin, Warner, *The Defence of Warner Mifflin Against Aspersions cast on him on Account of his Endeavours to promote Righteousness, Mercy and Peace Among Mankind*, Philadelphia, 1796.

The Military Profession Unlawful for a Christian, Norwich (England), n.d.

Minutes of the Annual Meeting of the Church of the Brethren, for 1911 and 1914, n.p.p.

Moomaw, Benjamin F., *Discussion on Trine Immersion . . . also, a Dialogue on the Doctrine of Non-Resistance*, Singer's Glen (Va.), 1867.

Morgan, P. B., *The Coming Conflict: With the Inquiry,—Ought Christians to bear arms?*, Boston, 1861.

Mott, James, Sr., *The Lawfulness of War for Christians, examined*, New York, 1814.

Musser, Daniel, *Non-Resistance Asserted: or the Kingdom of Christ and the Kingdom of this World separated, and No Concord between Christ and Belial*, Lancaster (Pa.), 1864.

Noyes, John H., *The Berean: A Manual for the Help of those who seek the Faith of the Primitive Church*, Putney (Vt.), 1847.

Observations on the Natural and Constitutional Rights of Conscience, In Relation to Military Requisitions on the People called Shakers, Albany, 1816.

XV. *Papers relating to Quakers and Moravians*, n.p.p., n.d. [in Columbia University Library].

Peabody, Andrew P., *Lessons from Our Late Rebellion. An Address delivered at the Anniversary of the American Peace Society, May 19, 1867*, Boston, 1867.

———, *The Nature and Influence of War. An Address delivered before the American Peace Society at its Annual Meeting, May 29, 1843*, Boston, 1843.

———, *The Triumphs of War. A Sermon preached on the Day of the Annual Fast, April 15, 1847*, Portsmouth (N.H.), 1847.

"Philalethes," *Tribute to Caesar, How paid by the Best Christians, And to What Purpose*, [Philadelphia], n.d.

Phillips, Catherine, *Memoirs of the Life of Catherine Phillips*, London, 1797.

Pilkington, George (ed.), *Testimonies of Ministers, of Various Denominations, shewing the Unlawfulness to Christians of All Wars, Offensive or Defensive*, London, 1837.

Proceedings of the First Anniversary of the Universal Peace Society Masonic Hall New York, May 8th & 9th, 1867, Philadelphia, 1867.

The Proceedings of the First General Peace Convention: held in London, June 22 1843 and the Two Following Days, London, 1843.

Proceedings of the Peace Convention, held in Boston, in the Marlboro' Chapel, September 18, 19 & 20, 1838, Boston, 1838.

Proceedings of the Peace Conventions held in Boston, March 14 & 15, 1866; and in Providence, May 16th, 1866, [Philadelphia], 1866.

Proceedings of the Pennsylvania Yearly Meeting of Progressive Friends, held at Longwood, Chester County, for 1862 and 1864, New York.

Proceedings of the Second Anniversary of the Universal Peace Union, . . . held in Dodsworth's Hall, New York, May 15th, 1868, Philadelphia, 1868.

Proud, Robert, *The History of Pennsylvania . . .* , vol. I (1797) and vol. II (1798), Philadelphia.

959

The Question of War Reviewed, New York, 1818.

Radical Peace Resolutions, n.p.p., 1867.

Reckitt, William, *Some Account of the Life and Gospel Labours of William Reckitt*, London, 1776.

Remarks by a Member of the Society of Friends on the Subject of War, in reply to A.M., who addressed the Society on that Subject, n.p.p., n.d. [1847?].

Report on the Injustice and Inequality of the Militia Law of Massachusetts, with Regard to the Rights of Conscience, Boston, 1838.

Report of the New-York Peace Society, at the Anniversary, Dec. 25, 1818, New York, 1818.

Report on the Tendency and Effects of the Pacific Principle, and also on Military Establishments in Time of Peace, Boston, 1838.

Resolutions Adopted at the Annual Conference of the Mennonite Church. 1909, n.p.p., [1909].

Richardson, John, *An Account of the Life of that ancient Servant of Jesus Christ, John Richardson*, London, 1757.

Rules of Discipline and Advices of Illinois Yearly Meeting of Friends, Chicago, 1878.

Rules of Discipline and Christian Advices of the Yearly Meeting of Friends for Pennsylvania and New Jersey, . . , Philadelphia, 1797.

Saur, Christopher, Sr., *Ein Grundliches Zeugnusz Gegen das Kurtzlich herausgegebene Buchlein, Genandt: Plain Truth. Oder Lautere Wahrheit*, Germantown, 1748.

———, *Klare und Gewisse Wahrheit*, . . . *Betreffend den eigendlichen Zustand, so wohl der Wahren Friedliebenden Christen und Gottesfurchtigen, als auch der verfallenen, Streit-oder Kriegs-Suchtigen, zusammt ihrer beyder Hoffnung und Ausgang*, Germantown, 1747.

———, *Verschiedene Christliche Wahrheiten, und Kurtze Betrachtung Uber das kurtzlich herausgegebene Buchlein, Gennant: Lautere Wahrheit*, Germantown, 1748.

Sayre, John, *From the New-York Journal*, n.p.p., [1776].

Scott, Job, *Journal of the Life, Travels and Gospel Labours of that Faithful Servant and Minister of Christ, Job Scott*, Wilmington (Del.), 1797.

A Serious Expostulation with the Society of Friends in Pennsylvania, and Parts Adjacent, being a Sincere Endeavour, in the Spirit of Christian Duty and Affection, to point out the Propriety and Necessity of Preserving, in their Political Conduct, a Consistency with their Religious Opinions. By Pacificus, Philadelphia, 1808.

Sewell, E. G., "Reminiscences of the Civil War. Again" and "Reminiscences of Civil War Times. No. 3" in the *Gospel Advocate* (Nashville, Tenn.), vol. XLIX, no. 29 (18 July 1907) and no. 30 (25 July 1907).

Shaker-Russian Correspondence between Count Leo Tolstoi and Elder F. W. Evans, Mt. Lebanon (N.Y.), 1891.

Smith, Gerrit, *Gerrit Smith to Mr. Garrison. Let us deal impartially with the Sinning South and the Sinning North*, n.p.p., 1867.

———, *Peace better than War. Address delivered before the American Peace Society, at its Thirteenth Anniversary held in the City of Boston, May 24, 1858*, Boston, 1858.

————, *Sermons and Speeches of Gerrit Smith*, New York, 1861.

————, *Speeches of Gerrit Smith in Congress*, New York, 1855.

Smith, John, *The Doctrine of Christianity, as Held by the People called Quakers, Vindicated: In Answer to Gilbert Tennent's Sermon on the Lawfulness of War*, Philadelphia, 1748.

Smith, Samuel, *Necessary Truth: Or Seasonable Considerations for the Inhabitants of the City of Philadelphia and Province of Pennsylvania. In Relation to the Pamphlet call'd Plain Truth: And Two Other Writers in the News-Paper*, Philadelphia, 1748.

Smith, William, *A Brief State of the Province of Pennsylvania*, London, 1755.

————, *A Brief View of the Conduct of Pennsylvania, for the Year 1756*, London, 1756.

Spear, J. A., *Remarks, offered in a Non-Resistance Convention, held in East Bethel, February 24th and 25th, 1841*, Brandon (Vt.), [1841].

Spofford, Jeremiah, *A Vindication of the Right of Civil Government and Self-Defense; A Lecture Delivered at Bradford, Ms. in reply to several Itinerant Lecturers, on Non-Resistance, &c*, Haverhill (Mass.), n.d.

Stebbins, Rufus S., *An Address delivered before the Peace Society of Amherst College, July 4, 1838*, Amherst, 1838.

————, *Address on the Subject of Peace, delivered at the Odeon, on Sabbath Evening, February 7, 1836. On the Anniversary of the Bowdoin Street Young Men's Peace Society.*, Boston, 1836.

Stone, Thomas T., *Sermons on War*, Boston, 1829.

Story, Thomas, *A Journal of the Life of Thomas Story*, Newcastle upon Tyne, 1747.

Sumner, Charles, *The True Grandeur of Nations: An Oration delivered before the Authorities of the City of Boston, July 4, 1845*, Boston, 1845.

————, *The War System of the Commonwealth of Nations*, Boston, 1849.

Taber, Joseph, *An Address to the People called Quakers*, Boston, 1784.

The Tenth Annual Report of the American Peace Society, Boston, 1838.

Testimonies concerning the Character and Ministry of Mother Ann Lee and the First Witnesses of the Gospel of Christ's Second Appearing; given by some of the Aged Brethren and Sisters of the United Society, including a Few Sketches of their own Religious Experience: Approved by the Church, Albany, 1827.

A Testimony and Caution to such as do make a Profession of Truth, who are in scorn called Quakers, and more especially such who profess to be Ministers of the Gospel of Peace, That they should not be concerned in Worldly Government, [Philadelphia], 1692.

The Testimony of the Society of Friends on the Continent of America, Philadelphia, 1830.

Thurman, W. C., *Non-Resistance, or the Spirit of Christianity Restored*, 2nd edn., Charlottesville, (Va.), 1862.

Tilden, W. P., *All War Forbidden by Christianity. An Address, to the Citizens of Dover, delivered on Thanksgiving Evening Nov. 25, 1847*, Dover (N.H.), 1847.

To Our Fellow Citizens of the United States. [Philadelphia Yearly Meeting], Philadelphia, 1814.

To Pacificus, in Reply to his Essay, entitled "A Serious Expostulation . . . ," showing wherein he has partially and unfairly represented Political Trans-actions, and answering the Aggravated Charges exhibited against the So-ciety. By Philo Veritatis, Philadelphia, 1808.

A *Treatise shewing the Need we have to rely upon God as sole Protector of this Province* . . . , Philadelphia, 1748.

Tryon, Thomas, *The Planter's Speech to his Neighbours & Country-Men of Pennsylvania, East & West-Jersey, and to all such as have transported themselves into New-Colonies for the Sake of a Quiet Retired Life*, London, 1684.

Tukesbury, T. F., *The Taking of Human Life incompatible with Christian-ity: with Remarks on the "Present Crisis,"* Boston, 1864.

The Unlawfulness of All Wars and Fightings under the Gospel, Baltimore, 1846.

Upham, Thomas C., *The Manual of Peace*, New York, 1836.

Verhandlungen der dritten jährlichen Diener-Versammlung der Deutschen Täufer oder Amischen Mennoniten, gehalten nahe bey Goschen, Elkhart County, Indiana. Im Juny 1864, Lancaster, 1864.

Verhandlungen der siebenten jährlichen Diener-Versammlung der Amischen Mennoniten-Brüderschaft, gehalten am 31. May, und den 1. 2. und 3. Juni, 1868, in der Nähe von Belleville, Mifflin Co., Penn., Lancaster, 1868.

Verhandlungen der zweiten jährlichen Diener-Versammlung der Deutschen Täufer oder Amischen Mennoniten, gehalten in Mifflin County, Pennsyl-vanien. Im May, 1863, Lancaster, 1863.

The Views of Seventh-Day Adventists relative to bearing Arms, as brought before the Governors of Several States, and the Provost Marshal General, with a Portion of the Enrollment Law, Battle Creek (Mich.), 1865.

Walker, Amasa, *Iron-clad War-ships: Or, the Prospective Revolution in the War System. Speech of Hon. Amasa Walker, before the American Peace Society, at its Anniversary in Boston, May 26, 1862*, Boston, 1862.

———, *Le Monde; or In Time of Peace Prepare for War*, London, 1859.

———, *The Suicidal Folly of the War System. An Address before the American Peace Society, at its Anniversary in Boston May 25, 1863*, Boston, 1863.

Warner, H. E., *The Ethics of Force*, Boston, 1905.

War Unchristian; or the Custom of War compared with the Standard of Christian Duty, Hartford, 1834.

Washburn, John M., *Reason vs the Sword, A Treatise*, New York, 1873.

Waterous, Timothy, Timothy Waterous, Jr., and Zachariah Waterous, *The Battle-Axe, and the Weapons of War, discovered by the Morning Light: aimed for the Final Destruction of Priest-Craft*, 2nd edn., Groton (Conn.), 1841.

Watson, Thomas, *Some Account of the Life, Convincement, and Religious Experience of Thomas Watson, Late of Bolton, Massachusetts. Written by Himself* . . . , New York, 1836.

Wayland, Francis, *The Duty of Obedience to the Civil Magistrate: Three Sermons preached in the Chapel of Brown University*, Boston, 1847.

———, *The Elements of Moral Science*, New York, 1835. Also 1963 edn., ed. Joseph L. Blau, Cambridge (Mass.).

Wellcome, I. C., *Should Christians Fight? A Pamphlet on War*, Boston, 1864.

Wells, J. I., *An Essay on War*, Hartford, 1808.

Wells, Seth Youngs, *A Brief Illustration of the Principles of War and Peace, shewing the Ruinous Policy of the Former, and the Superior Efficacy of the Latter, for National Protection and Defence; clearly manifested their Practical Operations and Opposite Effects upon Nations, Kingdoms and People. By Philanthropos*, Albany (N.Y.), 1831.

Wetherill, Samuel, *An Apology for the Religious Society, called Free Quakers, in the City of Philadelphia*, Philadelphia, n.d.

Whelpley, Samuel, *Letters addressed to Caleb Strong, Esq. late Governor of Massachusetts: showing War to be inconsistent with the Laws of Christ, and the Good of Mankind*, 2nd edn., Philadelphia, 1817.

Whelpley, Samuel W., *An Address delivered before the Peace Society of Hartford County in the Centre Church, Hartford*, Hartford, 1830.

Whipple, Charles K., *Evils of the Revolutionary War*, Boston, 1839.

————, *Non-Resistance applied to the Internal Defence of a Community*, Boston, 1860.

————, *The Non-Resistance Principle: With Particular Application to the Help of Slaves by Abolitionists*, Boston, 1860.

————, *The Powers that be are ordained of God*, Boston, 1841.

White, Anna, *Voices from Lebanon*, n.p.p., 1899.

————, and Leila S. Taylor, *Shakerism, Its Meaning and Message*, Columbus (Ohio), 1904.

Worcester, Leonard, *A Discourse on the Alton Outrage, delivered at Peacham, Vermont, December 17, 1837*, Concord (N.H.), 1838.

Wright, Henry C., *Anthropology; or the Science of Man: in its Bearing on War and Slavery, and on Arguments from the Bible, Marriage, God, Death, Retribution, Atonement and Government, in Support of these and other Social Wrongs: in a Series of Letters to a Friend in England*, Cincinnati, 1850.

————, *Ballot Box and Battle Field. To Voters under the United States Government*, Boston, 1842.

————, *Christian Church; Anti-Slavery and Non-Resistance applied to Church Organizations*, Boston, 1841.

————, *Declaration of Radical Peace Principles*, Boston, 1866.

————, *Defensive War proved to be a Denial of Christianity and of the Government of God: with Illustrative Facts and Anecdotes*, London, 1846.

————, *Dick Crowninshield, the Assassin, and Zachary Taylor, the Soldier: The Difference between Them*, n.p.p., 1848.

————, *The Employers of Dick Crowninshield, the Assassin, and the Employers of Zachary Taylor, the Soldier: The Difference*, Hopedale (Mass.), 1848.

————, *Henry C. Wright's Peace Tracts*, Dublin, 1843: no. 1, *The Heroic Boy*; no. 2, *Forgiveness in a Bullet!*; no. 3, *The Immediate Abolition of the Army and Navy*.

————, *A Kiss for a Blow*, Dublin, 1843.

————, *Man-Killing, by Individuals and Nations, Wrong-Dangerous in All Cases*, Boston, 1841.

————, *The Natick Resolution; or, Resistance to Slaveholders the Right and Duty of Southern Slaves and Northern Freemen*, Boston, 1859.

————, *No Rights, No Duties: Or, Slaveholders, as Such, have no Rights,*

Slaves, as such, owe no Duties. An Answer to a Letter from Hon. Henry Wilson, touching Resistance to Slaveholders being the Right and Duty of the Slaves, and of the People and States of the North, Boston, 1860.
———, *Six Months at Graeffenberg; with Conversations in the Saloon, on Nonresistance and other Subjects,* London, 1845.
Yale, Cyrus, *War Unreasonable and Unscriptural. An Address before the Hartford Peace Society; delivered on the Evening of November 11, 1832, in the Centre Church, Hartford,* Hartford, 1833.

4. Later Edited Works and Documentary Collections

Abdruck der Gesammt-Protokolle der Kansas und Westlichen Distrikt Conference der Mennoniten von Nord-Amerika 1877-1909, Newton (Kan.), 1910.
Ashbridge, Elizabeth, "Some Account of the Life of Elizabeth Ashbridge. Written by Herself" in *The Friends' Library,* vol. IV, Philadelphia, 1840.
Ballou, Adin, *Autobiography of Adin Ballou,* ed. William S. Heywood, Lowell (Mass.), 1896.
———, *Christian Non-Resistance in all its Important Bearings, Illustrated and Defended,* ed. W. S. Heywood, Philadelphia, 1910.
———, *History of the Hopedale Community from its Inception to its Virtual Submergence in the Hopedale Parish,* ed. W. S. Heywood, Lowell (Mass.), 1897.
———, *Primitive Christianity and its Corruptions,* ed. W. S. Heywood, vol. II, Lowell (Mass.), 1899.
Barnes, Gilbert H., and Dwight L. Dumond (eds.), *Letters of Theodore Dwight Weld, Angelina Grimké Weld and Sarah Grimké, 1822-1844,* 2 vols., New York, 1934.
Barnes, James A. (ed.), "Letters of a Massachusetts Woman Reformer to an Indiana Radical," *Indiana Magazine of History* (Bloomington, Ind.), vol. XXVI, no. 1 (March 1930).
Bender, Harold S. (ed.), "An Amish Bishop's Conference Epistle of 1865," *MQR,* vol. XX, no. 3 (July 1946).
———, "The Correspondence of Martin Mellinger," *MQR,* vol. V, no. 1 (Jan. 1931).
———, "New Source Material for the History of the Mennonites in Ontario," *MQR,* vol. III, no. 1 (Jan. 1929).
Brissot de Warville, J. P., *New Travels in the United States of America 1788,* tr. and ed. M. S. Vamos and D. Echeverria, Cambridge (Mass.), 1964.
"Bucks County Quakers and the Revolution," *The Pennsylvania Genealogical Magazine* (Phila.), vol. XXIV, no. 4 (1966).
Byrd, William, *The Secret Diary of William Byrd of Westover 1709-1712,* ed. Louis B. Wright and Marion Tinling, Richmond (Va.), 1941.
Cadbury, Henry J. (ed.), *John Farmer's First American Journey 1711-1714,* Worcester, 1944.
———, "A Quaker Travelling in the Wake of War, 1781," *NEQ,* vol. XXIII, no. 3 (Sept. 1950).
———, "Some Anecdotes of John Woolman: Recorded by John Cox," *Journal of the Friends' Historical Society* (London), vol. XXXVIII (1946).

964

Charter to William Penn, and Laws of the Province of Pennsylvania passed between the Years 1682 and 1700, ed. George Staughton, Benjamin M. Nead, and Thomas McCamant, Harrisburg, 1879.

Chronicon Ephratense; A History of the Community of Seventh Day Baptists at Ephrata, Lancaster County, Penn'a by "Lamech and Agrippa," tr. from German by J. Max Hark, Lancaster (Pa.), 1889.

Coffin, William H., "Settlement of the Friends in Kansas," *Transactions of the Kansas State Historical Society, 1901-1902*, Topeka, 1902.

Comstock, Elizabeth L., *Life and Letters of Elizabeth L. Comstock*, ed. C. Hare, London, 1895.

Conference Record containing the Proceedings of the Kansas-Nebraska Mennonite Conference 1876-1914, n.p.p., 1914.

Conyngham, Redmond, "An Account of the Settlement of the Dunkers at Ephrata, in Lancaster County, Pennsylvania" in *Memoirs of the Historical Society of Pennsylvania*, vol. II, pt. I, Philadelphia, 1827.

Copy of a Memorial and Petition of the Society of Friends, to the Legislature of Virginia: with a Letter of Benjamin Bates, on the Subject of Militia Fines, Providence (R.I.), 1863.

Correll, Ernest (ed.), "The Congressional Debates on the Mennonite Immigration from Russia, 1873-74," *MQR*, vol. XX, no. 3 (July 1946).

———, "Mennonite Immigration into Manitoba: Sources and Documents, 1872, 1873," *MQR*, vol. XI (1937): pt. I, no. 3 (July); pt. II, no. 4 (Oct).

———, "Sources on the Mennonite Immigration from Russia in the 1870's," *MQR*, vol. XXIV, no. 4 (Oct. 1950).

Correspondence Between William Penn and James Logan, Secretary of the Province of Pennsylvania, and Others, vol. I (1870) and vol. II (1872), ed. Edward Armstrong and included in *Memoirs of the Historical Society of Pennsylvania* as vols. IX and X, Philadelphia.

"Decisions of Virginia General Court, 1626-1628," *Virginia Magazine of History and Biography* (Richmond, Va.), vol. IV, no. 2 (Oct. 1897).

Dodge, David Low, *Memorial of Mr. David L. Dodge*, Boston, 1854.

———, *War Inconsistent with the Religion of Jesus Christ*, ed. Edwin D. Mead, Boston, 1905 edn.

Durnbaugh, Donald F. (ed.), *European Origins of the Brethren*, Elgin (Ill.), 1958.

Dwight L. Moody and War, n.d., n.p.p.

Egmont, First Earl of, *Diary of the First Earl of Egmont* (Viscount Percival), ed. R. A. Roberts, vol. II (Historical Manuscripts Commission: Manuscripts of the Earl of Egmont), London, 1923.

Ellery, William, "Diary of the Hon. William Ellery of Rhode Island.— October 20 to November 15, 1777," *PMHB*, vol. XI, no. 3 (1887).

Emerson, Ralph Waldo, *English Traits*, vol. V of *The Complete Works* (Autograph Centenary Edition), Cambridge (Mass.), 1903.

———, *The Journals and Miscellaneous Notebooks of Ralph Waldo Emerson*, ed. William H. Gilman and Alfred R. Ferguson, vol. III, Cambridge (Mass.), 1963.

———, *Miscellanies*, vol. XI of *The Complete Works* (Autograph Centenary Edition), Cambridge (Mass.), 1904.

965

Ettwein, John, "Fragments from the Papers of Bishop John Ettwein," *TMHS*, vol. IV (1895).

"Extracts from the Brethren's House and Congregation Diaries of the Moravian Church at Lititz, Pa., relating to the Revolutionary War," tr. Abraham Reincke Beck, in *The Penn-Germania* (Lititz, Pa.), vol. I (XIII), nos. 11-12 (Nov.-Dec. 1912).

"Extracts from the Records of the Moravian Congregation at Hebron, Pennsylvania, 1775-1781," *PMHB*, vol. XVIII, no. 4 (1894).

Fisher, S. R., "Journal of Samuel Rowland Fisher, of Philadelphia, 1779-1781," ed. Anna Wharton Morris, *PMHB*, vol. XLI, nos. 2-4 (1917).

Franklin, Benjamin, *The Autobiography of Benjamin Franklin*, ed. Leonard W. Labaree *et al.*, New Haven, 1964.

——, *The Papers of Benjamin Franklin*, ed. Leonard W. Labaree *et al.*, vol. 3, New Haven, 1961.

Frantz, Michael, "Writings of Michael Frantz," *Schwarzenau* (Chicago), vol. II, no. 2 (Jan. 1941).

Gibbons, A. H., *Life of Abby Hopper Gibbons told chiefly through her Correspondence*, ed. Sarah Hopper Emerson, vol. I, New York, 1897.

Gilpin, Thomas (ed.), *Exiles in Virginia: With Observations on the Conduct of the Society of Friends during the Revolutionary War*, Philadelphia, 1848.

Gurney, Eliza P., *Memoir and Correspondence of Eliza P. Gurney*, ed. Richard F. Mott, Philadelphia, 1884.

Hartman, Peter S., *Reminiscences of the Civil War*, Lancaster (Pa.), 1964 edn.

Heatwole, R. J., "Reminiscences of War Days," *Gospel Herald*, vol. IV, no. 28 (12 Oct. 1911).

Herr, John, *John Herr's Complete Works*, Buffalo (N.Y.), 1890.

Hershberger, Guy F. (ed.), "A Newly Discovered Pennsylvania Mennonite Petition of 1755," *MQR*, vol. XXXIII, no. 2 (April 1959).

Hobbs, William, *Autobiography of William Hobbs*, Indianapolis (Ind.), 1962 edn.

Holdeman, John, *A Mirror of Truth*, Hesston (Kan.), 1956.

Jordan, John Woolf (ed.), "Bethlehem during the Revolution," pt. I, *PMHB*, vol. XII, no. 4 (1888).

——, "Bishop Augustus Gottlieb Spangenberg," *PMHB*, vol. VIII, no. 3 (1884).

——, *Fragments of History and Biography relating to the Moravians in York County, 1744-1782*, n.p.p., n.d.

Das Klein-Geschichtsbuch der Hutterischen Brüder, ed. A.J.F. Zieglschmid, Philadelphia, 1947.

Kline, John, *Life and Labors of Elder John Kline the Martyr Missionary*, ed. Benjamin Funk, Elgin (Ill.), 1900.

Krehbiel, Christian, *Prairie Pioneer*, Newton (Kan.), 1961.

Ladd, William, *An Essay on a Congress of Nations for the Adjustment of International Disputes without Resort to Arms* (1840), ed. James Brown Scott, New York, 1916.

Lincoln, Charles H. (ed.), *Narratives of the Indian Wars 1675-1699*, New York, 1952 edn.

966

Logan, James, "James Logan on Defensive War, or Pennsylvania Politics in 1741." *PMHB*, vol. VI, no. 4 (1882).

———, "Two Logan Letters," ed. Amelia Mott Gummere, *Journal of the Friends Historical Society*, vol. IX, no. 2, April 1912.

Macy, Jesse, *An Autobiography*, ed. Katharine Macy Noyes, Springfield (Ill.) and Baltimore (Md.), 1933.

Mekeel, Arthur J. (ed.), "New York Quakers in the American Revolution," *BFHA*, vol. 29, no. 1 (1940).

Michener, Ezra (ed.), *A Retrospect of Early Quakerism; being Extracts from the Records of Philadelphia Yearly Meeting and the Meetings composing it*, Philadelphia, 1860.

Miller, J. B., "Some Reminiscences of the Civil War," *Family Almanac for . . . 1918* (Scottdale, Pa.).

Miller, Peter, "Letter of Peter Miller (Brother Jabez of the Ephrata Community) to James Read, 1776," *PMHB*, vol. XXXVIII, no. 2 (1914).

Minutes of the Annual Meetings of the Church of the Brethren. Containing All Available Minutes from 1778 to 1909, Elgin (Ill.), 1909.

Minutes of the Commissioners for detecting and defeating Conspiracies in the State of New York. Albany County Sessions, 1778-1781, ed. Victor Hugh Paltsits, vol. II, Albany (N.Y.), 1909.

Minutes of General Conferences of Brethren in Christ (River Brethren) from 1891-1904, Harrisburg (Pa.), 1904.

Minutes of the Indiana-Michigan Mennonite Conference 1884-1929, Scottdale (Pa.), n.d.

Moore, James W. (ed.), *Records of the Kingswood Monthly Meeting of Friends, Hunterdon County, New Jersey*, Flemington (N.J.), 1900.

"More Source Material for Ontario Mennonite History," *MQR*, vol. V, no. 3 (July 1931).

Myers, Alfred Cook (ed.), *Hannah Logan's Courtship*, Philadelphia, 1904.

Newcomer, Christian, *The Life and Journal of the Rev'd Christian Newcomer, Late Bishop of the Church of the United Brethren in Christ*, ed. and tr. from German by John Hildt, Hagerstown (Md.), 1834.

"An Ontario Mennonite Petition," *MHB*, vol. XXIII, no. 4 (Oct. 1962).

Osgood, Jacob, *The Life and Christian Experience of Jacob Osgood, with Hymns and Spiritual Songs*, ed. Charles H. Colby, Warner (N.H.), 1873.

Paine, Thomas, *The Writings of Thomas Paine*, ed. Moncure Daniel Conway, vol. I, New York, 1894.

Palmer, William J., *Letters 1853-1868: Gen'l Wm. J. Palmer*, ed. Isaac H. Clothier, Philadelphia, 1906.

The Paxton Papers, ed. John R. Dunbar, The Hague, 1957.

Pemberton, John, *The Life and Travels of John Pemberton, A Minister of the Gospel of Christ*, London, 1844.

Pennsylvania Archives:

1st ser., ed. Samuel Hazard: vols. II, III, VI, IX, Philadelphia, 1853-1854.

2nd ser., ed. John B. Linn and William H. Egle, vol. VII, Harrisburg, 1878.

4th ser., ed. George Edward Reed, vol. II, Harrisburg, 1900.

Pennsylvania Colonial Records:

Minutes of the Provincial Council of Pennsylvania,

vols. I-III, Philadelphia, 1852;
vols. IV-VII, Harrisburg, 1851.
Minutes of the Supreme Executive Council of Pennsylvania, vol. XV, Harrisburg, 1853.
Pringle, Cyrus, *The Civil War Diary of Cyrus Pringle,* Wallingford (Pa.), 1962.
Records of the Colony of Rhode Island and Providence Plantations, in New England, ed. John Russell Bartlett, vol. I (1856) and vol. II (1857), Providence.
Records of the Moravians in North Carolina, Raleigh (N.C.):
vols. I-VII, ed. Adelaide L. Fries, 1922-1947;
vol. VIII, ed. A. L. Fries and Douglas Le Tell Rights, 1954.
Reichel, William C., *Memorials of the Moravian Church,* vol. I, Philadelphia, 1870.
Report of the Eastern Amish Mennonite Conference from the Time of its Organization to the Year 1911, Sugarcreek (Ohio), 1911.
Rotch, William, *Memorandum written by William Rotch in the Eightieth Year of His Age,* Boston and New York, 1916.
Savery, William, *A Journal of the Life, Travels and Religious Labours, of William Savery,* ed. Jonathan Evans, London, 1844.
Scheuner, Gottlieb (ed.), *Inspirations-Historie oder historischer Bericht von der neuen Erweckung, Sammlung und Grundung der Wahren Inspirations-Gemeinde in Deutschland, so wie deren Auswanderung nach Amerika und spätere Uebersiedlung von Ebenezer nach Amana, und was weiter in und mit dieser Gemeine in dem Zeitraum von 1817-1867 sich begeben hat,* Amana (Iowa), 1891.
Shultze, David, *The Journals and Papers of David Shultze,* 2 vols., ed. Andrew S. Berky, Pennsburg (Pa.), 1952-1953.
Skeel, C.A.J. (ed.), "The Letter-book of a Quaker Merchant, 1756-8," *EHR,* vol. XXXI, no. CXXI (Jan. 1916).
Smith, John, *A Narrative of Some Sufferings for His Christian Peaceable Testimony, by John Smith, Late of Chester County, Deceased,* Philadelphia, 1800.
Smith, Samuel, *History of the Province of Pennsylvania,* ed. William M. Mervine, Philadelphia, 1913.
———, "The History of the Province of Pennsylvania" in *The Register of Pennsylvania* (Phila.), vol. VI, 1830.
Spangenberg, August Gottlieb, *An Exposition of Christian Doctrine, as taught in the Protestant Church of the United Brethren or, Unitas Fratrum,* 2nd edn., Bath, 1796.
Spotswood, Alexander, *The Official Letters of Alexander Spotswood,* ed. R. A. Brock, vol. I (1882), Richmond (Va.).
Taylor, Bayard, *Life and Letters of Bayard Taylor,* ed. Marie Hansen-Taylor and Horace E. Scudder, 5th edn., Boston, 1895.
Thoreau, Henry David, "Civil Disobedience" in *Miscellanies,* vol. X of *The Writings of Henry David Thoreau,* Cambridge (Mass.), 1893 edn.
"Three Letters written at Bethlehem, Pennsylvania, in 1778," *PMHB,* vol. XXXVI, no. 3 (1912).
Tolles, Frederick B. (ed.), "The Twilight of the Holy Experiment: A Contemporary View," *BFHA,* vol. 45, no. 1 (1956).

————, "Two Quaker Memorials for Abraham Lincoln," *BFHA*, vol. 46, no. 1 (1957).

Tolstoy, Leo, *The Kingdom of God and Peace Essays*, London, 1936 edn.

Trueblood, Benjamin F., *The Development of the Peace Idea and Other Essays*, Boston, 1932.

Tschetter, Paul, "The Diary of Paul Tschetter, 1873," tr. and ed. J. M. Hofer, pt. II, *MQR*, vol. V, no. 3 (July 1931).

Votes and Proceedings of the House of Representatives of the Province of Pennsylvania in *Pennsylvania Archives*, 8th ser., vols. I-V, ed. Gertrude MacKinney, Harrisburg (Pa.), 1931; vol. VIII, ed. Charles F. Hoban, Harrisburg (Pa.), 1935.

Western District A. M. Conference: Record of Conference Proceedings from the Date of its Organization, Scottdale (Pa.), n.d.

White, Mrs. E. G., *Testimonies for the Church*, 3rd edn., vol. I, Mountain View (Calif.), n.d.

Wichtige Dokumente betreffs der Wehrfreiheit der Mennoniten in Canada, Gretna (Manitoba), 1917.

Wilson, Lewis G. (ed.), "The Christian Doctrine of Non-Resistance: Unpublished Correspondence between Count Leo Tolstoi and the Rev. Adin Ballou," *Arena* (Boston), vol. III, no. XIII (Dec. 1890).

Woods, John A. (ed.), "The Correspondence of Benjamin Rush and Granville Sharp 1773-1809," *Journal of American Studies* (Cambridge, England), vol. I, no. 1 (April 1967).

Woolman, John, *The Journal and Essays of John Woolman*, ed. Amelia Mott Gummere, London, 1922.

————, "From a Letter from John Woolman to Abraham Farrington," *PMHB*, vol. XVII, no. 3 (1893).

Worcester, Noah, *A Solemn Review of the Custom of War*, Boston, 1904 edn.

Young, Gertrude S., "A Record concerning Mennonite Immigration, 1873," *AHR*, vol. XXIX, no. 3 (April 1924).

B. SECONDARY WORKS

Books, Articles, and Dissertations

Adams, Robert, "Nathaniel Peabody Rogers: 1794-1846," *NEQ*, vol. XX, no. 3 (Sept. 1947).

Albright, S. C., *The Story of the Moravian Congregation at York, Pennsylvania*, York (Pa.), 1927.

Allen, Devere, "Daniel Chessman: An Unheard Voice for Peace," *Friend* (Phila.), 10 Aug. 1952.

————, *The Fight for Peace*, New York, 1930.

Andrews, Edward Deming, *The People called Shakers*, New York, 1953.

Anscombe, Francis Charles, *I have Called You Friends: The Story of Quakerism in North Carolina*, Boston, 1959.

Archer, Adair P., "The Quaker's Attitude toward the Revolution," *William and Mary College Quarterly*, 2nd ser., vol. I, no. 3 (July 1921).

Arndt, Karl J.R., *George Rapp's Harmony Society 1785-1847*, Philadelphia, 1965.

Bainton, Roland H., *Christian Unity and Religion in New England*, Boston, 1964.

Barba, Preston A., *They Came to Emmaus*, Emmaus (Pa.), 1960.

Bardwell, Horatio, *Memoir of Rev. Gordon Hall, A.M.*, Andover, 1834.

Barksdale, Brent E., *Pacifism and Democracy in Colonial Pennsylvania*, Stanford (Calif.), 1961.

Barnes, Gilbert Hobbs, *The Antislavery Impulse 1830-1844*, New York, 1933.

Bartlett, John Russell, *History of the Wanton Family of Newport, Rhode Island*, Providence, 1878.

Baumgartner, Samuel H., *Brief Sketches of Eight Generations: Descendants of Ulrich Welty*, Indianapolis (Ind.), 1926.

Beales, A.C.F., *The History of Peace*, London, 1931.

Beatty, Edward Corbyn Obert, *William Penn as Social Philosopher*, New York, 1939.

Beck, Herbert H., "William Henry: Patriot, Master Gunsmith, Progenitor of the Steamboat," *TMHS*, vol. XVI, pt. II (1955).

Bell, J. P. (ed.), *Our Quaker Friends of Ye Olden Time*, Lynchburg (Va.), 1905.

Bender, Wilbur J., "Pacifism among the Mennonites, Amish Mennonites and Schwenkfelders of Pennsylvania to 1783," *MQR*, vol. I (1927), no. 3 (July) and no. 4 (Oct.).

Bert, Harry, "Notes on Non-resistance in the Brethren in Christ Church to the End of World War I," *Notes and Queries in Brethren in Christ History* (Grantham, Pa.), vol. VI, no. 1 (Jan. 1965).

Bess, Roger Bates, *Life of D. L. Miller*, Elgin (Ill.), 1921.

Bi-Centennial of Brick Meeting-House, Calvert, Cecil County, Maryland, 1701-1901, Lancaster (Pa.), 1902.

Biographical Sketches and Anecdotes of Members of the Religious Society of Friends, Philadelphia, 1870.

Birney, Caroline M., *The Grimké Sisters: Sarah and Angelina Grimké*, Boston, 1885.

Bishop, Martha H., "Ann Branson" in *Quaker Biographies*, 2nd ser., vol. II, Philadelphia, n.d.

Bittinger, Foster Melvin, *A History of the Church of the Brethren in the First District of West Virginia*, Elgin (Ill.), 1945.

Blackwelder, Ruth, "The Attitude of the North Carolina Moravians toward the American Revolution," *The North Carolina Historical Review*, vol. IX, no. 1 (Jan. 1932).

Blinn, Henry C., *The Life and Gospel Experience of Mother Ann Lee*, East Canterbury (N.H.), 1901.

Bodo, John R., *The Protestant Clergy and Public Issues 1812-1848*, Princeton (N.J.), 1954.

Boller, Paul B., Jr., "George Washington and the Quakers," *BFHA*, vol. 49, no. 2, 1960.

Bolles, John R., and Anna B. Williams, *The Rogerenes: Some Hitherto Unpublished Annals belonging to the Colonial History of Connecticut*, Boston, 1904.

Boorstin, Daniel J., *The Americans: The Colonial Experience*, New York, 1964 edn.

Bowman, Rufus D., *The Church of the Brethren and War 1708-1941*, Elgin (Ill.), 1944.

Brickenstein, H. A., "Sketch of the Early History of Lititz, 1742-75," *TMHS*, vol. II (1886).

Brigance, William Norwood (ed.), *A History and Criticism of American Public Address*, vol. II, New York, 1943.

Brinton, Ellen Starr, "The Rogerenes," *NEQ*, vol. XVI, no. 1 (March 1943).

Brock, Peter, "Colonel Washington and the Quaker Conscientious Objectors," *Quaker History* (Swarthmore, Pa.), vol. 53, no. 1 (Spring 1964).

———, "The Peace Testimony in 'a Garden Enclosed'," *Quaker History*, vol. 54, no. 2 (Autumn 1965).

———, "The Spiritual Pilgrimage of Thomas Watson: From British Soldier to American Friend," *Quaker History*, vol. 53, no. 2 (Autumn 1964).

Brodin, Pierre, *Les Quakers en Amérique au dix-septième siècle et au début du dix-huitième*, Saint-Amand (Cher), 1935.

Bromley, Ernest R., "Did Early Friends pay War Taxes?" *Friends Intelligencer*, vol. 105, no. 42 (16 Oct. 1948).

Bronner, Edwin B., *William Penn's "Holy Experiment": The Founding of Pennsylvania 1681-1701*, New York, 1962.

Brookes, George S., *Friend Anthony Benezet*, Philadelphia, 1937.

Brumbaugh, Martin Grove, *A History of the German Baptist Brethren in Europe and America*, 2nd edn., Elgin (Ill.), 1910.

Brunk, Harry Anthony, *History of Mennonites in Virginia*, vol. I (1727-1900), Harrisburg (Va.), 1959.

Brusewitz, Carl F., "The Mennonites of Balk, Friesland," *MQR*, vol. XXX, no. 1 (Jan. 1956).

Burkhardt, G., *Die Brüdergemeine*, 2nd edn., vol. I, Gnadau, 1905.

Burkholder, L. J., *A Brief History of the Mennonites in Ontario*, Toronto, 1935.

Busbey, L. White (ed.), *Uncle Joe Cannon*, New York, 1927.

Byrd, Robert O., *Quaker Ways in Foreign Policy*, Toronto, 1960.

Cadbury, Henry J., "History of Quakers in Jamaica" (*MS* in microfilm, F.H.L.S.C.).

———, "Nonpayment of Provincial War Tax," *Friends Journal* (Phila.), vol. 12, no. 17 (1 Sept. 1966).

———, "Penn as a Pacifist," *Friends Intelligencer*, vol. 101, no. 43 (21 Oct. 1944).

———, *Quaker Relief during the Siege of Boston*, [Wallingford (Pa.), 1943].

Cadbury, William W., "How Friends of Over a Century Ago addressed the Pennsylvania Legislature in Behalf of Conscientious Objectors," *Friend*, vol. 119, no. 10 (8 Nov. 1945).

Carroll, Kenneth Lane, *Joseph Nichols and the Nicholites*, Easton (Md.), 1962.

———, "Persecution of Quakers in Early Maryland (1658-1661)," *Quaker History*, vol. 53, no. 2 (Autumn 1964).

———, "Talbot County Quakerism in the Colonial Period," *Maryland Historical Magazine*, vol. 53, no. 4, Dec. 1958.

Cartland, Fernando G., *Southern Heroes or the Friends in War Time*, Cambridge (Mass.), 1895.

Cassel, Daniel K., *History of the Mennonites*, Philadelphia, 1888.

Census of Religious Bodies 1936, Washington (D.C.), 1939-1940: Christa-

971

delphians, Evangelistic Associations, Miscellaneous Denominations, Pentecostal Assemblies, River Brethren, Schwenkfelders.

Chapman, John Jay, *William Lloyd Garrison*, Boston, 1921 edn.

Chapman, J. Wilbur, *The Life and Work of Dwight L. Moody*, Denver (Colo.), 1900.

Chase, Daryl, "The Early Shakers: An Experiment in Religious Communism," Ph.D. diss., U. of Chicago, 1936—also a 22-page printed summary, Chicago, 1938.

Clewell, John Henry, *History of Wachovia in North Carolina*, New York, 1902.

Climenhaga, A. W., *History of the Brethren in Christ Church*, Nappanee (Ind.), 1942.

Coletta, Paolo E., *William Jennings Bryan*, vol. I, Lincoln (Neb.), 1964.

Commager, Henry Steele, *Theodore Parker*, Boston, 1960 edn.

"The Conduct of the Schwenkfelders during the Revolutionary War," *The Pennsylvania-German* (Lititz, Pa.), vol. XI, no. 11 (Nov. 1910).

Cooper, H. Austin, *Two Centuries of Brothers-Valley Church of the Brethren 1762-1962*, Westminster (Md.), 1962.

Cope, Gilbert, "Chester County Quakers during the Revolution," *Bulletins of the Chester County Historical Society 1902-3*.

Correll, Ernest, "President Grant and the Mennonite Immigration from Russia," *MQR*, vol. IX, no. 3 (July 1935).

Coulter, E. Merton, *John Jacobus Flournoy: Champion of the Common Man in the Antebellum South*, Savannah (Ga.), 1942.

Cox, John, Jr., *Quakerism in the City of New York 1657-1930*, New York, 1930.

Crenshaw, Margaret E., "John Bacon Crenshaw" in *Quaker Biographies*, 2nd ser., vol. III, Philadelphia, n.d.

Cressman, J. Boyd, "History of the First Mennonite Church of Kitchener, Ontario," pt. I, *MQR*, vol. XIII, no. 3 (July 1939).

Cromwell, Otelia, *Lucretia Mott*, Cambridge (Mass.), 1958.

Crosby, Ernest, *Garrison the Non-Resistant*, Chicago, 1905.

Crosfield, George, *Memoirs of the Life and Gospel Labours of Samuel Fothergill*, Liverpool (England), 1843.

Cross, Whitney R., *The Burned-Over District*, New York, 1965 edn.

Currey, Cecil B., "Quaker Pacifism in Kansas, 1833-1945," M.Sc. thesis, Fort Hays Kansas State College, n.d.

———, "Quaker Revivalism and the Peace Testimony," *Friends Journal*, vol. 8, no. 4 (15 Feb. 1962).

———. "Quakers in 'Bleeding Kansas'," *BFHA*, vol. 50, no. 2 (Autumn 1961).

Curti, Merle Eugene, *The American Peace Crusade, 1815-1860*, Durham (N.C.), 1929.

———, *Bryan and World Peace*, Northampton (Mass.), 1931.

———, *The Learned Blacksmith: The Letters and Journals of Elihu Burritt*, New York, 1937.

———, "Non-Resistance in New England," *NEQ*, vol. II, no. 1 (Jan. 1929).

———, "The Peace Movement and the Mid-Century Revolutions," *Advocate of Peace through Justice* (Washington, D.C.), vol. 90, no. 5 (May 1928).

972

———, *Peace or War: The American Struggle, 1636-1936*, New York, 1936.

———, "Poets of Peace and the Civil War," *World Unity* (N.Y.), vol. X, no. 3 (June 1932).

Davidson, Robert L.D., *War Comes to Quaker Pennsylvania 1682-1756*, New York, 1957.

Davison, Robert A., *Isaac Hicks, New York Merchant and Quaker 1767-1820*, Cambridge (Mass.), 1964.

Demos, John, "The Antislavery Movement and the Problem of Violent 'Means'," *NEQ*, vol. XXXVII, no. 4 (Dec. 1964).

Dillon, Merton L., *Elijah P. Lovejoy, Abolitionist Editor*, Urbana (Ill.), 1961.

Dingwall, E., and E. A. Heard, *Pennsylvania 1681-1756: The State without an Army*, London, 1937.

Donald, David, *Charles Sumner and the Coming of the Civil War*, New York, 1960.

Dorland, Arthur Garratt, *A History of the Society of Friends (Quakers) in Canada*, Toronto, 1927.

Dove, Frederick Denton, *Cultural Changes in the Church of the Brethren: A Study in Cultural Sociology*, Philadelphia, 1932.

Drake, Thomas E., *Quakers and Slavery in America*, New Haven, 1950.

Dunn, Mary Maples, *William Penn: Politics and Conscience*, Princeton (N.J.), 1967.

Durnbaugh, Donald Floyd, "Brethren Beginnings: The Origins of the Church of the Brethren in Early Eighteenth Century Europe," Ph.D. diss., U. of Pennsylvania, 1960.

———, "Relationships of the Brethren with the Mennonites and Quakers, 1708-1865," *Church History*, vol. XXXV, no. 1 (March 1966).

Elam, E. A., *Twenty-five Years of Trust: A Life Sketch of J. M. Kidwell*, Nashville (Tenn.), 1893.

Ellsworth, Clayton Sumner, "The American Churches and the Mexican War," *AHR*, vol. XLV, no. 2 (Jan. 1940).

Encyclopedia of American Quaker Genealogy, vol. VI: *Virginia*, ed. William Wade Hinshaw, Thomas Worth Marshall, and Douglas Summers Brown, Ann Arbor (Mich.), 1950.

Engle, Jesse S., "The United Brethren and War," *Religious Telescope*, Dayton (Ohio), vol. 107, no. 18 (3 May 1941).

Ensign, Chauncey David, "Radical German Pietism [c.1675-c.1760]," Ph.D. diss., Boston U., 1955.

Erbe, Hellmuth, *Bethlehem, Pa. Eine kommunistische Herrnhuter Kolonie des 18 Jahrhunderts*, Stuttgart, 1929.

Falk, Robert P., "Thomas Paine and the Attitude of the Quakers to the American Revolution," *PMHB*, vol. LXIII, no. 3 (July 1939).

Farrell, John C., *Beloved Lady: A History of Jane Addams' Ideas on Reform and Peace*, Baltimore (Md.), 1967.

Ferguson, LeRoy C., "The Quakers in Midwestern Politics," *Papers of the Michigan Academy of Science, Arts and Letters*, vol. XXXII (1946), Ann Arbor, 1948.

Filler, Louis, *The Crusade against Slavery, 1830-1860*, New York, 1960.

———, "Parker Pillsbury: An Anti-Slavery Apostle," *NEQ*, vol. XIX, no. 3 (Sept. 1946).

973

Fitzroy, Herbert William Keith, "The Punishment of Crime in Provincial Pennsylvania," *PMHB*, vol. LX, no. 3 (July 1936).

Flory, John S., *Flashlights from History*, Elgin (Ill.), 1932.

Forbush, Bliss, *Elias Hicks: Quaker Liberal*, New York, 1956.

Forbush, LaVerne Hill, "The Suffering of Friends in Maryland," *The Maryland and Delaware Genealogist* (Washington, D.C.), vol. 3, no. 2 (Winter 1961-1962) and no. 3 (Spring 1962).

Ford, Worthington Chauncey, "Sumner's Oration on the True Grandeur of Nations,' July 4, 1845," *Massachusetts Historical Society. Proceedings*, vol. L, Boston, 1917.

Foster, Ethan, *The Conscript Quakers, Being a Narrative of the Distress and Relief of Four Young Men from the Draft for the War in 1863*, Cambridge (Mass.), 1883.

Foulke, Joseph, *Memoirs of Jacob Ritter, a faithful Minister in the Society of Friends*, Philadelphia, 1844.

Fox, R. Hingston, *Dr. John Fothergill and His Friends*, London, 1919.

Franklin, Joseph, and J. A. Headington, *The Life and Times of Benjamin Franklin*, St. Louis (Mo.), 1879.

Freehling, William W., *Prelude to Civil War: The Nullification Controversy in South Carolina 1816-1836*, New York, 1966.

Friedmann, Robert, *Mennonite Piety through the Centuries*, Goshen (Ind.), 1949.

Friends in Wilmington 1738-1938, n.p.p., n.d.

Fries, Adelaide L., *The Moravians in Georgia 1735-1740*, Raleigh (N.C.), 1905.

Galpin, W. Freeman, "God's Chore Boy: Samuel Joseph May" (typescript [1939]).

————, *Pioneering for Peace: A Study of American Peace Efforts to 1846*, Syracuse (N.Y.), 1933.

Garrison, Wendell Phillips, and Francis Jackson Garrison, *William Lloyd Garrison 1805-1879: The Story of His Life told by His Children*, New York, vols. 1-2 (1885) and vols. 3-4 (1889).

Garrison, Winfred Ernest, and Alfred T. DeGroot, *The Disciples of Christ: A History*, St. Louis (Mo.), 1948.

Gary, A. T. [Pennell], "The Political and Economic Relations of English and American Quakers (1750-1785)," D.Phil. thesis, Oxford, 1935.

Gibson, Mary Webb, *Shakerism in Kentucky*, Cynthiana (Ky.), 1942.

Gill, John, *Tide without Turning: Elijah P. Lovejoy and Freedom of the Press*, Boston, [1958].

Gingerich, Melvin, "Leo Tolstoy and the Mennonite Author Daniel Musser," *MQR*, vol. XXXII, no. 3 (July 1958).

————, *The Mennonites in Iowa*, Iowa City (Iowa), 1939.

————, "The Military Draft during the American Civil War," *MHB*, vol. XII, no. 3 (July 1951).

Gipson, Lawrence H., "Crime and Its Punishment in Provincial Pennsylvania," *Pennsylvania History*, vol. II, no. 1 (Jan. 1935).

Given, Lois V., "Burlington County Friends in the American Revolution," *Proceedings of the New Jersey Historical Society*, vol. 69, no. 3 (July 1951).

Gratz, Delbert L., *Bernese Anabaptists and Their American Descendants*, Goshen (Ind.), 1953.

974

Gummere, Amelia Mott, *Friends in Burlington,* Philadelphia, 1884.

Hall, Arethusa, *Life and Character of the Rev. Sylvester Judd,* Boston, 1854.

Hallowell, Anna Davis, *James and Lucretia Mott. Life and Letters,* Boston, 1884.

Hamilton, J. Taylor, *The History of the Church Known as the Moravian Church, or the Unitas Fratrum, or the Unity of the Brethren, during the Eighteenth and Nineteenth Centuries,* Bethlehem (Pa.), 1900.

Hamilton, Kenneth Gardiner, *John Ettwein and the Moravian Church during the Revolutionary Period,* Bethlehem (Pa.), 1940 (in *TMHS,* vol. XII, pts. III and IV).

Hamilton, W. J. (ed.), *Two Centuries of the Church of the Brethren in Western Pennsylvania 1751-1950,* Elgin (Ill.), 1953.

Hamlin, C. H., "The Disciples of Christ and the War between the States," *The Scroll* (Chicago), vol. XLI, no. 4 (Dec. 1943).

Hanna, William S., *Benjamin Franklin and Pennsylvania Politics,* Stanford (Calif.), 1964.

Harder, Leland, and Marvin Harder, *Plockhoy from Zurik-zee: The Study of a Dutch Reformer in Puritan England and Colonial America,* Newton (Kan.), 1952.

Harlow, Ralph Volney, *Gerrit Smith: Philanthropist and Reformer,* New York, 1939.

Harrell, David Edwin, Jr., "Disciples of Christ Pacifism in Nineteenth Century Tennessee," *Tennessee Historical Quarterly* (Nashville), vol. XXI, no. 3 (Sept. 1962).

———, *Quest for a Christian America: The Disciples of Christ and American Society to 1866,* Nashville (Tenn.), 1966.

Hartzler, J. S., and Daniel Kauffman, *Mennonite Church History,* Scottdale (Pa.), 1905.

Hazard, Caroline, *The Narragansett Friends' Meeting in the XVIII Century,* Cambridge (Mass.), 1899.

Heatwole, L. J., *Mennonite Handbook of Information,* Scottdale (Pa.), 1925.

Hemleben, Sylvester John, *Plans for World Peace through Six Centuries,* Chicago, 1943.

Hemmenway, John, *The Apostle of Peace: Memoir of William Ladd,* Boston, 1872.

Hendrick, George, "The Influence of Thoreau's 'Civil Disobedience' on Gandhi's *Satyagraha,*" *NEQ,* vol. XXIX, no. 4 (Dec. 1956).

Henry, James, "Nazareth and the Revolution," *TMHS,* vol. II (1886).

Hershberger, Guy Franklin, "Pacifism and the State in Colonial Pennsylvania," *Church History* (Chicago), vol. VIII, no. 1 (March 1939).

———, "The Pennsylvania Quaker Experiment in Politics, 1682-1756," *MQR,* vol. X, no. 4 (Oct. 1936).

———, "Quaker Pacifism and the Provincial Government of Pennsylvania, 1682-1756," Ph.D. diss., U. of Iowa, 1935; summary in *University of Iowa Studies: Studies in the Social Sciences,* vol. X, no. 4 (1937): *Abstracts in History III* (Iowa City, Iowa); also typescript draft of book on this subject.

———, "Some Religious Pacifists of the Nineteenth Century," *MQR,* vol. X, no. 1 (Jan. 1936).

975

————, *War, Peace and Nonresistance*, Scottdale (Pa.), 1st edn., 1944.

Hinds, William Alfred, *American Communities* (1878), New York, 1961 edn.

Hirst, Margaret E., *The Quakers in Peace and War*, London, 1923.

History of the Amish Mennonite Conference (Conservative), Scottdale (Pa.), 1925.

A *History of the Church of the Brethren in the Middle District of Pennsylvania 1781-1925*, n.p.p., [1925].

History of the Philadelphia Bible-Christian Church for the First Century of its Existence from 1817 to 1917, Philadelphia, 1922.

Hoblitzelle, Harrison, "The War against War in the Nineteenth Century: A Study of the Western Backgrounds of Gandhian Thought," Ph.D. diss., Columbia U., 1959.

Holsinger, H. R., *History of the Tunkers and the Brethren Church*, Lathrop (Calif.), 1901.

Hopewell Friends History 1734-1934, Frederick County, Virginia, Strasburg (Va.), 1936.

Horst, Samuel, *Mennonites in the Confederacy: A Study in Civil War Pacifism*, Scottdale (Pa.), 1967.

Hostetler, John A., "Amish Problems at the *Diener-Versammlungen*," *Mennonite Life*, vol. IV, no. 4 (Oct. 1949).

Howe, M.A. DeWolfe, "Biographer's Bait: A Reminder of Edmund Quincy," *Proceedings of the Massachusetts Historical Society*, vol. LXVIII, Boston, 1952.

Huggard, William Allen, *Emerson and the Problem of War and Peace*, Iowa City (Iowa), 1938.

Hull, William I., *William Penn and the Dutch Quaker Migration to Pennsylvania*, Swarthmore (Pa.), 1935.

Illick, Joseph E., *William Penn the Politician*, Ithaca (N.Y.), 1965.

Ivie, Flora Kendall, "The Quest for Peace," *Annals of Iowa*, 3rd ser., vol. XX, no. 4 (April 1936).

Jacobson, Henry A., "Revolutionary Notes concerning Nazareth, Friedensthal and Christian's Spring," *TMHS*, vol. II (1886).

James, Sydney V., "The Impact of the American Revolution on Quakers' Ideas about Their Sect," *William and Mary Quarterly*, 3rd ser., vol. XIX, no. 3 (July 1962).

————, *A People among Peoples: Quaker Benevolence in Eighteenth-Century America*, Cambridge (Mass.), 1963.

Janzen, Cornelius Cicero, "A Social Study of the Mennonite Settlement in the Counties of Marion, McPherson, Harvey, Reno and Butler, Kansas," Ph.D. diss., U. of Chicago, 1926.

Jenkins, Charles F., "Joseph Hewes, the Quaker Signer" in *Children of Light*, ed. Howard H. Brinton, New York, 1938.

————, *Tortola: A Quaker Experiment of Long Ago in the Tropics*, London, 1923.

Jennings, Francis, "Thomas Penn's Loyalty Oath," *American Journal of Legal History* (Phila.), vol. 8, no. 4 (Oct. 1964).

Jericho Friends' Meeting and its Community, Ann Arbor (Mich.), 1958.

Johnson, Oliver, *William Lloyd Garrison and His Times*, Boston, 1880.

Jones, Louis Thomas, *The Quakers of Iowa*, Iowa City (Iowa), 1914.

976

Jones, Rufus M., *The Later Periods of Quakerism*, 2 vols., London, 1921.
————, *The Society of Friends in Kennebec County, Maine*, New York, 1892.
————, *et al.*, *The Quakers in the American Colonies*, London, 1911.
Justice, Hilda, *Life and Ancestry of Warner Mifflin*, Philadelphia, 1905.
Keith, Charles P., *Chronicles of Pennsylvania from the English Revolution to the Peace of Aix-la-Chapelle 1688-1748*, 2 vols., Philadelphia, 1917.
Kelsey, Rayner Wickersham, *Friends and the Indians 1655-1917*, Philadelphia, 1917.
Ketcham, Ralph L., "Conscience, War, and Politics in Pennsylvania, 1755-1757," *William and Mary Quarterly*, 3rd ser., vol. XX, no. 3 (July 1963).
King, Emma, "Rufus P. King" in *Quaker Biographies*, 2nd ser., vol. II, Philadelphia, n.d.
Kirby, Ethlyn Williams, *George Keith (1638-1716)*, New York, 1942.
Klein, Walter C., *Johann Conrad Beissel*, Philadelphia, 1942.
Knollenberg, Bernhard, *Pioneer Sketches of the Upper Whitewater Valley: Quaker Stronghold of the West*, Indianapolis (Ind.), 1945.
Knowles, James Purdie, *Samuel A. Purdie*, Plainfield (Ind.), [1908].
Kolb, Aaron C., "John Fretz Funk, 1835-1930: An Appreciation," pt. I, *MQR*, vol. VI, no. 3 (July 1932).
Konkle, Burton Alva, *Benjamin Chew 1722-1810*, Philadelphia, 1932.
Korngold, Ralph, *Two Friends of Man*, Boston, 1950.
Krahn, Cornelius (ed.), *From the Steppes to the Prairies (1874-1949)*, Newton (Kan.), 1949.
Kreidel, George C., *The Early Life of Professor Elliott*, Washington (D.C.), 1917.
Kriebel, Howard Wiegner, *The Schwenkfelders in Pennsylvania, A Historical Sketch*, Lancaster (Pa.), 1904.
Landis, George B., "The Society of Separatists of Zoar, Ohio" in *Annual Report of the American Historical Association for the Year 1898*, Washington (D.C.), 1899.
Landis, Ira D., "The First Lancaster Conference Printed Discipline," *Mennonite Research Journal*, vol. I, no. 1 (April 1960).
Leach, Douglas Edward, *Flintlock and Tomahawk: New England in King Philip's War*, New York, 1958.
Leach, Robert J., "Elisha Bates, 1817-1827: The Influence of an Early Ohio Publisher upon Quaker Reform," M.A. thesis, Ohio State U., 1939.
————, "Nantucket Quakerism 1661-1763" (typescript in F.H.L.S.C.).
Levering, Joseph Mortimer, *A History of Bethlehem, Pennsylvania 1741-1892*, Bethlehem (Pa.), 1903.
Lewis, Joseph L., *A Memoir of Enoch Lewis*, West Chester (Pa.), 1882.
Littrell, Mary P., Mary E. Outland, and Janie O. Sams, *A History of Rich Monthly Meeting of Friends, 1760-1960*, Woodland (N.C.), [1960].
Lokken, Roy N., *David Lloyd, Colonial Lawmaker*, Seattle (Wash.), 1959.
Loughborough, J. N., *Rise and Progress of the Seventh-Day Adventists*, Battle Creek (Mich.), 1892.
Ludlum, David M., *Social Ferment in Vermont 1791-1850*, New York, 1939.
Lunger, Harold L., *The Political Ethics of Alexander Campbell*, St. Louis (Mo.), 1954.

MacLean, J. P., *Shakers of Ohio*, Columbus (Ohio), 1907.

McPherson, James M., *The Struggle for Equality: Abolitionists and the Negro in the Civil War and Reconstruction*, Princeton (N.J.), 1964.

Mallott, Floyd E., *Studies in Brethren History*, Elgin (Ill.), 1954.

Martin, E. K., *The Mennonite*, Philadelphia, 1883.

Martin, John Hill, *Historical Sketch of Bethlehem in Pennsylvania*, Philadelphia, 1873.

Mast, C. Z., "Imprisonment of Amish in Revolutionary War," *MHB*, vol. XII, no. 1 (Jan. 1952).

May, Joseph, *Samuel Joseph May: A Memorial Study*, Boston, 1898.

Mekeel, Arthur J., "Free Quaker Movement in New England during the American Revolution," *BFHA*, vol. 27, no. 2 (1938).

———, "New England Quakers and Military Service in the American Revolution" in *Children of Light*, ed. Howard H. Brinton, New York, 1938.

———, "The Quakers in the American Revolution," Ph.D. diss., Harvard U., 1939 (copy in H.C.Q.C.).

Melcher, Marguerite Fellows, *The Shaker Adventure*, [Cleveland, Ohio], 1960 edn.

Memoir of Samuel Joseph May, Boston, 1873.

The Mennonite Encyclopedia, 4 vols., Scottdale (Pa.), 1955-1959.

Mennonite Year Book and Almanac, n.p.p., 1910.

Merrill, Walter M., *Against Wind and Tide: A Biography of Wm. Lloyd Garrison*, Cambridge (Mass.), 1963.

Mitchell, David, *Seventh-Day Adventists: Faith in Action*, New York, 1958.

Moody, William R., *The Life of Dwight L. Moody*, New York, 1900.

Moore, Emily E., *Travelling with Thomas Story*, Letchworth (Herts.), 1947.

Moore, J. H., *Some Brethren Pathfinders*, Elgin (Ill.), 1929.

Morgan, Robert H., "John Wells and Adna Heaton: Early American Exponents of Quaker Pacifism," *Friend*, vol. 114, no. 6 (19 Sept. 1940).

Morlan, Charles P., *A Brief History of Ohio Yearly Meeting of the Religious Society of Friends (Conservative)*, Barnesville (Ohio), 1959.

Morse, Kenneth S.P., *Baltimore Yearly Meeting 1672-1830*, n.p.p., 1961.

Munroe, James A., *Federalist Delaware 1775-1815*, New Brunswick (N.J.), 1954.

Murray, Augustus Taber, "Whittier's Attitude Toward War," *Present Day Papers* (Haverford, Pa.), vol. II, no. 7 (July 1915).

Myers, Albert Cook, *Immigration of the Irish Quakers into Pennsylvania, 1682-1750*, Swarthmore (Pa.), 1902.

Neal, Julia, *By their Fruits: The Story of Shakerism in South Union, Kentucky*, Chapel Hill (N.C.), 1947.

Nye, Russel B., *William Lloyd Garrison and the Humanitarian Reformers*, Boston, 1955.

Osgood, Herbert L., *The American Colonies in the Eighteenth Century*, vol. IV, New York, 1924.

Palimpsest (Iowa City, Iowa), vol. XLI, no. 1 (Jan. 1960): "John Brown among the Quakers."

Peare, Catherine Owens, *William Penn*, Philadelphia and New York, 1957.

Perkins, William Rufus, and Barthinius L. Wick, *History of the Amana Society or Community of True Inspiration*, Iowa City (Iowa), 1891.

Phelps, Christina, *The Anglo-American Peace Movement in the Mid-Nineteenth Century*, New York, 1930.

Pickard, Samuel T., *Life and Letters of John Greenleaf Whittier*, vol. II, Cambridge (Mass.), 1894.

Pierce, Edward L., *Memoir and Letters of Charles Sumner*, vol. II, Boston, 1877.

Piercy, Caroline B., *The Valley of God's Pleasure: A Saga of the North Union Shaker Community*, New York, 1951.

Pillsbury, Parker, *Acts of the Anti-Slavery Apostles*, Concord (N.H.), 1883.

———, "Stephen Symonds Foster," *Granite Monthly* (Manchester, N.H.), Aug. 1882.

Pomfret, John E., "West New Jersey: A Quaker Society 1675-1775," *William and Mary Quarterly*, 3rd ser., vol. VIII, no. 4 (Oct. 1951).

Pritchard, H. O., "Militant Pacifists: A Study of the Militant Pacifists of the Restoration Movement," *World Call* (Indianapolis, Ind.), vol. XVIII, no. 3 (March 1936).

Quincy, Josiah Phillips, "Memoir of Edmund Quincy," *Proceedings of the Massachusetts Historical Society*, 2nd ser., vol. XVIII (1905), Boston.

Reichel, Gerhard, *August Gottlieb Spangenberg, Bischof der Brüderkirche*, Tübingen, 1906.

Reichel, William C., "Friedensthal and its Stockaded Mill," *TMHS*, vol. II (1886).

Reimer, Gustav E., and G. R. Gaeddert, *Exiled by the Czar: Cornelius Jansen and the Great Mennonite Migration*, Newton (Kan.), 1956.

Renkewitz, Heinz, *Hochmann von Hochenau (1670-1721): Quellenstudien zur Geschichte des Pietismus*, Breslau, 1935.

Report of American Commissions of the Conference of All Friends. The Relation of the Life of the Society of Friends to the Peace Testimony. Being Report of Commission V, Philadelphia, 1920.

Richardson, Robert, *Memoirs of Alexander Campbell*, vol. II (1886), St. Louis (Mo.).

Roberts, Robert, *Dr. Thomas: His Life & Work*, 1st edn. (1884) and 3rd edn. (ed. E. C. Walker and W. H. Boulton, 1954), Birmingham (England).

Robinson, Charles Edson, *A Concise History of the United Society of Believers called Shakers*, East Canterbury (N.H.), 1893.

Root, Winfred Trexler, *The Relations of Pennsylvania with the British Government, 1696-1765*, New York, 1912.

Sachse, Julius Friedrich, *The German Pietists of Provincial Pennsylvania, 1694-1708*, Philadelphia, 1895.

Sanborn, F. B., and William T. Harris, *A. Bronson Alcott: His Life and Philosophy*, vol. I, Boston, 1893.

Sanders, Thomas G., *Protestant Concepts of Church and State*, New York, 1964.

Sanger, S. F., and D. Hays, *The Olive Branch of Peace and Good Will to Men*, Elgin (Ill.), 1907.

Sappington, Roger E., *Courageous Prophet: Chapters from the Life of John Kline*, Elgin (Ill.), 1964.

————, chapter on "Military Service and Wartime Activities" from book in preparation on the Brethren in Virginia.

Schultz, Selina Gerhard, *Caspar Schwenckfeld von Ossig (1489-1561)*, Norristown (Pa.), 1947.

————, "The Schwenkfelders of Pennsylvania," *Pennsylvania History*, vol. XXIV, no. 4 (Oct. 1957).

Schuster, Eunice Minette, *Native American Anarchism: A Study of Left-Wing American Individualism*, Northampton (Mass.), 1932.

Scott, Kenneth, "The Osgoodites of New Hampshire," *NEQ*, vol. XVI, no. 1 (March 1943).

Seibert, Russell Howard, "The Treatment of Conscientious Objectors in War Time, 1775-1920," Ph.D. diss., Ohio State U., 1936.

Semi-Centennial Anniversary Western Yearly Meeting of Friends Church 1858-1908, Plainfield (Ind.), 1908.

Semple, Robert B., *A History of the Rise and Progress of the Baptists in Virginia*, Richmond (Va.), 1810.

Shambaugh, Bertha M.H., *Amana: The Community of True Inspiration*, Iowa City (Iowa), 1908.

Sharpless, Isaac, *Political Leaders of Provincial Pennsylvania*, New York, 1919.

————, *A Quaker Experiment in Government*, 2 vols. in 1 edn. (vol. I: *History of Quaker Government in Pennsylvania 1682-1756*; vol. II: *The Quakers in the Revolution*), Philadelphia, 1902.

————, *Quakerism and Politics*, Philadelphia, 1905.

Shepard, Odell, *Pedlar's Progress: The Life of Bronson Alcott*, Boston, 1937.

Shetler, Sanford G., *Two Centuries of Struggle and Growth 1763-1963*, Scottdale (Pa.), 1963.

Sider, E. Morris, "Nonresistance in the Brethren in Christ Church in Ontario," *MQR*, vol. XXXI, no. 4 (Oct. 1957).

Skizzen aus dem Lecha-Thale, Allentown (Pa.), 1886.

Smith, C. Henry, *The Coming of the Russian Mennonites*, Berne (Ind.), 1927.

————, *The Mennonite Immigration to Pennsylvania in the Eighteenth Century*, Norristown (Pa.), 1929.

Smith, Elmer Lewis, John G. Stewart, and M. Ellsworth Kyger, *The Pennsylvania Germans of the Shenandoah Valley*, Allentown (Pa.), 1964.

Smith, H. E., *The Quakers, Their Migration to the Upper Ohio, Their Customs and Discipline*, n.p.p., 1928.

Smith, Joseph, *A Descriptive Catalogue of Friends' Books*, 2 vols., London, 1867.

Spalding, Arthur Whitefield, *Origin and History of Seventh-Day Adventists*, vol. I, Washington (D.C.), 1961.

Steckel, William R., "Pietist in Colonial Pennsylvania: Christopher Saur, Printer 1738-1758," Ph.D. diss., Stanford U., 1949.

Stewart, Frank H., "The Quakers of the Revolution," *Year Book. The New Jersey Society of Pennsylvania. 1907-1921*, n.p.p., n.d.

Stillé, Charles J., "The Attitude of the Quakers in the Provincial Wars," *PMHB*, vol. X, no. 3 (1886).

Stocker, Harry Emilius, *A History of the Moravian Church in New York City*, New York, 1922.

Sturge, Charles D., "Friends in Barbadoes," *Friends' Quarterly Examiner* (London), vol. XXVI, no. 104 (Oct. 1892).

Swalm, E. J., *Nonresistance under Test*, Nappanee (Ind.), 1940.

Swansen, H. F., "The Norwegian Quakers of Marshall County, Iowa," *Norwegian-American Studies and Records* (Northfield, Minn.), vol. X (1938).

Thayer, Theodore, "The Friendly Association," *PMHB*, vol. LXVII, no. 4 (Oct. 1943).

———, *Israel Pemberton, King of the Quakers*, New York, 1943.

———, *Pennsylvania Politics and the Growth of Democracy 1740-1776*, Harrisburg (Pa.), 1953.

———, "The Quaker Party of Pennsylvania, 1755-1765," *PMHB*, vol. LXXI, no. 1 (Jan. 1947).

Thistlethwaite, Frank, *America and the Atlantic Community: Anglo-American Aspects, 1790-1850*, New York, 1963 edn.

Thomas, Benjamin P., *Theodore Weld: Crusader for Freedom*, New Brunswick (N.J.), 1950.

Thomas, John L., *The Liberator: William Lloyd Garrison*, Boston, 1963.

Thompson, Mack, *Moses Brown: Reluctant Reformer*, Chapel Hill (N.C.), 1962.

Thorne, Dorothy Gilbert, "North Carolina Friends and the Revolution," *The North Carolina Historical Review*, vol. XXXVIII, no. 3 (July 1961).

Thrift, Minton, *Memoir of the Rev. Jesse Lee. With Extracts from his Journals*, New York, 1823.

Tolis, Peter, "Elihu Burritt: Crusader for Brotherhood," Ph.D. diss., Columbia U., 1965.

Tolles, Frederick B., *George Logan of Philadelphia*, New York, 1953.

———, *James Logan and the Culture of Provincial America*, Boston, 1957.

———, "A Literary Quaker: John Smith of Burlington and Philadelphia," *PMHB*, vol. LXV, no. 3 (July 1941).

———, *Meeting House and Counting House: The Quaker Merchants of Colonial Philadelphia 1682-1763*, Chapel Hill (N.C.), 1948.

———, *Quakers and the Atlantic Culture*, New York, 1960.

Tooker, Elva, *Nathan Trotter, Philadelphia Merchant, 1787-1853*, Cambridge (Mass.), 1955.

Two Centuries of Nazareth 1740-1940, Nazareth (Pa.), 1940.

Two Hundred Fifty Years of Quakerism at Birmingham 1690-1940, West Chester (Pa.), 1940.

Two Hundredth Anniversary of the Establishment of the Friends Meeting at New Garden, Chester County, Pennsylvania, 1715-1915, n.p.p., [1915].

Tyler, Alice Felt, *Freedom's Ferment*, New York, 1962 edn.

Uhler, Sherman P., *Pennsylvania's Indian Relations to 1754*, Allentown (Pa.), 1951.

Umble, John Sylvanus, *Mennonite Pioneers*, Elkhart (Ind.), 1940.

Unruh, John D., Jr., "The Burlington and Missouri River Railroad brings the Mennonites to Nebraska 1873-1878," pt. I, *Nebraska History* (Lincoln, Neb.), vol. 45, no. 1 (March, 1964).

Uttendörfer, Otto, and Walther E. Schmidt, *Die Brüder: Aus Vergangenheit und Gegenwart der Brüdergemeine*, 2nd edn., Herrnhut, 1914.

Villard, Fanny Garrison, *William Lloyd Garrison on Non-Resistance*, New York, 1924.

981

Walker, Amasa, *Memoir of Rev. Amos Dresser*, n.p.p., n.d.

Ward, A. Gertrude, "John Ettwein and the Moravians in the Revolution," *Pennsylvania History*, vol. I, no. 4 (Oct. 1934).

Ware, Henry, Jr., *Memoirs of the Rev. Noah Worcester, D.D.*, Boston, 1844.

Waterston, Elizabeth, *Churches in Delaware during the Revolution*, Wilmington, 1925.

Wayland, Francis, and H. L. Wayland, *A Memoir of the Life and Labors of Francis Wayland D.D., LL.D., late President of Brown University*, vol. II, New York, 1867.

Weaver, Glenn, "The Mennonites during the French and Indian War," *MHB*, vol. XVI, no. 2 (April 1955).

———, *The Schwenkfelders during the French and Indian Wars*, Pennsburg (Pa.), 1955.

Weeks, Stephen B., *Southern Quakers and Slavery*, Baltimore (Md.), 1896.

Wellcome, Isaac C., *History of the Second Message and Mission, Doctrine and People*, Yarmouth (Me.), 1874.

Wenger, John C., *History of the Mennonites of the Franconia Conference*, Telford (Pa.), 1937.

———, *The Mennonites in Indiana and Michigan*, Scottdale (Pa.), 1961.

Wertenbaker, Thomas Jefferson, *The First Americans 1607-1690*, New York, 1929.

West, Earl Irvin, *The Life and Times of David Lipscomb*, Henderson (Tenn.), 1954.

———, *The Search for the Ancient Order: A History of the Restoration Movement 1849-1906*, vol. I, Nashville (Tenn.), 1949; vol. II, Indianapolis (Ind.), 1950.

Wetherill, Charles, *History of the Religious Society of Friends called by some the Free Quakers, in the City of Philadelphia*, [Philadelphia], 1894.

Wherry, Noel M., *Conscientious Objection*, vol. I, Washington (D.C.), 1950.

White, Julia S., "The Peace Testimony of North Carolina Friends prior to 1860," *BFHA*, vol. 16, no. 2 (1927).

Whitney, Edson L., *The American Peace Society: A Centennial History*, Washington (D.C.), 1928.

Whitney, Janet, *John Woolman, American Quaker*, Boston, 1942.

Wilcox, Francis McLellan, *Seventh-Day Adventists in Time of War*, Tacoma Park (Washington, D.C.), 1936.

Willis, Frederick L.H., *Alcott Memoirs*, Boston, 1915.

Wisbey, Herbert A., Jr., *Pioneer Prophetess: Jemima Wilkinson, the Publick Universal Friend*, Ithaca (N.Y.), 1964.

Wright, Edward Needles, *Conscientious Objectors in the Civil War*, New York, 1961 edn.

Wyman, Lillie Buffum Chace, and Arthur Crawford Wyman, *Elizabeth Buffum Chace 1806-1899: Her Life and Its Environment*, vol. I, Boston, 1914.

Yoder, Edward, "Peace Principles from a Scriptural Viewpoint," *Gospel Herald* (Scottdale, Pa.), vol. XXXIII, no. 3 (18 April 1940).

Yoder, Richard B., "Nonresistance among the Peace Churches of Southern Somerset County, Pennsylvania, during the Civil War," paper at Goshen College Biblical Seminary, 1959.

Zigler, D. H., *History of the Brethren in Virginia*, 2nd edn., Elgin (Ill.), 1914.

Zimmerman, John J., "Benjamin Franklin and the Quaker Party, 1755-1756," *William and Mary Quarterly*, 3rd ser., vol. XVII, no. 3 (July 1960).

C. ADDENDA

The following items came to my attention too late for consideration in the text of this book:

Bronner, Edwin B., "The Quakers and Non-Violence in Pennsylvania," *Pennsylvania History*, XXXV, no. 1 (Jan. 1968), 1-22.

Durnbaugh, Donald F. (ed.), *The Brethren in Colonial America: A Source Book on the Transplantation and Development of the Church of the Brethren in the Eighteenth Century*, Elgin (Ill.), 1967, chap. 10.

Juhnke, James C., "J. G. Ewert—A Mennonite Socialist," *Mennonite Life* (North Newton, Kan.), XXIII, no. 1 (Jan. 1968), 12-15.

Lerner, Gerda, *The Grimké Sisters from South Carolina: Rebels against Slavery*, Boston, 1967, *passim*.

Pease, William H., and Jane H. Pease, "Freedom and Peace: A Nineteenth Century Dilemma," *Midwest Quarterly* (Pittsburg, Kan.), IX, no. 1 (Oct. 1967), 23-40.

Sappington, Roger E., "The Mennonites in the Carolinas," *MQR*, XLI, no. 2 (April 1968), 107, 108, 113, 114.

Schlissel, Lillian D. (ed.), *Conscience in America: A Documentary History of Conscientious Objection in America, 1757-1967*, New York, 1968, pts. 1-3.

Sowle, Patrick, "The Quaker Conscript in Confederate North Carolina," *Quaker History*, vol. 56, no. 2 (Autumn 1967), pp. 90-105.

Wagenknecht, Edward, *John Greenleaf Whittier: A Portrait in Paradox*, New York, 1967, chap. IV.

Windhausen, John D., "Quaker Pacifism and the Image of Isaac Norris II," *Pennsylvania History*, XXXIV, no. 4 (Oct. 1967), 346-60.

Index

985

987

994

995

996

997

998

999